The Queen of Katwe

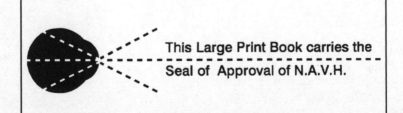

The Queen of Katwe

A STORY OF LIFE, CHESS, AND ONE EXTRAORDINARY GIRL'S DREAM OF BECOMING A GRANDMASTER

Tim Crothers

THORNDIKE PRESS
A part of Gale, Cengage Learning

GALE
CENGAGE Learning

Detroit • New York • San Francisco • New Haven, Conn • Waterville, Maine • London

GALE
CENGAGE Learning

Photo credits: Chapters 1, 2, 5, and 9: Tim Crothers; Chapters 3 and 10: courtesy of Robert Katende; Chapters 4, 7, and 11: David Johnson/Silentimages.org; Chapter 6: Courtesy of the Popp family; Chapter 8: Rodney Suddith.
Thorndike Press, a part of Gale, Cengage Learning.

Thorndike Press® Large Print Inspirational.
The text of this Large Print edition is unabridged.
Other aspects of the book may vary from the original edition.
Set in 16 pt. Plantin.

LIBRARY OF CONGRESS CATALOGING-IN-PUBLICATION DATA

Crothers, Tim.
The queen of Katwe : a story of life, chess, and one extraordinary girl's dream of becoming a grandmaster / by Tim Crothers.
p. cm.
Originally published: New York : Scribner, 2012.
ISBN-13: 978-1-4104-5455-3 (hardcover)
ISBN-10: 1-4104-5455-X (hardcover)
1. Mutesi, Phiona. 2. Women chess players—Uganda—Kampala—Biography. I. Title.
GV1439.M87C76 2013
794.1092—dc23
[B] 2012038812

Published in 2013 by arrangement with Scribner, a division of Simon & Schuster, Inc.

Printed in the United States of America
1 2 3 4 5 6 7 17 16 15 14 13

To Atticus and Sawyer,
the children of Uganda and beyond

CONTENTS

Prologue

She wins the decisive game, but she has no idea what it means. Nobody has told her what's at stake, so she just plays, like she always does. She has no idea she has qualified to compete at the Olympiad. No idea what the Olympiad is. No idea that her qualifying means that in a few months she will fly to the city of Khanty-Mansiysk in remote central Russia. No idea where Russia even is. When she learns all of this, she asks only one question: "Is it cold there?"

She travels to the Olympiad with nine teammates, all of them a decade older, in their twenties, and even though she has known many of them for a while and journeys by their side for 27 hours across the globe to Siberia, none of her teammates really have any idea where she is from or where she aspires to go, because Phiona Mutesi is from someplace where girls like her don't talk about that.

19th sept. 2010

Dear mum,

I went to the airport. I was very happy to go to the airport. this was only my second time to leave my home. When I riched to the airport I was some how scared because I was going to play the best chess players in the world. So I waved to my friends and my brothers. Some of them cried because they were going to miss me and I had to go. so they wished me agood luck. They told me that they will pray for me. So we board on europlane to go from Uganda to Kenya. The Europlane flew up the sky. I saw clouds looking niece. This time I thought that I was may be in heaven. I asked God to protect me. because who am I to fly to the europlane. so it was Gods power. We riched in kenya very well. I was very tired and they gave me acake it was like abread. I had never tested that before but it was very sweat and I liked it.

When we boad an europlane to Dubai it was very big. So they served us very many eats. I was very hungry. I prayed to God to protect us very well. and he did so. and we riched very well. What I surprised of people which I went with. They were like my parents. they treated me well and my coach treating me as if I was his babby. What I never expected before. That was my first day.

When we riched in Dubai things were different. every was on his own. After then we board the last europlane to take us in Roncha. we prayed so that we rich well. An europlane flew. This time we were along distance from the ground. I think this time I was nearly to tutch on heaven. the clouds were looking niece. then they served me food which I not seen and I was not used to that food. I felt bad. wanted to vomite. So we riched very well. We were welcomed at the airport.

Then they gave us rooms.

The opening ceremony at the 2010 Chess Olympiad takes place in an ice arena. Phiona has never seen ice. There are lasers and woolly mammoths and dancers inside bubbles and people costumed as chess pieces, queens and bishops and pawns, marching around on a giant chessboard atop the ice. Phiona watches it all unfold with her hands cupping her cheeks as if in a wonderland. She asks if this happens every night in this place and she is told, no, that the arena normally serves as a home for hockey, concerts, the circus. Phiona has never heard of any of those things.

She returns to the hotel, which at fifteen floors is by far the tallest building Phiona has ever entered. She rides the elevator with giddy trepidation like it is an amusement park roller coaster. She stares out her hotel room window for a half hour amazed by how tiny people on the ground look from six stories high. Then she takes a long, hot shower, trying her best to wash away her home in the slum.

The following afternoon when she first enters the competition venue, a vast indoor tennis stadium packed with hundreds of shiny new chessboards from baseline to baseline, she immediately notices that at 14 years old she is among the youngest competitors in a tournament that features more than 1,300 players from 141 countries. She is told this is the most accomplished collection of chess talent ever assembled. That makes Phiona nervous. How could she not be? She is playing for her country, Uganda, against other nations, but she isn't playing against kids anymore like she does in Katwe. She is playing against grown women, and as her first game approaches, as she struggles to locate her table because she is still learning to read, she keeps thinking to herself, "Do I belong here?"

Her first opponent is Dina Kagramanov, the Canadian national champion. Kagramanov, born in Baku, Azerbaijan, the hometown of former men's world chess champion Garry Kasparov, learned the game at age six from her grandfather. She is competing in her third Olympiad and at age 24 has been playing elite chess longer than Phiona has been alive. They could hardly be more different, this white woman playing black against this black girl playing white.

Kagramanov preys on Phiona's inexperience by setting a trap during the game's opening and gains a pawn advantage. Phiona sits forward in her chair, leaning over the board aggressively as she often does, with her hands pressed to her forehead, as if she might will her pieces into a better strategic position. Phiona stubbornly tries but fails to recover from her initial mistake. Still, it is the victor who comes away impressed. "She's a sponge," Kagramanov says. "She picks up on whatever information you give her and she uses it against you. Anybody can be taught moves and how to react to those moves, but to reason like she does at her age is a gift that gives her the potential for greatness."

21st sept. 2010

Dear mum,

I great you in the might name of Jesus crist. I have written this letter to inform you that this way it was not fine it was raining at morning and it is very cold now. I don't want to eat any thing. Iam not used to eat this type of food. Whenever it riches to break fast I feel like sick and I feel like I want to vomit. But let pray to God may be I will be ok. What I have like from this way they have given us so many gifts even if I have lost the first game but I will wine others I promise you mother. My coach is ecouraging to play very well. But I am sure I will not disapoite him. I am going to work for my best. I will make sure I wine five games even if I am playing strong women. I pray to at God to make my promise possible. In Jesus's name I have preyed amen.

Phiona is lucky to be here. The Ugandan women's team has never participated in a Chess Olympiad before because Uganda could never afford it. But this year the president of FIDE, the world's governing body of chess, has arranged funding for the entire Ugandan team to travel to the Olympiad in the hope of garnering the country's vote in his reelection campaign. Phiona needs breaks like that.

She arrives early for the second day of matches, because she wants to explore. She sees Afghan women dressed in burkas, Indian women in saris, and Bolivian women in ponchos and black bowler hats. She spots a blind chess player and wonders how that is possible. She notices an Iraqi suddenly kneel down and begin praying to someplace called Mecca.

As she walks toward her designated table, Phiona is halted by security and asked to produce her player credential to prove she is actually among the competitors, perhaps because she looks so young, or perhaps because with her short-cropped hair, baggy sweater, and sweatpants, she could be mistaken for a boy.

Before her next game, against Yu-Tong Elaine Lin of Taiwan, Phiona slips off her sneakers. She has never played chess wearing shoes. Lin is stoic, staring only at the board, as if Phiona is not even there. Midway through the game, Phiona commits a tactical error that causes her to lose two pawns. Later, Lin makes a similar blunder, but Phiona does not detect it until it is too late, missing an opportunity that could have turned the game in her favor. From that moment on, Phiona gazes into the distance, hardly able to bear looking at the pieces left on the board, crestfallen as the remainder of the moves play out predictably and she loses a game she knows she should have won.

Phiona leaves the table and runs straight out to the parking lot. Coach Robert has warned her never to go off on her own, but Phiona boards a shuttle bus alone and returns to the hotel, then goes straight to her room and bawls into her pillow like a typical teenager. Later that evening, her coach tries to comfort her, but Phiona is inconsolable. It is the only time chess has ever brought her to tears. In fact, despite the extraordinarily difficult life she has endured, Phiona cannot remember the last time she cried.

Opening

Chapter 1
Land of the Frogs

Hakim Ssewaya, who has lived 40 years in Katwe, stands in front of his shack. The structure fills with raw sewage during the slum's frequent floods.

She had no other choice. Nakito Jamidah had borne four children out of wedlock, including twins who died during childbirth, and she was no longer welcome at her parents' home in the tiny Ugandan village of Namilyango. Jamidah was working as a cook at the same Lugala Primary School where she'd dropped out a decade earlier at age eight, but she still could not afford to support her two surviving children, who lived with their grandparents. The father of Jamidah's children, who maintained relationships with several other women, was a former soldier and a violent drunk who often physically abused Jamidah until she finally left him. Then one day he came to the Lugala School in a drunken rage and kicked a saucepan full of scalding porridge over Jamidah, causing her severe burns. Jamidah feared for her life. She had to go.

So she came to the city.

When Jamidah arrived in Kampala, the sprawling, congested, dusty capital city, in 1971, Uganda was a mess and it was about to get a lot messier. The small East African nation, bordered by Kenya to the east, Sudan to the north, the Democratic Republic of Congo to the west and Tanzania, Rwanda, and Lake Victoria to the south, was nine years removed from its independence from Great Britain, and the former colony was falling victim to the same growing pains as nearly all of its fledgling African brethren. The colonial map of Africa had been drawn haphazardly, as if by children with crayons. Uganda's four primary tribes, who shared no culture, language, or custom, but had previously been bonded by a common colonial enemy, could no longer live in harmony inside the artificial borders. Uganda languished in a constant state of civil war.

The story of postcolonial Ugandan politics is that of a lieutenant who betrays his general. In the same year that Jamidah arrived in Kampala, Idi Amin, the commander of Uganda's army, deposed Uganda's president, Milton Obote, in a coup d'état. Amin would become the most malevolent dictator in African history.

A primary school dropout and former

national boxing champion, Amin had joined the colonial army's King's African Rifles in 1946 as an assistant cook before enlisting in the infantry and climbing through the ranks, proving his desire to triumph at any moral cost during brutal military campaigns in Kenya and Somalia. Immediately after the coup d'état, Amin promised free elections. They never occurred. One week after the coup, Amin declared himself his nation's president and eventually bestowed upon himself the title "His Excellency, President for Life, Field Marshal Al Hadji Doctor Idi Amin Dada, VC, DSO, MC, Conqueror of the British Empire in Africa in General and Uganda in Particular." Amin also famously referred to himself as the "Lord of All the Beasts on the Earth and Fishes of the Sea."

Amin was known to order white Ugandans to carry him on a throne and kneel down before him as news photographers captured the scene for the outside world to see. He praised Hitler's treatment of the Jews, threatened war against Israel, insulted other world leaders, and thumbed his nose at Uganda's former colonial overseers by offering to become King of Scotland and lead the Scots to their rightful independence from England. He allied with Libyan dictator Muammar Qaddafi and courted arms from the Soviet Union. Amin ruled through terror, his regime responsible for killing its political and ethnic enemies, both real and imagined, in a horrific slaughter that took the lives of an estimated 500,000 Ugandans. Amin was even rumored to be a cannibal who consumed the organs of his victims.

Amin's eight-year reign would devastate Uganda's economy. In 1972 Amin exiled tens of thousands of immigrant Indian merchants upon which the country's financial infrastructure depended and handed their shops over to his soldiers who sold size 17 shirts for 17 Ugandan shillings because they didn't know any better. Having banished its business class, the country's economy unraveled, leaving half of the population languishing below the international poverty line. Amin nationalized the country's land, evicting Ugandan villagers from their ancestral farms and prompting other tribes to revolt against Amin and his Kakwa tribe. People flooded into Kampala seeking any kind of security. Upon their arrival, many were shooed away to a slum called Katwe where nobody else wanted to be.

Jamidah and two of her sons, Hakim Ssewaya and Moses Sebuwufu (last names in Uganda are drawn from the father's clan), rented a tiny room in Katwe near a petrol station where Jamidah sold alcohol from a stall near the gas pumps. When she began falling behind on the rent and feared eviction, one of her customers told her about an old man down the hill in the swamp who was considering selling inexpensive plots of land. "As much as my mother wanted to come and meet this man," Hakim says, "she was fearing the area because it was wild bush and no one risked going there."

Eventually Jamidah arranged to meet the man, Qasim, instead along Nasser Road, where he was working splicing newspapers into cuttings that were compacted into burlap sacks to form mattresses. Qasim was a Tanzanian who told Jamidah that he'd once worked as a servant for the Kabaka, the king of the region of Buganda and its Baganda tribe, whose ancestral lands comprised Kampala and much of its surrounding area in southern Uganda, and from which the nation takes its name. Qasim explained to Jamidah that he had been working in the Kabaka's palace up high on the hill during the 1960s, when one of the Kabaka's chiefs offered this land to him, thinking it was worthless because any member of the Baganda possessed too much pride to ever sleep in a swamp.

Jamidah agreed to meet with Qasim again, this time on his land, where they surveyed a small spit of dirt, and in 1971 Jamidah became the first person ever to purchase a piece of the Katwe lowlands. She bought her plot for 1.2 cents, but she could only afford a down payment of .8 cents. Jamidah would work for months to pay off the balance.

Katwe was a bush area of about four square kilometers filled with elephant grass, mango trees, yams, and countless frogs. Every evening the frogs bellowed out such a cacophonous din that it was difficult for Hakim and Moses to sleep. Jamidah began referring to the area claimed by Qasim as Nkere, which translates to "land of the frogs," and would eventually be recognized as one of 19 zones that comprise the enormous slum known as Katwe.

Qasim was an eccentric old man who dressed in a ska made of sewn-together socks, stuck coins in his ears, and never wore shoes. His tiny house stood within a thicket of trees and was surrounded by beehives and green snakes. Hakim suspected that Qasim, who claimed to be more than 80 years old, was a witch doctor.

Jamidah's land was only a short distance from Qasim's house, so Qasim would often summon the young Hakim to fetch him fresh water or to help him prepare a freshly butchered cow's head for eating, all the while narrating stories for Hakim about how the Kabaka mobilized his forces for battle with other tribes. Every evening Qasim would build a fire in his small shack and sing songs in a mysterious language that Hakim did not understand.

One day Hakim's mother was suddenly forced to leave her stall at the petrol station because the station was purchased by an Indian immigrant who refused to let a black woman sell there. So Jamidah would instead hide beneath some nearby trees to peddle her alcohol. When Idi Amin banished the Indians from Uganda, that petrol station was handed back over to a black Ugandan, and Jamidah returned to work there again. Her business grew and she was able to upgrade the shack on her small plot to include three tiny rooms. She replaced the roof of papyrus leaves with tin sheets to better keep out the frequent rainstorms. She was even able to afford to send Hakim to St. Peter's Secondary School up the hill in Nsambya, where he played such skillful soccer that he became known as St. Peter's Pelé.

Then in 1980 one of Uganda's civil wars

spread into Katwe. Because Katwe is viewed by most Ugandans as a sort of blind spot, the slum became an ideal slaughtering ground. Ugandan troops would randomly kill anyone they so much as suspected might be a rebel. One day the soldiers shot Hakim's grandmother, Mariam Nakiwala, who laid outside the family's shack bleeding to death with Hakim powerless to help her. Hakim huddled inside the shack with his hand over the mouth of his two-year-old nephew, Simon, knowing that if either made a sound they would be killed as witnesses. Hakim and his family eventually fled to another area of Katwe for a year, where they regularly saw people burned alive. Soldiers burned one of Hakim's best friends so severely, all that remained was his leg.

But the most consistent menace in Katwe has always been the water. For his entire life in the slum, Hakim has looked at the sky with apprehension. Because Katwe is a natural swampland and the water table is so high, almost every rain floods the area. Sometimes the floods rise so high that Hakim must flee to his roof and it can be days before he's even able to enter his house to begin bailing out.

Jamidah, who died in 1994, would eventually bear ten children by three different fathers, but only Hakim and Moses survive. Hakim works for a taxi company and remains as desperately poor as the day he first arrived in the slum. His wife left him and their six children a few years ago after a particularly massive flood completely submerged their house for several days, but Hakim stays because it is the only real home he's ever known. "For my future time I really feel so concerned with my family that whenever I try to put my head down to sleep, sleep doesn't come," Hakim says. "I must wear torn shirts to save whatever I can for the family. What challenges me most is that I don't have any program for my children. When I die, I don't know how they will continue. Even the following morning, they will not be able to get sugar."

Hakim Ssewaya believes he is about 48 years old and he has lived in Katwe for four decades. During his first 15 years there he saw ten different transfers of power in Uganda's government. Each time a new leader took over, people from his tribe would stream into Katwe hoping to take advantage of having one of their tribesmen in power. Finally in 1986, in yet another coup, Yoweri Museveni became president and has remained in that position ever since — the people of Uganda hardly satisfied, but having grown weary of rebellion and war as failed change agents.

"When the war ended in 1986, people started running back to Nkere," Hakim says. "Many people had fled the area to someplace else in Katwe because of the war, but the moment they realized that the fighting had stopped, they came back. It seemed like they left as individuals, but they came back as three. You can ask yourself, 'Why would so many people experience this kind of miserable place and not vacate?' Because it is a place full of people with nowhere else to go."

They came. They came. They came.

By the time Qasim died, he had sold off all of his land, tiny parcel by tiny parcel, to hundreds of different owners, until there was hardly space left to bury him. His grave is now a sewer trench.

People from remote villages all over Uganda came to Kampala because they believed that life was better in the city where they had access to electricity and better hospitals and schools. They came because there are only so many times that a family's ancestral land can be deeded to the sons of a new generation before there is no land left to farm, or they came simply because Idi

Amin took their land and they were unable to reclaim it. They came because they learned that foreign aid reaches people in the city first and often never makes it to the countryside at all. They came to escape the wars that were usually fought in the bush. They came to find treatment for the AIDS virus that at its zenith had stricken an estimated 15 percent of Uganda's adult population, spread largely through unprotected sex. They came because money didn't exist in the villages and they felt rich somehow if they touched a few shillings every day, even if they earned less than was necessary to survive.

So they came. But then what?

"It is a trap," says John Michael Mugerwa, a Pentecostal bishop and native Ugandan who worked in Katwe for nearly three decades. "You leave your village with big dreams because you associate everything good and nice and successful and prosperous to the city and people will go to any lengths to get there, only to discover it is not as they thought. Money does not grow on trees in Kampala. The trap is that when you leave the village to come to the city, you've made a promise to the people at home that you're going to live a better life. Many times you've sold off everything you own to come, so there is nothing to go back to."

Then what?

"Imagine you literally have no skills except for subsistence agriculture, tilling the land, sewing seeds, weeding, and you have not been educated or taught other skills that translate to the city," Mugerwa says. "When you arrive in Kampala you almost become a fugitive, not because you've done anything wrong, but because you have nothing to do, so you need to go to a place where you will not be easily detected and you will not fall into the wrong hands of the law. Usually that will push you to a place where life is shadowy, where no one will ask who you are or where you are from or even notice that you exist."

So they came. And they stayed. And they needed a place to get lost.

Katwe.

The largest of eight slums in Kampala, Katwe (kot-WAY) is one of the worst places on earth. The slum is often so severely flooded that many residents sleep in hammocks suspended just beneath their roofs to avoid drowning. Raw sewage runs through trenches beside the alleyways of the slum and floods carry it inside people's shacks. The human waste from neighboring downtown Kampala is also dumped directly into Katwe. There is no sanitation service. Flies are everywhere. The stench is appalling.

When it isn't flooded, Katwe's land is packed dirt, fouled by the sewage. Nothing grows there. Stray dogs and rats and long-horned cattle all compete with humans to survive in a confined space that becomes more overcrowded every day. Homes exist wherever someone can find space to construct a makeshift shack, at least until a developer decides that land might have some value and the area is set afire. People are evicted from their dwellings by way of a controlled burn.

In Katwe they say that "running water" is the water you have to run through the slum to get, either from a dirty community well or a fetid puddle. Electricity is far too expensive for most Katwe residents where it is accessible at all. Landlords show up periodically with a sack full of padlocks and anyone who can't pay the rent is locked out of their home.

Katwe has no street signs. No addresses. It is a maze of rutted alleys and dilapidated shacks. It is a place where time is measured by where your shadow hits the ground. There are no clocks. No calendars. Because it lies just a few degrees from the equator,

Katwe has no seasons, which adds to the repetitive, almost listless, nature of daily life. Every day is just like the next. Survival in Katwe depends on courage and determination as well as guile and luck. During Amin's regime when Uganda suffered through a foreign trade embargo, Katwe became known as a mecca for spare parts. Anything that could be sold on the black market could be found in Katwe, where the people developed a vital resourcefulness amid the squalor.

If you live in Katwe, the rest of the Ugandan population would prefer that you stay there. In the more stable neighborhoods that surround Katwe, homes and petrol stations and supermarkets are patrolled by uniformed security guards with AK-47s. The skyscrapers of downtown Kampala are in view from any dwelling in Katwe, just steps away. Children of the slum venture to the city center daily to beg or pickpocket and then commute back to Katwe to sleep at night.

In Katwe, life is so transient that it is often hard to identify which children belong to which adults. It is a population of single mothers and their kids tossed randomly from one shack to another. Everybody is on the move, but nobody ever leaves. It is said that if you are born in Katwe, you die in Katwe. Death from disease or violence or famine or neglect touches everyone in the slum, yet individual tragedies are not dwelled upon because they occur so frequently. Most of the children of Katwe are fatherless and the men in their lives often beat or abuse them. The women of Katwe are valued by men for little more than sex and childcare. Many women in the slum are sex workers who eventually become pregnant, but can't afford to stop working in the trade. They must leave their children locked in the shack at night and it is not uncommon for them to return home in the early morning to find their kids have drowned in a flood or died in a fire after knocking over the kerosene lamp they were using as a night-light.

Bishop Mugerwa estimates that nearly half of all teenage women in Katwe are mothers. Due largely to the lack of access to birth control in Katwe and its neighboring slums, Uganda is now the youngest country in the world with an average age of 14 years. The prodigious birthrate produces legions of young children without an infrastructure strong enough to raise them or educate them. Many become homeless and hopeless, with no sense that if they disappeared they would even be missed. Katwe's youth endure an overwhelming stigma, a sense of defeat, and a resignation that they'll never do any better than anybody else in the slum. Achievement is secondary to survival. "What we have is children raising children," Mugerwa says. "It is known as a poverty chain. The single mother cannot sustain the home. Her children go to the street and have more kids and they don't have the capacity to care for those kids. It is a cycle of misery that is almost impossible to break."

By the time Harriet Nakku came to Katwe in 1980, the muddle of decrepit shacks overstuffed with people stretched as far as the eye could see in every direction.

All of the frogs were gone.

Harriet Nakku was not wanted. Not planned. A mistake, like so many other children in Uganda, if it is even reasonable to call a child born without the use of birth control a mistake. Better to say that Harriet was a child her parents hoped wouldn't be conceived. Her mother, Kevina Nanyanzi, was not married to her father, Livingstone Kigozi, who had several other wives. Nanyanzi used to meet Kigozi secretly. One of those meetings produced Harriet.

Harriet was born in Seeta, her father's village, 15 kilometers outside of Kampala. Harriet believes it was in about 1969. Because she was an illegitimate child, Harriet was born at Nanyanzi's sister's house. Nanyanzi then moved with Harriet to her aunt's home in the nearby village of Nantabulirirwa. Harriet stayed there with her mother until she was about six years old and ready to go to school, and that's when Nanyanzi handed the young girl back over to her father because she could not afford her daughter's school fees.

"I stayed at my father's house with my stepbrothers and stepsisters and my father used to leave us there with the stepmum for several weeks without any support, because he used to support other women of his elsewhere," Harriet says. "My father was a womanizer. He had such a bad character. He could only enjoy himself. Because I was not really part of that family, it was not all that easy, so my father chose to take me to the grandmother."

Harriet stayed with her grandmother, Miriam, until a point when Harriet fell sick. Harriet developed wounds and boils all over her body that Miriam could not afford to treat. So Harriet was sent back to her mother. Nanyanzi had since moved to

Katwe, where she worked cooking cassava, a nutrient-rich vegetable that is among Uganda's food staples, and selling it from a stall on the street in the evenings. When Harriet's health improved through medicine from a local free clinic, she began helping her mother boil maize and serve it to customers. Harriet began schooling but was twice forced to leave because her mother could not pay her tuition. Harriet studied only through her second year of primary school before Nanyanzi sent her back to her father in Seeta hoping he could continue to fund Harriet's education. Kigozi did not and Harriet languished in the village for several years. "Right from my childhood I used to not enjoy myself," Harriet says. "I wasn't that kind of person who could go and have fun. I don't remember ever being happy."

When Harriet was about 12 years old, her mother brought her back to Katwe. Harriet began the cycle again, in and out of school, constantly dogged by lack of funds, until she finally dropped out for good during her fourth year of primary school, known in Uganda as P4.

"As a child in school I desired to become a nurse," Harriet says. "I always admired them. The attire they used to put on and the lifestyle they led. I admired all their ways. I was very grieved when I had to drop out. I didn't have any hope of studying after I had become a big lady because I left school from a lower class. It could be embarrassing to study with the young ones."

Harriet dropped out of school before she had learned how to read or even to write her own name.

She returned to her mother's food stall. One of Harriet's regular customers was an older man, Godfrey Buyinza, who lived not far from her stall in Katwe. Buyinza would stop by daily to eat and talk with Harriet, often leaving her a little extra money in the transaction. The gratuity was an enticement, a form of seduction in the slums. Harriet began visiting Buyinza at his workplace and sometimes spending nights with him in the hope of continuing to curry his favor. In Katwe, there is often a fine line between courtship and prostitution.

At that time Buyinza was 37 years old, Harriet 15. Buyinza had a wife from whom he had separated and three children in a nearby village and just enough money to expand his family. In Uganda, men like Buyinza are known as "sugar daddies."

"That man could really be a good friend and I started spending more time with him," Harriet says. "Then I got him. I think it had come to six months when I was seeing him and that's when I got spoiled."

Harriet believes she was 16 when she gave birth to her first child. Her daughter was born around midnight, so Harriet called her Night. It was the time of the Bush War in Uganda, and Buyinza returned to his home village of Buyubu because Katwe was too unstable and men there were regularly abducted and forced to join the fighting. Harriet and Night stayed with Nanyanzi until months later when Nanyanzi spotted Buyinza back in Katwe. "My mother used to ask me, 'Where did the father of your child go?' " Harriet says. "So when the man had come back, my mother chased me away and I had to go and stay with the man."

Buyinza rented a house just outside of Katwe along Salaama Road and the three moved in as a family when Night was about a year old. Buyinza worked as a welder. Harriet found a job at a primary school called New African Child, where she cooked porridge and sold food in the school canteen.

"At first the situation was not very bad; though we were not well off at least we could meet some of the basic requirements to survive," Harriet says. "We lived well in our home and at times he could take me to his home village to visit. He didn't make much trouble because he was not a drug addict, he wasn't smoking or taking alcohol. He was just a soccer fan. By then we were all healthy. To me it was a good life."

Over the next ten years on Salaama Road, Harriet gave birth to three more children: Juliet, Brian, and Phiona. Buyinza proved to be a doting father who would often come home at lunchtime and take his children for a meal followed by a treat of sugarcane from a street vendor. In the evenings the family would sometimes go to the video hall to see a movie or take a walk to watch a neighborhood soccer game.

"One thing I remember about our father is that he loved us very much," Brian says. "At night I used to overhear him talking with our mother about how much he enjoyed his time with us."

Two months after giving birth to their fifth child, Richard, Harriet noticed Buyinza's appearance beginning to change. He was becoming gaunt. He stopped eating. Says Harriet, "I was worried and I asked him, 'Are you sick? Should you go to the hospital?' He wouldn't tell me anything. He said, 'Everything is fine.' But he kept changing for the worse. Then one day he disappeared. I had no idea where he was. He left us with nothing more than the money for one day. I became bitter because he said he wasn't sick, so I thought he'd abandoned us."

Harriet struggled on Salaama Road without her husband. The rent went unpaid and because she had left her job during her pregnancy, Harriet had no income. She was eventually evicted and took the kids to stay at her mother's house. Harriet sold the family's belongings to feed her children.

One day in the spring of 1999, about three months after Buyinza left, Harriet received a visit from one of Buyinza's daughters from his first marriage, who told Harriet that her husband was gravely ill. The daughter said that Buyinza was back in his home village, that Harriet and the children must go there right away, and she gave Harriet some money to transport the family to Buyubu. Everyone was shocked at how quickly Buyinza had deteriorated. He was a living cadaver, unable to speak, only able to weep as he extended a hand to touch the baby, Richard.

"I reached the village and I could not even recognize whether he was my husband because he had grown so thin," Harriet says. "I tried to take care of him, but the situation was hopeless. At that point I realized he had AIDS."

Buyinza had known he was dying of AIDS and could not bear to tell Harriet for fear she'd be worried that she had contracted the disease as well. Four days after his wife and children arrived in Buyubu, Godfrey Buyinza died.

"After the burial, my husband's family told me that I was not in position to look after the children," Harriet says. "Initially I refused, but they convinced me that I should leave the children there for some stability and I would go back to Katwe on my own to make plans for what we can do."

So Harriet returned to Kampala with Richard. She had been back in Katwe for just three weeks when Buyinza's daughter returned again to summon Harriet to Buyubu because her second child, Juliet, had fallen sick. By the time Harriet arrived, Juliet was dead. "Maybe Juliet was shocked by the death of her father because she loved him very much," Harriet says. "It may have been malaria, but I believe she didn't want to go on living without him." Juliet was buried beside her father in the family graveyard in Buyubu.

Harriet collected the rest of her family and brought them back to her mother's shack in the slum. Harriet feared for her life. She believed she too must have AIDS and wondered if she would live long enough to raise her four surviving children. Harriet had even begun to ponder suicide rather than suffer her husband's grisly fate. On the family's first night back together in Katwe, Harriet huddled with Night, Brian, Phiona, and Richard on the dirt floor of her mother's shack. "If I am to die," she whispered to them, "let me die with you, my children."

Chapter 2
Katende

Aidah Namusisi holds the only existing photograph of her daughter Firidah Nawaguma and grandson Robert Katende (far left). *The picture was taken shortly before Nawaguma's death.*

"I have no memory of my father," Katende says. "I am a bastard child. I don't know where I was born or when. My birth was not all that easy. My mom conceived me when she was still in secondary school. The man who is my dad was already married and had a family. I was told later that his wife was very angry. She said, 'If I get to see that kid, I will kill him.' "

Joseph Ssemakula was another sugar daddy. He was in his late 30s as he drove through the village of Kiboga, 125 kilometers north of Kampala, early one morning in 1981 and spotted Firidah Nawaguma walking with some friends down the side of the road toward Bamusuuta Secondary School. Ssemakula was smitten by the 14-year-old Firidah. He stopped his car and offered to give the children a ride to school.

"There was a valley the children used to

pass through before going up the hill to school," says Aidah Namusisi, Firidah's mother. "That man would put my daughter in the vehicle to help her go through that valley to reach school. He did that daily. It was a trick. Sometimes I would even be in bed sleeping and he would come and pick her up without me knowing and take her to school and that was the plan he laid."

Before long Joseph Ssemakula was arranging to meet Firidah Nawaguma after school and the young girl became pregnant. Fearing the wrath of her mother, Nawaguma ran away from home and began staying with an older brother.

"I tried to look for her and I could not find where she is and then this son of mine told me she is at his place," Namusisi says. "I continued to let her stay with her brother because I was concerned that she would run away again and she might go somewhere where I don't even know where she is."

So Nawaguma gave birth at her brother's home. She was 15 years old and she had a son. She called him Katende, the name taken from his father's clan. Ssemakula already had a wife and five children in another part of Kiboga and could not bring the boy into his home. So Nawaguma and the baby eventually moved in with Namusisi, but the teenage mother quickly became overwhelmed by the challenge of raising a child. "The moment she stopped breast-feeding him, then she gave him to me," Namusisi says. "She told me, 'Let me give you your grandson and you be with him.' "

Namusisi initially didn't understand why Nawaguma would give up her eight-month-old son, but then she learned that her daughter had met another man with a steady government job who wanted to marry her and help her resume her education, and Nawaguma feared that the man would not accept her baby.

So Katende lived with his grandmother in Kiboga, along with another infant boy, Julius Kiddu, a child that one of Namusisi's sons could not support. The trio lived a simple life. On most days Namusisi would wander deep into the bush, pick bananas, and then sell them in the village market to earn just enough money to feed the two children an evening meal that had to be finished before dark.

Namusisi, who was in her early 60s, had been caring for Katende and Kiddu in Kiboga for only a short time when she first heard gunfire in the distance. Rebel leader Yoweri Museveni and his forces, the National Resistance Army, were engineering an insurgency against Ugandan president Milton Obote, who had returned to power in 1980. The civil war would become known as Uganda's Bush War. The main theater of the war would be a region known as the Luwero Triangle. Kiboga rested smack in the center of that triangle. The menacing gunshots were quickly followed by the arrival of trucks carrying armed soldiers. "The rebels had just conquered our area," Namusisi says. "So we were all terrified. I was shaking. It was a war. I had never seen soldiers. I had these two tiny children. I didn't know where to go. I didn't know what to do with them. I called them to where I was and they sat close to me. I asked them, 'Where can we go and hide?' But they could not even talk because they were very young."

The following day dozens of Ugandan army vehicles full of soldiers began arriving from a nearby district. They came looking for Museveni and parked near Namusisi's home. The soldiers asked her questions and threatened her when she didn't answer, but they were not speaking her language, Luganda. Instead they were speaking Swahili, a language she did not understand.

After some time, Namusisi pointed to her children and then to her garden, pleading to be allowed to pick some vegetables to feed them. As she returned from the garden, a group of rebels entered the village and confronted the government troops. A firefight ensued. “I dropped the food, ran into a neighbor’s house, and started praying to God: ‘How about my children?’ ” Namusisi says. “I started crying because I thought those men had killed the children. But I found them alive. Then I told the children, ‘Okay, let us sit here. We can die from here together. They will find our bones here.’ ”

The fighting eventually shifted to another area and a local schoolteacher came to Namusisi’s shack imploring her to evacuate, insisting it would not be safe to spend the night in her home. Namusisi picked up a blanket and a saucepan and began walking, holding one child in each arm. She had initially planned to go to the local hospital, but there were government troops there looking for rebel casualties and Namusisi feared they might recognize her, so she kept walking until nightfall when she finally begged to be allowed into a stranger’s house. She and the two children stayed there for two weeks before she returned to her shack to find it had been ransacked by Obote’s troops. Namusisi began staying in her home again until one day when a Ugandan government soldier knocked on her door demanding that she lead him to a particular neighbor. Namusisi believed she would be killed if she refused. As she slowly walked toward the neighbor's home, soldiers shot at her feet to make her walk faster.

Says Namusisi, "The following morning a relative came and told me, 'You know this place is not really favorable to us. You saw how you were almost dying for nothing? We have to go and join another uncle. I will go first and try to find out where his hideout is and if I find him I will come back for you and we will join him.' He came back later and said, 'Let us go immediately.' "

Namusisi left Kiboga with the two infants, Katende and Kiddu. They encountered roadblocks from both sides of the war, but eventually reached the uncle in rebel territory.

"I had these two little children and we were running with the rebels through the bush," Namusisi says. "I had one piece of clothing that I used to carry with me to help me cover these kids. They would sleep on one portion then I used the other part to cover them up. If it rains, then it just rains on us until it stops raining. We used to look for grass to use for tea leaves and we ate nuts from the bush. The children were too small to know anything. Bullets were going over our heads and all they asked me is, 'Do you have food?' "

Namusisi, Katende, and Kiddu remained in the bush under rebel protection for two years, constantly on the move, flowing with the troop movements.

"We could camp in one area for some time and then the rebels would tell us that government soldiers were coming and the rebels would direct us to hide in another place," Namusisi says. "Sometimes we would go six or seven miles at a time, but I had to run to save our lives. I was always terrified and we used to pray together seriously because I knew we could be dying at any time."

Finally, one day the rebels began shooting their bullets into the sky. When Namusisi asked what was going on, the rebels told her that they had conquered the Luwero Triangle. Government troops had ceded the area and it was safe for her to go home to Kiboga. "When we returned to the village, people greeted us as ghosts," Namusisi says. "It was as if they assumed we were dead."

Whenever war refugees returned to Kiboga, they were told to register with the government in an attempt to determine who was still alive. Firidah Nawaguma, who had been working as a nurse at the hospital in

Kiboga, learned that her mother and son had returned. Dressed in her nurse's uniform, she rode a bicycle to meet them at the registrar's office. Initially, Nawaguma pedaled right past Katende, neither recognizing the other. But when Nawaguma spotted her mother, she knew which boy must be her son. Nawaguma sobbed as she ran to Katende, lifted him over her head with joy and hugged him. The young boy had no idea who the woman was until she said, "My son, I thought you were dead."

Holding her son for the first time in almost three years, Nawaguma carried him into the government office to register him. "This is Katende," Nawaguma told the registrar. "Robert Katende."

It was the first time Katende had ever heard his first name.

During the next year, Robert continued to live with his grandmother, rarely seeing his mother, even though she lived fewer than two kilometers away. He was a bastard child and his mother's husband would not permit Robert in his house.

After the war ended, Namusisi resumed selling bananas to earn a meager living. She would sometimes journey to Kampala by truck to sell her fruit to vendors at the outdoor markets in the city. Because she could not afford to send Robert and Julius to school and they would cry if she left them behind alone, Namusisi brought the two kids along. The three of them would ride atop the bananas in the back of the truck and when they needed a bathroom break, Robert would throw a banana over the top of the cab onto the road to signal the driver. Those trips were Robert's first connection to modern life in the city. Says Robert, "I found that you touch a wall and a light goes on. You touch a wall again and a light goes off. I thought, 'Eh, how is this possible?' " Another time during one of Kampala's regular power outages, Robert asked his grandmother, "When the power goes off, why do the cars still work?"

Nawaguma eventually left her husband and their four children and moved to Kampala, to the Nankulabye slum, in search of a better life. She also stopped working as a nurse, hoping to earn more money alongside her mother, shuttling back and forth between Kiboga and the capital city, supplying bananas to the Kampala markets. During one of Robert's trips to Kampala, Nawaguma told Namusisi, "You leave the boy here so he can start studying."

It took Robert some time to adjust to his

new life in the city. He had never before worn shoes, but his mother insisted he wear sandals so that he would not cut his feet on the broken glass and other debris that littered the slum. The boy complained bitterly about how the sandals made his feet feel. "This piece between my toes, it pains me," Robert told his mother.

Nawaguma valued education and sent Robert to school, where he began to learn English. Raised speaking only Luganda, the most widely spoken language in Uganda, it took Robert some time to catch up with the other children who had been in school for several years, but before long he started performing at their level. "My mom was proud of me, especially my math," Robert says. "I used to do numbers very well."

During the holidays, Nawaguma would send Robert to Kiboga to deliver goods to his grandmother and other relatives. While in the village, Robert would get a chance to act as a bushman. He was given a small spear and taught how to help with hunting warthogs. "The adults would place us children where they don't want an animal to pass and then tell us to make noise and we'd scare the animal toward where it is silent and where the trap is," Robert says. "They cautioned us if we don't make enough noise, the animal will come and kill us, so we had to ensure that we made enough noise. For us it was fun. It was like a game."

By the time Robert had reached P4 his mother could not afford his school fees. She arranged with a friend who taught at Robert's school to sneak him in through a back door. On Robert's first day of class, this teacher asked Robert to come with him for a math lesson in P5 before he could enroll him in P4. The teacher gave a lesson in long division, but before completing the lesson, he was called away from the room by another teacher. The other children began the exercise, so Robert pulled out his notebook as well, because it was math and he thought he might be able to do it.

When the teacher returned to the classroom nearly an hour later, he sat at his desk and called for the students to bring him their notebooks to be marked. Eventually Robert took his work to him. "The teacher said, 'Oh, Robert, I'm sorry, I forgot that you were in class. You have done the work? Let me have a look at it.' "

Robert handed him his book and the teacher was surprised to see that he had solved nine of the ten equations correctly.

"Then the teacher said, 'Okay, everyone

open your books and if you failed a number that this kid has got right, I'm going to cane you,' " Robert recalls. "He went to the first desk. 'You failed two numbers, two strokes. You failed five numbers, five strokes. This kid is supposed to be in P4 and you are failing them!' I was ahead of almost the whole class. It made my day unfavorable in the school. Everyone looked at me with a very ugly face and I had no friends."

The teacher then asked Robert if he would like to remain in P5 because that would be more convenient for him. Robert agreed, despite his unpopularity with the other students.

But skipping P4 proved problematic for Robert in subjects other than math. He struggled in science and social studies, mostly because he lacked a firm grasp of the English language, which was used for all of the lessons. "I remember one time we were asked to tell the internal parts of the body and I had never seen these before," Robert says. "I left the whole paper blank and I got caned. On my next test, in social studies, I didn't want to hand in a blank paper, so anything I could think of I wrote in. I didn't understand what the question was asking, but I wrote in: *President Museveni.* For another answer I just wrote in *Kam-*

pala. Whatever I could think of, just to fill in every space."

In P3 Robert had ranked first in his class. In P5 he was struggling near the bottom. By that time his mother had remarried and given birth to another child. Nawaguma and her new husband were selling timber and she was prospering financially. For Robert's P6 year, Nawaguma was planning to send Robert to boarding school because she was not comfortable with him staying at a house filled with her husband's children from a previous marriage.

When Nawaguma and Robert walked together around the slum, she had a difficult time convincing people that she was Robert's mother. They thought she must be his older sister because she was still so young. In time, the two developed a very close relationship. "At first I didn't know what a mother was or what a mother was supposed to do, but whenever we were together I knew it felt so good," Robert says. "We had a connection and I grew a great love for her, because I was having a better life."

A month before the end of his P5 year in 1990, eight-year-old Robert was studying for final exams when his mother began making regular visits to the hospital. She had been sick for several months and had tried various treatments, including local herbs from a witch doctor to combat a potential curse placed on her by the vengeful wife of Robert's father. Doctors at the hospital eventually diagnosed Nawaguma's condition as advanced breast cancer and Robert noticed that one of his mother's breasts was nearly detached from her body. Namusisi came from Kiboga to look after her daughter.

One day after school Robert was playing in the slum while his mother was at the hospital for treatment when a friend came to Robert and told him his mother had died. "All I can remember is I was shocked," Robert says. "I stopped playing and I just ran off crying until I reached home and my grandmother was there and she was also crying. She said, 'Katende, my son, who are you left with?' "

At his mother's funeral in her father's home village of Mubango, 20 kilometers outside of Kampala, Robert slowly approached Nawaguma's casket. "I reached her and it looked like she was just sleeping, so I shook her and tried to wake her up," Robert says. "When she didn't wake up, I cried at the top of my voice. I was in the deepest sorrow. I had a lot running in my mind. I felt like killing myself. When people put my mom in the ground, I knew all was over. I had lost everything I had. When she died, I believed that was the end of me."

Lying in a hospital bed just days before her death, Nawaguma turned to her cousin Jacent with a last request.

"I know I'm going to die," Nawaguma told Jacent. "I have five kids and I've just given birth to a sixth. I know the sixth one will be taken care of by the father. Even the other four, their dad is there. But I'm feeling so bad for my son Robert and I don't know how it will go for him when I die. I request if you do anything, don't allow Robert to go back to my mother in Kiboga. If you allow Robert to go back, he's just going to hunt wild animals."

"That is the sentiment which I think turned my life," Robert says. "Because of that statement, my Auntie Jacent took pity on me."

As Nawaguma's funeral concluded, Jacent had not yet decided what to do, but her late cousin's words kept ringing in her ears. She looked at the boy with no shirt and torn pants and she came to him and said, "Robert, I'm taking you to my place. You come."

Jacent was already caring for 12 children,

six of her own and six orphans who lived in a ramshackle bunkhouse in her backyard. She and her husband lived comfortably in a middle-class neighborhood in Kampala. Jacent worked in a bank and her husband had a job with the government. When Robert returned to Jacent's home he walked into a sitting room, sunk down into a comfortable couch with a rug beneath his bare feet and sat mesmerized for two hours by the first color television he had ever seen. When it came time for dinner, he was served a plate of meat and carrots, but because he didn't know what carrots were, he sorted them out. "After dinner I was so sorrowful, and I went out into the yard and cried because I didn't know what was next," Robert says. "Even though the house was nice, I felt very insecure. I don't remember how I stabilized."

For weeks, Robert would ask Jacent questions about why his mother was taken from him. He could not shake the feeling that evil forces were involved. "When she died I was convinced that it was because my dad's wife had gone to a witch doctor to put a curse on her and I felt like at that moment if I had seen that lady I would have killed her, even it meant I would be killed as well," Robert says. "I was ready to go. I couldn't find that lady and I had no way of finding out where she was. I was so small that I don't even know if I could have physically killed her, but my heart was strongly telling me to do it."

In her will, Nawaguma had left behind enough money to support her son through two years of school. Robert returned to P5 to complete his exams, but he couldn't concentrate through his grief. When he received the P5 report form, he was ranked in the 66th position out of 72 students in the class. He told himself, "This can't be."

On the day he received his report, Robert walked two kilometers to the city center. He walked rather than ride a bus so he would have enough money to buy a red pen; Robert was determined to improve his position. The red ink in the pen he bought was a lighter shade than the pen used to write the marks, but Robert went ahead and scribbled over one 6, thus upgrading him from 66th to 6th. Then he folded up his report form and walked home.

Robert had been staying with Aunt Jacent only for about three weeks and was nervous about her reaction to his report form. He placed it on the dining table and promptly left the room. When Jacent looked at the form, she noticed immediately that it had been altered. She confirmed her suspicion by examining the individual course grades and realizing they could not possibly add up. She called Robert into the room and asked, "What happened to your report?"

"What do you mean?" Robert said, growing more anxious.

"What happened to your report?"

"Auntie, I'm sorry, I rubbed my report."

"Tell me why and bring a cane."

Robert first ran to the bunkhouse and picked up his report form for P3. Then he got a cane. He had the stick in one hand and the report in the other. Jacent told Robert she was going to cane him, not because he performed poorly in school, but because he tampered with the form. Robert begged forgiveness, showing Jacent how he had finished first in P3, explaining how he had skipped P4, and reminding her that he had taken his final exams just days after the death of his mother. Jacent took pity on him and put the cane away.

During holidays with no school, Robert and the other orphans would wake up at 4 A.M. to travel to the family's farm to do what is locally known as "the digging." They would work all day in the fields, plowing and tilling with hoes and cutting the grass back with scythes, all the while hoping to avoid encounters with the venomous snakes that populate the Ugandan farmland. They would dig until dusk and then sleep six people in one tiny shack. They would often do this for a week before collecting enough food to carry back home for the rest of the family.

"Katende turned out to be a hard-working, obedient boy," Jacent says. "If you gave him a job, he would never say he was tired like the others. He would always finish his work on time."

Whenever Robert and the other orphans returned from the digging, they were reminded by Jacent's other kids that the orphans were a class below in the house hierarchy. "Instead of saying 'Welcome back,' they would say, 'Have you brought me back some maize?' " Robert says. "Then you go outside and cry and you endure. It would be really hard on you, but you had to swallow it up."

Robert viewed his situation as survival of the fittest. At breakfast, Robert was often served a banana, but the portion never filled his stomach, so one morning he pretended that bananas gave him a stomachache. Aunt Jacent started serving him cornmeal instead, which provided a more filling breakfast.

"It was all about *How do I keep going?*"

Robert says. "The first three months I would go in the corner and shed tears. I remember once when my aunt told me to give my clothes to some of the smaller kids because they didn't fit me anymore. Those were the clothes that my mom had bought for me new in the city center and so that was hard on me as a child. I knew those clothes would never be replaced. After that I had only one shirt that I wore every day and I became known as 'the kid in the red shirt.' "

Another orphan, Jacent, who was five years older than Robert, was so favored by Aunt Jacent that she had taken her name. The young Jacent was always abusing Robert. One time when she was preparing the daily tea, Robert found a cockroach in his cup. He knew Jacent had put it there, but he could not report her. He poured out his tea and didn't tell anyone.

"I don't like to remember such times," Robert says. "There were times when I asked myself, 'What will I be?' When you've lost a person you've been depending on entirely and then you are just moved to a different place, a lot of bad things happen when you are where you are not supposed to be. You have to submit to anyone who is in that place and they will never be wrong when you are there. You are always the one to blame. I remember one day someone said, 'There is not enough sugar for all of us and it is because of the new people who have come in. Go away, Robert. You shouldn't be here.' That was hard to hear when I had no place else. Every rebuke made me think, 'Is it because I don't belong here?' That really affected me. I prayed, 'Lord, I pray that I get a better life.' "

Says Aunt Jacent, "When Robert used to quarrel with my children he would tell them, 'Do you think I want to be like this? Do you think I wanted my mother to die?' That showed that he was suffering very much."

Robert sometimes considered surrendering to his pain. "Once I was almost tempted and if I had the money I would have left this life," Robert says. "I felt it was better for me to die than go on. I thought, 'This life is not worth anything to me. My mom is dead and now she is at peace. Why don't I join her?' I knew a way of accessing rat poison, but I could not afford it. I could not afford to die."

This is not who I am.

Robert kept repeating that phrase to himself every time he looked at his rubbed report from P5. He was at a crossroads. He needed a reason to live and it would have to come from within. Fortunately, he possessed the one trait so lacking in the other orphans, the one commodity that nobody, not even his tormentor, Jacent, could take from him. Pride.

It happened in an instant early in his first term of P6 while he was working on a math assignment. Robert worried that he had again fallen behind his schoolmates. On all of his exercises up to that point in P6, he had asked for help from friends, because he was not completely confident in himself.

"But that one I did myself," Robert says. "I thought, 'Let me just do what I know.' I thought I might fail, but it came back with eleven correct out of twelve. It was my comeback. I thought, 'Wow, am I the one who did this?' Now I thought I could do anything. I became even more serious. I started really working hard to reach my potential."

After the first term of P6, Robert ranked 37th in his class. By the end of his P6 year he had improved to third in his class. In P7 there were no grades, but he placed in the highest division of his class.

In 1993, 11-year-old Robert attended his first year of secondary school, S1, at Lubiri

Secondary School, part of a class of 240 students. When report forms were distributed at the end of the first term, Robert took a quick peek and saw "1ST." In his haste, he misread it as "15th." He was thrilled. He folded up the report and went to play after school with some friends. "At one point somebody said, 'Who was the first?' " Robert recalls. "Nobody knew. So everybody was showing their reports. I gave mine to them and then I continued playing, because I knew I was the fifteenth. One said, 'Hey, you guys. Robert's a thief. He was the first and he's just not telling us!' I said, 'What? No, I was fifteenth.' Then I looked again."

Robert quickly picked up his books and ran all five kilometers back to Aunt Jacent's house. When he got there he announced to everyone, "I was the first!" The other kids looked at his report form and said, "Wow, he was the first?" Some of them warned him that the second term would be much harder and if he did not perform well in that term everybody would assume he had been copying.

"My attitude was that every day I see 240 heads and I think they are all trying to take my spot," Robert says. "I must not rest." Robert finished first in the second term of

S1. First in S2. First in S3. First in S4.

He liked being first. Sure. Finishing first in his class felt like winning. He enjoyed the competition, even thrived on it, but Robert viewed academics clinically. He saw it as a means to an end. He earned those marks as much for other people, living and dead, as he did for himself. Math and science gave him satisfaction. They did not give him joy. Only one competition gave him joy. Only one competition helped him stave off his demons. Only one competition helped him truly escape. Only one competition was all for himself.

Soccer.

When Robert Katende ran down the soccer field, he felt as if he were running away from his troubles, leaving them far behind, and when he scored a goal, well, that was his personal bliss. Playing soccer was the only time he completely stopped thinking about the myriad problems in his life. "Growing up, soccer gave me all of my happiest moments," Robert says. "Whenever I was on the soccer field, it was the only time I felt at peace."

Robert had first played the game as a child in Kiboga when he and his grandmother repatriated there after the war. The soccer ball then was made with dried banana leaves bound together with vines. Robert and some friends would build two small piles of bricks or take off their shirts and use them to mark the goals. They had no idea what a real soccer goal looked like. They usually played on a dirt compound in the village pocked with trees in the middle of the field, which acted as extra defenders. When it came time to pick teams, Robert's friends always wanted to play on his side.

"I was very tiny and at first I always used my right leg to kick," Robert says. "I had a close friend and I admired him because he could kick with either leg. I used to try to imitate this guy and I kicked with my left leg and fell down badly and I believed the leg could never learn to kick that ball. Then one time I was playing and I hit a ball with my left leg and I scored and that was the end of my game. I ran right home to tell my grandma that I had scored with my left leg."

When Robert came to Kampala, his soccer balls became pint-size milk cartons softened by hot water that would be blown up and supported by rubber bands. Whenever that "pinter ball" struck the barbed wire that lined the schoolyard it popped and the game was over. Robert carried a small pinter ball in his rucksack and he and his schoolmates used to play during every break and every lunchtime. By the time Robert reached S5 he had a reputation as one of the best players in the school. Robert's friends told the school's games master about him, but when the games master came to recruit Robert for the school team, Robert declined because he had no soccer shoes and he had never played with a real soccer ball. He was afraid that kicking a real ball would hurt his bare feet. He also feared playing against much older and bigger boys. But when the games master caned him, Robert changed his mind.

In his very first intramural game, Robert, the only player on the field playing in bare feet, scored the only goal in a 1-0 victory for his team. "I became a celebrity in the school," Robert says. "I was a hero. Everyone at school assembly sang my name in praise."

A prolific scorer, Robert humbly explained to his teammates, "There are two goals on the field. I will handle the offense. You all handle the defense."

Robert scored as many as six goals in one match. He would even take requests to score goals. "If three kids in school would ask me to score a goal, I would score one for each of them," Robert says. "Sometimes I would score and then run to the side of the field to the person who requested a goal and say to them 'That is your goal.' Another time the school offered a full crate of soda if I scored, so I scored and shared the crate of twenty-four sodas with my whole team."

Robert's favorite move was to balance the ball on the toes of his bare foot, flip it over the head of an unsuspecting defender, and then break in alone on the goalkeeper. One day he arrived in class to see that one of his schoolmates had drawn a picture of him on the blackboard. In place of his right foot, a spoon was drawn. So Robert's nickname became *kajiiko,* "the spoon."

His skill became so well-known around Kampala that when Lubiri didn't have a game scheduled, he would sometimes play for other secondary schools on a mercenary basis. The other school would pay Robert a few shillings plus transport, and when he arrived the coach would pluck a uniform off of another player and give it to Robert, and he would usually lead that team to victory.

"Robert was a talented young player," says Barnabas Mwesiga, Uganda's former national team coach. "He had some speed. He had good shots. He could dribble. Those are the three attributes that make a good striker. According to our standards, he had the skill at that time to someday make our national team."

At one point, Robert was invited to a training camp for Uganda's Under-15 national team, but he couldn't attend because it was during the holidays and Aunt Jacent insisted that he do the digging. "At home there was no soccer allowed," Robert says. "They had no idea I was a good player. My Aunt Jacent did not approve of sports. For sure, when I was on the soccer field, I felt like I could do anything I wanted with the ball. If I had more support, I believe I could have played professionally."

Robert watched the World Cup every four years and Uganda TV's taped broadcasts of Bundesliga games from Germany on Saturdays with Aunt Jacent's husband, Amir, studying the moves of players like Jürgen Klinsmann and Rudi Völler.

"I used to have this vision where I could see myself walking up from a valley to a beautiful green soccer field like you just see in a dream and they are playing very well and I remember I could join other people and we would play very serious games and I was making goals. I always wondered where this field was, but I definitely know it was not in Uganda because we don't have fields like that. I looked forward for that always and I knew maybe it would happen."

Soccer allowed Robert to dream. It gave him joy. It became his identity.

"I remember one time after a soccer game I thought, 'If I had killed myself I would not have experienced the fun of scoring those goals. I think it was wise not to do what I was planning.' "

Soccer gave him life. Then soccer nearly took it away.

Moments before the game began, Robert walked over to his friend Allan Sayire and asked, "How many goals can I score for you?"

"If you score one goal," Sayire said, "that will be a blessing."

A 15-year-old three weeks into his first term of S5, Robert was his school's star striker. Early in an intramural game at Lubiri, Robert received a pass along the right wing. He spooned the ball over his defender at the edge of the goalkeeper's box and then sprinted to reach the ball before the goalie. The ball took one big bounce into the air. Robert leaped as high as he could. The goalkeeper lunged at the ball. Robert headed the ball over the goalkeeper's outstretched hands, just as the keeper attempted to punch the ball to safety. The goalkeeper's punch caught Robert's jaw instead, flipping Robert upside down. Robert landed on his head. He doesn't remember anything after that.

The ball trickled into the vacated goal and Robert's schoolmates stormed the field as they often did after goals to congratulate the scorer. But when they reached Robert still prone on the ground, they noticed blood on his face and backed off anxiously. Robert appeared to be unconscious, but his legs were still kicking in spasms. Robert's schoolmates feared that he was taking his last breaths.

The school van was quickly summoned and Robert was driven to nearby Rubaga Hospital. Doctors there were ill-equipped for the severity of Robert's injury, so they ordered that Robert be taken to Mulago, the government hospital. Robert's condition was so grave that they didn't even take the time to transfer him to an ambulance. The school van careened through the congested streets, barreling straight over roundabouts, the driver madly honking his way through Kampala's crawling traffic. By the time Robert arrived at Mulago, he had lapsed into a coma. The doctors did whatever they could to help keep him alive.

Before that school year began, Robert had

been forced to leave Aunt Jacent's home because she had retired from her job and could no longer support the orphans. Robert had moved back in with his grandmother, who had relocated to Kampala's Kasubi slum upon hearing rumors of another rebel insurgency in Kiboga. On the day of the soccer accident, Namusisi waited for Robert at home, but he never returned. Mulago had called Aunt Jacent instead, but she refused to come to the hospital, scared of what she might find there. "I feared to go because they said he was not going to live," Jacent says. "I told them to go to the other cousin of mine and let her look after him, because I had told Robert to stop playing sports and now you see what has happened."

Robert's Aunt Dez received a call from Mulago Hospital at around 8 P.M. "I will never forget that call," Aunt Dez says. "They told me, 'Your son has been in an accident. Come to the hospital right away. You are likely to find him dead.' "

Aunt Dez rushed to Mulago and found Robert in a critical state. She spent the night standing vigil at Robert's bedside, checking if he was still breathing. She kept touching his face to feel for warmth and wiping away blood that seeped out of his mouth and nose.

Suddenly at around 6 A.M., Robert's body began trembling. He emerged from the coma in agonizing pain. He had no idea where he was. "I woke up that following morning and saw a ceiling," Robert says. "My last memory was on the soccer field at school, so I thought maybe this was a classroom, but I realized that we did not have a classroom with such a ceiling."

As Robert looked around, he saw his Aunt Dez, a teacher from Lubiri, and several doctors wearing white. He also noticed his soccer uniform covered in blood. "Where am I?" Robert asked. "How did I come here?"

When Robert tried to sit up, his jaw throbbed in terrible pain. Doctors began injecting him with painkillers and rushed him off for an X-ray. He had suffered multiple fractures to his jaw. Doctors performed an operation to seal his jaw shut, after which Robert overheard one of the nurses say, "Wow, that kid is alive? We thought he was dead for sure."

That same morning at the Lubiri school assembly, the headmaster began with an announcement about Robert by saying, "Sad news . . ." Before he could finish, wails rang out throughout the audience from students who thought Robert had died. Then the schoolmaster continued: ". . . you know Robert our soccer player was injured badly and he's admitted at Mulago."

School was canceled and nearly 100 students made the trek across Kampala to Mulago to see if Robert was still alive. They were surprised to find him awake and in fair condition, although unable to speak because his jaw had been wired shut.

Robert had some friends at school who were born-again Christians and one of them asked him, "Robert, you are so talented, you are a good soccer player, you are a good mathematician, you are the best in class, God has gifted you, so why don't you get saved?"

Another visiting student told him, "We thought you were dead. We just thank God that you are alive. But Robert, do you know why you are still alive? If you had died, where would you have gone? Nobody knows the day, the hour when they will die. Why don't you get saved?"

Robert, who had attended church regularly since his days as a boy in Kiboga but had never taken religion very seriously, pondered those questions for some time. Then he nodded.

"That is when I gave my life to Christ and accepted Christ as my personal savior,"

Robert says. "Just in case I died, then I could go to Heaven. I was scared to go to Hell. I thought, 'I better do this and be ready because it seems like anytime I can die.' "

Robert's jaw would remain wired shut for a month. He would spend three months in the hospital.

Doctors told Robert he would never play soccer again.

Nine months later, Robert was juggling the ball. He regularly suffered excruciating headaches, but he wasn't about to give up soccer. He couldn't. Soccer sustained him, both emotionally and, more importantly, financially. Soccer was his passion. It was also his job.

After his injury, Aunt Dez couldn't stand by and watch Robert try to nurse himself back to health while living with his grandmother in the slum, so she took Robert home from the hospital, fulfilling a promise to look after him that she, like her cousin Jacent, had made to Nawaguma on her deathbed. Robert stayed with Aunt Dez for five months. Aunt Dez lived in a small but stable house at the edge of the bush in the outskirts of Kampala, where monkeys snuck in from the forest to raid the vegetable garden and could only be turned back by stones thrown by Robert and his three new "sisters." Robert cooked and cleaned the house daily. He worshipped Aunt Dez, who strongly resembled Nawaguma. He even called her "Mama," just as he always did Aunt Jacent.

Robert had missed a full year of school and couldn't return to Lubiri School because Aunt Jacent could no longer afford his tuition there. Jacent offered Robert 100,000 shillings, the equivalent of about $80 at that time, toward a new school.

Progressive Secondary School Bweyogerere was a private school that sought academically gifted students. The registrar there looked at Robert's report forms and offered him a place with a tuition of 180,000 shillings. Robert said he had only 100,000. Then the registrar was informed of Robert's talent on the soccer field, and he was enrolled.

At Progressive, Robert organized a soccer team that competed against other schools for the first time. When second term of S5 arrived, students could campaign for leadership positions, but the school didn't allow day schoolers to participate. The headmaster wouldn't bend the rules but recognized Robert's leadership potential, so he invited him to join the school's boarding section. Robert tied his mattress to a friend's bicycle and walked it five kilometers from Aunt Dez's home to the boarding house. Robert was elected the school's sports minister and was placed in charge of recruiting players, scheduling games, and arranging transportation.

Still, Robert had little money and was often hungry. Sometimes one of the school matrons, another woman who Robert referred to as "Mama," would give him a plate of food from her home within the school grounds. The school's headmaster came to admire Robert so much that he said, "If you lack sugar, come see me." Robert looked forward to visiting days because a friend's family would often invite him to eat with them. Robert never had any visitors on those days, except one afternoon when an uncle stopped by just to verify that Robert was actually attending the school. "My relatives thought I was deceiving them," Robert says. "They thought, 'How can he go to a school that is so expensive and moreover the boarding section?' "

The first time Robert played soccer for Progressive in S5 he led his team to victory in a regional tournament. During his two seasons there he acted as his team's captain, its leading scorer, and also its coach. During a game near the end of the second term of his S6 year, Robert was tripped and fell awkwardly, dislocating his right wrist. He was taken to Mulago Hospital, where doctors planned to operate, but fearing a mistake that could leave him lame, Robert asked instead that they pop the wrist back into place. He planned to rehabilitate it through massage. With his final exams quickly approaching — tests that would determine whether Robert could continue his education at university on a government scholarship — he trained his left hand to write the essays. But when it came time for the exams, he found the left hand to be too slow, so he endured the pain of writing with his right hand. Each time it swelled up, he would shake it out to restore the feeling in his fingers.

During an anxious six-month waiting period to learn his marks, Robert earned money by playing soccer for a club team sponsored by Pepsi. He also did the digging at Aunt Dez's garden, washed cars, and worked as a porter carrying huge loads of bricks up stairs at a building site. He even became an entrepreneur, purchasing a cheap mobile phone and selling calls to people without phones. Finally, Robert returned to Progressive one day to learn his fate and was greeted by fellow students who had already discovered through an announcement at morning assembly that Robert had qualified for a scholarship. When they saw him that day, Robert was mobbed by some of his former soccer teammates who told him, "Robert, you made it!"

Robert had earned free tuition and room and board at Kampala's Kyambogo University. What Robert did not have was a direction. He didn't know what to do with his life and didn't have anybody to ask. One day during his first term at Kyambogo, Aunt Dez showed up to inform Robert that his father was gravely ill and had come to Kampala. Robert went to visit him. Seeing his father for the first time in more than ten years, Robert felt no emotional connection. Ssemakula barely recognized Robert as one of his many children. Robert suspects that when his father died a few months later, the cause was AIDS. At his father's funeral, it struck Robert how much he lacked a male role model in his life.

"Even though I had rarely seen my dad over the years, I always took some comfort that he was there," Robert says. "His death bothered me a lot. Now I was truly an orphan. At the funeral, I prayed, 'Lord, you are my God, you are my Father. Perhaps you will send someone to help see me through.' "

Shortly after his father's passing, Miracle came. The Miracle Football Club showed up one day to play Robert's Pepsi Club in a friendly match. Miracle played very well that day, but what really captured Robert's attention occurred after the match. The Miracle players invited anyone within earshot to join them for testimony. They said they were recruiting for the Lord. Robert watched carefully as the Miracle players converted people right before his eyes. Afterward he asked some of them if he could get involved with their team. A meeting was arranged with Miracle's coach, Aloysius Kyazze.

Kyazze had once been the captain of the Ugandan national soccer team. A staunch defender. No nonsense. A coach on the field.

"Robert caught my eyes as a coach because I saw in him a great potential as a striker and I passed on whatever I could to help him become a better player, but what impressed me more is that he was very attentive whenever it came to spiritual discipline, devotions, hearing my testimony,"

Kyazze says. "He didn't ask for anything in exchange like other players who would ask me, 'What will I get? What can I expect?' Robert never thought he would get his daily bread from Miracle. He believed he was there to benefit spiritually, psychologically, and socially and that really touched my heart. I believe he could have played soccer for the national team, but he chose instead to be there for the Lord."

Robert played for Miracle during his two years at Kyambogo University. Because of his studies, he was never able to practice with the team, but in games he was the club's top scorer. He scored in almost every match, sometimes two or three goals, and the team improved significantly with his addition. He was also getting more and more comfortable with the proselytizing after the games and the club's overall brotherhood. "I'll never forget at halftime of one match with Miracle when Aloysius put his hands on my shoulders and drew me close," Robert says. "He was giving me words of encouragement and at that time it felt like I had found a home."

When Robert graduated from Kyambogo at age 20 with a diploma in civil engineering, he had been promised a job with Uganda's National Water Company, because he had done his training there as an engineer. However, when he went to the offices of the National Water Company asking for a job, he was told no positions were available. Once again Robert was homeless. He had to leave his room at the university and didn't want to go back to Aunt Dez's house because there was no steady work there. He had a small allowance from the university for his industrial training, so he was able to rent a room. He owned little more than a cup, a fork, a mattress, and a blanket. After several months, Robert was struggling to find enough money to eat. Following his games with Miracle, Kyazze would give Robert cab fare home and Robert would walk instead so he could afford to buy some food.

On Christmas Eve of 2002, Robert was at a low point. He wanted to visit his Aunt Dez, to be around the closest thing to family that he had left, but he had no money to travel there. He had nothing to eat. Kyazze called him that night and invited Robert to his house. Robert walked three kilometers to Kyazze's home, where he was given a meal and 10,000 shillings as a Christmas gift.

"Sometimes it's embarrassing to describe how far people's lives have fallen when they come to you," Kyazze says. "Robert came when he was almost having nothing, not even a coin for food. It was clear to me that this was a young man who greatly needed help. My heart was there to listen to the issues he was going through and I extended a hand to him because I love to share with people I see as my children."

Robert used some of the money to visit his Aunt Dez's home for Christmas. "The family was having fun and people were drinking beers and they gave me one," Robert says. "As a born-again Christian, I could not drink the beer, but I didn't want them to be unhappy that I wouldn't take the beer, so I kept it. I went home with the bottle of beer because I couldn't throw it out."

It wasn't long before Robert's Christmas money ran out. "I was very hungry and thirsty and I asked myself, 'What can I do?' " Robert says. "I couldn't drink water because I couldn't boil it without kerosene and I couldn't afford to fall sick. I was in a puzzle. Then I saw something. I saw the beer. I said, 'Lord can I take this beer?' I had heard some Christians say that if you are going to die, you do what you must to survive. I sat alone in my room and thought, 'Lord, I'm going to take this beer.' I poured it in my cup and I looked at it for some time. Then I just closed my eyes and swallowed it down. All of it."

The following day Robert recycled his empty beer bottle in exchange for two mangos that would sustain him for the next several days. It was at that point, when Robert had exhausted all of his resources and was beginning to lose hope, that Kyazze told him he wanted Robert to interview for a job with an American ministry called Sports Outreach Institute, an organization that works to provide relief and religion through sports to the world's poorest people. Kyazze worked for Sports Outreach and coached the Good News Football Club, which ministered after games, much like Miracle Football Club. Robert had found his lifeline.

"I saw Robert coming to the position as a raw material which God needed to be prepared," Kyazze says. "He was not a servant at the time he first came to me. No, no, no. He was a young boy. He needed shaping and guidance and direction. When we are called to serve, there must be a process and then later on we ascend."

After nearly a year under Kyazze's tutelage the boy had become a man. Robert had become Katende again. Katende and Kyazze made a good team. The striker and the defender. Kyazze became Katende's mentor. His surrogate father. Kyazze taught him how to teach. Katende would study Kyazze's every move, how he built relationships, his immense patience, how he solved problems. Katende recalls one day during a soccer game when a vicious tackle occurred. Kyazze stopped the game, brought the players together, and made it clear, without raising his voice, that reckless and dangerous play would not be tolerated. Katende admired how whenever Kyazze spoke, he captured the attention of everybody around him. Katende gradually learned how to command that level of respect. Katende also admired Kyazze's extraordinary compassion. On paydays, Kyazze would sometimes slip Katende 3,000 shillings when he knew he was only owed 1,000.

After Katende's training ended in 2003, he was assigned to Katwe to institute a program for children in the slum that involved ministering through soccer. Sports Outreach had designed a blueprint for the project. Kyazze had taught Katende the bullet points, but he'd also stressed that in sports ministry there is room for improvisation. He told Katende that he would have to constantly adjust to the needs of the kids.

Katende had never been to the Nkere district of Katwe where the project would be staged. On his first day there, he arrived with two brand-new red soccer balls provided by Sports Outreach. Walking through the alleyways of the slum carrying those balls, Katende attracted curious children who then followed him to a dump site which had been chosen for a makeshift soccer field. There were only a few children playing at first, but word spread quickly about the coach with the new red balls and before long 60 kids of all ages were showing up every afternoon to play soccer with Katende.

The games were followed by testimony, during which Katende would ask some of the kids to share the challenges they were enduring in their lives, and he would share stories from his own past. At the end of each session Katende distributed to each of the children small pieces of sugarcane, which he paid for from his own pocket. The project was full of street kids. Kids who didn't go to school. Many were orphans. Some were homeless. All of them were desperate for guidance in their own way.

"Some of the kids challenged me initially, but I was certain I could handle any bad behavior because I had lived in the situation they were in," Katende says. "I told them I was not there to judge them, but to love them. I found that if you treated them with respect, you could open up a lot in their hearts. I learned not to always do what I thought was best, but to follow the trend of the children. I thought I was teaching them, but they were also teaching me."

After about a year running the soccer project, Katende was troubled that some kids didn't participate in the games. Ivan Mutesasira was among the children who watched from the sideline every day. At one point Katende asked Ivan, "Why aren't you taking part in the game? No one cares if you are very good. We are just learning."

"Coach," Ivan said. "I fear soccer because I have been hurt before and I could easily break my bones and I don't have the money to take care of my medication."

Katende knew it was time for him to improvise as Kyazze had suggested. "That's when I asked myself, 'These children who are not interested in soccer, how can I involve them?' " Katende says. "I just needed a platform to build a relationship and, like soccer, I needed to be able to play it with them to build that trust stronger."

For about a month, Katende pondered other options. He considered draughts, a Ugandan board game, but it was considered a contest for gamblers. He thought of relay races, but decided that would quickly become monotonous. He thought of basketball, but he didn't have a ball or a goal. When he thought about what he did have available, an idea struck him. A game so foreign that there was no word for it in his native language. An idea so strange that he wondered if it was even possible. "I asked myself, 'Can this really work?' " Katende recalls. "With their education and their environment, can these kids really play this game?"

Chapter 3
Pioneers

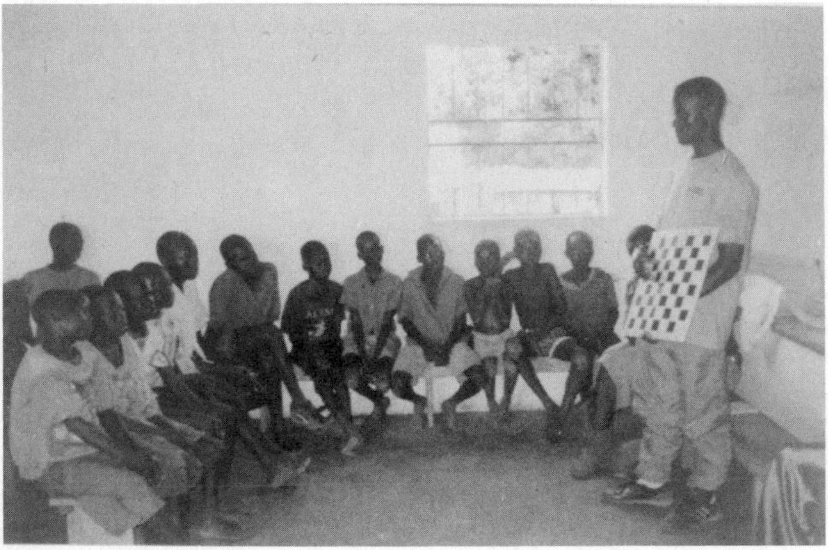

Robert Katende teaches children how to play the game in the early days of his chess project. He came to believe chess is the best tool to help slum kids learn how to overcome the many obstacles in their daily lives.

One day after soccer, Katende huddled the children of his Katwe project around him and asked them, "Would you like to learn a new game?"

Katende was pleased to see Ivan Mutesasira and many of the other soccer spectators among the 20 children who gathered.

"What game?" one child asked.

"Chess," Katende said.

There were blank stares. None of the children had ever heard of it.

Then one of them spoke up. "Oh, I know this game," he said. "You chase a person around the compound until you catch him."

"No," Katende said. *"Chess."*

Katende pulled a vinyl chessboard out of his back pocket and searched for a flat spot on the barren ground of the dump site. Then he produced a plastic bag and emptied its contents onto the board. The children examined the chessboard, counting eight squares on each edge, 64 total, alternating light and dark. They counted out the 32 pieces, 16 black and 16 white. Katende then picked up a knight and asked them what it looks like. "They said it was a goat," Katende recalls. "I told them that it looks like a horse, but they had never seen a horse. So we called it a dog. *Embwa* in Luganda. We were just having fun. They really did not learn anything that first day. I was just trying to capture their imagination so they would come back the following day excited to learn."

The next day's chess session began with one of the children asking, "Coach, how will we ever get to know all of these thirty-two pieces and how they move?"

Katende came up with a plan. He asked the children to group pieces together that looked the same, regardless of color. Six piles were formed. Katende then separated one piece from each pile and told them, "If you learn to move these six pieces, you shall have learned all of the remaining pieces."

The next day he told them the names of each piece, writing each of the names in the dirt for emphasis. Then he asked the kids to choose a piece and share its name. After learning the names, they talked about their positioning on the board. Katende kept the lessons slow. Simple. After soccer each day, he devoted only about 40 minutes to chess to try to avoid any potential burnout. Katende was in no hurry. Where else were these kids going to go?

The next day he started with the pawn. He showed them how a pawn can move forward either one or two spaces on its initial move and then only one space thereafter. Then he asked them to move the pawn and they each took a turn at the board. Finally, one exasperated child said, "Coach, we're just moving pieces around, there is no one who is eating another!"

Katende asked them to be patient. In time they had mastered how a pawn moves and then Katende taught them that it captures not by moving directly forward, but by moving forward one space diagonally.

"Some children tried to capture by moving the pawn the way a pawn is supposed to move and others moved the pawn the way it is supposed to capture," Katende says. "There were a lot of mix-ups."

It took three or four sessions just to cover the movement of the pawn, but to encourage the children, Katende told them that the pawn was the hardest piece to learn, because rules governed its movement that did not apply to any of the other pieces.

Using the pawn as a foundation, Katende taught them how the other pieces move. He told the children that the rook moves like the pawn, but it is not limited in its steps as long as there isn't any other piece in its way, and that it could move either vertically or horizontally.

Then Katende explained that the knight moves like the rook, except that it is limited to only two steps and then it turns for a single step. Knowing that the knight could be a frustrating piece for the children to understand, Katende created a phrase that the children eventually translated into a sort of dance step. *One-Two-Turn. One-Two-Turn.* Katende challenged them and eventually all of the students wanted to move the knight without showing the other kids that they had counted the steps. Katende then placed one black knight and one white pawn on the board and asked all of the children to try to capture the pawn with the knight.

"That was a good puzzle," Katende says. "It triggered them to think, one-two-turn, one-two-turn. The pawn was always there stationary, but how many times must you move the knight until it reaches the pawn? They might get right beside the pawn and then they fear moving away from it. It was a struggle, but eventually they mastered it."

Katende told them that the bishop is the only religious person on the board and they translated it into Luganda. *Munadiini.* It was easier to explain the bishop moving diagonally and always on the same color, because the piece moves very much the same way as the king in draughts, a game many of the children had previously played. The ones who knew taught the ones who did not know as Katende sat back and watched.

Learning the queen was simple. Katende took a bishop in one hand and a rook in the other and told them that the queen combines the movements of both pieces.

The day Katende reached for the final piece, the king, the children expected the king to be moving in an extraordinary way because of its size relative to the other pieces. Then Katende explained that the king could move only one space in any direction. When he sensed some disappointment among his pupils, he related the story of the king to their lives.

"I asked them, 'Who knows the Kabaka of Buganda and who has ever seen him running?' " Katende says. "No one had ever seen him running. I said, 'No, this is a very powerful person. He's a king. He does not run. He's a diplomat. He just takes one step here and he's through with his movement.'

They knew that the Kabaka does not run because he's a powerful person respected by everyone. They saw the king in a new way."

As Katende spent weeks painstakingly explaining each of the pieces, the number of children in attendance dropped. "One kid called Gerald after twenty minutes of each session he would be dozing with saliva coming out of his mouth," Katende recalls. "I would ask him if he was okay and he always snapped awake. By this point we had lost some kids because they saw learning chess as a long process."

The original group of 20 children eventually dwindled to only five boys. For several weeks, attendance even dropped as low as three and Katende wondered if his suspicions had been correct all along. *Can these kids really play this game?* He questioned if the chess project could survive.

After Katende had covered all of the pieces, the three remaining children convinced the two who had recently dropped out to return. When they came back, Katende asked the boys who knew how to move all of the pieces to teach the others. When the attendance finally stabilized at five, Ivan Mutesasira, Samuel Mayanja, Gerald Mutyaba, Julius Ssali, and Richard Tugume, Katende began referring to them as "The Pioneers." The Pioneers called Katende "Coach Robert."

"The Pioneers developed a very great interest in the game," Richard Tugume says. "Time came when we reduced our time of going to soccer because we really loved chess so very much. We saw how this game could develop our minds."

Katende identified Richard as a leader. Richard had been playing soccer on the dump site the day Katende first arrived to stage the soccer portion of his sports ministry there. Richard was among the first to join Katende's soccer project and had rarely missed a day since. One evening, in an effort to help empower Richard, Katende handed the boy the project's only chessboard to take home with him. Richard quickly gave it back.

"But why?" Katende asked. "Why don't you want to keep our board?"

Richard remained quiet until Katende pulled him aside and asked him again why he didn't want to keep the board.

"I am sorry, Coach," Richard said, "but when Daddy comes back home every evening he is drunk and he fights with Mommy and he will end up destroying our board."

Instead, that same day Richard rallied the rest of the Pioneers to search the dump site for bottle caps and a blank piece of cardboard. They drew the 64 squares on the cardboard and carefully shaded every other one and then etched the names of the 32 pieces on the bottle caps. For many evenings thereafter when it came time for Katende to leave Katwe, the Pioneers played their new favorite game, with bottle caps on cardboard, until it was too dark to see.

Coach Robert never had a coach. He figured out chess on his own simply by watching some of his friends play it in the schoolyard during his second year at Lubiri Secondary School.

"I saw students playing this strange game and I asked them, 'What is this?' " Katende says. "They told me that the game was only for guys who are really clever. I had to prove I was clever enough for this game."

Katende would watch his schoolmates play every evening and eventually asked if he could join them. He bought a cheap vinyl chessboard and pieces from a friend and played recreationally on and off for the next few years. He didn't really play chess competitively until he reached the engineering department at Kyambogo University, where he competed in tournaments against far more talented players who had grown up in affluent families playing the game more consistently. Throughout the odyssey of his childhood, one of the few possessions Katende held on to was the chess set he had purchased during secondary school, and it was that same set he brought with him to teach the children of Katwe.

Katende had learned the game primarily through trial and error and he taught it that way to the Pioneers. He admits that he didn't even know all of the rules of the game until several months into the chess project when a friend from Sports Outreach gave him a book titled *Chess for Beginners.* The book taught Katende some basic chess strategy and tactics. He learned the importance of controlling the central part of the board to gain a position of strength. While he had been taught "castling," a move where the king and rook exchange positions, the book taught him "long castling" and "short castling" and that a player should try to castle within the first ten moves of the game. He also discovered that chess could be divided into three stages: opening, middlegame, and endgame. "Reading that book was a turning point," Katende says. "I studied every word and then I used it as a reference to teach the children some things about the game that I was just learning myself."

Working without any depth of knowledge in chess theory, which is a means of approaching a game more as a whole than as a series of individual moves, Katende taught his students to analyze the board and try to make the best choice for each move. At first they all wanted to use every move to capture, whether it made sense for the long-term result or not. They thought only one move at a time. So Katende gradually taught them to plan, to think one move ahead, then two, then three, and beyond.

"I don't like the way players who say they have learned chess by theory make moves and they can't explain why they have even made those moves," Katende says. "My players must have a reason why they play each move. It might be a bad reason, but at least there's a reason."

Katende taught them to play one piece at a time. The Pioneers' first games involved only pawns. After they learned the rook, the four rooks were added to the board for play. "At first I just had them move any color piece they wanted to as long as they move it the way it's supposed to move," Katende says. "I didn't concern myself with white then black then white then black. White might make ten moves in a row without black making a single move. Someone might move the queen right beside the opposing king. Then some moves later the king might capture the queen. It wasn't very strict. I just wanted to see if they could move the pieces correctly and let them discover things slowly."

For the first few months, the Pioneers thought the game ended when one player captured all of his opponent's pieces. Then when Katende felt the Pioneers were ready, he explained that the game is actually won when an opponent's king is hopelessly cornered in "checkmate," which begins with the warning that that king is in "check," or what Katende called "target."

"It was an interesting moment for them when they first learned about their king in target," Katende says. "At first it was like a big scare. Their breathing rate changed. 'Where can I run? What can I do?' "

Initially the children struggled with the idea that the king didn't actually need to be captured for the game to end. Then Katende explained checkmate with another story to which the Pioneers could relate.

"The children would always ask me, 'Why should I tell you your king is in target when

I can just capture your king?' " Katende says. "I told them, 'No, you don't kill the president. The president is just arrested. Who has ever heard of a president being killed? He's a big person in the country. You only arrest him. Target is like you're telling a president, "You are in danger. Do you have any soldiers to protect you?" If he doesn't, then you arrest him and the game is over.' "

To further illustrate his point, Katende demonstrated what is known as "The Fool's Mate," which he'd learned from *Chess for Beginners.* The term refers to a series of simple moves at the opening of a game that can quickly checkmate an opponent.

Eventually Katende began playing against the Pioneers, usually rotating them through the seat opposite him, sometimes letting them team up to decide each of their moves, but always explaining why he made each of his moves and thoroughly evaluating each move made by the opponent as the children looked on with rapt attention. Katende was always searching for ways to challenge them.

"One time I was teaching them how to win when you have just two bishops and a king and your opponent just has a king," Katende says. "I did not tell them what to do. I just asked them, 'Who of you can checkmate me when I just have a king?' We played for over fifty moves and they failed to mate me. They said, 'Coach, it is not possible.' I told them that it is possible and I left it to them to figure out how. They discovered it by themselves."

As months passed, the chess project began to expand slightly beyond the Pioneers, possibly caused by word of mouth that the sugarcane had turned into a daily bowl of porridge. Katende began to realize the profound lessons the chessboard had for his congregation of children. They were slum kids. He was a slum kid. Their story was his story. They had all been in target for their entire lives.

"I came to appreciate that chess is the best tool for kids in the slums," Katende says. "I believe when they play the game they can integrate the principles used in the game into their daily life. The moment your opponent makes a move, it is like posing a challenge to you, and the whole issue is to think, 'What can I do to overcome this?' It is like the challenges they face every day. They must think how they can overcome those as well. I told them they can never resign in a game, never give up until they are checkmated. That is where the chessboard is like life. That is the magic in the game."

Before long it became harder and harder to differentiate the chess games from the spiritual guidance that followed. A teaching point could spring up anytime. Whenever Katende saw a player become frustrated during a game, he would share the biblical story of Joseph:

> "Joseph was in a family with his brothers and though he was not a bad behaved person, in a way they mistreated him. They ended up even selling him off to go and work as a slave. If Joseph were looking for someone to blame he would definitely be on wrong terms with his brothers, but this was God's plan. He went through all of that suffering, but it was a connection to another level. You need to develop that positivity in you so that problems do not affect you greatly. With every challenge you need to see what is the lesson out of this? Why has God allowed this to happen? How does He want me to grow from this? Is it endurance? Is it tolerance? You must develop that muscle to stand and know how to address it when something bad happens to you."

Whenever there was a crisis of confidence, Katende would tell his favorite story about an inept doctor.

"Think of a situation when you are sick and you have gone to the clinic for treatment and a doctor comes up and says, 'Young man, you're sick. I am going to inject you, but I don't know whether I still remember how to inject. Let me first see if I can remember.' Then he gets a sponge and he tries to inject it and says, 'I think I can remember. Okay, let's do the injection.' Can you allow yourself to be injected? Of course you can't. Why? Because the doctor does not believe in himself. Then how do you entrust your life to him? You cannot. If you don't believe in yourself, how do you expect anyone else to believe in you?"

Katende's lessons were designed to bond a bunch of desperate slum children into a community of chess players helping each other learn how to see into the future.

"Someday you will be able to read your opponent's mind many moves in advance," Katende told them. "You will see what is going to happen on the chessboard before it happens. You are all going to be prophets."

Brian Mugabi sat among them on that very first day when Katende placed the chessboard in the dirt and spilled the pieces over it. Brian had been playing in the soccer project from the beginning when he was about 11 years old, sneaking away from his chores whenever he could, at the risk of a caning from his mother. He was relatively small and sometimes grew frustrated playing soccer against boys who were bigger and stronger and more skilled. He kept coming, less for the soccer and more to hear what the young coach had to say, and, of course, for the food.

Brian embraced chess from the first day, because he recognized immediately that his size didn't matter. This game was contested with the brain and Brian thought there could be nobody better at plotting and scheming. He saw chess as a chance to be good at something for the first time in his life. The game reminded him of the days when his father took him to the video halls and he watched movies about soldiers on horseback with spears charging toward one another. The idea had always fascinated him. One army against another. Do or die. That's what he saw when he looked at the chessboard.

Brian escaped to the chess project whenever possible during its first several months, long enough to have learned how each of the soldiers attacked and captured, but not yet how to command his army successfully as a whole. One night after chess as he was walking home through Katwe, he was struck by a bicycle. Brian was knocked down and badly hurt. He had to be carried home and that night he noticed blood in his urine. The following day he was taken to the hospital, where doctors discovered he was bleeding internally. He was treated there for a week. As Brian was laid up in his family's shack recuperating, he couldn't stop thinking about returning to the chess project, seeing his friends again, reconnecting with the first sense of stability he'd ever experienced. He began to realize it wasn't the game that he craved as much as the people who played it with him. It would be three months before Brian recovered enough to return to the chess project, by which time Katende had dubbed some of the other boys he had first trained with "The Pioneers."

By that time, Katende had arranged to have the chess project moved from the dump site to a dusty veranda outside Bishop John Michael Mugerwa's office, where a roof would protect the children from the rain and enough dim light shone to allow them to continue playing on those evenings when dusk fell early over the slum. One day, probably in 2005, as Brian snuck away from his younger siblings, Phiona and Richard, and darted off to the chess project, he had no idea that he was blazing a trail and he could never have imagined where that trail might eventually lead. He certainly didn't know anyone was there when Katende spotted somebody at the edge of the veranda peeking around the corner.

A young girl.

CHAPTER 4
RESURRECTION

Phiona Mutesi prays inside her family's shack before leaving for her three-hour trek through the treacherous alleyways of Katwe to fetch fresh water.

> "I have no memory of my father," Phiona says. "I was so young I didn't even know how he died. After his funeral we stayed in the village for a few weeks and one morning when I woke up, my older sister Juliet told me she was feeling a headache. We got some herbs and gave them to her and then she went to sleep. The following morning we found her dead in the bed. That is what I remember."

Only God knows what day the child was born. There is no birth certificate. No documentation of any kind. They don't bother with that kind of paperwork at a clinic in Katwe. Many Africans trace their birthdays back to nothing more specific than a certain year marked by a landmark in their country's history. In Uganda, many people track their birthdays to a war. Harriet believes her third daughter was born in

1996, but she doesn't know her daughter's birthday and doesn't understand why anyone would need to know, because nobody celebrates birthdays in the slum.

Because she is illiterate, Harriet didn't bestow a name upon her newborn daughter, so much as a sound. Harriet's cousin, Milly Nanteza, had given all of her children names beginning with an *F* sound. Harriet liked that. Nanteza had named one of her daughters with the sound *FEE-OH-NUH*. It was never spelled out. When Harriet is asked how her daughter's name is spelled, she does not understand the question. The answer would not be determined in any official manner for many years.

Phiona was about three years old when her father died and her life turned upside down. She had been preparing to go to kindergarten. Suddenly she was no longer a child but a worker. The widowed Harriet needed all of her children to be part of her labor force.

By the time Harriet had returned home from Buyubu after the second family funeral she'd endured in three weeks, she had lost her job at the New African Child School and the family had been evicted from their home on Salaama Road. Night and Brian, who were about 13 and six years old, respectively, dropped out of school to help support the family. "After my husband's death I had so many children and I could not pay the rent," Harriet says. "Life was so, so, so terrible. I could not pay for their school fees and they were denied exams or report forms. Eventually I had to make a choice to either educate my children or to feed them."

One day after seeing a child walking through the slum selling boiled maize from a saucepan on her head, Harriet, believing she had no other choice, decided her family would do the same. Each morning she would walk to the Kibuye outdoor market and buy some maize, often on borrowed money. Harriet would then cook it and she and her children would wander around selling it in the slum.

"At times you could grow weary because you are walking long distances with the maize on your head without anyone buying," Brian says. "And personally I had bad feelings about what we were doing. We all wanted to be in school. It would come to around 5 P.M. and at that time most of my friends would be playing and I wanted to go and join them, but that is a time that our mother would tell us to go and sell the maize."

Beginning when Phiona was about five years old, Harriet sent her daughter out alone into the slum each day carrying a saucepan of maize on her head. She would sell during morning and evening teas. Phiona carried 20 corncobs and each was to be sold for 100 shillings (U.S. $.06), a supply worth 2,000 shillings, but a five-year-old girl rarely returned with that.

"There were some moments when you would come across some street children and they would beat you up and steal your maize and then they go," Phiona says. "At times they would even take the money you have so far earned and you go home with nothing. It was really very challenging because I could go home crying and I could not express anything to my mother because she is also feeling very bad about that and she is preparing to cane me. So it was such a terrible moment. That really affected us because when we were unable to raise enough money, we would end up not eating that day."

There were plenty of days when Harriet had no food for her children. They usually ate no breakfast in the morning. At times Harriet was able to scrape together some rice for a meal at midday. A cup of tea often would have to suffice as dinner. Whenever there wasn't enough food for the entire family, Harriet would fast. Once a year, on Christmas Day, Harriet allowed her children to skip selling maize and she would buy meat for their daily meal, which she would split among them while taking none for herself. Christmas was the only day of the year the children were permitted to eat until they were full.

Before her first run of maize each day, Phiona was expected to do much of the housework that her sister Juliet had once done. She was also required to fetch water. Phiona would wake up at five o'clock each morning to begin a three-hour roundtrip trek through Katwe to fill a jerry can with drinkable water. Sometimes she would even sling an extra jug over her shoulder for a neighbor in exchange for a few shillings she could give to her mother for food.

"We fetched water, sold maize, and did chores," Phiona says. "That was our day. In most cases we used to come back and we were really tired and our mother realized this and she used to help us to even wash our clothes because we were too tired to do that ourselves."

Understanding the value of the education that she could never get as a child, Harriet tried repeatedly to reenroll her children in school, but she could never keep up with the fees. She transferred them from school to school, but they were typically expelled before completing a full term. During a period of six years, Phiona completed less than two grades of school. Even when they were enrolled, Phiona and her siblings continued to sell maize in the evenings.

As she grew older, Phiona's behavior began to change. She would often fight with children around the neighborhood. Unlike most girls, she would even stand up to the boys. One time a boy teased her about how she had no father and her family slept on the ground and Phiona attacked him so aggressively that Harriet had to break up the fight before Phiona hurt the boy.

"I would do all sorts of bad things," Phiona says. "I would run around with the wild kids in the neighborhood abusing whoever we find. I did not even fear to quarrel with older people if anybody did anything that was not in line with what I wanted. I usually had nobody around telling me what to do and what not to do, so I wound up learning a lot of bad actions."

Phiona attributes her poor conduct to her family's constant state of desperation. "It affected us to a certain extent, but our mother used to encourage us so we didn't lose hope," Phiona says. "Many times the landlord would come to our home demanding his money for rent and we had no money even for food. Everything was really in a mess so we were really very much scared and we didn't know what was next."

When she is asked if there were any happy moments in her childhood during that time, Phiona shakes her head and for emphasis she responds in English: "No."

In her mind it would be best if it happened by car. Harriet wasn't exactly sure where or when, but that would be a quick way to go. It wouldn't require any planning, just a snap decision. A brief jolt of courage, or perhaps cowardice, and she would be gone.

"The life I was leading, I was fed up with it," Harriet says. "I had so many challenges and at times I lost hope. During that time for sure I had nothing in mind apart from looking for food to make us survive and I always wondered if God would ever remember us. I was so tired of living that kind of life. I was working very hard but all in vain. It was a real devil distressing me. It caused me to hate myself and I felt like it wasn't worth living. So time came when I said, 'Why don't I die and leave this kind of life?' "

Only her responsibility to her children had prevented Harriet from committing suicide. She would always think of them and wonder what would happen to them without her. In her most despondent moments she wondered if she wouldn't rather die than see her kids suffering. She wanted to let them go. At some point in Katwe, Harriet Nakku approached that dark point of no return when she began to think, "Could my children really be any worse off without me?"

Sometime around the year 2000, about a year after the death of her husband and daughter, a friend who was worried about Harriet's state of mind directed her to see a pastor. "Before 2000 I had a dream over and over and a voice spoke to me, 'Why don't you get saved?' " Harriet says. "But I would not pay attention."

That day Harriet confessed Christ as her savior. She was born-again. Then the pastor shared a prophecy.

Says Harriet, "When I went to church and I saw that man of God, he spoke to me and he said, 'You have been praying to God that a vehicle can hit you and you die. You go today and God will indicate something to you.' "

Later that afternoon, as Harriet was walking through Katwe carrying her infant,

Richard, near a place called Prayer Palace, she heard a car speeding around a bend in the road and it was headed directly toward her. The onlookers in Katwe that day drew in a collective gasp, certain they were about to witness yet another senseless death in the slum. Harriet said a quick prayer and braced for the impact.

"The vehicle came and suddenly stopped right where we are," Harriet says. "I saw the motorcar turning around and then facing where it had come from and I remembered the prophecy and realized that the man of God was referring to me. Maybe it was God's arrangement. I cannot explain that."

That single day changed Harriet's entire outlook on her life.

"At that time my heart was transformed," Harriet says. "I used to spend most of the time crying and worried before I got saved. Then I became strong and I gained hope and inner peace. Our situation was not all that good, but I began to meditate on what God had done for us, somehow keeping us alive. I wouldn't be here anymore if it wasn't for the power of God. And I thank him for that."

The first time Phiona died she was about seven years old. It happened suddenly one evening. Phiona fell sick with a fever and then she was gone. Her body was cold and still. Nobody could find a pulse.

Phiona's body was dressed for burial and cotton was placed in each nostril to stem any flow of blood. As is custom in Uganda, the family removed all of the possessions from the shack, placed the body in the center of the floor, and invited the neighbors to sit on mats along the walls and help the family mourn and pray for the deceased. Harriet went to church to solicit some funds for Phiona's body to be transported to the village for a funeral, while Phiona's youngest siblings were sequestered outside the shack unaware of what had occurred.

Several hours after Phiona had died, Night began to notice some sweating around her sister's legs. Before long, Phiona's entire body appeared to be perspiring, so Night removed some of the clothes she had put on her sister. By the time Harriet had returned from church, Phiona had resurrected. "Personally, I've never seen anything like that," Harriet says. "Even though the child was mine, I really feared her. I don't like even to talk about that, because I know people will be fearing her. For sure, there is no way I can explain that. It is God's glory. At that time, I was just praying and believing God, but I was not even praying for her to be brought back to life. I don't even know what happened to bring her back to life, but I believe there is a reason for it."

"All of a sudden we saw Phiona returning to life and all of the visitors scattered and ran out of the room because they believed this is a ghost," Night says. "We were also fearing her. We thought she was a ghost. Then our mother said, 'No, it is God who has brought back my daughter.' We went ahead and told Phiona, 'You were dead.' Phiona told us, 'No, I was just asleep.' She became better, but people feared her for some good time."

Some of the neighbors who had mourned Phiona that night refused to make any further contact with her and began referring to her as "the girl who feared the grave."

About a year later, Phiona died again. She fell gravely ill and Harriet begged one of her sisters for the money to take Phiona to the hospital. While Harriet was never informed of a diagnosis, she believes her daughter had an acute case of malaria, a malady that is contracted with the frequency of the common cold in Katwe, and which Phiona had endured many times before. Phiona lost consciousness and fluid had to be removed from her spine. Harriet was informed that her daughter's condition was life-threatening. "I was so terrified," Harriet says. "I was told that when someone gets some water removed from their spinal cord the chances are very small that they are going to survive. I knew Phiona was going to die, just like Juliet before her."

Harriet left Night at Phiona's bedside because she was so certain of Phiona's fate and could not bear the thought of losing another daughter. She took Brian and Richard with her to try to gather the money to bury Phiona. Several days later, Phiona baffled her doctors by making a sudden recovery.

"I was very surprised that Phiona stabilized," Harriet says. "Maybe her time had not yet come. That must have been God's plan. I believe there is divine intervention in my daughter's life."

Says Phiona, "I don't remember anything about that time except that when I came home my mother told me, 'You died for two days.' "

Harriet had lost everything that belonged to her, except for her children and a mattress. Now the mattress was gone. Harriet had offered her mattress as collateral for a loan, seed money for a job selling cassava in the Kibuye market. When the business failed within a week, the mattress was gone. Harriet and her children had nothing left to sleep on.

At that point they had moved in with Harriet's mother, into a tiny shack in Katwe barely fit for one person but sleeping six. One day the landlord showed up and told them that without a rent payment, they would have to leave immediately. They had no money.

So the family moved to another shack in the Kizungu zone which borders Katwe, a dwelling that had been abandoned because it was in such a decrepit state. Shortly after they arrived there, Harriet's mother died. They continued to stay there despite returning one day to find that their possessions had been stolen because they could not afford a lock for the door. Finally, the house collapsed. At that time, Harriet didn't have money to rent another house, so she begged her stepbrother, Juma Sserunkuma, to allow her family to stay with him in the two-room shack he rented in the nearby Nateete slum.

Harriet didn't know until they arrived there that Sserunkuma practiced witchcraft. On some nights Sserunkuma would wake up Harriet and the children at 3 A.M. and insist that they go outside while he performed rituals like slaughtering a chicken and spreading its blood around the shack. Sserunkuma constantly claimed that someone was urinating in his bedroom, even though he kept it locked. He would complain that he was no longer getting the money he used to earn and that Harriet's presence precluded him from obtaining a wife. "He would tell me that everything of his was in a mess," Harriet says. "There were some flowers he would irrigate with local brew and they all dried up. It seems he thought that we had disorganized his spirits."

Sserunkuma eventually ordered Harriet and her family to leave. "I told my children that it was not safe for us to stay with him," Harriet says. "I feared he could sacrifice us, slaughter us, so we had to leave his place and go on the street."

Because she had no other choice, Harriet and her children stayed on the roadside near the Kibuye market. The only other option for shelter was back in her father's village in Seeta, but Harriet didn't have the fare to transport everybody there and wasn't sure she'd even be welcome. "During that time when we slept on the street, I didn't know that we would ever be able to get another house to stay in," Phiona says. "We were sleeping in the road and people were laughing at us. Our mother's plan was for us to sometime go back to the village."

Day after day on the roadside, Harriet split a single cassava among her children while she fasted on water. Harriet survived on small donations from friends in the church, who eventually persuaded her that living in the street wasn't safe for the children and that she should take her family to sleep in the church once it had emptied each evening.

At that dire moment, the solution fell to Night. She left the family on the roadside and made a decision she'd been resisting for a long time, the same decision her mother once made in a similar moment of hopelessness. "I had to go and get a man and I started staying with that man," Night says. "So when I got that man, it wasn't the right thing to do because really I was not of age. I was fifteen years old. But I had no option and he was the one now giving me some money to support my family. So that's how God rescued us from the street."

After three weeks on the roadside, with a gift of 40,000 shillings from the man with whom Night was staying, Harriet rented a room in the nearby Masajja district, where the family stayed for four months until that structure was demolished because the landlord wanted to build a sounder structure. So once again Harriet moved her family to yet another shack in Katwe, the sixth time they had relocated in five years.

To help muster the rent for each of these humble dwellings, Harriet returned to work at the Kibuye market, a chaotic outdoor bazaar that offers everything from vegetables to underwear to toothpaste to dishes, much of which sits in the mud inside an entrance marked by cattle defecating in the street.

Harriet didn't give up after her first business failure at the market, but tried again after learning from her mistakes. She no longer sold cassava, which had proven to be expensive and had a short shelf life, instead choosing to sell curry powder, which was far cheaper and more durable.

Harriet would eventually expand her inventory to tea leaves, avocados, and eggplants, which she normally sells from a wobbly wooden stand under a feeble umbrella that offers virtually no protection from the blistering sun. Six days a week she leaves her home at 2 A.M. to make a five-kilometer walk to meet the farmers who bring their goods into Kampala for purchase, and then she resells those goods for a tiny profit that she hopes will amount to enough money each month to pay rent and feed her children a daily meal of rice.

Because of her work schedule, Harriet is usually gone from the family's shack and her children never know when she will return. Harriet sometimes passes several days without seeing them. "When I wake up in the morning I commit my kids to God's hands," she says. "I don't always know where my kids are. God is like their father."

One day when it came time to go out on the evening run selling maize, Brian was nowhere to be found. Before his accident with the bicycle he had begun a routine of wandering off at about the same time each day. Curious, his little sister would try to follow him. But Phiona would inevitably lose her big brother among the labyrinth of alleys in Katwe. She couldn't keep up with him.

But on this day, perhaps motivated by the possibility of finding a meal on a day when she'd had nothing to eat, Phiona was able to track Brian for five kilometers, all the way to an abandoned lot, a dump site that was being used as a soccer field. Phiona looked on from a safe distance as Brian began to play soccer with a group of boys, watched over by a young coach. She studied the coach and liked the way he joined in the game and seemed to genuinely care for the children. After about an hour, the soccer game ended. Brian and the other boys then walked deeper into the valley of Katwe, toward the heart of Nkere. Phiona continued to follow her brother until at one point a boy named Gerald turned, saw Phiona, and said, "Brian, your sister is coming."

Brian retreated to where Phiona was standing and insisted she go home. After initially resisting, Phiona turned and began to walk back toward home, but then turned again and continued her stealthy pursuit of her brother until she reached a dusty veranda across the alley from the shack of Hakim Ssewaya. Brian disappeared inside. Phiona carefully peeked around a corner to see where he had gone.

"I saw there were many children seated and they were all looking at some good things and I didn't know if it was a game because I had never seen it," Phiona says. "I looked at it some more and I just felt like I really wanted to go inside and touch the beautiful pieces. I thought, 'What could make all these kids so silent?' Then I watched them play the game and get happy and excited and I wanted a chance to be that happy."

Phiona kept peering around the corner, fascinated by the game. Suddenly she was spotted by the coach. "Young girl," said Katende. "Don't be afraid. You come."

Chapter 5
Teach Her What You Know

Gloria Nansubuga was four when Robert Katende selected her to become nine-year-old Phiona Mutesi's first chess tutor.

"Phiona," she responded, when Katende asked her name. But he couldn't hear her. Nobody could. She spoke at a whisper with her chin buried in her chest. Katende took a step closer. "Phiona," she said again, no louder.

She was dirty. Her skirt was soaking wet. Her blouse torn. Her bare feet caked in mud. She stunk.

She gradually eased her way onto the veranda, where many boys and a few girls were sitting on wooden benches or the floor, playing the strange game. She picked up a queen and caressed it with her fingers. Phiona had never felt anything like it.

The other children in the chess project did not welcome the new kid. Brian wasn't quite sure how to handle his sister among them. Even Katende stood back strategically to see if the community would embrace her without his influence. Phiona ate her bowl of porridge alone. Everybody refused to sit near her because of her stench. They laughed at her. They told her to leave. "Look at the dirty girl," one said. "You girl, you go away. You're not worthy to be with us here. We can't be with such a dirty girl."

Suddenly the quiet girl became more aggressive. Phiona walked over toward her primary tormentors with a bearing that she was ready to fight. The moment is what Katwe had trained Phiona for; an animalistic awareness that each day is survival of the fittest, that retaliation is demanded, that even the most naturally timid creature must fight when her existence depends on it. Phiona could sense that this day was a benchmark in her young life, a line drawn in the dust, and she could not, would not, be turned away from the beautiful pieces.

"They abused me, but they didn't know who they were joking with because I also abused them," Phiona says. "I said so many bad words. I told them, 'Look at your nose. Look at your teeth. You are not so good-looking, either.' "

Phiona threatened some of the other children until Katende and Brian stepped in to break them up. Brian dragged his sister off the veranda and walked her back to their shack, where he told their mother about how Phiona had quarreled with the other children and how much he hated to see his sister abused like that. "Our mother got angry with me and she even slapped me for my behavior," Phiona says. "She told me never to go there again."

On his way home that night, Robert Katende believed he had seen the last of Phiona Mutesi. "Because the day was so hard for her, for sure I did not expect to meet her again," Katende says. "When she came back the next day, I knew she had an enduring kind of spirit. I knew this girl had courage."

She may have come back for the porridge, but she came. The following day Phiona cleverly waited for the moment when her mother left their home for church and then sprinted to the chess project. She had rinsed herself with water and dressed in clothes that she had freshly cleaned in the wash basin. Luckily for her, Brian was not at the veranda that day.

Phiona was greeted by Katende, who scanned the room seeking a candidate to help tutor the new girl. He knew that her mentor must be another female, because none of the boys would deign to teach a brand-new girl, but there was only one other girl at the project that day: a four-year-old who knew nothing more than some basics about how to move the pieces. Katende introduced nine-year-old Phiona to the tiny girl and then said to the younger one, "Gloria, teach her what you know."

Gloria Nansubuga had been with the program for only a short time, convinced to join at the insistence of her older brother, Benjamin, if for no other reason than to get a free meal.

Initially, Gloria did not want to tutor Phiona, and Phiona did not want Gloria to tutor her. "I'm teaching an old lady," Gloria would complain. Phiona was embarrassed by the age difference as well.

"I thought to myself, 'How could this tiny girl teach me anything?' " Phiona says. "Whenever Gloria taught me, I really felt as if she was putting me down. But as much as I was despising her, I enjoyed what she was doing, because I wanted to learn the game."

Phiona eventually grew to feel comfortable around Gloria, who was the only girl in the project who seemed to accept her. "Whenever I assigned her to Gloria, Phiona could feel peace and she knew she was going to learn," Katende says. "It became a driving force for Phiona that if this young girl is able to learn the game, then she can also learn. Phiona could not be as comfortable with me as sometimes she was with Gloria. With Gloria she could ask four or five times until she understood something. With me she would fear to ask me so many times one thing."

Gloria showed Phiona the oddly shaped pieces and explained how each was regulated by different rules about how it could move. The pawns. The rooks. The bishops. The knights. The king. And finally the queen, the most powerful piece on the board. She told Phiona about the *embwa* and the *munadiini,* and about how the Kabaka, the king, is never killed but simply arrested, although Gloria didn't totally understand yet how that translated to the game. Gloria told Phiona that the most important point in many chess games is when a pawn reaches the opponent's back row, how it was called "queening," and how at that moment a pawn miraculously transforms into a queen. How could Phiona have imagined at the time how these 32 pieces and 64 squares could queen her?

What made Phiona come back day after day were the beautiful pieces that had attracted her in the first place. She desperately wanted to move these pieces just as the other children were moving them. She could see the excitement in their faces, but at first she was not feeling the same emotion. After several weeks under Gloria's tutelage, Phiona began to understand the basic strategy of the game. At one point, Phiona heard one of the other children tell her, "Ah, that was a great move." She felt happy and wanted to make more and more great moves, positive reinforcement being an unfamiliar but powerful incentive to a slum child.

"Phiona really grasped the game so easily," Gloria says. "Nothing disturbed her. When she started learning, she developed a very big interest in the game and she constantly continued to play and that's how she became better."

As the two became friends, Gloria also mentored Phiona about her conduct outside of the game.

Says Phiona, "One time when I got upset with Gloria, she told me, 'Phiona, don't abuse me. Coach Robert told us that the people who play chess are always good people. They are very well disciplined. They don't make trouble.' In a way Gloria was bringing out a very good lesson to me."

After about two months of training with Gloria, Phiona had caught up to her four-year-old tutor. Gloria had nothing left to teach, and Katende knew it was time for Phiona to move on to the opposite side of the veranda, to start actually playing the game, and to do it at a level of competition that had caused many other girls to flee from the program. It was time to start playing with the boys.

Ivan Mutesasira was about eight years old when his mother, Annet Nakiwala, told him and his four siblings that it was time to go. Nakiwala loaded all of her possessions onto her head and, trailed by her children, walked away from her husband and out into Katwe, vowing never to speak to him again.

"I never got to know what caused the divorce, because by then I was very young," Ivan says. "I remember seeing our mother carrying her things away from our home and she told us to follow her. We were five young kids and we did not know what was going on."

Nakiwala and her children relocated to another shack in Katwe, but she could not afford to raise five kids on her own. The family struggled to find food and their living conditions were miserable. "The place where we stayed, the water would come inside the room whenever it rained," Ivan says. "I could not even sleep at night because I had to be awake to be able to lift things from wherever the water level has reached and continue to put them upwards. Sometimes I could spend two days without sleep."

Like so many other kids in Katwe, Ivan bounced in and out of school because of lack of funds. "We faced several challenges that included starving at school because we were not paying the feeding fee so we could not eat," Ivan says. "I remember some days we could offer to go to wash the school saucepans and then we could eat what is left not eaten from the saucepans and the teachers' dishes."

Eventually Ivan dropped out of school in P7 and remained out of school for three years. Five years after she had taken Ivan from his father, with no other choice, Nakiwala sent him back. Ivan was another child of Katwe, blowing in the wind, when one day in 2003 his friend Richard Tugume told him he had met a coach who had come to Katwe with real soccer balls that they could use to play.

"At first we thought that Coach Robert had come for a short term because there were other people who used to come with those good balls, but always after a short while they would leave," says Ivan, who believes he is 20 years old. "We didn't know that he was serious to stay, but later we realized that he was really committed to us, that he was different from all of the others."

As one of the Pioneers, one the oldest players in the project and one of the few who was humble and well behaved from the outset, Ivan was identified by Katende as another potential leader. But Ivan lacked self-esteem, so Katende sought to empower him by calling on him to tutor younger players. Whenever Katende identified a new player with talent, he placed him with Ivan. One day Katende introduced Ivan to Benjamin Mukumbya and told Ivan, "Teach him what you know."

Benjamin was a street kid. A loner. As a young child, he used to be left at home alone all day while both of his parents scrounged Katwe for a few shillings to feed him. Then one day after thieves robbed the family's shack, Benjamin's mother, Jane Kobugabe, brought her son to stay at an aunt's place in a nearby village. Benjamin was not fed properly there and at one point when his mother discovered him gravely malnourished, she took him back to Kampala, where he fell victim to negative influences. "Actually, my father was not a Christian and he very much believed in witchcraft," Benjamin says. "I had also started to believe in that kind of thinking and became very badly behaved."

When Benjamin's parents split up over his father's infidelity, the boy was relegated to a life on the street. "I used to fight almost everyone no matter their age, including even stoning people." Benjamin says. "I spent many nights sleeping on the streets. I had a big shirt that was beyond my size and I could fold my arms and legs into it so it would cover me up. I remember some nights I spent in the church and other nights on the side of the road."

Benjamin's mother eventually began operating a small shop next door to Bishop John Michael Mugerwa's veranda, a grocery business she had taken over from her brother who had gradually been driven insane by the challenges of life in Katwe. Kobugabe was constantly borrowing money from various people to keep the shop open without any clear idea about how she was going to pay it back. When Kobugabe started working at the grocery, she brought Benjamin and his younger sister Gloria to live with her. Some nights they slept in a small room behind the grocery stall and others in a nearby shack.

At one point, Katende, who was running

his chess project next door, asked Kobugabe if he could store flour at her shop because it was being stolen from its previous location, and also to cook the daily porridge on her stoop. Kobugabe began noticing the enthusiastic children at the chess project and told Benjamin that he should join. Benjamin initially refused, convinced he wouldn't like chess, before he finally capitulated, like so many others, because it ensured him a meal every day.

It didn't take long for Ivan to realize that he was teaching a natural. Benjamin was the most instinctive chess player Ivan had met in the project. Benjamin's brain was wired for the game. Within months Benjamin was the best player in the program, eclipsing Ivan and the rest of the Pioneers. Benjamin could be beaten only by his own considerable hubris, which he'd developed over time to mask the pain of his childhood. Once after Benjamin lost a game against a clearly inferior opponent, Katende approached Benjamin and asked, "Do you know why you lost?"

"No," Benjamin said.

"You lost," Katende said, "because of too much pride."

"Because I had learned the game so easily I thought I knew everything about chess,"

Benjamin says. "I used to treat the other children in the project as if nobody else mattered. So I started changing my character and the other kids began seeing me as a model, began listening to me unlike before when no one even dared to be close to me because I was known as one of the notorious children in the slum."

Benjamin became an ambassador for the chess project, recruiting other kids to join, including his sister Gloria, Phiona's initial tutor. When Benjamin started teaching and practicing with Gloria, he found that it helped him understand the game even better.

In 2008, with debt collectors on her trail, Benjamin's mother suddenly disappeared. Benjamin heard through relatives that Kobugabe had gone to "the islands," some small shards of land that were part of Uganda's territory in Lake Victoria, an area known to be even more lawless than Katwe. Kobugabe said she was going to get a job there and then come back to repay her debts. Since then she has contacted Benjamin only once, saying she was leaving the country, again supposedly to find work. When Katende tried to speak to Benjamin's father, Wilson Mubiru, to ask him to be more responsible for Benjamin and his other children, Mubiru said he had remarried with three new children and that he was broke.

So Benjamin was left to take care of his two younger siblings, the three of them living in the room behind the grocery stall and Benjamin washing their clothes and cooking meals whenever food was available. "They greatly rely on me and I very much desire that I invest my life in them," says Benjamin, who believes he is 13 years old. "Luckily enough the sisters to my mother are not bad people. They try to support us as if we are their children. I don't know if I will ever see my mother again. You never know."

Benjamin says that Katende has taught him to seize any opportunity that is available and try not to be discouraged by his past. "The way that I grew up somehow trained me to be on my own," Benjamin says. "My younger brother does not even know who our mother is, but I very much believe that it really affects my young sister. Many times she even mentions it to me, 'I wish our mother was here.' When I am at home with them I feel somehow tormented, but I get courage and I say, 'No, if other people have been able to stand, can't I also stand?' "

Benjamin was the first boy ever to play chess with Phiona at the project. He normally didn't play against newcomers, who tended to segregate themselves in their own corner of the veranda, but he recognized that Phiona had initially trained with his sister, so he took an interest in her as well.

"The first time I played against Phiona I was surprised that she gave me some challenges and I thought she had a chance to be good with training," Benjamin says. "I told her, 'The big deal with chess is planning. What's the next move? How can you get out of the attack they have made against you?' We make decisions like that every day in the slum."

Says Ivan, "When Phiona first came I thought, 'What does she want here?' During those days we rarely played girls. When Phiona first arrived I took it for granted that girls are always weak, that girls can do nothing, but I came to realize that a girl can play good chess. Phiona wanted chess seriously. Her level of playing was like the level of boys. She played like a boy. She thought like a boy."

Ivan, several years older than Phiona, and Benjamin, several years her junior, would become Phiona's primary mentors in the project. Though the three played at different levels, they became bonded by a shared obsession with the game. With no other distractions and nowhere else to go, they would train together for hours and hours, day after day.

While other girls in the project were afraid to play against boys, Phiona relished it and her game matured quickly. "She was always saying that boys are very difficult to play, but she became used to that," Benjamin says. "It felt normal for her to play against boys and she wanted to play against boys because she thought that would make her a better player."

Phiona did not find it intimidating to play against boys because at home she was the only girl. During her early development in the game, influenced by her male opponents, she played too recklessly, attacking blindly without much thought to the consequences, just as she did in her neighborhood fights. She often sacrificed crucial pieces in risky attempts to capture pieces as quickly as possible, even when playing black — second in a chess game — which usually dictates a defensive posture in the opening.

"I learned that chess is a lot like my life," Phiona says. "If you make smart moves you can stay away from danger, but you know any bad decision could be your last. When I first started playing, I lost so many games before the boys convinced me to act more like a girl and play with calm and patience."

Phiona remembers almost nothing about the game, except the outcome. Joseph Asaba can recall every single move. It occurred sometime in 2006. Phiona had been at the chess project for several months. She isn't sure how many games she played and lost without ever winning, saying only that the number is too high to count.

Phiona was anxious as she sat down across the board from Joseph, who had specifically requested her as an opponent because he expected to beat her, and winners at the project are usually allowed to keep playing on a board until they are defeated. Phiona had played against Joseph a few times before and he had always won within a few moves. How could he do that? It seemed like magic to her. It wasn't. It was the Fool's Mate.

Joseph had learned the Fool's Mate from Katende and it was his favorite tactic. He used it in every game he played. So again in this game against Phiona, Joseph employed his customary opening, maneuvering his bishop and queen into position. He thought the trap was set as usual. But this time Phiona responded by moving her queen directly in front of her king. Joseph had never seen that before, but he still jumped at the opportunity to capture Phiona's pawn with his queen. Phiona then took Joseph's queen and his bishop, while forfeiting her queen and a pawn, an advantageous swap.

"By the time I laid my usual plan, it seemed that there was someone who revealed my plot to her because she recognized how to defend it and guard her king," Joseph says. "I knew I could not win with the Fool's Mate because there was someone who revealed to her my tricks."

"Coach Robert taught me how to defend the Fool's Mate," Phiona says with a sly smile. "Coach told me to bring the queen in front of the king and I would take two pieces from him and then the game could play on."

After the Fool's Mate failed, Joseph didn't know what to do next. He was never comfortable in the middlegame because he rarely had to play it.

"I started advancing my pawns and I captured her bishop and she took my knight," Joseph remembers. "Then she forked my pieces and I had never seen that before. She put my two pieces in target and I knew she would capture one and I had to ask myself which one I should defend. So I played a back move to try to guard the rook, but when I tried to guard it, she still captured it. I can't forget that game."

The problem for Phiona was that without her queen, she didn't have any idea how to win a game with the other pieces. She didn't believe she could mate without the queen. So the two continued playing. Phiona had two rooks on the board, and she used them to protect an advancing pawn until she executed a queening. Once she recovered her queen, she used that to try to mate.

Because Phiona had never successfully checkmated an opponent, she didn't really know how to do it. She kept putting Joseph in check without a clear strategy to finish the game. "At the end, I remember I didn't know that I had won the game," Phiona says. "Joseph might have known, but he did not reveal it. The other children watching were saying, 'Phiona has won the game! Phiona has won the game!' I didn't know what they were talking about, so I just played the move I had already planned and it was the right move to mate him."

Suddenly Phiona realized that Joseph's king had nowhere safe to go. He had been arrested. That's when she realized that maybe the game was over.

One of the game's spectators, Wilson

Mugwanya, said, "Eh, Joseph, you are not serious. A girl? A girl has mated you?"

Joseph slumped over the board and began to cry. Instead of celebrating, Phiona found herself consoling her first victim. Joseph told Phiona that he would never, ever, play her again.

"When she mated me, I felt so bad," Joseph says. "The person who all along I have been winning with the Fool's Mate and now she has won me? All along I teased her and I knew she was very weak and I felt very bad when I lost to her because I learned the game before her so I felt that a learner should not beat me. This was a person I used to teach. How can she now challenge me and be able to win?"

Phiona rarely left the project early, rarely left the place she felt most comfortable in her world before Katende kicked her out, but she didn't play any more games that day. She went straight home, five kilometers across Katwe at a giddy gallop to tell her mother that she had won a game of chess. And against a boy.

Harriet didn't understand chess. When she was told about the little pieces that looked like castles and animals moving around a board of different-colored squares, she assumed it was a child's game.

"At first when Phiona went to play chess with Brian, I didn't know what chess was and I didn't take it seriously," Harriet says. "I wasn't certain about what they were really doing there. She and Brian tried to explain the game to me, but my head was too weak."

All Harriet knew was that the chess program guaranteed her children a meal each day, which was more than she could do, so after initially resisting, and over Brian's repeated objections early on, Harriet began exempting Brian and Phiona from selling maize in the afternoons so they could play chess.

News eventually spread around Katwe that the chess project was part of an organization run by white people, known throughout much of Africa as *mzungu.*

One day Harriet had a disturbing conversation with some of the other mothers in her neighborhood who told her that they refused to let their children go to the project and warned her not to allow her children to attend.

"The neighbors said a lot that terrified me," Harriet says. "They told me that chess is the white man's game and if my kids go there and interact with them that the mzungu will steal them and never bring them back. But I could not afford to feed them. I had to trust the mzungu. What choice did I have?"

Chapter 6
Mzungu

Andrew Popp plays with children at a Chinese orphanage during his school year abroad in 2003.

Mzungu is a Swahili word that translates as "someone who wanders around without purpose." The term was initially used by Africans to describe European missionaries and explorers, then later traders, colonists, and eventually tourists. The word *mzungu* has come to encompass all white people and is usually tinged with distrust born of years of exploitation by those who fit the description. However, without mzungu there would be no Coach Robert and without Coach Robert, Phiona Mutesi would likely still be selling maize from a saucepan on her head, assuming there was still a Phiona at all. While the mzungu in Phiona's story come from far away and have lived vastly different lives, the disparity in their journeys from those of Phiona and Robert Katende aren't as stark as they might initially appear. They are all wanderers, but none without a purpose.

■ ■ ■ ■

Carl Russell Hammond, Jr. was born in suburban Boston on July 16, 1933, the son of an international banker. The Hammonds lived a cozy, upper-middle-class life in their white two-story colonial home until the day when the boy they called Russ was four years old and his life turned upside down. One evening, when his father, Carl, Sr., was away on a business trip, Russ's mother, Helen, told Russ and his older sister, Daphne, that they were moving to California where their grandmother lived. Helen didn't mention divorce. Russ didn't understand what was going on, but he didn't question his mother's authority. He just packed his belongings as she requested and boarded the train, unsure if he would ever see his father again.

Four days later, Helen and her two children arrived in California to a far less comfortable life. Russ and Daphne were taken in by their grandmother while Helen searched for work. It was the tail end of the Great Depression.

Shortly after the family arrived in California, Helen's mother moved to Bellflower, a hardscrabble suburb of Los Angeles, where for the next few months she and the two children lived in a small shack where they cooked over a wood stove and the kids bathed in a tin tub located in a storage shed behind the house.

At age five, Russ and his sister moved back to Los Angeles to live with their mother. A latchkey kid, Russ organized a bunch of local boys into a gang who used to hang out at the local Woolworth's and shoplift candy to fill their starving bellies. In 1940, Helen married C. Robert Carr, her children assumed their stepfather's last name, and the family moved to Santa Barbara, where they continued to struggle. "We were so poor that I remember making sandwiches day after day from the peanut butter that I could scrape off the lid," Russ says. "My clothes were threadbare and my shoes had holes in them." Russ's chores included caring for three dozen chickens penned up behind the garage and cleaning out the chicken coop. He wandered the neighborhood daily selling eggs.

Russ Carr was an ill-behaved child who often got into fights, until a coach at Harding Elementary School, Gordon Gray, began to develop Russ's athletic ability as a way to lure him off the streets. Progressing through grade school, Russ was named captain of every sport he tried, from baseball to football to basketball.

One summer during junior high, Russ was invited to participate in a program called Camp Conestoga that included an overnight camping trip. He and 14 other boys were bedded down for a night in the woods when sometime before dawn, Russ says he awoke to a bright light above him. He initially thought he was dreaming. "I heard a voice that I thought must be an angel speaking to me," Carr remembers. "The voice said, 'I have chosen you to follow me.' That moment began my spiritual journey."

During his senior year at Santa Barbara High School, Russ met Jay Beaumont, a student at local Westmont College, who recruited him to join the Christian group Young Life. After high school, the St. Louis Browns offered Carr a chance to play professional baseball, but he opted to concentrate on his education and seek his spiritual direction, eventually choosing to follow Beaumont to Westmont College, where Russ would meet his future wife, Sue. Russ enrolled with ten cents in his pocket. His mother couldn't believe he'd turned down a professional baseball contract as well as athletic scholarships to the University of Arizona and UCLA.

Russ graduated from Westmont in 1956

with plans to become a teacher, and the Carrs began an odyssey that included four children and 18 moves over three decades. At each stop, Carr took a personal interest in the most troubled students. At one Oregon school he met a girl who wore the same stained, dirty dress every day. Carr drove to her home, which consisted of two rooms and an outhouse, with no electricity or running water. The mother had abandoned the family. The father worked as a logger, and the responsibility of raising her three younger siblings fell to the girl in Carr's class. To bathe she had to go to a nearby creek, then carry water back for drinking and cooking. After Carr discovered her circumstances, the girl was given a locker in the women's dressing room at school, which was stocked with toiletries, and a job in the cafeteria where she was able to eat a square meal each day.

The Carrs eventually moved to Washington, to Germany, and to England, before coming full circle back to Santa Barbara in 1966 when Carr accepted a job at Westmont College as a teacher as well as the school's baseball and soccer coach. Carr had never played soccer in school but had developed an interest in the sport during his three years living in Europe.

At the end of the 1968 baseball season, Carr was faced with a decision. Both soccer and baseball were year-round programs and each team felt neglected when Carr coached the other sport. Carr gave up baseball and decided to pour his full energy into his soccer program. "Later, I could look back and realize how God had a hand in my decision," Carr says. "Soccer would ultimately lead me into the next phase of my life and serve as the vehicle to open doors to what would become my true calling."

Who knows when the light bulb actually turned on? The passage of time has obscured exactly when the idea first struck him. But for Russ Carr it may have happened in a park in Guatemala. Carr traveled to Guatemala City in 1974 as the coach of a collegiate all-star soccer team on a Christian barnstorming tour through Central America. He and two of his players left their hotel one afternoon to kick around a soccer ball in a local park, and before long, 50 Guatemalan children showed up out of nowhere wanting to play. As Carr and the two players scrimmaged with the kids and tried to communicate across the language barrier, Carr began to view it as a seminal moment. At one point he stepped out of the game to soak in the joy on the children's faces. That steamy afternoon in Central America felt like a beginning. The seed of sports outreach to underdeveloped countries had been planted.

In 1982, Carr chose to leave his job and friends behind in Santa Barbara and move across the country to Lynchburg, Virginia, where he and Sue purchased a farmhouse flanked by two five-acre meadows. Carr planned to use those meadows for soccer fields, staging areas for his future sports ministry. Shortly after he arrived in Lynchburg, Carr accepted a job at Liberty University, the Christian school founded by Rev. Jerry Fallwell, where he eventually met Vernon Brewer, the director of Liberty's Light Ministry, a student mission group. In 1987 Brewer was preparing to take his annual summer mission trip with Liberty students when he approached Carr about joining the group as a basketball coach.

Carr agreed and then asked, "Where will the first stop be?"

Brewer replied, "Uganda."

During his visit to Uganda with the team, Carr and his six players staged basketball clinics at schools and organized a workout program for the Ugandan national basketball team. They also shared their testimony at churches, hospitals, and a prison, as well as in the streets of Kampala. One afternoon a man who had been a student at Kampala University during the Idi Amin regime approached Carr and tearfully shared his story about returning home for lunch one day to find his father, mother, three brothers, and two sisters murdered by Amin's soldiers. Carr comforted the heartbroken man, who was inspired that day to convert to Christianity. At that moment, Carr decided to make a long-term commitment to do whatever he possibly could to fix what ailed Uganda.

By the time he and the Liberty team returned to Uganda the following year, Carr had officially founded Sports Outreach Institute. The organization's mission would be to use soccer as a catalyst to offer the guidance of religion to the country's most impoverished people. Uganda's National Council of Sports assigned a man named Barnabas Mwesiga to act as the group's host and guide. Mwesiga was one of the best strikers ever to play for the Ugandan national soccer team and also the team's former coach. Carr and Mwesiga struck up a friendship over their shared interest in soccer and coaching and Mwesiga would become the first Ugandan to accept a job with

Sports Outreach.

"They discovered me and I see it as a blessing," Mwesiga says. "I didn't know about sports ministry. My interest all along was to raise young people to accept soccer as a means of improving their lives. Then when the ministry came in, I found an additional tool."

In 1995 Mwesiga introduced Carr to Aloysius Kyazze, the former Uganda national team captain. Carr immediately saw that Kyazze shared his passion and offered him a position with Sports Outreach as well. At the time, Kyazze was coaching a soccer team of born-again Christians called Miracle, grooming several young sports ministers including a gifted striker by the name of Robert Katende.

One morning probably in 2002, with Barnabas Mwesiga at the steering wheel driving down a dirt road in Southern Uganda toward another village where he and Carr would preach, the two began talking about the burgeoning numbers of slum youth in Kampala. Suddenly an idea flashed through Carr's mind. He began to outline a plan on his yellow notepad that would ultimately become the blueprint for Sports Outreach in the city slums.

Carr plotted the foundation of the plan with Mwesiga that day. Soccer players with leadership potential would be selected to form a team called the Good News Football Club and then would be trained in how to implement Carr's program for children in the slums. The projects would ultimately include five components: sports, vocational training, community service, education, and meals — all under an umbrella of discipleship — and would first be implemented in three of Kampala's eight slums: Kibuli, Nateete, and Katwe.

Understanding that mzungu such as him would initially be viewed either with suspicion or as a target for a bribe, Carr sought ways to gain the respect and acceptance of the slum communities. His team would first contact the local leader elected by the people of that slum district and gain approval for some community service that would include collecting trash and clearing out drainage ditches. After several hours of cleanup, they would bring out soccer balls and encourage children to participate in a varicty of games.

Carr, who was nearly 70 by then, knew he was getting too old to spearhead his plan over the long term. He needed somebody who could take his vision and expand upon it. The Sports Outreach board asked Carr to find an American who would recruit the next generation of Ugandan leaders for the organization. One day Carr invited a local pastor named Rodney Suddith to visit his Virginia farm. During a tour of the grounds, Carr explained to Suddith his vision of sports ministry.

"Gosh, I guess I've kind of been working as a sports minister my whole life," Suddith told Carr in his syrupy Southern drawl. "I just never knew there was such a thing."

"I think I was raised in Camelot," Rodney Suddith says.

It was actually Newport News, Virginia, in the 1950s. Rodney's father, Joseph Buxton "Buck" Suddith, was a classic blue-collar World War II vet. Buck's father had been a timekeeper in the shipyard. Buck grew up by the water and loved sailing, and it was always understood he would follow his father to work in the shipyard as well. Buck finished high school and then joined the United States Merchant Marine in World War II. When he returned from the war, he married Lois Parker and they had four children, including Rodney, born in 1949.

Buck got a job as an electrician at the shipyard in Newport News and the Suddiths lived in a two-room bungalow on Gambol Street in a neighborhood called Green Oaks, not far from the docks. Every father in Green Oaks was a shipyard worker, the patron of a lower-middle-class family, and no one ever moved. Along Gambol Street the families had names like Ostrosky, Turnidge, Judkins, Smith, Pulley, Schaumberg, and Mackenzie. Their roots traced all over the world. They were all white.

"I was never in a classroom with a person of color all the way through high school, yet my parents taught me to be very sensitive to everyone," Suddith says. "We were never allowed to make any kind of negative statement about any ethnic group or person of color. It was a very segregated time in the South, so people all around us would, but never a Suddith. At the time I didn't understand what a powerful life lesson that was."

On Rodney's first day of first grade he and the other students were asked to count as high as they could. Some of the other kids had gone to preschool or kindergarten. Rodney had not, because no one in his neighborhood did. All of the other students in the class could print their names. Rodney didn't know how to write an *R*. Because he was sitting in the front row, Rodney was the first to stand up and count. He counted to six.

"I was six years old and I thought that was pretty good," Suddith says. "Well, right behind me there were kids counting to places I'd never heard of, counting beyond a hundred, and it was really kind of a humbling experience. I think that's when I began to realize there was a competitive streak in me. I felt embarrassed and I didn't want to be in that position again. I wanted to push myself a little bit more."

For most of his childhood Rodney did not own a bike. The yards along Gambol Street were small, so if the kids in the neighborhood wanted to play baseball, they needed to go to Deer Park, about two miles away. When the other kids pedaled off on their bikes for Deer Park, Rodney took off running on a shortcut through the woods and would usually be the first one to arrive. Those jogs developed in him an interest in running that blossomed as Rodney grew older. The sport clicked with him. Rodney was an introvert and running fit his personality.

Because he was not naturally fast, Rodney's track teammates at Warwick High School jokingly called him "Rocket." He eventually found his niche as a miler, thriving on guts and determination, driven by a visceral fear of losing to other runners that he knew possessed more talent.

"High school sports taught me what it is to live in-between," Suddith says. "I think that's the greatest lesson I ever learned from sports. Mentally most of us are in between where we would like to be and where we are. I had an idea what I wanted and I wasn't there yet, but I really wanted to get there. If I decided that I wanted to reach a certain level in a classroom or on the field then before I could achieve it, I would always raise the standard a little bit higher."

During many of his races in high school, Rodney would push himself well beyond his comfort zone and after the race he would urinate blood. The harder he ran, the more blood. "I knew my body was failing," Suddith says. "But in the neighborhood I grew up in, if you had a problem like that, you kept it to yourself."

When Rodney was a junior in high school, he was called to the guidance office where his counselor said, "We'd like you to start looking at colleges."

"College?" Rodney said. "I'm going to work in the shipyard."

"But you can go to William & Mary on a scholarship."

Rodney spent the rest of the day thinking for the first time about attending college, about leaving the predestined path of his life. That night Rodney discussed the idea with his father, who was clearly disappointed. Buck's circle believed that when you finished high school, you went to work. He spoke derisively about "college boys." Then Buck said, "Do you think you're too good for the shipyard?"

"No, I don't think that at all," Rodney said. "I just think there might be something else out there."

At William & Mary in the late 1960s there were still very few people of color in Rodney Suddith's class. Like so many college students at that time, he was trying to figure out the rapidly changing rules in American society. So he decided to spend a semester at Hampton University, leaving a campus that was nearly all white for a campus almost entirely black.

"I wasn't embraced for being different and that was really an eye-opener for me," Suddith says of Hampton. "I learned more about myself because although I'm an introvert by nature, I didn't really like being totally alone, feeling isolated just based on my appearance, especially when I didn't know how to cross that barrier to feel comfortable."

As an athlete at William & Mary, Suddith found himself firmly in-between. His team included two sub-4-minute milers. That was always Suddith's goal, breaking four minutes. In one dual meet in his sophomore year he was on pace to finally achieve it when, during a rough race, he was knocked off stride in the final turn and finished third in a time of 4:00.3. Suddith would never get that close again.

After his sophomore year, Suddith qualified for the 1972 Olympic Trials in the mile. As a 23-year-old, he figured those Olympics in Munich would likely be his only chance to run on that grand stage. When Suddith arrived at the trials in Eugene, Oregon, he found out just how small his pond was. He was intimidated and his body was failing him. He didn't make it past the first heat.

"That's when my kidney really started getting bad and I could tell I was coming undone," Suddith says. "That was the era when they were just starting to check pee and when they got a cup of my pee, I knew my running career was over."

Suddith underwent surgery that evening and doctors discovered he suffered from a birth defect. One of his kidneys had deteriorated to the point of failure. Competitive running was putting too much pressure on his renal system and the kidney had to be removed. Says Suddith, "I was haunted by the idea that I knew I'd never have another chance to chase my athletic dreams."

Suddith would become the first in his family ever to graduate from college. He then went to graduate school at Virginia Commonwealth University, where he earned a teacher's certificate and met his future wife, Janice. Suddith's first teaching job was at Thomas Jefferson High School, an inner-city school in Richmond. The student population consisted almost entirely of black students bused into a mostly white neighborhood. Suddith taught history and political science and became an assistant coach for the track team, which captured four state championships over the next seven years. "In some ways it was the most rewarding place to be because you were really giving people hands up," Suddith says. "I remember seeing kids graduate and go to Harvard, but I found out that most stories in the inner-city don't end as you'd like."

Suddith was particularly affected by the story of Sherrie Trent, one of the female runners on Jefferson High's team. Suddith used to drive his orange Volkswagen beetle into the projects each morning at 5 A.M. to pick up Sherrie for what was known as Dawn Patrol, the team's early-morning workouts. "One night I got a call that Sherrie's mother and her boyfriend had been in an argument and that he'd just murdered Sherrie with a shotgun right in front of her mother," Suddith says. "Going through that, I realized there are some things I can't control and that are beyond my comprehension. That just wore me down."

Sherrie's death helped trigger the end of Suddith's tenure at Jefferson High. On the day Sherrie's teammates won the state championship in her honor, Suddith received a job offer to teach and coach at E. C. Glass High School in Lynchburg. Suddith knew he needed a change. He took the job.

Suddith ended up coaching at Glass High for only a short time; at the end of one track season, he promptly quit. Suddith had a strong spiritual sense that he was supposed to be doing something else. He and Janice had four children and Suddith had become deeply involved in his church. Eventually the church asked him if he would do full-time service as the director of Christian education. Suddith had no real training other than his parents being Sunday school teachers and some knowledge of the Bible, but he accepted the job despite his fear that he might be underqualified.

The same year Suddith arrived in Lynchburg, Russ Carr bought his farm as a staging area for his new path in life. One of the elders at Suddith's church had helped Carr buy his property and suggested to Suddith that he meet Carr. Suddith asked why. "Remember when you told us we should use sports to help kids in the church?" the elder said. "Well, Russ is talking about that weird stuff, too. We don't get it, but you all might bond."

Eight years later, Rodney Suddith stood beside Russ Carr in Gulu, Uganda. Gulu was then Uganda's headquarters for horror. Thousands of children were being kidnapped by Joseph Kony and his vicious cadre of rebels known as the Lord's Resistance Army. Those children were either killed or forced to become child soldiers in the LRA. Suddith and Carr stared in amazement on their first night in Gulu as thousands of children, some as young as three years old and carrying only a blanket, walked from the surrounding villages into Gulu's many camps for internally displaced people, hoping to escape the LRA. Aloysius Kyazze, who directed Sports Outreach's operation in Gulu, told them these kids were known as "night commuters" or "the invisible children."

Kyazze shared stories about children who had been forced by the rebels to kill their parents as they were being abducted. Young girls were repeatedly raped and tortured while others were sold as slaves. When these children escaped the LRA or were liberated by government troops, their emotional state was in complete collapse. As Suddith surveyed this scene and listened to stories from survivors, he sensed his life was about to change again.

"It was horrific seeing thousands of kids in a fenced area just trying to feel safe because they were afraid they were going to be kidnapped or murdered," Suddith says. "I looked at my life and it was such a disconnect. I'd become so isolated and so secure that I was as boring as dirty water. I had gotten away from the in-between. When I got home from Uganda I talked to my wife and in an unfair way I used the ultimate Christian phrase on her: *I think God's calling me to this.*"

Suddith experienced a similar gut reaction the first time he visited Katwe. "I'd been to some pretty tough places on mission trips, but the face of hopelessness is a scary one to me because often times those faces turn to violence, either against themselves or against others," Suddith says. "My first experience in the Katwe slum was looking at a powder keg about to explode. Outsiders would tell me that the people there need Jesus. I would say, 'Yes, they do, but they also need education, they need job training, they need food.' "

Suddith realized that Uganda, like most developing countries, did not provide the same economic safety net for its poorest people that exists in America and he thought Sports Outreach should attempt to fill some of that void. Rather than take a purely evangelical approach, Suddith began with Carr's blueprint and devised his own holistic approach, leaning on six tenets: social, psychological, emotional, mental, physical, and spiritual.

"I thought there was no way to address this problem solely on a purely spiritual level," Suddith says. "We can't just tell these children, 'Don't fear, God is with you.' We've got to show them we can address all of their challenges. I would go to the slums and see where a Christian organization had come in and converted hundreds of people, but that didn't stick. Others fed people, but if that's all you do, then who's going to feed them tomorrow?"

Carr's mandate to Suddith was to help develop the young leaders mentored by Mwesiga and Kyazze. The first time Suddith met Robert Katende he immediately recognized his potential.

"There was something special about Robert, a certain dignity and awareness that just stood out," Suddith says. "Robert would have scared me if I had to compete against him. He had just begun the chess program and what amazed me about it was that he had a grand plan. The plan wasn't just that this was an alternative activity for the kids who don't want to play soccer. The plan was that these kids are going to learn from him, they're going to get better in school, become more socially interactive, become young people with a chance to succeed."

When some of the purists in the Sports Outreach community complained that chess wasn't really a sport and shouldn't take any time away from soccer, Suddith was there to back Katende. Suddith, who has shuttled between Virginia and Uganda dozens of times over the past decade, has become a valued mentor for Katende and the other two dozen young Ugandan Sports Outreach ministers.

"My goal is to help these poor children

grow and to do that I try to train Robert and the other leaders how to stay in-between," Suddith says. "If someday I went to Uganda and met the ministers and children that I'm blessed to work with and I thought that this was all that they would ever be, it would really crush me. People who know me best say that if there's any good quality I have, it is a way of helping people get from where they are to where they want to be. I believe I am called to help others who are not able to count past six, but really, really want to get to seven."

Santa Barbara, California, is one of the best places on earth. In many ways, it really is Camelot. It is beautiful, prosperous, and nurturing of children — everything Katwe is not. Andrew Popp grew up there.

Andrew's parents, Norm and Tricia, describe their only son as kind and thoughtful and sensitive and impressionable. As a young boy, Andrew loved to read. Possessed with a vivid imagination, Andrew would lose himself in stories. Once, after reading *Aladdin,* he had nightmares for a week about the villain Jafar. Andrew was a very driven child, who learned how to play guitar, piano, and drums. As a fourth grader he was asked to choose a younger child to counsel for his school's Big Buddy program. All of the other kids shied away from one particular child with Down syndrome. Andrew said that was the only kid he wanted to mentor. As a sixth grader during reading period, while the rest of the kids flipped through comic books or teen magazines, Andrew read the Bible.

Andrew was a dreamer. He grew up wanting to drive monster trucks and then he wanted to be a professional surfer and then he wanted to be seven feet tall, until he discovered girls and realized that his 6'9″ stature was plenty tall enough. His proud parents describe him as larger than life.

Andrew Popp was another person for whom sports had the potential to change his life. He and his father would play basketball for hours on their driveway hoop and Norm coached his son in the sport until high school. During Andrew's junior year at San Marcos High School, he studied in China, learning the language and playing on a basketball team there. He also taught the game to children while on a church mission to Guatemala during the following summer of 2004.

As a senior at San Marcos High, Andrew earned all-league honors in both volleyball as a middle blocker and basketball as his team's starting center. He also scored over 1500 on the SATs, which made him a model student-athlete for college recruiters. He could have his choice of college. Andrew was recruited by dozens of schools around the country for basketball, but his dream was always to attend an Ivy League school like Harvard or Yale. Those schools showed interest in him, but for reasons that his parents still cannot explain, Andrew began to unravel psychologically during his senior year and when it came time to submit his college applications, Andrew missed the deadlines and those schools eventually lost interest.

In 2005 — the same year that half a world away nine-year-old Phiona Mutesi first sat down at a chessboard and began to change her life — very early one summer morning just weeks after his high school graduation, 18-year-old Andrew Popp drove along San Marcos Pass Road up into the mountains to Cold Spring Canyon Bridge, a 1,200-foot-long steel arch along California State Route 154 that spans a valley connecting Santa Barbara to Santa Ynez. At about 5:15 A.M. a deputy sheriff driving to work spotted Andrew's car on fire at the bridge's north end and Andrew inching his way from the centerline of the bridge toward the thigh-high guardrail. When the policeman approached, Andrew, with a blank stare on his face, leaped backward and dropped 200 feet into a foggy wooded ravine.

Norm and Tricia Popp were devastated. They initially struggled with how to memorialize their son. Then they recalled one Sunday morning at Santa Barbara Community Church, when their family heard an evangelist named Russ Carr speak so passionately about his vision for Sports Outreach Institute. The Popps decided the organization's focus on children, sports, and academics perfectly reflected who Andrew was. Instead of flowers, the Popps requested that donations be sent to Sports Outreach in their son's name. When the Popps realized the potential of that money to help dozens of children in Uganda pay for school, they took the funds they had planned to spend on Andrew's college education and with Suddith's help they created the Andrew Popp Memorial Scholarship.

For years after his death, Andrew's parents could never bring themselves to witness the fruits of the scholarship. Suddith kept encouraging them to come to Uganda and on the five-year anniversary of their son's suicide, the Popps traveled to Kampala and met Phiona Mutesi and the 60 other slum children who would not be attending school were it not for the Andrew Popp Memorial Scholarship. It sounds like a simple story of redemption, but for the Popps, it is far more complicated than that.

Standing on the balcony at the Namirembe Guest House in Kampala, on the morning of September 18, 2010, Andrew's parents spoke about what visiting the children studying on the Popp Scholarship meant to them:

> **Tricia Popp:** "Coming to Uganda has crystallized my understanding of our experience. As a Westerner we don't like to face death and we don't like to face loss. We had difficulty navigating that experience because it was so foreign to us. Our life has been completely upended and so this experience has been amazing for me. Phiona's life brings us such joy. It's an incredible gift. I will never lose the sadness of losing Andrew and we would want him back in a heartbeat, but I'm so grateful to be able to celebrate Phiona's life. I think what I've learned is that's why we have two hands. There's life and there's death. This trip has helped me understand death and life and their interconnection.

"I think people want us to be who we were, but I don't want to ever be the same. I want to embrace Andrew's loss just as Phiona has had to embrace all the hardship in her life. I feel so much more a sense of wholeness despite my loss because this trip helps me understand that most of the world suffers so much more than we do. To infuse Phiona's life with some hope is a huge gift. Phiona's mom thanked us. Are you kidding me? I thanked her for having the courage to face every day taking care of Phiona. We're both moms. I have sadness in my life as a mom and she does, too. I felt such solidarity with her. I feel like we're partners. I'm in no way helping her any more than she's helping me. When Phiona's mom knelt and said, 'Thank you,' I had this overwhelming clarity that we were all part of the same family and who wouldn't do what they could to help their family?

"Our son listened to some dark voice that said that his life was better off ended. That's too bad. He was my sweet boy. That's the mystery that we hold. It's a puzzle we'll never resolve and I don't think we're made to make sense of it. We spent two years asking why and we finally realized that you ask why until you can live with the why. This is helping us live with the why."

Norm Popp: "I don't know if I've ever tried to verbalize this before, but no matter how sick someone is or whatever their circumstances are, while they are still living there's hope. For me and my wife, dealing with the fact that Andrew was gone and there was no hope has been one of the hardest things to come to grips with. On this trip there are sixty-one kids on Popp Scholarship and we hope to see every one of them. There's no question their circumstances are dire. It's gut-wrenching. But at least there is hope there.

"One thing that's tricky is that people like to put a ribbon on tragedy. People say that there must have been a reason that Andrew died. There's no way in my mind that I will ever think that the good things that have come out of this were worth his death. Nothing could ever be worth that. Nothing can replace him. It's not a mathematical equation. It's not one for sixty-one. It doesn't add up that way. But it is redemptive in another way, because had that not happened we wouldn't be here. We wouldn't have started this scholarship. We, in a unique way, appreciate life and what it means the way kids don't.

"The connection we feel with Phiona is not like we've given this kid some money and she's doing well. We're pulling for her life in a way that she wouldn't understand, in a much deeper way. It's so tricky because Andrew didn't value life, because he didn't have any kind of perspective. I know these kids don't either, but if we can somehow help get them through and keep them alive, they might have hope for a future.

"I think that one of the difficult things is that we can't make a hero out of Andrew and yet we love him as much as any parent could. What he did wasn't in any way exemplary or a courageous thing. It was an impulsive thing in dealing with his problems. That's the rub. But we did want to honor him. He made a mistake that was permanent. Fortunately, most people make mistakes that are redeemable. As long as you're still alive there's no reason not to have hope and we are trying to communicate that to the kids that we see here. We aren't able to talk about the circumstances of

Andrew's death particularly, but we are able to say, 'Hey, we lost our son and the life that he doesn't have, we'd like you to have. We'd like to have you alive with hope.' "

Phiona's annual school tuition, funded by the Andrew Popp Memorial Scholarship, is $75.

Middlegame

CHAPTER 7
LIKE A BOY, BUT NOT A BOY

Robert Katende at the chessboard in Katwe with Phiona Mutesi, the girl whom he believed he could teach to become a "prophet" and eventually a national champion.

Chess is generally believed to have originated in India sometime around the sixth century, where it was known by the Sanskrit name *chaturanga* and consisted of pieces divided into four divisions: infantry, cavalry, elephants, and chariotry. The game migrated through Persia, where it assumed the name *Shah Mat,* which translates to "the king is helpless" and is the origin of the English word "checkmate." The game then spread across Russia, where it would eventually be favored by the tsars, and into Western Europe, often transported to new regions by invading armies.

The pieces were named for roles in the courts of kings during the Middle Ages and play was modeled after how wars were contested in that period. In the 15th century the name *chess* first came into use and the game assumed the same general rules that have governed it ever since, with the queen as the most powerful piece on the board. By the early 1800s chess clubs and chess literature began to appear. In America, Thomas Jefferson and Benjamin Franklin both wrote about playing chess. The first modern chess tournament was staged in London in 1851. A few decades later, a Czech named Wilhelm Steinitz revolutionized the game by emphasizing the position of his pieces on the board to build strength and attack an opponent's weaknesses, utilizing his more theoretical approach to capture the first World Chess Championship in 1886.

Steinitz lost his title in 1894 to German mathematician Emanuel Lasker, who remained the world champion for a record 27 years. The epicenter of chess would gradually shift to the Soviet Union, where from 1948 until 2000 the world championship never left Russian hands, except between 1972 and 1975, when it was held by American Bobby Fischer. The International Olympic Committee officially recognized chess as a sport in 1999, but has yet to include it as part of the Olympic program because it lacks physical activity.

The highest ranking a player can achieve in chess is Grandmaster, a distinction earned primarily through consistently excellent play in events sanctioned by FIDE. In 1950 FIDE first awarded the title of Grandmaster to 27 players and there are now more than 1,300 male Grandmasters across the globe. Chess long being the provenance of men, very few women have ever broken into the top 500 rated players in the sport and it wasn't until 1991 that Susan Polgar became the first woman to earn a Grandmaster title on the same basis as her male counterparts. Polgar is currently among the 22 women who hold that title. There is also a gender-specific title, Woman Grandmaster, with lesser requirements, which has been achieved by more than 200 players.

Among the most popular sports in the world, chess infiltrated almost everywhere else on earth before it discovered sub-Saharan Africa. It needed 1,500 years to find Uganda. Initially introduced in Uganda through the country's colonial ties, chess was played only in homes and a few schools and clubs before the early 1970s. In 1972 a group of Ugandan doctors, inspired by the highly publicized world championship match between Fischer and Russian Boris Spassky, formed the Chess Association of Uganda. The group organized sporadic games in Kampala, often at Mulago Hospital or Makerere University, and would later become known as the Uganda Chess Federation after its affiliation with FIDE in 1976.

The first chess literature shared by the federation's players was a photocopied chess book given to Mathew Kibuuka, one of Uganda's trailblazers in the sport, as a wedding present. In the late 1970s the federation began publishing a small pamphlet called *Checkmate* that helped spread interest in the game. Uganda's chess evolution was further accelerated by an American chess administrator, Jerry Bibuld, who traveled to Uganda for a chess seminar in the early 1980s and subsequently began mailing issues of the United States Chess Federation magazine, *Chess Life,* to the Ugandan federation. "Reading *Chess Life* is how we learned the game," says current Ugandan national chess team coach Joachim Okoth, another of his nation's pioneers in the sport. "Before that we had read a few chess books and memorized some moves, but we didn't always know why we were making those moves. With Jerry's help, we learned why."

Of the 158 chess federations recognized by FIDE, Uganda's is among the most recently established. The first Ugandan national champion was an Englishman, a professor at Mbarara University. While

Uganda has occasionally produced a strong player — the most notable is Willy Zabasajja, who won the Ugandan national championship a record nine times and became the first East African to earn the title of FIDE Master — the nation has never been ranked among the top 100 in the world in the FIDE ratings. While there are six Grandmasters in Africa, Uganda has never produced a Grandmaster or even an International Master, the level below Grandmaster and above FIDE Master. Because there is no translation for the word "chess" in her native Luganda language, whenever Phiona Mutesi talks about the game, she must shift into English for any chess terminology.

The man who first brought chess into Ugandan schools was Damien Grimes, a white Catholic priest and missionary who in 1967 took over as headmaster at Namasagali College, one of the most prestigious middle and high schools in the country at that time. Grimes began a chess program at Namasagali that slowly spread to other schools. Eventually Father Grimes organized a chess tournament among a few schools in Kampala, many of which also had headmasters from Great Britain. That tournament has since expanded to schools across the nation and adopted his name.

It was on the 2005 Father Grimes tournament where Robert Katende set his sights. His chess project had been in existence for a little over a year and the coach was beginning to sense that his players needed a goal. "I was concerned that what we were doing had started to become monotonous," Katende says. "You come one day. You train. You go. You come the next day. You train. You go. The question became, after that, what? I thought we needed to be training to go somewhere."

So Katende appealed to the chairman of the Uganda Chess Federation at the time, Enoch Barumba, requesting to enter players from his chess project in the 2005 Father Grimes tournament. The idea was emphatically rejected.

"Barumba was asking me, 'How can they come?' " Katende says. "He told me, 'These are street children. They do not go to school. How can they play in a schools tournament? How can they come and play students from well-established families? This cannot be allowed.' When I talked of slum children he thought he knew who they are. He thought they were dirty. He thought they were badly behaved. He thought they were hooligans who will offend the other children in some way. So he had all the reasons to refuse me."

Katende knew he would have to dispel a long-standing class prejudice in Uganda. Many Ugandans consider street children irredeemable and resist their integration into more privileged society. Katende visited Barumba numerous times over a period of three months, offering various ideas for how his program's children could compete in the tournament. He suggested that his players could compete as guest participants. He told Barumba that his children were young and inexperienced and certainly would not win a trophy, but they needed a platform to learn more about competitive chess. Katende also appealed to Godfrey Gali, the federation's general secretary.

"Robert's request was politically sensitive," Gali says. "When I spoke to the chairman he asked me, 'How do they fit in here?' He didn't want to allow that kind of arrangement, but I had met some of these kids and I convinced the chairman that we need to show that one of our federation's objectives is to spread the game to the entire Ugandan society."

Barumba finally relented, but under a condition that he suspected would preclude the slum kids from playing. "The registration cost was high and he knew I didn't have the money, so he said we could play as guest participants if we paid the registration," Katende says. "It was like a hurdle that he believed would rule us out. So I talked to Sports Outreach and they released the money and then I went back to Barumba and he was surprised that I had the money, but he had no way of taking back his words."

When Katende explained to the Pioneers what had happened, they could not believe it. "Before that time children had been dropping out of the program because they thought that chess was a waste of time," Ivan Mutesasira says. "Many had actually lost hope because they didn't see any future in playing chess, but when Coach Robert told us we were going for a tournament we were all surprised and excited."

Katende's team included the Pioneers: Samuel, Richard, Ivan, Julius, and Gerald, along with Phiona's brother Brian. The boys ranged in age from seven to 13 years old. For most of them, the 2005 Father Grimes tournament at King's College Budo in Mpigi was their first-ever trip out of the Katwe slum. When they were picked up in a van for the ride to King's College, it was their first time in a vehicle. During the 45-minute drive out of Kampala to Mpigi, Katende briefed the children on basic life skills, like how to open a water bottle and how to eat with silverware. They arrived to a vast campus full of trees and walkways threading through landscaped flowers. The playing hall was an austere theater with ceiling fans and glassed windows, neither of which the children had seen before. After letting the children soak in this new environment, Katende had a message for them. "It is us who know who we are," Katende told them. "They don't know who we are. What we need to do is to behave as if we live their life."

Katende tried to anticipate anything that could reveal the children's sheltered background, but some things were beyond his control. His players did not own any clothes that were not stained or torn. They were competing against children dressed in pressed school uniforms. Some even wore blazers and knickers.

"At the tournament we were isolated, and some of the other competitors laughed at our team and thought we were dirty, when in fact my players were wearing their best clothes and looking as smart as they could," Katende says. "Some of the students asked, 'Which school is this one?' Because it was their first time to see kids in this state."

Eventually, word leaked out that

Katende's players were not schoolchildren at all. "They called us street kids," Ivan says. "We heard them say, 'Street kids? How do we play with street kids?' It was that kind of intimidation and torture. We were being shunned. They looked down on us."

When the tournament began, Katende's players were clearly affected by their treatment from the other players. They were all extremely nervous. "Gerald was shaking, the whole of himself shaking, so he could not even hold a piece," Katende says. "I told him, 'The people you are playing are not shaking. Just be confident. Don't mind if you lose. Just play as if we are still down there in Katwe training.' "

"Before the playing I would really feel good just to be in a new place I had never been," Samuel Mayanja says. "But as you go to play the game then you somehow develop some fear and many times I used to shiver at the board. Then I would remember coach telling me to be confident enough not to shiver. I could somehow gain some confidence. I could look at some of my other friends from the project and see them all stable and somehow playing very well and seated comfortably, so I somehow also developed that courage and started feeling better and better."

The tournament lasted for a week and Katende never let his players out of his sight. He was anxious about allowing them to interact with the other children because his players did not speak English well and he knew that could potentially lead to teasing and fights. While the students slept in dormitory beds, Katende and his children all slept on the dormitory floor sharing one mattress as a pillow. The kids from Katwe ate all of their meals together, marveling at their access to eggs, milk, bread, fruit, and the routine of three meals a day. "My kids would tell me, 'Coach, I am already satisfied and they are calling us for dinner,' " Katende says. "So they had to go for dinner with no room left in their stomachs. It was really something very exciting for them."

Katende's team finished the tournament ranked in the middle of the pack overall. They had outperformed many more-established chess programs, to the surprise of their coach. The certificate they received at the end of the tournament referred to them as "The Children's Team." They were given a tiny trophy and medals acknowledging them as the youngest team in the tournament.

"We sneaked the kids from the slum in there and fortunately they played well and they were very disciplined, even more disciplined than those who were formally in schools," Gali says. "When you asked them to assist with something, they rushed very fast to do it. In a way they touched my heart. They became darlings to us in the federation. Eventually even the other students realized that those kids were good, that they had potential, and they were eventually accepted."

While The Children's Team won some games at the 2005 Father Grimes Tournament, the lasting memory for Katende occurred when Ivan was playing a game in which he had a significant positional advantage and appeared certain to mate his opponent. Instead, Ivan committed a foolish blunder that forced him to settle for a draw.

"Ivan was sure that he would win and when it resulted in a draw he cried seriously, crying so loud that I had to get him out of the playing hall," Katende says. "The attitude from the school players was that this was an insult because this little kid is crying after he makes a draw against an older kid. I heard some people say, 'These street kids are funny. How do you cry over a game?' Those people didn't understand what the game meant to these children."

■ ■ ■ ■

Because she had no other choice, Harriet let her children go.

Brian and Phiona returned to the dusty veranda each day to play chess. Occasionally, they could even borrow a board from Katende and return to their shack to play at home, game after game after game, neither sibling wanting to leave the board having lost the last game to the other, so they would play on until the last drops of kerosene burned out in their lamp.

"I remember the first time Phiona defeated me," Brian says. "We were all training for a tournament and we were paired together and Phiona won me. I felt ashamed, so what Phiona did is she told everybody that I was the one who won instead. That is a good sister. Ever since that day whenever she beats me, she isn't happy. She tells me the mistakes I made so that I can fix them and try to beat her the next time. She doesn't like beating me."

The truth is that Brian doesn't beat Phiona very much anymore, due in part to the time he has invested in making her a better player. "Coach Robert once told us that because there are so few girls playing chess in Uganda that Phiona had a chance to rise quickly in the game in our nation," Brian says. "So the boys at the project began to take more of an interest in seeing how good we can make her. Benjamin, Ivan, Samuel, we all want to put ourselves in her and see how far she can go."

By the time Phiona had learned the game, the barriers had been breached, the trail to chess tournaments in the outside world had been blazed by the Pioneers. They shared their incredible story upon returning from their first Father Grimes tournament and word got out as it does in Katwe. Before long, attendance at the chess project tripled.

With the teaching assistance of the kids he'd mentored in Katwe, Katende gradually expanded his chess project to three other slums: Kibuli, Nateete, and Bwaise. Katende often visited two or three of the slum projects on the same day. Knowing that in the future he wanted his kids to be more battle tested for tournaments like the Father Grimes event, Katende created his own competition contested among his four slum programs and called it the "interproject tournament."

Katende's first interproject tournament was staged in August of 2006 in the dining hall at the Kampala School for the Physically Handicapped, which shares its compound with the main office of Sports Outreach Institute. Katende had borrowed a sack of wooden chess pieces from the Uganda Chess Federation that were carved so crudely that it was difficult to tell a rook from a bishop. The chessboards were drawn onto pieces of cardboard, the squares carefully constructed with rulers and pens. Each morning Katende drove to his four chess projects in the slums to pick up the competitors and transport them to the site where they would play a game, then take a lunch break, then play more games in the afternoon before Katende delivered them all back to the slums each evening. The tournament lasted for three days.

Katende paid Samuel Mayanja's grandmother 15,000 shillings (about $8) for the event's grand prize: a duck. Richard Tugume, one of the Pioneers, won the duck, and other high finishers received 10,000 shillings. For the rest of the competitors, Katende raided a box of used T-shirts donated by mzungu. On the back of each he silk-screened S.O.I. CHESS ACADEMY. In future years, Katende would track down a "champion's trophy" from a donation box. Over the brass plate previously engraved with 1973 MOST IMPROVED PLAYER,

Katende would glue a piece of paper on which he had written: INTERPROJECT CHESS TOURNAMENT CHAMPION. Nobody seemed to care that on top there was a baseball player catching a fly ball.

Barely noticed during that first interproject tournament was one shy and frightened girl competing in her first-ever tournament against a roomful of boys. Before her first game, Phiona stared around at the other tables and when she noticed she was the only girl among the two dozen players, she wondered if her being there was a mistake. She thought about asking Katende if she should simply watch the others play, but she was curious enough about what it would feel like to compete against all of these boys that she kept her seat and suppressed her anxiety.

"That day they told me we were going to play a tournament, I didn't even know what a tournament means," Phiona recalls. "For sure, I felt like I had some fear in me because I knew there were going to be other players from other places. I remember that first day I only won one game out of three, but it was in the last round. I somehow felt better and I thought, 'Tomorrow I'm coming back to challenge these people.' "

Phiona turned up the following day and

won all three of her games, which qualified her to play some of the best players in the tournament on the final day. She lost both of her games that last day but no longer felt intimidated the way she had been just two days earlier. At the end of the tournament, Katende handed Phiona an envelope containing 15,000 shillings for winning the "girls' championship." Phiona could not believe she had earned it by playing chess. She brought the money home to her mother.

"What really motivated me greatly was that they gave me that gift," Phiona says. "They didn't give me a gift because I had won. They gave me a gift because I was the only girl who had taken part in the tournament, but that greatly motivated me to continue to play chess."

In January of 2007, just five months after her initial tournament experience at the interproject event, Phiona entered Uganda's Under-20 national championship held at the Lugogo Sports Complex. The tournament was well organized with real chessboards and pieces, as well as clocks to time the moves. Phiona was one of 20 participants from Katende's chess project entered into a tournament field of 70. Phiona was just 11 years old. Most of her opponents were 18 or 19.

Katende didn't watch Phiona play a single game in that tournament. With 20 children to follow, he concentrated most of his time on Ivan, Benjamin, Richard, and Gerald, four boys he thought might have a chance to win. But Phiona did capture the attention of Godfrey Gali, the Uganda Chess Federation's general secretary. Gali was initially intrigued by the sight of tiny Phiona with her unkempt hair, torn skirt, and flip-flops playing a well-dressed university student twice her size. He assumed the game would be a mismatch, but the longer he watched, the more Gali became captivated by the little girl's chess ability. "I remember when the game was near the end and Phiona was walking in a minefield," Gali says. "The only safe move to avoid losing the game was her knight to a specific space and she made that move. Now I was really interested. The next time her only safe move was her bishop to one particular place and I thought she would never see that move. She made that move. She made four successive moves when any other move would have finished her and she slowly turned the game until she'd won. At that point, I knew this girl had some potential to be a champion."

Because it was a round-robin format that

mixed the boys and the girls, it was difficult to track the overall standings during the tournament. As the final results were tabulated, Phiona knew she had played well, but she never even considered the possibility that she might have won. Phiona waited anxiously as the names of the top female finishers were called. The winner was revealed last. That's when Phiona finally heard her name. She was the women's champion.

"It actually kind of blew my mind," Katende says. "Phiona had been playing only one year and she emerged the best girl against girls from well-established families. That's the first time I realized Phiona might be having something special."

Phiona won a gold trophy that stood almost as tall as she did. She had never held a trophy before, never really won anything in which there were other competitors.

"That was a very, very happy day," Phiona says. "I remember by the time I got home I felt like I was not the Phiona of always. I was a different Phiona."

In 2005 Robert Katende attended a chess tournament in Kampala with Godfrey Gali and as they watched a girl named Christine Namaganda win the championship, Katende shook his head incredulously. At that time,

Christine dominated the girls' division in all of the local tournaments, but Katende believed that Christine's skills were not extraordinary. He turned to Gali and said, "Give me three years and I will develop someone who can be the girls' champion."

Katende thought that girl would be Farida Nankubuge, but Farida soon dropped out of the Katwe chess project when her parents found out that their Muslim daughter was playing with a Christian organization. They ordered her to sell sugarcane on the street during the time she had been playing chess.

So Katende focused on Phiona instead. And somewhat to his amazement, it had taken him only two years to produce a champion.

Katende took an even more intense interest in developing Phiona's game after she won the 2007 national junior championship. He admired her courage. He admired her drive. He admired how she walked five kilometers to get to the project each day when she first started and how when her family had to move even farther away from the veranda, Phiona just kept walking. All of this was unique to any girl he'd ever met in the program. Phiona was like a boy, but because she was not a boy, her opportunity to advance quickly in the game was mind-boggling.

Phiona had never read a chess book. Never read a chess magazine. Never used a computer. Yet this girl was already a national champion.

Katende told Phiona she would be a prophet. He told her about the inept doctor and the injections and asked, "If you don't believe in yourself, how do you expect anyone else to believe in you?" He told her how he learned chess and challenged her to be clever enough to keep growing in the game. He told her chess was a sport played by masters that was impossible to master, and she didn't shrink from that challenge, but embraced it. Phiona nodded humbly after each lesson, soaking it all in without much audible response, just as Katwe had trained her to do.

"When we first met, Phiona did not believe in herself," Katende says. "She was nervous and hesitant. She had never had anyone to trust. No one to listen to her. No one to give her time and attention. I realized that her background was affecting her and she was convinced that she could not do anything good. I told her, 'Why do you look down? Look at the person you are talking to in the face. Be yourself. Be free. No one is going to penalize you. No one is going to beat you.' It took several years for her to open up. It wasn't easy."

Ever since the first day Phiona had watched Katende playing with Brian and the other kids in the soccer game at the dump site, she felt as if she could trust him. Katende and Phiona were both kids from the slums who grew up without fathers, struggled for meals, constantly relocated without any tether. He could see himself in her and he tried to make sure she could see herself in him.

"I understood what she was going through because I have gone through that as well," Katende says. "I have always told her what I am. I told her I washed vehicles. She didn't believe it. I told her I walked ten kilometers every day to go to school. She didn't believe it. I used my life experiences to show her a good example."

Katende used their time together at the chessboard to pose some challenging questions to Phiona about her place in the world.

"Are you happy with the life you are leading?" he once asked Phiona.

"No," Phiona said.

"Put yourself in your mom's place, would you like to lead a life like she's leading?"

"No," Phiona said.

"Would you like to make a change?"

"Yes," Phiona said.

"What do you need to do to do that?"

He explained about discipline and good behavior and seizing any opportunity that comes her way and using her past as motivation for her future.

"I told her what has helped me be who I am is that I knew who I was," Katende says. "Because of who I was, if I was not to work hard, I wouldn't be where I am."

They played the game together constantly, Phiona and Katende, often until it was just the two of them left in the project and long past the time when Katende had planned to go home.

While Katende often helped Phiona with advice on which move to play, during one game he deliberately told her to make a poor move. Phiona began to move the piece and then hesitated.

"I told you to do this and you are refusing?" Katende said. "Why?"

"Coach, I think it is a wrong move," Phiona said. "My piece would be captured."

"Have you ever done something wrong because someone else has told you to do it without thinking?" Katende asked her. "Before you do something, always think, 'What will be the repercussions? What will be the consequences?' "

At first, when he played games against Phiona, Katende played as a teacher. He would play her without his queen, or remove his bishops or some pawns from the board, until the time came when he needed all of his pieces to defeat her. Then Phiona started beating him. "Initially I sometimes would give her a chance to capture pieces to see if she can be in position to see a move," Katende says. "Can she capitalize on an advantage like that? I tested her with some tricky moves and she would see them all. I would leave my queen deliberately vulnerable to find out if she could see that it was a trap. Before long, I realized that Phiona could see everything."

Phiona grew more and more comfortable with the game, even teasing her coach, something she would never have felt comfortable doing with any of the boys in the project. She would say things like, "Coach, I see what you are planning and I'm very sorry, but I can't allow you to do that."

Chess began to make sense for Phiona. It is a game of survival through considered aggression. It is about finding some clarity among the confusion, some way to organize the chaos by always thinking several moves ahead of the danger. Phiona has even become a student of the game, writing down each move of her tournament games and reviewing them extensively with Katende afterward. She knows that the best way for her to keep learning is through practice. She is a tireless grinder. When asked to estimate how many games she has played since joining the project, Phiona says she can't imagine a number that high.

"I do believe why she's successful is because she has an open mind to learn," Katende says. "She admires better players and asks herself, 'Can I sometime be like this?' I always tell her it is not enough to want to be like them, you must work like them. Because you don't just wake up one day and you are there."

Katende taught Phiona to understand the game, then to appreciate the game, and then finally to love the game. "One thing I really enjoy about chess is it sharpens my brain," Phiona says. "Before I played chess I wasn't motivated to think, but when I learned the game I really liked how it gave me so many challenges. I feel so comfortable when I am at the board. Even when I lose, I don't want to leave the board. I feel a happiness whenever I am playing the game, doing what I do best."

"There were some dogs in a pack and

one of them was much faster than the other dogs. So these dogs would run after cats and eat them. Unfortunately there was a certain cat that was so fast and most of the dogs would run after it and fail to get it. So one time the fastest dog, who liked to show off his speed, was challenged by the other dogs.

" 'Hey, there is one cat who is very fast. Do you think you can catch it?'

" 'Many times before you have challenged me and I have always caught the cat,' the fastest dog said. 'This cat will be my meal for today.'

"So that day the cat came by. 'Hey, Mr. Cat is there,' said one of the dogs. 'That is the fast one.'

"The fastest dog ran after the cat. He was gone for a long time and finally came back and he hadn't caught the cat. So the other dogs asked, 'What happened?'

" 'Me, I was just running for a meal that I can get somewhere else. That cat was running for its life.' "

Katende tells the story with admiration for the unlikely hero, making it clear all along that he is rooting for the cat. "That cat was running to save his life and didn't have any other choice," Katende says. "Phiona looks at chess the same way. I feel maybe that is helping her reach her full potential, because she recognizes chess as a way to survive."

Phiona's game is still very raw. She plays almost entirely on instinct, instead of following the various opening, middlegame, and endgame theory utilized by more refined and experienced players. She succeeds because she possesses that precious chess gene that allows her to envision the board many moves ahead and she focuses on the game as if her life depends on it, which in her case it might.

When Phiona sits at a chessboard she reacts just as she once did when fighting with that abusive boy in the neighborhood or getting teased by the other children during her first day in the chess project. She reacts the way Katwe has taught her to react. She attacks.

"She likes to play what I call 'kill me quick' chess," Godfrey Gali says. "Phiona has a very aggressive plan. She surrounds you until you have nowhere to go and then she will squeeze you like a python until you are dead. That aggression in a girl is quite a treasure."

Still, Phiona's ardor can occasionally get

the best of her. "If she has a weakness, it's that she can be too eager to move forward, very eager to kill without ammunition," says Dr. George Zirembuzi, Uganda's former national team coach. "In chess if you try for a coup d'état and fail, you will be hung."

Phiona's game plan features aggression that has been honed over time to be more calculating, molded by her many games against Benjamin and Ivan, who taught her that while attacking, you must never neglect defending.

"In the beginning she was an aggressive player who didn't really know how to attack smartly," Benjamin says. "So we tried to teach her how to stop all the mistakes she was doing. Now she's not so aggressive as she was. She's more strategic. When I play with her I have to be so strict and so steady or she will destroy me."

While Phiona's strategy is to back her opponent into a defensive position as soon as possible, over time she has gradually learned how to handle a game that isn't won through her initial assault. "I think she is always planning her attack, but when she sees some responses that might be dangerous, she addresses them ahead of time," Katende says. "So by the time she is ready to attack, she has addressed everything. She is aware that if the opponent responds in this kind of way, I will do this. If he does this, I will do this. You won't see any serious concentration on her face. She looks very casual, but you better not take any moves she makes for granted because she is always ready to pounce."

Ivan believes Phiona's greatest strength is her patience. "Our games sometimes last many hours and most girls lose interest after thirty minutes," Ivan says. "Girls have lots of excuses. Phiona never loses interest or makes excuses. She's committed. She never gets tired like the other girls."

"One of the weaknesses we find among most kids we train is that they usually play too fast," Gali says. "Kids don't want to take their time to think through certain moves. But Phiona takes her time. Her opponent may make a move where they offer her some big piece like a queen and if you are the kind of player who plays by impulse without thinking through the moves, you'll lose that way. Phiona looks at all the options and then makes the best move. She makes moves that you don't expect from a kid of her age."

"I think she is developing into what we call a strategic player more than a tactical player," Dr. Zirembuzi says. "Strategic players last longer because they use fundamental principles and they aren't easily surprised, while tactical players have many tricks up their sleeves. She plays textbook chess, which leaves a lot of open road ahead."

Phiona is still so early in her learning curve that Uganda's most renowned chess experts like Dr. Zirembuzi and Joachim Okoth believe her potential is staggering. They talk about how most chess players begin with theory and never fully develop the instincts that Phiona relies upon. They marvel at how much better she can become once she learns to interpret and react to the theory that guides the elite players in the game.

"To love the game as much as Phiona does and already be a champion at her age means her future is much bigger than any girl I've ever known," Dr. Zirembuzi says. "When Phiona loses, she really feels hurt and I like that, because that characteristic will help her keep thirsting to get better."

Phiona captured the national junior championship again in 2008. And again in 2009. Then at Katende's 2009 interproject tournament she defeated Samuel Mayanja, the boys' national junior champion, who wept after losing the game, while the girls in the room shouted, "Phiona is now junior champion for boys *and* girls!"

Phiona didn't celebrate that victory, just as she didn't celebrate her first against Joseph Asaba, another boy she had brought to tears. While she is already implausibly talented at a game she has no business being good at, like most women in Uganda, Phiona is uncomfortable sharing what she is really feeling. She tries to answer any questions about herself with a shrug, but when Phiona is compelled to speak, she is unfailingly humble. She realizes that chess makes her stand out, which in Katwe makes her a potential target, so she is conditioned to say as little as possible.

"I'm very careful on how I live my life," Phiona says. "Chess is just a game. I am very aware that if I'm not behaving well, if I put out a lot of pride, I won't be favored by anyone. Life is not a game. In life I have to stay quiet to ensure I get favor from people."

It is a dilemma for Phiona. She is caught somewhere between trying to be better than everybody else and trying not to be better than everybody else.

"Her personality with the outside world is still quite reserved because she feels inferior due to her background," Katende says. "But in chess I am always reminding her that anyone can lift a piece because it is so light. What separates you is where you choose to put it down. Chess is the one thing in Phiona's life she can control. Chess is her one chance to feel superior."

Harriet experienced the prophecy for the first time in 2008. Phiona had qualified to attend the African Junior Chess Championship in South Africa and was supposed to leave in a week, when one night Harriet had a dream. In her dream Harriet saw a tiny child who was very dark and dirty sitting in her lap on top of Phiona's passport application papers. That child spoke to Harriet and said, *Your girl is not going.*

In the coming days, despite Katende's tireless efforts to accelerate the bureaucratic process, Phiona's passport was issued too late. Phiona did not go.

Then early in the summer of 2009, Harriet experienced a similar prophecy, though she wasn't sure why this time. She wasn't aware of any pending trips for her daughter and didn't really expect Phiona to ever leave Uganda, but once again Harriet found herself experiencing the same dream about a child sitting on some papers in her lap. This time the child's voice carried a different message.

Your girl is going.

CHAPTER 8
HEAVEN

Ivan Mutesasira, Robert Katende, Benjamin Mukumbya, and Phiona Mutesi (left to right) *on the day they returned to Katwe after representing Uganda at the 2009 International Children's Chess Tournament in Sudan.*

She didn't know if the world was round. Or flat. She knew nothing about the world. The outside world. The world beyond Katwe. The slum can seem endless in every direction and there are few landmarks to break up the endless muddle of shacks. Everything in the slum is "just there." And everything beyond that is unimaginable.

Even though Phiona can see the skyscrapers of downtown Kampala from almost anywhere in Katwe, she had spent the first dozen years of her life assuming that everybody else on earth lived just as she did, scrounging for one meal a day, just hoping to get home safely each day so they could try to survive the next one.

So when Katende informed Phiona that her 2009 national junior tournament victory had qualified her to go to Sudan for Africa's inaugural International Children's Chess Tournament later that summer, she didn't take him seriously. *Sudan? What is Sudan?* All Phiona knew was that Sudan was not "just there."

"When I told Phiona about going to Sudan, she looked at me like she knew this coach is joking," Katende says. "She believed she could not go to another country because she was not anyone in our country. She thought there must be some better people who could go there. She told me, 'How can I go to another country? This is impossible. It will never happen. It is not real.' "

"I remember the day Coach Robert told me that I was going, I thought, 'Who am I to be able to go on a plane?' " Phiona says. "I had never expected that I would go anywhere. For sure, I continued to do my training, as always, but I didn't really believe that I was to go anywhere."

The International Children's Chess Tournament was an event for children aged 16 and under organized by FIDE and the United Nations Security Council as part of a peacemaking effort to popularize chess among the children of East and Central Africa. The tournament, which took place in August of 2009, was underwritten by a local petroleum company that sponsored two boys and one girl from each participating country. From all of Uganda, the three children who qualified all came from Robert Katende's tiny chess project in the Katwe slum. Ivan and Benjamin would be Phiona's teammates at the tournament. Several other players who may have qualified dropped out of consideration, refusing to go with a slum kid.

During the summer of 2009, Phiona watched Ivan and Benjamin training intensely so she figured it must be nearing time for another tournament of some kind. On the night before she was to leave for Sudan, according to Katende's instructions Phiona packed all of the clothes she possessed into her tiny rucksack, expecting to go to a local event. Phiona and Brian were alone in the shack that evening. Harriet and Richard spent the night at the market awaiting the early morning purchase of vegetables to sell.

Brian woke up his sister while it was still dark and Phiona told him it was too early to leave. Brian was so excited he couldn't sleep. The two woke up again shortly after dawn and Brian could sense they were late, measuring time by the call to Muslim prayers cascading across the city. Brian told Phiona not to even go wash up, just to put on her clothes. He picked up Phiona's bag and they began walking, but Phiona was moving at her own pace. Brian kept jogging ahead and would sometimes grab his sister's hand to speed her up. He kept telling Phiona she was late, but she knew she had never gone to any tournament this early, so what was the rush? When they reached the veranda, they were 30 minutes late for the scheduled departure. They hustled onto the minibus, the two siblings quarreling over the fact that Phiona's nonchalance might cause her to miss the plane. Phiona still didn't believe she was flying anywhere.

It was only after Phiona boarded the bus and saw that other children from the chess project had come to escort them, that she thought maybe this trip was different. Then she spotted Ivan's mother, Annet Nakiwala, who used to babysit Phiona and her siblings when their families were neighbors in Katwe. "You are going to the airport in Entebbe," Nakiwala told Phiona. "You are going to board a plane. You are going to eat good food. You are going to win. We are going to be praying for you."

Many of Ivan's and Benjamin's other relatives refused to go to the airport because it was such an unfamiliar place and they were afraid of what might happen to them there.

Phiona stared out the window as the bus

exited the slums and connected to Entebbe Road. She knew about the road. She crossed that dusty and chaotic road every time she walked to the Kibuye market, but she had never before been inside a vehicle on that road. She'd once heard that the road led to the airport. Phiona had never been to the airport before. The only time Phiona had ever seen an airplane was in the sky.

The group arrived at the airport in Entebbe and met Godfrey Gali, who would be chaperoning the three children on the trip. Gali watched Phiona as she wandered around the airport awestruck.

"It felt like taking someone from the nineteenth century and plunging them into the present world," Gali says. "Everything at the airport was so strange to her; security cameras, luggage conveyors, so many white people."

Phiona passed through security and looked back through a window at the people who had escorted them to the airport. She waved to Brian and to her first chess tutor, eight-year-old Gloria Nansubuga. When Phiona saw both Brian and Gloria crying she realized that maybe she really was going to this place called Sudan.

"No one else in Katwe could believe they were going," Katende says. "The only way to make it real was to bring some people to the airport with the kids and even when those witnesses came back, they said it might not be true. I even requested to the driver not to leave the airport until they all see the kids' plane leave the ground."

As the plane took off, the three children felt scared and dizzy and Phiona nearly vomited. Then when the plane ascended above the clouds, Phiona looked out the window and asked, "Mr. Gali, are we about to reach Heaven?"

"No," Gali said. "Heaven is a bit higher."

When the flight attendants came by with sandwiches, none of the children had ever seen a sandwich before. They waited for Gali to eat as if he were a food taster and then they still chose not to eat.

"In the airplane I was smiling all the time because I could not believe that I was the one flying to another country," Phiona says. "I felt like I was going to a new world."

By the end of the 90-minute flight to Juba, Sudan, the three children were no longer apprehensive about the travel. They had completely embraced the adventure. Phiona's room at the hotel was like no place she'd ever seen in her life. She stared at the bed. She had never seen one like it. She could not believe she was the one who was going to sleep in that bed. The only one. She had never slept alone in a bed before. She had never seen a television screen attached to a wall and she thought the remote control was magical. It was the first time she'd experienced air-conditioning. The first time she'd ever seen a flushing toilet. She flushed it over and over, fascinated by how the water spun and disappeared. "I could never have imagined this place I was visiting," Phiona says. "I felt like a queen."

Benjamin and Ivan were placed next door to Phiona, who was rooming with a girl from Kenya. Phiona could not speak to her roommate because Phiona's English was not sufficient to carry on a conversation. The unfamiliar surroundings again filled all of the Ugandan kids with anxiety. "Whenever one of us got a bit nervous we would keep encouraging each other," Ivan says. "One of us would say, 'This is where we're going to stay. This is so good. This is where we're going to sleep.' Everyone was comforting each other."

When they went for lunch in the hotel restaurant, they were each handed menus and Gali told them they could ask for whatever they wanted. Phiona didn't understand that she was being given a choice about what to eat for the first time. The children pointed to everything they could recognize. Chicken. Fish. Pork. They wanted to order it all. Gali told them they should ask for only what they would be able to finish. When it came time for Phiona to order, she said, "Let me have a big fish."

The fish stretched across her plate and Phiona could not come close to finishing it, but Ivan told her she must. She gave the remainder to him, but Ivan could not eat it all. The portions were simply too large for children accustomed to rationed meals.

As the lunch ended, Phiona said, "Mr. Gali, I'm going to do my best playing chess so that I may come back to such a place."

The day before the three kids left Kampala for Sudan, Benjamin approached Robert Katende at the chess project with a worried look on his face. "Coach, I'm scared," Benjamin said. "What makes us think we can win any games when none of us has ever even reached the airport? What's going to happen if we lose?"

Katende gathered Benjamin, Ivan and Phiona around him and shared the story of Shadrach, Meshach, and Abednego from scripture:

"These three guys refused to worship

idols, so King Nebuchadnezzar passed a decree that said that all the people must submit to the king and to worship what he said should be worshipped. But these guys believed in God and they didn't want to worship any idols. These guys would not submit, so the king said if you're not willing to worship idols, I will set you in a furnace. So he commanded that they set afire a furnace and the guys said we must continue to believe in our God and we know he has the ability to save us, but even if he does not, we are not ready to submit to the idols. So the king was bitter and he commanded his people to set a furnace seven times hotter than it had ever been set and the three guys were sent into the furnace. The three guys didn't burn up and when the king looked in the furnace there was a fourth person inside. A divine person. It could have been God or an angel. It was a fearful moment, but these three put their trust in God no matter what comes and God was able to rescue them from the fire. If you have great fear the question is, 'Where do you put your trust?' You trust in God. Even if you lose, you honor yourself by competing and we're going to honor you."

Though he didn't share his expectations with the children, Katende wasn't at all concerned with their results in the tournament.

"The moment those three kids from Katwe were able to fly on a plane to another country, that was already the ultimate win I was looking for," Katende says. "I did not expect them to perform well in Sudan. I was just looking for them to be exposed to that kind of atmosphere."

"I know I didn't expect them to do much," Gali says. "I knew they would try their best. I knew they wouldn't be outclassed completely. Some of the other teams had better training and more experience in international events. Our team had none. I was trying to encourage them that even if you lose, don't give up. I was preparing them for the worst-case scenario."

In the tournament, the Ugandan trio, by far the youngest team in the competition, played against teams from 16 other African nations. When the pairings were announced, Phiona learned that she was going to play Isabelle Asiema from Kenya in the opening game. She'd heard the tournament administrators praise Asiema, believing that she was one of the most talented young female players in all of Africa and clearly the best girl in the tournament. At the time Phiona didn't realize that Asiema was also her roommate. "I was really very nervous," Phiona says, "I heard people talking about a Kenyan girl who was playing very well and I felt like it caused me to have a lot of fear and I felt discouraged to even go and play her."

The three Ugandans hatched a plan to engage the Kenyan team in friendly games on the day before the tournament officially began as a means of scouting them. Phiona played Kenya's top-ranked boy, Benjamin played their second-ranked boy, and Ivan played Asiema. "I beat their best boy and then I wondered if this guy was just trying to trick me," Phiona says. "Maybe he just wanted to see how I play and he was just fooling around. So I played a second game with him and I won again."

After the friendly games against the Kenyans, the three Ugandans huddled to discuss what they'd learned. Phiona anxiously asked Ivan, "How was their girl?"

Ivan said that he'd beaten her in every game they'd played. Then Ivan told Phiona, "You are going to beat that girl."

"But Ivan," Phiona said, "just because you've beaten her doesn't mean I will beat her."

"No, you are going to beat that girl," Ivan said. "I know how you play and now I have played that girl and I know you can beat her."

Phiona and Benjamin then reported that they had won their friendly games as well. "All of a sudden I realized that if they are not tricking us we will be in position to challenge these people," Benjamin recalls. "So in a way we tried to comfort each other that way."

The next morning, when the time came for the tournament to begin, Phiona's nerves had returned. Her hands shook whenever she lifted a piece. Her body shivered. Her legs quaked beneath the table. Asiema executed a well-trained opening. Phiona, who had little training in formal openings, simply pushed her pieces forward with her basic plan of how to defend them. When they reached the middlegame, Phiona had systematically built a position advantage and realized that she was actually squeezing her opponent. Feeling the pressure, Asiema then started making errors. "I could actually wonder, 'Is this move she made like a trick or is it actually a mistake?' " Phiona says. "I realized that they were blunders and I continued to pin her down and capture her pieces that were unprotected."

After a very long game, Phiona reduced Asiema to just her king on the board. Then Phiona cornered that king with a rook and several pawns until Asiema was finally checkmated.

"I got courage from beating that girl and how everyone was praising me," Phiona says. "That gave me the belief that I could beat the rest."

In the next game, Phiona played against the top-seeded Kenyan male player, and she beat him just as she had in the practice games. "That boy wanted to cry when she finished him," Gali said. "You could see the expression on his face and it looked like he couldn't believe it."

"The games got harder because the other coaches would tell their players about our tactics and give their players tactics to try to win or make draws," Benjamin says. "But we kept telling each other, 'We can make it. We can make it.' "

Benjamin recalls one game when he was in a very disadvantaged position against a strong player. Gali was speaking with somebody else watching the game and Benjamin overheard Gali say, "It seems that Uganda is going to lose this point."

"I made a move which I had not seen before that blocked his bishop and then he had no way of stopping my pawn from passing and I somehow won that game," Benjamin says. "For sure, I don't know how I made that great move, but I think it must be through the power of the Holy Spirit. I felt like it was not me making the moves."

"After three matches or so everyone in the tournament started talking about who was strong, so when they met them they knew they were facing a superior opponent and they became a bit timid," Gali says. "That's when I first thought we could be winning this. Everybody there was scared of ours. Ours were a class above."

None of the Ugandan players actually thought about winning the tournament. It never occurred to them. They just kept playing. Phiona played eight games without a loss. Benjamin and Ivan were undefeated as well.

After their final games, they returned to their rooms and soon after, Gali entered Ivan and Benjamin's room to tell them that Uganda had been declared the tournament champions. From her room next door, Phiona could hear Ivan and Benjamin shouting. She joined the others and the three started screaming and jumping up and down on the beds.

At the closing ceremonies the Ugandans

received gold medals, certificates, and a trophy. "Winning felt amazing," Ivan says. "We couldn't even believe it. It was such a surprise at first, but then we somehow reflected as if it was a normal thing because in Uganda we'd all experienced winning. I remember Phiona was thinking about her mother and brother and how good they would feel."

A stunned Russian chess administrator approached Phiona after the tournament and told her, "I have a son who is an International Master and he was not as good at your age as you are."

Meanwhile several of the opposing coaches approached Gali and asked, "How do you train these kids?"

"I thought to myself," Gali recalls with a chuckle, " 'if only they knew where these kids are coming from.' "

When the ceremony ended, Ivan asked Gali, "Now that we've won this one, where do we go next? Are we going to another country?" The children hoped there was another tournament, a new place to visit, but Gali told them it was time to go home. Ivan collected soap, shampoo, and a pen from his hotel room as gifts for his mother.

Through it all, Katende had received regular updates from Gali through text messages. Katende marveled at the progress of his players. One day he received a text that read, *Robert, I am surprised to tell you that these kids have got gold medals. They are the champions for this tournament.*

"When I learned that they had won I went and told some people at the Sports Outreach office and they didn't believe it," Katende says. "They thought it was a fake. They were suspicious. It was really very unbelievable. In Katwe some people said this is a lie. It cannot happen. They know these kids' situations and they ask, 'So how? How?' "

Katende concentrated on what the unlikely victory would mean moving forward. "To me I was so excited because I knew this was going to be a big landmark to restore hope and to inspire the minds of everyone in the chess project," Katende says. "Most people in the slums think they can't do something, but if success happens, then people have a reference to build on. I knew this would be a foundation for each and every thing that we will do in the future."

When the Ugandan delegation returned to Kampala the following afternoon, Katende met them at the airport. The three children were smiling and carrying a trophy that was too big to fit into any of their tiny backpacks. When Katende initially tried to congratulate Phiona, she was too busy laughing and teasing her teammates, something he had never seen her do before. For once, he realized, Phiona was just being the kid that she is.

If only that story could end there. Two slum kids, coach and pupil, each at some time left for dead, combining to win a most improbable championship. But happy endings are as rare as snow in Katwe.

"I remember when we arrived back at the airport in Uganda and the plane inside it is always conditioned to stay cool, but the moment I left the airport I felt the sun scorching me," Benjamin says. "I said to Ivan, 'Can we go back?' "

"I felt bad, too," Ivan says. "I just thought of where we were heading and I knew that things were about to be turned upside down because we are leaving this place that was so fantastic and we are coming back to Katwe. But I had no choice. I just had to endure it because this is our home."

"It felt like I was going back to a kind of prison," Phiona says.

As Phiona, Benjamin, and Ivan were driven back into Katwe for a victory celebration, the psychological shift began to take hold. They became apprehensive about what they were going to find when they arrived there. Windows in their van were reflexively shut and backpacks pushed out of sight. Ivan, who was holding the trophy in his lap, suddenly slid it under the seat in front of him. The faces that had been so joyful at the airport turned solemn, the mask of the slum. The three children discussed who would keep the trophy and decided none of them could because it would surely be stolen, so they asked Katende if he could lock it in the storage shed.

Arriving at the site of the chess project, they were surprised to find children waiting there singing and dancing and chanting: *Uganda! Uganda! Uganda!* The three champions looked embarrassed, totally unaccustomed to being treated as heroes. Brian lifted Phiona onto his shoulders and joyously carried her around in the street until she begged him to put her down. Rodney Suddith took a few photographs that reveal all of the children smiling and laughing except for Ivan, Benjamin, and Phiona, who each look as if they would rather be anywhere else. "It was as if they'd done something that they really thought was going to change their lives, but then it really doesn't,"

Suddith says. "The sense I got was their disappointment that they were right back where they started. They had had their moment. But that moment was gone."

The excitement in the crowd that afternoon existed not only because the three children from the slum had won an international chess tournament, but because some people from Katwe had gone away and come back. The children were greeted with some strange questions:

Did you fly on the silver bird?

Did you stay indoors or in the bush?

Why did you come back here?

"It struck me how difficult it must have been for them to go to another world and return," Suddith says. "Sudan might as well be the moon to people in the slum who have no point of reference. The three kids couldn't share their experience with the others because they just couldn't connect. It puzzled me at first and then it made me sad, and then I wondered, 'Is what they have done really a good thing?' "

As Phiona left the celebration headed for her home that evening, a mzungu excitedly asked her, "What is the first thing you're going to say to your mother?"

"I need to ask her," Phiona said, " 'Do we have enough food for breakfast?' "

CHAPTER 9
THE OTHER SIDE

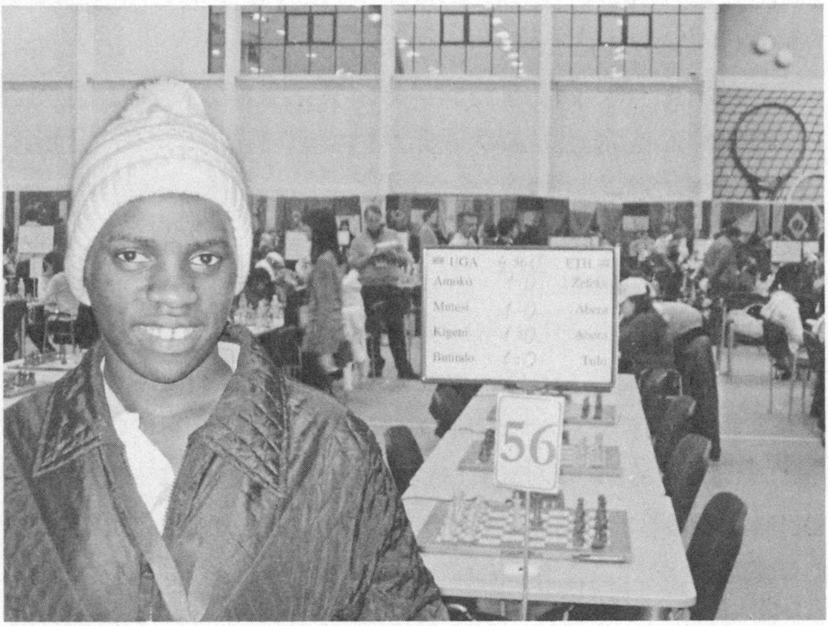

Phiona Mutesi relishes her first victory at the 2010 Chess Olympiad in Khanty-Mansiysk, Russia.

Phiona did not eat the night she returned from Sudan. Or the day after. Neither did Benjamin or Ivan. For once, it wasn't because they couldn't. It was because they didn't want to. A big fish was no longer an option. In fact, there were no options. They had sampled from the tree of knowledge and their appetites had changed forever. They didn't know it yet, but none of their lives would ever be quite the same.

There is a stubborn tolerance amid the misery of a place like Katwe. A subconscious defiance that is necessary to keep going. It is a peculiar disconnect between circumstance and attitude that creates a uniquely African peace of mind. Many have argued that the average African is more serene than the average American, and much of the reason has to do with access. Many people in Katwe do not know there is anything better for which to strive, which leads to an odd kind of tranquility, which some might call lethargy. Every day people like Phiona Mutesi walk a fine line between quiet forbearance and hopelessness, a line that had to be redrawn when Phiona saw what she saw in Sudan.

From her relatively plush hotel room in Juba, Phiona returned home to a 10 × 10 foot windowless room, its walls made of crumbling brick with a corrugated tin roof held up by some spindly wood beams and spiderwebs. Drawn across the doorway was a curtain, which must almost always remain open in the oppressive heat of a country dissected by the equator. Laundry hung on wash lines that crisscrossed the room. There was nothing on the walls, except where someone had etched some phone numbers in case of emergency. There was no phone.

The entire contents of the home were two jugs for water, a wash bin, a kerosene lamp, a tiny charcoal stove made from scrap metal, a teapot, a few plates and cups, one well-worn toothbrush, a tiny shard of a mirror, a Bible, and two musty mattresses stacked on top of each other, which were spread out at night to accommodate the four people who regularly slept in the shack: Phiona, Harriet, Brian, and Richard.

A piece of warped plywood covered the

only small window. There were a few intended air holes in the brick for ventilation and a few unintended holes in the roof that didn't provide much shelter from the torrential rains that often struck at night. Outside was a broom that Harriet used to sweep the pebbles off the mud stoop. Just beyond the stoop was a pit that served as a garbage dump where roosters pecked away at the debris of rotten banana peels and dung. Around the corner were three pieces of tin bent together to form a rudimentary bathing area just a few paces from a brick outhouse that drained into a hole in the ground and down the hill into the valley.

Four small pouches of rice, curry powder, salt, and tea leaves were the only hints of food in the house. There was no electricity because Harriet couldn't afford the 20,000 shillings a month it took to pirate it.

Back in the shack on the night she returned from Sudan, Phiona felt a fever as she watched Brian and Richard eat small bowls of rice. Brian asked Phiona, "What kind of food do people in Sudan eat?" Phiona changed the subject. Then Brian asked, "How does it feel to be in a plane?" Again, Phiona's answer was brief. Finally, Brian asked, "How do you pee in a plane?" Phiona couldn't resist smiling at the question and tried a bit harder this time to satisfy her brother's curiosity, but her heart was still not in it. Living in her shack felt different somehow. She was a changed person. "When Phiona came back there was a lot of work to be done at home, but we treated her like a big, important person in the family," Brian says. "I realized it was really very hard for Phiona to participate in any kind of work because she spent most of the time in Sudan not doing anything. She didn't want to do chores, so I and Richard had to endure about two weeks when we were doing all of her work for her."

Phiona didn't see Harriet her first night back from Sudan. Her mother was off at the market. Harriet didn't arrive home until very late that night and left again early the following morning before Phiona woke up. Phiona wouldn't see her mother for two days. When the family finally reunited, Harriet didn't know what had transpired in Sudan. "Mama," Brian said, "are you aware that when Phiona left that she had won?"

"What?" Harriet said, raising her arms to the heavens. "She won? Let me go to the church and testify. God is so good!"

Harriet immediately left for church. When she returned an hour later, she was still brimming with pride. "You see?" she told

Brian. "You wanted to stop your sister from going to the chess program. You see? You see now what she can do?"

It wasn't easy to return to school either. The morning after coming home from Sudan, Phiona grabbed the green plastic bag she used as her school backpack and walked five kilometers through Katwe to the Universal Junior Primary School, where she was a student in P7. Universal was a cramped, dusty place where the latrines dominated the schoolyard, their foul smell permeating the compound. The school bell was the rusty rim of a tire, with a crowbar attached on a string. At the beginning of each school day the children sang "We Shall Overcome."

On the morning Phiona returned, the school staged a brief ceremony to congratulate her. Phiona still had a little money left over from a small allowance she'd been given for the tournament in Sudan, so she quietly distributed some coins among the poorest classmates at her school. "When I saw that, I admired her heart," says Zakaba Al-Abdal, the school's headmaster. "I thought that this girl will make a very good future woman." After witnessing the positive effect of chess on Phiona, the headmaster added chess to Universal's curriculum, the classes taught by Benjamin three times a week.

Winning the tournament in Sudan prompted Phiona to become even more obsessed with chess. The next scheduled event was a national tournament beginning in November that would include all of the top players in Uganda. Phiona begged Katende to let her play, but he refused, knowing it was a qualifying tournament for the Chess Olympiad. Katende believed Phiona and his other chess apprentices weren't ready to handle that level of competition against much older and more experienced players. "I feared," Katende says. "I was sure Phiona could not qualify because I knew who those other girls are and I thought they were definitely stronger than she is. I thought it was a waste of time and finances."

But a week before the tournament began, Katende received a phone call from Godfrey Gali asking him to enter Phiona in the tournament field. Gali didn't view Phiona as a serious contender to qualify, but he wanted her to help strengthen the players who would qualify.

Says Katende, "I told Phiona, 'Mr. Gali is insisting that I enter you, but I'm doing so on grounds that you are going for training.

Those big ladies who are playing, they will be competing to see who represents the country, but you just go and that will be good training as they are preparing for that tournament.' "

Gali had sold Katende on the idea that it would benefit Phiona to be introduced to the tournament before she attempted to qualify for a future Olympiad. Katende was thinking two years ahead, to 2012. Then Phiona would be more comfortable in the pressurized atmosphere of an event like that. He believed her level at least approached that of her competition, so Phiona was the only player from Katende's chess project he would enter into the event, while other players like Ivan and Benjamin were held out.

"Coach knew I would have to play against those big ladies," Phiona says. "At first he was very sure that he would not allow me to go and play, but I really wanted to go there and try to improve my game, so he allowed it."

The qualifying tournament took place over a period of three months, one game each Saturday. The women's field included ten players who played a round-robin and the top five overall finishers would qualify for the Olympiad. Katende did not attend the early rounds. He sent Phiona with his assistant, Paul Mubiru, because Katende was busy tending to the other children in the chess project on Saturdays. On the first Saturday of qualifying, Phiona came back to the veranda and said, "Coach, I won."

"You won?" Katende said. "That is good."

Katende knew there were six women in the field who were clearly the best players and assumed that Phiona had played against a weaker opponent. The next Saturday Phiona returned to the project and reported that she'd won again. "I still wasn't taking it seriously," Katende says. "I took a look at the game she played on her recording sheet and I told her, 'This was a good game. You played well.' But I still knew she could not qualify."

Through five of the nine games of the qualifying tournament, Phiona produced three wins, one draw and one loss. At that point, Gali phoned Katende. "Robert, we are all surprised," Gali said, "but it seems this little girl might even qualify when we see the trend of this tournament."

"How?" Katende asked.

"She has played most of the strong people and she has actually challenged them," Gali said. "If she continues to play this way, there's no way she can miss to be among the five people who are needed."

"Are you sure?" Katende said. "Are you serious about that?"

He asked if Phiona had been told. Gali said she had not.

Katende later told Phiona, "You know that you might qualify to go to Russia? Now, it's a must. Let us intensify our training and make sure that you win all of the remaining games. If you win those games, you will qualify."

Katende reviewed all of the games Phiona had previously played in the tournament. He asked the strongest boys in the Katwe project, Benjamin, Ivan, and Richard, to play a game against Phiona every day. Katende also tried to play at least one game against her each day.

Katende received email updates on the standings each week. With three games remaining he calculated that even if Phiona lost all of her remaining games, she would still qualify. Phiona became the first to clinch qualification for the Olympiad and during her final games, she even had some of the older women begging her to draw with them so that they could qualify as well. Phiona finished in second place overall. Unaware that the tournament winner would also be considered Uganda's national champion, Phiona gave away a game at the end of the event that she thought had no meaning, but instead cost her the national title.

"The qualifying for the Olympiad was very tight because everybody who participated was very good, very strong, and everyone wanted to go so badly," says Rita Nsubuga, who also qualified. "I admit I feared Phiona. I would rather play someone I know than a young kid, because you get disappointed when a young kid beats you. All of the other girls were fearing her. They knew that this one is a threat."

"It was exciting, but with Uganda many things had happened before when qualifying for a tournament came to nothing," Katende says. "Because it is Uganda, I didn't really believe that Phiona was going to Russia. Uganda had never before been able to afford to send a women's team to the Chess Olympiad. I told her, 'If God makes it possible for you, you might go.' I never said she *will* go. I didn't think she would."

Several months passed before Gali informed Katende that FIDE would pay for all ten of Uganda's players to travel to Russia. When Katende shared that news with Sports Outreach, Rodney Suddith began raising funds to send Katende, because

Phiona was too young to travel to Russia without him. When those funds materialized, as one of the few Ugandan delegates who could afford the trip, Katende was nominated to be the women's team captain.

In early September, Universal Junior Primary School received a letter from the Uganda Chess Federation requesting Phiona's release from school for a month so that she could play in the Chess Olympiad. The school's headmaster made a dozen copies of the letter and posted them in each classroom as a means of inspiration.

On her final day at school before leaving for Russia, the school declared its own holiday. In Phiona's class 33 students were packed into a sweltering classroom. On the wall were posters of Africa and of the presidents of Uganda, and a map of the world. When the students were asked to point out where Phiona was going on the map, only one was able to correctly identify Russia. Phiona was among the rest who could not.

On the day before the Ugandan national team was due to leave for the Olympiad, the Uganda Chess Federation staged a send-off press conference. There were no microphones, so the reporters and players in the audience had to lean forward in their plastic chairs to try to hear the speeches from the dignitaries.

"You are ten Ugandans," said Jasper Aligawesa, the general secretary of Uganda's National Council of Sports, "but you leave behind thirty million Ugandans whose eyes are on you."

Federation chairman Joseph Kaamu told the players how in 1972 he remembered Idi Amin sending the Ugandan national boxing team off to an international competition by saying, "Don't try to win on points. Just knock the guy out and you will have no doubt who wins." Then Kaamu seemed to undercut his pep talk by saying, "When you get to the Olympiad, we know you will never beat the Russians, but try your best."

The following day a half dozen children from the chess project, many of whom had never ridden in a vehicle before, accompanied Phiona to the airport. When Night's three-year-old daughter Rita saw Phiona leave with white people, the alarmed child mimicked a common warning in Uganda about running off with strangers: "The mzungus have taken Phiona and they are going to cut off her head!"

On the bus to the airport Phiona teased Katende about how this would be his first time on an airplane, so Phiona would act as the coach for this journey.

Phiona's mother also accompanied her to the airport, her first ever trip there. Harriet had some final advice for her daughter. "Be careful," she told Phiona. "The country you are going to is not your own. If you behave well you will represent your country well. If not, you will have let your country down. Don't be misled by anyone, especially boys, and a lot of treasures lie ahead of you. God is remembering us."

Then after wiping away her tears with a rag, Harriet rubbed Phiona's shoulders and said something she had never said to her before: "Stay warm."

Harriet would later admit that she didn't believe she would ever see her daughter again.

They flew through one night and into the next, through Nairobi, Kenya, and Dubai in the United Arab Emirates, and didn't breathe fresh air again until the chill wind of Khanty-Mansiysk, Russia. Phiona had traveled from the only world she'd ever known to the middle of nowhere. From a place where she'd spent nearly every day of her life to a place she could never have imagined spending a single day of her life. Siberia.

As she stared out the airplane window during the final hours of the flight, she saw nothing in every direction. She couldn't believe there was so much open space with no people living there, nothing built on it. Khanty-Mansiysk is an oil town of about 75,000 stolid citizens on the stark Siberian steppe, so isolated, so far from any other metropolitan area that it has no bus station or railway.

The first thing Phiona noticed about Siberia was that her initial fear back when she'd first learned about the trip had been confirmed. It was cold there. Very cold. She was warned that on the warmest day she'd spend in Khanty-Mansiysk, the temperature wouldn't reach the coldest temperatures she'd ever experienced in Uganda. She also noticed that the streets were well paved, devoid of the dust that she had grown so accustomed to at home. There were traffic lights but no traffic. The people were all so smartly dressed. There were so many tall buildings. Even the bus she rode from the airport to the hotel was nothing like any vehicle she'd ever seen before. The hotel was so big it was hard to remember how to find her room. She took a shower and at first the water came out freezing cold and she wondered why anyone would ever want to do that, until it was pointed out to her that there was a faucet for hot water as well. In the lobby there were people of many races, all speaking languages she could not understand.

Katende sensed this was a much bigger culture shock for Phiona than her trip to Sudan and as he watched his pupil wander around wide-eyed he kept reminding her that while everything else may be different, when the tournament began the chessboard would still be familiar — the same 64 squares she tried to conquer every day in Katwe.

The Chess Olympiad is the world's premier international team chess championship. It began in 1927 and has been staged 39 times in all, including biennially since 1950. It comprises the best chess players in the world. Former world champions Anatoly Karpov, Garry Kasparov, and Bobby Fischer all competed in at least four Olympiads. Before 2010, the previous 15 Olympiads were all won by Russia or countries once part of the Soviet Union. Russia's leadership in the sport helped Khanty-Mansiysk develop into a chess hub in recent years, hosting the 2005, 2007, and 2009 Chess World Cups and earning the right to host the Olympiad through a bidding system similar to that of the Olympic Games.

Uganda has participated in every Chess Olympiad since 1980 except the 1990 Moscow Olympiad, but never had a Ugandan woman played in the tournament. The Uganda Chess Federation often struggled to finance a full men's team. A women's team had never seriously been considered until FIDE announced they would pay for both a men's and a women's team to travel to the 2010 event.

The Olympiad format consists of national teams competing against each other in one match per day. Four players compete for each team, beginning with the top players on Board 1 through the fourth-rated players on Board 4. Each player is awarded one point for a game won and a half point for a game drawn. Cumulative points in all four games determine which country wins the match. One player on each team sits out each day. For most of the Olympiad, Phiona would play Board 2 because that is where she ranked among the five women who qualified for the Ugandan team.

Uganda's big ladies knew nothing about the little girl. Phiona's Olympiad teammates were all from a different world. All of them grew up in more affluent neighborhoods of Kampala. All of them graduated from college, including three from Makerere University, one of the finest schools in all of East Africa. They were all groomed to have careers. None of them had ever been to Katwe.

Rita Nsubuga, 25, learned the game as a child from her father who had played against some of Uganda's elite players such as Dr. George Zirembuzi and Joachim Okoth. She won her first chess tournament in primary school, earning a small magnetic chessboard as a prize, and she became enamored with the game. Rita's father would place a 20,000-shilling note beside the family chessboard and tell his daughter that if she could beat him, the money was hers. Once when Rita won a tournament, her father rewarded her by taking her on a cruise. Eventually Rita began training under Zirembuzi and became the first girl ever to join his chess club, the Mulago Kings, which helped her to qualify for the 2008 Olympiad in Germany, but the funds were not there to send a women's team.

Joan Butindo, 27, started playing chess after spending many evenings watching her mother and father play games that sometimes spread out over three or four days. Joan often found herself driven by the urge to change one or two pieces from the positions where they were left overnight, which alerted Joan's father to her interest in the game. He gave her lessons and they played regularly. By the age of 11, Joan had become the best player in her family, telling all of her siblings that she was no longer interested in playing the "dirty games," only chess. By the age of 23, Joan had become Uganda's national women's champion.

Ivy Claire Amoko, 24, learned chess from her stepbrother when she was 11 years old, but she initially found it dull. Ivy didn't play again until age 14 during a competition at boarding school, where she lost her first game and promptly quit. She wouldn't return to chess until 2007, when the 19-year-old was invited to participate in an interhall competition at university. Ivy shocked herself by winning her first game and has continued in the sport ever since, viewing chess as a welcome diversion from her work as a law student. She distinctly recalls playing in a tournament, losing to Joan Butindo — then the national champion — and hearing later that Joan had said she was a weak player. Ivy dedicated herself to training, eventually beat Joan, and became the women's national champion in 2010, finishing ahead of Phiona at the Olympiad qualifying event.

Grace Kigeni, 24, learned the game from a friend during a school holiday when she was 13. She played in some tournaments during secondary school, but didn't dedicate herself to the game until joining Rita playing for a club at Makerere University and then the Mulago Kings.

When the big ladies were asked about Phiona before the Olympiad began, they all agreed that she possessed amazing potential, but there were times when Phiona didn't seem invested enough in the game, when she reacted to a loss with a dismissive shrug of the shoulders.

"I don't know her background or how she started in chess," Grace says. "I don't know if she wanted to play or if she was made to play. That is what is different with us. If I didn't want to play, I wouldn't play. Nobody is going to force me to play. I really see a difference for her. Maybe she feels like chess must save her. When I'm around her, she's just like any other child. A little carefree. I sense her passion is really sunk in. She knows how important chess can be for her, but she doesn't like to show it."

"The attitude Phiona gives us is that she doesn't care that much," Ivy says. "It's like she has a wall that she is always trying to hide behind so no one knows what she's thinking or what she's feeling. She's a tough person and she probably thinks breaking down will make her look weak, so she's blocking away so much emotion that would probably help her. I just wish she would show she cares."

Phiona admits that she doesn't reveal herself to her teammates very often. It is a product of Katwe and they wouldn't understand.

"Actually it is very true that no one can see me inside," Phiona says. "Sometimes when I lose I can even smile and put on a happy face, but inside I'm in real pain because I never want to lose any game. If you look at me, it is very hard to know that I am going through some challenges unless I have told you. It is part of living in the slums. At home we may not have much, but we remain proud, because we fear being abused for showing how we feel. That's how our mother brought us up. During bad times we just keep it to ourselves and we don't show it out. We swallow that pain."

Phiona cried. Sobbed uncontrollably. After her second game at the 2010 Chess Olympiad, a game against a Taiwanese player that she knew she should have won, Phiona Mutesi was inconsolable.

Phiona could not remember the last time she cried, but she couldn't control herself. She somehow felt it was safe to cry in Siberia, so far away from home, so she buried her head in her pillow and bawled. Let it all out. Her teammates, Rita and Grace and Ivy and Joan, they all tried to comfort her. Katende tried to reassure her. But Phiona's tears just kept flowing all through the night, as if because she was in a place where she was permitted to cry, she was going to make up for all of the sadness she had never been allowed to indulge in Katwe.

"When Phiona reached the Olympiad she may have thought the things she was doing to win games in Uganda would be the same things she'd do to win games there," Rita says. "But that was not the case. So maybe she got a bit disappointed. She made a mistake to lose that second game, but we tried not to say things that insult her. We tried to encourage her."

"When she lost that game it was kind of a shock to us because we knew she was good enough to win it," Grace says. "The environment was tough on her. She was so young. The board she was playing on was quite high. We were all talking about, 'How could you put such a young girl on such a board?' We were all scared and intimidated because we had not been exposed to that level of competition. Like all of us, I'm sure Phiona looked back at that game and some of the poor moves she made and thought, 'Oh my God, what was I thinking?' "

Katende decided that to relieve some stress on Phiona, he would sit her out of the next day's match against Japan. Phiona looked on as her team registered its first match victory by winning one game and drawing the other three. Katende believed that had he let Phiona play she would likely have won her game, which left him even more conflicted about whether to play Phiona in the next match against Brazil, a stronger opponent. Katende rested Phiona again, believing that she hadn't completely stabilized and hoping to bring her back against weaker competition.

Chess. Chess. Chess. Even when Phiona did not play, she did not escape. After a long day of chess at the Olympiad, the players would return to the hotel and talk about chess. If they were not talking chess, they were playing it and if a laptop computer was open, chances are that a chessboard was on the screen. Even when she was not playing, Phiona was engulfed by chess, interrupted only by visits to the hotel restaurant, where she dined on three meals a day at an all-you-can-eat buffet. At the first few meals, Phiona made herself sick by overeating. Even during dinners, chess moves were replayed with salt and pepper shakers.

Chess is not a spectator sport. Other than teammates and coaches, only a few family members and an occasional reporter watch the Olympiad matches play out. During games, it is not uncommon for 20 minutes to elapse without a single move. Players regularly leave the game for a bathroom break or to get a cup of tea or perhaps to psyche out an opponent by pretending it isn't even necessary to sit at the board to win. Phiona never left the board. She didn't know what it meant to psyche out an opponent or, fortunately for her, what it meant to be psyched out.

She was restless. Games at the Olympiad progressed too slowly for Phiona, nothing like chess back in Katwe. She had spent two games fidgeting and slouching in her seat, desperate for her opponents to get on with it.

Wary of Phiona's breakdown after the second game, Katende quietly rued the Uganda Chess Federation's decision to place Phiona as her team's Board 2 player. That meant Phiona must face elite players from other teams rather than lower-seeded competition with less experience whom he suspected she could be defeating.

Phiona's third game was against a Woman Grandmaster from Egypt, Mona Khaled. Pleased by Khaled's quick pace of play, Phiona got lured into her opponent's rhythm and played too fast, causing her to make critical errors. Khaled played flawlessly, winning the game in just 24 moves. When Phiona conceded after less than an hour, Katende looked worried, but Phiona recognized that on this day she was beaten by an exceptional player. Instead of being discouraged, she was inspired. Phiona walked straight over to Katende and said, "Coach, I will be a Grandmaster someday."

Phiona looked relieved, and a bit astonished, to have spoken those words.

Phiona's opponent in her fourth game was Sonia Rosalina, an Angolan, who kept staring at Phiona's eyes, which Rosalina would later say were the most competitive she has ever faced in chess. Phiona was behind for most of the game, but she refused to surrender. She battled back and had a chance to force a draw in the endgame, but at the pivotal moment, she played too passively, too defensively, not like herself. After more than three hours and 72 moves, Phiona finally grudgingly submitted, confessing that she didn't have her "courage" when she needed it most. She promised herself that she would never, ever, let that happen again.

The ninth day of the tournament, September 30, 2010, dawned cold and dreary, like every other day at the Olympiad. Phiona hated the Russian weather, but she loved the hotel room, the clean water, and the three meals a day, and she was already dreading her return home when she would begin scrounging for food again.

Phiona sat down at the chessboard for her fifth game wearing a white knit hat, a black overcoat, and woolly beige boots that were several sizes too large, all gifts from mzungu. Her opponent was an Ethiopian, Haregeweyn Abera, who, like Phiona, was an African teenager and an Olympiad rookie. For the first time in the tournament, Phiona saw someone across the table she could relate to. She saw herself. For the first time in the tournament, she was not intimidated at all.

Phiona played black, the defender in a chess game, but remained patient and gradually shifted the momentum during the first 20 moves until she created an opening to attack. Suddenly Phiona felt as if she were back on the veranda in Katwe, pushing and pushing and pushing Abera's pieces into retreat until there was nowhere left for Abera to move.

When Abera extended her hand in defeat, Phiona tried and failed to suppress her gap-toothed grin. Then Phiona skipped out of the hall, cocked her head back, and unleashed a blissful shriek into the frigid Siberian sky loud enough to startle some of the players still inside the arena. It was a shriek like Phiona had never shrieked before. The shriek of a 14-year-old who could not afford to buy her own chessboard vanquishing one of the better players on the planet and having no experience suppressing that kind of joy. The shriek of a dismissed girl from a dismissed world finally making herself be heard.

"She's only fourteen?" Rashida Corbin asked incredulously. "This is her first Olympiad? For a fourteen-year-old kid with no formal coaching to be playing that confidently on Board 2 at the Olympiad, that's fantastic. I commend that. That's got to mean something."

Corbin, the 24-year-old national champion of Barbados, had never played anybody quite like Phiona. After defeating her in Phiona's sixth game of the Olympiad, Corbin praised Phiona for playing so instinctively and "outside of the books." Books? Phiona had never opened a chess book. She didn't know what was *inside* the books.

Back at the hotel after the match, Corbin sought out Phiona and the two reviewed their game together move by move, breaking down the two minor blunders that cost Phiona the game. Corbin explained some tactics she used that Phiona had never seen before.

"Phiona has phenomenal potential for a fourteen-year-old," Corbin said. "I look forward to seeing her a few years from now. She looked like she was really beating herself up about this game. You see that in a player's eyes. You can see how competitive she is. She looks like she really has the heart of a champion."

On the shuttle bus from the hotel to the playing arena before Phiona's seventh and final game at the Chess Olympiad, Katende stared out the window into the Siberian mist and said, "Nobody here knows where this girl has come from. That God has picked this girl up from the slums in Katwe and has brought her to this place, it is not believable."

Phiona sat across the aisle lost in thought, but more resolute, older somehow than she seemed before any of her other six matches. Uganda's last match at the Olympiad was against Mozambique. Because Ivy was chosen to sit out the final match, Phiona was promoted to Board 1 for the first time in the tournament. She was pitted against 25-year-old Vania Fausto Da T. Vilhete, the Mozambique women's champion who was competing in her second Olympiad.

Playing more slowly, more deliberately, proving she'd learned from the previous games, Phiona eased into a positional advantage. The girl who on Day One did not understand anything about standard chess openings had clearly learned some of the nuances of a solid opening by the time she reached her final game. Phiona pressed her advantage throughout the middlegame until her opponent suddenly offered her a draw, essentially hoping to save face in a game that appeared to be a lost cause. Phiona's initial reaction was to keep playing, to finish her opponent off, but Katende leaned in to Phiona and whispered that because Uganda had already won two games and drawn the other, thus clinching victory in the overall match against Mozambique, that accepting a draw would be the proper etiquette. After the game, Katende playfully patted Phiona's head as he often does and joked, "Don't think you are a Board 1 player now."

Afterward Vilhete said, "My opponent is a very solid player. With help she can be a Grandmaster. I was fortunate to get a draw. I never saw any sign in her that she was only fourteen. The children of today grow up too fast."

Phiona's diary entries abruptly stopped after her second game at the Olympiad. She was too upset to write. She didn't even want her mother to know what she was feeling. Eleven days passed before she would pull out her diary again. Finally, on the team's last night in Khanty-Mansiysk, Phiona opened her diary and wrote one final entry from the Olympiad:

> Dear mum,
>
> I prayed my games very bad because I didn't know opens. I think that is why I was beaten. But there's agame I prayed I prayed very well and I thought I am going to wine. but they won me at the end. I was very disapointed and I went back to the hotel and I cried.

My feelings about the last game.

When we were going to pray the last game I was scared. What maked me to be so scared was the country I was playing. Although it is African country but I was scared because this time I was playing board one. Board one is where you find strong players from every country. I didn't want to take break fast because I new that lam meeting strong player any time. So I went back to the room to prepare my self. What I knew that I was not going to lose that game. We were playing against mosbique. So when I riched the playing hall I prayed to God so that I could pray well. So the games started. The girl was play very quickly but me I was playing slowly. The time riched when I was wining the girl, so she had to think a lot. After asmall time the girl baged me adraw so I had to ask my coach weather he can accept me to make adraw. I made adraw. But when I finished my team mates told that I was wining because I had abetter position.

So after agame we went to the museum we so things of long ago. we saw some guns and we saw bones of big mammals and I was very happy to see all of that because I have never gone to the museum so this was my first time.

After that we went to the closing celemony. It was big inside. Down there was abig board. I saw some pieces on it. But they were not pieces they were people. But they were wearing things like pieces they were very nice. avery thing was organised very well. When they started giving trofys I was jelus and I cried. I was very disapointed and when the closing celemony ended we went to the last party.

At that time very tired and disapointed. I took some drinks and some eats. After that I had to live the place to go to the hotel. So I went with my coach but we left our team mates to continue these drinks. And I came back to pack my cloth. Because the following day we were going back home.

They stayed up late, night after night after night, the three siblings, Brian, Richard and Phiona, lying beside each other on the mattress on the floor of their pitch-dark shack in Katwe. Each night Phiona told her brothers a new and wondrous bedtime story that often held them rapt until dawn. One night she told them about the glittering, gleaming airport in a place called Dubai and how if you had some money you could buy anything you could ever imagine without ever leaving the terminal, including a beautiful blue car that for some reason had no roof on it. She told them about the cold white flakes that fall from the sky like rain. She told them about how somebody had told her that there are places in Russia where some days the sun never comes up and others when night never comes. She told them about the strange taste of Irish potatoes and about people who wear wires on their teeth to make them straight. She told them about meeting Garry Kasparov, the former world champion, and how he actually wanted to know her name. She told them about the day when the Ugandan team was walking around the city and people kept stopping them, asking to take their photo.

"Why did those people want to take pictures of you?" Brian asked.

"Because of our color," Phiona said.

Then Brian asked her, "You mean that those people in Russia, they have not seen soccer players who are black? Does that mean there are no black people on the other side of the world?"

"Those people think that for us to get this color we just paint it on ourselves," Phiona said. "They think that we really look just like them, but we wake up in the morning and we paint ourselves before we go out."

The morning after she flew home from Siberia, Phiona returned to Universal Junior Primary School to a hero's welcome. The headmaster had planned to hire a car to drive her to school from her home, but for lack of funds, they could only afford to ride the last 500 meters from the corner petrol station. Students and teachers lined the rutted dirt road that leads into the school's compound. Phiona arrived to hear fellow students chanting her name, *Phi-o-na! Phi-o-na!* and holding up handmade posters, one of which read, LONG LIVE UGANDA, LONG LIVE UNIVERSAL JUNIOR, LONG LIVE PHIONA MUTESI, FOR GOD AND OUR COUNTRY.

Phiona said a few words and then distributed to her schoolmates some candies that she'd bought in the airport the day before with an allowance that all players received at the Olympiad. She would use much of that stipend to pay off her mother's debts, including back rent and money Harriet owed to suppliers at the Kibuye market. The little that was left over Phiona used to buy hair extensions, a teenage indulgence she had never heard of before going to Russia.

Once again Phiona felt profoundly affected by her time outside of Katwe. "Surely, the way I think really changed,"

Phiona says. "All along, all I knew was Africa. When I went to Russia my mind was broadened. I realized that another place was better than ours. I noted the way they behaved, what they feed on, the kind of life-style they lead, and they are totally different from ours here. Actually, that motivates me. Because if I'm in this kind of life and I see another person who is in a better state, then I get a sense that perhaps if I work hard I can also be able to achieve what other people are having as a better life."

Phiona has learned to sense the lessons on her own that Katende once needed to fill in for her.

"I will never forget how I lost the first Olympiad games," Phiona says. "I won't forget because some games I played badly and I made terrible mistakes. I learned from that. The way I played the first games was not the same way I played the games at the end. I have learned some of the openings and even the endgames and I can now play them much better. The Olympiad was so challenging. It has given me great power to work hard and practice so that the next time I go to an Olympiad I can win the games that I lost and then someday become a Grandmaster."

When she is asked how long becoming a

Grandmaster might take, she is confused. That sort of specific time frame question makes no sense to a kid from Katwe who never plans beyond the end of the day. Any goal is "just there."

Finally, Phiona replied, "How can I know when what will be will be?"

■ ■ ■ ■

ENDGAME

■ ■ ■ ■

CHAPTER 10
HURDLES

Phiona Mutesi's older sister Night (left) *and mother Harriet Nakku sell vegetables at Kampala's Kibuye Market, the life for which Phiona appeared destined until she discovered chess.*

He couldn't win. John Akii-Bua was not supposed to win. One of 43 children from his father's nine wives, Akii-Bua was born in 1949 and grew up in Lira, a small village in northern Uganda, where he struggled for one meal a day that he often had to hunt down in the bush. He dropped out of school when his father died and came to Kampala in his late teens seeking a better life. He found a job as a policeman, discovered competitive running while training for the police force, and joined the police track team. His training regime was rudimentary, partly because there was no modern athletic track in all of Uganda. Akii-Bua became a 400-meter hurdler, but unlike other runners who carefully plotted their steps between hurdles and always led with the same leg, Akii-Bua jumped the hurdles in however many steps were necessary to travel from one to the next and led with whichever leg happened to be closest to the hurdle at the time. The 23-year-old Akii-Bua was not a favorite at the 1972 Olympics because he lacked the proper experience in international competition. He was running the Olympic final from Lane 1, the last lane he would have chosen. Above all he was from Uganda. Ugandans don't win.

When Akii-Bua left the starting blocks at Munich's Olympic Stadium on September 2, 1972, hardly anybody in Uganda even knew who he was. A mere 47.82 seconds later, Akii-Bua was a national hero. Akii-Bua won the 400-meter hurdles, hunting down his rivals and then leaving them behind to stare at the bottom of his two-year-old track shoes, one of which, according to legend, was missing a spike. Akii-Bua set a new world record and captured Uganda's first Olympic gold medal. After the race, he joyously jogged a victory lap with a flag unfurled above his head, beginning a tradition at track events that endures to this day.

Very few Ugandans were able to watch Akii-Bua's race on television, but shortly after the race was over, Radio Uganda blared the news across the country.

"Uganda's athletics fraternity was following John and could see the progress in him, but the whole country did not know much about athletics because as a sport it was not known like football," says Daniel Tamwesigire, another 400-meter hurdler who became Akii-Bua's teammate shortly after the Olympics. "You could look at the seeding in terms of the lanes and it was not the lane you expect for a winner. The rest of the world was not expecting a medal for him. John told me later that his attitude was, 'Hey, I have nothing to lose here. Let me go and see what can I achieve.' "

Three days after the race, 11 Israeli athletes and coaches were killed by Palestinian terrorists and the world quickly forgot Akii-Bua, but Uganda's president Idi Amin made certain his country remained focused on its new conquering hero. When Akii-Bua returned to his country he was personally received by Amin. He was promoted in the police force. A house was built for him in one of the finest neighborhoods in Kampala. Even a major thoroughfare in the capital city was renamed Akii-Bua Road. Plans were announced for the construction of John Akii-Bua Stadium. Akii-Bua's stunning victory had provided a ray of hope for all Ugandans that success on that type of grand international stage was actually possible.

"John was a great role model," Tamwesigire says. "He loved to encourage his peers and those athletes lower than him in stature, which is not common among top athletes. His achievement would inspire all Ugandans that followed him to dream bigger."

In the ensuing years, Akii-Bua struggled to recapture the moment, though he was still among the 400-meter hurdles favorites leading up to the 1976 Olympics in Montreal — until the African nations chose to boycott those Olympics right before the Games began.

While many members of Akii-Bua's tribe were being murdered during the bloody years of the Amin regime, Akii-Bua was protected by his fame, though several attempts were made to evict his family from the house that Amin had built for him. When the regime collapsed in 1979, Akii-Bua fled to Kenya for fear of being jailed as a collaborator, despite the fact that three of his brothers had been murdered by Amin's forces. In Kenya, Akii-Bua was forced into a refugee camp, from which he and his family were rescued by his shoe sponsor and brought to Germany for several years before he eventually returned to Uganda and his job with the police.

Akii-Bua died in 1997 at the age of 47 as

a man of modest means and modest celebrity. Only in death was he properly remembered for his accomplishments. His body lay in state in Uganda's parliament and his funeral was a national event.

"As a sports hero John died when he was still very young and the country definitely needed him," Tamwesigire says. "His contemporaries in other countries are still alive and playing a big role in developing gold medalists in those countries. John would have been a leader in our Olympic movement, but his demise denies our country that type of advantage. He should still be here telling his story about winning the gold medal to young people to inspire them."

However, Akii-Bua does live on in the Ugandan schoolyards, on the tongues of young runners who invoke his name while sometimes having no idea who he is.

"When John won the gold medal, people in Uganda replaced the word 'running' with 'Akii-Bua,' " Tamwesigire says. "So even today you'll hear kids say that some boy *'akii-buas,'* meaning he 'runs.' That is his legacy."

Could she win? Ugandan women don't win, do they? Plenty of Ugandan men believe that women shouldn't even compete in sports. But both of Dorcus Inzikuru's parents were runners, father and mother, and they told their daughter often about a certain magical day in Munich. Inzikuru grew up idolizing Akii-Bua, who won his gold medal ten years before Inzikuru was born in the tiny town of Vurra in Arua district, tucked into the northwest corner of Uganda near the Sudanese border. Inzikuru was the oldest of six girls in her family. Both of her older brothers died in childhood.

Inzikuru's family was so poor that when she ran in school track meets, she did so barefooted. She couldn't afford running shoes. She won anyway, jumping out to early leads and never looking back, the tiny girl seeming to dance across the ground like a sprite, dominating all of her local competition until as a teenager she was spotted and brought to Kampala to train, like so many others dreaming of a better life.

She eventually had to leave Uganda for Italy because her home country simply didn't have the training facilities, the coaching, or the competitors necessary to prepare her for elite competition. Inzikuru began her career as a 5,000-meter runner, but that race proved a little too long for her. Then one day in 2003 her coach suggested she try her sport's most unusual race, the

3,000-meter steeplechase, an event that features five hurdles, including one with a water jump — all the deterrents that track has to offer. Inzikuru decided that she kind of enjoyed getting wet.

The 3,000-meter steeplechase would be contested for the first time ever at a World Championship during the 2005 meet in Helsinki, Finland, and while most of the athletics community didn't realize it yet, Inzikuru was among the best in the world. She was an unknown. Her name was misspelled on her passport and every story written about her dashing her way into the 3,000-meter steeplechase final perpetuated the error. Inzikuru didn't care. Her surname, Inzikuru, translates to "no respect."

Daniel Tamwesigire, at that time the president of the Uganda Athletics Federation, pinned Inzikuru's number to her chest before the gold-medal race and then asked her, "What are you going to do?"

"I am going to leave them," Inzikuru said.

When Inzikuru left the starting line at Helsinki's Olympic Stadium on August 8, 2005, many people across Uganda were just learning for the first time who she was. A little more than nine minutes later, Dorcus Inzikuru was a national hero.

"The race was playing in all of the bars

where they usually watch football," Godfrey Gali says. "People stood up on their seats. People were shouting. Tension was so high. People all over Kampala were watching the race with great anticipation."

Tamwesigire believes he may have been the most nervous person inside the stadium that day.

"When you are the president of the Federation, you can't sit," Tamwesigire says. "I had brought our national flag, but I left it on my seat and moved closer to the track. When Inzikuru won the race, I was looking for this flag to give to her, but I couldn't find it anywhere. Watching the race was very exciting. She was a very good distance ahead of the pack. She left them."

Preferring to pace the field, Inzikuru ran in front for the entire race, winning in a time 9:18.24, more than two seconds clear of the field. Inzikuru jogged her victory lap without a flag after winning Uganda's first international gold medal in any sport since her idol, Akii-Bua, 33 years before, thus joining him as only the second sports role model ever produced by their nation. By contrast, the United States has won more than 1,000 gold medals just in its Olympic history, and Uganda's neighbor Kenya has won 23 Olympic gold medals.

"When it came time for the medal award, Inzikuru was crying instead of smiling because she couldn't believe what she had done," Tamwesigire says. "She couldn't believe that the national anthem being played was for her. I didn't expect the level of excitement and knowledge back at home. People called me asking when her flight was coming back so the celebration could begin. I said, 'What? The lady is going somewhere first to continue her training.' They said, 'No, she must come here first.' "

The Ugandan government chartered a plane to bring Inzikuru home. A jubilant crowd of 10,000 people met her at the airport in Entebbe. The following morning a motorcade of 12 motorcycles followed by a Mercedes-Benz convertible carrying Inzikuru required five hours to carry her the 30 kilometers from Entebbe to Kampala as euphoric Ugandans lined up along the roadside. One elated young man ran the entire route beside Inzikuru's car. After touring all of the major streets of Kampala to more cheering crowds, Inzikuru was honored in a special session convened by Uganda's parliament and invited for dinner with the president.

"Inzikuru has become a national hero known all over, just like Akii-Bua," Gali says. “In schools now when they are teaching mathematics, they say, ‘If Inzikuru is running 10 kilometers per hour and she must run 50 kilometers, how long will it take Inzikuru to cover that distance?’ ”

Inzikuru would become known as “the Gazelle of Arua.” After winning the 3,000-meter steeplechase in the 2006 Commonwealth Games, she was slowed by injuries. Then she became pregnant and, after missing two years following the birth of her child, she has only recently begun to train again at an elite level.

“For many years Ugandan society was not positive about women in sport because they thought sport is masculine and while top sportswomen might be admired as great athletes, they were not admired as great family people because they were off the expected road,” Tamwesigire says. “Inzikuru has helped change that. People are proud of this lady. Because of Inzikuru, Ugandans are no longer saying that sport is not a woman thing.”

“Inzikuru has inspired and motivated so many women,” says Jasper Aligawesa, the general secretary of Uganda’s National Council of Sports. “When she won the medal every school wanted to invite her there to show kids that you can come from a very poor background and if you put in good effort you can still become a champion. Inzikuru has become synonymous with the word 'champion.' She may be a tiny woman but every Ugandan looks up to her."

She could win. Inzikuru helped her believe. Phiona Mutesi hasn't heard of all that much, but she has heard of Inzikuru. Everybody in Uganda has heard of the Gazelle of Arua. Phiona knows Inzikuru is the best female athlete in her country and she knows that they both began from nowhere with nothing and no respect.

"I know that she runs for Uganda and she's a world champion," Phiona says. "Inzikuru actually motivates me because I know she has gone through the same lifestyle I have gone through and so whenever I look at her I feel like I am encouraged. That I can also make it."

Phiona thought of Inzikuru on the eve of the Rwabushenyi Memorial Chess Championship staged in December of 2010 at the Lugogo Sports Complex in Kampala. All of the top Ugandan players were there. Seven games in three grueling days. After returning to the Katwe chess project from the Olympiad with a new level of confidence forged by competing day after day against the world's elite players, the annual Rwabushenyi tournament, one of the most coveted titles in Ugandan chess, would be Phiona's first opportunity to show how much her game had grown from her experience in Russia.

"I did not think I could become the champion at that event," Phiona says, "because all of the big ladies were there and they were telling me how they'd been training using their computers and personally I was just training with my friends in the project."

After winning her first-round game, Phiona found herself staring across the board in the second game at her Olympiad teammate Rita Nsubuga.

"Whenever I play Phiona I really focus because I have this fear in me about how will I resign to this young girl," Rita says. "I remember I was winning that game. I really focused and I had the game in my hands and she saw it."

Phiona admits she fell into a weak position against Rita and was on the verge of surrendering. "I remember that right from the start Rita was having an upper hand," Phiona says. "In the middle of the game I had no position whatsoever and actually I lost hope. I stood up and I had a chance to look at other games of other project children who were also taking part in the tournament and I saw some of them were also having very terrible positions, but we had agreed that this time we were going to compete and not just participate. So I sat down and I endured to continue to think and play and luckily enough the game turned to my advantage."

Says Rita, "I touched on a piece that I was not supposed to move, but by the rules I had to move it, and so Phiona ended up winning. I made a lot of blunders. So she ended up taking the game and she was so excited. I was so hurt, because it was my game. I felt so bad. It was so painful."

Later that afternoon, Phiona found herself facing Ivy Claire Amoko, her Board 1 teammate at the Olympiad, considered the country's national champion. Phiona was intimidated from the start. She again had thoughts of resigning early in the game. "She was winning right from the opening, so why would she resign?" Ivy says incredulously. "I was so beaten that I couldn't even understand where I went wrong. She beat me so badly I felt like I had not played in ten years."

The following morning Phiona faced Goretti Angolikin, another strong player whom Phiona had feared playing in the past. But whether or not Phiona knew it, she was not the only apprehensive player at the board. "To be honest, I was scared of her," Goretti says. "Phiona has a coach. She does more training than I do. I just had a feeling she would win. In chess, once you're scared, it's hard to get a good result."

Still, Goretti got off to a fast start and familiar doubts began to creep into Phiona's mind. "When I saw Coach Robert coming to look at my game I remembered how he had given us a caution never to resign, so when I saw him I feared to resign," Phiona says. "When I remembered that agreement, it somehow encouraged me and I just said, 'Okay, let me continue.' "

As Phiona and Goretti reached the endgame, the contest appeared destined for a draw. But Goretti made one small blunder and Phiona recognized it immediately and stole the game. It would be Goretti's only loss of the tournament.

At this point in the event, it occurred to Katende that Phiona was playing the best chess of her life and that if she finished strong in her final three matches she could well be the women's champion, but he chose not to share his thoughts with her.

He knew that Phiona never thinks that way, never thinks ahead, and it could be perilous to plant that idea in her mind.

In her next game, Phiona faced Grace Kigeni. "I remember she beat me easily, which was quite embarrassing," Grace says. "She played so well that I remember thinking, 'This girl is becoming such a strong and confident player. This girl is not the same girl who played at the Olympiad.' "

Later that evening, Phiona easily defeated Joan Nakimuli for her sixth straight win. Phiona wasn't aware that her victory in that game secured the tournament championship until all of the matches in that round had been completed. When Katende informed her of the news, Phiona's reaction was typically reserved, at least until Ivan, Benjamin, Samuel, and many of the other competitors from Katwe came to congratulate her and coaxed a shy smile. A win for anybody from Katende's project has always been treated as a victory for everybody, dating all the way back to the days of The Children's Team. Katende says he couldn't truly gauge Phiona's joy until she walked out of the playing hall with a subtle bounce in her step that he had noticed before following significant victories.

Even after clinching the Rwabushenyi

championship, there was still one challenge remaining for Phiona. In the final round, she was slated to face Christine Namaganda, the same girl from whom Katende had once drawn inspiration to train his own champion. Katende had never shared that story with Phiona, but Phiona was aware of Christine's championship pedigree, and before the game she came to Katende and told him, "Coach, I am nervous. That Christine is tough and she is experienced."

Katende tried to comfort Phiona. He reminded her that she had played against more talented players at the Olympiad. Then moments before the game was to begin, Christine approached Phiona and asked her if she would accept a draw, admitting she was reluctant to compete against Phiona after seeing how well she had played in the tournament to that point. Phiona consulted Katende, who insisted that she play for the experience but told her that because she did not need to win to be the tournament champion, she could accept a draw during the game. Phiona quickly jumped ahead of Christine with a strong opening and when Christine requested a draw early in the middlegame, Phiona granted it to help Christine save face. Suddenly there was nobody left to fear.

"A young girl like her shouldn't be able to win that tournament," Rita says. "But all of us made blunders against her and she took advantage of us. When you look at Phiona's background, she is totally different from the rest of us, so you have to feel happy for her when she wins."

"Maybe some people were surprised she won that tournament because she was so young, but those of us who know her were not shocked," Grace says. "She deserved it."

For the first time, Phiona was the undisputed best women's chess player in all of Uganda. For the first time, she was beginning to leave them.

The first 13 years of her life, she was somebody else. She was Fiona. Because her name was never formally spelled out for her, when Harriet's daughter began to learn to write in primary school, she spelled her name the way it sounded to her: F-I-O-N-A. When she reached P4, she met another student who shared her name, but spelled it P-H-I-O-N-A. She didn't really understand how their names could be spelled differently, so she kept using "Fiona" until the day she looked at her passport to travel to the chess tournament in Sudan. During the passport application process, Godfrey Gali filled out her documents without bothering to check how she spelled her name. Gali knew a woman with that name who spelled it "Phiona," so that is how he printed it on the application. When Fiona received the passport, she noticed the alternate spelling. Katende told her that from that point on she must begin spelling her name with a "Ph" or risk bureaucratic hassles whenever she used her passport for identification. And so Fiona became Phiona, through no choice of her own.

Phiona isn't Fiona. Less so every day.

Rodney Suddith remembers the first time he ever crossed paths with the girl back in 2006. He visited the chess project and asked Katende to point out some of the children who were rising above the others with their skill level. At that time, 10-year-old Phiona had been out of school for most of the last six years. She spoke Luganda but could neither read nor write in that language. She could not speak any English, could write only her name and a handful of other words, and could understand just the simplest phrases.

"The first time I met Phiona I think I may have glimpsed her face, but I basically just saw the top of her head because she wouldn't make eye contact," Suddith says. "Robert translated, so I'm assuming Phiona said something, but I never heard it. I was really taken by what an extreme introvert she was. She would answer a very direct question, but never with more than the most simple answer to get the conversation over. Unlike a lot of Ugandans who like a physical touch, a pat on the shoulder, she seemed to shy away from that as well. But each visit after that, I watched her progress and grow in confidence, not only in chess, but in life."

From the beginning, Suddith also noticed Phiona's compassion for the other kids. Each day when she arrived at the project she would tend to many of the younger children. While most of her peers would move straight for the chessboards and begin playing, Phiona would first make sure certain kids she was looking out for were there and often sat with them to help teach them how to play. She always volunteered to prepare the porridge and when she didn't cook, she was always appreciative of those who did. Following Katende's advice, Phiona never left the project without thanking everybody who had helped out that day.

Suddith could see himself in this girl. Phiona was another kid whose life had left its predestined path through sport. Another grinder who has lived the in-between. Another person from a sheltered background inspired by the idea that there might be something else out there. He particularly remembers the day when Phiona returned from Sudan with a different level of self-confidence.

"There was a newfound spark there and that comes from being competitive," Suddith says. "I asked her, 'Did you enjoy your trip?' Phiona told me, 'Yes, we won.' That wasn't even my question, but I liked her answer."

By that time, Phiona had embraced chess as her true calling. "I love chess with all of my heart," Phiona says. "And when you love something with all your heart, it brings many other things. I wouldn't have gone out of the country if it wasn't for playing chess. I wasn't schooling, but I began schooling again because of chess. I wouldn't have met Coach Robert and so many other people if it wasn't for chess. Because of the love I have for chess I am able to access all that."

"If you're a slum kid your personality is suffocated by the need to survive," Suddith says. "But what is so rare about Phiona as a kid in Katwe is that she doesn't ignore what's around her. She observes it and she absorbs it and she learns from it. And as she's seen some of the horror stories that are part of daily life in the slum, it strikes a deeper chord with Phiona than in her peers. It touches her. She's very sensitive to what other people are thinking and feeling and I think that plays well with her chess."

Katende attributes much of Phiona's personal transformation to the fact that she has found religion. "It is really hard to measure spiritual aspects because there are no parameters," Katende says. "You cannot really know whether the wind is blowing unless you see it shaking things. You need to see its effect. I can confidently say that Phiona was not good spiritually because of the way she used to quarrel and say vulgar things to the other children. But I would say that she has made a complete U-turn. Her conduct is totally different from the way she was before she joined the program. She has even developed grace in her."

Phiona worships every day either at a church near her school or at her mother's church closer to their home. One of Phiona's few regular possessions is a tiny dog-eared Bible that she carries with her almost everywhere she goes. She believes in God, even as she is still figuring out the impact religion can have on her life.

"Getting saved has really helped me greatly because sometimes I can have problems and I just put them in prayer requests and I've seen God able to rescue us," Phiona says. "I remember one time when I fell sick and I was almost dying and there was a certain pastor who came and made me confess some words and after confessing those words the following day I felt like I was getting better. In the days that followed I got healed, so I understand that being a born-again Christian has helped me a lot. I appreciate that God has helped me stay alive."

In January of 2011, Phiona's story was published in *ESPN The Magazine.* Until that point, Phiona's exploits were known only to those at the chess project and inside Sports Outreach. Though chess is not among the sports most closely followed in Uganda, suddenly the nation began to discover the prodigy in its midst.

When the story was published, Uganda's National Council of Sports increased its organization's annual funding for chess from two million to five million shillings and pledged even more support for the sport in the future.

Says Godfrey Gali, "That story caused our local media to say, 'Who is this person? We didn't know.' They came to me asking for interviews. Also, from the international media, they came around as well. It has opened up Phiona's story to the world. Our administrators in the ministry of sport, they were all asking me, 'Who is this kid? When did this happen? How did this happen? We had no idea this sport was this popular.' "

"Chess tends to be a sport that is mostly hidden indoors," says Daniel Tamwesigire, who is now Uganda's Commissioner for Physical Education and Sports. "The spectator population is very small. It is not a major story in our newspapers. But Phiona can make it so. What she needs is exposure. If the press picks up on chess as regular publicity material, the community will come to know, the schools will come to know, the young girls will come to know. We don't have a very good reading culture so we also need the electronic media, the radios and the televisions, to talk about this young lady. We just need to figure out how to focus the camera on her in Uganda. Then she can make a difference."

"Phiona's story reminds me of another teenage girl from nowhere," says Jasper Aligawesa. "I believe that Phiona could be another Inzikuru. If this girl goes to an international competition and wins a gold medal, she could have the same impact, because don't forget that track is not as popular as football. When we hold a track event in Uganda the entrance is free, but we don't see people. But when Inzikuru won a gold medal then everyone was in the streets. If you ask anybody, 'Who is Inzikuru?' they say, 'The Gazelle of Arua.' Someday maybe when you ask, 'Who is Phiona?' they will say, 'The Queen of Katwe.' "

Teopista Agutu was surfing online in the spring of 2011 when she stumbled upon an article in London's *Guardian* newspaper about Phiona Mutesi, a follow-up to the *ESPN* story. Agutu, who lives with her husband and two sons in one of Kampala's affluent gated communities known as Naalya Estates, phoned the city's daily newspaper, *New Vision,* and asked whether anyone there had heard of Phiona. *New Vision* had begun following Phiona's career and so one of the reporters gave Agutu a phone number for Robert Katende. She phoned Katende and told him she had always wanted her sons, 10-year-old Stefan and seven-year-old Samuel, to learn chess and asked if Phiona would be interested in tutoring them. Agutu offered to bring her children to Katwe, but because they had never been there before, Katende felt that Phiona should go to Agutu's home so that Phiona would not be embarrassed — and her teaching potentially compromised — by her students' finding out where she lives.

A week later, during a school holiday, Phiona boarded a taxi for the seven-kilometer ride to another world. She walked into a home with a brand-new flat-screen television, children's bedrooms the same size as her shack, and a sparkling clean toilet with Mickey Mouse stickers over the commode. There was a treehouse in the yard from which one could get a panoramic view of Kampala that did not include the low-lands of Katwe.

"Normally a community like Naalya would not allow a slum kid through the gate," Katende says, "but Phiona has developed a certain kind of potential that opens up a door."

"Phiona has a skill we value," Agutu says. "It's all about what she knows and not who she is or where she comes from."

As many as a dozen kids from the Naalya neighborhood show up on school holidays to meet Phiona and several other children from the chess project anxious to make the journey out of Katwe. They are paid only for their travel expenses.

Phiona began teaching chess with the pawn. Then the rook. Then the bishop, just as she had once learned from Gloria and Gloria had once learned from Benjamin and Benjamin from Ivan and Ivan from Katende himself. The curriculum is the same. In fact, Stefan executed the Fool's Mate on Samuel several times before Phiona taught Samuel how to combat it.

"Phiona was telling us about how she went to Sudan and Russia and she was playing chess and beating people from all over the world and I was amazed," Stefan says. "I was wondering, 'How could that happen?' She made very many articles in the newspapers until she became a very popular person in Uganda. Coming from where she comes from, it inspires me. I know she is the best player among girls in Uganda and that is a good teacher to have."

Phiona has also created her own informal chess project at her secondary school, tutoring 20 of her fellow female students in the game. Chess has become so popular that Phiona's teacher, Abbey Ssentogo, has often had to confiscate chessboards from students who are surreptitiously playing the game during class.

"What I know about Phiona is that she's

influential because when she started playing chess in school the number of girls playing started increasing every day," Ssentogo says. "They know that chess has taken Phiona to different countries. Many kids are getting interested because of that. Sometimes kids when they hear about something good happening to somebody they get encouraged. They are proud of her."

International publicity has also led Phiona to acquire pen pals around the world, including an American convict named Damion Coppedge, who is serving time for manslaughter at the Wende Correctional Facility in Alden, New York. Coppedge read Phiona's story and the two began a chess game through the mail. Coppedge has sent Phiona three chess books, a check for $25 that prompted Katende to open Phiona's first bank account, and the following note:

Dear Phiona,

I write to you happy to hear from you & your coach. I thought I would never get a letter back, and when I did I smiled with excitement.

Your letter was the very first one I ever received from my original home. I write to you and Robert not only as a fellow student of chess, but also a brother in a distant land. Captured long ago were my ancestors and as I descend from them I'm delighted to reconnect with you as a friend and brother. I thank you for agreeing to play with me. I absolutely love everything about chess. I have a small library of chess books in my cell along with 2 chess sets made of plastic. My father taught me to play when I was 8 years old. I've been hooked since. I am 34 and I don't have much competition here in this prison.

Don't worry about me defeating you. I read that you make everybody's pieces retreat until there is nothing for them to do but resign!

I have 6 1/2 years to come out of this place. I've been in here since 1997. When I was younger I was living without good in my life and I killed my best friend by playing with a loaded gun which went off & hit him & took his life.

Every day I wish I could bring him back. Every day I wish I could change the past. Every day I escape my wishes through an intricate maze of chess, prayer and deep thought. The prison life is like a chess game with many dimensions. Every day is an obstacle & challenge. A temptation to explode and attack. But like in chess sometimes restraint is better for your position than to attack. In prison the best position is to be walking out of the place and going home never to come back. So I work hard to restrain myself, not involving myself in nonsense. My king (ME) remains mostly castled (in my cell) and away from the center of the board where many empty-minded pawns roam.

Thank you very much for reaching out.

Take care, Damion

Phiona says that she can relate to Coppedge. Both are bound by tragic circumstances, both struggling to survive against the odds of their environment. Katende believes that Phiona is just beginning to realize the positive influence her life story can have on other people's lives.

"I want to say that Phiona understands what she's accomplished because she compares how she is with how she was," Katende says. "She was really proud to complete primary school. She is proud to begin speaking some English. Even when she's going through trauma and being at school with nothing, she still has that self-esteem. Other students don't come to her directly, but they know what she's done. They whisper, 'Oh, that's the girl.' In a way it gives her confidence. She may not have enough money to visit the canteen, but they look at her as though she is a hero. Still, according to the way she sees herself, she has not done what she wants to do. She is really still striving. All the time."

"I don't feel like I'm the best woman chess player in the country," Phiona says. "I realize thinking that could hold me back. The moment I feel like I'm the best, then I won't be able to add on, so I don't even in any way get close to that. I always work as though I'm not the one who is the champion and then I am able to continue to train."

Katwe is not a place where people trumpet their own success. Those instances are rare and thus can attract unwanted attention. Any personal celebration is best kept private. When Phiona was preparing to begin P7 in 2010, she had to fill out some forms that included her date of birth. She asked her mother. She asked Brian. Of course, nobody knew what to tell her. She wanted to fill in something, so she wrote March 28, simply because in P5 her English teacher had organized a party for her class on March 28, so Phiona chose that day as her birthday. "I had a happy memory of that day, so that is my birthday now," Phiona says. "On that day in 2011 when I turned fifteen I was at home on holiday and I called out to the children in my neighborhood and I gave them sweets. That is how I celebrated. I did that because I wanted it to be a special day."

Yet for all the positives that chess has brought to her life, Phiona still suffers just as Fiona once did. When Phiona returned from the Chess Olympiad in October of 2010, she discovered that her family had been evicted from their home again. Harriet was two months behind on the rent payments and when the landlord discovered that mzungu from America had visited Harriet's shack with their notepads and cameras, the landlord believed that Harriet must have some money. When Harriet insisted she did not, the family was tossed out. With money from the stipend that Phiona was allotted at the Olympiad, the family was able to relocate to another shack.

Phiona is in boarding school at St. Mbuga Secondary School through the Popp Scholarship and lives at home only during the holidays. She is reminded every day by the hunger that often grips her gut and the rotten stench that permeates the school compound that some things have not changed. She is still a slum kid in Katwe, constantly confronted by an environment that conspires against her on so many levels.

So many hurdles.

There is a well-known story in Uganda about a mzungu who watches a Ugandan man fishing in a lake. The Ugandan catches a fish, cooks it, and eats it while sitting under a shady tree. The mzungu asks him, "Why don't you catch more fish and sell them to make money?"

"Then what?" the Ugandan fisherman asks.

"You can use that money to start a business," the mzungu says.

"Then what?"

"You can use money from your business to build yourself a home."

"Then what?"

"You can become a rich man and relax."

"If the ultimate goal is to relax, then why should I go through all of that work?" the Ugandan says. "I am already relaxing now."

Phiona must defy Uganda, defy the sentiment that surrounds her, tugs at her, whether it be lethargy or hopelessness. She must defy the paradox of a country so fertile that many Ugandans spend their entire days chopping down tall grass that seems to grow almost as fast as it can be cut, but still struggles to properly feed its population.

She must defy her country's rampant inflation, because Phiona's chess career needs sponsorship and so Uganda's economic future is tied to hers. For the first time, it actually matters to her what is going on beyond "just there."

Uganda's future lies in the hands of Yoweri Museveni, the man who once protected Katende and his grandmother in the bush of the Luwero Triangle and then became president. Like all Ugandan presidents, Museveni, the former rebel, is dogged by rebels. Uganda is a nation struggling with a lingering civil war that compelled the United States to send special advisers to the country in 2011 to help the Ugandan military hunt down Joseph Kony and his Lord's Resistance Army and bring them to justice for the atrocities they have committed over the last 25 years.

"Sometimes it makes me want to shed tears when I think of our future in Uganda," Katende says. "That's why I invest my life in the children. The only way to break the chain of poverty is to do it with the children. It is too late for the adults. We have to let that generation go and start from here."

Because Uganda's economy has still yet to recover from the damage done by Amin and his successors, both John Akii-Bua and

Dorcus Inzikuru often had to leave the country to train in places with more modern facilities. It is galling to Ugandans that a neighboring country like Kenya collects gold medals routinely in international competition, yet Akii-Bua and Inzikuru are the only gold medal winners in any sport in Uganda's history. Ugandans revere soccer above all other sports, yet the country has never qualified for the World Cup. It is a nation so starved for recognition on the world stage that many of its people have begun to long for the time of Idi Amin, whose megalomania pushed Uganda into the international consciousness both on and off the field.

"General Amin, among all the presidents that the country has ever had, promoted sport more than any other, although he is not known for that," Daniel Tamwesigire says. "In sports you realize that most of Uganda's achievements came in the 1970s, the reason being that we had stable physical education and a good follow-up system for athletes who performed well in sports. Comparing us with other African nations, at that point we were ahead, but there came a time when our systems were interfered with while the others continued, and we have never recovered."

"Our current president needs to be better educated on the issue so we can get more funding," Godfrey Gali says. "To Museveni sports is nothing more than leisure. A pastime. I remember once he told us that Uganda must spend all of its money on roads and hospitals. Sports is not a priority for him. He has the wrong perspective of the contributions that sports could make to our national pride."

Because of lack of funding, Ugandan chess players rarely take part in tournaments outside of their own country. Even a tournament inside Uganda requires money for registration, transportation, and meals, which is often too much for the chess federation to underwrite on its own. In September of 2011 Phiona qualified to play in the All-Africa Games in Mozambique, but the funds never materialized to send her. Over the last two years, Phiona has had to turn down invitations from tournaments all over Africa, and even some inside Uganda, because the trips were too expensive. The Uganda Chess Federation could not even afford to stage its own national junior championship in 2010.

"Uganda used to be a force in chess inside Africa," says former national team coach Dr. George Zirembuzi. "There was a time when we were third on the continent with only Egypt and Tunisia ahead of us, but now Botswana and Zambia and Zimbabwe and South Africa have moved so fast ahead of us. They even have Grandmasters. We have really fallen behind."

"It is a struggle," says Joachim Okoth, Uganda's current national chess coach. "We lack facilities. We play our chess at an old tennis club. We have gotten the permission to take chess to the schools, but we don't have the equipment. We don't have the boards."

"The way we train our players in Uganda is crude and rudimentary," Gali says. "We don't have many coaches so our children will just play the game and someone will tell them what they think is a good move and what is not."

It makes sense that Uganda's two most celebrated athletes are runners. Hurdlers. That's what you do in Uganda, run until you reach the next hurdle. Both Akii-Bua and Inzikuru eventually had to run away from their country and the question remains whether Phiona, too, would have to somehow leave Uganda to reach her full potential in chess.

Uganda's best chess player is currently living in England. Stephen Kawuma is part of what is becoming his nation's lost generation of chess. Stephen's father, Medi, was one of the pioneers of the Uganda Chess Federation and taught his three sons to play the game. The Kawumas bought chess books for the boys to study, which was all Stephen needed to reach the top level of Ugandan chess. Stephen is a FIDE Master who has played in every Chess Olympiad since 2000, but has never performed as well as he would like. He evolved in the game by playing whatever competition was presented to him in Uganda along with games on the Internet. But like every Ugandan before him, he has never had a true coach. Many chess players believe that it takes a Grandmaster to make one, and there simply isn't access to that in Uganda.

"We have had a coach, Dr. Zirembuzi, who once trained in Russia, but he has given us everything he can," Stephen Kawuma says. "To reach the next level we need a Grandmaster or an International Master who could sit down and analyze our games and give us the needed boost. For so many years, Uganda's top players have done their own work. Today I read this book. Tomorrow another book. You have knowledge, but that's haphazard knowledge and that doesn't help against the world's top players. I'm twenty-nine and my game is the same as it was ten years ago."

Stephen works as a refrigeration engineer in Southampton, England. Without any sponsorship money, chess has become more of a hobby, just a small part of his life. He could train with a chess coach 75 miles away in London, but that would cost 50 pounds an hour. There is an American Grandmaster offering him coaching online, but Stephen has to consider the endgame. How long can he continue to invest energy and money in chess?

"Chess demands a lot of time," Stephen says. "I got to a point where there was no time for chess. Now I'm married and from observation, when you get married your chess goes down. I don't regret that. I'm happy to be married and to have a job."

While FIDE Master is the highest ranking ever achieved by any Ugandan, Stephen says he would need to reach the next level, International Master, to start potentially receiving a regular stipend to play in tournaments. He rarely plays in FIDE-rated tournaments other than the Olympiad. He does play in club tournaments, but they do nothing to help his rating. He is close to a level where he could sustain himself as a chess player, but he has begun to question whether he has the drive and the resources to keep climbing.

Stephen's older brother, Moses, was once Uganda's best player, but he also left Uganda for England. Moses also achieved the rating of FIDE Master before reaching a point where he could sense his dream of becoming a Grandmaster was no longer possible and he basically retired from the sport, playing only recreational online chess. He has offered to be Stephen's coach, but Moses cannot take his brother to greater heights.

Stephen's younger brother, Patrick, is 20 years old and benefits from the road map provided by his older brothers. They supply him with the books and the computer software that he needs to reach their level. Stephen believes that Patrick, who ranks one rung below his brothers as a Candidate Master, is already capable of playing at his level and believes that in a few years Patrick could be an International Master if only he could find the proper coaching and competition.

"When our best players leave the country that's a brain drain for Ugandan chess," says Stephen Kisuze, vice chairman of the Uganda Chess Federation. "Because there is so little funding to travel to tournaments outside the country we must count on our own players to make each other better."

There are only two tournaments staged each year for national team players in Uganda, far fewer than most countries with a chess federation. Ugandan chess players are a family and they gather often in Kampala to play in the national league, but they are no longer able to push each other to become better in the game because they all know each other's tactics too well. Their regular competition is with club teams, the Mulago Kings and the Mulago Queens, which comprise many of the 2010 Olympiad participants, and is staged at Kampala's upscale Hotel Africana, where during breaks between games Phiona and the other players gaze curiously at the vast swimming pool that occupies the courtyard.

Harold Wanyama, who played Board 1 at the 2010 Olympiad and is the top player still living in Uganda, admits that he has become complacent because there isn't enough competition in his country to challenge him. He has twice missed out after qualifying for the Olympiad because Uganda could not afford to send him and he says he would move to another country if he could afford to do so.

"You play in a cocoon in Uganda," Wanyama says. "There is so little contact with the outside world in chess that it is hard to improve relative to the better players elsewhere, because you don't get the competition outside of the Olympiad. There is a ceiling here and if you grow tall enough in the game you just keep banging your head."

All four of Phiona's female Olympiad teammates acknowledge serious doubts about their futures in chess. Joan Butindo married Stephen Kawuma in 2011, moved to England, and says she'd like to compete in future Olympiads, but it will depend largely on her husband's level of interest in the game. Ivy, Grace, and Rita all graduated in the same class from Kampala's Makerere University in 2011 and now must support themselves financially.

"There are many hurdles," Ivy says. "Time is a problem. Money. Attitude is a very big issue. You look into the future and you ask yourself, 'Why am I suffering for chess?' The only motivation that makes us come to most tournaments is hoping we can win some money, but then if we lose on the first day, sometimes we don't show up on the second day. We are the biggest obstacles to ourselves. You have to have an overly positive attitude and once that falters, you're finished. It's a hard world."

Like many women in Uganda, Ivy has not always been encouraged to pursue sports, even by members of her own family.

"When I started shining in chess my dad could not accept that," Ivy says. "I told him I was going to Russia to play in the Chess Olympiad and he said, 'Yeah, you can do chess, but I want you to excel more in your studies.' It's very disheartening. Just once say you're proud of me without bringing in the 'but.' Every time I dream about chess, he has to say 'but.' I could be so much better with some support."

Some talented female players in Uganda have given up chess after getting married because their husbands forbid them to play. It is also telling that none of Phiona's teammates on the national team are older than their mid-20s because that is the age when most women in Uganda can no longer concentrate as intently on the sport.

Grace is diverted from the game by an interest in music and the need to find a job. "I have gone to school and studied accounting, but that's not my passion," Grace says. "I must do it to earn a living. The most common thing that takes a Ugandan chess player away from the game is work. I am one of a number of women in Uganda who would love to focus on chess alone and take it on as a career, but in our country chess cannot put food on the table."

Ivy plans to become a lawyer because she also sees no future in chess.

"I won't base my career on chess because realistically in Uganda what can you become? A chess coach? A chess teacher? Maybe as a side job. You get a few students. But career-wise, no. Uganda won't allow it."

Like Grace, Rita also has a degree in accounting and talks dreamily about how she will earn money as an accountant and use it to form a club to teach young girls the game of chess. She, too, wants to go to more Olympiads, if time permits, but she recognizes the difference between her situation and that of Phiona. "Phiona grew up on the streets and she stays in the slum and that's why I try to treat her like my own sister," Rita says. "I absolutely pray that Phiona continues to play chess, because I think chess is a light for her. It's like a torch that can take her out of the slum to people who may be able to look after her. I always tell Phiona not to ever leave chess."

There has never been a titled female chess player in Ugandan history. When it comes to their futures in chess, the big ladies don't dream of titles or ratings, just more trips out of Uganda. Only Phiona has aspirations to be great in the game. All of Phiona's Olympiad teammates agree that Phiona is blessed by her youth to continue to pursue the game and that her potential is immense, but that her biggest hurdle is herself.

"It's tricky to figure her out because one day Phiona will play and you won't be that impressed and the next day she'll play and you'll think, 'Oh my God this girl is so incredibly talented,' " Grace says. "She lacks consistency and that's probably because her background is so inconsistent."

Says Rita, "When I look at Phiona she just needs attention. She needs love. She needs people who care about her and encourage her. I look at her and I think that once I get a big job in a few years, I will sponsor Phiona in each and every tournament in the world."

"Phiona is a very good player, but she could be even better if she really believed in herself," Ivy says. "It's hard for someone to step out of the slum thinking that the world is at my feet and I'm going to conquer it. That takes a big, big, big heart to have such an attitude. We all know how good Phiona is. Sometimes I think we know it more than she does."

The magazine covers stuck up on the walls inside shacks around Katwe are usually there to cover a hole, but the faces pictured on them are significant. Beyonce. Serena Williams. Michelle Obama. For the most part, the girls of Katwe need to be told who these people are and once they learn, they want to be just like them. For Phiona Mutesi and the other teenage girls of Katwe, there are no true female role models to follow. Nothing realistic. Nothing attainable. No solid businesswoman or stable homemaker. There is no in-between for Phiona to grab onto during a very impressionable time in her life, a time when she needs a lot of guidance about becoming an adult.

"Phiona is beginning to blossom into a woman, but she wears loose clothes and covers herself up because it's such a hard thing in the slum to be single and be a young woman," Rodney Suddith says. "It would help if Phiona could find a female role model to help her figure out who she is."

Instead, Phiona seems guided by a man. More of a phantom, really. Phiona has been told by those who knew him that she is her father's daughter, strong and resilient and fierce when challenged. But she never knew her father. She has no memories of him. She doesn't even know what he looked like. The only photograph Harriet once had of Godfrey Buyinza was lost long ago in a Katwe flood.

"There are times when I feel I miss my father," Phiona says. "For example my mother has not bought me any clothes since I was nine years old. If my father was there, I think he would have bought me clothes since I was nine. I love my mother and I sympathize with her. She struggles to look for food and pay for rent, so how can I ask her for money for clothes? But I believe my father would have met all that."

Harriet never talks about her late husband. It is only when one of her children asks her for something that she cannot afford, that she says, "Did your father leave me with any money?"

Phiona has learned not to ask her mother about her father and she discourages any talk about him from her older siblings.

"I don't really know anything concerning my father and I don't want to know," Phiona says. "Sometimes my older brother and sister will try to tell me things concerning our dad and they could tell me the kind of life that was there before he died. I really even end up sad and tell myself I wish he was still alive. If he was still alive then we wouldn't be suffering the way we are suffering. So that's why I don't want anyone to talk about him."

Part of Buyinza's legacy for his daughter is a threat of AIDS. Phiona learned several years ago that her father died of AIDS, which makes her wonder if she might also have the virus. There are 1.2 million people in Uganda infected with HIV and more than 100,000 Ugandans die of AIDS every year. For years Harriet refused to be tested because she feared the stigma that a positive result carries in Uganda, shunning from her community and possibly even her own family. But Harriet says that in recent years she has been tested three times and has always tested negative for the HIV virus. Harriet has never spoken to Phiona about HIV and while the subject is discussed in school, Phiona is still relatively naive to the causes of the disease.

"I know a bit about AIDS," Phiona says. "I know this kind of disease you can get through adultery or sharing piercing instruments. When you love a man and you don't go for a blood test you can give birth to children who can end up also becoming victims."

While Phiona is well aware of the possibility that she has the virus, she has not been tested because children in Uganda are rarely tested before the age of 18. Katende may encourage her to be tested sooner so that she might begin treatment with the necessary medicine if she is found to be positive.

Phiona has known dozens of people in Katwe who have died of AIDS. She is surrounded by tragedy daily. Inside the chess project alone she has observed as a fellow player, Alawi Katwere, became ill with a mysterious disease that first discolored his skin and then stopped his heart. She knows another girl from the project who was gang-raped and then abandoned by her family because her medical treatment cost too much money. She knows another girl from the project who twice aborted her own children with a coat hanger and nearly died of the trauma.

"These kids in Katwe are at the bottom and many Ugandans want them to stay at the bottom," Suddith says. "It's a form of prejudice. People in the slums are recognized as human, but that's about it. For anyone in Katwe to achieve anything is a big thing. So as much as we're excited about Phiona's accomplishments, there's a deep concern over how she'll handle all of this. The fact that she's a teenager now, many believe she should already be a mother. Warding off guys who just want to sleep with her is part of her daily routine. Phiona's life is so fragile. Katwe is a fallen world. It is a war zone and you can only dodge bullets for so long."

As long as Phiona is in the slum, she must keep dodging those bullets. Clearing those hurdles. She's a girl who must avoid becoming the woman who every single day Katwe keeps pushing her to be. She must keep struggling to heed the cautionary tale she has witnessed so clearly and painfully in her own sister.

Night's daughter Rita was kidnapped sometime toward the beginning of 2011, though it seems so much longer ago than that to her mother. Night isn't exactly sure how long her daughter has been gone. She knows only that Rita was four years old when she was abducted and that she is older now. And still gone.

Days before Rita was abducted, Night ran into a man that she once knew when she lived in the Nateete slum. The man greeted her and asked, "Where do you stay?" Then one afternoon, when Night was away working with her mother at the Kibuye market and had left her children at home, that man came to her shack. He brought a gift of popcorn for her children. Then he took Rita.

"When I arrived home, one of my older daughters, Winnie, showed me the way the man had left with Rita and I tried to follow him up," Night says. "When I reached where he used to stay, they told me that they knew the man but he had already been chased away from the village. When I reached the police they told me that they too knew the man and they had many cases against him."

Unable to find the man, Night sought out his wife. With some support from other members of the wife's village, Night was able to lead her to the police station and the woman admitted that her husband had taken Rita, but that they had gone to Kasese district, which is more than 300 kilometers from Kampala.

"So when the policemen heard the woman confess that my daughter is there, they told the woman to take me to where Rita is staying," Night says. "But this woman suggested that unless I had 200,000 shillings for transport that I won't be in position to go there. So I tried my best to look for the money and I failed to get it. I think about

Rita all the time, but what can I do? I cannot afford to go try to find her. So I look after the other three children as best I can."

Rita is the third oldest of the four children Night has conceived with two different men, along with Eva, 10, Winnie, 7, and two-year-old Grace. Night has stayed with each of the men in the hope of supporting her children and sometimes her mother and siblings. Night also works at the market, where Harriet has subcontracted her business so that Night can sell curry powder and tea leaves while her mother sells vegetables. Night's other job is with a local tailor who makes children's clothes. The tailor prices a dress at 1,000 shillings and if Night is able to hawk it on the street for 1,500 shillings, she keeps the difference.

Night is now about 27 years old. She has walked a very similar path as her mother, often sacrificing herself to try to save the rest of her family. Phiona is at the crossroads age when Night's life turned for the worse, when Night committed herself to help get her family off the street at the risk of her own future. Harriet's two surviving daughters maintain a complicated relationship.

"I remember there were times when we were younger and I would tell Night, 'Stop giving birth to children,' because when she gave birth their fathers often denied them, so we had nothing to do apart from still allowing them to stay with us," Phiona says. "I realized that the food we were using for four people couldn't be enough for us and for Night and her children, but she continued to have more children."

Night believes that Phiona doesn't understand her situation, doesn't grasp the sacrifices she has made, and worries that her younger sister doesn't respect her.

"I try to advise her, but personally I believe Phiona despises me in a way because she sees me as though I'm really low in status to her," Night says. "I rarely see her because I stay in a different place, but if I somehow find her home, I'll tell her, 'Phiona, the opportunity you have, make good use of it, because I did not have such an opportunity. Make sure you study hard, because you can see the kind of life I have now. I don't have any chance and I will never be happy as you are.' Whenever I advise her, she says to me she has understood what I have told her, but I don't know whether she leaves everything there. I don't know."

Night is on the wrong side of the dividing line, born too early to potentially have been rescued by Robert Katende's chess project.

Now she must be saved by her sister, just as she saved Phiona from the streets many years ago in a very different way.

"I remember one day one of my daughters was sick and I didn't have any money on me and Phiona gave me money she won playing chess and I was able to take that kid to the hospital," Night says. "Whenever Phiona gets money, she buys items for my children and promises me that if it is possible she will make sure that they go to school. For sure, when I'm having serious problems and she has some money she does not hesitate to extend support to me."

When Night is asked about her dreams for the future, a sadness envelops her. "The way I see it, I don't have any hope," Night says. "I have no dreams. All I need is to see my children studying. And maybe have someplace to live where they can find me."

When Night is asked about her dreams for Phiona, she simply says, "That she would not lead my life."

Chapter 11
Dreams

Phiona Mutesi in front of the Agape Church where she trains to realize her dream of becoming a Grandmaster.

Agape Church could collapse at any moment. It is a ramshackle structure that lists alarmingly to one side, barely held together by scrap wood, rope, a few nails, and faith. It is disposable, like everything else around it.

Inside Agape on this Saturday morning are 37 children whose lives are equally rickety. They dribble in from all over Katwe to play a game that none of them had ever heard of before they met Robert Katende. When the children walk through the door, grins crease their hardened faces. This is home as much as any place in their lives. It is a refuge, the only community they know. These are their friends, their brothers and sisters of chess, if not of blood, and there is relative safety and comfort here. It is a place to be that they can count on, a place that is predictable, a place where the competition is not to survive but simply to win a game.

Inside Agape it is almost possible to forget the chaos outside the doorway.

Now in its eighth year, Katende's chess project relocated to Agape at the beginning of 2010 from its roots at Bishop John Michael Mugerwa's veranda. There are only seven chessboards inside and chess pieces are so scarce that sometimes an orphan pawn must stand in for a king. A child sits on each end of a wobbly bench, which acts as a pew for Sunday services, both straddling the board between their knobby knees with captured pieces guarded in their laps. Those who aren't playing gather around the boards to study players they admire. A five-year-old kid in a threadbare Denver Broncos jersey with #7 on the back competes against an 11-year-old in a T-shirt that reads J'ADORE PARIS. One of the game's spectators wears a discolored shirt that reads S.O.I. CHESS ACADEMY. Most of the kids are barefoot. Some wear flip-flops. One has on black wingtips with no laces.

It is rapid-fire street chess. When more than a few seconds elapse without a move, there is a palpable restlessness. It is remarkably quiet except for the violent thud of one piece slaying another and the occasional dispute over location of a piece on a board so faded that the dark squares are barely distinguishable from the light. Surrender is signaled by a clattering of the opponent's captured pieces onto the board. There is rarely any celebration from the victor, more often a humble piece of advice to the vanquished on how best to avoid the trap that decided the game, always the more experienced players teaching the others what they know. It is an individual sport being played by kids who have been forged by their harsh environment to look out only for themselves, yet these children are a team. The Children's Team. Each one of them contributing to a greater whole.

Phiona Mutesi arrives without ceremony and takes her place in the audience of her brother Brian's game. The girl who was initially spurned by the other children for being too dirty has become a sort of den mother for the chess project. Phiona is a patient teacher who, whenever she's asked, will share remarkable stories of her travels. The younger children in the project sit close to her, watching and listening intently. They often ask why she has made a specific move. Phiona explains it to them and tells them that if they work hard they can someday exceed her in the game.

Katende wanders from board to board, sometimes sitting to play, sometimes suggesting moves, always searching for a teaching point, whether it be in chess or in life. There is no timetable at the project. After several hours of chess, a few of the kids volunteer to cook the porridge in three rusty saucepans. When it is ready and poured into bowls, the children who are not involved in a game line up to eat, while those playing don't leave their boards until their games are over. Because there are no spoons, everybody eats with their hands. Many of the kids consume their porridge ravenously because they have not eaten anything since this same bowl of porridge the previous day.

Katende sits among a small group of children who are licking porridge from their fingers. He agrees to tell them their favorite story, the one about St. Peter from the Bible. The other kids gradually gather around, one by one, from all corners of the church, until all of them are huddled around Katende, even though most have heard this tale before. When Katende speaks, his words take on the power of a sermon:

> "One time when Jesus was with his disciples, one of his disciples called St. Peter walked on water. St. Peter was with all of his other friends on the boat and he saw Jesus coming on the water walk-

ing and someone asked, 'Master, are you telling me to come?' The rest feared. But St. Peter was the one who stepped out of the boat. It wasn't an easy situation. It is extraordinary. Unrealistic. How do you get out of the boat then step on the water when you know you are definitely going to drown? But that's when you realize it was a miracle. He could do it. If he hadn't stepped out, there would be no miracle. So that's why sometimes we need to get out of our boats to realize a miracle. We can't just sit back and wait for a miracle to happen.

"We don't have. But if we don't have what we desire to have, then we realize we have to think, 'What can we do with the little we have?' Because no one is here without anything. But the issue is, how can I work with the little I have to go to another level? Because many times people spend a lot of time thinking about what they don't have and this has also changed my life. If you ask me how was I able to keep sponsoring myself for school, I can't tell you because I don't know. A miracle happened. But it was after I took a step and then a miracle occurred. I got a loan and I started studying and I played soccer for the school and after the first semester that's when the dean said this guy is playing very well and we can give him some money for schooling. It didn't find me. I had to take the bold step. Then after the second semester, they said that this guy is a good player, other schools will give him a full scholarship, we must do that or they will take him. My aim was not to go there to play soccer, it was to achieve my academics. All these miracles started happening, but only after I took the first step. If I had not taken the first step, I would have been nowhere.

"We shouldn't have excuses. Personally my life is a testimony and I've shared my life story with all of you. Some of you think you are suffering but you have not yet gone through what I went through. But I'm here. You all say, 'Coach is well off,' but I'm not yet where I want to be, but at least where I am is not where I would have been if I had not really worked hard. It depends on you, but there is always a way out, but how do we make it happen?

"So St. Peter stepped out of the boat and he went to where Jesus was. For all of you, learning chess has not been a walkover. For all of you it involved diligence, commitment, determination, faith, and then being here day after day. But through that because you turned up for the program, someone came in and said, 'Hey, these kids are doing well in chess, but they are not studying. If they can do well in chess, then given an opportunity to study they can do well in school.' This education has not come because someone found you out there. It is because you took a step to come for the program. Other people dropped off, but you kept on coming.

"If you show that kind of character, you need no excuses. Even when there is tragedy you know life must continue still. You just recorrect yourself and say, 'What next? I need to go on. Life needs to continue. I don't have this, I don't have this, I don't have this, but what do I have?' You cannot even complete the list of what you don't have. It is huge. Now forget that. Don't even think about what you don't have. Ask yourself, 'What do I have?' After having that list of what you have, then assess yourself and ask, 'What are my abilities? What can I do to live? Where can I apply this?' Then you use what you do have to get what you don't have on the list. Each one of you is realizing a miracle because you had the courage to step out of the boat. All of you can walk on water."

Benjamin and Ivan sat on either end of a bench one day at Agape, a chessboard in between them, when Benjamin first told Ivan about his dream to be a Grandmaster.

The more cautious of the two, Ivan said, "You know, Benja, those Grandmasters, they spend a lot of time on training. They have all the facilities. For us we have to struggle for what we eat, so it will be so hard for us to make it there."

"We have been to Sudan and become champions when we didn't think that was possible," Benjamin said. "Why can't we also be Grandmasters?"

Rather than dwell on who they are, the children of the chess project like to talk about who they want to be. They dream. The biggest difference between the children inside Agape Church and those outside is the capacity to dream.

Benjamin, who like most of the children in the chess project attends school on a Popp Scholarship, dreams of becoming a doctor. Ivan dreams of becoming a telecommunications engineer. Joseph Asaba dreams of becoming a bank manager. Richard Tugume dreams of becoming an electrical engineer. Gloria Nansubuga dreams of becoming a GM. When Gloria, who is about 11 years old, is asked what a GM is, she admits that she doesn't really know. She just knows that is the goal that everyone else in the chess project aspires to, but not what the letters actually stand for. It doesn't matter to her. Gloria wants to be a GM, and considering her blossoming talent, her age, and her accomplished tutor, she may have the best chance of them all. "That Phiona has been able to go to other countries and she has won, that is my inspiration," Gloria says. "She is not only very masterful in the game, but she is very kind. Phiona is now my role model. I was first her teacher, but she is now the one teaching me. Phiona believes I can become a GM."

Ever since Phiona's brother Brian was seriously injured in the bicycle accident, he has dreamed of becoming a doctor. "I realize that if I become a doctor then from that I can open up a hospital someday. If anyone in my family ever had to be fixed, I would not have to worry about paying for it. I believe the chess program in the slum will still be running by then and I want to be in position to support the children who will be in that program. When they are coming to the hospital, I will be treating them for free."

Phiona's 13-year-old brother, Richard, who joined the Katwe chess project shortly after his sister, attends primary school and often sleeps in the project's storage shed to be closer to school. He dreams of becoming an electrical engineer.

"When I grow up I want to be many things," says Samuel Mayanja, one of the Pioneers. "First, I want to be a medical doctor. I want to be a Grandmaster. I want be an engineer and I want also to be a movie producer."

Overhearing this list, Katende smiled and asked, "Mayanja, have you ever heard of any one person succeeding in all of those fields?"

Samuel's resolve was unshaken. "Why not?" Samuel says. "Why can I not be the first?"

Inspired by the success of Phiona and Benjamin and Ivan, they all want to stick with chess, to join the national team, to travel to future Olympiads. The slum kids, who were initially rejected by the country's chess establishment, now are considered the backbone of Uganda's promising future in the game.

"In the years to come I believe Coach Robert's kids will fill our national team,"

Godfrey Gali says. "The wealthier kids in the school system cannot win games against them. They complain to me that they don't receive the same training. In future Olympiads, I believe our teams will be made up entirely of kids from the slums. They are driven by the kind of life they lead. There is a desperation in the way they play that you don't see in the other kids. You play harder when the outcome may decide if you eat that night."

Most of Katende's chess children also aspire to someday teach the game, to follow in their mentor's footsteps. They hope to mirror and honor the man who has helped save them by saving others like them in the slums.

"I want to train many, many children to play chess because I remember when Coach told me to train Benjamin and now I see Benjamin is a very good player and a very good person," Ivan says. "That motivates me and I feel I can also train other players to be successful, just as Coach Robert does."

Katende has dreams as well. Based on the model he has established with Phiona and the children she tutors at Naalya Estates, Katende aspires to open a chess academy where the children of the project can teach the children of more affluent families how to play the game. It is part of his ultimate dream to open a Children's Home that will provide a place to live for disenfranchised kids, orphans, and abused children, including children from the chess project.

After passing on potential opportunities several years ago to play soccer professionally in Argentina, Denmark, and Vietnam because he could not afford to travel to those places to try out for interested clubs, Katende says he no longer dreams of soccer. He no longer dreams of playing on that lush green field. He plays only on the Good News Football Club, where his greatest fulfillment occurs after the games.

He has dedicated his life to backing up a vow he made one day as a student in S2 during his five-kilometer walk home from school, when he turned to a friend and said, "We have to make sure we study hard so that our children won't have to walk the way we have walked. My children will not suffer the way I have."

In 2008 Katende handed over the soccer portion of his project to other Sports Outreach ministers so he could concentrate all of his efforts on the chess program, which he continues to expand to more slum areas in Kampala. With the help of Aloysius Kyazze, Katende has even brought the program to Sports Outreach's other headquarters in Gulu, in the northern part of Uganda, where 40 children competed in their first chess tournament in 2010. That tournament was run by Gerald Mutyaba, a former Pioneer, who acts as Gulu's version of Coach Robert.

The 30-year-old Katende sees himself as an example of what a little hope and help and some exposure to a more stable life can produce.

"I have experienced many lives," Katende says. "I was in a poor state and when I left my grandma I came to a moderately better place where my mother and I were renting in the slums. Then when she died I moved to my auntie's place, which was a better place again, and with her I saw many new things and I asked myself, 'That means people can live like this?' With my grandma, when it rained I got a banana leaf to cover myself, but Aunt Jacent had a vehicle and when it rained they could just drive to school. I wanted to do whatever I could to make sure that I could be like those people who live a better life. That's where my drive comes from and I want these children to follow my lead."

To that end, Katende has invited Phiona and the other chess children to landmark events in his life, so that they can see for themselves what living a more normal life looks like. "I took four of the chess children to my introduction to my wife's family," Katende says. "I wanted them to see that. It is easy to tell them, 'You must wait until time comes when you find the right person to marry and then you get introduced properly to the family.' But that's mere talking. They can ask, 'Coach, have you done that?' It is now more clear to them. They've witnessed it and now they tell me they want to do that as well."

About 20 children from his Katwe project attended Katende's wedding in June of 2010 to Sarah Ntongo, whom he'd met three years earlier when she volunteered as a teacher at the Kampala School for the Physically Handicapped, which shares its compound with Sports Outreach Institute. During school holidays, Katende has also invited many of the children to stay with him and his wife at the modest two-room house they rent in the Mengo-Lungujja district, less than three kilometers from Katwe.

Katende also tries to provide some financial support to his extended family whenever possible.

"Robert is my Lord," says Katende's

grandmother, Aidah Namusisi, who believes she is 93 years old and still lives in the Kasubi slum with other relatives. "He is the one who takes care of me. He's the one who looks after all of us. Whatever good things we are to get, he is the one who can get it for us."

Katende has become the role model for his entire family. The same framed photograph of Katende dressed in cap and gown graduating from university is prominently displayed in the sitting rooms of both Aunt Jacent and Aunt Dez.

"I believe Robert's mother looks down on him from above and she is very, very happy to see the way he is right now," Aunt Dez says. "She died lamenting and crying because of her son, but you cannot really refuse God's plan. Right before she died, Robert's mother told me, 'That son of mine. I don't want him to become a hooligan. I don't want him to become a thief. I want him to become a son who our country is proud of.' Knowing what he's done for these children, I believe her last wish has been granted."

Katende's first child arrived in dramatic fashion when his wife was taken to the hospital delivery room, but the baby would not come. Doctors allotted Sarah a half hour, after which they said they would need to perform a Caesarean section. Katende anguished over that possibility because he did not have enough money to pay for the expensive procedure. Thirty minutes elapsed without change, but doctors were delayed for another half hour. Just as they arrived to take Sarah to the operating room, she went into labor and had a normal birth, sparing her family the anguish and expense of an operation that they could not afford. Katende's daughter was born on April 26, 2011.

He named her Mercy.

In Uganda it is said, "Giving birth to a daughter is like giving birth to sugar." Female children are viewed by many Ugandans as assets. Dowry. When it comes time for marriage, they are worth a negotiable number of cattle, which explains why many Ugandan men see women as property. Some fathers have even been known to forbid daughters from marrying until they find a husband wealthy enough to pay a dowry that can help the rest of the bride's family survive.

Women in Uganda don't often get to dream for themselves. It's a male-dominated society, so everything Phiona has accomplished has come with the assistance of men.

When Bishop Mugerwa was approached by Robert Katende years ago and asked about the use of his veranda to shelter his chess program, Mugerwa had never heard of chess.

"I never expected chess to catch on," Mugerwa says. "I thought it was promoting laziness because I saw the kids just sat there for hours and hours. I am shocked at what has happened. By using chess to travel out of Katwe, Phiona is carrying a message to the other kids that slum children are not a waste, not forgotten, not a lost generation. These kids just lack leadership because there is usually no one successful to imitate. Phiona is their role model. We are a neighborhood full of children who think they are nobodies and she is making kids believe they can be somebody. Phiona is my hero and I believe she can be all of Uganda's hero."

Katende chuckles about how some of the same mothers in Harriet's neighborhood who feared the mzungu and forbade their children from joining the chess program at its inception, sheepishly approached Harriet a few years later asking how their children could attend. He acknowledges that he never expected this level of success or exposure. It was never his goal. He was just looking for a forum to relate to the children at his project who didn't play soccer. Now he has created a pipeline for them to potentially escape the slum.

"Frankly, I never imagined Phiona making the national team," Katende says. "My purpose was not for Phiona to be great at chess, but to have a way that I could share my faith with her, make her a good citizen, and see her life transformed through fear of the Lord. Now I see that maybe she can be more."

Because she had dropped out of school completely for two years along with parts of four others before the Popp Scholarship opportunity arose in 2006, Phiona has only reached S2 at St. Mbuga Secondary School and has four years remaining there. Phiona is in the top 20 percent of her class academically and Katende believes that if she continues to concentrate on her studies she has a chance to earn a government scholarship to university just as he once did.

"I want Phiona to understand that her way out of the slum is a combination of studying very hard and pursuing chess greatly," Katende says. "Ask most kids when they finish secondary school what they want to become and they don't know. Ugandan kids are not trained to do jobs. There is no path. Studying alone is not a sure deal. You need to have contacts. In Uganda it is more about *know who* than know how. Nobody is certain how they will survive, but Phiona's chess can possibly produce a contact. It is the only advantage she has."

"The goal is that chess will help her find a way out of that slum and she will have an improved life and when that is witnessed by other kids it will be profound," Rodney Suddith says. "If Phiona can escape, the others will follow. Then if they can find their way out, they are going to want the same for their brothers and sisters and cousins and eventually their kids. This chess program could be an ongoing means for kids to not only grow in the game, but a means to an education, a means to a job, which is a means to a healthy family. With this chess program of forty kids in it, you think, 'What if twenty of these kids went to university because of this? That means that there are twenty parents who went to school who now have kids that are living a better life.' "

While Katende says he hopes through her chess that Phiona can begin to blaze a trail out of the slum for his other chess kids to follow, he remains realistic. He knows that for her to accomplish that, Phiona likely must produce success in chess on a world stage like no other Ugandan, man or woman, has ever achieved.

"That path has a lot of struggles," Katende admits. "Unless an opportunity comes up where she has a chance to train at a higher level, she may put in a lot but it may not match the standard out there in the rest of the world. If she gets funds, I believe she can go to another level. That is just a dream. Sometimes you don't even want to talk about it because it seems impossible. But we have to move by faith. If we've already been able to achieve things that we never expected, then we don't lose the hope. Surely, we cannot know the end because there are so many questions left to answer."

Can she keep improving in chess without a more advanced coach?

Can she improve without books or a computer?

Can she improve without sponsorship?

Can she really become a Grandmaster?

Can the attention to her story make her a target in Katwe?

Can she avoid the pressure to become a mother?

Can she still thrive if she has HIV?

Can she get out of Katwe?

Can she stay out?

The true magic of Phiona's journey lies in the remarkable breadth of possibilities. Even if Phiona can somehow produce the means to leave Katwe, then history has proven that her struggle is just beginning. Nearly all of the stories of people leaving Katwe end with their return. Can Phiona really break the chain?

"She's got this pull in two directions and that's a dilemma for her," Suddith says. "For Phiona to succeed, realistically she has to separate from the slums and that's going to be harder than people think. She's so sensitive and she is going to have a very hard time moving away from her family, who may pressure her to stay. I've learned that you can't pull someone out of Katwe. You have to walk out with them side by side. Phiona could walk out with Robert, but she can't pull her sister out. She can't pull her mother out. If they are not willing to walk, they may pull her back."

Both Suddith and Katende express concern that Phiona is a role model without a role model. They understand that the further Phiona strides from the life she's known, the more they may have to fill that void.

"Phiona's eyes have really opened to the idea that she has a gift and she's become very curious about how to handle that," Suddith says. "She asks me questions like 'What would I do if I worked in the big city?' or 'How do you go shopping?' It's fascinating. She's seeking information. For the first time she is starting to ask questions about life that her mother cannot answer. Harriet is not a life teacher. She's lived a very hard life and she knows she doesn't want the same life for her daughter, but her experiential reality is that she can't really help her."

Harriet is just another denizen of Katwe who once dreamed of getting out, but tragic circumstances prevented her from leading a better life than those before her. She arrived in Katwe as a young child and has never left and she doesn't see beyond "just there." Harriet simply aspires to be a religious servant and hopes her daughter will do the same.

"I want Phiona to be a child that is pleasing to God," Harriet says. "I am also very sure that if she continues with chess she will meet good people and live a good life."

When Harriet is asked if she believes that her daughter will leave Katwe, she pauses for a moment and then says, "I have never thought about that."

■ ■ ■ ■

Phiona Mutesi is the ultimate underdog. To be African is to be an underdog in the world. To be Ugandan is to be an underdog in Africa. To be from Katwe is to be an underdog in Uganda. To be a girl is to be an underdog in Katwe.

When asked about her dreams, Phiona ponders the question for a long time, as if it is necessary to inventory them all in her mind. "Okay, what I think is to study hard and perform well in chess in order to be able to get the money to lift up my family," Phiona says. "That is where my dreams begin."

Phiona says that she dreams to someday be married to a man of her choosing, married in the true sense of the word, unlike her mother and her sister who have referred to themselves as "married" but were never officially wed. Phiona dreams of having children, but not for many years and not, she has vowed to her family, until she and her husband are secure enough financially to support those children. "I expect that to happen many years ahead," Phiona says. "I dream to have two children, a boy and a girl, but only after I have planned for them, not like the way we are at home when you give birth to many children you can't take care of. Me, I expect to take the best care of my children."

Phiona dreams to someday be a Grandmaster, but considering the hurdles involved, Katende has impressed upon her the need for a backup plan.

Phiona dreams to someday be a nurse. When Harriet learns of this, she smiles proudly and places both hands over her heart. "Phiona never told me that," Harriet says. "One time when we were in the house we were talking and I said to her that I had once dreamed of being a nurse because those people looked so nice to me and the way they conduct themselves fills my heart with joy. My dream was not able to be fulfilled, but God has again revealed it through my daughter."

Phiona's favorite place to dream is at home late at night with her brothers, Brian and Richard, lying down beside her. Their fondest shared dream is about building a house. A place that doesn't flood. A place where they will no longer fear an angry landlord's knock on the door. A place they own.

"There is one dream I have beyond all others," Phiona says. "I imagine living in a home where all the suffering, all the challenges we have been through would be over."

During their many discussions, the three siblings have devised a mental blueprint for their house. It will have eight rooms with windows made of glass, including a dining room with flowers on the table and a sitting room with a comfortable sofa and chairs, and everyone will have their own bedroom with their own bed. The house will not have stairs because it is assumed that by that time Harriet will be too old to climb them. The plans also include a large compound filled with trees where Night's children can play, surrounded by a secure gate and fencing and tiles in the ground between the gate and the front door so that visitors will not have to step in mud to reach the house. There will be fans on the ceilings to regulate the air and there will be toilets to sit on that flush with water. And a television that plays DVDs. And a water tap inside the house. And some electric lamps. And a fridge. There is a continuing disagreement among the siblings over whether a swimming pool will be affordable.

"Our dream is about our whole family living a better life there, a life that we deserve to be in," Brian says. "So we want someplace where we could really feel so secure when we are staying there."

All that is left undecided is where the building will stand.

"We are not bothered about the location," Phiona says. "As long as it is anywhere else apart from the slums and it belongs to us."

When the sermon is over, the porridge dishes cleaned and stored away, an early evening rainstorm beating on the tin roof of the Agape Church and beginning to flood Katwe, they come back to chess.

Katende is still there, much later than he'd planned to be as usual, along with Ivan and Benjamin and Samuel and Richard and Brian and tiny Gloria, and up beside the pulpit there is 16-year-old Phiona Mutesi, one of the best chess players in the world, juggling three games at once and dominating them all. Phiona stalks her young opponents as ruthlessly yet compassionately as she can, while drawing a flower in the dirt on the floor with her toe, plotting her next move.

ACKNOWLEDGMENTS

One of the first questions I'm asked whenever I speak to anyone about the story of Phiona Mutesi is, "How did you ever hear about her?"

The gentleman who shared Phiona's story with me, Troy Buder, learned of it by reading an article written by Rodney Suddith in a Sports Outreach newsletter. Buder skimmed through the story about three slum children winning a chess tournament in Sudan and then threw out the newsletter. Later that day, Buder retrieved it out of his office trash can, because he couldn't get the story out of his mind. Buder tells me that scenario occurred several more times until one day in March of 2010 when he attended an event where I was speaking. Buder approached me afterward to share Phiona's extraordinary story, and I can't thank him enough for doing so.

I promptly wrote a proposal and sent it to

ESPN, where it wound up in the hands of brilliant *ESPN The Magazine* editor J. B. Morris, who assigned me to travel to Uganda to meet Phiona in September of 2010. Within hours of my arrival at Agape Church in Katwe, I realized that Phiona's story was much bigger than just a magazine article. I knew I needed to write this book.

The logistics of conducting interviews in a Ugandan slum are daunting, and frankly, *The Queen of Katwe* would not exist without the herculean efforts of Robert Katende. Not only did Katende spend countless hours sharing his personal story with me, but he also arranged and acted as my translator for almost every interview featured in this book. Since my most recent trip to Kampala in August of 2011, I have spoken with Katende regularly, asking for his help with everything from tournament results and historical research to coordinating a photo shoot. Thank you so much, Robert.

I also offer my heartfelt thanks to Harriet Nakku, her children, and all of the other Ugandans I had the pleasure to meet and talk to for this project. While their names are too numerous to include here, their courage is inspirational, and without them I would not have been able to tell this story. I also want to thank Patrick Wolff, an American chess Grandmaster who generously shared his expertise, and especially Russ Carr, Rodney Suddith, and Norm and Tricia Popp for their participation in this book, but more importantly, for everything they have done, and continue to do, to help the people of Uganda.

I am also deeply thankful to my editor at Scribner, Paul Whitlatch, for his exceptional instincts in helping me chisel this story from a boulder, as well as his Simon & Schuster colleagues Nan Graham, Susan Moldow, Roz Lippel, Lauren Lavelle, Brian Belfiglio, and Rex Bonomelli. I also owe an enormous debt of gratitude to my agent, Chris Parris-Lamb, whose initial unbridled excitement about the story of a Ugandan chess player encouraged me to pursue it.

Of course, thank you to my amazing wife, Dana, my awesome kids, Atticus and Sawyer, and the rest of my family for enduring two years of near-total preoccupation, when my mind was often in Katwe even if my body was at home.

During my most recent trip to Uganda, I will never forget sitting on the porch of the Pope Paul Memorial Hotel in Kampala each night with Rodney Suddith reveling in the remarkable story unfolding before me. At the end of each evening, we shared our favorite moment, what Suddith called the "snapshot of the day," and I am so grateful to him for always finding a blessing where I had merely seen an interview.

Finally, my most essential thanks must go to Phiona Mutesi for trusting me to share her remarkable story in this book that someday soon, as her English continues to improve, I expect she will be able to read herself. Phiona's narrative evolves daily. I am still reporting, still speaking regularly with Katende in preparation for a future postscript, because I know there are many more snapshots to come for Phiona, and I am eager to discover what happens next.

The employees of Thorndike Press hope you have enjoyed this Large Print book. All our Thorndike, Wheeler, and Kennebec Large Print titles are designed for easy reading, and all our books are made to last. Other Thorndike Press Large Print books are available at your library, through selected bookstores, or directly from us.

For information about titles, please call:
(800) 223-1244

or visit our Web site at:
http://gale.cengage.com/thorndike

To share your comments, please write:
Publisher
Thorndike Press
10 Water St., Suite 310
Waterville, ME 04901

Allison —

To a true partner in the Gospel and one who knows the cost of thinking — and writing — theologically. With great affection.

שלום καὶ εἰρήνη

[illegible] 10 August 1993

THE NEW INTERNATIONAL COMMENTARY ON THE OLD TESTAMENT

R. K. HARRISON, *General Editor*

The Book of NUMBERS

by

TIMOTHY R. ASHLEY

WILLIAM B. EERDMANS PUBLISHING COMPANY
GRAND RAPIDS, MICHIGAN

255 Jefferson Ave. S.E., Grand Rapids, Mich. 49503

Printed in the United States of America

Library of Congress Cataloging-in-Publication Data:

Ashley, Timothy R., 1947-
The book of Numbers / by Timothy R. Ashley.
p. cm. — (The New international commentary on the Old Testament)
Includes bibliographical references and indexes.
ISBN 0-8028-2354-8
1. Bible. O.T. Numbers — Commentaries. I. Title. II. Series.
BS1265.3.A845 1992
222′.14077 — dc20 93-7095
CIP

To
David H. Wallace
and
the Memory of
Robert B. Laurin (1927–77)
Christian Gentlemen
and Scholars, Both

CONTENTS

PREFACE

The book of Numbers will never replace the Psalms at the heart of Christian devotion nor the Gospel of John and the Epistle to the Romans at the heart of Christian theology, nor should it. The book of Numbers tells a story. The story has two main characters, God and Israel. The way the story is told sounds odd and often times harsh to modern ears. For example, I suspect that the opening four chapters with all their names and numbers have defeated many folk who have decided to read through the whole Bible and have just emerged from the rigours of Leviticus. I suspect, as well, that the brutal nature of such passages as the end of the Korah story (ch. 16), the story of Phinehas (ch. 25), and the war with Midian (ch. 31) are repellent to many.

In spite of all these difficulties, and others, that confront modern readers, the point of the book of Numbers is important for God's people in any age: Exact obedience to God is crucial. Numbers makes the point most especially through examples of *dis*obedience such as those found in chs. 11–21. Although it is clear that God punishes disobedience, at the heart of the book of Numbers is the God who, while demanding exact obedience, is constantly revealing ways in which Israel can render that obedience through new torah (i.e., teaching; see chs. 5–9, 15, 17–19, 27–30, 32–36). It is notable that the invitations to new obedience often come right in the midst of Israel's failure and rebellion. Israel thought that the story of its disobedience and failure was important enough to tell. By claiming the Bible (including Numbers) as our standard of faith and conduct, Christians have implicitly said that the story of Numbers is worth *re*-telling. It is important that God's people re-learn the fact that their rebellion will still lead to "death in the wilderness." Numbers is the story of a people who did what they ought to have known better than doing and suffered for it (see also Paul's lament in Rom. 7:15). The failure of others may be salutary for us all.

The book of Numbers has been my companion now for the better part of a decade. It has been a comfort, a judgment, a joy, and a frustration all at the same time. Through the years many resources have come across my desk. Never far away has been George Buchanan Gray's great commentary. Although it is now nearly 70 years old and, in many respects, out-of-date, Gray's grasp of Hebrew philology is indispensable. He is still "the" commentator on Numbers with whom one agrees or disagrees. If I have done a considerable amount of the latter, it is no sign of disrespect. Quite the contrary, it is a mark of Gray's erudition that long after his death his work should still be used. The commentary by Philip Budd in the Word Biblical Commentary has also been indispensable because of its discussions of the (supposed) redactional history of the various sections of the book. These discussions really form a summary of most critical work on the book from the middle of the last century to the early 1980s. The reader of the present work will note how little these redactional histories are discussed here. The reason is not that such matters are unimportant, but that I am quite sure that no one knows these things nor really can know them. I am, therefore, committed to explaining the final form of the text as the primary job of a commentary for the Church. No one knows better than I do now how difficult it is to explain the text. The reader is directed to Budd if she/he wishes to read on these critical matters as a primary concern. The many articles and, in the last stages of this work, the commentary by Jacob Milgrom have also been of assistance to me in matters of research on the sacrificial system and much more.

The manuscript of this commentary was submitted to the publishers in August 1990. During a delay in publication due to editorial changes at least three major commentaries on Numbers have appeared. Milgrom's (in the Jewish Publication Society Torah [1990]), R. K. Harrison's (in the Wycliffe Exegetical Commentary [1990]), and R. B. Allen's (in the Expositor's Bible Commentary, vol. 2 [also 1990]). I have only been able to use these works in the proof-reading stage, and, so, in a less thorough way than they deserve. In the case of Milgrom, this problem is partially offset by the many articles of his that have been available.

Only those who have tried to write commentaries know the difficulties involved. Commentaries are never wholly satisfactory documents (this one is certainly no different). I would thank my colleagues and students at Acadia Divinity College and Acadia University for their understanding. Craig and Jacqueline Hiebert deserve thanks for compiling the indexes. Special thanks goes to the Principal of the Divinity College, the Rev. Dr. Andrew D. MacRae, for his willingness to release me from some teaching and administrative duties in the interests of research and writing. Last of all, I thank my wife and colleague in ministry, the Rev. Maxine F. Ashley, for encouragement in untold ways while enduring the long hours of my preoccupation with the book of Numbers. These contributions and many others make her help the most precious of all.

It is hoped, however, that, with its weaknesses, the commentary will be of some use to those who wish better to hear and re-tell the story of exact obedience in the book of Numbers.

TIMOTHY R. ASHLEY
Wolfville, Nova Scotia
August 1992

ABBREVIATIONS

AASOR	Annual of the American Schools of Oriental Research
AB	Anchor Bible
ADAJ	*Annual of the Department of Antiquities of Jordan*
AfO	*Archiv für Orientforschung*
AJSL	*American Journal of Semitic Languages and Literatures*
AJT	*American Journal of Theology*
Akk.	Akkadian
AnBib	Analecta Biblica
ANET	J. B. Pritchard, ed., *Ancient Near Eastern Texts Relating to the Old Testament.* 3rd ed. Princeton: Princeton Univ. Press, 1969
AOAT	Alter Orient und Altes Testament
Arab.	Arabic
Aram.	Aramaic
Assyr.	Assyrian
ASTI	*Annual of the Swedish Theological Institute*
ATDA	J. Hoftijzer and G. van der Kooij, eds., *Aramaic Texts from Deir ʿAlla*. Leiden: Brill, 1976
AusBR	*Australian Biblical Review*
AV	Authorized (King James) Version
BA	*Biblical Archaeologist*
BASOR	*Bulletin of the American Schools of Oriental Research*
BDB	F. Brown, S. R. Driver, and C. A. Briggs, *Hebrew and English Lexicon of the Old Testament.* Repr. Oxford: Clarendon, 1959
BHK	R. Kittel, et al., eds. *Biblia Hebraica.* Stuttgart: Württembergische Bibelanstalt, 1937
BHS	K. Elliger and W. Rudolph, eds., *Biblia Hebraica Stuttgartensia.* Stuttgart: Deutsche Bibelstiftung, 1967–77
Bib	*Biblica*
BJS	Brown Judaic Studies

BK	*Bibel und Kirche*
BR	*Biblical Research*
BT	*The Bible Translator*
BTB	*Biblical Theology Bulletin*
BWANT	Beiträge zur Wissenschaft vom Alten und Neuen Testament
BZ	*Biblische Zeitschrift*
BZAW	Beihefte zur *ZAW*
CBQ	*Catholic Biblical Quarterly*
DJD	Discoveries in the Judaean Desert
DOTT	D. Winton Thomas, ed., *Documents from Old Testament Times.* Repr. New York: Harper & Row, 1961
EBC	Expositor's Bible Commentary
Eng.	English
EvT	*Evangelische Theologie*
ExpTim	*Expository Times*
FOTL	Forms of the Old Testament Literature
GKC	*Genesius' Hebrew Grammar.* Ed. E. Kautzsch. Tr. A. E. Cowley. 2nd ed. Oxford: Clarendon, 1910
GNB	Good News Bible (Today's English Version)
HALAT	W. Baumgartner, et al., *Hebräisches und aramäisches Lexikon zum Alten Testament*
HDB	*Hastings' Dictionary of the Bible*
Heb.	Hebrew
HKAT	Handkommentar zum Alten Testament
HSM	Harvard Semitic Monographs
HTR	*Harvard Theological Review*
HUCA	*Hebrew Union College Annual*
IB	G. A. Buttrick, et al., eds., *Interpreter's Bible.* 12 vols. Nashville: Abingdon, 1953–56
ICC	International Critical Commentary
IDB(Sup)	G. A. Buttrick, et al., eds., *Interpreter's Dictionary of the Bible.* 4 vols. Nashville: Abingdon, 1962. *Supplementary Volume.* Ed. K. Crim, et al. 1976
IEJ	*Israel Exploration Journal*
Int	*Interpretation*
ISBE	J. Orr, et al., eds., *International Standard Bible Encyclopedia.* 2nd ed. 5 vols. Grand Rapids: Eerdmans, 1939. Rev. ed. Ed. G. W. Bromiley, et al. 4 vols. 1979–88
JAOS	*Journal of the American Oriental Society*
JB	Jerusalem Bible

JBL	*Journal of Biblical Literature*
JCS	*Journal of Cuneiform Studies*
JNES	*Journal of Near Eastern Studies*
JPOS	*Journal of Palestine Oriental Society*
JPST	The JPS Torah Commentary
JQR	*Jewish Quarterly Review*
JSOT	*Journal for the Study of the Old Testament*
JSOTSup	*JSOT* Supplement Series
JSS	*Journal of Semitic Studies*
JTS	*Journal of Theological Studies*
KB	L. Koehler and W. Baumgartner, *Lexicon in Veteris Testamenti Libros.* Leiden: Brill, 1958
LS	*Louvain Studies*
LSJ	Liddell, Scott, Jones, *Greek-English Lexicon*
LXX	Septuagint
Mish.	Mishnah
Moffatt	James Moffatt, *The Moffatt Bible*
ms(s).	manuscript(s)
MT	Masoretic Text
NASB	New American Standard Bible
NBD	J. D. Douglas, et al., eds., *New Bible Dictionary*
NCBC	New Century Bible Commentary
NEB	New English Bible
NICOT	New International Commentary on the Old Testament
NIDNTT	C. Brown, et al., eds. *New International Dictionary of New Testament Theology.* 3 vols. Grand Rapids: Zondervan, 1975–78
NIV	New International Version
NJPS	New Jewish Publication Society Version
NKJV	New King James Version
OBT	Overtures to Biblical Theology
OTL	Old Testament Library
OTS	*Oudtestamentische Studiën*
PEFQS	*Palestine Exploration Fund Quarterly Statement*
PEQ	*Palestine Exploration Quarterly*
Pesh.	Peshitta
PJ	*Palästina-Jahrbuch*
Proceedings, 1989	J. Hoftijzer and G. van der Kooij, eds. *The Balaam Text from Deir 'Alla* . . . Leiden: Brill, 1990
RB	*Revue biblique*
RevQ	*Revue de Qumran*

RSV	Revised Standard Version
RV	Revised Version
Sam. Pent.	Samaritan Pentateuch
SB	Sources bibliques
SBLDS	Society of Biblical Literature Dissertation Series
SBLMS	Society of Biblical Literature Monograph Series
SBLSP	Society of Biblical Literature Seminar Papers
SBOT	Sacred Books of the Old Testament
SBT	Studies in Biblical Theology
ScrHier	Scripta hierosolymitana
SEÅ	*Svensk Exegetisk Årsbok*
Sem	*Semitica*
SJLA	Studies in Judaism in Late Antiquity
SJT	*Scottish Journal of Theology*
SNTSMS	Society for New Testament Study Monograph Series
SOTSMS	Society for Old Testament Study Monograph Series
Syr.	Syriac
Targ(s).	Targum(s)
T.B.	Babylonian Talmud
TBT	*The Bible Today*
TDNT	G. Kittel and G. Friedrich, eds., *Theological Dictionary of the New Testament.* Tr. and ed. G. W. Bromiley. 10 vols. Grand Rapids: Eerdmans, 1964–76
TDOT	G. Botterweck and H. Ringgren, eds., *Theological Dictionary of the Old Testament.* Tr. D. Green, et al. Vols. 1–6 (to date). Grand Rapids: Eerdmans, 1974–90
TGUOS	*Transactions of the Glasgow University Oriental Society*
THAT	E. Jenni and C. Westermann, eds., *Theologisches Handwörterbuch zum Alten Testament.* 2 vols. Munich: Kaiser; Zurich: Theologischer Verlag, 1971–76
TLZ	*Theologische Literaturzeitung*
TOTC	Tyndale Old Testament Commentaries
TPQ	*Theologisch-praktische Quartalschrift*
TWOT	R. Harris, et al., eds., *Theological Wordbook of the Old Testament.* 2 vols. Chicago: Moody, 1980
TynBul	*Tyndale Bulletin*
UF	*Ugarit Forschungen*
Ugar.	Ugaritic
VT	*Vetus Testamentum*
VTSup	Supplements to *VT*

Vulg.	Vulgate
WBC	Word Biblical Commentary
WEC	The Wycliffe Exegetical Commentary
WMANT	Wissenschaftliche Monographien zum Alten und Neuen Testament
WO	*Die Welt des Orients*
ZAW	*Zeitschrift für die alttestamentliche Wissenschaft*
ZDPV	*Zeitschrift des deutschen Palästina-Vereins*
ZPEB	M. Tenney, et al., eds., *Zondervan Pictorial Encyclopedia of the Bible.* 5 vols. Grand Rapids: Zondervan, 1975–76
ZTK	*Zeitschrift für Theologie und Kirche*

INTRODUCTION

I. TITLE AND CONTENTS

The title of the book in English comes through the Vulgate from the LXX, which used the title "Numbers" (Vulg. *Numeri;* LXX *Arithmoi*). The variant Hebrew titles come from the first word of the text (*wayᵉḏabbēr,* "and he spoke") or, more commonly, the fourth (*bᵉmiḏbar,* "in the wilderness [of]").[1] "In the wilderness" describes the contents of the book much better than "numbers," which is derived from the census takings of chs. 1–4, 26.

The story is rather simple. Israel is counted by Moses, Aaron, and the leaders in order to prepare for the march to Canaan and life in the land following the conquest (chs. 1–4). After further exhortations to holy living and preparations to depart from Mt. Sinai (5:1–10:10), Israel leaves the holy mountain for Canaan (10:11–12:13). Spies are sent out from the oasis of Kadesh-barnea to reconnoiter. When they return to Moses and the people, their report is split. The majority say that the land and its inhabitants are too mighty to be taken. The minority (Caleb and Joshua) say that, since God had promised victory, he would bring victory for Israel, despite the strength of the land and its people. The people of Israel choose to believe the majority and are ready to go back to Egypt (thus rebelling against the leadership of Yahweh as well as that of Moses and Aaron) when God intervenes and punishes their disbelief and disobedience. Because of their sin, every person over the age of twenty would wander and die in the wilderness without coming into possession of Canaan. They would wander forty years, until the whole generation was dead (chs. 13–14).

The Israelites decide to try to make things better on their own. Unassisted by God (or Moses), they try to conquer the land but are

1. Counting *'el-mōšeh* ("to Moses") as one word, since they are joined by a maqqeph, which deprives the first word of its independent accent.

humiliated in defeat (14:40–45). So for nearly forty years the people wander around Kadesh-barnea in the wilderness until all that generation dies (chs. 16–19). They then return to Kadesh-barnea, and are told to set out once again for Canaan. They depart from Kadesh-barnea and travel to the plains of Moab, just outside the land of promise (chs. 20–21). Along the way, they win some battles, showing that the tide is turning (21:1–4, 21–35). Just outside Canaan, the people are blessed by Balaam, a foreign seer (chs. 22–24). After his blessing, they sin further at Peor and are punished again (ch. 25). On the plains of Moab a new census is taken to mark the new beginning (ch. 26). The people wait for further instructions for life in the land of Canaan, where Joshua will lead them after the death of Moses (chs. 27–36).

II. STRUCTURE

One may analyze the structure of any book in several ways. The kind of structure one sees depends on the questions one asks. Most commentators have structured Numbers in three sections related to geographic locale: section I at Mt. Sinai (1:1–10:10); section II at and around Kadesh-barnea (10:11–19:22), and section III on the plains of Moab (20:1–36:13). This kind of structure involves two travel sections: the first from Sinai to Kadesh-barnea (10:11–12:13), and the second from Kadesh-barnea to the plains of Moab (20:1–21:35). The venue of section I is the same as that for Exod. 20–Lev. 27 and hence links Numbers with the central books in the Pentateuch.[1]

D. T. Olson has proposed an alternate structure that divides the book into two sections of unequal length: section I: The Death of the Old Generation; the first Exodus generation fails in the wilderness (1:1–25:19); and section II: The Birth of the New; the second Exodus generation prepares to take the land of Canaan (26:1–36:13). This view sees the two census documents (chs. 1 and 26) as forming the pillars of the book's structure, and the theme of the book as two-generational: the failure of one generation and the promise of another.[2] Section I is broken down into a cycle of preparation for departure and inauguration of it (1:1–10:36),

1. For discussion and criticism of this structure for Numbers see D. T. Olson, *The Death of the Old and the Birth of the New: The Framework of the Book of Numbers and the Pentateuch,* BJS 71 (Chico, Calif.: Scholars Press, 1985), pp. 31–37.

2. Ibid., pp. 83–124.

and a cycle of rebellion, death, and deliverance, ending in ultimate failure (11:1–25:19). Section II is broken down into a large and disparate group of passages dealing with preparation and organization of the second Exodus generation as it prepares to enter the land of Canaan (26:1–36:13). The fate of that second generation is left open at the end of the book, and is a matter of conjecture — perhaps a promise of great success, perhaps a warning of great danger.[3]

Although Olson's analysis has much to recommend it, the more traditional analysis of Numbers connects the book more closely with the Pentateuch, in which it is, after all, set. With most commentators on the book, I follow such an analysis here.

III. AUTHORSHIP AND COMPOSITION

The book of Numbers does not name its author. In 33:2 Moses is said to have written down the "starting points" of the Hebrews' journey, "stage by stage," which probably indicates at least the framework for the itinerary of ch. 33, but, as is well known, this is the only reference to Moses' writing in the book. One cannot discuss the question of authorship and composition of Numbers in isolation from that of the other books of the Pentateuch. The history of pentateuchal criticism is too lengthy to rehearse here, but some brief words of representative positions on the matter are in order.

Scholars who believe that Moses had a significant role to play in the composition of the Pentateuch appeal to the following evidence. First, the text itself claims that Moses wrote some of the material of the Pentateuch.[1] Second, the Pentateuch refers hundreds of times to Moses' receiving communications from Yahweh.[2] Third, much of the material in the book of Numbers makes good sense in the Mosaic age, indeed, better sense than in the postexilic age (see further below).[3] Those who espouse this view usually maintain the theological presupposition that the Bible is

3. Ibid., esp. pp. 123–24.

1. In addition to Num. 33:2, see Exod. 17:14; 24:4; 34:27; Deut. 31:9, 22.

2. E.g., see the clause "Yahweh said/spoke to Moses (and Aaron)," which occurs over 60 times in the book of Numbers alone (1:1; 2:1; 3:1, 5, 11, 14, 40, 44; 4:1, 17, 21; 5:1, 5, 11; 6:1, 22; 7:4; 8:1, 5, 23; 9:1, 9; 10:1; 11:16, 23; 12:4; 13:1; 14:11, 20, 26; 15:1, 17, 37; 16:20; 17:1, 9, 16 [Eng. 16:36, 44; 17:1]; 18:1, 8, 25; 19:1; 20:7, 12, 23; 21:8, 34; 25:4, 10, 16, 19; 26:52; 27:6, 12, 18; 28:1; 31:1, 25; 34:1, 16; 35:1, 9). The same clause occurs in Exodus 63 times.

3. See the discussion in R. K. Harrison, *Introduction to the Old Testament* (Grand Rapids: Eerdmans, 1969), pp. 614–22.

authoritative. Hence, when the text claims that, for example, Moses wrote something or received a communication from God, it is not just a literary convention but a description of historical fact.

The position that most commonly stands over against the so-called traditional theory of Mosaic authorship is associated with the name of Julius Wellhausen, who, in his *Prolegomena to the History of Ancient Israel,* defended and refined the view that the Pentateuch was made up of a series of written documents: J (Jahwist or Yahwist), E (Elohist), D (Deuteronomist), P (Priestly), originating from the early monarchy (J) to the postexilic period (P).[4] The editing of the whole of the Pentateuch occurred at the hands of a Priestly redactor (not necessarily the same Priestly author as the P source) in the postexilic age (perhaps 5th cent. B.C.).

The criteria scholars used to divide the sources were, first, the alternation between the divine names (Yahweh and Elohim especially); second, different names for the same reality (such as Horeb/Sinai); third, double or triple narratives of the same event (e.g., passing off one's wife as one's sister; Gen. 12:10–13:1; 20:1–18; 26:6–11); and, fourth, vocabulary that occurs only in one document or another (e.g., the word *kind,* Heb. *mîn,* said to occur only in P).[5] These scholars assumed that all institutions, writings, and other manifestations of human civilization moved along a unilinear evolutionary scale from simple to complex. For example, if an institution was simple, free, and anthropomorphic, it must be early; if it was complex, institutional, liturgical, and less anthropomorphic, it must be late.

Although scholars have continued to refine and modify the basic scheme,[6] it stands today on these same four criteria. Thus even scholars who developed new approaches, such as Gerhard von Rad, who used the form-critical approach that emphasized the oral transmission of smaller

4. See J. Wellhausen, *Prolegomena to the History of Ancient Israel,* tr. J. S. Menzies and A. Black (repr. Gloucester, Mass.: Peter Smith, 1983).

5. For discussions of these criteria, see, e.g., S. R. Driver, *Introduction to the Literature of the Old Testament,* 12th ed. (New York: Scribner's, 1906), esp. pp. 116–59; C. A. Simpson, *The Early Traditions of Israel* (Oxford: Blackwell, 1948); O. Eissfeldt, *The Old Testament: An Introduction,* tr. P. Ackroyd (New York: Harper & Row, 1965), pp. 158–212, esp. 182–88; G. Fohrer, *Introduction to the Old Testament,* tr. D. Green (Nashville: Abingdon, 1968), pp. 103–95.

6. See, e.g., the differences between the charts on the formation of the Pentateuch in the 2nd and 3rd eds. of B. W. Anderson, *Understanding the Old Testament,* 2nd ed. (Englewood Cliffs, N.J.: Prentice-Hall, 1966), p. 382; 3rd ed. (1975), p. 424.

textual units, and Martin Noth, who used the so-called traditio-historical approach that emphasized the shaping and reshaping of traditions rather than written documents, assumed the basic correctness of the documentary hypothesis in its main outlines.[7]

More recently, however, other scholars, like Rolf Rendtorff, have recognized that the traditio-historical approach cannot be reconciled with the documentary hypothesis and have abandoned the latter in favor of a scheme based on the editing together of the larger units of the Pentateuch (i.e., such units of tradition as the patriarchal material in Gen. 12–50 or the Balaam stories in Num. 22–24). The whole was given its definitive stamp by an editor more or less closely aligned to the viewpoint of Deuteronomy.[8]

The view connected with the name of Y. Kaufmann, and carried forward by such scholars as M. Weinfeld, A. Hurvitz, J. Milgrom, and others, also deserves mention here.[9] While not denying the basic correctness of the written documents as such, this group of scholars has attempted to show that the so-called Priestly materials in the Pentateuch are preexilic rather than postexilic. They thoroughly criticize the unilinear evolutionary theory on which the dating of the documents rests. The laws and institu-

7. See G. von Rad, "The Form-Critical Problem of the Hexateuch," in *The Problem of the Hexateuch and Other Essays,* tr. E. W. Trueman Dicken (London: Oliver & Boyd, 1966), pp. 1–78; M. Noth, *A History of Pentateuchal Traditions,* tr. B. W. Anderson (Englewood Cliffs, N.J.: Prentice-Hall, 1972), esp. pp. 5–62. The traditio-historical approach is also assumed in Noth's commentary on the book of Numbers.

8. See R. Rendtorff, *Das überlieferungsgeschichtliche Problem des Pentateuch,* BZAW 147 (Berlin: de Gruyter, 1977), esp. pp. 1–28, 70–74, 147–73; a convenient summary of Rendtorff's view may be found in R. Rendtorff, *The Old Testament: An Introduction,* tr. J. Bowden (London: SCM, 1985), pp. 160–63.

9. Y. Kaufmann, *The Religion of Israel,* tr. and abridged by M. Greenberg (Chicago: Univ. of Chicago Press, 1961), pp. 153–211, esp. pp. 175–200 on the antiquity of the Priestly Code on such matters as the chosen site for worship, the festivals, the tent of meeting, the high priest and congregation, the clergy generally, as well as a discussion of priests and Levites. See, e.g., A. Hurvitz, "The Evidence of Language in Dating the Priestly Code," *RB* 81 (1974) 24–57. See also the work of Jacob Milgrom, e.g., in "Priestly Terminology and the Political and Social Structure of Pre-Monarchic Israel," *JQR* 69 (1978) 65–81; "The Term *ʿAboda,*" in Studies in Levitical Terminology 1 (Berkeley: Univ. of California, 1970), pp. 60–87; "The Priestly Doctrine of Repentance," *RB* 82 (1975) 186–205. These three articles are now reprinted in *Studies in Cultic Theology and Terminology,* SJLA 36 (Leiden: Brill, 1983) ix–66. See also Milgrom's *Jewish Publication Society Torah: Numbers B^{e}Midbar* (Philadelphia/New York: Jewish Publication Society, 5750/1990), pp. xxxii–xxxv et passim. On Weinfield see below, note 12.

tions discussed in the Priestly legislation and narrative simply do not fit in the postexilic age.[10] Specific studies of Priestly vocabulary also show that words long thought to be postexilic may more probably be dated in the preexilic period.[11] Also, these scholars show that Deuteronomy, which they date in the 7th cent., cites material from P, but P does not cite Deuteronomy.[12]

Although scholars from a wide variety of critical and theological perspectives have subjected every aspect of the documentary hypothesis to searching criticism,[13] it is unlikely that most scholars will return to the traditional position, since many would conclude that there is too much evidence for a long period of transmission standing behind the present text to return to a theory of Mosaic authorship. The present author includes himself in this group of many. On the other hand, the text itself is undeniably connected to Moses and this, too, must be taken into account.

In other words, to ignore lessons learned from either basic approach would be to ignore data presented by the text of Numbers itself. On the one hand, the traditional theory affirms the many and basic unifying features of the book, which are anchored in the person of Moses. It seems difficult to deny his role in the origin of the book. On the other

10. See, e.g., A. Hurvitz, "The Evidence of Language in Dating the Priestly Code," *RB* 81 (1974) 24–57.

11. See, e.g., J. Milgrom, *Studies in Cultic Theology and Terminology,* SJLA 36 (Leiden: Brill, 1983), pp. ix–66.

12. See M. Weinfeld, *Deuteronomy and the Deuteronomic School* (Oxford: Clarendon, 1972), pp. 180–81.

13. From the conservative theological position see W. H. Green, *The Higher Criticism of the Pentateuch* (New York: Scribner's, 1895); O. T. Allis, *The Five Books of Moses* (Nutley, N.J.: Presbyterian & Reformed, 1941); and R. K. Harrison, *Introduction,* pp. 19–82, 351–61, 495–541. From the so-called Uppsala School, see I. Engnell, "Methodological Aspects of Old Testament Study," in VTSup 7 (Leiden: Brill 1960), pp. 13–30; idem, "The Traditio-Historical Method in Old Testament Research," in *Critical Essays on the Old Testament,* tr. J. Willis and H. Ringgren (London: SPCK, 1970), pp. 3–11; idem, "The Pentateuch," in ibid., pp. 50–67. See also U. Cassuto, *The Documentary Hypothesis,* tr. I. Abrahams (Jerusalem: Magnes, 1961); M. H. Segal, *The Pentateuch: Its Composition and Its Authorship and Other Studies* (Jerusalem: Magnes, 1967), pp. 1–170. An interesting study of one part of the Pentateuch is I. M. Kikawada and A. Quinn, *Before Abraham Was: The Unity of Genesis 1–11* (Nashville: Abingdon, 1985). One of the most recent and trenchant criticisms of the documentary approach (as well as the traditio-historical approach) is R. N. Whybray, *The Making of the Pentateuch: A Methodological Study,* JSOTSup 53 (Sheffield: JSOT Press, 1987). Whybray himself opts for a single sixth-century author for the whole Pentateuch who used earlier source materials.

hand, a great deal of evidence suggests a long period of transmission for some materials in the book. Most of the book presupposes a time later than the conquest, and particularly materials from ch. 22 on point to a time significantly later.[14] The evidence given especially by Kaufmann, Milgrom, et al., seems convincing, however, that one does not need to posit so late a date as the postexilic era for the book in its more-or-less final form; a preexilic date is most likely, possibly in the time of the united monarchy.

It seems best to take the materials of the text itself as offering some clue to the sources and composition of the book. Moses may be seen as having a key role in the origin of some of the material in Numbers, though we have no way of knowing how much of it goes back to him. Much of what is in the book bears marks of antiquity, but there are also undoubted signs of a long period of transmission. The book probably went through a more complex history of transmission than is recoverable. The most reasonable and practical approach to specific texts in Numbers is to explain what they mean as they stand in the final form of the text. The book did not simply fall together, and does make sense as it stands. Demonstration that the text makes sense will, of course, be more difficult in some cases than in others. I do not object to a literary theory of sources as such, but to the assumption that these sources were not compiled into a cogent text. When the text presents a literary difficulty, I will attempt to find a literary solution from within the text itself, having to do with the function of the text, rather than simply positing a combination of sources by an editor who had little appreciation for logic, cogency, and literary style. I believe that, through all the complexities of the transmission of the text of Numbers, God was at work to bring to his people the final form of the text. Inspiration should not be limited to any one stage in the composition of the biblical text (e.g., the earliest) as opposed to other stages. The Church and the Synagogue confess the whole OT text as God's Word, not just one stage in its composition.

14. E.g., the Balaam stories (chs. 22–24) would take some time to come into Israelite hands and, if they were genuinely non-Israelite, to be translated into Hebrew. Ch. 26 discusses clans of people rather than individual families, which suggests some time later than Moses. Ch. 36 assumes 27:1–11, etc. (see the commentary below on these chapters).

IV. THEOLOGICAL THEMES

The themes of obedience, disobedience, holiness, and the presence of God are keys to understanding the book of Numbers. For purposes of thematic discussion it will be helpful to break the book into three constituent parts: Orientation (1:1–10:10), Disorientation (10:11–22:1), and New Orientation (22:1–36:13).[1] The travel sections (10:11–12:16; 20:1–22:1) are transitional.

The opening section (1:1–10:10) stresses the importance of exact obedience to Yahweh in the census (cf. 1:54), the camp (2:34), the presentation of offerings (ch. 7), and Israel's encampment/decampment (9:23). Yahweh's will is that Israel be *oriented* toward him as a holy people, separated from the uncleanness of the rest of the world, as seen in the separation of the Levites (chs. 3–4) and the Nazirites (ch. 6) from the people and the priests from the Levites (ch. 8). Yahweh's camp is also a place where no uncleanness (e.g., leprosy) is allowed (5:1–4). Wrongs that are not atoned for (5:5–10) and suspicions between husbands and wives (5:11–31) also bring uncleanness to Yahweh's holy people. The first section concludes with the recognition that uncleanness will in fact exist, but it also shows Yahweh's gracious provision that feasts (e.g., Passover) may be postponed until cleanness is regained (9:1–14). The camp as ideally constituted will have the numinous presence of Yahweh with his people as they move toward their destiny in Canaan (9:15–22).

After the command to depart is given (10:11–13), the people leave the sacred mountain in exact obedience to the instructions in ch. 2 (10:14–36). This obedience to Yahweh is the way for Israel to maintain holiness and orientation. What happens next, however, is almost instantaneous complaining and *dis*obedience. In three scenes the complaints involve the people in general, the rabble (the non-Israelites who had come along with them; cf. Exod. 12:38), and even the family of Moses itself. Each disobedience brings immediate judgment from Yahweh (11:1, 3;

1. These categories are drawn from W. Brueggemann's work on the Psalter, e.g., in "Psalms and the Life of Faith," *JSOT* 17 (1980) 3–32; cf. J. Goldingay, "The Dynamic Cycle of Praise and Prayer," *JSOT* 20 (1981) 85–90; W. Brueggemann, "Response to John Goldingay's 'The Dynamic Cycle of Praise and Prayer,'" *JSOT* 22 (1982) 141–42. The scheme is also worked out in Brueggemann's *Praying the Psalms* (Winona, Minn.: St. Mary's Press, 1982), and *The Message of the Psalms: A Theological Commentary,* Augsburg OT Studies (Minneapolis: Augsburg, 1984). I am not applying these terms in exactly the same way as Brueggemann does.

12:9–12). In this transitional section the paradigm of the central section of the book is set: painful disorientation for God's people.

The story of the spies (chs. 13–14) is extremely important to understand the disorientation of the Israelites. In these chapters the people decide that Moses and Aaron (God's chosen leaders) are not to be trusted to lead. Then, through fear, the people decide that, in spite of God's promise to give them Canaan, they are not strong enough for the task, and, further, that they need to select a new leader who will take them back to Egypt. In effect they choose to go back to a time before Yahweh had revealed himself to them at Sinai, when they were choosing "other gods," and God sees this act as rebellion. God's response to this rebellion is a curse on the entire generation. The old generation had been afraid to go forward; now they would not go forward. They had been afraid that their children would die in the wilderness; now, *they* would die there. Not one of the Exodus generation over twenty years of age (except Caleb and Joshua) would go into Canaan. It was not possible to go back to Egypt. Rebellion against Yahweh would, instead, lead to forty years' wandering in the wilderness, making no progress toward the goal of God's promise of land in Canaan (14:20–35), but it could not lead back to Egypt. The people were God's in spite of their rebellion.

In ch. 15 God shows his continued care for Israel by giving supplementary laws for cereal and drink offerings, first fruits, and purification offerings. God is still working with the people in spite of their rebellion, but that the supposedly holy people are by this time truly disoriented is seen in the further rebellions of Korah, Dathan, and Abiram (ch. 16). These men are not satisfied with the leadership as God had given it; they want more power. The result is tragic and fatal (16:31–35; 17:6–15 [Eng. 16:41–50]). Yahweh's presence brings awful judgment in the narratives of the spies and of Korah, in contrast to the cloudy pillar, which was to provide leadership on the way to Canaan in 1:1–10:10. In spite of the judgment, however, God affirms that the people are his (chs. 17–18). Once again he appoints the tribe of Levi in general and the family of Aaron in particular to stand as leaders of the people and intercessors between God and Israel (17:17–28 [Eng. 1–13]). Also, in response to the people's terror, God changes the duties of both the priests and the Levites so as to protect the people from future outbreaks of divine wrath. God moves to work with his people in their disorientation in order to reorient their lives.

In 20:1–22:1 the people begin moving back toward Canaan, and so toward a new orientation to God's will for them. At the beginning of this transitional section is the note of Miriam's death (20:1), followed immediately by a situation in which both Moses and Aaron commit a fatal sin (20:2–13). Following the announcement of the impending doom of the Exodus leaders Moses and Aaron, the situation begins to move toward a better day. The king of Edom denies a request to pass through his land, but Israel suffers no defeat (20:14–21). When Aaron the high priest dies at Mt. Hor (20:22–29), it is the end of an era.[2]

After his death Israel gains a victory at Hormah (21:1–3) in contrast to the old and painful defeat there in 14:39–45 at the beginning of the period of disorientation. The incident of the fiery serpents shows that, although the people continue to complain and rebel, intercession is now quick and effective, and the presence of God is both for judgment (21:6) and for salvation (21:8–9). The travel itinerary (20:10–20) sees even the wilderness wandering as making progress toward a goal, that is, God is involved in the process to bring about his purposes even in the face of human rebellion. Further evidences that the people are moving toward a new orientation are the two victories over Sihon the Amorite (21:21–32) and Og of Bashan (21:33–35).

As the Israelites arrive on the plains of Moab (22:1), they are on the threshold of a new orientation. The dominant theme in the last section of the book becomes the blessing of God in Canaan. The paradigm for this blessing is set by a non-Israelite seer named Balaam, who is hired to curse the Israelites by Balak of Moab (with the complicity of the Midianites), but instead blesses them four times (22:7–12, 13–26; 23:27–24:13; 24:14–19) and outlines God's promise for the future of this people (24:20–25).[3] It has been apparent in chs. 13–19 that Israel can bring a curse upon themselves, but in spite of that curse, if the people obey, the future will lay open to them. None of their enemies could curse them, for Yahweh was intent on blessing a newly oriented Israel.

The incident concerning the Baal of Peor (ch. 25) is the last disorientation narrative in the book. Because of idolatry, once again, God's presence becomes a consuming fire in the form of a plague (25:1b–5). The plague is stemmed when Phinehas acts in zeal to defend Yahweh's honor (25:6–9). The response of God is the future establishment of Phinehas's priestly line (25:10–15), thus showing, again, the future orientation of the whole last section of Numbers.

2. See the discussion on the death of the high priest in the commentary below on 35:25–28.

3. See the commentary below on these chapters, which contain many problems of interpretation.

Evidently the plague killed the last of the cursed Exodus generation. It was now time for a new beginning in earnest. A new census (26:1–51) reasserts the people's exact obedience to Yahweh's command through Moses. This is not, however, a simple return to the old orientation, but a *new* orientation because it is a *new* generation.

From this point on the vast majority of material concerns the new land. The matters of daughters' inheritance rights (27:1–11; 36:1–13), of the commissioning of Joshua as leader for the new day (27:12–23), of the calendar of feasts for regular celebration of Yahweh's presence in the new land (28:1–29:40), of vows (30:1–16), of the division of certain parts of the Transjordan (32:1–42) and Canaan proper (34:1–49), of the ideal boundaries of Canaan (34:1–29), of the Levites' cities (35:1–8), and of the cities of refuge (35:9–34) all point toward the good future in the land that Yahweh will give. Punishment of Midian (31:1–54) and destruction of the other Canaanites (33:50–56) are reaffirmations of the importance of orientation toward Yahweh and Yahweh alone. The long list of campsites (33:1–49) puts the whole journey from Egypt to Canaan under the direction of Yahweh, who has guided even through the rebellions of Israel.

The obvious fact is that Numbers ends on the plains of Moab with Moses alive. The death of Moses is postponed until Deut. 34, which serves to link Numbers with Deuteronomy. The story of Numbers is a story without a conclusion. The future is open to God's people, but it is unsure. It will depend on whether his people maintain their orientation toward him and him alone. Every new generation of God's people faces the same uncertainty, but also has the same promise of blessing.[4]

Minor themes in the book of Numbers will be discussed as they are met in the commentary proper (e.g., the theme of leadership in 11:4–35; 16:1–17:28 [Eng. 16:1–17:13]; etc.).

V. TEXT AND VERSIONS

Because of the importance of the Torah to Judaism, the Hebrew text of the Pentateuch, including that of the book of Numbers, is on the whole well preserved and free from problems.[1] Most of the textual difficulties

4. On the theology of the book, see esp. Olson, *Death of the Old,* pp. 179–98.

1. See P. K. McCarter, *Textual Criticism: Recovering the Text of the Hebrew Bible,* Guides to Biblical Scholarship, OT Series (Philadelphia: Fortress, 1986), p. 88. On general textual criticism, in addition to McCarter, see the

arise in the poetic bits of ch. 21 and in the Balaam oracles of chs. 22–24.[2] Since neither the Sam. Pent. nor the LXX renders much help in reconstructing the original text of these passages, these textual problems are probably older than either of these versions (see below).

The Masoretes produced a text (MT) that, with the exception of the above-named passages, shows little significant variation among the extant mss. At several points in the text of Numbers the Masoretes inserted readings or notes that are significant. The so-called *special points (puncta extraordinaria)* mark particular words in the text to show Masoretic awareness of textual or doctrinal reservations about that word (or passage) in the tradition of their community.[3] The *inverted nuns* that mark off 10:35–36 probably show that these verses were considered to be out of place.[4] The *Sebir notes* (Aram. *s*^{e}*ḇîr,* "supposed") occur over twenty times in the book (and often elsewhere) and seem to be used as a sign that the marginal reading is the more usual or commonly occurring form.[5]

The Sam. Pent. is a different Hebrew recension from the MT, written in a special Hebrew script.[6] The date of this recension is unknown;

---

following: for an introduction to *BHS,* E. Würthwein, *The Text of the Old Testament: An Introduction to the Biblica Hebraica,* tr. E. Rhodes (Grand Rapids: Eerdmans, 1979); more briefly, see S. K. Soderlund, "Text and MSS of the OT," *ISBE,* rev., IV:798–814; B. K. Waltke, "The Textual Criticism of the Old Testament," in *EBC,* vol. I: *General Articles* (Grand Rapids: Zondervan, 1979), pp. 211–28; and B. K. Waltke and M. O'Connor, *An Introduction to Biblical Hebrew Syntax* (Winona Lake, Ind.: Eisenbrauns, 1990), §§ 1.5–6.

2. See the commentary below on Num. 20:14–15, 17–18, 27–30; 23:7–10, 19–24; 24:3–9, 15–19, 20–24.

3. E.g., the point at 3:39 shows Masoretic awareness of the difference between the number of Levites given in the text itself (22,000) and the actual sum of adding the figures found in ch. 3 (22,300). See the commentary below on 3:39. The special points occur in *BHS* at Gen. 16:5; 18:9; 33:4; 37:12; Num. 3:39; 9:10; 21:30; 29:15; Deut. 29:28; 2 Sam. 19:20; Isa. 44:9; Ezek. 41:20; 46:22; Ps. 27:13.

4. Some scholars think that these verses came from another source, or were themselves another source. On these inverted *nun*s, see S. Z. Leiman, "The Inverted *Nuns* at Num. 10:35–36 and the Book of Eldad and Medad," *JBL* 93 (1974) 348–55; for a critique of Leiman, see B. Levine, "More on the Inverted *Nuns* at Num. 10:35–36," *JBL* 95 (1976) 122–24. The LXX has 10:35–36 before 10:34.

5. *Sebir* notes occur in *BHS* at Num. 4:3, 19, 36; 7:3; 8:4, 16; 11:10, 21; 13:22; 14:25; 18:23; 22:5, 12; 23:18; 26:51; 31:50, 52; 32:23, 25, 32; 33:8; 34:2; 35:5. For more on the special points and *Sebir* notes, as well as other Masoretic notes, see Würthwein, *Text of the OT,* pp. 17–21. See also the notes to the translations of each of the passages listed above in the commentary.

6. The primary edition of the Sam. Pent. is A. von Gall, ed., *Der he-*

estimates range from the 4th to the 1st cent. B.C.[7] The Sam. Pent. differs from the MT some 6,000 times, 1,900 of these in agreement with the LXX. It is a full text in that it tends to expand on the MT, not only in the direction of giving special place to the theology of the Samaritan sect, but also in the direction of incorporation of readings from similar texts elsewhere in the OT into the text. In the book of Numbers the longest and perhaps most significant variants are additions from Deut. 1–3 (e.g., Deut. 1:6–8 is inserted after Num. 10:10; Deut. 1:20–23a after Num. 12:16).[8] Especially interesting are the interpolations from Deut. 2 into the travel narrative of Num. 21.[9] These add bits of dialogue to the rather colorless MT, but none of these readings should be considered original.

The Pentateuch of the LXX (or Old Greek version) is usually dated in the 3rd cent. B.C.[10] In Numbers, as in the rest of the Pentateuch, the LXX offers for the most part a translation of the MT into idiomatic Greek.[11] Most of the variant readings in the LXX are in the spellings of names; in a few cases the LXX order of verses differs from the MT.[12] The LXX is quite frequently longer than the MT, but occasionally it is shorter.[13] While it is

---

bräischer Pentateuch der Samaritaner, 5 vols. (Berlin: de Gruyter, 1914–18; repr. 1966). On this recension see Würthwein, *Text of the OT,* pp. 42–44; B. Waltke, "The Samaritan Pentateuch and the Text of the Old Testament," in *New Perspectives on the Old Testament,* ed. J. B. Payne (Waco: Word, 1970), pp. 212–39; and, more briefly, J. D. Purvis, "Samaritan Pentateuch," *IDBSup,* pp. 772–75.

7. See Würthwein, *Text of the OT,* p. 42; Purvis, "Samaritan Pentateuch," p. 775.

8. See Gray, p. xl.

9. Deut. 2:9 is inserted after Num. 21:11; Deut. 2:17–19 after Num. 21:12; Deut. 2:24–25 after Num. 21:20; Deut. 2:28–29a after Num. 21:22; and Deut. 2:31 after Num. 21:23a. For more, see Gray, p. xli.

10. On the LXX see H. B. Swete, *An Introduction to the Old Testament in Greek,* rev. A. Ottley (Cambridge: Cambridge Univ. Press, 1902; repr. New York: KTAV, 1968); S. Jellicoe, *The Septuagint and Modern Study* (Oxford: Clarendon, 1968); idem, *Studies in the Septuagint: Origins, Recensions and Interpretations* (New York: KTAV, 1973); R. Klein, *Textual Criticism of the Old Testament: From the Septuagint to Qumran,* Guides to Biblical Scholarship, OT Series (Philadelphia: Fortress, 1974); more briefly, R. A. Kraft, "Septuagint," *IDBSup,* pp. 807–15; S. K. Soderlund, "Septuagint," *ISBE,* rev., IV:400–409.

11. See McCarter, *Textual Criticism,* p. 88; Klein, *Textual Criticism,* p. 1.

12. A different order occurs as follows: LXX 1:26–37 = MT 1:26–37, 24–25; LXX 26:15–47 = MT 26:19–27, 15–18, 44–47, 28–43 (these two passages show a different order of the tribes in the two census documents); LXX 6:22–26 = MT 6:22–23, 27, 24–26.

13. The LXX is longer, e.g., in 2:7; 3:10; 7:88; and shorter, e.g., in 9:20–23. For more examples, see Gray, p. xli.

possible that some LXX readings preserve a different (perhaps older) text-tradition than the MT, each LXX reading must be assessed to determine this.

The Qumran materials do not yield much in the way of significant textual variants.[14] Most of what has been published consists of scattered words and lines of text, some of which show affinity with the Sam. Pent. and LXX readings.[15] A single ms. found in Cave 4 gives portions of 3:30–4:14 in a Greek version that generally follows the LXX text, but with some variants.[16]

The Vulg. on the book of Numbers was translated by St. Jerome sometime between A.D. 390 and about 405. Although Jerome undertook to translate the Hebrew OT rather than the LXX into Latin, he also admitted to using the LXX as well as the other Greek Versions (Aquila, Symmachus, and Theodotion). Scholars have also detected traces of the conclusions of some rabbinic exegesis in the translation. B. J. Roberts concluded his summary of the nature of the Vulg. OT in the following way:

> Our conclusion, then, regarding the nature of Jerome's translation is that, when due allowance is made for all external influecnes, it must be admitted that his method was neither straightforward nor consistent.[17]

In sum, the MT is generally preferable to the variant readings of Sam. Pent., LXX, Vulg., or the Qumran materials. The translation in the

14. The texts from Qumran are: 1QLev (fragments of 1:48–50 and possibly 36:7–8), published in D. Barthélemy and J. T. Milik, *Qumrân Cave I,* DJD 1 (Oxford: Clarendon, 1955), pp. 51–54; MurNum (fragments of 34:10 and about 8 partial lines from 36:7–11), published in P. Benoit, J. T. Milik, and R. de Vaux, eds., *Les grottes de Murabbaʿat,* DJD 2 (Oxford: Clarendon, 1961), p. 78. The very interesting 2QNum[a] (3:38–41; 3:51–4:3), along with 2QNum[b] (33:47–53), 2QNum[c] (7:88), and 2QNum[d] (18:8–9), is published in M. Baillet, J. T. Milik, and R. de Vaux, eds., *Les "petites grottes" de Qumrân,* DJD 3 (Oxford: Clarendon, 1962), pp. 57–60. For the preliminary publication of 5/6 ḤevNum (20:7–8) see Y. Yadin, "Expedition D — The Cave of the Letters," *IEJ* 12 (1962) 229. The preliminary publication of parts of 4QLXXNum (fragments of 3:38–4:14) is found in P. W. Skehan, "The Qumran Manuscripts and Textual Criticism," in VTSup 4 (Leiden: Brill, 1957), pp. 155–57.

15. See Skehan, "Qumran Manuscripts," p. 149.

16. Ibid., pp. 155–57.

17. B. J. Roberts, *The Old Testament Text and Versions: The Hebrew Text in Transmission and the History of the Ancient Versions* (Cardiff: Univ. of Wales, 1951), p. 258; the whole section on the Vulg. (pp. 247–65) may be consulted with profit. See also Würthwein, *Text of the OT,* pp. 91–95. Especially helpful is J. Gribomont, *IDB(Sup),* pp. 527–32.

commentary below is based on the MT and adheres to it as far as possible, although variants will be mentioned in the notes.

VI. ANALYSIS OF CONTENTS

I. PREPARATION FOR DEPARTURE (1:1–10:10)
- A. Matters Concerning the People and the Camp (1:1–6:27)
  - 1. The Censuses and the Arrangements of the March (1:1–4:49)
    - a. First Lay Census (1:1–54)
      - (1) The Leaders (1:1–16)
      - (2) The Census Itself (1:17–47)
        - (a) Introduction (1:17–19)
        - (b) The census lists (1:20–47)
      - (3) Levites Are Excepted (1:48–54)
    - b. Placement of the Camp and Marching Order (2:1–34)
    - c. Levitical Censuses (3:1–4:49)
      - (1) General Census (3:1–39)
        - (a) Introduction: Family of Aaron (3:1–13)
        - (b) The census itself (3:14–39)
      - (2) Levites for Firstborn (3:40–51)
      - (3) Census of Working Levites (4:1–49)
  - 2. Various Legal Enactments (5:1–6:21)
    - a. Camp Must Be Kept Free from Those with Serious Skin Disease (5:1–4)
    - b. Restitution When There Is No Kinsman (5:5–10)
    - c. The Jealous Husband (5:11–31)
    - d. Law of the Nazirite (6:1–21)
    - e. Conclusion: Aaronic Benediction (6:22–27)
- B. Various Matters concerning the Tabernacle (7:1–10:10)
  - 1. Offerings by Tribal Leaders (7:1–89)
  - 2. Lamps in the Tabernacle (8:1–4)
  - 3. Consecration of Levites (8:5–22)
  - 4. The Levites' Work (8:23–26)
  - 5. Supplement to the Passover Law (9:1–14)
  - 6. Preparations to Depart (9:15–10:10)
    - a. Fiery Cloud (9:15–23)
    - b. Silver Trumpets (10:1–10)

II. THE JOURNEY FROM MT. SINAI TO KADESH-BARNEA (10:11–12:16)
- A. Departure from Mt. Sinai (10:11–36)

- B. Crises of Authority on the Way (11:1–12:16)
  1. At Taberah (11:1–3)
  2. At Kibroth-hattaavah (11:4–35)
  3. At Hazeroth (12:1–16)

III. IN AND AROUND KADESH-BARNEA (13:1–19:22)

- A. The Spies (13:1–14:45)
  1. Spies Are Selected (13:1–16)
  2. Spies Go and Return (13:17–33)
  3. Responses to the Spies' Reports (14:1–45)
     - a. Responses by People and Leaders (14:1–10a)
     - b. Yahweh Responds (14:10b–38)
     - c. The People Attempt to Enter Canaan (14:39–45)
- B. Cultic Legislation (15:1–41)
  1. Supplementary Laws of the Offerings (15:1–16)
  2. First of the Dough (15:17–21)
  3. Purification Offering (15:22–31)
  4. Case Law on Capital Punishment for Sabbath Violation (15:32–36)
  5. Tassels on Garments for Remembrance (15:37–41)
- C. Legitimation of Aaron's Priesthood (16:1–17:28 [Eng. 13])
  1. Rebellions of Korah, Dathan, and Abiram (16:1–35)
  2. Aftermath of Rebellions (17:1–15 [Eng. 16:36–50])
  3. Aaron's Budding Rod (17:16–28 [Eng. 17:1–13])
- D. Further Cultic Legislation (18:1–19:22)
  1. Redefined Role for Priests and Levites (18:1–32)
     - a. Responsibilities of Priests and Levites (18:1–7)
     - b. Support of Priests (18:8–20)
     - c. Support of Levites (18:21–24)
     - d. Tithe of the Tithe (18:25–32)
  2. The Red Cow (19:1–22)
     - a. Making the Waters of Impurity (19:1–10)
     - b. Using the Waters of Impurity (19:11–22)

IV. THE JOURNEY FROM KADESH-BARNEA TO THE PLAINS OF MOAB (20:1–22:1)

- A. Death of Miriam and Disaster at Meribah (20:1–13)
- B. Request to Pass through Edom (20:14–21)
- C. Death of Aaron (20:22–29)
- D. Second Battle of Hormah (21:1–3)
- E. Fiery Serpents (21:4–9)
- F. Travel Itinerary (21:10–20)

- G. Wars against Sihon and Og (21:21–22:1)

V. ON THE PLAINS OF MOAB (22:2–36:13)

- A. Story of Balaam (22:2–24:25)
  1. Encounter between Balak and Balaam (22:2–40)
     - a. Messengers Find Balaam (22:2–21)
     - b. Balaam and the Donkey (22:22–35)
     - c. Balak Meets with Balaam (22:36–40)
  2. First and Second Oracles (22:41–23:30)
     - a. Introductory Preparations (22:41–23:6)
     - b. First Oracle (23:7–12)
     - c. Second Oracle (23:13–26)
  3. Third, Fourth, and Final Oracles (23:27–24:25)
     - a. Third Oracle (23:27–24:13)
     - b. Fourth Oracle (24:14–19)
     - c. Final Oracles (24:20–25)
- B. Incident of Baal-Peor (25:1–18)
- C. Second Census (25:19–26:65 [Eng. 26:1–65])
- D. Daughters of Zelophehad (27:1–11)
- E. Joshua Named as Moses' Successor (27:12–23)
- F. Further Legislation (28:1–30:17 [Eng. 16])
  1. Cultic Calendar (28:1–30:1 [Eng. 28:1–29:40])
  2. Women's Vows (30:2–17 [Eng. 1–16])
- G. War with Midian (31:1–54)
- H. Transjordanian Inheritance (32:1–42)
- I. Travel Itinerary (33:1–49)
- J. Regulations for Living in Canaan (33:50–36:13)
  1. Introduction: Canaanites Must Be Expelled (33:50–56)
  2. Borders of the Land (34:1–15)
  3. Leaders to Draw Israel's Borders (34:16–29)
  4. Cities of the Levites (35:1–8)
  5. Cities of Refuge (35:9–34)
  6. Additional Legislation for Daughters of Zelophehad (36:1–13)

VII. SELECT BIBLIOGRAPHY

Abba, R. "The Origin and Significance of Hebrew Sacrifice," *BTB* 7 (1977) 123–38.

———. "Priests and Levites in Deuteronomy," *VT* 27 (1977) 257–67.

———. “Priests and Levites in Ezekiel,” *VT* 28 (1978) 1–9.

Aberbach, M., and L. Smolar. “Aaron, Jeroboam, and the Golden Calves,” *JBL* 86 (1967) 129–40.

Aharoni, Y. “The Province List of Judah,” *VT* 9 (1959) 225–46.

———. “The Solomonic Temple, the Tabernacle and the Arad Sanctuary,” AOAT 22 (1973) 1–8.

Aharoni, Y., and R. Amiran. “Arad: Its Inscriptions and Temple,” *BA* 31 (1968) 1–32.

Albright, W. F. “The Administrative Divisions of Israel and Judah,” *JPOS* 5 (1925) 17–54.

———. “From the Patriarchs to Moses: 2. Moses out of Egypt,” *BA* 36 (1973) 57–58, 63–64.

———. “The Home of Balaam,” *JAOS* 35 (1915) 386–90.

———. “Jethro, Hobab and Reuel in Early Hebrew Tradition,” *CBQ* 25 (1963) 1–11.

———. “The List of Levitic Cities.” In *L. Ginzberg Jubilee Volume.* New York: American Academy for Jewish Research, 1945. Pp. 49–73.

———. “Midianite Donkey Caravans.” In *Translating and Understanding the Old Testament: Essays in Honor of Herbert Gordon May.* Ed. H. Frank and W. Reed. Nashville: Abingdon, 1970. Pp. 197–205.

———. “The Oracles of Balaam,” *JBL* 63 (1944) 207–33.

———. *The Proto-Sinaitic Inscriptions and Their Decipherment.* Harvard Theological Studies 22. Cambridge: Harvard Univ., 1969.

Allegro, J. M. “The Meaning of the Phrase *šetūm hāʿayin* in Num. 24:3, 15,” *VT* 3 (1953) 78–79.

Allen, R. B. “Numbers.” In *EBC* 2. Grand Rapids: Zondervan, 1990. Pp. 657–1008.

———. “The Theology of the Balaam Oracles.” In *Tradition and Testament: Essays in Honor of Charles Lee Feinberg.* Ed. J. S. Feinberg and P. D. Feinberg. Chicago: Moody, 1981. Pp. 79–119.

Allis, O. T. *The Five Books of Moses.* Nutley, N.J.: Presbyterian & Reformed, 1941.

Alter, R. *The Art of Biblical Narrative.* New York: Basic Books, 1981.

Ap-Thomas, D. R. “Some Notes on the Old Testament Attitude to Prayer,” *SJT* 9 (1956) 422–29.

Arden, E. “How Moses Failed God,” *JBL* 76 (1957) 50–52.

Auerbach, E. “Die Feste im alten Israel,” *VT* 8 (1958) 1–18.

———. “Die Herkunft der Sadokiten,” *ZAW* 49 (1931) 327–28.

Auld, A. G. “Cities of Refuge in Israelite Tradition,” *JSOT* 10 (1978) 26–29.

———. *Joshua, Moses, and the Land: Tetrateuch, Pentateuch, Hexateuch in a Generation Since 1938.* Edinburgh: T. & T. Clark, 1980.

Avi-Yonah, M. *The Encyclopedia of Archaeological Excavations in the Holy Land.* 4 vols. London: Oxford Univ. Press, 1975.
Baentsch, B. *Exodus–Leviticus–Numeri.* HKAT 2. Göttingen: Vandenhoeck & Ruprecht, 1903.
Bamberger, B. J. "Revelations of Torah after Sinai," *HUCA* 16 (1941) 97–113.
Barnouin, M. "Les Rscensements du Livre des Nombres et l'Astronomie Babylonienne," *VT* 27 (1977) 280–303.
———. "Tableaux numériques du Livre des Nombres," *RB* 76 (1969) 351–64.
Bartlett, J. R. "The Brotherhood of Edom," *JSOT* 4 (1977) 2–27.
———. "The Conquest of Sihon's Kingdom: A Literary Re-examination," *JBL* 97 (1978) 347–51.
———. "The Historical Reference of Numbers 21:27–30," *PEQ* 101 (1969) 94–100.
———. "The Land of Seir and the Brotherhood of Edom," *JTS* 20 (1969) 1–20.
———. "The Moabites and Edomites." In *Peoples of Old Testament Times.* Ed. D. J. Wiseman. Oxford: Clarendon, 1973. Pp. 229–58.
———. "The Rise and Fall of the Kingdom of Edom," *PEQ* 104 (1972) 26–37.
———. "Sihon and Og, Kings of the Amorites," *VT* 20 (1970) 257–77.
———. "The Use of the Word *rōʾš* as a Title in the Old Testament," *VT* 19 (1969) 1–10.
———. "Zadok and His Successors at Jerusalem," *JTS* 19 (1968) 1–18.
Begrich, J. "Das priesterliche Heilsorakel," *ZAW* 52 (1934) 81–92.
Beltz, W. *Die Kaleb-Traditionen im Alten Testament.* BWANT 98. Stuttgart: Kohlhammer, 1964.
Ben-Barek, Z. "Inheritance by Daughters in the Ancient Near East," *JSS* 25 (1980) 22–33.
Bennett, C. "Excavations at Buseirah, Southern Jordan," *Levant* 5 (1973) 1–11.
———. "Tawilân," *RB* 76 (1969) 386–90; 77 (1970) 371–74.
———. "Ummel-Biyara-Pétra," *RB* 71 (1964) 250–53; 73 (1966) 372–403.
Bentzen, A. "Zur Geschichte der Sadokiten," *ZAW* NS 10 (1933) 173–76.
Bergmann, A. "The Israelite Tribe of Half Manasseh," *JPOS* 16 (1936) 224–54.
Bertman, S. "Tasseled Garments in the Ancient East Mediterranean," *BA* 24 (1961) 119–28.
Bewer, J. A. "The Literary Problems of the Balaam Story in Numbers, Chapters 22–24," *AJT* 9 (1905) 238–62.
Binns, L. E. *The Book of Numbers: With Introduction and Notes.* Westminster Commentaries. London: Methuen, 1927.

———. “Midianite Elements in Hebrew Religion,” *JTS* 31 (1930) 337–54.

Bird, P. “To Play the Harlot: An Inquiry into an Old Testament Metaphor.” In *Gender and Difference in Ancient Israel.* Ed. P. Day. Minneapolis: Fortress, 1989. Pp. 75–94.

Blank, S. H. “The Curse, the Blasphemy, the Spell, and the Oath,” *HUCA* 23/1 (1950–51) 73–95.

———. “Men against God — The Promethean Element in Biblical Prayer,” *JBL* 72 (1953) 1–14.

———. “Some Observations concerning Biblical Prayer,” *HUCA* 32 (1961) 75–90.

Bodenheimer, F. W. “The Manna of Sinai,” *BA* 10 (1947) 1–6.

Boeker, H. J. *Law and the Administration of Justice in the Old Testament and the Ancient East.* Tr. J. Moiser. Minneapolis: Augsburg, 1980.

Bowman, J. “Did the Qumran Sect Burn the Red Heifer?” *RevQ* 1 (1958) 73–84.

Brenner, A. *Colour Terms in the Old Testament.* JSOTSup 21. Sheffield: JSOT Press, 1982.

Brichto, H. C. “The Case of the *Sota* and a Reconsideration of Biblical Law,” *HUCA* 46 (1975) 55–70.

———. “Kin, Cult, Land and Afterlife: A Biblical Complex,” *HUCA* 44 (1973) 1–54.

———. *The Problem of “Curse” in the Hebrew Bible.* Philadelphia: Society of Biblical Literature and Exegesis, 1962.

Brin, G. “The Formula ‘From . . . and Onward/Upward,’ ” *JBL* 99 (1980) 351–54.

———. “Numbers XV 22–23 and the Question of the Composition of the Pentateuch,” *VT* 30 (1980) 351–54.

Brown, F., S. R. Driver, and C. A. Briggs. *A Hebrew-English Lexicon of the Old Testament.* Oxford: Clarendon, 1907.

Brueggemann, W. “From Hurt to Joy, from Death to Life,” *Int* 28 (1974) 3–19.

Buchanan, G. W. “Eschatology and the ‘End of Days,’ ” *JNES* 20 (1961) 188–93.

Budd, P. J. *Numbers.* WBC 5. Waco, Tex.: Word, 1984.

Buis, P. “Les Conflits entre Moise et Israël dans Exode et Nombres,” *VT* 28 (1978) 257–70.

———. “Qadesh, un Lieu Maudit?” *VT* 24 (1974) 268–85.

Buit, M. du. “Quelques contacts bibliques dans les archives royales de Mari,” *RB* 66 (1959) 576–81.

Burns, R. J. *Has the Lord Indeed Spoken Only Through Moses? A Study of the Biblical Portrait of Miriam.* SBLDS 84. Atlanta: Scholars Press, 1987.

Burrows, E. *The Oracles of Jacob and Balaam.* London: Burns, Oates and Washbourne, 1938.

Buttrick, G. A., et al., eds. *The Interpreter's Dictionary of the Bible.* 4 vols. Nashville: Abingdon, 1962. *Supplementary Volume.* Ed. K. Crim, et al. 1976.

Canney, M. A. "Numbers 22:21–31," *ExpTim* 27 (1917) 568.

Cassuto, U. *The Documentary Hypothesis.* Tr. I. Abrahams. Jerusalem: Magnes, 1961.

Cazelles, H. "David's Monarchy and the Gibeonite Claim," *PEQ* 87 (1955) 165–75.

———. "La Dîme Israélite et les Textes de Ras Shamra," *VT* 1 (1951) 131–34.

Cheyne, T. K. "Some Critical Difficulties in the Chapters on Balaam," *ExpTim* 10 (1898–99) 399–402.

Childs, B. S. "The Etiological Tale Re-examined," *VT* 24 (1974) 387–97.

Christensen, D. L. "Num. 21:14–15 and the Book of the Wars of Yahweh," *CBQ* 36 (1974) 359–60.

Clark, R. E. D. "The Large Numbers in the Old Testament," *Journal of the Transactions of the Victoria Institute* 87 (1955) 82–92.

Clines, D. J. A. *The Theme of the Pentateuch.* JSOTSup 10. Sheffield: JSOT Press, 1978.

Coats, G. W. "Balaam: Sinner or Saint?" *BR* 18 (1973) 21–29.

———. "Conquest Traditions in the Wilderness Theme," *JBL* 95 (1976) 177–90.

———. "An Exposition of the Wilderness Traditions," *VT* 22 (1972) 288–95.

———. "Legendary Motifs in the Moses Death Reports," *CBQ* 39 (1977) 34–44.

———. "Moses in Midian," *JBL* 92 (1973) 3–10.

———. *The Murmuring Motif in the Wilderness Traditions of the Old Testament: Rebellion in the Wilderness.* Nashville: Abingdon, 1968.

———. "The Wilderness Itinerary," *CBQ* 34 (1972) 135–52.

———. "The Way of Obedience: Traditio-Historical and Hermeneutical Reflections on the Balaam Story," *Semeia* 24 (1982) 53–79.

Cody, A. *A History of the Old Testament Priesthood.* AnBib 35. Rome: Pontifical Biblical Institute, 1969.

Cook, F. C., and T. E. Espin. *The Fourth Book of Moses Called Numbers.* The Holy Bible According to the Authorized Version. Vol. I/II. London: Murray, 1871.

Coppens, J. "Les Oracles de Bileam: Leur Origine Littéraire et leur Portée Prophétique." In *Mélanges Eugene Tisserant.* Ed. P. Hennequin et. al. Vol. 1. Cittá del Vaticano: Bibliotheca Apostolica Vaticana, 1964. Pp. 67–80.

Cox, S. *Balaam: An Exposition and a Study.* London: Kegan Paul, Trench, 1884.

Craigie, P. C. "The Conquest and Early Hebrew Poetry," *TynBul* 20 (1969) 76–94.

Cross, F. M. *Canaanite Myth and Hebrew Epic.* Cambridge: Harvard Univ. Press, 1973.

———. "The Priestly Tabernacle in the Light of Recent Research." In *Temples and High Places in Biblical Times; Proceedings of the Colloquium in Honor of the Centennial of Hebrew Union College-Jewish Institute of Religion.* Jerusalem: Nelson Glueck School of Biblical Archaeology, 1981. Pp. 170–72.

———. "The Tabernacle," *BA* 10 (1947) 1–68.

Cross, F. M., and G. E. Wright. "The Boundary and Province Lists of the Kingdom of Judah," *JBL* 75 (1956) 202–26.

Daiches, S., "Balaam, a Babylonian *bārû:* The Episode of Num. 22.2–24.24 and Some Babylonian Parallels," *Assyriologische und Archaeologische Studien Hermann von Hilprecht gewidmet* (Leipzig: Hinrichs, 1909), pp. 60–70.

David, M. "Die Bestimmungen über die Asylstädte in Jos. 20," *OTS* 9 (1951) 30–48.

Davidson, A. B. *Hebrew Syntax.* 3rd ed. Edinburgh: T. & T. Clark, 1902.

Davies, E. W. "Inheritance Rights and the Hebrew Levirate Marriage," *VT* 31 (1981) 138–44.

Davies, G. I. *The Way of the Wilderness: A Geographical Study of the Wilderness Itineraries in the Old Testament.* SOTSMS 5. Cambridge: Cambridge Univ. Press, 1979.

———. "The Wilderness Itineraries," *TynBul* 25 (1974) 46–81.

Dever, W. G. "The EB IV–MB I Horizon in Transjordan and Southern Palestine," *BASOR* 210 (1973) 37–63.

De Vries, S. J. "The Origin of the Murmuring Tradition," *JBL* 87 (1968) 51–58.

Digges, M. L. "Balaam: A Man in a Corner," *Bible Today* 13 (1964) 869–74.

Dillmann, A. *Die Bücher Numeri, Deuteronomium und Joshua.* Kurzgefasstes exegetisches Handbuch zum Alten Testament. 2nd ed. Leipzig: Hirzel, 1886.

Douglas, C. E. "The Twelve Houses of Israel," *JTS* 37 (1936) 49–56.

Douglas, M. *Purity and Danger: An Analysis of the Concepts of Pollution and Taboo.* London: Routledge and Kegan Paul, 1966.

Driver, G. R. "Two Problems in the Old Testament Examined in the Light of Assyriology," *Syria* 33 (1956) 70–78.

———, and J. C. Miles. "Ordeal by Oath at Nuzi," *Iraq* 7 (1940) 132.

Driver, S. R. *Introduction to the Literature of the Old Testament.* 12th ed. Oxford: Clarendon, 1906.
———. *A Treatise on the Use of the Tenses in Hebrew and Some Other Syntactical Questions.* 2nd ed. Oxford: Clarendon, 1881.
Dumbrell, W. J. "Midian — A Land or a League?" *VT* 25 (1975) 323–37.
Dus, J. "Herabfahrung Jahwes auf die Lade und Entziehung der Feuerwolke," *VT* 19 (1969) 290–311.
Eichrodt, W. *Theology of the Old Testament.* Tr. J. A. Baker. 2 vols. OTL. Philadelphia: Westminster, 1961–67.
Eising, H. "Balaams Eselin," *BK* 13 (1958) 45–47.
Eissfeldt, O. *Hexateuch-Synopse: Die Erzälung der fünf Bücher Mose und des Buches Josua mit dem Anfange des Richterbuches.* Leipzig: J. C. Hinrichs, 1922.
———. "Die Komposition der Bileam-Erzählung," *ZAW* 57 (1939) 212–41.
———. *The Old Testament: An Introduction.* Tr. P. Ackroyd. New York: Harper & Row, 1965.
———. "Protektorat der Midianiter über ihre Nachbarn im letzten Viertel des 2. Jahrtausends v. Chr.," *JBL* 87 (1968) 383–93.
———. "Sinai Erzählung und Bileamsprüche," *HUCA* 32 (1961) 179–90.
Elhorst, H. J. "Das Ephod," *JBL* 30 (1910) 154–76.
Elliger, K. "Sinn und Ursprung der Priesterliche Geschichtserzählung," *ZTK* 49 (1952) 121–43.
Emerton, J. A. "Priests and Levites in Deuteronomy," *VT* 12 (1962) 129–38.
Engnell, I. "Methodological Aspects of Old Testament Study," VTSup 7. Leiden: Brill, 1960. Pp. 13–30.
———. "The Pentateuch." In *Critical Essays on the Old Testament.* Tr. J. T. Willis. London: SPCK, 1970. Pp. 50–67.
———. "The Traditio-Historical Method in Old Testament Research." In *Critical Essays on the Old Testament.* London: SPCK, 1970. Pp. 3–11
———. "Wilderness Wandering." In *Critical Essays on the Old Testament.* London: SPCK, 1970. Pp. 207–14.
Erdman, C. R. *The Book of Numbers: An Exposition.* Westwood, N.J.: Revell, 1952.
Fensham, F. C. "Malediction and Benediction in Ancient Near Eastern Vassal-Treaties and the Old Testament," *ZAW* 74 (1962) 1–9.
Fichtner, J. "Die etymologische Ätiologie in den Namengebungen der geschichtlichen Bücher des Alten Testament," *VT* 6 (1956) 372–96.
Finesinger, S. B. "Musical Instruments in the Old Testament," *HUCA* 3 (1926) 21–76.
———. "The Shofar," *HUCA* 8–9 (1931–32) 193–228.

Fisch, S. "The Book of Numbers." In *The Soncino Chumash: The Five Books of Moses with Haphtaroth.* Ed. A. Cohen. London: Soncino, 1947. Pp. 793–987.

Fishbane, M. "Accusations of Adultery: A Study of Law and Scribal Practice in Numbers 5:11–31," *HUCA* 45 (1974) 25–46.

Fisher, L. R. "A New Ritual Calendar from Ugarit," *HTR* 63 (1970) 485–501.

Flack, E. E. "Flashes of New Knowledge, Recent Study and the Book of Numbers," *Int* 13 (1959) 3–23.

Flanagan, J. W. "History, Religion and Ideology: The Caleb Tradition," *Horizons* 3 (1976) 175–85.

Fohrer, G. *Introduction to the Old Testament.* Tr. D. Green. Nashville: Abingdon, 1968.

Foote, T. C. "The Ephod," *JBL* 21 (1902) 1–47.

Franken, H. J. "Texts from the Persian Period from Tell Deir ʿAlla," *VT* 17 (1967) 480–81.

Freedman, D. N. "Archaic Forms in Early Hebrew Poetry," *ZAW* 72 (1960) 101–7.

———. "Pottery, Poetry, and Prophecy: An Essay on Biblical Poetry," *JBL* 96 (1977) 5–26.

Fretheim, T. E. "The Priestly Document: Anti-Temple?" *VT* 18 (1968) 313–29.

Frick, F. S. *The City in Ancient Israel.* SBLDS. Missoula, Mont.: Scholars Press, 1977.

Fritz, V. "Arad in der biblischen Überlieferung und in der Liste Schoschenk I," *ZDPV* 82 (1966) 331–42.

———. "Erwägungen zur Siedlungsgeschichte des Negeb in der Eisen 1-Zeit (1200–1000 v.Chr.) im Lichte der Ausgrabungen auf der Ḥirbet el-Mšaš," *ZDPV* 91 (1975) 30–45.

———. *Israel in der Wüste: Traditionsgeschichtliche Untersuchungen der Wüstenüberlieferung des Jahwisten.* Marburg: Elwert, 1970.

Frymer-Kensky, T. "The Strange Case of the Suspected Sotah (Numbers V 13–31)," *VT* 34 (1984) 11–26.

Gaster, T. H. "The Name *lēwî*," *JTS* 38 (1937) 250–51.

Gemser, B. "Der Stern au Jacob (Num. 24:17)," *ZAW* 45 (1925) 301–2.

Gibson, J. C. L. *Canaanite Myths and Legends.* 2nd ed. Edinburgh: T. & T. Clark, 1978.

Gillischewski, E. "Die Geschichte von der 'Rotte Korah' Num. 16," *AfO* 3 (1926) 114–18.

Glueck, N. "The Boundaries of Edom," *HUCA* 11 (1936) 141–57.

———. "The Civilisation of the Edomites," *BA* 10 (1947) 77–84.

Golka, F. W. "The aetiologies in the Old Testament," *VT* 26 (1976) 410–28; 27 (1977) 36–47.

Gottwald, N. K. *The Tribes of Yahweh.* Maryknoll, N.Y.: Orbis, 1979.
Gowan, D. E. "The use of *ya'an* in biblical Hebrew," *VT* 21 (1971) 168–85.
Gradwohl, R. "Das 'fremde Feuer' von Nadab und Abihu," *ZAW* 75 (1963) 288–96.
Gray, G. B. *A Critical and Exegetical Commentary on Numbers.* ICC. Edinburgh: T. & T. Clark, 1903.
———. "The Nazirite," *JTS* 1 (1899–1900) 201–11.
———. *Sacrifice in the Old Testament.* Oxford: Clarendon, 1925.
Gray, J. "The Desert Sojourn of the Hebrews and the Sinai Horeb Tradition," *VT* 4 (1954) 148–54.
———. *The Legacy of Canaan: The Ras Shamra Texts and Their Relevance to the Old Testament.* VTSup 5. 2nd ed. Leiden: Brill, 1965.
Green, W. H. *The Higher Criticism of the Pentateuch.* New York: Scribners, 1895.
Greenberg, M. "The Biblical Conception of Asylum," *JBL* 78 (1959) 125–32.
———. "Idealism and Practicality in Numbers 35:4–5 and Ezekiel 48," *JAOS* 88 (1968) 59–66.
———. "A New Approach to the History of the Israelite Priesthood," *JAOS* 70 (1950) 41–46.
Greenstone, J. H. *Numbers, with Commentary.* Philadelphia: Jewish Publication Society, 1948.
Gressmann, H. *Mose und Seine Zeit.* Göttingen: Vandenhoeck & Ruprecht, 1913.
Gross, W. *Bileam: Literar- und Formkritische Untersuchung der Prosa im Num. 22–24.* Munich: Kösel, 1974.
———. "'Ein Zepter wird sich erheben aus Israel' (Num. 24:17): Die messianische Hoffnung im Alten Testament," *BK* 17 (1962) 34–37.
Guillaume, A. "A Note on Num. 23:10," *VT* 12 (1962) 335–37.
Gunn, D. M. "The 'Battle Report': Oral or Scribal Convention," *JBL* 93 (1974) 513–18.
Gunneweg, A. H. J. *Leviten und Priester.* Göttingen: Vandenhoeck & Ruprecht, 1965.
———. "Mose in Midian," *ZTK* 61 (1964) 1–9.
Guyot, G. H. "Balaam," *CBQ* 3 (1941) 235–42.
———. "The Prophecy of Balaam," *CBQ* 2 (1940) 330–40.
Hackett, J. *The Balaam Text from Deir 'Allā.* HSM 31. Chico, Calif.: Scholars Press, 1980.
———. "Some Observations on the Balaam Text at Deir 'Allā." *BA* 49 (1986) 216–22.
Halpern, B. "Levitic Participation in the Reform Cult of Jeroboam I," *JBL* 95 (1976) 31–42.

Hanson, H. E. "Num. XVI 30 and the meaning of *bārā'*," *VT* 22 (1972) 353–59.

Haran, M. "From Early to Classical Prophecy: Continuity and Change," *VT* 27 (1977) 385–97.

———. "The Levitical Cities: Utopia and Historical Reality," *Tarbiz* 27 (1957–58) 421–38.

———. "The Nature of the *''ohel mo'edh'* in Pentateuchal Sources," *JSS* 5 (1960) 50–65.

———. "The Passover Sacrifice." In *Studies in the Religion of Ancient Israel.* VTSup 23. Leiden: Brill, 1972. Pp. 86–116.

———. "The Priestly Image of the Tabernacle," *HUCA* 36 (1965) 191–226.

———. "Studies in the Account of the Levitical Cities," *JBL* 80 (1961) 45–54.

———. *Temples and Temple Service in Ancient Israel.* Oxford: Clarendon, 1978.

———. "The Uses of Incense in the Ancient Israelite Ritual," *VT* 10 (1960) 113–29.

Harrelson, W. "Guidance in the Wilderness: The Theology of Numbers," *Int* 13 (1959) 24–36.

Harrison, R. K. *Introduction to the Old Testament.* Grand Rapids: Eerdmans, 1969.

———. *Numbers.* WEC. Chicago: Moody, 1990.

Heinisch, P. *Das Buch Numeri, Übersetzt und Erklärt.* Die Heilige Schrift des Alten Testament. Bonn: Hanstein, 1936.

Hempel, J. "Die israelitischen Anschauungen von Segen und Fluch im Lichte altorientalische Parallelen." In *Apoxsymata: Vorarbeiten zu einer Religionsgeschichte und Theologie des Alten Testaments.* Festgabe J. Hempel. Ed. W. Baumgartner, et al. BZAW 81. Berlin: Töpelmann, 1961. Pp. 30–113.

Henke, O. "Zur Lage von Beth Peor," *ZDPV* 75 (1959) 155–63.

Hertz, J. H. "Numbers 23:9b, 10," *ExpTim* 45 (1933–34) 524.

Hoftijzer, J. "The Prophet Balaam in a 6th Century Aramaic Inscription," *BA* 39 (1976) 11–17.

Hoftijzer, J., and G. van der Kooij, eds. *The Balaam Text from Deir 'Alla Re-Evaluated: Proceedings of the International Symposium held at Leiden, 21–24 August 1989.* Leiden: Brill, 1990. (*Proceedings,* 1989).

———, eds. *Aramaic Texts from Deir 'Alla. With Contributions by H. Franken, V. R. Mehra, J. Voskuil, J. A. Mosk. Preface by P. A. H. de Boer.* Documenta et Monumenta Orientis Antiqui 19. Leiden: Brill, 1976 (*ATDA*)

Holzinger, H. *Numeri, Erklärt.* Kurzer Hand-Commentar zum Alten Testament 4. Tübingen: J. C. B. Mohr, 1903.
Hooke, S. H. "Theory and Practice of Substitution," *VT* 2 (1952) 2–17.
Horne, S. H. "The Excavations at Tell Hesban, 1973," *ADAJ* 18 (1973) 87–88.
Horst, F. "Recht und Religion im Bereich des A.T.," *EvT* 16 (1956) 49–75.
Hort, G. "The Death of Qorah," *AusBR* 7 (1959) 2–26.
Hurvitz, A. "Evidence of Language in Dating the Priestly Code: A Linguistic Study in Technical Terms and Terminology," *RB* 81 (1974) 24–56.
Jacob, E. *Theology of the Old Testament.* Tr. A. W. Heathcote and P. Allcock. New York: Harper & Row, 1958.
James, E. O. *The Ancient Gods: The History of the Diffusion of Religion in the Ancient Near East and the Eastern Mediterranean.* London: Weidenfeld and Nicholson, 1960.
Jirku, A. "Wo Stand Ursprünglich die Notiz über Hebron in Num. 13:22?" *ZAW* 39 (1921) 312.
Jobling, D. "The Jordan a Boundary: A Reading of Numbers 32 and Joshua 22." In SBLSP, 1980. Ed. P. J. Achtemeier. Chico, Calif.: Scholars Press, 1980. Pp. 183–207.
Johnson, A. R. *The Cultic Prophet in Ancient Israel.* Cardiff: Univ. of Wales, 1962.
Joines, K. R. "The Bronze Serpent in the Israelite Cult," *JBL* 87 (1968) 245–56.
———. "Winged Serpents in Isaiah's Inaugural Vision," *JBL* 86 (1967) 410–15.
Judge, H. G. "Aaron, Zadok, and Abiathar," *JTS* NS 7 (1956) 70–74.
Kallai-Kleinmann, Z. "The Town Lists of Judah, Simeon, Benjamin, and Dan," *VT* 8 (1958) 134–60.
Kapelrud, A. "How Tradition Failed Moses," *JBL* 76 (1957) 242.
———. *The Ras Shamra Discoveries and the Old Testament.* Oxford: Blackwell, 1962.
Kaufmann, Y. "Der Kalendar und der Priester-Kodex," *VT* 4 (1954) 307–13.
———. *The Religion of Israel.* Tr. and abridged by M. Greenberg. Chicago: Univ. of Chicago Press, 1960.
Kautzsch, E., ed. *Gesenius' Hebrew Grammar.* 2nd ed. Tr. A. E. Cowley. Oxford: Clarendon, 1910.
Keil, C. F. *The Book of Numbers.* Biblical Commentary. Tr. J. Martin, et al. Edinburgh: T. & T. Clark, 1869.
Kellermann, D. "'Āšām in Ugarit?" *ZAW* 76 (1964) 319–22.
———. "Bermerkungen zum Sündopfergesetz in Num. 14:22ff." In *Wort und Geschichte: Festschrift für Karl Elliger zum 70. Geburtstag.*

Ed. H. Gese and H. P. Rüger. Neukirchen: Kevelaer, 1973. Pp. 107–14.

———. *Die Priesterschrift von Numeri 1,1 bis 10,10.* BZAW 120. Berlin: de Gruyter, 1970.

Kennedy, A. R. S. *Leviticus and Numbers.* New Century Bible. London: Caxton, n.d. Pp. 185–391.

Kennett, R. H. "The Origin of the Aaronic Priesthood," *JTS* 6 (1905) 161–86; 7 (1906) 620–24.

Kosmala, H. "Form and Structure in Ancient Hebrew Poetry," *VT* 14 (1964) 423–45.

Kraus, H.-J. "Zur Geschichte des Passah-Massot-Festes im AT," *EvT* 18 (1958) 47–67.

Kselman, J. S. "A note on Numbers 12:6–8," *VT* 26 (1976) 500–504.

Kuschke, A. "Die Lagervorstellung der priesterschriftlichen Erzählung," *ZAW* 22 (1951) 74–105.

Kutsch, E. "Erwägungen zur Geschichte der Passafeier und des Massotfestes," *ZTK* 55 (1958) 1–35.

Lagrange, M. J. "L'Itinéraire des Israélites," *RB* 9 (1900) 63–86.

Latley, C. "Vicarious Solidarity in the Old Testament," *VT* 1 (1951) 267–74.

Laughlin, J. C. H. "The Strange Fire of Nadab and Abihu," *JBL* 95 (1976) 559–65.

LaVerdiere, E. A. "Balaam Son of Peor," *TBT* 89 (1977) 1157–65.

Lehmann, M. R. "Biblical Oaths," *ZAW* 81 (1969) 74–92.

Lehming, S. "Versuch zu Num. 16," *ZAW* 74 (1962) 291–321.

Leiman, S. Z. "The Inverted *Nuns* at Num 10:35–36 and the Book of Eldad and Medad," *JBL* 93 (1974) 348–55.

Lemaire, A. "Le 'Pays de Hépher' et les 'Files de Zelophehad' à la lumière des ostraca de Samarie," *Sem* 22 (1972) 13–20.

Levine, B. "The Descriptive Tabernacle Texts of the Pentateuch," *JAOS* 85 (1965) 307–18.

———. *In the Presence of the Lord: A Study of Cult and Some Cultic Terms in Ancient Israel.* SJLA 5. Leiden: Brill, 1974.

———. "More on the Inverted *Nuns* of Num 10:35–36," *JBL* 95 (1976) 122–24.

———. The Plaster Inscriptions from *Deir ʿAllā:* General Interpretation." In *Proceedings, 1989.* Pp. 58–72.

Liebreich L. J. "The Songs of Ascents and the Priestly Blessing," *JBL* 74 (1955) 33–36.

Lindblom, J. "Lot-casting in the Old Testament," *VT* 12 (1962) 164–78.

Lipiński, E. "*b'ḥryt hymym* dans les textes préexiliques," *VT* 20 (1970) 445–50.

———. "ʾŪrīm and Tummīm," *VT* 20 (1970) 495–96.

Liver, J. "Korah, Dathan, and Abiram." In *Studies in the Bible*. ScrHier 8. Ed. C. Rabin. Jerusalem: Magnes, 1961. Pp. 189–217.
Lock, W. "Balaam," *JTS* 2 (1901) 161–73.
Loewe, H. "Numbers 22:6," *ExpTim* 26 (1914–15) 378.
Loewenstamm, S. E. "The Death of Moses," *Tarbiz* 27 (1957–58) 142–57.
Lohfink, N. "Die Ursünden in der priesterlichen Geschichtserzählung." In *Die Zeit Jesu*. H. Schlier Festschrift. Ed. G. Bornkamm and K. Rahner. Freiburg: Herder, 1970. Pp. 38–57.
Löhr, M. "Bileam, Num. 22:2–24:25," *AfO* 4 (1927) 85–89.
Long, B. O. "The Effect of Divination upon Israelite Literature," *JBL* 92 (1973) 489–97.
———. *The Problem of Etiological Narrative in the Old Testament*. BZAW 108. Berlin: Töpelmann, 1968.
Loretz, O. "Die Herausführungsformel in Num. 23:22 und 24:8," *UF* 7 (1975) 571–72.
Lucas, A. "The Number of Israelites at the Time of the Exodus," *PEQ* 76 (1944) 164–68.
McCarthy, D. J. "An Installation Genre?" *JBL* 90 (1971) 31–41.
———. "The Symbolism of Blood and Sacrifice," *JBL* 88 (1969) 166–76.
———. "Further Notes on the Symbolism of Blood and Sacrifice," *JBL* 92 (1973) 205–10.
McEvenue, S. E. *The Narrative Style of the Priestly Writer*. AnBib 50. Rome: Pontifical Biblical Institute, 1971.
Mackay, C. "The North Boundary of Palestine," *JTS* 35 (1934) 22–40.
McKeating, H. "The development of the law on homicide in Ancient Israel," *VT* 25 (1975) 46–68.
Mackensen, R. S. "The Present Form of the Balaam Stories." In *The MacDonald Presentation Volume*. Princeton: Books for Libraries Press, 1933.
McNeile, A. H. *The Book of Numbers in the Revised Version*. Cambridge Bible for Schools and Colleges. Cambridge: Cambridge Univ. Press, 1911.
MacRae, G. W. "The Meaning and Evolution of the Feast of Tabernacles," *CBQ* 22 (1960) 251–76.
Maier, J. "Urim und Tummim. Recht und Bund in der Spannung zwischen Königtum und Priestertum im alten Israel," *Kairos* NF 11 (1969) 22–38.
Malina, B. J. *The Palestinian Manna Tradition*. Leiden: Brill, 1968.
Mann, T. W. "Theological Reflections on the Denial of Moses," *JBL* 99 (1979) 481–94.
Margaliot, M. "The Transgression of (Moses and) Aaron at Mey Merivah," *Beth Mikra* 58 (1974) 375–400, 456.

Marsh, J. "Exegesis of the Book of Numbers." In *IB,* 2. New York: Abingdon, 1953. Pp. 137–308.
Martin-Achard, R. *Essai biblique sur les fêtes d'Israël.* Geneva: Labor et Fides, 1974.
Mauchline, J. "The Balaam-Balak Songs and Saga." In *Studie Semitica et Orientalia. Vol. 2. Presentation volume to William Barron Stevenson.* Ed. J. C. Mullo-Weir. Glasgow: Glasgow Univ. Oriental Society, 1945.
———. "Gilead and Gilgal: Some Reflections on the Israelite Occupation of Palestine," *VT* 6 (1956) 19–33.
May, H. G. "The Relation of the Passover to the Feast of Unleavened Cakes," *JBL* 55 (1936) 65–82.
Mays, J. L. *The Book of Leviticus, the Book of Numbers.* Layman's Bible Commentary. Richmond: John Knox, 1963.
Mazar, B. "The Cities of the Priests and Levites." In VTSup 7. Leiden: Brill. Pp. 193–205.
———. "The Sanctuary of Arad and the Family of Hobab the Kenite," *JNES* 24 (1965) 297–303.
Meek, T. J. "Aaronites and Zadokites," *AJSL* 45 (1929) 149–66.
———. "Moses and Levites," *AJSL* 56 (1939) 113–20.
———. "Some Emendations in the Old Testament," *JBL* 48 (1929) 167–68.
Mendenhall, G. E. "The Census Lists of Numbers 1 and 26," *JBL* 77 (1959) 52–66.
———. " 'Change and Decay in All Around I See': Conquest, Covenant, and *The Tenth Generation,*" *BA* 39 (1976) 152–57.
———. "The Hebrew Conquest of Palestine," *BA* 25 (1962) 66–87.
———. *The Tenth Generation.* Baltimore: Johns Hopkins Univ. Press, 1973.
Meshel, Z., and C. Meyers. "The Name of God in the Wilderness of Zin," *BA* 39 (1976) 6–10, 148–51.
Meyers, C. L. *The Tabernacle Menorah: A Synthetic Study of a Symbol from the Biblical Cult.* AASOR 2. Missoula, Mont.: Scholars Press, 1976.
Milgrom, J. "Akkadian Confirmation of the Meaning of the Term *tĕrûmâ,*" *Tarbiz* 44 (1974/75) 189. Repr. in *Studies in Cultic Theology and Terminology.* Pp. 171–72.
———. "The Alleged Wave-offering in Israel and the Ancient Near East," *IEJ* 22 (1972) 33–38. Repr. in *Studies in Cultic Theology and Terminology.* Pp. 133–38.
———. "The Biblical Diet Laws as an Ethical System," *Int* 17 (1963) 288–301. Repr. in *Studies in Cultic Theology and Terminology.* Pp. 104–18.
———. "Concerning Jeremiah's Repudiation of Sacrifice," *ZAW* 89

(1977) 274–75. Repr. in *Studies in Cultic Theology and Terminology.* Pp. 119–21.
———. *Cult and Conscience: The* asham *and the Priestly Doctrine of Repentance.* SJLA 18. Leiden: Brill, 1976.
———. "The Cultic *Šᵉgāgāh* and Its Influence in Psalms and Job," *JQR* 58 (1967) 115–25. Repr. in *Studies in Cultic Theology and Terminology. Pp. 122–32.*
———. *"Hattĕnûpâ."* In *Zer Li' gevurot.* Festschrift for Z. Shazar. Ed. B. Z. Luria. Jerusalem: Kiryat Sepher, 1972. Pp. 93–110. Repr. in *Studies in Cultic Theology and Terminology.* Pp. 139–58.
———. "Israel's Sanctuary: The Priestly 'Picture of Dorian Gray'," *RB* 83 (1976) 390–99. Repr. in *Studies in Cultic Theology and Terminology.* Pp. 75f–84.
———. *The JPS Torah Commentary: Numbers Bemidbar.* Philadelphia/New York: The Jewish Publication Society, 5750/1990.
———. "The Literary Structure of Numbers 8:5–22 and the Levitic kippûr." In *Perspectives on Language and Text: Essays and Poems in Honor of Francis I. Andersen's Sixtieth Birthday July 28, 1985.* Ed. E. Conrad and E. Newing. Winona Lake, Ind.: Eisenbrauns, 1987. Pp. 205–9.
———. "The Paradox of the Red Cow (Num. xix)," *VT* 31 (1981) 62–72. Repr. in *Studies in Cultic Theology and Terminology.* Pp. 85–95.
———. "The Priestly Doctrine of Repentance," *RB* 82 (1975) 186–205. Repr. in *Studies in Cultic Theology and Terminology.* Pp. 47–66.
———. "Priestly Terminology and the Political and Social Structure of Pre-Monarchic Israel," *JQR* 69 (1978) 65–81. Repr. in *Studies in Cultic Theology and Terminology.* Pp. 1–17.
———. "A Prolegomenon to Lev 17:11," *JBL* 90 (1971) 149–56. Repr. in *Studies in Cultic Theology and Terminology.* Pp. 96–103.
———. "The *Šôq hattĕrûmâ:* A Chapter in Cultic History," *Tarbiz* 42 (1972–73) 1–14. Repr. in *Studies in Cultic Theology and Terminology.* Pp. 159–70.
———. "Sin-offering or Purification-offering?" *VT* 21 (1971) 237–39. Repr. in *Studies in Cultic Theology and Terminology.* Pp. 67–69.
———. *Studies in Cultic Theology and Terminology.* SJLA 36. Leiden: Brill, 1983.
———. *Studies in Levitical Terminology.* Vol. I. University of California Publications, Near Eastern Studies 14. Berkeley: Univ. of California Press, 1970.
———. "Two Kinds of *ḥaṭṭā't,*" *VT* 26 (1976) 333–37. Repr. in *Studies in Cultic Theology and Terminology.* Pp. 70–74.
Miller, P. D. "The Blessing of God: An Interpretation of Numbers 6:22–27," *Int* 29 (1975) 240–51.

Mitchell, T. C. "The meaning of the noun *ḥtn* in the Old Testament," *VT* 19 (1969) 93–112.
Mittmann, S. "Num. 20:14–21 — eine radaktionelle Kompilation." In *Wort und Geschichte: Festschrift für Karl Elliger zum 70. Geburtstag*. Ed. H. Gese and H. P. Rüger. Neukirchen-Vluyn: Neukirchener, 1973.
Möhlenbrink, K. "Die levitischen Überlieferungen des Alten Testament," *ZAW* 52 (1934) 184–231.
Moore, M. *The Balaam Traditions: Their Character and Development*. SBLDS 113. Atlanta: Scholars Press, 1990.
Morgan, D. F. "The So-Called Cultic Calendars in the Pentateuch (Ex. 23:10–19, 34:18–26, Lev. 23, Nu. 28–29, Deut. 16:1–17). A Morphological and Typological Study." Ph.D. diss., Claremont School of Theology, 1974.
Morgenstern, J. *The Ark, the Ephod, and the "Tent of Meeting."* Cincinnati: Hebrew Union College, 1945.
———. "A Chapter in the History of the High Priesthood," *AJSL* 55 (1938) 1–24, 360–77.
———. "The Three Calendars of Ancient Israel," *HUCA* 1 (1924) 13–78; 3 (1926) 77–107; 10 (1935) 1–148.
———. "Trial by Ordeal among the Semites in Ancient Israel," *HUCA Jubilee Volume* (1925) 113–43.
———. "Two Ancient Israelite Agricultural Festivals," *JQR* 8 (1917–18) 39–50.
Mowinckel, S. *Tetrateuch—Pentateuch—Hexateuch. Die Berichte über die Landnahme in den drei altisraelitischen Geschichtswerken*. BZAW 90. Berlin: Töpelmann, 1964.
———. "Der Ursprung der Bileamsage," *ZAW* 48 (1930) 233–71.
Müller, H.-P. "Die aramäische Inschrift von *Deir ʿAllā* und die älteren Bileamsprüche." *ZAW* 94 (1982) 214–44.
———. "Einige alttestamentliche Probleme zur aramäische Inschrift von *Deir ʿAllā*." *ZDPV* 94 (1978) 56–67.
Mullen, E. T. *The Assembly of the Gods: The Divine Council in Canaanite and Early Hebrew Literature*. HSM 24. Chico, Calif.: Scholars Press, 1980.
Murtonen, A. "The Use and Meaning of the Words *L^E^Bareḳ* and *B^E^raka^H^* in the Old Testament," *VT* 9 (1959) 158–77.
Nestlé, E. "Num. 23:19," *ZAW* 28 (1908) 228–29.
Neusner, J. *The Idea of Purity in Ancient Israel*. Leiden: Brill, 1973.
Newing, E. G. "The Rhetoric of Altercation in Numbers 14." In *Perspectives on Language and Text: Essays and Poems in Honor of Francis I. Andersen's Sixtieth Birthday July 28, 1985*. Ed. E. Conrad and E. Newing. Winona Lake, Ind.: Eisenbrauns, 1987. Pp. 211–28.

Nielsen, E. "The Levites in Ancient Israel," *ASTI* 3 (1964) 16–27.
Noordtzij, A. *Numbers.* Bible Student's Commentary. Tr. E. van der Maas. Grand Rapids: Zondervan, 1983.
North, F. "Aaron's Rise in Prestige," *ZAW* 66 (1954) 191–99.
Noth, M. *A History of Pentateuchal Traditions.* Tr. B. W. Anderson. Englwood Cliffs, N.J.: Prentice-Hall, 1981.
———. "Israelitische Stämme zwischen Ammon und Moab," *ZAW* 60 (1944) 11–57.
———. *Die Israelititischen Personennamen im Rahmen der Gemeinsemitischen Namengebung.* BWANT 3/10. Stuttgart: Kohlhammer, 1928.
———. *The Laws in the Pentateuch and Other Essays.* Tr. D. R. Ap-Thomas. Philadelphia: Fortress, 1967.
———. "Num. 21 als Glied der 'Hexateuch' Erzählung," *ZAW* 58 (1940–41) 161–89.
———. *Numbers: A Commentary.* Tr. J. D. Martin. OTL. Philadelphia: Westminster, 1968.
———. *Das System der zwölf Stāmme Israels.* BWANT 4/1. Stuttgart: Kohlhammer, 1930.
———. "Der Wallfahrtsweg zum Sinai," *PJ* 36 (1940) 5–28.
Nyberg, H. S. "Korahs Upror (Num. 16f.)," *SEÅ* 11 (1946) 214–36.
Olávarri, E. "Sondages à "Arôʿer sur l'Arnon," *RB* 72 (1965) 77–94; 76 (1969) 230–59.
Olson, D. T. *The Death of the Old and the Birth of the New: The Framework of the Book of Numbers and the Pentateuch.* BJS 71. Chico, Calif.: Scholars Press, 1985.
Orlinsky, H. M. "Numbers XXVIII 9, 12, 13," *VT* 20 (1970) 500.
———. "*Rābás* for *Šākáb* in Num. 24:9," *JQR* 35 (1944–45) 173–77.
Pákosdy, L. M. von. "Theologische Redaktionsarbeit in der Bileam-Perikope." In *Von Ugarit nach Qumran.* Festschrift for O. Eissfeldt. Ed. J. Hempel and L. Rost. BZAW 77. Berlin: Töpelmann, 1958. Pp. 161–76.
Paradise, J. "A Daughter and Her Father's Property at Nuzi," *JCS* 32 (1980) 189–207.
Parker, I. "The Way of God and the Way of Balaam," *ExpTim* 17 (1905) 45.
Parker, S. B. "Possession trance and prophecy in pre-exilic Israel," *VT* 28 (1978) 271–85.
Paterson, J. A. *Book of Numbers.* SBOT. Leipzig: Hinrichs, 1900.
Patrick, D. *Old Testament Law.* Atlanta: John Knox, 1985.
Pedersen, J. *Israel: Its Life and Culture.* 4 vols. repr. in 2. London: Oxford, 1926–40.
Perles, F. "Zu Numeri 24:23," *ZAW* 29 (1909) 73.

Péter, R. "L'imposition des mains dans l'Ancien Testament," *VT* 27 (1977) 48–55.

Petrie, W. M. F. *Egypt and Israel.* New York: Macmillan, 1923.

———. *Researches in Sinai.* London: Murray, 1906.

Phillips, A. "The Case of the Woodgatherer Reconsidered," *VT* 19 (1969) 125–28.

Porter, J. R. "The Role of Kadesh-barnea in the Narrative of the Exodus," *JTS* 44 (1943) 139–43.

Press, R. "Das Ordal im alten Israel," *ZAW* 51 (1933) 121–40, 227–55.

Rabe, V. W. "The Origins of Prophecy," *BASOR* 221 (1976) 125–28.

Rackman, E. "Jewish Philosophy of Property," *JQR* 67 (1976–77) 65–89.

Rad, G. von. *Old Testament Theology.* Trans. D. Stalker. 2 vols. New York: Harper & Row, 1962, 1965.

———. "The Story about Balaam." In *God at Work in Israel.* Tr. J. Marks. Nashville: Abingdon, 1980.

Rainey, A. F. "The Order of Sacrifices in Old Testament Ritual Texts," *Bib* 51 (1970) 485–98.

Ramsay, G. W. "Speech Forms in Hebrew Law and Prophetic Oracles," *JBL* 96 (1977) 45–58.

Reif, S. C. "A note on a neglected connotation of *ntn*," *VT* 20 (1970) 114–16.

———. "What Enraged Phinehas?" *JBL* 90 (1971) 100–106.

Rendtorff, R. *Die Gesetze in der Priesterschrift: Eine Gattungsgeschichtlichen Untersuchung.* Göttingen: Vandenhoeck & Ruprecht, 1954.

———. "Traditio-historical Method and the Documentary Hypothesis," *Proceedings of the World Congress of Jewish Studies* 5 (1969) 5–11.

———. *The Problem of the Process of Transmission in the Pentateuch.* Tr. J. Scullion. JSOTSup 89. Sheffield: JSOT Press, 1990. (Orig. *Das überlieferungsgeschichtliche Problem des Pentateuch.* BZAW 147. Berlin: de Gruyter, 1977.

———. "The Yahwist as Theologian: Dilemma of Pentateuchal Criticism," *JSOT* 3 (1977) 2–45.

———. "Zur Lage von Jaser," *ZDPV* 76 (1960) 124–35.

Richter, G. "Die Einheitlichkeit der Geschichte von der Rotte Korah," *ZAW* 39 (1921) 123–37.

Riggans, W. *Numbers.* Daily Study Bible. Philadelphia: Westminster, 1983.

Roach, C. C. "The Camp in the Wilderness: A Sermon on Numbers 2:2," *Int* 13 (1959) 49–54.

Robertson, E. "The 'ūrīm and tummīm; what were they?" *VT* 14 (1964) 67–74.

Robinson, G. "The Prohibition of Strange Fire in Ancient Israel," *VT* 28 (1978) 301–17.
Rofé, A. *The Book of Balaam* (Hebrew). Jerusalem: Simor, 1979.
Rost, L. "Fragen um Bileam." *Beiträge zur alttestamentlichen Theologie: Festschrift für Walther Zimmerli zum 70. Geburtstag*. Ed. H. Donner, et al. Göttingen: Vandenhoeck & Ruprecht, 1977. Pp. 377–87.
———. "Zu den Festopfervorschriften von Numeri 28 u. 29," *TLZ* 83 (1958) 329–34.
Rouillard, H. "L'ânesse de Balaam," *RB* 87 (1980) 5–36.
Rowley, H. H. "Zadok and Nehushtan," *JBL* 58 (1939) 113–41.
Ruppert, L. "Das Motiv der Versuchung durch Gott in vordeuteronomistischer Tradition," *VT* 22 (1972) 55–63.
Sabourin, L. "The Biblical Cloud: Terminology and Traditions," *BTB* 4 (1974) 290–311.
Sakenfeld, K. D. "The Problem of Divine Forgiveness in Num. 14," *CBQ* 37 (1975) 317–30.
Sasson, J. M. "A 'Genealogical Convention' in Biblical Chronography?" *ZAW* 90 (1978) 171–85.
———. "Nu. 5 and the Waters of Judgment," *BZ* 16 (1972) 249–51.
Saydon, P. P. "Sin-Offering and Trespass-Offering," *CBQ* 8 (1946) 393–98.
St. Clair, G. "Israel in Camp: A Study," *JTS* 8 (1907) 185–217.
Scharbert, J. "Fluchen und Segnen im Alten Testament," *Bib* 39 (1958) 1–26.
Schedl, C. "Biblische Zahlen unglaubwürdig?" *TPQ* 107 (1959) 58–62.
Schmidt, L. "Die alttestamentliche Bileamüberlieferung," *BZ* 23 (1979) 234–61.
Schmidt, W. "*miškan* als Ausdruck Jerusalemer Kultsprache," *ZAW* 75 (1963) 91–92.
Schottroff, S. *Der altisraelitische Fluchspruch.* WMANT 30. Neukirchen: Kreis Moers, 1969.
Schulz, H. *Leviten im vorstaatlichen Israel und im Mittleren Osten.* Munich: Chr. Kaiser, 1987.
———. *Das Todesricht im Alten Testament.* BZAW 114. Berlin: Töpelmann, 1969.
Schunk, K.-D. *Benjamin. Untersuchungen zur Entstehung und Geschichte eines israelitischen Stammes.* BZAW 86. Berlin: Töpelmann, 1963.
———. "Ophra, Ephron und Ephraim," *VT* 11 (1961) 188–200.
Seebass, H. "Num. xi, xii und die Hypothese des Jahwisten," *VT* 28 (1978) 214–23.
———. "Zu Num. X 33f.," *VT* 14 (1964) 111–13.

Segal, J. B. "The Hebrew Festivals and the Calendar," *JSS* 6 (1961) 74–94.
———. *The Hebrew Passover.* London: SPCK, 1963.
———. "Intercalation and the Hebrew Calendar," *VT* 7 (1957) 250–307.
———. *The Pentateuch: Its Composition and Its Authorship and Other Studies.* Jerusalem: Magnes, 1967.
———. "The Settlement of Manasseh East of the Jordan," *PEFQS* 50 (1918) 124–31.
Sellin, E. O. "Zu Efod und Terafim," *ZAW* 55 (1937) 296–98.
Seybold, K. "Das Herrscherbild des Bileamorakels, Num. 24:15–19," *BZ* 29 (1979) 1–19.
Simons, J. *Geographical and Topographical Texts of the Old Testament.* Leiden: Brill, 1959.
———. "Two Connected Problems Relating to the Israelite Settlement in Transjordan," *PEQ* 79 (1947) 27–39, 87–101.
Simpson, C. A. *The Early Traditions of Israel.* Oxford: Blackwell, 1948.
Smick, E. B, "A Study of the Structure of the Third Balaam Oracle (Num. 24:5–9)." In *The Law and the Prophets: Old Testament Studies in Honor of Oswald T. Allis.* Ed. J. Skilton. Nutley, N.J.: Presbyterian & Reformed, 1974.
Smith, W. R. *The Religion of the Semites.* 2nd ed. London: Black, 1907.
Snaith, N. H. "The Daughters of Zelophehad," *VT* 16 (1966) 124–27.
———. *The Hebrew New Year Festival.* London: SPCK, 1947.
———. *Leviticus and Numbers.* NCBC. London: Nelson, 1967.
———. "A Note on Numbers XVIII 9," *VT* 23 (1973) 373–75.
———. "Numbers XXVIII 9, 11, 13," *VT* 19 (1969) 374.
———. "Sacrifices in the Old Testament," *VT* 7 (1957) 308–17.
———. "The Sin Offering and the Guilt Offering," *VT* 15 (1965) 73–80.
Snijders, L. A. "The Meaning of *'zar'* in the Old Testament," *OTS* 10 (1954) 1–154.
Sonsino, R. *Motive Clauses in Hebrew Law.* SBLDS 45. Chico, Calif.: Scholars Press, 1980.
Speiser, E. A. "Census and Ritual Expiation in Mari and Israel." In *Biblical and Oriental Studies.* Ed. J. J. Finkelstein and M. Greenberg. Philadelphia: Univ. of Pennsylvania Press, 1967. Pp. 171–86.
———. "Unrecognized Dedication," *IEJ* 13 (1963) 69–73.
Stade, B. "Die Eiferopferthora," *ZAW* 15 (1895) 166–78.
Stephens, F. J. "The Ancient Significance of Ṣiṣith," *JBL* 50 (1931) 59–71.
Stevenson, W. R. "Hebrew Olah and Zebach Sacrifices." In *Festschrift für A. Bertholet.* Ed. W. Baumgartner, et al. Tübingen: Mohr, 1950. Pp. 488–97.
Strack, H. L. *Die Bücher Genesis, Exodus, Leviticus und Numeri.* Kurzge-

fasster Kommentar zu den Heiligen Schriften Alten und Neuen Testamentes sowie zu den Apokryphen. Nordlingen: C. H. Beck, 1894.

Sturdy, J. *Numbers.* Cambridge Bible (NEB). New York: Cambridge Univ. Press, 1976.

Sumner, W. A. "Israel's encounters with Edom, Moab, Ammon, Sihon, and Og according to the Deuteronomist," *VT* 18 (1968) 216–28.

Sutcliffe, E. F. "De Unitate Litteraria Num. 22," *Bib* 7 (1926) 3–39.

———. "A Note on Num. 22," *Bib* 18 (1937) 439–42.

Talmon, S. "Divergencies in Calendar Reckoning in Ephraim and Judah," *VT* 8 (1958) 48–74.

Thiersch, H. "Ependytes und Ephod," *ZAW* 53 (1935) 180–85.

Thomas, D. W. "The Word *rōḇaʿ* in Numbers 23:10," *ExpTim* 46 (1934–35) 285.

———. "Some Further Remarks on Unusual Ways of Expressing the Superlative in Hebrew," *VT* 18 (1968) 120–24.

Thompson, H. C. "The Significance of the Term *ʾAsham* in the Old Testament," *TGUOS* 14 (1953) 20–26.

Thompson H. O. "The Ammonite Remains at Khirbet al-Hajjar," *BASOR* 227 (1977) 27–34.

Thompson, R. J. *Moses and the Law in a Century of Criticism Since Graf.* Leiden: Brill, 1970.

———. *Penitence and Sacrifice in Early Israel Outside the Levitical Law: An Examination of the Fellowship Theory of Early Israelite Sacrifice.* Leiden: Brill, 1963.

Tosato, A. "The Literary Structure of the First Two Poems of Balaam (Num. 23:7–10, 18–24)," *VT* 29 (1979) 98–106.

Tucker, G. M. "Covenant Forms and Contract Forms," *VT* 15 (1965) 487–503.

Tunyogi, A. C. "The Rebellions of Israel," *JBL* 81 (1962) 385–90.

———. *The Rebellions of Israel.* Richmond: John Knox, 1969.

Tushingham, A. D. "The Excavations at Dibon (Dhiban) in Moab, the Third Campaign 1952–53," AASOR 40 (1972) 93.

Urie, D. "Officials of the Cult at Ugarit," *PEQ* 80 (1948) 42–47.

Valentin, H. *Aaron. Eine Studie zur vorpriesterschriftlichen Aaron Überlieferung.* Göttingen: Vandenhoeck & Ruprecht, 1978.

van der Kooij. "Book and Script at Deir ʿAlla." *Proceedings, 1989.* Pp. 239–62.

van der Ploeg, J. "Studies in Hebrew Law," *CBQ* 12 (1950) 248–59, 416–27; 13 (1951) 28–43, 164–71, 296–307.

van Goudoever, J. *Biblical Calendars.* Leiden: Brill, 1959.

Van Seters, J. "The Conquest of Sihon's Kingdom: A Literary Examination," *JBL* 91 (1972) 182–97.

———. "Once Again: The Conquest of Sihon's Kingdom," *JBL* 99 (1980) 117–19.
———. "Recent Studies on the Pentateuch: A Crisis in Method," *JAOS* 99 (1979) 663–72.
———. "The terms 'Amorite' and 'Hittite'," *VT* 22 (1972) 64–81.
Vaulx, J. de. *Les Nombres.* SB. Paris: J. Gabalda, 1972.
Vaux, R. de. *Ancient Israel. Its Life and Institutions.* Tr. J. McHugh. 2 vols. London: Darton, Longman and Todd; New York: McGraw-Hill, 1961.
———. "Ark of the Covenant and Tent of Reunion." In *The Bible and the Ancient Near East.* Tr. D. McHugh. Garden City, N.Y.: Doubleday, 1971. Pp. 136–51.
———. *The Early History of Israel.* Tr. D. Smith. Philadelphia: Westminster, 1978.
———. "L'Itinéraire des Israéliens de Cadès aux Plaines de Moab." In *Hommages à André Dupont-Sommer.* Ed. A. Caquot and M. Philonenko. Paris: Librairie d'Amerique et d'Orient, 1971. Pp. 136–51.
———. "Notes d'histoire et de topographie transjordaniennes," *RB* 50 (1941) 16–47.
———. "Le Pays de Canaan," *JAOS* 88 (1968) 23–30.
———. "Reflections on the Present State of Pentateuchal Criticism." In *The Bible and the Ancient Near East.* Tr. D. McHugh. Garden City, N.Y.: Doubleday, 1971. Pp. 31–48.
———. *Studies in Old Testament Sacrifice.* Tr. J. Bourke and R. Potter. Cardiff: Univ. of Wales Press, 1964.
Vermes, G. "The Story of Balaam: The Scriptural Origin of Haggadah." In *Scripture and Tradition in Judaism.* Leiden: Brill, 1955. Pp. 127–77.
Vetter, D. *Seherspruch und Segensschilderung. Ausdruckabsichten und sprachliche Verwirklichungen in den Bileam-Sprüchen von Numeri 23 und 24.* Stuttgart: Calwer Verlag, 1975.
Wagner, S. "Die Kundschaftergeschichten im Alten Testament," *ZAW* 76 (1964) 255–69.
———. "Offenbarungsphänomenologische Elemente in der Bileam-Geschichte von Num. 22–24," *Theologische Versuche* 5 (1975) 11–31.
Walsh, J. T. "From Egypt to Moab: A Source Critical Analysis of the Wilderness Itinerary," *CBQ* 39 (1977) 20–33.
Walters, S. D. "Prophecy in Mari and Israel," *JBL* 89 (1970) 78–81.
Wanke, G. *Die Zionstheologie der Korachiten.* BZAW 97. Berlin: Töpelmann, 1966.
Waterman, L. "Some Determining Factors in the Northward Progress of Levi," *JAOS* 57 (1937) 375–80.

Watson, J. *Leviticus-Numbers.* Expositor's Bible. New York: Armstrong, 1903.
Wefing, S. "Beobachtungen zum Ritual mit der roten Kuh (Num 19:1–10a)," *ZAW* 93 (1981) 341–64.
Weinberg, J. P. "Das Beit 'Abot im Jh. v.u.Z.," *VT* 23 (1973) 400–414.
Weingreen, J. "The Case of the Daughters of Zelophehad," *VT* 16 (1966) 518–22.
———. "The Case of the Woodgatherer (Numbers XV 32–36)," *VT* 16 (1966) 361–64.
Weippert, H. "Das geographische System der Stämme Israels," *VT* 23 (1973) 76–89.
Weippert, M. *The Settlement of the Israelite Tribes in Palestine.* SBT 2/21. London: SCM, 1971.
———. "The Balaam Text from *Deir ʿAllā* and the Study of the Old Testament." In *Proceedings, 1989.* Pp. 151–84.
Weisman, Z. "The Biblical Nazirite, Its Types and Roots," *Tarbiz* 36 (1967) 207–20.
Wellhausen, J. *Prolegomena to the History of Ancient Israel.* Tr. J. S. Black and A. Menzies. Gloucester, Mass.: Peter Smith, 1973 .
Wenham, G. J. *Numbers: An Introduction and Commentary.* TOTC. Downers Grove: Inter-Varsity, 1981.
Wenham, J. W. "Large Numbers in the Old Testament," *TynBul* 18 (1967) 19–53.
Westphal, G. "Aaron und die Aaroniden," *ZAW* 26 (1906) 201–30.
Wharton, J. A. "The Command to Bless: An Exposition of Numbers 22:41–23:25," *Int* 13 (1959) 37–48.
Whybray, R. N. *The Making of the Pentateuch: A Methodological Study.* JSOTSup 53. Sheffield: JSOT Press, 1985.
Williams, R. J. *Hebrew Syntax.* 2nd ed. Toronto: Univ. of Toronto Press, 1976.
Wilson, R. R. "Between 'Azel' and 'Azel,' Interpreting the Biblical Genealogies," *BA* 42 (1979) 11–22.
———. *Genealogy and History in the Biblical World.* New Haven: Yale Univ. Press, 1977.
———. "Early Israelite Prophecy," *Int* 32 (1978) 3–16.
———. "The Old Testament Genealogies in Recent Research," *JBL* 94 (1965) 169–89.
Wiseman, D. J. "Flying Serpents," *TynBul* 23 (1972) 108–10.
Wright, G. E. "The Levites in Deuteronomy," *VT* 4 (1954) 325–30.
Wright, G. R. H. "The Bronze Age Temple at Amman," *ZAW* 78 (1966) 350–56.
Wüst, M. *Untersuchungen zu den siedlungsgeographischen Texten des Alten Testaments.* Vol. I: *Ostjordanland.* Wiesbaden: Reichert, 1975.

Yahuda, A. S. "The Name of Balaam's Homeland," *JBL* 64 (1945) 547–51.

Zannoi, A. E. "Balaam: International Seer/Wizard Prophet," *St. Luke's Journal of Theology* 22 (1978) 5–19.

Zohar, N. "Repentance and Purification: The Significance and Semantics of *ḥṭ't* in the Pentateuch," *JBL* 107 (1988) 609–18.

Zuckschwerdt, E. "Zur literarischen Vorgeschichte des priesterlichen Nazir-Gesetzes (Num 6:1–8)," *ZAW* 88 (1976) 191–205.

TEXT AND COMMENTARY

I. PREPARATION FOR DEPARTURE (1:1–10:10)

These chapters deal with the Hebrews' preparation to leave Mt. Sinai for the land of promise. Since the events recounted here take place at Sinai, these chapters link with the material that has gone before in the books of Exodus and Leviticus.[1] The fact that the setup of the camp is given makes it clear that this material narrates the final preparation for departure, which occurs in what follows.

At first glance these chapters may seem to be a miscellany, but closer attention reveals that the central theme around which they turn is holiness.[2] Although on one level these chapters simply narrate preparations to leave Sinai, on another level they show the importance of holiness in the camp (e.g., ch. 2), in dealing with the tabernacle (e.g., chs. 3–4; 5:1–4), and with various incidents in the life of the people (e.g., 5:5–10, 11–31).

One may divide this unit into subsections in various ways. In this commentary the division comes between chs. 6 and 7, for ch. 1 begins with a chronological indicator (v. 1), ch. 6 ends with a benediction (vv. 22–27), ch. 7 also begins with a chronological indicator (v. 1), and 10:10 concludes with the statement *I am Yahweh your God,* a typical concluding formula. Further, 10:11 begins with a new chronological note.

That this unit has sources is undeniable. Those who adhere to the so-called documentary hypothesis along lines classically set down by J. Wellhausen would agree that Numbers comes from the P source. Other less hypothetical sources may underlie 1:1–10:10, such as the lists of

1. This link is also seen in that, in Hebrew, the book begins with a *waw*-consecutive construction, which is dependent (at least supposedly) on a previous verb (i.e., in Leviticus) for its meaning; cf. GKC, § 49b n. 1.

2. See B. S. Childs, *Introduction to the Old Testament as Scripture* (Philadelphia: Fortress, 1979), p. 196.

names and of tribes, census lists, and legal enactments (or narratives about such enactments) found in the present text.

A. MATTERS CONCERNING THE PEOPLE AND THE CAMP (1:1–6:27)

1. THE CENSUSES AND THE ARRANGEMENTS OF THE MARCH (1:1–4:49)

The first subsection deals with God's people and their camp. In everything they are to be a holy nation. The first four chapters deal with the selection of Moses' helpers, the first lay census, the marching order, and two Levitical censuses.

a. First Lay Census (1:1–54)

(1) The Leaders (1:1–16)

1 *And Yahweh spoke to Moses in the wilderness of Sinai, in the tent of meeting, on the first day*[1] *of the second month in the second year after the exodus from the land of Egypt, saying,*

2 *"Calculate the total of all the congregation of the children of Israel, as regards their clans, as regards their fathers' houses, according to the number of their names, every male, individually*

3 *from twenty years old upward, all in Israel going out to the army, you will number them by their companies, you and Aaron.*

4 *And with you shall be one man for each tribe,*[2] *each man head of his father's house.*

5 *And these are the names of the men who will stand with you: From Reuben, Elizur the son of Shedeur;*

6 *from Simeon, Shelumiel the son of Zurishaddai;*

7 *from Judah, Nahshon the son of Amminadab;*

8 *from Issachar, Nathanel the son of Zuar;*

9 *from Zebulun, Eliab the son of Helon;*

10 *from the sons of Joseph: from Ephraim, Elishama the son of Ammihud; from Manasseh, Gamaliel the son of Pedahzur;*

1. MT has no word for "day"; Biblical Hebrew commonly omits such terms after numerals (GKC, § 134n).

2. *'îš 'îš lammaṭṭeh* expresses the distributive thought, "one man for each tribe." *'îš* is also used distributively in the next clause: *'îš rō'š lᵉḇêṯ-'ᵃḇōṯāyw hû'*, "each man the head of his father's house"; cf. GKC, § 124d.

11 *from Benjamin, Abidan the son of Gideoni;*
12 *from Dan, Ahiezer the son of Ammishaddai;*
13 *from Asher, Pegiel the son of Ochran;*
14 *from Gad, Eliasaph the son of Deuel;*[3]
15 *from Naphtali, Ahira the son of Enan."*
16 *These are the ones called*[4] *from the congregation, exalted ones*[5] *from their fathers' tribes, heads of the clans of Israel.*

1 This verse gives the basic setting for what follows: who said it, to whom it was said, where it was said, and when it was said. First and foremost, these words are the words spoken by Yahweh himself to Moses the mediator. The plan was not one that Moses worked out, but one delivered to him by the revelation of God.

wilderness (Heb. *miḏbār*). This translation (so AV, RV, RSV, etc.) seems preferable to "desert" (NIV). The latter connotes a land devoid of life and water, and this is not always the meaning of the Hebrew word, which refers to three kinds of country: pastureland (e.g., Josh. 2:22; Ps. 65:13 [Eng. 12]), uninhabited land (e.g., Job 38:26; Jer. 2:24; 9:1), and large tracts of such land (e.g., "the wilderness of Judah," Josh. 15:61–62). Cities and towns could be located in the *miḏbār* (e.g., Josh. 15:61–62; Isa. 42:11).[6]

Sinai. The people were still at the foot of the holy mountain (see Exod. 19:1). The location of Mt. Sinai is debated among scholars. The

3. Here LXX reads *Ragouēl,* presupposing Heb. *r^{e}ʿûʾēl* instead of MT *d^{e}ʿûʾēl.* In Hebrew the *d* and *r* are quite similar, and are thus easily confused. Since elsewhere MT has Deuel (7:42, 47; 10:20; but cf. 2:14), MT should be retained here.

4. The Ketib is *q^{e}rîʾê,* the Qere is *q^{e}rûʾê.* The latter is a masc. pl. passive construct participle from *qārāʾ,* "to summon." An adj. *qārîʾ* is found in the pl. *(q^{e}rîʾê),* which is the same as the Qere in this verse. Both Ketib and Qere may be by-forms of *qārîʾ*, pl. construct *q^{e}rîʾê.* See BDB, p. 896b; Gray, p. 9. The construct (genitive) relationship here may express origin, or it may be a partitive genitive; cf. GKC, § 128i.

5. The word *naśîʾ* has often been taken as one of the terms marking the P stratum (cf. Driver, *Introduction,* p. 134). This kind of argumentation is at least in doubt in the present case in the light of the probable discovery of the term *na-se,* "a ruler," at Ebla in the 3rd millennium B.C.; cf. M. Dahood, "Ebla, Ugarit, and the Bible," in G. Pettinato, *The Archives of Ebla: An Empire Inscribed in Clay* (Garden City, N.Y.: Doubleday, 1981), pp. 278–79; also K. A. Kitchen, *The Bible and Its World* (Downers Grove: InterVarsity, 1977), p. 50.

6. E. S. Kalland, *TWOT,* I:181; Wenham, p. 57; Noordtzij, p. 18.

traditional site is in the southern Sinai Peninsula at Jebel Mûsā, which is part of a short ridge of granite, about 2½ mi. long, with Ras eṣ-ṣafṣafeh at the northwest (about 6,500 ft. high) and Jebel Mûsā at the southeast (about 7,500 ft. high). Since Mt. Sinai is also called Horeb in the OT, some identify Jebel Mûsā with Sinai and Ras-eṣ-ṣafṣafeh with Horeb. The probability is that Sinai and Horeb are synonyms. It is also possible that the author has the whole granite ridge in mind here.[7]

Yahweh is said to have spoken *in the tent of meeting (bᵉ'ōhel mô'ēḏ)*. The word *mô'ēḏ* is derived from a verb meaning "to appoint" *(yā'aḏ)*. This tent may therefore be either the place "appointed" by God or the place of "appointment" with God (possibly both).[8] The tabernacle (*miškān,* from *šāḵan,* "to dwell") is a tent shrine, which the Hebrews thought of as the temporary abode of God.[9] The tent of meeting may have preceded the tabernacle (see, e.g., Exod. 33:7, which refers to a time before the tabernacle was built).[10] The primary description of the Israelite tent shrine is found in Exod. 25–40, where the tent shrine is called the "tent of meeting" *('ōhel mô'ēḏ)* 32 times and the "tabernacle" *(miškān)* 49 times. These references do not seem to distinguish between these terms, and passages such as Exod. 39:39 and Num. 3:38 suggest that the terms were considered synonymous at the time these books received their final form. The probability is, then, that the function and place of an earlier tent shrine (the tent of meeting) was absorbed into that of the tabernacle. It is at least possible that the two shrines coexisted for a time, but that either name may have been used for the tent shrine by the time of the final editing of the Pentateuch.

A great deal of ink has been spilled over whether the tent of meeting (tabernacle) ever existed or was an idealization of the temple

7. See further G. E. Wright, "Sinai, Mount," *IDB,* IV:376–78; G. I. Davies, *The Way of the Wilderness,* SOTSMS 5 (Cambridge: Cambridge Univ. Press, 1979), pp. x–xii; J. Day, ed., *The Oxford Bible Atlas,* 3rd ed. (New York: Oxford Univ. Press, 1984), pp. 58–59. The matter of the location of Sinai is not settled and the position taken above is tentative. For a discussion of modern scholarly debate on the subject, see Davies, *Wilderness,* pp. 63–69.

8. J. P. Lewis, *TWOT,* I:387–89.

9. V. P. Hamilton, *TWOT,* II:925–26 (with bibliography).

10. "And Moses used to take [*yiqqaḥ,* past frequentative] the tent and pitch it outside the camp at a distance, and he called it the tent of meeting. And anyone who would inquire of Yahweh would go out to the tent of meeting which was outside the camp." On the verb *yiqqaḥ* see Williams, *Syntax,* § 168; GKC, § 107g; see also the verbs in Num. 11:16–30; 12:4–10.

projected back into the wilderness period. The critical opinion of many scholars has shifted from the day when J. Wellhausen offered the critical orthodoxy: "hitherto it had only been *asserted* that the tabernacle rests on a historical fiction. In reality it is proved."[11] Today, on the basis of the archeological discoveries of prefabricated tent shrines in ancient Egypt, and on a general reassessment of the monolinear evolutionary tenets of much of earlier scholarship, one cannot deny the possibility that the tabernacle could have existed in the Mosaic age.[12]

The time of God's speaking is placed at *the first day of the second month in the second year after the exodus from the land of Egypt.* The chronological note at Num. 10:11 marks the twentieth day of the same month; that is, the time frame of 1:1–10:10 is nineteen days. The events of 7:1–10:10 take place one month earlier, on the day in which the tabernacle was set up. The Hebrews arrived at Sinai on the third new moon after the Exodus (Exod. 19:1), so they had been at the mountain some eleven months by the first day of the second month in the second year.

the exodus (*ṣē'ṯām,* lit., "their going out"). Two theories on the date of the Exodus are popular: the early (ca. 1445 B.C.) and the late (ca. 1290 B.C.). On balance the archeological evidence and historical data may be said to favor the later date, but the case is far from proved.[13]

11. J. Wellhausen, *Prolegomena to the History of Ancient Israel,* tr. A. Menzies and J. S. Black (1885; repr. New York: Scribner's, 1957), p. 39; also C. H. Toy, *History of the Religion of Israel* (Boston: Unitarian Sunday School Society, 1882), p. 39; I. Benzinger, "Tabernacle," *Encyclopaedia Biblica* (London: Black, 1903), cols. 4861–75; A. Bentzen, *Introduction to the Old Testament* (Copenhagen: Gad, 1949), II:34; and many others.

12. See K. A. Kitchen, "Some Egyptian Background to the Old Testament," *TynBul* 5–6 (1960) 7–11; R. K. Harrison, *Introduction,* pp. 403–8; see also B. Childs, *The Book of Exodus: A Critical, Theological Commentary,* OTL (Philadelphia: Westminster, 1974), pp. 529–52, for an excellent discussion of the whole matter.

13. One of the more recent attempts to argue for a 15th-century date is J. Bimson, *Redating the Exodus and Conquest,* rev. ed. (Sheffield: Almond Press, 1981); a more traditional defense of the early date may be found in G. Archer, *A Survey of Old Testament Introduction,* rev. ed. (Chicago: Moody, 1974), pp. 223–34 (this summary is rather strident at points). For a defense of the 13th-century date see, e.g., R. K. Harrison, *Introduction,* pp. 175–77, 315–25; also K. Kitchen, *Ancient Orient and Old Testament* (Downers Grove: InterVarsity Press, 1966), pp. 57–75. For two reviews of the literature on the subject, see H. H. Rowley, *From Joseph to Joshua* (London: Oxford, 1950); T. L. Thompson, "The Joseph and Moses Narratives," in *Israelite and Judaean History,* ed. J. H. Hayes and J. M. Miller, OTL (Philadelphia: Westminster, 1977), pp. 149–66, esp. 150–54.

2 *Calculate the total* (*śeʾû ʾeṯ-rōʾš,* lit., "lift up the head"). The term *head (rōʾš)* is used metaphorically for the "top" (e.g., of a mountain, Gen. 8:5). The "sum" is the top amount of cumulative numbers, and so the meaning of "total" is not far from the spatial meaning of the word. The idiom is found elsewhere (Exod. 30:12; Lev. 5:24; Num. 1:49; 4:2, 22; 5:7; 26:2; 31:26, 49; Ps. 119:160; 139:17).

Congregation (ʿēḏâ) — this term is related to the verb *yāʿaḏ*, "to appoint," and the noun *môʿēḏ*, "meeting." It is found 149 times in the OT, just over half of these occurrences in the book of Numbers. Depending on the context, the exact make-up of the *ʿēḏâ* varies. In the present verse the congregation is the whole people of Israel — men, women and children.[14] In other contexts, specific groups of Israelites, which nonetheless represent the whole people, are meant.[15] In places where *ʿēḏâ* means the whole people of Israel, it is synonymous with the term *qāhāl* ("the assembly"; 10:7), but not when *ʿēḏâ* takes on the narrower meaning of a representative group.[16] The legislative function of the congregation may be seen in Num. 35:12, 24–25 as well as in Josh. 9:18–19; 20:6, 9; 22:16; Judg. 21:10, 22; 1 K. 12:20.

clans (mišpeḥôṯ) and *fathers' houses (bêṯ ʾāḇôṯ)* are tribal subdivisions, the larger being given first. The *father's house* comes close to what might be described as a nuclear family: mother, father, brothers, sisters. The *clan* is a wider term, including other blood relatives as well. The widest term is "tribe" *(maṭṭeh, šēḇeṭ).* Of course, the usage of all these terms varies in different contexts.[17]

14. E.g., Exod. 16:1; Num. 17:11 (Eng. 16:46); 20:1, 7–8; 27:17; 31:16; 32:4; Josh. 22:16–18, 20.

15. E.g., adult male Israelites: Num. 14:1–4; 31:26, 28, 43; tribal leaders in an assembly met for governmental decisions: Exod. 12:3, 21; Num. 8:7; Josh. 22:13, 16; Judg. 20:12, 27; 21:10, 13, 22.

16. J. Milgrom, "Priestly Terminology and the Political and Social Structures of Pre-Monarachic Israel," *JQR* 69 (1978) 65–81. The earlier study of B. Luther attempted to use the terms *ʿēḏâ* and *qāhāl* as tools to sort out strata within the P document; see "'Kahal' und 'edah' als Hilsmittel der Quellenscheidung im Priesterkodex und in der Chronik," *ZAW* 56 (1938) 44–63. It is doubtful whether Luther made his case here, although he does demonstrate that *ʿēḏâ* in its wider sense and *qāhāl* are synonyms. This whole section owes much to Milgrom's article, which was reprinted in his book *Studies in Cultic Theology and Terminology,* SJLA 36 (Leiden: Brill, 1983), pp. 1–17.

17. See the lexica (esp. BDB, *HALAT*) under these words; see also T. C. Mitchell, "Family, Household, Old Testament," *NBD,* 2nd ed. (Wheaton: Tyndale, 1982), pp. 370–71; N. Gottwald, *The Tribes of Yahweh: A Sociology of the Religion of Liberated Israel, 1250-1050* B.C.E. (Maryknoll, N.Y.: Orbis, 1979), pp. 257–70, 285–315.

individually (*l^egulg^elōṯām,* lit., "with regard to their skulls"; viz., "with regard to themselves"). Since each person has only one skull, the idiom comes to refer to each individual.[18] The command is to count the males of Israel, by clans, families, and right down to the individual names. The census is to be as complete as practical.

3 The census is further defined by limiting it to males from twenty years of age and older — all, that is, who were eligible to serve in the army. The word *army* (*ṣāḇā'*; cf. 31:48, RSV) can mean "host" (2:4, RSV), or "war" or "battle" (e.g., 3:3–4, RSV). Most scholars have seen the groups of Israelites designated as *ṣāḇā'* as military groups.[19] Ch. 4 consistently uses the term to refer to the community of Levites serving in the tent of meeting (e.g., vv. 1, 23, 30). It is probable, however, that even in this matter the military image is to the fore, since the chief duty of the Levites is "guard duty" *(šāmar mišmereṯ),* as will be seen, e.g., in 1:53, 3:8, etc. Since the military usage seems more common in Hebrew and the cognate languages, and since the age of an able-bodied male (twenty years) is included in the census instruction,[20] the least that can be said is that the pattern used for this census was a military pattern. No doubt such a numbering would be invaluable in military planning.

The census commanded here is not the first one during the stay at Sinai. Exod. 30:11–16 gives a command that when a census is taken, each one counted should be liable for a half-shekel assessment (to be used in the building of the tabernacle; see Exod. 38:25–28). One might simply assume that the two censuses were separate were it not that the total of persons counted in 38:26 is 603,550, precisely the total given for the census in Num. 1:46. These identical totals cannot merely be coincidental. These data have led some scholars to conclude that the command to take the census is given in Exod. 30:11–16 and that the census is not carried out until Num. 1.[21]

Exodus 30:11 has no command to take a census immediately. The command is that, "when you calculate the total of the children of Israel"

18. See also vv. 18, 20, 22; 3:47; 1 Chr. 23:3, 24; BDB, p. 166a.

19. See, e.g., the commentaries of Wenham, p. 58; Snaith, p. 121; Noth, p. 20.

20. See, KB, p. 790b; BDB, p. 838b; J. E. Hartley, *TWOT,* I:750–51. According to Lev. 27:3 age twenty began the most valued time of life. The monetary valuation on a male between the ages of twenty and sixty is the highest of any person. It seems reasonable that twenty years was the earliest age at which a young male was eligible for military service.

21. See, e.g., Noordtzij, pp. 18–19.

(i.e., when that time should come), then there must be a half-shekel redemption price paid for each person twenty and older who is counted. The text does not say that this counting was carried out immediately, but 38:25–28 does state that 603,550 people paid 100 talents and 1,775 shekels of silver for the fitting of the tabernacle.[22]

Although biblical data on the chronology of this specific period are limited, there are difficulties in the assumption that the censuses of Exodus and Numbers are the same. Num. 1:1 is dated one month after the tabernacle was erected (cf. Exod. 40:2). Exod. 38 indicates that the first census was completed and the redemption price levied in order to make fittings for the tabernacle. That census, of course, had to take place before the tabernacle was erected. Thus, on the chronology of the text itself, the two cannot be seen as the same event. The census of Exod. 30 was concluded at least one month before the one in Num. 1 was commanded, and probably some time before that. It is hard to believe that the final editor of the Pentateuch would not have smoothed out such differences if the intent had been to see the census command of Exod. 30 carried out in Num. 1.

Another approach to the problem assumes that Exod. 30 and 38 are later insertions into the text derived from the book of Numbers or elsewhere. For example, Budd argues this way and states that Exod. 30 and 38:21–31 could have been from the hand of the author of Numbers.[23]

It is, of course, true that the Pentateuch was edited together at a period after the events it narrates. It is also true that the Pentateuch is not arranged consistently in chronological order (see, e.g., Num. 1:1; 7:1). Although theoretically the kind of editing Budd proposes may have occurred, one cannot demonstrate that it never took place. To say that Exod. 38:21–31 is an insertion based on material in Numbers does not necessitate any greater distance from the events narrated than a time after the material in Num. 4 (supposedly some time between the first and nineteenth days of the second year after the Exodus), although it may be later than this time by an indeterminate period.

What does the final form of the text wish the reader to make of these two obviously related but separate censuses? They are similar in that they

22. 100 talents = 300,000 shekels (3,000 shekels per talent) plus 1,775 shekels = 301,775 shekels or 603,550 half-shekels.

23. Budd, p. 9. Of course, Budd is not alone in seeing Exod. 30 and 38:21–31 as supplementary to the text; see also M. Noth, *Exodus: A Commentary*, tr. J. Bowden, OTL (Philadelphia: Westminster, 1962), pp. 234, 278; J. P. Hyatt, *Exodus*, NCBC (Grand Rapids: Eerdmans, 1980), pp. 291, 331.

give totals of Israelite males twenty years of age and up.[24] But the purpose of the two seems different. The first has a religious purpose (a levy for the tabernacle), and the second an administrative or military purpose. The technique was also different. The first census reports only the grand total. The census in Num. 1 numbers the people by tribe, clan, and father's house, in addition to a count of individual names. That twelve leaders are appointed to help Moses and Aaron in this numbering indicates the much greater scope of this census. The total figure of the census checked with that of the earlier one, so that, although these countings were distinct, they were so close in time that they were related. Data from the first were probably used in the second. They stand as two halves of one act, the religious half (Exodus) and the military or administrative half (Numbers). Perhaps to remind the Israelites of the religious dimension of all life — even the supposedly administrative details — Aaron is included in the census of Num. 1.

4 Twelve men were appointed to assist Moses and Aaron in the work of counting. God appointed one man from each tribe. Each one of these men was (at least) the head of his father's house, the more immediate family group.

5–16 These verses are nominal sentences that emphasize the names of the men involved. The nominal clause or sentence usually emphasizes the subject and expresses a constant condition.[25] The function of these leaders, who are called *exalted ones* in v. 16, is to lead the tribes, especially on the march (see 2:3–31; 10:11–38).

The names of these same leaders are found again in 2:3–31; 7:12–83; and 10:14–27.[26] Although the names are the same in these later lists, the order of the tribes is different. Numbers has seven lists of the Israelite tribes (1:5–16, 20–46; 2:3–31; 7:12–83; 10:14–27; 13:4–16; 26:5–62), none of which includes the tribe of Levi.

The listings of the tribes seem to have three different orders. Those narratives dealing with the choice of leaders (1:5–16 and 13:4–16) have similar orders,[27] apparently based on a genealogical principle: the sons of Leah (minus Levi), followed by the sons of Rachel, followed by the sons

24. Although the census of Exod. 30 and 38 does not state that it was of *males,* the total of people counted is the same as that in Num. 1:46, which does state that it was a total of males twenty years of age and older.

25. Cf. Davidson, *Syntax,* § 104; GKC, § 141.

26. Num. 13:4–16 has a list of different leaders, and 34:19–29 has a partial list.

27. On the order of 13:8–10, see the commentary below on these verses; also see Gray, p. 136; Noth, pp. 98, 103.

of the two handmaidens Zilpah and Bilhah (the last in a flexible order).[28] In the census lists (1:20–46 and 26:5–62) Gad, the son of Zilpah (Leah's handmaiden), takes the place of Leah's son Levi. The census list of 1:20–46 (followed in most respects by that of ch. 26) is set up to facilitate the division of the Israelites into four camps of three tribes each (as is accomplished in ch. 2). If the order of the old list in 1:5–16 were followed the result would be four camps (L = Leah's sons; R = Rachel's sons; HL = sons of Leah's handmaid; HR = sons of Rachel's handmaid):

Reuben (L)	Issachar (L)	Manasseh (R)	Asher (HL)
Simeon (L)	Zebulun (L)	Benjamin (R)	Gad (HL)
Judah (L)	Ephraim (R)	Dan (HR)	Naphtali (HR)

The sons of Rachel are thus split into two camps. If, however, one moves Gad up to the third place, as is done in the census list of 1:20–46, the following is the result:

Reuben	Judah	Ephraim	Dan
Simeon	Issachar	Manasseh	Asher
Gad	Zebulun	Benjamin	Naphtali

The camps are broken into two Leah groups, one Rachel group, and one handmaidens group. The marching order (2:3–31; 7:12–83; 10:14–27) maintains the same basic four-group structure, except that pride of place on the east side of the tabernacle is given to the Judah-Issachar-Zebulun group.[29]

Scholars have been divided on the question of which form of the list is original (i.e., presumably, which form is archetypal, the one from which all the others have been derived — not simply the first in order of appearance). Noth posits that ch. 26 is the original form, while Mayes argues for the list in 1:5–16.[30] In addition to being captive to other critical

28. The sons of Leah: Reuben, Simeon, (Levi), Judah, Issachar, Zebulun; the sons of Rachel: Joseph (i.e., Manasseh and Ephraim), Benjamin; the sons of Zilpah (Leah's handmaiden): Asher, Gad; the sons of Bilhah (Rachel's handmaiden): Dan, Naphtali.

29. This reconstruction owes much to the discussions in D. Kellermann, *Die Priesterschrift von Numeri 1,1 bis 10,10,* BZAW 120 (Berlin: de Gruyter, 1970), pp. 11–17; also R. de Vaux, *The Early History of Israel,* tr. D. Smith (Philadelphia: Westminster, 1978), pp. 723–27; and A. D. H. Mayes, *Israel in the Period of the Judges,* SBT 2/29 (London: SCM, 1974), pp. 16–22.

30. M. Noth, *Das System der zwölf Stämme Israels,* BWANT IV/1 (1930), pp. 29ff.; A. D. H. Mayes, *Israel,* pp. 18–20.

presuppositions,[31] these views presuppose that all the lists derived from one original list in an "official" order. This assumption is not necessary. It seems as likely that, from ancient times, different orders existed for different purposes. The final form of the text reflects these different orders, and we have no objective way of getting behind this text. Therefore, 1:5–16 is original only in the sense that it comes first in the book.[32]

The list of names in vv. 5–15 contains quite a few theophoric elements (i.e., elements relating to God): *'ēl* (God, 9 times), *šadday* (Almighty [?],[33] 3 times), *ṣûr* (Rock, 3 times), *'āḇ* (Father, 2 times), *'āḥ* (Brother, 2 times). For many years Gray's approach to this list has been the standard: "several of the names are unquestionably ancient, but the *list* is certainly unhistorical."[34] By contrast, Noth sees the list as an old traditional list of names that goes back to the time after the conquest.[35] Each one argues diligently for his own point of view on the basis of which kinds of grammatical constructions are found in "early" or "late" names, and which names have extrabiblical parallels in early and late periods of Hebrew history. From a literary perspective, however, it is very difficult to construct valid arguments for the date of a piece of literature in terms of vocabulary of any kind, especially proper names. Early names could be put into a late list by an editor. Furthermore, one can draw parallels only from the extant literature. What fraction of ancient Near Eastern literature has been discovered, and what fraction of what has been discovered has been deciphered? The argument from silence is a weak argument, which may be overturned by the next spade of dirt from the Near East. Nothing prohibits any of the names found in this list from appearing in a document of the late 2nd or early 1st millennium B.C., but there is also no proof that the list is ancient.[36]

31. For example, Noth's view is really dependent on the documentary approach to the biblical literature; see Mayes, *Israel,* p. 18.

32. For another view, cf. Mayes, *Israel,* p. 20. For further discussion see D. T. Olson, *Death of the Old,* pp. 55–70.

33. The term *šadday* goes back at least as far as the LXX's *pantokratōr* ("all-powerful"). Many scholars, such as Albright and Walker, have rejected this translation. See W. F. Albright, "The Names Shaddai and Abram," *JBL* 54 (1935) 173–193; M. Walker, "A New Interpretation of the Divine Name 'Shaddai,'" *ZAW* 72 (1960) 64–66. V. P. Hamilton, *TWOT,* II 907.

34. Gray, p. 6.

35. Noth, pp. 18–19.

36. Kellermann (*Priesterschrift,* pp. 155–59) shows the tenuousness of some of the evidence. He opts for a late date for much of the material in the list; see also the excellent summary in Budd, pp. 4–6.

Both Noth and de Vaux have stated (but not explained in any detail) that 1:5–15 (or 16) sits awkwardly in its context. This awkwardness, they claim, marks the list as an insertion in a later context.[37] That a list of names is a free-standing composition that may be eliminated without doing a great deal of damage to the context is true. The same could be said of most lists both inside and outside the Bible. In fact, the text proceeds quite smoothly: God commands Moses and Aaron to take the census (vv. 2–3), God tells Moses (and Aaron) that twelve leaders will assist (v. 4), God gives Moses and Aaron the names of the men he has chosen to assist them (vv. 5–15), and a concluding formula rounds off the section (v. 16). Much of the so-called roughness of the section may be attributed to the nominal sentences in which it is written, and which are, by nature, rather terse.

16 These men, chosen by God to help with the census and lead the tribes, are described in three terms: *called, exalted,* and *head.* These persons are called out by God and chosen by him. They are also *exalted ones from their fathers' tribes (nᵉśîʾê maṭṭôṯ ʾᵃḇôṯām).* This expression indicates that the divine choice of these men exalted them from the tribes of their fathers (i.e., their ancestors). The phrase is unique. E. A. Speiser held that the term *exalted one* (*nāśîʾ*, from *nāśāʾ*, "to lift up") is a technical term for one who has been elevated in the assembly or elected to serve.[38] This may well form the background of this technical term, although it is God who does the electing here.

The function of these men who were called and exalted was to be *heads of the clans of Israel.* The word *clans* here is not *mišpᵉḥôṯ* (as in 1:2), but *ʾalᵉp̱ê* (lit., "thousands"). That *ʾelep̱* may mean "company, clan," is shown by Judg. 6:12, which states that Gideon's *ʾelep̱* (clan) is the weakest in Manasseh.[39] Thus the *ʾelep̱* may be equivalent to the *mišpᵉḥâ* in v. 2, but we do not know the exact size. One could imagine that the *ʾelep̱* was larger than the father's house and smaller than the (father's) tribe. These leaders were to exercise their function by, first, assembling the people for the census (1:18); second, leading in the encampment and departure of Israel (e.g., 2:3; 10:14); and, third, spying out the land of Canaan (although this was a different specific group, 13:4).

37. Noth, p. 18; de Vaux, *Early History,* p. 724. The two do not agree in their dating of this list, however.

38. E. A. Speiser, "The Background and Function of the Biblical *Nāśîʾ*," *CBQ* 25 (1963) 111–17.

39. See the excursus below on the large numbers in the census lists.

(2) The Census Itself (1:17–47)

Numbers 1:17–46 contains the story of the first lay census. The story has been prefaced by the appointment of leaders to help in the process (vv. 4–16). The passage is introduced in vv. 17–19, followed by the heart of the passage, the census list itself in vv. 20–43. The passage closes with a summary in vv. 44–46. V. 47 is a summary statement about the Levites' census and forms a transition to vv. 48–54. The narrative passages that surround the list serve only to frame it.

(a) Introduction (1:17–19)

17 *And Moses and Aaron took*[1] *these men who had been designated by name,*

18 *and they assembled the whole congregation on the first day of the second month, and they set down their family ancestry*[2] *according to their fathers' houses, by the number of names, from twenty years of age and up, one by one.*

19 *As Yahweh had commanded Moses, so he numbered them in the wilderness of Sinai.*

The verb indicates that the leaders fulfilled God's command to number themselves with regard to their tribal connections. Noth takes the verb to refer to the entering of the names in a register; this, although possible, is speculative.[3]

Some scholars have posited that v. 19a *(As Yahweh had commanded Moses)* should be connected to the end of v. 18 rather than starting a new thought.[4] Generally this formula concludes sections rather than

1. The sing. verb *wayyiqaḥ* agrees in gender and number with the grammatical subject nearest to it. Subsequent verbs are in the pl. (as here in *niqq^{e}ḇû, hiqhîlû, wayyiṯyal^{e}ḏû*); see Davidson, *Syntax,* § 114b; GKC, § 146f. Other examples of this common phenomenon are found in Gen. 7:7; 9:23; 21:32; 24:50, 55; 31:14; 44:14; Num. 12:1; Judg. 5:1; 8:21; 1 Sam. 11:15; 18:3; 27:8, etc.

2. The verb rendered *they set down their family ancestry (hiṯyālaḏ)* is a denominative verb from *tôl^{e}ḏôṯ,* "family history" (cf. vv. 20, 22, 24, etc.).

3. Noth, p. 20; cf. the Eng. versions: AV "declared their pedigree" (cf. BDB, p. 409a); RSV "registered themselves"; NIV "indicated their ancestry"; NEB "registered their descent."

4. *BHS* conjectures this reading; RSV, NIV, and NEB follow this reading, while AV, RV, and NKJV do not. More modern commentators (e.g., Budd, p. 3) note the possibility that the clause attaches to v. 18. See the similar issue in the second census document at 26:4b.

beginning them (see, e.g., Num. 2:33; 3:51; 8:3; 15:36; 27:11). If this be true, then v. 19b *(so he numbered them in the wilderness of Sinai)* should be taken as a preface to the list that follows.[5]

In a sense all of vv. 1–19 form an introduction to the census list that follows in vv. 20–46. At the beginning and the end of this introduction (vv. 1 and 19) only Moses is named as the recipient of God's command, while in the detailed material (see vv. 3 and 17) Aaron is also brought into the picture. This must mean that, while Moses was ultimately responsible to God for the execution of the census, Aaron (and the leaders as well) had a helping role. This is further evidence of the wisdom of the counsel given to Moses by his father-in-law in Exod. 18:13–37 to the effect that leadership tasks need to be shared.

(b) The census lists (1:20–47)

20 *The sons of Reuben, firstborn of Israel, their family histories, by their clans, by their fathers' houses, by the number of names, one by one*[1] *every male from twenty years and upward, everyone who is eligible to go in the army.*

21 *Those numbered from the tribe of Reuben: 46,500.*

22 *As regards*[2] *the sons of Simeon, their family histories, by their clans, by their fathers' houses (those of his counting),*[3] *by the number of names, one by one, every male from twenty years and upward, everyone who is eligible to go in the army.*

23 *Those numbered from the tribe of Simeon: 59,300.*

24 *As regards the sons of Gad, their family histories, by their clans, by their fathers' houses, by the number of names, from twenty years and upward, everyone who is eligible to go in the army.*

25 *Those numbered from the tribe of Gad: 46,500.*[4]

26 *As regards the sons of Judah, their family histories, by their clans, by their fathers' houses, by the number of names, from twenty years and upward, everyone eligible to go in the army.*

5. The difference in meaning is not great either way; cf. Gray, p. 9.

1. Lit., "with regard to their skulls"; cf. BDB, p. 166a.

2. The preposition *l*[e] is the basic particle of relationship in Hebrew. Its general meaning is often clarified by the translation "as regards" or "in relation to"; Williams, *Syntax,* §273; GKC, §119r.

3. MT has *p*[e]*qudāyw,* "those of his counting" (referring to the tribe as an individual). The word is missing from a number of Hebrew mss., LXX, Pesh., and Targ. Pseudo-Jonathan. On the basis of this textual evidence, *BHS* conjectures tht the word should be deleted; so also, e.g., Gray, p. 10; Budd, p. 3.

4. LXX places the section on Gad after v. 37.

27 *Those numbered from the tribe of Judah: 74,600.*

28 *As regards the sons of Issachar, their family histories, by their clans, by their fathers' houses, by the number of names, from twenty years and upward, everyone eligible to go in the army.*

29 *Those numbered from the tribe of Issachar: 54,400.*

30 *As regards the sons of Zebulun, their family histories, by their clans, by their fathers' houses, by the number of names, from twenty years and upward, everyone eligible to go in the army.*

31 *Those numbered from the tribe of Zebulun: 57,400.*

32 *As regards the sons of Joseph: As regards the sons of Ephraim, their family histories, by their clans, by their fathers' houses, by the number of names, from twenty years and upward, everyone eligible to go in the army.*

33 *Those numbered from the tribe of Ephraim: 40,500.*

34 *As regards the sons of Manasseh, their family histories, by their clans, by their fathers' houses, by the number of names, from twenty years and upward, everyone eligible to go in the army.*

35 *Those numbered from the tribe of Manasseh: 32,200.*

36 *As regards the sons of Benjamin, their family histories, by their clans, by their fathers' houses, by the number of names, from twenty years and upward, everyone eligible to go in the army.*

37 *Those numbered from the tribe of Benjamin: 35,400.*

38 *As regards the sons of Dan, their family histories, by their clans, by their fathers' houses, by the number of names, from twenty years and upward, everyone eligible to go in the army.*

39 *Those numbered from the tribe of Dan: 62,700.*

40 *As regards the sons of Asher, their family histories, by their clans, by their fathers' houses, by the number of names, from twenty years and upward, everyone eligible to go in the army.*

41 *Those numbered from the tribe of Asher: 41,500.*

42 *As regards the sons of Naphtali, their family histories, by their clans, by their fathers' houses, by the number of names, from twenty years and upward, everyone eligible to go in the army.*

43 *Those numbered from the tribe of Naphtali: 53,400.*

44 *These are those persons numbered, who were numbered by Moses and Aaron —and also the exalted ones of Israel, twelve men, one man for each father's house.*[5]

5. The phrase *'îš-'eḥāḏ l^{e}ḇêṯ-'^{a}ḇōṯāyw* ("one man for each father's house") raises the problem of the meaning of the term *father's house* here. In 1:4 the task was to use *one man for each tribe* in the census process. *BHS* emends by

45 *And all those who were numbered of the children of Israel — by their fathers' houses, from twenty years and upward, everyone eligible to go in the army in Israel —*
46 *all those numbered totaled 603,550.*
47 *But the Levites were not numbered together with them by their fathers' houses.*

The individual census reports recorded here are all structured along the same lines: the name of the tribe and the total number are inserted into two formulae.[6] The first formula is based on the wording of vv. 2–3. The second is: "those numbered of the tribe of *x:* (total number)." On the one hand, the redundancy of the formulae is just what one would expect in a list. On the other hand, the small variations that do occur introduce a small amount of literary variety.[7]

20-44 The contents of this list are rather straightforward. The major difference from 1:5–16 is that Gad is moved from eleventh to third place.[8] The LXX is unsure of where to place Gad. In the current census document Gad is in ninth place (after Benjamin), while in ch. 26 he is in sixth place (after Zebulun). At the very least this shows that the LXX translator was unsure of the criterion by which Gad had been moved from eleventh place in the MT of 1:14 to third in the current list. In 1:5–16 and in chs. 2, 7, and 10, the LXX follows the MT in the order of the tribes — even in putting Gad in sixth place. It is likely that because Gad is in sixth place in the lists of chs. 2, 7, and 10, he is placed sixth also in the census list of ch. 26.[9]

With the slight exception of Gad (son of Leah's handmaiden), the list in 1:20–46 still proceeds in a more-or-less chronological fashion, with

---

deleting the words *'îš-'eḥāḏ* ("one man") and inserting the words *l^e^maṭṭeh 'eḥāḏ 'îš rō'š* ("for one tribe, a man head of [his father's house]"), thus yielding a reading similar to 1:4. The LXX and Sam. Pent. also make changes that would smooth out the problem of identifying a father's house and a tribe. If one chooses to retain MT, then it is hard to avoid the conclusion that, in some contexts, the term *bêṯ-'āḇ* is thought of as equivalent to *maṭṭeh/šēḇeṭ.* Gottwald is probably right when he sees evidence of the equivalency in the mixed term *their fathers' tribes (maṭṭôṯ 'aḇôṯām)* in 1:16. N. Gottwald, *The Tribes of Yahweh,* pp. 288–89.

6. On the minor variations see Gray, p. 10.

7. The variations are as likely the result of intention or textual corruption as they are of the splicing of sources or additions to the text.

8. For a suggested reason for this movement, see the commentary above on 1:5–15.

9. In ch. 13 the LXX shares the confusion of the texts of MT; see the commentary below on 13:8.

the sons of Leah first, the sons of Rachel second, and the sons of the handmaidens third. Thus, Reuben, the firstborn, initiates this list (and the other census list, as well as the lists for the selection of leaders). He is replaced by Judah in those lists that deal with the arrangement of the camp or the march.

their family histories (tôl^{e}ḏōṯām) is found in each of the sections (e.g., vv. 20, 22, 24, 26, 28). This word may have been suggested by the denominative verb "to set down a family ancestry" *(hiṯyallaḏ)* in v. 18. Both words go back to the root *yld,* "bear a child." The *tôl^{e}ḏôṯ* include the genealogical descent of a family, and this is no doubt the emphasis here. *Tôl^{e}ḏôṯ* is used in Genesis to indicate the histories of the origins of particular patriarchal families.[10] Here the term is likely a replacement for "tribe" *(maṭṭeh),* the widest family connection, tracing the family line back to one of the sons of Jacob the patriarch. This judgment is confirmed by the fact that the rest of the designations are arranged from the larger to the smaller units.

In sections dealing with Reuben and Simeon the phrase *one by one (gulg^{e}lōṯām)* clarifies the phrase *by the number of names (b^{e}mispār šēmôṯ).* The people are counted by the number of their names, viz., individually. Since the *one by one* does not occur after v. 22, one may assume that the compiler of the list felt confident that readers would take for granted after that point that *by the number of names* meant one by one.

45-47 These verses continue the conclusion of the unit. The words *fathers' houses* is picked up from v. 44 and used in a way more strictly appropriate to it as "an extended family."[11] Phrases on the acceptable age limit and eligibility for military service are repeated here. These repetitions round off the unit (see vv. 20, 22, 24, 26, 28, 30, 32, 34, 36, 38, 40, 42).

603,500 — The compiler of the present text simply added the total of people found in the attached twelve tribal census reports to get this total. The same procedure is used in ch. 26. After the period of the wilderness wandering the total was 601,730, a difference of 1,280 people.

V. 47 forms a brief summary and transition to the section on the excepting of the Levites from the general census process (see 1:48–54).

10. See Gen. 5:1; 6:9; 10:1; 11:10, 27; 25:12, 19; 36:1, 9; 37:2; also Harrison, *Introduction,* pp. 543–47.

11. Gottwald, *Tribes of Yahweh,* pp. 285–87.

EXCURSUS ON LARGE NUMBERS

The numbers in Num. 1:20–46 appear rather straightforward. The totals are clear and there are no significant textual problems. The only problem is that these numbers (just over 600,000 fighting men) seem much too large for a variety of reasons. We meet the issue of large numbers in the Bible as early as, e.g., Gen. 5:5, 7, 11, etc., in the ages given for Adam, Seth, Enosh, etc. Exod. 12:37 reports that 600,000 "men on foot, besides women and children," came out of Egypt. After our text the Chronicler reports that the combined figures for Israel and Judah at the time of David was 1,570,000 men (1 Chr. 21:5).

Some evangelical scholars have held that the easiest solution is simply to take the numbers at their face values, as the compiler of the present text (and others) obviously has done, since simple addition of the totals for the individual tribes yields the same grand total as in the text.[1] But this solution is not without problems, and the problems are real and persistent. Here is a selection of them:

(1) Such a number of males from twenty years of age and up would give a total populace of about two to two and one-half million. It is hard to believe that such a number could be sustained for forty years in the wilderness without constant, day-to-day, miraculous intervention. The miraculous intervention and provision that do occur seem to be the exception rather than the rule (see, e.g., Num. 11).

(2) Such a number would have, indeed, caused Egypt's Pharaoh consternation, for not only would there have been very little room for them in Egypt, but a group of this size could likely have taken over Egypt with or without weapons.[2] They would hardly have had to fear Pharaoh's army, which was probably at most about 20,000 men.

(3) Current estimates of the population of Canaan at the time of the Exodus are well below three million. Exod. 23:29 and Deut. 7:7, 17, 22 indicate that the Israelites were far fewer in number than the Canaanite population that they were to conquer.

(4) It is well known that two midwives are said to have served the entire number of Hebrews (Exod. 1:15), that the entire number could gather

1. See, e.g., E. J. Young, *An Introduction to the Old Testament* (Grand Rapids: Eerdmans, 1960), p. 85; G. Archer, *Survey of OT Introduction,* pp. 246–49; Keil, pp. 5–15.

2. For some comparative figures on ancient Near Eastern armies, see G. Mendenhall, "The Census Lists of Numbers 1 and 26," *JBL* 77 (1958) 64–65; Wenham, p. 62.

around the tent of meeting to hear Moses (Exod. 16:9; 19:17; 33:18; Deut. 1:1; etc.), and that the whole number could march around Jericho seven times in one day (Josh. 6:15) with enough time left in the day to fight a battle.

(5) According to Num. 3:40–43 the number of firstborn males among the people was 22,273, out of a population of about 600,000 adult males. This is a ratio of about 27:1. This means that a firstborn male must had had, on average, 26 brothers, not to mention sisters. Unless polygamy was the common practice in this period (and no evidence suggests that it was), this kind of ratio is not likely on a wide scale.

(6) Such a massive group would have taken up a great deal of space on the march, especially when one considers their animals and possessions.[3]

This group of problems has been admitted by scholars across the theological spectrum.[4] In the light of these, and other obvious and serious problems, various scholars have attempted to understand these figures in a way that does not take them at face value. Some of the options have included the following.

(1) One group of scholars has held that these figures and others throughout the OT are fabrications of the author or compiler of the material. The numbers have no relation to fact.[5] Why these tables of figures should have been invented in just this way is not clear, and the impression is often given that solutions grow more from the minds of modern scholars than from a treatment of ancient texts in their own worlds.

(2) A second group of scholars has held that the numbers in the text are fairly accurate for a later date in Israel's history, and have been transposed to the wilderness period to show that, in a theological sense, all Israel was present.[6] G. Wenham holds that the figures in Num. 1 and 26 would still be high for David's time.[7] But the biblical figures in 2 Sam. 24:9 are 800,000 warriors for Israel and 500,000 for Judah, while, as reported above, the Chronicler's figures are 1,100,000 for Israel and

3. See J. Bright, *A History of Israel,* 3rd ed. (Philadelphia: Westminster, 1981), p. 134.

4. See, e.g., Gray, pp. 13–15; Wenham, pp. 61–62; Harrison, *Introduction,* p. 632.

5. See, e.g., Gray, p. 13; de Vaux, *Early Israel,* p. 725 n. 22; cf. Sturdy, p. 16.

6. See W. F. Albright, *From the Stone Age to Christianity,* 2nd ed. (New York: Doubleday, 1957), pp. 253, 290–91; it incorporates portions of his article "The Administrative Districts of Israel and Judah," *JPOS* 5 (1925) 17–24, esp. 20–25.

7. Wenham, p. 62.

470,000 for Judah (1 Chr. 21:5). 2 K. 15:19–20 reports that King Menahem of Israel (ca. 738 B.C.) paid Pul (Tiglath-pileser III) of Assyria 1,000 talents of silver by assessing all the wealthy men of the land 50 shekels apiece. A talent equals 3,000 shekels. Thus there must have been about 60,000 men of means in Israel toward the end of the 8th century.[8] The relationship of the figures in such a passage as 2 K. 15:19–20 to the figures in Num. 1 and 26 is unclear, but it is known that Israel was quite well-off during the years of Jeroboam II (ca. 782–753 B.C.; see Amos 6:1–7), so that the number of wealthy men in Israel might well have been higher at that time than in some other periods. But these figures do not enhance one's confidence in the figures in Numbers.

(3) Other scholars have seen the numbers as symbolic in some way. Some see the figures as partaking of gematria, that is, making the numbers represent a name or a saying by their combined numerical values.[9] For example, using a system (widely used after the Maccabean age) wherein the first nine letters of the Hebrew alphabet represented the units, the next nine the tens, and the last four the hundreds, G. Fohrer derives the number 603 from the letters of the words "the sons of Israel" *(bny yśr'l)*, which is then multiplied by 1,000.[10] The words "every head" *(kl r'š)* give a total of 551. The two numbers added together give a total of 603,551, which is then rounded off to the appropriate 603,550.

The weaknesses of such an approach are multiple. (a) There is no reason why the first set of numbers should be multiplied by 1,000 other than the fact that one needs to do so to come out with the desired number. (b) There is no clear reason why certain Hebrew words are treated in this way in this case (or in any other), other than the fact that they make the theory work. In fact, the last number does not work, but has to be rounded off. In cases like this one, one might as well round off many numbers as one. (c) Even the words that are chosen work only for the total of 603,550 in Num. 1:46. They do not work for the total in Num. 26. It is also difficult to relate these symbolic totals to the various individual tribal totals. (d) Although some have claimed to derive meaning from a few other biblical texts by using gematria (e.g., Gen. 14:14), virtually the only clear example of such is Rev. 13:18, with the mysterious meaning of 666.[11]

8. See Kellermann, *Priesterschrift,* p. 160.
9. See, e.g., W. T. Smith, *ISBE,* IV:2162; Holzinger, e.g., pp. 5–6.
10. Fohrer, *Introduction,* p. 184.
11. See the comments of G. E. Ladd, *A Commentary on Revelation* (Grand Rapids: Eerdmans, 1972), p. 186.

(e) The common Hebrew system of representing numbers by successive letters of the alphabet, as mentioned above, is not the only possible system that could have been used. In later times, the Jewish Kabbala used no fewer than nine systems based on the Hebrew alphabet.[12] (f) The first extant examples of the commonly used system of numerical equivalents are not until the 2nd cent. B.C.[13]

M. Barnouin has proposed a different symbolic key based on Near Eastern mathematics and astronomy. His system is carefully worked out, but seems more clever than convincing. It is doubtful whether persons in ancient Israel would have been able to get this meaning from the text. Most certainly, it is not plainly in the text.[14]

(4) The other proposed solutions have in common the feature that they take Heb. *'elep̄*, translated in most English versions as "thousand," in some other sense, thus considerably reducing the numbers involved. The first to suggest such a solution appears to be W. M. Flinders Petrie.[15] He held that the consonants *'lp* could also be translated as "group" or "clan" (as in 1 Sam. 10:19; Judg. 6:15; etc.).[16] Thus, for Reuben, whose tribe has "forty-six *'elep̄* and five hundred," one should read forty-six "groups" with a total of five hundred men. This leads to a grand total of 5,550 men in 598 groups in Num. 1, and 5,730 men in 596 groups in Num. 26. These numbers are reasonable amounts of fighting men, and would be an adequate size to answer the problems set out at the beginning of this excursus. Although many problems may be solved by using this system, not all are. Flinders Petrie himself admitted that his system did not have all the answers. For example, this system does not work for the Levites, who would have twenty-two groups with a total of no men. Flinders Petrie treated the narratives dealing with the Levites as later additions to the text.

In 1958 G. Mendenhall refined and updated the Flinders Petrie hypothesis.[17] Mendenhall used materials from Mari especially to hold that

12. Kellermann, *Priesterschrift,* p. 161.

13. Ibid.; see also GKC, § 5k.

14. Indeed, the meaning Barnouin suggests is very obscure; see M. Barnouin, "Les recensements du Livre des Nombres et l'astronomie babylonienne," *VT* 27 (1977) 280–303; idem, "Remarques sur les tableaux numeriques du Livre des Nombres," *RB* 76 (1969) 351–64. See the excellent summary of the former article in Wenham, pp. 64–66.

15. W. M. Flinders Petrie, *Researches in Sinai* (London: Murray, 1906), pp. 208–21.

16. According to KB, p. 57a, the word means a "(numerical) part of a tribe" in about a dozen places in the OT.

17. Mendenhall, "Census Lists," pp. 52–66.

the census lists of chs. 1 and 26 contained the quotas of contingents sent to war from each group rather than the whole number of fighting men.[18] He then used the Flinders Petrie hypothesis (*'lp* = "tribal division"). The same term was used to describe both the tribal subsection itself and the fighting units levied from that tribal subsection. Mendenhall's numbers are therefore the same as those of Flinders Petrie. He does give a different explanation of the figures, as has been seen. These tribal subsections varied in size from about five men for Simeon to about fourteen for Gad in Num. 1. The figures in ch. 26 range from about five men for Issachar to about seventeen for Reuben. According to Mendenhall the tendency toward larger subsections in the latter passage shows that the texts are in the right order.[19] Mendenhall dated the census lists in the period of the Judges.

The Flinders Petrie/Mendenhall solution has much to commend it, although one may differ on points of detail, such as date. The most serious objection to the theory is that it does not deal with the number of the Levites either in chs. 3–4 or in 26:57–62.

N. Gottwald assumed much in the Flinders Petrie/Mendenhall hypothesis. He gave some of the Hebrew terms content related to their social functions. Secondary social divisions begin with the *mišpāḥâ,* "a protective association of extended families." The *'elep̱* is simply "men at arms." A number of men are mustered from each group, and this group is called an *'elep̱.* Other times an *'elep̱* seems equivalent to a *mišpāḥâ,* but with a different social function. Gottwald assumes, with Mendenhall, that the P traditionist misunderstood the term *'elep̱* as "thousand" instead of a tribal unit.[20]

J. W. Wenham argued that *'lp* may not only be vocalized as *'elep̱,* but also as *'allup̱,* "chieftain," as in Gen. 36:15.[21] Wenham criticized Flinders Petrie and Mendenhall: "If the numbers of *'ᵃlap̱îm* and the numbers of *me'ôṯ* are two different ways of saying the same thing, there should be at least some correspondence between them."[22] This is not the case. The "group" numbers vary from as few as five to as many as seventeen, as was seen above. Wenham set up a rather complicated scheme for figuring out the number of "captains" *('allûp̱îm)* and the

18. Ibid., p. 60.

19. Ibid., p. 63.

20. See N. Gottwald, *The Tribes of Yahweh: A Sociology of Religion of Liberated Israel, 1250–1000 BCE* (Maryknoll, N.Y.: Orbis), pp. 257–84.

21. J. W. Wenham, "The Large Numbers in the Old Testament," *TynBul* 18 (1967) 19–53.

22. Wenham, "Large Numbers," p. 29.

number of units *(mēʾôṯ)*. For example, Reuben has forty-five *ʾallûpîm* and 1,500 men, Simeon has fifty-seven *ʾallûpîm* and 2,300 men. Wenham's work, based on R. E. D. Clark's theory, gives a steady number of between two and three leaders per unit.[23] He considered an *ʾallûp* to be a specially trained warrior who would be either a captain of a contingent of one hundred or a captain of a contingent of fifty men. In his scheme some *ʾallûpîm* would be left over to act as captains of the contingents of one thousand or as "super-numerary captains of fifty."[24] The total fighting force would be about 18,000 men on this reckoning, and the total population about 72,000. This compares with the 2–2½ million of the text on face value, about 20,000 in the Flinders Petrie/Mendenhall scheme, and about 140,000 on R. E. D. Clark's theory.

The problem of the Levites must be worked out another way. The difficulty is that the Levites have 22,000 men according to Num. 3:39. As pointed out above, this would be read as twenty-two groups of no men each. Obviously something is amiss. That the Levites' census must be worked out in another way from the semimilitary census of the lay tribes is not a surprise, since the Levites were not to go to war but to serve the religious needs of the community. It does not seem reasonable to expect *ʾlp* to mean either "trained warrior" (J. Wenham) or "tribal subsection" (Flinders Petrie, Mendenhall). J. Wenham explained the number of Levites by noting that biblical texts are often corrupted by the simple addition of zeros to the numbers.[25] If, in fact, this is the case in the book of Numbers, the total figure should read 2,200 Levite males. This amount compares favorably to the other tribes.

What can be said in conclusion? No one system answers all the questions or solves all the problems. Rather than assuming this complex (mis-)use of *ʾlp,* one might be better served to assume that a zero needs to be dropped from all the figures involved. This would give a fighting strength of 60,355 and a total population of between 200,000 and 250,000 (still quite high by ancient standards).[26] The flaw in this suggestion is that

23. See the chart in ibid., p. 37; see R. E. D. Clark, "The Large Numbers of the Old Testament," *Journal of the Transactions of the Victoria Institute* 87 (1955) 82–92.

24. Wenham, "Large Numbers," p. 31.

25. Ibid., p. 21.

26. Reducing the numbers further by dropping two zeros would give a more reasonable total but would run into the problem of an odd five on the grand total as well as an odd five (or fifty) for Gad in ch. 1, and an odd three (or thirty) for Reuben in ch. 26.

the mistake in zeros would easily occur only where numbers were represented by figures rather than by words. We have little or no evidence that figures were used in the biblical texts during the biblical period.

A weak point in all the solutions that understand *'lp* as "tribal subgroup" is that the text of Numbers understands it as "thousand." The editor simply totals the figures to get 603,550. Using the *'lp* = "group" solution, the total is (according to Flinders Petrie and Mendenhall) 598 groups of 5,550 men. To understand *'lp* in any other way than "thousand" assumes a misunderstanding and mistransmission of the text in all the census lists of Exodus and Numbers (not to mention other texts). Since both the LXX and the Sam. Pent. basically agree with the MT, the misunderstanding must have taken place as early as the 5th or 4th cent. B.C.

In short, we lack the materials in the text to solve this problem. When all is said and done one must admit that the answer is elusive. Perhaps it is best to take these numbers as R. K. Harrison has done — as based on a system familiar to the ancients but unknown to moderns. According to Harrison the figures are to be taken as "symbols of relative power, triumph, importance, and the like and are not meant to be understood either strictly literally or as extant in a corrupt textual form."[27]

(3) Levites Are Excepted (1:48–54)

48 *And Yahweh spoke to Moses, saying:*

49 *"Only[1] the tribe of Levi you will not number, you will not calculate their total among the children of Israel;*

50 *rather, you appoint the Levites over the tabernacle of the testimony and over all its vessels and over all that pertains to it. They are to carry the tabernacle and all its vessels, and they are to attend to it and encamp around the tabernacle.*

51 *When the tabernacle is to move, the Levites will take it down, and when the tabernacle is to be erected, the Levites will put it up. The unauthorized party who encroaches will be put to death.*

52 *And the children of Israel shall make camp, each one beside his encampment, and each one beside his standard, by their armies.*

27. Harrison, *Introduction,* p. 633.

1. Heb. *'aḵ* is an adverbial particle found 159 times with two meanings; first, "but" or "only," introducing a condition contrary to what has been discussed previously; second, an asseverative particle, "surely." This is an example of the first usage. LXX reads *hora,* "see to it!" See BDB, p. 36b; Williams, *Syntax,* §§ 388–89; GKC, § 153.

53 *And the Levites will encamp around the tabernacle of the testimony that there should be no wrath against the congregation of the children of Israel. And the Levites will guard the tabernacle of the testimony."*

54 *The children of Israel did so; according to all that Yahweh commanded Moses, so they did.*

This section is an expansion of the previous verse. It explains why the Levites have no place in the previous two lists. They have been set aside for special treatment and will therefore have a special census. Instead of going into the army, the Levites will serve by carrying, attending, and guarding the tabernacle. The tabernacle was the place where God met the people and was thus a holy place. Humans were not ordinarily in the holy sphere. Thus special persons (the Levites) had to be set apart *(appointed),* by God through Moses, to do the work of the service of the tabernacle. The Levitical camp surrounded the tabernacle so that that which was holy did not contact that which was unclean. The specific plan for setting up the Levitical camp is given in 3:21–39.

50 *you appoint.* The pronoun emphasizes that Moses is personally to appoint these Levites. The verb *pāqaḏ* has the sense "to appoint" here; it is the same verb translated "number" earlier in the chapter.[2]

the tabernacle of the testimony is, in this text, identical with the tent of meeting (1:1). The structure is also called the tent of the testimony in 9:15; 17:22–23; 18:2; and 2 Chr. 24:6. Similar phrases are "the ark of the testimony," "the tables of the testimony," and "the veil of the testimony."[3]

testimony (ʿēḏâ) is related to the root *ʿwd,* which has to do with repetition. A testimony is that which affirms the continuing relevance of something through repetition.[4] The particular testimony in mind here may be the written law of God (e.g., the Decalogue), which acted as a repeated testimony or witness to God's covenant with Israel.[5] Also the tent, the ark, and the veil are themselves all testimonies that speak of God and his desire

2. The verb is translated "to number" in, e.g., 1:3; see BDB, p. 823; *TWOT,* II:731–33.

3. For "ark of the testimony" see Exod. 25:22; 26:33–34; 30:6, 26; 31:7; 39:35; 40:3, 5, 20–21; Num. 4:5; 7:8–9; Josh. 4:16. For "tables of the testimony" see Exod. 31:18; 32:15; 34:29. For "veil of the testimony" see Lev. 24:3.

4. See C. Schultz, *TWOT,* II:648.

5. See W. J. Harrelson, "Testimony," *IDB,* IV:579.

to have a people unto himself, his election of his people in Egypt, and his covenant at Sinai.[6]

51 When the tabernacle is to be moved the Levites are to do the dismantling and reconstruction. They are appointed as guardians over all the paraphernalia of the tabernacle. Any *unauthorized party* or "stranger" *(zār),* in this case a non-Levite, who approaches in order to usurp the role of guardian over these holy things will be put to death by the Levitical guards.[7]

52 The Israelites are to encamp by tribal groups (see ch. 2), *each one beside his standard.* The traditional interpretation of *standard (degel)* has been a colored flag to designate each group. Rashi thought that each flag was a color matched to a stone in the high priest's breastplate (cf. Exod. 28:17–21). Ibn Ezra saw each flag with a different symbol: Reuben, a man; Judah, a lion; etc.[8] We have no idea on what basis these comments were made. Gray preferred to translate *degel* as "company" on the basis of the LXX, Pesh., and Targ. renderings.[9] The only occurrence of the related verbal form *(dāgal)* is a passive participle in Cant. 5:10, usually translated as "conspicuous," or "easily distinguished." In the light of this related form and the cognate Akkadian verb *dagālu,* "to see," the traditional translation seems preferable.

6. For the NT development of the concept of testimony and witness, see A. A. Trites, *The New Testament Concept of Witness,* SNTSMS 31 (Cambridge: Cambridge Univ. Press, 1977).

7. For the usage of the terms *stranger, approach,* and *put to death (zār, qārēḇ, yûmaṯ),* see the important study by Milgrom, *Studies in Levitical Terminology,* I: 1–8, 16–18.

8. See A. Cohen, ed., *The Soncino Chumash,* Soncino Books of the Bible (London: Soncino, 1947), p. 798.

9. LXX *tagma;* Pesh. *twlq;* Targ. *ṭqm;* see Gray, p. 20. Gray's rendering is also supported by the meaning of *degel* in postbiblical Hebrew, though in postbiblical Aramaic it means "standard, flag" (see M. Jastrow, *Dictionary of the Targumim, Talmud Babli, Yerushalmi and Midrashic Literature* [New York: Judaica, 1971], p. 280a). In Modern Hebrew *degel* can mean either "group" or "standard" (R. Alacalay, *The Complete Hebrew-English Dictionary* [Jerusalem: Massada, 1970], col. 407). Gray's appeal to LXX is problematic, however. While *tagma,* which means "group, detachment," occurs in ch. 2, here in 1:52 LXX reads a related word, *taxis.* But *taxis* is surely the translation of *maḥᵃneh,* "camp." See Hatch and Redpath, *Concordance to the Septuagint* (Oxford: Clarendon, 1897), I:603. LXX uses *hēgemonian* to translate *degel.* This Greek word is generally a word for leadership or a leader. In Gen. 36:30 LXX uses *hēgemonian* to translate *'allûp,* "chief." It is possible that here and in Num. 2:17 LXX understood *degel* to refer to the *nᵉśî'îm* elected in vv. 5–16.

53 The Levites were to form a cordon around the tabernacle in order to keep other Israelites from coming in contact with the holy objects housed in it. If anyone were to encroach upon the holy precinct, the wrath of God would be let loose on the whole camp. In the incident with Korah (ch. 16), the wrath of God goes forth in the form of a plague that strikes the whole people.[10] This result may also be seen in the incident with the Philistines in 1 Sam. 5:6–12. The Levites' duty was to keep the wrath of God from striking all concerned, whether primarily guilty or not.[11]

Therefore the main task of the Levites was to *guard* the tabernacle. Jacob Milgrom has shown that the expression *šāmar mišmereṯ* meant "guard duty."[12] The Levites were known as a warlike tribe (cf. Gen. 49:5–7); they were charged with the execution of 3,000 men who had sinned by worshiping the golden calf (Exod. 32:25–29). It is not surprising that the same term *(ṣāḇā')* is used of their service (which included guarding the tabernacle) and the military service of the rest of the tribes (4:23).

The actual setup of the camp, with the Levites around the tabernacle, is not related until ch. 2; the Levites' other tasks regarding the tabernacle are not set out until chs. 3 and 4. The intention of this section is only to summarize why the Levites are not involved in the lay census (they have been appointed to special service) and the primary task involved in this special service (guarding the tabernacle, thus keeping the camp safe).

b. Placement of the Camp and Marching Order (2:1–34)

1 *And Yahweh spoke to Moses and to Aaron, saying:*

2 *"Let the children of Israel encamp, each man by his standard, with the standards of their fathers' houses. They shall encamp at a distance from the tent of meeting, on every side.*

3 *Those who are to camp to the east, toward the sunrise, are to be of the standard of the camp of Judah, by their armies. And the leader of the sons of Judah was Nahshon the son of Amminadab.*

4 *His host, that is, those numbered: 74,600.*

5 *And encamping next to him were those of the tribe of Issachar. And the leader of the sons of Issachar was Nethanel the son of Zuar.*

10. See, e.g., 16:46: "wrath has gone forth from Yahweh, the plague has begun."

11. Milgrom, *Studies in Levitical Terminology,* I:17 n. 75; p. 30 n. 109.

12. Ibid., pp. 8–16.

6 *His host, that is, those numbered: 54,400.*

7 *[Then][1] the tribe of Zebulun; and the leader of the sons of Zebulun was Eliab the son of Helon.*

8 *His host, that is, those numbered: 57,400.*

9 *All those numbered, by their hosts, in the camp of Judah: 186,400. They are the first to depart.*

10 *The standard of the camp of Reuben, by their hosts, is to be to the south. And the leader of the sons of Reuben was Elizur the son of Shedeur.*

11 *And his host, that is, those numbered: 46,500.*

12 *And encamping next to him were those of the tribe of Simeon. And the leader of the sons of Simeon was Shelumiel the son of Zurishaddai.*

13 *And his host, that is, those numbered: 59,300.*

14 *Then the tribe of Gad, and the leader of the sons of Gad was Eliasaph the son of Deuel.[2]*

15 *And his host, that is, those numbered: 46,650.*

16 *All those numbered, by their hosts, in the camp of Reuben: 151,450. They are the second to depart.*

17 *Then the tent of meeting is to depart, the camp of the Levites being in the midst of the camps. As they encamped, so they are to depart, each one in his place, by their standards.*

18 *The standard of the camp of Ephraim, by their hosts, is to be to the west. And the leader of the sons of Ephraim was Elishama the son of Ammihud.*

19 *And his host, that is, those numbered: 40,500.*

20 *And encamping next to him were those of the tribe of Manasseh. And the leader of Manasseh was Gamaliel the son of Pedahzur.*

21 *And his host, that is, those numbered: 23,200.*

22 *Then the tribe of Benjamin, and the leader of the sons of Benjamin was Abidan the son of Gideoni.*

23 *And his host, that is, those numbered: 35,400.*

24 *All those numbered, by their hosts, in the camp of Ephraim: 108,100.*

1. A few mss. of Sam. Pent. and Pesh. add *w*^{e}-, "and," here, which conforms with vv. 14, 22, 29. *BHS* prefers this reading. The reading is probable.

2. *BHS* proposes to read *d*^{e}*'û'ēl* instead of *r*^{e}*'û'ēl* here, as in 1:14, and in many mss. of the Hebrew as well as Sam. Pent. and Vulg. The Hebrew *d* and *r* are easily confused in both the square script and its predecessors. There seems no reason not to follow *BHS* at this point.

25 *The standard of the camp of Dan, by their hosts, is to be to the north. And the leader of the sons of Dan was Ahiezer the son of Ammishaddai.*
26 *And his hosts, that is, those numbered: 62,700.*
27 *And encamping next to him were those of the tribe of Asher. And the leader of the sons of Asher was Pagiel the son of Ochran.*
28 *And his host, that is, those numbered: 41,500.*
29 *Then the tribe of Naphtali, and the leader of the sons of Naphtali was Ahira the son of Enan.*
30 *And his host, that is, those numbered: 53,400.*
31 *All those numbered, by their hosts, in the camp of Dan: 157,600. They shall depart in the last place, by their standards.*
32 *These were those numbered of the children of Israel, by their fathers' houses, all those numbered in the camps, by their hosts: 603,550.*
33 *But the Levites were not counted among the children of Israel. Just as Yahweh had commanded Moses,*
34 *so the children of Israel did. According to all that Yahweh commanded Moses, they encamped by their standards, and they departed the same way, each one by his clans, according to his father's house.*

Chapter 2 uses the figures developed in ch. 1 (hence once again, the reader is faced with the problem of large numbers)[3] and gives the formation of the camp and the order of departure for the march. The arrangement of the tribes differs slightly from ch. 1. The tribal group belonging to Judah (Judah, Issachar, and Zebulun) are moved from the fourth, fifth, and sixth places to the first, second, and third.

The east side is the natural place to begin because that is the side in which the opening into the tabernacle was placed, and thus the way into the presence of God. The east was generally the primary direction in the ancient Near East. Since it is the direction of the rising sun, it is usually called the "front" *(qdm)* or the direction of "the dawn" *(mzrḥ)*.[4] From this basic (and common) eastward orientation, one would proceed to one's right hand (the south), one's back (the west), and one's left hand (the north). This is the pattern of ch. 2.[5]

But why should Judah's group be moved from its place as found

3. See the "Excursus on Large Numbers" above.
4. Both terms are used in 2:3.
5. See B. S. Childs, *IDB*, III:608–9.

in the census document of 1:20–46? One possibility is that the author of this passage wished, for his own theological reasons, to emphasize the preeminence of Judah. This solution is common among those who analyze and explain the Pentateuch along the lines of the documentary hypothesis. This passage belongs to source stratum P. The provenance of P is usually thought to be the Babylonian diaspora,[6] at a time when any thought of preeminence for a group other than Judah was impossible. P was concerned to elevate the status of Judah.[7] Looking back on the history of Israel from the standpoint of the Exile, one can see that the kingdom of Judah (and hence the tribe of Judah) was the one that had become preeminent. This passage is an attempt to show that this postexilic preeminence had a theological basis in the Mosaic age.[8]

Another approach assumes that Judah comes first in this list simply because his group did encamp on the east side of the tabernacle. Judah and his host are given the first place because of the prophecy in the Testament of Jacob (Gen. 49:8–12), which, in spite of its many obscurities, clearly gives Judah preeminence over his brothers. The same passage associates Issachar and Zebulun with Judah as they are in the current passage. Everyone agrees that the Testament of Jacob is earlier than the list here in Num. 2.[9] It could easily have provided the theological rationale for giving Judah and his camp the first place at the east side of the tabernacle.[10]

A simpler solution than either of these commends itself here. Judah was allowed pride of place on the east with Aaron and the priests because its census figures are the largest of any of the tribes and its camp was also the largest.[11]

1-2 In the introduction to the chapter, God gives the command

6. See, e.g., Fohrer, *Introduction,* p. 185.

7. See, e.g., Gray, pp. 14, 18.

8. See also Budd, pp. 24–25; Noth, p. 24; etc.

9. The Testament of Jacob is usually assigned to J, the oldest of the documentary sources (ca. 900 B.C.), or to JE; see Driver, *Introduction,* p. 147. But neither G. von Rad (*Genesis,* tr. J. Marks, OTL [Philadelphia: Westminster, 1961], p. 417) nor E. A. Speiser (*Genesis,* AB [New York: Doubleday, 1964], p. 371) is willing to assign Gen. 49 to J. Speiser thinks it is much older than J; he prefers a date no later than the end of the 2nd millennium B.C.

10. See Keil, p. 18; R. Allen, "Numbers," *EBC*, II (Grand Rapids: Zondervan, 1990), 714.

11. See T. E. Espin, T*he Holy Bible: According to the Authorized Version (1611),* Vol. I, Part. II: *Leviticus-Deuteronomy* (London: Murray, 1871), p. 658; R. K. Harrison, *Numbers,* WEC, pp. 55–56.

to place the camp in a certain order. Once again, the biblical author sees a detail of administration as the direct command and will of the Almighty. The formula *And Yahweh spoke to Moses (and to Aaron), saying,* commonly begins a unit in the book of Numbers.[12]

The tribes are to encamp by their *standard,* which is the flag or banner marking off each camp of three tribes.[13] They are also to encamp *with the ensigns of their fathers' houses (b*^{e}*'ōṯōṯ l*^{e}*ḇêṯ '*^{a}*ḇōṯām).* The *ensign ('ôṯ)* means a "sign" or "token," and must be some sort of insignia of a father's house. The simplest way of visualizing the camp is to picture each of the four subcamps gathered under a *standard* (thus, by synecdoche, the camps are called standards), with each subcamp further divided by the ensigns or insignia of each father's house.

The Israelites are to encamp *at a distance [minnegeḏ] from the tent of meeting* (or tabernacle), *on every side [sāḇîḇ]* of it. The basic meaning of *minnegeḏ* is "away from the front of," which is how many commentators translate it.[14] Some Jewish exegesis connects the current passage with Josh. 3:4, which stipulates 2,000 cubits (a little over ½ mi.) as the distance between the marching people and the ark, and posits that each camp was 2,000 cubits from the tabernacle.[15]

3–31 The four camps were set around the tent of meeting in a rectangle. Protecting the tabernacle on the east end were Aaron and the priests, while the Levites formed a protective cordon about the holy precinct on the other three sides. It is interesting that this rectangular form of encampment is similar to one Pharaoh Ramses II (perhaps a contemporary of Moses) used in his campaigns in Syria.[16]

12. Moses alone, 30 times (1:48; 3:5, 11, 44; 4:21; 5:1, 5, 11; 6:1, 22; 8:1, 5, 23; 9:9; 10:1; 13:1; 15:1, 17; 16:23; 17:1, 9, 16; 18:25; 20:7; 25:10, 16; 26:52; 28:1; 31:1; 34:1, 6; 35:9). Moses and Aaron, 6 times (2:1; 4:1, 17; 14:26; 16:20; 19:1). Aaron alone, once (18:8). In other pentateuchal books the formula is also common, e.g., with Moses alone: Exodus, 9 times; Leviticus, 28 times, etc.

13. See the commentary above on 1:52.

14. E.g., Wenham, p. 67; Snaith, pp. 123–24. So also AV, NASB, NIV, NKJV, and JB. See BDB, p. 617b. LXX translates the Hebrew as *enantioi,* "opposite, facing," which reading is followed by, e.g., RSV, NEB, and Budd, p. 20.

15. See Cohen, *Soncino Chumash,* p. 798. In NT times the Sabbath day's journey (cf. Acts 1:12) was probably thought of as 2,000 cubits. See Mish. *Erubin* 4:3; 5:4.

16. See K. A. Kitchen, "Some Egyptian Background to the Old Testament," *TynBul* 5–6 (1960) 11. His source is Ch. Kuentz, *La Bataille de Qadech* (1928–34), plates 34, 39, 42.

The syntax of the various sections describing the tribal arrangement (i.e., vv. 3–9, 10–16, 18–24, 25–31) is as follows (using the first group as an example): *on the east (are) . . . the tribe of Judah . . . next to him (are) . . . Issachar . . . (and) Zebulun.* In other words, the camp leader is in the center flanked by the other two tribes, as is seen in the following diagram.[17]

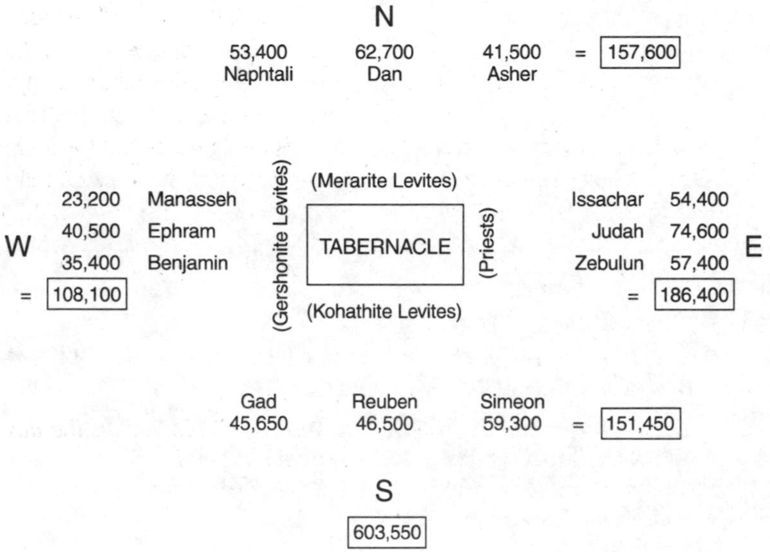

32–34 These verses conclude the unit, and again summarize information given in ch. 1. The total of men is 603,550. The Levites are not counted in this census, but the reader is not burdened, at this point, with the reason for the omission (cf. 1:47–54). *as Yahweh had commanded Moses* refers to 1:49–53. The concluding formula in v. 34 is similar to the one that rounded off the previous chapter. Thus, this passage begins with the command of God and ends with its execution by the people of Israel.

17. See also Gray, p. 20.

c. Levitical Censuses (3:1–4:49)

When the lay census had been taken, it had been made clear that the Levites' service was to be different (see 1:47–54). The tent of meeting had to be protected from contact with that which was not holy, and thus special persons (the Levites) were appointed to guard it in ch. 1. Chs. 3–4 expand on this Levitical guard duty, their other duties, their numbers, and the camp arrangement.

Two censuses are reported here (3:14–39; 4:1–49), but they are neither repetitions nor parallel accounts. The purpose of the first census was to number all male Levites from one month of age and up. The second census was to number the working Levites — those from thirty to fifty years of age. The two censuses had ancillary purposes as well. The first also provided the camp arrangement, thus completing what was begun in ch. 2. The second also set forth specific kinds of work for the different Levitical clans. In between these two censuses (3:40–51) is a small unit that picks up a number of commands from the book of Exodus and works out specifics of the principles set forth in 3:11–13.

(1) General Census (3:1–39)

(a) Introduction: Family of Aaron (3:1–13)

1 *These are the family histories of Aaron and Moses, on the day Yahweh spoke to Moses on the mountain of Sinai.*

2 *And these are the names of the sons of Aaron: the firstborn Nadab, and Abihu, Eleazar, and Ithamar.*

3 *These are the names of the sons of Aaron, the anointed priests, whom he consecrated to minister as priests.*

4 *But Nadab and Abihu died before Yahweh, when they presented unacceptable fire before Yahweh in the wilderness of Sinai, and they had no sons. So Eleazar and Ithamar ministered as priests in the presence of Aaron their father.*

5 *And Yahweh spoke to Moses, saying:*

6 *"Bring the tribe of Levi near and present them before Aaron the priest that they might serve him.*

7 *And they will stand guard for him and for the whole congregation before the tent of meeting, in doing*[1] *the work of the tabernacle.*

8 *And they will guard all the furnishings of the tent of meeting, and*

1. The infinitive construct plus l^e- should be read as a gerund with the word *in;* see, e.g., GKC, § 114o; Williams, *Syntax,* § 195; Milgrom, *Studies in Levitical Terminology,* I:72.

this[2] guard duty is on behalf of the children of Israel,[3] in doing the work of the tabernacle.

9 *And you will give the Levites to Aaron and his sons; they are wholly given[4] to him from among the children of Israel.*

10 *And you shall appoint Aaron and his sons, and they shall watch over their priesthood. And the unauthorized persons who encroach will be killed."*

11 *And Yahweh spoke to Moses, saying:*

12 *"I, even I, have taken the Levites from the midst of the children of Israel instead of each firstborn who opens the womb from the children of Israel; therefore the Levites will belong to me,*

13 *because every firstborn is mine. On the day when I smote every firstborn in the land of Egypt I consecrated to myself every firstborn in Israel, from human and animal; they will belong to me. I am Yahweh."*

1–3 This short section contains genealogical formulae: *These are the family histories of* (*'ēlleh tôl^{e}d̲ōt̲*) and *these are the names of* (*'ēlleh š^{e}môt̲*). The first formula is the same one that divides Genesis into a number of family histories, as many commentators have recognized.[5] The second formula is also common in OT genealogical contexts, especially in the Pentateuch.[6]

This passage is the first one in the book of Numbers to introduce the family of Aaron: firstborn Nadab and his brothers Abihu, Eleazar, and Ithamar.[7] Aaron and his four sons had been consecrated as priests before God,[8] but the two older sons Nadab and Abihu had been killed when they

2. The particle *'et̲* here is to be taken as virtually equivalent to the relative (i.e., *zō't̲*); GKC, § 117m.

3. See Milgrom, *Studies in Levitical Terminology,* I:72.

4. The idiom "wholly given" is produced by the repetition of the Qal passive participle *n^{e}t̲ûnîm;* see GKC, § 123e.

5. E.g., J. Skinner, *A Critical and Exegetical Commentary on Genesis,* ICC (Edinburgh: T. & T. Clark, 1910), pp. xxxiii–xxxiv, 39–40, etc.; D. Kidner, *Genesis,* TOTC (Downers Grove: InterVarsity, 1967), pp. 23, 59.

6. The formula is found 14 times in the Pentateuch (Gen. 25:13; 36:10, 40; 46:8; Exod. 1:1; 6:16; Num. 1:5, 3:2–3, 18; 13:16; 27:1; 34:17, 19), and only 6 times in the rest of the OT (Josh. 17:3; 2 Sam. 5:14; 23:8; Ezek. 48:1; 1 Chr. 6:2; 14:4).

7. The family of Aaron has already been traced out in Exod. 6:20–25. In contrast to the present text, Exod. 6 traces the family to Aaron's grandson Phinehas (see Num. 25).

8. This consecration is commanded in Exod. 29 and carried out in Lev. 8.

had performed an unauthorized ritual (Lev. 10). This story, one of the few narratives in Leviticus, is placed after the election of Aaron and his sons to the privilege and service of the priesthood (Lev. 8) and immediately before a discussion of clean and unclean animals (Lev. 11). Nadab and Abihu offered incense in an improper manner before Yahweh and were consumed by fire from his presence. The problem was not that they offered incense when they were not qualified to do so. Ch. 8 relates their ordination as priests with all the rights and privileges of priests. The problem was that they offered incense "that Yahweh had not commanded them" (Lev. 10:1). They made this offering on their own, of their own free will, not in response to God's command. Thus the fire was *unacceptable* or "unauthorized" *(zārâ)*. This word is related to the one used for the encroacher who is to be killed if he attempts to pass into the tabernacle in Num. 1:51. In Lev. 10 there were presumably no Levitical guards to keep interlopers out of the sacred precincts, so God had acted directly to protect his holiness. This act left Aaron with only two sons.

4 *in the presence of Aaron their father (ʿal pᵉnê ʾaḥᵃrōn ʾᵃḇî-hem)*. Some render this phrase "in the lifetime of Aaron their father."[9] The literal rendering of *ʿal pᵉnê* is "upon" or "against the face of." The idiom may only indicate one who is in the presence of another (which must be during his or her lifetime). Others translate it as "under the oversight of," i.e., directly in front of Aaron's face.[10] The phrase probably indicates both contemporaneity and oversight, and so the translation *in the presence,* which implies both.

5–10 The Levites are presented to Aaron to serve the priesthood, and, by doing so, to serve the whole community.

6 Moses is charged by God to *Bring the tribe of Levi near (haqrēḇ ʾeṯ-maṭṭēh lēwî)*. The term *bring near* is a technical one that can mean "to offer (an offering, sacrifice, etc.)."[11] Moses is to *present* (lit., "cause to stand") the Levites to Aaron and to God as offerings (as will be seen in due course). The idiom "to make someone stand before someone" is used of presenting an inferior to a superior, e.g., Jacob before Pharaoh (Gen. 47:7), a poor person before a priest (Lev. 27:8). In Esth. 4:5 it has the thrust of "to make a servant to."[12]

9. E.g., RSV, NIV; so also BDB, p. 818b.
10. See BDB, p. 898a.
11. Contra Gray, p. 25.
12. Milgrom, *Studies in Levitical Terminology,* I:52 n. 201: "*ʿmd lpny* is the language of subordination."

The purpose of the Levites' being brought near and put under Aaron's authority is *that they might serve him.* The word *serve* (*šērēṯ,* Piel) is a general word for the work and ministry that the Levites are to undertake. According to Gray, the verb is used absolutely only of the priests. When the verb is used of the Levites, it always has an object, e.g., the priest (as here), the assembly (16:9), or the tabernacle (1:50).[13]

Both specific kinds of service to be rendered have already been set out in 1:50–53, viz., guard duty and the work of dismantling, carrying, and reassembling the tabernacle. Vv. 7–8 further describe these duties.

7 As in 1:53, the idiom here is *šāmar mišmereṯ,* which Milgrom has shown to mean "guard duty."[14] Here the standard English translations muddy the waters considerably by translating the terms for the duties of the Levites in these verses as equivalents when they are in fact quite distinct. V. 7 tells of the duties of the Levites when the tribes are in camp, since this is the only time when one can keep watch in front of or *before (lip̱nê)* the tent of meeting. V. 6 has said that the Levites were to serve Aaron and the priests, and one of the ways in which the Levites serve is by *standing guard for him before* [i.e., in front of] *the tent of meeting.* The Levites are to stand guard in front of, i.e., outside, the tent of meeting, and the priests are to guard the inner precincts, as will be seen.[15]

the whole congregation. As the allusion to Nadab and Abihu illustrated, even priests can incur Yahweh's killing wrath by offering "unauthorized fire." As will be seen in ch. 16, it is also, of course, possible for others to trespass and for the *whole congregation* to suffer God's wrath, whether or not they had physically taken part in the trespass (cf. 17:6–15 [Eng. 16:41–50]). Therefore, by keeping the congregation out of the holy precincts, the Levites are rendering a protection and a service to the community.

A second way in which the Levites are to serve Aaron is by *doing the work of the tabernacle.* Milgrom has shown conclusively that the word *ʿaḇōḏâ* means physical *work.* Since this verse applies to the work of the Levites *before* (i.e., "out in front of") the tent of meeting, i.e., in camp, the physical work required here is general.[16]

13. See Gray, p. 25.
14. See the commentary above on 1:53.
15. See Milgrom, *Studies in Levitical Terminology,* I:9–10 and n. 33.
16. See ibid., pp. 60–87, esp. 72–76. Milgrom gives three definitions of *ʿaḇōḏâ:* (a) general physical labor, (b) the task of transport of the tabernacle, (c) a portion of that task, either dismantling and reassembling or carrying (p. 61).

8 Although some consider the last half of this verse an addition to the text, since it repeats the last part of v. 7,[17] this is doubtful. This verse is not simply a doublet. V. 7 deals with the Levites' work in the camp and v. 8 deals with their work on the march. This is shown by the reference to the *furnishings (kᵉlî)* that the Levites guard. When the camp is set up these *furnishings* are inside the tabernacle enclosure, guarded by the priests (3:38; 18:5). The Levites guard the area out in front of *(lip̄nê)* the tabernacle (3:7; cf. vv. 23, 29, 35). The only time the holy object would be exposed is on the march. Here the general word *work (ʿᵃḇōḏâ)* refers to the erecting, disassembling, and carrying that will be assigned to the various Levite groups later in this chapter and in the next.[18] The two verses are distinct in their references and both are necessary to provide information on the duties of the Levites. The phrase *and this guard duty is on behalf of the children of Israel* interrupts the flow of the sentence in order to reinforce the idea, already present elsewhere in the text, that the Levites' guard duty is really on behalf of and for the benefit of the whole community.[19]

9 The Levites are *wholly given* to Aaron and his sons, i.e., the priests. This verse is similar to 8:16, which states that the Levites are wholly given to God. Some versions attempted to harmonize the two verses,[20] but the difference between them is more important than their similarity. Here Moses gives the Levites to the priests while in 8:16 God gives them to himself. Furthermore, in this verse the Levites are given to the priests *from among (mēʾeṯ),* i.e., "on the part of," or "representing," the children of Israel, while in 8:16 they are given by God *from the midst of (mittôḵ)* the children of Israel, representing the firstborn.

10 This verse states that the priests have a part to play in guarding the tabernacle. Aaron and his sons are to *watch over [šāmar] their priesthood [kᵉhunnāṯām],* i.e., over their priestly functions.[21] This verse contains the second occurrence of the formula *the unauthorized person who encroaches will be killed.*[22]

11–13 These verses refer to the laws of Exod. 13:2; 22:29–30; and 34:19–20. The principle is that every firstborn belongs to God

17. See *BHS.*

18. The specifics will be spelled out in 3:25–26, 31–32, 36–37; 4:15, 24–28, 31–33.

19. See the commentary above on v. 7 and on 1:53.

20. See LXX and Sam. Pent., as well as a number of Hebrew mss.

21. See also 18:7; Milgrom, *Studies in Levitical Terminology,* I:17–18.

22. See the explanation above on 1:51.

(13:2).[23] Every firstborn animal must be either sacrificed or redeemed and the substitute sacrificed (22:30; 34:19–20a). The firstborn son was to be redeemed by a substitution (34:20b). After the sin of the golden calf, the Levites were substituted without a formal statute (32:25–29). Their substitution is made formal here and spelled out in greater detail in 3:44–51.

To summarize what has been introduced here concerning the priests and Levites: The priesthood was reduced with the deaths of Nadab and Abihu (vv. 1–4), so that augmentation of those standing guard over the tabernacle was desirable. This resulted in the Levites' being dedicated to the service of the priests (v. 6). The Levites would be responsible for guard duty outside the tent when it was set up and (some of them) for the other physical work connected with setting up, taking down, and carrying the structure (vv. 7–8). The Levites are given over to Aaron and the priesthood as representatives of Israel (v. 9). The priests also have a guard duty over their own priestly duties (v. 10). The Levites stand as God's replacement for the firstborn in Israel (vv. 11–13).

(b) The census itself (3:14–39)

14 *And Yahweh spoke to Moses in the wilderness of Sinai, saying:*
15 *"Number the sons of Levi by their fathers' houses, by their clans; you shall number every male from one month of age and up."*
16 *And Moses numbered them according to the command of Yahweh, as he had been commanded.*[1]
17 *And these are the sons of Levi, by their names: Gershon and Kohath and Merari.*
18 *And these are the names of the sons of Gershon, by their clans: Libni and Shimei.*
19 *And the sons of Kohath, by their clans: Amram and Izhar, Hebron and Uzziel.*
20 *And the sons of Merari, by their clans: Mahli and Mushi. These are the clans of the Levites by their fathers' houses.*

23. At the tenth plague in Egypt, the death of the firstborn, a firstborn male yearling lamb was substituted for the Hebrew firstborn male. See Exod. 11:1–12, 32.

1. On the basis of evidence in Sam. Pent., *BHS* suggests that the first word of v. 17 *(wayyihyû),* which is awkward in its context there, be repointed and read as the divine name Yahweh. The adjusted text would then read *ka'ᵃšer ṣiwwāhû YHWH,* which is more common in similar contexts. Since the other clauses beginning with *'ēlleh* do not include the copular verb, it is quite possible that this suggestion is correct. The present translation simply renders the MT's *ṣuwwâ,* a Pual (passive), as a pluperfect; Davidson, *Syntax,* §39c.

21 *To Gershon belonged the clan of the Libnites and the clan of the Shimeites; these are the clans of the Gershonites.*
22 *Those numbered, according to the number of all males, from one month of age and older, those numbered: 7,500.*
23 *The clans of the Gershonites: They will encamp behind the tabernacle, to the west,*
24 *and the leader of the father's house of the Gershonites: Eliasaph the son of Lael.*
25 *And the guard duty of the sons of Gershon in the tent of meeting: the tabernacle, the tent, its covering, the screen of the door of the tent of meeting,*
26 *the hangings of the court, and the screen*[2] *of the door of the court that is around the tabernacle and around the altar; also its cords, and any work concerning these things.*
27 *And to Kohath belonged the clan of the Amramites and the clan of the Izharites and the clan of the Hebronites and the clan of the Uzzielites. These are the clans of the Kohathites.*
28 *According to the number of all males, from one month of age and up: 8,600,*[3] *standing guard over the holy things.*
29 *The clans of the sons of Kohath will encamp at the side of the tabernacle to the south.*
30 *And the leader of the father's house of the households of the Kohathites: Elizaphan the son of Uzziel.*
31 *And their guard duty: the ark, the table, the lampstand, the altars, the holy objects with which they assist, and the screen, as well as their removal.*[4]
32 *And the leader of the leaders of the Levites was Eliezar the son of Aaron the priest. He was overseer of those who stood guard over the holy things.*

2. MT here reads *w^{e}'eṯ-māsaḵ*. Here (and also below, "also its cords," *w^{e}'ēṯ mêṯārayw*) the particle *'eṯ* does not strictly depend on a verb and mark the definite direct object. This duty (and the one concerning the cords in this same verse) adds new items to the list of duties of the Gershonites. For this usage of *'eṯ*, see Davidson, *Syntax*, § 72 Rem. 4. In a sense these particles depend upon the verbal idea inherent in *mišmereṯ* (guarding) in v. 25 (cf. GKC, § 117l). *BHS* eliminates both these particles for inadequate textual reasons.

3. *BHS* proposes reading *š^{e}mōnaṯ '^{a}lāp̄îm ûš^{e}lōš mē'ôṯ* (8,300) on the basis of a few Hebrew mss., Pesh., Vulg., and the Lucianic recension of LXX *(triakosioi)*, instead of MT *š^{e}mōnaṯ '^{a}lāp̄îm w^{e}šēš mē'ôṯ* (8,600). See the commentary below.

4. See Milgrom, *Studies in Levitical Terminology*, I:64 n. 237, and the references cited there.

33 *To Merari belonged the clans of the Mahlites and the Mushites. These are the clans of the Merarites.*

34 *And those numbered, by the number of every male from one month of age and up: 6,200.*

35 *And the leader of the fathers' houses of the clans of Merari: Zuriel son of Abihail. They are to encamp on the north side of the tabernacle.*

36 *The appointed guard duty of the sons of Merari: the boards of the tabernacle, its crosspieces, its pillars, its sockets, and all their accessories, as well as all their removal,*[5]

37 *the pillars surrounding the court, their sockets, their tent pegs, and their cords.*

38 *And those who encamp before the tabernacle, toward the east, before the tent of meeting, toward the rising sun, will be Moses and Aaron and his sons, standing guard over the holy things*[6] *—a guard duty on behalf of the children of Israel—and the unauthorized person who encroaches will be killed.*

39 *All those Levites numbered, whom Moses and Aaron*[7] *numbered, according to the command of Yahweh; by their clans, every male from one month of age and up: 22,000.*

This section gives some specific duties of the three Levite groups. It is important to keep the census of ch. 3 separate from the one in ch. 4. The present census, on all Levites from one month of age and up, emphasizes *guard duty (mišmereṯ); work (ʿ*^{a}*ḇōḏâ)* is barely mentioned. By contrast, the stress in ch. 4 is on the *ʿ*^{a}*ḇōḏâ*. This census in ch. 3 is the more important of the the two since 22,000 Levites, at least potentially, keep guard, while only 8,580 are engaged in the work of assembly, disassembly, and cartage.

14 Again, this census is not merely an administrative detail but a fulfillment of the command of Yahweh.

5. An alternate translation for the phrase *w*^{e}*ḵol-kēlāyw w*^{e}*ḵol ʿaḇōḏāṯô* would be to take it as a hendiadys, "their work tools"; see the similar *l*^{e}*ḵol-k*^{e}*lēhem ûl*^{e}*ḵol ʿ*^{a}*ḇōḏāṯām* in 4:32. Milgrom takes the latter verse in this way but not the present verse (*Studies in Levitical Terminology,* I:77 n. 279).

6. The word *hammiqdāš ("the holy things")* can also mean the sacred area; see Milgrom, *Studies in Levitical Terminology,* I:23 n. 78.

7. The word *w*^{e}*ʾaḥ*^{a}*rôn* is missing from a number of mss. as well as from Sam. Pent. and Pesh. In MT the word has extraordinary punctuation above it to show that the Masoretes knew of the difficulty in the text here. Another problem here is that the figures in the text add up to 22,300. See the Introduction above, section V, "Text and Versions," and the commentary below on the passage itself.

15–20 These verses tell, once again, about the three branches of the Levites: the Gershonites, the Kohathites, and the Merarites, named after the three sons of Levi.[8] The further subdivisions of these groups are given in vv. 18–20 in virtually the same order as found in Exod. 6 and 1 Chr. 6 and 23. Vv. 14–20 comprise two smaller sections, both of which end with concluding formulae: vv. 14–16, ending with Moses' carrying out of the command he had been given, and vv. 17–20, ending with the summary *and these are the clans of the Levites by their fathers' houses.*

21–39 The census account itself is made up of a number of stock phrases arranged in virtually identical order:

(1) An introduction, which repeats the various groups within the clan, and concludes with the formula "these are the clans of the *x*" (vv. 21, 27, 33).[9]

(2) A formula introducing the number of males counted, from one month of age and up (vv. 22a, 28a, 34a), followed by the number itself (vv. 22b, 28b, 34b).

(3) A statement of the place of encampment, to the west, south, or north (vv. 23, 29, 35b).[10]

(4) The naming of the leader of the particular group (vv. 24, 30, 35a).[11]

(5) The actual items that the group is to guard (vv. 25–26, 31, 36–37). The last section is very important and will be discussed below.

21, 27, 33 The names of the clans of the different Levitical groups are, for Gershon, the Libnites and the Shimeites; for Kohath, the Amramites, the Izharites, the Hebronites, and the Uzzielites; for Merari, the Mahlites and the Mushites. The clan names are derived from the names

8. Cf. Exod. 6; 1 Chr. 6; 23. Also called the Gersho*m*ites in 1 Chr. 6; 23.

9. This construction uses a noun clause where the "far" demonstrative *(hēm)* substitutes for the copular verb. See GKC, § 136d; Williams, *Syntax,* § 115.

10. This component is varied in several ways. First, the order (place, leader) of the first two lists is reversed by the third. Then the groups themselves are named in a variety of ways — with or without the word *clans (mišpᵉḥôṯ),* the definite article, or the word *sons (bᵉnê).* These small verbal differences are perhaps for variety, as they amount to saying the same thing in different ways. In the discussion on 2:3–9 above we posited that the group with the most honor is listed first (Gershon), while the group with the most important job is named second (Kohath). Since the Gershonites do not encamp on the east or even the south, but the west, the Hebrew word order places *'aḥᵃrê hammiškān* in a position of emphasis, before the verb.

11. This component is, again, varied in the third group, the Merarites, and the sections have small verbal differences for variety.

of the children of Gershon, Kohath, and Merari, and are listed in Exod. 6 and 1 Chr. 6 and 23. Little is known about the men themselves, but enough time must have passed for the name of individual son of Aaron to be understood as a clan name.

22, 28, 34, 39 The individual figures (Gershonites, 7,500; Kohathites, 8,600; Merarites, 6,200) add up to 22,300. V. 39 gives the figure as 22,000. Either the total figure is meant only to represent a round number, or, more likely, at least one of the individual group numbers is incorrect. The individual total most likely to be textually corrupt is usually held to be the 8,600 for the Kohathites. In the consonantal Hebrew text the word "three" is *šlš,* while "six" is *šš.* Thus, the "extra" three hundred is accounted for by the loss of one Hebrew consonant. This solution is simplest and is probably correct.[12]

In v. 28 the phrase *standing guard over the holy things* is added to the standard formula. The term *the holy things (haqqōḏeš)* cannot refer to the sanctuary proper (as in RSV, NIV, etc.) because the Levites do not guard the sanctuary itself — that is the job of the priests (cf. 3:38). The Kohathites guard only the ark, altars, holy vessels, etc., and this only in transit (see 3:7).

23, 29, 35b The various groups of Levites will station themselves on the west (Gershonites), the south (Kohathites), and the north (Merarites) sides of the tabernacle. The group with the most important guard duty (the Kohathites) is placed on the south, near to the priests. All through this census description the Kohathites have been described in more detail because their guard duty (the holy things) is more dangerous.

24, 30, 35a The heads of the various groups are named next. *Eliasaph* here is probably not the same person named as a leader in Gad (e.g., 1:14). *Lael* is a name that occurs only here in the Bible. A variant of the name *Elizaphan* (Elzaphan) is found in Exod. 6:22 and Lev. 10:4. El(i)zaphan was one of the persons Moses called on to carry away the corpses of Nadab and Abihu. *Uzziel* is one of the sons of Kohath and is mentioned often in the OT (e.g., Exod. 6:18, 22; Lev. 10:4; 1 Chr. 6:2, 18). *Zuriel* also occurs only here in the Bible. Thus the only names in this list to occur elsewhere in the Bible are El(i)zaphan and Uzziel.

25–26, 31, 36 The next part of the description is the assigned duty of the groups with an emphasis on their guard duty. All that is said about the work of dismantling, assembling, and carting the tabernacle

12. E.g., Gray, p. 28; Noordtzij, p. 38; Noth, p. 27; Snaith, p. 125; Sturdy, p. 31; Wenham, p. 71; Budd, p. 28; Riggans, p. 32.

seems almost an afterthought here.[13] This work will be more clearly detailed in the next chapter. It is possible that the comment is part of the process of editing chs. 3 and 4 together.

The Gershonites are to guard the coverings and the fabric or skin coverings of the sanctuary, i.e., the *tabernacle* and the *tent.* These structures are identified many times, but here they are listed separately, as in Exod. 26. The Gershonites are to be in charge of the coverings. The *tabernacle* itself *(hammiškān)* consisted of ten curtains made of fine linen (Exod. 26:1–6). The *tent* (*'ōhel*) was made of goats' hair and consisted of eleven curtains to go over the top of the tabernacle (Exod. 26:7–14). The Gershonites were also responsible for guarding the *covering (miśkeh)* that covered the whole structure (Exod. 26:14; cf. Num. 4:6–14). They were also to watch over *the screen of the door of the tent of meeting* (*māśāḵ peṯaḥ 'ōhel mô'ēḏ,* Exod. 26:36), *the hangings of the court* (*qal'ê heḥāṣer,* Exod. 27:9), *the screen of the door of the court* (*maśak peṯaḥ heḥāṣer 'ašer 'al hammiškān we'al hammizbēaḥ sāḇîḇ,* Exod. 27:16), and the *cords (mêṯār)* that were connected with these items. To this guard duty is added a note about the *work ('aḇōḏâ)* connected with this task. Since *specific* work has not yet been assigned to the Gershonites (see ch. 4), the term may be taken as general here.[14]

The Kohathites have the most holy things as their guard duty assignment. These include *the ark* (*hā'ārōn,* Exod. 25:10–22), *the table* (of the bread of the Presence, *haššulḥān,* Exod. 25:23–30), *the lampstand* (*hammenōrâ,* Exod. 25:31–40), *the altars* (*hammizbeḥôṯ,* Exod. 27:1–8; 30:1–10), *the holy objects* (*kelê haqqōḏeš,* e.g., Exod. 30:17–21; 31:7–11), and *the screen (hammasaḵ).* This last term is used to refer to three items: *the screen of the door of the tent of meeting* (v. 25), *the screen of the court that is around the tabernacle and around the altar* (v. 26), and the screen that divided the Most Holy Place from the Holy Place in the tabernacle proper (see, e.g., Exod. 26:31–33). Since the Gershonites guard the first two of these screens, and since the Kohathites carry the holy things, the screen referred to here must be the third screen. As will be seen in ch. 4, the Kohathites are responsible only for carrying these items. The priests pack them up for moving (see 4:4–14). Therefore, one may understand *work ('aḇōḏâ)* here as "cartage."

13. On the construction *we-* (or *le-*) *kōl 'aḇōḏāṯô* see Milgrom, *Studies in Levitical Terminology,* I:64 n. 237, and the references cited there.

14. For two fine older treatments, see A. R. S. Kennedy, "Tabernacle," *HDB,* IV:653–68; T. Whitelaw, "Tabernacle," *ISBE,* V:2887–98. See also the more modern treatments by G. Henton Davies, *IDB,* IV:498–506; S. Westerholm, *ISBE,* rev., IV:698–706; and Harrison, *Introduction,* pp. 403–8.

The Merarites are responsible for guarding the framework of the tabernacle, including the outer structure (Exod. 26:15–30) and the supports for the court (Exod. 27:9–19). Their *work (ʿăḇōḏâ)* included dismantling, reassembling, and carrying these materials to the carts.

38–39 On the east side of the tabernacle, at the preeminent position,[15] Moses (presumably with his family) and Aaron and his sons were to encamp. The priests, too, have a guard duty to perform. They stand guard over the holy things. This guard duty is to be differentiated from that of the Kohathites, who stand guard over the holy things when the sanctuary has been erected. The construction *a guard duty on behalf of the children of Israel* interrupts the flow of the sentence. This guard duty is on behalf of and for the benefit of Israel. The reason why it is beneficial is seen in the next clause, the formula *and the unauthorized person who encroaches will be killed* (see also 1:51; 3:10; 18:7). The priests here have only guard duty, no "work" *(ʿăḇōḏâ)* as such.

The sacred shrine is called the *tabernacle* and the *tent of meeting* in apposition here.[16] The structure may be referred to in a technical way (as in v. 25 above), in which case tabernacle and tent may be differentiated, or, as here, the general structures may be identified.

The total number of Levites, from one month of age and up, is 22,000, which includes the 7,500 Gershonites, 8,300 Kohathites, and 6,200 Merarites.[17]

EXCURSUS ON THE PRIESTS AND LEVITES

According to the biblical narratives, both priests and Levites were descended from Levi, the third son of Jacob and Leah (Gen. 29:34). Levi had three sons: Gershon (or Gershom), Kohath, and Merari (Gen. 46:11; Exod. 6:16; 1 Chr. 6:2). Aaron and Moses were descendants of Kohath (Exod. 6:16–20; 1 Chr. 6:2–3). Their descent from him is probably corroborated by the fact that, although the Kohathites are not descendants of the firstborn, they are given more responsibility and honor than the other Levites. The priests were the only ones who were allowed to offer sacrifices and preside at the sacred rites of the tabernacle (see, e.g., Num. 3:38; 18:1–32). The Levites included all other descendants of Levi, i.e.,

15. See the commentary above on 2:3–9.
16. See also the commentary above on 1:1.
17. See the "Excursus on Large Numbers" above.

the non-Aaronite Kohathites, the Gershonites, and the Merarites. The Levites' duties had to do with guarding the outside of the tabernacle ("guard duty," *šāmar mišmereṯ*) and the physical work of erecting, dismantling, and carrying it *(ʿāḇaḏ ʿ^{a}ḇōḏâ)*.

From the point of view of the text as it stands, Levi was originally a "secular" tribe that was later set apart for sacred service. Genesis paints Levi as a bloodthirsty man (tribe?) who, along with Simeon, avenged their sister Dinah's assault by killing all the men of Shechem (Gen. 34), a fact noted with disapproval in the Testament of Jacob (Gen. 49:7). The Levites were chosen by Moses to execute the death sentence on 3,000 idolators after the incident with the golden calf (Exod. 32:28). That Moses and Aaron were brothers and Levites probably explains, at least in the first instance, why this tribe was chosen for special service.

The question that has arisen, however is, Is this the way it really happened? Since the time of Julius Wellhausen the answer of a great portion of critical scholarship has been negative. As is well known, Wellhausen fixed the date of the Priestly Code of the Pentateuch in the postexilic age. This meant that the assignment of duties of priests and Levites here in Numbers did not really belong to the time of Moses, but rather was a projection of the concerns of the time of the second temple back into the Mosaic age.

As is widely admitted today among all varieties of scholarship, Wellhausen assumed much of what he wrote rather than demonstrating it to be true. One of his major assumptions was the unilinear evolution of religious institutions from simple to complex. The complexity of regulations in Num. 3 and 4 meant that in all probability the material was very late, and in hardly any cases could belong to the Mosaic period, or even that of the united monarchy.[1]

According to the common theory that has become connected with the names of Graf and Wellhausen, the earliest narrative sources in the Pentateuch speak little about the Israelite priesthood at all. What may be said is that the complex legislation of Numbers left minimal or no traces in the time, e.g., of the judges. In the early days most anyone could become a priest, although a Levite might be preferred. During the time of the monarchy the priesthood became more settled in families, notably the (supposedly) non-Levitical family of Zadok that officiated at the Jerusalem temple.[2]

1. The commentary by Gray, which is a classic example of this line of approach, is clear in this assertion. See, e.g., pp. xlii–xlvii.

2. The Zadokites are not called Levitical until the time of the Chronicler.

In the 620s, when Josiah tore out the local sanctuaries in favor of the Jerusalem temple, some of the local priests, of course, lost their jobs. He brought them to Jerusalem to assist the Zadokite priests. It is usually assumed that the programmatic document for Josiah's reforms was Deuteronomy (or some part of it). It is also assumed that Deuteronomy makes no differentiation between Levites and priests by its formula "the priests, the Levites" (RSV "the Levitical priests"; e.g., Deut. 17:9).

Priests and Levites were first sharply distinguished only later, in Ezekiel's plan of the restored temple (chs. 40–44). The Priestly Code projects all this innovation back into the Mosaic age as existent from the beginning.[3] The clearly postexilic books of Ezra-Nehemiah and Chronicles agree more fully with the Priestly Code in Numbers than with any other literature. In this literature the priests are traced back to Aaron rather than merely to Zadok (e.g., Ezra 8:2). A clear difference is also made between priests and Levites (e.g., Ezra 2:36–42), again, as in the Priestly Code.

The biblical text, when read as it stands, would seem to hold that the postexilic interest in religious, cultic, and priestly matters was a revival of an interest that existed at the beginning of the history of the people and originated in divine revelation. Why is it not likely that in the age of Ezra and Nehemiah, when the whole question of national identity and goals was transposed from a political into a religious key (since the Jews' political fortunes were not in their own hands), interest would not revive in the priesthood, worship, and temple service? What better programmatic document for such goals could be found than the Priestly Code? The picture given by the present text (i.e., the antiquity of this priestly material and the priesthood) is just as likely as the very complex (overly complex?) reconstructions offered by modern followers of Wellhausen. This is especially so in the light of the methodological problems that plague such reconstructions.[4] For example, the only reason why Ezekiel must precede the Priestly Code is surely a prior decision to that effect. It is just as likely that Ezekiel used the Priestly material in his proposals. Whereas Ezekiel's program fits well in the postexilic age, the

---

Many have seen this to be a late attempt to make all priests descendants of Levi; see, e.g., Wellhausen, *Prolegomena,* p. 126 n. 1.

3. See Wellhausen, *Prolegomena,* p. 124.

4. See, e.g., Rendtorff, *Das überlieferungsgeschichtliche Problem des Pentateuch;* Whybray, *Making of the Pentateuch;* Allis, *Five Books of Moses;* Harrison, *Introduction,* pp. 3–82, 495–541; Kitchen, *Ancient Orient,* pp. 112–50.

program of the Priestly material is locked into the wilderness period and would have more limited immediate usefulness in a sedentary environment. For example, Ezekiel makes provision for the priests near the sanctuary rather than in priestly/Levitical cities around the countryside, as in Num. 35. To their credit, a growing number of scholars affirm the antiquity of the Priestly material.[5]

Of course, the case must be argued on its merits and on the details of individual texts rather than on general feelings and principles (as important as the latter may be). This is not the place to engage in a full-blown discussion of the case of Wellhausen's school, but a few points can be made.

First, the contention that D (the Deuteronomist) made no differentiation between priests and Levites is open to question.[6] Every Levite was, at least potentially, a priest. Levites are mentioned 19 times in Deuteronomy, in 10 of which the people are adjured to care for the Levites along with other "homeless" classes such as the sojourner, widow, and fatherless.[7] In 27:14 the Levites declare the curses found in the following verses. In 31:25 the Levites are responsible for carrying the ark, in agreement with such passages as Num. 3:31 and 4:15.[8] In Deut. 18:6–7 a group of Levites is responsible for ministering along with other Levites. This last passage is within a pericope crucial to the question, and will be dealt with in a moment.

In five cases the Levites are mentioned in the formula "the priests, the Levites," i.e., "the Levitical priests" (RSV) or "the priests, who are

5. Conservative scholars have usually affirmed this — not always for the most convincing reasons. One exception to this was the work of Allis, *Five Books of Moses.* See also R. Abba, "Priests and Levites," *IDB,* III:888–89; and more fully in his articles "Priests and Levites in Deuteronomy," *VT* 27 (1977) 257–67; and "Priests and Levites in Ezekiel," *VT* 28 (1978) 1–9. On the Jewish side, see, e.g., Kaufmann, *Religion of Israel,* esp. pp. 153–211; Milgrom, *Studies in Levitical Terminology,* I:46–59; idem, *Studies in Cultic Theology,* pp. 1–66; M. Haran, *Temples and Temple Service in Ancient Israel* (Oxford: Clarendon, 1978), pp. 58–111. This list is not by any means exhaustive, nor do all the scholars listed take the same positions. It is, however, a sign that OT scholarship is showing some willingness to reopen the questions of origins of this part of the biblical text.

6. See, e.g., G. E. Wright, "The Levites in Deuteronomy," *VT* 4 (1954) 325–30; J. A. Emerton, "Priests and Levites in Deuteronomy," *VT* 12 (1962) 129–38; Abba, "Priests and Levites in Deuteronomy," pp. 257–67.

7. See Deut. 12:12, 18–19; 14:27, 29; 16:11, 14; 26:11–13.

8. It is true that the priests are also said to carry the ark in 31:9. On this see Abba, "Priests and Levites in Deuteronomy," pp. 260–61.

Levites" (NIV).[9] This construction has, at the very least, confirmed the widespread assumption that in Deuteronomy "priest" and "Levite" are equivalent terms. It should be remembered that, according to, e.g., Exod. 28; Lev. 8; and Num. 16–18, only the sons of Aaron the Levite could officiate at cultic ceremonies in Israel. In other words, all priests had to be Levites descended from Aaron. It is possible that in the light of this fact, the phrase "the priests, the Levites" *(hakkōhᵃnîm halᵉwîyim)* simply points to the fact that each *legitimate* priest had to be a Levite. That this is a possible meaning can be further shown from another similar phrase used for the priests, "the priests, the sons of Levi" (*hakkōhᵃnîm bᵉnê lēwî,* 21:5; 31:9). Otherwise these functionaries are simply called "the priests" (17:12; 18:3 [twice]; 19:17; 20:2; 26:3, 4).

Deuteronomy 18:1–8 is crucial to the discussion. One cannot even outline all the problems here, but only sketch some proposed solutions. The text begins: "None of the priests, the Levites, all the tribe of Levi, will have a share or inheritance with Israel." The question is whether "the priests, the Levites" is the same as "all the tribe of Levi" here, as J. A. Emerton holds, or whether, as G. E. Wright suggested, the latter is a larger group that makes the former designation, "the priests, the Levites," more expansive.[10] R. Abba gave important support to Wright's reading of the verse,[11] but, in fact, the syntax of the verse is not clear and no final decision can be rendered on it. The conclusions one comes to here will likely be influenced by one's own view of the problem in the first place. Suffice it to say that Emerton does not appear to shut the door on the Wright/Abba case, and their reading of the verse remains possible.

The rest of the pericope seems to favor Abba's position. Vv. 3–5 prescribe that dues be received not by "the priest, the Levite," but simply by "the priest." Vv. 6–8 outline the ministry simply for "the Levites." If there is no difference between the terms *priest* and *Levite,* why not use one term throughout the passage? This is not a simple matter of using different terms for literary variety. It, rather, seems more likely that vv. 1–2 use a general term encompassing both priests and Levites (for neither has a land inheritance); vv. 3–5 deal with the priests, and vv. 6–8 with the Levites.[12]

9. See Deut. 17:9, 18; 18:1; 24:8; 27:9.

10. Emerton, "Priests and Levites in Deuteronomy," pp. 133–34; Wright, "Levites in Deuteronomy," p. 326.

11. Abba, "Priests and Levites in Deuteronomy," p. 264.

12. P. Craigie, *The Book of Deuteronomy,* NICOT (Grand Rapids: Eerd-

Attention might now be drawn to the terminology used to describe the Levites' work in Numbers, Chronicles, and Ezekiel. In Numbers the work is described as guard duty *(šāmar mišmereṯ)* and the physical work of assembly, disassembly, and cartage of the tabernacle *(ʿaḇōḏâ)*. In Chronicles the first duty is still understood and given to the Levites, as is shown by 1 Chr. 9:27: "They [the Levites] spent the night surrounding the house of God because the guard duty *[mišmereṯ]* was upon them." The most likely reason that the Chronicler does not explain *mišmereṯ* is that he knew "guard duty" to be the original and proper meaning of the term.[13] When it came to the other duty, however, Milgrom has shown that the Chronicler shifted the meaning of *ʿaḇōḏâ* from physical work to cultic service.[14]

In Numbers the Levites simply do not play the role in the cult that they do in Chronicles. For example, the Levites' work with the utensils in 1 Chr. 9:28–32 is very different from the hands-off attitude of Num. 4:4–14. There is also no comparison between the great number of other types of functionaries (e.g., the singers) in Chronicles and in Numbers. In short, the book of Numbers is wholly geared to Levitical service in a mobile tent shrine, while Chronicles shows the more cumbersome mechanisms of a permanent temple. To place the composition of Numbers, even in its final form, within 50 to 100 years of Chronicles seems unlikely.

Ezekiel's program for the reestablishment of the temple service (chs. 40–44, esp. 44:6–31) is an ideal plan that divided the Levites from the priests (the latter were descended only from Zadok). That his plan was not put into practice after the return from exile (as a comparison with Chronicles shows it was not) must be left aside as beside the present note. Ezekiel uses *mišmereṯ* as "guard duty," but expands it to mean "guarding by will power."[15] He uses the word *ʿaḇōḏâ* only once (44:14), in a paraphrase (midrash?) on Num. 18:4a (where *ʿaḇōḏâ* occurs in the text of Numbers), and to this he adds an extra phrase ("that is, everything that is to be done in it," *ûlᵉḵol ʾašer yēʿāśeh bô*) to explain what it means to him.

---

mans, 1976), p. 258, also takes the view expressed above. For the other view, in addition to Emerton and the sources he mentioned, see H. Wheeler Robinson, *Deuteronomy, Joshua,* Century Bible (Edinburgh: E. C. & T. C. Jack, 1907), p. 146; and, less clearly, A. D. H. Mayes, *Deuteronomy,* NCBC (Grand Rapids: Eerdmans, 1981), p. 275.

13. Milgrom, *Studies in Levitical Terminology,* I:12–15.

14. Ibid., pp. 83–84. See also pp. 76–83.

15. Ibid., p. 11.

It is clear that the duties of slaying the whole burnt offering and the sacrifice, assigned to the Levites in 44:11, is a task reserved for the laity in Lev. 1:5, 11; 3:2, 8, 13; 4:24, 29, 33.

In sum, neither Ezekiel nor Chronicles uses either the term *mišmereṯ* or *ʿᵃḇōdâ* in just the way Numbers does. Numbers is, again, tied to the wilderness-wandering period. Only the desire to agree with a particular school of interpretation forces one to the necessity of seeing the material in Numbers as later than Ezekiel. If anything, Ezekiel shows traces of having used Numbers (and Leviticus) rather than the other way around.[16]

(2) Levites for Firstborn (3:40–51)

40 *And Yahweh said to Moses, "Number every firstborn male of the children of Israel from one month of age and up, and calculate their total by names,*
41 *and take the Levites for me — I am Yahweh — instead of each firstborn among the children of Israel, as well as the Levites' cattle, instead of every firstborn among the cattle of the children of Israel."*
42 *So Moses numbered every firstborn among the children of Israel as Yahweh had commanded him.*
43 *And it was*[1] *that every firstborn male, by the number of names, from one month of age and up, numbered 22,273.*
44 *And Yahweh spoke to Moses, saying:*
45 *"Take the Levites instead of every firstborn of the children of Israel and the cattle of the Levites instead of their cattle, and the Levites shall be mine — I am Yahweh.*
46 *And, as for the ransoming of the 273*[2] *from the firstborn of the*

16. Abba, *IDB,* IV:888; idem, "Priests and Levites in Ezekiel," pp. 8–9.

1. The word *wayᵉhî* should be understood as the narrative formula ("and it was," "came to pass," or "happened") followed by a noun clause (GKC, § 111f) rather than the verb of which "every firstborn male" *(kol-bᵉḵōr zāḵār)* is the subject. If the latter were the case, one would probably have found the pl. here (as is found in Sam. Pent., etc.); cf. *BHS.*

2. In "as for the ransoming . . ." *(wᵉʾēṯ pᵉḏûyê haššᵉlōšâ wᵉhaššiḇʿîm wᵉhammāṯāyim),* the particle *ʾēṯ* is to be thought of as introducing and emphasizing the numbers that follow. See GKC, § 117m (see also Num. 5:10; 35:6; etc.); J. Blau, "Zum Angeblichen Gebrauch von ʾēṯ von dem Nominative," *VT* 4 (1954) 7–19. The definite article on each one of the numbers has the effect of referring to a definite 273 persons that have been mentioned before (i.e., in v. 43). See Davidson, *Syntax,* § 37 Rem. 5; GKC, § 134k; cf. Williams, *Syntax,* § 97.

children of Israel, who are over and above the number of the Levites,

47 *you shall take five shekels for each one individually*[3] *(you shall take this in the shekel of the sanctuary, the twenty-gerah shekel),*

48 *and you shall give the silver that has ransomed these over and above them*[4] *to Aaron and his sons."*

49 *So Moses took the silver of the ransom*[5] *from those who were over and above those ransomed by the Levites,*

50 *from the firstborn of the children of Israel he took the silver, 1,365 shekels by the shekel of the sanctuary.*

51 *And Moses gave the silver of the ransom to Aaron and to his sons according to the command of Yahweh, just as Yahweh had commanded him.*

The firstborn male Israelites of one month of age and up are counted and found to total 22,273. This total exceeded the total number of Levites by 273. Thus there were 273 unreplaced and unredeemed Israelite males in this count, since the Levites were meant to replace the firstborn males of Israel (see, e.g., 3:11–13). These unredeemed males were redeemed at a cost of five silver shekels apiece, and the total ransom price of 1,365 shekels was given to the priests.

This section contains two subsections, each begun by a formula that relates what follows as Yahweh's word ("Yahweh said . . . ," v. 40; "Yahweh spoke . . . ," v. 44). The first subsection deals with two subjects: the count of the firstborn males, and their replacement by the Levites (vv. 40–43). The second subsection repeats the replacement theme and then discusses the ransom of the 273 extra firstborn males (vv. 44–51).

40 *Number . . . calculate by names.* Again, as in 1:2 (where the same idiom occurs), the counting of Israelites is not seen as an unimportant detail, but is placed in the will and command of Yahweh.

3. The clause "you shall take five shekels for each one individually" *(w*^{e}*lāqaḥtā ḥ*^{a}*mēšeṯ ḥ*^{a}*mēšeṯ š*^{e}*qālîm lagulgōleṯ)* has repeated construct forms (*ḥ*^{a}*mēšeṯ ḥ*^{a}*mēšeṯ,* lit., "five of, five of"). The first form may have become a construct by attraction to the second. The whole repeated construction forms the single distributive idea "five shekels for each one." See Davidson, *Syntax,* § 28 Rem. 6. For the repetition of numbers as distributives, see ibid., § 28 Rem. 5 (2); Williams, *Syntax,* §§ 15, 100. On *gulgōleṯ,* see the commentary above on 1:2.

4. The pronoun here refers to the Levites.

5. For "silver of the ransom" *(kesep̱ happiḏyôm)* Sam. Pent. reads *hap-p*^{e}*ḏûyim,* "ransom," as in v. 51. This requires the change of only two letters and is probably correct. MT *happiḏyôm* is a hapax legomenon. The meaning is the same.

41 *for me* means "for my use." This verse reiterates that all the Levites belonged to Yahweh as a replacement for the firstborn sons of Israel who became Yahweh's at the time of the tenth plague in Egypt.[6]

The text also makes clear that the firstborn animals belong to Yahweh: *take . . . the Levites' cattle, instead of every firstborn among the cattle of the children of Israel.* The text cannot mean (and does not say) that the Levites' cattle replaced the sacrifice of firstlings of other cattle. In fact, 18:5, 7 forbid cows, sheep, or goats to be redeemed. Rather than seeing the whole construction as artful theorizing long after the fact,[7] the text should be considered an expansion of the statement of 3:11–13 — that the Levites and all they have belonged to Yahweh.[8] In the light of the priestly exclusivity of v. 38, a restatement of the special status of the Levites as over against the priests is quite natural and timely.

42–43 Moses did as Yahweh commanded him, and the total was 22,273. The problem of the number of firstborn males in a male population of over 600,000 has already been referred to above.[9]

44–45 The second subsection is also that which Yahweh said, and begins with the main theme of the previous subsection (the divine possession of the Levites), thus linking the two units. The firstborn cattle are mentioned here only to indicate that all the Levites' possessions truly belonged to God.

46–48 *ransoming, ransomed.* The Hebrew words *p*^{e}*ḏûyê, hap-p*^{e}*ḏûyyîm* (v. 51), and *happiḏyôm* (v. 49) are derivatives of *pāḏâ,* the basic meaning of which is to transfer ownership of someone or something to another.[10] All contain the idea of ransoming. In Num. 3 the ransom price is a life for a life: the Levites for the firstborn male Israelites.[11] Thus the *kesep̱ happiḏyôm* (lit., "the silver of the ransom") is the "ransom price" (v. 49).

6. See Exod. 13:2; 22:29b–30; 34:19–20; Lev. 27:26–27; Num. 8:17–18.

7. See, e.g., Noth, p. 41; Snaith, p. 125.

8. See Budd, p. 38: "The point at issue is the dignity of the Levitical office, not the operation of the law of the firstborn."

9. See the "Excursus on Large Numbers" above. Noordtzij (p. 41) presents the case that "firstborn" here refers only to the first male children in a family, not simply to the first male child of a particular father and mother. This means that there was only one firstborn no matter how many parents might have been involved; e.g., Reuben is the one and only firstborn of Jacob, although four different mothers were involved.

10. In Arabic *fida*^{n} is a ransom paid for a prisoner.

11. For more on the concept of "ransom," see O. Procksch, *TDNT,* IV:330–35; W. B. Coker, *TWOT,* II:716–17, and the references contained in these articles.

47 Each of these firstborn males is ransomed, not at the cost of a life, but for *five shekels* of silver. This five-shekel redemption price, according to Lev. 27:6, is the price of redemption for a male from one month to five years of age. The regulation of 18:15–16 establishes the principle that each firstborn is to be redeemed at the age of one month (as is appropriate for the five-shekel price).

It is not certain what is intended by the *shekel of the sanctuary.* Although the term *shekel* was a common unit of weight all across the ancient Near East, its actual value differed from place to place and time to time.[12] Scholars usually assume that the sanctuary shekel was different in some way from other shekels.[13] All that can be said with certainty is that the shekel here was measured on the standard then current and in force at the sanctuary. This standard is listed as *twenty gerahs* to the shekel. A gerah is usually thought to have weighed about half a gram, so that a twenty-gerah shekel would weigh about 0.4 oz.

48 At the time of this first redemption, the reader is not informed which 273 had to pay the price or how it was collected. The collected silver, like the Levites for which it was to be a substitute, belonged to the priests. Wenham may well be right in concluding that the valuations of Lev. 27:2–8 and the current passage come from the average price that a slave would bring on the ancient Near Eastern market.[14]

This chapter shows, first, that the Levites were set aside by God for divine and priestly use. The Levites aid the priests by standing guard over various items connected with the tabernacle while the camp is on the march, and by guarding the gate of the holy shrine when the camp is set up. The Levites also have physical work (as yet undesignated) that is connected with the tabernacle service. The Levites belong to God as replacements for the firstborn males of Israel. Once the number of the Levites became known through a census, the number of firstborn males could also be calculated. When it was found that there were 273 more firstborn males than Levites, a five-shekel ransom price was set for each one. Thus God's holiness is insulated from the people and the people are insulated by the Levites from the fatal holiness of God. The Levites keep watch over both the priests and the people to make sure that no unauthorized person encroaches upon the sanctuary and the holy things in it.

12. See, e.g., O. R. Sellers, *IDB,* IV:829–39, esp. 832–33.

13. Cf., e.g., Noordtzij, p. 41; D. J. Wiseman, *NBD,* p. 1247.

14. G. Wenham, "Leviticus 27:2–8 and the Price of Slaves," *ZAW* 90 (1978) 254–65.

49–51 These verses form the conclusion to the present unit. *Silver of the ransom* — see the note on the translation above. *1,365 shekels* — this figure is obtained by multiplying the number of unredeemed and unreplaced Levites (273) by the five-shekel ransom price for each. V. 51 is a conclusion which, once again, states that all was done exactly as Yahweh had commanded Moses (see also 1:54; 3:33–34; 4:42).

(3) Census of Working Levites (4:1–49)

1 *And Yahweh spoke to Moses and to Aaron, saying:*
2 *"Calculate the total of the sons of Kohath from the midst of the children of Levi, by their clans, by their fathers' houses,*
3 *from the age of thirty years to the age of fifty years, all who are qualified to go to the service, to do work in the tent of meeting.*
4 *This is the work of the sons of Kohath in the tent of meeting: the holiest things.*
5 *When the encampment is to move, Aaron and his sons will go in and take down the veil of the screen, and cover the ark of the testimony in it,*
6 *and they shall put over it a covering of porpoise skin,*[1] *and spread out over it a wrapping entirely of blue-violet, and put its poles in place.*
7 *And over the table of the Presence they will spread out a blue-violet covering, and put upon it the dishes, the spoons,*[2] *the sacrificial bowls,*[3] *and the jars*[4] *for the drink offering. The continual bread will also be upon it.*

1. This translation finds its basis in the Arab. *taḥas* $(^{un})$, "porpoise." See R. F. Youngblood, *TWOT*, II:967b. The LXX takes the term as relating to the color of the skins (*dermata hyakinthina*, "hyacinth-colored skins"), e.g., in Exod. 25:5.

2. Presumably the *kap* was a flattened spoon since the word is primarily used to designate the palm of the hand or sole of the foot. AV translates "spoon" both here and in ch. 7. According to ch. 7 these vessels were used to contain incense, thus RSV "dishes for incense."

3. The term *m*^{e}*naqqîyâ* occurs also in Exod. 25:29; 37:16; Num. 4:7; and Jer. 52:19. According to LXX these vessels were ladles for drawing wine from bowls (LSJ, I:1003), and this may well be correct. Also see the note in A. MacAlister, *HDB*, II:41a; M. C. Fisher and B. K. Waltke, *TWOT*, I:598.

4. Heb. *qaśwâ*. This term, found only in the pl., occurs in Exod. 25:29; 37:16; Num. 4:7; and 1 Chr. 28:17. Here and in Exod. 37:16 these vessels are connected with libations. In Exod. 25:29 the order of the bowls and the *qaśwâ* is reversed and the latter term is connected with the libation. Possibly both vessels may have been so used.

8 *And they will spread out over them a wrapping of scarlet, and cover it in a covering of porpoise skin, and put its poles in place.*

9 *And they will take a wrapping of blue-violet and cover the lampstand of the light, and its lamps, and its tongs,*[5] *and its trays,*[6] *and all its oil vessels with which they service it.*

10 *And they will put it and all its accessories into a covering of porpoise skin, and put it on the carrying frame.*

11 *And upon the altar of gold they will spread out a wrapping of blue-violet, and cover it in a covering of porpoise skin, and put its poles in place.*

12 *And they will take all the accessories of service with which they serve in the sanctuary, and put them into a wrapping of blue-violet, and cover them in a covering of porpoise skin, and put them on the carrying frame.*

13 *And they will take away the ashes from the altar, and spread out over it a wrapping of purple.*

14 *And they will put on it all its accessories with which they service it, namely, the trays, the implements,*[7] *the shovels,*[8] *the basins,*[9] *that is, all the accessories of the altar, and they will spread out over them a covering of porpoise skin, and put its poles in place.*

15 *When Aaron and his sons have finished covering the sanctuary and the accessories of the sanctuary, when the camp is ready to move and after this is done,*[10] *the sons of Kohath may come to*

5. Heb. *melqāḥayim* (a dual form) comes from *lāqaḥ,* "to take." It is used once of a device used to remove a coal from the altar (Isa. 6:6). Elsewhere it is always connected with the menorah as something that "takes" something (viz., the flame) from it — a snuffer. Because the term occurs only in the dual, it is best to think of it as a two-part device of some kind, hence "tongs."

6. Heb. *maḥtâ* comes from *ḥāṯâ,* "to snatch up." It is used to describe a receptacle of some sort. Such receptacles held ashes from the altar (Exod. 27:3) or incense (Lev. 10:1; Num. 16:6).

7. Heb. *hammizlāḡōṯ,* lit. "the prongs." In 1 Sam. 2:13 a masc. form of this same word is described as a three-tined implement, i.e., a fork. See S. R. Driver, *Notes on the Hebrew Text and Topography of the Books of Samuel,* 2nd ed. (Oxford: Clarendon, 1912), p. 30 (also n. 1).

8. Heb. *yāʿîm* (found only in the pl.) is related to the verb "to sweep together" found only in Isa. 28:17. The contexts of the nine usages of the noun make it clear that this item was used for cleaning the altar; see KB, pp. 388–89.

9. Heb. *mizrāqōṯ* is related to a word which means "throw, sprinkle," and is used of the priest throwing blood against the altar (e.g., Exod. 29:16). These basins were vessels used for collecting the blood that was to be so used.

10. The syntax of this verse in Hebrew is difficult. The first *waw* (i.e., *w^{e}ḵillâ ʾah^{a}rōn ûḇānayw*) should be understood to introduce a temporal clause, "when Aaron and his sons have finished . . ." (see Williams, *Syntax,* § 496), which

carry these things, but they must not touch that which is holy or they will die. These things are the burden of the sons of Kohath in the tent of meeting.

16 *That which is the oversight of Eleazar the son of Aaron the priest is: the oil for the light, the sweet incense,*[11] *the regular meal offering, and the oil for anointing; also the oversight of all the tabernacle and everything that is in it, that is, the holy place and its accessories."*

17 *And Yahweh spoke to Moses and to Aaron, saying:*

18 *"You shall not cut off the tribe of the clans of the Kohathites from the midst of the Levites,*

19 *but do this for them that they might live and not die when they make contact with*[12] *the holy things. Aaron and his sons will go in and set them, each one, to his work and to his carrying.*

20 *But they must not enter to see the holy things even for an instant or they will die."*

21 *And Yahweh spoke to Moses, saying:*

22 *"Calculate the total of the sons of Gershon, as well, by their fathers' houses, by their clans.*

23 *You shall number them from the age of thirty years up to the age of fifty years, all those who are qualified to go to do service, to do work in the tent of meeting.*

24 *This is the work of the Gershonites, as relates to packing and carrying:*

25 *They will carry the curtains of the tabernacle, and the tent of meeting, its covering, and the covering of porpoise skin that is over the top of it, and the screen of the door to the tent of meeting,*

26 *also the hangings of the court, the screen for the door of the gate of the court that is around the tabernacle and around the altar, their cords, and all the accessories for transporting them. And all that is done for them, they shall do.*

27 *All the work of the sons of the Gershonites will be at the command*

---

is continued by the further temporal construction *'aḥ^a rê-ḵēn* ("after this," i.e., "then afterward"). The *waw* on the verb *mēṯû* ("they will die") is best translated by "or." The consequence of touching the holy things is death.

11. See Budd, p. 42, "sweet incense"; RSV "fragrant incense"; etc.

12. Milgrom has shown that the verb *nāgaš,* "to make contact with," is a rough synonym for *qāraḇ,* which can have the negative sense "to encroach" and the positive sense "to be admitted to." The Levites incur death when they touch the holy things, not when they simply come into proximity with them. See Milgrom, *Studies in Levitical Terminology,* I:60-66.

of Aaron and his sons, as regards all their carrying and all their packing. And you shall appoint them as a guard for all that they are to carry.

28 *This is the work of the clans of the sons of the Gershonites in the tent of meeting. And their guard duty is to be under the authority of Ithamar, the son of Aaron the priest.*

29 *As for the sons of Merari, by their clans, by their fathers' houses, you shall number them,*

30 *from thirty years of age up to fifty years of age you shall number them, all who are qualified to go to the service to do the work of the tent of meeting.*

31 *This is their guard burden, as regards their packing work in the tent of meeting: the boards of the tabernacle, its crosspieces, its pillars, and its sockets,*

32 *also the pillars surrounding the court, their sockets, their tent pegs, their cords, and all their accessories for all their work. And you shall specify all the items by name that are their charge to carry.*

33 *This is the work of the clans of the sons of Merari, as regards all their work in the tent of meeting. They are under the authority of Ithamar, the son of Aaron the priest."*

34 *So Moses and Aaron and the leaders of the congregation numbered the sons of Kohath by their clans and by their fathers' houses,*

35 *from the age of thirty years up to the age of fifty years, everyone who was eligible to go to the service, for work in the tent of meeting.*

36 *And those numbered, by their clans, were 2,750.*

37 *These are those numbered of the clans of the Kohathites, all who would work in the tent of meeting, whom Moses and Aaron numbered according to the commandment of Yahweh by the agency of Moses.*

38 *And those numbered of the sons of Gershon, by their clans and by their fathers' houses,*

39 *from the age of thirty years up to the age of fifty years, everyone who was eligible to go to the service, for work in the tent of meeting.*

40 *And those numbered, by their clans, were 2,630.*

41 *These are those numbered of the clans of the sons of Gershon, all who would do work in the tent of meeting, whom Moses and Aaron numbered according to the commandment of Yahweh.*

42 *And those numbered of the clans of the sons of Merari, by their clans, by their fathers' houses,*

43 *from the age of thirty years up to the age of fifty years, everyone who could go to the service, for work in the tent of meeting.*
44 *And those numbered, by their clans, were 3,200.*
45 *These are those numbered of the clans of the sons of Merari, whom Moses and Aaron numbered according to the commandment of Yahweh by the agency of Moses.*
46 *All those numbered of the Levites, whom Moses and Aaron and the leaders of Israel numbered, by their clans, and by their fathers' houses,*
47 *from the age of thirty years up to the age of fifty years, everyone who was eligible to go to do the work of packing and the work of bearing burdens in the tent of meeting.*
48 *And those numbered were 8,580.*
49 *According to the commandment of Yahweh by the agency of Moses he numbered them, each one to his labor or his burden. And they were appointed just as Yahweh had commanded Moses.*

Several points about this census record have already been made in connection with the last chapter, but a further general comment is in order. Although it has not been the normal custom in English Bible translation to do so, the interpreter should be careful to define just what it is that the Levites are charged to do here. In ch. 3 the most common duty was "guard duty" *(mišmereṯ)*. Here three other words come into play: *work* in the sense of "skilled labor" *(m^{e}lāḵâ), work* in the sense of "physical work" (*ʿ^{a}bōḏâ* or the verbal form *ʿāḇaḏ*), and a general term for *service* or "ministry" *(šērēṯ)* in which the Levites assist the priests.[13] The following chart shows the distribution of these words:

Guard Duty	Ministry	Physical Work	Skilled Work
3:7	3:6	3:7	3:—
8	31	8	
25		26	
28		36	
31			
32			
36			
38			

13. On *m^{e}lā'ḵâ,* see ibid., I:77–79. On *ʿ^{a}bōḏâ* and *ʿāḇaḏ,* see ibid., pp. 60–66. On *šērēṯ,* see ibid., p. 67 n. 245.

4:27	4:12	4:3	4:3
28	14	19	
31		23	
32		24	
		26	
		27	
		28	
		30	
		31	
		32	
		33	
		35	
		37	
		39	
		41	
		43	
		47	
		49	

Of course, specific meanings of these words will depend upon individual contexts, but the general meanings hold. This chart shows that one major purpose of ch. 4 is to detail the physical work for each of the Levitical clans involved in the dismantling, carrying, and reassembling of the tabernacle. The purpose of ch. 3 was to discuss the guard duty the Levites were to exercise around the tabernacle. This explains why ch. 4 limits the age range from 30 to 50 years (adults at the peak of physical power), whereas ch. 3 allows guard duty to be carried out by most any age group, including, at least theoretically, those only one month old.[14] In the

14. The age requirement is stressed seven times in ch. 4 (vv. 3, 23, 30, 35, 39, 43, 47). A different lower age limit is given in 8:24. The reason for this seeming contradiction is not clear, but it strains credibility that any ancient redactor, clumsy or otherwise, would have let such a contradiction stand only four chapters apart if he had not understood the two passages to be functioning differently. To assume these kinds of things would not have been smoothed out had the editor understood them to be referring to the same thing implies that the book was not edited together at all, but exists as it "fell together" on its own. Of course, it may be objected that ancient editors did not care about textual consistency. This, it is said, is a modern concern rather than an ancient one. There is no way to enter into the ancient mind to discover the motivations for seeming inconsistencies in texts, but the *overall* consistency of many OT passages would seem to point to some concern in the direction of the smoothing out of texts in ancient times.

case of the very young Levites, this guard duty would only be potential. It is ipossible that older children were thought of as in-training for their actual guard-duty, which would come later.

The order of the Levitical clans differs here from ch. 3. The reason for the difference is not hard to find. Kohath, who had charge of the holy things, is first, followed by the one who has the next most important task, etc. The census is not introduced as a whole, but only by the clans. The introduction of each of the clans is basically the same (vv. 1–3, 21–23, 29–30). This is followed by an outline of the work each clan was to do (vv. 4–15, 24–27, 31–32). Next comes a statement as to which of Aaron's sons had authority over the particular work (vv. 16, 28, 33). The Kohathite section has a special note on the delicate nature of their work with the holy things (vv. 17–20), which is naturally missing from the other sections. A group of totals follows the individual lists of clan responsibilities (vv. 34–49).

1–4 After setting forth the introductory qualifications in vv. 1–3, the Kohathites are given the task of *the holiest things* (*qōḏeš haqqᵒḏāšîm,* v. 4). In fact, the physical work *(ʿᵃḇōḏâ)* of the Kohathites consists solely in carrying the holiest things, because the priests must prepare them for transit. That the Kohathites only carry the holiest things is shown by reference to the priests in v. 15 and the death penalty for even seeing the holy things in v. 20.

5–15 These verses deal with the way in which Aaron and his sons (not the Kohathites) will pack up the holiest things. These things are to be prepared for transport in a certain order, beginning with the holiest place and moving outward to the court. The assumption is that the reader will be familiar with the contents of the tabernacle (Exod. 25–31; 35–40).

The first item to be taken down is the *veil of the screen (pārōḵeṯ hammāsāḵ).*[15] This is also called "the veil" (e.g., Exod. 26:31), "the veil of the testimony" (e.g., Lev. 24:3), "the veil before the testimony" (Lev. 27:21, because of its proximity to the ark of the testimony/covenant), or "the veil of the sanctuary" (Lev. 4:6). It is different from the "screen" *(hammāsāḵ)* that was the door of the tabernacle (e.g., Exod. 26:36).

In this three-colored cloth the most holy thing, *the ark of the testimony,* was wrapped.[16] According to Exod. 25:10–15 this box was to

15. So also in Exod. 35:12; 39:34; 40:21. According to Exod. 26:31, this veil was made of blue-violet, purple, and scarlet stuff twined together with gold cherubim embroidered on it. These three colors are the same three colors as the wrappings for the various holy things in Num. 4:5–15.

16. The name "ark of the testimony" is common in the narrative about the

be made of acacia wood and be 2.5 cubits long by 1.5 cubits wide and 1.5 cubits high (about 44 by 26 by 26 in.). It was to be covered in gold inside and out, and to be furnished with a gold molding around it and four gold rings in its feet so that two gold-covered acacia wood carrying *poles* could be inserted. On the ark was the golden mercy seat from which Yahweh spoke to Moses and Israel (e.g., Exod. 25:22; Num. 7:89).

The ark and the veil were wrapped in a sheath of *ʿôr taḥaš,* here translated *porpoise skin* (see NEB and NIV; see also note on translation). The bottle-nosed dolphin is found in the eastern Mediterranean, while the dugong (another kind of dolphin) is plentiful in the Red Sea and Gulf of Aqaba. Modern bedouin women use the skin of the dugong to make sandals. A related word for women's sandals occurs in Ezek. 16:10. This skin would conceivably have been available in the locality, and it would be waterproof and tough.

The word here translated *blue-violet (tᵉḵēlet)* is translated "blue" by most modern English versions.[17] According to A. Brenner, this term and *'ārgāmān* ("red-purple") are variant shades of purple.[18] The ark is wrapped in the veil and the sheath of porpoise skin and blue-violet cloth. This procedure is reversed for the other objects (i.e., the porpoise skin is on the outside; see vv. 8, 10, etc.). This clearly sets the ark apart from all the other items to be carried.

Outside the veil of the most holy place, on the north side of the tabernacle, stood the *table of the Presence.*[19] The top of this table was about 3 ft. square, and the table itself was about 2 ft. high. It was covered with gold and had four gold rings attached to its legs. Through these rings were inserted the gold-covered acacia wood *poles (baddîm)* upon which

---

plan of the tabernacle and its construction (Exod. 25:22; 26:33–34; 30:6, 26; 39:35; 40:3, 5, 21; cf. Num. 7:89; Josh. 4:16). Other common names for this ark are simply "the ark" (Exod. 25:14 and 54 times), "the ark of Yahweh" (Josh. 4:11 and 32 times), "the ark of God" (1 Sam. 4:13 and 32 times), and "the ark of the covenant (of Yahweh)" (e.g., Num. 10:33; 14:44; Deut. 10:8; 31:9, 25).

17. So AV, NKJV, RSV, NIV, NASB; cf. NEB "violet." It is also so translated in G. W. Thatcher, *HDB,* I:457.

18. A. Brenner, *Colour Terms in the Old Testament,* JSOTSup 21 (Sheffield: JSOT Press, 1982), pp. 145–48.

19. The directions for constructing this table are found in Exod. 25:23–29. They are not wholly clear (see J. Hyatt, *Exodus,* NCBC [Grand Rapids: Eerdmans, 1971], pp. 268–69). One may get some idea of how the table may have looked from an illustration of the table that the Roman governor Titus took from the temple (see H. F. Beck, *IDB,* I:464, fig. 49), although there is no proof that this table was exactly like the one discussed in Exod. 25.

the table was carried (see Exod. 25:13–15; 35:12; 37:4–5; 39:35; 40:20). The various utensils on the table are noted in Exod. 25:29 and 37:16. The order here is according to the latter verse. These utensils are *the dishes* or plates *(qeʿārōṯ),* which were presumably for the continual bread (see below); the *spoons (hakkappōṯ), the sacrificial bowls (hammenaqqîyōṯ),* and the *jars for the drink offering (qeśôṯ hannāseḵ).*

The term *continual bread (leḥem hattāmîḏ)* is unique, but the meaning is clear enough from Exod. 25:30, where the original legislation is given. There the bread is called "the bread of the Presence that is always before me" *(leḥem pānîm lepānay tāmîḏ).* Thus, this bread is always to be on the table in Yahweh's presence. The directions for its preparation are given in Lev. 24:5–9. Twelve loaves, perhaps representing the twelve tribes of Israel, were set in two rows. The bread was replaced each Sabbath. The old loaves were eaten by the priests.[20]

The table, which had previously been wrapped in blue, with all its contents on it, is now wrapped in a scarlet cloth *(beḡeḏ tôlaʿaṯ šānî).*[21] Thus, as the only item wrapped in scarlet, the table of the Presence is also clearly marked.

Next a blue cloth is put over the seven-branched menorah and all its accessories. This golden lampstand is called *the lampstand of the light (menōraṯ hammā'ôr)* here and in Exod. 35:14. *its lamps (nērōṯeyhā)* refers to each individual light on the lampstand. The pattern for the menorah is given in Exod. 25:31–40. It is located opposite the table of the bread on the south side of the structure outside the most holy place. The accessories named are *tongs* (or "snuffers," *malqāḥayim*), *trays (maḥtôṯ),* and *oil vessels (kelê šemen).* The lamp and accessories will be wrapped in an outer covering of porpoise hide and put on the *carrying frame* (or "pole," *hammôṭ*). This last-named article is to be distinguished from the gold-covered acacia wood poles that were inserted into the golden carrying rings in the ark and the table. The menorah and accessories had no such provisions for carrying so that they had to be transported on this carrying pole. Num. 13:23 uses this same word to describe the pole carried by two men upon which was suspended a huge cluster of grapes from the Valley of Eshcol in Canaan.[22]

20. See C. L. Feinberg, *ZPEB,* V:420–21; Beck, *IDB,* I:464.

21. On the color, see Thatcher, *HDB,* I:457–58; Brenner, *Colour Terms,* pp. 143–45.

22. Heb. *môṭ* is related to a verb meaning "totter," and takes its name from the springlike action of the pole when carried between two people. Just how the menorah and its accessories were attached to this pole is not said.

11–12 Among the holy things are two more items of furniture, and both are altars. These verses speak of the *altar of gold* that stands in front of the veil outside the most holy place, also called the altar of incense.[23] The golden altar was wrapped in porpoise hide and its poles inserted. Next, all the accessories for it were placed in porpoise hide, and, since they had no provision for being carried on poles, they were placed on a *carrying frame (môṭ),* as was the menorah.

13–14 These verses discuss the other altar that stood in the court of the tabernacle along with its accessories.[24] After taking away the ashes of the whole burnt offerings from this altar, the priests were to spread over it a wrapping of purple cloth.[25] The accessories of the altar of whole burnt offerings were the *trays (maḥtōṯ),* the *implements* (or "forks," *hammizlāḡōṯ*), the *shovels (hayyāʿîm),* and the *basins (hammizrāqōṯ).* These accessories were placed on the altar of burnt offerings, the entire assemblage covered with porpoise hide, and the carrying poles slid into the bronze rings.

Only after Aaron and his sons finished dismantling and covering all the holy things are the sons of Kohath permitted to enter to carry these things. They are allowed to touch the carrying poles but not the holy things themselves on pain of death. Again, the holiness of God's sanctuary (which is the holiness of God himself) is not to be treated lightly.

16 Eleazar, Aaron's older surviving son, is given oversight of four holy things not previously mentioned as well as administrative oversight of the tabernacle and its furnishings as set out in the previous verses. It is possible that Eleazar himself was responsible for carrying the four holy things since all of them were holy and thus had to be handled only by a priest.

the oil for the light (šemen hammāʾôr). This oil was mentioned in Exod. 25:6 and put into the hands of the priests in Exod. 27:20–21. The latter text specified that Aaron and his sons would have charge of it.

23. The plan for the construction of this altar is not given until Exod. 30:1–10, which has led some scholars to posit that it was a later addition (e.g., Budd, p. 49; Snaith, p. 127). The size of this altar was about 17.5 in. square and 35 in. high. It was covered in gold and had one ring on each side into which gold-covered acacia wood poles could be inserted.

24. This altar was used for the sacrifices and was located in the court. The directions for its construction are found in Exod. 27:1–8. It was to be approximately 7.5 ft. square and 4.4 ft. high, covered with bronze, with four bronze rings, one at each corner, into which bronze-covered acacia wood poles could be inserted.

25. On the color purple *(ʿargāmān),* see Thatcher, *HDB,* I:457; Brenner, *Colour Terms,* p. 145.

the sweet incense (lit., "incense of spices," *q^e ṭōreṯ hassammîm*) was also mentioned in Exod. 25:6. The recipe is given in Exod. 30:34–38, which also makes plain that this incense is holy to Yahweh, and therefore only the priests are to handle it.

the regular (or continual) *meal offering (minḥaṯ hattāmîḏ)* is not mentioned elsewhere in the Pentateuch, although the meal or cereal offering *(minḥâ)* of Lev. 6:7–10 (Eng. 14–17) is probably the same offering. That offering is most holy and is to be offered and consumed only by priests.

Finally, *the oil for anointing (šemen hammišḥâ)* is discussed in Exod. 30:22–33. It is holy to Yahweh and must be handled by priests. Eleazar's administrative oversight includes both the packing work of the priests and the carrying work of the Kohathites.

A second-millennium-B.C. Hittite document is similar in many ways to the texts regarding the work of the priests and Levites in the Pentateuch. In the Hittite document, as here, two classes of people watch over and tend the temple — a priestly class and a nonpriestly class of keepers. The latter group is under the watchcare of the priests. This kind of parallel in a nonbiblical text of pre-Mosaic times shows the possibility of such a thing in Israel.[26]

17–20 This section grows out of all that has been said in ch. 4 to this point. If all that has been legislated is true, then the danger to the Kohathites from accidental exposure to the holy things is great. These verses underline that danger and warn Moses, and especially Aaron, to take care in the packing and preparation of the holy things for transport. These items must be properly prepared before any Levite can be allowed even to catch a glimpse of them: *even for an instant (k^e ḇallaʿ),* describing the slightest glimpse of the holy things, is literally "as a swallowing," i.e., even the time it takes to swallow.[27] For the Levite any exposure, no matter how slight, to the holy things brings death. The priests are to make sure that their work is well done so that lethal contact for the Levites is eliminated. This warning is given only to the Kohathites, since the other clans do not risk contact with the holy things in the same way.

26. See A. Goetze, "Instructions to Temple Officials," *ANET,* pp. 207–10; Milgrom, *Studies in Levitical Terminology,* I:50–53.

27. The only parallel that is suggested is in Job 7:19: "will you not leave me alone long enough to swallow my spittle?" *(lōʾ-ṯarpēnî ʿaḏ-bilʿî ruqqî),* viz. "for a moment." See, e.g., J. Hartley, *The Book of Job,* NICOT (Grand Rapids: Eerdmans, 1988), p. 162. Hartley refers to a contemporary Arabic idiom "let me swallow my spittle" = "wait a minute."

21–28 The duties of the Gershonites concern the cloth, fabric, and skin items that cover and enclose the tabernacle structure. Three words are used in connection with their tasks. The first is *ʿăḇōḏâ,* which, in this case, describes the physical work of dismantling the curtains, etc., loading them on wagons, and reassembling them in due course. One month earlier the Gershonites had been given two wagons and four oxen to carry their burdens (see Num. 7:1–11). The second word, here translated as *carrying (maśśāʾ),* is literally "a burden."[28] The third word is *mišmereṯ,* which, once again, means *guard duty,* and indicates that the Gershonites were responsible for watching over these curtains, etc., as these things traveled on the wagons (as has already been set out in 3:25–26).

The list of items to be packed and loaded by the Gershonites is found in more or less the same order in 3:25–26. This is also the same order as found in the first commands regarding these things in Exod. 26–27.

the curtains of the tabernacle and the tent of meeting (ʾeṯ-yᵉrîʿōṯ hammiškān wᵉʾeṯ-ʾōhel môʿēḏ). The original command for these is found in Exod. 26:1–14. The two coverings for the tent are set out in 26:14. The first covering was to be of "tanned ram's skin" (RSV) *(ʿōrōṯ ʾêlim mᵉʾāḏāmîm),* and the second was to be of "porpoise skin" *(ʿōrōṯ tᵉḥāšîm).* Next came the *screen (māsaḵ)* of the holy place (Exod. 26:36–37). The *hangings of the court (qalʿê heḥāṣer)* were to be 100 cubits long (approximately 146 ft.) on the north and south sides of the tabernacle, and 50 cubits long (approximately 73 ft.) on the west (Exod. 27:9, 11–12). On the east side the hangings were in two parts, each 15 cubits long (approximately 22 ft.; Exod. 27:14–15), with *the screen for the door of the gate of the court (māsaḵ peṯaḥ šaʿar heḥāṣēr)* (i.e., the whole structure) made of blue, purple, and scarlet embroidered linen covering the gap of 20 cubits (approximately 29 ft.) between the hangings (Exod. 27:16).

After the holy things have been removed from the tabernacle, the next logical step was the the removal of the coverings, thus exposing the framework. This led on to the work of the Merarites, which follows in vv. 29–33. The work of both the Gershonites and the Merarites was to be done under the supervision and authority of Ithamar, Aaron's younger surviving son.

29–33 After the standard introduction of the Merarites in vv. 29–30, their work is set forth, but in an unusual way. The text uses all three

28. The word comes from *nāśāʾ*, "to lift up." See Milgrom, *Studies in Levitical Terminology,* I:60–66.

terms for work (discussed above: *mišmereṯ, maśśā', ʿᵃḇōḏâ*) in the same sentence (v. 31). The guard duty of the Merarites is the same as their *burden* and their *packing work*. In general this task involves the framework of the tabernacle and the court. These materials have already been assigned to the Merarites in 3:36–37 as their *guard duty (mišmereṯ)*.

Briefly, their work consisted in packing, guarding, and unpacking the following: *the boards of the tabernacle (qaršê hammiškān)*. These were 48 in number (20 on the north-south sides and 8 on the west side), each measuring about 14 ft. long and 2 ft. wide, and made of gold-covered acacia wood (Exod. 26:15–25). Each board had gold rings in it (Exod. 26:19) through which were inserted gold-covered acacia wood *crosspieces (bᵉrîaḥ)*. There were five of these on the north, south, and west sides of the tabernacle. The center crosspiece ran from end to end while the other four were broken in the middle (Exod. 26:26–29). At the bottom of each board were two tenons or projections (lit., "hands") that fitted into silver *sockets* or "bases" *('ᵃḏānîm)*, each made of one talent of silver (Exod. 26:19, 21, 25; 38:27). Four *pillars (ʿammûḏîm)* of gold-covered acacia wood, each in a silver socket, divided the holy place from the most holy place (Exod. 26:32–33). The outer court also had pillars *(ʿammûḏê heḥāṣer)*, 60 in number (20 on the long sides, 10 on the short), each one resting in a bronze *socket ('eḏen,* Exod. 27:9–19). Bronze *pegs (yaṯēḏôṯ)* held the pillars in place (Exod. 27:19), and *cords (mêṯrîm)* were used in erecting and securing the tabernacle and its court. Also mentioned are the *accessories (kēlîm)* (possibly the tools) necessary for performing their labors.

Ithamar the priest is to oversee each item the Merarites are to load and unload. In Num. 7:1–11, which relates events that had taken place one month before the current text,[29] four wagons and eight oxen were given to the Merarites to transport these materials. Their work consisted in dismantling the framework, etc., packing it on the carts, guarding it on the journey, and reassembling it upon arrival at the destination.

34–49 These verses finally give the census figures for the Levites from age 30 to 50. The clans are dealt with in the same order in which they have already been named (Kohath, vv. 34–37; Gershon, vv. 38–41; Merari, vv. 42–45; grand totals, vv. 46–49). The numbers are: Kohath, 2,750; Gershon, 2,630; Merari, 3,200. This gives a grand total of 8,530 Levites between 30 and 50 years of age.[30]

29. See the chronological indicators in 1:1 and 7:1 (cf. Exod. 40:17).

30. For these numbers themselves, see the "Excursus on Large Numbers" above.

2. VARIOUS LEGAL ENACTMENTS (5:1–6:21)

a. Camp Must Be Kept Free from Those with Serious Skin Disease (5:1–4)

1 *And Yahweh spoke to Moses, saying:*

2 *"Command the children of Israel that they should send out of the camp everyone with a serious skin disease, everyone with a bodily discharge, and everyone who is unclean by reason of contact with a corpse;*

3 *both male and female you shall send, to the outside of the camp you shall send them, that they might not defile the camp in the midst of which I am dwelling."*

4 *And the children of Israel did so and sent them to the outside of the camp. As Yahweh had spoken to Moses, so they did.*

1–4 The structure of this unit is clear. Following the introduction, which claims divine authority for the legislation (v. 1), comes the legislation proper (vv. 2–3), followed by a concluding formula, which details faithful performance of the legislation (v. 4). The subject is the removal of that which is unclean *(ṭāmē')* from the *camp* —the dwelling of holy Yahweh. Although a full discussion of the concepts of "clean," "unclean," and "holy" is not possible here, a few comments are in order.[1]

That God is holy is a commonplace assertion of the Pentateuch (e.g., Lev. 11:44–45; 19:2). That which is unclean is the antithesis of that which is holy; it is impure and abnormal for its class. That which is clean is in a middle state; it is pure and normal for its class. That which is holy is made so by sanctification and is fitted for the divine use in the divine presence.[2] Therefore a basic principle is that the holy must not come into contact with the unclean (e.g., Lev. 7:19–21; 22:3). The three disorders named in the present passage all bring about communicable uncleanness.[3] The alternatives are being isolated from the camp where the holy Yahweh dwells or being "cut off."[4]

1. See further G. J. Wenham, *Leviticus,* NICOT (Grand Rapids: Eerdmans, 1978), pp. 18–25. See also Mary Tew Douglas, *Purity and Danger: An Analysis of the Concepts of Pollution and Taboo* (London: Routledge & Kegan Paul, 1966).

2. Wenham, *Leviticus,* pp. 19–25.

3. Skin disease, Lev. 13:45; discharges, Lev. 15:2, 16, 19, 25; contact with a corpse (a dead animal, Lev. 11:24, 29; a dead human body, Lev. 21:1–3; Num. 6:6–12; 19:1–22).

4. Wenham, *Leviticus,* pp. 241–42.

Whatever the precise meanings of the terms *serious skin disease (ṣārûaʿ)* and *bodily discharge (zāḇ),* the current passage advances the Levitical code only in that persons afflicted with these complaints are to be expelled from the camp. Those who have skin disorders are legislated out of the camp in Lev. 13:46, and although those with bodily discharges are not excluded in so many words, Lev. 15:31 legislates a "separation from their uncleanness" in the camp. The very least this means is that such people are forbidden to participate in worship.

Contact with a corpse is said to defile the priest (Lev. 21:1–3) and the high priest (21:11), and, in just a few verses, will be said to defile the Nazirite (Num. 6:6–12). The current passage extends defilement by a corpse from the priesthood to the laity.[5] The same alternatives apply to these unclean people as to the first two classes.

The term *ṣārûaʿ* has commonly been translated as "leprosy,"[6] but modern lexical and medical studies have widened the term to include a variety of complaints such as vitiligo.[7] In Leviticus this malady affects not only people but also houses and clothes, so that the reference must be to spots that affect part of the object and make it unclean.

In Lev. 15 and here the term *zāḇ* refers to a bodily discharge, particularly from the sexual organs.[8]

unclean by reason of contact with a corpse (ṭāmēʾ lāneḇeš) — here *neḇeš* is used of a dead body. The term usually refers to living creatures.[9] The current usage is, however, also found in several other texts (e.g., Num.

5. See the later legislation on purification after contact with a corpse, Num. 19:1–22.

6. The most common Greek translation was *lepra;* cf. BDB, pp. 863b–64a.

7. See *HALAT,* pp. 988b–89. On the derivation of this term see J. F. A. Sawyer, "A Note on the Etymology of SARAʿAṮ," *VT* 26 (1976) 241–45. On the analogy of other Hebrew medical terms, Sawyer contends that the root meaning of *ṣrʿ* is not, as is sometimes argued, connected with Arab. *ṣaraʿa,* "to prostrate," but rather is derived from a description of an obvious symptom of the disease (cf. *ṣāheḇeṯ,* "jaundice," related to *ṣahoḇ,* "yellow"). He then points to Heb. *ṣirʿâ,* which, in its three biblical occurrences, is rendered "hornet(s)." Sawyer concludes that the person afflicted with *ṣāraʿaṯ* (i.e., a *ṣārûʿâ*) had pain similar to a hornet's sting. See also L. Koehler, "Aussatz," *ZAW* 67 (1955) 290–91. Many scholars deny that *ṣāraʿaṯ* includes modern leprosy (Hansen's disease): e.g., E. Hulse, "The Nature of Biblical 'Leprosy' and the Use of Alternate Medical Terms in Modern Translations of the Bible," *PEQ* 107 (1975) 87–105. R. K. Harrison, *Leviticus,* TOTC (Downers Grove: InterVarsity, 1980), pp. 136–39, disagrees. Cf. Wenham, *Leviticus,* p. 192.

8. See Harrison, *Leviticus,* pp. 158–66; Wenham, *Leviticus,* pp. 217–25.

9. The literature on *neḇeš* is enormous. See, e.g., B. K. Waltke, *TWOT,* II:587–91; N. W. Porteous, *IDB,* IV:428–29.

9:6–7, 10), and is perhaps explained as a reference to the "person" *(nep̱eš)* who has died and not to a dead *nep̱eš*. One can see this in such a passage as Num. 19:13: "whoever touches a corpse, that is the *nep̱eš* of a person who has died" *(nōḡēaʿ* b^{e}*mēṯ* b^{e}*nep̱eš hāʾāḏām ʾ*^{a}*šer-yāmûṯ)*.[10]

b. Restitution When There Is No Kinsman (5:5–10)

5 *And Yahweh spoke to Moses, saying:*

6 *"Speak to the children of Israel: When a man or woman commits any human sin, thereby trespassing against Yahweh, when that person feels guilty,*

7 *then they shall confess their sin that they have committed, and he will make reparation in full, adding a fifth to it, and give it to the injured party.*

8 *But if there is no kinsman to whom reparations may be made, the reparation that is paid back is to be given to Yahweh for the priest, in addition to the ram of atonement by which he*[1] *makes atonement on his behalf.*

9 *And every gift, that is, all the holy things of the children of Israel that they offer to the priest, shall belong to him,*

10 *that is, each man's holy things shall belong to him; whatever each man gives to the priest will belong to him."*

This case law is related in subject matter to the laws found in Exod. 22:7–15. The passage in Lev. 5:20–26 (Eng. 6:1–7) seems to form the basis for the heart of the current passage, which supplements and applies it. The structure of vv. 5–10 moves from divine authorization (vv. 5–6a) to the condition or the "when" clause (the protasis, v. 6b) to the action to be taken or the "then" clause (the apodosis, v. 7). To this basic law a condition (no kinsman) and an action are added (v. 8). To the whole unit a clarification is added on the priest's share of gifts (vv. 9–10).

At the same time the present text and Lev. 5:20–26 (Eng. 6:1–7) differ in a number of ways. First, this text generalizes, whereas the Leviticus text adds specific crimes (i.e., in Lev. 5:21–23a, 23c–24 [Eng. 6:2–4a, 4–5c]). Second, the current text adds the section on payment to the priests when no kinsman is available (v. 8). Third, this text adds the section on confession of the wrong prior to and as part of the restitution

10. See E. Jacob, *TDNT*, IX:620–21.

1. I.e., the priest.

(v. 7a).[2] Finally, the Numbers text adds the statement about gifts to the priest (vv. 9–10).

Although virtually all commentators see the relationship of this text to the Levitical one, the relationship of it to what immediately precedes is disputed. On the one hand, for example, Gray, Noth, and Snaith see very little connection here, or indeed, within the whole of chs. 5–6.[3] On the other hand, scholars such as Sturdy have made the connection between ceremonial purity (5:1–4) and ethical purity (5:5–10) in God's camp.[4] Wenham has pointed to the literary fact that in the current section we have a series of three pairs of laws (5:5–10, 11–31; 6:1–21) all introduced by the formula "And Yahweh spoke to Moses, saying: 'Speak to the children of Israel.' " Two of these pairs deal with "trespass" (5:6, 12, 27). Also the priest is given the right to share in the gifts/sacrifices in all three (5:8–10, 25; 6:10–12, 14–20).[5]

5 *And Yahweh spoke to Moses, saying.* As is quite common in Numbers, this formula marks a new section.[6] It also reminds the people that this material is Yahweh's revealed word to them through Moses.

6 The heart of the present passage (vv. 6b–7) stipulates that one who has transgressed against God by taking a false oath in addition to defrauding another human being, and who feels remorse about the act, may rectify it only by confession of sin. That person may then proceed to restitution plus one-fifth, which is to be paid to the wronged party.

any human sin (mikkol-ḥaṭṭō'ṯ hā'āḏām). The question is whether this construction is to be understood as a subjective genitive ("sins that humans commit," so RSV) or an objective genitive ("sin toward a fellow human," so NJPS). The Hebrew text is ambiguous, but, assuming a relationship to Lev. 5:22b (Eng. 6:3b; "any of the things humans do and sin thereby"), then the subjective genitive seems the better choice. Noth remarked that this line in Numbers looks like a contraction of that phrase in Leviticus.[7]

2. On these three see J. Milgrom, *Cult and Conscience: The* asham *and the Priestly Doctrine of Repentance,* SJLA 18 (Leiden: Brill, 1976), p. 106. This study is also found, in modified form, in *RB* 82 (1975) 192–93; and in *Studies in Priestly Theology,* pp. 53–54.

3. So Gray, p. 39; Noth, p. 44; Snaith (p. 128) calls chs. 5–6 Miscellaneous Regulations.

4. See Sturdy, p. 42.

5. See Wenham, p. 78. For other triple laws in the Pentateuch, see G. Wenham and J. McConville, "Drafting Techniques in the Deuteronomic Laws," *VT* 30 (1980) 248–52.

6. E.g., 3:5, 11, 44; 5:1, 11; 6:1, 22; etc.

7. Noth, p. 46. Budd, p. 57, and Gray, p. 43, also opt for the subjective

These are *human* sins against Yahweh that are at the same time against other human beings. *thereby trespassing against Yahweh* (*limᵉʿōl maʿal bYHWH,* lit., "to trespass a trespass against Yahweh." See Lev. 5:21–22 (Eng. 6:2–3): "If a person should sin and trespass against Yahweh *(ûmāʿᵃlâ maʿal bYHWH)* and deceive his comrade in the matter of a deposit or property or a robbery, or should extort his comrade, or find that which was lost and deceive him concerning it, and swear falsely. . . ." Two categories of sin are noted here. All the sins are against human beings except the last one (the false oath), which is a trespass against Yahweh. This trespass is to be seen as accompanying each of the other crimes so that the human crimes are compounded by lying on oath, thus making Yahweh a party to these other crimes. Although the passage here in Numbers does not specifically speak of a lie on oath, neither does it specify any human sin, and this lying on oath to God is probably in the author's mind.[8]

and feels guilty (wᵉʾāšᵉmâ). This verbal form of the root *'šm* is usually translated as "be guilty" (so RSV). It seems hardly necessary to add, however, that the one who commits sin *(ʿaśâ ḥāṭṭāʾṯ)* and trespasses against Yahweh *(māʿal maʾal bYHWH)* is, or becomes, guilty. It can hardly be conceived that such a person would be innocent. A different translation of the term is in order. J. Milgrom's research has given a new translation to all occurrences of the root in cultic contexts in the Pentateuch. He speaks of the "consequential *'āšām,*" which means that, in cultic contexts, the root does not refer to the act so much as to the consequence of the act, the guilt.[9] For *'šm,* Milgrom gives four meanings: as a noun it means either "reparation" or "reparation offering"; as a verb with a personal object (plus the preposition *lᵉ-*) it means "to incur liability to (someone)," and without such a personal object, as here, it means "to feel guilty."[10]

7 *then they shall confess their sin that they have committed (wᵉhiṯwaddû 'eṯ-ḥaṭṭā'ṯām 'ᵃšer 'āśû).* The act of confession for deliberate

---

genitive. Milgrom argues the case for the objective genitive (*Cult and Conscience,* p. 105 n. 388).

8. For the argument that the trespass against Yahweh is the false oath, see Milgrom, *Cult and Conscience,* pp. 16–35, 84–104.

9. The basic connotation of the root *'šm* has to do with guilt. On this, see D. Kellermann, *TDOT,* I:429–37. As with other terms in the OT (e.g., *ḥṭ',* "sin"), the same word serves for the act and its cause. E.g., *ḥāṭṭā'ṯ* means "sin" in Num. 5:6, but the "sin offering" in Lev. 7:37. The usual translation of *'āšām* can be either "guilt" (e.g., Gen. 26:10, RSV) or "guilt offering" (Lev. 5:24 [Eng. 6:5]). On this usage of the noun, see Milgrom, *Cult and Conscience,* pp. 1–14.

10. See Milgrom, *Cult and Conscience,* p. 11.

sin (as the sin outlined here must be) is a necessary accompaniment to the forgiveness of the act. This is an important addition to the law of Lev. 5:20–26 (Eng. 6:1–6), although confession of the sinful action does play a role in Lev. 5:1–5. Lev. 5:23 (Eng. 6:4) does include a sense of remorse (*weʾāšēm,* "and he feels guilty"), but no explicit articulation of responsibility for the sin *(hiṯwaddâ).*[11] Of course, confession as a part of the atoning act of the contrite individual becomes an important theological principle. For example, in Num. 15:30 it is the unrepentant sinner who is condemned. Later, Israel's confession of deliberate sins committed against God forms an important part of Nehemiah's mission (Neh. 1:4–11). In the NT one finds a passage like 1 John 1:9. Here in Numbers the confession is only the first step in the forgiveness process; reparation and sacrifice must follow.[12] The Christian is also enjoined to repair wrongs that have been done to fellow creatures (e.g., Matt. 5:23–24). As for the offering of a sacrifice, one could argue that the Christian depends upon the once-for-all sacrifice of Jesus for this part of the procedure.[13]

In vv. 6–7 the verbs vary from singular to plural forms (which the translation above endeavors to show). The reason for the mixture is the alternation between the thought of the Israelites as a group (e.g., "when they commit any human sin," v. 6; "then they shall confess," v. 7) and as single examples of that group (e.g., "when that person feels guilty," v. 6; "then he will make reparation in full," v. 7). The LXX simplifies the situation by using singulars throughout. Gray called this mixture of singulars and plurals "remarkable, but scarcely unparalleled."[14] From

11. The only other usage of *hiṯwaddâ* in a legal context in the Pentateuch (Lev. 16:21) also refers to deliberate sin. Lev. 26:40 enjoins confession but in the context of narrative and exhortation rather than in a legal context. Confession as a qualification for sacrificial forgiveness is not unique to Israel, but is also found in the ancient Near East more generally. For parallel Hittite materials, see Milgrom, *Cult and Conscience,* pp. 106–8.

12. LXX uses *exagoreuein* to translate *hiṯwaddâ* here and in Lev. 5:5; 16:21; 26:40. This verb means "to divulge" (LSJ, 580a). The reason why this Greek word is chosen rather than the far more common *exomologein* (or the simpler *homologein,* used in 1 John 1:9) may be to emphasize the verbal nature of this confession. Whereas *ʾāšām* (remorse) was sufficient for unintentional sins, only a verbal confession was sufficient for intentional sins. See Milgrom, *Cult and Conscience,* p. 109 n. 407.

13. For more on confession see the following articles and bibliographies: D. Fürst, *NIDNTT,* I:344–48; O. Michel, *TDNT,* V:199–220; W. A. Quanbeck, *IDB,* I:667–68; V. C. Grounds, *ZPEB,* I:937–39.

14. See Gray, p. 43.

time to time the Hebrew OT uses the plural as a device to express a general or unspecified subject.[15]

he will make reparation in full (w^{e}hēšîḇ 'eṯ-'^{a}šāmô b^{e}rō'šô). In Lev. 5:20–26 (Eng. 6:1–7) the noun *'āšām* refers to that which may be returned (hence the verb *hēšîḇ,* "to return," is used) or repaid (thus the verb *šillēm,* "to repay," is used) to the wronged person to compensate that one for what has been misappropriated. Here *hēšîḇ* is used again with *'āšām,* thus indicating that, here too, the *'āšām* is that which gives recompense or *reparation* to the wronged party. "Reparation" is therefore a better translation than RSV "guilt" or "guilt offering."[16] The added words *in full (b^{e}rō'šô)* bear a similar meaning to the term *rō'š* (lit., "head") in 1:2, 49; 4:2, 22, etc. In addition to the value of the original object, one-fifth of its value is to be given to the wronged party, as in Lev. 5:24 (Eng. 6:5).

and give it to the injured party (w^{e}nāṯan la'^{a}šer 'āšām lô). The verb *'āšam* with a personal object plus the preposition *l^{e}*- means "to incur liability to (someone)," i.e., to incur that which needs reparation as regards someone. Thus the repentant sinner must give the reparation to the one to whom *(la'^{a}šer)* he has incurred liability *('āšam lô).*[17]

8 This verse adds a case not included in the original legislation. Such a case would not be long in presenting itself. It can be assumed that if the original injured party died between the crime and the reparation, that his kinsman *(gō'ēl)* would receive the reparation on behalf of the family.[18] But what if the injured party had no kinsmen left at all? Num. 5:8 legislates that, in this case, the reparation for the original property plus

15. See GKC, § 144g. One could also understand this construction as a circumlocution of the passive, i.e., "the sins committed must be confessed." This construction is more common in Aramaic than in Hebrew. See GKC, § 114g. Cf. F. Rosenthal, *A Grammar of Biblical Aramaic,* Porta Linguarum Orientalium (Wiesbaden: Harrassowitz, 1967), § 181.

16. See Milgrom, *Cult and Conscience,* pp. 11–14, 137–40; also R. de Vaux, *Studies in Old Testament Sacrifice* (Cardiff: Univ. of Wales Press, 1964), p. 98. Heb. *hēšîḇ* is the special verb used most commonly with *'āšām;* see Milgrom, *Cult and Conscience,* pp. 6, 13–14.

17. Also see Lev. 5:19: "he has incurred liability to Yahweh" *('āšôm 'āšām lYHWH);* cf. Milgrom, *Cult and Conscience,* pp. 6 n. 23, 12.

18. The *gō'ēl* would refer, first, to a person's brother, and then to an uncle, cousin, or other male kinsman. These kinsmen would take legal responsibility to see that the family's rights were upheld. For a complex example of the *gō'ēl,* see Ruth 3–4. See also H. Ringgren, *TDOT,* II:350–55; R. L. Harris, *TWOT,* I:144–45, and the bibliographies there.

twenty percent was to be given to Yahweh for the priest. This is over and above the ram for the reparation offering itself, which the priest would normally have received (Lev. 7:6–7). The last clause of the verse refers to this ram as *the ram of atonement by which he makes atonement on his behalf ('êl hakkippurîm 'ᵃšer yᵉḵapper-bô).* The description of this ram as *'êl hakkippurîm,* although unique here, is best understood as a contraction of the longer formula of Lev. 5:25b–26a (Eng. 6:6b–7a): "a perfect ram or its equivalent to be a reparation offering. The priest shall make atonement for him before the Lord."[19] The tendency to give slightly rephrased contractions of the passage in Lev. 5:20ff. (Eng. 6:1ff.) has been noticed before in v. 6.

9–10 These verses are linked with v. 8 by the appearance of the catchwords "to (or for) the priest" *(lakkōhēn)* in all of them. V. 8 has stated that the priest is to receive the reparation sum of the one who dies without a kinsman before reparation can be made. But what about the support of the priest in more normal cases? Vv. 9–10 teach that the people have a responsibility to look after the priest.[20]

That which is given to the priest is called *tᵉrûmâ,* which is a general term that means literally "that which is lifted off, separated." The word is used to describe contributions including a portion of cereal offerings (Lev. 7:14), animal sacrifices (Lev. 7:20; Num. 6:20), the Levites' tithe and the priests' tenth of the Levites' tithe (Num. 18:24–29), booty taken in a raid (Num. 31:29), contributions for the building of the tabernacle (Exod. 25:2, 3, 5), or contributions for the half-shekel tax to keep the service of the tabernacle going (Exod. 30:13–15). The common denominator in all these seems to be that all are gifts or contributions to God or his priests (or both).[21] Here the *tᵉrûmâ* is a term for any gift to the priest for his support.

The question arises, however, whether these gifts are the same as *all the holy things of the children of Israel (kol-qoḏšê ḇᵉnê-yiśrā'ēl),* which follows (thus, "every gift, namely, all the holy things"), or whether the gifts are specially denominated objects from the wider sphere of holy things (thus, "every gift of all the holy things").[22] The determining factor

19. This translation is from G. Wenham, *Leviticus,* p. 104. See his excellent discussion of the nature of this sacrifice.

20. The Pentateuch addresses this situation elsewhere as well, e.g., Lev. 7:7–9; Num. 6:20; etc.

21. See, e.g., Gray, p. 42; Budd, pp. 56, 58; Noordtzij, p. 51. Further confirmation of this sense can be found, once again, in the work of Milgrom, *Studies in Cultic Theology,* pp. 159–72.

22. For the former, see Gray, pp. 42–43. This interpretation takes the

will be the way in which the author has used the term *holy things (qoḏāšîm)* in other contexts.

In some passages the term defines exactly what is holy as opposed to that which is most holy (e.g., Lev. 21:22). It appears, however, that with regard to the priests, *qoḏāšîm* most often in the Pentateuch refers to portions of the offerings and sacrifices that have become holy as a result of their being offered *(qāraḇ)* to God, but have not been consumed on the altar and are used to support the priesthood. The priests have a share in all the sacrifices except for the whole burnt offering (the *'ōlâ*).[23] Lev. 22, which discusses danger to the priests from eating these holy portions while in an unclean state, uses *qoḏāšîm* in this way often. In addition, Num. 18:8 appears to equate the gifts and the holy things. Using these passages as analogies, we can take v. 10 as the required clarification. This verse simply eliminates the term *t^erûmâ* and uses only *qoḏāšîm: each man's holy things* shall belong to him (i.e., the priest), *whatever each man gives to the priests will belong to him.*[24]

c. The Jealous Husband (5:11–31)

11 *And Yahweh spoke to Moses, saying:*

12 *"Speak to the children of Israel and say to them, 'Any man, if his wife should turn aside and transgress against him,*

13 *in that another man has sexual intercourse with her,*[1] *and this is concealed from the eyes of her husband, and it remains undetected though she has defiled herself, since there is no witness against her and she has not been caught;*

14 *and if a spirit of suspicion passes over him, and he becomes suspicious of his wife, and she has been defiled; or if a spirit of*

---

preposition *l^e-* as equivalent to "namely, that is." See BDB, p. 514b; *HALAT,* p. 485a. In the latter interpretation, *l^e-* is simply the normal way of keeping the noun *t^erûmâ* from being construed as definite with the following definite construct-genitive, "the holy things of the children of Israel." See, e.g., Williams, *Syntax,* § 270. One might have, rather, expected the partitive *min* had this been the intent; see Williams, *Syntax,* § 324.

23. The priest has a portion of the cereal offering (Lev. 2:3, 10), the peace offerings (Lev. 7:31–36), the purification offering (or sin offering; Lev. 6:19, 22 [Eng. 26, 29]), and the reparation offering (Lev. 7:6, 9).

24. So, in various ways, RSV, NEB, NIV; Gray, pp. 42–43; Budd, p. 56; Milgrom, *Cult and Conscience,* p. 37 n. 137.

1. Heb. *w^ešāḵaḇ 'îš 'ōṯāh šiḵ^eḇaṯ zera',* lit., "a man bedded her, a lying of seed" (or "with an emission of semen"). See BDB, p. 1012b; Holladay, p. 368b. On *'ōṯāh,* see BDB, p. 1012a, s.v. *šāḵaḇ* 3. See also Driver, *Samuel,* p. 298.

suspicion should pass over him, and he should become suspicious of his wife, but she has not been defiled,

15 *in either case the man may bring his wife to the priest along with the appropriate offering for her, that is, one-tenth ephah of barley flour. He shall not pour oil on it and he shall not put incense on it because it is a meal offering of suspicion, an evocatory offering, evoking sin.*

16 *Then the priest shall bring her near and present her before Yahweh.*

17 *And the priest shall take holy water*[2] *in an earthen vessel. And the priest will take some of the dust that may be found on the floor of the tabernacle and put it into the water.*

18 *Then the priest will present the woman before Yahweh, and he will unbind the hair of*[3] *the woman's head, and he will put into her hands the evocatory meal offering, which is a meal offering of suspicion. And in the hand of the priest will be the waters of distress, which bring the curse.*

19 *And the priest will adjure her and he will say to the woman: "If a man has not lain with you and if you have not turned aside to uncleanness while under your husband's authority, then be free from the effects of these waters of distress, which bring the curse.*

20 *But, as for you, if you have turned aside while under your husband's authority, and have become defiled and a man has had sexual relations with you, other than your husband. . . ."*

21 *(Then the priest will adjure the woman, in the oath of the curse, and the priest shall say to the woman) "May Yahweh make you for a curse and an oath in the midst of your people, as Yahweh makes your thigh*[4] *fallen and your belly swollen,*

22 *and may these waters that bring the curse enter into your inward parts, and cause your belly to swell and your thigh to fall." And the woman will say: "This is fitting and proper."*

23 *And the priest will write these curses in the book and wash them into the waters of distress.*

24 *And he will cause the woman to drink the waters of distress, which*

2. MT *mayim qᵉḏōšîm* is a unique expression, which has led some to question its correctness. LXX reads *hydōr katharon zōn,* "pure living (i.e., running) water," which might reflect an original Hebrew text *mayim ḥayyîm.* But MT makes sense, and the construction is not unparalleled; see GKC, § 128p. See also Gray, pp. 51, 53; Budd, p. 61.

3. Lit., "unbind the woman's head."

4. "Thigh," Heb. *yārēḵ,* is probably a euphemism for womb. See the commentary below.

bring the curse, and the waters that bring the curse will enter into her for the purpose of distress.

25 *Then the priest shall take from the hand of the woman the meal offering of suspicion, and he shall dedicate the meal offering before Yahweh, and shall offer it on the altar.*

26 *And the priest shall take a handful of the meal offering as a memorial offering and put it to smoke on the altar; only then will he cause the woman to drink the waters.*

27 *And he will cause her to drink the waters, and it will be, if she has defiled herself and trespassed against her husband, that the waters that bring the curse will enter into her for the purpose of causing distress, and her belly will swell up and her thigh will fall, and then the woman will become a curse in the midst of her people.*

28 *And if the woman has not been defiled and she is clean, then she shall be free from punishment and shall bear children.*

29 *This is the legal procedure for suspicion when a woman may have turned aside while under authority of her husband and become defiled,*

30 *or for him upon whom a spirit of suspicion should come, and he should become suspicious of his wife. The priest will present the woman before Yahweh and he shall do to her according to this entire procedure.*

31 *Now, the husband shall be free of punishment, but that woman shall bear her punishment.' "*

This passage forms the basis for the tractate *Sotah* in the Mishnah, and has probably been debated since well before the time of the Mishnah.[5] It occasions problems on literary, sociological, and theological levels. A single reading of the passage from most modern translations suffices to show the literary difficulties. For example, repetitions abound. It seems that the woman is brought near to Yahweh twice (vv. 16, 18), that she is given the water to drink at least twice and perhaps three times (vv. 24, 26, 27),[6] an oath is administered by the priest twice (vv. 19, 21), but the woman never repeats it herself. Three rituals seem to be intertwined here: the meal offering, the drink offering, and the oath/curse. The literary problems are increased by the obscurity of certain key terms.[7]

5. The Mishnah contains the Jewish oral law. It was written down by the end of the 2nd cent. A.D. The traditions upon which the Mishnah is based are of unknown age, but parts may easily predate the written text by several centuries. See H. Danby, T*he Mishnah* (London: Oxford, 1933), pp. xvii–xxiii.

6. Notice the debate on this already in Mish. *Sotah* 3:2.

7. E.g., the feeling (or spirit) of suspicion (vv. 14, 29–30), the meal

A complete review of scholarly study of this passage is not possible here.[8] Suffice it to say that scholars have chosen two major paths to the solution of the literary problems. The first course has been to posit a number of different sources that have been woven together. On the basis of the parallels and differences between vv. 12–14 and 29–30, B. Stade long ago posited a source A dealing with a meal offering of remembrance (vv. 11–12, 13aα, b, 15–17, 18aβb, 19–20, 22a, 23–24, 25bβ, 26a, 31), and a source B dealing with a meal offering of jealousy (suspicion) (vv. 13aβ, 14, 18aα, 21, 22b, 25abα, 27–30).[9]

Although scholars have differed in points of detail and rationale for source division down the years, the uniting factor in all such approaches is their explanation of the literary phenomena of the text in a nonliterary way, viz., the present text came about by the historical occurrence of the conflation of two (or more) separate strands.[10] This conclusion meant that an editor had the responsibility of connecting two (or more) originally unconnected sources into one document of a composite nature. Many scholars of the 19th and early 20th cents. thought that the discovery of multiple sources behind biblical texts answered the most important questions about these texts (at least to judge from the amount of space taken up by such studies in the works of many of this period).

Another group of scholars have recognized that a text is best explained in literary terms, i.e., in terms of the style and content of the

---

offering of suspicion (vv. 15, 25), the meal offering evocative of sin (v. 15), the waters of distress (vv. 18–19, 23–24), the guilty woman's punishment, i.e., a fallen "thigh" and a swollen belly (vv. 21–22, 27), etc. On the meaning of these terms see the commentary below.

8. See, e.g., Gray, pp. 43–49; Budd, pp. 62–64.

9. B. Stade, "Die Eiferopferthora," *ZAW* 15 (1895) 166–78.

10. In addition to the work of Stade, see, e.g., Gray, pp. 43–49, esp. 46–49; Holzinger, pp. 16–17, 19–21. Holzinger claimed that the text had two sources: Source A, which deals with the meal offering, in part of v. 15, part of v. 18, and in vv. 21, 22b, 25–26a, 27a, 29–30. Source B deals with a "magical potion" and is found in vv. 16–17, 19, 22a, 24, and part of v. 27. Vv. 12b–14, 15a, and 28 were common to both sources. R. Press ("Das Ordal im alten Testament," *ZAW* 51 [1933] 122–26) finds two sources as well. Source A deals with the "ordeal" (vv. 12b, 13aβ, 15a, 17, 19–20, 22–24, 27aβb–28, 31). Source B deals with the offering (vv. 14, 15b–16, 18, 21, 25–26, 29–30). The Priestly writer added some verses of editorial material to all this. Noth (p. 49) suggested a lightly edited text made up of a variety of elements, each one of which has a preliterary history. Kellermann (*Priesterschrift,* esp. pp. 79–83) saw one basic document supplemented by two expansions. Many others have followed this kind of explanation with differences in detail.

present text, not in terms of a hypothetical earlier text that is no longer extant. The second path to a solution of the literary problems of this (or any) text lies in this direction. This way of approaching the text begins by looking on it as a unity. The text makes sense if one can understand the language as it is; figures of speech, repetitions, parallel names and phrases, etc., are viewed as literary devices. The question is not whether texts can have sources (obviously they can and do), but whether understanding these putative sources is the best way to understand a text.

Studies by scholars like Michael Fishbane, H. C. Brichto, Jacob Milgrom, and Tikva Frymer-Kensky have not begun with a need to dissect the present text into sources.[11] The obviously repetitive language of this text is not seen as a mark of diverse origin of sources, but as a literary device to make a point. Fishbane's study has clarified the nature of the framework of the passage (vv. 12–14, 29–30). Long ago, Stade had observed that one case was set forth in vv. 12–13 and another in v. 14. Along with the repetition in vv. 29–30, this recognition became crucial to his delineation of sources. In vv. 12–13 the woman is said to be guilty, while in v. 30 the door is open to her innocence. Vv. 29–30, then, gave a summary of the elements of the cases. This so-called concluding subscript is a regular feature of cuneiform law and, as Fishbane showed, is also common in biblical law.[12]

Frymer-Kensky carried Fishbane's insights further when she found the repetitive summary not only in the framework of the passage but also at major points throughout. This device of summary repetition of the beginning at the end is called *inclusion.*[13] Because of the complex

11. See M. Fishbane, "Accusations of Adultery: A Study of Law and Scribal Practice in Numbers 5.11–31," *HUCA* 45 (1974) 25–45; H. C. Brichto, "The Case Law of the *ŚŌṬĀ* and a Reconsideration of Biblical Law," *HUCA* 46 (1975) 55–70; J. Milgrom, "The Case of the Suspected Adulteress, Numbers 5:11–31: Redaction and Meaning," in *The Creation of Sacred Literature,* ed. R. Friedman (Berkeley: Univ. of California Press, 1981), pp. 69–75; T. Frymer-Kensky, "The Strange Case of the Suspected Sotah (Numbers V 11–31)," *VT* 34 (1984) 11–26.

12. See Fishbane, "Accusations," pp. 31–35. Frymer-Kensky ("Strange Case," p. 17 n. 11) pointed out that the two cases set forth in the text are probably not the ones Fishbane saw (i.e., one case where a husband's suspicion is aroused by the public [vv. 12–13], and one where the husband's suspicion was a private matter [v. 14]). The public does not come into the picture anywhere in vv. 12–14. The two cases are: the woman is guilty (vv. 12–14a), and the woman is innocent (v. 14b).

13. On the *inclusio* or repetitive literary device, see already C. Kuhl, "Die Wiederaufnahme — ein literarkritisches Prinzip?" *ZAW* 64 (1952) 1–11. Also see Frymer-Kensky, "Strange Case," p. 12 nn. 8–10.

nature of the present text, which both describes what happened and at the same time prescribes the proper ritual, the device of inclusion serves to set each section of the text off by itself in the interests of clarity.

Each section in the present text is framed by a repetition of the main action. In the middle a coordinate action is set forth. The first section (v. 15) has the husband bringing *(hēšîḇ)* both his wife and the appropriate offering to Yahweh.[14] In the second section (vv. 16–18), the main action is stationing the wife before Yahweh (*heʿĕmîḏ,* repeated in vv. 16, 18). The coordinate action is the preparation of the liquid (v. 17). In the third section (vv. 19–23) the main action is the priestly adjuration of the woman (*hišbîaʿ,* repeated in vv. 19, 20–23). The coordinate action is promised acquittal (v. 19b). In the fourth section (vv. 24–28) the main action consists in giving the woman the liquid to drink (*hišqâ,* repeated in vv. 24, 27) and the coordinate action is the meal offering (vv. 25–26).[15] In each case the final repetition of the main action contains more detail than the original statement of it. Therefore the structure of each unit as we have it is *A* (main action) plus *B* (coordinate action) plus *A′* (repeated main action in more detail). The structure of the whole unit is also *A* (vv. 12–14) plus *B* (vv. 15–28) plus *A′* (vv. 29–30).[16] The introductory statement (v. 11) on the divine source of what is written is balanced by the concluding statement on the certainty of the postritual outcome being in divine hands (v. 31).[17]

On the sociological level this passage raises concerns about the fairness of the so-called trial by ordeal as well as the unjust treatment of women that this passage prescribes (since no procedure is recorded for the suspicious wife). First, we must recognize that this passage is not a product of modern Western concerns. The cultural life of the ancient Near East was very different from modern life as regards societal roles, etc., and we must not make the text into something it is not just because what it is grates on our twentieth-century consciences. But, once we have issued

14. The first section repeats the verbs only. A short section such as this has no real need for repetitive resumption. This verse has not occasioned much debate. The repetitions in vv. 16–28 have caused the most discussion.

15. See Frymer-Kensky, "Strange Case," pp. 13–16.

16. For a more complex view of the literary structure of this passage see J. Milgrom, "Suspected Adulteress."

17. On "bearing one's punishment" *(nāśāʾ ʿāwōn)* in v. 31 indicating divine rather than human punishment, see W. Zimmerli, "Die Eigenart der prophetischen Rede des Ezechiel," *ZAW* 66 (1954) 1–26, esp. 8–11; see also below on v. 31.

this warning, let us also be careful that this text is not made into an antiwoman trial by ordeal on the basis of a surface reading.

The trial by ordeal was a common feature of the ancient world.[18] This method was "an appeal to divine judgment to decide otherwise insoluble cases that cannot be allowed to remain unresolved."[19] Thus the ordeal was related to divination as a method for discovering the divine will for a course of action.[20] The most common ordeals in the ancient world seem to be by water (e.g., plunging into rivers), by heat (e.g., carrying a red-hot object or plunging the hand into boiling liquid), and by the action of some potion. It must be admitted that the current passage is similar to certain features of the trial by ordeal, viz., the imbibing of the liquid and the fact that the verdict is, in effect, left in God's hands. These similarities have led virtually every modern commentator to call the ritual in Num. 5:11–31 a trial by ordeal.[21]

As in any investigation, differences between institutions, texts, etc., are likely to be at least as significant as similarities. The present ritual differs in important ways from the typical trial by ordeal. First, in the ancient Near Eastern ordeal the agent of the ordeal (the fire, water, etc.) was dangerous to innocent and guilty alike. Here the water probably poses no threat at all to the innocent party. Second, in the ordeal the accused had to *survive* something inherently harmful. If the accused was harmed by an inherently harmful agent, that person was guilty. Thus, the accused was guilty until proven innocent. Here the case is genuinely open, as vv. 12–14 show. Perhaps the woman is guilty, perhaps she is not. Third, in the ancient Near Eastern ordeals the guilt of the party was determined by the ordeal procedure, but the punishment was pronounced separately by the court. Injury to the guilty party was separate from the legal penalty.[22] Here the penalty is the outcome of the ritual. Finally, the punishment in the ancient Near Eastern ordeal is manifest immediately. Here we have no statement of how long it will take for the liquid to do its work.[23]

18. See Gray, p. 41; T. H. Gaster, *Myth, Legend, and Custom in the Old Testament* (New York: Harper & Row, 1969), pp. 280–300.

19. See T. S. Frymer, "Ordeal, judicial," *IDBSup,* p. 639.

20. See ibid. for the differences between ordeal and divination (and oath).

21. E.g., Gray, p. 43; Kennedy, pp. 214–15; Binns, pp. 30, 35–36; Snaith, p. 128; Marsh, p. 166; Sturdy, p. 43; Noordtzij, p. 52; Wenham, p. 79; Budd, p. 60. Not all authors mean exactly the same thing when they use the term *ordeal.*

22. Of course, if the accused was killed (drowned, etc.), the declaration of guilt and the penalty for it may be the same.

23. Frymer-Kensky, "Strange Case," p. 24.

In the present case the whole matter, from beginning to end, is placed in God's hands. There is no human punishment on top of divine punishment. The punishment for the *adulteress* prescribed by the Torah is death (Lev. 20:10). Neither the term *adulteress (nō'āpet)* nor the death penalty is mentioned here. Rather, the divine punishment is limited to the "fallen thigh" and the "swollen belly," whatever those expressions may mean. This text, in fact, supplements that of Lev. 20:10. It prevents a jealous husband from punishing his wife on the basis of suspicion alone. This complex ritual must be exactly performed (v. 30b) so that the woman might be protected from a husband's whim in an age in which protections for women were admittedly few and far between. To call this ritual an ordeal, however, is misleading and confusing.[24]

Theologically one must affirm the theocentricity of this passage in order to keep it from slipping into the realm of magic. It would be an erroneous reading of the present text to affirm that these *mārîm* waters functioned in a magical way, i.e., by themselves and apart from divine action. The whole of the ritual is God's revelation (v. 11); it is to God that the woman is brought (vv. 16, 18, 30); it is God who metes out punishment to the guilty (v. 21); and it is God to whom the meal offering is given. The potion is made up of holy water (so called because it has been taken from God's presence in the tabernacle), plus dust from the tabernacle floor (hence also from the realm of the holy), plus the words of a negative oath (curse) sworn before God. God is the major actor in this ritual drama and none of it takes place without him.[25]

Therefore the danger to the guilty (unclean) woman is real. Contact between that which is holy and that which is unclean brings disaster to the latter.[26] Any "naturalistic" view that sees the potion as harmless water and "more likely to acquit a hundred guilty wives than convict one innocent one," or that the punishment happens merely by the power of suggestion, or that the ritual is a "transparent charade" to unmask a jealous husband, must be rejected.[27] It must be seen as an operation of divine grace that the punishment on the unclean woman is limited in this case.

12–14, 29–30 The framework of the passage gives the reader

24. Cf. Brichto, "Case of the *ŚŌṬĀ*," p. 66; Frymer-Kensky, "Strange Case," pp. 24–25.

25. Brichto, "Case of the *ŚŌṬĀ*," p. 65.

26. See, e.g., Exod. 19:7–13; Lev. 10:1–11; Num. 1:51; 3:10; etc. Also see Wenham, *Leviticus,* pp. 18–29.

27. See Brichto, "Case of the *ŚŌṬĀ*," pp. 66–67. W. McKane was right when he connected the effectiveness of the waters of *mārîm* with their holiness ("Poison, Trial by Ordeal and the Cup of Wrath," *VT* 30 [1980] 476–78).

two cases. First, the case of a wife whose husband suspects her of infidelity and who is, in fact, guilty (vv. 12–14a, 29). Second, the case of a wife who is so suspected but is innocent (vv. 14b, 30a).[28] These two cases are similar to one found in the Code of Hammurabi: "If the wife of a citizen is accused by her husband, but she was not caught lying with another male, she shall take an oath of the god and return to her house."[29]

Fishbane has also posited a connection with the following law from the Code of Hammurabi: "If the finger is pointed at the wife of a citizen on account of another man, but she has not been caught lying with another man, for her husband's sake she shall throw herself into the river [i.e., for a trial by ordeal]."[30] As Frymer-Kensky rightly saw, however, the condition of the latter law was public suspicion ("the finger is pointed"), and the Numbers passage has no stated public suspicion. The ground for bringing the charge is the husband's suspicion both in vv. 12–14a and in v. 14b. The difference between these passages is the guilt or innocence of the woman.[31] In addition, it is also problematic to connect the ritual in vv. 15–28 with a trial by ordeal, as was pointed out above.

The same phrase is used in both vv. 6 and 12 for transgressing against someone *(māʿal maʿal bᵉ-)*. These words are the verbal link between the previous passage and the present one. Both misappropriation and adultery can be seen as *transgression (maʿal)*. In discussing *maʿal* in 5:6 we concluded that the actual transgression consisted in lying on oath to God. How does adultery fit into this situation (especially since it is her husband against whom the woman is said to have transgressed in 5:12)? It would be tempting to conclude that Israelite betrothal/marriage involved an oath sworn to God (as many modern marriages do).[32] But the Bible (and the ancient Near East) offers little direct evidence that this was the case. It remains only a possibility. The prohibition of adultery is incorporated into the Decalogue, the most basic of Israel's covenant documents, and one to which every faithful Israelite must be considered to have agreed before God.[33] The violation of marriage is a violation of a basic characteristic of Israel's nature as a people, similar to the violation

28. See Frymer-Kensky, "Strange Case," pp. 16–18.

29. Code of Hammurabi, § 131; see W. J. Martin, *DOTT,* p. 31; T. J. Meek, *ANET,* p. 171.

30. Code of Hammurabi, § 132; see Martin, *DOTT,* p. 31; Meek, *ANET,* p. 171; also Fishbane, "Accusations," pp. 35–38.

31. See Frymer-Kensky, "Strange Case," p. 17 n. 11.

32. For betrothal/marriage portrayed in terms of covenant, see Gen. 31:43–54; Prov. 2:17; Ezek. 16:8; Mal. 2:13–16.

33. See Exod. 20:14; also Milgrom, *Cult and Conscience,* pp. 133–37.

of the prohibition against idolatry. Marriage within the covenant community has a divine dimension (as does all of life). The shattering of part of the community relationship was violation of an oath to God and, so, being false to God. The relationship between God and Israel is, from time to time, pictured as a marriage relationship.[34] Analogous to the false oath to God involved in adultery is the false oath to the husband. When adultery occurs, one party transgresses the other in the biblical sense of oath violation.

The first case continues in v. 13 with the fact that another man (i.e., other than the woman's husband) *has sexual intercourse with her.* This act has been done in complete secrecy, as v. 13 shows: *this is concealed . . . it remains undetected . . . there is no witness . . . she has not been caught.* Even though the act is done in secret, the woman is truly *defiled (niṭᵉmā'â),* i.e., guilty before God and unclean. The point here is that the basis for the husband's bringing his wife to judgment is his suspicion and nothing else. It is unlikely that the woman is visibly pregnant at the time of the ritual since this would hardly be "undetected."[35]

Nonetheless, in spite of the lack of concrete evidence, a *spirit* (or "mood") *of suspicion (rûaḥ qin'â)* sweeps over the husband, and he can neither gainsay nor dispel it. In this case, he is allowed[36] to bring his wife to the tabernacle for the ritual that would determine her innocence or guilt. A common translation of *qin'â* (and its verbal form *qinnē',* vv. 14, 30) is "jealous" (or "to be [or become] jealous").[37] The word *suspicion* seems preferable here since, in more modern times, the primary connotation of "jealousy" is resentfulness and possessiveness. Although these qualities may, from time to time, be found in Heb. *qinā',* they are altogether inappropriate for the present context. The biblical word is also to be thought of more in terms of the action growing out of the emotion (in this case the action is the ritual) rather than the emotion itself.[38]

34. See, e.g., Hos. 2:14–23.

35. McKane ("Poison," p. 475) holds that the woman is pregnant and the man doubts that he is the father. This interpretation also does not fit the statement of the text that there is no evidence of guilt.

36. The verbal tenses in the main verbs in the passage are all either imperfects or perfects consecutive. These tenses may denote potential action; they need not denote a mandated action. See Brichto, "Case of the *ŚŌṬĀ,*" pp. 57 n. b, 58 n. i.

37. So RSV, NIV, NEB, NJPS, etc.

38. See L. J. Coppes, *TWOT,* II:802–3; Brichto, "Case of the *ŚŌṬĀ,*" pp. 58–59 n. i.

15 The suspicious husband *may* (i.e., he is not forced to) bring his wife to the ritual, but if he does he must bring along an appropriate offering as well. This offering is called by the general title *qorbān.*[39] The offering consists of one-tenth ephah (about two quarts) of coarse barley meal or flour.[40] Whereas most other meal offerings were made up of "fine flour" *(sōleṯ),* this offering is made up of the less expensive barley flour.[41] In Lev. 2, where the ordinances for the meal offerings were given, these offerings were normally accompanied by oil and incense. Here, however, they are offered dry. The only other dry meal offering is the poor person's purification offering in Lev. 5:11. Perhaps the potential sin in both instances is the reason for the prohibition of oil and incense in both offerings.[42]

The *meal offering of suspicion* is mentioned only here; thus it is not possible to know all one might wish to know about it. Two terms are offered to clarify its meaning: *an evocatory offering (minḥat zikkārôn),* and *evoking sin (mazkereṯ ʿāwōn).* The term *zikkārôn* usually means something like "a reminder," or "that which brings something to memory," as if it were derived from the Hiphil (causative) stem of the root *zkr (hizkîr),* meaning "to cause to remember, mention, call upon, accuse." If this be the case, the meal offering of suspicion is either to act as a reminder (passively) or to call to memory (i.e., "to evoke" something). Brichto has opted for the latter (effective) meaning of the term.[43] According to him, this offering is to bring the husband's suspicion into prominence before God.

Furthermore, this offering is said to evoke sin. Every other instance of a remembrance *(zikkārôn)* before Yahweh in the OT is for good, so that this phrase *evoking sin (mazkereṯ ʿāwōn)* is added to show the difference here. The verbal form *mazkereṯ* is a Hiphil participle of *zāḵar,* and in certain limited circumstances with the noun *sin (ʿāwōn)* the Hiphil

39. Heb. *qorbān* is derived from the verb *qāraḇ,* and is lit. "that which is brought near (to God)." In the OT the term is found only in Leviticus, Numbers, and Ezekiel. Lev. 2:1, 4, 13 have the compound *qorbān minḥâ* ("offering of a meal offering"). See de Vaux, *Ancient Israel,* II:417; also J. J. Reeve, "Sacrifice, Old Testament," *ISBE,* IV:2639a; A. F. Rainey, "Sacrifices and Offerings," *ZPEB,* V:200a.

40. An ephah is about 20 quarts. The regular amount for the meal offering was one-tenth of an ephah (Lev. 6:20; Num. 28:5).

41. Heb. *sōleṯ* ("fine flour") is found, e.g., in Lev. 2:1, for the regular meal offerings. It is possible that *sōleṯ* was fine flour milled from wheat as opposed to the barley flour of the present offering. See Exod. 29:2; Mish. *Sotah* 2:1.

42. Without hard data upon which to proceed, it is not wise to find symbolism for the oil and incense. See, e.g., Keil, p. 775.

43. See Brichto, "Case of the *ŚŌṬĀ,*" p. 59 n. j.

of *zāḵar* can mean "to accuse."[44] This offering, then, is meant to bring the husband's suspicion of his wife's (potential) sin into Yahweh's presence. One can only guess as to the further purpose of the meal offering itself. The nearest parallel offering, as has already been stated, is the poor person's purification offering in Lev. 5:11. If Milgrom is right and the purification offering purifies the sanctuary, then perhaps the present offering is to purify the sanctuary if the woman is guilty.[45]

16–18 The discussion of the meal offering is discontinued for the moment (see v. 18b) so that two other actions can be mentioned. The main action, repeated at the beginning and the end, is the stationing of the woman before God. The coordinate action is the preparation of the special water for the ritual. In v. 16 the priest is charged with two important acts: he is to *bring her near and present her before Yahweh (wᵉhiqrîḇ 'ōṯāh wᵉheʿᵉ miḏāh lip̄nê YHWH).* The first term may indicate that the priest is admitting the woman to God's presence on the basis of the meal offering — even though she is potentially unclean and thereby in danger.[46] The second term indicates that the woman is formally presented in Yahweh's presence, i.e., in the tabernacle.[47]

17 The coordinate action of preparing the special water takes place. As has been pointed out above, the water is holy because it has been dedicated to God and is in his presence. The most likely source for such water would be the laver in the tabernacle, and the Mishnah so identifies the source.[48] The laver was made of bronze and was placed in the tabernacle to make water available for ritual cleansing.[49] An amount of

44. See, e.g., 1 K. 17:18: "And she said to Elijah, 'What do you have against me, O man of God, that you *accuse* me of my sin and kill my son?' "

45. See J. Milgrom, "Sacrifices and Offerings, OT," *IDBSup,* pp. 766–67; idem, "Sin-offering or purification-offering," *VT* 21 (1971) 237–39; idem, "Two Kinds of *ḥaṭṭā'ṯ,*" *VT* 26 (1976) 333–37. This proposal is accepted by Wenham, *Leviticus,* pp. 88–89, etc.

46. See Milgrom's discussion of the root *qrb* in *Studies in Levitical Terminology,* I:33–43, esp. 37–38 n. 141.

47. See Mish. *Sotah* 1:5, which names the site as the Nicanor Gate in the second temple. The location of this gate is debated: either between the Court of the Women and the Court of Israel (W. S. LaSor, *ISBE,* rev., II:1025a) or between the Court of the Gentiles and the Court of the Women (W. F. Stinespring, *IDB,* IV:556). On *present* see above on 3:6 and below on 27:19.

48. Cf., e.g., Mish. *Sotah* 2:2–3; of course, one cannot verify the date of these comments.

49. See Exod. 30:18, 28; 31:9; 35:16; 38:8; 39:39; 40:6, 11, 30; cf. B. K. Waltke, *ZPEB,* III:881–83.

dust from the tabernacle floor is mixed with this water. Since this dust has been in God's presence, it is holy. As has been said before, one who is unclean is in great danger in the presence of the holy. The holy water and the dust from the tabernacle floor are mixed together in an ordinary earthen bowl, i.e., not one of the special vessels used in the tabernacle service.

18 The procedure of stationing the woman before God is repeated and expanded to include further details. The priest first *will unbind the hair of the woman's head.* The exact meaning of this ritual is unknown. Unbound hair is a sign of mourning in Lev. 10:6 and 21:10. Lev. 13:45 prescribes that the person with a serious skin disease must wear the hair unbound as a sign of uncleanness or, again, perhaps mourning. The phrase here (*pāraʿ rōʾš,* lit., "unbind the head") also occurs in all these passages in Leviticus. One possibility, therefore, is that the woman's hair is loosed to indicate that, if guilty, she will be placed in mourning (thus a visual aid to the oath in v. 22). Another possibility is that the unbound hair marks out her (again, potential) uncleanness (like the leper). A third possibility is that her unbound hair is a sign of shame. This suggestion is as old as Philo and, although the Mishnah does not pronounce on the meaning of the unbound hair, the other marks of shame (the fact that the woman is bound, her breasts are exposed, she is dressed in black, etc.) might lead one to assume that this last possibility is how the Mishnah understood the unbinding.[50]

The priest then hands the woman the meal offering (thus bringing that offering back into the picture). Meanwhile the priest keeps the mixture of water and dust in his own possession. This potion is called, for the first time here, *the waters of* mārîm, *which bring the curse (mê hammārîm hamᵉʾārᵃrîm).* The exact translation of these words is debated. The last Hebrew word, *hamᵉʾārᵃrîm,* means simply that these waters bring with them the curse uttered in v. 22 (whatever *hammārîm* is determined to mean).[51]

The word *hammārîm* causes difficulty. The traditional derivation of the term from the root *mrr* ("bitter, be bitter") has been widely questioned. The LXX rendered it *hydōr tou elegmou,* "waters of proof, testing." G. R. Driver suggested a root *mry,* meaning "rebel, rebellion."[52]

50. See Mish. *Sotah* 2:5–6 for the Mishnah's view. See also Gray, p. 52; Philo (c. 20 B.C.–A.D. 50), *The Special Laws* (*De specialibus legibus*), ch. 10.

51. See BDB, p. 76b; *HALAT,* p. 88b. The Piel means "to lay under a curse" in Gen. 5:29, the only other occurrence of *ʾārâ* outside the present passage. See Frymer-Kensky, "Strange Case," p. 25.

52. G. R. Driver, "Two Problems in the Old Testament Examined in the Light of Assyriology," *Syria* 33 (1956) 73–74; cf. BDB, p. 598a.

It is not surprising that NEB adopted this reading, but it is hard to see how "waters of rebellion," which is what the root *mry* (i.e., *mrh*) means in Hebrew, is superior to the traditional meaning. Snaith used the Arabic cognates *mārar* ("to pass by") and *marmara* ("to cause to flow") to suggest that these waters led to an abortion of the sinfully conceived fetus.[53] There is, however, no evidence that this ritual was given (at least exclusively) to pregnant women. H. C. Brichto traced *hammārîm* to the root *yrh* ("to throw"). His derived meaning is "oracular waters."[54] This view has grammatical difficulties.[55] Jack Sasson found an Ugaritic root *mrr* ("bless"), which then yields a meaning of "waters that bless and bring the curse," a merismus for "waters of judgment."[56] This Ugaritic root has left no trace of a cognate in Hebrew, however; hence this solution must remain conjectural.

In the light of these conjectural solutions, it remains to be seen what the traditional derivation has to offer. As stated above, this proposal derives *hammārîm* from the root *mrr,* "bitter, be bitter." Opponents of this derivation usually point out that water plus dust or ink (v. 23) is not bitter to the taste.[57] One only need look at the uses of the root *mrr,* however, to discover that both noun and verb are used to indicate more than an unpleasant taste. Both indicate a hard and stressful life.[58]

A significant variant name for these waters is found in the clause *and the waters that bring the curse will enter into her for the purpose of distress* (*ûḇā'û ḇāh hammayim ham^{e}'ār^{a}rîm l^{e}mārîm,* vv. 24 and 27). McKane argued that the meaning of *mārîm* here is "poison," so that the

53. Snaith, p. 129. Frymer-Kensky ("Strange Case," p. 26) emphasizes that the ritual procedure is not limited to pregnant women (see also p. 19 n. 15).

54. See Brichto, "Case of the *ŚŌṬĀ,*" p. 59 n. 1.

55. Brichto (ibid., p. 59 n. 1) traces *hammārîm* to a root *yrh* on the analogy of *mem*-formation nouns such as *maddā'* (root *yd'*). But any meaning such as "oracle" from the root *yrh* would be derived from the Hiphil rather than the Qal; thus the noun would be built on the analogy of *tôrâ* or *môreh* (from *yrh,* "teaching" and "teacher" respectively), and *môrîm,* not *mārîm,* would be the expected form (see BDB, p. 435a).

56. J. Sasson, "Numbers 5 and the Waters of Judgment," *BZ* n.f. 16 (1972) 249–51. Merismus is a figure of speech in which a totality is expressed in two contrasting parts. Old and young, near and far are typical examples. See A. M. Honeyman, "Merismus in Biblical Hebrew," *JBL* 71(1952) 11–18.

57. See, e.g., Frymer-Kensky, "Strange Case," p. 25.

58. For the verbal form with this meaning see *nap̄šāh mārâ lāh* (1 K. 4:27; also Ruth 1:13). For the noun form see *mārê nep̄eš* (Job 3:20), and *yôm mār* (Amos 8:10). Cf. BDB, p. 600.

waters have a harmful effect on the guilty. He connects the poisonous potion with other mentions of poison in what he takes to be similar contexts in the book of Jeremiah.[59]

The traditional meaning of "bitterness" or "distress," however, fits just as well. On the basis of the traditional rendering of "bitterness" or "distress" the meaning is this: if the woman is guilty, the waters will make her life bitter and distressful by carrying out the curse of making her thigh fall and her belly swell. Thus the water is meant to have the same effect as the unbinding of her hair; both point to the curse that follows. According to the Mishnah the suspected adulteress could refuse to continue the procedure at certain points,[60] and perhaps these preliminary "visual aids" were to force a confession from the guilty party before a curse was actually pronounced and the woman was brought into contact with holy water.

19–23 The main action of this section is the administration of the oath in v. 19a (repeated in vv. 20–23). The coordinate action is the promise of weal accompanying innocence (v. 19b). Most modern translations make it clear that the first part of v. 21 interrupts the curse with a repeated instruction to the priest.[61] If v. 21a is seen as a parenthetical repetition for exactness as well as effect, the general situation becomes clear, even if the details do not. The undefiled woman will be free from any harm by the curse-bearing waters (v. 19b), but the guilty woman will be punished by God. V. 21 clearly emphasizes the divine agency of her punishment. Twice God is the subject who acts in punishment: He makes the woman a curse *('ālâ)* and an oath *(šᵉḇuʿâ)* among her kin; he causes her thigh to fall and her belly to swell. Thus any magical view of waters as effectual all by themselves is eliminated. *God* punishes the guilty.

The two punishments belong together and are related, but one needs to separate them for analysis. In biblical thought a *curse ('ālâ)* and an *oath (šᵉḇuʿâ)* are often related.[62] The oath carries with it an implicit

59. See McKane, "Poison," pp. 477–87.

60. Mish. *Sotah* 3:3, 6, etc.

61. See, e.g., RSV, NIV, NEB, NJPS. On the whole relationship between the oath and the curse (and the blessing), see F. C. Fensham, "Malediction and Benediction in Ancient Near Eastern Vassal Treaties and in the Old Testament," *ZAW* 74 (1962) 1–9; M. R. Lehmann, "Biblical Oaths," *ZAW* 81 (1969) 74–92. Milgrom pointed out the strategic nature of this verse, which places God not only at the center of the action but also at the center of the passage literarily ("Suspected Adulteress," pp. 71–72).

62. See Gen. 26:28; 1 Sam. 14:24; Ezek. 17:19; Neh. 10:30; Dan. 9:11. Cf. Lehmann, "Biblical Oaths," p. 77.

curse that will fall on the oath breaker.[63] The curse for oath violation would be understood by the guilty woman's kin. She would be held up as an example of the way in which God punishes oath violators.

Yahweh makes your thigh fallen and your belly swollen. The rendering of the second punishment has been much debated. Most modern English translations agree on a rendering something like "a fallen thigh and a swollen belly."[64] The Mishnah offers the following comments: "With what measure a man metes out it shall be measured to him again. . . . She began transgression with the thigh first and afterward with the belly; therefore the thigh shall suffer first and afterward the belly; neither shall aught else of the body go free."[65] Since the blessing connected with the innocent woman is the ability to bear children (*w^enizr^eʿâ zāraʿ*, v. 28), most commentators connect the curse with the stoppage of childbearing. The word *thigh (yārēḵ),* in addition to its literal meaning of the upper part of the leg, seems to be used euphemistically of the seat of procreative power in men, due perhaps to the thigh's proximity to the sexual organs.[66] This passage is the only place where such a usage is found for a female.[67] A *fallen thigh,* therefore, seems to indicate the falling or atrophying of the sexual organ so as to make childbearing impossible.[68]

The coordinate term *belly (beṭen)* is a general term for internal organs. Because of its coordination with *yārēḵ (thigh)* here, some scholars have taken it to mean "womb."[69]

The verb translated *swollen (ṣāḇâ)* occurs only here in Biblical Hebrew, although it is frequent in postbiblical Hebrew.[70] The usual translation, "swell" or "swollen," agrees with the LXX, which reads *prēthō.* Brichto accepts the meaning "to swell," and points out that a

63. Thus the reversal of the conditional particles, i.e., *'im lō'* for a positive oath and *'im* or *kî* for a negative one. The first looks to the curse if the oath is not kept; the second for a curse unless the oath is kept. See Lehmann, "Biblical Oaths," pp. 86–91.

64. See, e.g., RSV, NIV, NJPS; but cf. NEB, which depends upon Driver's conjectures, mentioned above, for its translation.

65. Mish. *Sotah* 1:7.

66. See, e.g., Gen. 46:26: "who were his own offspring" is lit. "those who go out (from) his thigh" *(yōṣ^e'ê y^erēḵô).*

67. Unless the reference to the female "thigh" be considered a euphemism in Cant. 7:2 (Eng. 1).

68. See Brichto ("Case of the *ŚŌṬĀ,*" pp. 60–61, 62 n. r), who translates it "a shrivelled pubis."

69. See, e.g., Gray, p. 54.

70. See Jastrow, *Dictionary,* p. 1258a.

swollen belly is not the mark of sterility but of pregnancy. He concludes that the fallen thigh and the swollen belly are marks of what is called pseudocyesis or hysterical pregnancy.[71]

Other scholars have searched the cognate lexica for help in explaining the term *ṣāḇâ.* For example, G. R. Driver related it to the Syriac term *sbʿ,* "to be dry and hot," and connected this to the supposedly ancient medical notion that barren women were unable to conceive because their wombs were too dry and hot.[72] Frymer-Kensky proposed an interesting solution based on an Akkadian verb *ṣabû/ṣapû,* "to flood." The uterus is flooded by the curse-bearing waters, thus distending it and leading to the ancient versions' translations of "swell."[73] On the basis of the text itself, it is impossible to decide among these options. The text implies a curse of sterility and a blessing of childbearing, without entering into detail.

22 The emphasis shifts between vv. 21 and 22. Whereas the former verse has the power of God central, the latter emphasizes the work of the waters. The result is the same if the above arguments are followed: the guilty woman will be punished with sterility of some sort.

The woman responds with *This is fitting and proper* (lit., "amen, amen"). This formula of accepting a curse upon oneself with the word *amen* (i.e., "let it be this way") also occurs in Deut. 27:15–26 and Neh. 5:13.[74] The purpose of the double "amen" is probably to emphasize the seriousness of the oath and the solemn determination of the woman to declare her innocence before God.[75]

23 The words of the curse (lit., *these curses*) that have just been uttered by the priest and accepted by the woman are now written *in the book* (or "in the scroll"),[76] and then washed off into the mixture of water and dust. This is a further powerful symbol that the very words of the curse itself will penetrate the innermost parts of the woman along with the waters.

24–28 The main action in this section is the administration of the potion (vv. 24, 26b–28), and the coordinate action is the meal offering

71. See Brichto, "Case of the *ŚŌṬĀ,*" p. 66.

72. Driver, "Two Problems," p. 75.

73. Frymer-Kensky, "Strange Case," pp. 20–21.

74. The double amen without a copula occurs only in Neh. 8:8, in a different context from the present one.

75. Cf. A. Jepsen, *TDOT,* I:320–21. See Mish. *Sotah* 2:5.

76. Heb. *bassēper* has the definite article, which indicates that this is a specific scroll to be used for *this* purpose (only?); see GKC, § 126s. Mish. *Sotah* 2:3–4 gives more definite instructions for the scroll and the writing.

(vv. 25–26a). Both these actions have been discussed above. The wording here makes it plain that the potion is given to the woman only after the meal offering has been given.[77] Thus it is possible that, in the previous sections, the main actions also happen after the coordinate actions (although the wording in the previous sections is ambiguous). In vv. 16–18 this would mean that the woman is stationed before God only after the water-and-dust mixture has been prepared (a proposal that makes certain administrative sense),[78] and in vv. 19–23 it would mean that the woman is given the oath only after she is promised acquittal if she is innocent. The sequence for these previous sections remains uncertain, however.[79]

That the meal offering is offered to God before the potion is administered means that the offering is the preliminary to the whole matter and has the effect of negating, once again, a magical view of the waters as efficacious apart from Yahweh's power. Before the priest puts the memorial portion *('azkārâ)* to smoke on the altar, he *dedicates (hēnîp̱)* the offering to God. Although the traditional translation of the latter term has been "to wave," the translation adopted here is probably more accurate. The basic meaning of this verb is "to elevate" (viz., in dedication or consecration to God).[80] Milgrom thinks of the action of elevation (or "waving," *tᵉnûp̱â*) as necessary with gifts that belong to the worshiper when they are brought to God as well as with gifts that are different from others in their class.[81]

77. See the word *wᵉ'aḥar,* "only then," in v. 26 to describe the drinking *after* the offering. See Brichto, "Case of the *ŚŌṬĀ*," p. 61; BDB, pp. 29b–30a.

78. Although it would add considerably to the drama of the whole occasion if this potion were to be prepared "before her eyes" in the tabernacle.

79. The first section (v. 15) is too short to judge whether one action comes before the other. It makes sense, however, to assume that both the woman and the offering arrive at the same time. See Frymer-Kensky, "Strange Case," p. 16.

80. The traditional translation, which comes from rabbinic tradition, is explained as a sideways movement toward and away from the altar. This translation is accepted, e.g., by AV, RV, RSV, NIV, NASB. The noun *tᵉnûp̱â* is related to the verb *hēnîp̱* and is explained as "the wave offering," in modern times by, e.g., W. Brueggemann, *IDB,* IV:817; see also N. Snaith, "The Wave Offering," *ExpTim* 74 (1962–63) 127. G. R. Driver ("Three Technical Terms in the Pentateuch," *JSS* 1 [1956] 100–105) argued that the Babylonian exiles took over an Akkadian term for a gift to God. This thought is incorporated into NEB's translation, "special gift." Milgrom has reexamined the whole concept thoroughly and concluded that *tᵉnûp̱â* is a term used for dedication of gifts to God. See Milgrom, "Wave Offering," *IDBSup,* pp. 944–46; idem, *"Hattĕnûpâ,"* in *Studies in Cultic Theology,* pp. 139–58; idem, "The Alleged Wave Offering in Israel and in the Ancient Near East," in ibid., 133–38.

81. See Milgrom, *"Hattĕnûpâ,"* pp. 156, 158.

31 The latter view is made more likely by v. 31. Although the husband who accused his wife in the way described herein is *free of punishment (niqqâ ʿāwōn),* the guilty woman (lit., *that woman, hāʾiššâ hahîʾ*) *shall bear her punishment (tiśśāʾ ʾeṯ-ʿᵃwōnāh).* A careful study of the idiom *nāśāʾ ʿāwōn* has shown that "to bear one's punishment" means that the punishment is left to God.[82] The sanctions of the curse are simply brought to bear on the guilty party by God. The community has no role in determining the punishment. Thus time alone will suffice to mark out the guilty party, and God alone will suffice to punish her. This legislation forbids human punishment of a woman on the basis of suspicion alone, and, in fact, protects her from what could be a death sentence at the hands of the community.

d. Law of the Nazirite (6:1–21)

1 *And Yahweh spoke to Moses, saying:*

2 *"Speak to the children of Israel and say to them, 'If a man or woman should vow the special vow*[1] *of the Nazirite,*[2] *to become a Nazirite belonging to Yahweh,*

3 *he must separate himself*[3] *from wine and strong drink. He must not drink the vinegar from wine or the vinegar from strong drink, any juice of grapes,*[4] *and he must not eat grapes, either fresh or dried.*

4 *All the days of his consecration he must not eat anything that is made from the grapevine, from the seeds to the skin.*[5]

5 *All the days of his vow of consecration no razor must go over his*

82. See Zimmerli, "Die Eigenart der prophetischen Reden des Ezechiel," pp. 8–11; Frymer-Kensky, "Strange Case," pp. 22–24.

1. *BHS* and *HALAT,* p. 876b, suggest that the Hiphil *yap̄liʾ* ("to vow") should be repointed as a Piel, *yᵉpallēʾ,* which then could be taken with *neḏer* to mean "to make a votive offering," as in Lev. 22:21 and Num. 15:3, 8. NKJV so translates here.

2. Heb. *nāzîr,* from *nzr,* "dedicate, dedication, consecration"; see BDB, p. 634a; *HALAT,* p. 646.

3. Heb. *yazzîr,* Hiphil of *nāzar;* the reflexive pronoun (himself) is added for a smooth translation. It is also possible to translate it "he will abstain from wine. . . ."

4. The term *mišrâ* is a hapax legomenon from *šārâ,* "to water, be moist." Hence it may mean "juice"; see BDB, p. 1056; *HALAT,* p. 617a.

5. The meaning of *ḥarṣannîm* (here translated "seeds") and *zāḡ* ("skin") is uncertain. They are usually taken to refer to a small and insignificant part of the grape. For the first term BDB, p. 359a, and L. J. Coppes, *TWOT,* I:326, suggest "grape seeds"; *HALAT,* pp. 342b–343a, "unripe grapes"; RSV and NIV, "seeds"; NEB, "shoots." For the second, both BDB, p. 260a, and *HALAT,* p. 253a, offer "skin."

head; he will be holy until the fulfillment of the days which he has separated to Yahweh, thus allowing the locks of the hair of his head to grow long.

6 *All the days of his consecration of himself to Yahweh he must not approach a dead body.*

7 *He must not defile himself for his father or his mother or his sister or his brother when they die because his dedication to God is upon his head.*

8 *All the days of his consecration he is holy to Yahweh.*

9 *And if one near him should die suddenly,*[6] *so that he defiles his consecrated head, he must shave his head on the day of his cleansing; he will shave it on the seventh day.*

10 *On the eighth day he must bring two turtledoves or two young pigeons to the priest at the gate of the tent of meeting.*

11 *And the priest shall offer one for a purification offering and one for a whole burnt offering. And he will make atonement for him, since he sinned concerning the dead body.*[7] *And he will sanctify his head on that day,*

12 *that is, he will consecrate to Yahweh the days of his consecration, and bring a yearling lamb for a reparation offering. But the former days will not count*[8] *because his consecration was defiled.*

13 *And this is the regulation*[9] *for the Nazirite on the day of the fulfillment of his Nazirite vow. He shall bring it to the door of the tent of meeting*

14 *and shall offer his gift to Yahweh: one perfect yearling lamb for a whole burnt offering and one perfect yearling ewe lamb for a purification offering, one perfect ram for a peace offering,*

15 *and a basket of unleavened bread, cakes of fine flour mixed with oil, and wafers spread with oil, along with their meal offering and their drink offerings.*

16 *And the priest shall offer these before Yahweh and make his purification offering and whole burnt offering.*

6. Heb. *b*^{e}*peṯaʿ piṯʾōm*, lit., "in suddenness, suddenly." For a similar idiom, see Isa. 29:5: *w*^{e}*hāyâ l*^{e}*peṯaʿ piṯʾōm*, "and it will happen very suddenly." See BDB, p. 837a.

7. See the commentary above on 5:2 for this meaning of *nep̄eš*. Note that in 6:6 the fuller expression *nep̄eš mēṯ* occurs; here in v. 11 perhaps the author simply abbreviated the expression.

8. Heb. *w*^{e}*hayyāmîm hāriʾšōnîm yipp*^{e}*lû*, lit., "but the first days will fall." See BDB, p. 657b s.v. *npl*, Qal, no. 5.

9. On *tôrâ* as "regulation" see Lev. 6:2, 7, 18; 7:1, 7, 11, 37; 11:46; 12:7; 13:59; 14:2, 32, 54, 57; Num. 5:29, 30; 6:21; 15:16, 29; 19:2, 14; 31:21. BDB, p. 436a; *HALAT*, pp. 1575–76; J. E. Hartley, *TWOT*, I:403–5, esp. 404a.

17 *And the ram he shall offer as a sacrifice, a peace offering, to Yahweh together with the basket of unleavened bread. And the priest will make its meal offering and its drink offering.*
18 *And the Nazirite shall shave his consecrated head at the door of the tent of meeting. And he shall take the hair of his consecrated head and put it on the fire that is under the sacrifice of the peace offering.*
19 *And the priest shall take the boiled shoulder from the ram, one cake of unleavened bread from the basket, and one unleavened wafer, and put it in the hands of the Nazirite, after he has shaved himself of his consecration,*[10]
20 *and the priest shall elevate it as a dedication offering before Yahweh. It is a holy portion for the priest together with the breast of dedication (which was elevated) and with the thigh of the offering (which was offered). Afterward the Nazirite may drink wine.*
21 *This is the regulation for the Nazirite who takes a vow, his offering to Yahweh for his Nazirite vow—besides whatever else he can afford. He must do, in proportion to the vow which he vowed, according to the regulation for his consecration.*

A majority of modern critics have attributed Num. 6:1–21 to P or a supplement to P.[11] According to the formulation of the documentary hypothesis in the 19th cent., the P stratum was composed no earlier than 500 B.C., with supplements coming as much as two centuries later.[12] While modern proponents of source analysis have been willing to concede that each "document" is really a stream of tradition containing some ancient material,[13] this concession rarely means that much of a preexilic nature

10. I.e., of his hair.

11. E.g., see S. R. Driver, *Introduction to the Literature of the Old Testament* (12th ed.; New York: Scribner's, 1906), p. 159; O. Eissfeldt, *The Old Testament: An Introduction,* tr. P. Ackroyd (New York: Harper & Row, 1965), p. 189; and G. Fohrer, *Introduction to the Old Testament,* tr. D. Green (Nashville: Abingdon, 1968), p. 180, to name only three. Of individual commentaries on Numbers, see, e.g., Gray, pp. xxxiii–xxxiv; Noth, pp. 53, 55 (also idem, *History of Pentateuchal Traditions,* p. 18); and Budd, pp. xviii–xxvi, 39–71. As usual, Budd gives an excellent overview of previous studies.

12. See, e.g., Gray, p. 39.

13. Gray admits that parts of P (what he calls P^x) were possibly written down as early as the 6th or 7th cents. B.C. (p. 39). See J. A. Soggin, *Introduction to the Old Testament,* tr. J. Bowden, OTL (Philadelphia: Westminster, 1976), pp. 85–96. Or compare the charts in the 2nd and 3rd eds. of B. W. Anderson, *Understanding the Old Testament* (Englewood Cliffs, N.J.: Prentice-Hall, 1966,

(let alone Mosaic) is credited to P. The postexilic redactor who put the P stream together has so reshaped his material that it might as well be considered late, whatever its roots might be. To confirm this judgment with regard to the present passage one has only to consult many modern commentaries.[14] The assumption is that passages such as Judg. 13:5, 7; 16:17; 1 Sam. 1:11 (LXX); and Amos 2:11–12 are all earlier both in substance and in literary shape than Num. 6:1–21; consequently, the picture of the Nazirite found in these other passages is more ancient than the picture in Num. 6.[15]

According to the dominant explanation, the ancient Nazirite was consecrated for life (like Samson and, probably, Samuel). The emphasis in this early period was on the divine call of the Nazirite (again, Samson, as well as the Nazirites of Amos 2). Only later did the Hebrews initiate the Nazirite vow for a specific period or task as reflected here in Num. 6 and continued in such literature as 1 Maccabees, Josephus, and the Mishnah.[16] Gray was confident of this conclusion, and scholars since Gray have evinced much of the same confidence.[17]

Turning to the biblical text itself, however, one is confronted with a different picture. Num. 6 does not institute the office of Nazirite, but only seeks to regulate it in certain (not exhaustive) ways.[18] Num. 6:13–20 regulates the termination of the Nazirite vow. Except for the case of Samson and the possible case of Samuel, the rest of the literature agrees

---

1975), pp. 382 and 424 respectively. The 4th ed. (1986) differs in no way at this point. The admission of ancient material in P, however, seldom gets beyond the theoretical stage.

14. See, e.g., Budd, pp. 69–71; Noth, pp. 53–55; also R. Klein, *1 Samuel,* WBC (Waco: Word, 1983), p. 8.

15. There is no conclusive, universally agreed, way to demonstrate the age of any biblical text, whether early or late. If Num. 6 has received a later redaction (viz., in the post–exilic period) as, e.g., Gray, pp. 56–61 (also "Nazirite," p. 202), Noth, pp. 53–55, and Budd, pp. 69–71, have argued, it must also be remembered that texts in Joshua, 1 Samuel, and Amos have also received a redaction later than their compositions. See, e.g., M. Noth, *The Deuteronomistic History, JSOTSup* 15, tr. J. Doull et al. (Sheffield: JSOT, 1981), esp., pp. 27–99. Such later redactions will make it impossible to judge which texts are based on which with any degree of surety.

16. See 1 Macc. 3:49; Josephus, *Ant.* 19.6.1; Mish. *Nazir.*

17. G. B. Gray, "The Nazirite," *JTS* 1 (1899–1900) 202. This opinion has also been offered in more modern sources such as J. C. Rylaarsdam, *IDB,* II:526; Klein, *1 Samuel,* p. 8; as well as both Budd, pp. 73–74, and Noth, pp. 53–55.

18. The office of Nazirite must therefore (from the point of view of the text) be older than Mosaic times. When and why it was established is unknown.

that the Nazirite vow may be terminated.[19] The common assumption that there was "a large class of life-long devotees" in the early period of Israel must be disputed.[20] The texts give us the case of one, possibly two, in the whole expanse of the history of Israel.

Amos 2:11–12 says nothing about the Nazirite's length of service. It merely compares the prophet and the Nazirite and states that God's people have made both ineffective. That the office of prophet could be temporary is not inconceivable; Amos himself may be a good example of one who was called from another profession. Furthermore, to say that the earlier Nazirite was marked by the call of God and the later by the human vow must mean that, if Samuel was a Nazirite, he belonged to the later period since Hannah made a very human promise to give her hoped-for son to God. Surely a divine call and a human vow are not mutually exclusive in either the ancient or the modern world.

Numbers 6 assumes that the Nazirite vow will normally be taken by a person on his or her own behalf. Although one might reasonably expect this to be the case the majority of the time, Num. 6 by no means legislates that a person must take the vow for her/himself. Both Samson and Samuel are given to God before their births, and Num. 6 does not prohibit such a practice.[21]

It remains to look at the two examples of the so-called permanent Nazirites to see what the texts themselves say. 1 Sam. 1:11 says only that Samuel's mother gave him to Yahweh for life and that no razor would touch his head. The Hebrew text does not state that Samuel was a Nazirite, although it has been so interpreted by the LXX, the Qumran exegetes, and the Mishnah.[22] The text says only that Samuel was "given" *(nāṯan)* to Yahweh as long as he lived *(ûnᵉṯattîw lYHWH kol-yᵉmê ḥayyāyw)*. It does not say that no razor would go over his head as long as he lived. Therefore, one would have to demonstrate that everyone "given" to Yahweh must have been a Nazirite, which is not possible.[23]

19. 1 Macc. 3:49; Josephus, *Ant.* 19.6.1; Mish. *Nazir* 1:3–7; 3:1–7; etc. *Nazir* does recognize a permanent Nazirite vow in 1:2, 4–5, but few regulations are given for it.

20. Gray, "Nazirite," p. 205.

21. Although Mish. *Nazir* 4:6 does forbid a woman to take a vow for her son, Num. 6 contains no such prohibition.

22. See Klein, *I Samuel,* p. 8; Mish. *Nazir* 9:5.

23. The Levites, e.g., were given to God (Num. 8:16), but that did not make them Nazirites. If the genealogy of 1 Chr. 6:25–28, 33 is generally correct, it means that Samuel was a Levite. The Levites were given to God from age 25 to age 50 (Num. 8:24–25). Samuel was given for life.

The remainder of Samuel's story certainly does not mention his being a Nazirite, and he did not keep thc vow as regards contact with a corpse when he "hacked Agag in pieces before Yahweh" (1 Sam. 15:33). If Samuel was a Nazirite, his being a Nazirite was lifelong only because the nature of his task was so immense (i.e., the transition from theocracy to monarchy) and his role so complex (i.e, both prophet and judge).

Samson was almost certainly a Nazirite.[24] He was called by God before his birth (Judg. 13:3–7). In the story God forbids Samson's mother from imbibing wine (forbidden in Num. 6:1–4) and eating unclean food (no parallel in Num. 6). She is furthermore told not to cut his hair because he is to be God's Nazirite from conception (Judg. 13:5, 7; 16:17). God also tells Samson's mother her sons's mission: "and he will begin to save Israel from the hand of the Philistines" (13:5), and, most importantly here, that he will be a Nazirite until the day of his death (*ʿaḏ-yôm môṯô,* 13:7). What do these words mean within the context of the Samson cycle of narratives?

The whole Samson cycle can be seen as the story of the disintegration of a Nazirite who breaks his vow. In the end, the accomplishment of his God-given task ("beginning to save Israel from the hand of the Philistines") costs him his life. Therefore Samson was a Nazirite for life only because his life ended in the accomplishment of his task. From this point of view, one may understand God's statement in 13:7 ("until the day of his death") not as an indication that being a Nazirite was permanent but as a sign of divine foreknowledge of the outcome of the story (which the reader only learns at the end). This kind of double meaning of a prediction is not unique to this passage, but is also found in Judg. 4.[25] By far, later literature (chiefly Mish. *Nazir* but also 1 Macc. 3:49 and Josephus) reflects more commonly the temporary character of the Nazirite, although the permanent Nazirite is also mentioned.[26]

Therefore, it appears that the norm was for one to take a Nazirite vow for oneself for a specific task. This is seen in both early (Num. 6) and late periods (e.g., Mishnah). In two possible cases (Samson and Samuel) God called people to be Nazirites for longer periods because of the

24. Unless one takes *nāzîr* in 13:5, 7; 16:17 in its generic sense of "consecrated," which is unlikely since the statement that no razor was to touch his head is also made.

25. See, e.g., Deborah's statement to Barak that the Canaanite general Sisera will fall to a woman (Judg. 4:9). This prediction is fulfilled not by Deborah herself but by the treacherous act of Jael (4:17–22).

26. See Josephus, *Ant.* 19.6.1.

complexity or difficulty of the task involved. It is, of course, possible (some would say likely) that Samson and Samuel were not the only long-term Nazirites. The text of Num. 6 does not forbid this kind of Nazirite. A person who was called for a lifetime would simply not fall under the last section of the regulations of Num. 6 dealing with exit from the Nazirite vow. Thus seeing Num. 6 as an early text does not mitigate the possibility of long-term Nazirites.

1–8 These verses define the Nazirite vow. The verb *vow* (*yap̱li'*, Hiphil of *pl'*) is related to the word *pele'*, "miracle," "wonder," which indicates something out of the ordinary. In Lev. 27:2 the same verb is used with the word *vow (nēḏer)* as a "special vow."

Several of the regulations governing the Nazirite are related to those concerning the priest or high priest. The priests are forbidden to drink wine while they are serving in the tent of meeting (Lev. 10:9), and the Nazirite is forbidden wine at all times (Num. 6:3). The Nazirite must also not imbibe any strong drink or grape products for the extent of his or her vow (vv. 3–4). The priest may not pollute himself by contact, with corpses, except for immediate family members (Lev. 22:1–3); the high priest and the Nazirite may not come into contact with any corpse, even that of immediate family members (Lev. 22:10–12; Num. 6:6). The major difference between the priest and the Nazirite is that, while only males could become priests, either males or females could become Nazirites. Furthermore, the Nazirite is clearly a layperson. In ancient Israel God called a group of laypeople who would be especially consecrated to him.

The most important positive characteristic of the Nazirite is that she or he is *holy* (or separated, consecrated) *to Yahweh* (vv. 5, 8). The word *holy* carries with it the idea of a special relationship to Yahweh, of being marked out for Yahweh's service.[27] Three distinctives mark out the Nazirite from the rest of Israelite society; all three mark abstinence (vv. 3–7); and all three are prefaced by the phrase *all the days of (kol-y*^{e}*mê).*[28]

3–4 The first mark of the Nazirite is complete abstinence from wine, strong drink, and all grape products. These verses give as complete

27. The literature on the concept of "holiness" in the OT is immense. See, e.g., W. Eichrodt, *Theology of the Old Testament,* tr. J. Baker, 2 vols., OTL (Philadelphia: Westminster, 1961–67), 1:137, 270–80, etc.; T. E. McComiskey, *TWOT,* II:786–89 (plus bibliography); O. Procksch, *TDNT,* I:89–97; H. Seebass, *NIDNTT,* II:224–29.

28. Three times the term used for the Nazirite vow is changed (perhaps for literary variety): "his consecration" (*nizrô,* v. 3); "his vow of consecration" (*neḏer nizrô,* v. 5), and "his consecration to Yahweh" (*hizzirô lYHWH,* v. 6).

a catalogue of grape products as can be given in short compass. The Nazirite must abstain from *wine (yayin)* and *strong drink (šēḵār).* The latter term most probably means any intoxicant made from fruit or grain. The term is usually found in connection with wine (23 of 25 times).[29] The Nazirite must also abstain from the *vinegar* of wine and strong drink, which was produced when the grapes or other fruit fermented too long. It was also made by pouring water over the squeezed-out fruit and allowing the mixture to ferment. It could be used either as a refreshing drink or as a condiment.[30] Even unfermented *juice of grapes (mišraṯ ʿᵃnāḇîm),* or *grapes* themselves *(ʿᵃnāḇîm), either fresh [laḥ] or dried* (i.e., raisins, *yᵉḇēš*), must be avoided, right down to the most minute parts of the grape *(from the seeds to the skin).*

It is not possible to recapture the rationale behind the prohibition of grape products. The Nazirites were asked for a higher level of consecration in this matter than the priests. Many scholars have seen this prohibition as a rejection of the evils of sedentary life in Canaan, which was known for its viticulture. Scholars often interpret the prohibition this way because of their assumption that the Nazirite office reflected in Num. 6 is a later, post-conquest phenomenon.[31] But one can as easily see it as God's preparation of these people to live in a Canaanite culture as a different (i.e., a holy) people. The norm, not only in Canaan but elsewhere, was to drink wine and eat grapes. The Nazirites were marked out as special people, consecrated to Yahweh only; they were not to conform to the norms of everyday life. The same basic reason may lie behind the other two prohibitions.

29. See, e.g., Lev. 10:9; Isa. 5:11; Prov. 20:1. The verb *šāḵar* means "to be drunk," e.g., in Gen. 9:21. Cf. BDB, p. 1016; KB, pp. 971–72.

30. See J. F. Ross, *IDB,* IV:786.

31. So Gray, p. 62; Riggans, p. 52; Budd, p. 74. If the prohibition against grape products is to be seen as a rejection of Canaanite life and viticulture, it seems odd that only the Nazirites are forbidden grapes, etc., and not the whole of Israel, who are to be "a kingdom of priests and a holy nation." The figure of speech of wine and vineyards is also used as a standard image for divine blessing in the OT, which is strange if they are to be rejected by those truly consecrated to God. See, e.g., 1 K. 4:25; Amos 9:14; Isa. 36:17; 65:21; Jer. 32:15; Ezek. 28:26; Neh. 9:25. See also Num. 16:14 and Deut. 6:11.

5 The second prohibition is against cutting or trimming the hair. The hair was a living, growing part of the human person and, as such, represented the life-force of the person very well, since hair will keep growing, for a while, even after death. Nothing external was to disturb the hair, representing as it did the power and life of the dedicated human being, until the accomplishment of the vow. At that time, and only then, the head would be shaved and the hair offered to God by being burnt on the altar (as in v. 18). Therefore, the hair can be seen as the most visible badge of the Nazirite. Not even the priests, and surely no other laypeople, had this special mark of consecration. It is interesting that both the high priest's diadem and the Nazirite's hair are called *nēzer* (lit., "consecration"). Both the diadem and the hair are special marks of the wearer's consecration to Yahweh.[32] To dedicate one's hair to the deity was not a uniquely Israelite practice but was common in the Semitic world.[33]

6–7 The third prohibition is not to *approach a dead body.* A corpse rendered those who came in contact with it unclean, hence unacceptable in Yahweh's camp, as 5:1–4 described. The ritual for cleansing the ordinary layperson is found in 19:1–22. That the prohibition was absolute is seen both by the reference to the Nazirite's immediate family and also by the regulation that follows in vv. 9–12, which is designed to cleanse the Nazirite after accidental pollution. The prohibition of casual contact with the dead (even a dead mother or father, v. 7) effectively reduced or eliminated the Nazirite's participation in mourning for the dead. This is important because of the pagan practice of shaving one's head in mourning for the dead. Such pagan practice is excluded for Israel in Lev. 19:27 and, more explicitly, in Deut. 14:1, but such mourning practices existed in Israel, as is evident from many OT passages.[34] The temptation to take part in such shaving of the head explains why the text says: *he may not defile himself* [even for family members] . . . *because his dedication to God is upon his head.*

8 Finally, the key characteristic of the Nazirite is repeated: *he is holy to Yahweh.* This special status obtains for the length of his or her vow, however long or short that might be (the text is not specific: *all the days of his consecration*).

32. For the high priest, see Exod. 29:6; 39:40; Lev. 8:9; for the Nazirite, see Num. 6:9, 18.

33. See W. Robertson Smith, *The Religion of the Semites,* rev. ed. (London: Black, 1901), pp. 327–35, 481–85.

34. See, e.g., Deut. 21:2; Jer. 7:29; Job 1:20.

9–12 These verses take up the case of accidental pollution by a corpse. No regulations for accidental pollution by wine drinking or by hair cutting were necessary, since these things do not happen accidentally.

9 The accidental nature of this case is seen by the use of the word *suddenly.* One who is *near him (ʿālāyw),* perhaps another Nazirite, dies suddenly. The dead body brings uncleanness upon the Nazirite, even though contact with it was accidental. That it is an accidental pollution means that the ritual in Lev. 5:14–16 for accidental trespass of holy things (and people) can be applied. The legislation here also uses the regulations for purification of those who have become unclean by means of physical disorders in Lev. 12–15. The regulation concerning shaving the head on *the seventh day* (which is the day of purification) parallels the timetable of Lev. 14:2, 9, for the cleansing of the leper.[35]

10 *On the eighth day.* Again here we have the same timetable for cleansing as in Lev. 14:10. The sacrificial victims for the purification offering and whole burnt offering are either two *turtledoves or two young pigeons (š^{e}tê ṯōrîm ʾô š^{e}nê b^{e}nê yônâ).* These birds are found together as sacrificial victims in Lev. 1:14; 5:7, 11; 12:6, 8; 14:22, 30; 15:14, 29.[36] One of these birds is used for a purification offering *(ḥaṭṭāʾṯ),* which purifies the sanctuary of the uncleanness brought into it by the contaminated Nazirite. The second bird is used by the priest as a whole burnt offering *(ʿôlâ),* which probably invokes the presence of God.[37] Only after these sacrifices have been offered is the Nazirite free to reconsecrate his or her head (i.e., hair) and take a new Nazirite vow. In fact, this vow and consecration should be seen as part of the reparation offering *(ʾāšām).*

The reparation offering of a male yearling lamb is unique. Elsewhere, when a lamb is offered, it is a female (Lev. 5:6), or the age of the male animal is not stated (Lev. 14:21). As mentioned above, the model for the reparation offering here is Lev. 5:14–16, which deals with unwit-

35. Compare *bayyôm ṭah^{o}rāṯô* here and in Lev. 14:2; also *w^{e}hāyâ ḇayyôm hašš^{e}ḇîʿî y^{e}gallaḥ (ʾeṯ-kol-ś^{e}ʿārô) ʾeṯ-rōʾšô* in Lev. 14:9 with *w^{e}gillaḥ rōʾšô . . . bayyôm hašš^{e}ḇîʿî* here.

36. The name *tōr* for this group of birds is probably onomatopoeic, like the Latin generic name *turtur.* See W. S. McCullough, *IDB,* IV:718–19. The *pigeon* (or *dove, yônâ*) is a member of the subfamily *columbinae;* see W. S. McCullough, *IDB,* III:810. These same two birds may be substituted by an impoverished leper in Lev. 14:22.

37. On the *ḥaṭṭāʾṯ* and the *ʿôlâ,* see, e.g., Milgrom, *IDBSup,* pp. 766–69. On *ʿôlâ* as an invocation, see B. Levine, *In the Presence of the Lord,* SJLA 5 (Leiden: Brill, 1974), pp. 22–27.

ting trespasses of holy things and holy people. The sacrificial victim itself is different here (presumably because of the different status of the offerer), but the procedure is the same. For unwitting trespass, in addition to the reparation offering itself the offerer must "make restitution for what he has done amiss in the holy thing" (Lev. 5:16, RSV; *wᵉʾēṯ ʾᵃšer ḥāṭāʾ min-haqqōḏeš yᵉšallēm*). Similarly, the Nazirite must resanctify his or her hair and repledge a new Nazirite vow to make restitution for that holy thing (the Nazirite vow), which has been defiled by contact with the dead. Only then is the Nazirite able to offer the reparation offering with any success.[38] In effect, the Nazirite starts the Nazirite vow all over again. *But the former days will not count* because the Nazirite became polluted by accidental exposure to a dead body.

13–21 This section deals with the voluntary termination of the Nazirite vow. The *regulation* (*tôrâ,* vv. 13, 21) does not necessarily mandate the termination of the vow; hence it is possible to be a lifelong Nazirite. The existence of such a regulation does assume, however, that many, if not most, Nazirite vows were temporary. This was the procedure for the Nazirite's transition from the state of special consecration to the normal state of the ordinary layperson.

The order of the sacrifices is different in vv. 14–15 and vv. 16–17. This variance reflects not a conflation of sources, but, as A. F. Rainey saw, two different purposes. The text as a whole fits into the genre of what he called "descriptive-administrative" texts.[39] In his study of Lev. 6–7 (Eng. 6:8–7:38), Rainey pointed out that the texts are framed by *tôrâ* statements (Lev. 6:2 [Eng. 9]; 7:37), much as the text here is (vv. 13, 21). The order of the sacrifices in this kind of text is not procedural but logical, beginning with the whole burnt offering because it belongs *wholly* to God (i.e., it is consumed on the altar), and ending with the peace offerings because they are shared by the worshipers.[40]

Inserted into the administrative text is one that gives the procedural order (vv. 16–17), beginning with the purification offering, to deal

38. On *ʾāšām,* see the commentary above on 5:5–10; see also Milgrom, *IDBSup,* p. 768; idem, *Cult and Conscience.* The order of the text in Lev. 5:16 is telling: first, restitution must be made; then, one-fifth penalty must be paid; and finally, the priest "makes atonement" for the offerer. No fine of one-fifth is appropriate in this case. See Milgrom, *Cult and Conscience,* pp. 66–70.

39. A. F. Rainey, "The Order of the Sacrifices in Old Testament Ritual Texts," *Bib* 51 (1970) 485–98. Rainey built on the work of B. Levine, "The Descriptive Tabernacle Texts of the Pentateuch," *JAOS* 85 (1965) 307–18.

40. Rainey, "Order," pp. 487–89.

with impurities that have been brought into the sanctuary and so on. Even these verses do not deal with the precise description of the rituals; rather they preserve the order for administration of the rituals.[41]

These rituals take place *at the door of the tent of meeting* (*peṯaḥ 'ōhel mō'ēḏ*, i.e., in the outer court, v. 13), the same place as those for the unclean Nazirite (v. 10). The difference is that whereas the former rituals climaxed in a reparation offering to compensate for the Nazirite's defiled hair and vow, the present ritual climaxes in the joy of the so-called *peace offering* (*zeḇaḥ šelāmîm*, v. 14). The purification offering *(ḥaṭṭā'ṯ)* and the whole burnt offering *('ôlâ)* have already been discussed. The regulations for the peace offering are given in Lev. 3:1–17 and 7:11–36. The *zeḇaḥ šelāmîm* appear to be offered on three occasions: the thank offering (*tôḏâ*, Lev. 7:12–15), the votive offering *(neḏer),* and the freewill offering (*neḏāḇâ*, Lev. 7:16–18).

The meaning of *šelāmîm,* along with the plural formation, are debated.[42] The *šelāmîm* appear to be a subgrouping of the slain offering *(zeḇaḥ),* all of which are to be eaten. According to Milgrom, the common denominator of all these peace offerings (whether thank, votive, or freewill) was that they were done with rejoicing.[43] Rejoicing is certainly appropriate in the current case. According to Levine, the *šelāmîm* ought to be understood as a "gift of greeting," related etymologically and perhaps procedurally to the Ugar. *šlmm* and the Assyr. *šulmānu,* "gift."[44] While one might not agree with all of Levine's historical assumptions and conclusions, his argument about the basic meaning of the term is attractive, and ties in with what others (e.g., Milgrom) have said about the celebrative nature of the peace offerings.[45] The rejoicing Nazirite comes into Yahweh's present at the conclusion of the vow with a present for God.

15–17 The *basket of unleavened bread (sal maṣṣôṯ)* is made up of *cakes of fine flour (sōleṯ ḥallōṯ)* and *wafers (reqîqîm;* cf. *raq,* "thin") covered or spread with oil. Virtually the same description of the offering is given in Lev. 2:4.

The last phrase of v. 15 *(their meal offering and their drink offerings)* and the last sentence of v. 17 *(And the priest will make its meal offering and its drink offering)* cause several problems.

41. Ibid., pp. 494–98.
42. See Milgrom, *IDBSup,* p. 769; Levine, *Presence,* pp. 3–52.
43. See Deut. 27:7; Milgrom, *IDBSup,* p. 770.
44. Levine, *Presence,* pp. 8–20.
45. Milgrom, *IDBSup*, p. 770.

First, by their brevity, these words assume that the correct amounts for both these offerings were well known. The detailed legislation for meal and drink offerings to accompany sacrifice is not found until Num. 15. The answer to this problem on a historical level is probably that the correct procedures *were* well known. Several texts previous to Num. 6 speak of meal and drink offerings, and two of them even give proportions.[46] On a literary level one must not assume that because a text does not speak of something until later it was unknown earlier. Obviously the book of Numbers was edited after the events narrated. If earlier parts of the book assume later parts, it means nothing more than that the parts must be read in the light of the whole. This is surely not unusual for literature in general and religious literature in particular.

The second problem concerns the suffixes of the two nouns. In v. 15 the suffixes are plural, but in v. 17 they are singular. This difference leads the reader to suppose that, in v. 15, the meal and drink offerings are thought of as accompanying all previous sacrifices and are to be thought of as additional to the meal offering. In v. 17 the meal and drink offerings accompany only the peace offering (*its meal offering,* etc.). The purification offering was usually not accompanied by either a meal or drink offering,[47] so that its linkage with these offerings is problematic.

Because of this problem (and the different suffixes) Gray has suggested that both vv. 15b and 17b are glosses.[48] This may be so, but one would assume that a glossator who put the words "their meal offering and their grain offerings" in v. 15 and "its meal offering and its grain offerings" in v. 17 would have made the suffixes consistent within the compass of two verses. A more likely solution is to remember that we have here a narrative about the ritual, not a detailed prescription for it. To repeat, the purpose of the paragraph is not to give detailed instructions but to give a general impression of what was involved. In this case it is possible that the plural suffixes in v. 15 referred in a general way to the sacrifices to

46. The texts have to do with the whole burnt offering. Exod. 29:23, 40–41 (the ordination of Aaron; cf. Lev. 8:26), and Lev. 23:13 give amounts for the whole burnt offering at the first fruits. Other passges such as Lev. 23:18, 37 mention the meal and drink offerings; hence they were known. The legislation in Num. 15 codifies in one place that which was probably known and followed earlier.

47. It is possible that meal and drink offerings accompanied purification offerings in Lev. 14:10–20, the cleansing of a leper (which shows other parallels with the current passage as well). It is more probable, however, that the meal and drink offerings in Lev. 14 were offered only with the whole burnt offering.

48. See Gray, p. 67; also Noth, p. 56.

which they were relevant. In v. 17 the topic is only the peace offering, as a careful study of the verse shows.[49]

18 This verse deals with the shaving of the Nazirite's hair. The ceremony takes place at the door of the tent of meeting. Scholars debate whether this ritual is another offering to God (i.e., the Nazirite offers the special mark of consecration on the altar along with the peace offering), or whether it simply gets rid of something holy, hence dangerous (i.e., it marks a step in the process of desacralization).[50] Since no ceremony is described, it is probable that the latter is the case.

19–21 These verses deal with the priest's portion (as does, e.g., 5:9–10). The *breast that was elevated (ḥᵃzê hattᵉnûp̄â)* and the *thigh that was offered (šôq hattᵉrûmâ)* are part of the priests' share of the peace offering according to Lev. 7:28–34. Because of the special nature of the Nazirite's consecration, an added portion is given: *the boiled shoulder (hazzᵉrōaʿ bᵉšēlâ),* from the same offering.[51] The *boiled shoulder* is still in the Nazirite's possession, and to transfer it to God's ownership the priest puts the shoulder, along with one unleavened cake and one unleavened wafer, into the Nazirite's hands. These are elevated *(hēnîp̄)* before Yahweh to consummate the transfer.[52] The shoulder, the breast, the thigh, and the meal offering (minus the memorial portion, Lev. 2:2–3) are *holy portions (qōḏeš)* for the priest.

Verse 21 is called a Torah subscript, which summarizes the section (using the word *tôrâ,* "regulation, law, instruction," also found in v. 13).[53]

e. Conclusion: Aaronic Benediction (6:22–27)

22 *And Yahweh spoke to Moses, saying:*

23 *"Speak to Aaron and to his sons, saying: 'Thus you shall bless the children of Israel, saying to them:*

49. E.g., the verb *ʿāśâ* is repeated three times in vv. 16–17, once for the purification offering and the whole burnt offering, once for the peace offering, and once for the meal and drink offerings. With each occurrence a new point of departure is reached.

50. For the former, see, e.g., Gray, p. 68. For the latter, see, e.g., Noth, p. 57; Sturdy, p. 53; Noordtzij, pp. 62, 65; cf. de Vaux, *Ancient Israel,* II:436.

51. See the commentary above on 5:25. Cf. Milgrom, *"Hattĕnûpâ,"* in *Studies in Cultic Theology,* pp. 156, 158.

52. See the following studies by Milgrom: "Wave Offering," *IDBSup,* pp. 944–46; *"Hattĕnûpâ,"* pp. 139–58; "Alleged Wave Offering," in *Studies in Cultic Theology,* pp. 133–38; *"Šôq hattĕrûmâ,"* in ibid., pp. 159–70; "Akkadian Confirmation of the Meaning of the Term *tĕrûmâ,*" in ibid., pp. 171–72.

53. See the commentary above on 5:29–30.

24 *"May Yahweh bless you and keep you.*
25 *May Yahweh make his face to shine upon you and be gracious to you.*
26 *May Yahweh lift up his face to you and give you peace."'*
27 *So they shall put my name on the children of Israel and I will bless them."*

Aaron's blessing (vv. 24–26) is surrounded by a framework that identifies the divine author of the directive and the human mediator of it (v. 22), states the priestly duty to pronounce blessing on the people (v. 23), and tells the outcome of such a blessing (v. 27). The blessing itself is a prayer that God would grant his gracious presence and watchcare to his people.[1] This is expressed in three poetic lines of unequal, increasing length. In the liturgical tradition of Israel (and of the Church) the blessing (or benediction) concludes the service of worship and serves as a promise of God's blessing on the worshipers as they go into the world. An example of a concluding benediction is Lev. 9:22, which climaxes the worship service that culminates the whole revelation of the tabernacle, the sacrificial system, and the priesthood (Exod. 25–Lev. 9).[2] Lev. 9:22 refers to a blessing by Aaron but does not give the words of that blessing. It is possible that Num. 6:22–27 contains these words, although why they should be given here rather than in Leviticus is unknown.

As it stands, Num. 6:22–27 concludes the section of mainly legal materials that stretches from Lev. 1 to Num. 6. At Num. 7:1 the chronological indicator reverts to the day when Moses set up the tabernacle (first day, first month, second year after the Exodus). This date is the same as the material headed by Exod. 40:17. Thus the Aaronic blessing concludes the section of text dealing with the bulk of Israel's priestly legislation, and,

1. For the definition and description of the genre of blessing, see, e.g., B. O. Long, *1 Kings; with an Introduction to the Historical Literature,* FOTL (Grand Rapids: Eerdmans, 1984), p. 245.

2. See C. Westermann, *Blessing in the Bible and the Life of the Church,* tr. K. Crim, OBT (Philadelphia: Fortress, 1978), pp. 42–45; for a bibliography, see p. 24 n. 3 and pp. 26–27 n. 14. It may be that the liturgical placement of a blessing at the end of a worship service is related to the last (i.e., deathbed) blessings of the patriarchs and other ancient leaders; see, e.g., Jacob (Gen. 48–49), Moses (Deut. 33), Joshua (Josh. 23). Other examples of final blessings are found in Josh. 22:6 (Joshua dismisses the people); 2 Sam. 6:18 (= 1 Chr. 16:2) (David); 1 Chr. 30:27 (priests and Levites).

implicitly, promises that if these laws are kept, the blessing of God will follow. The material in this major section (Lev. 1–Num. 6) comes between the date of the erection of the tabernacle and the movement of the camp some fifty days later (Num. 10:11).[3]

22–23, 27 The framework fits the blessing itself (vv. 24–26) into its present context. As before, God is the author and Moses the mediator. The priests *(Aaron and his sons)* are to be the ones in Israel who pronounce these blessings (seen already in Lev. 9:22 and to be seen again in Deut. 21:5). The framework uses the third-person masc. pl., while the blessing itself shifts to second-person masc. sing. forms. This shift probably indicates that the blessing had already attained a fixed liturgical form that was not to be changed.[4] The third-person masc. pl. is resumed in the last part of the framework,[5] which tells of the blessings that will ensue if this benediction is pronounced and all the laws of the preceding section are appropriately followed. The priests' instructions are to *put* Yahweh's *name on* the people, in a narrow sense, by pronouncing the words of this blessing. In a wider sense, however, God's name would be put on the people if they kept the priestly law as revealed in Lev. 1–Num. 6.

Blessings in the OT vary widely in their construction and contents.[6] One should distinguish between the *blessing,* which calls for future goodness, and the *beatitude,* which looks to the blessings that presently exist (Ps. 1:1–2); one should also distinguish between the *blessing* in which God is the giver of the good gifts and the *praise speech* in which he is the receiver of praise for those good gifts.[7] Even within the remaining blessings the person and number differ. Many blessings use the second-person masc. sing. (as here; see also, e.g., Deut. 7:13–14; 28:3–6; 1 Sam. 2:20), while others use the second-person masc. pl. (e.g., Deut. 1:1; Josh. 23; 1 Sam. 23:21), or the third-person masc. sing. (e.g., Deut. 33:8–11).

3. For a chart of the dated events between Exod. 40 and Num. 10, see Wenham, p. 91.

4. Most patriarchal blessings (Gen. 12–50) are pronounced on individuals, so the use of the sing. is perhaps to be expected. An exception is Gen. 48:20 (Jacob's blessing of Ephraim and Manasseh), where the same shift between third-person masc. pl. and second-person masc. sing. occurs (see also Jer. 31:23).

5. V. 27a, *wᵉśāmû,* "so they shall put."

6. See, e.g., the twelvefold categorization of A. Murtonen in "The Use of the Words LᴱBAREK and BERAKAH in the Old Testament," *VT* 9 (1959) 158–77.

7. See Long, *1 Kings,* pp. 244–45, 255.

Some even mix the second and third persons (e.g., Deut. 33:24–25), or second sing. and pl. (e.g., Deut. 7:12–14).[8]

That God is the one who is able to bless his faithful people is seen in v. 22 by the fact that it is Yahweh who is the author of the revelation. In v. 27 he makes the emphatic statement *I will bless them (wa'ᵃnî 'ᵃḇārᵃḵēm).*[9] That this same God is the source of all the blessings here set forth is seen in the body of the blessing by the threefold repetition of Yahweh as the subject.

24–26 Each verse of the blessing itself contains a first clause whose subject is explicitly Yahweh and a second clause whose subject is implicitly Yahweh. The verses get progressively longer (in Hebrew, 3, 5, and 7 words respectively). Thus, the impression is given of a stream of blessing that begins as a trickle but flows ever more strongly. According to P. Miller, the first clause of each verse invokes God's movement toward his people, while the second asks him to act on behalf of his people. The emphasis on the singular subject in the blessing indicates that God's blessings come to individuals in the community and to the community thought of as a unity.[10]

Some of the terms of the priestly blessing are connected theologically and literarily with many passages in the OT, but none is so striking as the relationship with the so-called Songs of Ascent (Pss. 120–134). The exact literary relationship between these psalms and the present passage is not clear, but it is close enough for there to be some justification for the contention that these psalms were composed under the influence of at least four of the major terms in Num. 6:24–26.[11] The four terms taken up in the Psalms of Ascent are *bless* (*bērēḵ,* e.g., Ps. 128:5; 133:3; 134:3), *keep* (*šāmar,* e.g., Ps. 121), *be gracious* (*ḥānan,* e.g., Pss. 123; 130), and *peace* (*šālôm,* e.g., Ps. 122:6–8; 125:2, 5; 128:5–6; 133:1).

24 In the first line the priest is to pray that God will *bless* and *keep* the faithful community. The first term is a general summary of

8. The third person examples here and in Deut. 33:8–11 might be separated as a class and called *reports of blessings.* See Westermann, *Blessing,* pp. 42–45.

9. This construction is emphatic because the personal pronoun *I* is not grammatically necessary in Hebrew. See GKC, §§32b, 135a.

10. See P. Miller, "The Blessing of God," *Int* 29 (1975) 243.

11. See, e.g, L. J. Liebreich, "The Songs of Ascent and the Priestly Blessing," *JBL* 74 (1955) 33–36. See also some hints at the same connection in F. Delitzsch, *Commentary on the Psalms,* tr. D. Eaton, rev. ed. (London: Hodder & Stoughton, 1889), III:282, 287, 321.

everything else in the blessing. The basic meaning of *bless* relates to the power to be fertile and abundant or prosperous.[12] God, it is prayed, will give the faithful community (and the individuals in it) abundance and fertility in all areas of life.

keep. The keeping or preserving power of God (basic to the root *šmr*) can be seen in widely separated contexts in the OT.[13] God has the power to guard and preserve his faithful servants alive, no matter where their paths lead (see, e.g., Gen. 28:15; Exod. 23:30; Josh. 24:17; Ps. 12:7; most of the stories in Dan. 1–6 have this as one of their themes). God can watch over his servants in battle (1 Sam. 30:23), and gives his watchcare for his own (e.g., Ps. 91:11; 127:1). God is also faithful to keep *(šmr)* his covenant with his people and his steadfast covenant loyalty and love *(ḥesed)* with them (Deut. 7:12; Neh. 1:9; 9:32; etc.), not because he must but because of his grace (see further below).

25–26 The initial clauses of these verses are identical except for the verbs.[14] Both clauses ask, in slightly different terms, that Yahweh show his benevolent presence to his faithful people. The first clause is a prayer that he take action to make his *face* (i.e., his presence) shine forth in benevolence on his people. The second verb, *lift up,* is not elsewhere used with God as a subject. When God "hides his face" he is angry (see, e.g., Deut. 31:17–18; Ps. 30:8 [Eng. 7]; 104:29; etc.).[15] So when God elevates his face he looks on his people for good. The "shining forth" and "lifting up" of Yahweh's face are more closely defined by the second two clauses. God's positive presence with his people issues in grace and peace.[16]

"Grace" describes the attitude that issues in kindly action of a superior party to an inferior one in which the inferior has no claim on the superior. Graciousness is a fundamental aspect of Yahweh's character, as

12. So J. Pedersen, *Israel: Its Life and Culture* (London: Oxford, 1926), I–II:162–212; also Murtonen, "Use of L^E^BAREK and BERAKAH," pp. 176–77; and H. Mowvley, "The Concept and Content of 'Blessing' in the Old Testament," *BT* 16 (1965) 74–80.

13. Cf. the "guard duty" (*mišmereṯ,* from the root *šmr*) of the Levites in ch. 4.

14. I.e., *yā'ēr YHWH pānāyw 'ēleyḵā,* v. 25; *yiśśā' YHWH pānāyw 'ēleyḵā,* v. 26.

15. See also the example of Cain, whose "face fell" when he was angry (Gen. 4:5–6).

16. I.e., *wîḥunnekkā,* v. 25; *w^e yāśēm l^e ḵā šālôm,* v. 26. "Grace" *(ḥēn)* and "gracious" *(ḥannûn)* are nominal and adjectival forms from the root *ḥnn,* which is found in the verb *wîḥunnekkā,* "and may he be gracious to you" (v. 25).

both Old and New Testaments abundantly witness.[17] Even though the placement of this passage emphasizes the keeping of various laws and rituals, the keeping of the law does not force God to be gracious. In fact, if the inferior party deserves the kindness, it would not be grace but payment. Yahweh is sovereign and he will show his grace when and to whom he wills (Exod. 33:19).[18]

God's gracious presence leads, in the end, to *peace (šālôm)*. By ending with *šālôm* the Aaronic Blessing ends as generally as it began. *Šālôm* is fundamentally not merely the absence of conflict, although that may be a part of it. In essence, *šālôm* means fullness of life and wholeness in all areas of life: material, familial, societal, and religious.[19] One might say that the motive for God's gift of wholeness is his grace, which in turn points back to the light of his presence and his will to bless.[20]

B. VARIOUS MATTERS CONCERNING THE TABERNACLE (7:1–10:10)

A new section of text begins with 7:1 and extends through 9:23 (with 10:1–10 as a transition passage). The date given at the beginning of this section is one month earlier than the date of 1:1, to "the day when Moses finished the erection of the tabernacle," the first day of the first month of the second year after the Exodus (cf. Exod. 40:17). Chs. 7–9 contain materials not found in Lev. 1–Num. 6, which is mainly a legal section. These supplemental materials are important for a full appreciation of the preceding legal chapters.

Many scholars have dated chs. 7–9 in the late postexilic age.[1] This dating derives from the conclusion that the basic P stratum is postexilic, and any supplement to it must be later than that. Chs. 7–9 are clearly

17. See Exod. 22:28 (Eng. 27); Ps. 86:15; 103:8: 111:4; 116:5; 145:8; Joel 2:13; Jon. 4:2; 2 Chr. 30:9; Neh. 9:17, 31; Luke 2:40; 1 Cor. 1:3–4; 3:10; 15:10; 2 Cor. 12:9; 1 Pet. 5:10; etc.

18. See W. Zimmerli, *TDNT,* IX:376–81; E. Yamauchi, *TWOT,* I:302–4, and the accompanying bibliographies.

19. See G. von Rad, *TDNT,* II:402–6; G. L. Carr, *TWOT,* II:931, and the accompanying bibliographies.

20. "Grace and peace" becomes an important greeting in the NT Epistles (Rom. 1:7; 1 Cor. 1:3; 2 Cor. 1:2; Gal. 1:3; Eph. 1:2; Phil. 1:2; Col. 1:2; 1 Thess. 1:2; 2 Thess. 1:2; 1 Tim. 1:2; 2 Tim. 1:2; Titus 1:4; Phlm. 3; 1 Pet. 1:2; 2 John 3; Rev. 1:3).

1. See, e.g., Gray, p. 74; Noth, p. 63; for ch. 7, see Kellerman, *Priesterschrift,* p. 89.

supplemental,[2] but this does not commit one to such a late dating, at least for the materials in the chapters. As is well known (if not widely appreciated), the criteria for a postexilic dating of the Priestly materials in the Pentateuch are highly questionable and ought not to be maintained.

It is possible that the (or an) author of the developing Pentateuch wished to add important materials to what was found in Lev. 1–Num. 6 without disturbing the order of these chapters as they stood. This, of course, must remain a conjecture, but it is possible to see a literary logic in allowing the text of Lev. 1–Num. 6 to remain rather than breaking into the legal exposition of the sacrificial system, etc., with the details of the tribal leaders' gifts (Num. 7). This important detail, therefore, was added after the reader had the opportunity to appreciate the significance of the tabernacle, the sacrificial system, the duties of the priests and Levites, etc. The same literary logic can be seen in the insertion of the note about wagons for the Gershonite and Merarite Levites after the exposition of their tasks and responsibilities had been expanded by some laws of purity and special service in the camp (chs. 5–6). It is also understandable that the narrative about the appointment of the Levites (8:5–26) should not interrupt the census materials of Num. 1–4, but should be placed in a supplementary position. One may always inquire why a particular text (ancient or modern) is the way it is and not some other way. But such inquiry should not obscure the fact that Num. 7–9 do make literary sense where they stand.

1. OFFERINGS BY TRIBAL LEADERS (7:1–89)

1 *And it happened on the day when Moses finished erecting the tabernacle and had anointed and sanctified it, along with all its accessories, the altar, and all its accessories —he anointed and sanctified them,*

2 *that the leaders of Israel, the heads of their fathers' houses (they were the leaders of the tribes who were standing over those who had been numbered), made an offering.*

2. That chs. 7–9 are placed after chs. 1–6 and yet are dated before them shows that they are supplementary. Some evidence suggests that chs. 7–9 were edited to be read where they appear in the current text. E.g., the names of the tribal leaders are simply given in ch. 7; the reader is to assume these names as already given in ch. 1. Thus ch. 7 has been accommodated to ch. 1. The order of the tribes is the same in ch. 7 as in ch. 2, and yet the logic of this arrangement of tribes comes out only in ch. 2 (which, again, is later than ch. 7). The conclusion is that, while ch. 7 is said to occur before chs. 1–2, it is meant to be read after them. This evidence suggests an editing of this section of Numbers as a whole.

3 *And they brought their offering before Yahweh, six covered wag-*
ons[1] *and twelve oxen, a wagon for every two of the leaders and an*
ox for each one, and they offered them before the tabernacle.
4 *And Yahweh said to Moses, saying:*
5 *"Take these things*[2] *from them, and let them be for doing the*
service of the tent of meeting, and you shall give them to the
Levites, each one according to his work."
6 *And Moses took the wagons and the oxen and gave them to the*
Levites.
7 *Two of the wagons and four of the oxen he gave to the sons of*
Gershon in proportion to their work.
8 *And four of the wagons and eight of the oxen he gave to the sons*
of Merari in proportion to their work, under the authority of[3]
Ithamar son of Aaron the priest.
9 *But to the sons of Kohath he gave nothing because the cartage of*
the holy things was their responsibility; on their shoulders they
carried them.
10 *And the leaders made an offering for the dedication of the altar*
on the day when it was anointed, that is, the leaders made their
offering before the altar.
11 *And Yahweh said to Moses, "They shall give their offering, one*
leader per day, for the dedication of the altar."
12 *And it happened that the one who gave his offering on the first day*
was Nahshon son of Amminadab of the tribe of Judah.
13 *And his offering was: one silver dish weighing one hundred thirty*
shekels and one silver bowl weighing seventy shekels, according
to the sanctuary shekel, both of them full of fine flour mixed with
oil for a meal offering;
14 *one golden spoon, ten shekels in weight, full of incense;*
15 *one young bull,*[4] *one ram, one male yearling lamb for the whole*
burnt offering;

1. *Covered wagons ('eglaṯ ṣāḇ)* — This translation is unsure, especially the latter word. The current translation depends on the versions, viz., LXX (*lampēnikas,* "covered chariot"), Vg. (*tecta,* "canopy"), Tg. Onkelos (*mḥpyn,* "covered"), etc. On the other hand, the Peshitta translates as "readied" and Symmachus as "(for) military service." See Gray, p. 76.

2. MT *qaḥ mē'ittām,* lit., "take from them."

3. MT *b*^{e}*yad,* lit., "in the hand of," often has the sense of "in the power of, in the care of, under the authority of" (much like the English expression); see BDB, pp. 390b–91a.

4. MT *par 'eḥaḏ ben-bāqār,* lit., "a young bull, one, son of cattle"; the seemingly redundant "young bull, son of cattle," is a common expression. See BDB, pp. 121b, 133a, 830b.

16 *one male goat for a purification offering;*
17 *and for the peace offering, two oxen, five rams, five male goats, five male yearling lambs. This was the offering of Nahshon son of Amminadab.*
18 *On the second day Nethanel son of Zuar, leader of Issachar, made an offering.*
19 *He made his offering: one silver dish weighing one hundred thirty shekels and one silver bowl weighing seventy shekels according to the sanctuary shekel, both of them full of fine flour mixed with oil for a meal offering;*
20 *one golden spoon, ten shekels in weight, full of incense;*
21 *one young bull, one ram, one male yearling lamb for the whole burnt offering;*
22 *one male goat for a purification offering;*
23 *and for the peace offering, two oxen, five rams, five male goats, five male yearling lambs. This was the offering of Nethanel son of Zuar.*
24 *On the third day, leader of the children of Zebulun, Eliab son of Helon,*
25 *his offering was: one silver dish weighing one hundred thirty shekels and one silver bowl weighing seventy shekels according to the sanctuary shekel, both of them full of fine flour mixed with oil for a meal offering;*
26 *one golden spoon, ten shekels in weight, full of incense;*
27 *one young bull, one ram, one male yearling lamb for the whole burnt offering;*
28 *one male goat for a purification offering;*
29 *and for the peace offering, two oxen, five rams, five male goats, five male yearling lambs. This was the offering of Eliab son of Helon.*
30 *On the fourth day, leader of the children of Reuben, Elizur son of Shedeur,*
31 *and his offering was: one silver dish weighing one hundred thirty shekels and one silver bowl weighing seventy shekels according to the sanctuary shekel, both of them full of fine flour mixed with oil for a meal offering;*
32 *one golden spoon, ten shekels in weight, full of incense;*
33 *one young bull, one ram, one male yearling lamb for the whole burnt offering;*
34 *one male goat for a purification offering;*
35 *and for the peace offering, two oxen, five rams, five male goats,*

five male yearling lambs. This was the offering of Elizur son of Shedeur.

36 *On the fifth day, leader of the children of Simeon, Shelumiel son of Zurishaddai,*

37 *his offering was: one silver dish weighing one hundred thirty shekels and one silver bowl weighing seventy shekels according to the sanctuary shekel, both of them full of fine flour mixed with oil for a meal offering;*

38 *one golden spoon, ten shekels in weight, full of incense;*

39 *one young bull, one ram, one male yearling lamb for the whole burnt offering;*

40 *one male goat for a purification offering;*

41 *and for the peace offering, two oxen, five rams, five male goats, five male yearling lambs. This was the offering of Shelumiel son of Zurishaddai.*

42 *On the sixth day, leader of the children of Gad, Eliasaph son of Deuel,*[5]

43 *his offering was: one silver dish weighing one hundred thirty shekels and one silver bowl weighing seventy shekels according to the sanctuary shekel, both of them full of fine flour mixed with oil for a meal offering;*

44 *one golden spoon, ten shekels in weight, full of incense;*

45 *one young bull, one ram, one male yearling lamb for the whole burnt offering;*

46 *one male goat for a purification offering;*

47 *and for the peace offering, two oxen, five rams, five male goats, five male yearling lambs. This was the offering of Eliasaph son of Deuel.*

48 *On the seventh day, leader of the children of Ephraim, Elishama son of Ammihud,*

49 *his offering was: one silver dish weighing one hundred thirty shekels and one silver bowl weighing seventy shekels according to the sanctuary shekel, both of them full of fine flour mixed with oil for a meal offering;*

50 *one golden spoon, ten shekels in weight, full of incense;*

51 *one young bull, one ram, one male yearling lamb for the whole burnt offering;*

52 *one male goat for a purification offering;*

5. LXX and Pesh. have *r^{e}ʿûʾēl* here (and in v. 47) for MT *d^{e}ʿûʾēl;* see the discussion above at 1:14.

53 *and for the peace offering, two oxen, five rams, five male goats, five male yearling lambs. This was the offering of Elishama son of Ammihud.*
54 *On the eighth day, leader of the children of Manasseh, Gamaliel son of Pedahzur,*
55 *his offering was: one silver dish weighing one hundred thirty shekels and one silver bowl weighing seventy shekels according to the sanctuary shekel, both of them full of fine flour mixed with oil for a meal offering;*
56 *one golden spoon, ten shekels in weight, full of incense;*
57 *one young bull, one ram, one male yearling lamb for the whole burnt offering;*
58 *one male goat for a purification offering;*
59 *and for the peace offering, two oxen, five rams, five male goats, five male yearling lambs. This was the offering of Gamaliel son of Pedahzur.*
60 *On the ninth day, leader of the children of Benjamin, Abidan son of Gideoni,*
61 *his offering was: one silver dish weighing one hundred thirty shekels and one silver bowl weighing seventy shekels according to the sanctuary shekel, both of them full of fine flour mixed with oil for a meal offering;*
62 *one golden spoon, ten shekels in weight, full of incense;*
63 *one young bull, one ram, one male yearling lamb for the whole burnt offering;*
64 *one male goat for a purification offering;*
65 *and for the peace offering, two oxen, five rams, five male goats, five male yearling lambs. This was the offering of Abidan son of Gideoni.*
66 *On the tenth day, leader of the children of Dan, Ahiezer son of Ammishaddai,*
67 *his offering was: one silver dish weighing one hundred thirty shekels and one silver bowl weighing seventy shekels according to the sanctuary shekel, both of them full of fine flour mixed with oil for a meal offering;*
68 *one golden spoon, ten shekels in weight, full of incense;*
69 *one young bull, one ram, one male yearling lamb for the whole burnt offering;*
70 *one male goat for a purification offering;*
71 *and for the peace offering, two oxen, five rams, five male goats, five male yearling lambs. This was the offering of Ahiezer son of Ammishaddai.*

72 *On the eleventh day, leader of the children of Asher, Pagiel son of Ochran,*
73 *his offering was: one silver dish weighing one hundred thirty shekels and one silver bowl weighing seventy shekels according to the sanctuary shekel, both of them full of fine flour mixed with oil for a meal offering;*
74 *one golden spoon, ten shekels in weight, full of incense;*
75 *one young bull, one ram, one male yearling lamb for the whole burnt offering;*
76 *one male goat for a purification offering;*
77 *and for the peace offering, two oxen, five rams, five male goats, five male yearling lambs. This was the offering of Pagiel son of Ochran.*
78 *On the twelfth day, leader of the children of Naphtali, Ahira son of Enan,*
79 *his offering was: one silver dish weighing one hundred thirty shekels and one silver bowl weighing seventy shekels according to the sanctuary shekel, both of them full of fine flour mixed with oil for a meal offering;*
80 *one golden spoon, ten shekels in weight, full of incense;*
81 *one young bull, one ram, one male yearling lamb for the whole burnt offering;*
82 *one male goat for a purification offering;*
83 *and for the peace offering, two oxen, five rams, five male goats, five male yearling lambs. This was the offering of Ahira son of Enon.*
84 *This was the dedication offering of the altar by the leaders of Israel on the day when it was anointed: twelve silver dishes, twelve silver bowls, twelve golden spoons.*
85 *Each one of the silver dishes weighed one hundred thirty shekels, and each one of the bowls weighed seventy shekels, according to the sanctuary shekel.*
86 *Twelve golden spoons full of incense weighing ten shekels per spoon, according to the sanctuary shekel. All the gold of the spoons weighed one hundred twenty shekels.*
87 *All the cattle for the whole burnt offering: twelve bulls, twelve rams, twelve male yearling lambs; also their meal offering; also twelve male goats for a purification offering.*
88 *And all the beasts of the peace offering: twenty-four bulls, sixty rams, sixty male goats, sixty male yearling lambs. This was the dedication offering of the altar after its anointing.*
89 *And when Moses went into the tent of meeting to speak with*

> *him,[6] then he heard the Voice speaking to him[7] from upon the mercy seat, which was on the ark of the testimony, from between the two cherubim, and he spoke to him.*

This chapter breaks down into three parts: first, the wagons assigned for the work of the Levites (vv. 1–9); second, the offerings of the tribal leaders (vv. 10–88); third, the result of these offerings — communion between Moses and Yahweh.

1–9 As mentioned in the introduction to this section, the chronological note in 7:1 places this chapter one month prior to the census begun in 1:1. The men that are called *leaders* in v. 2 (lit., "exalted ones," *n^e^śî'îm*) are the same ones called by this title in 1:16, i.e., those who helped Moses with the census.[8] Although the action described by the current chapter preceded the action of ch. 1, the present text has been edited so as to appear dependent upon that chapter.

In v. 3 these leaders brought an offering of six *covered carts* and twelve oxen to present before the tabernacle. Although the text does not say that God commanded the offering, it makes sense to assume that he did, for he then showed Moses what to do with the carts and oxen. Moses gave the wagons and oxen to the Gershonite and Merarite Levites to assist them in their work of cartage and tabernacle construction. The Gershonites, whose job it was to deal with the curtains and hangings of the tabernacle, were given two carts and four oxen. The Merarites, whose responsibility was the heavier framework of the tabernacle, were given four carts and eight oxen (see 4:24–33). Only the Kohathite Levites were given no carts or oxen. It was their job to carry the holiest things of the sanctuary *on their shoulders* (4:15; 7:9). The text makes clear that the physical *work* (*'^a^ḇōḏâ*) of the Gershonite and Merarite Levites involved carrying parts of the tabernacle to and from the carts as well as constructing and dismantling the structure itself, but not carrying it. Only the Kohathite Levites carried the sacred things, although they themselves did not prepare them for cartage (this was the prerogative of the priests; see 4:5–14).

6. I.e., Yahweh; see the commentary below.

7. MT here is *wayyišma' 'eṯ-haqqōl middabbēr 'ēlāyw.* Although the Hithpael of *dbr (middabbēr)* is found with a reflexive meaning in the OT (e.g., Ezek. 2:2), the use of the Piel elsewhere in this verse *(way^e^ḏabbēr),* as well as the sense, suggests that the emendation in *BHS* to *m^e^ḏabbēr* (Piel) is correct; hence, *wayyišma' 'eṯ-haqqôl m^e^ḏabbēr 'ēlāyw,* "and he heard the voice speaking to him" (i.e., Moses). The emendation is supported by LXX *(lalountos),* "speaking."

8. On the term *nāśî',* see the commentary above on 1:16.

The *covered carts (ʿeglōt ṣāb)* were each pulled by two oxen. Both Hebrew words mean "cart" or "wagon," so the translation is uncertain.[9] If this is the correct translation of the terms, the holiness of the objects transported explains the covering. No unconsecrated person would defile these holy objects by looking on them (cf. the matter of the Kohathite Levites and holy objects in the tabernacle, 4:17–20). These carts may have had two or four wheels.[10] Although only the Levites and priests were responsible for the assembly and cartage of the tabernacle, all twelve tribes participated in its service, not only by supplying the carts and oxen, but also by the offering that accompanied the tabernacle's dedication (see below).

10–88 This passage is one of the most repetitive and, consequently, one of the most ignored passages in the OT. B. Levine sees the repetition as a literary device that derives from the origin of the text itself in an archival account set up as a two-dimensional chart with columns, totals, etc. He describes these verses as a formulaic descriptive ritual text.[11] The formulaic nature of the text is seen in the repetition of the names of the tribal leaders at the beginning and end of each section. The descriptive nature of the text is seen in its summary nature (i.e., it does not give details of what happened, only a summary of the numbers involved and their purpose). The text is also descriptive in that it tells what happened at a point in the past rather than being prescriptive of what was always to happen in the future. The cumulative effect of the repetition is that readers are assured that each tribe had an identical share in the support of the ministry of the tabernacle.

A. Rainey established that OT ritual texts use more than one order of sacrifices.[12] The usual order is the whole burnt offering *(ʿôlâ),* the meal offering *(minḥâ),* the purification offering *(ḥaṭṭāʾṯ),* the reparation offering

9. This translation is found, e.g., in RSV, NIV, NEB, NKJV, and in *HALAT,* p. 933a, which also suggests "freight-wagons" *(Last-karren).*

10. D. J. Wiseman (*NBD,* p. 180) sees them as two-wheeled, while W. S. McCullough (*IDB,* I:540) implies a four-wheeled cart.

11. See B. Levine, "The Descriptive Tabernacle Texts of the Pentateuch," *JAOS* 85 (1965) 307–18; see p. 316 for the two-dimensional chart. By two-dimensional Levine simply means that the tables are to be read both horizontally and vertically. On his designation of these verses as a formulaic descriptive ritual text, see pp. 312–13 n. 24.

12. See A. Rainey, "The Order of Sacrifices in Old Testament Ritual Texts," *Bib* 51 (1970) 487–89 for the administrative order, pp. 494–98 for the procedural order.

(ʾāšām), and finally the peace offering *(zeḇaḥ šᵉlāmîm).* Rainey showed that the sacrifices were probably offered in a different order. In the present text the meal offering is moved to first place because of its connection with the silver and gold vessels that contained its components.[13] The reparation offering is effective for specific offenses and would not be required in this particular instance.[14]

Except for minor verbal variations, the description of each tribal leader's gift is identical. These leaders are the same as those in 1:5–15 (see above). The name of each leader is given at the beginning and the end of an individual section (e.g., Nahshon at 7:12, 17). In the extant two-dimensional charts from the ancient Near East, the name of the receiver or donor occurs, most times, at the end. Thus the name references here at the beginning of each unit may be part of the so-called narrativization of the original archival text.[15] However that may be, the name references frame each day's offering as a formula.

At the beginning of each offering a *silver dish,* a *silver bowl,* and a *golden spoon* are mentioned. The two silver utensils contained *fine flour (sōleṯ)* mixed with *oil (šemen)* for the meal offering, and the *golden spoon* contained *incense (qᵉṭōreṯ),* also for the meal offering.[16]

One cannot be sure of the exact nature of these vessels. The word *dish (qᵉʿārâ)* is related to words that, in the cognate languages, mean "to be deep,"[17] hence a "deep dish." The word *bowl (mizrāq)* is related to the verb *zāraq,* "to toss," hence a recepticle used for tossing liquids.[18] Most texts connect this vessel with the service of the tabernacle (e.g., Exod. 27:3; 38:3; Num. 4:14) or the temple (e.g., 1 K. 7:40, 45; Jer. 52:18; Zech. 14:20). These utensils were used for the ceremonial tossing of sacrificial blood against the altar.[19] The word *spoon (kaṗ)* means a slightly cupped surface; it is also used for "the palm of the hand."[20] The

13. Ibid., p. 495 n. 2: "Variations of this sort that stem from practical considerations are exactly what one would expect in an *administrative* system."

14. For the reparation offering, see Lev. 5:14–26 (Eng. 5:14–6:7) and the commentary above on Num. 5:5–10. Reference should be made, once again, to Milgrom, *Cult and Conscience.*

15. See Levine, "Descriptive Tabernacle Texts," p. 316.

16. The basic texts for the meal offering are Lev. 2:1–16 and 6:14–18.

17. See BDB, p. 891a.

18. See BDB, p. 284b.

19. See, e.g., Lev. 1:5, 11; 3:1; etc., where the verb *zāraq* is used to describe this tossing action.

20. See BDB, pp. 496a–97a.

small weight of this vessel compared to the others has led to the translation *spoon.*[21]

These vessels are weighed in *shekels,* which was the standard unit of weight across the Semitic world. The verb *šāḵal* means simply "to weigh." The MT omits the word *shekel* for both the dish and the spoon, but since it was the standard unit and is already given in the context, it is to be understood in both cases. The shekel weighed approximately 0.4 oz., so the dish weighed over 3 lbs., the bowl 1.75 lbs., and the spoon about 4 oz. The term *sanctuary shekel* probably refers to the standard shekel weight, which was kept at the sanctuary, or even to a weight used to measure sacred offerings. Some scholars have held that the sanctuary shekel was a different weight than the standard shekel, but this is uncertain.[22]

Verses 13–88 enumerate the offerings of the various leaders by giving the name of the item first, followed by the number (e.g., "oxen, two," 7:17, etc.). This order of enumeration is more common in Semitic texts that use numerical figures (as in Eng. 1, 2, 3) rather than words representing numbers ("one, two, three"). The almost exclusive use of the item-plus-number order in this text may be adduced as further evidence for its derivation from an earlier archival record of a type already suggested that did use figures rather than words.[23]

The details of the various sacrifices here follow the general regulations laid down by the book of Leviticus, although in the cases of the whole burnt offering and the peace offering the information is more specific here than in Leviticus. The basic texts outlining procedures for the whole burnt offerings are Lev. 1:3–17 and 6:2–6 (Eng. 9–13). The purification offering is discussed in Lev. 4:1–5:13 and 6:17–23 (Eng. 24–30). *One male goat* is the purification offering (Lev. 4:22–26). The peace offering is discussed in Lev. 3:1–17 and 7:11–36.

Modern readers may wonder why an ancient author would reproduce the same detail twelve times. Would not a summary statement such as is found in vv. 84–88 have been sufficient?[24] While we have argued

21. See the various English translations: e.g., AV, RV "spoon"; RSV "dish"; NEB "saucer"; NASB "pan"; NIV, NJPS "ladle."

22. E.g., R. B. Y. Scott, "Weights, Measures, Money and Time," *Peake's Commentary on the Bible,* rev. ed. (London: Nelson, 1962), p. 38.

23. See the texts mentioned in Levine, "Descriptive Tabernacle Texts," pp. 314–15 and nn. 31–33. The exceptions are found in 7:87–88 with "twelve bulls" and "twenty-four bulls."

24. In the modern age we are especially impatient with repetition. See, e.g., GNB, which summarizes the whole of vv. 12–88 in a few lines.

above that this text may be derived from a two-dimensional archival chart, which — at least presumably — contained all the data here reproduced,[25] this supposed origin still does not answer the question of why the author chose to use it so completely when summaries are found at other points.

The answer must surely be that the author wanted the cumulative effect that results from a reading of the account of twelve identical offerings. By repetition the author showed that each tribe had an equal stake in the support of the sacrificial ministry of the tabernacle. No tribe had a monopoly on the responsibility for support and no tribe was unnecessary. That the support came from the tribes themselves rather than from the priests or Levites is also significant. The outcome of a partnership in the support of the ministry is seen in the last verse of the chapter.

89 Commentators often assert that 7:89 is an independent fragment of another tradition.[26] Admittedly the verse is difficult and obscure. One difficulty is that the reference to God as *him ('ittô)* has no clear antecedent in the rest of the chapter. Even if the pronoun *'ittô* refers to the noun *Voice,* the sentence is obscure and awkward in syntax.[27] The LXX solved the problem by reading "the voice of the Lord" *(tēn phonēn kyriou),* but this reading is almost surely a secondary interpretation designed to ease the problem.

The verse is further complicated by the pointing of the MT, which reads "he heard the voice speaking to himself" *(wayyišmaʿ 'eṯ-haqqôl middabbēr 'ēlāyw).* The above translation, *he heard the Voice speaking to him,* is based on a slight change (*m*ᵉ*ḏabbēr,* the more common Piel participle, for *middabbēr,* the Hithpael — reflexive — participle).[28]

As the text stands, the verbal tenses (imperfect consecutive) do not allow it to be understood as an event that happened again and again, but rather to refer to an event that happened at a specific point, viz., after the proper dedicatory rites for the tabernacle. The outcome of the leaders' offering was the fulfillment of God's promise of Exod. 25:22: fellowship and communion between God and Moses, the people's representative.

25. See the discussion on pp. 161-62 above and Levine, "Descriptive Tabernacle Texts," esp. p. 317 and nn. 42–43.

26. E.g., Gray, p. 77; McNeile, p. 43; Noordtzij, p. 75; Noth, p. 65; Sturdy, p. 63.

27. Deut. 4:12 speaks of God's voice in roughly the same way. Later the rabbis used the term *baṯ-qôl* (lit., "daughter of a voice") as a circumlocution for God's revealing presence. Cf. G. Dalman, "Bath Kol," *The New Schaff-Herzog Religious Encyclopedia* (New York: Funk & Wagnalls, 1908), II:4a; also idem, *Words of Jesus,* tr. D. M. Kay (Edinburgh: T. & T. Clark, 1902), pp. 204–5.

28. See *BHS* and the notes to the translation above.

Linking the last verse of ch. 7 with what has gone before (as the effect of what was done) thus makes better sense than setting it with what follows (as Budd does), or leaving it hanging on its own (as Gray, Noth, Sturdy, Noordtzij, and others have done).

God spoke to Moses from atop *the mercy seat that was on top of the ark of the testimony, from between the two cherubim.* The regulations for the construction of the so-called *mercy seat (kappōreṯ)* are found in Exod. 25:17–22. It consisted in a golden slab 2.5 cubits long by 1.5 cubits wide (approximately 44 × 26 in.), placed on top of the ark. This slab formed the base for the two golden cherubim (and was of one piece with them). The *cherubim* were winged creatures upon whom Yahweh's throne was conceived to sit. This is the place from which God promised to speak in Exod. 25:22, a promise fulfilled here.[29]

2. LAMPS IN THE TABERNACLE (8:1–4)

1 *And Yahweh spoke to Moses, saying:*

2 *"Speak to Aaron and say to him, 'When you set up the lamps, the seven lamps shall shed light toward the front of the lampstand.' "*

3 *And Aaron did so. He set up the lamps toward the front of the lampstand, just as Yahweh had commanded Moses.*

4 *Now this was how the lampstand was made: hammered work of gold, from its base to its flowers it was hammered work. According to the pattern that Yahweh showed Moses, thus he made the lampstand.*

The last verse of ch. 7 took the reader to the tent of meeting, where Moses, the people's representative, communicated with God. The connection between 7:89 and 8:1–4 is not so rough as one might think if one remembers that the lampstand (or menorah) was also inside the tent of meeting. This lampstand has already been mentioned in 3:31 and 4:9,[1] and is, of course, the familiar seven-branched lampstand. The symbolic meaning that the menorah carried for Israel is nowhere specified in the Bible, so that any suggestion must be made with caution. The shape of the menorah is that of a stylized tree, which might suggest a connection with

29. On the mercy seat, see, e.g., G. Henton Davies, *IDB,* III:354; C. Armerding et al., *ISBE,* rev., I:291–94; on the cherubim, see R. K. Harrison, *ISBE,* rev., I:642–43.

1. See the commentary above on 4:9 and articles on the lampstand: L. E. Toombs, *IDB,* III:64–66; R. H. Smith, *ISBE* rev., III: 69–71.

the tree of life (Gen. 3:22, 24). The light suggests illumination. Zech. 4:1–4 speaks of the seven lamps as the seven eyes of God (see also Rev. 1:14). The number *seven* is almost universally the ancient number of perfection or completeness.[2] The whole menorah might be said to symbolize God's perfect presence and life illuminating his sanctuary and, through Moses, his people. The topics of 7:89 and 8:1–4 are therefore basically the same, although the introductory formulae at 8:1 and 8:5 make it impossible for them to be formally linked. The time frame of these verses is assumed to be that of 7:1, although that is not clear.

These verses summarize and offer a commentary on earlier material, viz., Exod. 25:31–40; 27:20–21; 37:17–24; Lev. 24:1–4.[3] The introductory section (vv. 1–2a) is of a type common in Numbers.[4] Vv. 2b–3 form a commentary on earlier material. At the center of the unit is the statement *And Aaron did so.* Here, as elsewhere in Numbers, it is important to notice that God's instructions were carried out exactly.[5] Exod. 27:20–21 and Lev. 24:1–4, which name Aaron as responsible for the lamps, do not state that he did what God commanded.

Verses 2b–3a summarize the material that is much more completely dealt with in Exod. 25:31–40 and 37:17–24. The detail is not the point upon which the author wishes to comment. Rather, he wants to focus on the direction in which the lamps are to be set up and the fact that Aaron is to set up these lamps. To take the latter first, Exod. 27:21 and Lev. 24:3 make it clear that Aaron (or Aaron and his sons) is responsible for "arranging" *(ʿāraḵ)* the lamps. Exod. 27:20 and Lev. 24:2 leave vague just who is to "set up" *(heʿĕlâ)* these lamps. Num. 8:2 clarifies this point: *when you* [Aaron] *set up the lamps (beha ʿalōṯeḵā ʾeṯ-hannērôṯ).*

Verses 2b–3a also bring to prominence the direction in which the seven lamps are to throw their light (viz., to the front of the lampstand). A comparison between vv. 2b–3a and Exod. 25:37 shows that the author of Numbers has made the words indicating the direction more prominent by repeating them, by making them precede the verb (thus emphasizing them), and by changing the unique phraseology of Exod. 25:37 to a synonymous but more common one.[6]

2. See de Vaulx, p. 117; Toombs, *IDB,* III:64–66.

3. The summary nature of this passage is well known. See, e.g., Gray, pp. 77–78; Budd, p. 86. The nature of this text as commentary is less generally appreciated.

4. E.g., 5:1–2, 5–6, 11–12; 6:1–2, 22–23; etc.

5. See also, e.g., 1:19, 54; 2:33–34; 3:42, 51; etc.

6. The phrase "toward [or upon] the front of (the lampstand)" in Exod.

4 This verse summarizes Exod. 25:31–40, emphasizing that the whole lampstand was made of golden hammered work, from its base to its *flowers* (probably flower-shaped ornaments).[7] The details are not in view here, but the whole. Furthermore, the lampstand was built exactly according to the pattern that God had showed Moses on Mt. Sinai. Once again, all is done in precise fulfillment of God's command.

3. CONSECRATION OF LEVITES (8:5–22)

5 *And Yahweh spoke to Moses, saying:*

6 *"Take the Levites from the midst of the children of Israel and purify them.*

7 *Thus you will do to them in order to purify them: sprinkle upon them the waters of purification, and let them bring a razor over their whole body, and let them scrub their garments, and thus purify themselves.*

8 *Then let them take a young bull and its meal offering of fine flour mixed with oil, and you shall take a second young bull for a purification offering,*

9 *and present the Levites before the tent of meeting, and gather all the congregation of the children of Israel,*

10 *and you shall present the Levites before Yahweh. Then the children of Israel shall lay their hands upon the Levites,*

11 *and Aaron shall elevate the Levites as a dedicatory offering before Yahweh out of the children of Israel that they may do Yahweh's work.*

12 *Then the Levites will lay their hands on the heads of the bulls, and you shall sacrifice the one for a purification offering and the other for a whole burnt offering to Yahweh to make atonement for the Levites.*

13 *And you shall present the Levites before Aaron and before his sons, and you will make them a dedicatory offering to Yahweh.*

25:37 is *ʿal ʿēḇer p*^{e}*nê,* which is unique in Biblical Hebrew (although Ezek. 1:9, 12; 10:22 have a similar expression: *ʾel ʿēḇer p*^{e}*nê*). The synonymous phrase used here (and in Exod. 26:9; 28:25, 37; 39:18; Lev. 8:9; 2 Sam. 11:15) is *ʾel mûl p*^{e}*nê.*

7. For a discussion of the various parts of the lampstand, see the articles in Bible dictionaries and commentaries on the relevant sections of the book of Exodus, e.g.: J. Durham, *Exodus,* WBC (Waco, Tex.: Word, 1987), 362–65; U. Cassuto, *A Commentary on the Book of Exodus,* tr. I. Abrahams (Jerusalem: Magnes, 1983), 340–45; also A. Kennedy, *HDB,* IV: 653–68; E. Goodenough, "The Menorah among the Jews of the Roman Period," *HUCA* 23 (1950–51), 449–92.

14 *And you will separate the Levites from the midst of the children of Israel, and the Levites will be mine.*

15 *Afterward the Levites will qualify to enter into the work of the tent of meeting, and you will cleanse them and offer them as a dedicatory offering.*

16 *For each of them has been given to me out of the midst of the children of Israel. Instead of every firstborn who breaks the womb*[1] *from among the children of Israel, I have taken the Levites to myself.*

17 *For every firstborn among the children of Israel is mine, among both human and beast. In the day I struck every firstborn in the land of Egypt, I separated them to myself.*

18 *And I have taken the Levites instead of every firstborn among the children of Israel.*

19 *And I have given the Levites as gifts to Aaron and his sons from the midst of the children of Israel, to do the work of the children of Israel in the tent of meeting and to make atonement for the children of Israel, that there might be no plague among the children of Israel when they encroach on the sanctuary."*

20 *So Moses and Aaron and all the congregation of the children of Israel did concerning the Levites. According to all that Yahweh commanded Moses concerning the Levites, so the children of Israel did concerning them.*

21 *And the Levites purified themselves from uncleanness, and scrubbed their garments. Then Aaron elevated them as a dedicatory offering before Yahweh, and Aaron made atonement on their behalf in order to cleanse them.*

22 *And after this the Levites were qualified to begin their work in the tent of meeting before Aaron and his sons. As Yahweh had commanded Moses concerning the Levites, so they did concerning them.*[2]

This section should be compared and contrasted with Lev. 8, which deals with the dedication ceremony for the priests. The most obvious point of

1. For MT *piṭraṯ kol-reḥem* b^{e}*ḵôr kol* Sam. Pent. and the Sebir note read *kol-*b^{e}*ḵôr peṭer reḥem.* Parallel texts (Exod. 13:2; Num. 3:12) have *peṭer reḥem* before b^{e}*ḵôr.* This and the unique fem. form *piṭrâ* cause one to suspect either corruption or glossing here. The words "breaker of the womb" would be understood as in apposition with "every firstborn." *BHS* proposes moving the second *kol* before b^{e}*ḵôr.* Either reading clarifies the meaning of the text. The simplification of the text in v. 18 may show either that the difficulty of the phrase *piṭraṯ kol-reḥem* was known early in the history of the text, or that *piṭraṯ kol-reḥem* b^{e}*ḵôr kol* is an early gloss on the text.

2. The pronoun "they" refers to the Israelites; "them" refers to the Levites.

comparison is that both narratives deal with ceremonies of dedication. The most obvious point of contrast, visible in several separate matters, is that, while the Levites are brought into the sphere of the ritually clean *(ṭāhôr),* the priests are brought into the sphere of the holy *(qāḏôš)*. Thus, while the Levites are purified (*ṭihar,* Num. 8:7), the priests are sanctified (*qiddēš,* e.g., Lev. 8:12). While the Levites may serve within the court of the tabernacle because they are ritually clean, they still may not handle the sacred objects themselves, but must depend upon the priests to wrap up the objects and place them on poles and frames before they can dare to carry these objects on their shoulders (see Num. 4:5–14). It should also be clear that 8:5–22 is connected with the material in 3:5–13, which summarizes some of the same basic information without setting forth the ceremony involved.

The whole of vv. 5–22 is connected by a complex series of repetitions and other structures that will be mentioned in due course. The passage is tripartite: (a) the divine command (vv. 5–13), (b) the historical rationale for the sacrifice (vv. 14–19), and (c) an obedience formula and summary (vv. 20–22).

5–8 The comparison between the Levites and other sacrificial offerings is developed for the first time in this passage. This is the fundamental comparison in vv. 5–19. After a typical introductory formula (v. 5), the command to *purify (ṭihar)* the Levites is given. To *purify* the Levites means to move them into a sphere of purity where they can enter into proximity with holy objects and, indeed, with God himself, without danger to themselves or to the community.[3]

This purification is accomplished by a threefold ritual of cleansing. As in 5:11–31, the text of 8:6–7 makes use of the literary device of inclusion to underline the major point (the ritual purification of the Levites) at both the beginning and the end. First, Moses is commanded to sprinkle the Levites with the *waters of purification (mê ḥaṭṭā'ṯ);* second, the Levites are commanded to shave themselves completely; third, the Levites are to scrub their clothes. Similar requirements, although with some different terminology, are found for the cleansing of the leper in Lev. 14:8–9. The exact procedures for, and the meaning of, these rituals are not known.

The phrase *waters of purification* is unique here,[4] but since the purpose of the purification offering is the purification of the sanctuary,

3. For a discussion of these "spheres" of "unclean," "clean," and "holy," see Wenham, *Leviticus,* pp. 18–24; and on the danger of encroachment on the sanctuary, see Milgrom, *Studies in Levitical Terminology,* I:5–59.

4. The phrase is related to the "waters of impurity" *(mê niddâ ḥaṭṭā'ṯ)* in 19:9, and perhaps to "clean water" *(mayim ṭᵉhōrîm)* in Ezek. 36:25.

and since the purpose of the whole section is ceremonial cleanness, one may assume that, whatever the source of these waters, their purpose was cleansing.[5] The connection between removal of hair and removal of uncleanness is not known, although this ritual is mentioned elsewhere in the OT (e.g., Lev. 14:8–9) and in other parts of the ancient world as well.[6] The easiest ritual of the three to interpret may be the scrubbing of the clothes, which signifies the ritual cleansing of the person who wears them.[7] V. 8 mentions the parallel offerings, which involve the young bulls for the purification and whole burnt offerings.

9–13 This section clarifies the parallel between the Levites and the animal sacrifices. Vv. 9–10a and 13 form another inclusion, repeating the main points of the text. Beginning in v. 10b the procedures for offering both the Levites and the animal sacrifices are given in parallel form: hands are laid on the offerings (vv. 10b, 12a), a proper person offers the sacrifices (vv. 11a, 12b),[8] and the outcome of the offerings is given (vv. 11b, 12c). The laying on of hands possibly denotes the identification of the Levites with the people and the animal sacrifices, but more probably denotes the substitution of the one for the other.[9] Of course, the difference between the Levites and the animal sacrifices is clear, since the animals are slain while the Levites have the role of living sacrifices. The Levites are dedicated or made a *t^erûmâ,* i.e., they are set aside and dedicated to Yahweh's realm and work.[10] That this is the case is seen in the clause *that they may do Yahweh's work* (v. 11b).

The bulls are sacrificed to cleanse the sanctuary (the purification offering or *ḥaṭṭā'ṯ*) and to atone for human sin (the whole burnt offering

5. Some have suggested that these waters were drawn from the laver in the tabernacle or were simply pure water; see, e.g., Wenham, p. 96; Gray, p. 79. See the commentary below on 8:21.

6. This ceremony was not the same as everyday shaving, for which a different word is used *(gillaḥ).* It may be similar to an Egyptian practice noted by Herodotus (*Hist.* 11.37).

7. The term *kibbēs* is used of scrubbing clothes, whereas *rāḥaṣ* is used of cleansing the body; see, e.g., Lev. 14:9 for both terms together. The exceptions to this usage are Jer. 2:22 and 4:14, where *kibbēs* is used in a poetic text for the cleansing of the body from sin.

8. In v. 11b Aaron offers the Levites. V. 12b says that "you" shall offer the animals. The natural referent of "you" might seem to be Moses, but as v. 21 makes clear it refers to Aaron.

9. See R. Péter, "L'imposition des mains dans l'Ancien Testament," *VT* 27 (1977) 48–55, esp. 53–55; also E. Leach, *Culture and Communication* (Cambridge: Cambridge Univ. Press, 1976), p. 89.

10. This was possible only after the Levites had been ceremonially cleansed. On the *t^erûmâ,* see the commentary above on 5:25.

or *ʿōlâ*). These sacrifices are said *to make atonement for the Levites* (*l^ekappēr ʿal hal^ewîyim*). The term *kippēr* varies in meaning according to the particular sacrifice involved. In the case of the *ḥaṭṭāʾṯ*, the purpose of which is cleansing the sanctuary, the translation "to purge" is preferable.[11] In the *ʿōlâ*, the purpose was "to pay a ransom" (i.e., a *kōp̄er*) or to substitute a lesser penalty for a greater one.[12] Here the term refers to both kinds of sacrifices so that some general expression such as *to make atonement* is necessary in order to include both meanings of *kippēr.*[13]

14–19 These verses add a complex chiasm to the inclusio pattern of vv. 5–13, thus linking the two major sections of the passage.[14] The chiastic structure is:

A. To make atonement for the Levites (v. 12)
B. To do the work of the tent of meeting (v. 15)
C. The Levites are given to God (v. 16a)
D. They are given instead of the firstborn (v. 16b)
E. Events from the time of the Exodus (v. 17)
D.′ They are given instead of the firstborn (v. 18)
C.′ The Levites are given to Aaron (v. 19a)
B.′ To do the work of the tent of meeting (v. 19b)
A.′ To make atonement for Israel (v. 19c)

That the present chiasm is interwoven with the previous section in vv. 9–12 shows that the subject of the comparison between the Levites and the sacrifices is continued. First, the two bulls offered *to make atonement* for the Levites may be compared with the Levites offered *to make atonement* for the Israelites.[15] Just as the animal sacrifices atone for the Levites by purging the sanctuary (in the case of the purification offering) and by being the ransom price (in the case of the whole burnt offering), so the Levites themselves become a substitute (i.e., a ransom price, *kōper*) for the Israelites.[16]

11. See Milgrom, "Two Kinds of *ḥaṭṭāʾṯ*," *VT* 26 (1976) 337; also idem, *IDBSup*, pp. 78–79.

12. See Milgrom, *Studies in Levitical Terminlogy,* I:28–31; also Wenham, *Leviticus,* pp. 28, 59–61.

13. For further parallels between the Levites and the sacrificial animals, see the commentary below on v. 19.

14. I am indebted to Wenham (pp. 95–96) for noting the chiasm.

15. See v. 12: *l^ekappēr ʿal hal^ewîyim.* Cf. v. 19: *ûl^ekappēr ʿal b^enê yiśrāʾēl.*

16. See above and Wenham, *Leviticus,* pp. 28, 57–61; Milgrom, *Studies in Levitical Terminology,* I:28–31.

Second, from the preliminary comparison linking vv. 9–13 with vv. 14–19, the passage moves to the center point of the chiasm in v. 17: that God had owned every firstborn Israelite from the time of the tenth plague in Egypt (see Exod. 13:2; 22:29–30a; 34:19–20). Num. 3:5–13 has already alluded to these events, though setting forth only the divine command and the human response. Here the text details the way in which the Levites were set apart. Thus, the purpose of the two texts is different. Here, as in ch. 3, God's gift of the Levites to Aaron is based on the formative national events of Exodus and Passover. From v. 17, the text works out forward to v. 19 and backward to v. 12 in the chiasm. It is best to discuss the parallel themes together.

16b, 18 These verses are virtual duplicates. V. 18 begins with a verb in the imperfect consecutive rather than the perfect (as in v. 16b) and does not have the somewhat difficult phrase *piṭraṯ kol-reḥem* (lit., "opener of every womb"). The lines mean that the Levites are the divinely ordained substitutes for the firstborn of Israel.

16a, 19a Both these sentences state that the Levites were given to someone. In v. 16a the recipient is Yahweh (as in Exod. 22:28b and Num. 3:12–13). In v. 19a Yahweh gives the Levites to Aaron and his sons. The Levites are God's special possession, which he, in turn, gives to help Aaron and his sons.

15, 19b Here the Levites are charged with their work. It is the work of the tent of meeting. Readers know from 3:10 that the Levites will be in the tent to do work. If one takes the chronological note at 7:1 as applicable to this text, the current text is chronologically prior to the texts in chs. 3 and 4. V. 15 emphasizes the qualification of the Levites to do the work.

qualified to enter. Here and in chs. 3–4 the Heb. *bōʾ* carries this meaning.[17] After they were cleansed and made a dedicatory offering, the Levites were qualified for labor in the tent of meeting. The character of the work in all cases in ch. 8 is the work of carrying the holy things. The other task of the Levites ("guard duty," *mišmereṯ*) is not done in the sanctuary but outside it and thus would require no cleansing. Only the work of carrying the holy tabernacle required indirect contact with the holy objects.

The emphasis in v. 19b is on the substitutionary nature of the

17. See Milgrom, *Studies in Levitical Terminology,* I:73 n. 265; see also the phrase *kol-habbāʾ laṣṣāḇāʾ* and its variants in 4:3, 23, 30, where *bōʾ* again means "to be qualified."

Levites' work. It is *the work of the children of Israel in the tent of meeting ('eṯ-ʿᵃḇōḏaṯ bᵉnê yiśrāʾēl bᵉʾōhel mōʿēḏ).* Had it not been for the Levites, the Israelites themselves would have had to undertake this work in the tent. The mention of a *plague* in v. 19c tells the reader what the outcome would have been had the Israelites attempted this work in their state of uncleanness.[18] Just as the sacrificial bulls paid the ransom price on behalf of the Levites, the Levites, by a different procedure, paid the ransom price for the rest of Israel.[19] They were living sacrifices.

20–22 This paragraph combines the typical obedience formula (vv. 20, 22b) with a summary account of the cleansing of the Levites (vv. 21–22a). The obedience formula is not unlike other closing formulae in the book. Moses, Aaron, and all the people did exactly as God outlined to Moses. Thus, once again, the importance of an exacting obedience to God's word is underlined. The summary (vv. 21–22a) contains bits and pieces from vv. 7, 11, and 12, but leaves out the parallel between the Levites and the sacrificial offerings, which has already been drawn out at length in vv. 5–19. The summary is to support the obedience formula. The theological point of the sacrificial and substitutionary nature of the Levites has already been sufficiently made in vv. 5–19.

21 *And the Levites purified themselves from uncleanness (wayyiṯḥaṭṭᵉʾû halᵉwîyim).* This clause summarizes the rituals of sprinkling with the waters of purification and shaving the body in v. 7. The scrubbing of the clothes is the only ritual that is actually named here. Elsewhere in the OT the Hithpael of *ḥṭʾ* refers to the ritual cleansing of one's body from contact with a corpse (Num. 19:12, 13, 20; 31:19, 23).[20] Most other contexts also mention cleansing waters (which could be inferred where they are not specifically mentioned). It is possible, therefore, that the

18. For a connection between a plague or the wrath of God and encroachment on the holy things, see, e.g., Exod. 30:12; Num. 25:9, 18; 31:16; 1 Sam. 4:17; 6:4.

19. The Levites were the divinely established means by which the plague of God's wrath concerning the trespass of the sanctuary would strike only the guilty party and not the whole community. Milgrom states that the Levites were the "lightning rod to attract God's wrath upon themselves whenever an Israelite trespassed upon the sancta" (*Studies in Levitical Terminology,* I:31; see also pp. 28–31).

20. The Hithpael of *ḥṭʾ* occurs 8 times in the OT. Seven of these occurrences may be translated "to cleanse oneself from uncleanness." The exception is Job 41:17 (Eng. 25), which is probably best translated as "to withdraw" (so, e.g., J. Hartley, *Book of Job,* NICOT [Grand Rapids: Eerdmans, 1988], p. 529) or "to be beside oneself." See BDB, p. 307b; *HALAT,* p. 293b.

sprinkling with water was to purify contamination derived from contact with the dead. Since the Levites had to consent to the process of sprinkling, and since they shaved their own bodies, the act of purification could be said to be self-accomplished (as here), although it is recognized that God is the source of the purification.

4. THE LEVITES' WORK (8:23–26)

23 *And Yahweh spoke to Moses, saying:*

24 *"This is that which pertains to the Levites: From twenty-five years of age and up, one shall be qualified to enter on doing service in the work of the tent of meeting,*

25 *and from fifty years of age, one shall retire from the service of the work, he shall do no more work,*

26 *although he may assist his brothers in the tent of meeting by standing guard duty, he will do no more work. You will do accordingly concerning the Levites' guard duties."*

23–26 This little section contains a major problem. Before discussing the problem, however, let us turn to what is clear. The Levites have two kinds of *work:* *ʿaḇōḏâ,* physical labor (dismantling, carrying, and reassembling the tabernacle structure), and *mišmereṯ,* guard duty around the tabernacle.[1] Whereas ch. 4 has made it clear that Levites have primary duties until fifty years of age, the current passage makes it clear that after fifty years of age the Levites may stay on to assist their younger fellows in guard duty, but not in physical labor. One might also make a similar point concerning the duties of those who were under age, viz., that they assisted their fellows in guard duty but did no physical labor.

The problem in the unit concerns the lower age limit for physical work in the tent of meeting. A few chapters earlier (e.g., 4:3 — a month previously), the age had been given as between thirty and fifty. How is one to undertand the five-year discrepancy at the lower age limit? The problem was recognized at least as early as the LXX, which simply harmonized the readings of ch. 4 to agree with those of ch. 8. Ancient rabbinic exegesis pointed to a five-year apprenticeship period.[2] No textual evidence supports this view, however.

Keil reasoned that the law of ch. 8 was binding for all time,

1. See the commentary above on chs. 3 and 4.

2. See Cohen, ed., *Soncino Chumash,* p. 841; also G. Archer, *Encyclopedia of Bible Difficulties* (Grand Rapids: Zondervan, 1982), pp. 134–35.

whereas that of ch. 4 was temporary legislation for the tabernacle on the move.[3] This explanation carries with it the assumption that all the lifting, carrying, etc., was done by those thirty to fifty years of age, while the service of the standing tabernacle was given to those between twenty-five and fifty years. One must surely question this view, as well as Keil's contention that men of thirty years have more vigor and strength than those of twenty-five. Noordtzij simply comments that the different texts reflect changed circumstances.[4] What could these changed circumstances be? Wenham has suggested that the census results showed that the need for Levites was not as great as originally thought, thus leading to the rise in age from twenty-five to thirty years (remembering that ch. 8 is chronologically prior to ch. 4, although literarily subsequent to it).[5]

For other scholars, the discrepancy reflects different traditions, sitting side by side in the final form of the text and possibly reflecting different time periods in the postexilic age.[6] Noth argues that vv. 23–26 were an appendix to ch. 8. This appendix loosened the rule of ch. 4 at a time when few Levites were to be found.[7] Kellermann also thinks of vv. 23–26 as a later appendix, which modifies the earlier tradition of ch. 4.[8] All these approaches simply take ch. 8 as later than ch. 4, and thus either ignore the chronological statement of 7:1 or think it irrelevant to the present text.

But what is the literary function of 7:1 (repeated in 9:1, 15) if it does not intend to set off the material in chs. 7–9 as prior to chs. 1–6? Furthermore, simply to assert that in 4:3, 20, 23, 25, 39, 43, 47 we have a different tradition than in ch. 8 means that the final redactor of the text allowed these apparent contradictions to exist within 200 verses of one another. It is hard to see how this can be called redaction, clumsy or otherwise. Little evidence (apart from the conclusions derived from theories) indicates that editors of the biblical period transmitted mistakes and contradictions just because they were in the traditional text. To make sense out of the change in age here, one must assume that something happened, or was perceived to have happened.

Again, as in other places in Numbers, we do not have the information to resolve this problem. The age of entry into Levitical service

3. Keil, pp. 789–90.
4. Noordtzij, p. 81.
5. Wenham, pp. 97–98.
6. E.g., Gray, pp. 32–33.
7. Noth, pp. 69–70; so also Budd, p. 94.
8. Kellermann, *Priesterschrift,* p. 124.

apparently changed from time to time. Thus 1 Chr. 23:24, 27; 2 Chr. 31:17; and Ezra 3:8 give the lower limit as twenty years and give no retirement age at all. One assumes that this change reflected the small number of Levites available in the postexilic age. Here in Numbers the originally lower age is raised. The rise in the minimum age of the Levites would reduce the number in service significantly.[9] Perhaps Israel found that men of thirty years of age were generally more spiritually mature than men of twenty-five, and that this spiritual maturity was necessary in the work of carrying the holy things (the job for which the age limits apply).

In addition to Wenham's suggestion tying the difference to the census (which seems plausible), I offer the following possibility. Perhaps the Nadab and Abihu incident recorded in Lev. 10:1–20 caused the Levitical minimum serving age to be raised. Though the age of Nadab and Abihu at their deaths is not known, this incident had to have occurred after the tabernacle was set up and before the departure from Sinai, or within a fifty-day period.[10] This terrible event might well have caused the age limit to be raised more fully to insure against an immature individual assuming the (at least potentially) dangerous role of Levite.

5. SUPPLEMENT TO THE PASSOVER LAW (9:1–14)

1 *And Yahweh spoke to Moses in the wilderness of Sinai, in the second year after their exodus from the land of Egypt, in the first month, saying:*

2 *"Let the children of Israel observe the Passover at its appointed time.*

3 *On the fourteenth day of this month, between the two evenings, you shall observe it at its appointed time. According to all its statutes and according to all its ordinances you shall observe it."*

4 *And Moses spoke to the children of Israel to observe the Passover.*

5 *And they observed the Passover in the first month, on the fourteenth day of the month, between the two evenings, in the wilderness of Sinai. The children of Israel did according to all that Yahweh commanded Moses.*

6 *And it happened that there were men who were ritually unclean because of a dead body, and not able to observe the Passover on that day. And they came before Moses and Aaron on that day,*

9. Wenham (pp. 97–98 n. 2) estimates the reduction to be at least 20%.

10. I.e., between the first day of the first month of the second year and the twentieth day of the second month of that same year.

7 *and those men said to him, "We are unclean because of a dead body; why should we be restrained so that we might not offer Yahweh's offering at its appointed time, among the children of Israel?"*
8 *And Moses said to them, "Stand here that I may surely hear what Yahweh will command regarding you."*
9 *And Yahweh spoke to Moses, saying:*
10 *"Speak to the children of Israel, saying, 'If anyone of you is unclean because of a dead body, or is on a distant journey —you or your descendants — then he may still observe the Passover of Yahweh.*
11 *Let him observe it in the second month on the fourteenth day, between the evenings. Let him observe it with unleavened bread and bitter herbs.*
12 *Let them not leave any of it over until the morning, and let them not break a bone in it. They shall observe it according to every statute of the Passover.*
13 *But the one who is ritually clean and who is not on a journey and fails to observe the Passover, then that life shall be cut off from his people because he did not offer Yahweh's offering at its appointed time. That one shall bear his sin.*
14 *And if a sojourner should sojourn with you, then he may observe the Passover of Yahweh. According to the statute of the Passover and according to its ordinance, so he must keep it. There will be one statute for you, both for the sojourner and the native of the land."*

This passage concerns the celebration of the second Passover. It begins with a summary of current Passover regulations (vv. 1–5), follows with the exceptional case (vv. 6–8) and the new legislation based on this case (vv. 9–13), and concludes with the case of the sojourner (v. 14). The passage is recorded because of the new legislation in vv. 6–14, much of which looks forward to settled life in the land of Canaan.

1–5 These verses simply summarize the ordinances for the observance of the Passover (the first Passover had been observed in Egypt) as given in Exod. 12:2–11, 21–27, 43–49 and Lev. 23:5–8, and apply these ordinances to the celebration of the second Passover one year later.[1]

1. Many scholars agree that the Passover and Feast of Unleavened Bread may have had pre-Exodus, agricultural connections. Although this may be true, the OT text itself looks back to these feasts only as shaped by the historical events of the tenth plague and deliverance from Egypt. The literature on the background

The phrase *its appointed time* (*mô'ᵃḏô,* vv. 2–3) refers to the divinely selected time for the event as previously legislated (the fourteenth day of the first month). This divinely appointed time is more closely defined as *between the two evenings (bên hā'arbayim).* This phrase is usually translated as "in the evening" (RSV), "between dusk and dark" (NEB), or "at twilight" (NIV, NASB, NJPS). The exact time of day is considered important, but unfortunately it is difficult to know precisely what time is indicated. Rashi placed the time between the darkness of the day and that of the night, or between about noon and 6:00 P.M. Ibn Ezra argued for the approximately 1⅓ hours between sunset and darkness.[2] Deut. 16:6 places the Passover "in the evening, at the going down of the sun" *(bā'āreḇ kᵉḇô' haššemeš),* which seems to favor the explanation of Ibn Ezra.

The *statutes (ḥuqqôṯ)* and the *ordinances (mišpāṭîm)* of the Passover are the enactments that God has revealed previously. As elsewhere in Numbers, meticulous obedience of these regulations is necessary. V. 5 takes words and phrases from vv. 1–4 to show that Israel took great care to do what Yahweh had commanded through Moses. *The children of Israel did according to all that Yahweh commanded* is the obedience formula that occurs commonly (e.g., with minor verbal variations, Exod. 39:32, 42; 40:16; Num. 1:54; 2:34; 8:20).

6–8 This section raises an issue not covered by the original Passover legislation of Exodus or Leviticus. A group of Israelites had become *ritually unclean (ṭāmē')* via contact with a corpse. The assumption was made that such contact rendered one incapable of observing the Passover. These people raised the question whether their temporary uncleanness should bar them from the observance of the Passover that year. The only legislation prior to this time that had stated that contact with the dead defiled one is in Lev. 21:1–12, which concerns only the priests. Subsequent legislation (Num. 5:1–4; 6:6–7, 9–12; 19:1–22) applies this principle more widely. One may assume that previously given general legislation on uncleanness (e.g., Lev. 7:19–21, concerning the peace offerings, and 11:1–15:33) was interpreted to mean that unclean-

---

of the Passover and the Feast of Unleavened Bread is enormous. See, e.g., J. B. Segal, *The Hebrew Passover* (London: SPCK, 1963); R. de Vaux, *Studies in Old Testament Sacrifice,* tr. J. Bourke and R. Potter (Cardiff: Univ. of Wales Press, 1964), pp. 1–26; idem, *Ancient Israel,* II:484–93; H.-J. Kraus, "Zur Geschichte des Passah-Massot-Festes im AT," *EvT* 18 (1958) 47–67.

2. See Cohen, ed., *Soncino Chumash,* p. 387; also see Mish. *Pesahim* 5:1.

ness via contact with a corpse barred one from observance of the Passover, even though this feast was to be observed in the homes rather than in the tabernacle. In any case, these Israelites raised this question to clarify the situation. Moses did not have an immediate answer for the question, and asked the people to *stand,* or wait, for an answer from Yahweh.[3]

9–13 *And Yahweh spoke.* As elsewhere, this legislation is seen as the word of Yahweh.[4] It is applied not only to the immediate situation but also to future generations, and not only to the question that gave it rise but to a further (and seemingly unrelated) question. The enactment confirms the notion that uncleanness via contact with a corpse does bar one from keeping the Passover at the appointed time. This specific uncleanness need not prevent participation in this most fundamental community celebration for an entire year, however. God provided that such people as were disqualified here could observe a Passover one month later than normal. In every other way this observance of the Passover would be identical. To this provision is added another, dealing with one who is *on a distant journey* (*b*ᵉ*ḏereḵ r*ᵉ*ḥōqâ,* v. 10).

The logic of the inclusion of this second provision in the current context is hard to see. Kellermann sees the exemption of travelers as the original legal enactment (vv. 10b–12) to which the exemption of unclean persons was added.[5] This interpretation does nothing but turn the passage on its head. It does not answer the difficulty of the relationship of uncleanness and long journeys. Why would any later editor associate these two? In addition to the lack of connection with the context, the references to travelers would seem to have little application to the wilderness period, but would apply only later, after the people were settled in the land. Is it possible that the reference to travelers in vv. 10 and 13 is a later application inserted in this text?

Since the holy and the unclean are antithetical, they must never be brought into contact (as has been argued above on 5:1–4). Between the states of "holy" and "unclean" is the state of "clean." Cleanness is a neutral, or normal, state for Israelites.[6] From the regulations concerning the states of cleanness and uncleanness in Lev. 11–15, one can see that

3. For parallel situations earlier, see Lev. 24:10–23; for a later parallel, see Num. 15:32–36.

4. See, e.g., Num. 1:1; 2:1; 3:5, 11, 14, 44; 4:1, 17, 21; 5:1, 5; 6:1, 22; 7:4; 8:1, 5, 23; 9:1.

5. Kellermann, *Priesterschrift,* pp. 124–33.

6. See further in Wenham, *Leviticus,* pp. 18–25.

the unclean person is to be separated from the camp so as not to pass the contagion of uncleanness on to the rest.[7] Here when one is unclean from contact with a corpse, he or she is to be separated from the community (which is clean). The person who is away on a *distant journey,* i.e., a journey that takes him or her outside the covenant community of Israel, is also in the realm of the unclean, separated from the community. In this way the two regulations are similar — both deal with people who are outside the covenant community, at least temporarily. Such people are eligible to observe the Passover one month late. Whether the phrases concerning the traveler are later additions to the text or not, both regulations have the same basis.

11–12 These regulations are meant to be representative of the statutes that had already been given for the observance of the Passover in Exod. 12. For the phrase *unleavened bread and bitter herbs (maṣṣôṯ ûm^e rōrîm),* which connects Passover with the Feast of Unleavened Bread, see Exod. 12:8. For the clause *let them not leave any over until the morning (lō' yaš'îrû mimmennû 'aḏ-bōqer),* see Exod. 12:10.[8] For *let them not break a bone in it (w^e 'eṣem lō' yišb^e rû bô)* see Exod. 12:46.[9] All three of these ordinances would still be relevant in the wilderness period. The regulation concerning the blood on doorposts and lintels (Exod. 12:21–27) would be less so, and is not repeated here.

13 In the context of the last plague in Egypt, the penalty for failing to observe the Passover was death at the hands of the Destroyer (Exod. 12:23). In the changed circumstances of the wilderness (and looking forward to settlement in Canaan), the penalty for nonobservance is restated: that person *shall be cut off (kāraṯ)* and *shall bear his sin" (niśśā' 'āwōn).* Late observance of the Passover was an extension of God's grace to the person who was suffering temporary separation from the community. The person who was clean and present in the community at Passover time and who simply chose not to observe it (for whatever reasons) was liable to punishment.

The exact meaning of the phrase *be cut off from the people* has been much debated. Some have argued that it probably meant excommunication from Israel, which, at least in the wilderness period, could

7. See, e.g., Lev. 12:4; 13:4–5, 46; 15:31; also Num. 5:1–4.

8. One change in these regulations is the substitution here of the verb *šā'ar* for its synonym *yāṯar* in Exod. 12:10.

9. On this regulation, see the discussion in de Vaux, *Studies in OT Sacrifice,* pp. 9–10.

have meant almost certain death.[10] Others have posited that the expression meant "to put to death judicially."[11] Still others have seen in it the ominous threat that, in some way, at some unknown time, God himself would destroy the offender.[12] The probability is that, in specific contexts, the idiom could mean any of the three, especially the last. This judgment is reinforced by the phrase that the author used to interpret "to be cut off," viz., *bear one's sin (niśśāʾ ʿāwōn)*. As we pointed out in dealing with 5:11–31, this clause refers to a judgment left entirely to God.[13] Together the two idioms indicate that the one so punished has lost Yahweh's protection and, in essence, operates outside the sphere of the covenant relationship.

14 This regulation (like that on the traveler in v. 10) is only marginally relevant to the wilderness community and clearly looks to life in Canaan. The *sojourner (gēr)* is the one who lived among the Israelite community, although not a native-born Israelite, and who had chosen to live according to Israelite law and custom, much like landed immigrants or resident aliens in modern North America. The *gēr* is distinguished from the "foreigner" *(ben-nēḵār)*, the temporary resident *(tôšāḇ)*, and the "hired worker" *(śāḵîr)*, all of whom are forbidden to observe the Passover in Exod. 12:43, 45.

A whole group of laws in the Torah have the interests of the *gērîm* as their focus (e.g., Exod. 12:19 puts the *gēr* on the same level as the native-born Israelite regarding the celebration of the Feast of Unleavened Bread).[14] The rationale behind the care and concern for sojourners in Israel's midst is to be found, e.g., in Exod. 22:20 (Eng. 21): "For you were sojourners in the land of Egypt" (cf. Deut. 23:8 [Eng. 7]). All Israelites had their roots in sojourning, and should remember these roots as they deal with those who sojourn in their midst. In the regulation of Exod. 12:48 the sojourner is required to receive circumcision before being allowed to participate in the Passover. Although this condition is not repeated here,

10. E.g., J. P. Hyatt, *Exodus,* NCBC (Grand Rapids: Eerdmans, 1971), p. 135; R. Cole, *Exodus,* TOTC (Downers Grove: InterVarsity, 1973), p. 109; Budd, p. 98.

11. Keil, p. 173; Gray, pp. 84–85; E. Smick allows such a meaning in *TWOT,* I:457.

12. See the discussion in Wenham, *Leviticus,* pp. 241–42; McNeile, p. 48; Milgrom, *JPST,* pp. 405–8.

13. See the commentary above on 5:31.

14. See other examples in Exod. 22:20 (Eng. 21); 23:9; Lev. 17; Num. 15:11–31; etc.

it is probably to be assumed as part of the *statute (ḥôq)* and *ordinance (mišpāṭ)* concerning the Passover: "No uncircumcised man shall eat of it" (Exod. 12:48).

6. PREPARATIONS TO DEPART (9:15–10:10)

a. Fiery Cloud (9:15–23)

15 *And on the day when the tabernacle was erected, the cloud covered the tabernacle of the tent of the testimony. And in the evening something like the appearance of fire used to come over the tabernacle until morning.*

16 *So it used to be continually; the cloud covered it,*[1] *and the appearance of fire by night.*

17 *Whenever the cloud was lifted up from upon the tent, then the children of Israel departed. And in the place where the cloud settled down, there the children of Israel encamped.*

18 *According to the command of Yahweh the children of Israel departed, and according to the command of Yahweh they encamped; all the days in which the cloud was sitting over the tabernacle they encamped.*

19 *And when the cloud remained over the tabernacle many days, then the children of Israel kept the watch of Yahweh and did not depart.*

20 *And when it happened that the cloud remained over the tabernacle a few days, according to the command of Yahweh they encamped and according to the command of Yahweh they departed.*

21 *And when it happened that the cloud remained from evening until morning, when the cloud was taken up in the morning, then they departed; or if it remained a day and a night, when the cloud was taken up, then they departed;*

22 *whether two days or a month or any number of days,*[2] *whenever*

1. On the basis of the versions (LXX, Pesh., Vulg., Pal. Targ.), *BHS* and some commentators (e.g., Budd, p. 101) assert that *yômām,* "by day," should be added here. While the sense of the sentence seems to require this addition, MT is the more difficult reading.

2. The translation of *yāmîm,* lit., "days," here is a problem. One would expect it to be a period of longer than one month. Most modern English translations render the term "one year" (AV, RV, NASB, NEB, NIV, NKJV, NJPS, JB). Gray (p. 87) denied the possibility of such a translation, despite Lev. 25:29, which is usually used to support the contention. In the Leviticus passage, the term *days* parallels the term *year,* and the derived meaning comes from that parallelism, nothing else. BDB, p. 399b, gives examples of the term *yāmîm* being used for an indefinite period of time (e.g., Gen. 40:4; 1 K. 17:15; Neh. 1:4). The phrase is

the cloud remained over the tabernacle, to rest over it, the children of Israel encamped and did not depart. Then, when it was taken up, they departed.

23 *According to the command of Yahweh they encamped, and according to the command of Yahweh they departed. They kept the watch of Yahweh according to the command of Yahweh through Moses.*

This passage expands the obedience formula of Exod. 40:36–38, thus framing the legislation that issued from the tabernacle (Lev. 1:1–Num. 9:14) with the theme of God's presence with his people in the cloud and the fire. Added to the theme of divine presence is the further statement of the people's exact and complete obedience to Yahweh.

The passage itself is bipartite and can be divided along thematic lines. Vv. 15–16 bring forth the old theme of God's presence in the sanctuary in the midst of the people. The elevated prose section of vv. 17–23 emphasizes the theme of exact obedience to God. This section (along with 10:1–10) rounds off the material about the sojourn at Mt. Sinai, although the point of view of the section is already that of the march and encampment. Vv. 17–23, while not actually poetry, share with poetry such features as parallelism and repetition. The most outstanding feature of the section is the repeated formula "according to the command of Yahweh" *(ʿal pî YHWH),* which is expanded in various ways in vv. 18, 20, 23a, and 23b.[3]

The passage amounts to expository sections on faithful obedience in departure and encampment tied together by means of obedience formulae. The following diagram illustrates the chiastic structure.[4]

DF + EF + ET + EF + DF + DT + EF + DF

18a 18b 20a 20b 21–22 23a

probably equivalent to an indefinite time period; hence something like RSV "a longer time" is preferable.

3. For a more complete discussion of this expansion, see below; see also Wenham, pp. 100–101.

4. In the diagram the following codes are used: DF = departure formula: "According to the command of Yahweh, they departed"; EF = encampment formula: "According to the command of Yahweh, they encamped"; DT = exposition of departure theme; ET = exposition of encampment theme; the obedience formula is made up of either DF + EF or EF + DF.

15–16 These verses introduce the topic of the cloud in words reminiscent of Exod. 40:2, 34–38. The whole purpose of these verses is to state that the tabernacle was covered *(kiśśē')* by cloud in the daytime and by fire at night. This covering emphasizes the presence of God with the people. The perfect tense of the verb *(kiśśē')* should be taken here to describe a single act. Beginning with the verb translated *used to come (yihyeh),* the verbs are imperfects and should be taken as indicating frequentative past acts.[5]

The tent shrine is called by its full name, *the tabernacle of the tent of the testimony (hammiškān lᵉ'ōhel-hāʿēḏuṯ).* The thought is probably that the tent of the testimony enclosed the tabernacle (as in Exod. 26:7 and probably Num. 3:26–27).

God's presence has been previously portrayed using the images of *cloud* and *fire.* Some texts use the word *pillar (ʿammûḏ)* to describe the theophany in cloud and fire (e.g., Exod. 13:21–22; 14:19, 24; 33:9–10) and some do not (e.g., Exod. 19:9; 40:34, 38).[6] God met the people in cloud and fire just outside Egypt in the wilderness; he led them through the wilderness to Mt. Sinai, where the "thick cloud" *(ʿaḇ heʿānān)* descended, representing the divine presence on the mountain. Here, as well as in Exod. 40:34–38, the presence of God finds a new dwelling place — the tabernacle. From Exod. 40 through Num. 9:15 the site of revelation is not the mountain but the sanctuary. God is preparing to be with the people as they leave Sinai for the land of Canaan.

17 This verse introduces the second theme of the passage, treated in vv. 17–23. The people moved their camp only in response to Yahweh's command, which was seen in the ascent or descent of the cloud. Although the present context does not address it, the final text of Numbers leads the reader to conclude that the ascent and descent of the cloud was used to guide the Israelites on the march (14:14). The theme of the text moves from departure to encampment because the Israelites were already encamped at Sinai. The next logical step was departure. The order will be reversed, however, as the passage progresses.

18a The order of elements in this first occurrence of the obedience formula *(According to the command of Yahweh the children of*

5. For this use of the imperfect tense, see, e.g., Driver, *Treatise on the Use of the Tenses in Hebrew,* § 30.

6. The use of the word *pillar* to describe the cloud/fire theophany has been seen as marking the putative documents JE and P. See, e.g., G. Henton Davies, *IDB,* III:817.

Israel departed, and according to the command of Yahweh they encamped) is the same as in v. 17. This formula will be repeated but in reversed order in vv. 20b and 23a.

18b–20a Since the formula of v. 18a ends with the theme of encampment, the author places like themes with like themes and expands on "encampment" in these verses. The basic thrust of the section is that the Israelites remained encamped *all the days in which the cloud sat over the tabernacle* (*kol-yᵉmê-ʼᵃšer yiškōn heʻānān ʻal hammiškān,* v. 18b), whether that time was *many days* (*yāmîm rabbîm,* v. 19) or *a few days* (*yāmîm mispār,* v. 20). The occupation of the people during their encampment is summarized by the clause *the children of Israel kept the watch of Yahweh (wᵉšāmᵉrû ḇᵉnê yiśrāʼēl mišmereṯ YHWH).* The expression *kept the watch of Yahweh,* when connected with the sanctuary or the Levites, means "guard duty."[7] Here the term is more general because the "keepers" of this "guard duty" are the Israelites generally and not only the Levites. Even so, the term should be allowed to keep its connotation of a special guarding or watching to make sure that obedience to Yahweh was exact and complete.[8]

20b The second occurrence of the departure formula places like with like again. Thus the formula begins with encampment. In addition to knitting the section together, this wording shifts the emphasis in the later part of the verse to the theme of departure, which the next section expands.

21–22 In some ways these verses combine the themes of encampment and departure. Parts of vv. 21–22 deal with the cloud's remaining over the tent, but the most common verbs are "to be lifted up" (*ʻālâ,* Niphal, twice) and "to depart" (*nāsaʻ,* four times), thus giving some emphasis to the latter. No matter how long the cloud remained over the tent, whether it was only *from evening until morning* (v. 21), *two days* (v. 22), *a month* (v. 22), or even longer, as soon as the cloud was lifted from the tabernacle, the people departed.

23 The third formula is in the same form as the previous one. Although this breaks the pattern of placing like with like, the verse does conclude with the theme of departure, which is the same theme with which the passage began in v. 18a. This verse thus completes a chiasm. V. 23b repeats the obedience formula *at the command of Yahweh,* but this time it is expanded by the addition of the phrase *through* (lit., "by the hand of")

7. See the commentary above on 1:53; 3:7.
8. See Milgrom, *Studies in Levitical Terminology,* I: 8–12.

Moses. The command of Yahweh that is mediated through his servant Moses is that *the watch of Yahweh* is to be kept. Again, this formula emphasizes the careful and exact obedience to Yahweh that is so important to the author of Numbers.

b. Silver Trumpets (10:1–10)

1 *And Yahweh spoke to Moses, saying:*
2 *"Make for yourself two silver trumpets. Of hammered work you shall make them, and they will be for the convoking of the congregation and the breaking up of the camp.*
3 *When they blow them, then all the congregation will gather to you, to the door of the tent of meeting.*
4 *But when they blow one, then the leaders, the heads of the clans of Israel, will gather to you.*
5 *When you blow an alarm signal, then the camps which are encamped to the east will depart.*
6 *And when you blow a second alarm signal, the camps which are encamped to the south will depart. An alarm signal will be blown for their departing.*
7 *And when the assembly is to gather, you will blow but not give the alarm signal.*
8 *Now the sons of Aaron, the priests, will blow on the trumpets. And they will be for you a perpetual ordinance through your generations.*
9 *And when you go to war in your land, against the foe who harasses you, then you shall give the alarm signal on the trumpets, that you may be remembered before Yahweh your God and be saved from your enemies.*
10 *Also, in your day of joy, in your appointed feasts, and in your month's beginning you shall blow on the trumpets over your whole burnt offerings, and they will be for you for a remembrance before your God. I am Yahweh your God.*

The verses concerning the silver trumpets conclude the first major section of the book. They fit well into the context of the divine presence and guidance as set forth in 9:15–23. The tribal groups would need a device to direct their movements on the march, and these silver trumpets would meet such a need. They were tools to aid the people in following God's instructions. The section is marked off by the typical introductory formula in v. 1. The formula *I am Yahweh your God* (v. 10) is used elsewhere to conclude units of priestly legislation.[1] Thus this pericope is framed by the identity of the divine lawgiver.

2 *trumpet (ḥ^a^ṣōṣ^e^râ).* This term refers to a different instrument from the *šôp̄ār,* which the AV sometimes translated "trumpet," but which was made from a ram's horn. Later, Josephus described these instruments as slightly less than a cubit in length (i.e., between 18 and 20 in.) and constructed of a narrow tube ending in a bell.[2] Similar instruments are known to have existed in Egypt from at least the beginning of the 15th cent. B.C. A particularly well-known example, also made of silver, was discovered in Tutankhamen's tomb (mid-14th cent. B.C.). Thus such instruments did exist in the Mosaic age.[3]

The trumpets are to be made of *silver.* Further, they are to be of *hammered work (miqšâ),* like the cherubim as well as the menorah in the tabernacle.[4] The basic meaning of *miqšâ* is unknown, but scholars agree for the most part on the translation itself.[5]

Verse 2b sets out the function of these trumpets. First, they are to be used to assemble the congregation *(hāʿēḏâ),* all the adult males representing the whole people, or the assembly *(haqqāhāl),* the worshiping community. Second, a special signal (or alarm, *t^e^rûʿâ,* from a verb meaning "to shout") is to be blown to indicate that the tribes were to break camp and move out, following the order set forth in ch. 2.

3–8a The first function of the trumpets was to gather the people to the tabernacle (vv. 3–4). When a certain sound was produced on both

1. For the opening formula, see, e.g., Num. 1:1; 2:1; 3:5, 11, 14. For the closing formula, see, e.g., Lev. 18:30; 19:25, 31, 34, 36; 20:7, 24; 23:22, 43; 25:7, 38, 55; 26:13; Num. 15:41. For a shorter formula, "I am Yahweh," see, e.g., Lev. 18:6, 21; 19:12, 14, 16–17, 28, 32, 37.

2. Josephus, *Ant.* 3.12.6.

3. See, e.g., F. W. Galpin, *Music of the Sumerians and Their Immediate Successors the Babylonians and the Assyrians* (1936; Freeport, N.Y.: Books for Libraries Press, repr. 1970), p. 21. See also plate XI, 25. The dimensions of the horn from Tutankhamen's tomb are: length 22⅞ in.; narrow width, ½ in.; width of bell 3¼ in. (ibid., p. 90 n. 14). See also E. Werner, *IDB,* III:473, illustration 87; C. C. J. Polin, *Music of the Ancient Near East* (New York: Vantage, 1954), pp. 40 (fig. F), 41–42, 66; C. Sachs, *Real Lexicon der Musikinstrumente* (1912; repr. New York: Dover, 1964), p. 77; S. Marcuse, *Musical Instruments: A Comprehensive Dictionary* (Garden City, N.Y.: Doubleday, 1964), p. 238; Harrison, *Introduction,* p. 623; de Vaulx, p. 130; Sturdy, p. 74.

4. For the cherubim, see Exod. 25:18; 37:7. For the menorah, see Exod. 25:13; 37:17, 22; Num. 8:4.

5. See, e.g., BDB, p. 904b; KB, p. 562a; Budd, p. 105.

trumpets (the verb is simply *tāqaʿ*, "to blow"), then all adult males of the congregation, representing the whole people, were to gather. If only one trumpet was blown, then only the leaders *(neśîʾîm)* were to attend at the entrance of the tabernacle. Another sound, an *alarm signal* (*terûʿâ* again), was sounded to indicate that the tribes were to set out on the march. The Hebrew text gives as an example the departure of the groups on the east and the south of the tabernacle. One assumes that the departure of the other groups is summed up in v. 6b.[6]

The two functions are outlined by way of summary in v. 7, and in v. 8a the priests are given the responsibility for sounding the trumpets (for a later example of this function, see 2 Chr. 29:26). Throughout vv. 3–7 the text makes clear that two different signals were used. The exact difference between the two is not known; it may have been a difference in tone, duration, or both. Jewish tradition is that the convocation sound (vv. 3–4) was a long steady blast, while the alarm signal (vv. 5–6) was a succession of three shorter notes.[7]

8b–10 The trumpets are said to be given as a *perpetual ordinance* (*leḥuqqaṯ ʿôlām,* v. 8a). This term is used elsewhere in Exodus, Leviticus, and Numbers to refer to a legal enactment that is underlined as particularly relevant or important. Other perpetual ordinances deal with matters such as the Passover (Exod. 12), the Day of Atonement (Lev. 16), and the ritual of the red heifer (Num. 19), all of which concern the priests in a special way, although the laity are also involved.[8]

That this particular enactment is called a *perpetual ordinance* led to the addition of two extensions to the use of the trumpets that would

6. LXX gives an account of the third and fourth trumpet blasts, but there seems to be no reason to accept LXX's reading as original (contra Budd, p. 105). MT gives an example only of the march, the full text of which has already been developed in ch. 2. In fact, LXX leaves the departure of the tabernacle itself out of its translation (see 2:17).

7. See Snaith, p. 137; Wenham, p. 102. Mish. *Roš Haššana* 4:9 indicates that the convocation sound *(tqʿ)* was actually three times longer than the departure signal *(terûʿâ);* cf. Polin, *Music of the Ancient Near East,* p. 66, for further material on the difference between the two sounds.

8. In addition to the priestly involvements mentioned above, note the following perpetual ordinances: Exod. 27:21; Lev. 24:3 (tending the lamp); Exod. 28:43 (priests' vestments); 29:9 (the priesthood itself); Lev. 3:17 (no fat or blood to be consumed with the peace offerings); 7:36 (priests' portion of the peace offerings); 10:9 (no priestly drunkenness in the tabernacle); 17:7; Num. 15:15 (sacrifices); Lev. 23:14, 21, 31, 41 (cultic calendar). All of these matters directly concern the priests. Num. 18:23 redefines the Levites' function.

become relevant only as Israel came into Canaan. The *alarm signal* is to be used in future battles in the land (v. 9; see also Num. 31:6 and 2 Chr. 13:12–16). The convocation signal is to be used in the land to summon the people to worship at festal occasions (v. 10; see also 1 K. 11:14; 2 Chr. 5:12–14; Ezra 3:10–11; Ps. 98:6). Thus, these trumpets were to summon the people to action even after the situation of the wilderness was no longer relevant. The use of the trumpets for war and for worship is also paralleled by the use of trumpets in New Kingdom Egypt. This parallel may also serve to anchor the materials of this passage in the Mosaic period.[9]

9. See H. Hickman, "Die kultische Verwendung der altägyptischen Trompete," *WO* 1 (1950) 351–55. Of course, because such instruments are found at a time around that of Moses does not prove that this portion of Numbers was written then.

II. THE JOURNEY FROM MT. SINAI TO KADESH-BARNEA (10:11–12:16)

The second major section of Numbers begins with the people's departure from the wilderness of Sinai and ends with their arrival in the wilderness of Paran. It consists of the first of two travel sections in the book (the second occurs in 20:1–22:1). Many commentators attach these travel sections to the ones that precede or follow, but since these times of travel form distinct sections of narrative where important happenings take place, it seems better to distinguish them as main sections.

These chapters break into two major parts; 10:11–36 and 11:1–12:16. After a reaffirmation of the people's identity (10:11–28, which is mostly a recapitulation of material from ch. 2), and the incident between Moses and Hobab (10:29–32), the people set out for the land of promise (10:33–36). Chs. 11–12 deal with three crises of authority along the way, all connected with specific sites (Taberah, 11:1–3; Kibroth-hattaavah, 11:4–35; Hazeroth, 12:1–16). These various subsections are all clearly marked either by formulae (e.g., 10:11, 28) or by shifts in subject matter (e.g., 10:29).

It is possible that a number of sources underlie the present text. Scholars who accept the documentary hypothesis have assigned 10:11–28 to P and 10:29–12:16 to JE.[1] Whether these documents ever existed is an issue that is, once again, being debated within OT studies. Other sources, such as an order of tribes on the march (10:11–36; cf. ch. 2) or lists of campsites (chs. 11–12) may also underlie the present text. Whatever sources may have been used have been made into a cogent whole by the editor of the material. What is important for purposes of commenting on a text is its final form, not hypothetical predecessors of it.

1. See, e.g., Gray, pp. xxvii, xxxi; Sturdy, pp. 76, 78, 80, 83–84, 88–89; Snaith, pp. 138–46; Budd, pp. xxi–xxii, 109–10, 113–14, 117, 124, 126, 133.

A. DEPARTURE FROM MT. SINAI (10:11–36)

11 *And it happened that in the second year, in the second month, on the twentieth day of the month, the cloud was taken up from upon the tabernacle of the testimony,*

12 *and the children of Israel embarked on their journeyings from the wilderness of Sinai. And the cloud settled down in the wilderness of Paran.*

13 *They moved out initially at the command of Yahweh through*[1] *Moses.*

14 *The standard of the camp of the sons of Judah moved out first, by their hosts. Over its host was Nahshon son of Amminadab.*

15 *Over the host of the tribe of the sons of Issachar was Nathanel son of Zuar.*

16 *And over the host of the tribe of the sons of Zebulun was Eliab son of Helon.*

17 *Then the tabernacle was dismantled, and the sons of Gershon and the sons of Merari set out as bearers of the tabernacle.*

18 *Then the standard of the camp of Reuben set out, by their hosts. Over its host was Elizur son of Shedeur.*

19 *Over the host of the tribe of the sons of Simeon was Shelumiel son of Zurishaddai.*

20 *And over the host of the tribe of the sons of Gad was Eliasaph son of Deuel.*[2]

21 *Then the Kohathites, bearers of the sacred things,*[3] *set out, so the tabernacle could be erected by the time of their arrival.*

22 *Then the standard of the camp of the sons of Ephraim, by their hosts, and over its host was Elishama son of Ammihud.*

23 *Over the host of the tribe of the sons of Manasseh was Gamaliel son of Pedahzur.*

24 *And over the host of the tribe of the sons of Benjamin was Abidan son of Gideoni.*

25 *Then the standard of the camp of Dan set out, as a rear guard for all the camps, by their hosts. And over its host was Ahiezer son of Ammishaddai.*

26 *Over the host of the tribe of the sons of Asher was Pagiel son of Ochran.*

1. MT *b^{e}yaḏ*, lit., "by the hand of," as, e.g., in 9:23.

2. LXX renders *Ragouel* (i.e., Reuel) here as well as in 1:14; 7:42, 47; MT has Reuel at 2:14, but Deuel everywhere else. Reuel is possibly a copyist's error for the more commonly found Deuel.

3. On this translation of *hammiqdāš,* see Milgrom, *Studies in Levitical Terminology,* I:23–24 n. 78.

27 *And over the host of the tribe of the sons of Naphtali was Ahira son of Enan.*
28 *These were the orders of march for the children of Israel, by their hosts. And they set out.*
29 *And Moses said to Hobab the son of Reuel the Midianite, the father-in-law of Moses, "We are setting out for the place about which Yahweh has said, 'I will give it to you.' Come with us and we will do good for you, for Yahweh has said good things concerning Israel."*
30 *But he said to him, "I will not go; rather, I will go to my own land and kindred."*
31 *And he said, "Do not leave us, I pray, for you know the way wherein we are to encamp in the wilderness, and you can be our eyes for us.*
32 *And it will be that, if you come with us, then the good that Yahweh does for us, we will do for you."*
33 *And they set out from the mountain of Yahweh a three days' journey. And the ark of the covenant of Yahweh set out ahead of them on the three days' journey to find a place of rest for them.*
34 *Also the cloud of Yahweh was over them by day as they departed from the camp.*
35 *And it happened when the ark departed that Moses said, "Arise, O Yahweh, and let your enemies be scattered and let those who hate you flee before you."*
36 *And when it rested he said, "Return,*[4] *O Yahweh, to*[5] *the myriads*[6] *of clans*[7] *of Israel."*

11 *in the second year.* The departure date here is over eleven months after their arrival at the mountain, nearly fourteen months after their departure from Egypt, and nineteen days after the census of 1:1.

4. Some scholars (e.g., Noordtzij, p. 96; Noth, pp. 79–80; cf. *BHS*) have chosen to read "descend" *(šᵉḇâ)* rather than "return" *(šûḇâ),* but no textual evidence supports such a change. The form of the latter also provides a better parallel to *qûmâ,* "arise," the first word of v. 35.

5. MT has no preposition, but the verb *šûḇ* followed by an accusative of direction is a relatively common feature of the language. See Gray, p. 97; GKC, §§ 118d, f.

6. Several emendations of MT *riḇᵉḇôṯ* have been suggested, including reading *ûḇēraḵtā,* "and bless," or *wᵉraḇtā,* "and increase" (see *BHS*). The whole verse, as reconstructed, e.g., by Noordtzij, then reads, "Return, O Yahweh, and bless the thousands of Israel" (cf. p. 96). But these suggestions are without adequate textual evidence, and MT should be retained.

7. On the word *clans (ʾalᵉp̱ê),* see the commentary above on 1:16.

12 This verse is a summary description of all the narratives through ch. 12. The stations on the way to the wilderness of Paran (at which place they arrive in 12:16) are Taberah (11:1–3),[8] Kibroth-hattaavah (11:4–35), and Hazeroth (12:1–16a).

the wilderness of Paran. The identification of geographical sites is difficult because often no trace of a biblical name remains on a site. Since the Hebrews did not occupy or hold this territory to any great extent, one would not expect the name they gave to a site to leave any trace. *Paran* is mentioned in Gen. 14:6; 21:21; Num. 12:16; 12:3, 26; Deut. 1:1; 33:2; 1 Sam. 25:1; 1 K. 11:18; and Hab. 3:3. These texts indicate that Paran was north of the traditional site of Mt. Sinai and west of Midian (see 1 K. 11:18). It may have extended as far north as Kadesh-barnea, since Num. 13:26 identifies Kadesh as a site within it.[9] It may be that Paran was a general term descriptive of most of the wilderness areas of the Sinai.[10] This conclusion would have the advantage of explaining the double identification of the location of Kadesh-barnea (Zin and Paran, Num. 20:1; 27:14; 33:36, etc.), and also the absence of Paran in the itinerary list of Num. 33, since, on this hypothesis, many or most of the sites would be located within the wilderness of Paran.

13 *through Moses.* Once again Moses is the mediator between Yahweh and Israel. The reference here may be to Moses' initiation of the procedure with the trumpets described by 10:5–6.

14–27 On the list of the tribes and leaders, see the commentary above on 1:5–15, 20–47.[11] The order of the tribal organization is that of 2:3–31 and 7:10–83. The list is used at this point to show both continuity with the past and the development of new elements for the future. From a human standpoint the leadership of the tribes is the same as that in ch. 1, thus showing stability and continuity with what has already come to pass. The new element in this list, compared with the list of ch. 2 — and, one might argue, the reason why this text has been transmitted — is found

8. Taberah is not counted as a separate station by Num. 33:16–17, and some (e.g., Keil, pp. 64–65) have thought it identical with Kibroth-hattaavah. See below.

9. The borders of Paran must have been fluid, for Num. 20:1; 27:14; 33:36; etc., put Kadesh within the wilderness of Zin. For a good summary of the data here, see T. V. Briscoe, "Paran," *ISBE,* rev., III:662.

10. See Y. Aharoni, *Land of the Bible: A Historical Geography,* tr. and ed. A. F. Rainey, rev. ed. (Philadelphia: Westminster, 1979), p. 199.

11. On these lists as the crucial part of the structure of the book see Olson, *Death of the Old,* esp. chs. 4–5 (pp. 55–125).

in 10:17. This verse narrates the fact that the Gershonite and Merarite Levites dismantled the structure of the tabernacle and set out after the first group of tribes departed.[12] The rationale for this change in operations is obvious, and is set forth by the text itself in 10:21: *so the tabernacle could be erected by the time of their* (i.e., the Kohathites with the holy things) *arrival.* Gray's comment that the holy things would thus be left unsheltered before the march is beside the point, since Aaron and his sons would already have covered all these items before the tabernacle itself was dismantled.[13]

21 *the sacred things (hammiqdāš)* include items such as the lampstand, table, altar, and the various utensils. Are we to include the ark of the covenant as one of *the sacred things,* as it was in 4:4–20? If so, then this verse contradicts vv. 33–36 below, which place the ark at the head of the whole people on the march. Some scholars accept this contradiction and explain it as the result of different sources being set side by side.[14] One could hardly use the word *editing* for such a procedure. The alternative is to read all of vv. 12–36 as a unity. There is no reason to conclude that the ark must be included in the sacred things of 10:21, especially since it is mentioned specifically as in a different place in 10:33–36. Were the solution to be found along source-critical lines, one would have to explain why the final editor of Numbers (who is usually thought to have been at least under the influence of the standpoint of P) would allow verses such as 33–36, which contradict his earlier view (2:17) that the ark was moved in the midst of the tribes, to remain here. Vv. 33–36 make more sense as the announcement of a change in the position of the ark, perhaps on the basis of Hobab's refusal to lead the people.[15] While many scholars still accept the source-critical solution, it seems that it does not answer the questions of the present form of the text.

28 This verse forms a concluding summary to the preceding section, a literary device that has been seen before (e.g., in 2:32–34; 3:20b; 5:29–30; 6:21).

29–32 This unit concerns Moses' request of Hobab, the son of Reuel the Midianite, to help provide guidance through the wilderness on the basis of his knowledge of the logistics of encamping in the wilderness

12. Cf. 2:16–17, where the tabernacle and its furnishings depart after the second group of tribes.

13. Gray, p. 92.

14. E.g., Gray, pp. 90–97; Snaith, pp. 138–39; Budd, pp. 109–16, etc.

15. See the commentary below on 10:29–32.

(see v. 31). Hobab declines, however, preferring to return to his own people in Midian. Some commentators have concluded from Hobab's statement that Midian and Canaan lay along completely different routes from Sinai, thus telling against a southern location for the mountain. This conclusion misses the point of Hobab's statement, which is no more than his wish to go his own way to his homeland (perhaps via a shortcut not traversable by the many Hebrews with all their belongings). This text does not disclose whether Hobab was convinced by Moses' entreaties, but if Hobab's name is original to the text of Judg. 1:16, as is possible, then his descendants were still with the Israelites in the conquest period.[16]

Verse 29 is ambiguous; was Hobab or Reuel the *ḥōṯēn* (usually translated "father-in-law") of Moses? Hobab is clearly called his *ḥōṯēn* in Judg. 4:11, and, although Reuel never is called Moses' *ḥōṯēn* (at least in the MT), Exod. 2:16–18 implies that he was. The problem is compounded by Exod. 3:1; 4:18; 18:1–2, 5–6, 12, which name Moses' *ḥōṯēn* as Jether or Jethro. The situation is complicated even further by the fact that, in Judg. 4:11, Hobab is called a Kenite, while here (by implication) he is a Midianite. Many scholars simply echo Snaith's statement that we have "three separate traditions and three distinct names" regarding the identity of Moses' father-in-law.[17] Thus many solve this difficulty by assigning the various names to the various putative documents of the Pentateuch, e.g., Hobab to J and Jethro to E. It is also common to assume that the name Reuel is a gloss in Exod. 2:18 on the basis of a mistaken reading of the current verse in Num. 10.[18]

Many scholars, both those who have assumed the classical documents thought to underlie the present Pentateuch and those who have not, have posited that two of these three individuals are the same man. The question is, Which two? Some have said that Reuel/Jethro is the father-in-law of Moses and Hobab is Reuel/Jethro's son. This view requires that one translate *ḥōṯēn* in Judg. 4:11 (and 1:16) in some other way than "father-in-law" (see below). Others have posited that Hobab and Reuel

16. The reading with the name Hobab in the text of Judg. 1:16 is supported by Codex Alexandrinus (LXX) and by a wide range of commentators, including J. A. Soggin, *Joshua: A Commentary,* tr. J. Bowden, OTL (Philadelphia: Westminster, 1981), pp. 19, 23. For a discussion of the data, see also J. Gray, *Joshua, Judges and Ruth,* rev. ed., NCBC (Grand Rapids: Eerdmans, 1986), pp. 237–38.

17. Snaith, p. 138. Snaith is echoing others.

18. E.g., S. R. Driver, *Introduction,* pp. 22–23; A. H. McNeile, *The Book of Exodus,* Westminster Commentaries (London: Methuen, 1917), p. 11; also idem, "Midianite Elements in Hebrew Religion," *JTS* 31 (1930) 340.

are the same man and that Jethro is his father. At first sight, this solution is attractive, since both Hobab and Jethro are called the *ḥōṯēn* of Moses (e.g., Judg. 4:11 and Exod. 3:1). One problem with this view is Exod. 2:16–22, which makes clear that the priest of Midian had seven daughters (v. 16), that the name of this man was Reuel (v. 18), and that this man gave Zipporah to Moses for a wife (v. 22). The only way around this difficulty is to see the word *father* used in v. 18 as indicating "grandfather" or "head of the house," as it sometimes does.[19]

Another problem with this view is W. F. Albright's contention that Jethro and Hobab are portrayed as very different persons: Jethro being old enough to give Moses advice (Exod. 18) and Hobab young and energetic enough to lead the people in the wilderness (Num. 10).[20] In fairness, it should be said that much of the difference between Hobab and Jethro must be read into the texts, since neither Exod. 18 nor Num. 10 says anything about the relative youth, age, or energy of either person. A more serious objection to this view is found in Exod. 18:27, which states that Moses' father-in-law "went away into his own country." Did he change his mind and stay for nearly one more year? Did he come back? Probably not. Thus it seems difficult to hold that Hobab and Jethro were one individual.[21]

Other solutions assume that the three named characters may be three different personae; any of these solutions requires a wider meaning than "father-in-law" for *ḥōṯēn,* since both Hobab and Jethro are called the *ḥōṯēn* of Moses. The simplest solution seems to be that if Reuel is the father of Hobab and the father-in-law of Moses (Exod. 2:16–22), then Hobab must be the brother-in-law of Moses, and Reuel and Jethro must be the same man. A whole range of scholars have translated *ḥōṯēn* in this way.[22] T. C. Mitchell has attempted to show that the root *ḥtn* (regardless of the vowels) meant something like "a relative by marriage"; hence "father-in-law," "brother-in-law," or "son-in-law" (see below) would be possible, as the context required.[23]

19. E.g., Gen. 28:13; 32:10; 2 K. 15:3; see *bêṯ-'āḇ* in Num. 3:30, 35, etc.

20. W. F. Albright, "Jethro, Hobab and Reuel in Early Hebrew Tradition," *CBQ* 25 (1963) 7.

21. Very few modern commentators have held this view.

22. See the list in G. F. Moore, *A Critical and Exegetical Commentary on the Book of Judges,* ICC (Edinburgh: T. & T. Clark, 1895), p. 33; also Keil, p. 60; and idem, more clearly, on Exod. 2:16–18 (*Pentateuch,* I:434).

23. T. C. Mitchell, "The meaning of the noun *ḥtn* in the Old Testament," *VT* 19 (1969) 93–112.

Albright offered a more complex solution.[24] He attempted to show that, first, Reuel is not a personal name but a clan name; second, Jethro and Hobab are different persons, and *ḥōṯēn*, "father-in-law," should be vocalized *ḥāṯān*, "son-in-law," in Hobab's case; and third, in those texts that called Hobab a Kenite, the word translated "Kenite" should be rendered by the root's original meaning of "smith, metalworker."[25] One problem that this view produces is the need to create a daughter for Moses of whom we otherwise know nothing.

From the foregoing survey, it is clear that no proposed view is entirely satisfactory or free from difficulties. One needs to be careful not to expect too much of solutions proposed for ancient documents that were not designed to give the information needed for a solution. No solution to any literary or historical problem is entirely free from objection. On the basis of the proposals here mentioned, the simplest would be to read *ḥōṯēn* as Keil, Wenham, and many others have done. The slightly more complex view of Albright is also attractive.

Verses 29–32 suggest that Moses desired to have Hobab's special expertise in the wilderness — since Israel's immediate future lay in the wilderness. This text pictures shared human leadership. (The ark narrative that follows suggests a change in the position of the ark, hence a modification in the way divine leadership is shown for the immediate future as well.) The picture of Moses is thus one of a leader who does not dictate all alone, but one who shares the leadership (see below on 11:4–35). The verses give the reader important information so that the complaints of chs. 11–12 can be seen in their proper contexts (especially Miriam and Aaron's complaint in ch. 12). Moses' special status is God's will, not Moses'.

In a literary sense this narrative returns to the theme of a Midianite advisor to Moses with which the whole Sinai story began (i.e., Jethro and Moses in Exod. 18), and thus forms an inclusio with Exod. 18. The Midianite theme provides continuity between the beginning and the end (Exod. 18; Num. 10), but there is also development for the future because the Midianite is no longer Jethro the father-in-law, but his son Hobab, the brother-in-law of Moses.

33–36 This passage functions in a number of ways. First, its

24. Albright, "Jethro, Hobab and Reuel," pp. 1–11.

25. On the first point, see ibid., p. 5, esp. n. 14 (at this point Albright followed Gray, p. 93). On the second point, see p. 7, esp. n. 22. On the third point, see pp. 8–9; the passages are Judg. 1:16 and 4:11.

initial words *(And they set out, wayyisᵉʿû)* look back to the same words in the summary statement of v. 12 and bring the description of the departure to completion. All the material in vv. 12–32 happened before the actual departure. Second, the passage informs the reader of the change in the position of the ark from within the tribes to a position at their head (cf. 2:17). This shift shows the inadequacy of mere human leadership (even Moses') to bring the people to victory in Canaan. Third, this new position of the ark is shown not to cancel or make unnecessary the presence of the cloud. Here again, the theme of continuity and development is seen. In the previous journey from Egypt to Sinai the people had been led by the cloud of Yahweh.[26] The new stage of the journey would have not only the continuity of the old cloud, but also the development of the ark's leadership, symbolizing Yahweh on his throne, to assure the people of divine leadership in the days ahead. Fourth, growing out of what has already been said, the passage sets the leadership of Yahweh and the rebellion of the people in stark contrast. According to Yahweh's will the people would be fortunate and well-off (see 10:29), but almost immediately the people begin to complain about their misfortune (chs. 11–12). Finally, vv. 35–36, although somewhat different in form, function in the same way as Aaron's blessing in 6:22–27, i.e., they conclude a major section of text with a wish for an act of Yahweh on behalf of the people.

33 *a three days' journey (dereḵ šᵉlōšeṯ yāmîm).* This phrase occurs twice in the verse. The first instance has to do with the length of the journey from Sinai to the first stopping place.[27] One cannot be sure of the actual distance of such a journey, with the whole company of Israel unaccustomed to travel in the wilderness. The second occurs as part of a longer clause describing the ark's position for the journey. One can be fairly sure that the ark was not three days' journey ahead of the whole people, for it would be out of sight and hence useless for guidance and assurance. It is tempting simply to excise the phrase as an inadvertent repetition that entered the text from the first part of the verse, but there is little textual evidence for such a change.[28] The temporal sense of the

26. Heb. *ʿᵃnan YHWH;* see Exod. 13:21–22; 14:19–20, 24–25; 16:10; 33:7–11; summarized in Num. 9:15–23 and mentioned again in 10:11.

27. Probably Kibroth-hattaavah; cf. 11:34; 33:16.

28. So, e.g., *BHS;* Gray, p. 95; Noordtzij, p. 94; Snaith, p. 139; Noth, pp. 74, 78; Budd, p. 112. The only textual evidence comes from Pesh., which reads "one day's journey" instead of "three days' journey."

phrase seems best; it describes the duration of the journey, during the whole of which the ark went before *(lip̱nê)* the people.[29]

34 *Also the cloud of Yahweh was over them (waʿanan YHWH ʿalêhem).* In addition to the ark, the cloud that had accompanied them in their sojourn heretofore continued to be over them. Some scholars wish to make much of the preposition *over (ʿal)* here. They say that this position of the cloud is much different from others, which state that the cloud goes "before" *(lip̱nê)* the people or rests "on" *(bᵉ)* the tabernacle.[30] Surely it is pedantic to expect rigorous exactitude of expression of any author, ancient or modern, every time a subject is discussed. This point is especially obvious since the preceding passage has used the preposition "before" *(lip̱nê)* to discuss the position of the ark. Nothing in this verse contradicts the summary of past movements of the cloud in 9:15–23 (which uses the preposition *ʿal* to describe the position of the cloud while on the march). Obviously, when the people were in the camp, the position of the cloud was different. Surely a cloud that is said to be "over" a people can also, from a slightly different viewpoint, be said to be "before" them without involving differences and contradictions in the story. It is simply a matter of the point-of-view of the observer.

35–36 These verses are enclosed in so-called inverted *nun*s in the MT. The meaning of these marks of punctuation, which also occur seven times in Ps. 107, is debated, but scholars generally agree that they indicate that the early scribes thought verses so enclosed were displaced from their original context.[31] Conjecture on a better or original context for these verses is fruitless, because they are found in *this* context, and hence one must explain how they fit here. They seem to function as a poetic conclusion to the whole passage concerning departure and, in a sense, to the whole of the Sinai story (Exod. 19–Num. 10).

Return, O Yahweh, to the myriads of clans of Israel (šûḇâ YHWH riḇᵉḇôṯ ʾalᵉp̱ê yiśrāʾēl). When the ark "rests," it symbolizes Yahweh's presence with his people. *Myriad clans (riḇᵉḇôṯ ʾalᵉp̱ê)* — The second word may also be translated as "thousand," although one might, then,

29. See GKC, §§ 118i, k; Williams, *Syntax,* § 56; so also many English versions including AV, NASB, NIV, NKJV, NJPS.

30. See, e.g., Gray, p. 96; cf. Snaith, p. 136.

31. See, e.g., the standard manual by B. J. Roberts, *The Old Testament Text and Versions* (Cardiff: Univ. of Wales Press, 1951), p. 34; and E. Würthwein, *The Text of the Old Testament,* tr. E. Rhodes (Grand Rapids: Eerdmans, 1979), p. 17.

expect the word order to be reversed. The theme of this passage is Israel's glorious leadership by Yahweh as the people depart from the Mountain of God for an immediate conquest of Canaan. There is no sense here of the impending doom that awaits Israel's rebellion in the wilderness. In this context the word *'elep* may more easily be thought to have its meaning as "clan-unit," especially a clan-unit for military purposes. The word *myriad* is a hyperbole that suggests that Israel's forces are invincible.[32]

B. CRISES OF AUTHORITY ALONG THE WAY (11:1–12:16)

Numbers 11:1–12:16 can be considered a literary unit. After a brief, schematic introduction in 11:1–3, two themes are interwoven: the specific problem of food for the people (11:4–13, 18–20, 31–34), leading to the problem of leadership for the people (11:16–17, 24–30; 12:1–15), connected by appropriate (but not identical) transitions (11:14–15, 21–23, 35; 12:16).

1. AT TABERAH (11:1–3)

1 *And the people took up murmuring[1] about their misfortune[2] in the ears of Yahweh, and Yahweh heard it and his anger burned. Then the fire of Yahweh burned among them and consumed the outskirts of the camp.*

2 *Then the people cried out to Moses, and Moses prayed to Yahweh, and the fire abated.*

3 *So he called the name of that place Taberah because the fire of Yahweh had burned among them there.*

Since Taberah is not listed in either 11:35 or 33:16–17 as one of the stations on the journey, and since the traditional formula for arriving at one of these stations is missing here, it is doubtful that Taberah should be counted as

32. See above, Excursus on Large Numbers; also Gottwald, *Tribes of Yahweh,* p. 281; J. Milgrom, *JPST,* pp. 335–39.

1. The *k*^{e} in *k*^{e}*miṯ'ōn*^{e}*nîm* is probably an asseverative particle, which indicates that, from the point of view of the narrator, the people were, in every respect and truly, murmuring. Cf. Gray, pp. 99–100; GKC, § 118x; Williams, *Syntax,* § 261.

2. *BHS* proposes (as does Snaith, though indirectly, p. 139) that, instead of MT *ra',* "evil, misfortune," *ra'aḇ,* "hunger," should be read. The text would then assert that the people are complaining from hunger, as in 11:4ff. There is no textual evidence for this emendation.

a separate campsite. The incident happened somewhere between Sinai and Kibroth-hattaavah.[3]

What is the purpose of this little story? It would seem that, rather than simply being an etiological tale to explain the name of a place in the memory of post-conquest Israel,[4] it is better seen as the first, and schematic, example of the disaffection and rebellion of Israel in the wilderness in response to Yahweh's clear provision of leadership on the way to the land of promise in the preceding narratives. This story may have an etiological motif, but this in no way jeopardizes the historicity of the place or the incident. The etiological element is subsumed under the general theme of "Rebellion and Murmuring in the Wilderness."[5]

1 *And the people took up murmuring about their misfortune* (*wayᵉhî hāʿām kᵉmiṯʾōnᵉnîm raʿ,* lit., "the people became like those murmuring of misfortune"). The immediate context gives no cause for this murmuring; indeed, it occurs in the context of Yahweh's gracious provision for the guidance and leadership of his people on the way (esp. in 9:15–10:35). Thus the complaining is more striking and contrasts with the murmuring found in the book of Exodus (e.g., 14:11–12; 15:24; 16:2–3; 17:2–3) and that which follows in Num. 11:4–34, both of which had external causes. Here the problem is left undefined. In contrast with the good *(ṭôḇ)* purposes of Yahweh for the people in the new land (see esp. Num. 11:29–32), this people murmurs about *misfortune* (*raʿ,* lit., "evil").

The people murmured *in the ears of Yahweh (bᵉʾoznê YHWH).* He heard it and was not indifferent to this uncaused rebellion: *his anger*

3. These formulae have been briefly discussed, e.g., in G. W. Coats, "The Wilderness Itinerary," *CBQ* 34 (1972) 135–38. Some scholars have identified Taberah and Kibroth-hattaavah (e.g., Keil, pp. 64–65), or suggested that the former was in the vicinity of the latter (e.g., Wenham, p. 106), but the text does not tell us that much. The literary function of introducing the narratives of rebellion in a general way is more important for this narrative than fixing where it happened.

4. So, e.g., Noth, pp. 83–84; Budd, p. 118; B. O. Long, *The Problem of Etiological Narrative in the Old Testament,* BZAW 108 (Berlin: Töpelmann, 1968), pp. 42–43.

5. See, e.g., J. F. Priest, "Etiology," *IDBSup,* pp. 293–95; B. Childs, "The Etiological Tale Re-examined," *VT* 24 (1974) 393–97. For general material on the etiological narrative, in addition to the literature just listed, see Long, *Problem,* pp. 42–47; F. Golka, "The Aetiologies in the Old Testament," *VT* 26 (1976) 410–28; 27 (1977) 36–47. On the theme of rebellion and murmuring, see G. Coats, *The Murmuring Motif in the Wilderness Traditions of the Old Testament: Rebellion in the Wilderness* (Nashville: Abingdon, 1968), pp. 21–264.

burned, and he sent a judgment: *the fire of Yahweh ('ēš YHWH).* Fire is a common biblical image for God's presence, as at the burning bush (Exod. 3:2) or at Mt. Sinai (19:18), and especially common as an image for God's judgment.[6] A further contrast here is between the fire of God used for divine guidance (as in the fiery pillar, e.g., Num. 9:15–16) and the fire of God used for judgment, as here. Since the fire led to the naming of the place as "the burning place" *(Taberah),* and since the fire is said to have *consumed* part of the camp, it is better to take this judgment as literal fire rather than as a metaphor for some other divine punishment.[7]

The fire consumed *the outskirts of the camp (biqṣēh hammaḥ^{a}neh).* Although this phrase is unique, *qaṣeh* is used elsewhere to describe an outer boundary.[8] Most times a contrast is drawn between that which is inside the camp (*b^e* or *'el hammaḥ^{a}neh*), hence ceremonially clean, safe, and permissible, and that which is outside the camp *(miḥûṣ hammaḥ^{a}neh),* hence ceremonially unclean, unsafe, and forbidden.[9] Here what is consumed by Yahweh's judging fire are those marginal areas, i.e., those areas near the outside of the camp where danger and uncleanness lurk.[10]

2 The people, seeing the fire of Yahweh, turn from their complaining and cry out, not directly to God, but to God's appointed leader, apparently to intercede with Yahweh for them. This appeal to Moses only underlines his special role, which Numbers has made abundantly clear already and which will be restated climactically in 12:4–8. It may also be one reason why the burden of the leadership was too great for Moses to bear.

and Moses prayed to Yahweh (wayyitpallēl mōšeh 'el YHWH). The verb "to pray" does not indicate general prayer here, but intercession. This

6. See, e.g., Lev. 9:24; 10:2; Num. 16:35; 21:28; 26:10; Deut. 9:3; Jer. 49:27; 50:23; Ezek. 28:18; 30:8, 14, 16; 36:5; 38:19; and esp. Amos 1:4, 7, 10, 12, 14; 2:2, 5; 5:6; 7:4. The NT also uses this image, e.g., in Matt. 13:40, 42, 50; 18:8–9; 25:41; 1 Cor. 3:13, 15; 2 Thess. 1:8; and frequently in Revelation.

7. While possible, the common assertion that this fire was caused by lightning (e.g., Gray, p. 99; Binns, p. 65; Noordtzij, p. 96; Milgrom, *JPST,* p. 82) cannot be supported from the text.

8. E.g., the end of a field, Gen. 23:9; the end of a valley, Josh. 15:8; the farthest border of a tribal holding, 15:21; the outer border of Moab, Num. 20:16; 22:36; the outskirts of a city, 1 Sam. 9:27; etc. See BDB, p. 892a.

9. For the former, see, e.g., Exod. 19:16; Lev. 14:8; 16:26, 28; as well as the detailed rules for the camp in Num. 1–9. For the latter, see, e.g., Lev. 14:3, 8; 16:27; 17:3.

10. See M. Douglas, *Purity and Danger: An Analysis of the Concepts of Pollution and Taboo* (London: Routledge & Kegan Paul, 1966), esp. chs. 6–10.

verb is not often used with Moses as the subject, and all of the occurrences are in response to a request from the people after rebellion.[11]

3 *Taberah (tab̲ʿērâ).* Noth has suggested several different roots from which the name may derive, none of them the one suggested by the text itself. His assumption is that this narrative exists to explain the name of a site in the Sinai that was "still known to the Israelites in the period after the conquest."[12] It is more likely, however, that the narrative is intended to introduce the series of rebellion narratives, and that the name Taberah is a specifically Hebrew one, given to the site by the Israelites. Thus the root from which Taberah is derived (*bʿr,* "burn") as given by the text is appropriate.[13] Since the Israelites left behind no sedentary population to carry on the memory of this place-name, one cannot expect that the name would have survived and come into popular usage at all. Thus the only places where Taberah is mentioned are in this passage and in Moses' remembrance of this incident in Deut. 9:22.

2. AT KIBROTH-HATTAAVAH (11:4–35)

4 *Now the rabble*[1] *that was in their midst had a craving, and the children of Israel also wept again, and they said, "Who will feed us meat?*[2]

5 *We remember*[3] *the fish we ate in Egypt for free as well as the cucumbers, the watermelons, the leeks, the onions, and the garlic,*

6 *but now our strength is dried up, there is nothing at all! Our eyes are only on the manna."*

11. Other occurrences are at Num. 21:7 and Deut. 9:20, 26 (the last two recalling the present incident). Of course, Moses interceded for the people on other occasions, but different verbs were used (e.g., Exod. 14:15; 15:25; 32:11–14, 31–33; Num. 14:5, 13–14).

12. Noth, p. 84.

13. Heb. *tab̲ʿērâ is a tau*-formation noun drawn from the Piel of the root *bʿr;* cf. S. Moscati, ed., *An Introduction to the Comparative Grammar of the Semitic Languages,* Porta Linguarum Orientalium (Wiesbaden: Harrassowitz, 1969), § 12.7.

1. MT *hāʾsapsup̲* is a hapax legomenon, apparently derived from the root *ʾsp,* "gather," hence "a gathering, group." See BDB, p. 63b; *HALAT,* p. 73a.

2. The interrogative sentence with *mî* may also express a wish, "O that we might have meat to eat." See Davidson, *Syntax,* § 135; GKC, § 151a n. 3. The current translation is more directly confrontal of Moses' leadership, which is the crux of the passage.

3. The perfect tense is used in verbs of remembering as an action, complete in any moment, yet ongoing; GKC, § 106g.

7 *Now the manna was like the seed of coriander, and its appearance was like the appearance of bdellium.*

8 *The people used to go about, gather it, grind it in mills or crush it in a mortar, boil it in a pot, and make cakes of it. And its taste was like the taste of dainty morsels with oil.*[4]

9 *When the dew fell upon the camp at night the manna fell along with it.*[5]

10 *Now Moses heard the people weeping, in their clans, each one at the door of his tent, and the anger of Yahweh burned exceedingly, and it was a bad thing in Moses' sight.*

11 *And Moses said to Yahweh, "Why have you dealt badly with your servant, and why have I not found favor in your sight, that you have placed*[6] *the burden of all this people on me?*

12 *Did I conceive this whole people, did I give them birth,*[7] *that you should say to me, 'Carry them in your bosom, as a nurse carries a suckling child, to the land that I swore to their fathers'?*[8]

13 *Where can I find meat to give to this whole people? For they weep against*[9] *me, saying, 'Give us meat that we might eat.'*

14 *I alone am not able to bear this whole people, for it is too heavy for me.*[10]

15 *If you*[11] *will deal in this way with me, kill me here and now,*[12] *if I find favor in your sight, that I might not see my misfortune."*

16 *And Yahweh said to Moses, "Gather*[13] *to me seventy men from the*

4. Note the perfects plus w^{e} following a perfect for past frequentative action; Davidson, *Syntax,* § 54 Rem. 1.

5. On this use of *ʿal* as "together with," see BDB, p. 755b; Williams, *Syntax,* § 293.

6. Heb. l^{e} plus infinitive can be a phrase of consequence or result. See Williams, *Syntax,* § 198.

7. The first part of the question here uses h^{a}, while the second, by large measure repetitive, uses *'im.* See Davidson, *Syntax,* § 124.

8. According to GKC, § 122f n. 1, the gender of *'ōmēn* here is only grammatical and the word should be translated as "nurse." Cf. *HALAT,* p. 62a.

9. The *ʿal* here is probably adversative. See Davidson, *Syntax,* p. 143 (note); Williams, *Syntax,* § 288.

10. The *min* in *mimmennî* is an elative, expressing the ultimate degree, "too heavy." See Williams, *Syntax,* § 318.

11. The pronoun *'at* is masc. only here, Deut. 5:24, and Ezek. 28:14 (GKC, § 32g). *BHS* suggests reading *t*^{ʿa}*śeh* or *'attā ṯa*^{ʿa}*śeh* to eliminate this rare (seemingly incorrect) form, but no textual evidence supports such a change.

12. *hār*^{e}*gēnî nā' hārōḡ* — The infinitive absolute after the imperative here indicates emphasis, certainty, or immediacy (unlike most usages with the finite verb). See Davidson, *Syntax,* § 86c; Williams, *Syntax,* § 205.

13. On the use of the emphatic imperative, see GKC, § 48i.

elders of Israel, whom you know to be elders of the people and
their officials, and you will take them to the tent of meeting, and
they will station themselves there with you.
17 *Then I will descend and I will speak with you there; and I will set*
apart some of the spirit that is upon you and I will place it upon
them; and they will bear a share of the people's burden with you,
and you will no longer bear it alone.
18 *And you will say to the people, 'Sanctify yourselves for tomorrow,*
and you will eat meat, because you have wept in the ears of
Yahweh, saying, "Who will feed us meat? It was good for us in
Egypt." So Yahweh will give you meat and you will eat it.'
19 *You will not eat one day, nor two days, nor five days, nor ten days,*
nor twenty days,
20 *but until a month of days, until it comes out from your nostrils and*
becomes a loathsome thing for you, on account of the fact[14] *that*
you have rejected Yahweh who is in your midst and wept before
him, saying, 'Why did we go out of Egypt?' "
21 *And Moses said, "The people in whose midst I am numbers*
600,000 men on foot, and you have said, 'I will give to them and
they will eat for a month of days'?
22 *Will flocks and herds be slaughtered for them, and so enough be*
found for them, or will all the fish of the sea be gathered for them,
and so enough be found for them?"
23 *And Yahweh said to Moses, "Is Yahweh's hand cut short? Now you*
will see whether[15] *my word will happen to you or not."*
24 *So Moses went out and he spoke to the people the words of Yahweh,*
and he gathered seventy men from the elders of the people and
stood them around the tent.
25 *And Yahweh descended in the cloud and spoke to him and set apart*
some of the spirit that was upon him and put it upon the seventy
men, the elders. And it happened that when the spirit settled down
on them they prophesied, but they did not continue to do so.[16]
26 *And two men were left behind in the camp. The name of the first*
was Eldad, and the name of the second was Medad. And the Spirit
of Yahweh rested on them. Although they were among those

14. Heb. *ya'an kî* is a way of introducing a causal sentence. See Davidson, *Syntax*, § 147; Williams, *Syntax*, § 363.

15. On h^{a}- used in indirect questions meaning "whether," see BDB, p. 210a; Davidson, *Syntax*, § 125; Williams, *Syntax*, § 543; GKC, § 150i.

16. MT w^{e}*lō' yāsāp̱û*, lit., "and they did not add"; cf. Sam. Pent. *y'spw*, "they did not gather"; Vulg. and Targs. presuppose *yāsup̱û*, "they did not cease" (followed by AV), which is the opposite sense of MT. As *BHS* indicates, MT should be retained.

registered, yet they did not go out to the tent, and they prophesied in the camp.

27 *And a certain*[17] *young man ran and told Moses, and said, "Eldad and Medad are prophesying in the camp."*

28 *And Joshua son of Nun, Moses' servant, one of his chosen young men, answered and said, "My lord Moses, prevent them!"*

29 *And Moses said to him, "Are you jealous on my account? O that Yahweh*[18] *would make all Yahweh's people prophets and that Yahweh would put his Spirit on them."*

30 *And Moses and the elders of Israel went back to the camp.*

31 *And a wind went up from Yahweh, and he brought quail from the sea; and they flew over the camp, about a day's journey on the one side and about a day's journey on the other side, round about the camp, and about two cubits above the surface of the ground.*

32 *And the people rose up all that day and all night and all the next day and gathered the quails. He who gathered the least gathered ten homers. And they spread*[19] *them out for themselves around the camp.*

33 *While the meat was still between their teeth, before the supply had been exhausted, Yahweh's anger burned among the people and Yahweh struck the people with a very great plague.*

34 *And the name of the place was called Kibroth-hattaavah, for there they buried the people who had the craving.*

35 *From Kibroth-hattaavah the people departed for Hazeroth, and they remained in Hazeroth.*

In the present passage the specific problem of dissatisfaction with food (11:4–6) leads Moses to question his own role as leader (before Miriam and Aaron do in ch. 12) and his leadership style (11:10–13). From this point on, the two themes of food and leadership are intertwined throughout the passage, and in the end the punishment (bad meat?) is brought about on the basis of the people's rejection of Yahweh's leadership (not Moses'; cf. 11:18–20). The three themes are interwoven as follows (A = Food Theme, B = Leadership Theme, T = Transition):

17. The definite article on *naʿar* indicates a certain young lad who was in the author's mind. In English the indefinite article might be more common in this case (i.e., *a* certain young man). See GKC, § 126r.

18. Here *mî* is a desiderative particle, "O that. . . ." See GKC, § 151b; Davidson, *Syntax,* § 135 Rem. 3.

19. The Qal infinitive absolute here with the finite verb indicates continuous action. See Davidson, *Syntax,* § 86c; Williams, *Syntax,* § 206.

A 11:4–13	A 11:18–20	A 11:31–34
T 11:14–15	T 11:21–23	T 11:35
B 11:16–17	B 11:24–30	B 12:1–15

Although it is possible to attempt to disengage one theme from the other, the result of such analysis is not two complete tales but fragments. The unitive factor in the narrative is the person of Moses himself. As the text stands the themes are related, and the primary task of the exegete is to explain the text, not its putative ancestor.[20]

The food theme has parallels in the stories of Exod. 16 (which took place in the wilderness of Sin between Elim and Sinai). The major thrust of this earlier narrative is the provision of the manna, although quails are mentioned in 16:13. At the end of Exod. 16 the narrator relates that manna was provided from that time until the Israelites came to the land of Canaan, and Josh. 5:12 confirms this provision. One major difference between the present narrative and Exod. 16 is that in the latter the murmuring brought about food as a blessing, whereas in Numbers the food is a punishment. The likelihood is that the author of Num. 11 assumes that readers will be familiar with the Exodus narrative. Whereas in Exodus the complaint was because of no food, in Numbers it is because the divinely provided manna is considered unsuitable or insufficient (see Num. 11:6), and this complaint is taken as rebellion against Yahweh's gracious provision. The people are punished with the very meat they wept to receive.

The leadership theme finds a parallel in the account of Jethro's visit to the Israelites in Exod. 18. According to 18:24–26, Moses had already appointed elders to help him in the legal administration. The major difference between that narrative and the one here in Numbers lies in the sharing of the spirit, with the resultant "prophesying" *(hiṯnabbē')*, and this difference should not be underplayed (see below).[21]

4–6 *the rabble.* This group seems to be set over against *the children of Israel (b^{e}nê yiśrā'ēl)*, and thus probably refers to the non-

20. The artificial separation of so-called documents was shown to be inadequate literary methodology long ago by W. H. Green's parody of the method. He divided two of Jesus' parables into sources, with interesting results (*Higher Criticism of the Pentateuch,* pp. 118–25).

21. Scholars generally assign both Exod. 18 and Num. 11 to JE (see, e.g., Gray, p. 116). The incidents, although similar, are clearly different. That similar tasks, in this case the appointment of elders to share the load with Moses, must be done more than once in a relatively short period of time can surprise no one who has been in a position of oversight — even among God's people!

Israelite element that came out of Egypt with the Hebrews.[22] This rabble *had a craving* (lit., "craved a craving," *hiṯ'awwû ta'ᵃwâ*). Both words come from the root *'wh,* which means "incline toward, desire." The verb occurs fifteen times in the Hithpael, meaning "to desire, crave, lust for," as here. The *tau*-formation noun *ta'ᵃwâ* means "desire" seven times in the negative sense of "craving, lust," as here (and about nine times in the neutral sense of "appetite").[23] The noun becomes the basis of the name given to the site in v. 35: Kibroth-hattaavah *(qiḇrôṯ hatta'ᵃwâ)*.

The Israelites *also wept again (wayyāšuḇû wayyiḇkû gam).* In combination with other verbs, the verb *šûḇ* ("to turn, return") lends an iterative sense to the construction, i.e., "to do something [e.g., weep] again."[24] Although no previous weeping *(bāḵâ)* is mentioned in this story, in the context the reference is probably to the murmuring and complaining of 11:1–3, or more distantly, to the narratives of Exod. 15:23–25 or 17:2–7. While the author may have wished ultimately to blame the non-Israelite element (who are not mentioned again by name), the people of Israel themselves soon took up the complaint, and thus deserved Yahweh's response.

The people contrasted *the fish (haddāgâ),* which they had eaten *for free (ḥinnām)* in Egypt, and various other foodstuffs ("cucumbers," *qiššu'îm;* "watermelons," *'ᵃḇaṭṭiḥîm;* "leeks," *ḥāṣîr;* and "onions," *bᵉṣālîm*) with what was available to them in the wilderness.[25] The act of looking back and remembering the good old days had one major flaw. The people remembered eating, but it was hardly *for free.*[26] In fact, the cost of that plenty had been slavery, and the contrast drawn by the people between the plenty of slavery and the *nothing at all* (except manna) of their freedom (given by Yahweh) is seen as rebellion against God the Liberator (see vv. 18–20).

our strength is dried up (napšēnû yᵉḇēšâ). The verb *yāḇaš,* "to be dried up," is common, e.g., in the Psalms, for a waning or withering of

22. Cf. Exod. 12:38; Deut. 29:11; Josh. 8:35 for references to the mixed character of the people.

23. See BDB, p. 16.

24. See ibid., pp. 996b, 998a; GKC, §§ 120d, g; Davidson, *Syntax,* §§ 82–83. Cf. 11:1–3.

25. On these plants, see, e.g., J. Trever, *IDB,* I:748; III:107, 344, 604; R. K. Harrison, *ISBE,* rev., I:833; III:100, 314, 606; and Gray, pp. 103–4. Some of these plants would have been abundant in Egypt, as would the fish.

26. Heb. *ḥinnām* is derived from *ḥēn,* "free favor," plus the adverbial sufformative *-ām.* Cf. BDB, p. 336b; GKC, §§ 100g, h, and nn. 1–2.

heart, strength, or life itself.[27] The word *nep̱eš* here is a good summary of all these qualities, i.e., the whole physical-spiritual person.[28]

7–9 These verses are an aside from the author to explain the nature of manna, and are paralleled by Exod. 16:14–21, 31, although with many differences of detail.

7 The manna is compared to the *seed of coriander (zᵉraʿ-gaḏ)* and *bdellium (bᵉḏōlaṯ)* in appearance. According to J. Trever, seed of coriander is the fruit of the plant *Coriandrum sativum,* and is used as a condiment, much as poppy, caraway, and sesame seeds are today.[29] *Bdellium* is a loanword in English and is of uncertain character; evidence can be adduced for its being a gumlike resin, a precious stone, or a pearl, with the preponderance of evidence pointing to the resin.[30]

8 Manna was prepared by being ground up, boiled, and made into cakes. *its taste was like the taste of dainty morsels with oil (wᵉhāyâ ṭaʿmô kᵉṭaʿam lᵉšaḏ haššāmen).* The noun *lᵉšaḏ* is found only here and in the difficult text of Ps. 32:4 (where emendation may be necessary); hence the meaning is obscure. The LXX renders it *enkris ex elaiou,* "a cake made with oil," and Vulg. *panis oleatus* is similar. The same Greek word *enkris* translates Heb. *ṣappîḥiṯ,* "cake," in Exod. 16:31, where the taste of manna is described as "like a cake made with honey" *(kᵉṣappîḥiṯ biḏᵉḇāš).* Most lexicons and commentaries agree that *lᵉšaḏ* and *ṣappîḥiṯ* are equivalents.[31]

9 Enough manna fell each night only for the next day (cf. Exod. 16:18–19, 21–24), thus pointing, day by day, to the loving watchcare and providence of Yahweh.[32]

10–13 This subsection describes the reaction of God to the people and the reaction of Moses to both God and the people. As Moses listened to the people weeping their complaints, first, God's wrath burned exceedingly *(wayyiḥar 'ap̱ YHWH mᵉ'ōḏ),* then Moses himself became

27. See, e.g., Ps. 22:16 (Eng. 15); 90:6; 102:5, 12 (Eng. 4, 11); 129:6.

28. Cf. BDB, pp. 659–61; *HALAT,* pp. 671–74; E. Jacob, *TDNT,* IX:617–22; B. Waltke, *TWOT,* II:587–91, and the bibliographies in these entries.

29. J. Trever, "Coriander Seed," *IDB,* I:681–82; also idem, "Flora," *IDB,* II:289.

30. See, e.g., I. H. Marshall, "Bdellium," *NBD,* 2nd ed., p. 127; also W. Staples, *IDB,* I:367; D. Bowes, *ZPEB,* I:494.

31. See BDB, pp. 545, 860; *HALAT,* p. 509 *(Gebäck);* KB, p. 813; Gray, pp. 106–7; Budd, pp. 122, 127, etc.

32. On the whole question of manna, see G. L. Carr, "Manna," *ISBE,* rev., III:239–40; F. S. Bodenheimer, "The Manna of Sinai," *BA* 10 (1947) 2–6 (repr. in *Biblical Archaeologist Reader* [Garden City, N.Y.: Anchor, 1961], I:76–80).

distressed (*it was a bad thing in Moses' sight, ûḇeʿênê mōšeh rāʿ*, lit., "in the eyes of Moses [it was] evil"). As the following verses indicate, however, Moses does not react against the people's rejection of God's provision but against the people for making his job as leader more difficult, and against Yahweh for giving him the task as leader.

11–12 Moses addresses a group of angry questions to Yahweh, leading up to the real problem: his inadequacy as a leader to find meat for the whole company in response to their demands (v. 13).

nurse. The word *'ōmēn* is problematic, for it is masculine in form but its linkage with *suckling child (hayyōnēq)* seems to require a feminine meaning. Since *'ōmēn* may mean "foster father,"[33] it is possible to interpret this passage as saying that Moses, the foster father, is incapable of providing for this suckling child Israel as demanded. But the context (note in the previous line, "did I give them birth") seems to favor the usual translation, *nurse* (so RSV, etc.).

14–15 These verses form a transition from the specific problem of food (and the people's rebellion in demanding it) to the more general problem of shared leadership. The personal pronouns *I* (*'ānōḵî*, strengthened by *leḇaddî*, "alone") and *you* (sing., *'at*) are emphasized. Moses sees his loneliness in leadership as a judgment of God, and requests that, if he has found any favor in God's sight, he be killed now rather than carrying on as he has been and being seen as inadequate to find food for the people (i.e., *my misfortune*). The reader is not told why Moses cannot share the leadership with those elders who were appointed while still at Mt. Sinai (Exod. 18:25–26). God must deal with the leader of the people before he can deal with the people.

16 Moses is instructed to appoint seventy elders, who were known to be *leaders (šōṭēr)* of the people.[34] These elders were to go with Moses to the tent of meeting — the place where God would speak with Moses.[35] The center of God's revelatory meeting with the people has shifted from the mountain to the tent. God was still intending to speak only with Moses (see the charge made by Miriam and Aaron and God's reply in 12:8 below).

17 *I will set apart some of the spirit that is upon you, and I will place it upon them (we'āṣaltî min-hārûaḥ 'ašer 'āleyḵā weśamtî 'alêhem).*

33. LXX has *tithēnos,* "one who nurses, foster father." See LSJ, 1792a.

34. The term *šōṭēr* is used, e.g., in Exod. 5:6, 10, 14–15, 19, for the Israelite foremen appointed over the people by the Egyptians. In Josh. 1:10; 3:2 it describes those who are to organize the people for march. It parallels the word *šōpṭîm,* "judges," in Deut. 16:18. See BDB, p. 1009b.

35. On the tent of meeting, see the commentary above on 1:1.

The sharing of spirit here indicates that this narrative is not a simple doublet of Exod. 18:25–26. The purpose here is not just administrative sharing, but sharing also in spiritual matters, in *the people's burden* (see also 11:25–29).

The question arises whether this *spirit (rûaḥ),* part of which is transferred by Yahweh from Moses to the elders, is Moses' spirit or Yahweh's Spirit that is upon Moses. On the side of it being Moses' spirit is the fact that this spirit is already *upon (ʿal)* Moses, and not a special imbuement poured from on high on these elders. This phrasing is probably meant to keep clear the distinction between Moses' status and that of the elders. It is precisely this special status that will be at stake in ch. 12.[36] On the other side, of the approximately forty instances in the OT where the word *rûaḥ* is used with the preposition *ʿal* meaning "upon," twenty-five are clearly references to God's Spirit, seven are references to other "spirits" sent by or from God, and eight are references to other "spirits," six of these clearly the human spirit.[37] It was common in the period of the Judges and the early monarchy that mighty deeds (including prophesying) were the result of God's Spirit being or coming upon a person.[38] All this would make one lean toward interpreting the spirit here as being Moses' only in the sense that it was upon him. The source of this Spirit is Yahweh; he sent it. Certainly Moses himself understands the Spirit as Yahweh's (11:19, "his [God's] Spirit," *rûḥô*).[39]

18–20 This unit gives Yahweh's response to the people's demand for meat. At first sight, these verses are confusing, because v. 18 might lead one to believe that Yahweh is simply granting the demand —

36. This case is only partially parallel to 2 K. 2:15, which deals with the succession of Elijah by Elisha. Compare the phrasing of Num. 11:17 with 2 K. 2:15 *(rûaḥ 'ēlîyāhû ʿal-'ĕ lîšāʿ).* The spirit here is not simply *rûaḥ mōšeh* but *rûaḥ 'ᵃšer ʿal mōšeh,* i.e., the Spirit is not only *upon* the elders, but also *upon* Moses (i.e., it is not his).

37. For God's spirit, see Gen. 1:2; Num. 11:29; 24:2; Judg. 3:10; 11:29; 14:6, 19; 15:14; 1 Sam. 10:6, 10; 11:6; 19:20, 23; Isa. 11:2; 32:15; 42:1; 44:3; 59:21; 61:1; Ezek. 11:5; 39:29; Joel 3:1 (Eng. 2:28); 2 Chr. 15:1; 18:23; 20:14. For spirits sent from God, see Gen. 8:1; 1 Sam. 16:16, 23; Isa. 11:2 (3 times); 29:2. For other spirits, see Num. 5:14, 30; 2 K. 2:15; Isa. 28:6; Ezek. 20:32; Ps. 142:2; 143:4; Eccl. 1:6.

38. See Judg. 3:10; 11:29; 14:6, 19; 15:14; 1 Sam. 10:6, 10; 11:6; 19:20, 23; also Ezek. 11:5; Joel 3:1 (Eng. 2:28).

39. On this issue of the spirit — human or divine — see, e.g., F. Baumgärtel, *TDNT,* VI:359–67; J. Payne, *TWOT,* II:836–37; Eichrodt, *Theology of the OT,* II:46–68 (esp. p. 48 n. 3), 131–34.

i.e., because the people have rebelled and rejected Yahweh's leadership, he capitulates and gives them what they desire. Even v. 19 might support such a view. Only v. 20 makes it clear that Yahweh is going to punish the people by giving them what they asked for — to excess (this punishment finally comes to pass and is clarified in vv. 33–34). If one compares the two motives for Yahweh's reaction to the people (e.g., vv. 18 and 20), what stands out in the second is the clause *you have rejected Yahweh who is in your midst (mᵉʾastem ʾeṯ-YHWH ʾᵃšer bᵉqirbᵉḵem).* Yahweh had come to be in the midst of his people; he desired to be there (cf., e.g., Exod. 25–30; 35–40; Num. 2:17; also Deut. 7:21), and had purposed to lead them to the new land (e.g., Num. 9:15–22; 10:33). The wish to go back to Egypt was a wish to go back to a time before Yahweh was in their midst, and thus was rebellion against him.

Sanctify yourselves for tomorrow (hiṯqaddᵉšû lᵉmāḥār). Here and elsewhere, this formula functions in a situation of confrontation between Yahweh and the people as the time frame for a coming, decisive act of God. The people are, literally, "to make themselves holy" today because *tomorrow (māḥār)* Yahweh will act.[40]

The people will eat meat — will be forced to eat it — for a whole month, until it becomes *loathsome (zārāʾ)* to them. The word *zārāʾ* is a hapax legomenon; hence its meaning is uncertain. The LXX reads *cholera,* "nausea," which cannot be far off.[41]

Note the play on words between *your nostrils (mēʾappᵉḵem)* and *you rejected (mᵉʾastem).* The punishment is directly related to the rejection of Yahweh.

21–23 This unit is another transitional passage. In it Moses questions Yahweh's ability to provide the great company of the Hebrews with the superabundance of meat just promised. Not only God's people question his power, but from time to time God's leaders do as well.

The people in whose midst I am (hāʿām ʾᵃšer ʾānōḵî bᵉqirbô). Moses uses similar words for being among the people (*bᵉqereḇ* plus pronominal suffix) that Yahweh has used in v. 20. He has not seen in what

40. Cf. also, e.g., Exod. 19:10; Josh. 3:5; 7:13. See S. J. De Vries, "The Time Word *Māḥār* as a Key to Tradition Development," *ZAW* 87 (1975) 73–79. One does not have to agree with De Vries's presuppositions or his methodology to benefit from this article.

41. Heb. *zārāʾ* seems to be related to the root *zûr,* "be strange," participle *zār,* "stranger," as in Num. 1:51; 3:10, 38; etc. (see BDB, p. 266b). Something loathsome may well be something that was foreign to a prescribed norm. See Milgrom, *Studies in Levitical Terminology,* I:5.

God has said that Yahweh is the leader and in the midst. Moses sees only his own condition.

He states that the people *number 600,000 men on foot (šēš-mē'ôṯ 'eleṗ raglî)* plus, of course, women, children, and the Levites.[42]

Is Yahweh's hand cut short? (hᵃyaḏ-YHWH tiqṣār). The word *hand (yāḏ)* is used many times in the OT as an anthropomorphism for God's strength.[43] The use of the verb "to cut off" *(qāṣar)* with "hand" *(yāḏ)* indicates impotence in God (e.g., Isa. 50:2; 59:1) or in humankind (2 K. 19:26; Isa. 37:27). The proof of the true God is whether his word comes to pass (cf., e.g., Isa. 41:21–29; 46:8–11). Here God simply says, *Now you will see whether my word happens to you or not.* In the present context this word of Yahweh applies not only to feeding the multitude, but also to appointing elders to share the leadership.

24–30 Even though Moses has expressed his doubts to Yahweh in one area, he goes out and obeys him in another, i.e., the appointment of elders (see 11:16–17). In this unit Yahweh's promise of shared leadership is realized. The section falls into two main parts: vv. 24–25, which simply fulfill the word of vv. 16–17 (with some development), and vv. 26–29, which tell of the further incident concerning Eldad and Medad. V. 30 forms a conclusion to the unit.

The vocabulary of vv. 24–25 is similar to that of vv. 16–17. In v. 25 Yahweh is said to descend *in the cloud (bᵉʿānān)*. A different verb for "to put, place" is used in v. 25, describing the impartation of the Spirit to the elders.[44]

The outcome is that *when the Spirit settled down on them they prophesied (kᵉnôaḥ ʿᵃlêhem hārûaḥ wayyiṯnabbᵉ'û)*. It is hard to know exactly what is meant here. The verb "to prophesy" *(hiṯnabbē')* occurs twenty-nine times in the Hithpael, and is a denominative verb from the noun "prophet" *(nāḇî')*.[45] It means, literally, "to act the prophet." In such

42. This is a round number, perfectly consistent with the figure of 603,550 in 1:46. See the excursus on large numbers above.

43. See, e.g., Gen. 49:24; Exod. 9:15; etc.; BDB, pp. 389b–90a; *HALAT,* pp. 370b–71a; G. Mayer, *TDOT,* V:418–26; R. H. Alexander, *TWOT,* I:362–64.

44. V. 25 uses *nāṯan* rather than *śîm* (v. 17). These two verbs are often parallel and are nearly synonymous; cf. BDB, pp. 680–81. The change probably signifies no more than literary variety, although *nāṯan* (lit., "to give") may emphasize the nature of the origin of the Spirit (i.e., it was a gift of God) more than *śîm*.

45. The Niphal form *(nibbā')* is used some 88 times in the OT with no discernible difference in meaning from the Hithpael.

passages as 1 Sam. 10 and 19 the verb is clearly connected with behavior that might be called abnormal or, better, "ecstatic."[46] In other passages the verb just as clearly indicates speaking Yahweh's word without any hint of such behavior.[47] Can any choice be made here, the only passage in the Pentateuch to use the verb? Since the text itself gives no message or word from Yahweh derived from this prophesying, the more natural meaning seems to be the former, i.e., that these elders behaved in some way that accredited them as prophets. They were under the influence of Yahweh's Spirit, which had been upon Moses. More specific than this we cannot be.[48]

The question also arises as to what is meant by *they did not continue to do so* (lit., "they did not add," *wᵉlōʾ yāsāp̱û*). The verb *yāsap̱* is used in combination with other verbs to indicate a continuous or repeated action. With the negative, the meaning is that the action (here "prophesying") did not continue beyond this one occurrence.[49] All that is meant by this phrase, if the conclusion drawn above is correct, is that these elders engaged in the activity that accredited them as prophets under the influence of Yahweh's Spirit only on this occasion. Nothing at all is said about their continuing to function as spiritual leaders, but one may assume that they did.

26–30 In the case of Eldad and Medad, who are mentioned only at this point in the story,[50] the Spirit rested on them while they were still in the camp because, for unstated reasons, they did not go to the tent of meeting with Moses and the elders. They were *among those registered* (lit., "written down," *bakkᵉṯuḇîm*). Nowhere else does this narrative say

46. See, e.g., 1 Sam. 10:6; 19:24. Also Jer. 29:26, where the one who prophesies (in this case, Jeremiah) is virtually equated with a madman (*ʾîš mᵉšuggâ*). The prophets of Baal also engaged in this ecstatic behavior (1 K. 18:29).

47. E.g., Ezek. 37:9; Jer. 26:20. In Jer. 26:26–28 the meaning of proclaiming is placed next to the meaning of ecstatic behavior (v. 26).

48. The treatment here concurs with E. J. Young, *My Servants the Prophets* (Grand Rapids: Eerdmans, 1953), pp. 66–75, esp. 68–70.

49. See also Deut. 5:19 (Eng. 22) for another example. See GKC, § 120d n. 2.

50. *The Stiochometry of Nicephorus* (a list of OT, NT, and apocryphal books) refers to a book of Eldad and Medad (or Modad). See E. Hennecke and W. Schneemelcher, eds., *New Testament Apocrypha,* tr. and ed. R. McL. Wilson, 2 vols. (Philadelphia: Westminster, 1963, 1965), I:50; *The Shepherd of Hermas* 2.34 also cites this work. See E. J. Martin, "Eldad and Modad," in *The Old Testament Pseudepigrapha,* ed. J. Charlesworth, 2 vols. (New York: Doubleday, 1983, 1985), II:463–65 (with bibliography).

that any names were written down. Either one may assume that the word is used loosely here to indicate those chosen (i.e., by Moses),[51] or a written record must have been made. The censuses taken earlier in the book are not said to have been written down, but the narratives are impossible to understand apart from some assumption of writing.[52] The other alternative is that this writing was not a list of the seventy elders, but of some other group, since v. 24, taken literally, states that Moses gathered all seventy elders around the tent. In this case we do not know who Eldad and Medad were or what "being written down" meant.[53] Since the later complaint is not that people outside the chosen seventy are prophesying, but solely that these two men are prophesying in the wrong place (vv. 26–27), it is better to assume that "being written down" is equivalent to being one of the seventy elders and that the "seventy men from the elders" in v. 24 refers to the group more loosely.

Some scholars read vv. 26–30 to imply that the tent was outside the camp, as in Exod. 33:7–11, rather than in the center of the camp, as in, e.g., Num. 2. The words said to indicate the former are: *left behind in the camp* and *they did not go out to the tent* in v. 26; *Eldad and Medad are prophesying in the camp* in v. 27; and *Moses and the elders of Israel went back to the camp* in v. 30.[54] But it is questionable that one would reach such a conclusion from reading this narrative had the theory of sources not existed. All that is meant is that Moses gathered the elders around the tent. To be there, they had to go out from among the people to the tent in the center of the camp. Eldad and Medad did not go to the tent but remained in the camp around the tent, perhaps at some distance. When the incident was over, Moses and the elders went back into the camp from the tent.[55]

An unnamed *young man (hannaʿar)* came upon Eldad and Medad prophesying in the wrong place and ran to the tent of meeting to report this to Moses (v. 27). It is impossible to determine the chronological age of this young man, since the Hebrew term can refer to males from infancy (Exod. 2:6) through mature manhood (2 Sam. 14:21). It is possible that the term here refers to the man's immaturity. In, e.g., Jer. 1:6 the prophet speaks of himself as "only a young man" *(naʿar)* who does not know how

51. See Gray, p. 114.
52. On this point see the commentary above on chs. 1–4.
53. See, e.g., Gray, p. 114; Budd, pp. 128–29.
54. See, e.g., Gray, pp. 114–16.
55. So Noordtzij, p. 104.

to speak, i.e., he is immature.[56] Joshua asked Moses to stop this unauthorized activity. Joshua is called Moses' *servant (mᵉšārēṯ)* four times (see Exod. 24:4; 33:11; Josh. 1:1). This term is a general one for service.[57]

Joshua is also called *one of his chosen young men (mibbᵉḥurāyw).* The word *baḥûr* is probably derived from the root *bḥr,* "choose."[58] Scholars are divided on whether the plural noun *baḥûrîm* should be taken with *min* as a partitive ("one of his chosen [or 'choice'] young men") or as an abstract noun for an age group ("from his youth").[59] Joshua is first mentioned in Exod. 17:9 without introduction, as if he were already known. In Exod. 33:11 he is called a "young man" *(naʿar).* The time of Exod. 33 would have been just a matter of months before the time of the present narrative. Thus, while we do not know the precise difference between the age of a *baḥûr* and that of a *naʿar,* it is unlikely that it could be significant. The difference between the two terms seems to be that *naʿar* is a more general designation; *baḥûr* emphasizes the prime nature of the young man. Another possibility is that this comment is a later gloss on the text, made from the point of view of the whole life of Joshua.

The response of Moses in v. 29 is interesting. The word *jealous* (*mᵉqannēʾ*, a Piel participle from the root *qnʾ*, the same root found in the ritual of 5:11–31), indicates basically a strong desire to possess something another possesses. Thus it may be translated as "envy," "jealousy," or "zeal," depending on the context. In Gen. 26:14 the Philistines envy Isaac's possessions. Here Joshua strongly desires that Moses be the leader; he is devoted to him as his servant. He sees the unauthorized actions of Eldad and Medad as a challenge to Moses' leadership.[60]

Moses himself, who earlier in this passage had been very concerned with his own role as leader (see 11:14–15, 21–22), even when speaking to

56. See M. Fisher, *TWOT,* II:585–86. S. Blank hypothesized that the various valuations on age groups in Israel found in Lev. 27:1-8 might point to the age of twenty as the time when one passed from being a "young man" to being a mature man (*IDB,* IV:925).

57. See the commentary above on 3:6. The term is also found in 8:26.

58. E.g., *HALAT,* pp. 114–15, derives *baḥûr* from a second root *bḥr,* which is related to an Akkadian word for "man"; but see H. Seebass, *TDOT,* II:74; and J. Oswalt, *TWOT,* I:101.

59. For the former see GKC, § 119w n. 2; Davidson, *Syntax,* § 101 (p. 141); Williams, *Syntax,* § 324; so AV, RV, RSV, NKJV. For the latter see *zᵉqûnîm,* "old age," Gen. 37:3; *nᵉʿûrîm,* "youth," Gen. 8:21; GKC, § 124d; Davidson, *Syntax,* § 16; Williams, *Syntax,* § 7; so NEB, NIV, NASB, GNB, JB, Moffatt, NJPS.

60. See L. J. Coppes, *TWOT,* II:802–3; E. Good, *IDB,* II:806–7.

Yahweh, responds strangely: *O that Yahweh would make all Yahweh's people prophets and that Yahweh would put his Spirit on them (ûmî yittēn kol-ʿām YHWH nᵉḇîʾîm kî-yittēn YHWH ʾeṯ-rûḥô ʿᵃlêhem).* One wonders what made Moses respond so differently. Perhaps the experience of the shared Spirit is ever the antidote for the weary, harried, threatened leader.

At the conclusion of this section, Moses and the elders simply go back from the tent of meeting (where Yahweh had indeed met them) to the everyday life of the camp. One problem (leadership) has come to a satisfactory conclusion.

31–34 This unit gives the unfortunate outcome of the second issue in the passage — food for the people. Like previous units, it also breaks into two sections: vv. 31–32 simply tell of the coming of the quails, and vv. 33–34 give the judgment and its aftermath. V. 35 is a travel note that both concludes the present passage and forms a transition to the next.

31 *And a wind went up from Yahweh (wᵉrûaḥ nāsaʿ mēʾēṯ YHWH).* This section of text is bound to the previous one by the recurrence of the word *rûaḥ* (11:17, 25–26, 29, translated "Spirit"), this time with another common meaning, "wind."[61] The *rûaḥ* of Yahweh settled the leadership problem; now the *rûaḥ YHWH* will bring a solution to the food problem.

quail from the sea (śalwîm min-hayyām). Quails had previously been used to feed the Israelites in the wilderness (see Exod. 16:13a). Heb. *śᵉlāw* ("quail") is possibly a loanword.[62] Most modern scholars agree that a bird of the genus *coturnix* is meant, the most abundant of which is the common quail *(coturnix coturnix, coturnix vulgaris),* which migrates from Europe and West Asia to North Africa.[63]

The *sea* is probably the Gulf of Aqabah. Some ancient evidence for the migration of the quail on the wind comes from Aristotle:

> The quail also migrates. . . . When quails come to land, if it be fair weather or if a north wind is blowing, they will pair off and manage pretty comfortably; but if a southerly wind prevail they are greatly distressed owing to the difficulties in the way of flight. . . . For this reason bird-catchers trap them in southerly winds but not during fine weather. They fly badly because of their weight for their body is heavy.[64]

61. According to BDB, pp. 924–25, *rûaḥ* means "breath" some 33 times, "wind" 117 times, and "spirit" (human or divine) 230 times.

62. See BDB, p. 969a.

63. See the brief but helpful articles in W. McCullough, *IDB,* II:973; and G. Cansdale, *ZPEB,* V:2, for further information and bibliographies.

64. Aristotle, *The History of Animals,* in *The Complete Works of Aristotle:*

Thus a migration of quails on the wind is possible, though the numbers of quail in the biblical text are extraordinary, even miraculous. *about two cubits above the surface of the ground (kᵉʾammāṯayim ʿal-pᵉnê hāʾāreṣ).* It is not clear whether this is the height at which the quails were flying or the height of the pile into which the quails fell.[65] One cubit equals about 17.5 in., so two cubits is about 35 in. The former meaning is supported by the practice of netting quails in flight, reported in the Sinai until relatively recent times.[66] The latter reading seems based on understanding MT *yṭš* as from the verb *nāṭaš* (usually "leave, forsake"), meaning "to allow to fall," and the difficulty of trapping by net ten homers of quail in two days and an intervening night (see below on v. 32).[67] G. R. Driver proposed that MT *wyṭš* should be repointed to read *wayyāṭōś,* from *ṭûś,* a rare word in Biblical Hebrew, meaning "to fly, flutter, swoop" (only Job 9:26).[68] This solution seems plausible.

32 In any case, the language here is intended to give the impression that the number of quails captured was exceedingly large: the people took two days and a night to gather them all, and *He who gathered the least gathered ten homers.* The *homer* is a dry measure, the name for which is related to the Akkadian word for "donkey," hence presumably "a donkey-load." Estimates of its modern equivalence vary between 3.8 and 6.5 bushels; thus 10 homers would equal at least 38 bushels, a very large amount.[69]

And they spread them out for themselves (wayyišṭᵉḥû lāhem šāṭôaḥ). Most commentators, agreeing that the purpose of spreading the dead quails out on the group was to dry them, cite Herodotus as evidence for the Egyptian practice of drying quails after first salting them, and assume that the Israelites picked up this practice from the Egyptians.[70]

The Revised Oxford Translation, ed. J. Barnes, Bollingen Series LXXI.2 (Princeton: Princeton Univ. Press, 1984), I:934, lines 6–15. The assumption is, of course, that Aristotle and Numbers refer to the same bird, which is unprovable at present. On the identification of these birds, see Gray, p. 117; and J. Gray, "The Desert Sojourn of the Hebrews and the Sinai/Horeb Tradition," *VT* 4 (1954) 148–54.

65. For the former, see, e.g., Noordtzij, p. 105; Budd, p. 129; Snaith, p. 144; cf. Vulg., NEB. For the latter, see, e.g., Keil, p. 73; Wenham, p. 109; and most English versions.

66. Wenham, p. 109.

67. Ibid.

68. G. R. Driver, *PEQ* 90 (1958) 57–58; *HALAT,* p. 357b; the NEB follows Driver's proposal here as elsewhere.

69. See O. R. Sellers, "Weights and Measures," *IDB,* IV:834–35.

70. "Some fish they dry in the sun . . . and of birds they eat quails, ducks,

The verb *šāṭaḥ* means only "to spread out," however; it does not imply the drying process. If the plague that followed was in any way connected with food poisoning (as, from a human perspective, seems reasonable), then the Israelites probably did not take care to preserve the quails, perhaps counting on God to make provision for that as well as for the abundant supply itself.[71]

33–34 These verses tell of Yahweh's judgment on the people, thus fulfilling the threat of 11:20. Two related questions arise: first, the nature of the plague, and, second, its timing. The word *plague* (lit., "blow, stroke," *makkâ*) is used in this sense in seven other places in the OT. In Deut. 28 and 29 the term parallels words for "sickness" or "disease" (*ḥ^{o}lî, taḥ^{a}lu'îm*). In 1 Sam. 4 the term describes the plagues of Egypt. The cognate verb occurs in Exod. 3:20 and 9:15 to describe these plagues. In the present context (a large supply of meat), the most natural thought is of some form of food poisoning.

If this is the case, one must translate the temporal clause differently than some English versions do, e.g., "While the meat was still between their teeth, before it was chewed" (so NKJV; cf. AV, RV, NASB), because such a translation would indicate that the plague descended at the first taste of the meat. The problem is the translation of the verb *kāraṯ* (Niphal, lit., "be cut") as "be chewed." This translation is unique for *kāraṯ*.[72] Much more common would be the translation "to fail, be exhausted."[73] If the latter translation is adopted, the passage indicates that the plague came upon the people before the great supply of fresh quails had been exhausted.

The plague took many lives. The incident was memorialized by calling the place *Kibroth-hattaavah* ("the graves of the craving"). Again as before, the Israelites left no people behind to carry on the tradition of this name; hence it is not surprising that it has left no trace on the map, although sites for Kibroth-hattaavah and Hazeroth have been proposed.[74]

35 This verse is simply a transition that takes the Israelites from

---

and smaller birds after, first, salting them" (*Herodotus,* ed. H. Cary [London: George Routledge & Sons, 1892], 2.77, p. 106). Vulg. reads *siccaverunt,* "they dried." See Gray, p. 118; Wenham, p. 109; Binns, p. 74; Keil, p. 73; Noordtzij, p. 105; Noth, p. 91; cf. Snaith, p. 145.

71. Snaith, p. 145.

72. BDB, p. 504a, may be behind this translation, which it admits is unique to this passage.

73. Ibid. See also Gray, p. 118; Josh. 1:5–6, 16; 3:13, 16; 4:7; etc.

74. See, e.g., G. I. Davies, *The Way of the Wilderness,* SOTSMS 5 (Cambridge: Cambridge Univ. Press, 1979), pp. 41, 88–89.

the scene of their last conflict to the scene of their next one — Miriam and Aaron's challenge to Moses' leadership at Hazeroth.

3. AT HAZEROTH (12:1–16)

1 *And Miriam and Aaron spoke*[1] *against*[2] *Moses because of the Cushite woman he had married, for he had married a Cushite woman.*

2 *And they said, "Is it true that God has spoken exclusively*[3] *through*[4] *Moses? Has he not also spoken through us"? And Yahweh heard them.*

3 *Now the man Moses was the meekest of all humans who were upon the face of the earth.*

4 *Suddenly,*[5] *Yahweh said to Moses and to Aaron and to Miriam, "Come out, you three,*[6] *to the tent of meeting." And the three of them went out.*

5 *And Yahweh came down in a pillar of cloud and stood at the door of the tent, and he called to Aaron and Miriam; and the two of them went out.*

6 *And he said:*

"Hear my words:
If there is a prophet of Yahweh among you,[7]

1. Before a compound subject the verb often agrees in number and gender with only the first. See GKC, §§ 146f, g; Davidson, *Syntax,* § 114; Williams, *Syntax,* § 230.

2. The preposition *b*^{e} is adversative here (and again in v. 9); see Williams, *Syntax,* § 242.

3. The two adverbs *raq* and *'aḵ* are placed together for emphasis, "Simply and solely"; see GKC, § 133k n. 1; Davidson, *Syntax,* § 153; Williams, *Syntax,* § 390.

4. The preposition *b*^{e} here shows the agent; see Williams, *Syntax,* § 245.

5. Heb. *piṯ'ōm* derives from a substantive meaning "suddenness" (*HALAT,* pp. 924, 930; cf. Num. 6:9, *b*^{e}*peṯa';* BDB, p. 837), with the sufformative *-m* (see GKC, § 100g; Moscati, ed., *Introduction to Comparative Grammar,* § 15.2).

6. The suffixes here are properly genitives: *š*^{e}*laštem,* "your triad," "you three"; see GKC, § 97i; Davidson, *Syntax,* § 36 Rem. 4.

7. Although it is a common practice to modify the MT from *n*^{e}*ḇî'*^{a}*ḵem* to *nāḇî-ḇāḵem* (so *BHS;* J. Kselman, "A note on Numbers XII 6–8," *VT* 26 [1976] 500–504; F. M. Cross, *Canaanite Myth and Hebrew Epic* [Cambridge: Harvard Univ. Press, 1973], p. 203 n. 36; Budd, p. 133; Gray, p. 126; etc.), MT may be retained once it is recognized that this construction is the so-called broken construct chain, with a pronominal suffix intervening between the construct and its genitive. The meaning of such a construction would be "if there is among you a prophet of Yahweh." See GKC, § 130; D. N. Freedman, "The Aaronic Benediction (Num. 6:24–26)," in *Pottery, Poetry, and Prophecy* (Winona Lake, Ind.: Eisenbrauns,

I may make myself known to him in a vision;
In a dream I may speak to him.
7 *Not so my servant Moses,*
He is entrusted with my whole house.
8 *Mouth to mouth I speak with him,*
And neither in vision[8] *nor in riddles,*
The form of Yahweh he beholds.
How does it happen that you were not afraid,
To speak against my servant, against Moses?"
9 *Then Yahweh's anger burned against them and he departed.*
10 *When the cloud departed from over the tent, just then, Miriam became leprous, as white as snow. When Aaron turned to Miriam, at that moment, she became leprous.*[9]
11 *And Aaron said to Moses, "O my lord, do not, I beg you, lay the penalty of the sin that we have foolishly committed*[10] *against us.*
12 *Please do not let her be like a dead one,*[11] *half of whose flesh is consumed when he comes from his mother's womb."*
13 *So Moses cried to Yahweh, saying, "O God,*[12] *please heal her, I pray."*

1980), p. 237; idem, "The Broken Construct Chain," *Bib* 53 (1972) 534–36, repr. in *Pottery, Poetry, and Prophecy,* pp. 339–41. For examples of the phenomenon in the Psalter, see M. Dahood, *Psalms,* 3 vols., AB (Garden City, N.Y.: Doubleday, 1965, 1968, 1970), III:381–83, esp. 381–82. Recognition of the broken construct chain also alleviates the need to move the word *YHWH* to a place after *wayyō'mer* in v. 6a (as, e.g., in *BHS;* and Cross, *Canaanite Myth,* p. 203 n. 37).

8. Emending MT *ûmar'eh,* lit., "and an appearance," to *b^{e}mar'eh* on the basis of Sam. Pent., LXX, Pesh., and Vulg. See *BHS;* Freedman, "Aaronic Benediction," p. 237; Cross, *Canaanite Myth,* p. 204 n. 39.

9. On the use of *hinnēh* (usually, "behold") to convey a sense of immediacy, see T. O. Lambdin, *Introduction to Biblical Hebrew* (New York: Scribner's, 1971), § 135.

10. The two verbs *nô'alnû* and *ḥāṭā'nû* combine to express one idea; hence MT, which is lit. "the sin that we were foolish and that we sinned," means "the sin that we foolishly committed." Cf. Davidson, *Syntax,* §§ 82–83; Williams, *Syntax,* §§ 223–24.

11. The definite article refers to a specific class — dead people. In English one more properly uses the indefinite article here. See GKC, § 126o; Davidson, *Syntax,* § 22 (e); Williams, *Syntax,* § 92.

12. *BHS* suggests reading *'al* (a negative) for *'ēl* (God), as in vv. 11–12. GKC, § 105b n. 1 (p. 308), supports the emendation because of the unique instance of the particle *nā'* coming after the noun *'ēl.* What meaning does such an emendation yield, however? "Please do not heal her"! In addition, the negative is usually followed by the jussive. Gray (p. 128) sees the construction as an interjection, "Nay, now" (cf. Gen. 19:18; BDB, p. 39a), hence "Nay, now, heal her, I pray." The change in meaning from MT is slight.

14 *But Yahweh said to Moses, "If her father had but spit in her face would she not be humiliated for seven days? Let her be shut up for seven days on the outside of the camp, and after this, she may be restored."*
15 *So Miriam was shut up outside the camp for seven days, and the people did not depart until Miriam was restored.*
16 *And afterward the people departed from Hazeroth and encamped in the wilderness of Paran.*

Chapter 12 concludes not only the discussion of leadership begun in ch. 11 but also the first travel section of the book. The theme of rebellion against proper authority again comes to the surface. In ch. 11 the people, led by the rabble, rebelled against Moses and ultimately against Yahweh, but the people's leaders were not involved in this struggle (other than Moses himself). The present narrative widens the rebellion to include Moses' own family.

Although Moses himself may have wished that Yahweh's Spirit were upon all his people, and that all might have a share in that spirit of prophecy, in Yahweh's eyes Moses is unique. Yahweh speaks to Moses in a direct way, unlike any other divine communication with other humans (prophets or otherwise, 12:6–8). Miriam and Aaron have forgotten this special relationship and are rebuffed by Yahweh for their impertinence. The root of their problem may be that they, the siblings of the leader, were not included in the sharing of Yahweh's Spirit with the elders (11:4–35 does not mention Aaron).

The narrative breaks into two main sections. Vv. 1–8 give the challenges to Moses' position and authority; Yahweh responds to these challenges in vv. 9–15 (v. 16 is a travel note). Within this narrative, unified around the person of Moses, are two incidents which are the bases for the development of two themes (much as in ch. 11). The first theme (Moses' Cushite wife) is more mundane than the second (Moses' unique status), and forms a point of entry to it. The complaint about Moses' foreign wife is brought by Miriam with Aaron's complicity (see the order of the names in v. 1), and leads to punishment of Miriam in vv. 10–15. The complaint concerning Moses' status as sole interpreter of God's words is brought by Aaron with Miriam's complicity (see the order of the names in vv. 3–4) and leads to Yahweh's harsh words to both (v. 8).

Again, it will not do to make independent strata or documents out of these two elements in the one story united around the person of Moses; they merely form themes in the story.[13] V. 9 is a transition between the

13. Gray, pp. 98–99; Noth, pp. 92–96; Coats, *Rebellion in the Wilderness,*

two thematic elements, and v. 16 is a travel note that places the Israelites in the wilderness of Paran. The unit is marked by a poetic section contrasting the way in which Yahweh communicated with Moses as over against all other prophets. This section contains numerous textual problems. The unit is also marked by the narrator's frequent confirmatory or informational comments to add vividness to the descriptions.[14]

1 *the Cushite woman (hāʾiššâ hakkušîṯ)*. Commentators have puzzled over the identity of this woman for centuries. The solutions boil down to two: Zipporah (so, in the medieval period, Ibn Ezra), or some other woman, about whom we know nothing save that she was a Cushite (most English translations read "Ethiopian") (so, in the same period, Rashbam).[15] In the first instance, the confirmatory comment *for he had married a Cushite woman (kî ʾiššâ kušîṯ lāqāḥ)* means that it is legitimate, from the narrator's perspective, to call Zipporah a Cushite. In the second instance the comment means simply that Moses had indeed taken a Cushite woman as a wife. Modern commentators are as divided on the issue as their forebears were.[16]

In the OT *kûš* can refer to (1) a Nubian or, less accurately (in modern terms), an Ethiopian (cf. Ezek. 29:10); (2) a Kassite (cf. Gen. 10:8), or (3) an inhabitant of *kûšān* (Cushan), which parallels Midian in Hab. 3:7.[17] Although Zipporah, a Midianite, could not qualify as a Cushite under the first or second options, she might just qualify in the third. One does wonder, however, why Miriam would wait this long to complain

pp. 261–64; de Vaulx, pp. 158–59. The analyses of these scholars differ, but they agree in seeing the thematic differences as explained by different sources; see Budd, pp. 133–36.

14. E.g., "because of the Cushite woman he had married" (*kî-ʾiššâ ḵušîṯ lāqāḥ,* v. 1); "And Yahweh heard them" (*wayyišmaʿ YHWH,* v. 2); "And the three of them went out" (*wayyēṣᵉʾû šᵉlōštām,* v. 4); "and the two of them went out" (*wayyēṣᵉʾû šᵉnêhem,* v. 5); "When Aaron turned to Miriam, at that moment, she became leprous" (*wayyip̄en ʾahᵃrōn ʾel-miryām wᵉhinnēh mᵉṣōrāʿaṯ,* v. 10); "and the people did not depart until Miriam was restored" (*wᵉhāʿām lōʾ nāsaʿ ʿaḏ-hēʾāsēp̄ miryām,* v. 15).

15. See Cohen, ed., *Soncino Chumash,* p. 855. LXX is the likely source of the reading "Ethiopian" for "Cushite" here.

16. Those who favor an identification with Zipporah include Binns, pp. 75–76; Sturdy, pp. 89–90 (slightly); and de Vaulx, p. 159. Those who do not favor such an identification include Keil, pp. 75–76; Budd, p. 136; Gray, pp. 106–7; Noordtzij, pp. 121–22; and Wenham, pp. 110–11. Other commentators (e.g., Noth, p. 94; and Snaith, p. 145) simply credit the two stories to different traditions.

17. On the second possibility, cf. W. S. LaSor, *ISBE,* rev., I:839. On the third, see Gray, p. 121 note; Noth, p. 94.

about Zipporah; one would have expected earlier complaints if Miriam was referring to Zipporah here.

Since Cushites were not Israelites, perhaps the Cushite woman referred to was a part of the mixed multitude of Exod. 12:38, or even one of the rabble of Num. 11:4. If the latter speculation is true (and it is speculation), then a complaint from Miriam may not be surprising, especially in the light of what had just happened at Kibroth-hattaavah. Another basis for this complaint may well be the fact that Miriam and Aaron were not included in the sharing of the Spirit in ch. 11, and this complaint about a foreign wife was really only a surface issue that concealed the deeper problem of jealousy over their brother's unique status before God in the community (see v. 2).

2 The connection between v. 1 and what Moses' siblings say in this verse is not clear. The issue here seems to be a different one, unless one assumes that Moses' unique status was threatened because of his foreign wife (the text draws no such conclusion), or, as mentioned above, that the issue of a foreign wife was a subterfuge. Aaron and Miriam are concerned to point out that God also spoke through them. In a sense, of course, they were right, and the charge here may not seem very serious. But *Yahweh heard them* and took it upon himself to defend Moses' unique position.

3 *Now the man Moses was the meekest.* That this statement should come from Moses himself is not likely (at least if it is true). The narrator wishes the reader to know that Moses himself would probably have let this challenge go unanswered. It was Yahweh who heard it and who took it upon himself to answer it.

4 Yahweh spoke *Suddenly (piṯ'ōm).* This word is used frequently of an invasion or judgment coming without great warning.[18] Yahweh called Moses, Aaron, and Miriam to come out from among the people to the tent.

5 There Aaron and Miriam are summoned into Yahweh's presence, leaving Moses out of the matter until v. 11. It is far more common for Moses to be in God's presence. Although one assumes that Aaron was often alone in Yahweh's presence in his role of high priest, the Pentateuch itself does not speak much about this. Lev. 9:23 and Num. 16:43 speak of Aaron coming "before the tabernacle," but in both texts Moses accom-

18. See Isa. 47:11; Jer. 4:20; 6:26; 15:8; 18:22; 51:8; Job 5:3; Ps. 64:8 (Eng. 7); etc.; see also D. Daube, *The Sudden in the Scriptures* (Leiden: Brill, 1964), pp. 1–8; V. Hamilton, *TWOT,* II:744.

panied him. In most contexts Aaron does not receive the direct communication of Yahweh, but, in his role as "prophet," he transmits what God has said to Moses on to the people (cf. Exod. 7:1–2).[19] Miriam is scarcely mentioned in the Pentateuch (only four times outside this narrative). Exod. 15:20 calls her a "prophetess," but never discusses her role as such. In any case, the reader is left in suspense as to why God would call Aaron and Miriam to the tent of meeting. Was it, indeed, an oversight that they were left out of the sharing of Moses' spirit? The poem of vv. 6–8 leaves no doubt that this is not the case.

6–8 The first question to be settled is the extent of the poem. F. M. Cross and, following him, J. Kselman have seen it as containing eight poetic lines (i.e., vv. 6b–8c).[20] But since v. 6a and v. 8de are in the same poetic form as the rest of the unit, there seems no reason to excise these lines from consideration (the fact that they do not fit Kselman's proposed chiastic structure for the unit is insufficient grounds for eliminating them from the poem). As it stands in the text, the poem consists of eleven lines (each having between six and nine syllables).[21]

Verses 6cd and 8abc mention the different kinds of revelation received by an "ordinary prophet" (e.g., Aaron and Miriam) as over against Moses. Yahweh *may*[22] reveal himself to prophets via *vision (mar'â)* or *dream (ḥ^{a}lôm),* v. 6cd. But he speaks *Mouth to mouth* (*peh 'el-peh,* i.e., personally) with Moses.

The question remains as to how one should understand *And neither in vision nor in riddles* (*ûmar'eh w^{e}lō' b^{e}ḥîḏōṯ ût^{e}munaṯ YHWH yabbîṭ,*

19. In a few passages God speaks to Aaron alone (Exod. 4:27; Lev. 10:8; Num. 18:1, 8, 20), but this is rare. The usual formula is "God spoke to Moses and to Aaron" (e.g., Exod. 6:1, 31; 7:8; Lev. 11:1; 13:1; Num. 2:1; 4:1, 17; etc.).

20. See Kselman, "Note on Numbers XII 6–8," pp. 500–504. Kselman's text follows the reconstruction of the text by Cross in *Canaanite Myth,* pp. 203–4. Kselman's structure is:

A	*'m yhyh nby' bkm*	(6b)
B	*bmr'h lw 'twd'*	(6c)
C	*bḥlwm 'dbr bw*	(6d)
D	*l' kn 'bdy mšh*	(7a)
D′	*bkl byty n'mn hw'*	(7b)
C′	*ph 'l ph 'dbr bw*	(8a)
B′	*bmr'h wl' ḥdyt*	(8b)
A′	*tmnt yhwh ybyṭ*	(8c)

21. See Cross, *Canaanite Myth,* pp. 203–4; Freedman, "Aaronic Benediction," pp. 236–38. Freedman's analysis differs from both Cross and Kselman.

22. The verb is here in the imperfect (potential) aspect.

v. 8bc). The word *t^e^mûnâ* occurs ten times in the OT, and all but once (Job 4:16) describes the visible manifestation of Yahweh.[23] Thus the last line, *the form of Yahweh he beholds,* is a further poetic description of personal communication, perhaps leaning on the description of the events in Exod. 24:15–18; 33:7–11,[24] 17–23; 34:5–9, 29–35; etc. One can reasonably expect that the phrase *ûmar'eh w^e^lō' b^e^ḥîḏōṯ* is in the same general semantic field. By pointing the word *mar'eh,* "visible appearance," the Masoretes distinguished it from *mar'â,* "vision," in v. 6. D. N. Freedman has proposed that the two words should be taken as equivalents and that *w^e^lō' b^e^-* in v. 8b should be taken with both *mar'eh* and *ḥîḏōṯ,* thus yielding the translation "and neither in vision nor in riddles." The terms *bammar'â* and *baḥ^a^lôm* are, then, parallel to *ûmar'eh* and *b^e^ḥîḏōṯ.*[25]

At the center of the passage is v. 7. As it stands, this verse is made up of two synthetically parallel lines.[26] Kselman has made a case for reading *lō'-ḵēn* (usually, "not so") as the Qal participle of *kûn* plus the asseverative or emphatic *l'*. The two lines would then be synonymous: "My servant Moses is surely loyal/In all my house he is faithful."[27] It would seem, however, that the poem is designed to contrast Moses with others (including Aaron and Miriam). Kselman's translation removes that element of contrast at the center of the poem. Therefore the traditional translation seems preferable.

The conclusion of the poem turns back to Aaron and Miriam (v. 8de). On the basis of the contrast here, they have overstepped themselves in issuing a challenge to Moses' unique status by claiming parity with him. As in v. 7, Moses is spoken of as Yahweh's *servant (ʿeḇeḏ),* which, in the light of the rest of what is said about the relationship between

23. The Joban passage may well refer to the visible manifestation of God as well, but it is vague. In addition to the current passage and Job 4:16, *t^e^mûnâ* is found in Exod. 20:4 (= Deut. 5:8); Deut. 4:12, 15–16, 23, 25; Ps. 17:15. See BDB, p. 568.

24. See Exod. 33:11: *w^e^ḏibber YHWH 'el-mōšeh pānîm 'el-pānîm ka'^a^šer y^e^ḏabbēr 'îš 'el-rēʿēhû,* "and Yahweh spoke to Moses face to face, as one might speak to his friend."

25. See Freedman, "Aaronic Benediction," p. 237.

26. For the syllable count see either ibid., p. 236, or Cross, *Canaanite Myth,* p. 204. The conclusions drawn from this syllable count vary between the two scholars (as is not surprising to those who follow their debates on these matters).

27. See Kselman, "Note on Numbers XII 6–8," pp. 502–3. He also furnishes parallel passages from Samuel, the Psalter, and extrabiblical sources.

Yahweh and Moses, lifts the role of his servant to a very high position indeed.[28]

9 *Then Yahweh's anger burned against them and he departed (wayyiḥar 'ap̱ YHWH bām wayyēlaḵ).* Rather suddenly after Yahweh's statement in v. 8de, he becomes angry and departs the camp, thus exposing it to danger. Since only Miriam is punished in v. 10, it may be that v. 9 forms a transition back to the complaint in v. 1 (in which Miriam is mentioned first, which suggests that she was primary in the complaint).

10 As Yahweh departs and the cloud lifts, at that very time, Miriam is smitten with *ṣāraʿaṯ.* The disease leaves her *white as snow (kaššāleg̱).* The same description is used of a skin disease (leprosy?) in Exod. 4:6 (Moses at Sinai) and 2 K. 5:27 (Gehazi, Elisha's servant).[29] In both these passages the disease is a sign of God's judgment (in the former case only as a demonstration for Moses). It is literarily interesting that Yahweh's judgment on Miriam made her skin very white, since her complaint against her brother's Cushite wife concerned a woman whose skin was probably dark.[30] This judgment by reversal is another reason to connect this judgment with the original complaint in which Miriam took the lead (v. 1), rather than the assertion of equality with Moses, in which Aaron took the lead (vv. 4–5). This reversal is not the only ironic element in the story.

11–13 Aaron intercedes with Moses who, in turn, intercedes with Yahweh for Miriam's restoration. Here again, the irony is obvious. Aaron, who had wanted to be able to be like his brother in the latter's role as a speaker for Yahweh, is forced to intercede with Moses who intercedes with God. Thus the theme of equality and the complaint over Moses' wife (issuing in this judgment) come together at this point. Yahweh is right — Moses is special!

14 But Yahweh does not simply agree to heal Miriam in response

28. Moses is called God's (Yahweh's) servant 36 times in the OT (Exod. 14:31; Num. 12:7–8; Deut. 34:5; Josh. 1:1–2, 7, 13, 15; 8:31, 33; 9:24; 11:12, 15; 12:6 [twice]; 13:8; 14:7; 18:7; 22:2, 4–5; 1 K. 8:53, 56; 2 K. 18:12; 21:8; Mal. 3:22; Ps. 105:26; Dan. 9:11; Neh. 1:8; 9:14; 10:30; 1 Chr. 6:34; 2 Chr. 1:3; 24:6, 9).

29. On the noun *ṣaraʿaṯ* and what is indicated by it, see the commentary above on 5:1–4.

30. See Gk. *Aithiops,* "burnt face," "dark skinned" (LSJ, I:37a). That the skin of these people was dark does not necessarily indicate that they were Negroid; see W. S. LaSor, *ISBE,* rev., I:838–39.

to Moses' plea in v. 13. Rather, he sets conditions on Miriam's cleansing. *If her father had but spit in her face would she not be humiliated for seven days? (wᵉʾāḇîhā yārōq yāraq bᵉp̄āneyhā hᵃlōʾ ṯikkālēm šiḇʿaṯ yāmîm).* Yahweh sets up a hypothetical situation: if Miriam's father had shown some unspecified contempt for her by spitting in her face, she would be held in a state of public humiliation for seven days. The reference here may be to a community practice the legislation for which is not in the Bible, although Deut. 25:9 refers to spitting in the face as a sign of contempt (in a legal framework), and Isa. 50:6 connects it with insult or shame *(kᵉlimmâ).*[31]

Let her be shut up for seven days outside the camp. Num. 5:2–4 underlines the holiness of the camp. Unclean persons must be put out. The period of isolation varied with the uncleanness involved. Here the punishment, described as "being humiliated" *(nikkālēm),* which is a general word for being dishonored or put to shame,[32] is qualified by the word *sāḡar,* "to be shut up, confined," which indicates isolation, but outside the camp *(miḥûṣ lᵉmaḥᵃneh),* for a period of *seven days.* Lev. 13 and 14 prescribe seven-day periods for both the detection of and the cleansing from "leprosy" *(ṣāraʿaṯ).*[33] Again, the basic thought of the clause is that seven days would be required even to reinstate one in whose face his or her father had spit. That, surely, is the least period of isolation required of Miriam here. The seven days can be thought of as a short period during which time Miriam's "leprosy" could be cleansed and she could atone for her crime.

15 This verse simply reports the fact that the people waited in camp for Miriam's cleansing and restoration before setting out on the journey again. Although she had transgressed, her transgression did not permanently bar her from her people, and the fact that they waited in camp until she was restored witnesses to her status as a leader of the people.

16 After the seven-day period had expired, the people broke camp and departed Hazeroth (another disaster), and came, at last, into the wilderness of Paran.[34] Num. 10:11 gave a summary account of the trip, which has taken from 10:12 to the end of ch. 12 to narrate in more detail. This is the end of the first travel section of the book.

31. Cf. Job 30:10; being spat upon and becoming unclean are connected in Lev. 15:8.

32. See BDB, pp. 483b–84a.

33. On the detection, see Lev. 13:4, 26–27, 31, 50; 14:38; a second period of seven days is prescribed in Lev. 13:5, 33, 54. On the cleansing, see Lev. 14:8.

34. On the possible location of Paran, see the commentary above on 10:11.

III. IN AND AROUND KADESH-BARNEA (13:1–19:22)

With Israel's arrival at Kadesh-barnea the third major section of the book begins. Only chs. 13 and 14 center on Kadesh-barnea itself. The final author or editor has attached chs. 15–19 (legal and narrative material) to the site presumably because he wanted the reader to make the connection with Kadesh and environs. The rebellions of chs. 11–12 are continued in the spies' reconnaissance of Canaan and their report (13:1–14:10a), which leads to Yahweh's punishment of the entire Exodus generation except Caleb and Joshua (14:10b–38). This, in turn, leads to Israel's attempt to conquer the land from the south without Yahweh's help, issuing in disaster (14:39–45). The case is not hopeless, however, because Yahweh gives the people further legislation to supplement that which he had given in Leviticus (Num. 15), showing that, although Israel is rebellious, God is still seeking to communicate his will to them. The response to God's revelation is again rebellion, this time by a group of Levites and Reubenites led by Korah, Dathan, and Abiram, and this rebellion also leads to a punishment (ch. 16). God further responds to the rebellion by designating, in a miraculous way, Aaron and his descendants as leaders (ch. 17), and by changing the role of the other Levites in the community (ch. 18). The final piece of cultic legislation is the rather elaborate ritual of the red heifer, used to cleanse the great uncleanness brought about by contact with a corpse (ch. 19).

A. THE SPIES (13:1–14:45)

Chapters 13 and 14 are of central importance in the book. The campaign for which the census of 1:20–45 was taken is about to begin. In fact, all the preparations of chs. 1–10 are now to be brought to bear for the first real foray into the promised land. The failure of the people to trust in Yahweh and their consequent punishment (wandering and dying in the wilderness) has a direct connection with the census of ch. 1, since the very phrase used to number the tribes is used to describe those who will be punished in 14:29 (i.e., those "from twenty years and up").[1] Later, in the census of ch. 26, the spy story is mentioned (26:64–65). Other connections with chs. 13–14 are found in ch. 32, where the requests of the Reubenites and Gadites to settle in Transjordan are met with reflections of this story (32:10–15), and in ch. 34 in the division of the land, the boundaries of which are similar to those of 13:21–29 (see 34:3, 12, 29).[2]

The great rebellion at the climax of the spy narrative is related to the previous rebellions against Moses and Yahweh in chs. 11 and 12. The first ten chapters of Numbers are positive in tone, setting forth God's plans for his people on the march. The human response to God's revelation here in the wilderness is rebellion, just as it had been at Sinai.[3] The change of venue from Sinai to the wilderness does not bring a change in the rebellious human heart. In ch. 11 the people rebelled; in ch. 12 two of the leaders rebel. Here leaders and people unite and choose a new leader to take them back to Egypt — to a time before Yahweh had shown them his mighty nature (14:4).[4] Furthermore, the people charge that God brought them out of Egypt only to abandon them to a sure death in Canaan (14:3). This charge shows a fundamental misunderstanding of Yahweh's nature and actions. When Joshua and Caleb attempted to interpret the spies' report differently, the people were ready to kill them until Yahweh himself intervened (14:10). So great a rebellion led to a great punishment — death for an entire generation (14:20–38).

The punishment of the people was, like that at Kibroth-hattaavah (11:19–20, 33–34) and at Hazeroth (12:10), related directly to the words of the people involved.[5] The people had expressed the wish to have died

1. Heb. *pᵉquḏêḵem . . . mibben ʿeśrîm šānâ wāmāʿlâ;* see 1:3, 18, 20, 22, 24, 26, 28, 30, 32, 34, 36, 38, 40, 42, 45.

2. For a stimulating discussion of this section of the book, see Olson, *Death of the Old*, pp. 129–52, esp. 138–52. The discussion here is indebted to Olson's work.

3. Compare the current narrative with the incident of the golden calf in Exod. 32. There as here the human response to God's revelation was rebellion.

4. See the commentary above on 11:5–6.

5. I.e., the people had demanded meat (11:5) and Miriam had condemned Moses for marrying a Cushite (dark-skinned) wife (12:1). Miriam was turned "white as snow" (12:10).

in the wilderness or in Egypt rather than having to undergo their current difficulties (14:2). So their punishment is "out of their own mouths": "As I live, an utterance of Yahweh, as you have spoken in my ears, so shall I do to you." Furthermore, their wish to go back to Egypt in 14:3–4 is fulfilled when Yahweh sends the people back by the way of the Reed Sea (*derek̲-yām sûp̲*, 14:25). The fear that they would fall by the sword (14:3) is fulfilled at the first encounter with the Amalekites and Canaanites (14:45). The statement that "our wives and our little ones will become spoil" (14:3) finds its unfortunate fulfillment in the fact that "your children will become shepherds in the wilderness forty years" (14:33).

The magnitude of the rebellion meant that the whole generation would die in the wilderness and that the fulfillment of God's promise would be delayed by an entire generation. This judgment is finished at the end of ch. 25 with the death of the last of the rebellious generation in a plague. The census of ch. 26 signals a new starting point, and the fact that a new generation is discussed at all in Num. 14 (after some negotiation between Moses and Yahweh) is a mark of God's grace. The old generation will indeed die out in the wilderness rather than being eradicated immediately (only the ten faithless spies die immediately, 14:37). The promise of God will still be fulfilled. Later in the book (ch. 32) it will become clear that the promise to the new generation is not automatic but depends upon their faithfulness and obedience. Thus, the promise for future generations is open ended.[6]

1. SPIES ARE SELECTED (13:1–16)

1 *And Yahweh spoke to Moses, saying,*

2 *"Send men and let them spy out the land of Canaan, which I am giving to the children of Israel; you will send one man*[1] *from each of the tribes of their fathers — each one a leader among them."*

3 *So Moses sent them from the wilderness of Paran according to the command of Yahweh. All of them were men who were heads of the children of Israel.*

4 *And these are their names: For the tribe of Reuben, Shammua son of Zaccur.*

5 *For the tribe of Simeon, Shaphat son of Hori.*

6. See Olson, *Death of the Old*, pp. 144–52, for a discussion of these themes.

1. The whole phrase *'îš 'eḥād̲* is repeated to show distributive force. See Davidson, *Syntax*, § 38 Rem. 4.

6 *For the tribe of Judah, Caleb son of Jephunneh.*

7 *For the tribe of Issachar, Igal son of Joseph.*[2]

8 *For the tribe of Ephraim, Hoshea son of Nun.*

9 *For the tribe of Benjamin, Palti son of Raphu.*

10 *For the tribe of Zebulun, Gaddiel son of Sodi.*

11 *For the tribe of Joseph,*[3] *for the tribe of Manasseh, Gaddi son of Susi.*

12 *For the tribe of Dan, Ammiel son of Gemalli.*

13 *For the tribe of Asher, Sethur son of Michael.*

14 *For the tribe of Naphtali, Nahbi son of Vophsi.*

15 *For the tribe of Gad, Geuel son of Machi.*

16 *These are the names of the men whom Moses sent to spy out the land. Now Moses called Hoshea son of Nun Joshua.*

1–15 For a summary of the forms of the lists of Hebrew tribes in Numbers, see above on 1:5–15. The leaders chosen here are different from those chosen at 1:5–15; thus, of the men listed here, only Hoshea (Joshua) and Caleb are mentioned elsewhere in the OT. The names Gaddiel, Sethur, Nahbi, and Geuel are unique in the OT. The pivotal nature of what was supposedly about to happen is shown by the fact that new leaders are chosen to represent each tribe. Perhaps leaders who were appropriate for the tasks connected with 1:5–15 were not appropriate for purposes of spying out the land. No objective judgment on the date of this list can be made on the basis of these names.[4] There is no evidence to suggest that these leaders were to replace the leaders chosen in 1:5–15.

Some scholars question the order of this list. As it stands, the order of ch. 13 is unique in the book, and it is not easy to see the logic by which it was constructed (of course, this point does not militate against its originality). If one assumes that vv. 10 and 11 originally followed v. 7,[5] the only difference between this list and that of 1:5–15 is the order of Ephraim and Manasseh. Though there is no textual support for this change, Gray, among others, proposes that it be made on the basis of the

2. According to *BHS*, vv. 10–11 should follow v. 7, giving the usual order of Issachar (v. 7), Zebulun (v. 10), Manasseh (v. 11), Ephraim (v. 12).

3. For *lᵉmaṭṭeh yôsēp̱ BHS* proposes to read *liḇnê yôsēp̱*. The reconstructed text would then be *liḇnê yôsēp̱ lᵉmaṭṭeh mᵉnaššeh.*

4. See the commentary above on 1:5–15.

5. So *BHS*; Gray, p. 136; Noth, pp. 98, 103; Noordtzij, p. 113.

unique separation of Issachar from Zebulun and Ephraim from Manasseh, and this seems reasonable.[6]

Caleb, the representative from Judah, is also called a Kenizzite in, e.g., Num. 32:12; Josh. 14:6, 14. The Kenizzites were an Edomite clan descended from Kenaz, the youngest son of Eliphaz, the oldest son of Esau (Gen. 36:10–11). Gen. 15:19 states that this group lived in Canaan. Since the book of Numbers makes it clear that Caleb was chosen as a leader of Judah (13:6; 26:65; 34:19), at some point the Kenizzites must have become related to or absorbed by the tribe of Judah (probably generations before Caleb's time). Indeed, Josh. 14:6 mentions both groups together.[7]

16 As is consistent with the genealogical lists in Numbers (and elsewhere), v. 16 forms a concluding summary that completes the list and allows the lists to be read as a chart.[8]

The note in v. 16 that Moses renamed *Hoshea son of Nun Joshua* is possibly a later gloss on the text. The text does not say that it was at this point that the renaming took place. The author here wished the reader to note that the Hoshea of the list just previous is the famous *Joshua.* At some unknown point, Moses put the Yahwistic element in *hôšēaʿ* ("he saved") by changing it to *y*ᵉ*hôšuaʿ* ("Yahweh saves").

2. SPIES GO AND RETURN (13:17–33)

17 *And Moses sent them to spy out the land of Canaan, and he said to them, "Go up into this*[1] *Negeb and go up*[2] *into the hill country,*

6. E.g., Gray, p. 136; Noth, p. 103; Sturdy, p. 95 (a confused comment?); Noordtzij, p. 113.

7. See R. K. Harrison, *ISBE,* rev., III:7; L. Hicks, *IDB,* III:6. The Caleb mentioned in 1 Chr. 2:18–19, 24 was probably the grandfather of the Caleb in Numbers. Cf. Noordtzij, p. 114; H. G. M. Williamson, *1 and 2 Chronicles,* NCBC (Grand Rapids: Eerdmans, 1982), pp. 52–53; J. M. Myers, *I Chronicles,* AB (Garden City, N.Y.: Doubleday, 1965), p. 14.

8. For the nature of this text, see the commentary above on 7:10–88; see also B. Levine, "The Descriptive Tabernacle Texts of the Pentateuch," *JAOS* 85 (1965) 307–18; A. Rainey, "The Order of Sacrifices in Old Testament Ritual Texts," *Bib* 51 (1970) 485–98. For other concluding formulae on the lists of names in Numbers see 1:16, 44; 2:32; 7:17b, 23b, 29b, 35b, 41b, 47b, 53b, 59b, 65b, 71b, 77b, 83b, 84–88; 10:28; 26:7a, 14a, 22a, 25a, 27a, 34a, 37a, 41a, 42b, 47a, 50a, 51a; 34:29. Cf. also Gen. 35:26b; 49:28; Exod. 6:26a.

1. The demonstrative *zeh* is used here as an enclitic indeclinable particle for emphasis; see Williams, *Syntax,* § 118.

2. The perfect consecutive follows and continues the flavor of the imperative; see GKC, § 112r.

18 *and see what the land is, and whether the people who are dwelling in it are strong or weak, whether*[3] *they are few or many,*

19 *and whether the land in which they are dwelling is good or bad, and whether*[4] *the cities in which they are dwelling are in camps or in strongholds,*

20 *and whether the land is fertile or barren. Is there wood in it or not? Now take courage and take some of the fruit of the land" (for the time was the days of the first fruits of the grapes).*

21 *And they went up and spied out the land, from the wilderness of Zin to Rehob by Lebo-Hamath.*

22 *And they went up into the Negeb and arrived at Hebron. And there were Ahiman, Sheshai, and Talmai, the offspring of Anak. (Now Hebron was built seven years before Zoan in Egypt.)*

23 *And they arrived at the Valley of Eshcol, and they cut down a branch with one cluster of grapes. And they carried it on a pole between two of them. They also took some of the pomegranates and some of the figs.*

24 *That place was called the Valley of Eshcol because of the cluster that the men of Israel cut down from there.*

25 *So they returned from spying out the land at the end of forty days.*

26 *And they came to Moses and to Aaron and to the whole congregation of the children of Israel, to the wilderness of Paran at Kadesh. And they brought a report to them and to the whole congregation; and they showed them the fruit of the land.*

27 *And they recounted it to him, and said, "We went to the land to which you sent us; it flows with milk and honey, and this is its fruit.*

28 *Nevertheless,*[5] *the people who dwell in the land are mighty, and their cities are very great strongholds, and also we saw the offspring of Anak there.*

29 *Amalekites dwell in the land of the Negeb, the Hittites, the Jebusites, and the Amorites dwell in the hill country, and the Canaanites dwell by the sea and along the Jordan."*

3. The question that sets forth alternatives (the disjunctive question) rarely, as here, has the *hê* interrogative in the second clause. It is more common to have *'ô, 'im,* or *w^e;* see Davidson, *Syntax,* § 126 Rem. 1; Williams, *Syntax,* § 544. See n. 4 below.

4. The last member of the question in v. 18 and those in the current verse have the more common *h^a* in the first clause followed by *'im* in the second; see Davidson, *Syntax,* § 124.

5. The construction *'epes–kî* serves as an adverb of limitation (used only five times in the OT) with the meaning "except that," "nevertheless"; cf. Davidson, *Syntax,* § 154; Williams, *Syntax,* § 558.

30 *But Caleb stilled the people before Moses and he said, "Let us surely go up and possess it, for we are surely able to do it!"*
31 *But the men who went up with him said, "We are not able to go up against*[6] *the people because they are stronger than we are."*
32 *So they brought forth an evil report to the children of Israel concerning the land that they spied out, saying, "The land into which we crossed over to spy out is a land that devours its inhabitants, all the people whom we saw in it were men of great stature.*
33 *We even saw the Nephilim" (the sons of Anak came from the Nephilim). "And we seemed, in our eyes, as grasshoppers, and so we must have seemed to them."*

The purpose of this section (which is really two sections, treated together for convenience) is to narrate the mission of the spies to Canaan (vv. 13–24) and their report to Moses, Aaron, and the people (vv. 25–33). Many commentators divide chs. 13 and 14 into the documents J (or JE) and P.[7] Whatever the background of the text, and however it came to be edited together, it was in the end formed into a single story that was meant to be interpreted as a whole. Of course, the editing of the text took place after the events narrated, and events of the past may well be described in ways that are more relevant to the time of the editor than to the time of the original text.

17–20 These verses form Moses' instructions to the spies. His topographical instructions are vague, as befits one with no independent knowledge of the land of Canaan. He includes only the Negeb immediately before them and the hill country beyond it. One should interpret the scope of these instructions in the light of what actually happened in the mission itself.

In modern times the *Negeb* is a roughly triangular piece of territory bordered by Wadi Arabah on the east, the Sinai on the south and west, and a line running roughly from around Gaza to the west shore of the Dead Sea, a bit north of Beer-sheba, on the north. The term *negeḇ* means "dry

6. For *'el* used of disadvantage or an adversarial relationship, see Williams, *Syntax,* § 303.

7. J(E): 13:17b–20, 22–24, 26b–31; 14:4, (11–23a), 23b–24, 39–45; P: 13:1–17a, 25–26a, 32–33; 14:1–3, 5–10, 26–38. Earlier scholars (e.g., Holzinger, pp. 43–44; Gray, pp. 130–65) see it as possible to separate J and E. More recent scholars (e.g., Budd, pp. 141–44; Noth, 101–12; de Vaulx, pp. 164–69, 171–75) are less eager to separate them and see the older stratum as a combination JE. One problem with such an approach is its atomistic view of the text.

land," which it surely is, although not in the sense of a desert. From within Canaan, the Negeb was to the south; hence in many biblical texts the term means simply the south (e.g., Gen. 13:14). In the Bible itself, the Negeb is smaller than in modern times, being mainly confined to the area east and west of Beer-sheba and north of Kadesh-barnea.

As one travels to the north and west through this dry land, one eventually comes to the *hill country (hāhār)*. Many times this term is taken to mean the north-south strip, about 30 mi. long and 15 mi. wide, bordered by the lower hills of the Shephelah ("lowlands")[8] on the west and the wilderness of Judah on the east. Hebron is in this territory (v. 22), at an altitude of about 3,000 ft. above sea level. This territory is surely included in *hāhār (hill country)* in the text, but since the spies' mission took them far to the north of this, the term *hill country* should be taken in a more general sense, as an indication of the whole land beyond the Negeb. How Moses knew that hill country lay beyond the Negeb is not stated in the text, nor the source of his knowledge (whatever it was) of the topography of Canaan. There is no reason to think that he had detailed information about it; these general instructions were the best he could give.

Moses then charged the spies to bring back detailed information that would be useful in military operations to conquer the land, and, beyond that, in settling in it. Whether the people were strong enough to defend their cities, whether the land would support the invading armies of Israel, whether the dwellings of the inhabitants of Canaan were in unfortified camps or in walled cities, all these facts would be important in drawing plans for the forthcoming conquest.

At the end of his instructions, Moses ordered the spies to bring back a sample of the fruit of the land. An explanatory note, which some take as an editorial gloss,[9] gives the time of year: *for the time as the days of the first fruits of the grapes (wᵉhayyāmîm yᵉmê bikkûrê ʿᵃnāḇîm)*, i.e., midsummer (mid to late July).

21–24 These verses summarize the scope of the mission and what was found. Other than the general itinerary, only two comments are made: one concerning the Anakim at Hebron (v. 22), and the other about the grape cluster at Eshcol (vv. 23–24).

8. The Shephelah is the country to the west of the Judean hills. It is usually distinguished from *the hill country* and the *Negeb*. See G. A. Smith, *The Historical Geography of the Holy Land* (25th ed.; London: Hodder & Stoughton, 1931; repr. New York: Harper & Row, 1966), pp. 143–67.

9. The purpose and origin of this editorial note are uncertain; some see it as a later addition (see Gray, p. 139), though most do not discuss it at all.

21 This verse is a summary of the geographical dimensions of the entire mission.[10]

the wilderness of Zin (miḏbar-ṣin). According to 13:26 Kadesh-barnea was in the wilderness of Paran, and according to 20:1 it was in the wilderness of Zin; it is likely that the border between the two areas was fluid and that Kadesh-barnea was near this border. Thus this territory was immediately north of the encampment in Kadesh and formed the southern border of the reconnaissance.

The northernmost extension of the spies' travels was *rᵉḥōḇ,* an unknown site, but probably to be identified with Beth-rehob *(bêṯ-rᵉḥôḇ)* near Dan (Laish; Judg. 18:28). The site is clarified by the addition of another place-name, *Lebo-Hamath (lᵉḇōʾ-ḥᵃmāṯ),* which is probably to be identified with modern Lebweh on the Orontes River below Riblah.[11] Whatever the precise location, this same Lebo-Hamath is cited as part of the northern border of Canaan in 34:8. The spies went through the whole land, from south to north.

The text itself does not tell us the place from which Moses sent out the spies (vv. 17–20), although it does say that the spies came to Moses and the Israelites at Kadesh (barnea, v. 26) on the return from their mission. The alternatives seem to be that Moses made an appointment to bring the Israelites to Kadesh to meet the spies on their return, or that he sent the spies out from Kadesh and waited there with the Israelites until the spies came back. The latter choice is easier to imagine from a logistical point of view. If, then, the spies did go up from Kadesh-barnea (probably to be connected with modern Ain-Qedeis and Ain Qudeirat),[12] it was possibly by a route that N. Glueck called the "Way of the Wells," an irregular diagonal line of wells and springs that had been used from ancient times.[13]

22 *Hebron (ḥeḇrôn)* is ancient Kiriath-arba, about 18 mi. southwest of Jerusalem. It is in the vicinity of Mamre (Gen. 13:18), which is connected with the Abraham traditions, hence particularly important to

10. For a parallel summary, see that of the trip from Sinai to Paran in 10:12, at the beginning of the travel section.

11. Wenham, p. 231; Sturdy, p. 95; H. G. May, *IDB,* II:516–17; M. Liverani, "The Amorites," in *Peoples of Old Testament Times,* ed. D. J. Wiseman (Oxford: Oxford Univ. Press, 1973), p. 124 n. 91.

12. Cf., e.g., S. Cohen, *IDB,* III:1–2; Davies (*Way of the Wilderness,* pp. 74–75) mentions only the former.

13. N. Glueck, *Rivers in the Desert,* rev. ed. (New York: Norton, 1968), pp. 85–90, 111–15. This whole book may still be consulted with profit.

the Israelites (see esp. Gen. 23). The people who lived around Hebron in Abraham's day were called Hittites (Gen. 23:5). That *Hebron was built seven years before Zoan in Egypt* makes it very ancient indeed. For the name Zoan corresponds to the Egyptian *dʿn(t)* (Greek Tanis), the capital of the Hyksos pharaohs, built sometime in the first half of the 2nd millennium B.C.

At Hebron the spies encountered Ahiman, Sheshai, and Talmai *(ʾaḥîman šēšay wetalmay).* These names probably designate three clans who were living in the area. Later, Caleb and the Judahites would defeat these three groups and take Hebron from them (Josh. 15:14; Judg. 1:10). The three are said to be *the offspring of Anak* (*yelîḏê hāʿănāḵ,* lit., "children of the neck"). *Anak* also probably designates a group named after an eponymous ancestor or chieftain. The Anakim are noted for their height in Num. 13:28 (also Deut. 2:21 and 9:2), and Num. 13:33 relates them to the Nephilim, the offspring of the union between the "sons of God" and the daughters of men in Gen. 6:4. Most of the biblical evidence connects the Anakim with Hebron,[14] although Josh. 11:21–22 states that there were Anakim beyond Hebron in such places as Debir (Tell Beit Mirsim) and Anab (Khirbet Anab), which are in the general vicinity (12 and 15 mi. to the southwest respectively), and as far removed as the cities of Gaza, Gath, and Ashdod (between 18 and 36 mi. distant).

the Valley of Eshcol (naḥal-ʾeškōl). The word *naḥal* (here *valley*) refers to the wadi or seasonal torrent-valley in the dry land.[15] This valley was named for the *cluster (ʾeškōl)* of grapes found there. Since v. 24 makes clear that the spies themselves called the valley Eshcol, it is not surprising that the actual site is unknown. Some scholars have assumed that Eshcol was in the Hebron area, perhaps around Ramet el-Amleh.[16] The biblical text probably means that the spies left Hebron and went on their way, coming to Eshcol at some point north of the town, but how far north is unknown.

25–26 The journey from the wilderness of Zin to the north and back took *forty days,* a well-known biblical phrase for an indefinite shorter time period.[17] Such a mission on foot would take about forty days.

14. Num. 13:22, 28, 33; Deut. 9:2; Josh. 15:13–14; 21:11; Judg. 1:20.

15. BDB, p. 636.

16. Glueck, *Rivers in the Desert,* p. 112. This is a traditional site mentioned already by Jerome in *Epistle* 108. See further *IDB,* III:142b.

17. The number can, of course, mean the literal figure, but often carries with it a less exact sense of an indefinite time period. See, e.g., "forty days" in Gen. 7:17; 8:6; 50:3; Num. 14:23; 1 K. 19:8; Jon. 3:4; etc.; "forty days and forty

At the close of this period they returned to Moses and the people at Kadesh-barnea.

27–29 These verses are probably a summary of the spies' report. The general report was that the land was very good: *it flows with milk and honey (zāḇat-ḥālāḇ ûḏ^e^ḇaš hîʾ).*[18] Although vv. 27ff. concentrate on the report to Moses (*they recounted it to him,* v. 27), the text makes clear that the report was in the hearing of the whole congregation (v. 26).

28 *Nevertheless (ʾep̱es-kî).* Even though the land was very good, the people that inhabited it were very strong, their cities were well fortified, and the Anakim (tall people) dwell there.

29 This verse lists the different groups that the spies either heard about or encountered during their mission. *Amalekites dwell in the land of the Negeb (ʿ^a^mālēq yôšēḇ b^e^ʾereṣ hanneg̱eḇ).* Amalek was the offspring of Eliphaz son of Esau by the concubine Timna (Gen. 36:12), and so was related to the Kenizzites (of which group Caleb was a member) in a way analogous to that in which Judah (son of Leah) was to Gad or Asher (sons of Leah's handmaid Zilpah). According to Gen. 14:7 the Amalekites were already entrenched around Beer-sheba in the 2nd millennium B.C. The Amalekites attacked Israel, but were defeated at Rephidim on the way to Sinai (Exod. 17:8–16). Later, they attacked stragglers on their way through the wilderness (Deut. 25:17–19). From the earliest times the Amalekites are portrayed as the enemies of Israel.[19] That the Amalekites were powerful adversaries is indicated by the command to avoid them in Num. 14:25.

The *Hittites (haḥittî),* along with the Jebusites and the Amorites, *dwell in* (i.e., are inhabitants of) the hill country. Just who these Hittites were is not known. They were inhabitants of part of Canaan in the time of Abraham, who purchased the cave at Machpelah from one Ephron the Hittite.[20] The Hittites are connected with others as inhabitants of pre-

---

nights" in Gen. 7:4, 12; Exod. 24:18; etc.; "forty years" in Judg. 3:11; 1 Sam. 4:18; Amos 2:10; 5:25; etc. B. Birch calls forty "the most frequently used round number in the Bible" (*ISBE,* rev., III:558).

18. A standard description of Canaan: Exod. 3:8, 17; 13:5; 33:3; Lev. 20:24; Num. 13:27; 14:8; 16:14; Deut. 6:3; 11:9; 26:9, 15; 27:3; 31:20; Josh. 5:6; Jer. 11:5; 32:22; Ezek. 20:6, 15. See BDB, pp. 185a, 316.

19. See the later confrontation between Samuel and King Agag the Amalekite (1 Sam. 15), in which the former hacked the latter in pieces before the Lord, i.e., "in the presence of Yahweh."

20. Cf. Gen. 15; 23; 25–26; 36; 49.

Israelite Canaan often in the OT.[21] The Bible is well aware of thc great Anatolian power called the Hittites (ca. 1650–1200 B.C.; see Josh. 1:4; Judg. 1:26), but the connection between the Anatolian Hittites and the Canaanite Hittites is a mystery.[22] The names of these Canaanite Hittites are, like Ephron in Genesis, Semitic names, which would not be true of the non-Semitic Anatolian Hittites. This and other factors have led some scholars to identify the Canaanite Hittites as a native Semitic group. Heb. *ḥittî* is not identical with *ḫat,* which is the name used by the Anatolian Hittites, and may be due to chance conflation.[23]

the Jebusites (hayᵉḇûsî). This name is usually given to the pre-Israelite inhabitants of Jerusalem and environs.[24] Although raided by the Israelites (Judg. 1:8) the city of Jerusalem did not fall until David's time (2 Sam. 5:6–7).

the Amorites (ha'ĕmōrî) . . . the Canaanites. Here the Amorites are distinguished from the Canaanites, who *dwell by the sea and along the Jordan;* elsewhere the term *Amorite* is an inclusive term for the populace of Canaan.[25] The *amurru* are first attested in Mesopotamian cuneiform sources in the late 3rd millennium B.C. The term indicated Northwest Semitic groups of people who lived in the area west of Mesopotamia (*amurru* means "west" in some texts). In the Amarna correspondence (14th–13th cents. B.C.) the name is applied to a Syrian province or geographical area stretching from the Mediterranean Sea to the Orontes River, but not including Canaan proper. M. Liverani cites Josh. 13:4–5 as the only OT reference to the Late Bronze Age Syrian region of Amurru.[26] According to him, this text in Joshua "keeps the exact memory of the situation during the fourteenth and thirteenth centuries, that is, of the period to which the passage refers."[27] It is worth noting that Lebo-Hamath (or the entrance to

21. Cf. Exod. 3:8, 17; 13:5; 23:23, 28; 33:2; 34:11; Deut. 7:1; 20:17; Josh. 3:10; 9:1; 11:3; 12:8; 24:11; Judg. 3:5; 1 K. 9:20; 11:1; Ezra 9:1; Neh. 9:8.

22. Cf. F. F. Bruce, *ISBE,* rev., II:720–23, esp. 723; also see J. Van Seters, "The terms 'Amorite' and 'Hittite' in the Old Testament," *VT* 22 (1972) 64–81.

23. The whole question of the Hittites is complex; see Bruce, *ISBE,* rev., II:720–23; H. A. Hoffner, "The Hittites and the Hurrians," in *People of OT Times,* pp. 197–228, esp. p. 214.

24. E.g., Josh. 15:8; 18:16.

25. E.g., Gen. 15:16; Josh. 10:5; Judg. 6:10; cf. 1 Sam. 7:14.

26. Liverani, "Amorites," pp. 123–24.

27. Ibid.

Hamath) is mentioned in both Josh. 13:5 and Num. 13:21. May not the same "exact memory" be operative in both texts?[28]

the Canaanites (hakk^{e}na^{ʿa}nî). In the current text, these are the dwellers along the seacoast and the banks of the Jordan, as opposed to the inhabitants of the whole land.[29]

One must consider whether the tradition reported here is intended to reflect the ethnic or political groups in Canaan in the late 2nd millennium B.C., or whether its inclusion here reflects a later perspective. Many scholars simply tend to assume the latter to be true. Those scholars still committed to a documentary explanation of the Pentateuch usually attribute 13:29 to J(E), which means a date as early as the 9th or, perhaps, even the 10th cent. B.C., with a chance that earlier material is reflected.[30] Others have seen 13:29 as an exilic addition to J.[31] In fact, J. Van Seters denies that these names identify historical entities in any important way for the author of this text. Rather, they are used for rhetorical purposes, i.e., to suggest the evil, pagan powers present all around Israel.[32] The above paragraphs show that it is difficult to know just what is meant by the names here recorded. The stability of the list of names, however, may as well point to historical fact as to purely literary use (as if the two were opposed by necessity). If this and other lists of pre-Israelite inhabitants of Canaan were used only rhetorically or ideologically, as Van Seters suggests, it would seem that in addition to a standard number of nations, a standard order would have been adopted. Among the sixteen lists of foreign nations in Canaan, the members (some have 5, 6, 7, 8, 9, and 10 members) and the order (13 different orders) vary.[33] It is virtually certain that these spies would use terms in a popular way rather than a scientific one (in either ancient or modern senses of the word *scientific*).

One must also ask where these spies would get the information of

28. Cf. H. B. Huffmon, "Amorites," *IDBSup,* p. 21; A. H. Sayce and J. A. Soggin, "Amorites," *ISBE,* rev., I:113–14; Liverani, "Amorites," pp. 123–26.

29. As also in Deut. 1:7; Josh. 5:1; 13:3; 17:15–18; Judg. 1:1–36. See C. G. Libolt, "Canaan," *ISBE,* rev., I:585–91, esp. 586–87; A. R. Millard, "The Canaanites," in *Peoples of OT Times,* pp. 29–52.

30. E.g., Gray, pp. 130–31, 146; Budd, p. 142.

31. E.g., Van Seters, "The terms 'Amorite' and 'Hittite,'" esp. p. 81; also Noth, p. 107.

32. Van Seters, "The terms 'Amorite' and 'Hittite,'" p. 81.

33. The lists are found in Gen. 10:15; 15:19–21; Exod. 3:8; 13:5; 23:23; 33:2; 34:11; Num. 13:29; Deut. 7:1; 20:17; Josh. 3:10; 13:8; Judg. 3:5; 1 K. 9:20; Ezra 9:1; and Neh. 9:8.

v. 29, and of what use it would have been to Israelites who had never been in Canaan before. Did the people have lists of peoples in Canaan from Egyptian or other (Midianite?) sources? The present state of knowledge does not permit answers to these questions, although the probability is strong that such a list might be more valuable after the settlement of the land than before.

30–33 This section gives the account of the first conclusions drawn by the spies on the basis of the data in their report. The spies have two distinct reactions. Caleb speaks in favor of going into the land and conquering it. Here Caleb alone speaks; after the reaction of the people not only against Moses but also against God, Joshua joins with him (14:6ff.). The majority of the spies, however, are clearly against attacking the land (at least from the south) because of the strength of the inhabitants. Thus these verses begin a contrast between faith (Caleb and Joshua) and the lack thereof (the other spies and the rest of the people). This lack of faith will lead to the end of the whole Exodus generation in the wilderness. That old generation will finally die out, except for Caleb and Joshua (and Moses), at the end of ch. 25. These men will lead the new generation into the land, beginning with the new census in ch. 26.

30 *Caleb stilled the people (wayyahas kālēḇ 'eṯ-hā'ām).* The verb *hāsâ* usually occurs in the form of an interjection, "Hush!" This leads one to suspect that the spies' report evoked a vocal reaction from the people. Caleb simply asserted that, although the report as given was true — many mighty peoples lived in Canaan — Israel should *go up ('ālâ)* and *possess (yāraš)* the land. These words are used in, e.g., Exod. 3:8, 17; 33:3; and Lev. 20:17 of God's promises to the people concerning the land.

32 The contrast between faith and the lack of faith comes out clearly, even here at the beginning, in the word used to describe the majority interpretation of the reconnaissance mission. It is called *an evil report (dibbâ).* This term contains within it the idea of negativity, falsehood, and strife. When 14:27 adds the word *evil (rā'â)* to *dibbâ* it is merely clarifying what is already implicit.[34]

Whereas Caleb has attempted to quiet the people, the evil report of the majority attempts to stir them up and instill fear. It is an exaggerated interpretation of the dangers. The land itself *devours its inhabitants,* a vivid word-picture not designed to instill confidence. Whether this phrase

34. Heb. *dibbâ* is also used in 14:36 with the same sense. It may also be used of a true report of evil deeds; cf. Gen. 37:2. Prov. 12:22 parallels *dibbâ* to *śip^{e}ṯê–šāqēr,* "lying lips," and 20:19 to *rāḵîl,* "slander." See BDB, p. 179; H.-J. Fabry, *TDOT,* III:72–79, esp. 78.

meant that the land was infertile, or unstable, warlike, and unforgiving, or even comparable with Sheol,[35] the real point is that the phrase is designed rhetorically to frighten the people and win them to the majority view. The land itself was destructive, not to mention the inhabitants, who were equally frightening: they were *men of great stature ('anšê middôṯ)*.

33 The spies connect these tall men with the *Nephilim.* These creatures were, at least in part, the "mighty men" *(gibbôrîm)* resulting from the union between the "sons of God" and the daughters of men in that difficult and tantalizing passage, Gen. 6:1–4.[36] The simplest way to take the text here is that, although the Israelites would not have known who the Anakim were, since Num. 13:22 is the first mention of them in the Bible, they would be familiar with the story of the Nephilim. Connecting the *men of great stature* with the *Nephilim* is an exaggeration for rhetorical effect.

The Hebrew text clarifies the name Nephilim with an added note: *the sons of Anak came from the Nephilim (b^enê ʿ^anāq min-hann^epilîm).* This note makes explicit the connection between the current statement and Gen. 6:4, whether this note is to be taken as a later gloss (it is missing from LXX), or as the interpretation offered by the spies themselves (which is more likely). The spies' self-description as *grasshoppers (ḥ^agāḇîm)* is a figure of speech called meiosis, which diminishes one thing to increase the size or importance of another.[37]

The entire argument by the majority in vv. 31–33 is woven together to interpret the data in the report in a way that would lead the people to the conclusion that the conquest of the land was not feasible. Although it may be that the original majority report was meant only to reject an entrance into Canaan from the south,[38] as the text stands it is clear that the majority report is condemned as false and faithless. It should be noted that nowhere in ch. 13 does the name of God or his promise of the land figure as a prominent theme. It is only after the reaction of the

35. For the first see Gray, p. 151. For the second see, e.g., Keil, p. 91; Noth, p. 107; Noordtzij, p. 120; Coats, *Rebellion in the Wilderness,* pp. 140–41. For the last see McEvenue, *Narrative Style,* pp. 135–36.

36. On Gen. 6:1–4, see, e.g., U. Cassuto, *A Commentary on the Book of Genesis, Part I: From Abraham to Noah,* tr. I. Abrahams (Jerusalem: Magnes, 1961), pp. 290–300; G. von Rad, *Genesis: A Commentary,* tr. J. Marks, OTL, rev. ed. (Philadelphia: Westminster, 1972), pp. 113–16.

37. See E. W. Bullinger, *Figures of Speech Used in the Bible* (London: Eyre & Spottiswoode, 1898), p. 155.

38. So Glueck, *Rivers in the Desert,* pp. 113–14.

people, which in the light of their recent history (chs. 11–12) was predictable, that ch. 14 develops the theme of divine promise and help. Ch. 14 gives the reactions of various groups of people to this majority interpretation of the reconnaissance mission and to one another in the light of Yahweh's promises and concern for his people.

3. RESPONSES TO THE SPIES' REPORTS (14:1–45)

a. Responses by People and Leaders (14:1–10a)

1 *And the whole congregation raised their voices*[1] *and the people wept that night.*

2 *And all the children of Israel murmured against Moses and against Aaron, and the whole congregation said to them, "If we had only died*[2] *in the land of Egypt or if we had only died in this wilderness.*

3 *Now why is Yahweh bringing us into this land to fall by the sword? Our wives and our little ones will become prey. It seems better*[3] *to us to return to Egypt."*

4 *And they said to one another, "Let us choose a leader and let us return to Egypt."*

5 *And Moses and Aaron fell*[4] *on their faces in front of the whole congregation of the children of Israel.*

6 *Then Joshua son of Nun and Caleb son of Jephunneh, who were among those who spied out the land, tore their garments,*

7 *and they said to the whole congregation of the children of Israel, "The land*[5] *into which we have crossed over to spy out is a very good*[6] *land.*

1. Heb. *wattiśśâ kol-hāʿēḏâ wayyittᵉnû ʾeṯ-qôlām,* lit., "and the whole congregation raised and gave their voices." The first verb is fem. sing., in agreement with its subject. The second is pl. in agreement with the plural/collective nature of the subject; cf. Gray, pp. 152–53.

2. Heb. *lû-maṯᵉnû.* With a verb in the perfect, *lû* expresses an unfulfilled desire, usually in past time. With an imperfect, *lû* is a wish for the present or immediate future; cf. GKC, §§ 106p, 151e; Davidson, *Syntax,* § 39d; 134; Williams, *Syntax,* §§ 166, 460, 548; Driver, *Tenses,* § 140.

3. For *ṭôḇ* alone as a comparative adjective, see Gray, p. 153; it would be more normal to expect the definite article as in Gen. 1:16: *hammāʾôr haggāḏôl,* etc.; cf. GKC, § 133f.

4. Heb. *wayyippōl mōšeh wᵉʾaḥᵃrōn.* Occasionally, when the predicate precedes the subject, as here, the verb is in the third masc. sing. in spite of a pl. subject (or fem., 2 K. 3:26); see Davidson *Syntax,* § 113b; GKC, § 145o.

5. On the construction *hāʾāreṣ . . . hāʾāreṣ,* cf. Driver, *Tenses,* § 197, Obs. 2.

6. On the construction *ṭôḇâ mᵉʾōḏ mᵉʾōḏ,* "very good," see Gen. 7:19;

8 *If Yahweh delights in us then he will bring us into this land and he will give it to us —a land flowing with milk and honey.*
9 *Only do not rebel against Yahweh, and, you, do not fear*[7] *the people of the land, for they are our bread. Their protection has turned aside from over them and Yahweh is with us. Do not fear them!"*
10a *But the whole congregation said to stone them with stones.*

1–4 *And the whole congregation raised their voices and the people wept (wattiśśâ kol-hāʿēḏâ wayyitt^e^nû 'eṯ-qôlām wayyiḇkû hāʿām)* — Two verbs, literally "to lift" *(nāśâ')* and "to give" *(nāṯan),* are combined into an idiom meaning "to shout aloud."[8] The author uses three different names for the people: *the whole congregation* (*kol-hāʿēḏâ,* vv. 1a and 2b), *the people* (*hāʿām,* v. 1b), and *all the children of Israel* (*kol b^e^nê yiśrā'ēl,* v. 2a). By the use of these designations he emphasizes that all the people were, indeed, involved in the rebellion that is to follow.

Four successively more specific and climactic clauses make it clear that the whole people complained about their present situation. They not only raised their voices (*wattiśśâ . . . wayyitt^e^nû 'eṯ-qôlām,* v. 1a), they also wept (*wayyiḇkû,* v. 1b); their weeping consisted in murmuring (*wayyillōnû,* v. 2a), and their murmuring was specifically that they wished to have died in Egypt or in the wilderness (*wayyō'm^e^rû . . . lû-maṯ^e^nû . . . ,* v. 2b). Their complaint issues in attributing an evil motive to Yahweh (*YHWH mēḇî' 'ōṯānû 'el-hā'āreṣ hazzō'ṯ linpōl . . . ,* v. 3) and a desire, if not a decision, to reject God's leader and choose a new one to take them back to Egypt (*h^a^lô' ṭôḇ lānû šûḇ miṣray^e^mâ . . . nitt^e^nâ rō'š w^e^nāšûḇâ miṣrāy^e^mâ,* vv. 3b–4). The verbs used in vv. 1–4 tie this account of rebellion to others already narrated in Exod. 15–17 and Num. 11–12. In fact, these verses allow the whole spy mission of ch. 13 to be seen as the preamble for one more great rebellion in the wilderness.[9] Although the numbers of words used for the Israelites and

---

30:43; 1 K. 7:47; 2 K. 10:4; Ezek. 37:10; Williams, *Syntax,* § 16; GKC, § 123e; Davidson, *Syntax,* § 29 Rem. 8.

7. The prohibition with *'al* plus the jussive *(tim^e^rōḏû, tîr^e^'û, tîrā'ûm)* indicates a strong negative entreaty or wish; cf. Davidson, *Syntax,* § 127 (a); Williams, *Syntax,* §§ 401–2.

8. See note to the translation above. Other verbs of saying are used in combination to make up one idiom; e.g., "to answer and say," *'ānâ wayyō'mer,* Gen. 18:27; Exod. 4:1; Num. 11:28; 22:18; 23:12; etc.

9. E.g., *lûn* is used of murmuring in Exod. 15–17, *bāḵâ* of the weeping of the Israelites at Kibroth-hattaavah in Num. 11, and *'āmar* of Miriam's rebellion

the different verbal expressions for their complaining, etc., are numerous in this text, these factors may be explained rhetorically as easily as they are as indicators of a composite text.[10]

that night (ballay^e^lâ hahû') is the night after the spy report of ch. 13.

As we have seen before, the words of the people are connected to Yahweh's judgment on them: compare vv. 2b and 29, 32, 33b, 35b (dying in the wilderness), vv. 3a and 43–45 (falling by the sword), and vv. 3b, 31, 33 (the children becoming prey). The irony is obvious.

The sins of the people are multiple. First, they have implicitly denied Yahweh's salvation and providential care by wishing to have died in Egypt or in their journey thus far. The reason for Israel's death wish is their fear of death at the hands of the Canaanites. This lack of faith is foisted on Yahweh himself and is made to be his purpose in bringing the people into Canaan, where he will allow the Canaanites to slaughter the men and take the women and children as booty.[11] This conclusion, of course, shows a further, fundamental misunderstanding of Yahweh's character. Israel's fear issues in the decision that it was surely better to go back to Egypt, the place of slavery and death, rather than forward to face the Canaanites.

4 *And they said to one another (wayyōm^e^rû 'îš 'el-'āḥîw,* v. 4). It is hard to know whether these words mean that the Israelites said this privately or publicly. In any case, Yahweh knew the whole story, and Moses and Aaron knew enough to cause them to fall on their faces in front of the people (v. 5).

The Israelites themselves wanted to choose a *leader* (*rō'š,* lit., "head"), as opposed to Moses and Aaron, whom Yahweh had chosen. Although the term *leader* is not carefully defined here, in Numbers leaders

---

in ch. 12. The idiom "to give the voice and weep," *nāṯan 'eṯ-haqqôl w^e^ḇāḵâ* ("to weep aloud"), is found in Gen. 21:26; 27:38; 29:11; 1 Sam. 24:17; 30:4; 2 Sam. 3:32; Ruth 1:9, 14; etc.

10. Gray, p. 152, explains the literary phenomena in this text by recourse to a combination of three different sources.

11. The noun *baz,* "prey," and the verb *bāzaz,* "to make prey, spoil of," are mainly used in military contexts to designate persons or things that have become part of the victors' prize (see, e.g., Ezek. 29:19; 38:12–13). In Ezek. 34:8, 22, 28 the noun is used in a figure of speech in which the nations fall like wild animals upon the Israelites, who are compared to helpless sheep. The noun parallels other words for booty: *šālāl* (e.g., Isa. 10:6) and *m^e^šissâ* (e.g., 2 K. 21:14; Isa. 42:22). Cf. BDB, pp. 102–3; H. Ringgren, *TDOT,* II:66–68.

are generally those men who headed up the tribal units.[12] Yahweh chose these leaders directly (1:4) or through Moses (13:3). The office was not hereditary; rather it was based on God's choice, and presumably some competence on the part of the potential leader.[13] The people wanted to appoint a leader who would carry out their desire to go back to Egypt. The Latter Prophets especially consider "returning to Egypt" a synonym for rebellion against God.[14]

5 *And Moses and Aaron fell on their faces (wayyippōl mōšeh wᵉʾaḥᵃrōn ʿal-pᵉnêhem).* This idiom is used 25 times in the OT.[15] Other than its literal meaning, this idiom generally indicates the deference shown by a lesser party to a greater, whether human or divine.[16] The inferior party occasionally has a request to present before the superior.[17] Since Yahweh does not make his presence known until v. 10b, it is impossible to judge whether the purpose of the present action is to be seen as primarily intercessory or simply obeisant before Yahweh, the Judge of all the earth, who will punish rebellion now as in the past (see 14:2–4). Both motives are probably present. Note the feeling of suspense that the narrator maintains. The sin occurs in vv. 1–4, but God does not even appear until v. 10b.

in front of the whole congregation . . . (lip̄nê kol-qᵉhāl). The inferior party sometimes falls "before" *(lip̄nê)* the greater.[18] If that is the case here, the meaning would be that Moses and Aaron fell down in deference to the people, perhaps because they were afraid for their lives.[19]

12. Many times the "fathers' houses," e.g., 1:4, 16; 10:4; 13:3; 14:4; 17:18 (Eng. 3); 25:4, 15; 31:26; 32:28; 36:1; also the whole tribe, 30:2 (Eng. 1).

13. On the term *rōʾš,* cf. J. R. Bartlett, "The Use of the Term *rōʾš* as a Title in the Old Testament," *VT* 19 (1969) 1–10.

14. See, e.g., Isa. 30:1–7; 31:1–3; Jer. 2:18; Ezek. 17:15.

15. Gen. 17:3, 17; 50:1; Lev. 9:24; Num. 14:5; 16:4, 22; 17:10 (Eng. 16:45); 20:6; Josh. 7:6, 10; Judg. 13:20; 1 Sam. 17:49; 2 Sam. 9:6; 14:4; 1 K. 18:7, 39; Ezek. 1:28; 3:23; 9:8; 11:3; 43:3; 44:4 (the last two with *ʾel*); Ruth 2:10; Dan. 8:17.

16. For the literal meaning, see Gen. 50:1; 1 Sam. 17:49. For deference to humans, see, e.g., 2 Sam. 9:6; 14:4; 1 K. 18:7. For deference to God, see, e.g., 1 K. 18:39; Ezek. 1:28; 3:23. Sometimes the presence of God is taken as imminent, as in Num. 17:10 (Eng. 16:45) and the present text.

17. E.g., Num. 16:4, 22; Josh. 7:6, 10; Ezek. 9:8.

18. With the present idiom, only in Josh. 7:6. A similar idiom without the words "on the face" *(ʿal pānîm)* uses *lip̄nê* attached to the name of the greater party, e.g., "And Shimei . . . fell down before the king" *(wᵉšimʿî . . . nāp̄al lip̄nê hammeleḵ),* 2 Sam. 19:19 (Eng. 18); see also Lev. 26:8; 2 Sam. 3:34; Esth. 6:12.

19. Cf. de Vaulx, p. 175.

This meaning is not likely because, in fact, neither Moses nor Aaron intercedes with the people on his own behalf, but rather with God on behalf of the people (14:13–19). The preposition *lip̱nê* here, then, expresses the positions of Moses and Aaron *in front of* the people.[20] The two leaders were aware of the great sin of the people before God and hence prostrated themselves before his imminent presence.[21]

6 *Then Joshua . . . and Caleb . . . tore their garments (wîhôšuaʿ . . . w^{e}ḵālēḇ . . . qār^{e}ʿû big̱^{e}ḏêhem).* Tearing garments is a mark of distress, which is sometimes specified as mourning for the dead.[22] Both Joshua and Caleb now come to the forefront of the debate. Again, those scholars who see the text as composite argue that only Caleb's name is found in JE, while Joshua's is found alongside Caleb's in P. Even if this were true (and this is far from certain), explaining the pedigree or redactional layers of a text does little to elucidate that text in its final form. The composite hypothesis also does not explain why any editor would leave such untidiness in a text. If one reads the text holistically, one sees that Caleb speaks alone first (13:30) and then together with Joshua (14:6–9). Yahweh responds first to Caleb alone (14:24) and then to both Caleb and Joshua (vv. 30, 38), so that the response is patterned on the speeches of the men themselves. From the point of view of the whole text as it stands, it makes sense for Joshua to have kept silent until this point. Before this point the dispute had simply been over whether the land was conquerable. God's leadership had only tacitly been involved. Caleb had expressed the positive point of view well enough without the need for additions from Joshua (or Moses, for that matter). But in 14:1–4 the people had responded in a way that challenged not only the human leadership but also the divine leadership. This response changed the situation significantly and called for the leaders to tell where they stood. Moses, Aaron, and Joshua added their voices to Caleb's at this point.[23]

20. BDB, p. 817b.

21. See also Num. 17:10 (Eng. 16:45) and 20:6.

22. For distress see Gen. 37:29; 1 K. 21:27; 2 K. 5:7, 8 (twice); 6:30; 11:14 (par. 2 Chr. 23:13); 18:37 (par. Isa. 36:22); 19:1 (par. Isa. 37:1); 22:11 (par. 2 Chr. 34:19); 22:19 (par. 2 Chr. 34:27); Jer. 36:24; Joel 2:13; Ezra 9:3, 5; Esth. 4:1. For mourning see Gen. 37:34; 2 Sam. 1:3, 11; 3:31; 13:31; Jer. 41:5.

23. Olson criticizes Wenham for "bringing more to the text than is there" in explaining the alternation of speakers on the basis of a psychologizing explanation similar to the one adopted here. One might level similar charges at those who find sources in the text — including Olson. See Olson, *Death of the Old,* p. 132; Wenham, p. 121; cf. pp. 124–26.

7–9 Caleb and Joshua use the good rhetorical devices of surprise and reversal to argue against the evil report of the other spies. The language of their speech contains many reflections of the report in 13:25–29, 31–33. For example, both speeches begin with the clause *the land into which we crossed over to spy out* (*hā'āreṣ 'ašer 'āḇarnû ḇāh lāṯûr 'ōṯāh,* 13:32; 14:7). The conclusion of the clause is opposed in the two interpretations, however; in the original report *the land devours its inhabitants ('ereṣ 'ōḵeleṯ yôšeḇeyhā hî'),*[24] while Caleb and Joshua conclude by saying that the land *is a very good land (ṭôḇâ hā'āreṣ me'ōḏ me'ōḏ).* The inhabitants of this all-devouring land who, according to the other spies, are *strong ('az), the descendants of Anak,* i.e., *the Nephilim* (13:28, 33), and who make mere Israelites look *like grasshoppers* (*kahagāḇîm,* 13:33) are, in the minority report, simply *our bread (laḥmēnû).*[25]

The land of Canaan was described as good *(ṭôḇâ)* in Exod. 3:8. One of the purposes for which the spies were sent into the land was to discover whether it was good or bad (*ṭôḇâ hî' 'im rā'â,* 13:19). "The (or this) good land" *(hā'āreṣ [hazzō'ṯ] haṭṭôḇâ)* becomes a standard description of Canaan in Deuteronomy.[26]

8 For Yahweh to give the people success, he must *delight (ḥāp̄ēṣ)* in them, which requires that Israel obey him.[27] If Yahweh delights in the people *he* will bring them into the land of Canaan in triumph. The land is here described by the common epithet *a land flowing with milk and honey ('ereṣ 'ašer hî' zāḇaṯ ḥālāḇ ûḏeḇāš).*[28]

9 Rather than being a delight to Yahweh, Israel has rebelled against him. V. 9 begins with the adverb *'aḵ,* which is restrictive and

24. In the consonantal text of the Pentateuch there is only one form for both masc. and fem. 3rd person pronouns, *hw'*. When the pronoun should be a fem. the Masoretes pointed the consonants with the vowel of the usual fem. form *(ḥireq; hî'),* the resulting impossible form being called *Qerê Perpetuum.* See Waltke and O'Connor, *Hebrew Syntax,* p. 292 n. 13; GKC, §17c.

25. For the image of eating up enemies as positive, see (in addition to 13:32 and 14:7) Deut. 7:16; Jer. 10:25; Ps. 14:4/53:4. See Wenham, p. 121 n. 1, for an interesting list of these parallels.

26. See Deut. 1:25, 35; 3:25; 4:21–22; 6:18; 8:7, 10; 9:6; 11:17; see also Josh. 23:16; Judg. 18:9; 1 Chr. 28:8.

27. See 1 K. 10:9 (par. 2 Chr. 9:8); Ps. 22:9 (Eng. 8); Ps. 41:12–13 (Eng. 11–12); 147:10–11; Jer. 9:24. See G. J. Botterweck, *TDOT,* V:92–107, esp. 101–6.

28. On milk and honey as descriptive of Canaan, see Exod. 3:8, 17; 13:5; 33:3; Lev. 20:24; Num. 13:27; 16:14; Deut. 6:3; 11:9; 26:9, 15; 27:3; 31:20; Josh. 5:6; Jer. 11:5; 32:22; Ezek. 20:6, 15; the same expression is used once of Egypt (Num. 16:15).

emphasizes the importance of the prohibitions that follow — "do not rebel, do not fear."[29] It would be rebellion if the Israelites carried through on the decision to return to Egypt (v. 4). Since Yahweh looks on motivations as well as actions, the people's very desire to go back to Egypt is considered sinful and punishable (see vv. 11–12, 21–23, 26–37).[30]

The rebellion against Yahweh is also directly connected to the fear of the inhabitants of Canaan. It is rebellion to disbelieve what Yahweh had promised. In their own strength the Israelites may not have been able to meet the Canaanites, but the latter's *protection has turned aside from over them (sār ṣillām mēʿᵃlêhem)* and Yahweh is with the Israelites. The noun *ṣēl* (lit., "shadow") is used metaphorically of protection from, e.g., the sun (Isa. 25:4; Ps. 121:5) or enemies (Isa. 30:2–3; 32:2; 49:2; Jer. 48:25; Ps. 91:1),[31] and is an apt image for protection in the hot climate of the Near East. The metaphor here indicates that God has been protecting the Canaanites up to this point, but will do so no longer, so that the Canaanites would become prey (food, *bread,* v. 7) for the Israelites.[32] Israel need not fear either the Canaanite gods[33] or the Canaanite armies. According to Dillmann the theological reason for the removal of divine protection from the Canaanites was their sin, which has defiled the land itself (see, e.g., Lev. 18:24).[34]

10a *But the whole congregation said to stone them with stones (wayyōʾmᵉrû kol-hāʿēḏâ lirgôm ʾōṯām bāʾᵃḇānîm).* Crimes for which stoning had been prescribed prior to the present text are: transgression of God's holiness at Sinai (Exod. 19:13), manslaughter by an ox (21:28), sacrifice of children to Molech (Lev. 20:2), spirit divining (20:27), and blasphemy (24:13–23). Later the following would be added: sabbath breaking (Num. 15:32–36), enticement to idolatry (Deut. 13:11 [Eng. 10]), rebellion against parental authority (21:18–21), idolatry (17:2–7), premarital sexual relations (22:13–24), and violation of the ban (*ḥērem,* Josh. 7:25). Stoning is also a frequent expression of public anger (cf., e.g., Exod. 17:4; 1 Sam. 30:6; 1 K. 12:18; 2 Chr. 10:18).

29. See BDB, p. 36; GKC, §§ 100i, 153; Davidson, *Syntax,* § 153.

30. Since the jussive with *ʾal* is used for the prohibition here, it is probably the actual carrying out of the plan to return to Egypt (still hypothetical, thus the jussive) that is in sight.

31. BDB, p. 853a.

32. Keil, p. 92; Milgrom, *JPST,* p. 109.

33. Noth, p. 108; Gray, p. 154; and Binns, p. 92, see the meaning of *ṣēl* as protection of Canaanite gods.

34. Dillmann, p. 75.

Wenham posits that the people's reaction here is a judicial reaction to what they perceive as false witness on the part of Joshua and Caleb.[35] But two points tell against this explanation. First, it is doubtful that their words *do not rebel* (*'al-timrōḏû,* v. 9) in the jussive may be taken as false witness. Second, although the Torah forbids false witness (Exod. 20:16; 23:1; Deut. 5:17 [Eng. 20]) the punishment for it is set forth only in Deuteronomy and is a *talion,* i.e., doing to the false witness what he had planned for the accused (Deut. 19:16–21); no punishment of stoning is set forth. Therefore, the reaction of the crowd here is more likely to be a reaction of anger than a perceived judicial sentence.

b. Yahweh Responds (14:10b–38)

10b *Then the glory of Yahweh appeared to all the children of Israel at*[1] *the tent of meeting.*

11 *And Yahweh said to Moses, "How long will this people spurn me and how long will they disbelieve in spite of all*[2] *the signs I have done in their midst?*

12 *I will strike them with a pestilence and will disinherit them and will make you into a greater and stronger nation than they."*

13 *And Moses said to Yahweh: "If the Egyptians hear of this —since you brought this people up in your strength from among them —*

14 *then they will tell it to the inhabitants of this land. They have heard that you, O Yahweh, are in the midst of this people, for you, O Yahweh, are seen eye to eye, and your cloud stands over them and in a pillar of cloud you go up before them by day, and in a pillar of fire by night.*

15 *If*[3] *you kill this people as one man, then the nations who have heard report of you*[4] *will say:*

35. Wenham, p. 122.

1. The preposition b^e- carries the basic notion of rest "in" or "at" a place. The former usage is more common (e.g., Gen. 4:16, "in the land of Nod"), but the latter is also found (e.g., 1 Sam. 29:1, "at the spring"); see BDB, pp. 88–91; Davidson, *Syntax,* §101, Rem. 1a. LXX recognizes the difficulty of Yahweh's glory being seen by all the children of Israel if it appeared "in(side) the tent of meeting." It reads *en nefēlē epi tēs skēnēs,* "in a cloud upon the tabernacle." BHS suggests the equivalent Hebrew *(be'ānān al-'ōhel mô'ēḏ),* but the present translation seems a better option.

2. Heb. *b^eḵōl;* for b^e as an adversative, see Williams, *Syntax,* § 242.

3. The conditional sentence here has no distinctive particle. Usually, as here, sentences of this type have perfect consecutive in both protasis and apodosis. Also see Gen. 44:22; Exod. 4:14; cf. Davidson, *Syntax,* § 132.

4. Lit., "the nations will have heard hearing of you." The noun *šema'* is related to the verb *šāma',* "to hear." LXX reads *w^ešim^{e}ḵā,* "your name."

16 *'Since Yahweh was not able to lead this people to the land which he swore to them, he has slaughtered them in the wilderness.'*
17 *And now, I pray, let the power of my Lord become great, as you have spoken, saying:*
18 *'Yahweh is slow of anger and great of covenant loyalty, bearing iniquity and rebellion, but who will never completely leave them unpunished, visiting the iniquity of the fathers upon the children to the third and fourth generation.'*
19 *Please forgive the iniquity of this people according to the greatness of your covenant loyalty, just as you have already borne with this people from Egypt until now."*
20 *And Yahweh said, "I have forgiven according to your word,*
21 *but for a fact, as I live, and as the whole earth will be filled with Yahweh's glory,*
22 *none*[5] *of the men who have seen my glory and my signs that I did in Egypt and in the wilderness but have tested me these ten times and have not listened to my voice*
23 *will see the land which I promised to their fathers, and all those who spurn me will not see it.*
24 *As for my servant Caleb, because a different spirit is in him, and he followed fully after me,*[6] *therefore I will bring him to the land into which he went, and his descendants shall inherit it,*
25 *even though the Amalekites and the Canaanites are inhabiting*[7] *the valley. Tomorrow turn and depart into the wilderness by the way of the Reed Sea."*
26 *And Yahweh spoke to Moses and Aaron, saying:*
27 *"How long*[8] *will this wicked congregation keep murmuring against me? I have heard the murmurings of the children of Israel that they are murmuring*[9] *against me.*

5. The *kî* simply introduces the oath, as is common in OT usage; see, e.g., Gen. 42:16; 1 Sam. 14:39; 20:3; Isa. 49:18; BDB, p. 472a.

6. The construction *way^{e}mallē' 'aḥ^{a}rāy* is equivalent to *way^{e}mallē' lāleḵeṯ 'aḥ^{a}rāy;* see GKC, § 119gg; Gray, p. 159; Keil, p. 95.

7. The verb *yôšēḇ* is sing. with a pl. subject construed with the first member of that subject; cf. Davidson, *Syntax,* § 114a.

8. Heb. *'aḏ-māṯay* is a different particle than that found in v. 11 *('aḏ-'ānâ),* but it has the same meaning. The particle is composed of the temporal interrogative *māṯay,* "when," compounded with *'aḏ,* "unto, until," hence "until when?" or "how long?" The particle generally refers to future time in the OT, and is found in rhetorical questions. See BDB, p. 607b; *HALAT,* p. 618; V. Hamilton, *TWOT,* I:536b.

9. In both instances of the Hiphil participle *mallînîm,* the first consonant of the root is doubled (Aramaic doubling); see GKC, § 27ee.

28 *Say to them, 'As I live,' an utterance of Yahweh, 'as you have spoken in my ears, so shall I do to you.*
29 *Your corpses will fall in this wilderness, and not one of all your number that you counted from twenty years of age and up who murmured against me*
30 *will enter into the land in which I swore to make you dwell,*[10] *except for Caleb son of Jephunneh and Joshua son of Nun.*
31 *And your children, whom you said would become prey, I will bring them in and they will know the land that you have rejected.*
32 *But your corpses will fall in this wilderness!*
33 *And your children will be shepherds in the wilderness forty years, and they will bear the penalty for your fornications until the last of your corpses lies in the wilderness.*
34 *According to the number of days in which you spied out the land, forty days, a day for every year,*[11] *you shall bear your iniquity forty years and know my opposition.*
35 *I Yahweh have spoken. I will surely do this to this whole wicked congregation who are gathered*[12] *against me. In this wilderness they come to an end,*[13] *and they will die there.' "*
36 *And the men whom Moses sent to spy out the land and who returned and caused the whole congregation to grumble*[14] *against him by bringing an evil report against the land,*
37 *the men*[15] *who brought an evil report on the land, died in a plague before Yahweh.*
38 *Only Joshua son of Nun and Caleb son of Jephunneh remained alive of those men who went to spy out the land.*

10b–12 On this whole section, compare Exod. 32:7–14.

10 *Then the glory of Yahweh appeared (ûḵ^e^bôḏ YHWH nir'â).* The word *glory (kāḇôḏ)* can be used of wealth (Gen. 31:1), or a throne

10. The verb *šikkēn* (Piel) is a causative; cf. Williams, *Syntax,* § 142.

11. The repetition of *yôm laššānâ* (lit., "a day for the year") carries distributive force; cf. GKC, § 123d; Williams, *Syntax,* § 15.

12. The sing. (collective) noun *hāʿēḏâ* has the pl. verbal complement *ad sensum.* See Davidson, *Syntax,* § 115.

13. For the somewhat unusual pointing of the verb *yittammû* as a Qal rather than a Niphal see, e.g., GKC, § 67g.

14. The Ketib is *wayyilônû* (Qal); read with the Qere *wayyallînû* (Hiphil, again with Aramaic doubling of the first consonant of the root, as in v. 27); see *BHS.* Here the Hiphil has a causative meaning; see BDB, p. 534a.

15. The whole of v. 36 qualifies the word *hā'^a^nāšîm,* which is the subject of the sentence and which the verse repeats for clarity; cf. Isa. 49:5–6; Davidson, *Syntax,* § 127a.

(1 Sam. 2:8), or chariots (Isa. 22:18). God crowned humans with "honor and glory" (Ps. 8:6 [Eng. 5]). In many pentateuchal texts Yahweh's glory, as here, is the visible manifestation of his presence.[16] Exod. 24:17 states that this glory is "like a devouring fire" *(kᵉʾēš ʾōḵelet)* on Mt. Sinai. It is no wonder that the appearance of Yahweh's glory stopped the people in their tracks.

The glory appeared *at the tent of meeting (bᵉʾōhel môʿēḏ).* See note 1 on p. 251. If one insists on taking *bᵉ-* in the sense of "in" here, then one must assume that the door of the tent is meant, as in 16:19; 20:6, so that it could be seen by all. It is also possible, of course, that the glory simply filled the tent and then overflowed into the area outside (see Exod. 40:34–35). Again, the simplest course is to take *bᵉ-* as *at.* The meaning is, then, "in the court."

11 *How long (ʿaḏ-ʾānâ).* This temporal particle is found twice in the present verse.[17] The point is not so much that the rebellion has been a long one as that the end of it has now been reached and Yahweh will endure it no longer. The people have *spurned* or "despised" (RSV) and *disbelieved* or refused to trust Yahweh for long enough! To *spurn* (Piel of *nāʾaṣ*) in places means "to reject" (cf. Isa. 1:4; 5:24), and the Israelites had in fact rejected Yahweh and their covenant with him in v. 4.[18]

they disbelieve (lōʾ-yaʾᵃmînû) does not mean that they have not assented to correct propositions about Yahweh; rather, it means that they have refused to trust or rely on him,[19] in spite of *the signs (hāʾōṯôṯ)* that he has done in their midst. A *sign* is a person or thing that points to something or someone beyond itself. In the OT both the rainbow (Gen. 9:12) and circumcision (Gen. 17:11) are called signs. In the events surrounding the Exodus, the signs were the miracles and acts of Yahweh

16. See Exod. 16:7, 10; 24:16–17; 40:34–35; Lev. 9:6, 23; Num. 14:10; 16:19; 17:7 (Eng. 16:42); 20:6. Milgrom (*JPST,* p. 109) equates the *kāḇôḏ* here with the "cloud" that covered the tabernacle, e.g., in 9:15–23. He cites a number of rabbinic sources that make the equation. The equation may explain the LXX's translation of *kāḇôḏ* with "in a cloud upon the tabernacle." See the note to the translation of 14:1.

17. See the related, and more common, expression *ʿaḏ-māṯay* in v. 27. The expression *ʿaḏ-ʾānâ* is found 11 times in the OT. The only other place in the Pentateuch is Exod. 16:28, also in the context of rebellion against God; cf. BDB, p. 33a.

18. For an excellent discussion of *niʾeṣ,* see K. D. Sakenfeld, "The Problem of Divine Forgiveness in Num. 14," *CBQ* 37 (1975) 321–22.

19. See *ʾᵉmûnâ,* "firmness," "steadfastness," "reliability"; also *ʾᵉmeṯ,* "firmness," "truth," from the same root. Cf. BDB, pp. 52–54.

for the salvation of his people.[20] Here God's mighty acts in the wilderness (e.g., crossing the Reed Sea, the manna) are in view.

12 *with a pestilence* (*baddeḇer,* lit., "with the pestilence"). This term may be defined as a divine judgment that may destroy either animal or human life (Exod. 9:3, 15). The term parallels "the sword" in Exod. 5:3 and Lev. 26:25, as well as other curses (Deut. 28:21). In Exod. 9:15 a pestilence is set over against the plagues *(maggēpôṯ)* of Egypt. A pestilence is that which would have obliterated the Egyptians from the earth, as over against the plagues that left at least some alive. In the prophets (esp. Jeremiah and Ezekiel) "pestilence" is commonly used in connection with "the sword" and "famine" to sum up the total experience of divine judgment.[21] The definite article on *deḇer* here may point to "pestilence" as a general class with well-known characteristics, such as those which would be found in 11:1, 33 in this context.[22]

Yahweh parallels his threat to strike the people with a pestilence with the threat to *disinherit them (wᵉʾôrišennû).* In the light of this parallel the verb *hôrîš* ("to disinherit") may be taken to imply destruction (see Exod. 15:9) as well as its more common meaning of "to cause someone else to possess"[23] (in this case the land of Canaan). As in Exod. 32:9–10 God threatens to wipe out the people and start over again with Moses. Such destruction would set the timetable for fulfillment of Yahweh's promises back to the time of Abraham (Gen. 12:2). This threat shows the seriousness with which God takes rebellion on the part of his people.

13–19 Here, as in Exod. 32:11–14, Moses intercedes on behalf of the people. He bases his appeal to God on the reputation of Yahweh among the nations if he destroys the people (vv. 13–16) and, more importantly, on Yahweh's faithfulness as a forgiving God (vv. 17–19). Vv. 13–14 are difficult and may be corrupt.[24]

13–14 These verses alternate the verbs "to say" *(ʾāmar)* and "to hear" *(šāmaʿ),* and this alternation passes into v. 15. The subjects of these verbs are clear in v. 13 *(Moses said, wayyōʾmer mōšeh; if the Egyptians*

20. See, e.g., Exod. 4:8–9; 7:3; 8:19 (Eng. 23); Snaith, p. 150.

21. See Jer. 14:12; 21:6, 9; 24:10; 27:8, 13; 29:17–18; 32:24, 36; 34:17; 38:2; 42:17, 22; 44:13; Ezek. 6:11–12; 7:15; 12:16; cf. 28:23. See G. Mayer, *TDOT,* III:125–27.

22. See Davidson, *Syntax,* § 22 Rem. 1; Williams, *Syntax,* §§ 83–84, 92.

23. The latter meaning is found 55 times, e.g., Num. 21:32; 32:31; 33:52–53, 55. See BDB, p. 440a; *HALAT,* p. 421b.

24. See, e.g., Noth, p. 109; Budd, p. 150; Gray, pp. 156–57, 159.

hear, wešāmeʿû miṣrayim).[25] In v. 14, however, the subjects are not clear. If the MT is correct, the subject of "to say" is probably Egypt (*they will tell it to the inhabitants of this land, weʾāmerû ʾel-yôšēḇ hāʾāreṣ hazzōʾṯ),* while the subject of "to hear" may be either the Egyptians or the Canaanite nations (*They have heard that you, O Yahweh, are in the midst of this people, šāmeʿû kî-ʾattâ YHWH beqereḇ hāʿām hazzeh).* Keil took the subject to be both the Egyptians and the Canaanites.[26] An alternative is to follow the LXX, which solves this problem by offering "but now all those dwelling in this land have heard" *(alla kai pantes hoi katoikountes epi tēs gēs tautēs akēkosin),* thus making "the nations" the subject of both verbs and assuming a Hebrew text of *wegam kol-yôšēḇ hāʾāreṣ hazzōʾṯ šāmeʿû.*[27]

The syntax is further complicated by v. 13b *(wešāmeʿû miṣrayim).* Why does the clause begin with the conjunction *we*, "and" (*we* plus the perfect consecutive)? It may be, as Keil suggested, that the words *wešāmerû . . . weʾāmerû* (vv. 13–14) are to be understood as "they not only hear . . . but also tell."[28] Alternatively, v. 13b may begin the protasis of a conditional sentence with *we* plus the perfect consecutive.[29] Since v. 15 is widely admitted to be such a conditional statement, it seems wise to see vv. 13–14 as a parallel condition. The first condition (i.e., when Yahweh does as he has said and destroys Israel, *if* the Egyptians, out of whose midst Yahweh had brought these people, hear of it, *then* they will tell the Canaanites who had heard of Yahweh's presence among, and might on behalf of, his people) lays the groundwork for the second in vv. 15–16, which is linked to the present condition by the same alternation of verbs for "to hear" and "to say." The conditional statement in v. 15a (*if you kill this people as one man . . . wehēmattâ ʾeṯ-hāʿām hazzeh keʾîš ʾeḥāḏ)* simply restates in conditional form what Yahweh has purposed to do in v. 12, after the intervening material of vv. 13–14. If Yahweh were to smite his people in the same way he did the Egyptians,[30] then those same

25. Also in v. 15: "the nations who have heard report of you will say," *weʾāmerû haggôyim ʾašer-šāmeʿû ʾeṯ-šimʿaḵā.*

26. Keil, p. 93.

27. See *BHS;* Budd, pp. 148–50.

28. See Keil, p. 93; GKC, § 154a n. 1; BDB, p. 253a.

29. So Snaith, p. 151; Budd, pp. 148, 150; cf. Davidson, *Syntax,* § 132. If this meaning is correct, then *kî ʾattâ YHWH beqereḇ hāʿām hazzeh ʾašer-ʿayin beʿayin nirʾâ* should be taken as a parenthetical report of the content of what has been heard, and *kî* should be taken as a particle introducing direct narration; see GKC, § 157b.

30. The same verb *nāḵâ,* "to smite," is used in Num. 14:12 and, e.g., Exod. 9:15.

Egyptians would hear of it and would spread the story among the Canaanites. Heretofore these Canaanites had heard that Yahweh was intimately concerned with the Israelites.

The idiom *eye to eye (ʿayin beʿayin)* refers to closest personal contact, and is found again in the OT only in Isa. 52:8.

The last part of v. 14 *(your cloud . . . by night)* looks like standard confessional language and has close verbal parallels to other "cloud" passages.[31]

15–16 The second condition grows out of the first and begins with a restatement. To *kill this people as one man (wehēmattâ ʾeṯ-hāʿām hazzeh keʾîš ʾeḥāḏ)* means to kill the whole group as if it were simply a single entity, hence to wipe out the whole number. This is one more indication that the rebellion was by the entire people (cf. 14:1, etc.).[32]

These verses appeal, once again, to the damage that will be done to Yahweh's reputation among the nations if he carries through on his purpose to destroy the people. *The nations who have heard report of you (haggôyim ʾašer-šāmeʿû ʾeṯ-šimʿaḵā)* will then credit this destruction to Yahweh's lack of power: he *was not able to lead this people to the land that he swore to them.*

17–19 In the light of the preceding argument, Moses makes a second appeal to Yahweh, based not on the nations' perceptions of Yahweh's reality, but on the reality of Israel's perception of Yahweh, viz., his mercy, covenant loyalty, and forgiveness. Vv. 17 and 19 are pleas to Yahweh that frame a standard summary of Yahweh's character in v. 18, which is the high point of the unit.

And now let the power of my Lord become great (weʿattâ yigdal-nāʾ kōaḥ ʾaḏōnāy). This request might be misunderstood in the light of what has gone before. What Moses means is that Yahweh should show his great power by revealing, once again, his heart of mercy and forgiveness. Moses asks Yahweh to make good on what he has said in revelation of his character (v. 18).

18 The confession here is probably an old liturgical one; it is reflected at points throughout the OT.[33] In fact, it is a shortened version of Exod. 34:6–7, which is part of the story of God's forgiveness of the people after the incident of the golden calf.

31. E.g., Exod. 13:21–22; 33:9; Num. 10:34.

32. See de Vaulx, pp. 175–76. For the same idiom see Judg. 6:16; 20:1, 8, 11; 1 Sam. 11:7; 2 Sam. 19:15; Ezra 3:1; Neh. 8:1.

33. E.g., Jer. 32:18; Jon. 4:2; Ps. 103:8; Neh. 9:17, 31.

The similarities between Exod. 34:6–7 and Num. 14:18 are far too great to be explained by chance, though the text in Numbers is several words shorter (see below). The verbs in both versions are participles, as is usually the case in confessions. Two balanced constructions describing Yahweh's character begin the confession: he *is slow of anger* (*'ereḵ-'ap-payim,* lit., "long of nose") and *great of covenant loyalty (raḇ-ḥeseḏ).* The term *ḥeseḏ* is one of the most studied terms in the Hebrew language. The basic meaning is faithfulness within a covenant structure, e.g., covenant loyalty. It is a relational term used to express both God's loyalty to Israel and human loyalty both to Yahweh and to other humans.[34] Exod. 34:6 adds *'ĕmeṯ,* "truth, dependability,"[35] as well as the clause "keeping covenant loyalty with thousands" *(nōṣēr ḥeseḏ lā'alāp̱îm)* in v. 7, neither of which is in Numbers, perhaps because the author wished to hasten on to the forgiving nature of God.

bearing iniquity and rebellion (nōśē' 'āwōn wāp̱āša'). When *nāśā' 'āwōn* is used with a human subject the meaning is usually that the person will bear the penalty of divine punishment.[36] Can one say here that God has himself borne the penalty for sin or has taken it away? One cannot be certain of the dynamics of the divine forgiveness, but a meaning such as this may not be wide of the mark.[37] The terms for sin are *iniquity ('āwōn),* which usually has to do with willful destructive behavior, and *rebellion (peša'),* which speaks of the breaking of a relationship.[38] Exod. 34:7 adds a third term for sin, *ḥaṭṭā'â,* which usually refers to missing a goal.[39]

34. For a summary of the work on *ḥeseḏ* see H.-J. Zobel, *TDOT,* V:44–64 (including bibliography). To this list add three titles by K. D. Sakenfeld: *The Meaning of Hesed in the Hebrew Bible,* HSM (Missoula, Mont.: Scholars Press, 1978); *Faithfulness in Action: Loyalty in Biblical Perspective,* OBT (Philadelphia: Fortress, 1985); "The Problem of Forgiveness in Num. 14," *CBQ* 37 (1975) 323–26. Cf. the important article by F. I. Andersen, "Yahweh, the Kind and Sensitive God," in *God Who Is Rich in Mercy: Essays Presented to Dr. D. B. Knox,* ed. P. T. O'Brien and D. G. Peterson (Homebush West, Australia: Lancer, 1986), pp. 41–88.

35. For "truth" *('emeṯ)* as "dependability" see A. Jepsen, *TDOT,* I:309–16.

36. See the commentary above on 5:31. Cf. W. Zimmerli, "Die Eigenart der Prophetischen Reden bes Ezechiel," *ZAW* 66 (1954) 9; T. Frymer-Kensky, "The Strange Case of the Suspected Sotah (Num. V 11–31)," *VT* 34 (1984) 22–24.

37. So Snaith, p. 152.

38. On the former see KB, p. 689; E. Jacob, *Theology of the Old Testament,* tr. A. Heathcote and P. Allcock (New York: Harper, 1959), p. 281. On the latter see KB, p. 785; cf. H. W. Wolff, *Joel and Amos,* tr. W. Janzen, S. MacBride, and C. Muenchow, Hermeneia (Philadelphia: Fortress, 1977), pp. 152–53.

39. See Jacob, *Theology,* p. 281.

but who will never completely leave them unpunished (weṇaqqēh lō' yenaqqeh). This translation, as well as NJPS ("yet not cancelling all punishment"), has the advantage of not requiring the insertion of the word *guilty,* which, though as old as the LXX, is not in the MT.[40] The construction of the infinitive *(naqqēh)* plus the finite verb of the same root *(yenaqqeh)* is a common way of sharpening or emphasizing the verbal idea; in the case of *niqqeh,* "to declare innocent, leave unpunished."[41]

visiting (pōqēḏ). This verb has various meanings in Numbers (as elsewhere). In addition to its current sense of "visiting" or "inflicting," it can mean "appoint" and "number."[42] *Fathers . . . children . . . third and fourth generation* — in Exod. 34:7 and the current verse the purpose of this seemingly harsh language is to affirm Yahweh's right to judge as he sees fit. There seems little reason to try to make this language seem less threatening, although as early as Deut. 5:9–10 it is interpreted to mean that God punishes to the fourth generation those who "hate him," i.e., those who continue to live in rebellious ways. Just as God's mercy is great and his anger slow to kindle, because God is a just God, the guilty will be punished, even if this takes several generations. God's mercy and his punishment are both awe-inspiring and to be taken earnestly. In the present context, although Moses does not wish to deny Yahweh's awful judgment, he wishes to emphasize the divine mercy and covenant loyalty.

19 Moses asks Yahweh to *forgive [selaḥ] the iniquity [ʿāwōn] of this people* based on Yahweh's own *covenant loyalty (ḥeseḏ)* as exemplified in his bearing with the people *(nāśā')* from the time of the Exodus until the present moment. By forgiveness neither Moses (v. 19) nor Yahweh (v. 20) means to indicate that Israel's punishment will be avoided or cancelled, but only that the fundamental covenant relationship between Yahweh and Israel will be maintained from Yahweh's side.[43]

20–25 In this unit one sees that divine forgiveness does not cancel divine punishment. The punishment postponed by God in Exod. 32:34 is put off no longer. God's mercy is seen in that he does not wipe

40. LXX *Kai katharismō ou katharieī ton enochon;* so also AV, RV, RSV, NIV, NASB, NKJV.

41. See GKC, § 113n; Davidson, *Syntax,* § 86; Williams, *Syntax,* § 205; cf. BDB, p. 667b. NEB takes the verb to mean "to be swept clean away," which is possible but less likely.

42. See BDB, p. 823. The text of Exod. 34:7 increases the punishment of the children by adding "and to sons' sons" *(weʿal-benê ḇānîm)* before the words "to the third and fourth generation" *(ʿal-šillēšîm weʿal-ribbēʿîm).*

43. See, e.g., Sakenfeld, "Problem of Forgiveness," 327–28.

out the Israelites immediately. A general statement of punishment in vv. 22–23 is all that is said for the moment. Vv. 26–35 specify the details of the punishment. There Yahweh swears an oath by his own person. The words *ḥay-'ānî* are common in oaths, but are found in the Pentateuch only in vv. 21 and 28.[44] The adverbial particle *w^e'ûlām (but for a fact)* is rare in the OT, being found mostly in the book of Job.[45] It is a strong adversative particle that contrasts what follows with what has gone before.[46]

21 The clause *as the whole earth will be filled with Yahweh's glory (w^eyimmālē' k^eḇôḏ-YHWH 'eṯ-kol-hā'āreṣ)* as the basis for an oath is unique here, although the thought is parallel to that of Hab. 2:14.[47]

22 *My glory* — see above on v. 10. The presence of Yahweh is meant. *My signs* — see above on v. 11. These *signs* are the mighty acts of God surrounding the Exodus events. *Have tested me (way^enassû 'ōṯô)* — the verb can mean "to attempt" (e.g., Deut. 4:34), or "to test, try" (as here). In Gen. 22 God "tests" Abraham (v. 1) by demanding the sacrifice of Isaac. Through this experience Abraham is proved to be worthy. In Exod. 16 God "tests" Israel by withholding food in the wilderness. By their dependence upon God (finally), Israel is proved to be faithful. Here, however, it is God who is "tested" by Israel. God has already proved himself to be faithful and powerful many times by giving the divine presence (God's *glory*) and by working miraculous acts (God's *signs*) before Israel's eyes. Yet, the Israelites continue to "test" God by disbelieving that he can bring the people into Canaan. *ten times ('eśer p^e'āmîm).* Most commentators take this to be a round number, or an idiomatic expression for "over and over," much as "a dozen" is used in English.[48] The Talmud lists the following ten occasions of rebellion: at the Reed Sea (Exod. 14:11–12), at Marah (15:23), in the wilderness of Sin (16:2), twice

44. Cf., e.g., Isa. 49:18; Jer. 46:18; Ezek. 5:11; 14:16, 18, 20; 16:48; 17:16; 18:13; 20:31; 33:11; 34:8; 35:6, 11. A related saying, "as Yahweh lives" *(ḥay-YHWH)* is also common, e.g., Judg. 8:19; 1 Sam. 14:39; 19:6; 20:3; 25:34; 26:10, 16; 28:10; Jer. 4:2; Ruth 3:13.

45. It occurs only 3 times without *w^e* (Job 2:5; 5:8; 13:3) and 16 times with *w^e* (Job 11:5, 11; 12:7; 13:4; 14:18; 17:10; 33:1). The other occurrences are: Gen. 28:19; 48:19; Exod. 9:16; Judg. 18:29; 1 Sam. 20:3; 25:34; 1 K. 20:23; Mic. 3:8.

46. See BDB, p. 19b; *HALAT,* p. 21b; H. Wolf, *TWOT,* I:23a.

47. Cf. also Isa. 11:9. On the glory of Yahweh, see the commentary above on v. 10b.

48. So, e.g., Budd, p. 158; Gray, p. 158; Noordtzij, p. 126; Snaith, p. 152; Sturdy, p. 103; Binns, p. 95; Heinisch, p. 58; Dillmann, p. 97.

at Kadesh (16:20, 27), at Rephidim (17:2ff.), at Sinai (ch. 32), at Taberah (Num. 11:1), at Kibroth-hattaavah (11:4ff.), and the present situation (chs. 13–14).[49]

23 Some scholars take *and all those who spurn me will not see it (w*^{e}*ḵol-m*^{e}*na'*^{a}*ṣay lō' yir'ûhâ)* as redundant, hence pointing to the beginning of another document at v. 23b.[50] All the intervening material in vv. 11b–23a is then seen to interrupt the flow of the narrative between the first occurrence of "to spurn" *(ni'ēṣ)* in v. 11 and the second occurrence here. An alternative is to see the text holistically and to assume that the clause is intended to round off the first section on punishment running from v. 11 to v. 23. This section begins by mentioning those who spurn Yahweh and ends here with a clause to explain that spurning Yahweh is to be identified with seeing his glory and his signs in Egypt and the wilderness and yet not listening to his voice. This reading would mean that the conjunction "and" *(w*^{e}*)* has its explicative or epexegetical sense here, meaning *that is* (or namely).[51]

24 Only Caleb is noted for commendation in v. 24, whereas later, in vv. 30 and 38, Joshua is included. As noted above on 14:6, this pattern follows the actual speeches in the text — only Caleb speaks in 13:30, while in 14:6 Joshua joins in. It is also true that when Caleb alone speaks the struggle with the other spies is quite general in tone, while when Joshua comes in, the case becomes more specific and serious. The announcements of punishment follow the specificity in the reasons for punishment; only a general punishment is announced here (and only Caleb is named), while a much more detailed announcement is made about the overt rebellion against which both Joshua and Caleb struggle. It makes as much sense to see this as a conscious literary pattern as it does a patchwork of edited documents or oral sources.

a different spirit (rûaḥ 'aḥereṯ). For the word *rûaḥ* indicating a psychological reality, see, e.g., 11:17.

25 *the Amalekites and the Canaanites (hā'*^{e}*mālēqî w*^{e}*hak-k*^{e}*na'*^{a}*nî)*. In 13:29, the Amalekites and the Canaanites were located in different parts of the land (Amalekites in the Negeb, Canaanites along the coast and along the Jordan), which seems to contradict what is said here.

49. T.B. *Arakin* 15b; cf., e.g., Keil, p. 94; Dillmann, p. 77; Gray, p. 158.

50. See, e.g., Noth, p. 109: "The original J-narrative reappears at v. 23b with a verbal reference to its last occurrence (v. 11a)."

51. See GKC, § 154a n. 1 (b); Davidson, *Syntax*, § 136 Rem. 1 (c); BDB, p. 252b.

One assumes that an editor would not allow blatant contradictions to exist in the usage of the same terms in such close proximity.[52] Closer attention to context helps clarify the problem. Reference here is to the Amalekites and Canaanites living in the immediately relevant area, i.e., *in the valley (bā'ēmeq),* which could be part of the Jordan Valley in a particular locale in the Negeb.[53]

Several scholars have assumed that the whole sentence concerning the Amalekites and Canaanites is out of place here,[54] and, were it simply a historical or geographical note, one might easily agree. But it is not merely such a note. Two explanations of this sentence are possible. The first is to translate the conjunction "and" *(wᵉ)* as "since" and to understand the sentence to form the basic reason why the Israelites were told to turn and go into the wilderness (i.e., since God is punishing them and since the Amalekites and Canaanites are already in the valley).[55] The second, followed here, is to connect the first clause of v. 25 with the promise to Caleb and his descendants in v. 24. This requires a concessive translation of *wᵉ (even though),* and a new sentence beginning with "Tomorrow."[56]

Tomorrow turn and depart into the wilderness by the way of the Reed Sea (māḥār pᵉnû ûsᵉ'û lāḵem hammiḏbār dereḵ yam-sûp̱). Although some commentators see this as a general directive to turn back south, others have realized that it is not likely that so large a group as the Israelites could hope to survive in the wilderness apart from a well-known road or path; the *way of the Reed Sea* was such a road.[57] It stretched from the area of Kadesh to the north shore of the Gulf of Aqabah.[58] God's command here is another aspect of Israel's punishment that had come out of its own mouth. The people get their wish to turn around and go in the opposite direction from the promised land (cf. 14:3–4). God will not (immediately, at least) bring them into the good land, but will allow them to remain outside it where, in fact, they have chosen to be.

52. The gentilic form *ha'ᵃmalēqî* (here and 11 other times in the OT), and the proper name *(ha)'ᵃmālēq* (13:29 and 36 other times). One assumes that the two terms are equivalent.

53. See the commentary below on 14:45.

54. See, e.g., Noth, p. 109; Budd, pp. 149–50.

55. See, e.g., Exod. 4:8–9; 7:3; 8:19 (Eng. 23); Snaith, p. 150.

56. So Noordtzij, p. 127; cf. NEB's paraphrastic translation. On the flexibility of *wᵉ*, see BDB, pp. 252–54; Driver, *Tenses,* §§ 156–60; GKC, § 141e.

57. For the former see, e.g., Gray, pp. 160–61; Binns, p. 96. For the latter see, e.g., Budd, p. 159; Wenham, p. 123.

58. See Davies, *Way of the Wilderness,* p. 77.

26–35 In this section the general judgments of vv. 22–23 are specified in terms of the people's own complaints against Yahweh in 14:2–4.

27 Like v. 11, this verse is an introductory rhetorical question. The first half of the verse is difficult. A literal translation might be, "How long with regard to this wicked congregation, which they are murmuring against me" (*ʿaḏ-māṯay lāʿēḏâ hārāʿâ hazzōʾṯ ʾᵃšer hēmmâ mallînîm ʿālāy*). If the text is correct, then one must either supply a verb such as "I forgive" (i.e., "How long shall I forgive this wicked congregation in their murmuring against me"), or, as above, think of the words *ʾᵃšer hēmmâ* as referring to the subject, which is also named in *lāʿēḏâ hārāʿâ hazzōʾṯ*.[59] Neither solution is convincing; the latter seems preferable because in the parallel v. 11 the "how long" (*ʿaḏ-ʾānâ*) refers to an act of the people, not of Yahweh.

The verb *to murmur (lûn)* is found only in Exod. 15–17; Num. 14, 16–17; and Josh. 9:18 in reference to specific complaints in the wilderness.[60]

I have heard. God states that he has taken note what the Israelites said in 14:2–4.

28–30 *an utterance of Yahweh (nᵉʾum-YHWH).* This formula identifies the speaker as Yahweh; although extremely common in the OT prophetic literature,[61] it is rare in the Pentateuch (here and Gen. 22:16).

as you have spoken in my ears, so shall I do to you. The judgments of Yahweh will come out of the Israelites' own mouths.[62]

Your corpses (pigrēḵem). This general word does not always even indicate a human corpse (see Gen. 15:11, referring to animals), although most times it does (cf. Lev. 26:30; Isa. 34:3; 66:24; etc.). A related verb (Piel of *pāgar*) occurs in 1 Sam. 30:10, 21, with the meaning "to be faint, weak," so that the basic meaning of the word may well be "a weak or lifeless thing."

59. Gray (p. 164) has suggested that *ʾᵃšer hēmmâ mallînîm ʿālay* is possibly dittography from the end of the verse. Even if this is true and the clause is eliminated, what remains is very difficult. Those who supply a verb, e.g., *ʾeslaḥ* (cf. v. 19) or *ʾeśśāʾ*, include AV, RV, NEB, NASB; see Budd, pp. 95–96; Keil, p. 149. Those who follow the above view include RSV, NIV, NJPS; see Heinisch, pp. 58–59, etc.

60. The term is found in Exod. 15:24; 16:2, 7–9; 17:3; Num. 14:2, 27, 29, 36; 16:11–12; 17:6, 20, 25; Josh. 9:18. See BDB, p. 534a.

61. The formula is found, e.g., some 162 times in Jeremiah alone.

62. See the commentary above on 14:2–4.

in this wilderness (bammiḏbār hazzeh). The word order emphasizes the words *in this wilderness,* which are found in Israel's heretofore unfulfilled wish to have died *in this wilderness* (14:2). Yahweh will grant their wish! Even though it may have been only a figure of speech on the people's lips, it will now come to pass.

and not one of all your number that you counted from twenty years of age and up who murmured against me (wᵉḵol-pᵉquḏêḵem lᵉḵol-misparᵉḵem mibben ʿeśrîm šānâ wāmāʿlâ ʾᵃšer hᵃlînōṯem ʿālāy). This clause simply clarifies who will be punished. The reference is to the census of ch. 1,[63] and those counted in it, i.e., all able-bodied men of Israel. It is unclear whether the clause *who murmured against me* is meant to delimit this group further or simply to describe all those who were counted in the census. Although it may seem natural to assume the latter in the light of the text's emphasis on the guilt of the whole people (e.g., 14:1–2, 7), some people must be excluded from that *all* since Moses, Aaron, Caleb, and Joshua are excepted (although the former two do not go into the land).

The Levites are also not to be counted in the number of those who murmured and spurned Yahweh (v. 23). This conclusion is probable for two reasons. First, Eliezar (Aaron's son and successor) was probably over twenty years old at the first census, and he survived to enter Canaan (cf. Josh. 14:1; 17:4; 20:24, 33). Second, and more importantly, the Levites are exempted from the punishment because they were not involved in the general census of ch. 1, but were set over against Israel and given their own censuses in chs. 3–4, with different age ranges than *from twenty years of age and up.*[64]

30 *the land in which I swore to make you dwell* (*hāʾāreṣ ʾᵃšer nāśāʾṯî ʾeṯ-yāḏî lᵉšakkēn ʾeṯᵉḵem bāh,* lit., "the land which I lifted my hand to make you dwell there"). The idiom "to raise the hand," meaning "to swear," is common (e.g., Gen. 14:22; Exod. 6:8; Ezek. 20:5–6, 15, 23, 28, 42).

except for Caleb son of Jephunneh and Joshua son of Nun (kî ʾim-kālēḇ ben-yᵉpunneh wîhôšuaʿ bin-nûn). The lineage of these men is

63. The formula "from twenty years of age and up" occurs in 1:3, 18, 20, 22, 24, 26, 28, 30, 32, 34, 36, 38, 40, 42, 45.

64. The Levites and Israel are separated from one another in 1:47–54. The age limit in 3:15, 22, 28, 34, 39 is "from one month of age and up" *(mibben-ḥōḏeš wāmaʿlâ),* and in 4:3, 23, 30, 35, 39, 43, 47 it is "from thirty years up to fifty years of age" *(mibben šᵉlōšîm wāmaʿlâ wᵉʿaḏ ben-ḥᵃmiššîm šānâ).* Cf. Keil, pp. 95–96; Binns, p. 97; Noordtzij, pp. 128–29. The Levites are also counted separately from the other Israelites in the second census (see 26:62).

given first in Num. 13:6 (Caleb) and Exod. 33:11 (Joshua). On both men being included here, see above on v. 24.

31–33 This section refers to the fear and complaint concerning the children becoming prey in the wilderness (v. 3). The wives of v. 3 are not mentioned here; it is useless to speculate as to their fate. Whereas the judgment of vv. 28–30 is, in effect, a granting of the people's wish to die in the wilderness (however real this wish was), here the judgment is a reversal of the people's fears. They had feared that their children would *become prey (yihyû lāḇaz),* but, in fact, Yahweh will bring these very children into the land and they will know (i.e., experience) the land that the current generation had *rejected.*[65] The only other text that mentions the land as rejected or despised (RSV) is Ps. 106:24, which refers to the current incident in hymnic form. By rejecting Yahweh (Num. 11:20) the people are also rejecting Yahweh's land, which he swore to them. Entrance to the land is commonly tied to obedience to Yahweh.[66]

32 This verse contrasts the two judgments — life for the children, but death for the parents — in the same words as v. 29a, but with a different word order and different emphasis. This time the emphasis is not on the wilderness, but on the corpses, i.e., death.[67]

33 This verse gives a further specification of v. 31. Not even the children will inherit the land immediately. They must wait until v. 32 is fully accomplished. *shepherds (rōʿîm).* Some English versions (e.g., RV, NEB) have followed an ancient Jewish tradition, probably based on 32:13, and read the text as "wanderers."[68] Although the MT, supported by the LXX, is probably correct, it is very likely that the aspect of shepherding in the author's mind was its wandering, nomadic life-style, so that the ancient interpretation of the text is on the right track.[69]

The period involved is *forty years,* which is often a round number in the OT (e.g., 14:25; probably Gen. 7:17; Ezek. 4:6; etc.), and is also

65. The verb *mā'as* is found again here, as it was in 11:20, of the people's rejection of Yahweh.

66. Cf. 14:7–9; Deut. 4:1–40; 7:1–8:20; Josh. 1:10–18; etc.

67. The emphasis is seen not only by the word order *(ûpigrēḵem 'attem yippᵉlû),* but also in the presence of the pronoun *'attem,* which, from a strict grammatical point of view, is not necessary; see GKC, §135a, c.

68. The suggested Hebrew text is either *tōʿîm* (from *tʿh*) or *nāʿîm* (from *nwʿ;* cf. 32:13), both meaning "wanderer" or "vagabond." The interpretation is at least as old as the tradition behind Targ. Jonathan (*tʿyym,* "wanderer") picked up in Vulg. (*vagi,* "wanderer").

69. Cf. de Vaulx, p. 174.

often thought of as the length of a generation (see, e.g., Deut. 2:14; Josh. 5:6). Here it is a round number, for Deut. 2:14 gives the time as thirty-eight years.[70]

they will bear the penalty for your fornications (*wᵉnāśᵉû 'eṯ-zᵉnûṯēḵem,* lit., "they will bear your fornications"). The verb "to bear" *(nāśā')* in conjunction with a noun for good or bad behavior (such as *'āwōn, ḥāṭṭā'*, or, as here, *zᵉnûṯ*) can mean "to bear the penalty of such an act."[71] Fornication is just one more image to add to *spurning* (*ni'ēṣ*, vv. 11, 23), *disbelieving* (*lō' he'ĕmîn,* v. 11), *testing* (*nissâ,* v. 22), *not listening* (*lō' šāma',* v. 22), and *murmuring* (*lûn,* v. 27) to describe the rebellious, disloyal spirit of what v. 35 calls *this whole wicked congregation.* The verb *zānâ,* "to engage in sexual relations outside of or apart from marriage,"[72] and its derivative nouns (*zᵉnûnîm, zᵉnûṯ,* etc.) are common words to describe apostasy and idolatry,[73] but the present context emphasizes lack of commitment and loyalty to Yahweh rather than loyalty to other gods. That the noun *fornications* is plural is a reference to Israel's repeated rebellion and disloyalty (cf. 14:22, *ten times*).[74]

until the last of your corpses lies in the wilderness (*'aḏ-tōm pigrêḵem bammiḏbār,* lit., "until the completing of your corpses in the wilderness"). The verb *tāmam* means "to be finished, complete,"[75] and

70. To be precise, the time was from the second month, twentieth day, of the second year after the Exodus (10:11) until sometime in the middle of the fortieth year. Cf. the story of Aaron's death (20:22–29; 33:38) and Deut. 2:14. For forty as a round number, cf. S. McEvenue, "A Source Critical Problem in Num. 14,26–38," *Bib* 50 (1969) 454–56.

71. See 14:34; 5:31 (with *'āwōn*); 9:13 (with *ḥāṭā'*). See Milgrom, *Cult and Conscience,* pp. 3–4; BDB, p. 671b.

72. S. Erlandsson, *TDOT,* IV: 99–104, esp. 100.

73. For the verb see, e.g., Ezek. 16:15; Hos. 2:7; Isa. 57:3; for *zᵉnûnîm* see 2 K. 9:22; Ezek. 23:11, 29; Hos. 2:4, 6; 4:12; 5:4; for *zᵉnûṯ* see Jer. 3:2, 9; 13:27; Ezek. 43:7, 9; Hos. 6:10. See BDB, pp. 275b–76a; Erlandsson, *TDOT,* IV: 99–104. P. Bird has argued that the prophet Hosea provided the primary literary and religio-historical context that connects the verb *zānâ,* which primarily means "to fornicate or engage in illicit extramarital relations," to a figurative application to Israel's worship of other gods. It is a valuable insight that the verbal sense is primary over the nominal sense of "prostitute" *(zônâ).* Bird really assumes that Hosea is primary in this matter of the figurative application of *zānâ.* She does not mention the current text at all. P. Bird, "To Play the Harlot": An Inquiry into an Old Testament Metaphor," in P. Day, ed., *Gender and Difference in Ancient Israel* (Minneapolis: Fortress, 1989), pp. 75–94.

74. Cf. Gray, p. 163.

75. BDB, p. 1070; KB, p. 1032a.

what is completed is the full number of corpses, not the complete rotting away of these corpses (cf. AV, RV, NKJV). Once again, death in the wilderness is mentioned (vv. 29, 32), and the emphasis this time is the completeness of the judgment of death. The children will be shepherds in the wilderness until every last one of the old rebellious generation dies there.[76]

34 This verse forms a natural continuation of v. 33b, which gives a figure of forty years until the completion of punishment. Here the formula by which forty years is reached is given; i.e., one *year* for every *day* of the spies' mission in Canaan (cf. 13:25), which mission had formed the basis for the latest episode of Israel's rebellion against Yahweh. As before, "to bear an iniquity" *(nāśā' 'āwōn)* means to take the brunt of the punishment for iniquity.[77]

know my opposition (wîḏa'tem 'eṯ-tᵉnû'āṯî). This difficult clause has long exercised interpreters.[78] LXX reads "you shall know the passion of my wrath" *(gnōsesthe ton thymon tēs orgēs mou),* and other versions paraphrase as well.[79] The verb *nw'* means "to hinder, restrain, frustrate."[80] The likelihood is that God is saying that Israel will, by their dying in the wilderness, experience a frustration brought about by Almighty God,[81] and perhaps that they will feel frustrated as Yahweh has felt with them.

One must contrast the two generations here. The verb "to know" is used of both groups. The children, in due course, will *know* (i.e., experience) *the land* (v. 31), while the older generation will *know* Yahweh's frustration and opposition so that they may not go forward, but only in circles until the punishment is fulfilled. The use of the noun *opposition (tᵉnûa')* has led at least one scholar to conclude that v. 34 is a gloss based on 32:7.[82] Other scholars have, for different reasons, con-

76. For a parallel usage of the verb *tāmam,* see Deut. 2:14: "until the completion of the generation" *('aḏ-tōm kol-haddôr);* the full meaning is spelled out in 2:15: "For, indeed, the hand of Yahweh was against them to destroy them from the midst of the camp until their extinction" *(wᵉgam yaḏ-YHWH hāyᵉṯâ ḇām lᵉhummām miqqereḇ hammaḥᵃneh 'aḏ tummām).*

77. See the commentary above on 14:33.

78. See R. Loewe, "Divine Frustration Exegetically Frustrated — Num. 14:34 *tnw'ty,*" in *Words and Meanings: Essays Presented to D. Winton Thomas,* ed. P. Ackroyd and B. Lindars (Cambridge: Cambridge Univ. Press, 1968), pp. 142–57.

79. Ibid.

80. BDB, p. 626a; *HALAT,* p. 640a; McEvenue, "Source Critical Problem," pp. 457–58.

81. Loewe, "Divine Frustration," p. 158.

82. McEvenue ("Source Critical Problem," pp. 457–58) argues that *tᵉnû'â*

sidered the verse to be a later composition, which it may be, of course.[83] One must finally admit, however, that this verse is in the final form of the text, as witnessed not only by MT but also by the ancient versions, however it may have gotten there. The verse relates the punishment to former experiences of the people in a way consistent with other places in the book.

35 This verse concludes and rounds off the judgment speech by reiterating that (a) it is Yahweh who has spoken and will perform his word (cf. vv. 11, 21–22, 26, 28); (b) the whole generation is to blame and will die (cf. vv. 1–2, 5, 7, 10, 22, 29); and (c) this whole generation will die in the wilderness (cf. vv. 12, 22, 29, 32).

In this wilderness they will come to an end (bammiḏbār hazzeh yittammû). This clause has great similarities with previous death sayings and sums up this judgment.[84] Once more the wilderness is emphasized. *and they will die there (wᵉšām yāmuṯû)* makes the judgment crystal clear and brings discussion of it to a close.[85]

36–38 At the conclusion of this narrative concerning the judgment of death on the whole congregation (vv. 10b–35), the original judgment of immediate destruction is carried out, except that, in keeping with Moses' intercession and Yahweh's response (vv. 13–19, 20–35), the scope of the original judgment is narrowed.

36 This verse carefully characterizes the ones who were destroyed: *the men whom Moses sent* [*haʾᵃnāšîm ʾᵃšer šālaḥ mōšeh,* 13:3, 17, 27] *to spy out the land* [*lāṯûr ʾeṯ-hāʾāreṣ,* 13:1, 16–17, 21, 25, 32; 14:7] and who *caused the whole congregation to grumble* (*wayyillînû ʿālāyw ʾeṯ-kol-hāʿēḏâ,* 14:2, 27, 29) by bringing *an evil report against the land* (*dibbâ ʿal-hāʾāreṣ,* 13:32).

---

in 14:34 takes its meaning from 32:5–15, where God "reproaches Reuben and Gad for 'opposing' Israel's intentions to enter the promised land" (32:7), paralleling that incident to the one in Num. 13–14. Ch. 32 is called a "late text" (postexilic). Speculation on the date of this or that fragment or section of a book is just that. Certainly the text here may, as McEvenue argues, take its meaning from the text in ch. 32. Equally, it may be the other way round. What is required is that the text of Numbers be seen as a whole — originating as a composition after the events narrated. How long after is, again, a matter for speculation.

83. E.g., Noth, p. 110. Coats (*Rebellion in the Wilderness,* p. 139) rejects Noth's claim.

84. Cf. *bammiḏbār hazzeh yittammû* here and *bammiḏbār hazzeh tōm* in v. 33.

85. The two clauses together form a hendiadys — "they shall come to an end by dying there." See Gray, p. 163.

37 The next verse summarizes by referring only to the *evil report* (this time *dibbaṯ-hā'āreṣ rā'â*). This narrows the judgment to the ten spies who brought this report. They were slain by a *plague (maggēp̱â)*.[86] For plagues as the judgment of God, see, e.g., 17:13–15 (Eng. 16:48–50); 25:8–9, 18–19; 31:16; Exod. 9:14; 1 Sam. 6:4; Zech. 14:18.

38 This verse states that only Joshua and Caleb escaped death. The death by plague (v. 37) may be seen as the judgment that God intended to bring upon the whole nation in v. 12. Only the ten spies who had brought in the evil report died in the plague. The survival of Joshua and Caleb is based on their actions reported in 13:30 and 14:6–9, which were judged as worthy of life by Yahweh (see 14:24, 30). At the beginning of this unit (vv. 10b–12) and at the end (vv. 36–38) this theme of immediate judgment on disobedience is emphasized. The judgment of death here may be contrasted with the units in which Yahweh's commandments were followed exactly (see, e.g., 1:54; 2:34; 3:51; 4:49; 5:4; 8:20–22; 9:23).

d. The People Attempt to Enter Canaan (14:39–45)

39 *And Moses told these words to all the children of Israel, and the people lamented greatly.*

40 *And they rose up early in the morning and went up into the height of the hill country, saying, "Behold, we are here! We will go up to the place of which Yahweh has spoken, for we have sinned."*

41 *And Moses said, "Why are you transgressing the utterance of Yahweh? This will not prosper."*[1]

42 *"Do not go up that you may not be smitten before your foes, for Yahweh is not in your midst."*

43 *"For the Amalekites and the Canaanites are there before you, and you will fall by the sword; because you turned from going after Yahweh, Yahweh will not be with you."*

44 *But they heedlessly ascended to the height of the hill country, although neither the ark of the covenant of Yahweh nor Moses went from the midst of the camp.*

86. BDB, p. 620a. The noun *maggēp̱â* comes from the root *ngp,* "to strike"; see BDB, p. 619b. A related noun *neḡep̱* describes the judgment against the firstborn in Egypt (Exod. 12:13). Plague is threatened if there are unauthorized encroachers on the sanctuary in Num. 8:19. Cf. Milgrom, *Studies in Levitical Terminology,* I:30 n. 109.

1. The verb *ṯiṣlāḥ,* "prosper," is fem. sing. The fem. is sometimes used to refer to the general idea contained in the preceding sentence. The fem. verb here is in concord with the pronoun *hî',* "This"; see GKC, § 135p; Davidson, *Syntax,* § 1 Rem. 2.

45 *And the Amalekites and the Canaanites who were dwelling in that hill country descended, and they defeated them and put them to rout all the way to Hormah.*

39–45 In spite of difficulties in points of detail, the thread of the story is clear enough here. When Moses tells Israel the words of Yahweh (14:11–35), they engage in mourning and seek to change Yahweh's mind, since they are either unwilling or unable to accept the seriousness of their rebellion. They now compound their sin of rebellion with arrogance in trying to capture the land on their own. They are like children who had broken a valuable vase and decided to "make it better" by gluing it back together. The result of such action looks nothing like the original. Moses attempts to tell the Israelites that Yahweh would not go with them and that his absence would mean disaster for them, but as elsewhere the people do not show a willingness or ability to listen either to God or to his servants. When they go into the hill country to face the Amalekites and the Canaanites, neither Moses nor the ark goes with them (thus changing the pattern of 10:32), and the engagement with these native peoples ends in disaster. The Israelites are pursued as far as Hormah (see below on v. 45). The fear of 14:3 has become a reality.

The details of this story are difficult to follow in several ways. For example, what is the connection between v. 40, which seems to indicate that the Israelites went up into the highlands, and vv. 41–43, where Moses addresses the people? Did he go with them and then return with the ark to camp? Further, what is the relation of the Amalekites and Canaanites in v. 45 with previous mentions of these people as living *in the valley* (14:25; cf. 13:29)? Also, where and what is Hormah and how is the present narrative to be related to 21:3 and Judg. 1:16–17? All these questions must be addressed.

Some scholars have posited the existence of several sources in the story that have been put together roughly. Others see one source that has grown and developed in the history of the tradition.[2] While one cannot

2. For a discussion of the various source divisions, see, e.g., Gray, pp. 164–65. Many contemporary scholars simply assign the passage to J or JE and account for the difficulties by means of various modifications of the tradition for theological purposes; cf. O. Eissfeldt, *Hexateuch Synopse* (Leipzig: Hinrichs, 1922), p. 102, pp. *172–73. Others have seen v. 40 (minus the words *we have sinned*) as being a pre-Yahwistic link between 13:30 (which related Caleb's encouragement to conquest) and 21:3 (which tells of victory at Hormah), which the J author has interpreted within his framework of Israel's unfaithfulness and punishment. See, e.g., Budd, pp. 154–55; Noth, pp. 111–12.

deny that such a process may have taken place, it is doubtful that modern scholars can recover it with certainty. Again, one wonders what the final editor of the piece thought it said as a whole.

39 The first part of the verse rounds off the previous narrative as well as forming a transition to the present one. The clause *And Moses told these words (wayᵉḏabbēr mōšeh 'eṯ-haddᵉḇārîm hā'ēlleh)* simply indicates that he faithfully reported Yahweh's command in 14:28.[3] The second part of the verse begins the present narrative proper.

And the people lamented greatly (wayyiṯ'abbᵉlû hā'ām mᵉ'ōḏ). The verb *'āḇal* refers not to an inner sadness but to an outer action demonstrating it. The verb is often connected with mourning rites for the dead (e.g., Gen. 37:34; 2 Sam. 13:31–37; etc.). Where, as here, there is no explicit connection with these rites, the emphasis is still on external actions designed to turn a disaster aside.[4] The mourning was inefficacious, as Moses' response in vv. 41–43 shows.

40 The children of Israel *rose up early in the morning (wayyaškimû ḇabbōqer),* i.e., the morning of the day in which they had been commanded to *turn and depart into the wilderness by the way of the Reed Sea* (v. 25). They have thus disobeyed God once again, and mistaken the seriousness of his judgment for something amenable to change if only they will do what was originally commanded. Perhaps they thought that the "mourning rites" would change Yahweh's judgment. In their overweening arrogance (see v. 44) they now decide to go *into the height of the hill country* (*'el-rō'š-hāhār,* lit., "into the top of the mountain"; so AV; see 13:17). The action narrated here should be thought of as a summary of what the rest of the narrative will contain, much as 10:12 summarizes the Israelites' trip into the wilderness of Paran.[5] The speech of Moses in vv. 41–43 should be thought of as happening in the camp before the people depart, as should v. 40.

The action proceeds as follows. First, the people announce their presence to Moses: *Behold, we are here (hinnennû),* and then they simply declare that they will go into the land of which Yahweh has spoken (10:29). They seem to assume that atonement for their sin, which they admit (*we have sinned, ḥāṭā'nû),* requires nothing more than a confession.

3. See other similar idioms indicating a report by Moses, e.g., Exod. 6:9; Lev. 24:23; Num. 9:4; 17:21.

4. See A. Baumann, *TDOT,* I:44–48. Cf. 1 Sam. 15:35; 16:1; 2 Sam. 12:22ff.; Ps. 35:13–14; Ezra 10:6; Neh. 1:4; etc.

5. See the commentary above on 10:12. The tense of the verbs both here and there is imperfect consecutive.

In their view, it was only a matter of changing their minds and going up into the land. What they have failed to recognize is that it is Yahweh's mind that needs to be changed. Atonement for their sin will be made only by wandering for forty long years in the wilderness. The time for easy repentance has passed. Judgment is inevitable.

41–43 Moses tries to dissuade the people from their idea that going into the land of Canaan is all that is required for them to do Yahweh's will. In going into the land now the people are *transgressing the utterance of Yahweh* (*'ōḇ^{e}rîm 'eṯ-pî YHWH,* lit., "going beyond the mouth of Yahweh").[6]

The verb *prosper (ṣālaḥ)* means "to succeed" here.[7] The proposed foray into Canaan, in the light of Yahweh's judgment, is seen as disobedience. In vv. 42–43 this foray is foretold as an undoubted disaster for the people because Yahweh is not in their midst. In 14:14 Moses had spoken of Yahweh as in the midst of Israel *(b^{e}qereḇ yiśrā'ēl).* Here this protecting presence is withdrawn. Lack of divine protection will mean that the inhabitants of the hill country, the Amalekites and Canaanites, will destroy the Israelites. The reason is underlined in v. 43b: *because you turned from going after Yahweh (kî-'al-kēn šaḇtem mē'aḥ^{a}rê YHWH).* The idiom "to turn from going after" *(šûḇ mē'aḥ^{a}rê)* is used of defection from Yahweh's way (e.g., in 32:15; Deut. 7:4; Josh. 22:16, 18, 23, 29; 1 Sam. 15:11).[8] Moses' speech ends with the ominous *Yahweh will not be with you.*

44 In spite of Moses' clear warning about the consequences of an unassisted expedition into Canaan from the south, the Israelites *heedlessly ascended (wayya'pilû la'^{a}lôṯ).* The hapax legomenon *'āpal* is problematic. The parallel text in Deut. 1:41 reads "they made light to ascend" *(wattāhînû la'^{a}lôṯ).* The ancient versions guessed at the meaning of *'pl* (e.g., LXX *diabiasamenoi anebēsan,* "going in, they ascended").[9] In Hebrew the letter *'ayin* represents the falling together of two Semitic phonemes (*'ayin* and *ghayin*), which appear, e.g., in Arabic. Thus there are two lexical possibilities for *'pl,* and cognate Arabic words may be found for both. The first is *'afala* (with *'ayin,* "swell"?), connected perhaps with Heb. *'ōpel,* meaning either "hemorrhoid" (Deut. 28:27) or "hill, mound" (1 K. 5:24). The second is *ghafala,* which means "to be heedless, reckless." If one relates *'pl* here to the first, one gets a meaning

6. Cf. BDB, pp. 804b–5.
7. Ibid., p. 852.
8. Ibid., p. 30a.
9. For further discussion on the ancient versions, see Gray, p. 167.

such as "in their arrogance they ascended" (cf. RSV, etc.). The present translation follows Snaith, who holds the second as the more likely root of the verb here.[10] The flow of the story emphasizes that Israel did not listen to the words of Moses. This meaning also parallels the sense of Deut. 1:41.

Here the Amalekites and the Canaanites are said to dwell in *that hill country (hāhār hahû')*, i.e., that to which Moses has just referred in v. 40. These two peoples are said to dwell *in the valley* in 14:25, and in 13:29 the Amalekites are said to dwell in the Negeb and the Canaanites by the sea and along the Jordan. Again, the term *hill country (hāhār)* is probably used generally here as in 14:40 and 13:17 to describe most of the land north of the Negeb. One must also assume that 13:29 describes only part of the Amalekites and that some of them also lived north of the Negeb in the hill country. In ancient times, when boundaries were inexact at best, this situation is not hard to imagine. One must also say that, even armed with the information the spies brought back, Moses' knowledge of the geographic description of the peoples of Canaan would likely be imperfect. No precise ethnic description is intended here, but rather a general description of the inhabitants of the land. Deut. 1:44 substitutes the general term *Amorite* for Amalekite and Canaanite.[11]

The site of *Hormah* is unknown. The OT mentions the place seven other times, and specifies that it was on the west side of Jordan (Josh. 12:7) toward the south (Deut. 1:44; Josh. 12:14; 15:30), in the tribal holdings shared by Judah and Simeon (Josh. 15:30; 19:4), and near Ziklag in the Negeb (Judg. 1:17). The site was at one time called Zapheth and was around Arad (Judg. 1:17). Many modern scholars have identified the site as Tell el-Meshash east of Beer-sheba, although other locales in this general vicinity have been posited as well.[12] More important than the location of Hormah is the use of the name here. The definite article is

10. See Snaith, p. 153; see also BDB, p. 779.

11. Other scholars find that the texts of 13:29; 14:25, 48 conflict with one another; cf. Noth, pp. 109–10. Comparison should be made between Num. 14:38–45 and Deut. 1:41–44. The deuteronomic text is clearly intended as a summary. The differences are: (a) In Deuteronomy there is no ascending the heights of the hill country (Num. 14:40); (b) Moses' speech (Num. 14:41–42) is put into God's mouth in Deuteronomy 1; (c) 14:43, 44b find no parallel in Deuteronomy; (d) Deuteronomy uses the term *Amorite* for "Amalekite and Canaanite"; (e) Deuteronomy follows this narrative with the sojourn at Kadesh-barnea.

12. Budd, p. 160; Noth, p. 111; E. G. Kraeling, ed., *The Rand-McNally Bible Atlas,* 3rd ed. (New York: Rand-McNally, 1966), p. 117; Y. Aharoni in the *Encyclopedia of Archaeological Expeditions in the Holy Land,* I:88. For other sites see, e.g., W. Albright, *BASOR* 15 (Oct. 1924) 6–7; B. Mazar, *JNES* 24 (1965) 297–303.

attached to the name *(haḥōrmâ).* The noun *ḥōrmâ* comes from a root meaning "devoted, under the ban of destruction" (cf. *ḥērem*). It is at least possible that the definite article means that, although a place-name, Hormah is to be taken in its generic sense as "a place of the ban" (destruction), so that the Israelites were pursued to Hormah, i.e., to destruction. In 21:1–3 the Israelites again encounter the Canaanites at Hormah, this time victoriously. It is possible that the narrative of punishment in the wilderness is framed by battles leading to destruction *(ḥōrmâ),* here at the beginning of the period for Israel, and toward the end of it (21:1–3) for the Canaanites.

B. CULTIC LEGISLATION (15:1–41)

1. SUPPLEMENTARY LAWS OF THE OFFERINGS (15:1–16)

1 *And Yahweh spoke to Moses, saying,*

2 *"Speak to the children of Israel and say to them: 'When*[1] *you come into your dwelling land that I am about to give you,*[2]

3 *when you make a fire offering to Yahweh, a whole burnt offering, or a blood sacrifice, to fulfill a vow or in a freewill offering or in your appointed feasts, to make a pleasing aroma to Yahweh, from the cattle or the sheep,*

4 *then the one who presents his offering to Yahweh shall offer a meal offering of one-tenth ephah of fine flour mixed with one-quarter hin of oil.*

5 *And you will also use one-quarter hin of wine for the drink offering for each lamb, with the whole burnt offering or for the blood sacrifice.*

6 *Or, for a ram, you shall use this meal offering: two-tenths of an ephah of fine flour mixed with one-third hin of oil.*

7 *And for the drink offering you shall offer one-third hin of wine, a pleasing aroma to Yahweh.*

8 *And when you offer a bull, a whole burnt offering or a blood sacrifice, to fulfill a vow or for peace offerings to Yahweh,*

9 *then one will offer with the bull a meal offering of three-tenths of an ephah of fine flour mixed with one-half hin of oil.*

10 *And you shall offer one-half hin of wine for a drink offering, a fire offering of pleasing aroma to Yahweh.*

1. For the temporal use of *kî,* see Williams, *Syntax,* § 445.
2. For the imminent use of the participle, see Williams, *Syntax,* § 214.

11 *Thus shall it be done for each bull or ram, for each one among the male lambs*[3] *or among the male kids.*
12 *According to the number that you use, so you will do with each one according to their number.*
13 *Any native shall do thus in these matters in presenting a fire offering of pleasing aroma to Yahweh.*
14 *And, if a sojourner should sojourn with you, or one should be in your midst through your generations, and that one wishes to make a fire offering of pleasing aroma to Yahweh, he will do just as you do.*
15 *As for the assembly, there shall be one statute for you and for the sojourner who is sojourning with you, a perpetual statute, throughout your generations; as you are, so the sojourner will be before Yahweh.*[4]
16 *One law and one ordinance shall be for you and for the sojourner who sojourns with you.' "*

While Lev. 2 deals with the independent meal offering,[5] and several previous passages in the Pentateuch mention the meal or drink offerings (e.g., Gen. 35:14; Exod. 29:40; Lev. 23:13, 18, 37; Num. 6:15, 17), the present passage establishes a scale or tariff for both these offerings based on the size of the sacrificial animal (vv. 3–10). In addition, this passage establishes a time for this tariff to take effect (v. 2), an ordinance requiring that the meal and drink offerings be added to every appropriate animal sacrifice (esp. vv. 11–12, but cf. vv. 3–10) and the application of this ordinance both to the Israelite and the sojourner (vv. 13–16).

Ezekiel 46:5–7, 11, 14 set up a different tariff, which both increases the amounts of flour and oil and simplifies the scale, but says nothing at all about the drink offering. Many scholars have concluded that the Numbers passage is later than the Ezekiel passage (or, indeed, than Lev. 2) and belongs to "one of the very latest sections of the Pentateuch."[6] The major reason for this dating seems to be that the Numbers passage is

3. The *Sebir* note reads *bkśbym* rather than MT *bkbśym.* The meaning of the two is the same: *kśb* is a synonym for *kbś* that arose from the metathesis of *ś* and *b.* Heb. *kśb* is found 13 times while *kbś* is found 107 times in the OT. See BDB, p. 461a.

4. GKC, § 161c, speaks of *kāḵem kāggēr* as "virtual substantives with a following genitive . . . , *the like of you shall bē the like of the stranger,* i.e. *your duty shall be* (also) *the stranger's duty;* cf. Lv 24:22."

5. See also Lev. 6:7–18 (Eng. 14–23) and 7:9–10.

6. Noth, p. 114.

more universal in scope and definite in prescription.[7] It is an assumption, however, not a proved fact, that all documents must proceed from informal to formal. It is just as logical to assume that Ezekiel modified the rules of the Pentateuch on the basis of the needs of the exilic age as it is to assume that the author of Numbers modified Ezekiel on the basis of the needs of the postexilic age. Both meal and drink offerings in conjunction with other sacrifices are attested in the ancient Near East.[8] Other portions of the OT also show that such offerings were known in Israel apart from the legislation of the Pentateuch (cf. Judg. 9:9, 11; 1 Sam. 1:24; 10:3; Hos. 9:4; Mic. 6:7; 2 K. 16:13–15; etc.).

Another reason why many scholars have concluded that this passage is late is that other texts in the Pentateuch,[9] indeed, those texts concerned with the establishment of the whole burnt offerings and the blood sacrifices, seem to know nothing of the accompanying meal and drink offerings, while the narrative texts mentioned above show that the combination of meal and drink offerings with other sacrifices was known. This apparent contradiction may result from different passages having different focuses; the focus of the legislative passages in Leviticus is the establishment of a particular rite, not all possible accompanying details.[10] Indeed, Num. 15 nowhere explains the meal or drink offerings, but rather simply details amounts to be used in particular cases. There seems to be no objective reason to doubt that these offerings were practiced in ancient Israel, although it is uncertain whether the details of the legislation of the Pentateuch were followed to the letter at all times and places.

The most difficult literary feature of the section is the shift in person. The author starts and finishes in the second person plural (vv. 2b–3, 12–16), sections which address the whole community. The main part of the tariff uses the second person singular (vv. 5–8, 10–11), but two verses have the third person singular (vv. 4 and 9). The singular number (vv. 4–11) may be said to be natural in sections that address worshipers as individuals. The shift between second and third person seems to create difficulties, but it should be noted that Lev. 2 (also dealing with meal offerings) has a similar shift (third sing. in vv. 1–3, second sing. in 4–8a,

7. See, e.g., Gray, pp. 169–70; Binns, p. 99; Budd, pp. 166–67.

8. See the evidence of the Ugaritic KRT text, lines 156–71 (e.g., in *ANET*, p. 144); cf. R. de Vaux, *Studies in Old Testament Sacrifice,* tr. J. Bourke and R. Potter (Cardiff: Univ. of Wales Press, 1964), p. 47; cf. de Vaulx, pp. 179–80.

9. See, e.g., Lev. 1; 3; 6:1–6 (Eng. 8–13); 7:11–21; 22:21–25; 23:19.

10. See Noordtzij, p. 135.

third sing. in 8b–10, and second sing. in 11–14). Both verses with the third person singular in the present passage deal with the amount of a meal offering (v. 4 for a lamb and v. 9 for a bull). Why these verses should be in the third person is unknown. Perhaps it was either for literary effect or for variety.[11]

In spite of this difficulty the vocabulary remains fairly constant throughout the whole section, thus speaking for the unity of the piece, at least as a final composition: e.g., "a pleasing aroma to Yahweh" (*rêaḥ nîḥōaḥ lYHWH;* vv. 3, 7, 10, 13–14), "fire offering" (*'iššeh;* vv. 3, 10, 13–14), "blood sacrifice" (*zeḇaḥ;* vv. 3, 5, 8), "whole burnt offering" (*'ōlâ;* vv. 3, 5, 8), "meal offering" (*minḥâ;* vv. 4, 6, 9), "drink offering" (*neseḵ;* vv. 5, 7, 10), etc. Thematic indicators also go all through the chapter, showing that it too may be best taken as a unity.[12]

The whole of ch. 15 is best seen as a response to the rebellion of chs. 13–14. At the end of those chapters the future of the people is in doubt, the whole people has been disobedient to Yahweh; an entire generation will die in the wilderness as a payment for sin. Ch. 15 begins with a word of hope to the new generation: *When you come into your dwelling land . . .* (v. 2; cf. v. 18). What follows is for the new generation in the new land. Furthermore it is still Yahweh who speaks. God is still determined to bring them into the land (v. 2b). The whole chapter shows that fullness of life is still to be had by exact obedience to Yahweh's word. When the people come into the land of Canaan they will have enough agricultural abundance to afford these offerings of fine flour, oil, and wine for every appropriate sacrifice.[13]

1–2 Yahweh has not stopped speaking through Moses, even though the Israelites have rebelled and are under a sentence of death.

When you come into your dwelling land . . . (kî ṯāḇō'û 'el-'ereṣ môšᵉḇōṯêḵem). Although this chapter has few time indicators, the present

11. Budd concludes that the shift in person marks the assimilation of material by the compiler of the present text. Vv. 1–3 and 12–16 (second person pl.) are the compiler's own framework for the passage. The oldest portions of the text are the two laws in the third person sing. (vv. 4 and 9). These have been subject to accretions distinguishing various amounts and adding the drink offering placed in the second person sing. (vv. 5–8 and 10–11; cf. Budd, p. 167). This account does not explain why a compiler should simply transmit a text already in mixed persons and complicate the issue by adding his own work in yet another person.

12. See, e.g., the remarks by Wenham (pp. 126–27), who finds similarities in phrasing at the beginning of units ("and Yahweh said to Moses, say to the children of Israel," vv. 1–2, 17–18, 37–38).

13. See the excellent comments by Wenham, p. 127.

clause indicates that Israel is still in the wilderness. In the light of 14:29, the ordinance that follows is obviously directed to the new generation, and, since it appears to be directed at adults rather than children, one might assume a time well into the wilderness-wandering period (although the nature of the case forbids a firm statement on this matter). The use of the words *dwelling land ('ereṣ môš^e^ḇōṯêḵem)* as a synonym for Canaan is unique in the OT, although the word for "dwelling" is found frequently, both by itself (e.g., Num. 35:29) and in other combinations (e.g., Ezek. 34:13).

3–10 It should be stressed again that this tariff explains neither the meal offering *(minḥâ)* nor the drink offering *(neseḵ),* but assumes that the meaning of these offerings is already known to the Israelites.[14]

fire offering ('iššeh). Although the original meaning and the etymology of the term are debated,[15] the simplest explanation (and probably the popular etymology) derives the term from *'ēš,* "fire," and sees in it a general term for offerings consumed on the altar. The *fire offering* is further delineated by the terms *whole burnt offering ('ōlâ)* and *blood sacrifice (zeḇaḥ).*[16]

Although *zeḇaḥ* may be used as a general term to summarize all blood sacrifice both inside and outside Israel, its most common use is as an abbreviated term for *zeḇaḥ š^e lāmîm,* "peace offerings."[17] That *zeḇaḥ* is here contrasted with *'ōlôṯ,* "whole burnt offerings" (cf. Lev. 1), would also give the impression that the peace offerings are intended. One basic difference between the two is that the whole burnt offering is wholly consumed on the altar while the peace offerings are only partially consumed.[18]

14. See the commentary above on 6:15, 17 for the editing of this text and the meal and drink offerings.

15. For a convenient summary of the debate, see Wenham, *Leviticus,* p. 56 n. 8. NEB and GNB translate as "food offering," relating the term to Sumerian *eš,* "food." On this see, e.g., de Vaux, *Studies,* p. 31 n. 14.

16. For more on these two offerings, see the commentary above on 6:14–17.

17. As a general term, see, e.g., Gen. 46:1; Exod. 34:15. In Lev. 3 the longer expression *zeḇaḥ hašš^e lāmîm* is used uniformly for the peace offerings (vv. 1, 3, 6, 9), but in 7:11–36 the rite is also called simply *zeḇaḥ* (v. 16 [twice], 17) or *š^e lāmîm* (vv. 14, 33). In ch. 7 *zeḇaḥ hašš^e lāmîm* occurs in 7:1, 13, 15, 18, 20–21, 29 (twice), 32, 34, 37. In other sections of the OT, *zeḇaḥ* substitutes for the longer expression, e.g., in Lev. 17:5, 7–8; 19:6: 23:37; *š^e lāmîm* substitutes, e.g., in Exod. 20:26; 32:6; Lev. 6:5 (Eng. 12); 9:4, 22; Num. 6:14; 15:8. This evidence suffices to show that the terms are often interchangeable.

18. For a discussion of the *zebaḥ š^e lamîm* and the *'ōlôṯ,* see, e.g., Milgrom, *IDBSup,* pp. 764–71, esp. pp. 769–70.

It is also unclear whether the phrases *to fulfill a vow or in a freewill offering or in your appointed feasts* refer to both the whole burnt offerings and the blood sacrifices (i.e., the peace offerings) or only to the latter.[19] The likelihood is that these three phrases give reasons to celebrate either or both together.[20] The present ordinance regulates meal and drink offerings only with whole burnt or peace offerings; the purification offering *(ḥaṭṭā'ṯ)* and the reparation offering *('āšām)* are excluded here, as are any whole burnt or peace offerings not of the bovine *(from the cattle, min-habbāqār)* or goat *(from the flock, min-haṣṣō'n)* types. These fire offerings are said *to make a pleasing aroma to Yahweh (la'ᵃśôṯ rêaḥ nîḥōaḥ lYHWH).* Although the origin of the clause was probably in the ancient idea that a god was attracted to a sacrifice and pleased by its odor, in the OT the meaning is generally that a particular sacrifice is acceptable to and efficacious with Yahweh.[21]

19. E.g., Noordtzij, pp. 134–35; Milgrom, *IDBSup,* pp. 764–71; and de Vaux, *Studies in Sacrifice,* pp. 27–51, esp. pp. 33, 37–42, favor the former; Gray, pp. 172–73, and McNeile, pp. 79–80, the latter.

20. Votive offerings and freewill offerings are two occasions for the presentation of the peace offerings (Lev. 7:16). The third phrase ("in your appointed feasts") is not, unless one argues that this phrase indicates the thank offering (Lev. 7:11–15), which is unlikely. Most scholars consider appointed feasts *(mō'ēḏîm)* to consist of the fixed festivals of the Hebrew calendar as codified in Lev. 23 and Num. 28–29. At these festivals both whole burnt offerings and peace offerings were made (cf., e.g., Lev. 23:4, 18–19, 37–38; Num. 29:39). Therefore, "in your appointed feasts" may apply to both kinds of offerings discussed here. Ezek. 46:12 refers the freewill offering to either the whole burnt offering or the peace offering. See the resources referred to in the previous note.

21. E.g., in the laws establishing the fire offerings in Lev. 1–3, the term is so used 8 times (1:9, 13, 17; 2:2, 9, 12; 3:5, 16); cf. Sturdy, p. 108, and the discussion of the first occurrence of the term (Gen. 8:21) in G. Wenham, *Genesis 1–15,* WBC (Waco: Word, 1987), p. 189. A good example of this ancient idea occurs in the Gilgamesh Epic, tablet XI, lines 155–61:

> (Then) I sent forth (everything) to the four winds and offered a sacrifice.
> I poured out a libation upon the peak of the mountain.
> Seven and (yet) seven kettles I set up.
> Under them I heaped up (sweet) cane, cedar, and myrtle.
> The gods smelled the savor,
> The gods smelled the sweet savor.
> The gods gathered like flies over the sacrificer.

(A. Heidel, *The Gilgamesh Epic and Old Testament Parallels,* 2nd ed. [Chicago: Univ. of Chicago Press, 1949], p. 87; cf. also *ANET,* p. 95; Gray, p. 173.)

The materials for the offerings are *fine flour* (*sōleṯ*, probably finely milled wheat flour),[22] *oil (šemen),* and *wine (yayin).* The liquids are measured in fractions of a hin. The fine flour is probably measured in fractions of the ephah, although no unit of measurement is given in the text. It is difficult to determine modern equivalents for these measurements; scholarly estimates vary widely.[23] A fair consensus might be that the *ephah* equals about 16 dry quarts, and the *hin* about four liquid quarts. The amounts for the fine flour increase at a ratio of 1:2:3, while the liquids increase at only 1:1.3:2. The following chart illustrates the scale of the meal and drink offerings:

Animal	Amount of Fine Flour	Amount of Wine/Oil
lamb	1/10 ephah? (1.6–2 dry qts.)	1/4 hin (.8–1 liq. qt.)
ram	2/10 ephah (3.3–4 dry qts.)	1/3 hin (1–1.4 liq. qts.)
bull	3/10 ephah (4.9–6 dry qts.)	1/2 hin (1.6–2 liq. qts.)

As was said above, no procedure for either offering is given here. One might conjecture that a procedure similar to that of Lev. 6:7–18 (Eng. 14–23) obtained for the meal offering. As for the drink offering, some have been prepared to conjecture that, since it is called *a fire offering of pleasing aroma to Yahweh* in v. 10, it may have been poured over the sacrifices, much as was done in Greece.[24] Others have seen in the clause *a fire offering* . . . a general description of the whole procedure rather than a description of the drink offering as such. These scholars usually point to the much later practice of pouring the drink offering at the foot of the altar (Sir. 50:15).[25] The evidence is insufficient to make a decision on this point.

11–12 These verses simply state that the specific amounts for each offering obtain for each animal offered as a sacrifice; i.e., the meal

22. As in the other meal offerings; cf., e.g., Lev. 2:1, 4–5, 7; Num. 6:15; 7:13, 19, 25, 31, 37, 43, 49, 55, 61, 67, 73, 79; 8:8.

23. See the cautious remarks of de Vaux, *Ancient Israel,* I:201–2 (his entire ch. 13 may be consulted with profit). Cf. the equivalents given, e.g., by de Vaulx, p. 181, which are three times greater than those given by Wenham, p. 128.

24. E.g., Binns, p. 101; Noordtzij, p. 135.

25. This is the more common position; cf. Gray, p. 175; Budd, p. 168; Sturdy, p. 109. See Sir. 50:14–15: "Finishing the service at the altars, and arranging the offering to the Most High, the Almighty, he reached out his hand to the cup and poured a libation of the blood of the grape; he poured it out at the foot of the altar, a pleasing odor to the Most High, the King of all." Also, see Josephus, *Ant.* 3.9.4.

and drink offerings were offered for individual animals (*According to the number that you use, kammispār ʾ^{a}šer taʿ^{a}śû)*.

13–16 Both the regulation requiring the offering of the meal and drink offerings (the *law, tôrâ*) and the tariff setting forth specific amounts (the *ordinance, mišpāṭ*) shall be binding for all time (*a perpetual statute, throughout your generations, ḥuqqaṯ ʿôlām l^{e}ḏōrōṯêḵem*) on all native Israelites. The same *law* and *ordinance* are also extended to the *sojourner (haggēr),*[26] as well as to the one who simply dwells with the Israelites without the formal status of *sojourner* (i.e., *one* who *should be in your midst through your generations, ʾ^{a}šer-b^{e}ṯôḵ^{e}ḵem l^{e}ḏōrōṯêḵem*).[27]

2. FIRST OF THE DOUGH (15:17–21)

17 *And Yahweh spoke to Moses, saying:*

18 *"Speak to all the children of Israel and say to them: 'When you come into the land into which I am about to bring you,*[1]

19 *and when you eat the bread of the land, you will set aside a contribution to Yahweh.*

20 *Of the first of your dough you shall set aside a loaf as a contribution; as a contribution of the threshing floor, so shall you set it aside.*

21 *From the first of your dough you will give a contribution to Yahweh throughout your generations."*

The present unit is bound to the previous unit by a similar introduction (vv. 1–2, 17–18, with minor variations), by the phrase *through(out) your generations* (*l^{e}ḏōrōṯêḵem,* vv. 15–16, 21), and by a similar structure, although with enough difference for literary variety (*when . . . [then] you will . . . ,* vv. 3, 8, 19). Vv. 17–31 form one complete unit, as is demonstrated by the single introductory formula ("and Yahweh said to Moses") for this unit (v. 17; cf. vv. 1, 31). As mentioned above, vv. 1–16 respond to the rebellion of chs. 13 and 14 with new divine legislation for

26. This is only one of a whole series of statutes that put the native and the sojourner on a par; cf. Exod. 12:19; Lev. 16:29–31; 17:8, 10–12, 15–16; 18:26; 20:2; 22:18–20; 24:6; Num. 9:14; 15:26, 30; 19:10–12; 35:15. For a definition of the "sojourner," see the commentary above on 9:14.

27. Both NEB and GNB see only one category here, applying both "sojourning" and "being in your midst" to the sojourner; but cf. Gray, p. 176; McNeile, p. 81; Budd, p. 168; etc.

1. The imminent use of the participle, as in 15:2; see Williams, *Syntax,* § 445.

the new land; in the present passage this legislation is taken down to the level of everyday life (i.e., baking bread). Vv. 22–31 give an example of what might happen if one fails to keep God's law. Finally, vv. 32–36 give a specific example of sinning with a high hand (see below). The verses are broken into sections here for convenience.

The regulation about dough, like the previous one, comes into effect only in the new land (v. 18), when the Israelites *eat the bread of the land (ba'ᵃḵālᵉḵem milleḥem hā'āreṣ),* i.e., after they settle into the land and begin to produce crops. When that happens, they are to *set aside* (*hērîm,* vv. 19–20) some of the *first of the dough* (*rē'šîṯ ʿᵃrisōṯêḵem,* v. 20; cf. v. 21) for a *contribution,* or gift *(tᵉrûmâ),* to Yahweh *as a contribution from the threshing floor* (*kiṯrûmaṯ gōren,* v. 20) as a permanent statute (i.e., *thoughout your generations, lᵉḏōrōṯêḵem,* v. 21).

On *tᵉrûmâ* as *contribution* or gift (vv. 19–21) and on *hērîm* as *to set aside a contribution,* see the commentary above on 5:9. The *contribution for Yahweh* really goes to the priest, so that a blessing might come on individual houses (Ezek. 44:30; cf. Neh. 10:38 [Eng. 37]).

Both terms in the phrase *first of your dough* (*rē'šîṯ ʿᵃrisōṯêḵem,* v. 20; cf. v. 21) need clarification. The first term simply identifies something as "first in time or prominence."[2] It is used, most especially, to describe the earliest parts of the crops (Exod. 23:19; 34:26; Lev. 23:10; Deut. 26:2, 10; Ezek. 44:30), of grain (Deut. 18:4; 2 Chr. 31:5), of wool or fleece (Deut. 18:4), and of all the produce (Prov. 3:9). Like the firstborn human male (Exod. 13:12–15; Num. 18:15–16) and the firstborn male animal (Exod. 12:12–13; Lev. 27:26–27; Num. 18:16–18; Deut. 15:19–23) these first crops are dedicated to Yahweh. The current passage, along with Ezek. 44:30 and Neh. 10:38 (Eng. 37), adds another "first" to the lists of dedicated quantities, the first of the *ʿᵃrisōṯ*.

Each year the Israelite was expected to set aside the first portion of the harvest to Yahweh fifty days before the beginning of the Feast of Weeks. This is called the first-fruit offering (Lev. 23:10). During the Feast of Weeks another offering of first fruits is made.[3] The question is whether the "first of the *ʿᵃrisōṯ*" is offered just once per annum, at the time of the first fruits, or whether "first" indicates something more general here. To answer this question, one must define the second term. Some translate it

2. See BDB, p. 912a; it occurs over 50 times in the OT.

3. I.e., at the end of the harvest in addition to at its beginning. Other passages seem to summarize the situation and only mention first fruits in connection with the Feast of Weeks (Exod. 23:16; 34:22; Num. 28:26).

"coarse meal."[4] The translation *dough* is based on a cognate word in the Talmud, which means "kneading trough, the dough of one kneading trough, batch," and LXX *phyrama,* "dough."[5] Here, then, *first of the dough* probably means not that once per annum a first pinch of dough is set aside before any baking is done with a new crop, but that an amount is offered before every new batch of baking as a contribution toward the support of the priest.[6]

In any case, the *ʿarisâ* must be capable of being made into a *loaf (ḥallâ).* The root of the word is *ḥll,* "pierce, perforate,"[7] so that one may think of a perforated wafer. Exod. 29:23 and Lev. 8:26 mention the use of oil,[8] so these perforations may be for the penetration of this substance. The loaf may be either leavened (Lev. 7:13) or unleavened (8:26), and made of "fine flour" (Lev. 24:5) or not (as here). It is also spoken of together with the flat *maṣṣâ* (Lev. 8:26); thus *ḥallâ* probably describes the shape and kind, not the content, of the loaf.[9]

The phrase *gift of the threshing floor (tᵉrûmaṯ gōren)* occurs only here in the Bible. The meaning of *gōren* is simply "the flat place where grain was ground."[10] In Num. 18:27, the Levites' tithe to the priests is reckoned as if it were "the grain of the threshing floor" *(kaddāgān min-haggōren).* Since the priests have no inheritance in the land (18:20), and since the Levites' inheritance is only the tithe (18:21), the Levites have no crops of their own to be offered to Yahweh for support of the priest. Nonetheless, the tithe of the tithe that they contribute to the priests is counted as if it were such an agricultural gift (18:27). The phrase *tᵉrûmaṯ gōren* here probably indicates that this contribution is made from the produce of the threshing floor and counted as such an agricultural gift.

4. RSV; NASB mg.; cf. NIV "ground meal."

5. See Jastrow, *Dictionary,* pp. 1117–18; LSJ, 1962b. See also NEB; cf. NJPS.

6. So Gray, p. 177 (also see his note on pp. 225–29, esp. 227–28), McNeile, p. 81; Sturdy, p. 111; Wenham, p. 129. Note the pl. *(ʿarisōṯ),* which may suggest that this happens more than once. LXX translates *rēʾšîṯ* as *aparchē,* "first fruits."

7. *HALAT,* p. 304.

8. Also in Exod. 29:2; Lev. 2:4; 7:12; Num. 6:15.

9. BDB, p. 319b. A whole tractate in the Mishnah is called *Ḥalla,* based on this word and explicating the so-called dough offering (see esp. 1:1; 2:7; H. Danby, *The Mishnah* [Oxford: Oxford Univ. Press, 1933], pp. 83–88).

10. Cf. BDB, p. 175a.

3. PURIFICATION OFFERING (15:22–31)

22 *"But if you err and do not do all these commandments that Yahweh spoke to Moses,*

23 *all that Yahweh commanded you by Moses from the day that Yahweh commanded and onward throughout your generations,*

24 *then it shall be, if it was done without the knowledge*[1] *of the congregation, that is, inadvertently,*[2] *then all the congregation shall offer one young bull for a whole burnt offering, for a pleasing aroma to Yahweh, and its meal offering and its drink offering, according to the statute, and one male goat as a purification offering.*

25 *And the priest will make atonement for the whole congregation of the children of Israel, and they will be forgiven, for it was an inadvertence and they have brought their offering, a fire offering to Yahweh and a purification offering before Yahweh for their inadvertence.*

26 *And the whole congregation of the children of Israel will be forgiven as well as the sojourner who sojourns in their midst, for the whole people acted inadvertently.*

27 *And if one person should sin inadvertently, that one will offer a female goat one year old for a purification offering.*

28 *And the priest shall make atonement before Yahweh on behalf of the person who was inadvertent, since he sinned by inadvertence, to make atonement for him, that he might be forgiven.*

29 *For the native among the children of Israel and for the sojourner who sojourns in their midst —there will be one law for any of you who acts inadvertently.*

30 *But the person who acts with a high hand, from the native or from the sojourner, reviles Yahweh and that person will be cut off from the midst of his people.*

31 *Because he disdained the word of Yahweh and broke his commandment, that person will be completely cut off, his iniquity is with him.*

Leviticus 4:1–5:13 already has legislation on similar matters. In Lev. 4, four classes of sinners are delineated: the anointed priest (vv. 1–12), the whole community (vv. 13–21), the leader (*nāśî,* vv. 22–26), and the

1. GKC, § 119w, explains *mēʿênê hāʿēḏâ* as expressing separation, "far away from the eyes of the congregation."

2. The term *lišgāgâ* ("with regard to inadvertence") here and the similar term *bišgāgâ* ("in/with inadvertence") in vv. 26–29 should be translated adverbially, "inadvertently."

individual (vv. 27–35). In the present passage these classes are reduced to two more general ones: the community (vv. 22–26) and the individual (vv. 27–29). Lev. 4 requires the following purification offerings *(ḥāṭṭā'ṯ):* for the priest or community, one young bull (vv. 3, 14); for the leader, one male goat (v. 23); and for the individual, one female goat (v. 28).[3] Num. 15 requires a purification offering of one male goat for the community plus a young bull as a whole burnt offering (*'ōlâ,* v. 24); for the individual, the purification offering is one female goat, with no whole burnt offering prescribed (v. 27).

The relationship between the two passages is problematic. It used to be common to hold that Lev. 4–5 deal with sins of commission while Num. 15 deals with sins of omission.[4] It is easy to see why such could be held in the light of passages like Lev. 4:2, 13, 22, 27; 5:17; Num. 15:22. Lev. 5:2 speaks of a sin of omission, however, and Num. 15:24, 29–30 clearly imply that something is done against Yahwheh and not simply that something is left undone. Thus modern scholars are virtually unanimous that the passages are not related along these lines.[5] Since Num. 15 appears to be simpler in some ways than Lev. 4, many scholars assumed that the former was earlier than the latter.[6] It makes at least as much sense, however, to see in Num. 15 a later modification of and addition to the laws of Lev. 4–5.[7] Both the overall aim and therefore the details of the two passages differ. In general, Lev. 4 details the purification offering, while Num. 15 assumes that offering and gives special cases of it.[8] The main purposes of Num. 15 are the addition of the whole burnt offering in the case of the individual (v. 24), the application of the law to the sojourner (vv. 26, 29), and, most importantly, the explicit statement that *sins with a high hand,* i.e., sins of open rebellion (such as those of ch. 14), are not sacrificially expiable (vv.

3. According to Lev. 5:7–13, a poor person may substitute a cheaper offering for the female goat.

4. Cf., e.g., Keil, p. 101; F. C. Cook, ed., *The Holy Bible with Commentary,* I/2 (London: J. Murray, 1871), p. 706. An ancient tradition of the rabbis also held to this view; see J. Greenstone, *The Holy Scriptures: Numbers with Commentary* (Philadelphia: Jewish Publication Society of America, 1939), p. 158; Milgrom, *JPST,* pp. 402–5.

5. E.g., Dillmann, p. 84; Holzinger, p. 64; Gray, p. 178; Budd, p. 173.

6. E.g., Dillmann, p. 84; Gray, pp. 178–80; Binns, p. 103.

7. E.g., Holzinger, p. 61; Noth, p. 116; Sturdy, p. 112; de Vaulx, p. 185; Wenham, p. 130; Budd, pp. 172–73.

8. The two categories of Numbers are as comprehensive as the four of Leviticus. The different purposes of the two passages account for this variance.

30–31).[9] That such laws might be modified and supplemented over time is seen elsewhere in the biblical text.[10]

22–23 This section forms the introduction to the whole unit and sets forth the basic condition of which the cases of the community (vv. 24–26) and the individual (vv. 27–29) are examples. *But if you err (wᵉḵî ṯišgû).* This verb and the word *šᵉgāḡâ,* drawn from the related root *šgg,* are the most common words in the central part of the passage.[11] Both roots carry the meaning of "inadvertence," i.e., the act was intentional, but not known to be sinful.[12]

all these commandments ('ēṯ kol-hammiṣwōṯ). In the present context this phrase might be taken to indicate only the ordinance on the dough offering, which immediately precedes, or perhaps the whole of vv. 1–21.[13] V. 23, which explains this phrase, indicates that it means far more than this, however. In fact, it includes *all that Yahweh commanded you by Moses from the day that Yahweh commanded ('ēṯ kol-'ᵃšer ṣiwwâ YHWH 'ᵃlêḵem bᵉyaḏ-mōšeh min-hayyôm 'ᵃšer ṣiwwâ YHWH)* —i.e., from the first legislation at Mt. Sinai — *and onward throughout your generations (wāhālᵉ'â lᵉḏōrōṯêḵem),*[14] i.e., not only for the present, but into the future.

24–26 This section deals with the inadvertent sin of the community. It is not known just how the whole community could sin and at the same time be *without the knowledge of the congregation* (*mē'ênê hā'ēḏâ,* lit., "away from the eyes of the congregation"); the text explains this

9. That "inadvertence" *(šᵉgāgâ)* is the presupposition of Lev. 4 is clear from vv. 2, 13, 22, 27. Num. 15 makes this presupposition explicit and sets forth a penalty for sins with a high hand. For the meaning of *šᵉgāgâ,* see below.

10. Cf., e.g., Exod. 13:2 with Num. 3:12–13; Num. 2:17 with 10:17; Lev. 27:30–33; Num. 18:21–32 with Deut. 14:22–29.

11. In the present passage, the verb *šāgâ* occurs only at this verse, while the noun *šᵉgāgâ* occurs in vv. 24, 25 (twice), 26–27, 28 (twice), 29. Gray (p. 181) suggests that one should read *tāšōgû* (from *šgg*), instead of MT *ṯišgû* (from *šgh*), for consistency. But this change is unnecessary. It is often the case that biconsonantal Hebrew roots expand in a number of directions with basically the same meaning. So the roots *šgh, šgg,* and *šwg* all carry the meaning "inadvertent sin"; cf. BDB, pp. 992b–93a, 1000b; GKC, § 77.

12. See esp. V. Hamilton, *TWOT,* II:903–5; J. Milgrom, "The Cultic *Šᵉgāgāh* and Its Influence in Psalms and Job," *JQR* 58 (1967) 115–25, esp. 118; repr. in *Studies in Cultic Theology,* pp. 122–32, esp. 125.

13. As, e.g., Snaith (p. 155) suggests.

14. The phrase "throughout your generations" *(lᵉḏōrōṯêḵem)* is also found in 15:14–15, 21, and is one of the linking phrases of the whole chapter.

obscure reference by the term *lišgāḡâ, inadvertently* (see above on vv. 22–23 for this term).

The normal order for the offerings is the purification offering first (e.g., Lev. 5:7–10; 15:15–30; Num. 6:11, 16), although the present order is not unknown (Lev. 12:8). It may be that the whole burnt offering is listed first here simply because it is an additional offering to the rule of Lev. 4. It is impossible to say whether the male goat of the purification offering prescribed here is to substitute for the young bull prescribed in Lev. 4:14 or to be added to it, the latter not being improbable.[15]

according to the statute (kammišpāṭ). Of course, in order to follow the statute given in 15:8–9, both meal and drink offerings must accompany the whole burnt offering. This phrase shows that v. 24 assumes the legislation of vv. 1–16.

25 *And the priest will make atonement for the whole congregation (wᵉḵipper hakkōhēn ʿal-kol-ʿᵃḏaṯ bᵉnê yiśrāʾēl).* The verb *kāp̄ar* (usually Piel, as here) has been variously derived. The most likely derivations are from a word similar to Akk. *kuppuru,* "to wipe off," or from the noun *kōp̄er,* "ransom price."[16] In the latter case, "to make atonement" on behalf of *(ʿal)* someone would mean "to pay a ransom" or "to substitute" something (viz., a sacrifice) for them. Here *kipper* is a summary term for priestly sacrificial manipulation to secure forgiveness *for the whole congregation.*

26 This procedure extends beyond the native Israelite to the *sojourner (gēr).*[17] Both together go into making *the whole congregation* that finds forgiveness by the grace of God through the sacrificial offerings.

27–29 This passage concerns the inadvertent sin of one individual. Most of the key terms are the same as in the previous section. Note that the purification offering here is the same as in Lev. 4:28, a *female goat (ʿēz),* although the terminology differs slightly.[18] No whole burnt offering accompanies the purification offering here as was the case for the community. One reason for this difference may well be that it is a very

15. De Vaulx, p. 185; Dillmann, p. 85.

16. See R. Harris, *TWOT,* I:452–53; Milgrom, *Studies in Levitical Terminology,* I:28–33; but cf. J. Herrmann, F. Büchsel, *TDNT,* III:302–10, 312–15.

17. On *gēr,* see the commentary above on 15:15–16.

18. The differences are: in Leviticus the animal is *śᵉʿîraṯ ʿizzîm,* lit. "a female goat of goats," while here in Numbers the female gender is indicated by the qualifying phrase *baṯ-šᵉnāṯāh,* lit., "a daughter of her (first) year." No age for the animal is mentioned in Leviticus, but it is to be a "perfect" *(tᵉmîmâ)* animal.

serious sin of the community (Num. 13–14) that gave rise to the current modification in the law, so that the regulation for the individual was left pretty much alone. Again, after the appropriate offering has been brought, the priest uses it *to make atonement* for the individual, so that this individual *might be forgiven (w^e nislaḥ lô).*[19]

30–31 These brief verses form the climax of the passage and, indeed, point back to the sin of the community in chs. 13–14. The sins hitherto discussed have all been inadvertent and are expiable by the appropriate sacrifice. All this is in sharp contrast to the sins that are said to be *with a high hand (b^e yaḏ rāmâ).* The same phrase describes the attitude of the Israelites to Pharaoh and the Egyptians at the time of the Exodus (e.g., Exod. 14:8; Num. 33:3, usually translated as "boldly," or even "defiantly").[20] The Israelites thought themselves quite beyond the sphere of interference by Pharaoh, and they were confident that he was irrelevant for their future.[21] While the passages in Exod. 14 and Num. 33 provide a positive evaluation of such an attitude, and the context here clearly calls for a negative evaluation, there are parallels in the attitude: the sinner *with a high hand* considers Yahweh irrelevant for the future; this one sins in an open-eyed and rebellious way, knowing full well what he or she is doing. This kind of rebellion therefore differs from the intentional sin described in Lev. 5:20–26 (Eng. 6:1–7) for which a reparation offering may be made, "when the offender feels guilty" (5:23, 26).[22] The sinner with a high hand feels no guilt; therefore the offense is not sacrificially expiable.

When such an individual (for it seems that it is only an individual rather than a whole community in mind here), whether native or sojourner, sins with such an attitude, only one outcome is possible: *that person will be cut off from the midst of his people (w^e nikr^e tâ hannep̄eš hahî' miqqereḇ 'ammāh).*[23] Although the verb *be cut off* is vague, if one considers vv.

19. See above on vv. 24–26.

20. For the former see NIV, NASB, NJPS; cf. NJKV "with boldness." For the latter see NEB and RSV at Exod. 14:8.

21. Cf. J. Durham's translation of Exod. 14:8: "but the sons of Israel went out disregarding Pharaoh's attitude"; Durham comments, "as vv 10–12 show, the Israelites thought themselves beyond Pharaoh's interest and reach" (*Exodus,* WBC [Waco: Word, 1987], pp. 188, 191). Cf. U. Cassuto, *A Commentary on the Book of Exodus,* tr. I. Abrahams (Jerusalem: Magnes, 1967), p. 164.

22. On the translation of the verb *'āšam* by "to feel guilty," and on the reparation offering (the *'āšām*), see the commentary above on 5:5–10.

23. On this term, see the commentary above on 9:13.

32–36 as an example of a sin with a high hand, then one may say that death at the hands of the congregation is included as a possible meaning of the term. A further statement in v. 31 enlarges the concept of being cut off: *his iniquity is with him (ʿᵃwōnâ ḇāh),* which, most simply put, means that such a person's sin is not carried away by sacrifice, but remains clinging to the sinner and causing uncleanness to persist, which, according to 5:1, cannot be permitted in Yahweh's camp.[24]

Three further clauses specify this type of sin. First, such a one *reviles Yahweh* (*'eṯ YHWH hû' mᵉgaddēp̱,* v. 30). The position of the name *Yahweh* shows that the emphasis is not only on the abuse, but also on the identity of the one abused, the Almighty God. The verb *gāḏap̱* occurs only here in the Pentateuch, and means "revile," "abuse."[25]

Second, the sinner with a high hand *disdained the word of Yahweh* (*dᵉḇar-YHWH bāzâ,* v. 31). Although the verb "to disdain, despise" is fairly common in the OT, it is rare in the Pentateuch (only here and 25:34). It means "to regard with contempt."[26] The *word of Yahweh* includes the legislation that Yahweh has given, but this legislation is the communication of God, designed to bring humans into a relationship with him. Treating that personal communication with contempt means rejecting the relationship with God as well.

Third, such a sinner *broke his* [i.e., Yahweh's] *commandment* (*wᵉ'eṯ-miṣwāṯô hēp̱ar,* v. 31), which means that he or she had not done those things that Yahweh had directed.[27] It is not surprising, therefore that *that person will be completely cut off* (*hikkārēṯ tikkārēṯ hannep̱eš hahî',* v. 31), he or she will be punished by God.[28]

24. Cf. the similar term *niśśā' ʿāwōn* in 9:13 above.

25. The word is related to a cognate Arabic one meaning "be ungrateful." It occurs 6 times in the OT. A related noun *gᵉḏûp̱â* means "a taunt" in Ezek. 5:15, and a pl. noun built on the Piel stem, *giddûp̱îm,* means human "revilings" in Isa. 43:28; 51:7; and Zeph. 2:8. See BDB, p. 154b; G. Wallis, *TDOT,* II:416–18.

26. The term occurs 43 times in the OT. Only here is the word of Yahweh said to be despised. See BDB, p. 102; M. Görg, *TDOT,* II:60–65. On the word of Yahweh, cf. G. Mayer, *TDOT,* III:111–27.

27. The verb occurs some 50 times in the OT, only in the Hiphil. It is used of breaking or frustrating Yahweh's commandment only here and in Ezra 9:14, although Ps. 119:126 speaks of despising Yahweh's *tôrâ.* It means "reneging on revealed truth." See V. Hamilton, *TWOT,* II:738b; cf. BDB, p. 830.

28. On the term "to be cut off," see the commentary on 9:13 above and Milgrom, *JPST,* pp. 405–8. The infinitive absolute preceding the cognate finite verb *(hikkārēṯ tikkārēṯ)* adds emphasis; Williams, *Syntax,* §205.

4. CASE LAW ON CAPITAL PUNISHMENT FOR SABBATH VIOLATION (15:32–36)

32 *While the children of Israel were in the wilderness, they found*[1] *a man gathering sticks*[2] *on the Sabbath day.*
33 *And those who found the one gathering sticks brought him to Moses, Aaron, and the whole congregation.*
34 *And they placed him in custody, for it had not been made clear what should be done to him.*
35 *And Yahweh said to Moses, "That man must surely be put to death; all the congregation will kill him with stones*[3] *outside the camp."*
36 *And the whole congregation brought him outside the camp and they stoned him with stones, and he died, just as Yahweh had commanded them.*

32–33 The third subsection of this central portion of the chapter (vv. 17–36) consists of a law based on an incident that happened *While the children of Israel were in the wilderness (wayyihyû b̲ᵉnê yiśrā'ēl bammid̲bār).* This note indicates that the passage looks back to that time as past.[4] More importantly for what follows, this setting shows that, unlike the laws of vv. 1–21, the basic commandment of Sabbath keeping is not reserved for the new land, but is in force at all times.[5] This story is similar in both language and content to the story of the blasphemer in Lev. 24:10–14, 23, and, in a less exact sense, to other stories in Numbers.[6]

1. The verb *wᵉyimṣᵉ'û (they found)* may be taken as an impersonal circumlocution for the passive voice, hence "they found a man" can mean "a man was found"; see Williams, *Syntax,* § 160.

2. The verb *qōšēš* (only Poel) occurs six times in the OT. It is a denominative verb coming from a root that probably means "chaff," hence "to gather chaff"; see BDB, p. 905b. The verb is used with the pl. of "wood" *(ʿeṣîm)* as an object again in the story of Elijah and the widow of Zarephath (1 K. 17:10, 12). The word *ʿēṣîm* is the pl. of the common word for "wood" (over 300 times in the OT). This pl. shows that this natural product is in an artificial state according to GKC, § 124m; cf. Williams, *Syntax,* § 2; Davidson, *Syntax,* § 17 Rem. 1.

3. The infinitive absolute may substitute here for the imperfect (i.e., potential) tense of the verb (see Williams, *Syntax,* § 209), but it is as likely that it is a defective construction that stands for the infinitive absolute plus the finite verb as a substitute for the emphatic imperative; see GKC, § 113bb; cf. Davidson, *Syntax,* § 88 Rem. 5.

4. Cf., e.g., Binns, p. 105; Gray, p. 182; Heinisch, p. 64; Noordtzij, p. 139.

5. See Cook, *Holy Bible,* p. 707.

6. For a comparison and contrast of Num. 15 and Lev. 24, see Gray, p. 182. See also Num. 9:6–13; 27:1–11; 36:1–12.

This passage assumes the laws on Sabbath keeping found in Exod. 20:10–11, and especially 31:12–17 and 35:2–3. The first passage is the part of the Decalogue that commands observance of the Sabbath; the second and third passages spell out this command more generally by prescribing death for a profanation of the Sabbath by work (31:14–15), including even the kindling of domestic fires (35:3). The placement of the current verses after Num. 15:30–31, which deal with the "sins with a high hand," shows that vv. 32–36 are probably meant to serve as an example of such sin.

34 *And they placed him in custody, for it had not been made clear what should be done to him (wayyannîḥû 'ōṯô bammišmār kî lō' pōraš mah-yēʿāśeh lô).* It is common to assert that the punishment for the Sabbath breaker was well known, and that it was only uncertainty about the mode of execution that caused the people to keep the wood-gatherer in custody until further instructions could be received on the matter. While this assertion is plausible, J. Weingreen's comment that, if this had been the case, one would have to conclude that this was the first occasion of a public profanation of the Sabbath, is apposite.[7] The text has no trace of this kind of information. It seems more likely that a deeper question was at issue: whether a man who was *gathering sticks* (*meqōšēš ʿēṣîm,* v. 32) on the Sabbath, presumably to make a fire in contravention of the law, was as guilty as if he had actually built the fire.

The verb *pōraš* ("to make clear") is more common in extrabiblical Aramaic than in Biblical Hebrew.[8] The passive voice (*pōraš* is a Pual perfect) indicates that the people were awaiting clarity from some outside source. As it happens, that outside source was Yahweh himself (v. 35).[9]

35 Yahweh's response is that the wood-gatherer is, indeed, worthy of death. The penalty prescribed is stoning at the hands of the whole congregation. In the OT stoning is prescribed as the penalty for the ox who kills a person (Exod. 21:28–32), child sacrifice (Lev. 20:2–5), spirit

7. J. Weingreen, "The Case of the Woodgatherer (Numbers XV 32–36)," *VT* 16 (1966) 362; cf. the reply by A. Phillips, "The Case of the Woodgatherer Reconsidered," *VT* (1969) 125–28.

8. Found once in the Qal (the parallel passage in Lev. 24:12), once in the Niphal (Ezek. 34:12), and twice in the Pual (Num. 15:34; Neh. 8:8). Biblical Aramaic has the cognate verb (Pael passive ptcp.) in Ezra 4:18. For the extra biblical evidence see Jastrow, *Dictionary,* pp. 1242–43.

9. According to Paterson, p. 51, the Hebrew root *prš* may be related to Akk. *pirištu,* "oracular decision," so that some contact between Moses and Yahweh may be insinuated in the vocabulary as well as the plot itself.

divination (20:27), blasphemy (24:15–16), Sabbath breaking (Num. 15:32–36), inducement to worship other gods (13:7–11 [Eng. 6–10]), insubordination by a son (21:18–21), adultery (22:23–24), and violation of the sacred ban (*ḥērem,* Josh. 7:25). It is the most commonly prescribed Israelite capital punishment because it supposedly does not shed blood, and thus does not bring blood-guilt on the community.[10]

36 Stoning is conducted *outside the camp (miḥûṣ lammaḥ^{a}neh)* to avoid the uncleanness of a corpse in Yahweh's camp (cf. Num. 5:2).[11] Stoning is carried out by *the whole congregation* (*kol-hā'ēḏâ,* vv. 35–36), to show community solidarity in rejecting the sin in its midst.[12]

just as Yahweh had commanded them. It is emphasized here, as it has not been since the end of ch. 9, that the people obeyed Yahweh exactly.[13]

5. TASSELS ON GARMENTS FOR REMEMBRANCE (15:37–41)

37 *And Yahweh said*[1] *to Moses, saying:*

38 *"Speak to the children of Israel and say to them that they are to make for themselves tassels for the corners of their garments throughout their generations, and they are to put on the tassel of the corner a cord of blue.*[2]

39 *And it shall be for you a tassel that you will look on and remember all the commandments of Yahweh and do them and not go after your own heart and after your own eyes, after which you are prostituting yourselves,*

40 *so that you will remember and do all my commandments and may be holy to your God.*

10. Snaith, p. 156; the procedure for stoning is set forth in Mish. *Sanhedrin* 6:1–4. How far this tractate reflects the OT practice is uncertain.

11. See Lev. 24:14, 23 for the identical phrase; cf. "outside the city" in Deut. 21:19; 22:24.

12. See Lev. 24:16 for the same words (cf. vv. 14, 23). See the same idea in Lev. 20:2, 4 ("the people of the land"); Deut. 13:10 (Eng. 9; "the hand of all the people"); 21:21 ("all the men of the city").

13. The clause "just as Yahweh had commanded them" is last found at 8:22, although ch. 9 indicates that the people followed Yahweh's directives.

1. Here the word is *wayyō'mer,* rather than the more common *way^{e}dibbēr* ("spoke"), as in vv. 2, 17, and very often in Numbers.

2. The word is related to the rare verb *pāṯal* (Niphal and Hithpael), which means "to twist." The breastpiece was bound to the ephod and the golden signet on the high priest's turban by a "cord of blue" (Exod. 28:28, 37; 39:21, 31). See BDB, p. 836b.

41 *I am Yahweh your God who brought you out of the land of Egypt
to be your God; I am Yahweh your God."*

It is better to remember Yahweh's commandments than to violate them and be found guilty thereby. But how may that be done? The current passage gives one method of remembering the divine Torah, and should be seen together with passages such as Deut. 6:6–9 as commandments to prevent sins of inadvertence before they begin.

37 The opening formula *And Yahweh said to Moses, saying (wayyōʾmer YHWH ʾel-mōšeh lēʾmōr)* is similar to that in vv. 1, 17 and marks the beginning of a new section. The change of person between v. 38 and vv. 39–41 is comparable to that in vv. 1–16 above.

38 *they are to make tassels for themselves for the corners of their garments (w^{e}ʿāśû lāhem ṣîṣiṯ ʿal-kan^{e}p̱ê ḇig^{e}ḏêhem).* This passage is parallel to Deut. 22:12: "You shall make yourself tassels for yourselves for the four corners of your garment with which you cover yourself" *(g^{e}ḏilîm taʿ^{a}śeh-lāḵ ʿal-ʾarbaʿ kan^{e}p̱ôṯ k^{e}sûṯ^{e}ḵā ʾ^{a}šer t^{e}ḵasseh-bāh).* The Deuteronomy passage uses different words for "tassels" *(g^{e}ḏilîm)* and "garment" *(k^{e}sûṯ),*[3] specifies four corners of the garment, and gives no motive for the regulation.[4]

Several terms call for clarification. First, the term *tassels (ṣîṣiṯ)* occurs elsewhere only at Ezek. 8:3, where it means a "lock of hair." The basic meaning may be simply "a projection, protuberance."[5] On the basis of ancient pictorial evidence showing tassels on garments in the 2nd and 1st millennia in the Near East,[6] the parallel word used in Deut. 22:12, and

3. The root meaning of *g^{e}ḏilîm* is "twist together," hence a twisted or knotted cord; see BDB, p. 152a. Heb. *k^{e}sûṯ* occurs only eight times in the OT, and comes from a root that means "cover, hide," hence a covering; see BDB, pp. 491a–92a.

4. Scholars who explain the Pentateuch by means of some form of the documentary hypothesis usually see the Numbers passage as P and therefore later than the passage in Deuteronomy, and find the lack of a motive in the latter somewhat of a puzzle. If the Numbers passage is earlier, however, then the Deuteronomy passage did not give a motive for the regulation because it assumed that of the earlier passage. Cf. A. D. H. Mayes, *Deuteronomy,* NCBC (Grand Rapids: Eerdmans, 1981), pp. 308–9.

5. See F. Stephens, "The Ancient Significance of *Ṣîṣîth,*" *JBL* 50 (1931) 67. This word may be related to the word *ṣîṣ,* "flower, blossom" (e.g., of Aaron's rod in Num. 17:23 [Eng. 8]; also, e.g., of all flesh in Isa. 40:7–8), and the mysterious homonym *ṣîṣ,* usually translated "wing," in Jer. 48:9 (so AV, RV, RSV, NIV mg., NASB; but cf. NEB, NIV).

6. See S. Bertman, "Tassled Garments in the Ancient East Mediterranean," *BA* 24/2 (1961) 119–28.

the later Jewish practice of twisting tassels on the bottom of garments, the term should probably be translated as *tassels* rather than (a continuous) "fringe."[7] The *corner* (*kānāp̱,* lit., "wing") is anything that forms a winglike appendage.[8] The *garment (beged̠)* is probably the outer garment, worn as a cloak.[9]

This regulation, like others in this chapter, is to be observed *throughout their generations* (*l^e^d̠ōrōṯām;* cf. vv. 14–15, 21, 23), i.e., forever.

The Israelites were then to place a *cord of blue (p^e^ṯîl t^e^ḵēleṯ)* in or on the tassel. Presumably the color of this cord contrasted to the tassel itself. It is doubtful that the language of v. 38b *(and they are to put on the tassel of the corner . . .)* is sufficient to indicate that this cord was used to fasten the tassel onto the corner;[10] rather, it probably indicates that this blue cord was somehow attached or woven into the tassel.

The significance of the color of this cord is hard to determine. *blue (t^e^ḵēleṯ)* is one of the three special colors used in various parts and accessories of the tabernacle as described in Exodus ("blue and purple and scarlet [material]").[11] The curtains of the tabernacle have blue loops (Exod. 26:4; 36:11); a blue cord binds the high priest's breastplate to the ephod and the golden signet to his headdress (28:28; 39:21; 28:37; 39:31); the high priest's robe is also blue (28:31; 29:22). In none of these passages is the significance of the color made clear, perhaps because it was common knowledge. In the Prophets and Writings the color blue seems to indicate power, riches, and royalty, but how far back this symbolization can be read is unknown.[12] In Numbers itself blue material is used to cover the sancta from the most holy place (i.e., the ark and the veil of the screen) as well as table of bread, lampstand, golden altar of incense, and the various vessels from the holy place.[13] The very least that one can argue from all this is that the color blue marked something as important. It is likely that

7. For "tassels" see RSV, NIV, NASB, GNB, NEB; Gray, p. 185. For "fringe" see AV, RV, NJPS.

8. See BDB, p. 489.

9. This is the most common OT term for garment, occurring over 200 times; *HALAT,* p. 104.

10. Cf., e.g., Dillmann, p. 86.

11. The ten curtains (Exod. 26:1; 36:8), the veil (26:31; 36:35; cf. 2 Chr. 3:14), the door screen (Exod. 26:36; 36:37), the gate screen (27:16; 38:18), the high priest's ephod (also uses gold, 28:15; 39:8), the band on the ephod (gold, 28:8; 39:5), the breastplate of judgment (gold, 28:15; 39:8), and the high priest's skirts (gold, 28:33; 39:24).

12. Cf. Ezek. 23:6; 27:7, 24; Esth. 1:6; 8:15.

13. See Num. 4:6–7, 9, 11–12.

it was the mark of royalty. The king of Israel was Yahweh. The color blue therefore marked that which belonged especially to him. One showed divine ownership by fulfilling the role of "a kingdom of priests and a holy nation" (Exod. 19:6). Holiness of life was the hallmark of Yahweh's person ("be holy as I am holy," Lev. 11:44, etc.).

39–41 Whether the function of tassels on garments in the ancient Near East generally was purely decorative or religious,[14] in Israel their use is defined in vv. 39–41. They will be a visual reminder, in order that *you will look on [them] and remember all the commandments of Yahweh and do them (ûzᵉḵartem 'eṯ-kol-miṣwōṯ YHWH wa'ᵃśîṯem).* To *remember (zāḵar)* does not mean simply bringing something to mind, but using whatever means necessary to make real in the present what was real in the past: the power and love of Yahweh shown in statutes and ordinances for the guidance of his people (cf. Deut. 6:24; 10:13). Remembering in this sense includes doing. On the one hand, it is contrasted with going after one's own heart and eyes (v. 39).[15] The word *go after* is *tûr,* which was translated as "to spy out" in chs. 13–14.[16] Here the verb means "to explore" what the senses dictate rather than following what God has revealed; this word therefore includes doing the opposite of what God wants. On the other hand, remembering and doing Yahweh's commandments is compared with being holy, i.e., set apart for God's use.

The passage ends with a reminder to the people that Yahweh is their God, and that he has brought them out of bondage in Egypt to freedom. Therefore he has the right to command their obedience as his people (cf. Exod. 20:2).

C. LEGITIMATION OF AARON'S PRIESTHOOD (16:1–17:28 [Eng. 13])

In 16:1–17:28 (Eng. 13), three stories illustrate the need for and legitimacy of the Aaronic priesthood. As there had been challenges to Moses' leadership in chs. 11–14, so here there are challenges to Aaron's. The central point around which these chapters turn is the relationship of the Aaronic priesthood to the rest of the Levites. That is the problem broached

14. See Bertman, "Tasseled Garments," pp. 119–28, esp. 128; Stephens, "Ancient Significance," pp. 59–70, esp. 61–65.

15. On the term *zāḵar,* see B. Childs, *Memory and Tradition in Israel,* SBT 37 (London: SCM, 1962); H. Eising, *TDOT,* IV: 64–82.

16. See 13:2, 16–17, 21, 25, 32; 14:7, 34, 36, 38.

by Korah's rebellion in ch. 16. That there is a separation between priest and Levite is clear from chs. 16–17. The function of the Levite in Israelite society is clarified, or redefined, in ch. 18. These stories assume such previous pentateuchal materials as set forth the divine choice of Aaron and his family for the priesthood (e.g., Exod. 28–29; Lev. 8–10), and the difference between the priests and the other Levites (e.g., Num. 3:5–10; 8:13, 19). This position was not attained without struggle.

The first of the three stories is the complex narrative about the rebellions of the Kohathite Levite Korah and of the Reubenites Dathan, Abiram, and On. The stories are developed separately, by scenes, which necessitates some repetition, until the outcome in which both groups are put together. Korah's complaint (16:3–11) is that a priesthood restricted to Aaron's family is too limited in a people where the whole congregation is holy, every one of them! (16:3). This complaint shows a clear tie to the previous passage in which Israel was to use tassels on their garments as a reminder to do Yahweh's will and to be holy (15:40). It is unlikely that Korah wished to abolish the priesthood or even to open it to anyone. More probably he only wanted the privilege for all the Levites, or perhaps really only for himself.

Moses responds, first, by proposing a test. If one is a chosen priest, one ought to, at least, be able to offer incense to Yahweh. This was a priestly function, the incorrect observance of which had cost Aaron two of his own sons (Lev. 10). The next day, Korah and his company are to offer incense before Yahweh along with Aaron. Yahweh would decide who was the legitimate priest (16:5–7). Second, Moses told Korah that he was privileged to be a Levite, the implication being that it was only greed and ambition that would lead one so privileged to seek the priesthood as well (16:8–10).

The complaint of the Reubenites is really a reminder of the complaints against Moses in chs. 11–14. It is interesting that they call Egypt "the land of milk and honey," which is usually the expression for the land of Canaan. Moses has taken Israel out of the security of Egypt and has not been able, thus far, to lead them into the new land. He will lead them into death in the wilderness (cf. 14:2–3). Furthermore, they object to Moses' continuing to exercise leadership over them ("will you keep playing the prince over us," 16:13).

It is unclear just how much common ground there was between Korah and these Reubenites, except that both were unhappy with the leadership. Nonetheless, in 16:14, Dathan and Abiram seem to stand together with Korah in spite of this seeming lack of agreement.

In any case, God has a single reaction against both groups: to slay the whole congregation in an instant. This reaction leads Moses and Aaron to intercede on behalf of the people, and God limits his judgment (16:20–27). Both groups suffer a common fate, presumably at the time of the offering of the incense on the next day. God opens the ground, it swallows them up, and the people end up crying out to God in their distress (16:28–35).

The second story (17:1–15 [Eng. 16:36–50]) is related to the first and grows out of it. It tells what happened to the censers of incense from the test in the first story. Because these had been offered to God, they had become holy and had to be disposed of by a legitimate priest. Aaron's son Eliezar is told to gather these censers and to make a brass cover for the altar as a reminder that only an authorized priest was permitted by God to offer incense (17:1–5 [Eng. 16:36–40]). This visible sign does not, however, remind the people of the importance of the Aaronic (i.e., authorized) priesthood, but rather that Moses and Aaron "have killed Yahweh's people" (i.e., Korah and his followers, 17:6 [Eng. 16:41]). This response again causes God to decide to destroy the whole people, which he sets about doing, and it is only the second intercession of Moses and Aaron, particularly the latter, that stops the plague that Yahweh has sent (17:7–13 [Eng. 16:42–48]). Before Aaron's intercession stops the plague a great number of Israelites have already been slain (17:14–15 [Eng. 16:49–50]). Thus, again, Aaron's priestly work is effective with Yahweh.

The third story (17:16–28 [Eng. 1–12]) concerns a test that Yahweh proposes to the people in order to show that the Aaronic priesthood is the only legitimate one. Rods or staffs *(maṭṭeh)* are collected from each tribe and from Aaron and are left in the tabernacle overnight (vv. 16–19 [Eng. 1–4]). The rod that Yahweh chooses will bloom (v. 20 [Eng. 5]). The next day only Aaron's rod had put forth growth; it "had, indeed, sprouted, put forth growth, grown blossoms, and borne ripened almonds" (v. 23 [Eng. 8]). This sign to the people brings great fear and an outcry that no one at all could expect to approach the tabernacle, and thus the God of the tabernacle (vv. 27–28 [Eng. 12–13]).

Thus, all three of these scenes or stories end with the statement — implicit or explicit — that there was a need for intercession between the people and Yahweh that only the Aaronic priesthood could provide.

1. REBELLIONS OF KORAH, DATHAN, AND ABIRAM (16:1–35)

1 *Now Korah the son of Izhar, the son of Kohath, the son of Levi, and Dathan and Abiram the sons of Eliab, and On the son of Peleth,*[1] *the sons of Reuben, became arrogant*[2]

2 *and rose before Moses along with two hundred fifty of the children of Israel, leaders of the congregation chosen from the assembly, important men,*

3 *and they gathered themselves together against Moses and against Aaron, and they said to them: "You have gone too far! The whole congregation is holy, every one of them!*[3] *And Yahweh is in their midst! Now why do you exalt yourselves over the assembly of Israel?"*

4 *When Moses heard this he fell on his face.*[4]

5 *And he spoke to Korah and to his whole congregation, saying: "In the morning*[5] *Yahweh will make known who is his and who is holy and he will bring that one near to himself, that is, he will choose him whom he will bring near to himself.*

6 *Do this. Take for yourselves censers, Korah and all his congregation,*

1. Since On the son of Peleth is not mentioned elsewhere in this story or in texts which refer to this story, some scholars have posited that the name On (*'ôn)* should be eliminated as a corruption of the last letters of the preceding name Eliab (*'yb)*. The name Peleth should be read as Pallu (*pallû'*; so LXX here) in line with the census of 26:5. The text would then read: "Dathan and Abiram the sons of Eliab, the sons of Pallu, the sons of Reuben" (*dāṯān wa'ᵃḇîrām bᵉnê 'ĕlî'āḇ bᵉnê pallû' bᵉnê lēwî)*. See Gray, pp. 194–95 (also p. 190); Budd, p. 180. These suggestions make sense

2. MT is difficult here. The transitive verb *wayyiqqaḥ* must have an object, so, e.g., RSV supplies "men" and Binns (p. 109) suggested "offerings." The various readings of the versions, ranging from "and he said" (LXX) to "and he separated himself" (Pesh. and Targ.), witness to the difficulty of MT. Several scholars have proposed *wayyāqom,* "and he arose," as in v. 2, etc. (e.g., Dillmann, pp. 89–90; McNeile, p. 86). A more fruitful solution may be suggested by Origen's translation *hyperēphaneuthē,* "he became haughty (or arrogant)," which Snaith, among others, takes as presupposing *wayyēqaḥ,* from *y(w)qḥ,* "be bold, insolent," as in Arab. *waqaḥa.* This root also occurs, most likely, at Job 15:12. See Snaith, pp. 157–58; Budd, p. 180; Noth, p. 123; de Vaulx, p. 188; etc.

3. For the structure of this translation of *ḵol-hā'ēḏâ kullām qᵉḏōšîm,* see Driver, *Tenses,* § 199.

4. *BHS* proposes to read *wayyippᵉlû pānāyw,* "his face (countenance) fell," for MT *wayyippōl 'al-pānāyw,* but there is no textual evidence for it (as Budd, p. 181, acknowledges, though he accepts the emendation).

5. On *bōqer* meaning "in the morning," cf. Davidson, *Syntax,* § 57 Rem.

7 *and put fire in them and place incense on them before Yahweh tomorrow. And it will be that the man Yahweh will choose, he will be the holy one. It is you who have gone too far, O sons of Levi!"*

8 *And Moses said to Korah, "Hear now, O sons of Levi,*

9 *Is it too small a thing for you that the God of Israel has distinguished you from the congregation of Israel to allow you near to himself that you might do the work of the tabernacle of Yahweh and that you might stand in the presence of the congregation to minister to them?*

10 *Or that he has brought you and all your brothers, the sons of Levi, near with you? And do you now also seek*[6] *the priesthood?*

11 *Therefore you and all your congregation are the ones who are gathering*[7] *against Yahweh; and, as for Aaron, what is he that you should murmur against him?"*[8]

12 *And Moses sent to call Dathan and Abiram, the sons of Eliab, and they said, "We will not come up.*

13 *Is it too small a thing that you have brought us up out of a land flowing with milk and honey to kill us in this wilderness, that you will also keep playing the prince*[9] *over us?*

14 *You have not even brought us to a land flowing with milk and honey or given*[10] *us an inheritance of field and vineyard. Will you put out the eyes of these men? We will not come up!"*

15 *And Moses became very angry, and he said to Yahweh: "Do not have regard for their meal offering, I have not taken a single*[11] *donkey from them and I have not harmed even a single one of them."*

6. Driver (*Tenses*, § 119γ) proposes that *ûḇiqqaštem* should be taken as a perfect consecutive without a preceding imperfect as well as continuing the flavor of the *hê* interrogative of v. 9. The current translation reflects this suggestion.

7. *BHS* proposes that MT has suffered from faulty word division, and instead of reading *ʿ^{a}ḏāṯ^{e}ḵā hannōʿăḏîm* ("your congregation are the ones who are gathering"), we should read simply *ʿ^{a}ḏāṯ^{e}ḵâ nōʿāḏîm* ("your congregation is gathering"), with the definite article *(ha-)* attached as a plene spelling of the second masc. sing. pronominal suffix.

8. The last clause of this verse is a result clause; see Williams, *Syntax*, § 527.

9. On this use of the Hithpael *(ṯištārēr . . . hištārēr)*, see GKC, § 54e; BDB, p. 979a.

10. The negative sense of the previous clause continues in this clause, as in 23:19; see GKC, § 152z; cf. Davidson, *Syntax*, § 129 Rem. 6.

11. In the phrase *'eṯ-'aḥaḏ mēhem*, the *'eṯ* may indicate "a single (definite) one"; see GKC, § 117d; Davidson, *Syntax*, § 72 Rem. 4.

16 *And Moses said to Korah: "You and all your congregation be present before Yahweh, you and they and Aaron, tomorrow.*
17 *Each of you take his censer, and put incense upon them, and offer it before Yahweh, each one his censer, two hundred fifty censers, you and Aaron, each one his censer."*
18 *And each one took his censer, put fire upon them, and placed incense upon them; and they stood at the door of the tent of meeting along with Moses and Aaron.*
19 *And Korah gathered all his congregation against them to the door of the tent of meeting, and the glory of Yahweh appeared to the whole congregation.*
20 *And Yahweh spoke to Moses and to Aaron, saying:*
21 *"Separate yourselves from the midst of this congregation that I may devour them in a moment."*
22 *And they fell on their faces and said, "O God, the God of the spirits of all flesh, will one man*[12] *sin and you will be angry with the whole congregation?"*
23 *And Yahweh spoke to Moses, saying:*
24 *"Speak to the congregation, saying: 'Get away from around the tent of Korah, Dathan, and Abiram.' "*
25 *And Moses rose up and went to Dathan and Abiram, and the elders of Israel went after him.*
26 *And he spoke to the congregation, saying: "Please*[13] *turn aside from next to the tents of these evil men and do not touch anything that belongs to them lest you should be swept away*[14] *with all their sins."*
27 *So they went up from around the dwelling of Korah, Dathan, and Abiram. And Dathan and Abiram went out, standing at the door of their tents along with their wives, their sons, and their infants.*
28 *And Moses said, "In this way you may know that Yahweh has sent me to do all these works, that it is not on my own.*

12. MT *hā'îš 'eḥāḏ* is odd (the definite article *hā-* should be on both words; see Sam. Pent.). The easiest solution, as pointed out long ago by Gesenius (GKC, § 100m; followed, e.g., by Dillmann, p. 93; Holzinger, p. 65; Gray, p. 204; *BHS*), is to assume that the Masoretes mistook the *hê* interrogative *(ha-)* for the definite article *(hā-)*. The interrogative flavor is continued for the remaining clause (GKC, § 150m). The current translation reflects this suggestion.

13. On the particle *nā'* see the commentary below on v. 8 and GKC, §§ 105b, 110d.

14. Heb. *tissāp̄û,* Niphal of *sāp̄â,* is cognate with Arab. *safā*[w], which is used of "the wind which raises dust and carries it away" (BDB, p. 705a; cf. *HALAT,* p. 721a). LXX reads *synapolēsthe,* "to be destroyed with," possibly reading Heb. *sûp̱,* "to come to an end."

29 *If these men die*[15] *like the death of all humans, and if the visitation that comes on all humans comes on them, Yahweh has not sent me.*[16]

30 *But if Yahweh should do something new,*[17] *and the ground should open up its mouth and swallow them and all they have, and they should descend alive to Sheol, then you will know that these men have spurned Yahweh."*

31 *And it happened, as he finished speaking all these words, that the ground underneath them was split open.*

32 *And the earth opened its mouth and swallowed them and all their houses and all the people who belonged to Korah and all their belongings.*

33 *And they and all they had went down to Sheol alive; and the earth covered them over, and they perished from the midst of the assembly.*

34 *And all Israel who were around them fled at their voice, for they said, "Lest the earth swallow us!"*

35 *And fire went out from Yahweh and devoured the two hundred fifty men who were offering incense.*

As has been pointed out above, this story is complex. It deals with at least two groups: Korah and his supporters, and Dathan, Abiram, and On (?) and their followers. Here these two stories are combined into one narrative. Many scholars have explained the origin of these stories by means of the hypothesis that diverse documentary sources from various circles and time periods were combined to make a story different from the separate ones.[18] These documentary sources are usually said to be three. The first source is JE, which tells the story of a civil rebellion against the authority of Moses by the Reubenites Dathan and Abiram (vv. 12–15, 25, 26b–34). The second is the basic Priestly source (P_g), which tells of Korah and his group, who were not Levites but were rebelling against the Levites

15. For the *-ûn* termination on *y^e^muṯûn,* cf. GKC, §§ 47m, 159c n. 2. For the impersonal passive construction, cf. Davidson, *Syntax,* § 109.

16. MT *lō' YHWH š^e^lāḥānî,* lit., "not Yahweh sent me." The placement of the negative *lō'* before *YHWH* emphasizes the name and so the identity of Yahweh; Gray, p. 206; GKC, §152e.

17. The expression *b^c^rî'â yiḇra',* lit., "to create a creation," is uniquc here, although similar clauses are used elsewhere to express the novel and extraordinary (Exod. 34:10; Jer. 31:22); see BDB, p. 135.

18. See the excellent summary of the work in the 19th cent. in Gray, pp. 186–93. A more up-to-date, but less clear, summary is found in Budd, pp. 181–86, esp. 184.

Moses and Aaron for priestly privileges for all (vv. 3–7, 18–24, 26a, [perhaps 27a], 35). The third is a supplement to the Priestly source (P_s), which, late in the 5th cent. or early in the 4th, was added to make Korah a Levite and thus make the struggle appear to be one among the Levites for priestly privileges (vv. 8–11, 16–17).[19]

This view of the origin of the text, although common, seems artificial and based on the cleverness of the interpreter rather than on the text itself. The literary complexities of this text, including a certain roughness in transitions between sections, may be explained by literary or stylistic reasons for so-called tensions such as repetitions, rather than seeking refuge in putative documents not one of which can be proved to have existed. That the text confronts us with two rebellions, Korah's and the Reubenites', is patent. One point the text makes by uniting these stories is that these different rebels, with different agendas, made common cause in order to overthrow the order as ordained by God. One or two examples must suffice to indicate the inner coherence of this text.

In Dathan and Abiram's response to Moses in v. 13 (JE), they respond by saying, "is it too small a thing that you have brought us out" *(ham^{e}ʿaṭ kî he^{ʿĕ}lîṯānû)*, which clearly bases itself on (and is a sarcastic echo of) Moses' own indictment of Korah in v. 9 (*ham^{e}ʿaṭ mikkem kî-hiḇdîl,* P_s). Further, one should compare the language of v. 16a (P_g) with v. 17a (P_s) upon which it depends, rather than the language of P_g itself in vv. 6 and 7.[20] This story develops in scenes that alternate between Moses' confrontation with Korah (vv. 3–11, 16–19) and with the Reubenites (vv. 12–15, 25–30). The introduction (vv. 1–2) and the sections dealing with judgment (vv. 20–24, 31–35) seem to deal with both groups together (since these rebels have made common cause, they share a common punishment). There seems little doubt that the story, complex though it may be, is intended to be read as a single narrative with a continuity between the scenes. That an editor may have put stories from diverse sources together is, of course, possible. If such an editor (rather than a creative author) is a reality, then he has done the job very neatly, in spite of a certain difficulty in sorting out details. It is less likely that these

19. Although many years have passed since Gray's commentary was published, many moderns do not depart significantly from his conclusions; cf., e.g., Noth, pp. 120–22; Sturdy, pp. 115–16; Budd, pp. 181–86; de Vaulx, pp. 189–95. The most up-to-date study is Milgrom, *JPST*, pp. 414–23.

20. V. 17: *ûq^{e}ḥû ʾîš maḥtāṯô ûn^{e}ṯaṯem ʿ^{a}lêhem q^{e}ṭōreṯ*
V. 18: *wayyiq^{e}ḥû ʾîš maḥtāṯô wayyitt^{e}nû ʿ^{a}lêhem ʾēš*
Vv. 6–7: *q^{e}ḥû lāḵem maḥtôṯ . . . ûṯ^{e}nû ḇāhēn ʾēš*

sources can be dissected with the neatness suggested by the majority of scholars who follow the method discussed above. As in the rest of this commentary, the final text here is treated as a unity.[21]

1–2 In these verses two stories about two groups of rebels are introduced together. Rather than an accident, it seems that this is an intentional device to link these different people in one cause. The first rebel group is led by *Korah the son of Izhar, the son of Kohath, the son of Levi (kōraḥ ben-yiṣhār ben-q*^{e}*hāṯ ben-lēwî).* This genealogy is confirmed by Exod. 6:16, 18, 21 and 1 Chr. 5:27–28; 6:7, 22–23 (Eng. 6:1–2, 22, 37–38). Kohath had four sons: Amram (the ancestor of Moses and Aaron), Izhar (the ancestor of Korah), Hebron, and Uzziel (Exod. 6:18). According to the Levitical census of Num. 3:27–32, the leader of the Kohathites was Elizaphan of the family of Uzziel, the youngest (3:30). Perhaps Korah was indignant that his family, which might have a better claim to the leadership, had been overlooked.

The other group of rebels was led by *Dathan and Abiram the sons of Eliab, and On the son of Peleth, the sons of Reuben (dāṯān wa'*^{a}*ḇîrām b*^{e}*nê '*^{ĕ}*lî'āḇ w*^{e}*'ôn ben-peleṯ b*^{e}*nê r*^{e}*'ûḇēn).* Of these, On the son of Peleth is never mentioned again. (Ps. 106:16–18 mentions Dathan and Abiram but not On.) This has led scholars to conjecture that either he withdrew from the plot early on, or, more likely, the text is corrupt at this point.[22] These Reubenites may have felt slighted that the rights of the firstborn had been lost by the tribe of Reuben (see Gen. 49:3–4), and wanted a bigger role in the nation. These two groups of rebels camped nearby one another and marched one in front of the other. They would have ample opportunity to commiserate on their mutual loss of power and influence. By putting them together at this point, the author sets them on common ground — even though the specifics may have been different — in that they rebelled against the order of Israelite society as God had ordained it.

These men *became arrogant . . . and rose up before Moses (wayyiqqaḥ . . . wayyāqumû lip̄nê mošeh),* that is, they "created an uproar

21. This method is followed by, e.g., Keil, pp. 105–11; Noordtzij, pp. 141–56; Wenham, pp. 133–39; Harrison, pp. 231–43; and Allen, *EBC,* pp. 833–45, but was also suggested many years ago by G. Richter, "Die Einheitlichkeit der Geschichte von der Rotte Korah," *ZAW* 39 (1921) 128–37, which may still be consulted with profit.

22. Keil, p. 105, and Cook, p. 708, held that On withdrew from the plot. Other scholars (notably Bacon) have attempted to see in On a parallel rebel to Dathan and Abiram (E) from source J; see Gray, pp. 190–91.

before his eyes."[23] This expression means that they were rebelling against his authority.

Although vv. 17 and 35 seem to attach the *two hundred fifty men from the children of Israel* more to Korah's side of the rebellion than to Dathan and Abiram's, the text as it stands is rather unclear on whether this number refers to the followers of both groups together or just one. Since Zelophehad the Manassite is said not to have been one of Korah's company (27:3), the likelihood is that this group of two hundred fifty was made up from other tribes than the Levites as well as an undetermined number of Levites. These men were not run-of-the-mill Israelites. The text piles up three appositives to show their preeminence: they were *leaders of the congregation (n^eśî'ê 'ēḏâ),* they were *chosen from the assembly (q^eri'ê mô'ēḏ),* and they were *important men* (*'anšê-šēm,* lit., "men of a name"). This last term describes men who are acknowledged to be prominent in the community (e.g., in 1 Chr. 5:24; 12:30). The first two terms are similar to those used of the leaders given to Moses in Num. 1:16. The first term states simply that these men have been chosen from the congregation of Israel. The term *congregation* here probably indicates the adult males of Israel as representatives of the whole people (see on 1:2 above). The second term is unique, and its exact meaning is unknown. The term *mô'ēḏ* means "that which is appointed,"[24] and depending on its context may mean an appointed time or place, preeminently as in the *'ōhel-mô'eḏ,* "the tent of meeting," where Yahweh and his representatives meet. The term is not defined further here and may be taken as meaning either "chosen *for* a meeting," with either Moses or Yahweh, or "chosen *by* a meeting," i.e., by an assembly of the people. LXX here reads "called together for counsel" *(synklētoi boulēs),* i.e., these men were those who had a special function for advice or counsel. It is doubtful that these terms should be taken in a rigidly technical sense, the first two being, in fact, very similar to the last.

3–11 This complex section consists mainly of two addresses by Moses to Korah and two different groups (vv. 5–7, 9–11) in response to the latter's complaint (v. 3). This complaint, which is couched in very general terms in order to garner support from as many Israelites as possible, is that Moses and Aaron have excluded the people from full participation in the priestly affairs of the people. Korah begins by telling

23. Keil, p. 106; for the verb *qûm* as "to rebel," see, e.g., 2 K. 12:21; 2 Chr. 13:6.

24. BDB, pp. 417–18a.

Moses, *You have gone too far! (raḇ-lāḵem).* This same phrase is found in Deut. 1:6 and 2:3 in reference to enough time having been spent at Horeb (1:6) and in the wilderness (2:3). In 3:26 the phrase is used (in the sing.) by God when Moses begs to enter Canaan: "But Yahweh was angry with me on your account and he would not hear me, and Yahweh said to me, 'Enough! *[raḇ-lāḵ].* Do not speak to me again on this matter.' " A speaker might use this phrase to show that the one addressed should go no further in a particular direction.

Korah supports his charge against the leadership with two specifics: *the whole congregation is holy, every one of them! And Yahweh is in their midst.* The first clause echoes Exod. 19:6 and is a great truth. The grammatical construction means that not only is the whole congregation holy, but every individual in the congregation is holy. The second clause reflects God's promise in, e.g., Exod. 29:45: "and I will dwell in the midst of the children of Israel and I will be their God." Since these two statements are accepted truths, Korah concludes that he has grounds for his next question (which is rhetorical): *Now why do you exalt yourselves over the congregation of Israel?* In fact, it is unlikely that Korah wanted to abolish a special priesthood; rather, he wanted its privileges for other Levites than the Aaronic priests — at least that is the way Moses ultimately responds to him (vv. 8–11). *Assembly (qāhāl)* — Milgrom has held that the term *assembly* here is a synonym for *congregation (ʿēḏâ),* probably in the interests of literary variety.[25] Were this the case, one would expect to find *qāhāl* more than twice (vv. 3, 33) and *ʿēḏâ* fewer than fourteen times (vv. 2, 3, 5, 6, 9 [twice], 11, 16, 19 [twice], 21, 22, 24, 26). In addition, the two occurrences of *qāhāl* are at the introduction and conclusion of the story rather than integrated into the story itself where *ʿēḏâ* is consistently used. Further still, the term *congregation (ʿēḏâ)* itself is used for both the congregation of Israel *and* the rebel group of Korah.[26] Although the suggestion must be made tentatively, it is probable that the *assembly (qāhāl)* here and in v. 33 indicates the whole people of Israel, while the *congregation* is an unnamed group representative of the whole assembly, but more select.[27]

25. J. Milgrom, "Priestly Terminology and the Political and Social Structures of Pre-Monarchic Israel," *JQR* 69 (1978) 76.

26. Korah's congregation is differentiated from the congregation of Israel by the pronoun *his* (vv. 5, 6, 11) or *your* (v. 16).

27. Obviously Korah's congregation is a smaller group than the whole. On the *congregation* see above on 1:2; Milgrom's article "Priestly Terminology," pp. 65–81; and *JPST,* pp. 335–36.

4 In reaction to Korah's charges Moses *fell on his face (wayyippōl ʿal-pānāyw).* The probability is that here, as in ch. 14, motives of intercession and obeisance before God are present. Moses also undoubtedly needed instruction from Yahweh on how to deal with this crisis. The text does not say how long Moses is prostrate, but when he rises, he has two replies to make, the first to the specific charge raised by Korah and the second to the motive behind it.

5–7 The first reply comes in vv. 5–7. It is important to see that the narrator has informed us of those whom Moses addressed: *And he spoke to Korah and to his whole congregation (wayyōʾmer ʾel-qōraḥ waʿᵃḏāṯô).* This group is also addressed in vv. 6, 11, and 16,[28] and includes Korah himself and the two hundred fifty Israelite leaders, not all of whom (or none of whom) were Levites. Since it was Korah's contention that *all* the people were holy, the whole *congregation (ʿēḏâ)* must be put to the test (see vv. 17, 35). The term *ʿēḏâ* commonly describes the whole cultic community of Israel,[29] and its use here to describe the group of Korah's followers is hardly accidental. This was an alternate cultic community based on different regulations, and was a parody of the real community of Yahweh headed by Moses and Aaron. This congregation will be put to the test.

The test will be offering incense before Yahweh, which was a basic and exclusively priestly prerogative, and which, in the light of what happened to two ordained priests (Aaron's sons Nadab and Abihu) who offered incense improperly in Lev. 10, could be quite dangerous. If Korah's whole congregation was indeed holy, then they should have no trouble offering incense. This test, like the events of the stories in 17:1–15 (Eng. 16:36–50) and 17:16–28 (Eng. 1–13) took place over a two-day period.

But before the procedure for the test is proposed, the result is given. *In the morning Yahweh will make known who is his and who is holy.* At the start of a new day, the God of Israel would choose the ones who

28. V. 6: *qōraḥ wᵉḵol-ʿᵃḏāṯô;* vv. 11, 16: *ʾattâ wᵉḵol-ʿᵃḏāṯᵉḵa.* Also see 17:5 (Eng. 16:40); 26:9; 27:3.

29. So used about 115 times in the OT. Simply called "the congregation" *(hāʿēḏâ)* in Lev. 8:4 and 29 times. In other places it is defined by other terms, e.g., "the congregation of Yahweh" *(ʿᵃḏaṯ-YHWH),* Num. 27:17; 31:16; Josh. 22:16–17; "the congregation of Israel" *(ʿᵃḏaṯ-yiśrāʾēl),* Exod. 12:3, 6, 19, 47; Lev. 4:13; Num. 16:9; 32:4; Josh. 22:18, 20; "the congregation of the children of Israel" *(ʿᵃḏaṯ-bᵉnê-yiśrāʾēl),* Exod. 16:1–2, 9–10; 17:1; 35:1, 4, 20; Lev. 16:5; 19:2; Num. 1:2, 53; 8:9, 20; 13:26; 14:5, 7; 15:25–26; 17:6; 19:9; 25:6; 26:2; 27:20; 31:12; Josh. 18:1; 22:12; etc. See BDB, p. 417a; *HALAT,* p. 746b; J. Lewis, *TWOT,* I:388.

would belong to him. Much as the case of the spies was left in the hands of Yahweh, so this case is left there. Only he is wise enough to choose. The expressions *who is his (ʾeṯ-ʾ^{a}šer-lô)* and *who is holy (w^{e}ʾeṯ-haqqāḏôš)* certainly have to do with priestly functions here, as the following clause, *and he will bring that one near to himself (w^{e}hiqrîḇ ʾēlāyw),* makes clear. The verb *hiqrîḇ,* "to bring near," in this context means to admit into the immediate presence of God, something permitted only for Moses and the priests.[30] Thus Yahweh himself will choose the one who is holy in this case. The test itself is described in vv. 6–7a. V. 7b recapitulates the outcome of the test, so that the procedure itself is literarily surrounded by its outcome.[31]

First, Korah and all his congregation are to take *censers (maḥtôṯ).* In the OT this term is used to describe several different specific receptacles. Exod. 25:38 (cf. 37:23; Num. 4:9) refers to the golden pans used with the snuffers for the menorah, and Exod. 27:3 (cf. 38:8; Num. 4:14) to the bronze trays used to catch the ashes from the altar of burnt offerings. Only two passages, in addition to the current one, mention these trays as receptacles for incense: Lev. 10:1 and 16:12. In the latter passage the high priest uses a golden *maḥtâ* (Exod. 25:38) for the ritual of the Day of Atonement. In the former, Nadab and Abihu offer strange fire and die for their efforts. The current passage has much in common with Lev. 10 in that unacceptable incense is offered in both cases, and that in both cases the *maḥtâ* is not a piece of sanctuary furnishing, but a private receptacle.[32] The outcome of both incidents is also similar (cf. Lev. 10:2; Num. 16:35).

Korah and all his company (qōraḥ w^{e}ḵol-ʿ^{a}ḏōṯô). This phrase is probably a direct address (vocative), albeit a somewhat awkward one. The alternative is that it is a gloss on the text, using the same formula as in the previous verse to make sure the reader understands who the participants in this test were.[33]

30. As in 5:16. See the comments of Milgrom in *Studies in Levitical Terminology,* I:33–43, esp. pp. 37–38 n. 141. Also note 3:16: 18:2, where the term is used of the relationship of the priests and the Levites.

31. Another inclusion; see the commentary above on 5:11–31.

32. That they are private property may be seen by the fact that each censer is called "his censer" *(maḥtāṯô)* in Lev. 10:1. In the current passage, it is clear that the two hundred and fifty must "take for themselves *[q^{e}ḥû lāḵem]* censers." In addition to the fact that nothing is said about removing censers from the tabernacle in this story, it is surely obvious that there were not two hundred and fifty holy censers in the tabernacle in the first place!

33. See Gray, p. 199.

The procedure to be followed is the same as that found in Lev. 10:1: first fire is put into the censers, then incense is added.[34] These instructions were to be carried out *tomorrow (māḥār)*. As S. J. De Vries has shown, this term accompanies announcements of decisive acts of Yahweh; *today* is the day of preparation, *tomorrow* is the day of performance, action, or judgment.[35] Then, as mentioned above, v. 7b recapitulates the outcome: *And it will be that the man Yahweh will choose, he will be the holy one,* viz., the one fit to be the priestly intercessor for Israel.

The paragraph ends with Moses' statement using the very words of Korah (v. 3) against him: *It is you who have gone too far, O sons of Levi.* The last phrase is strange, since the group Moses is addressing is not made up wholly of Levites. Some scholars conclude that these words are out of place here, and should be moved to the end of the clause *you have gone too far* in v. 3.[36] This is a rather extensive displacement, although it is conceivable. Literarily these words of address identify the whole of Korah's congregation with him and also provide a transition to Moses' address to the Levites in the next verses.

8–10 Moses' second reply (vv. 8–10) is addressed to a different group, although Korah is also involved here. In these verses Moses goes beyond the externals of Korah's complaints and gets to the motive behind them.

Moses begins his address to Korah and the rebellious Levites with an imperative *(Hear, šimᵉʿû)* plus the particle *nāʾ*, which adds a certain strength of entreaty or exhortation to it.[37] He then asks, rhetorically it seems, whether it is *too small a thing,* i.e., unimportant, that Yahweh had set them apart from the other Israelites and accepted them into his presence (*to bring them near to himself,* v. 9). When he accepted them he did so in order that they might *do the work of the tabernacle,* i.e., the general job of moving the tent.[38] The purpose of all this was so that the Levite might

34. Lev. 10:1 and Num. 16:7a are comparable verses:

35. See also Num. 11:18; 14:25 (also Exod. 8:6, 19, 25; 9:5, 18; 10:4; etc.). S. J. De Vries, "The Time Word *māḥār* as a Key to Tradition Development," *ZAW* 87 (1975) 65–79, esp. the summary on pp. 78–79.

36. E.g., Dillmann, p. 91; Gray, pp. 197, 199; Noth, pp. 118, 123 note. *BHS* proposes the emendation on the basis of critical suggestion, not textual evidence (of which none is cited). A more likely place to look for the source of these words, if they are displaced, would be in the identical words *sons of Levi* in v. 8.

37. See GKC, §§ 105b, 110d; BDB, p. 609.

38. On the terms *ʿāḇaḏ* and *ʿᵃḇōḏâ,* see the commentary above on ch. 4.

stand in the midst of the other Israelites to serve or *to minister to them* (*l^e^šār^e^ṯām,* v. 9b). This last term may be a general one for service, but also may include aid to the priests in the sacrificial rituals.[39] Further, this is not the prerogative of only a few Levites (e.g., the Kohathites), but of all (v. 10a).

In v. 10b Moses comes to the nub of the matter — not being satisfied with the position to which God has called one, but wanting more for the sake of power and prestige. It is clear that the Levites' call was to ministry or service of the people, not to power and position over them. This misunderstanding is near the heart of that which makes Korah's rebellion so tragic: a misunderstanding of God's call as to privilege and not to service.

11 This verse forms the conclusion to this section, as is shown by the particle *lāḵēn, Therefore,* with which it begins. Based on what has been said, what follows is the only conclusion Moses can draw. The word is addressed, once again, to Korah and his whole congregation, which includes the Levites addressed in vv. 8–10, but also the wider group addressed in vv. 5–7.

The first clause is clear enough; it is Korah and company (not Moses and Aaron) who *are gathering [hannōʿāḏîm] against Yahweh.*[40] But the last clause, *and as for Aaron, what is he that you should murmur against him?* does not go smoothly with the rest of the verse. The meaning is that in rebelling against the priesthood, Korah is not really rebelling against Aaron, but against Yahweh himself, since Aaron did not put himself over the people, nor did Moses. It was Almighty God who

---

According to Milgrom, the term here refers only to the general removal work. This is because the term for that guard duty is usually *šāmar mišmereṯ,* which is not found here. It would also not be necessary for the Levites to be admitted into God's presence (i.e., "brought near") to do the guard duty since that took place outside the tabernacle. See Milgrom, *Studies in Levitical Terminology,* I:60–76, esp. p. 74 n. 272.

39. It certainly came to mean aid to the priests in sacrificial rituals in undoubtedly exilic or postexilic texts: Ezek. 44:11; 2 Chr. 29:34; 30:17; 35:11 (although the Chronicles texts concern temporary measures). In these texts the Levites slaughter and flay the sacrifices. Num. 16:9 is vague on this point, and it is impossible to be definitive. Milgrom, *Studies in Levitical Terminology,* I:60–76, esp. p. 74 n. 272.

40. The participle *nōʿāḏîm* is a Niphal (reflexive) form from the root *yʿd,* "assemble." This is the same root from which the term for Korah's "congregation" (*ʿēḏâ*) is derived. In rebelling against the Aaronic priesthood, Korah and his followers are "being a congregation against Yahweh." See BDB, pp. 416b–17a.

ordained things to be so, and disregarding the Aaronic priesthood is rebellion against him.

12–15 The scene shifts briefly to the complaint of Dathan and Abiram that is embedded in the story of the test of Korah and all his congregation (this story resumes with a summary in vv. 16–17). As has already been seen elsewhere in ch. 16,[41] this section begins and ends with the same words, i.e., *we will not come up* (vv. 12, 14). The whole section is patterned in a rather balanced way.[42] After the phrase just noted, the question *is it too small a thing?* is balanced with *will you put out the eyes of these men?* (vv. 13–14). The sentence on *bringing* the people *out* of Egypt (v. 13) is balanced with the one about not *bringing* them *to* Canaan (v. 14), and both lands are described as *a land flowing with milk and honey.* The central complaint of these Reubenites seems to be that Moses is *playing the prince (hiśtārēr)* over them, i.e., exerting an illegitimate authority over them.

The term to *come* (or go) *up* is used to indicate going to a higher authority or even a judge in Gen. 46:37; Deut. 25:7; and Judg. 4:5, and this is the likely meaning here.[43]

13 *Is it too small a thing.* As mentioned above, the repetition of this clause links these episodes.[44]

milk and honey. These are common epithets for the fertility of Canaan (see the commentary above on 13:27). It it used uniquely here of Egypt, the land of slavery. In 11:5 the fertility of Egypt's produce is recalled as "leeks and onions." That Dathan and Abiram would use the common description for Canaan to describe Egypt shows the seriousness of their rebellion. Painting the land of slavery as a paradise is the same kind of rebellion that has already been met and punished in chs. 11, 13–14.

to kill us in this wilderness. A similar complaint is found in 14:2–3; 20:4 (cf. Exod. 14:11; 16:3; and esp. 17:3). Life is hard now, so the complaint against the leadership is that the intent is to make it so. In this situation the past begins to look like the good old days, even when that past included slavery in Egypt.

that you will also keep playing the prince over us (kî ṯiśtārēr ʿālênû gam-hiśtārēr). Moses is asked a similar question in Exod. 2:12 by a

41. E.g., "You have gone too far," vv. 3, 7; also the inclusion in v. 7b, summarizing what has been said in v. 5.

42. Wenham (p. 136 n. 1) calls this a "concentric structure."

43. This suggestion is more likely than Keil's other suggestion that the tabernacle is the "high point" of the camp, hence the reference is to that (Keil, p. 108).

44. For other uses of *hamᵉʿaṭ,* see Gen. 30:15; Josh. 22:17–18; Isa. 7:13; Ezek. 34:18; Job 15:11; BDB, p. 590a.

Hebrew in Egypt. The verb *śārar,* which occurs only here in the Hithpael, is a denominative from *śar,* which is a general term for "captain, vassal leader, prince."[45]

14 Dathan and Abiram continue to paint a picture of Moses' failed leadership. Not only has he taken them out of the paradise of Egypt, he has not provided them with a new one to take its place. They begin with a taunt: *You have not even brought us to a land flowing with milk and honey,* now using this expression in its normal sense to refer to Canaan. This kind of complaint would have become particularly acute during the long period of wilderness wandering when it seemed as if no progress toward the goal was being made. One cause of this lack of progress was rebellions such as by Dathan and Abiram (cf. 14:29–34), a fact that neither man seems to consider.

field and vineyard. These collective singular nouns are used here and elsewhere to describe wealth and property.[46]

Will you put out the eyes of these men? The literal meaning of "to bore out the eyes" is found at Judg. 16:21 (Samson); 1 Sam. 11:2; Prov. 30:17. Virtually all commentators agree that the phrase in the present case is a metaphor for "to mislead" (see NEB "to hoodwink"). Deut. 16:19 states that a bribe makes the eyes blind, and, although the specific words are different there, both passages make the same point. According to Dathan and Abiram, Moses has been blinding the people to the actual facts of their situation in the wilderness. These two Reubenites, and any who would listen to them, are not going to be deceived any longer. They are giving notice of their intent not to follow Moses any longer. Once again, the call toward the land of promise is rejected.

15 Even Moses, the meek man (cf. 12:3), *became very angry* at this attack. Moses attempts to vindicate himself, not in the presence of Dathan and Abiram, but in the presence of Yahweh. He prays: *Do not have regard for their meal offering (ʾal-tēp̱en ʾel-minḥāṯām).* Although the term *minḥâ* elsewhere in the book means "meal offering," commentators are virtually unanimous that here it means something like "an offering (in general)," as in Gen. 4:3–5.[47] The problem is that there is no offering of

45. In Exod. 18 the term is used to describe those overseers of groups of 1,000, 100, 50, and 10. The term commonly has a military connotation. See BDB, p. 978; G. Cohen, *TWOT,* II:884–85.

46. See Exod. 22:4; Num. 20:17; 21:22; 1 Sam. 22:7.

47. Also 1 Sam. 2:17, 29; 26:19; Isa. 1:13; Ps. 96:8; Zeph. 3:10; see BDB, p. 585a. Even such usual opposites as Keil, Gray, and Budd agree on this point.

any kind elsewhere in the story to which this *minḥâ* might refer. It is also strange that an editor would choose to leave this term for a general offering in a context where it might be confused with the meal offering. Snaith suggests that this *minḥâ* might be understood as part of the "daily regular offering" (*tāmîḏ,* Exod. 29:41).[48] If *minḥâ* does carry its more common meaning of "meal offering," what would this mean? In addition to the regular daily offering, an independent meal offering is prescribed, e.g., in Lev. 2:7. Num. 15:1–16 also spelled out amounts of meal offerings to accompany whole burnt offerings and peace offerings — in other words, all the sacrifices except the guilt offering and the reparation offering. Both these offerings would require an admission of guilt on the part of the sacrificer. Since such an admission would be unlikely in Dathan and Abiram's cases, by praying that their *minḥâ* not be accepted, Moses was praying that they would have no part in the sacrifices that made access to Yahweh possible.

For Moses' statement *I have not taken a single donkey from them and I have not harmed even a single one of them,* see 1 Sam. 8:16; 12:3. This was evidently some kind of idiomatic statement that meant that one party had not taken tribute from another nor exalted himself over another.

16–19 These verses round off the first part of the story. In vv. 16–17 the procedure for the test is repeated with a few more details than in vv. 6–7a: there will be two hundred fifty censers for Korah's congregation, thus explicitly identifying this group with the two hundred fifty Israelite leaders of v. 2, and Aaron and Moses will also be expected to take part in the test.[49] This repetition has the literary effect of surrounding the narrative of Dathan and Abiram (vv. 12–15) with that of Korah and his congregation (vv. 5–11, 16–22), and effectively shows that the two rebellions were contemporaneous and related.

Verses 18–19 form the turning point of the story. In v. 18 Korah and his congregation (along with Moses and Aaron), each one, carry out the command of vv. 6–7a, 16–17. V. 18 also gives the site of the test as *the door of the tent of meeting* (i.e., *before Yahweh,* vv. 7, 16–17). Perhaps

48. Snaith, p. 159.

49. Participation by Moses and Aaron may be implied in the clause "he will choose him whom he will bring near to himself" (v. 3). Noordtzij, p. 149, comments that the words "and Moses" in v. 18a are probably later additions to the text made by a redactor who thought that, since Moses was present in v. 20, he would have to have taken part in the test as well, forgetting that Moses was not authorized to fulfill priestly functions, such as burning incense, and never did. There is no textual evidence to support excising these words.

assuming that he will be vindicated, Korah *gathered the whole congregation (wayyaqhēl . . . 'eṯ-kol-hā'ēḏâ).* Considering the fact that the people were already under a death sentence (viz., death in the wilderness), it is somewhat surprising to find that the *congregation* (the people) responded to Korah's call. The text says that they gathered *against them* (i.e., against Moses and Aaron, *'alêhem*). One must carefully differentiate the two uses of the word *congregation ('ēḏâ)* in this chapter. When the group of two hundred fifty under the leadership of Korah is meant, it is called *his* or *your* (i.e. Korah's) *whole congregation* (vv. 5–6, 11, 16), but where it indicates the whole of the sacred congregation of Israel, the expression *the whole* (or *this whole*) *congregation* (vv. 2–3, 9, 19, 21, 24, 26, 33). It was the latter group that Korah assembled against Moses and Aaron.

At the end of v. 19 *the glory of Yahweh (keḇôḏ-YHWH)* appeared to them.[50]

20–24 Here the judgment is announced before it is carried out (cf. 14:22–23, 28–34). God has again determined to destroy the group, but unlike 14:10–12, where all the people (the men, women, and children) were threatened, here the *congregation (hā'ēḏ â),* perhaps to be understood as a representative group of the whole people, is threatened. It should be remembered that the whole people over age twenty is already under a death sentence in the wilderness (14:29–30). The death promised here, in contrast, is instant: *in a moment (kerāḡa'),* which may have originally referred to quick back and forth movements.[51]

22 Again, as in ch. 14, Moses and Aaron intercede for the people: *they fell on their faces* (cf. 12:11–13; 14:13–19). In prayer they address God, here simply as *God ('ē l),* the generic Semitic name for deity. The reference may be general, rather than using the more specifically Hebrew name Yahweh, in order to emphasize God's role as creator of everything. This role is seen even more clearly in the appositional phrase: *the God of the spirits of all flesh.* This title is found only here and at Num. 27:16 in the OT, although it is quite common in the postbiblical literature.[52] The

50. See the commentary above on 14:10b.

51. Cf. 17:10 (Eng. 16:45); also Exod. 32:9–10; 33:5. The word means something like "to move to and fro"; BDB, p. 921a; W. White, *TWOT,* II:832b; *HALAT,* p. 1109b. On the *congregation* see above on 16:3 and 1:2.

52. The title is found over 100 times in the book of Enoch; cf. Jub. 10:3; 2 Macc. 3:24; 14:46. In Num. 27:16 the appositional title is Yahweh, not *'ēl.* On *'el,* see, e.g., M. Pope, *El in the Ugaritic Texts,* SVT 2 (Leiden: Brill, 1955); F. M. Cross, "Yahweh and the God of the Patriarchs," *HTR* 55 (1962) 225–59; W. F. Albright, *Yahweh and the Gods of Canaan* (Garden City, N.Y.: Doubleday, 1968),

clause recognizes not only that God is the creator of all life (as *all flesh, kol-bāśār,* probably means here),[53] but also the sovereign over it all (i.e., with the right of life and death over his own creation). After setting forth God's right to deal with creation as he sees fit, Moses appeals to God's mercy and grace (again as in 14:17–20).

will one man sin (hā'îš 'eḥāḏ yeḥṭā'). This *one man* is evidently Korah, in the light of this whole narrative, which tends to subsume Dathan and Abiram's sin under that of Korah. One should not be too quick to see in this statement a plea for individual retribution for sin, which fits into our modern context far better than it did into the ancient Near East. That there is still solidarity in sin is seen by the fact that Dathan and Abiram's families die with them (v. 32). For the danger of God's wrath breaking out against the people generally, see Lev. 10:6; Num. 1:58; 18:5; Deut. 9:19. In several contexts God's wrath *(qeṣep̱)*[54] is parallel to a plague *(negep̱) that breaks out against both the sinner and the community at large.*[55]

24 Yahweh purposes to turn his wrath on the whole congregation (cf. 14:12). He instructs Moses to tell the congregation to *get away from around the tent of Korah, Dathan, and Abiram (hē'ālû missāḇîḇ lᵉmiškān qōraḥ dāṯān wa'ᵃḇîrām).* Many English translations mask the difficulty here by translating Heb. *miškān* (sing.) by the pl. "tents" or the collective "dwelling."[56] Korah, Dathan, and Abiram did not live in one "tent" (see 16:27), though both the Kohathites and Reubenites lived near one another on the south side of the tabernacle. The word *miškān* cannot bear the meaning "vicinity," which it must in order to hold that all three lived in one *miškān.* In fact, this word in the sing. is never used of a human habitation, with the possible exception of Isa. 22:16, where it parallels the word *grave.* The sing. is reserved for Yahweh's "dwelling," especially the tabernacle or the temple.[57]

---

pp. 119–21; P. Miller, "El the Warrior," *HTR* 60 (1967) 411–31; most recently F. M. Cross, *TDOT,* I:242–61.

53. See Snaith, p. 159. In various contexts the phrase *kol-bāśār* can mean all living things (Lev. 17:14; Num. 18:15; etc.); animal life only (Gen. 7:15, 21; 8:17; etc.), or human life only (Deut. 5:26).

54. This noun is derived from the same stem as the verb used here, *qāṣap̱,* "to be angry, wrathful"; BDB, p. 893a.

55. See Milgrom, *Studies in Levitical Terminology,* I:17, esp. n. 75, also n. 109. The two words *wrath* and *plague* are parallel, e.g., in 17:11 (Eng. 16:46).

56. "Tents" (GNB, NIV, NKJV); "dwellings" (NEB, NASB); "abodes" (NJPS); "dwelling" (RSV); only AV, RV translate "tabernacle."

57. Num. 24:5 uses the pl., "tents of Jacob," parallel to the other word for "tent," *'ōhel.* See BDB, pp. 1015b–16a.

The case is made more complicated when it is realized that Korah has assembled the congregation around the door of the tent of meeting (i.e., Yahweh's tabernacle) in v. 19. If, in fact, they are now told to get away from the tent (even in the sense of "dwelling") of Korah, Dathan, and Abiram, they are told (in Gray's words) "to depart from a place in which they are not."[58] The LXX handles the difficulty by making two changes: It eliminates Dathan and Abiram's names both here and in v. 27a, and it uses the word *synagogē* to translate *miškān,* which elsewhere in ch. 16 has been used to translate *'ēḏâ (congregation),* either of Israel or of Korah.

Scholars have offered several solutions to these difficulties. (1) Some take the word *miškān* to mean "tabernacle," and posit that Korah, Dathan, and Abiram had set up their own rival shrine.[59] While not impossible, this option is less likely because such a blatant sin would surely have been made clearer in a text that has as one of its main purposes to detail the sins of these rebels. (2) Others go a step further than the LXX and eliminate all three names from the text as a later addition. The reason for such an addition would be the editorial wish to make the two rebellions appear together as one.[60] The reading of the text is then: "tell the congregation to move away from around the tabernacle." This emendation makes some sense out of a difficult case here, but makes the excision of v. 27a all but necessary.[61] (3) Still others posit that *miškān* here simply means "dwelling," and assumes that Korah, after he had summoned the congregation of Israel to the tent of meeting, withdrew to the tent of Dathan and Abiram. This option proposes a unique meaning for the sing. *miškān,* and also hypothesizes what Korah must have, or might have, done. The text is silent on the matter.[62]

The first option is the least likely for the reason set forth above. The second option is attractive because it makes some sense out of a

58. Gray, p. 204.

59. Budd, pp. 181, 183.

60. The text has already gone some way toward putting the two rebellions together by its literary shape, which surrounds the story of Dathan and Abiram (vv. 12–15, 25–34) with the story of Korah (vv. 5–11, 16–19, 35).

61. Unless, like Noordtzij, one moves v. 27a (without the names Korah, Dathan, and Abiram) to a place between vv. 24–25 (see Noordtzij, pp. 149 n. 3, 150). So, e.g., Dillmann, pp. 93–94; Gray, p. 204; McNeile, p. 89; Binns, p. 113; Heinisch, p. 67; Noordtzij, p. 148.

62. See Wenham, p. 137. This proposal raises a further question as to whether Dathan and Abiram were summoned to the tent of meeting by Korah, and, if so, when they returned to their own tent (cf. Keil, p. 109).

seemingly confused and conflated text, but does nothing to explain how the final editor of the text wanted that text to be understood. In other words, it eliminates perceived tensions by ascribing them to one who misunderstood that the two stories were originally separate (the clumsy redactor). By eliminating these tensions, one of the major points that this editor wishes the stories to make, viz., that the rebellions, although twofold, were basically the same — they were rebellions against Yahweh — is also eliminated. This is a very dubious process if the goal is to understand the text as it is rather than to hypothesize how it got that way. The third option, although it has considerable problems, not the least of which is living with a certain ambiguity in the text, may be the best of this list. By identifying Korah with Dathan and Abiram, the text unifies the two rebellions into one, and also makes a transition back to the story of Dathan and Abiram in vv. 25–34.[63]

25–30 The story returns to the rebellion of Dathan and Abiram against Moses. In vv. 12–15 Moses had summoned these men to himself and they had refused to come. V. 25 follows immediately upon this with Moses' attendance on Dathan and Abiram. That *the elders of Israel* went with him probably meant that he had some support from the leadership, in spite of what has been said in v. 19, or he forced them to accompany him.

26 When he arrived at the tents of Dathan and Abiram, Moses addressed *the congregation (hāʿēḏâ)*. This group is ubiquitous in ch. 16. Here the term refers to the group addressed in vv. 28–30, which is either the congregation of Israel (as in, e.g., v. 19), which must then have followed Moses from the tent of meeting where they had been to the tents of Dathan and Abiram; or a new congregation made up of the followers of Dathan and Abiram and others who were, naturally enough in the crowded camp, living around their tents. This group includes *all Israel who were around them* in v. 34, which may speak for the latter being the case here.

Moses' message begins with an entreaty, *Please turn aside (sûrû nāʾ). these evil men* are Dathan and Abiram here, although Moses will include Korah in the group in v. 27. Moses also urges the congregation, *do not touch anything that belongs to them,* since uncleanness was contagious and a holy God would not allow uncleanness in his camp (cf.

63. A similar phenomenon is the mention of the Levites in v. 7b, which makes a transition between Moses' address to Korah's congregation (vv. 5–7) and to the Levites (vv. 8–10).

5:1–4). A similar case of being infected by the sin of others is seen in the case of Achan (Josh. 7). If the people kept up contact with the rebels they would *be swept away with all their sins (tissāpû bᵉkol-ḥaṭṭ'ōṯām).* The verb *sāpâ,* "to be swept away," is associated with destruction in Gen. 19:15, 17; 1 Sam. 12:25; 26:10; cf. Prov. 13:23. This term gives readers a glimpse of what is in store for the rebels (vv. 31–33).

27 Verse 27a is the fulfillment of v. 24b, and the solution to the problem there will determine what is said here. By having the command including all three names in the Korah section (v. 24) and the fulfillment here in the Dathan/Abiram section, once more these two separate stories of rebellion are wed into one. In v. 27b Dathan, Abiram, and their families come out of their tents to meet Moses. One can imagine a confrontation as Moses (with the backing of the elders) speaks to them.

28 In a parallel to vv. 5–7, 16–17, Moses proposes a test to show *that Yahweh has sent me to do all these works (kî YHWH šᵉlāḥanî la'ᵃśôṯ 'ēṯ kol-hamma'ᵃśîm hā'ēlleh),*[64] and *that it is not on my own* (*kî-lō' millibbî,* lit., "that not from my heart"). The heart is the seat of emotion, will, and action in Hebrew thought. Moses is saying that he was not acting on his own impulse, but at the call of Yahweh.[65]

29–30 Moses announces the test itself, taking the negative possibility first: Yahweh has not sent him *If these men die like the death of all humans, and if the visitation that comes on all humans comes on them.* These two parallel clauses simply refer to death from natural causes. The term *visitation (pᵉquḏâ)* is related to the verb *pāqaḏ,* which has a variety of meanings, including "to number" (as in the census document in 1:3, 19; etc.) and "to visit" for different purposes (e.g., Gen. 21:1; Exod. 32:34; Jer. 6:15). The noun *pᵉquḏâ* here covers a similar semantic range (e.g., Num. 4:16; Hos. 9:7). Generally "visitation" indicates the intrusion of a higher person (usually God or the king) on a lower, most times for punishment (cf. Isa. 10:3; Mic. 7:4; etc.).[66] If these men die the same way

64. See, e.g., Exod. 3:10–15; 4:28; 5:22; 7:16; cf. Josh. 24:5.

65. As others have said and continue to say; cf. Balaam in Num. 24:13; Jeremiah in Jer. 20:9 (cf. 23:16, 21); Peter and John in Acts 4:19–20. On the Hebrew conception of the heart, see, e.g., J. Pedersen, *Israel: Its Life and Culture* (London: Oxford Univ. Press, 1926), I–II:102–8; W. Eichrodt, *Theology of the Old Testament,* OTL, tr. J. Baker (London: SCM, 1967), II:142–45; H. W. Wolff, *The Anthropology of the Old Testament,* tr. M. Kohl (London: SCM, 1974), pp. 40–58, 63–77.

66. It may, however, also be a gracious visitation; see Job 10:12; BDB, p. 824a; *TWOT,* II:731–32. Snaith calls God's "visitation" of people in this world

that all human creatures do, and the same blessings and punishments from God attend them, then Moses has not been sent by Yahweh.

30 The other possibility is that *Yahweh should do something new* —act in a way other than the way as set out in v. 29. This *something new* that Yahweh might do is expanded in two ways: *and the ground should open up its mouth and swallow them and all they have;* and *they should descend alive to Sheol.* The first clause is reminiscent of Gen. 4:11. The word *mouth* is here a metaphor for an opening or hole (as also in v. 32; Deut. 11:6; cf. Isa. 5:4; Ps. 69:16 [Eng. 15]).[67] *Sheol* is the realm of the dead.[68] It is difficult to know from this passage the concept of Sheol at this time, except to say that it was conceived of as "down" under the earth (thus the word *descend*) and that it was a place where someone would not normally go while still alive. That these men might go to Sheol alive may indicate that they would suffer in a way more intense than those who were dead.

The most surprising matter in this test, however, is the last clause. One might expect to read "if the ground opens up and swallows these men, and they go alive to Sheol, then *I* will be vindicated." What Moses says, however, is that if these men die in an unnatural way as outlined, *then you will know that these men have spurned Yahweh.* The word *spurned* is *ni'ēṣ*, which here, as in 14:11, 23, means ultimately to reject Yahweh. Moses makes no mention of his own personal vindication and triumph; it is the people who are shown to have been in the wrong, and, by implication, Yahweh who is shown to be right. The point is that rebellion against those whom Yahweh has chosen is rebellion against him. This does not mean simply that leaders are always right. It says that *if* the leader is appointed by God, rebellion against the leadership is rebellion against God.

"vertical time," by which an active God "visits men and women for good and for ill" (N. Snaith, "Time in the Old Testament," in *Promise and Fulfilment: Essays Presented to S. H. Hooke in Celebration of His Ninetieth Birthday,* ed. F. F. Bruce [Edinburgh: T. & T. Clark, 1963], pp. 175–86, esp. 181–82).

67. The word for "ground" is *'ᵃḏāmâ* both here and in Gen. 4:11; in v. 32 and in Deut. 11:6 the word is *'ereṣ*. The verb "to open" is *pāṣâ* here, in Gen. 4:11, and in Deut. 11:6, but in v. 32 it is *pāṯaḥ*. See BDB, p. 804a.

68. Most of the passages descriptive of Sheol are probably later than the current passage and are in poetry; e.g., Job 3:17–19; 21:23–26; Isa. 14:9–11; Ps. 6:6 (Eng. 5). Sheol was evidently thought of as dark (e.g., Job 7:9–10; 10:21; 38:17; Ps. 88:11–13 [Eng. 10–12]) and silent (Ps. 94:17). For a good summary see, e.g., Eichrodt, *Theology of the OT,* II:95–96, 210–16, 221–23. For another perspective see R. Harris, *TWOT,* II:892–93.

31–34 Unlike the test described for the congregation of Korah that took place over two days, this test comes to a conclusion immediately, *as he finished speaking all these words* (v. 31). The *ground* (*'ᵃḏāmâ,* the same word as in the prediction of the event in v. 30) *was split open.*[69]

32 For literary variety, v. 32 uses a synonymous term *earth* (*'ereṣ*):[70] *the earth opened its mouth and swallowed them* (as in v. 30). The *them* includes *their houses,* i.e., their households (cf. Gen. 42:19, 33; 45:18 for a similar use of *bayiṯ,* "house"), i.e., their wives and children (v. 27).

Also included are *all the people who belonged to Korah and all their belongings.* Many scholars simply assume that this group is the same as Korah and his whole congregation (vv. 5–6, 11, 15) and, in turn, the same as the two hundred fifty men who offered incense (vv. 2, 17). This view conflicts with the text itself, since this group is dealt with in v. 35. It is questionable whether any editor, ancient or modern, clumsy or otherwise, would allow such a contradiction to stand only words apart.[71] It is far more likely that *all the people who belonged to Korah* is *not* meant to include those who are clearly identified elsewhere as belonging to the group of two hundred fifty which made up Korah's congregation.[72] Since it is clear that v. 35 intends to dispose of the two hundred fifty men who offered incense, it makes sense to conclude that this verse does not. Thus the identity of these people is vague. Ch. 26 clarifies this point somewhat

69. The form is a Niphal (passive), which may suggest that the action was by God.

70. Several scholars (e.g., Gray, p. 207; Budd, pp. 181–86) have suggested on the basis of these differences in vocabulary that two sources are conflated here. Surely literary variety explains the differences, and good Semitic repetition of thought (seen more clearly in poetic parallelism, but not missing in Hebrew prose) explains the similarities sufficiently well without positing a conglomeration of sources.

71. But see the assumption of, e.g., Gray (p. 207): "an unskilful attempt of the editor to unite in death the two sets of rebels who, even in his form of the story, had in life been constantly divided" (cf. also Binns, p. 115); or Noth (p. 128), who speaks of v. 32b introducing v. 35 "in a completely unthinking way." These assumptions assume that modern scholars know more about how the story should be told than the author/editor who put the text together.

72. I.e., the text makes sense as it stands. The language used to identify Korah's congregation is quite exact: "Korah and his whole congregation" (*qōraḥ wᵉḵol-ʿᵃḏāṯô,* vv. 5–6, 11, 16). The two hundred fifty men of v. 2 are identified with this group in v. 17. It is reasonable to assume that if the author/editor had wished to indicate that Korah's congregation had been destroyed with Dathan and Abiram, he would have used one of these identifications of it.

by saying that Korah himself was included in this group, but that his sons were not (v. 11); they became the ancestors of the later Korahite guild of temple singers (v. 58; also 1 Chr. 6:16–23 [Eng. 31–38]). The group probably included the members of Korah's household (parallel to those of Dathan and Abiram) as well as any other followers he had managed to attract who were with him.

33 All these people fell into the chasm that was opened in the ground, and, in fulfillment of Moses' words (v. 30), *went down to Sheol alive.* That the *earth ['ereṣ] covered them over* means that after the incident there was no sign to mark the site. It is remarkable that no site-name marks this place in the light of such places as Taberah (11:3) and Kibroth-hattaavah (11:34), which mark the site of other rebellions. Perhaps no one wished to be reminded to this place (cf. Ps. 103:16: "and its place knows it no more"). These people perished *from the midst of the assembly,* i.e., the gathered people of Yahweh (the *qāhāl*).

Those Israelites who were in the vicinity fled in fear lest they too be consumed by the open earth. It is typical of the Israelites at this period that they did not take the issue of God-given leaders seriously (though chs. 11–18 speak of this issue repeatedly).

The text makes clear that what happened was *something new* (i.e., unique), a direct intervention of Yahweh in contrast with the normal workings of the world (vv. 28–30). It is natural to speculate on the exact nature of this event. Of course, God is capable of using natural phenomena for his purposes (e.g., the quails, ch. 11). Greta Hort has posited that the most likely natural phenomenon that would answer to the need of the text is the *kewir,* a muddy bog that, due to climatic conditions, can develop a crust over it, which makes it look dry and solid, but may split open if it rains and become hazardous.[73] Again, however, the text stresses not so much the natural event as its causation as an act of judgment by Yahweh.

35 The last verse of the section returns to the story of Korah's congregation, the two hundred fifty men who offered incense. Like Nadab and Abihu before them (Lev. 10:1–2), these leaders were consumed by fire from Yahweh. Once again the Dathan/Abiram story (vv. 25–34) is enclosed within the Korah story (vv. 16–24, 35). The likelihood is that the judgment took place immediately following the offering of incense in v. 18. The text suggests this in two ways. First, these men *were offering incense* (*maqrîḇîm haqqᵉṭōreṯ;* the participle usually indicates continuing

73. G. Hort, "The Death of Korah," *AusBR* 7 (1959) 2–26, esp. 19–26. The whole article may be consulted with profit.

action). Either they were still offering it after the judgment on Dathan and Abiram, or the text is not in chronological order. There seems little evidence that we are to read the text in the latter way. Second, in the similar account in Lev. 10:1–2, the fire that went out from Yahweh was immediate. If that were the case with priests who offered illegitimate offerings, how much more so with these nonpriests.

In commenting on this whole incident, Num. 26:11 states that Korah was swallowed up with Dathan and Abiram. This is the only mention in Numbers of Korah's fate; this chapter tells us nothing directly. That Korah should have suffered the punishment of Dathan and Abiram is surprising at first glance, because he surely committed the same crime as the two hundred and fifty leaders. But this is one more way in which the author/editor of the passage has shown that, although the rebellions may have included separate incidents, they were really one. They both in the end were a spurning of Yahweh by rejecting his chosen leaders.

After this rebellion was put down, one would think that both the Aaronic priesthood and Moses' leadership were well established. The sequels (17:1–28 [Eng. 16:36–50; 17:1–13]) show that more was needed to convince Israel beyond a merely temporary situation of the legitimacy of the leadership.

2. AFTERMATH OF REBELLIONS (17:1–15 [ENG. 16:36–50])

1 (16:36) *And Yahweh spoke to Moses, saying:*

2 (37) *"Say to Eleazar the son of Aaron the priest, 'Let the censers be taken up*[1] *from the midst of the burning, and scatter the fire at a distance,*[2] *for they have become holy.*[3]

1. Heb. *w*^{e}*yārēm,* lit., "and they took them up." Sometimes the third person (sing. or pl.) is used as a circumlocution for the passive voice. Cf. Williams, *Syntax,* § 160; GKC, §§ 144b, c, f. This is also the case with *w*^{e}*ʿāśû* in v. 3 (Eng. 16:38) and *way*^{e}*raqq*^{e}*ʿûm* in v. 4 (Eng. 16:39). RSV has simply translated *ʾ*^{e}*mōr* as "tell" and the verb *rûm* as a complementary infinitive (i.e., "tell Eleazar the priest to take up"). The basic thrust of the present translation is the same, although it translates the jussive *yārēm* more exactly than RSV.

2. Heb. *hāl*^{e}*ʾâ* is an adverb made up of *hāl*^{e}*ʾ* plus the *hê* locale. It means "out there, onward, further"; it is used temporally in Num. 15:23. See BDB, p. 229.

3. The syntax of the last two Hebrew words of v. 2, *kî qāḏēšû* (Eng. 16:37, "for they have become holy") and v. 3 (Eng. 16:38) through *wayyiqdāšû,* "and they have become holy," is difficult. The way in which the text has been translated above attempts to take the Masoretic punctuation seriously. The clause in v. 3

3 (38) *As for the censers of these men who sinned mortally, let them be made*[4] *into beaten plates as plating for the altar, for they have offered them before Yahweh and they have become holy. And they will become a sign for the children of Israel.' "*

4 (39) *And Eleazar the priest took the bronze censers which those who had been burned had offered and they were beaten*[5] *into plating for the altar*

5 (40) *as a reminder for the children of Israel that*[6] *no outsider, who is not of the seed of Aaron, would encroach by offering incense before Yahweh, lest that one become like Korah and his congregation, as Yahweh had spoken to him through Moses.*

6 (41) *But the whole congregation of the children of Israel murmured on the next day against Moses and against Aaron, saying, "You*[7] *have killed Yahweh's people."*

7 (42) *And it happened, as the congregation gathered against Moses and against Aaron, that they turned toward the tent of meeting and the cloud covered it, and the glory of Yahweh appeared.*

(Eng. 16:37), *kî qāḏēšû* (*qāḏēšû* being a pausal form of *qāḏ^ešû*), refers to the censers in that verse. V. 3 (Eng. 16:38) begins with a hanging nominative *(casus pendens)* introduced by the particle *'ēṯ*, "as for the censers of these men who sinned mortally" (see Driver, *Tenses,* § 197 [6]). This clause is picked up by the masc. pronoun *'ōṯām* ("them") after the verb *w^e'āśû* (on the masc. pronoun referring to the fem. *maḥtōṯ,* "censers," see the commentary above on 16:17–18; cf. Davidson, *Syntax,* §§ 1 Rem. 3, 113). The verb of the clause follows in the perfect consecutive, *w^e'āśû,* which carries on the force of the imperative *z^erēh* in v. 2 (Eng. 16:37) (see Driver, *Tenses,* § 123 [a]). On the impersonal third person, see n. 1 above.

Other scholars have concluded that *kî qāḏēšû* in v. 2 (Eng. 16:37) should be taken as supplying the verb for the first clause of v. 3 (Eng. 16:38), and translated "for the censers have become holy." This solution requires eliminating the particle *'ēṯ* marking the direct object, and making "censers" the subject rather than the object: "for the censers of these men who sinned at the cost of their lives became holy." (Dillmann, pp. 95–96; Gray, p. 209; McNeile, pp. 90–91; etc.).

Yet another option comes from LXX (followed by the Syr. and Vulg.), which reads *hoti hēgiasan ta pyreia tōn hamartōlōn toutōn en tais psychais autōn,* "for they had made the censers of the men who had sinned mortally holy" (probably reading the Piel *qidd^ešû* for the Qal in MT). See further Gray, pp. 209, 211.

4. See nn. 1, 3 above.

5. See n. 1 above.

6. On the position of *'^ašer,* see Davidson, *Syntax,* § 9 Rem. 2. The phrase *l^ema'an '^ašer* introduces a telic or purpose clause (Davidson, *Syntax,* § 149; Williams, *Syntax,* §§ 367, 524).

7. The position of the personal pronoun *'attem* is emphatic here. Davidson, *Syntax,* §1.

8 (43) *When Moses and Aaron came to the front of*[8] *the tent of meeting,*
9 (44) *then Yahweh spoke to Moses,*[9] *saying,*
10 (45) *"Get up and away*[10] *from the midst of this congregation that I might devour them in a moment." And they fell on their faces.*
11 (46) *And Moses said to Aaron, "Take the censer, put fire upon it from the altar, place incense on it, and take it quickly to the congregation and make atonement for them, for the wrath has gone out from before Yahweh, the plague has begun."*
12 (47) *And Aaron took it as Moses had spoken, and ran to the midst of the assembly, and, indeed, the plague had already begun, and he placed incense on it and made atonement on behalf of the people.*
13 (48) *And he stood between the dead and the living, and the plague was checked.*
14 (49) *But fourteen thousand seven hundred were dead in the plague, besides the dead ones in the affair of Korah.*
15 (50) *And Aaron returned to Moses at the door of the tent of meeting when the plague was checked.*

The second story in the section grows immediately out of the previous one and draws a lesson from it. It breaks down into two constituent scenes (17:1–5, 6–15 [Eng. 16:36–40, 41–50]). The first scene answers the question of what happened to the two hundred fifty censers used by Korah and his congregation. The assumption might be made that they were destroyed by fire (16:35), but the text explains that they were holy and hence a holy priest needed to dispose of them. These vessels are made into a bronze cover for the alter of incense. This cover is to function as a "sign" *('ôt)* and a "reminder" *(zikkārôn)* that only Aaronic priests may offer incense. Those who violate this prescription risk suffering like Korah. Therefore, the primary lesson of the whole of 16:1–35 is drawn here.

A further aftermath is found in 17:6–15 (Eng. 16:41–50). This subsection plays on two common themes: the disobedience or rebellion of the Israelites and the intercession of the leaders for the people. A

8. On *'el-pᵉnê* meaning "to the front of," after a verb of motion, cf. Lev. 6:7; 16:2; Num. 20:10; BDB, p. 816b. It may indicate that Moses and Aaron went into the court of the tabernacle; see Keil, p. 111.

9. Because both Moses and Aaron appear in v. 8 (Eng. 16:43), and because of the pl. verb *hērōmmû*, "get up and away," in v. 10 (Eng. 16:45), LXX adds the words "and Aaron" here.

10. Heb. *hērōmmû* is found in the Niphal only here and three times in Ezek. 10. Without the preposition *min* it means "to rise," but with the preposition it means "to get up and away from." Cf. KB, p. 895a.

familiar scenario is followed: the people murmur against Moses and Aaron (17:6–7 [Eng. 16:41–42]), Yahweh decides to kill them all instantly (17:8–10a [Eng. 16:43–45a]), but Moses and Aaron intercede for them (17:10b [Eng. 16:45b]). The difference in this story, however, becomes clear in 17:11–15 (Eng. 16:46–50). First, although Moses instructs Aaron to intercede for the people (17:11 [Eng. 16:46]), it is Aaron himself who does the interceding. Second, this intercession is not done through direct prayer to Yahweh, but by an incense offering. Third, this time it is too late to stop Yahweh from beginning to carry out the death sentence ("the plague has begun," 17:11 [Eng. 16:46]). Fourteen thousand seven hundred Israelites died before Aaron could get the plague under control (17:12–15 [Eng. 16:47–50]). These two scenes function together as a demonstration of the sole sufficiency of the Aaronic priesthood to deal with God for the people.

1–5 (16:36–40) Eleazar, rather than Aaron the high priest, was dispatched to dispose of the *fire* (i.e., the burning coals) as well as the censers left by the men of Korah's congregation. Why Eleazar should be the one chosen to do this is not entirely clear. The usual explanation is that it was not appropriate for the high priest to expose himself to the uncleanness of the corpses of the two hundred fifty leaders (Lev. 21:10–15; 22:1–4), but, since he is sent "to stand between the dead and the living" later on (17:13 [Eng. 16:48]), a broader principle must be in mind. Perhaps not only the unclean nature of the corpses, but the unclean nature of their act should be taken into account.

In any case, Eleazar was to take the censers *from the midst of the burning (mibbēn haśśᵉrēp̱â).* The usual meaning of *haśśᵉrēp̱â* is "that which is burning." If the remains of the corpses had been meant, one might have expected *haśśᵉrup̱îm* ("those who had been burned"), as in v. 4 (Eng. 16:39).[11] Eleazar is sent into the midst of the still burning material. He is to *scatter the fire at a distance,* i.e., far and wide, not only so that it would be outside the camp and less concentrated, but also so that it might not be put to some common purpose, since both coals and censers had been offered before Yahweh and hence were holy (i.e., belonged to him).[12]

3 (16:38) The syntax of this verse is difficult, and many scholars conclude that some textual corruption has occurred, although MT is just intelligible. *these men who sinned mortally (haḥaṭṭā'îm hā'ēlleh*

11. Cf. Amos 4:11; Isa. 9:4 (Eng. 5) for similar uses of *śᵉrēp̱â.*

12. An extremely helpful discussion of holiness is found in Wenham, *Leviticus,* pp. 18–25.

b^e napšōṯām, lit., "these men who sinned by their lives"). With the word *nep̱eš* ("life"), the preposition *b^e*- also indicates the cost in 2 Sam. 23:17 and 1 K. 2:23; viz., the cost of a life *(nep̱eš).* The whole phrase means "those men who sinned mortally," i.e., their sins caused their deaths.

The word *riqquʿê, beaten,* occurs only here, though related words make clear that it is fundamentally a metal-working term and refers to something beaten into very thin sheets.[13] The word *plates (paḥîm)* occurs only here and in Exod. 39:3 (the description of the high priest's ephod).[14] The word *plating (ṣippûy)* occurs also in Exod. 38:17, 19 (describing the silver-plated capitals of the pillars in the tabernacle), and in Isa. 30:22 (describing idols).

These thin metal plates are *for the altar (lammizbēaḥ),* though it is not clear which altar is intended. The alternatives are, of course, the altar of burnt offerings (Exod. 27:1–8; 38:1–7) and the altar of incense (30:1–10; 37:25–28). Both were made of acacia wood, but while the former was plated with bronze (27:2; 38:2), the latter was plated with gold (30:3; 37:26). Most scholars have concluded that, since bronze plating for the golden altar of incense would be inappropriate, the altar spoken of here must be the altar of burnt offerings. According to Exod. 27:2; 38:2, this altar was plated with bronze at its manufacture.[15] Thus some commentators consider this passage simply a parallel tradition of how the altar became covered in bronze. Why such a fragmentary tradition should be transmitted at this point is not clear, but it is taken to be more evidence for the composite nature of the Priestly narrative.[16] Others have seen this as a re-covering of the altar.[17] Another option (though with little support

13. It is well known that the "firmament" in Gen. 1:6–8 is called *rāqîaʿ*, "that which is beaten out," and pictured as a thin covering.

14. RSV "gold *leaf,*" the verbal cognate of *riqquaʿ (rāqaʿ),* occurs in Exod. 39:3 as well.

15. LXX inserts a note at 38:22 (= MT 38:2) that attempts to reconcile these two accounts by stating that Bezalel made the original plating for the altar of burnt offerings from the censers used by Korah and his congregation. The problem is how a wooden altar would function without a covering from the time of Exod. 38 until that of Num. 16. The LXX translator makes no attempt to deal with this anachronism, which causes more problems than it solves. Nonetheless, it shows that in ancient times there was an awareness of supposed difficulties between texts and that authors, editors, or translators were not always content simply to transmit them.

16. So, e.g., Dillmann, p. 96; Gray, p. 208; McNeile, p. 91; Snaith, p. 161; Budd, pp. 193–95.

17. So, e.g., Heinisch, p. 68; Noordtzij, p. 154; Wenham, p. 138; Greenstone, p. 179.

among scholars) is to see this plating as designed for the altar of incense.[18] Anyone who saw bronze covering on a golden altar would mark it as unusual, which would bring to mind that no outsider was to *offer incense* before Yahweh (the crime of Korah and his congregation, v. 5 [Eng. 16:40]). If one were forced to choose, the second option seems to have the fewest difficulties.

The clause *for they* (i.e., the two hundred fifty men) *had offered them* (i.e., the censers) *before Yahweh and they have become holy* explains what is meant by the last two words of v. 2 (Eng. 16:37), *for they have become holy.*

The purpose of the covering was as a *sign ('ôṯ)* for the Israelites.[19] Unlike the "signs" in Num. 14, which were positive indicators of God's goodness and salvation (e.g., the Exodus events), this one is negative — a warning of what one ought not to do. It will be a *reminder* (*zikkārôn,* v. 5 [Eng. 16:40]), a visual aid, of what not to do and who not to imitate, viz., Korah and his congregation.

5 (16:40) This verse summarizes the lesson the author wishes the reader to deduce from the whole Korah narrative that precedes. It is simply that no *outsider ('îš zār),* i.e., one who does not belong to Aaron's offspring,[20] is to *encroach* (*lō'* plus *qrb*) on the prerogatives of the Aaronites to make incense before Yahweh, i.e., to engage in priestly duty on behalf of the people. With the negative *lō'* the verb *qāraḇ* does not mean "to draw near" in this literature, but rather "to intrude" on other people's prerogatives, in this case the Aaronic priesthood's.[21]

The phrase *to become like Korah and his congregation* carries with it the thought of sharing his fate.[22]

6–15 (16:41–50) Neither awe nor terror brought about a change in the Israelites' behavior. On the day after the judgment on Korah, Dathan, and Abiram, apparently after the gathering of the censers, *the whole congregation of the children of Israel* once again *murmured* against Moses and Aaron. This same phrase described the murmurers in 14:7; it indicates the whole lay leadership of Israel. Here again, as consistently in

18. Although de Vaulx, p. 197, refers these verses to Exod. 27:2; 38:2, which deal with the altar of burnt offerings, he says that these beaten plates were used as a covering for the altar of incense *(l'autel des parfums).*

19. For *'ôṯ,* "sign," see the commentary above on 14:11.

20. See Milgrom, *Studies in Levitical Terminology,* I:5 and n. 6.

21. For the definitive study of this important idiom see ibid., pp. 5–59, esp. 16–21, 33–43.

22. Keil, p. 111.

the spy narrative in chs. 13–14, the point is made that the whole congregation was involved.[23] (On the verb *lûn,* "to murmur," see the commentary above on 14:2–3.)

Their complaint against their leaders is that *you have killed Yahweh's people ('attem h^{a}mittem 'et̲-'am YHWH).* The congregation blamed Moses and Aaron for these deaths, forgetting that it had been Yahweh himself who punished the rebels, and that their very survival as a congregation was due to the intercession of the leaders (16:4, 22). That they called Korah's congregation by the title *Yahweh's people* shows how completely they misunderstood what it meant to be his people.[24]

7 (16:42) As the people gathered against their leaders, they turned to look at the tent of meeting. *the cloud* had descended to cover it, and *the glory of Yahweh* had appeared. This is the last mention of the cloud in the narrative. The glory of Yahweh was intermittent in the tent. When it appeared it did show that God's presence was directly in the midst of Israel.[25]

8–10 (16:43–45) After Moses and Aaron came *to the front of ('el-p^{e}nê)* the tent, Yahweh spoke. He told Moses and Aaron to *get up from the midst of this congregation that I might devour them in a moment.* With the exception of the verb, the wording is the same as in 16:21. For the third time (16:4, 22), Moses and Aaron *fell on their faces.* Once again, we are not told why, but it has been argued above that intercession was at least one motive. This time when Moses and Aaron arise the judgment of God is already on the people (cf. 16:4, 22).

11 (16:46) This verse is both the center and the turning point of the passage. Aaron is told to take *the* (i.e., a particular) *censer* and to *make atonement* on behalf of the Israelites. The censer that Aaron took may have been the one mentioned in Lev. 16:12 in the ritual of Yom Kippur. Aaron

23. Different terms are used to identify those who complain against their leadership: *hā'ām (hazzeh),* "the (or this) people," 11:1; 14:1, 11; *hā'sapsup,* "the rabble," 11:4; *kol-hā'ēd̲â,* "all the congregation," 14:1, 10; *kol-q^{e}hal '^{a}d̲āt̲ b^{e}nê yiśrā'ēl,* "all the assembly of the congregation of the children of Israel," 14:5; *kol-'^{a}d̲at̲ b^{e}nê yiśrā'ēl,* "all the congregation of the people of Israel," 14:7. Of course, individuals also complain (e.g., Aaron and Miriam, ch. 12; Korah, Dathan, and Abiram, ch. 16).

24. Moses himself uses these words to describe Israel in 11:29. The expression occurs also in Judg. 5:11; 1 Sam. 2:24; 2 Sam. 1:12; 6:21; 2 K. 9:6; Ezek. 36:20; Zeph. 2:10.

25. For more on the cloud, see the commentary above on 9:15–23. For more on the glory of Yahweh, see the commentary above on 14:10.

was to prepare this censer in the normal way with coals from the altar (they would be holy) and incense (cf. 16:6–7, 17), and to avert the disaster by this means. It is unclear why this means was chosen, since it is unusual to *make atonement* without a blood sacrifice (but cf. Exod. 30:15). One explanation is that Yahweh gave these instructions to Moses and Aaron during prayer. Since the original offense had been given by an illegitimate incense offering (16:17), the remedy would be a legitimate offering of the same kind. Since no rationale is mentioned in the text itself, this remains a conjecture.

I previously suggested that the verb "to make atonement" *(kipper)* must have a meaning that varies with the particular sacrifice offered (see the commentary above on 8:19). Here the term clearly has the general meaning of averting the wrath of Yahweh, which has already begun its lethal work in the form of a plague. One must, of course, explain the term in the light of its individual contexts, and any searching for a "primary meaning" may be doomed to fail.[26]

the wrath has gone out from before Yahweh (yāṣā' haqqeṣep millipnê YHWH). It is as if God's wrath has an independent existence here in this vivid figure of speech. The kind of *plague* is not specified.[27] Two words, both drawn from the Hebrew root *ngp,* "smite," are used. The first, "the smiting" *(hannegep),* occurs in vv. 11–12 (Eng. 16:46–47), while the second, "the blow" *(hammaggēpâ),* is used (probably for literary variety) in vv. 13–15 (Eng. 16:48–50).

12–13 (16:47–48) Aaron successfully carries out Moses' instructions. *He stood between the dead and the living.* Aaron stationed himself on the leading edge of the advancing plague (between those who were living and those who were dying) and limited its destruction to one section of the camp. It is interesting to note that Aaron had to violate the statute concerning the high priest's contact with the dead in order to carry out this remedy, i.e., the offering carried with it a cost as far as for Aaron's ceremonial cleanness was concerned. The text does not say what part of the camp was destroyed, but 14,700 died before the plague could be *checked ('āṣar).* The verb, here in the passive voice (Niphal), means basically "to be held in" or "to be contained."[28]

26. See Budd, p. 196.

27. On "plague," see the commentary above on 14:37. On the parallel between wrath and plague, see the commentary above on 16:22. Other passages in which God's wrath is averted by sacrifice seem to be Gen. 8:21; Exod. 29:25; 1 Sam. 26:19. On the first of these see G. Wenham, *Genesis 1–15,* WBC (Waco: Word, 1987), pp. 189–91.

28. The Niphal of this verb is not too common. Most times it is used with

14 (16:49) *fourteen thousand seven hundred.* This number is in addition to the two hundred fifty-three (plus?) deaths associated with the narratives in 16:1–35.[29] The number is just under 2.5% of the totals listed in 1:46 and 3:39.

15 (16:50) After the plague was checked Aaron came back to Moses at the door of the tent of meeting.

3. AARON'S BUDDING ROD (17:16–28 [ENG. 1–13])

16 (1) *And Yahweh spoke to Moses, saying,*

17 (2) *"Speak to the children of Israel and take from them rods, one rod for each father's house, from all their leaders as regards their fathers' houses, twelve rods; you will write each man's name*[1] *upon his rod.*

18 (3) *Write the name of Aaron on Levi's rod, since there shall be one rod for the head of their fathers' house.*

19 (4) *And you will deposit them in the tent of meeting in front of the testimony where I meet*[2] *you by appointment.*

20 (5) *And it will be that the man whom I shall choose,*[3] *his rod will sprout. And I will stop the murmurings of the children of Israel that they are murmuring against you."*

21 (6) *And Moses spoke to the children of Israel, and all their leaders gave him a rod—one for each leader—as regards their fathers' houses, twelve rods; and Aaron's rod was in the midst of the rods.*

22 (7) *And Moses deposited the rods before Yahweh in the tent of the testimony.*

23 (8) *And it happened, on the next day, that Moses went into the tent of the testimony and Aaron's rod of the tribe of Levi had indeed sprouted, and put forth growth, and grown blossoms, and it bore ripened*[4] *almonds.*

---

reference to averting a plague: Num. 17:13, 15 (Eng. 16:48, 50); 25:8 (cf. Ps. 106:30); 2 Sam. 24:21 (= 1 Chr. 21:22), 25. In 1 K. 8:35 (= 2 Chr. 6:26), it refers to the sky being shut up for lack of rain. 1 Sam. 21:8 (Eng. 7) uses the term for "being in detention."

29. See the excursus on large numbers above.

1. The word *'îš,* "man," here is used with the idea of "each"; see GKC, §139c.

2. Driver (*Tenses,* § 33a) discusses *'iwwā'ēḏ* as a fact of definite occurrence within a longer or shorter period; in this case a generic or repeated custom.

3. On the syntax of the first clause of the verse *(wᵉhāyâ hā'îš 'ᵃšer 'eḇḥar-bô maṭṭēhû yiprāḥ),* see Driver, *Tenses,* § 121 Obs.

4. Heb. *gāmal;* see BDB, p. 168a.

24 (9) *And Moses brought out all the rods from before Yahweh to all the children of Israel; and they looked, and each one took his rod.*

25 (10) *And Yahweh said to Moses, "Return Aaron's rod to before the testimony to keep as a sign for the children*[5] *of rebellion so that you might put an end to their murmurings against me, that they might not die."*

26 (11) *And Moses did so; as Yahweh had commanded him, so he did.*

27 (12) *And the children of Israel said to Moses, saying, "Behold, we die! We perish! All of us perish!*[6]

28 (13) *Anyone who draws near to the tabernacle of Yahweh —anyone who draws near —must die! Are*[7] *we to die out*[8] *entirely?"*[9]

This third account in the series on the justification of the Aaronic priesthood narrates the story of the event that finally makes an impression on the people. It should not be separated from the other two stories in the series, because the final effect (vv. 27–28 [Eng. 12–13]) is a reaction not only to this miracle but also to the other dramatic interventions of God since 16:1. Wenham aptly points out that while the structure of ch. 16:1–17:15 (Eng. 16:1–50) begins each narrative with a reaction of the people and proceeds through a divine test, this one begins with the divine test and ends up with the reaction from the people.[10] This difference in structure also reveals another difference in the present passage. The point of 16:1–35 was the superiority of the Aaronic priesthood over the other Levites. Although that point is alluded to in 17:18 (Eng. 3), the main point here is the necessity for a divinely appointed priesthood to intercede for the laity. This story, then, balances out the division between the Aaronic priests and other Levites created by 16:1–35, by exalting the Levites (esp. the family of Aaron) above the lay tribes in the matter of service of God. This brings us back to the perspective of chs. 1–4.

5. The word *bēn,* "son," here indicates the class to which someone belongs ("rebels"); see GKC, § 128v.

6. The verbs are in the perfect tense to express a fact that is undoubtedly thought to be imminent and thus already accomplished; hence they are called "perfects of certainty"; see GKC, § 106n (cf. Williams, *Syntax,* § 165; Davidson, *Syntax,* § 41a).

7. The particle *hᵃ'im* is a compound of the interrogatives *hᵃ* and the conditional *'im.* With the word *tamnû,* it means "are we finished dying," i.e., "to die out entirely"; see Davidson, *Syntax,* § 126 Rem. 2 (cf. GKC, § 150g n. 1).

8. See GKC, §§ 67e, dd, for the formation of *tamnû.*

9. Again, note the perfects of certainty as in v. 27 (Eng. 12); cf. also Driver, *Tenses,* § 19 (2).

10. Wenham, p. 139.

16–17 (1–2) Again, Yahweh speaks to Moses his servant. *rod (maṭṭeh)* can mean either "rod, stick," or "tribe."[11] Here the play on the two meanings of the word is important in the story. Even a dead, dry stick can be made to blossom by the blessing of Yahweh. Even so, even the most inauspicious tribe can be made to blossom, flourish, and lead by the election and blessing of Yahweh.[12] The text itself does not say whether these rods are official staffs of office (as in Gen. 49:10; Num. 21:18) or everyday walking sticks (as in Gen. 38:15, 25; 1 Sam. 14:43).[13] Most scholars assume the former, and there is nothing unlikely about this conclusion.

one rod for each father's house (maṭṭeh lᵉḇêṯ 'āḇ). The term *father's house* here is used in a way different from, e.g., 1:2, where it indicates a subgroup of a clan *(mišpᵉḥâ).*[14] Since there are only *twelve rods* here, *father's house* must be a synonym at this point for the whole tribe. The probable reason for this unusual usage is the double meaning for the word *tribe (maṭṭeh),* which might have led to confusion in the narrative had it been used here.[15]

The *leaders (nᵉśî'îm),* then, may be the same people named in 1:5–15; 2:3–31; 7:12–83; 10:14–27, or at least their successors in office.[16] On each rod Moses is to inscribe the name of the tribal leader.

18 (3) The name of Aaron is to be inscribed on Levi's rod. This verse is meant to show that Aaron was God's choice to be the leader of the Levites. This is an interesting choice since Aaron is a descendant of Levi's *second* son, Kohath, and because Moses himself was also a Levite. Thus the leadership in view here is only the priesthood; it is not a challenge to Moses' own role as leader.

The question that this verse (and v. 21 [Eng. 6]) raises is whether

11. The word occurs over 250 times in the OT. The meaning "rod" is found, e.g., in Gen. 38:18, 25; Exod. 4:2, 4, 17; 7:15, 17, 20; 9:23; 10:13; 17:5 (Moses' staff); 7:9–10, 12, 19; 8:1, 12–13 (Aaron's staff). The meaning "tribe" is found, e.g., in Num 1:4 (and 89 times in Numbers); Josh. 7:1 (plus 56 times in Joshua). The synonym *šēḇeṭ* carries a similar double meaning.

12. Budd, p. 196; Snaith, p. 162.

13. For the former see, e.g., Dillmann, p. 97; Holzinger, p. 69; McNeile, p. 93; Heinisch, p. 69; Noordtzij, p. 157; Sturdy, p. 124; Budd, p. 197. For the latter see Gray, p. 215; and perhaps Noth, p. 131 ("bare branches").

14. See the commentary above on 1:2.

15. Snaith, p. 162.

16. On *nāśî'* see the commentary above on 1:16. The leaders listed in 13:4–16 were killed by plague (14:37), except for Joshua and Caleb (14:38). There is also a partial list of leaders in 34:19–29.

Aaron's rod was one of the twelve or an additional, thirteenth rod. The text does not say in so many words, and some scholars have simply assumed that the whole number is twelve, and that the half-tribes of Manasseh and Ephraim are counted as one tribe of Joseph (as in Deut. 27:12).[17] The consistent practice of Numbers, however, is to count twelve secular tribes in addition to Levi,[18] and unless one wishes to suppose a standpoint at odds with the rest of the book, one should probably see Levi as a thirteenth tribe (and rod) here. In this case v. 21b (Eng. 6b) makes better sense when it reports that Aaron's rod was "in the midst of their [i.e., the other twelve tribes'] rods" *(bᵉṯôḵ maṭṭôṯām)*.

since there shall be one rod for the head of their fathers' house (kî maṭṭeh 'eḥāḏ lᵉrō'š bêṯ 'ᵃḇôṯām). To what does the pronoun *their* refer? Virtually all modern translations have concluded that the idiom (lit., "for the head of their fathers' house") should be translated with the distributive "each" (e.g., RSV "for the head of each father's house").[19] It is certainly possible to read this construction in this way.[20] The clause may then be taken as a summary of v. 17 (Eng. 2), referring to the whole group of twelve (or thirteen) tribes. This kind of summary statement or inclusion is not unknown elsewhere in Numbers, but, after one small clause (v. 18a [Eng. 3a]), hardly seems necessary. V. 6b (Eng. 21b) would also become redundant.

The other alternative is to take *their* as referring to the singular collective noun Levi (as in 18:23).[21] *their fathers' house,* then, is a collective reference to the clans and families that make up the whole tribe of Levi. In this case the meaning of vv. 17–18 (Eng. 2–3) is "take one rod from each of the leaders of the twelve tribes, and write on them the names of these leaders. Take another rod from the Levites and write Aaron's name on it, since there must be one rod for each leader of a tribe (including Levi)."

17. Among those scholars who see only twelve tribes here are Keil, p. 113, and Noth, p. 131. Those who see thirteen include Dillmann, p. 97; Holzinger, p. 70; Gray, pp. 214–15; McNeile, p. 93; Heinisch, p. 69; Noordtzij, p. 157; and Wenham, p. 140.

18. In spite of the different orders of tribes, the counting of Levi in addition to the twelve other tribes is seen in every tribal list in the book: 1:5–15, 20–46; 2:3–31; 7:12–83; 10:14–27; 13:4–16; 26:5–62. This viewpoint seems to be unique to Numbers.

19. So also, RV, NIV, NEB, NASB, NJPS, NKJV, GNB, etc.

20. See GKC, §§ 123c, 134q; contra Gray, p. 215.

21. See GKC, § 145g; cf. Gray, p. 215, for further material.

19–20 (4–5) The *testimony (hāʿēḏûṯ)* is the Decalogue, written on the two stone tablets, which were kept in the ark.[22] The phrase *in front of the testimony (lip̱nê hāʿēḏûṯ)* is a synonym for "before the ark."[23]

I meet you by appointment. See the note on the translation above.

the man whom I shall choose (hāʾîš ʾᵃšer ʾeḇḥar-bô). Cf. 16:5. This test, like that of Korah and his congregation, is designed to show which leader Yahweh chooses to minister as priest before him. Unlike the test of Korah, this one is not precipitated by an overt challenge from the Israelites.

his rod will sprout (maṭṭēhû yip̱rāḥ). The verb *pāraḥ* occurs 23 times in the OT, most commonly with the general meaning of "to sprout, bud, grow," as here. The whole growth process (expanded by v. 23 [Eng. 8] below) is probably encompassed in this word.[24]

By this test Yahweh says, *I will stop the murmurings of the children of Israel that they are murmuring against you (wahᵃšikkōṯî mēʿālay ʾeṯ-tᵉlunnôṯ bᵉnê yiśrāʾēl ʾᵃšer hēm mallînim ʿᵃlêḵem).* On *murmurings* see the commentary above on 14:2–3. The verb *stop (šāḵaḵ)* is found only here in the Hiphil, but is used in the Qal for receding waters (Gen. 8:1) and lessening wrath (Esth. 2:1; 7:10).[25] The Hiphil here seems truly causative — Yahweh will cause the roaring breakers of dissent against Moses and Aaron (note the pl. suffix on *ʿᵃlêḵem*) to subside once and for all by showing in a dramatic way that Aaron is his chosen intermediary. The original act has *Yahweh* causing the murmuring against *the leaders* to stop. In the remembrance of the act (v. 25 [Eng. 10]), it is *Moses* who is to stop the people's murmuring against *God.* Murmuring against God's chosen leaders is murmuring against him.

21–24 (6–9) Moses carries out God's instructions. As argued

22. The tablets are called "the testimony" in Exod. 25:16, 21; 40:20, and by the longer title "tablets of the testimony" *(luḥōṯ hāʿēḏut)* in 31:18; 32:15; 34:29. The ark is called the "ark of the testimony" *(ʾᵃrôn hāʿēḏut)* in Exod. 25:22; 26:33–34; 30:6, 26; 39:35; 40:3, 5, 21; Num. 4:5; 7:89; Josh. 4:16; cf. Exod. 31:7 *(hāʾārōn lāʿēḏuṯ).*

23. The phrase is found in Exod. 16:34; 30:36 and in Num. 17:25 (Eng. 10) with this meaning. Also see the parallel phrase "before Yahweh" in Exod. 16:33 and in Num. 17:22, 24 (Eng. 7, 9), where that phrase means "before the ark." Keil, p. 113; Dillmann, p. 97; Holzinger, p. 70; Gray, p. 216; and Budd, p. 197, all of whom make this point.

24. See Gray, pp. 216–17.

25. The only other occurrence of *šāḵaḵ* is Jer. 5:26, which is problematic. Commentaries should be consulted, e.g., R. P. Carroll, *Jeremiah: A Commentary,* OTL (Philadelphia: Westminster, 1986), p. 188.

above, the clause *and Aaron's rod was in the midst of the rods* (*ûmaṭṭēh 'ahᵃrōn bᵉṯôḵ maṭṭôṯām,* v. 21 [Eng. 6]) makes more sense if thirteen rods are in view here. The Vulg. attempts to clarify matters by rendering "there were twelve rods besides Aaron's rod";[26] although paraphrastic, it gives the probable meaning.

Moses places the rods *before Yahweh,* i.e., he follows the instructions of v. 19 (Eng. 4), placing them in front of the ark.

23 (8) This verse is the turning point of the story. It takes place *on the next day (mimmāḥᵒrāṯ),*[27] when Moses went to the tent of the testimony and found that *Aaron's rod of the tribe of Levi had indeed sprouted, and put forth growth, and grown blossoms, and it bore ripened almonds (wᵉhinnēh pāraḥ maṭṭēh-'ahᵃrōn lᵉḇêṯ lēwî wayyōṣē' peraḥ wayyāṣēṣ ṣîṣ wayyigmōl šᵉqēḏîm).* The process of growth is described fully and rhetorically. The verb *pāraḥ* ("to sprout") has already been discussed. The Hebrew particle *hinnēh* is usually translated as "behold." The particle "emphasizes the immediacy, the here-and-nowness, of the situation."[28] The word *indeed* is meant to reflect this flavor. The cognate noun *peraḥ,* "growth," occurs in the second clause.[29] As with the verb, the noun is a general word for growth, especially as seen in the bud or immature blossom. The third clause contains a cognate noun and verb, *wayyāṣēṣ ṣîṣ* (lit., "and it flowered flowers").[30] Most of the biblical

26. *Fuerunt virgae duodecim absque virga Aaron.*

27. For the term *māḥār,* "tomorrow," see above on 16:16.

28. T. O. Lambdin, *Introduction to Biblical Hebrew* (New York: Scribner, 1971), p. 168. See also the discussion in Waltke and O'Connor, *Biblical Hebrew Syntax,* §40.2.1a–b.

29. The noun occurs 16 times. Twelve times it describes bud-shaped ornaments on the golden lampstand in the tabernacle or temple (Exod. 25:31, 33 [twice], 34; 37:17, 19 [twice], 20; Num. 8:4; 1 K. 7:49 [= 2 Chr. 4:5]) or the so-called molten sea in the temple (1 K. 7:26). Isa. 5:24 has a poetic contrast between the root and the *peraḥ* (RSV "blossom"), and 18:5 speaks of the growth of a vine (parallel to "flower" *[niṣṣâ]*). In Nah. 1:4 the word is symbolic of the fertility of Lebanon.

30. The noun occurs 14 times. Three occurrences describe flower-shaped ornaments on Aaron's headdress (Exod. 28:36; 39:40; Lev. 8:9), and four describe such ornaments in Solomon's temple (1 K. 6:18, 29, 32, 35). The remaining seven occurrences are in poetry: Isa. 28:1 describes a "fading flower" (*ṣîṣ nōḇēl,* probably v. 4 as well; see, e.g., J. Oswalt, *The Book of Isaiah Chapters 1–39,* NICOT [Grand Rapids: Eerdmans, 1986], pp. 501–8; J. D. W. Watts, *Isaiah 1–33,* WBC [Waco: Word, 1985], pp. 358–60), as does 40:6–8 (and Ps. 103:15 on which Isa. 40 is probably based). Job 14:2 speaks of the transitory nature of life as a flower that withers *(kᵉṣîṣ yāṣā' wayyimmāl).*

passages that use the noun stress the transitory nature of the flower, thus making one think of the full blossom, which, although lovely, is short-lived.

The last clause brings the description to its natural conclusion with the discussion of ripe fruit. Why almonds should be chosen is unknown. The almond comes to maturity early, hence its name "the watcher" (cf. Jer. 1:11–12).[31] Its fruit was highly prized (Gen. 43:11). Wenham also points to the whiteness of its flower, symbolizing purity and holiness. The qualities of Aaron and the Levites (for his tribe is named here in a way which is, strictly speaking, redundant) were not unlike those of the almond, watchful over God's word, holy, and pure (although not without fault; cf. ch. 12), and valuable to Israel.[32]

Thus the text describes the stages in the growth of the plant. It is not clear whether it means that all these stages were present simultaneously on the rod or only that the rod went through these stages, but the former is not impossible.

24 (9) After Moses discovered that Aaron's rod had grown overnight, he brought all the other rods out from their place in the tent and each leader looked at his rod. It must have been obvious that only Aaron's had sprouted, although this is not said in the text.[33] The divine miracle had been witnessed by the chosen leaders of Israel.

25 (10) Next, Moses is instructed to return Aaron's rod to the place before *the testimony* (i.e., the ark) where he had found it. It was to be kept as a *sign ('ôt)*[34] in order to stop the murmuring of rebellious Israelites (in present and future times), so that they might not die by God's hand, as those who had rebelled against him in chs. 11, 14, and 16 already had.

31. There is a play on words between "almond" *(šāqēḏ)* and the verbal form "watching" *(šōqēḏ)*.

32. Wenham, p. 140.

33. Many scholars (e.g., Dillmann, p. 98; Gray, p. 217) have listed legendary parallels to the present account. As Snaith (pp. 161–62) points out, however, many of these stories are similar only on the surface; great and important differences exist. One must also guard against the encroachment of a so-called modern worldview that searches for natural explanations for every supernatural event in the Bible. Cf. Noth, p. 131: "It is difficult to imagine that Aaron's rod ever really existed, even symbolically"; also, Sturdy, p. 124: "More probably it [i.e., Aaron's rod] never in fact existed." Such a worldview, which cannot accept the irruption of God into the history of his world, scarcely fits the witness of Scripture or an objective description of the world.

34. On *sign* see the commentary above on 14:11.

26 (11) The account ends with an obedience formula. Moses obeyed Yahweh to the letter.[35]

27–28 (12–13) These verses should be seen as a conclusion not only to the present narrative but also to the whole passage beginning at 16:1. They raise the issue to which ch. 18 offers the divine solution. Because of the deaths of Korah and his congregation, Dathan, Abiram, and their families (16:1–35), along with 14,700 other Israelites (17:1–15 [Eng. 16:41–50]), the people burst out in panic. The jerky, interjectional style of the verses supports this: *Behold, we die! We perish! All of us perish! (hēn gāwaʿnû 'āḇaḏnû kullānû 'āḇaḏnû)*. The terms *gāwaʿ* and *'āḇaḏ* are synonyms for dying.[36]

28 (13) *Anyone who draws near to the tabernacle of Yahweh — anyone who draws near! — must die! (kōl haqqārēḇ haqqārēḇ 'el-miškan YHWH yāmûṯ)* — As has been pointed out at 1:51; 31:10, 38 above, the noun *qārēḇ* in these contexts means "an encroacher (on the tabernacle)," i.e., one who has no right to be where he or she is. In the present verse, the same word is put into the mouths of Israelites who are panicked at the outbreak of a plague caused by God. That the present verse is not simply a restatement of the passages in 1:51; 3:10, 38 is seen, first of all, in the double occurrence of the noun *(haqqārēḇ haqqārēḇ)*. It is not the encroacher these Israelites have in mind, but the one who draws near, and, what is more, anyone *(kōl)* who draws near. This means that, in their panic, the Israelites hold that anyone who comes to the tabernacle is in danger of death.[37] The verb *must die* (*yāmûṯ,* Qal imperfect) is the most common word in the OT for dying, found over 730 times. Milgrom has shown that this verb in the Qal usually means "to die by divine agency" (as above in v. 27 [Eng. 12]), while in the Hophal it means "to die by human agency" with the apparent exception of this passage and 18:22.[38] The reality is, however, that, since the Israelites have been experiencing death by divine agency in the immediate context, their fear is that Yahweh will now not

35. See similar obedience formulae already in the book: 1:19, 44, 54; 2:33; 3:42, 51; 4:37, 41, 45, 49; 5:4; 8:4, 20, 22; 9:23; 11:24; 13:3; 15:36; 17:5 (Eng. 16:40); cf. Exod. 7:6; 40:16; Lev. 8:4. The formulae will also occur again, e.g., in Num. 20:27; 27:22.

36. Heb. *gāwaʿ* occurs 24 times in the OT; see H. Ringgren, *TDOT,* II:438–39. Heb. *'aḇaḏ* occurs over 180 times in the OT; see B. Otzen, *TDOT,* I:19–23.

37. See above on 1:51; 3:10, 38; Milgrom, *Studies in Levitical Terminology,* I:5–59; *JPST,* pp. 342–43.

38. See Milgrom, *Studies in Levitical Terminology,* I:5–8.

limit punishment to those who encroach on the tent of meeting, but will send it to anyone who simply comes near. This usage of the verb is further evidence that this verse is the desperate outcry of a terrified people. If God is going to kill anyone who comes near to the tent, then the sanest conclusion would be to separate oneself from the tent altogether.[39] This outcry, leading as it could to the separation of Israel and Yahweh, gives rise to the new legislation that follows in ch. 18.

D. FURTHER CULTIC LEGISLATION (18:1–19:22)

1. REDEFINED ROLE FOR PRIESTS AND LEVITES (18:1–32)

Many commentators see ch. 18 (esp. vv. 1–7) as a repetition of material already given in 1:50–53; 3:10–15, 38, and imperfectly joined to its context.[1] It is possible, however, to see the chapter as containing a striking innovation in the role of priest and Levite in Israel, which, although built on the earlier foundation of chs. 1, 3–4, is anything but unnecessary repetition. Ch. 18 is given in response to the Israelites' outcry in 17:27–28 (Eng. 12–13) that any and all who came near to the sanctuary are doomed, as in the plague in which 14,700 Israelites were killed by the mighty wrath of God (17:6–15 [Eng. 16:41–50]). God would kill not only sinners such as Korah — and even his family — but God might slay the entire nation. The gracious response of God was to remind them of the hierarchy of responsibility for encroachment on the sanctuary and to modify the roles of priests and Levites so that only they, not the Israelite community at large, would henceforth suffer death at the hand of Yahweh for encroachment (18:1, 3, 7, and esp. 22–23). The priests and the Kohathites together will now be responsible for trespass by the lay Israelites (v. 1a), the priests alone for encroachment by other priests (v. 1b), and the priests and all the Levites for that of Levites (v. 3).[2]

39. Milgrom translates, "all who merely seek access to the Lord's tabernacle must die." See *Studies in Levitical Terminology,* I:17–22, 31–32.

1. For the idea of repetition see, e.g., Gray, p. 218; McNeile, p. 94; Binns, p. 120; Noordtzij, p. 160; Sturdy, p. 126; cf. Dillmann, pp. 98–100. On context see Noth, p. 134; but cf. Budd, p. 202.

2. See the commentary below. The treatment here is heavily indebted to Milgrom, *Studies in Levitical Terminology*, I:5–59, esp. 16–36.

a. Responsibilities of Priests and Levites (18:1–7)

1 *So Yahweh said to Aaron, "You and your sons and your father's house with you shall bear the guilt for the holy objects,*[1] *and you and your sons with you shall bear the guilt for your priesthood.*
2 *But also you shall associate with your brothers, the tribe of Levi, your father's tribe,*[2] *that they might be joined with you and assist you, you and your sons with you, before the tent of the testimony.*[3]
3 *And they will stand guard for you, that is, guard duty on the tent in general, but they will have no access to the sacred vessels, or to the altar, so that neither they nor you might die.*
4 *And they will be joined with you and will stand guard over the tent of meeting — indeed, all the work of the tent*[4] *— but no outsider shall be associated with*[5] *you.*
5 *But you will stand guard over the holy objects and over the altar that wrath may not again come upon the children of Israel.*
6 *And I*[6] *have taken your brothers the Levites from the midst of the children of Israel, a gift to you, given to Yahweh, to do the work of the tent of meeting.*
7 *But you and your sons with you will keep your priesthood for all*

1. On *hammiqdāš* meaning "holy objects" rather than the "sanctuary" as in, e.g., RSV, cf. Milgrom, *Studies in Levitical Terminology,* I:23–24 n. 78.

2. Two words are used for "tribe" here: "the tribe *[maṭṭeh]* of Levi," your father's tribe *[šēḇeṭ].*" The use of two different words is not evidence of a composite text (contra Gray, pp. 219–20), but of simple literary variety. Further evidence is found here for the point made below on v. 1, that "father's house" meant the Kohathites, in that "father's tribe" here is obviously identified with Levi. Unless one is prepared to argue that v. 2 repeats v. 1 (for what reason?), then the terms are intended to contrast.

3. Heb. *lip̄nê 'ōhel hā'ēḏûṯ* may indicate "at the door of the tent of testimony." The Levites were not allowed to encroach on the sanctuary, but along with laymen they could go to the area known as "the entrance of the tent of meeting" *(peṯaḥ 'ōhel mô'ēḏ)* to perform rituals (e.g., Lev. 1:3–6; Num. 16:18) and to observe (8:3–4; etc.).

4. It is possible that the *l* on *lᵉḵol* here is not to be taken as a preposition with the meaning "with regard to," but as a conjunctive particle with an inclusive force, "including" (see Milgrom, *Studies in Levitical Terminology,* I:64 n. 237; p. 72 n. 262; p. 77 n. 279; P. Joüon, *Grammaire de l'hébreu biblique,* rev. ed. (Rome: Pontifical Biblical Institute, 1965), § 125l [1–2]). Alternately, it may be taken as an emphatic particle related to Arab. *lu,* "surely," or Assyr. *lû.* With *kōl* it means "in short," according to GKC, § 143e (cf. Williams, *Syntax,* § 283).

5. See Milgrom, *Studies in Levitical Terminology,* I:33–34.

6. The construction *wa'ᵃnî hinnēh* emphasizes both Yahweh and the reality of the subject. See T. O. Lambdin, *Introduction to Biblical Hebrew* (New York: Scribner's, 1971), pp. 168–70.

that concerns the altar and for that within the veil, you will also do work—I will give your priesthood valuable work. But the unauthorized person who encroaches will be put to death."[7]

1 The instruction comes from Yahweh to *Aaron*. This is unusual (only here and Lev. 10:8); elsewhere the word comes either to Moses and Aaron (e.g., Num. 2:1; 4:1; 16:20; 19:1; cf. 12:4), to Moses alone (e.g., 1:1; 3:5, 11, 14, 40, 44; 4:21; 5:1, 5, 11; 6:1; 9:1, 9), or for Aaron through Moses (18:25; Lev. 8:1; 16:2; 21:1; Num. 6:22–23; 8:1–2; etc.). The charge comes, first, to Aaron and his sons, i.e., the Aaronic priesthood. To this group is added *your father's house (bêṯ-'āḇîkā)*. Most scholars see this expression as a reference to the whole tribe of Levi.[8] But the pl. *bêṯ 'āḇôṯ* usually means a subdivision smaller than the clan *(mišpāḥâ)*.[9] Occasionally the expression is a synonym for the full tribe (Num. 17:17–18, 21 [Eng. 2–3, 6]). In the sing., as here, it means "tribe" only in 17:17 (Eng. 2), because of the play on the word *maṭṭeh*, "rod, tribe," in that passage. In the discussion of the census of the Levitical families in 3:14–37, the sing. designates the three Levitical groups: the Gershonites (3:24), the Kohathites (3:30), and the Merarites (3:35). It seems a sound conclusion that, except where the context demands otherwise for clarity, the term in either the sing. or the pl. indicates a tribal subunit. Thus *your father's house* here should probably be identified as Aaron's family group, the Kohathites.[10] This identification gains weight when it is realized that v. 2 brings the whole tribe of Levi into the picture prefixed with the words *and also (w^{e}gam)*. In 4:1–20 it is the Kohathites who cooperate with the priests in the preparation and carrying of the holiest things. This identification also agrees with the task assigned here

7. For an exegesis of this difficult verse, see the commentary below and Milgrom, *Studies in Levitical Terminology*, I:75–76 n. 275. LXX reads: "And you and your sons with you will watch over your priesthood in all matters of the altar and that inside the veil and you will do the service as a gift of your priesthood, and the stranger who approaches will be killed."

8. So, e.g., Dillmann, p. 99; Holzinger, p. 72; Gray, p. 219; McNeile, p. 95; Binns, p. 120; Noordtzij, p. 161; Noth, p. 134; Snaith, p. 163; Sturdy, p. 126; Wenham, p. 143. See also N. Gottwald, *The Tribes of Yahweh*, pp. 288–90 on the possibility of "father's house" meaning "tribe."

9. Cf., e.g., Exod. 6:14; 12:3; Num. 1:2, 4, 18, 22, 24, 26, 28, 30, 32, 34, 36, 40, 42, 45, 47; 2:2, 32; 3:15, 20; 4:2, 22, 29, 34, 38, 40, 42, 46; 7:2; 26:2, 55; 34:14.

10. So, according to Greenstone, p. 187; Rashi and Ibn Ezra; Keil, p. 115; and Milgrom, *Studies in Levitical Terminology*, I:24 n. 79 and *JPST*, p. 146.

for *the holy objects,* which, as in 10:21, is the proper translation of *hammiqdāš.*[11]

To *bear the guilt (nāśā' 'āwōn)* means to bear the divine punishment growing out of that guilt.[12] The particular subject matter at hand is encroachment on the sanctuary and the wrath it causes to break out (17:27–28 [Eng. 12–13]). Thus v. 1a states that the priests and the Kohathites are to bear guilt for future Israelite trespass against the holy objects. But only the Aaronic priests will *bear the guilt* for future encroachment on the priesthood (v. 1b).

2 This verse adds a responsibility for the rest of the tribe of Levi to that just set forth for the Aaronites and Kohathites. The latter are to *associate with (haqrēḇ 'eṯ)* their brothers in their father's tribe of Levi. The verb *qāraḇ* (lit., "to draw near") in the Hiphil has been used in a negative sense to mean "to encroach" (e.g., 17:5 [Eng. 16:40]). In a positive sense, however, it means "to be qualified for," or, as here, *to associate.*[13] The family relationship is stressed *(your brothers)* because, in part, chs. 16–17 have done much to isolate the Levites from the priests.

Although they are related to the priests, the Levites are in a subordinate role to them, as is already obvious from, e.g., 3:6, but reemphasized here in a number of ways. First, the rest of the Levites are to *be joined (wᵉyillāwû)* to the Aaronites. The verb *lāwâ,* "to join," is linked by either a play on words or popular etymology to the name Levite *(lᵉwî).*[14] The point is that the Levites are not independent but are linked to the priests. The second way in which subordination is suggested is by the word *assist (šērēṯ),* which is used of the general tasks of guard duty

11. See Milgrom, *Studies in Levitical Terminology,* I:23–24 n. 78. Many modern translations render *hammiqdāš* in 10:21 as "holy objects" (RSV, NIV, NEB, NASB, GNB, NJPS, NKJV), but none does in the current verse.

12. So NEB "They shall be fully answerable for"; NIV "They shall bear responsibility for." On the divine nature of such a punishment, see the commentary above on 5:31.

13. See also Exod. 28:1. See Milgrom, *Studies in Levitical Terminology,* I:33–37, esp. 33–34.

14. The Niphal may also be translated "to join themselves." The folk etymology is used to make a point here, and it is unlikely that it provides the actual etymology of the name Levi. For suggestions on the etymology of the word, cf. BDB, p. 532a; *HALAT,* p. 497b; de Vaux, *Ancient Israel,* II:358–59; A. Cody, *A History of the Old Testament Priesthood,* AnBib 35 (Rome: Pontifical Biblical Institute, 1969), pp. 29–33; for a convenient summary, see G. Pratico, *ISBE,* rev., III:108.

and physical labor (cf. 1:50, 53; 3:6–7).[15] The venue for this assistance is *before* (i.e., in front of) *the tent of meeting*. A third way in which the subordination of the Levites to the priests is suggested is in the use of the words *gift (mattānâ)* and *given (n*e*ṯunîm)* in v. 6 (see below).

3 On *guard duty (šāmar mišmereṯ),* see the commentary above on 1:53. The necessity of guard duty for the tabernacle is restated here in the light of Korah's rebellion and the panic that ensued after the plague. The topic here is again sanctuary encroachment. Since it is clear from both the present verse and 4:15 that the Levites *have no access* to the inner sanctuary,[16] their guard duty must be outside the sanctuary. Since *they will stand guard duty for you* (i.e., for Aaron and the priests),[17] one may assume that the outer guard duty is assistance of the priest's guard duty inside the sanctuary. The Levites, then, are charged with responsibility for trespass of the sanctuary by other Levites or laypersons.

*so that neither they nor you might die (w*e*lō'-yāmuṯû gam-hēm gam-'attem)*. The penalty for failure to stop encroachment on the sacred vessels and the altar is death at the hand of God. The Qal of the verb *mûṯ* ("to die") is used of death by divine agency. This penalty might seem strange since the punishment for offenses that have a disastrous effect on society is usually death by human agency.[18] But once a person breaks through the protective guard of Levites and priests, no one could stop the offense without endangering himself and the community in the process; hence only God could carry out the death sentence. The ones upon whom this death comes are *they* (the antecedent for which must be "the Levites" — all of them) and *you* (the antecedent for which is not just Aaron, since it is pl., but all the priests). Encroachment by a single Levite, then, would bring the death of the whole group of priests and Levites. This principle is harsh, but prior to this time such encroachment (without intercession) would bring the death of the whole community (e.g., the plague in 17:6–15 [Eng. 16:41–50]).

15. On *šērēṯ,* see Milgrom, *Studies in Levitical Terminology,* I:67 n. 245. Milgrom (p. 52 n. 201) also sees the subordination of Levi to the priests in the use of the preposition "with" *('ēṯ)* in vv. 1–2, which he translates as "under." This translation of *'eṯ* is not, however, accepted by anyone else.

16. Heb. *'aḵ 'el-k*e*lê haqqōḏeš w*e*'el-hammizbēaḥ lō' yiqrāḇû,* "not be admitted to the sacred vessels or to the altar"; see the commentary above on v. 2.

17. Lit., "stand your guard," *w*e*šām*e*rû mišmart*e*ḵā.*

18. See above on 17:28 (Eng. 13). Death by human agency is usually expressed by the Hophal *yûmaṯ,* Exod. 31:14–15; Lev. 19:20; Num. 15:35. See Milgrom, *Studies in Levitical Terminology,* I:5–7, esp. Tables A and B.

4 Again, as in v. 2, the Levites are said to *be joined (wᵉnilᵉwû)* to the priests. The purpose of this joining (indicating subordination, see above on v. 2) is *guard duty (šāmar mišmereṯ)* and *all the work of the tent (lᵉḵol ʿᵃḇōḏaṯ hā'ōhel).*[19] The *work (ʿᵃḇōḏâ)* here is general, referring to all the physical labor in the tent, including guard duty. The work of the Levites is further spelled out in v. 6, while vv. 5, 7 speak about that of the priests (see below).

The *outsider (zār)* is a non-Levite here,[20] who is not allowed access to this subordinate relationship with the priests that the Levites enjoy.

5 Once again, as if to emphasize it in the strongest possible terms, Aaron is instructed that only priests[21] will perform guard duty inside the sacred precincts to watch over the *holy objects (haqqōḏeš)* and *the altar (hammizbēaḥ).* As in 3:31, *haqqōḏeš* here seems to refer to the objects in the sanctuary, though the term is quite flexible and may also indicate the "sacred area" itself (e.g., Exod. 28:43). The contrast here is between the duties of the priests within the sanctuary and that of the Levites without. The subject is encroachment on the holy things, which encroachment can bring wrath. The reason for this clear division of labor is so that *wrath (qeṣeḇ)* may no longer come on the Israelites as it did, e.g., in Lev. 10:2, 6; Num. 17:11 (Eng. 16:46).

6 Yahweh reminds Aaron of the fact that he himself has taken the Levites out of the tribes of Israel and given them to the priesthood and, by that means, to himself. The verse has verbal similarities to 3:9; 8:16a, and especially 19a. In 3:9 Yahweh gives Moses the privilege of giving the Levites to Aaron, while 8:16, 19, and the present verse emphasize the ultimate source of this gift. In ch. 8 Yahweh receives the Levites and gives them to Aaron and the priests *out of the midst of the children of Israel (mittôḵ bᵉnê yiśrā'ēl)* as here. This verse is a reminder of God's choice of the Levites (3:5–10; cf. 1:47–53) and their ordination to his service (8:5–22).

Again, as in v. 2, the ties of kinship between Aaron and the Levites

19. On the two terms *guard duty* and *work,* see the commentary above on 3:7; cf. Milgrom, *Studies in Levitical Terminology,* I:8–16, 60–76 (esp. 72–76).

20. On *zār* see the commentary above on 1:51; cf. Milgrom, *Studies in Levitical Terminology,* I:5 n. 6.

21. Some, e.g., Gray, pp. 220–21 ,and McNeile, p. 95, claim that this verse addresses priests and Levites. But, as I argued above, this verse is clearly addressed only to priests. This passage twice (vv. 3, 5) attempts to keep the Levites from encroaching on the role of the priests.

are stressed *(your brothers, ʿaḥêḵem)* in order to place the priests and Levites together before God in corporate solidarity and responsibility. The purpose of God's gift of the Levites is so that they might *do the work of the tent of meeting (laʿaḇōḏ ʾeṯ-ʿaḇōḏâ ʾōhel môʿēḏ),* i.e., the general labor involved in serving the priests and guarding outside the stucture.[22]

7a The subject returns to the Aaronic priesthood once more (as in vv. 1, 3b, 5). *But you and your sons with you (weʾattâ ûḇāneyḵā ʾitteḵā)* contrasts with, sets off, and balances with *and I (waʾanî)* in the previous verse.

you will keep (tišmerû), i.e., as a matter of guard duty. The priests' guard duty, here as in v. 5, concerns the holy objects, specified as *all that concerns the altar (leḵol-deḇar[23] hammizbēaḥ)* and *that within the veil (ûlemibbêṯ lappārōḵeṯ).* The former includes all things in the place where the altar was. The meaning of the latter is debated. The *veil* is the curtain that separates the holy place from the most holy place.[24] The only priest who had access to the most holy place was the high priest, and that only once per year, on Yom Kippur (Lev. 16). Since no one but the high priest could enter, some scholars have thought that *pārōḵeṯ* here referred to the screen rather than the veil.[25] But the screen is called *hammāsaḵ* and is different from the veil. The question here is not of entering behind the veil, but of guarding what was behind it against encroachment. By definition this encroachment would have had to have been on the part of other priests since laypeople and Levites had no access to the inner shrine. It might be possible, of course, that a Levite/Israelite could elude the Levite guard outside the holy area, but this would be exceptional.

7b *I will give your priesthood valuable work (ʿaḇōdaṯ mattānâ ʾettēn ʾeṯ-kehunnaṯeḵem).* This sentence is difficult not only because of its abruptness but also because this is the only mention of priestly *work (ʿaḇōḏâ).* LXX renders: "and you shall perform the service, a gift of your priesthood" *(kai leitourgēsete tas leitourgias doma tēs heirateias hymōn).* This is at best paraphrastic of MT. Most English translations paraphrase as well; RSV has "I give you your priesthood as a gift," and suppresses the word ʿaḇōḏaṯ (lit., "work of," RSV "service of") to the margin.[26]

22. See Milgrom, *Studies in Levitical Terminology,* I:72–76.

23. *All that concerns . . . (leḵol- deḇar)* is literally "as regards every matter of . . ."

24. See the commentary above on 4:5.

25. E.g., McNeile, p. 96; Binns, p. 121.

26. See also NIV, NEB, NASB, all of which paraphrase in their own ways.

Many scholars have apparently simply accepted these paraphrases and explained the clause as meaning that the Aaronic priesthood is a divine gift.[27] E. A. Speiser suggested that, in the first part of the verse, the verbs "you will keep" (*tišmᵉrû,* translated as "to take care") and "you will work" (*wᵉʿa̲ḇaḏtem)* be translated as a hendiadys: "you will take care to perform."[28] In addition to the grammatical difficulty of having the members of the hendiadys separated at such a distance from one another in the text, Speiser did not recognize the technical nature of the terms *watch, keep (šāmar)* and *work (ʿa̲ḇōḏâ)* as developed here.[29] These words describe two elements of (to this point) Levitical duties at the tabernacle. Can the use of these (elsewhere) technical words for "guard duty" and "physical labor" be accidental here? Furthermore, Speiser translated *ʿa̲ḇōḏaṯ mattānâ* (lit., "work of a gift," here translated "valuable service") as "a service of dedication."[30] As Milgrom points out, however, the root *ntn* (lit., "give") indicates subordination (as above in v. 6 on the Levites), and nowhere are the priests ever given to anyone; rather, Levites and payments are given *to them* (3:9; 8:16, 19; 18:6; 1 Chr. 6:33; for payments, see below, vv. 8, 11–12, 19).[31] It is probable that the word *valuable* (*mattānâ,* lit., "gift") refers to the payments that will be detailed more fully in vv. 8–20.

I have already suggested that the verb "to keep" in v. 7a referred to the priests' guard duty, which clearly concerned the holy objects. The use of the term *work* here[32] must refer to the priests' dangerous tasks of dismantling, covering, and, in due course, unpacking the holy objects (4:5–15), for which they receive compensation (see below). The likelihood is that, just as the terms for "guard duty" and "physical labor" are contrasted for the Levites in 3:31, 35, so here they are are contrasted for the priests.

But the unauthorized person who encroaches will be put to death. On this formula see the commentary above on 1:51; 3:10, 38. The *unauthorized person (hazzār)* here is, of course, the nonpriest, as opposed to the non-Levite in v. 4.

27. So, e.g., Gray, p. 221; McNeile, p. 96; Snaith, p. 163; Sturdy, p. 127.

28. E. A. Speiser, "Unrecognized Dedication," *IEJ* 13 (1963) 69–73 (his translation is on p. 73).

29. See further the critique of Speiser in Milgrom, *Studies in Levitical Terminology,* I:75–76 n. 275.

30. Speiser, "Unrecognized Dedication," p. 73.

31. Milgrom, *Studies in Levitical Terminology,* I:75–76 n. 275.

32. The term "work" occurs in verbal form *ʿa̲ḇaḏtem,* "they will do work," and in nominal form *ʿa̲ḇōḏ aṯ mattᵉnâ,* "valuable work."

b. Support of Priests (18:8–20)

8 *And Yahweh said to Aaron, "And I have indeed given to you the keeping of my contributions, I give*[1] *to you and to your sons as an everlasting statute all the sacred things of the children of Israel*[2] *as a perquisite.*[3]

9 *This will belong to you from the holiest things, that which is from the fire; each of their offerings, namely, each of their cereal offerings, each of their purification offerings, each of their reparation offerings that they give back to me, they are most holy to you and to your sons.*

10 *You will eat it in the way of the most holy things;*[4] *any male may eat it, it is holy to you.*

11 *Also belonging to you is all the contribution of their gift, all the dedicated offerings of the children of Israel, I give them to you and to your sons and to your daughters with you as an everlasting due. All who are clean in your house may eat of it.*[5]

12 *All the best of fresh oil and all the best of new wine and grain, the first fruits that they give to Yahweh, I give them to you.*

13 *The first fruits of all that is in their land that they bring to Yahweh belong to you; any who is clean in your house may eat it.*

14 *Every devoted thing in Israel belongs to you.*

15 *Everyone who opens the womb of all flesh that they offer to Yahweh, from humans or beasts, belongs to you, except that you*

1. Heb. *n^e^ṯatîm,* lit., "I gave them." The proleptic pronomial suffix "them" on the verb refers to the "sacred things of the children of Israel" *(qoḏšê ḇ^e^nê yiśrā'ēl).* I have omitted this suffix in the translation for smoothness.

2. The clause *l^e^ḵol-qoḏšê ḇ^e^nê-yiśrā'ēl,* "all the sacred things of the children of Israel," may be taken as a casus pendens; see GKC, § 143e.

3. The noun *mošḥâ* is probably related to Akk. *masaḫu,* "to measure," and Arab. *masaḥa,* "a measure," rather than to the common Hebrew word *māšaḥ,* "to anoint" (contra BDB, p. 603), although the two words look identical in Hebrew. See Gray, p. 233; Snaith, p. 163; *HALAT,* 608b–9a.

4. Heb. *b^e^qōḏeš haqq^o^dāšîm tō'ḵ^a^lennû* is ambiguous. RV, NEB, NIV, NASB, NJPS, Cook, p. 714; Sturdy, p. 129; and de Vaulx, p. 210 render it similarly to the above. But it could also mean "you will eat it in a most holy place"; so, e.g., AV, RSV, GNB, Moffatt, Dillmann, p. 101; Gray, p. 223; McNeile, p. 97; Binns, p. 122; Heinisch, p. 71; Noordtzij, p. 162. See the discussion below.

5. On the meaning of terms in this verse, see the discussion below and several studies by J. Milgrom: "The Alleged Wave-offering in Israel and the Ancient Near East"; *"Hattĕnûpâ"*; "The *Šôq hattĕrûmâ*"; "Akkadian Confirmation of the Meaning of the term *tĕrûmâ,*" all repr. in his *Studies in Cultic Theology,* pp. 133–72.

will surely receive the ransom price[6] *for the firstborn of humans; you will receive the ransom price for the firstborn of unclean animals as well.*

16 *And its ransom price (at one month you shall ransom them) will be set at five shekels of silver; in the sacred shekel, this is twenty gerahs.*

17 *But you will not receive the ransom price for a firstborn bull or a firstborn lamb or a firstborn goat; they are holy; their blood you will toss against the altar, and their fat you will make smoke by fire for a sweet savor to Yahweh.*

18 *But the flesh belongs to you, just as the elevated breast and the right thigh belong to you.*[7]

19 *All the holy contributions that the children of Israel set aside to Yahweh I give to you and to your sons and to your daughters with you for an everlasting due; it is an everlasting covenant of salt*[8] *before Yahweh, for you and your descendants with you."*

20 *Yahweh said to Aaron, "You will not inherit in their land, and no share belongs to you in their midst. I am your share and your inheritance in the midst of the children of Israel."*

Based on the fact that the priests (as well as the Levites) have been given new and dangerous responsibilities to forbid encroachment and to be responsible for it on pain of death in vv. 1–7, God grants the priests special dues in order to compensate them in vv. 8–20. At the end of the unit (v. 20) a further theological rationale is added for these priestly contributions; the priests have no territorial inheritance in the land of Canaan. God himself (and the gifts that normally accrue to him) are their inheritance. These gifts to the priests are broken down into the categories of "most holy," which may only be eaten by the priests themselves within the sacred precincts (vv. 9–10), and "holy," which may be eaten by any ceremonially clean member of the priests' families in any ceremonially clean place (i.e., outside the sanctuary, vv. 11–19). The main point of the unit is the assignment of these dues, not a statement on the performance of offerings. Several terms are used in a less technical

6. The construction of infinitive absolute plus finite verb indicates surety or emphasis. See Williams, *Syntax,* § 205.

7. On *tᵉnûp̱â* see Milgrom, *Studies in Cultic Theology,* pp. 133–58 (also 159–72).

8. The obscure expression "covenant of salt" occurs only here and in 2 Chr. 13:5 (a rather different context); cf. "salt of the covenant" in Lev. 2:13. See the commentary below.

sense than elsewhere in the Pentateuch (e.g., "most holy place," "holy place").

8 Yahweh continues to address Aaron alone in this passage (see the commentary above on v. 1). *I have indeed given (wa'ᵃnî hinnēh nāṯattî).* The construction emphasizes the giver, Yahweh, and this emphasis is continued in the repetition of the word (with the pronomial suffix) *my contributions (tᵉrûmōṯāy).* These *contributions* have been assigned to Aaron (i.e., *to you, lᵉḵā*) as the representative of the priests. On *indeed (hinnēh),* see above on 18:6.

the keeping of my contributions ('eṯ-mišmereṯ tᵉrûmōṯāy). Several scholars propose taking *keeping (mišmereṯ)* in a concrete sense, "that which is kept," with a reference to a similar construction in 1 Sam. 22:23. This sense would be unusual for this noun, and would mean that the priests were being given the portion of the following dues that were not consumed on the altar.[9] At best, these portions might include the offerings in v. 9, but would not fit several enumerated in vv. 11–18. The better alternative is to give the word its more normal meaning of "keeping" (cf. NEB "control"), which then means that God assigned these contributions to the priests, and that they were to be allowed to keep what they would not normally have kept.[10]

These contributions are then described as *the sacred things of the children of Israel (qoḏšê bᵉnê yiśrā'ēl).*[11] Those things both belong to God *(my contributions)* and are donated to him (see NEB "contributions to me"). These assignments are called *a perquisite* (*mošḥâ,* lit., "a share"). A perquisite, from which we get our English noun "perk," indicates an additional benefit, over and above one's normal pay, to which a person may be entitled by his or her position.

9–10 The *meal offering (minḥâ), purification offering (ḥaṭṭā'ṯ),* and *reparation offering ('āšām)* have already been called *the holiest things (qōḏeš-haqqᵒḏāšîm)* by the author of Leviticus.[12] These are also defined here as *from the fire (min hā'ēš).* LXX understands this designation as "fire offering" *(hā'iššeh),* as at 15:3. The more probable meaning is that these

9. E.g., Dillmann, p. 100; Gray, pp. 221–22; McNeile, p. 97; Binns, p. 121; Sturdy, p. 129; Harrison, p. 248.

10. E.g., Keil, pp. 116–17; Holzinger, p. 73; Budd, p. 205.

11. On the words *contribution (tᵉrûmâ)* and *sacred things (qōḏᵉšîm)* and their relationship, see the commentary above on 5:9–10.

12. E.g., Lev. 2:3 (meal offering); 6:10 (Eng. 17) (purification offering); 7:1 (reparation offering). The purification offering is discussed in depth in Milgrom, *Studies in Cultic Theology,* pp. 67–95.

are the portions of the holiest things not consumed by the fire of the altar. The basic Levitical legislation gives these portions to the priests to be eaten by males of the household only, and with this the current text simply agrees.[13]

You will eat it in the way of the most holy things (bᵉqōḏeš haqqᵒḏāšîm tō'ḵᵃlennû). As noted above, the text may also be rendered "You will eat it in a most holy place"; it is impossible to tell which translation is correct. If the reference is to place, then what place? It surely cannot be the most holy place in the tabernacle, to which only the high priest had access on the Day of Atonement. Lev. 6:9, 19 (Eng. 16, 26) specify that these offerings must be eaten in a "holy place," which is more fully defined as "in the court of the tent of meeting" *(baḥᵃṣar 'ōhel-mô'ēḏ).* Since vv. 9–10 already seems unclear about the two terms *most holy* and *holy,* perhaps these two terms should be considered equivalents here. If the reference is to the manner of eating,[14] one must say that this is defined only by the fact that priests alone (v. 9), who are by definition males (v. 10), may eat it. Perhaps other criteria for eating the "most holy things" were common knowledge in the ancient world but have been lost to us.

11 This verse introduces the lesser holy contributions in vv. 12–18. *the contribution of their gift (tᵉrûmaṯ mattānâ)* is an odd phrase; some scholars have taken it to refer to the right thigh and breast that come to the priest from the peace offerings (Exod. 29:28; Lev. 7:34; 10:14–15),[15] although no one has been able to explain satisfactorily why the peace offerings should be designated as *their gift* here. The term may be a general term for contributions *(tᵉrûmôṯ),* given as gifts *(mattᵉnôṯ)* to God, and designated by him *(nāṯan)* for the priest and his family.

These contributions are further defined as *all the dedicated offerings of the children of Israel (lᵉḵol-tᵉnûp̄ōṯ bᵉnê yiśrā'ēl).* Heb. *tᵉnûp̄â* is a term used to describe a ceremony that removes an offering from the realm of the profane to that of the sacred, i.e., dedicates it to God.[16] These gifts will be spelled out in vv. 12–18.

13. For the meal offering see Lev. 2:3, 10; 6:9–11 (Eng. 16–18); 7:9–10. For the purification offering see Lev. 5:13; 6:26, 29. For the reparation offering see Lev. 7:6.

14. *bᵉ-* can be used in this way; see BDB, p. 88b (§ 7); Williams, *Syntax,* § 249.

15. E.g., Gray, p. 223; McNeile, p. 97; Binns, p. 122.

16. See the commentary above on 5:25 for more on *tᵉnûp̄â.*

for an everlasting due (lᵉḥoq-ʿôlām). The root *ḥqq* means "to inscribe, cut in"; hence an idiomatic rendering of *ḥoq-ʿôlām* might be "something carved in stone." The term takes on a technical meaning of a "prescribed due" for the priests from various offerings.[17] That one has passed into a different category from vv. 9–10 can be seen in the fact that both sons and daughters can eat of these gifts if they are ceremonially clean (cf. Lev. 22:3–7, 10–13). These contributions may be eaten in the priest's home rather than being limited to the sanctuary.

12–13 These verses deal with the first fruits, which God assigns to the priests here. *best (ḥēleḇ)* is lit. "fat," which carries this same meaning in other texts.[18]

fresh oil . . . new wine . . . grain (yiṣhār . . . tîrôš . . . dāgān). These are raw produce before any processing, as contrasted with "oil" *(šemen),* "wine" *(yayin),* and "meal" *(šeḇer)* thereafter.

the first of which they give to Yahweh (rēʾšîṯām ʾᵃšer-yittᵉnû lYHWH). The question is whether *first (rēʾšîṯ)* here indicates quality or time, since it may indicate either.[19] That the word many times means "first fruits" does not help to decide the issue here.[20] Perhaps it is used intentionally because of its ambiguity as a term for "the best" *(ḥēleḇ)* in v. 12a and "the first" *(bikkûrîm)* in v. 13.

first fruits (bikkûrîm) occurs seventeen times in the OT to describe the first-ripe grain and fruit crops that were brought to Yahweh.[21] In later times the *bikkûrîm* were apparently small offerings of raw produce directed to the priests after a temple ceremony (Neh. 10:36 [Eng. 35]; Mish. *Bikkurim* 1:3, 10), whereas the *rēʾšîṯ* were directed straight to the treasury (Neh. 10:37a [Eng. 36a]).[22] At the time that Numbers was written, it is improbable that such a division existed; therefore the two terms are probably synonymous.[23] Any priestly family member who was ceremonially clean could partake of these dues.

14 *Every devoted thing (kol-ḥērem).* Things that were "placed

17. BDB, p. 349.

18. BDB, pp. 316b–17a.

19. For quality see, e.g., Deut. 33:21; 1 Sam. 2:29; for time see, e.g., Gen. 1:1; 10:10; Exod. 23:19; Deut. 11:12.

20. See, e.g., Exod. 23:19; 34:26; Lev. 23:10; Num. 15:20–21; Deut. 18:4; etc.

21. See Exod. 23:16, 19; 34:22, 26; Lev. 2:14; 23:17, 20; Num. 13:20; 28:26; 2 K. 4:42; Ezek. 44:30; Nah. 3:12; Neh. 10:36 (Eng. 35); 13:31.

22. See Gray, p. 224. For a discussion of the firstfruits see pp. 225–29.

23. See Budd, p. 205.

under the ban" *(heḥ^{e}rîm)* were given wholly to God and could not be redeemed (Lev. 27:21, 28). In time of war Israel might take an oath to put people, cities, or nations under the ban (Num. 21:1–3), and people so banned were put to death (Lev. 27:29; Deut. 7:1–2; Josh. 6:17, 21; 1 Sam. 15:3). Wealth not banned (e.g., silver and gold) might be put in the treasury (Josh. 6:19). Although Lev. 27:21 hints that the priest might be in control of a field that was *ḥērem,* the current verse explicitly assigns *devoted things* (given wholly to God) to the use of the priests.

15–18 These verses deal with the firstborn of all human and animal life. These creatures belong to Yahweh, but are here assigned to the priest. V. 15 states the principle that is elaborated in vv. 16–18.

15 *Everyone who opens the womb (kol-peṭer reḥem)* is lit. " the splitter of the womb," hence the firstborn.[24] Cf. 3:12, where the concept is used to establish the principle of substitution of the Levites for the firstborn, based on the fact that every firstborn Israelite belonged to God as the result of God's mercy at the time of the tenth plague in Egypt (Exod. 13:2; 22:29–30; 34:19–20). Here the author does not develop that argument, but simply states that every firstborn in Israel belongs to Yahweh, hence to the priests. The text does not limit itself explicitly to males here, although 3:40–41 does (also Exod. 13:12–13; 34:19–20; Deut. 15:19); but since the redemption price (v. 16) is that of a male from one month to five years of age (Lev. 27:6), one may assume that only males are meant here.

that they offer to Yahweh (ʾ^{a}šer yaqrîḇû lYHWH) must refer to clean animals, since humans and unclean animals are mentioned as being ransomed (see v. 17 below).

you will surely receive the ransom price . . . will receive the ransom price (pāḏōh tiḇdeh . . . tiḇdeh). The construction emphasizes the ransoming of humans and thus perhaps contrasts their ransoming with that of the unclean beasts, which is simply stated. The verb *pāḏâ* usually means "to ransom,"[25] but here it means "to receive the ransom price of," since the point of the whole section is not what the priests will *do* but what they will *receive.*[26]

24. For other examples of this term see BDB, p. 809b.

25. Snaith (p. 164) distinguishes between *pāḏâ,* which indicates ransom of that which did not originally belong to one, and *gāʾal,* which indicates buying back what originally was one's own.

26. "We must either assume a sense for the Kal here which it nowhere else possesses, or point *taḇdeh*" (Gray, p. 233), i.e., a Hiphil, as in Exod. 21:8 (see

you will receive the ransom price for the firstborn of unclean animals as well. Exod. 13:13 speaks about the possibility of redeeming the firstling of a donkey for the price of one lamb, but nothing is said about who received this lamb. The purpose of this legislation was to decree the possibility of redemption. The discussion in Num. 18:15 does not focus on that point at all, but on the point of who receives the redemption price. There is no need to see a contradiction between Exod. 13:13 and Num. 18:15, as Gray seems to do.[27] This text indicates that when the firstling of an unclean animal is ransomed (no specific animal is mentioned), then the priest will receive the ransom price.

16–18 Verse 16 is a parenthetical statement that interrupts the sequence of vv. 15 and 17. It could be an explanatory gloss,[28] although this is conjecture.

16 *its ransom price (pᵉḏûyāw).* It is impossible to tell to what *its* (lit., "his") refers here. If the pronoun refers to the collective sing. *firstborn (bᵉḵôr)* in v. 15, then the firstborn of unclean beasts must also be ransomed at five shekels, thus providing a new regulation that goes far beyond Lev. 27:11–12, 27. It is possible, however, that the pronoun refers only to the *firstborn of humans (bᵉḵôr hā'āḏām)* in v. 15, which would then match 3:47 and Lev. 27:6. It is unlikely that such a high ransom price would be set on an unclean animal (according to Wenham's estimate, about six months' wages), or that an unclean animal would be set on a par with the value of a firstborn human male.[29] As stated above, the ransom price itself is that of a male from one month to five years (Lev. 27:6). The priests are to receive this price immediately following redemption at one month of age.

in the sacred shekel, this is twenty gerahs (bᵉšeḵel haqqōḏeš 'eśrîm gērâ hû'). On the sacred shekel see the commentary above on 3:47.

17–18 Firstborn bulls, lambs, or goats are not to be ransomed. They are clean animals, and as such belong to Yahweh as other firstborns do. They are here treated in a way similar to the sacrifice of the peace

---

also *HALAT,* pp. 862b–63a). At Exod. 21:8, however (the only Hiphil example in the OT), the meaning is "to permit to be redeemed," which is hardly more fitting in this context. It is better to assume a unique meaning for the Qal brought about by the needs of this context. This view is strengthened by the use of the cognate word *pᵉḏûyāw,* "its ransom price," in v. 16.

27. Gray, p. 230.

28. So, e.g., Dillmann, p. 101; Gray, p. 231; Noth, p. 136; Sturdy, p. 130.

29. Wenham, p. 144. Many scholars conclude that the five-shekel price applies only to the firstborn humans, e.g., McNeile, p. 98; Wenham, p. 144; Budd, p. 206.

offerings *(zebaḥ šᵉlāmîm)* concerning their blood and fat (cf. Lev. 3:1–17; 7:11–36; esp. 3:2–5), but not concerning the disposition of their flesh. The peace offering is eaten by the worshiper, and only the elevated breast and right thigh belong to the priest (Lev. 7:32–35); while in the present case the whole of the flesh belongs to him.

19 This verse summarizes vv. 12–18 by calling all of the above *holy contributions (tᵉrûmōṯ haqqᵒḏāšîm).* Again, these lesser holy contributions are differentiated from the holiest by permitting the former to be consumed by other members of priestly families (i.e., *your sons and daughters with you*). These contributions will belong to the priests as *an everlasting due* (*ḥoq-ʿôlām,* as in v. 11).

an everlasting covenant of salt (bᵉrîṯ melaḥ ʿôlām). This phrase is obscure. Exod. 30:35 speaks of salt being in the mixture for the holy incense, and Lev. 2:13 commands that salt be used in all meal offerings, but whether these passages clarify the idiom is unknown.[30] That most commentators take it to refer to an everlasting or inviolable covenant could be deduced from the words "everlasting covenant" *(bᵉrîṯ ʿôlām)* without reference to salt. 2 Chr. 13:5 is the only other OT text to connect the words "everlasting," "covenant," and "salt": "Is it not for you to know that Yahweh the God of Israel gave the kingship over Israel to David forever — to him and to his sons, a covenant of salt?"[31] The reference is clearly to the permanence of the covenant, since the word *forever (ʿôlām)* occurs in both texts.[32] W. Robertson Smith suggested that the origin of the idiom was in the old nomadic custom wherein if the smallest morsel of food be shared (e.g., a grain of salt), an alliance of mutual support and friendship existed.[33] Perhaps the preservative nature of salt pictures the permanence of such a covenant.[34]

30. In Ezekiel's vision of the restored temple, salt is used with the whole burnt offering (43:4). This use is reflected even later in Josephus, *Ant.* 3.9.1; Mish. *Zebaḥim* 6:5.

31. If the position on the date of Numbers taken in this commentary is correct, then the Chronicles passage is a later interpretation of the idiom, which may or may not be identical to the earlier.

32. See, e.g., R. B. Dillard, *2 Chronicles,* WBC (Waco: Word, 1987), p. 107; H. G. M. Williamson, *1 and 2 Chronicles,* NCBC (Grand Rapids: Eerdmans, 1982), p. 252.

33. W. Robertson Smith, *Religion of the Semites,* 2nd ed. (London: Black, 1901), p. 270; cf. Gray, p. 232.

34. Milgrom points to the preservative nature of salt as making it a good symbol of permanence (also Harrison, p. 250). Milgrom refers to a neo-Babylonian treaty that speaks of "all who have tasted the salt of the Jakin tribe," referring to

20 This verse provides a further theological rationale for the fact that the priests receive these dues. As already suggested, their added guard duty in vv. 1–7 is one reason for the change in these contributions. The one put forth here is that the priests (represented by Aaron) have no land inheritance in Canaan; their inheritance is Yahweh himself. Just as the other Hebrews will be supported from their *share (ḥēleq),*[35] so the priests will be supported by theirs, i.e., Yahweh. Although one must be careful not to limit this rationale to the dues, one may suppose that they were the tangible sign that the priests had Yahweh for their share. In this way the priests would be made to depend on God rather than on the land.

c. Support of Levites (18:21–24)

21 *"And I give to the sons of Levi every tithe in Israel for an inheritance, in exchange for*[1] *their work which they do, the work in the tent of meeting.*

22 *And the children of Israel shall henceforth not encroach on the tent of meeting, thus incurring guilt and dying.*

23 *Now the Levite will do the work of the tent of meeting, and they will bear their guilt; it shall be an everlasting due through your generations, that in the midst of the children of Israel they shall have no inheritance.*

24 *For I have given the tithe of the children of Israel that they set as a contribution to Yahweh to the Levites as an inheritance; therefore I have said to them: in the midst of Israel they will have no inheritance."*

Although Aaron is still presumably addressed in these verses, the subject changes from the priests to the Levites. In the Korahite rebellion the difference between priests and Levites had been clearly emphasized. In

---

the tribe's covenant partners; Milgrom, *JPST,* p. 154. See also Ezra 4:14, where to taste "the salt of the palace" means loyalty (cf. H. G. M. Williamson, *Ezra, Nehemiah,* WBC [Waco: Word, 1985], p. 56).

35. The word is commonly used for the tribal shares of Canaan (e.g., Josh. 15:13; 18:5–7, 9; 19:9). No "share" is given to the entire tribe of Levi (not just the priests; see vv. 23–24 below), Deut. 10:9; 12:12; 14:27, 29; 18:1; Josh. 14:4; 18:7. The term is used of Yahweh as the priests' portion only here, but this idiom is generalized in Ps. 16:5; 73:26; 119:57; Lam. 3:24.

1. The noun *ḥēlep̱* is used as a preposition only here and in v. 31 in the OT, meaning "in exchange for" (*ḥlp,* "pass on, away, through"); see BDB, p. 322a; cf. Milgrom, *Studies in Levitical Terminology,* I:76 n. 276.

18:1–7 the two groups have been set together once again as complementary. Vv. 8–20 have dealt with the priests' dues, and now it is time to say a word about the Levites' dues and to address a further word to the reason for them. What has been worked out in vv. 1–7 about corporate Levitical responsibility for Israelite encroachment on the sanctuary must be kept in mind in interpreting this section. Vv. 21a, 23b–24 deal with the tithe, which now is to be given to the Levite.[2] The middle section of the pericope (vv. 21b–23a) is centered on the work that the Levites do in exchange for this tithe.[3] At the center of the passage is the crux *they will bear their guilt* (v. 23a).[4]

21a, 23b–24 *the sons of Levi (b^{e}nê lēwî).* In the light of the context, this term must indicate the nonpriestly members of the tribe.

every tithe (kol-ma῾^{a}śēr). Tithing (i.e., giving one-tenth of something to someone else) is attested as practiced by Abraham (Gen. 14:20) and Jacob (28:22). The tithe was given not only to God (as in Jacob's case), but to God's priest (as in Abraham's); both cases probably reflect the same principle. Lev. 27:30–33 assumes the practice of tithing in its discussion of redemption of the tithe. Both there (v. 30) and in the current passage (Num. 18:24) the tithe is said to belong to Yahweh, which again probably means that it belonged to his priest. Yahweh himself assigns these tithes from the priests to the Levites in this passage.[5] The Leviticus passage mentions a tithe of both animals and crops (Lev. 27:32). The present context compares the tithe only to the latter (Num. 18:27, 30; recognized also in Neh. 10:38 [Eng. 37]; 12:44), hence it is uncertain what happened to the animal tithe (it reappears in 2 Chr. 31:6). *every tithe* may mean nothing more than every one that was offered, whatever its kind. The purpose of the present passage is not necessarily to set forth a wholly new tithe law, but to change the recipients of the tithe; thus it does not clarify what it took for granted.[6]

2. These verses are tied together by the use of such common vocabulary elements as "tithe" (*ma῾^{a}śēr,* vv. 21, 24); "inheritance" (*naḥ^{a}lâ,* vv. 23b, 24 [twice]); "to inherit" (*nāḥal,* vv. 23b, 24).

3. Common vocabulary in these verses: "work" (*῾^{a}ḇōḏâ,* vv. 21b, 23a); "to work" (*῾āḇaḏ,* vv. 21b, 23a); "tent of meeting" (*ʾōhel mô῾ēḏ,* vv. 21b, 22, 23a).

4. Such common vocabulary terms as "(children of) Israel" (*[b^{e}nê] yiśrāʾēl,* vv. 21, 23–24) and "sons of Levi/the Levite/the Levites" (*b^{e}nê lēwî/hallēwî/hal^{e}wîyim,* vv. 21, 23–24) tie the whole passage together.

5. If the current passage does transfer these tithes from the priests to the Levites, then Lev. 27:30–33 may be earlier than the current passage.

6. There are difficulties in understanding how the tithe here prescribed is

inheritance (naḥ^a^lâ). Cf. v. 20 above, which states that Yahweh is the priests' inheritance. Here the Levites' inheritance is the tithe (vv. 21a, 24a) rather than an inheritance of land *in the midst of the children of Israel (b^e^ṯôḵ b^e^nê yiśrā'ēl,* v. 24b) in Canaan. Because of the regulation in 35:1–8 that gives the Levites forty-eight cities *to dwell in,* Milgrom sees the term *inheritance (naḥ^a^lâ)* here as limited to farmlands.[7]

21b–23a The tithes that are transferred to the Levites here are clearly not simply a gift, but are looked on as a wage given *in exchange for (ḥēlep̱)* their work in the tent of meeting.[8] *their work (ʿ^a^ḇōḏāṯām)* that they accomplished in the tent of meeting has heretofore been defined as the physical work of dismantling and erecting the tabernacle, as well as the "guard duty" *(šāmar mišmereṯ)* to keep the encroacher out (cf. vv. 1–7 above).[9] The latter is most clearly in mind here, since it is encroachment and its dangers (growing out of 17:27–28 [Eng. 12–13]) that gave rise to this whole chapter, and since v. 22 raises that specific issue.

henceforth (*ʿôḏ,* i.e., from this time on) ordinary Israelites will not be faced with death at God's hand for the encroachment of one (like Korah) on the sanctuary, as was the case in the recent plague (17:6–15 [Eng. 16:41–50]).[10] The reason is that *the Levite will do the work of the tent of meeting (w^eʿ^āḇaḏ hallēwî hû' 'eṯ-ʿ^a^ḇōḏaṯ 'ōhel môʿēḏ),* i.e., because the individual Levite is on guard to stop it.

But that is not all; *and they will bear their guilt (w^e^hēm yiś^e'^û*

---

to be related to that of Deut. 12:17–19; 14:22–29; 26:12–15. The main difficulty seems to be that Deuteronomy says that the tithes are to be enjoyed by the worshipers and every third year shared with the poor of the land in addition to the Levites. This difficulty led in postbiblical times to a recognition of more than one tithe (Tob. 1:6–9; Josephus, *Ant.* 4.8.8, 22; Mish. *Maaseroth* and *Maaser Sheni*). On the tithe in Deuteronomy, see, e.g., Craigie, *Deuteronomy,* pp. 233–34, 323. On the tithe, see M. Weinfeld, "Tithe," *EncJud,* XIV:1156–62; Kaufmann, *Religion of Israel,* pp. 189–93; Milgrom, *Cult and Conscience,* pp. 55–62; de Vaux, *Ancient Israel,* I:140–41; II:380–82, 403–5.

7. Milgrom, *JPST,* pp. 155, 232, 288–89. But see below on 35:2.

8. In v. 31 below (the only other place to use *ḥēlep* as a preposition) the tithe is actually called a "wage" or "reward" *(śāḵār).* See BDB, p. 969a.

9. The question of whether this regulation applies immediately or only when the people come into Canaan is not directly relevant here. Even if the latter is the case, it is not clear that the OT text assumes that the tabernacle will not remain movable and that the Levites' work of dismantling and erecting will not continue indefinitely. Cf. Milgrom, *Studies in Levitical Terminology,* I:66–72 for a discussion of the point.

10. This is parallel to what was said in v. 5b: "that wrath may not again *[ʿôḏ]* come on the children of Israel."

ʿᵃwōnām, v. 23a).[11] This clause is difficult. What is the antecedent of the pronouns *they* and *their?* First, one must remember that the priests and Levites will share the fate of (i.e., *bear the guilt of*) the encroacher (see the commentary above on vv. 1–7). There are four possibilities: that the first refers to the Israelites and the second to the Levites; that both refer to the Israelites; that both refer to the Levites; and that the first refers to the Levites and the second to the Israelites. The first option is patently absurd in the context. The second is possible (see, e.g., NJPS); it draws its main cogency from the fact that v. 23 has two strictly superfluous pronouns: *he (hûʾ)* and *they (hēm)* (the former sing. and the latter pl.). Since the former clearly refers to the Levite, the latter (on this argument) must refer to Israel (v. 22), so that *they* refers to the Israelites. The crucial objection to this solution, however, is that it hardly answers the panic of 17:27–28 (Eng. 12–13) to tell the Israelites that they will be responsible for bearing their own guilt. It also directly contradicts the way in which vv. 1–7 have been interpreted.[12]

By process of elimination, then, the first pronoun, *they (hēm),* refers to the Levites. This is unusual since the earlier part of the verse refers to *the Levite* by the sing. pronoun *hûʾ* ("he"). In the present context, however, it is this sing. pronoun that is unusual. Everywhere else in the passage the Levites are referred to in the pl. (vv. 21, 23b, 24). The text says that the individual Levite ("he") will do the work of the tent and that all the Levites *(they)* will bear someone's guilt.[13] The question remains, Whose guilt?

The third option (i.e., that the Levites will bear their own guilt) is the most common exegesis.[14] The context allows that the Levites are here made responsible for lay encroachment, and so bear their own guilt for transgressions. The fourth option (i.e., that the Levites will bear Israelite guilt) is grammatically sound and also agrees closely with what has been worked out in vv. 1–7. Following this option, the passage states that the

11. The following paragraphs, once again, owe much to Jacob Milgrom's seminal work, "The Encroacher and the Levite," in *Studies in Levitical Terminology,* I:5–59, esp. 22–33.

12. Ibid., p. 25.

13. Ibid., pp. 25–26. That the last clause of the verse ("in the midst of the children of Israel they shall have no inheritance") contains no separate subject and nonetheless must refer to the Levites is further evidence for the reading adopted here.

14. NIV, NEB, GNB, Moffatt; Dillmann, pp. 102–3; Gray, pp. 234–35; Noordtzij, p. 166; Allen, *EBC,* p. 856.

Levites are themselves responsible for the encroachment on the sanctuary by lay Israelites.[15] If the third option is selected, the passage affirms that the Levites will answer for their own mistakes in allowing Israelite encroachment. The difference is slight.[16] Further encroachment on the sanctuary by Israelites will no longer bring the death of many (as in the recent plague), but only the death of the Levites.[17] Of course, this consequence made it necessary for the Levitical guard to kill an encroacher for self-preservation. It is for this reason that the Levites are given the tithes as *an everlasting due through your generations* (*ḥuqqaṯ ʿôlām lᵉḏōrōṯêḵem*, v. 23b); viz., as a permanent perquisite to offset this added duty.

d. Tithe of the Tithe (18:25–32)

25 *And Yahweh spoke to Moses, saying:*

26 *"You will also speak to the Levites and you will say to them, 'When you take the tithe that I have given you from them, as your inheritance from the children of Israel, you shall set aside from it a tithe of the tithe as a contribution to Yahweh.*

27 *And your contribution shall be accounted to you as grain from the threshing floor and like the fullness of the wine vat.*

28 *So you shall set aside a contribution to Yahweh from all your tithes that you take from the children of Israel, and you will give from it a contribution to Yahweh for Aaron the priest.*

29 *From all your gifts you will set aside a contribution to Yahweh, some of all its best part,[1] the consecrated part of it.'*

15. Cook, p. 716; Greenstone, p. 197; Harrison, p. 252; Milgrom (see next note).

16. Milgrom would disagree that the difference is slight. He argues for the fourth option by comparing "to make atonement for the children of Israel that there might be no plague among the children of Israel when they encroach on the sanctuary" (8:19) with "and they will bear their guilt" (in the current passage). He concludes that "bearing guilt" *(nāśāʾ ʿāwōn)* means "making atonement" *(kipper),* and that the latter meant "paying the ransom price" *(kōp̱ēr).* The Levites, then, are responsible for paying the ransom price with their own lives for encroachment on the holy things. See Milgrom, *Studies in Levitical Terminology,* I:28–32, and *JPST,* pp. 155, 423–24. But Milgrom rearranges the text slightly to make his point, and this rearrangement vitiates his argument.

17. For a connection between "wrath" and "plague," cf. Exod. 30:12; Num. 25:9, 18; 31:16; 1 Sam. 4:17; 6:4.

1. Commentators who have trouble with this verse do so because they insist that *miqdāš* means "sanctuary" (but see the commentary above on v. 1). The pointing

30 *And you will say to them, 'When you set aside the best part of it, then the rest will be accounted to the Levites as the produce of the threshing floor and as the produce of the wine vat.*
31 *And you may eat it in any place, you and your household, for it is a wage for you in exchange for your work in the tent of meeting.*
32 *And you will bear no penalty on its account when you set aside the part from it, but you will not pollute the holy things of the children of Israel, lest you die.' "*

The Korahite rebellion put the question of the Levites' role in Israel at the center of controversy. The way in which that rebellion had been put down emphasized the exclusive role of the priests, and finally many Israelites died in a plague brought about by encroachment on the holy things. At last the people understood the great danger inherent in sanctuary trespass (chs. 16–17). Although these happenings defined what the role of the Levites was not, it left open what positive role they had to play in Israel. Ch. 18 speaks of the function of the Levites as complementary to that of the priests (cf. vv. 1–7, 21–24). Though the Levites were vital to Israel's survival since they were to act as those who would save the people from extermination, they were still not to be confused with the priests. At the end of this chapter the author makes it clear that, just as every ordinary Israelite was required to bring a tenth of his or her produce to Yahweh, so the Levite had to do so. Since Yahweh had granted the people's tithes to the Levites, the Levites' tithes would go to the priests.

25–29 A new formula marks the beginning of a new section of text. Indeed, vv. 1–24 have been addressed to Aaron, but beginning with v. 25 the addressee is Moses once again. The reason for this change is that Aaron and the priesthood are to be the beneficiaries of the current legislation. In modern terms, the address to Moses avoids a conflict of interest.

25–27 *When you take the tithe (kî-ṯiqᵉḥû mē'ēṯ . . . 'eṯ-hammaʿᵃśēr).* The word *take (lāqaḥ)* here means "to take possession of," as in Lev. 25:36 and Num. 3:47.

---

of the word is unusual and one would have expected *miqdāšô.* BDB, p. 874a, wants to read *qoḏšô,* dropping the *m* as dittography (but from what?). Budd (pp. 201, 206, following Paterson, p. 52) proposes revocalizing so as to yield "which you hallow" (presumably either *tiqdᵉšû* or *taqdîšû*). This reading requires much more than a mere revocalization, however; it requires the assumption of faulty spacing between *'eṯ* and *miqdᵉšô* and the elimination of two consonants (' and *m*). It is better to look at the phrase as an irregularly pointed appositive to *ḥelbô,* "its best part."

from them, i.e., from the Israelites (vv. 21–24).

as your inheritance. The Levites have no land inheritance, and the tithes are treated as a substitute (cf. vv. 21, 24).

you shall set aside from it a tithe of the tithe as a contribution to Yahweh (wahᵃrēmōṯem mimmennû tᵉrûmaṯ YHWH maʿᵃśēr min-hammaʿᵃśēr). Just as other Israelites are expected to set aside a contribution *(tᵉrûmâ)* to Yahweh from the abundance of their inheritance (i.e., in the land of Canaan), so the Levites are to set aside such a contribution from their inheritance (i.e., the tithe). This contribution will be counted as the Levites' equivalent to the Israelites' contributions *from the threshing floor and like the fullness of the wine vat* (v. 27), i.e., like the tithe of their agricultural produce. As already stated, the tithe of the flock from Lev. 27:30 is not mentioned here.

28 This verse repeats much of what has already been said, adding that this contribution to Yahweh is for *Aaron the priest.* Aaron is not only a historical individual here, but also the representative of the priesthood as a whole (as in vv. 1, 8, 20).

29 On *your gifts (mattᵉnōṯêḵem),* see the commentary above on v. 11. These are the gifts that the Israelites have given to the Levites, hence "gifts to you" is also an appropriate translation.[2]

Just as the Israelites' tithes are to be from the "best" (*ḥēleḇ,* lit., "fat," v. 12) parts of their crops, so the Levites' tithes are to be the *best part (ḥēleḇ)*: This *best part* is further defined as *the consecrated part of it (ʾeṯ-miqdᵉšô mimmennû),* i.e., that part of the tithe to the Levites which is consecrated to the priests' use.

30–31 Verse 30 is difficult. It begins with a new formula *And you will say to them.* What is the antecedent of *them?* The most natural assumption is that this verse is further instruction to the Levites, since the preceding instruction was directed to them (v. 26). But then one would expect "then it will be accounted *to you* as the produce" later in the verse rather than *it will be accounted to the Levites (wᵉneḥšaḇ lalᵉwîyim).* The group named by the verb *hērîm, you set aside,* seems to be different from *the Levites.*

One solution sees the priests addressed here. But this solution requires the adoption of a translation such as "demanded"[3] or "received" for *hērîm,* which does not elsewhere have such a meaning. It is unlikely that, after having used *hērîm tᵉrûmâ* in vv. 19, 24, 26, 28–29 with the

2. See Williams, *Syntax,* § 110.
3. So Noth, p. 138; Sturdy, pp. 132–33.

technical meaning "to set aside a contribution" (cf. vv. 8, 11, 28 for *tᵉrûmâ* alone), the author would use it in a unique sense in the present verse. Furthermore, it is unlikely that the priests' tithe, which had been *consecrated* (i.e., "made holy," v. 29), would be eaten *in any place* (*bᵉḵol-māqôm*, v. 31), i.e., outside the holy precincts, or that it would be called *a wage for you in exchange for your work in the tent of meeting* (*śāḵār lāḵem ḥēlep ʿᵃḇōḏaṯᵉḵem bᵉʾōhel môʿēḏ*, v. 31), a phrase very similar to that describing the Levites' tithe in v. 21. Thus, although the words *to the Levites* in v. 30 make it difficult to suppose that they are the addressees of the verse, the alternative is even more difficult.

As far back as the Vulg., this awkwardness has been felt.[4] Several modern English translations have sought to alleviate the problem. NEB and NIV move the words *to the Levites* to the address: "[You shall] say to the Levites." NJPS makes "Levites" a term of direct address: "you Levites may consider it." What is being said is that, when the Levites have set aside the tithe of the tithe for the priests, the remainder may be considered as if it were agricultural produce and be enjoyed by the worshipers. One must insert the words *the rest* in the text, either here in v. 30 or in v. 31, because it is this remainder that is counted as produce for the support of the Levite and his family (v. 31).[5] Once this holy portion is set aside and given as a contribution to the priests, the rest is looked upon as *a wage in exhange for your work in the tent of meeting,* i.e., it is not holy and may be consumed anywhere by the Levite's whole family.

The particular *work (ʿᵃḇōḏâ)* here is undoubtedly the guard duty during which the Levite is in mortal danger.[6]

32 *And you will bear no penalty (wᵉlōʾ-ṯiśᵉʾû ʿālāyw ḥēṭʾ).* The word translated as *penalty* is lit. "sin" *(ḥēṭʾ),* but it often carries the connotation of "guilt caused by sin" or, as here, "the punishment for sin."[7] When the Levites follow the divine regulation and set aside the tithe of the tithe, consecrating this portion to the use of the priests (v. 29), then there is no penalty for consuming the remainder outside the sacred precincts. But if this consecrated portion is not removed, then by consum-

4. Vulg. reads *vobis,* "to you," rather than "to the Levites." Paterson (p. 52) concluded that the Vulg. reading was original.

5. RSV, NEB, NASB, NJPS, GNB, NKJV, and Moffatt insert it in v. 30; NIV in v. 31.

6. See Milgrom, *Studies in Levitical Terminology,* I:76 n. 277.

7. For the former see Num. 27:3; Deut. 15:9; 23:22–23; 24:15; 2 K. 14:6 (= 2 Chr. 25:4). For the latter, with *nāśāʾ*, Lev. 20:20; 24:15; Num. 9:13; 18:22; and with *nāśāʾ ʿal,* as here, Lev. 19:17; 22:9; cf. Isa. 53:12.

ing it as a nonpriest and by consuming it outside the sacred precincts (into which the Levites cannot go in any case), then the Levites are polluting holy things, which is a capital offense (i.e., encroachment).

2. THE RED COW (19:1–22)

Num. 11–14, 16–17 detail several incidents of Israelite rebellion against human and divine leadership. Punishment for rebellion finally culminates in the plague at the end of ch. 17. The plague so frightened the Israelites that they were convinced that any who even approached the tent of meeting would be slain (17:27–28 [Eng. 12–13]). Yahweh responded to Israelite fear by redefining the role of the priests and especially the Levites, making them the ones who would die for encroachment on the sanctuary (18:1–7, 22–23).

All through this period rebellion had been met with death. Death for sin is surely one of the lessons of the wilderness wandering period. Num. 19 gives a procedure by which the pollution brought by contact with a corpse may be countered. The Israelites were at one with the ancient world in the view that death brought with it pollution, and that in this pollution lay a great danger.[1] Defilement by a corpse is the presupposition behind such texts as Lev. 5:2; 11:8, 24–25; 21:1–4, 11; Num. 5:2; 6:6–12; 9:6–7, 10–11. The present passage does not legislate that death brings uncleanness and that contact with a corpse transmits that uncleanness. Such was already believed by Israel (on the basis of the just-named passages) and Israel's world. This passage gives a procedure to deal with the uncleanness.

Although ch. 18 had dealt with the immediate problems growing out of the plague by redefining Levitical roles, it left unresolved the problem of what to do with the massive pollution and uncleanness created by the deaths of more than 14,700 people. In modern times, we might be more likely to worry about matters of public (physical) health and not take the ceremonial/religious aspects of uncleanness very seriously. It was not so in the ancient world in general, nor Israel in particular. To be *ṭāmē'*, "unclean," meant to be in a state antithetical to that holiness in which fellowship with God and God's community was impossible. Therefore the pollution caused by the mass-deaths in the plague would have been a primary concern to Israel.[2]

1. For parallels outside Israel, see the summary in Gray, pp. 243–44.
2. On the issue of clean and unclean in Israel, see, e.g., G. von Rad, *Old*

According to 5:2 everyone who had contact with a dead body was to be excluded from the camp. Individuals or small groups might be easily expelled following such a regulation, but, following the plague, death was all around, almost everyone would have been in contact with a corpse, and virtually all could have been excluded. Ch. 19 gives a relatively simple procedure to cleanse the uncleanness of death. Such a procedure would be important not only in the immediate context, but also in coming days when more and more of the older generation would die in the wilderness. It thus becomes a way of making progress toward Canaan for the younger generation, the generation that would still inherit the land, but not until the older generation was dead. This chapter forms a fitting conclusion to the section on the causes and consequences of rebellion in chs. 11–19. Death is the final consequence, but those heirs of the promise may have fellowship with God by following the divinely given procedure here included.

The chapter breaks into two main parts, vv. 1–10 and 11–22. The first part gives the procedure for making the "waters of impurity," which are used for cleansing people from the impurity of contact with a corpse. The second part begins with the general rule (vv. 11–13), is followed by two specific cases (vv. 14–16) and the procedures for using the "waters" (vv. 17–19), and concludes with a statement on the importance of following the procedure (vv. 20–22).

a. Making the Waters of Impurity (19:1–10)

1 *And Yahweh spoke to Moses and to Aaron, saying:*

2 *"This is the statute of the ordinance that Yahweh commanded, saying: 'Speak to the children of Israel, let them bring to you a perfect red cow that has no blemish and that has never had a yoke.*[1]

3 *And you will give it to Eleazar the priest; and it will be brought outside the camp and slaughtered in his presence.*[2]

Testament Theology, 2 vols., tr. D. Stalker (New York: Harper & Row, 1962, 1965), I:272–79; H. Ringgren, *TDOT,* V:287–96; G. Andre and H. Ringgren, *TDOT,* V:330–42.

1. Heb. *lō'-'ālâ 'āleyhā 'ōl,* lit., "not gone up on it a yoke." It may be that this unusual way of putting the matter is the result of a play on words between *lō'* ("not") and *'ōl* ("yoke") as well as between *'ālâ* ("to go up") and *'āleyhā* ("up on it"). In fact, there is a play on the consonants *'aleph, 'ayin,* and *lamed* throughout the clause.

2. Since both verbs here are masc. sing. (*wᵉhôṣî',* "he will bring"; *wᵉšāḥaṭ,* "he will slaughter"), some (e.g., Harrison, p. 254) have taken them to have Eliezar

4 *And Eleazar the priest will take some of the blood on his finger and sprinkle some of the blood seven times toward the front of the tent of meeting.*
5 *And the cow will be burned in his presence, its skin and its flesh and its blood, along with its dung, shall be burned.*[3]
6 *And the priest will take a cedar stick and hyssop and scarlet material and will fling it into the midst of the burning of the cow.*
7 *Then the priest will scrub his garments and wash his body with water; afterward he may enter the camp, although he will be unclean until the evening.*
8 *And, as for the one who burns it, he shall scrub his garments in water and wash his body in water, and be unclean until the evening.*
9 *And a man who is clean will gather the ashes of the cow and put them outside the camp in a clean place, and they will be kept for the community of the children of Israel for the waters of impurity. It is a purification offering.*
10 *And the one who gathered the ashes of the cow will scrub his garments and be unclean until the evening. And this*[4] *will be an everlasting statute for the children of Israel and for the sojourner who sojourns in their midst.*

1–2 The addressees are both Moses and Aaron, although, as before, Moses seems primary (note the sing. verbs and pronouns in v. 2).

the statute of the ordinance (ḥuqqaṯ hattôrâ). This phrase is found elsewhere only in 31:21, again in a context dealing with the cleansing of corpse contamination. The phrase is similar to "a statute of a judgment" (*ḥuqqaṯ mišpāṭ,* 27:11; 35:29). The double phrase emphasizes the definitive nature of the law. In order to cleanse a person from the impurity of contact with a corpse, one must first find a *red cow (pārâ ʾaḏummâ).* The noun *pārâ* has been translated "heifer,"[5] mainly on the basis of the LXX

as subject. The question then becomes, To whom do the words *before him* refer? The only possible referent in the text is Eliezar, but this rendering becomes awkward (unless one takes the unlikely course of imagining that he is doing this "before himself"). It is better to take both verbs here as examples of the third masc. sing. impersonal ("and one will bring it out and slaughter it in his presence"), i.e., as passives. See Davidson, *Syntax,* §§ 108a, 109; GKC, § 144d; Budd, p. 209. LXX and Vulg. read pl. in both verbs here and in v. 5.

3. Heb. *wᵉśārap . . . yiśrōp̱,* lit., "he will burn . . . he will burn." As in v. 3, these verbs are best understood as having a passive sense; see n. 2 above.

4. I.e., the cow (*pārâ,* a fem. form), hence the fem. verb; see GKC, § 144b.

5. E.g., AV, RV, RSV, NASB, NIV, NKJV.

damalis, but it means a female bovine without reference to age,[6] although the other qualifying phrases make it likely that a young cow is in view. The color *red ('ᵃḏummâ)* does not refer to an artificial color, but probably a reddish-brown, as in Gen. 25:30 (Esau's stew) or Zech. 1:8 (a horse).[7] The word *perfect (tᵉmîmâ)* means "whole" or "faultless," but is here qualified by the clauses *that has no blemish* (as with sacrificial victims generally, Lev. 22:20; Deut. 17:1) and *that has never had a yoke on it* (i.e., the cow has been used for no profane purpose and is in full strength, Deut. 21:3). That it is a female animal indicates that the rite is to be looked upon as a purification offering of the individual, since these offerings are females.[8] This conclusion is fully borne out in vv. 9, 17 (see below).

3–5 This red cow is brought to Eleazar, Aaron's son. *you will give it (ûnᵉṯattem).* The verb is pl., indicating that, while the cow is brought to Moses only (*you,* v. 2, a sing. pronoun), both Moses and Aaron present the cow to Eleazar. The text does not say why Eleazar should be selected to deal with the matter rather than Aaron himself. The majority of commentators conclude that it is because it is unfitting for the high priest to deal with a dead body (Lev. 21:11). Budd has posited that Eleazar is appointed to do this work because the high priest could not come out of the sanctuary (Lev. 21:12).[9] As has been mentioned already, however, Aaron was sent to stand "between the dead and the living" (17:13 [Eng. 16:48]) as the only one who could stop the plague, and this action clearly occurred outside the sanctuary. Perhaps stopping the plague is to be seen as a special case, done at the direct command of God himself.

6. E.g., 1 Sam. 6:7 makes it clear that a *pārâ* may have calved, thus eliminating the translation "heifer" as necessarily proper. But see BDB, p. 831a. NEB, NJPS, and GNB translate simply as "cow."

7. For further information on the color, see A. Brenner, *Colour Terms in the Old Testament,* JSOTSup 21 (Sheffield: JSOT Press, 1982), pp. 62-65.

8. Lev. 4:28, 32; 5:6; 14:10; Num. 16:4; 15:27 show that the purification offering of the individual was a female animal. The case is well argued by J. Milgrom, "The Paradox of the Red Cow," in *Studies in Cultic Theology,* pp. 85–95 (repr. from *VT* 31 [1981] 62–72); *JPST,* pp. 438–43: "A bovine is required in order to provide the maximum amount of ashes. However, the bull cannot be chosen since it represents the *ḥatta't* either of the high priest (Lev. 4:1–12; 16:11) or of the community (Lev. 4:13–21). The red cow, on the other hand, is intended for the exclusive use of the individual Israelite, and, according to the priestly code, the individual may bring only a female of the flock for a *ḥatta't* (Lev. 4:22–35; Num. 15:27–29). Thus, since the ashes of the red cow must theoretically supply the purificatory needs of the entire population, the largest female animal is selected — a cow" (*JPST,* pp. 439–40).

9. See Budd, p. 212.

The passage itself hints at the reason why Eleazar was given the duty of officiating. In the passage the job passes from Moses (and Aaron, vv. 1–3) to Eleazar (vv. 3–5) to "the priest" (vv. 6–7). The passing of the task emphasizes that this ordinance is to be *an everlasting statute* (*ḥuqqaṯ ʿôlām,* v. 10b), i.e., it is to be carried on long beyond the time of Aaron or even Eleazar to the tenure of "the priest" (whoever that one may be) in the indefinite future.

The cow is brought outside the camp and slaughtered by someone other than Eleazar but under his supervision (i.e., *in his presence, lᵉpānāyw*).[10] Eleazar dips his finger in the blood of the slain cow and sprinkles it seven times. This is the method of a purification offering of the priest or the congregation (Lev. 4:6, 17), except that in the purification offering the blood is sprinkled "before the veil" *(ʾeṯ-pᵉnê pārōḵeṯ)* in the sanctuary and here *toward the front of the tent of meeting (ʾel-nōḵaḥ pᵉnê ʾōhel-môʿēḏ)* because this ritual takes place outside the camp. That the blood is sprinkled in the direction of the sanctuary is as close as can be, given the location, to dedication on the altar.

The location of the rite has led many scholars to deny its sacrificial character, though they generally refer to parallels with the purification offering.[11] Many modern commentators have been willing to see the ritual of the red cow as what the text most clearly claims it to be in vv. 9, 17 — a purification offering.[12] There are differences between this ritual and the normal purification offering, to be sure. Indeed, the current ritual is closer to the one for the cleansing of the leper and the contaminated house (Lev. 14:1–9, 49–53) than any other.[13] The cow is burnt in its entirety outside the camp, again like the purification offering (Exod. 29:14; Lev. 4:11; 8:17; 16:27). Differences from other purification offerings are: only the skin is burnt in Lev. 4:11, 20, and the blood is burnt only here. The reason why the blood is burnt here is not hard to find. Blood is the primary agent for the cleansing function of the purification offering. By burning the blood with the cow, the ashes will have a powerful cleansing effect (see

10. This is also shown by the impersonal verbs, taken as equivalents to the passive. See nn. 2–3 above.

11. Gray, pp. 248–50; McNeile, p. 103; Binns, p. 127; Noth, pp. 140–41. The term here translated purification offering is more usually translated "sin offering."

12. E.g., Snaith, p. 167; Wenham, pp. 145–47; Budd, p. 213. This position is strongly defended by Milgrom, "Paradox," pp. 86–95, and *JPST,* pp. 160, 162, 438–43.

13. Milgrom, "Paradox," pp. 92–93.

below, vv. 12, 18–19). The reason why the blood of the cow is not offered on the altar is that it is needed in the ashes as a continuing purification offering.[14]

its dung (piršāh) probably refers not to excrement but to the contents of the intestines.[15]

6 The name Eleazar is dropped here in favor of the more generic *the priest* (see above).

a cedar stick and hyssop and scarlet material (ʿēṣ ʾerez wᵉʾēzōḇ ûšᵉnî ṯôlāʿaṯ) are added to the burning carcass of the cow. These same items are used in the narrative concerning the cleansing of lepers (Lev. 14:4, 6, 49, 51–52), although they are used in a different way there. Their use in both these rituals of cleansing leads to the conclusion that these three items are what might be called ritual detergents. Commentators have speculated on the specific conceptions behind them, but the text does not give us a clue.[16] It is most likely that the *scarlet material* is selected for its conformity to the general color of the cow. Suffice it to say that, in some way, these items are thought to strengthen the cleansing potency of the burnt cow.

hyssop (ʾēzôḇ). The traditional translation comes from the Gk. *hyssōpos,* but it is unlikely that the Hebrew indicates true hyssop, which is not native to Israel. A more likely plant may be marjoram *(origanum marjorana/maru),* the characteristics of which make it ideal for being an aspergillum or sprinkler as required by, e.g., Lev. 14:7, 51; Ps. 51:9 (Eng. 7).[17]

7–10 The main characters in this section are the priest who officiates at the rite (v. 7), a layperson who burns the cow (v. 8), and a second layperson, ceremonially clean *(ṭāhôr),* who gathers the ashes of the burnt cow and stores them outside the camp in a clean place for future use (vv. 9–10). All three of these men become ceremonially unclean *(ṭāmēʾ)* and thus ineligible to reenter the camp.

14. Ibid., p. 86.

15. As in Arab. *farṯ* and Assyr. *piršu.* See Gray, p. 252; Binns, p. 127; *HALAT,* p. 918b.

16. E.g., Keil, p. 124; Gray, p. 251; McNeile, p. 102, all hold that the cedar stick stands for continuance of life; Binns, p. 127, notes pagan parallels to the use of cedar for medicinal purposes. Most commentators see hyssop as purgative (cf. Ps. 51:9 [Eng. 7]). The scarlet material is the same color as the cow with the same symbolism (whatever that may be), probably that it is the color of blood.

17. See, e.g., R. K. Harrison, *ISBE,* rev., II:790b; L. Baldensperger and G. M. Crowfoot, "Hyssop," *PEQ* 63 (1931) 89–98.

Different levels of uncleanness are apparent. The less serious is cleansed by scrubbing one's garments, washing one's body, and remaining unclean until evening (see Lev. 11:24–25, 27–28, 31–32, 39–40; 14:16–18, 46; 17:15; 22:6; cf. Deut. 23:12). The more serious is cleansed by a seven-day waiting period and the sacrifice of a purification offering (cf. Lev. 14:10–47; 15:13–14, 28–30). The uncleanness here is the less serious variety.

scrub his garments (wᵉḵibbes bᵉḡāḏāyw). The verb is usually used of clothes. Occasionally it is used of scrubbing the human body, and where it is so used it is significant (e.g., Jer. 2:22; 4:14; Ps. 51:4, 9 [Eng. 2, 7]).

afterward he may enter the camp. This clause is not repeated for the ones who burn the cow and gather the ashes, although it may, of course, be assumed for them as well, since returning to the community as a cleansed person is one purpose of the ritual.

9 The one who gathers the ashes puts them in a clean place to store them for later when they will be put into a solution called *the waters of impurity (mê niddâ).* Just as the so-called waters of purification *(mê ḥaṭṭā'ṯ)* in 8:7 were for *removal* of pollution *(ḥaṭṭā'ṯ),* so here the waters are for the removal of *niddâ,* which comes from a word meaning "flee," and hence may mean "that which makes one flee," "an abominable thing,"[18] "an impurity." This same word is used of bodily discharges such as menstruation.

It is a purification offering (ḥaṭṭā'ṯ hû'). Here *It* refers to the collected ashes of the burned cow. The simplest meaning of the clause in the present context is that these burnt ashes count as a purification offering, even though a unique one.

10a Even the one who had started out as ritually clean *(ṭāhôr)* is made *unclean (ṭāmē')* by handling these dedicated ashes (like both the priest and the one who slaughtered the cow). His uncleanness seems less serious than the other two, however, since he has to wash only his clothes — not his body — and remain unclean until the evening.

The offering of the red cow raises what Milgrom calls a paradox — it cleanses the polluted (the one who has contacted a corpse), but pollutes the clean (the priest and the two laypeople). He solves the problem by identifying the rite with the purification offering, which does

18. This is the meaning the word has in Aramaic (cf. BDB, p. 622a) and in postbiblical Hebrew (cf. Jastrow, *Dictionary,* p. 878a). Cf. also the similar terms *the waters that bring the curse (mê hammārîm hamᵉ'ārᵃrîm)* and *the meal offering of suspicion (minḥaṯ qᵉnā'ōṯ)* in 5:15, 18–19, 23–25 above.

defile those who handle it (Lev. 16:28). The blood of this sacrifice absorbs the impurity of that which it cleanses and so contaminates anything that touches it (Lev. 6:20 [Eng. 27]). Thus, anyone who touches the cow after it is slain becomes unclean and must undergo purification (i.e., by the rituals here in vv. 7–10a).[19]

10b *And this will be an everlasting statute for the children of Israel and for the sojourner who sojourns in their midst (wehāyeṯâ liḇnê yiśrāʾēl welaggēr haggēr beṯôḵām leḥuqqaṯ ʿôlām).* Some scholars assert that this sentence goes with what follows and introduces it in much the same way as v. 2b introduces the first part of the chapter.[20] Although it is possible to read the clause in this way, one may also see this sentence as rounding off what has gone before (cf. 9:14). Perhaps it is best seen as a transition passage that belongs with both the preceding and following sections.

b. Using the Waters of Impurity (19:11–22)

11 *The one who touches any*[1] *dead human body, he will be unclean*[2] *for seven days.*

12 *He will purify himself with it*[3] *on the third day and on the seventh day, then he will be clean. But if he does not cleanse himself on the third day and on the seventh day, he will not be clean.*

13 *Anyone who touches a dead human body, one who has died, and does not cleanse himself pollutes the tabernacle of Yahweh, and that person should be cut off from Israel, for the waters of impurity were not tossed*[4] *upon him.*

14 *This is the regulation for a human who dies in a tent:*[5] *Anyone who comes into the tent and everyone in the tent will be unclean for seven days.*

19. Milgrom, "Paradox," pp. 86–87.

20. E.g., Noth, p. 141.

1. Lit., "with regard to any" *(leḵol).* The preposition in combination with *kol* here has a generalizing sense, "namely." See BDB, p. 514b; GKC, § 143e.

2. For the verb *weṭāmēʾ* see Driver, *Tenses,* § 123a.

3. Here "it" must refer to the waters of impurity; see the commentary below.

4. For the Pual verb *zōraq* with an object, see GKC, §§ 121a, b; Davidson, *Syntax,* §§ 79–80.

5. The use of the word *tent (ʾōhel)* here is a mark of the wilderness venue of the original law. The wilderness was long past for the LXX translator, who held that the law was valid beyond that period by translating "tent" as "house" *(oikia).*

15 *And every open vessel, which does not have a cover twisted*[6] *on it, it is unclean.*

16 *In open country anyone who touches one slain by the sword, or a dead body, or a human bone, or a grave will be unclean for seven days.*

17 *For the unclean one, some of the burned dust of the purification offering will be taken,*[7] *and fresh water in a vessel will be poured over*[8] *it.*

18 *And a clean person will take hyssop, dip it in the waters, and sprinkle it on the tent, on all the vessels, on the persons who are there, and on the one who touched the bone or the slain one or the corpse or the grave.*

19 *And the clean one will sprinkle it on the unclean one on the third day and on the seventh day, and he will decontaminate him on the seventh day; and he will scrub his garments and wash in water, and he will be clean in the evening.*

20 *And the person who is unclean and does not cleanse himself, that person should be cut off from the midst of the assembly, for he has polluted the holy place of Yahweh; the waters of impurity were not tossed upon him, he is unclean.*

21 *And this will be an everlasting statute for them. The one who sprinkles the waters of impurity will scrub his garments, and the one who touches the waters of impurity shall be unclean until the evening.*

22 *And everything that the unclean one touches becomes unclean; and the person who touches that one becomes unclean until the evening.*

6. MT reads *pāṯîl,* a masc. sing. noun meaning "cord" or "thread" (BDB, p. 836b). Keil (p. 125) explained *pāṯîl* as an appositive to *ṣāmîḏ,* "cover." As Gray (p. 256) points out, however, the meaning of "stopper, lid," for *ṣāmîḏ,* although common enough in Arabic, is not common elsewhere, and is unique here in the OT (the word usually means "bracelet"). Perhaps *pāṯîl* is a gloss on the unfamiliar word *ṣāmîḏ.* It is also possible that both words refer to the way in which the jars in question were sealed, viz., with a ringlike seal (*ṣāmîḏ,* "bracelet") consisting of string *(pāṯîl).* LXX reads *katadedetai* (perfect passive indicative third sing. from *katadeō,* "to fasten down"). *BHS* proposes to read *pāṯûl* (Qal masc. sing. passive absolute participle from *pāṯal,* "to twist"); cf. *HALAT,* pp. 929b, 969a. This reading seems to make the most sense and requires only a slight change; hence it is adopted here.

7. Heb. *lāqᵉḥû,* a third masc. pl. verb, also to be taken in an impersonal or passive sense; see Davidson, *Syntax,* § 108b.

8. H. J. van Dijk pointed to the meaning of the root *ntn* in certain contexts as "to pour over" ("A Neglected Connotation of Three Hebrew Verbs," *VT* 18 [1968] 16–30). S. C. Reif applied van Dijk's insight to the present verse ("A note on a neglected connotation of *ntn,*" *VT* 20 [1970] 114–16, esp. 115).

The latter part of this chapter gives specific instructions for the use of the waters of impurity that were prepared in vv. 1–10. A general statement of the regulation (v. 11) is followed by a general statement of the remedy (v. 12a) and the penalty for failure to comply with the ritual (vv. 12b–13). Then a more detailed procedure follows, including the manner of the ritual, in vv. 14–22. The heading of the latter unit is "This is the regulation . . ." *(zō'ṯ hattôrâ)*. The same kind of structure (general regulations followed by more detailed procedures), with the same heading, is found, e.g., in the laws for sacrifice in Lev. 1–6.[9]

11–13 The basic ordinance is given in summary form. *any dead human body* (*mēṯ lᵉḵol-nep̄eš 'āḏām,* lit., "a dead one with regard to any human life"). The noun *nep̄eš* can mean "life," or "a life," but here, with its supposed opposite, "a dead one" *(mēṯ),* it indicates a "corpse."[10]

Any person who comes into contact with a corpse *will be unclean for seven days.* This longer term for ritual uncleanness is also found in vv. 14, 16, and 19. The shorter term, until sundown, is found in vv. 7–8, 10, and 21–22. Other examples of the longer period of uncleanness are found in Lev. 12, 14–15.

12–13 The general procedure is stated: *He will purify himself with it* (i.e., the waters) *on the third day and the seventh day, then he will be clean (hû' yiṯḥaṭṭā'-ḇô bayyôm haššᵉlîšî ûḇayyôm haššᵉḇî'î yiṭᵉhār).* On *purify oneself* (Hithpael of *ḥāṭā'*, lit. "to sin [or go wrong] oneself") see the commentary above on 8:21. The antecedent for *it* must be the waters of impurity (v. 9), thus binding vv. 11–13 with 1–10. There is no attempt to describe the procedure of decontamination in anything but the most general terms at this point. It may not be legitimate, therefore, to compare the present description with that of vv. 17–19 in points of detail (e.g., it may be true that a person may "decontaminate himself" by the work of another, as in vv. 17–19).

The text should be translated to convey the fact that there were

9. For the whole burnt offering (Lev. 1:3–17), see the formula in 6:2 (Eng. 9) and the procedures in 6:1–6 (Eng. 8–13); for the meal offering (2:1–16), see the formula in 6:7 (Eng. 14) and the procedures in 6:7–11 (Eng. 14–18); for the peace offerings (3:1–17), see the formula in 7:11 and the procedures in 7:11–36; for the purification offering (4:1–5:13), see the formula in 6:18 (Eng. 25) and the procedures in 6:17–23 (Eng. 24–30); for the reparation offerings (5:14–26 [Eng. 5:14–6:7), see the formula in 7:1 and the procedures in 7:1–10.

10. BDB, p. 660b (4.c.[5]). Sometimes *nep̄eš* has this meaning without *mēṯ* (e.g., Lev. 19:28; 21:1; 22:4; Num. 5:2; 6:11; 9:10; Hag. 2:13). See the commentary above on 5:2.

two applications of the waters, one on the third day (i.e., midway through the period) and the other on the seventh, rather than one on the third day that would then lead to cleanness on the seventh.[11] This double application of the waters may indicate the seriousness of the pollution of contact with a corpse. Vv. 12b–13 give the negative side of the picture. Anyone who does not undergo the ritual of the waters of impurity on the third and seventh days will not (naturally enough) be decontaminated. Furthermore, however, such a one *pollutes the tabernacle of Yahweh,* and is to be *cut off from Israel.* Lev. 15:31 uses the first phrase to indicate something that will surely bring death. Uncleanness was something that was clearly transferable to the sanctuary itself, thus the need for the purification offering in the first place.[12] On the meaning of "to be cut off" *(niḵraṯ),* see the commentary above on 9:13; 15:30–31.

The clause *and that person should be cut off from Israel (wᵉniḵrᵉṯâ hannep̱eš hahî' mîyiśrā'ēl)* occurs only here and in Exod. 12:15. That Lev. 15:31 speaks of death for defilement of the tabernacle suggests that death is also the meaning of *cut off* here.

14–16 These verses list two particular instances for the application of the rule: in a tent or dwelling (vv. 14–15) and in open country (v. 16). In the first instance all those who are present in the tent with the corpse, as well as all who come into the tent while the corpse is there, are unclean. Any vessel whose lid is not securely attached will also pick up the uncleanness of death (cf. Lev. 11:32–34).[13]

In *open country* (*'al pᵉnê haśśāḏeh,* lit., "upon the face of the ground"; cf. 1 Sam. 11:11), where one is likely to run into a wider variety of occurrences, care is taken to differentiate types of pollutants: *one slain by the sword (ḥᵃlal-ḥereḇ),* i.e., one who has died by violent means; *a dead body (mēṯ),* i.e., one who has died (perhaps of natural causes); *a human bone ('eṣem 'āḏām),* perhaps a single bone, perhaps an entire skeleton; *a grave (qāḇer),*[14] where any of the above may lie buried. There seems to be no differentiation between intentional and accidental contact, although

11. For the former, see, e.g., RSV, NIV, NEB, NASB, NJPS; for the latter, see, e.g., AV, RV.

12. See Milgrom's articles on the purification offering repr. in *Studies in Cultic Theology,* pp. 67–84, esp. "Israel's Sanctuary: The Priestly 'Picture of Dorian Gray,' " pp. 75–84.

13. For early Jewish interpretation of the passage, including the proper stoppers for vessels, etc., see Mish. *Kelim* 10:1–8.

14. This law led to such practices as whitewashing tombs to make them more visible (cf. Matt. 23:27; Acts 23:13).

one may assume the latter as more common in the face of the widespread fear of pollution from corpses in the ancient world.

17–19 These verses relate some details for the ritual of decontamination. In the light of the seriousness of the situation, several factors are surprising.

First, no priest is involved, only *a clean person* (*'îš ṭāhôr,* lit., "a clean [or pure] man"). This regulation is in contrast to the ritual for the preparation of the water, which was done under the watchcare of the priest. Perhaps the priest's watchcare is intended to be understood here as well, although, as careful as the prescription seems to be, it is unlikely that this information would be excluded. There is no proof of this from the text, however.

Second, there is no mention of banishment from the camp during the period of uncleanness, as in 5:2; 31:19. Noordtzij concludes that this is perhaps to be taken for granted here.[15] Note that there is likewise no mention of banishment in the law dealing with the Nazirite (6:9–12), where one might, above all, expect it. The present passage focuses on the waters of impurity rather than making any claim to be a law that supersedes and includes all others on the subject. It may well be that this passage is intended to be taken together with others in order to have the complete ordinance for decontamination from corpse defilement.

Third, it is surprising that the word used to describe the ritual action is "to sprinkle" *(hizzeh)* in vv. 18–19 (the participle of this verb is also found in v. 21), whereas the summary in v. 13 (and also again in v. 20) uses "to throw" *(zāraq)*. It is hard to see these two words as describing the same ritual.[16]

Some scholars conclude that vv. 14–19 are from a different source than vv. 11–13, 20–22.[17] Others conclude that vv. 11–13 are intrusive into

15. Noordtzij, p. 172.

16. The verb *zāraq* (Qal) occurs 34 times, most commonly to describe throwing blood from a bowl (called a *mizrāq*) on the altar (Exod. 24:6; 29:16, 20; Lev. 1:5, 11; 3:2, 8, 13; 7:2; 8:19, 24; 9:12, 18; 17:6; Num. 18:17; 2 K. 16:13, 15; Ezek. 43:18). See BDB, p. 284b. The verb *nāzâ,* "sprinkle," occurs 4 times in the Qal and 20 times in the Hiphil (as here, *hizzâ*). In sacrificial contexts it describes sprinkling small amounts of blood, oil, or water (e.g., Exod. 29:21; Lev. 4:6, 17; 5:9; 8:11; 14:7, 16, 27, 51; 16:14, 19; Num. 19:4). See BDB, p. 633. The latter verb is used of small amounts of liquid, whereas the former is used for large amounts. It is interesting that LXX uses the term *perirrainō* for *hizzâ* and the virtual equivalent *perirrantizō* for *zōraq;* these related terms seem to mean both "to pour over" and "to sprinkle"; see LSJ, 1385a; cf. Hatch and Redpath, *Concordance,* II:1126a.

17. Snaith, p. 168.

vv. 1–10, 14–22.[18] But if any verses are intrusive in the context, they are as likely to be vv. 13, 20, with their mention of the waters "being thrown upon" the unclean party (the only Pual occurrences of the verb *zāraq* in the OT), as vv. 17–19, 21. Perhaps a general formula was used at the beginning and end (vv. 13, 20) into which the detailed prescription (vv. 14–19) was inserted. Of course, this text may be composite, but one must still question the meaning of the text's final form.

The formula *the waters of impurity were not tossed upon him (mê niddâ lōʾ zōraq ʿālāyw)* occurs in vv. 13, 20. The simplest reading takes this expression as consistent with *a clean person will . . . sprinkle it on the tent . . . on the unclean one (ʾîš ṭāhôr . . . wᵉhizzâ ʿal-hāʾōhel . . . ʿal haṭṭāmēʾ).*

some of the burned dust of the purification offering (mēʿᵃp̄ar śōrēp̄aṯ haḥaṭṭaʾṯ). The word for *dust* here *(ʿāp̄ār)* is different from the word used in v. 9 to describe the "ashes" *(ʾēp̄er)* of the burnt red cow, and both are different from the usual word used for the ashes of sacrifices *(dešen).* On the *purification offering* see the commentary above on v. 9.

fresh water (*mayim ḥayyîm,* lit., "living water"). A similar regulation exists for cleansing from "leprosy" (Lev. 14:5–6, 51–52) and bodily discharges (15:13).

hyssop (ʾēzôḇ). As already mentioned (see v. 6), the hyssop is used here in its more normal sense as an aspergillum or sprinkler.

clean person, the clean one. Although it may be surprising that a clean layperson rather than a priest is involved in the ritual here (see above), the reason may be that the person who sprinkles the unclean people and possessions becomes unclean in the process, and the desire was to save God's priest from as much uncleanness as possible.

In addition to the cleansing on the third and seventh days in the manner prescribed in vv. 12 and 18, v. 19 adds the ritual of scrubbing the clothes and washing the body in water, which is usually reserved for the lesser kinds of uncleanness. Thus the uncleanness of death is met by both types of cleansing.

20–22 Some scholars have concluded that v. 20 simply repeats v. 13.[19] Although only one clause is identical in the two verses *(and he does not cleanse himself, wᵉlōʾ yiṯḥaṭṭāʾ),* the other clauses are very close and the differences may only be for variety. However, the order of the

18. E.g., Noth, pp. 141–42. A good summary of the researches of modern scholars is found in Budd, pp. 209–12.

19. E.g., Dillmann, p. 109; Budd, p. 211; cf. de Vaulx, pp. 213–15.

clauses in the two verses is different. V. 20 moves the clause *that person should be cut off from the midst of the assembly* (*from Israel* in v. 13)[20] from fourth place to third, thus giving the clause more prominence.

The reason for the punishment (introduced by *kî*) varies in the two verses as well. In v. 13 the punishment is continued uncleanness brought about because the person has not been affused with the waters. In v. 20 the punishment is being cut off because such a one has defiled the tabernacle of Yahweh. One might conclude that the movement between vv. 13 and 20 is toward more specificity and more emphasis on the punishment. The reason may be that the ritual for cleansing intervenes in vv. 14–19 (esp. 17–19), therefore leaving those who hear the ritual described without excuse.

The first clause of v. 21 is parallel to v. 10b, and should be seen as concluding the unit vv. 11–20. There may, however, be some sense in which such a formula forms a transition between units (as was also suggested above on v. 10b).

The last part of the passage continues to deal with uncleanness. The cases here, however, do not issue from direct contact with the dead, but rather from contact with the waters of impurity or with one who has contacted the dead. For this reason these regulations fall outside the main body of the passage, and look like an appendix. The one who has sprinkled the waters of impurity on the unclean persons and their possessions himself becomes unclean, because the procedure is a purification offering, which does make the officiator unclean (Lev. 16:28). Any person who even *touches the waters of impurity shall be unclean.* This is because the purification offering absorbs the uncleanness of the one cleansed.[21] Anyone *who touches that one* (i.e., the one who is unclean) *becomes unclean,* along with *everything that the unclean one touches.* This derivative or secondhand uncleanness is of the less serious variety; it is effective only *until the evening* and may be cleansed by scrubbing garments.

20. *The assembly (haqqāhāl)* in v. 20 is probably a variant for the whole people of *Israel* in v. 13. See above on 1:2 and 16:3.

21. See the discussion above on the purification offering, as well as Milgrom, "Paradox," p. 87.

IV. THE JOURNEY FROM KADESH-BARNEA TO THE PLAINS OF MOAB (20:1–22:1)

The second so-called travel section of Numbers (cf. 11:1–12:13) focuses on a number of further incidents on the way from the area around Kadesh-barnea (from the vicinity of which it is only assumed that much of the material in chs. 13–19 comes) to the plains of Moab, where chs. 22–36 take place. Several of these incidents are given only a brief note (e.g., the death of Miriam, 20:1b; various campsites known by name only, 21:10–20), but seven are told in longer narratives: the incident at Meribah (20:2–13), the request for passage through Edom (20:14–21), the death of Aaron (20:22–29), another battle at Hormah (21:1–3), the fiery serpents (21:4–9), and the defeats of Sihon (21:21–32) and Og (21:33–35).

The focus of the narratives in chs. 13–19 has been the sin of the people and the trouble caused by it. In chs. 20–21 this focus is still present, to be sure (20:2–13; 21:4–9), but it is beginning to shift to victories given by Yahweh as the people approach Canaan (21:1–3, 21–35). It should be remembered that these victories were given to the old generation that was under a death sentence in the wilderness. A new day is coming for the Israelites.

A comparison of the campsites in chs. 20–21 and 33 shows that, while neither list is complete, the final author/editor of the book probably intended that the narratives in these chapters be read as chronologically serial. The exception may well be 21:1–3 (the second battle of Hormah), which from a geographical point of view should probably occur after the departure from Kadesh (20:22a) and before the arrival at Mt. Hor (v. 22b). This seeming misplacement may be explained by the fact that ch. 20 tells why the leaders of the people did not go into Canaan. The chapter begins with Miriam's death (v. 1), and ends with Aaron's death (vv. 22–29), with the beginning of the end for Moses narrated in between (vv. 2–13). The battle at Hormah did not fit into this scheme. In a sense these chapters form a miscellany of stories from the end of the wilderness-wandering years.

The Balaam stories (chs. 22–24) differ from the previous narratives in that they occur on the plains of Moab, the final campsite outside the land of promise. The link between the Balaam stories and the current chapters is the old, dying generation, which is present in both sections. The new generation comes on the scene with the second census in ch. 26.

A. DEATH OF MIRIAM AND DISASTER AT MERIBAH (20:1–13)

1 *And the children of Israel, the whole congregation, came into the wilderness of Zin in the first month, and the people stayed at Kadesh. And Miriam died there and was buried there.*
2 *And there was no water for the congregation, so they assembled themselves against Moses and against Aaron.*
3 *And the people contended with Moses, and they said, saying,*[1] *"O that we had perished when our brothers perished*[2] *before Yahweh.*
4 *And why have you brought the assembly of Yahweh into this wilderness to die there, we and our cattle?*
5 *And why have you brought us up from Egypt to bring us into this*

1. The words *and they said, saying (wayyō'm^{e}rû lē'mōr)* seem redundant, and the construction is unusual (but see Num. 17:27 [Eng. 12]; Exod. 15:1; 2 Sam. 5:1; 20:18; Jer. 29:24; Ezek. 33:10; Zech. 2:4). The more common construction would use the verb *dibbēr* ("to speak") with *lē'mōr* ("to say"); e.g. (in the pl.), Gen. 34:2; Num. 36:1; (sing.), Num. 1:48; 3:5, 11, 44; 4:21; 5:1, 11; 6:1, 22; 8:1, 5, 23; etc. The combination of two verbs of speaking is simply a feature of Hebrew prose writing. Though *lē'mōr* often introduces direct speech, other words usually come between it and the finite verb (see, e.g., 2 Sam. 3:18; 1 K. 12:23; 1 Chr. 21:18); see BDB, p. 56a. *BHS* suggests *wayyim^{e}rû* (for MT *wayyō'm^{e}rû*), "and they rebelled" (cf. v. 10), but with no textual support.

2. Heb. *w^{e}lû gāwa'nû bigwa' 'aḥênû.* Heb. *lû* is an optative particle that, with the perfect, expresses an unrealized wish, much as in 14:2 (Davidson, *Syntax,* § 134; Driver, *Tenses,* § 140). The *w^e* ("and") on the particle may simply be the result of the impassioned speech (so Driver, *Tenses,* § 119γ note; cf. GKC, § 154b). More likely it is consequential, i.e., it introduces that which flows from what has gone before. This kind of construction occurs especially when an interrogative follows (as in vv. 4–5) (Davidson, *Syntax,* § 136 Rem. 1d). Further examples may be found in Gray, p. 264.

evil place; it is not[3] *a place of seed and fig tree and vine and pomegranate tree —and there is no water*[4] *to drink"!*

6 *And Moses and Aaron went from before the assembly, into the door of the tent of meeting, and they fell upon their faces. And the glory of Yahweh appeared to them.*

7 *And Yahweh spoke to Moses, saying:*

8 *"Take the rod and assemble the congregation, you and Aaron your brother,*[5] *then you will speak to the rock before their eyes and it will yield some of its water. And you will bring out water for them from the rock, and you will cause the congregation and their cattle to drink."*

9 *And Moses took the rod from the presence of Yahweh as he had commanded him.*

10 *And Moses and Aaron assembled the assembly to a place in front of the rock, and he said to them, "Hear, now, you rebels, must we bring forth water from this rock for you?"*

11 *And Moses raised his hand and struck the rock twice with his rod, and many waters came out; and the congregation*[6] *and their cattle drank.*

12 *And Yahweh said to Moses and to Aaron, "Because you have not trusted in me to hold me as holy before the eyes of the children of Israel, therefore you will not lead this assembly into the land that I gave to them."*

13 *These were the waters of Meribah where the children of Israel contended with Yahweh and he showed himself holy among them.*

As ch. 20 stands in the text, it consists mainly of a discussion of the reasons why Israel's first-generation leaders were not able to go into Canaan. It begins with a brief notice of Miriam's death, followed by what was, in retrospect, a death-sentence for both Moses and Aaron (v. 12, see below),

3. Heb. *lō'* negates a noun in the construct state *(m^{e}qōm)* with several genitives (i.e., *zera'*, "seed"; *t^{e}'ēnâ,* "fig tree"; *gep̱en,* "vine"; *rimmôn,* "pomegranate tree"), all taken in a collective sense.

4. The normal position of *'ayin* is before the word that it negates in the construct state (thus it is usually *'ên*). Here it stands after a noun in the absolute state (i.e., in apposition), in order to emphasize the thing denied. See Davidson, *Syntax,* § 127 (b).

5. On the compound subject with a singular verb, see, e.g., Davidson, *Syntax,* § 114.

6. The looseness of the collective sense of the noun is seen in the fact that *hā'ēḏâ* is construed with a sing. verb *(wattēšt),* although *ûḇîrām* ("their cattle") has a pl. suffix. See Davidson, *Syntax,* § 115.

and closes with the account of Aaron's death. Moses does not actually die until Deut. 34. The question is whether this chapter is structured chronologically or topically. Three of its four sections are marked out as centering on Kadesh-barnea (vv. 1, 14, 22). It seems strange that what is arguably the centerpiece of the chapter (vv. 2–13) would be the only section not so marked. The lack of a specific locale for vv. 2–13 draws attention to this section in contrast to the other three sections. Vv. 2–13 are also made more universal in their significance by the lack of a specific site for the story. The note of v. 1 is possibly, however, meant to apply to vv. 2–13 as well; in fact, the note on Miriam's death is probably placed here only because it happened at Kadesh. If one so understands the structure of the passage, then one must still wonder how the people could have been without water at the plentiful springs of Kadesh-barnea (if, in fact, Ain Qudeirat is the correct site, as many assume). Perhaps it is because, as Wenham suggests, Kadesh-barnea may be the name of a larger area and the Israelites were in a less well-watered area when the incident in vv. 2–13 happened.[7]

Because of the similarities between the current passage and Exod. 17:1–7, many scholars have concluded that both are variants on the same tradition, with Exod. 17 usually attributed to JE and Num. 20 to P. This analysis carries with it the assumption that the P writer, or whoever composed Num. 20, simply utilized and modified an earlier tradition to explain why Moses and Aaron did not lead the people into Canaan, and that the separate event narrated in vv. 2–13 never occurred. A detailed comparison of the stories indicates that the similarities between the two are no more striking than would be expected in two accounts of different events about the same subject (i.e., lack of water).[8]

The differences between the stories are more striking than the similarities. First, in Exod. 17, only Moses is an actor, whereas in Num. 20 it is Moses and Aaron. Second, the people mention the previous death of their "brothers" (20:3), which probably refers to the deaths of the rebels of Korah's day (16:31–17:14 [Eng. 16:31–49]).[9] Third, the rod that Moses is commanded to take is probably Aaron's rod, which in ch. 17 was put

7. Wenham, p. 150 n.

8. Noth's comments (pp. 145–46) are typical of attempts to show that Exod. 17 and Num. 20 refer to the same event told differently. A careful reading of what Noth says will show that the only real similarity is in the outlines of the two stories, which, again, one would expect. Noth minimizes anything that does not fit with his theory as an editorial extra.

9. Keil (p. 150) sees the reference as to those who had died in the sojourn in the wilderness.

"before Yahweh" (v. 22 [Eng. 7]) or "before the testimony" (v. 25 [Eng. 10]; cf. 20:8–9). Fourth, the methodology that Moses is commanded to follow in Exod. 17:6 is to strike the rock, whereas in Num 20:8 it is to speak to it.

These differences, along with many other minor ones,[10] although not disproving that the author of Numbers simply reshaped Exod. 17 for a different purpose, are sufficient to show that he wished his readers to consider this a separate incident. In fact, one must assume that the author knew that readers of the account would find similarities between Exod. 17 and Num. 20, and these are not accidental. For example, it is not an accident that the Israelites complain of a lack of water and are miraculously supplied before coming to "the mountain." The difference is that the mountain in Exodus is Sinai, where God's life-giving Torah is revealed, while in Num. 20 it is Mt. Hor, where Aaron the high priest of the old generation dies and Eleazar (of the new generation) takes over as high priest. It is possible that similarity between the two incidents may have led Moses to follow God's instructions less carefully, i.e., he assumed that what had worked in Exod. 17 (striking the rock) would work again. It is certainly possible that a reader might draw the conclusion that, since all this had been done before, care in following God's instructions in each case was less important. Such a conclusion is dangerous, as vv. 2–13 will show.

1 *The children of Israel, the whole congregation.* This designation is not common, being found again only in 20:22. The usual designation would be "the congregation of Israel" (e.g., Exod. 12:3, 47; Lev. 4:13) or "the whole congregation of the children of Israel" (e.g., Exod. 16:1–2,

10. E.g., the incident in Exod. 17:1–7 takes place in the wilderness of Sin *(sîn),* while that in Num. 20:1–13 occurs in Zin *(ṣin).* In Num. 20:2 the people "assemble themselves against" *(wayyiqqāhᵃlû ʿal)* their leaders, while in Exod. 17:2 they "find fault with Moses" *(wayyāreḇ . . . ʿim-mōšeh).* In Exod. 17:2 Moses responds to the people's demand for water with a twofold "why?" while in Numbers he gives no response at this point. The response of the people is very different in Exod. 17:3 and Num. 20:5. In Exod. 17:4 Moses remonstrates with God for the acts of the people, whereas in Num. 20 nothing is said (was he used to their complaints by this time?). Different words are used for cattle (Exodus, *miqnay;* Numbers, *bᵉʿîr*) and rock (Exodus, *ṣûr;* Numbers, *selaʿ*). These differences can, of course, be explained as differences between discrete documents (e.g., Gray, pp. 256–59; McNeile, pp. 105–6). They can also be explained as well or better by the assumption that the author wished his readers to understand, in subtle ways (as well as the bigger ones explained in the text), that although Exod. 17:1–7 and Num. 20:1–13 relate similar events, they are discrete incidents.

9–10; 17:1; 35:1, 4, 20, 25; Lev. 16:5; 19:12; Num. 8:20; 17:6 [Eng. 16:41]).

came into the wilderness of Zin (wayyāḇō' û . . . miḏbar-ṣin). On Zin, see the commentary above on 13:21.

the first month. The day and year are missing. If the conclusions drawn above about the structure of the chapter are correct, then arrival at Kadesh comes after many years of wilderness wanderings. As the people had begun their wilderness wanderings at Kadesh (14:25), so they ended them there. According to 33:36–38, the Israelites came from Kadesh to Mt. Hor, where Aaron died on the first day of the fifth month of the fortieth year. According to Deut. 1:3, it was on the first day of the eleventh month of that same year that Moses began speaking to the people on the plains of Moab. The year in the current verse should probably also be the fortieth year after the exodus from Egypt. Support for this conjecture may be drawn from the fact that the people were soon to be allowed to make progress toward Canaan again (beginning in 20:14), which would only happen at the close of the wilderness wandering (cf. 14:22–35). Also, as was pointed out above, ch. 20 gives the rationale for Moses' and Aaron's deaths outside Canaan, and this story would be most relevant close to the events narrated.

and the people stayed at Kadesh. 13:26 places Kadesh in the wilderness of Paran; see the commentary there and on 10:12.

Miriam died and was buried there. The note simply records her death as that of the first of the old-generation leaders. Perhaps the author felt it important to mention her death here before the events of vv. 2–13. Although the text does not mention mourning (cf. the death of Aaron, 20:24; and of Moses, Deut. 34:8), this does not mean that there was no period of mourning for her. Perhaps the only tradition available concerned the fact that she died at Kadesh. Miriam was last mentioned in 12:1–16. She had been preeminent in the rebellion of Israel's leaders against Moses (Aaron, Korah, and others followed). Rebellion against God brings death.

2–5 The revolt here is against Moses and Aaron, although Moses, as usual, takes the lead. The beginning and end of this unit state the basic problem in slightly different terms, perhaps for literary variety (v. 2: *there was no water, w^e^lō' hāyâ mayim;* v. 5: *there is no water to drink! ûmayim 'ayin lištôṯ*). The narrator states the problem in v. 2, but the people state it in v. 5.

It is interesting that even after all that had happened in chs. 16–18, the people still complained in familiar form: *they assembled themselves together against Moses and against Aaron (wayyiqqāh^a^lû 'al-mōšeh wᵉʿal-ʾahᵃrōn).* The same idiom describes the rebellions of the golden calf (Exod. 32:1) and especially of Korah (Num. 16:3, 19; 17:7 [Eng. 16:42]).

the people contended. The verb "to contend" *(rîḇ)* is often used in legal contexts, but it is not limited to these (e.g., Exod. 23:18; Deut. 33:7).[11] The same expression *(rîḇ ʿim,* "contend with") introduces the conflict between the people and Moses over water at Rephidim (Exod. 17:2) and between the shepherds of Isaac and those of Gerar (Gen. 26:20). With a change of preposition (from *ʿim* to *ʾeṯ*) it is used in 20:13 to conclude the present scene with an etymological explanation, where, of course, the verb *rîḇ,* "to contend," is the basis for the place-name *Meribah* (*mᵉrîḇâ,* "contention").

Also familiar from other complaints are the wish to have died before this time (14:2), the questions put to Moses (11:5; 14:2–4; 16:12–14), and the title *the assembly of Yahweh* (*qᵉhal-YHWH;* 16:3).[12] *O that we had perished when our brothers perished before Yahweh (wᵉlû gāwaʿnû biḡwaʿ ʾaḥēnû lip̄nê YHWH).* Most scholars conclude that this is a reference to those who died in the aftermath of Korah's rebellion (16:32–33; 17:14 [Eng. 49]), although Keil thought that the word used here for "to perish" *(gāwaʿ)* was not suitable for this reference, and applied instead to the Israelites who had simply died in the wilderness. In the light of the use of this verb in 17:27–28 (Eng. 12–13), however, the reference to Korah's rebellion and its aftermath is more probable. The comparison of the wilderness with Egypt is reminiscent of 11:5–6, and like that complaint, this one comes to its real point at the very end (11:6b: *our eyes are only on the manna;* 20:5b: *there is no water to drink!*).

6 As in other accounts of complaints, the leader(s) go to God for the answer to the difficulty. The site of their inquiry is *the door of the tent of meeting.* This is the only complaint narrative that gives the site of the complaint, although Num. 14:10b probably implies that Moses and Aaron were in the tent.

they fell upon their faces (wayyippᵉlû ʿal-pᵉnêhem). On this expression see the commentary above on 14:5; 16:4, 22; 17:10 (Eng. 16:45). There is no report of what Moses and Aaron said to God at this point, but this is common enough in these complaint narratives; only 16:22 reports

11. In the definition of this word, BDB (p. 936) and *HALAT* (pp. 1141b–43a) are much more flexible than KB (pp. 888b–89a), which defines the word in an almost wholly legal sense.

12. The same term is used positively in Deut. 23:2–4; 31:30; Mic. 2:5; 2 Chr. 28:8.

any speech by the one who has fallen on his face before Yahweh. When other formulae than "falling on the face" are used to describe the prayer of the leader(s), then the content of the prayer is reported four times (Exod. 17:4; Num. 11:11–15; 12:13; 16:22) and not given twice (Exod. 15:25; Num. 11:2).[13]

And the glory of Yahweh appeared to them (wayyērā' k̲ᵉb̲ōd̲-YHWH 'ᵃlêhem). Of the complaint stories only 14:4–45 mentions God's glory appearing as a prelude to the answer (in 14:10b). Both that story and (probably) this one took place at Kadesh, one at the beginning of the wandering and the other at its end. Perhaps the similarities point up the congruity of the two episodes.

7–8 Yahweh gives his instructions to Moses. He is to take the rod, he and Aaron are to gather the people together, then he is to speak to the rock, which will yield some of its water to slake the thirst of the Israelite people and their animals.

the rod (hammaṭṭeh). This instrument is referred to in vv. 8–9, 11. Is it Aaron's rod that budded (17:23 [Eng. 8]) or Moses' own rod with which he, e.g., struck the Nile in Egypt (Exod. 7:17, 20) and the rock at Rephidim (Exod. 17:6)? The most logical choice would seem to be the former, since the phrase *from the presence of Yahweh (millip̲nê YHWH)* in v. 9 is probably a direct reference to the fact that this rod had been placed "before Yahweh" *(lip̲nê YHWH)* and had been taken "from Yahweh's presence" *(millip̲nê YHWH)* and replaced "before the testimony" *(lip̲nê hā'ēd̲ût)* in the tent of meeting (17:22, 24–25 [Eng. 7, 9–10]). The question of whose rod it is would probably not have come up were it not called *his* (Moses') rod in v. 11. This phrase implies only that Moses was in possession of the rod. This is the interpretation of both LXX and Vulg., neither of which transmits the word *his* in v. 11 in order to make it clear that this was Aaron's rod.[14] Yahweh gives no further instructions for the use of the rod, so that it may be seen here simply as a visible sign of Moses' authority, rather than as something with which to strike the rock.

then you will speak to the rock before their eyes (wᵉd̲ibbartem 'el-hassela' lᵉ'ênêhem). The word for *rock* here *(sela')* is different from that of Exod. 17, and indicates a cliff or crag. Most interpret the fact that

13. In the case of Exod. 16:1–36, Moses does not seem to pray at all.

14. Commentators who identify the rod as Moses' include Keil, p. 130; Cook, p. 721; Snaith, p. 168; Sturdy, p. 140; de Vaulx, p. 222; those who identify it with Aaron's are Paterson, p. 53; Gray, p. 262; McNeile, p. 106; Binns, p. 132; Noordtzij, p. 176; Wenham, p. 149; Budd, p. 218.

the noun has the definite article to indicate that it was well known, which may be true, of course, whether that rock may be located today or not. The last phrase means "in their presence" or "in their full view," but does it modify the verb "to speak" or the noun "the rock"? Most commentators do not pronounce on the matter, but Keil cites the opinion of Nachmanides that it should modify the latter and be read *the rock-before-their-eyes,* i.e., "to the rock in front of them, and standing in their sight."[15] The alternative, that the speaking is to be done "in the presence of the people" (lit., "before their eyes") makes better sense, however, because, in God's sentence on the leaders in v. 12, they are accused of not relying on God by holding him as holy "before the eyes of *[lᵉʿênê]* the children of Israel."

And you will bring out water . . . and you will cause the congregation . . . to drink. These words surely indicate that Moses was God's chosen instrument through which these particular miraculous acts (i.e., bringing forth water and causing the congregation to drink) were to be performed. Moses' response in v. 10 *(must we bring forth water from this rock for you?)* may well indicate that, in his frustration with the people, Moses forgot that he was only God's instrument, not the performer of the miracle.

9–11 In vv. 9–10 Moses proceeds to follow Yahweh's instructions (v. 8), but in v. 11 he departs from those instructions. These verses contain a restrained and laconic description of the leaders' sin, and A. Kapelrud may be correct that the story has been transmitted in its current vague form in order to inform readers that Moses and Aaron were kept from the land of promise by their sin without incriminating these heroes of the faith with very specific crimes.[16] The identity of this sin has been the subject of debate; some see it as disobedience, others as anger or self-centeredness,[17] or perhaps a combination of these. De Vaulx thinks

15. Keil, p. 131. This opinion is also found in W. Jones, *Numbers, A Homiletical Commentary on the Old Testament* (London: Dickinson, 1880), p. 361.

16. A. Kapelrud, "How Tradition Failed Moses," *JBL* 76 (1957) 242.

17. Some (e.g., Gray, pp. 261–62; McNeile, p. 107; Binns, pp. 131–32) are pessimistic about knowing what the sin was at all on the basis of Num. 20:8–11. The theory is that the original story has been suppressed here. For the best explication of this view, see Gray, pp. 261–62. Those who see it as disobedience include Noordtzij, pp. 176–78; Sturdy, pp. 139–40; Wenham, pp. 150–51 (Wenham also stresses anger); P. Buis, "Qadesh, un Lieu Maudit?" *VT* 24 (1974) 268–85; S. Lemming, "Massa und Meriba," *ZAW* 73 (1961) 71–77. Those who see it as anger or self-centeredness include Keil, pp. 130–31; Noordtzij, pp. 176–78; Wenham, pp. 150–51; Budd, pp. 218–19; E. Arden, "How Moses Failed God," *JBL* 76 (1957) 50–52.

that striking the rock was sacrilege because it represented God.[18] In fact, all these suggestions may be true.

What is clear is that Moses was commanded to take Aaron's rod, assemble the people, and speak to the rock (v. 8); what he did was to take Aaron's rod, assemble the people, speak to them harshly, and strike the rock twice (vv. 9–11). The text of Numbers has mentioned many times that Moses did exactly as God commanded. Here he did not, and inexact obedience on the part of leaders (and others) is the same as disobedience.

The key element in Moses' sin, however, goes beyond this disobedience. He was commanded to speak to the rock, and by that means alone to bring forth water for the people. His speech to the people is telling. Although the people have complained again and again throughout their sojourn from Egypt to Kadesh, and although God has been displeased with them for their constant whining and murmuring, the present passage implies only Moses' anger with them — it is he who reacts negatively; God simply makes arrangements to quench their thirst (v. 8).[19] Moses' anger causes him to assume that these people are *rebels (hammōrîm),* a term used mainly to describe reaction against God. The only text using the word that does not deal with reaction against Yahweh is the case of the rebellious son in Deut. 21:18, 20.

It may also have caused him to say, *must we bring forth water from this rock for you? (hᵃmin-hasselaʿ hazzeh nôṣîʾ lāḵem māyim).* The clause *nôṣîʾ māyim* may be translated "shall we bring forth water?" "can we bring forth water?" or "must we bring forth water?" The first option would indicate that Moses was unsure whether it was right that he should do so, the second that he was unsure whether it was possible that he should do so, and the third that he was reluctant to do so. The matter cannot be decided on philological or grammatical grounds. That Moses would be either unsure of the morality of carrying forth the command of God or of the power of God to accomplish his promise through him would be totally out of keeping with what is known of Moses elsewhere. The remaining choice *(must we bring forth . . .)* is therefore the best; it alone fits the mood

18. De Vaulx, pp. 226–27. He notes that this interpretation is in line with the Targs. and rabbinic interpretation. It is also similar to Paul's interpretation of the rock as Christ in 1 Cor. 10:4.

19. Arden posits that the purpose of this incident, beyond satisfying thirsty people, is simply to show Yahweh's glory and to sanctify his name among his people. In this purpose the incident differs from 14:4–45, when God had punished the people for complaining about manna. See Arden, "How Moses Failed God," pp. 50–51.

set by Moses' words *you rebels.*[20] The simplest reading of the verb *nôṣîʾ (must we bring forth)* is that Moses thought that he and Aaron were being called on to perform a miracle for people who were defectors from God's ways.

V. 12 calls the leaders' sin a lack of trust (see below). V. 24 and 27:14 call it rebellion; Ps. 106:33 calls Moses' reaction "rash words." If, as has been held above, Moses thought that he and Aaron were the miracle workers, he was diverting the people's attention from God, the true miracle worker, to himself. This diversion fits the description of the act as rebellion. Moses not only spoke rash words to the people, but acted violently by striking the rock rather than speaking to it in obedience to Yahweh's instruction. The text is silent concerning Aaron's specific sin here. It is clear that he had been involved in rebellion against God in the incident of the Golden Calf (Exod. 32:1–6, 21–29, 35). He had also been involved in a less clear way in Miriam's rebellion against Moses' leadership (Num. 12:1–19, 11–12).

12 It appears that modeling an illegitimate type of leadership (disobedience, anger against God's people issuing in rash words, pointing to oneself as the source rather than God, violence) or complicity in such action is enough, in the current case, to keep Moses and Aaron from going into the land of promise and to keep them from leading the Israelites into it.

Yahweh's specific charge is *you have not trusted in me to hold me as holy before the eyes of the children of Israel (lōʾ-heʾᵉmantem bî lᵉhaqdîšēnî lᵉʿênê bᵉnê yiśrāʾēl).* To trust in Yahweh means basically to find that he is worthy of reliance.[21] In Num. 14, parallels to which have already been suggested, *lōʾ-heʾᵉmîn* describes the rebellion of the Israelites, who, in spite of the many signs Yahweh had done in their midst, refused to rely on him to fulfill his further promises (see the commentary above on 14:11). Here Moses and Aaron succumb to the same sin; they have refused by their actions to rely on God to quench his people's thirst

20. I owe this point to Noordtzij, p. 176.

21. In Exod. 4, when Moses and Yahweh are discussing returning to Egypt, Moses objects that, when he tells the Hebrews that Yahweh has sent him, the people will not believe (*heʾᵉmîn,* "rely on") him (v. 4). Therefore Yahweh gives him signs that will allow them to rely on him (vv. 5, 8–9), and later they do (vv. 30–31). In Exod. 14:31, when Israel had passed through the sea, they are said to have gained confidence and trust in God ("and they believed in Yahweh and in Moses his servant," *wayyaʾᵃmînu bYHWH ûbᵉmōšeh ʿaḇdô*). Cf. A. Jepsen, *TDOT,* I:298–309, esp. 303–4.

without their aid in spite of all that he has done. They therefore disobeyed what God had commanded, culminating with Moses' striking the rock twice. As the people had refused to rely on Yahweh in their first sojourn at Kadesh and were condemned to die outside the land of promise (14:11, 22–35), so here in the second sojourn there (many years later), the leaders make the same mistake and are sentenced to the same fate.

to hold me as holy. Yahweh's second charge consists of an infinitive construct *(lᵉhaqdîšēnî),* which in this case shows an action consequent on the relying or trusting. The verb *qāḏaš* means "be set apart, consecrated, holy," and in the Hiphil "to make separate, holy," i.e., "to consecrate" or "treat as sacred." Moses and Aaron have not treated Yahweh as sacred *before the eyes of the children of Israel,* i.e., openly, as they were commanded to do in v. 8 ("speak to the rock before their eyes"). Instead, by their lack of reliance on Yahweh, they have proved to be impediments to the manifestation of Yahweh's power and holiness before the eyes of his people. When this happens, leaders of God's people have lost their ability to lead.

This second charge also contains a play on the place-name Kadesh (*qāḏēš,* from *qdš,* the same root as *haqdîš,* "to hold as holy"). The place was to be known by what the people did there, viz., "holding Yahweh as holy." It will be known, however, first of all, by another name.

13 That name is *Meribah* ("contention, strife") because at this place *the children of Israel contended with Yahweh (rāḇû ḇᵉnê-yiśrā'ēl 'eṯ-YHWH).* This explanation is drawn from the use of the verb "to contend" *(rîḇ)* here and in v. 3. This site is remembered by a place-name that memorialized this contention rather than the sin of Moses and Aaron. The name Meribah was also given to a site near Rephidim in the Sinai (Exod. 17:7), and scholars continue to identify the two narratives (but see the discussion above).[22]

and he showed himself holy among them (wayyiqqāḏēš bām). Yahweh showed his own holiness (thus the reflexive verb) — his separateness, power, in short, everything that made him God — in two ways. First, he showed it by giving water to his thirsty people and their animals. Second, he judged the sin of his trusted leaders Moses and Aaron. In doing so, he showed that everyone must fulfill his commandments, even (especially!) his leaders.

As has been pointed out above, the root of the word *holy* in vv. 12

22. See, e.g., Coats, *Rebellion in the Wilderness,* pp. 71–82; de Vaulx, pp. 221–24; Budd, pp. 216–17.

and 13 are the same as that of the place-name Kadesh. This site is elsewhere called Meribah of Kadesh or Meribath-kadesh (*m^e rîḇaṯ-qāḏēš,* Num. 27:14; Deut. 32:51; Ezek. 47:19;[23] 48:28) in order to differentiate it from the other Meribah. Meribah is referred to in 20:24; Ps. 81:8 (Eng. 7); 106:32, and Meribah by Rephidim in Exod. 17:7; Deut. 33:8; Ps. 95:8.

B. REQUEST TO PASS THROUGH EDOM (20:14–21)

14 *And Moses sent messengers from Kadesh to the king of Edom: "Thus says your brother Israel, you know all the misfortune that has found us.*
15 *How[1] our fathers descended into Egypt and stayed in Egypt many days, and how Egypt did harm[2] to us and to our fathers.*
16 *And how we cried out to Yahweh and he heard our voice and sent an angel and brought us out from Egypt. And behold, we are in Kadesh, a city on the outskirts[3] of your border.*
17 *Now let us pass over into your land. We will not trespass into field or vineyard, and we will not drink well water, we will go on the King's Highway, we will not turn right or left until we have crossed over your border."*
18 *And Edom said to him, "You may not cross over me, lest I come out with the sword against you."[4]*
19 *Then the children of Israel said to him: "We will go up by the highway, and if we should drink your waters, I and my cattle, then*

23. MT reads *m^e rîḇôṯ-qāḏēš,* but *BHS* proposes to read *m^e rîḇaṯ-qāḏēš* on the basis of readings found in fragments from the Cairo Geniza and a few mss. of Pesh., Targ., and Vulg. Cf., e.g., G. A. Cooke, *A Critical and Exegetical Commentary on the Book of Ezekiel,* ICC (Edinburgh: T. & T. Clark, 1936), pp. 528, 531.

1. On *w^e* as "how," see Harper, *Syntax,* § 24.2.f.

2. The imperfects consecutive in this verse mark an expansion on the "misfortune" *(hatt^e lā'â)* of v. 14 rather than time sequence. See Driver, *Tenses,* § 76a.

3. Heb. *q^e ṣēh* (absolute *qāṣeh*) is related to a verb that means "cut off," "separated," hence "remote." See BDB, p. 891b. It is used of the "end" of something, e.g., the tip of a rod (Judg. 6:21; 1 Sam. 14:27, 43) or the ends of the tabernacle curtains (Exod. 26:5; 36:12). It may also be used to describe the "extremity" of a field (Gen. 23:9) or a valley (Josh. 15:8). It may also describe the "outskirts" of a town (1 Sam. 9:27) or of the Israelite camp (Num. 11:1). See BDB, p. 892a.

4. On this construction with *pen,* "lest," the clause that precedes the *pen* clause contains that which will prevent the clause with *pen* from coming to be. See GKC, § 152w.

I will give their price to you. Only —it is nothing —let me cross over on my feet."[5]

20 *But he said, "You may not cross over." And Edom came out against him with numerous people and with a mighty hand.*

21 *So Edom refused to allow*[6] *Israel to cross over into his territory, and Israel turned aside from near him.*

This passage deals with Israel's approach to Edom. Since the disastrous attempt to enter Canaan from the south had failed (14:39–45), another way of approach was sought. The easiest way to get to Canaan from Kadesh-barnea (other than the southern route) was to travel straight east, which would have taken them into Edom. The territory of Edom takes in basically the approximately 70 mi. from the Brook Zered on the north to the scarp of the *Neqb esh-Shtar* overlooking the *Ḥismeh* Valley on the south. The width is about 15 mi. from the Arabah in the west to the hills facing the desert in the east.[7] It is likely that Edom exerted influence over a wider area than this from time to time during its history.[8] Although there are traces of civilization in this area from as early as 4000 B.C., and a high degree of it from about 2200–1900, there is a gap in cultural remains from about 1900 to 1300 B.C. During these centuries bedouin seem to have been the major inhabitants of the land.[9] One first hears of Edom in Egyptian texts from the late 13th and early 12th centuries.[10] Bartlett has shown that

5. This sentence is difficult. LXX *alla to pragma ouden estin* supports MT. Sam. Pent. reads *nāsûr* (cf. Deut. 2:27), hence "only in nothing will we turn aside" (i.e., neither to the right or the left, as in v. 17). See BDB, p. 956b (2b); cf. Deut. 2:28 for the clause uncluttered by *'ên dāḇār*. The Eng. translations vary, though agreeing on the basic sense (e.g., RSV "nothing more," NIV "nothing else," NEB "simply").

6. The form of the infinitive construct *(n*ᵉ*ṯōn)* is unusual. One would expect *tēṯ* or *lāṯēṯ*. See GKC, § 66i.

7. These borders are somewhat indeterminate; cf. S. Cohen, "Edom," *IDB*, II:24; modified by C.-M. Bennett, "Edom," *IDBSup*, 251. Also see the older article of N. Glueck, "The Boundaries of Edom," *HUCA* 11 (1936) 141–57; and J. R. Bartlett, "The Land of Seir and the Brotherhood of Edom," *JTS* 20 (1969) 1–20.

8. See, e.g., Cohen, "Edom," p. 25; Bartlett, "Land of Seir," pp. 1–20, esp. 18–20, who differentiates Seir from Edom proper.

9. See N. Glueck, "The Civilization of the Edomites," *BA* 10 (1947) 77.

10. Edom and Seir are first mentioned by Pharaoh Merneptah (ca. 1224–1211 B.C.) and Ramses III (ca. 1183–1152 B.C.); see Glueck, "Civilization," 77; J. Bright, *A History of Israel*, 3rd ed. (Philadelphia: Westminster, 1981), p. 469.

the Edomites were an independent state of the organized type only in the 8th–6th cents. (much after the time of the conquest).[11] This kind of information affects the interpretation of these verses.

14 Moses sends a diplomatic mission to the *king of Edom (meleḵ-'ᵉḏôm)*. Gen. 36:31–39 (probably a gloss) holds that Edom had a king before Israel did. Indeed, the whole story of Jacob (= Israel) and Esau (= Edom) assumes that Esau is the elder brother (Gen. 25:19–34). It is doubtful, however, if Edom was organized into a centralized monarchy at this point, and there is no external evidence for kingship in Edom at this period.[12] Perhaps the Edomite kings who reigned at this time (Gen. 36:31–39) and the Edomite "chiefs" *('allûp̄îm,* vv. 15–19, 40–43) are not to be greatly differentiated.[13] The current text does not demand that Edom be a centralized monarchy, or even a place, only that there be some kind of Edomite ruler to which the request was made. The Israelites probably did not know what they would find in Edom; therefore a diplomatic letter addressed to "the king of Edom" could not fail in stroking the ego of a petty ruler in that territory.[14] The text also does not mention where the ambassadors were sent. It is not necessary to think of a national capital city; perhaps it was one of the Edomite outposts nearer to Kadesh.

your brother Israel. Texts that speak of a family relationship between Israel and Edom have already been referred to above (the patriarchal stories of Jacob and Esau, e.g., Gen. 25:19–34; 27:1–45; 32:1–33:20). Other passages are Deut. 2:4; 23:8; Amos 1:10. From time to time the Israelites and the Edomites were enemies; the bitterest opposi-

11. J. R. Bartlett, "The Rise and Fall of the Kingdom of Edom," *PEQ* 104 (1972) 26–37.

12. See, e.g., ibid., esp. p. 26.

13. Heb. *meleḵ,* "king," is flexible and may refer to great kings, such as those in Egypt (Gen. 39:20), Assyria (2 K. 15:19), Babylon (2 K. 24:1), or Persia (Ezra 1:1); to lesser national kings, such as those in Israel and Judah (2 Sam. 2:4; etc.); and to petty rulers of such local places as Sodom (Gen. 14:2), Gerar (Gen. 20:2), Jericho (Josh. 6:2), or Ai (Josh. 8:2)

14. Edom *('ᵉḏôm)* refers to Esau (Gen. 25:30; 36:1, 8, 19), the people descended from Esau, the Edomites (e.g., Gen. 36:9, 43; 1 Sam. 14:47 and 31 other times), or the land of Edom (Gen. 36:32, 43 and 32 other times). When the land is meant, *'ᵉḏôm* may be combined with *'ereṣ* ("land"; e.g., Gen. 36:16, 17, 21, 31; Num. 20:23; 21:4; 33:37). It is, quite often, unclear as to whether the people or the land is meant (as here; so also Exod. 15:15; Num. 24:18, etc.). The diplomatic note in vv. 14b–17, 19 has some remarkable parallels in form and content to some of the Amarna letters; cf. *ANET,* pp. 482–90. Also see the short letters (ca. 1000 B.C.) in W. Beyerlin, ed., *Near Eastern Religious Texts Relating to the Old Testament,* OTL (Philadelphia: Westminster, 1978), pp. 43–44.

tion was in the time of Jerusalem's fall to Babylon in 587/86 (see Obadiah).

the misfortune (hatt^{e}lā'â). The root meaning of the word is "weariness," hence "that which wears one out." In Exod. 18:8 the word refers to hardships suffered between Egypt and Sinai, in Neh. 9:32 to hardships suffered in the history of Israel. In Lam. 3:5 the word refers to the ignominy of the defeat of Jerusalem in 587/86 and is paralleled to "bitterness" or "venom" *(rō'š).*[15]

15–16 These verses contain a thumbnail sketch of events in the history of Israel that were deemed important for the king of Edom to know: the descent into Egypt, the bondage there, and the divine deliverance from that bondage. Many other things are left out of the picture because the point is to explain, in short compass, how the people got to Kadesh, and that they were brought there under divine leadership — a point designed to enhance the Israelite request for passage through Edom. While the reason why this divine leadership should be couched in terms of *an angel* is unknown, one may conjecture that such phrasing was designed to be both understood by and impressive to the Edomites. The Exodus story includes the presence of an angel of Yahweh at Exod. 14:19; 23:20; and 32:34, so the concept is not unheard-of in Israel at this time.

It is notable how often the Hebrew text of this passage switches between a sing. (collective) and a pl. verb or pronoun (the translation attempts to show this as much as possible). The reason for this seeming inconsistency is likely that Israelite thought was more fluid than modern Western thought in the matter of a people's being conceived of as present in an individual *or* in the group. This notion may also be seen in the fact that harm to the fathers meant harm to the present generation.

we are in Kadesh, a city on the outskirts of your border ('^{a}naḥnû ḇ^{e}qāḏēš 'îr q^{e}ṣēh g^{e}ḇûleḵā). Noth raises the question of why Kadesh, which was really only a series of wells, should be called a *city* here.[16] But this question does not take adequate account of the diplomatic nature of the present text. Its purpose is not preciseness in every detail, but a general impression of where the Israelites are, why they are there, and what they want from Edom. Since Kadesh-barnea is in what became Judah's territory (Num. 34:4), that Kadesh is called *a city on the outskirts of your border* has caused some commentators to conclude that Edom must have

15. If this is the right text; cf. *BHS* and, e.g., H. L. Ellison, "Lamentations," *EBC* (Grand Rapids: Zondervan, 1986), VI:719.

16. See Noth, p. 150.

exercised sovereignty west of the Arabah at this time, that the Kadesh mentioned here is not Kadesh-barnea but some Kadesh further east, or that the story is a late fabrication.[17] At present, no extrabiblical evidence confirms the first conclusion, the second conclusion assumes the existence of a site about which we know really nothing elsewhere, and the third comes from entrapment in philosophical presuppositions that are unnecessary.[18] Once again, the most likely solution seems to be to posit that the diplomatic message is not attempting scientific precision, and when Kadesh is called *a city on the outskirts of your border* it means no more than that the Israelites are near to Edom as opposed from far away from it.[19] Thus Gray's assumption that *g^eḇûl* here means "territory" (which the term does mean sometimes) rather than *border* is not necessary.[20]

17–18 These verses contain the actual request for passage, based on all that has gone before, and Edom's reply. It is interesting that the request does not divulge why the Israelites need passage through Edom, or their final destination. The pledge is that the Israelites will not go through Edom like a conquering army, much less like marauding bandits. Rather, they will act circumspectly by staying on the road. Of course, this is the language of diplomacy. The large number of Hebrews could not hope to cross through Edomite territory in one day, and one wonders where they planned to stay, what provisions they were to eat, etc. Whatever the answer to these questions, the gist of the message was that Israel will not be a burden on Edom.

the King's Highway (dereḵ-hammeleḵ) is an ancient roadway running north to south from Damascus to the Gulf of Aqabah through Bashan, Gilead, Ammon, Moab, and Edom. It was used by traders and was guarded by a line of fortresses from as early as the Early Bronze IV–Middle

17. For the first option see, e.g., Gray, p. 266; Binns, p. 134. For the second see Wenham, p. 152. For the third see, e.g., Sturdy, pp. 141–42.

18. On the first point see, e.g., Bartlett, "Rise and Fall"; earlier see N. Glueck, "Boundaries," pp. 141–57, esp. 152–57; idem, "Civilization," pp. 77–84. See also S. Cohen, *IDB,* II:24–26; C.-M. Bennett, *IDBSup,* pp. 251–52; B. MacDonald, *ISBE,* rev., II:18–21. On the third point, Noth's comments on this text (pp. 148–52) are so entangled in his presuppostions of what must have happened from a literary- and tradition-critical perspective that the text itself is virtually silenced. Sturdy's conclusion is likewise based on conclusions that he has already drawn (see pp. 141–42).

19. That the border of Judah touches the border of Edom is also stated in Num. 34:3–5; Josh. 15:1–12 (esp. v. 1), so that the current view of geography is found again.

20. See Gray, p. 269; BDB, pp. 147b–48a, agrees with Gray.

Bronze I (ca. 2200–1800 B.C.) and Iron I periods (ca. 1200–1000 B.C.). It may be along this route that Chedorlaomer's forces attacked (Gen. 14). One should not think of a paved highway built at the expense of the state (so Keil), but a well-marked track along which not only people on foot but also people with animals and in wagons and chariots (i.e., kings' armies) could pass.[21] The mention of *fields, vineyards,* and *wells* may speak of the fertility of the area. Again, however, one wonders where Israelite knowledge of the topography of the land came from, and whether these are not simply stock phrases. That the same phrases are used for completely different territory in 21:22 would seem to confirm the latter suspicion. The response of Edom (using a collective sing. for the ruler or chieftain) was refusal and a threat to come against the Israelites with a military force (v. 18).

19–20 That both vv. 17–18 and 19–20 deal with negotiations and refusal to grant passage has led some commentators to the conclusion that these verses are doublets and that the presence of these doublets confirms a composite text.[22] But negotiations are not always successful on the first try. After receiving a first refusal from Edom, the *children of Israel* (i.e., the messengers sent by Moses) offered to negotiate further. They say, *We will go up* (or "let us go up," *naʿᵃleh*) *by the highway (bammᵉsillâ).* The word *mᵉsillâ* is related to a word that means "lift up," and usually refers to a main country thoroughfare (not a city street) that will bear more than pedestrian traffic.

The second modification in the Israelite proposal is a recognition that both cattle and humans must have water. If any Edomite well water is taken, the Israelites will furnish adequate compensation for it.

it is nothing (ʾên dāḇār). This phrase interrupts the clause *only . . . let me cross over on my feet (raq . . . bᵉraḡlay ʾeʿĕḇōrâ).* If MT is correct here (and LXX follows it),[23] then it means that the matter of passage ought to be a simple one and need not cause any difficulties between the "brothers." The phrase *it is nothing,* then, means that Israel's request is a

21. See Keil, pp. 134–35; also, e.g., Glueck, "Boundaries," pp. 143–44; idem, "Civilization," p. 80; also J. Krautz, III, *ISBE,* rev., III:39. Both B. Oded ("Observations on Methods of Assyrian Rule in Transjordania after the Palestinian Campaign of Tiglath-pileser III," *JNES* 29 [1970] 177–86, esp. 182 n. 41) and Bartlett ("Rise and Fall," pp. 26, 33–34) think that this name reflects usage in the Assyrian period in the 8th–6th cents. B.C. This theory necessitates either a late redaction of the biblical text or a modernizing gloss in it.

22. E.g., Gray, pp. 264–68; Binns, pp. 132–34; Noth, pp. 150–51; O. Eissfeldt, *Hexateuch Synopse,* pp. 178–79.

23. See n. 5 above.

small thing. The small thing is, in turn, clarified by *only . . . let me cross over on my feet.* Because permission is sought to travel by the highway, Edom could be suspicious that Israel was moving both foot soldiers and chariotry through their territory. This clause is meant to assure the Edomites that Israel will not be bringing war materiel along the way, but only people walking on foot.

20–21 Edom refuses to negotiate the matter and again denies Israel permission to pass through its territory. Furthermore, Edom makes good on the threat of v. 18 and does take the field against Israel. The current verses are a summary to conclude the present narrative, and in a sense must be kept separate from v. 22, which tells of the departure from Kadesh.

The point is made that Edom took the field *with numerous people and with a mighty hand* (i.e., great power), which may imply that the Edomites greatly outnumbered the Israelites, hence the Israelites *turned aside* rather than to fight. But the Canaanites also outnumbered Israel (Deut. 7:1, 7), and God commanded Israel to fight against them. More important than numbers may be that Edom formed no part of the land of promise (Josh. 15:1); thus Israel did not feel compelled to fight, and turned aside to find another route to Canaan.

C. DEATH OF AARON (20:22–29)

22 *And the children of Israel, the whole congregation, set out from Kadesh and came to Mount Hor.*

23 *And Yahweh spoke to Moses and to Aaron at Mount Hor on the border of the land of Edom.*

24 *"Aaron is to be gathered to his kinfolk,*[1] *for he is not to enter the land that I have given to the children of Israel, since you rebelled against my word with regard to the waters of Meribah.*

25 *Take Aaron and Eleazar his son and bring them up on Mount Hor.*

26 *And strip*[2] *Aaron of his garments and put them on Eleazar his son, for Aaron will be gathered and die there."*

1. Sam. Pent., LXX, and Targs. read a sing. *ʿammô* (see *BHS*) for MT pl. *ʿammāyw,* "his peoples." This idiom occurs in Gen. 25:8, 17; 35:29; 49:33, where all texts and versions read the plural. In Num. 27:13; 31:2; and Deut. 32:50 (the same expression used of Moses) the versions also read the singular. Although one cannot be sure whether the sing. or pl. is original on the basis of this textual evidence, as Gray (pp. 270–71) points out, similar expressions use pl. forms, and MT may be retained; cf. also BDB, p. 3b (§ 4b).

2. Verbs of clothing usually take two objects, as here. See Davidson, *Syntax,* § 75.

27 *And Moses did as Yahweh commanded, and they went up on Mount Hor in the sight of the whole congregation.*
28 *Then Moses stripped Aaron of his garments and put them on Eleazar his son. And Aaron died there on the top of the mountain. Then Moses and Eleazar went down from the mountain.*
29 *When the whole congregation saw that Aaron had perished, the whole house of Israel wept for thirty days for Aaron.*[3]

With the death of Aaron the first fulfillment of the awful prediction of 20:12 comes to pass. In the midst of uncertainty about geographical details of the passage, one must not lose sight of the fact that it narrates the story of the death of Israel's first high priest. Since it is, in the end, a story of Aaron's failure, it should not be surprising that, like the story of the sin itself (20:2–12), it is almost reticent in its tone. It is also not surprising that this story has parallels to that of the death of Moses in Deut. 34: both take place on a mountain (20:22–23; Deut. 34:1), neither leader is to be allowed to enter the land (20:24; Deut. 34:4b); mourning lasts for thirty days (20:29; Deut. 34:8); and there is a transfer of leadership (20:25–26; Deut. 34:9). But the way in which the material in the two stories is developed and arranged, as well as the vocabulary, makes it highly unlikely that the Aaron narrative was simply modeled on Deut. 34.[4]

22–23 Verse 22 is a travel summary (cf. 10:12), into which may be fitted some of the events in vv. 14–21 and 21:1–3.

Mount Hor (*hōr hāhār,* lit., "Hor, the mountain"). The proper name precedes the title only with Mt. Hor (the usual form is, e.g., *har-sînay,* "Mount Sinai"). The actual site is unknown. The traditional identification, as old as Josephus,[5] is Jebel Nebi Harun ("Mount of the prophet Aaron") near Petra, which does not meet the criterion of being on Edom's border (v. 23). Jebel Nebi Harun is also too high a peak for the congregation to witness events there (see below). Scholars have suggested other possible sites: Jebel Meḏra, east-northeast of Kadesh; Jebel Murweile, about 9 mi. northwest of Kadesh; or Jebel Madurah, about 15 mi. northeast of Kadesh.[6] While the last location has the strongest scholarly support and

3. The Bomberg Rabbinic Bible begins ch. 21 with this verse.

4. Contra Noth, p. 153; cf. Binns, p. 136; H. Gressmann, *Moses und Seine Zeit: Kommentar zu den Mose-Sagen* (Göttingen: Vandenhoeck & Ruprecht, 1913), p. 343.

5. Josephus, *Ant.* 4.4.7.

6. For the first see, e.g., N. Glueck, *Rivers in the Desert* (New York: Norton, 1968), p. 206. For the second see, e.g., M. J. Lagrange, "L'Itinéraire des Israélites," *RB* 9 (1900) 280–81. For the third see, e.g., Gray, p. 270 (also contains

may be considered the most likely (not the least because it is partway to Arad [21:1–3]), certainty is not possible.[7]

24–26 *Aaron is to be gathered to his kinfolk (yēʾāsēp̱ ʾahᵃrōn ʾel-ʿammāyw).* This specific idiom is found with reference to Abraham (Gen. 25:8), Ishmael (25:17), Isaac (35:29), Jacob (49:33), and Moses (Num. 27:13; 31:12; Deut. 32:50). *kinfolk (ʿammāyw,* lit., "his peoples") may be understood in the sense of "clan." The meaning of this idiom for death is obscure. Since different verbs are used for dying *(mûṯ)* and being buried (Niphal of *qāḇar*), the idiom does not refer to dying or being buried per se. Neither Moses nor Aaron was buried in an ancestral grave, and this also separates the idiom from burial customs. In the end, it is best to admit that we do not have the information to know just what this idiom means in detail, although some kind of solidarity with one's kin after death is likely.[8]

The sin of both Moses and Aaron is here named as rebellion *(you rebelled, mᵉrîṯem).* The term is directly related to those in 17:25 (Eng. 10) and 20:10. The term indicates a conscious defection from God's will and

---

a list of older scholars who held this view); McNeile, p. 109; Snaith, p. 170; de Vaulx, p. 231; Budd, p. 227; cf. J. Mihelic, *IDB,* II:644; R. K. Harrison, *ISBE,* rev., II:755–56.

7. An alternative is that, although Hor has been taken as a proper name, it is really only an archaic form of *hār,* "mountain." The name Hor is applied to a mountain in Lebanon in 34:7. Here LXX translates *to oros to oros,* "the mountain (of) the mountain," or "the summit of the mountain." Some support for this sense may be found in the unique word order "Hor, the mountain." This view is at least as old as Jerome, who wrote: "it is possible to read, 'Aaron the priest ascended onto the summit of the mountain' " *(Epistula ad Fabiolam).* See Cook, p. 724; Budd, p. 227; cf. Gray (p. 270), who cites Jerome in support of the traditional location of Mt. Hor at Petra.

8. Wenham, p. 153, states that the idiom relates to the reunion of the family in Sheol (see also B. Alfrink, "L'expression *neʾᵉsap̱ ʾel-ammāyw,*" *OTS* 5 [1948] 118–31). Although it may be true that the idiom does, in some way, relate the union of a dead person with his ancestors, we must be careful not to assume that we know what the Hebrew view of life after death was at this period in Israel's history. Indeed, it is difficult to show that the Hebrews had one cogent view of life after death. Wenham uses 2 Sam. 12:23 in support of his contention about life after death. The passage in 2 Sam. 12:23 is as likely to be a statement about the immutability of death as it is a statement about life after death (H. W. Hertzberg, *I and II Samuel,* OTL, tr. J. Bowden (Philadelphia: Westminster, 1964), p. 316. Milgrom's view is that "being gathered" is the act between dying and being buried. He also connects it with a reunion with one's family in Sheol (Milgrom, *JPST,* pp. 169–70, 405–8). For a compact discussion of different views, see G. Lee, *ISBE,* rev., II:414. For other views, see, e.g., Binns, p. 135.

way. This statement ties the current passage to 20:1–13. Eleazar, Aaron's oldest suriving son (probably his third; Exod. 6:23; Num. 3:2), is to be invested with the high priesthood. He has already been given priestly responsibilities in Num. 3:2–4; 4:16; 17:1–5 (Eng. 16:36–40); 19:3–7. The ceremony for the transfer of the high priesthood consists in the transfer of the high priest's vestments (Lev. 8:7–9) from Aaron to Eleazar.[9] The regulation governing the transfer is found in Exod. 29:29–30. Whether the transfer involved more of a ceremony than is here reported (cf. Lev. 8) is unknown, but, since Eleazar had already been ordained to the priesthood, perhaps such would not have been thought necessary.

strip Aaron of his garments. The word *strip (pāšaṭ)* occurs over 40 times in the OT. In the Qal it means to strip something from *oneself* (e.g., 1 Sam. 19:24; Ezek. 26:16), while in the Hiphil (*hišpîṭ,* as here) it means to strip something from *someone else.* In no case does this stripping happen with the permission of the one stripped; an aspect of punishment or degradation is present as well.[10] From the choice of this verb, one may conclude that there is an aspect of demotion here for Aaron, but if that be the case, the matter is delicately handled by word selection only.

27–28 The command of Yahweh is carried out. *they went up on Mount Hor in the sight of the whole congregation (wayyaʿ^{a}lû ʾel-hōr hāhār l^{e}ʿênê kol-hāʿēḏâ).* This clause does not necessarily indicate that the whole congregation witnessed every aspect of the ceremony on the mountain, nor that they saw Aaron die. The text merely asserts that the people watched the party of leaders ascend Mt. Hor; i.e., the ascent was done in public. The public nature of this event may be contrasted to God's appearance on Mt. Sinai, when the cloud covered the mountain, not allowing the people to witness incidents happening there (cf. Exod. 19:9, 16, 18; 24:15–18; etc.). At this mountain, there is no cloud, so all can witness; but God does not appear, and a leader dies rather than a people being born.

9. There is no reason to hold to Noordtzij's view that the clothes involved here are simply Aaron's ordinary garments.

10. The verb is found 15 times in the Hiphil: Gen. 37:23 (Joseph's brothers strip him of his coat); Ezek.16:39 (lovers strip the unfaithful one); 23:26 (Oholibah is stripped by her lovers); 1 Sam. 31:9 (= 1 Chr. 10:9; Philistines strip Saul and sons of armor); Hos. 2:5 (Eng. 3; God strips his people naked like a harlot); Job 19:2 (God strips Job of his glory; i.e., God punishes Job); 22:9 (stripping people from their clothes, i.e., injustice; cf. Mic. 3:3). The only readings that do not have this punishment or demotion connotation are those passages (Lev. 1:6; 2 Chr. 29:34; 35:10) that speak of "flaying" the skin from the whole burnt offerings. See BDB, p. 833a.

According to Num. 33:38–39, Aaron died on the first day of the fifth month of the fortieth year after the Exodus at age 123. This information fits with the note in Exod. 7:7. Aaron was 83 at the time of the Exodus. According to Deut. 10:6, Aaron died at a site called Moserah, which is usually equated with Moseroth in Num. 33:30–31.[11] The easiest supposition is that Mosera/Moseroth was the campsite at the foot of Mt. Hor; 33:30–31 does not easily allow this assumption, however, since it sees Moseroth as six campsites before Kadesh and seven before Mt. Hor. Ewald long ago conjectured that Num. 33:36b–41a had fallen out of its correct place in the text, and ought to be inserted after 33:30a, so that the order of the campsites would be Hashmonah, Kadesh, Hor, Moseroth, etc.[12] But this conjecture has no proof. The theory of R. K Harrison that Moserah/Moseroth should be read as a common noun ("chastisement[s]") describing "the event, not the occasion of Aaron's death," still fails to deal with the placement of Moseroth in the list of Num. 33.[13] At this point it seems that the traditions behind the current text, and perhaps Num. 33:30–31, are not the same as those behind Deut. 10:6.

29 *When the whole congregation saw that Aaron had perished.* This clause supports the contention above that the congregation did not witness the whole matter, since it follows *Then Moses and Eleazar went down the mountain,* i.e., they knew that Aaron was dead when they saw Eleazar wearing Aaron's vestments (see v. 28).

thirty days. This is the same mourning period as for Moses (Deut. 34:8). The normal time for mourning is seven days (e.g., Gen. 50:10; 1 Chr. 10:12; cf. Job 2:13).[14] The prolongation of mourning shows the importance of the one who has died and the importance of the loss to Israel.

11. So, e.g., Keil, p. 136; Wenham, p. 153; Budd, pp. 227–28.

12. H. Ewald, *Geschichte des Volkes Israel* (3 vols.; Göttingen: Vandenhoeck & Ruprecht, 1843–52), I:285 n. 2; cf. S. R. Driver, *A Critical and Exegetical Commentary on the Book of Deuteronomy,* ICC (Edinburgh: T. & T. Clark, 1902), p. 119.

13. Harrison, *ISBE,* rev., II:755; cf. idem, *Introduction,* p. 639. See the commentary below on 33:30–31.

14. Gen. 50:3 tells of a 70-day mourning period for Jacob among the Egyptians. The normal period of mourning for a dead pharaoh was 72 days. See G. von Rad, *Genesis: A Commentary,* tr. J. Marks, OTL (Philadelphia: Westminster, 1961), p. 425. Joseph and the Hebrews mourned Jacob seven more days when they buried him (50:10).

D. SECOND BATTLE OF HORMAH (21:1–3)

1 *And the Canaanite, the king of Arad,*[1] *who was dwelling in the Negeb, heard that Israel was coming by the Way of Atharim, and he fought against Israel and took some of him captive.*[2]

2 *And Israel vowed a vow to Yahweh, and he said, "If*[3] *you will surely give*[4] *this people into my hand, then I will put their cities to the ban."*

3 *And Yahweh listened to Israel's voice, and he gave the Canaanites into his hand,*[5] *and he put them and their cities to the ban; and he called the name of the place Hormah.*

After Israel's defection from God's leadership following the report of the spies (14:1–10a), Yahweh condemned the old generation to wander forty years and to die in the wilderness without claiming the land of promise (14:10b–38). In a misguided attempt to put things right, the people then tried to go into Canaan from the south, only to be humiliated and pursued as far as a place called Hormah (*haḥōrmâ*, lit., "the destruction," 14:39–45). If one assumes that 21:1–3 took place around the time of Aaron's death, as the placement of texts seems to indicate, then the time is 38 years later (33:38). The Hebrews have returned to the same area, but this time it is not their own destruction that is related, but that of the Canaanites.

As Israel had begun at Kadesh-barnea before the death sentence in 14:20–24 and had come back to Kadesh-barnea to mark its end (20:1), so they traveled north from Kadesh, as they had foolishly done 38 years before, to the area of Hormah. On the way Aaron the high priest died at Mt. Hor. As being at Kadesh forms a framework for the wilderness wanderings, so does being at Hormah. After this victory at Hormah, where there had once been defeat, the Israelites are victorious regularly (21:21–

1. Heb. *hakkᵉnaʿᵃnî meleḵ-ʿᵃrāḏ* is difficult; not only does the gentilic (*hakkᵉnaʿᵃnî*) usually mean the collective, "the Canaanites," as in v. 3, but the gentilic also usually follows such titles (see BDB, p. 489a). Thus "the Canaanite king of Arad" would probably require *meleḵ ʿᵃrāḏ hakkᵉnaʿᵃnî* (see Budd, p. 229, who translates this way but sees "king of Arad" as a gloss). Cf. Gray, p. 273; Paterson, p. 54.

2. On the pointing of *wayyišb,* see GKC, § 75q.

3. When the condition has any possibility of coming to be, the simplest construction to express it is with the imperfect in the protasis and the perfect consecutive (or simple imperfect) in the apodosis; see Davidson, *Syntax,* § 130.

4. Heb. *'im-nāṯōn tittēn.* Often the protasis is strengthened by the addition of the infinitive absolute (here *nāṯōn*), but only with *'im* plus the imperfect (here *tittēn*), not with either *kî* or the perfect; see Davidson, *Syntax,* § 130 Rem. 3.

35). These victories occur before the old generation has completely died out. Although they will not claim the promise themselves, they will begin to see it fulfilled.

As suggested above at ch. 20, this passage is probably placed where it is because of subject matter rather than chronology, and may very well have happened on the way to Mt. Hor. But if Mt. Hor is identified with some of the places north of Kadesh (esp. Jebel Madurah), it is conceivable (if less likely) that the Israelites could have proceeded further north from Mt. Hor before meeting the resistance described here. The defect in such an explanation is that one must then explain why they turned south in v. 4 rather than continuing with a conquest from the south.

1 The opening verse relates an attack by the Canaanites on the approaching Israelites.

the king of Arad. In addition to the syntactic difficulties noted in the translation above, mention of this king is problematic in that he is not mentioned again in vv. 1–3, all reference being to "this people" (v. 2), "their cities" (vv. 2–3), "the Canaanites" (v. 3), and "them" (v. 3). Most modern scholars have therefore taken the words *the king of Arad* to be a gloss to the text (also found at 33:40) based on Josh. 12:14.[6]

Arad has been identified as Tell Arad, about 8 mi. south of Hebron. The major problem with this identification is the apparent lack of remains from either the Middle or Late Bronze Age. Y. Aharoni has suggested nearby Tell el-Milḥ (about 7 mi. south of Tell Arad), but this site does not seem suitable either.[7] Glueck's earlier suggestion may still have merit, viz., that the king of Arad here (and in 33:40) is only a tribal chieftain who encamped around Tell Arad, but had no fortified city there.[8] An invading Israelite might hardly be expected to know whether this person was a full-fledged king and what his city looked like.

5. Adding *b*^{e}*yāḏô,* "into his hand," with Sam. Pent. and LXX; so *BHS;* see Gray, p. 274, who also points out that the same expression occurs in v. 2.

6. E.g., Paterson, p. 54; Holzinger, p. 88; Gray, p. 273; McNeile, p. 110; Binns, p. 137; Noordtzij, p. 184; Noth, pp. 154–55; Sturdy, p. 146; de Vaulx, p. 234; Budd, pp. 229–30.

7. Y. Aharoni (and R. Amiran), "Arad: Its Inscriptions and Temple," *BA* 31 (1968) 31–32. Unfortunately there are no Late Bronze remains at Tell el-Milḥ either. Aharoni reports only "traces of a magnificent Middle Bronze age fortification" (p. 31). The Middle Bronze age runs from ca. 2000 to 1500 B.C. The whole article is interesting for the overview it gives to this important site.

8. N. Glueck, *Rivers in the Desert,* pp. 114–15.

the Way of Atharim (dereḵ ha'ᵃṯārîm). If this is a proper name,[9] it names an unknown road from the south toward Arad, a road that Israel may have taken from Kadesh-barnea to Mt. Hor. But others do not read it as a proper name. Aquila and Symmachus read *kataskopoi,* which assumes that the *aleph* on *'ᵃṯārîm* is prosthetic, hence the term *hattārîm,* "the spies" (as in ch. 13).[10] Dillmann connected *'ᵃṯārîm* with Arab. *'aṯar,* "footprint, track," hence "a way of tracks," i.e., a caravan route.[11] Snaith identifies *'ᵃṯārîm* with Tamar or Hazazon-tamar in the Arabah, just south of the Dead Sea, but this is uncertain.[12]

2 After the loss of some of their number to the Canaanites, *Israel vowed a vow (wayyiddar yiśrā'ēl neḏer),* i.e., made a solemn promise to God (cf. Jacob in Gen. 28:20–22).[13] The content of this solemn promise to Yahweh was that, if he would bring victory to Israel, Israel would *put their cities to the ban (wᵉhᵃḥᵃramtî 'eṯ-'ārêhem).* The Hiphil of *ḥāram,* "to put to the ban," means to give the conquered people (and things)[14] to Yahweh by destroying them, thus not claiming the spoils of victory for themselves, but for God, the real victor (cf. Deut. 7:1–2; 20:17; Josh. 6:17, 21; etc.).[15]

3 Yahweh hearkened to this vow and gave victory to Israel, and the Israelites put *them and their cities to the ban.* That Israel put certain Canaanite *cities* to the ban and that then the place of so doing was called *Hormah* ("the ban place") gives credence to the proposal that the place

9. See LXX *hodon Atharin;* RV, RSV, NASB, NEB, NIV, GNB, NJPS, NKJV; also Gray, p. 273; McNeile, pp. 110–11; Binns, p. 137; Heinisch, p. 81; Noth, p. 155; Snaith, p. 170; Sturdy, p. 146; de Vaulx, p. 234; Budd, p. 230; Milgrom, *JPST,* p. 172; Harrison, p. 274.

10. See AV, RV mg., NASB mg., NJPS mg.; also Keil, p. 137; Cook, p. 724.

11. Dillmann, p. 117; so also Moffatt.

12. Snaith, p. 170. This identification is also picked up by Budd (p. 230). Holzinger, p. 92, credits C. Steuernagel with the suggestion to link *hā'ᵃṯārîm* with *hattᵉmārîm* in Judg. 1:16 (this probably refers to Jericho).

13. Also see Judg. 11:30–31; 1 Sam. 1:11; 2 Sam. 15:8; etc. The same phrase is used of the Nazirite vow in Num. 6:21, although this vow is recognized to be a special one (v. 2).

14. Contrast Josh. 6:17, 21; 1 Sam. 15:3 with Deut. 2:34–35; 3:6–7.

15. See BDB, pp. 355b–56a; see also the commentary above on 18:14. On *ḥērem* (and its verbal forms), see, e.g., N. Lohfink, *TDOT,* V:180–99 (with bibliography); L. J. Wood, *TWOT,* I:324–25; de Vaux, *Ancient Israel,* I:260; Albright, *From Stone Age to Christianity,* pp. 279–81; Eichrodt, *Theology of the OT,* I:139–41; Gottwald, *Tribes of Yahweh,* pp. 543–50; for an extrabiblical description of the ban, see the Moabite Stone, translated in *DOTT,* pp. 195–98; *ANET,* pp. 320–21.

Hormah was a region, not a single town in this case. That Hormah was also a single site, and even in the vicinity of Arad, also need not be doubted.[16] In 14:45 the Israelites were pursued "to (their) destruction" (*ʿad haḥōrmâ),* and I suggested that the place-name there may serve two functions, the first to name a place and the second to give a description of the outcome of the battle (note the definite article on Hormah). Here a whole region is named Hormah as a similar description, but this time for the Canaanites, not for the Israelites. If one follows the history of this area from this point, it would seem that, although it was conquered, it was not easily held (cf. Josh. 12:14; Judg. 1:16–17).

E. FIERY SERPENTS (21:4–9)

4 *And they departed from Mount Hor by the way of the Sea of Reeds to go around the land of Edom, and the people became impatient*[1] *on the way.*

5 *And the people spoke against God and against Moses, "Why have you brought us up*[2] *from Egypt to die in this wilderness? There is no water and our souls are sick of this worthless food."*

6 *And Yahweh sent the fiery serpents*[3] *against the people, and they bit the people and many of the people of Israel died.*

7 *And the people came to Moses and they said, "We sinned when we spoke against Yahweh and against you. Pray to Yahweh that he might take away this serpent from upon us." And Moses prayed on behalf of the people.*

16. Cf. Gray, pp. 273–74. For references to the city see Josh. 12:14; Judg. 1:16–17 (where the site is also called Zephath); cf. Josh. 19:4; 1 Sam. 30:30; 1 Chr. 40:30. Deut. 1:44 may refer to a region, esp. if one reads "from Seir to Hormah" with LXX.

1. The verb *qāṣar* has the basic meaning of "to be/come short" (*HALAT,* pp. 1051b–52a). In Num. 11:23 Yahweh asked Moses whether the divine "hand" (power) was "short," i.e., whether it fell short of the power needed to feed the people. In the current verse the literal translation is "the *nep̄eš* of the people grew short" *(wattiqṣar nep̄eš-hāʿām).* The term *nep̄eš* might be paraphrased as "the inner self" (on *nep̄eš,* see, e.g., B. Waltke, *TWOT,* II:587–91; E. Jacob, A. Dihle, and E. Lohse, *TDNT,* IX:617–37). The same idiom is used of Yahweh's impatience in Judg. 10:16 and Zech. 11:8. (Cf. the similar idiom *qāṣar rûaḥ,* "to grow ill-tempered, impatient," in Job 21:4 and Mic. 2:7.)

2. The perfect attaches suffixes to the second masc. pl. in *-tû* (here written defectively; *heʿĕlîṯunû*) instead of *-tem.* Cf. Num. 20:5; Zech. 7:5. See GKC, § 59a.

3. MT *haśśerāp̄îm;* Sam. Pent. reads *haśśerûp̄îm;* LXX *tous thanatountas* (deadly); Pesh., Targ., *ḥrmn'* (cruel); Vulg., *ignitos* (fiery). Both *hanneḥāšîm* and

8 *And Yahweh said to Moses, "Make a fiery serpent and place it upon a pole. And it will be that any who have been bitten*[4] *and see it will live."*[5]

9 *And Moses made a copper serpent and he placed it on the pole. And it was,*[6] *if the serpent bit anyone*[7] *and he looked to the copper serpent he would live.*[8]

This narrative takes up where 20:21 left off. The Israelites turned south in order to circumvent Edom, and on the way the exigencies of life in the desert once again caused them to complain. The section shows that, even in the face of victories such as that in 21:1–3, the Israelites' basic character has not changed. They complain against both God and Moses because of a lack of acceptable water and food. Once more these people show themselves to be out of touch with reality as they long for Egypt and talk as if they had a choice about dying in the wilderness (cf. 11:4–6; 14:2–4; but see 14:33–35). In previous times complaints about food had brought a divine supply of their needs (11:4–35), but now the response of God is to send a scourge of fiery serpents that kills many people. Again as before, the Israelites repent (11:2; 12:11; 14:40) and ask Moses to intercede with Yahweh (11:2; 12:11–13). When he does, God instructs him to construct a copper image of one of the lethal snakes and to set it on a pole where it

---

haśśerāp̄îm are substantives with the definite article ("the serpents, the burning ones"). This is the normal position for attributive adjectives in Biblical Hebrew (cf., e.g., J. Weingreen, *A Practical Grammar for Classical Hebrew,* 2nd ed. [Oxford: Clarendon, 1959], pp. 32–34). The definite article on both nouns here is most probably generic (i.e., expressing that this is a group or a class of creatures; see Williams, *Syntax,* § 92; Davidson, *Syntax,* § 22 [c]) rather than either expressing the demonstrative or referring to a well-known group.

4. For the relative clause with the passive participle plus the definite article, cf. Davidson, *Syntax,* § 99.

5. Note that a perfect consecutive *(wāḥāy)* follows the (passive) participle *(hannāsûḵ)* in a contingent clause; see Davidson, *Syntax,* § 55 (c).

6. The clause with *wehāyâ* is inserted here, as often, to indicate future or frequentative actions; cf. Exod. 22:26; Judg. 6:3; etc. See Davidson, *Syntax,* § 57.

7. For MT *'eṯ-'îš,* Sam. Pent. has *hā'îš,* which is more common. According to GKC, § 117d, the *'eṯ* occurs with the undefined noun *'îš* perhaps "to avoid the cacaphony *nāšaḵ hannāḥāš 'îš.*" According to Davidson, *Syntax,* § 72 Rem. 4, the reason for the *'eṯ* is that a particular class of people is in mind (i.e., "anyone bitten").

8. With a pefect in the protasis *('im nāšaḵ)* the condition is to be thought of as realized or actual. Narratives of past frequentative actions are also often introduced by *'im* plus the perfect (Gen. 38:9; Num 21:9; Judg. 2:18; 6:3; etc.). See Davidson, *Syntax,* §130 (b).

can be seen. No one is saved from being bitten, but if one is bitten and chooses to obey God by looking at the copper snake, one will be cured from the lethal effects of the bite.

The connection between this passage and the note in 2 K. 18:4, in which King Hezekiah breaks in pieces a snake made by Moses, is a matter of debate among scholars.[9] The relationship between these two passages may be decided not only on objective scientific grounds but also on the more subjective assessments of the literary genre, date, etc., of both the Pentateuch and 2 Kings. The traditional view is that Num. 21 gives the story of the creation of a snake that over time became venerated in an idolatrous way and was finally removed by Hezekiah.[10] Those who believe that the Pentateuch is a product of the postexilic age argue that the story in Numbers is an etiology invented to explain what happened in Hezekiah's time.[11] Still others see the Mosaic incident as real enough, but not the story itself as it stands, which was written in the thought forms of the 9th/8th (or later) cent. B.C., and in a way that explains the incident in Hezekiah's time.[12]

Wenham has presented evidence of a copper snake of probable Midianite origin (ca. 1150 B.C.) at Timna, a site near the place where the Israelites must have been at this point, about 15 mi. north of the Gulf of Aqabah.[13] Again, one must be cautious in one's assessment of archeological material so as not to claim too much, but this material find at least confirms the possibility of just such a metal snake at a time and place very near to that of this story. The traditional view has not been overturned by any means.

4–5 *the way of the Sea of Reeds.* Whatever the specific meaning, this term must indicate a southerly route from Mt. Hor, because by it the Israelites intended *to go around (lisᵉḇōḇ)* Edom as they had been forced to do in 20:20–21.

9. See, e.g., G. H. Jones, *1 and 2 Kings,* 2 vols., NCBC (Grand Rapids: Eerdmans, 1984), II:562; T. R. Hobbs, *2 Kings,* WBC (Waco: Word, 1985), p. 252; J. Gray, *I and II Kings,* OLT (2nd ed.; Philadelphia: Westminster, 1970), pp. 670–71; etc.

10. E.g., Keil, p. 140; Noordtzij, pp. 186–87; Harrison, p. 278; Milgrom, *JPST,* p. 460.

11. E.g., Gray, pp. 274–76; Binns, pp. 139–41; H. H. Rowley, "Zadok and Nehushtan," *JBL* 58 (1939) 113–41, esp. 132–41; Sturdy, pp. 147–48; cf. Snaith, pp. 170–71.

12. E.g., K. R. Joines, "The Bronze Serpent in the Israelite Cult," *JBL* 87 (1968) 245–56, esp. 252–54; Budd, pp. 232–34; cf. Noth, pp. 156–57.

13. Wenham, pp. 156–57; for further descriptions of discoveries of metal serpents as cult objects see Joines, "Bronze Serpent," pp. 245–46.

and the people became impatient (*wattiqṣar nep̄eš–hāʿām,* lit., "the soul [or temper] of the people became short"). The verb *qāṣar* with either *nep̄eš* or *rûaḥ* ("spirit") means that they lost heart or, perhaps, patience.[14] The opposite may be seen in, e.g., Prov. 14:29, "slow to anger" *('erek̠ 'appayim).*

on the way (baddārek̠). This translation takes the preposition b^e as local. It could also be taken as causal, i.e., "because of the road," but, since the specific complaint in v. 5 does not have to do with the road but with food and water, this is less likely.

The hard life of the wilderness had again weighed heavily on the Israelites, with typical results. The complaint is similar to others (Exod. 14:11–12; 17:3; Num. 11:4–35; 14:2–4; 16:13–14; 20:4–5). The objects of the complaint are both Yahweh and Moses. The cause of the complaints is lack of water and acceptable food. *this worthless food (balleḥem haqq^elōqēl).* The adjective *haqq^elōqēl (worthless)* occurs only here. It is related to words indicating "lightness" and is sometimes used in the sense of "not to be taken seriously" or "treat with contempt."[15] Perhaps the closest cognate is *q^elālâ,* "curse" (Gen. 27:13; Deut. 28:15, 45; etc.).[16] Whether the complaint was about the manna (as in 11:6) or about the food available in the desert is not said. If the former is the case it amounts to a direct rejection of God's providence.

6–7 Unlike previous occasions of complaint (see above), the text has no verbal reaction from either Yahweh or Moses.[17] One reads only of the punishment. *the fiery serpents (hann^eḥāšîm haśś^erāp̄îm).* It is possible, in the light of v. 8 where only the word for *fiery* is found, that *śārāp̄,* "burner," is the name of this particular snake, and that the term *serpents* is only to clarify (it is used alone in v. 9). In ancient Greece certain snakes were called *dipsas* ("thirst") because their bites caused intense thirst; others were called *kausōn* and *prēstēr* because their bites caused inflammation and swelling.[18] Thus one might call these serpents "burners" because their bites inflicted a fiery inflammation.[19] (Cf. Deut. 8:15; Isa.

14. Cf., with *rûaḥ,* Prov. 14:29; Job 21:4; with *nep̄eš,* Judg. 16:16; also Exod. 6:9; Judg. 10:16; Mic. 2:7; Zech. 11:8.

15. The Hiphil of *qālal* means "to treat with contempt" in 2 Sam. 19:44; Isa. 23:9; Ezek. 22:7.

16. See BDB, pp. 886a–87a.

17. See the commentary above on 20:2–5.

18. See LSJ, 439b–40a, 932b, 1463a.

19. Keil, p. 139; Cook, p. 725; Dillmann, p. 119; Gray, p. 277; McNeile, p. 112; Binns, pp. 138–39; Heinisch, p. 82; Snaith, p. 171; Sturdy, p. 148;

14:29; 30:6 for similar references.) The noun *haśś^{e}rāpîm* is the same word found in, e.g., Isa. 6:2, to describe a heavenly being (i.e., a seraph). In the current incident, however, there is no reason to suppose that we are dealing with anything but actual snakes of a certain type, and therefore Noth's translation "seraph serpent" is unwarranted.[20]

7 This verse contains the people's confession of sin, their request for Moses' intercession, and a record of that intercession.

this serpent (*hannāḥāš,* lit., "the serpent"). The article here expresses a demonstrative sense, i.e., "this serpent." The singular number suggests the whole class of creatures under discussion.[21]

8–9 Yahweh commands Moses to make *a fiery serpent,* although here only the word *śārāp̱* is used.[22] This may be because, as suggested above, *śārāp̱* was the name for the particular species.

pole (nēs). This is some kind of conspicuous object high enough for a group to see and gather around. Elsewhere this noun means a "standard" (Exod. 17:15; 30:17) or a "signal flag" (Ezek. 27:7).[23] When this serpent is fashioned and placed on the pole it fulfills exactly this function.

9 The serpent is made of *n^{e}ḥōšeṯ,* which can mean copper (Deut. 8:9; Job 28:2) or bronze (e.g., Lev. 6:21 [Eng. 28]; Num. 17:4 [Eng. 16:39]; 1 Sam. 17:5, 6; 1 K. 14:27). The translation *copper* has been adopted here in the light of the Timna discoveries mentioned by Wenham. Copper may have been used because of its reddish color, which suggested the inflammation caused by these "burners." The apparent similarities between the words for *copper (n^{e}ḥōšeṯ)* and *serpent (nāḥāš)* should also not be overlooked.

In both the command (v. 8) and its fulfillment (v. 9), healing must be accompanied by an act of obedience to Yahweh: looking at the image

---

Wenham, p. 157. But Coats (*Rebellion in the Wilderness,* p. 117 n. 51) opts for them being called "fiery" because of their color; cf. Budd, p. 234. R. Wolff (*ISBE,* rev., IV:1209–10) argues that the animals were not snakes but worms *(dracunculus medinensis),* which infected the Israelites when the latter drank polluted water. Harrison, pp. 276–77 discusses Wolff's view and raises the following difficulties: (1) the worms live in water, an item of which the Israelites were usually short, (2) there is no evidence that Israel drank polluted water, (3) the infection brought on by these worms is usually not fatal, while the bite of a poisonous snake may be.

20. Cf. Noth, p. 157 note.

21. See Williams, *Syntax,* § 87. On the singular representing the class, see Waltke and O'Connor, *Biblical Hebrew Syntax,* §7.2.2a.

22. LXX fills out the text by adding the word *chalkoun,* "bronze," as in v. 9.

23. See M. R. Wilson, *TWOT* II:583.

of the snake. In the two verses two different words for "to see" are used, perhaps for literary variety, but also to stress that it was necessary to do more than simply "see" or "catch a glimpse of" the copper serpent; one actually had to "fix one's gaze" or "pay attention to" this figure — a definite act of the will — if one wanted to be healed.[24]

The temptation to treat this serpent in a magical (hence, to the OT, unacceptable) way can be seen in 2 K. 18:4 (mentioned above). One also suspects that it was against such a tendency that the author of Wis. 16:5–7 asserted that it was not the serpent itself that saved the Israelites, but God. In Christian circles, this passage is famous as the basis for Jesus' statement to Nicodemus in John 3:14 (cf. 8:28; 12:32; 19:37).[25]

F. TRAVEL ITINERARY (21:10–20)

10 *And the children of Israel set out and encamped at Oboth.*

11 *And they set out from Oboth and encamped at Iye*[1]*-abarim*[2] *in the wilderness that faces Moab from the rising of the sun.*

12 *From there they set out and encamped at Wadi Zered.*

13 *From there they set out and encamped on the other side of the Arnon, which is in the wilderness, that goes out from the border of the Amorites, for the Arnon is the border of Moab, between Moab and the Amorites.*

14 *Therefore it is said in the Book of the Wars of Yahweh:*

24. It would be difficult to show that *rā'â* always means physical sight and *nāḇaṭ* always means spiritual sight (or perception). Sometimes the former verb clearly has the meaning of understanding and perceiving (e.g., Gen. 1:10, 12; Exod. 3:4; 8:11; etc.) and of choosing to see (e.g., Gen. 9:22, 23; Lev. 13:3, 15; Num. 24:20, 21). On the other hand, *nāḇaṭ* (always found in either the Piel, or, as here, the Hiphil) indicates the physical process of looking (e.g., Exod. 3:6; etc.) as well as the deeper process of paying attention to (e.g., Isa. 22:8) or showing regard for (e.g., 1 Sam. 16:7). Statistical comparisons between the two verbs is difficult because *rā'â* occurs much more commonly than *nāḇaṭ*. What may be concluded here is that more than mere looking must be involved, there must be a willingness to pay attention. See, e.g., J. W. Simpson, Jr., *ISBE*, rev., IV:379–80; L. Coppes, *TWOT*, II:546; W. White, *TWOT*, II:823–24.

25. For Luther's thought on the passage, see Keil, p. 141; for a good summary of the typology, see Cook, p. 726; for a history of the Christian exegesis of the passage, see de Vaulx, pp. 237–38.

1. LXX (Vaticanus) reads *en Chalgaei* (others *Achelgai*, etc.); cf. 33:44, where LXX reads *Gai* (= Heb. *ʿay*). Pesh. reads *bʿyn'* (= Heb. *b*[e]*ʿên*); Targ. reads *bmgzt* ("at the ford [of] . . .").

2. LXX reads *ek tou* (or *tō*) *peran* ("from the far side").

"Waheb[3] *in Suphah and the wadis of the Arnon,*[4]

15 *and the cliff of the wadis that spread out*
to the seat of Ar,
and lean toward the border of Moab."

16 *From there they set out*[5] *for Beer. It is the well of which Yahweh*
said to Moses, "Gather the people and I will surely give them
water."

17 *Then Israel sang*[6] *this song:*
"Come up, O well —Sing to it —

18 *The well that princes dug,*
the nobles of the people dug out,
with staff of office, with their rods."[7]
From the wilderness they went to Mattanah.[8]

19 *And from Mattanah to Nahaliel, and from Nahaliel to Bamoth.*

20 *And from Bamoth they went to the valley that is in the region of*
Moab, at the top of the Pisgah, which overhangs[9] *the Jeshimon.*

3. Instead of MT *'eṯ-wāhēḇ,* a number of mss. read *'eṯwāhēḇ* (from *yāhaḇ*), "I will give." LXX reads *tēn Zōob,* which presupposes Heb. *'eṯ-zāhāḇ* and may be the same as Di-zahab in Deut. 1:1.

4. Note that *hann^{e}ḥālîm 'arnôn* is not a construct-genitive, but an independent construction of two nouns in apposition, "the valleys (i.e., those of) Arnon." See GKC, § 127f.

5. MT *ûmiššām b^e'ērâ,* lit., "and from there to Beer"; such elision of the verb is common, and occurs also in vv. 18–20.

6. The verb *yāšîr* is a preterite after the particle *'āz,* as also in Exod. 15:1; Deut. 4:41; Josh. 8:30; 10:12; 1 K. 8:1. With *w^e* this form is usually called the imperfect consecutive. See Williams, *Syntax,* § 177.

7. Sam. Pent. and Vulg. add "and" before "with their rods" (i.e., presupposing Heb. *ûḇm^{e}š‘^{a}nōṯām*); LXX reads *en tō kyrieusai autōn,* i.e., Heb. *b^{e}mošlām* ("by their rule"). See *BHS.*

8. LXX has *kai apo phreatos eis Manthanain,* "and from the spring [i.e., Beer] to Mattanah," instead of MT *ûmiḏbār mattānâ,* "and from the wilderness to Mattanah" (LXX also reads *phreatos* for MT Mattanah in v. 19). Perhaps the LXX translator thought that the Israelites had already departed from the wilderness when they reached Beer. K. Budde (*Preussische Jahrbücher* [1895] 491–580; Eng. tr. in *New World* [March 1895] 136–44; cited by Gray, p. 288) concluded that this phrase is to be translated "from the wilderness, a gift." This reading entails eliminating the conjunction "and" *(û-)* from the words *from the wilderness (mimmiḏbār)* and reading the place-name Mattanah as a common noun, "gift" (which is the meaning of Heb. *mattānâ*). This interpretation also requires reading "and from Beer" *(ûmibb^e'ēr)* instead of "and from Mattanah" *(ûmimmattānâ).* There does not seem to be adequate textual support to justify any of these emendations to MT (cf. *BHS*).

9. MT has the fem. sing. verb *w^{e}nišqāp̱â,* which probably refers to

This passage consists of a travel itinerary (vv. 10–13, 16, 18b–20) into which are placed two poetic bits (vv. 14–15, 17–18a), the first more fragmentary than the second. Both poetic pieces are songs; as the goal of the land of Canaan came nearer the songs increased, and the people began to anticipate the conquest.

Because the wording and style of vv. 10–11 are the same as that of ch. 33, scholars who hold to the documentary hypothesis have linked these two sections together as P material.[10] In fact, although the tense of the first verb is different, the same vocabulary is continued in vv. 12–13, which are usually attributed to JE.[11] Vv. 16, 18b–20 leave the verbs out entirely, so that, e.g., v. 19 reads: "and from Mattanah, Nahaliel, and from Nahaliel to Bamoth." The grounds for division into documents here are not to be found in the vocabulary.

The purpose of the list of campsites here is to summarize the campaign in the Amorite country, in which Israel fought battles against Sihon and Og (vv. 21–35). One might think that these battles should fit somewhere after v. 13, since all the sites beginning with v. 13 were in Amorite territory. Rather than split up the itinerary with these two battle reports, however, the author apparently decided to hold them (and the attached Amorite song in vv. 27–30) until after the itinerary, perhaps to maintain the integrity of the itinerary as a literary source.

The two poetic pieces function in distinct ways. The first (vv. 14–15) acts as a note to verify what the itinerary has said. It is quite fragmentary and obscure; in some ways it is more like Hebrew prose than poetry.[12] Its purpose in the narrative may explain its fragmentary nature (see below). The second poem (vv. 17–18a) is really more important than

happisgâ, the most obvious fem. noun in the context. Cf. *BHS,* which follows LXX, Pesh., Vulg., and Pal. Targ. in reading a masc. form (as in 23:28). One should probably read the fem. sing. participle plus the definite article *(hannišqāp̱â)* instead of the perfect consecutive as in MT (although Driver, *Tenses,* p. 162 n. 1, reads a frequentative, "and it used to overhang"). See Gray, p. 294.

10. See, e.g., Gray, pp. 279–81; Snaith, p. 172; etc. The common language is *wayyis*^{e}ʿ*û m(in) . . . wayyaḥ*^{a}*nû b*^{e} —.

11. I.e., *nāsāʿû.* The second verb remains the same *(wayyaḥ*^{a}*nû).* This section is usually claimed to be JE (see, e.g., the discussion in Budd, pp. 237–38).

12. The characteristic least like poetry is the presence of such so-called prose particles as the sign of the direct object (*'eṯ,* v. 14 twice), the relative particle (*'*^{a}*šer,* v. 15), and the definite article (*ha-,* vv. 14–15). See D. Christensen, "Num. 21:14–15 and the Book of the Wars of Yahweh," *CBQ* 36 (1974) 359 n. 4. His reference to "studies in the historical development of Hebrew poetry" probably refers to the work of F. M. Cross and D. N. Freedman, among others.

the campsite note to which it is attached. The site's name (Beer) simply means "well," and could refer to dozens of sites. One suspects that the song is a major part of the reason for the remembrance of Beer and its inclusion in the itinerary.

10–11 Comparing the campsites in the current passage with Num. 33:41–49,[13] one finds that ch. 33 lists more sites before Israel comes into Amorite country (five, counting Mt. Hor) than Num. 21 does (two); but ch. 21 names more sites in Amorite country (seven) than ch. 33 does (three). This difference may be due to the different purposes of the lists. The current list shows an interest in arriving at the eastern edge of Moab as quickly as possible and zeroing in on the Amorite land. It should, then, be linked with 21:21–35 as the story of the Amorite campaign. This itinerary (and that of ch. 33) probably list only a selection of campsites. The location of many of the sites listed throughout vv. 10–13, 16, 19–20 is unknown.

The site of *Oboth* is unknown. Many have identified it with ʿAin el-Weibeh south of the Dead Sea and west of Punon (= Feinan), although this identification is uncertain.[14] For the current list the mention of Oboth does little more than indicate that the Israelites traveled some distance before they came into Amorite land.

The reader is brought quickly to *Iye-abarim* ("the ruins of [the land] on the far side"). The situation of this site is *in the wilderness,* standing with one's back to the east *(from the rising of the sun)* and looking westward into Moab *(that faces Moab). Abarim* became the name for Transjordan (cf. 27:12; Deut. 32:9). These "ruins" (*ʿîyîm,* sing. *ʿāy*) are differentiated, then, from others (Ai, Iim) on the west side of the Jordan (e.g., Josh. 7:2; 15:29). Num. 33:44 says that Iye-abarim was "on the border of Moab."[15] Taking this text with the material here, one can say

13. In the present passage the sites are Oboth, Iye-abarim, Wadi Zered, other side of Arnon, Beer, Mattanah, Nahaliel, Bamoth, valley in the region of Moab near the Pisgah. In 33:41–49 they are Mt. Hor, Zalmonah, Punon, Oboth, Iye-abarim, Dibon-gad, Almon-diblathaim, mountains of Abarim.

14. E.g., G. E. Wright and F. V. Filson, eds., *The Westminster Historical Atlas to the Bible,* rev. ed. (Philadelphia: Westminster, 1956), p. 66 (the identification is uncertain in both the map and the index [p. 126] where ʿAin Ḥoṣob is given as an alternative). Less doubt on the identification is expressed by E. G. Kraeling, ed., *Rand McNally Bible Atlas,* 3rd ed. (New York: Rand McNally, 1966), pp. 121–22, 233. The identification is also made (tentatively) by, e.g., Binns, p. 141; Snaith, p. 172; Budd, p. 239; S. Cohen, *IDB,* III:582; but see W. LaSor, *ISBE,* rev., III:578.

15. Taking *g*ᵉ*ḇûl* in the sense of "border" (with Gray; cf. AV, RV, NEB,

that it was on the eastern edge of Moabite territory, and south of the Zered (the next stop on the northward journey, 21:12). Gray suggested a site near Wady el-Aḥsa on the southeast corner of Moab, although, again, this is uncertain.[16]

12–13 Scholars generally agree that *Wadi Zered* is Wâdī el-Ḥesā, which flows into the southern end of the Dead Sea from the east.[17] The Israelites were now in Moabite territory. Once again, the interest of the itinerary lies elsewhere, hence no further comment is made.

on the other side of the Arnon (mēʿēḇer ʾarnôn). The Arnon is Wâdī el-Mojib (or Mûjib), which flows (south to north) into the Dead Sea from the east a little north of its midpoint. It was a major river.[18] The *other side* of the Arnon is the north side, since the direction of the march was northward (as also in Judg. 11:18). Thus they were now in Amorite territory.

in the wilderness. This area is called the wilderness of Kedemoth in Deut. 2:26–27. According to Gray this phrase qualifies the Arnon rather than the territory over it.[19] The Arnon runs through the wilderness in its upper (more easterly) course, and together with the note that says that this wilderness *goes out from the border of the Amorites* (i.e., eastward), this phrase seems to indicate that the Israelites crossed the Arnon somewhere on its upper reaches, where the crossing would be more likely from a physical standpoint in any case.[20]

for Arnon is the border of Moab, between Moab and the Amorites.

NASB, NIV) rather than in the sense of "territory" (with Budd; cf. RSV, GNB, NJPS). See BDB, pp. 147b–48a.

16. Gray, p. 291.

17. Gray, p. 291; Noth, p. 159; Milgrom, *JPST,* p. 176; etc.

18. See G. A. Smith's description: "An enormous trench across the plateau of Moab. It is about 1700 feet deep, and two miles broad from edge to edge of the cliffs which bound it, but the floor of the valley down which the stream winds is only forty yards wide. About fifteen miles up from the Dead Sea the trench divides into branches, one running north-east, the other south-south-east, and each again dividing into two. The plateau up to the desert is thus cut not only across but up and down, by deep ravines, and a difficult frontier is formed" (*The Historical Geography of the Holy Land,* 25th ed. [London: Hodder & Stoughton, 1931; repr. New York: Harper Torchbooks, 1966], pp. 377–78).

19. Gray, pp. 283–84.

20. See the description of the lower course of the Arnon in n. 16 above. This crossing is consistent with vv. 4 and 11, which describe the journey as east of the lands of Edom and Moab. It also concurs with Judg. 11:18 (although this verse may well be dependent on the present text); see, e.g., J. M. Myers, "Judges," *IB,* II:766–68.

At some point the Amorite Sihon had taken territory between the Arnon and the Jabbok (about 50 mi. north) from the Moabites (21:26; cf. Judg. 11:22). This territory continued to be disputed for centuries. In later times the boundary shifted back and forth between Israel and Moab. In the days of Omri and Ahab, this territory belonged to Israel, but the Moabite king Mesha (cf. 2 K. 3:4–27) retook many of the cities north of the Arnon.[21] Jer. 49:1–3 may indicate that, still later, the territory belonged to Ammon. The text holds that the Moabites had been hemmed in south of the Arnon, i.e., that it formed a border between Amorite and Moabite country.

14–15 A citation from a source called *the Book of the Wars of Yahweh* supports the claim made in v. 13. The exact nature of this "book" is unknown, since the only fragment of it is the poetry cited in vv. 14–15, unless the poem in vv. 17–18a is also from it. The title of the work suggests that it contained songs celebrating Yahweh's victories against his enemies.[22] If the battles against Sihon and Og occurred sometime close to the Israelites' crossing of the Arnon, then a citation from this book would be appropriate here. The inclusion of this song at this point in the text serves to mark Israelite victories, and also to confirm geographical sites.

The citation is obviously fragmentary: it begins with a direct object, *Waheb in Suphah (ʾeṯ-wāhēḇ bᵉsûp̄â),* but has no verb. The fragmentary nature of the text may have to do with its use in the passage. To have included the verb would have made the song refer more definitely to warlike action,[23] which is clearly not its purpose. D. Christensen has

21. See the Mesha Inscription (the Moabite Stone), e.g., in Beyerlin, ed., *Near Eastern Religious Texts,* pp. 237–40; *ANET*, pp. 320–21; *DOTT,* pp. 195–99.

22. On the Yahweh war (sometimes called the holy war), see, e.g., F. Stolz, *Jahwes und Israels Kriege,* ATANT 60 (Zürich: Theologischer Verlag, 1972); G. von Rad, *Holy War in Ancient Israel,* tr. and ed. M. J. Dawn (Grand Rapids: Eerdmans, 1991); P. C. Craigie, *The Problem of War in the Old Testament* (Grand Rapids: Eerdmans, 1978).

23. Some commentators want to understand some verb such as *ʿāḇar,* "he went over," or *lāqaḥ,* "he took" (e.g., Gray); or *ʾāṯâ,* "he came" (Christensen, "Num. 21:14–15," pp. 359–60), with reference to Yahweh's action.

24. The text as Christensen reconstructs it is:

[Yahweh] came in a whirlwind	*ʾāṯā YHW bswph*
He came to the branch wadis of the Arnon	*ʾāṯā nḥlym ʾrnwn*
He marched through the wadis	*ʾšr nḥlym*
He marched (turned aside) to the sea of Ar	*ʾšr (nṭh) lšbt ʿr*
He leaned toward the border of Moab	*nšʿn lgbwl mwʾb*

Christensen notes the following changes from MT (among others): Read the poetic verb *ʾāṯā* (written defectively), "to come," instead of the sign of the direct object,

offered a reconstruction that has Yahweh as its subject and contains verbs referring to his action in war.[24] While possible, this reconstruction is less suitable to the purpose for which the citation is used than the present, admittedly obscure, text.[25]

Waheb in Suphah. Neither site is known, but the context places them in the vicinity of the Arnon.

the wadis of the Arnon. The pl. noun *wadis* shows that the reference is not just to the main stream of the Arnon, but to the whole system of streams that feeds into it, all of which were probably known by the one name Arnon (in addition to their own names).[26]

cliff ('ešeḏ). The word occurs in the sing. only here.[27] In the pl. it occurs in the phrase "the slopes *['ašdōṯ]* of Pisgah" (Deut. 3:17; 4:49; Josh. 12:3; 13:20). The translation *cliff* is an interpretative rendering based on the well-known geographical fact that the slopes of the lower Arnon are quite steep.[28]

to the seat of Ar (lᵉšeḇeṯ ʿār). The word *šeḇṯ (seat)* is a synonym for "dwelling." *Ar* is probably the same site mentioned in Deut. 2:9, 18, 29, and probably the same as Ar of Moab (Num. 21:28; Isa. 15:1) and "the city of Moab" (*ʿîr-mô'āḇ,* Num. 22:36; *ʿār* is cognate to *ʿîr,* "city," pl. *ʿārîm*).[29] These other texts are compatible with a location at the eastern end of the Arnon.[30] This territory is said to *lean toward (wᵉnišʿan),*[31] i.e., is adjacent to, or overlooking, *the border of Moab.* Again, this last phrase is the reason why this fragment has been included in the text.

16–18 The style of the itinerary now changes (vv. 16, 18b–20; see above). The song in vv. 17–18a is probably the reason why this campsite note was preserved (v. 16a).

16 The site of *Beer* ("well") is unknown. Sites with this word

---

'eṯ. Read the divine name *YHW* (written without the final *h*) instead of *wāhēḇ* (see Christensen, "Num. 21:14–15," p. 360 n. 6). Read the verb *'āšar,* "to march," instead of *'ešeḏ* and *'ᵃšer* (p. 360 n. 8).

25. Christensen admits that the purpose of the text is to note the boundary of Moab (ibid., p. 360). One should not deny any significance to the war theme here, but one should see it as secondary, in the background.

26. See Smith, *Historical Geography,* p. 378.

27. As Gray (p. 287) points out, it may be related to Assyr. *išdu,* "base."

28. See Gray, p. 286; Smith, *Historical Geography,* p. 378. NEB "watershed" is also preferred by Snaith.

29. It may be Medeyyene, Jerome's Madian; see Smith, *Historical Geography,* p. 373.

30. See, e.g., *Westminster Historical Atlas,* p. 65.

31. See KB, p. 1000; *HALAT,* pp. 1488b–89a.

as part of a compound name (e.g., Beer-sheba) are common. Many commentators think this site may be the same as Beer-elim (Isa. 15:8),[32] but since neither site is known, that identification is not much help. The general direction of the march seems to be northwest, and so one may suppose that Beer is some distance north-northwest of the upper Arnon. The site was remembered as the place where Yahweh provided water for the people by means of a well. The story of the digging of this well is not preserved, but it was probably a well-known story, since it could be brought to mind easily by the reference: *It is the well of which Yahweh said to Moses, "Gather the people and I will surely give them water,"* as if this was the only (famous) well where God gave them water.

17–18a O. Eissfeldt called these verses a "work song" that was used while digging a well, or at least a poem modeled on such a song.[33] But the song itself seems more like a "celebration song" for the completion of or dedication of a well.

It begins with an Israelite call for the waters of the well to continue to spring up (apparently as they have in the past), expressed in the form of an imperative (*come up, ʿalî*).

The song then celebrates the fact that the well was dug by the authority of *the princes (śārîm)* and *the nobles (nedîbîm)*. The former term is a general one for "leader," and is used, e.g., to describe those leaders appointed by Moses over groups of 1,000, 100, 50, and 10 men in Exod. 18:21, etc. The latter term, as an adjective, means "willing" or "noble," and as a noun means "a member of the noble class." The latter meaning is confined to two texts, both of which are poetry.[34]

staff (meḥōqēq). The usual understanding of this term (a Poel participle from *ḥāqaq,* "to cut in, decree") is the staff or mace of office (as in Gen. 49:10). AV has taken this participle in a substantival sense[35] as "the one who decrees," i.e., "the lawgiver" (as in Deut. 33:21) in order to refer it to Moses (v. 16b). This rendering is unlikely, for not only does it require an unusual sense of the preposition *be* (i.e., "by the direction of"),[36] but it also ignores the intended parallelism with the second word

32. Cook, p. 727; Gray, p. 288; Binns, p. 142; Noordtzij, p. 190.

33. O. Eissfeldt, *The Old Testament: An Introduction,* tr. P. Ackroyd (New York: Harper & Row, 1965), p. 88.

34. On *nāḏîḇ* as a class see Gottwald, *Tribes of Yahweh,* pp. 539–40.

35. This sense is common for the participle; cf. Williams, *Syntax,* § 217.

36. The NKJV returns to this reading.

(*b^e^miš^ʿa^nōṯām, with their rods)*. The term *mišʿeneṯ (rod)* refers to the staff used in everyday work and life (as a shepherd, Ps. 23:4).[37] The parallel favors a translation such as adopted above rather than that of AV or NKJV. Sturdy cites a relatively modern Bedouin well song as a parallel to the present text:

> Flow water, spread abundantly,
> Wood, camel, do not scorn it!
> With sticks we have dug it![38]

A number of commentators refer to K. Budde's conclusion that the current song may refer to the desert custom of covering a recently dug well, so as to allow an official of the community to uncover it with the ceremonial staff of office. Although this explanation may be possible, one cannot be sure how ancient this desert custom is.[39]

18b This part of the verse is most easily translated as the beginning of a new section of the itinerary (as above). It is parallel in form to vv. 19–20 *(and from the wilderness, Mattanah; and from Mattanah, Nahaliel; and from Nahaliel, Bamoth; and from Bamoth, the valley . . .)*.[40] The Israelites did not pass out of the wilderness immediately upon leaving the Arnon campsite. The text here says that they were in that wilderness until they left Beer and arrived at Mattanah. The site of *Mattanah* is unknown, although some have identified it with Khirbet el-Medeiyineh east-northeast of Jebel Attarus.[41]

19 The site of *Nahaliel* (lit., "wadi of God") is likewise unknown, although some have thought it to be at Wadi Zerqa-Maʿîn, which flows into the Dead Sea just north of Zareth-shahar.[42]

Bamoth (lit., "high place"). This site, although unknown, must be close to the Pisgah that overlooks the so-called plains of Moab (v. 20). Like Beer, the name Bamoth was frequently compounded with other elements, and many scholars have conjectured that Bamoth here is an

37. See also Exod. 21:19; Judg. 6:21; 2 K. 4:29, 31; Zech. 8:4; etc.

38. Sturdy, p. 151.

39. See, e.g., Gray, pp. 288–89; McNeile, p. 116; Binns, p. 143; Noordtzij, p. 190; Budde, *New World* (March 1895) 136–44.

40. So virtually all modern versions except NEB, which accepts Budde's emendation (no comment on this text by Sturdy, pp. 150–52). Noordtzij, p. 190, also accepts this emendation.

41. See *Westminster Historical Atlas*, p. 65 (map IX, J-7).

42. Ibid., p. 65 (map IX, H-7); also Davies, *Way of the Wilderness*, p. 92; Smith, *Historical Geography*, p. 380 (refers to healing springs at Wady Zerqa-Maʿîn); Gray, p. 291; McNeile; p. 116; Binns, p. 143; etc.

abbreviated form of Bamoth-baal (22:41), or perhaps of Beth-bamoth, which is found in the Mesha Inscription.[43]

20 The final campsite in the itinerary is in a *valley.* The most likely site for this valley is Wadi ʿAyûn Mûsā, which is about two mi. northeast of the Dead Sea.[44] This valley is defined by two terms in apposition. First, it is *in the region of Moab.* This is simply another way of saying "the land of Moab" (see, e.g., Gen. 36:25; Num. 15:20; Ruth 1:2, 6, 22; 2:6; 4:3; 1 Chr. 1:46; 8:8). This general description is specified further by *at the top of the Pisgah (rōʾš happisgâ). the Pisgah* is a collective term for the headlands of the Moabite plateau (23:14; Deut. 3:27; 34:1), which falls off quite sharply to the Dead Sea. This term may also refer to the north end of the Abarim range of mountains. From the west these headlands appear to jut up about 3,500–4,000 feet.

which overhangs the Jeshimon (ʿal-pᵉnê hayᵉšîmōn). Jeshimon means "wasteland." The term is used without the definite article to refer to the wilderness of wandering (Deut. 32:10; Ps. 68:8; 78:40), and with the definite article, as here, to indicate the wasteland in Judah north of the Dead Sea, on both eastern (Num. 33:49) and western (Isa. 23:19, 24; 26:1, 3) shores.

G. WARS AGAINST SIHON AND OG (21:21–22:1)

21 *And Israel sent messengers to Sihon king of the Amorites, saying:*

22 *"Let me cross over into your land. We will not turn into field and vineyard, we will not drink well water. We will go on the King's Highway until we cross over your border."*

23 *But Sihon did not let*[1] *Israel cross over into his territory, and Sihon gathered all his people and went out against Israel into the wilderness, and he entered Jahaz and fought against Israel.*

24 *And Israel smote him with the edge of the sword and took possession of his land, from the Arnon to the Jabbok, as far as the children of Ammon, for mighty*[2] *is the border of the children of Ammon.*

43. Line 27: "I built Beth-bamoth, for it was a ruin" (Beyerlin, ed., *Near Eastern Religious Texts,* p. 239); cf. *ANET,* p. 320; *DOTT,* p. 197.

44. So Gray, p. 291; McNeile, p. 117; Binns, p. 144. Noordtzij, p. 190, identifies the site as Ghor el-Belqa in the same general area (a bit to the south).

1. For *nāṯan* meaning "to allow," plus an infinitive, see GKC, § 157b n. 2.

2. MT reads *ʿaz; BHS* proposes to read *yaʿzēr* (Jazer). LXX has *Iazēr* here (which is different from *Iassa* [MT Jahaz] in v. 23).

25 *And Israel took all these cities. Israel settled in all the cities of the Amorites, in Heshbon and in all its villages.*[3]

26 *(For Heshbon was the city of Sihon king of the Amorites, who had fought*[4] *against the former king of Moab and had taken all his land from his hand,*[5] *as far as the Arnon.)*

27 *Therefore the bards*[6] *say:*[7]

Come to Heshbon, let it be built,
And let the city of Sihon be established.[8]

28 *For fire went out from Heshbon,*
and flame from the city of Sihon.
It devoured Ar[9] *of Moab,*
it swallowed[10] *the heights of Arnon.*

29 *Woe to you, O Moab!*
You have perished, O people of Chemosh!
He made his sons as fugitives,

3. The idiom *b^{e}nōṯeyhā,* lit., "her daughters," refers to the satellite villages of the main town (here, Heshbon). This idiom is also found in vv. 25, 32; Josh. 15:45, 47; etc.; see BDB, p. 123b (4).

4. The verb *wayyiqqaḥ* is best translated as a pluperfect here; see Davidson, *Syntax,* § 48 (c).

5. For "from his hand" *(mîyādô),* LXX reads "from Aroer" *(apo Aroēr).* Gray, p. 299, proposes to read "from Jabbok" *(mîyabbōq)* as in v. 24 (cf. Judg. 11:22). Since MT makes good sense, it should be retained.

6. The participle *hammōš^{e}lîm* is probably a *nomen agentis* (i.e., a word that names a "doer" or a "profession"). But its precise meaning is uncertain (*māšāl* usually means "proverb"). *HALAT* (p. 611b) identifies them as *(Spott)Redner* ("[taunt]speaker"). Cf. RSV "ballad singers"; NIV "poets"; NEB, NJPS "bards"; NASB "those who use proverbs." It is possible that *māšāl* has to do with the style of parallelism found in much biblical prose and poetry, and that, therefore, a *mōšēl* is one who works within this style, i.e., a "bard" or "poet." Cf. J. Kugel, *The Idea of Biblical Poetry: Parallelism and Its History* (New Haven: Yale Univ. Press, 1981), p. 69 n. 15.

7. The verb *yō'mer* is frequentative; see Williams, *Syntax,* § 168.

8. Most exegetes (e.g., BDB, p. 467b; Gray, p. 305) have taken *w^{e}ṯikkônēn* to be a Hithpoel imperfect consecutive with the elision of the *ṯ* infix to the following consonant (see GKC, § 54c). D. N. Freedman ("Archaic Forms in Early Hebrew Poetry," *ZAW* 72 [1961] 106) posits that it is a Niphal form, *tikkōn* plus the energic ending *-anna.* The meaning is the same.

9. Some commentators (e.g., Noordtzij, p. 193 n. 3; Noth, p. 161; Wenham, p. 162 and n. 2) and *BHS* read *ʿārê* ("cities of") rather than MT's proper name Ar *(ʿār),* but with no textual support.

10. For MT *baʿ^{a}lê,* "lords of" (so AV), LXX reads *kai katepien* ("and it swallowed up"), which presupposes Heb. *bal^{e}ʿâ,* with a simple metathesis of the consonants *l* and *ʿ*. This slight change is accepted here; see the discussion below.

his daughters as captives,
to a king of Amorites —Sihon.
30 *And we overthrew them,*[11]
Heshbon as far as Dibon perished!
And we ravaged[12] *as far as Nophah,*[13]
fire[14] *as far as Medeba!*[15]
31 *And Israel settled in the land of the Amorites.*
32 *And Moses sent to spy out Jazer, and they captured its villages*[16]
and dispossessed the Amorites who were there.
33 *Then they turned and went up by the way of Bashan. And Og the*
king of Bashan, he and all his people, came out against them for
battle at Edrei.
34 *And Yahweh said to Moses: "Do not fear him, for I have given him*
and all his people and his land into your hand. You will do to him

11. MT *wannîrām* is a doubtful reading (cf. GKC, § 69r), as a glance at the versions will show. LXX reads *kai to sperma autōn* ("and their descendants"), which presupposes Heb. *w^enînām* (root *nyn,* "offspring" [*HALAT,* pp. 657b–58a]; found in Gen. 21:23; Isa. 14:22; Job 18:19; all parallel to *neke̱ḏ,* "progeny"); see GKC, § 76r, which, in addition to explaining the vowel of the suffix (see also Exod. 29:30), advocates reading with LXX, as do *BHS,* Budd, p. 242; RSV, etc. This reading necessitates understanding the verb *'āḇaḏ,* "to perish," as a Piel, *'ibbaḏ,* "to destroy" (Gk. *apoleitai*). Vulg. (followed by Pesh.) reads *iugum ipsorum* ("their yoke," perhaps "their dominion"), which may reflect Heb. *w^enîrām.* Heb. *nîr* means "yoke" or, by extension, "dominion" in postbiblical Hebrew. The latter translation has been taken up by P. D. Hanson, "The Song of Heshbon and David's *Nir,*" *HTR* 61 (1968) 297–320. He translates the line: "the dominion of Moab has perished" *(nîr mô'āḇ 'āḇaḏ)* (p. 304). The present translation understands the verb *yārâ* as "to cast" down. See commentary on v. 30 below.

12. MT *wannaššîm,* "we ravaged." On the so-called Aramaic doubling in a double *'ayin* verb, see GKC, § 67g. LXX reads *kai gynaikes (autōn),* "their wives," which would be Heb. *w^enāšîm.*

13. MT reads a proper name, Nophah. Sam. Pent. reads *hinnāpaḥ* (Niphal, "to be heated"). LXX reads *prosexekausan,* "they blazed up," i.e., Heb. *nāp^eḥû.* Pesh. reads *l^enōḇaḥ,* "to Nobah" (as in Num. 32:42 and Judg. 8:11).

14. MT has a point over the *r* in *'^ašer,* which means the Masoretes doubted this letter. Both LXX and Sam. Pent. read *'ēš,* "fire." Budd, RSV, and NEB have adopted this reading. *BHS* suggests reading *šō'â,* a participle from a verb meaning "to make a crash" (BDB, pp. 980b–81a), hence "ruined."

15. LXX reads *Mōab.* The present translation is similar to NIV, NASB, NJPS. As the previous notes, the apparatus of *BHS,* and a comparison of modern English translations make clear, v. 30 is corrupt. As Budd has stated, "The only secure elements are Heshbon and Dibon" (p. 243).

16. MT *wayyilk^eḏû b^enoṯeyhā;* apparently on the basis of v. 2. LXX reads *kai katelabonto autēn kai tas kōmas autēs,* "and they took possession of it and its villages." Although *BHS* chooses to read with LXX, the MT may be retained.

just as you did to Sihon the Amorite who was dwelling in Heshbon."

35 *And they slew him and his sons and all his people until*[17] *no survivor was left to him. And they possessed his land.*

22:1 *And the children of Israel departed, and they encamped on the plains of Moab, on the other side of the Jordan of Jericho.*

21–22 The Israelites sent a request for safe passage through Sihon's land. The proposed terms of passage are quite similar to those of 20:17, although slightly shortened.[18]

Messengers (mal'āḵim) — this is a general term in Hebrew and the cognate Semitic languages for one sent to carry specific commissions and to represent those who sent him or her. Messengers announced either good news (e.g., 1 Sam. 6:21) or bad (e.g., 1 K. 19:2). Here the messengers announce a specific request (so also 20:14; 22:5; Judg. 7:24). Later in Israel's history such people could be in the official diplomatic service of the nation (Judg. 11:12–14; 2 Sam. 5:11; 11:4; 1 K. 20:2), and could even be spies (Josh. 6:25). The present text makes clear only that these messengers were charged to deliver a request to Sihon.[19]

Sihon king of the Amorites. He is called by this title again in 21:26 as well as in 32:33; 1 K. 4:19; Ps. 135:11; 136:19 (he is mentioned together with Og in Deut. 31:4; Josh. 2:10; 9:10). He is sometimes called "king of Heshbon," which was his capital city (cf. v. 26; Deut. 2:26, 30; 3:6; 29:6 [Eng. 7]; Josh. 12:5; 13:27; cf. Neh. 9:22). Still other places he is called by a combination of these titles (Deut. 1:4; 2:24; 3:2; 4:46; Josh. 12:2; 13:10, 21; Judg. 11:19). He is also mentioned in Jer. 48:45.

The term *Amorite* has various meanings in the OT: Canaanites generally (e.g., Gen. 15:16), inhabitants of the land west of the Jordan (e.g., Josh. 5:1), inhabitants of the regions of Judah (e.g., Josh. 10:5–6), inhabitants of the Negeb and the region to the southeast of the Dead Sea (e.g.,

17. See GKC, § 164d, for the temporal clause introduced by *ʿaḏ-biltî* (cf. Deut. 3:3; Josh. 8:22; 11:8). One would expect *haš'ēr* (i.e., the infinitive) as elsewhere with *biltî*.

18. The only real differences between the two verses are minor, although the changes are probably intentional. E.g., although the clause *lō' niṭṭeh yāmîn ûśᵉm'ôl* from 20:17 is missing in 21:22, the verb *niṭṭeh* is substituted for the verb *na'ᵃḇōr* in 20:17 to make up for the omission. In order to bring the two more into line, Sam. Pent. adds *bᵉḏereḵ hammeleḵ 'ēlēḵ lō' 'āsûr yāmîn ûśᵉm'ôl* ("I will go to the King's Highway, I will not turn to the right or the left"; cf. 20:17) to 21:22.

19. Many times the term *mal'āḵ* is used of supernatural messengers of God, viz., angels (e.g., Gen. 19:1, 15; Num. 22:22–27, 31–32, 34–35). A. Bowling, *TWOT,* I:464–65; *HALAT,* p. 554.

Gen. 14:7), and very often, as here, the inhabitants east of the Jordan under the rule of Sihon and Og (see the verses listed above under the titles of Sihon). The territory of Sihon apparently extended from the Jabbok on the north to the Arnon on the south and the Ammonite territory on the east (see below on v. 24). No extrabiblical texts confirm his kingship. One should not necessarily read the text to indicate any more than that Sihon was *an* Amorite king ("chieftain," as above on 20:14) who headquartered in and around Heshbon and controlled (to some extent) part of the countryside.

King's Highway. See the commentary above on 20:17.

23–24 Sihon's reaction was like that of the Edomite king earlier. The phraseology here is even similar to that in 20:20b, 21 (cf., e.g., 21:23a and 20:21a; 21:23b and 20:20b).

Jahaz. The location of this site is not certain. Ancient sources place it between Medeba and Dibon.[20] The Mesha Inscription (lines 18–21) mentions Jahaz next to Dibon, which may indicate their geographical proximity.[21] That Sihon *went out against Israel into the wilderness* clearly means that Israel was in the wilderness. That Sihon next *entered Jahaz and fought against Israel* must mean that at least some Israelites came into Jahaz. The text itself does not say that Jahaz itself is in the wilderness. The site is clearly on the Moabite plateau, as Jer. 48:21–25 shows, and is also called Jazrah.[22] Deut. 2:26 identifies this wilderness as Kedemoth. Israel may have come to meet Sihon as his forces went out toward the wilderness. In Gray's view, this means that Jahaz itself need not have been in the wilderness.[23] According to Snaith Jahaz is to be identified as Khirbet Umm-el-Idhâm, about 5 mi. north of Dibon.[24] Sturdy locates it east-southeast of Medeba, and Aharoni at Khirbet el-Medeiyineh, northeast of Dibon and southeast of Medeba.[25]

20. E.g., Eusebius, *Onomasticon* 131:17; Jerome, *Onomasticon* 262:29.

21. See Beyerlin, ed., *Near Eastern Religious Texts,* p. 239; *ANET,* p. 320; *DOTT,* p. 197. Also see Smith, *Historical Geography,* p. 378 n. 8.

22. Sometimes, as in the current passage and Deut. 2:32, the addition of the *-â* has a locative force (see the accents). In other places it is called Jazrah without any locative force (e.g., Judg. 11:20; Josh. 13:18; 1 Chr. 6:63 [Eng. 78]; Jer. 48:21). There are slight differences in pointing as well. The site is called Jazer (without *-â*) in Isa. 15:4; Jer. 48:34; and in the Mesha Inscription, lines 19–20. See Beyerlin, ed., *Near Eastern Religious Texts,* p. 239; *ANET,* p. 320; *DOTT,* p. 197.

23. Gray, p. 296.

24. Snaith, p. 173; followed by Budd, p. 246.

25. Sturdy, p. 145 (map); Y. Aharoni, *The Land of the Bible: A Historical Geography,* tr. and ed. A. Rainey, rev. ed. (Philadelphia: Westminster, 1979), pp. 204, 339, 437.

The Bible reports that Jahaz became a Levitical town in Reuben's territory (1 Chr. 6:63 [Eng. 78]).

The Israelite army smashed Sihon's force and *took possession of his land from the Arnon to the Jabbok, as far as the children of Ammon (wayyîraš 'eṯ-'ārṣô mē'arnōn 'aḏ-yabbōq 'aḏ-b^e^nê 'ammôn).* The borders are here given as the Jabbok River (Nahr Zerqâ) on the north and the Arnon (Wâdī Môjib; see on 20:13) on the south. The early course of the Jabbok runs east into the desert (south of Rabbath-ammon), then it turns north and west and runs to the Jordan about 45 mi. north of the Arnon.[26] The phrase *as far as the children of Ammon* is probably not to be taken as an appositive to *to the Jabbok,* but as referring to the Ammonites' territory as forming the eastern border of Sihon's kingdom.[27] The unnamed western border is undoubtedly the Jordan River.

for mighty is the border of the children of Ammon (kî 'az g^e^ḇûl b^e^nê 'ammôn). Commentators have used this clause to explain either why Sihon did not extend his territory further to the east, or why the Israelites stopped their own settlement at this point.[28] The first explanation would fit better if the clause had occurred in v. 26. The second has difficulty with Deut. 2:19, which gives the reason why Israel did not go further as a word from Yahweh forbidding conquest of the Ammonites because they were descended from Lot, and, therefore, were kin to the Israelites. The latter difficulty is not so great if one remembers that Moses plays no significant role in 21:21–31 at all, and that the present point of view — that the Israelites stopped because of the strength of the Ammonites — is enriched by Moses' own point of view in the matter in Deut. 2:19. The problem with such a theory is that the word for *mighty ('az)* does not elsewhere mean "well fortified," and this border is not "mighty" in the sense of imposing or geographically difficult.

This problem — an old one, to judge from the LXX — has led many scholars to follow that version in reading Jazer (*ya'zēr,* LXX *Iazēr*), a place-name, rather than *mighty ('az).*[29] Jazer is a site east of Jordan, often connected with Heshbon and other cities (Num. 21:32; 32:1, 3, 35; Josh. 13:25; 21:29; 2 Sam. 24:5; Isa. 16:8–9; Jer. 48:32). Again, the location of

26. Smith, *Historical Geography,* pp. 391–92; see also Keil, p. 151; Cook, p. 729; Holzinger, p. 98; Gray, pp. 296–97; etc.

27. Following Gray, p. 296.

28. See Keil, p. 151; Cook, p. 729. For the second problem see, e.g., Wenham, p. 161.

29. So BDB, p. 738b; Dillmann, p. 127; Holzinger, p. 98; Gray, pp. 297–98; McNeile, pp. 118–19; Binns, p. 145; Noordtzij, p. 192; Noth, p. 163; Snaith, p. 173; Budd, pp. 242, 246; etc. Also Moffatt, NASB, RSV.

this site is in doubt. Snaith locates it at Khirbet Jazzir near modern es-Salṭ, about 12 mi. south of the Jabbok; Binns has identified it as Ṣâr near Rabbath Ammon.[30] In any case, if one follows the LXX, then Jazer is fixed as the border of Ammonite territory. That the Israelites did not immediately settle down in these parts of Transjordan is shown by ch. 32. The statement here is a summary written from the point of view of a time after settlement in this territory.

25–26 Noth's literary judgment that vv. 25–26 form a transition to the song in vv. 27–30 is sound. The function of vv. 25–26 is to make the general note of conquest in v. 24 more specific.

25 *And Israel took all these cities.* The text has no antecedent for *these;* either a list of cities that were conquered (such as is found in 32:34–36) has been left out here,[31] or the demonstrative *these (hā'ēlleh)* refers to what follows. If the latter be the case, *these cities* are *all the cities of the Amorites* in the territory mentioned in v. 24, especially the city of Heshbon and *all its villages.*

Heshbon. Virtually all scholars are convinced that this is Tell Ḥešbân, located on a plateau about 3,000 ft. high, about 13 mi. east of the north end of the Dead Sea, and about 47 mi. east of Jerusalem. Excavations at Tell Ḥešbân have not found much from the Middle or Late Bronze Ages. In fact, there are only sparse remains at the site before the Iron II period (ca. 900–539 B.C.). One may account for this fact in three ways: (a) the remains of the conquest period have not been found yet, or have been destroyed by natural forces; (b) the narratives here are to be taken as much later projections of Heshbon's importance into the past; (c) the actual site of Heshbon has not yet been located.[32] Heshbon was a Levitical city (Josh. 21:39) and later came

30. Snaith, p. 173, again followed by Budd, p. 246; also *Oxford Bible Atlas,* p. 132. Cf. Binns, p. 144; followed by Noordtzij, p. 192; Aharoni, *Land of the Bible,* p. 38. Gray (p. 298) reports other options; e.g., near Jogbehah (T. K. Cheyne, "Jazer," *Encyclopaedia Biblica* [London: Black, 1901], II:2340–41).

31. Making for a rather poorly edited text; so, e.g., Gray, p. 298; McNeile, p. 119; Binns, p. 146; Noordtzij, p. 192.

32. Wenham (p. 161) argues for the last of these options, and mentions Arad as an analogy (later Arad is on a different site than the earlier city, although both share the same name). One could also argue that OT and NT Jericho are on different sites. Excavations at the site of Tell Ḥešbân were conducted by teams from Andrews University in Berrien Springs, Michigan. Reports of their discoveries are to be found in *Andrews University Seminary Studies* 9 (1971); 11 (1973); 12 (1974); 13 (1975); 16 (1978). Wenham refers to R. Ibach's article in this last issue, "Expanded Archaeological Survey of the Heshban Region," which mentions a wider number of (alternate) sites.

under Moabite control (Isa. 15:4; Jer. 48:2). It is somewhat surprising that a city of this importance is not named on the Mesha Inscription.

26 This verse identifies the subject of vv. 21–24 (Sihon) with the subject of the song in vv. 27–30 (Heshbon). It offers an explanation of Sihon's presence in Heshbon as well as in the surrounding territory (occupied by Israel in v. 24). The land had once belonged to Moab, but had been taken from *the former king of Moab* or, perhaps, "the first king of Moab" *(meleḵ mô'āḇ hāri'šôn).* The context offers little to determine which of these translations is preferable,[33] and little or nothing is known about early Moabite rulers. It is well known that the territory between the Arnon and Jabbok changed hands more than once; e.g., a bit later it became the territory of Reuben and Gad (ch. 32). For some of the later struggles over this part of the country, see Judg. 11:13; 2 K. 3 (and the Mesha Inscription);[34] Jer. 49:1–2.

27–30 These verses are difficult and ambiguous. Scholars have not been able to agree whether this poem or song is Amorite or Israelite, and when and for what purpose it was written.[35] One reason for these

33. For the meaning "former" see 2 K. 17:34; Mic. 4:8; Zech. 1:4; 7:7, 12; 8:11; Neh. 5:15; Ps. 79:8; etc. For the meaning "first" see Exod. 12:15–16; 40:2, 17; Lev. 23:5; Deut. 16:4; etc.

34. See Beyerlin, ed., *Near Eastern Religious Texts,* pp. 238–40; *ANET,* pp. 260–61; *DOTT,* pp. 196–98.

35. Although the traditional Jewish view of the song is that it was an Amorite victory song celebrating Sihon's victory over Moab north of the Arnon, the majority of scholars in the 19th and 20th cents. have not taken this view seriously. Gray's comment is typical: "The view . . . may be dismissed as inherently unlikely" (p. 300), and most scholars concluded that the poem was Israelite (e.g., Dillmann, p. 130; Keil, pp. 152–54; Noth, pp. 164–65; Sturdy, pp. 153–54; J. R. Bartlett, "The Historical Reference of Numbers 21:27–30," *PEQ* 101 [1969] 94–101). This view has most often been coupled with the view that the song is a satiric or ironic taunt of the Amorites (a view as old as H. Ewald according to Gray (p. 300), and as old as J. G. Herder (1744–1803) according to Binns [p. 146]); see, e.g., Keil, p. 154; Gray, pp. 300–301; Snaith, p. 174; Budd, p. 246; etc.). E. Meyer proposed that the song was intended to celebrate a victory of Israel over Moab, possibly in the days of Omri (cf. 2 K. 3; Mesha Inscription, lines 4–5; Beyerlin, *Near Eastern Religious Texts,* p. 238; *ANET,* p. 260; *DOTT,* p. 196; E. Meyer, "Kritik der Berichte über die Eroberung Palästinas," *ZAW* 1 [1881] 117–46, esp. 129–32; see also B. Stade, "Nachwort des Herausgabers," pp. 146–50; idem, "Der Krieg gegen Sichon und die zugehörigen Abschnitte," *ZAW* 6 [1886] 36–52). Although Dillmann rejected this view, B. Baentsch accepted it, as did A. R. S. Kennedy, *Century Bible,* in a simplified way (p. 313). This hypothesis requires the exegete to posit that the poem has been misunderstood and misapplied in the text itself, as well as calling for elimination of the last part of v. 29 (which deals

difficulties is that we have this song only in its biblical context, not in its original form. In the end exegetes cannot answer the question about the origin of this song; they can only examine its function in its present context, and even here there are ambiguities.

The reasons why the poem is cited in the first place are important. The first reason is probably to corroborate what has been reported in v. 26: that Sihon was an Amorite king in Heshbon and that he had taken over territory north of the Arnon from the Moabites. An important secondary reason is probably to corroborate that Israel had indeed taken all this territory at a stroke from this same Sihon (vv. 24–25). A citation from an Amorite victory song might fulfill the first purpose, but not the second. It is therefore possible that the author of the present text adapted an earlier Amorite song to fit into the present passage. Jer. 48:45–46 cites vv. 28–29 in a modified but recognizable form, which leaves vv. 27b and 30 (and perhaps the last part of v. 28, which identify Sihon as an Amorite king, hardly important in an Amorite song) as the modification to the poem made by the author of the present text.

Verse 27b begins with a summons to (re)build Heshbon, and vv. 28–29 continue with a justification for that call (initiated by *for [kî]*); v. 30 concludes the piece with a statement that Heshbon (and the whole surrounding region) is in ruins, and thus needs rebuilding. Thus vv. 27b and 30 (insofar as we can recapture what v. 30 is saying) call for Heshbon to be rebuilt because it has been conquered, while vv. 28–29 give a historical view of what the city had been under Sihon. In the background of all this is the knowledge that Israel was the conqueror of Sihon, who was the conqueror of Moab (v. 24). This victory would also establish Israel's firm claim on the land, which became important later when remembrance of this incident was used to attempt to stave off a land claim from the Ammonites (Judg. 11:12–28).

---

with Sihon the Amorite). It would also seem to require that Sihon was a Moabite king transformed into an Amorite by the later tradition (for what purpose is unclear); see Gray, p. 301; Smith, *Historical Geography,* Appendix III, pp. 444–45, refutes this thesis.

The view of the composition as a taunt-song depends upon reading a tone into the poem that is not obviously present. If we do not choose to read this tone into the composition, we are left with the old view that the song is an Amorite composition, which Budd (p. 245) admits is possible (although he does not adopt this view) and Gottwald supports (*Tribes of Yahweh,* pp. 215, 738 n. 153); so also Freedman, "Archaic Forms," pp. 101–7, esp. 106; Hanson, "Song of Heshbon"; Noordtzij, p. 193; de Vaulx, p. 245; Wenham, p. 161 n. 2; Milgrom, *JPST,* pp. 462–63.

27 *Therefore (ʿal-kēn)* might be paraphrased "since what has gone before [vv. 25–26 particularly] is true."[36]

the bards say. The text does not identify these bards.

Heshbon. When the city of Heshbon was mentioned in vv. 25–26, it was as the capital city of Sihon's territory, a capital city that had "daughters" (i.e., villages) dependent on it as a "mother." Why did such an independent, royal city need to *be built?* Why is there a call in v. 27b to have Heshbon of Sihon both built and established? The terms *be built (tibbāneh)* and *be established (wᵉṯikkônēn)* are clearly parallel (as are *Heshbon* and *the city of Sihon*). The first verb may mean either "to be built" (i.e., for the first time; e.g., Num. 13:22; 1 K. 3:2; 6:7; 1 Chr. 22:19), or "to be rebuilt" (Isa. 25:2; 44:26; Jer. 31:38).[37] Only the context (as Jer. 31:38) or accompanying particles (e.g., *ʿôḏ,* "again," Deut. 13:17 [Eng. 16]; Ezek. 26:14) can make the meaning clear. The second verb can mean "to be established" in the sense of "to be set up, founded" (and so parallel to "to be built for the first time"; e.g., Judg. 16:26, 29), or "to be made secure, enduring" (and so at least more parallel to the meaning "to be rebuilt"; e.g., 1 Sam. 20:31; 2 Sam. 7:16 [= 1 Chr. 17:14]; 1 K. 2:12, 45, 46).[38] The meaning of the terms is ambiguous here and is clarified only in v. 30. The hearer of the poem is, first, invited to *come.* This device is designed to attract the hearer's attention. The purpose for which the hearer is summoned is to build and establish Heshbon. The very ambiguity of these terms, as discussed above, forms an opening rhetorical device that draws the hearer (or the reader) into the rest of the poem.

28 *For (kî).* The particle introduces the ground for what has been said, and points to the past when, in the words of v. 26: "Sihon . . . had fought against the former king of Moab and had taken all his land from his hand as far as Arnon." The description here is more poetic. The parallel between Heshbon and the city of Sihon (v. 27) is repeated here. As pointed out above on v. 21, Sihon is often called king of Heshbon, so the parallel is apt.

fire (ʾēš) and *flame (lehāḇâ)* are also parallel terms. Fire may be used as an image for war (e.g., Amos 1:4). That this war fire had Heshbon as its source and not its end point[39] is shown by the use of the words *went*

36. See BDB, p. 487a.

37. See BDB, pp. 124–25a.

38. See BDB, pp. 465b–67a.

39. As claimed by Gray, pp. 302–3. Then the phrase would probably be as in Josh. 8:20 where smoke "went up from" *(ʿālâ min)* Ai.

out from (yāṣᵉʾâ min), as in Judg. 9:15, 20; Ezek. 19:14. The fire started in Heshbon and worked its destruction out from there as far as *Ar of Moab.* If the site suggested at the eastern extremity of the Arnon (see 21:15 above) is the right one, then the clause gives part of the scope of the conquest.

It swallowed the heights of Arnon. The translation *swallowed* is based on a slight change (metathesis of two consonants, reading *bālᵉʿâ* for MT *baʿᵃlê,* "lords of"), following LXX.[40] This change gives an admirable parallel to the verb *devoured (ʾāḵᵉlâ),* and continues the description of the scope of the conquest in a parallel clause. If MT is kept, then these "lords" were the so-called freeholders or citizens (NIV) in the land.

the heights of Arnon. The Targ. took *heights (bāmôṯ)* in the sense of "high places," i.e., Canaanite shrines, and the "lords" (in MT) to be Canaanite priests. But *bāmôṯ* here probably means only "high country" (Mic. 3:12; Jer. 26:18; Ezek. 36:2), or perhaps "the strategic places" (i.e., "the high ground"; Deut. 32:13; Isa. 58:14).[41]

29 Moab (above the Arnon) has been conquered. V. 29 speaks a word of woe to the vanquished Moabites. The Moabites are called the *people of Chemosh,* just as many times the Israelites are called "people of Yahweh" (Num. 11:29; 1 Sam. 2:24; etc.). *Chemosh,* the national god of Moab (and perhaps of Ammon; see Judg. 11:24), is mentioned seven times in the OT. Parallel to the present text, Jer. 48:46 calls the Moabites "people of Chemosh," and mentions "sons" and "daughters." Solomon erected a shrine to Chemosh near Jerusalem (1 K. 11:7) and worshiped him (11:33). This shrine was torn down in Josiah's time (2 K. 23:13). According to 2 K. 3:26, the king of Moab offered his own son as a sacrifice, presumably to Chemosh. The Mesha Inscription mentions Chemosh twelve times and speaks of him in ways similar to the ways in which Israel speaks of Yahweh, e.g., the "ban," which was similar to the Israelite *ḥērem,* in which Mesha (the son of Chemosh) dedicated the captives and spoils of war to his god by destroying them all.[42] That Chemosh is called Ashtar-Chemosh in line 17 of the inscription may mean that he was thought of as a local manifestation of the god Ashtar, known from Ugarit, among other places, but this point is disputed.[43]

40. So NEB, GNB; so also Noth, Wenham, Budd.

41. See BDB, p. 119a.

42. See Beyerlin, ed., *Near Eastern Religious Texts,* p. 239; *ANET,* p. 360; *DOTT,* p. 196.

43. For further discussion of the matter see the summary in P. Craigie, *ISBE,* rev., IV:95–101; W. F. Albright, *Archaeology and the Religion of Israel,* 4th ed. (Baltimore: Johns Hopkins Univ. Press, 1954), pp. 117–18.

He made his sons . . . his daughters. What is the antecedent of *He* here? Most have taken it to be the same as that for *his sons* and *his daughters,* viz., Chemosh, so that the meaning is that Chemosh as the god of Moab has given the Moabites into captivity (presumably because of their sin; the Mesha Inscription has a similar theological statement),[44] and this remains the most likely possibility. A few commentators have taken the antecedent of *He* to be Sihon, since, in an Amorite victory song, glory would not likely be given to a Moabite god.[45] Although it may be true that, according to the prose account of v. 26, it was Sihon who conquered the Moabites, it is grammatically and syntactically difficult to make him the antecedent in the poem of v. 29. If Sihon had been meant, one would expect some more conspicuous indication of it (there is not even a personal pronoun except the one inherent in the verb "he gave" *[nāṯan]* itself). This point is all the more telling because Chemosh is clearly meant as the antecedent in *his sons* and *his daughters* in the same part of the verse.

fugitives (pālêṭ/pālîṭ). This term usually refers to one who has managed to escape from a disaster (such as an enemy attack) alive, but through difficulty (Judg. 12:5; Ezek. 6:8–9; 7:16; 24:26–27; 33:21–22), and who is not necessarily out of danger (2 K. 9:15; Amos 9:1; Jer. 44:28). Occasionally *fugitive* is found together with "survivor" (*śārîḏ,* Josh. 8:22; Jer. 42:17; 44:14; Lam. 2:22).[46]

In addition to his sons being fugitives, *his daughters* will be made *as captives (baššᵉḇîṯ).* The children of Chemosh will barely escape death, and some who do will be placed into slavery.

To a king of Amorites —Sihon (lᵉmeleḵ ʾᵉmōrî sîḥôn). The absence of the definite article on the word *Amorite* is unusual in either prose or poetry. Gray sets out three options for accounting for this anomalous phrase: it is to be taken adjectivally ("an Amorite king"); it is done with poetic license; it is due to a glossator's brevity of style. Surely the first of these options is sufficient. While it is true that Hebrew poetic diction may eliminate the definite article, it does not always do so. Several commentators have concluded that this phrase is a gloss, primarily because it forms a ternary line in a poem made up otherwise of binary lines.[47] But Hebrew

44. So, e.g., Keil, p. 153; Dillmann, p. 131; Gray, p. 304; McNeile, p. 120; Binns, p. 147; Heinisch, p. 85. For the Mesha Inscription see Beyerlin, ed., *Near Eastern Religious Texts,* pp. 238–40; *ANET,* pp. 260–62; *DOTT,* pp. 196–98.

45. So Noordtzij, pp. 193–94; Wenham, p. 162.

46. See BDB, p. 812a.

47. E.g., Dillmann, p. 131; Gray, p. 304; McNeile, p. 121; Binns, p. 147; Paterson, p. 55; de Vaulx, p. 246; Budd, p. 242.

poetry does seem to alternate binary and ternary lines with no apparent scheme or regularity.[48] It is just as likely that the longer line was meant to attract attention to this phrase as significant. It is possible that the phrase is inserted by the author of the passage in order to draw attention to Sihon by name, because it is not likely that an Amorite poem would need to refer to an Amorite king in this way.

30 This verse is corrupt in nearly ever word; hence a wide range of options has been suggested, and definite conclusions are not possible. This is unfortunate because v. 30 contains the climax of the piece. MT seems to provide the answer to the question raised at v. 27b. Heshbon needs building and establishing because *we* destroyed not only it but the entire region. It is probable that the *we* here is the same speaker who called for building Heshbon in v. 27b. This speaker may be identified as the victorious Israelites in the present form of the poem.

Three site-names in Sihon's former territory are: *Heshbon* in the north, *Dibon* (identified with Dhibân, about 4 mi. north of the Arnon) in the south, and *Medeba* (identified as Madaba, about 20 mi. south of Rabbath-ammon) in between.

The MT begins each half-verse with a first person plural consecutive imperfect verb. The first, *we overthrew them* (*wannîrām,* from *yārâ*) may be literally translated as "to shoot" (arrows, Exod. 19:3) and more figuratively as "to cast down" (as in the Song of the Sea, Exod. 15:4). The second, *we ravaged* (*wannaššîm,* from *yāšaš*?) is less certain. The versions did not understand either word as a verb, and various translations have been suggested on the basis of the versions.[49] Although the text is in such a state of disarray that it is impossible to make a firm judgment, the verbs in MT do make some sense; the Israelites dislodged Sihon and his forces from the whole area north (Heshbon) to south (Dibon).

According to MT this "ravaging" continued *as far as Nophah* (*ʿaḏ nōp̄aḥ*). The site of Nophah is unknown. It might be possible, on the basis of Pesh., to read Nobah here, as in Judg. 8:11, but the location of Nobah is also unknown, though it may be near Jogbehah.[50]

fire as far as Medeba. The MT is *ʾašer ʿaḏ-mêḏᵉḇâ,* lit., "which is as far as Medeba." This makes little sense. The Masoretes themselves felt

48. See Kugel, *Idea of Biblical Poetry,* pp. 1, 26–27, 52, 72, etc.

49. See nn. 11–12 on the translation above.

50. For further possibilities for translating this word, see n. 13 on the translation above. For discussion of the Pesh. reading see, e.g., Dillmann, p. 132; Keil, pp. 153–54.

the difficulty, and put a special masorctic point (one of the *puncta extraordinaria*) above the last letter of *ʾᵃšer,* showing that they were doubtful how or whether this letter should be transmitted. If one leaves this letter off, one is left with *ʾēš,* the word for "fire," which is the reading of the Sam. Pent. and LXX. Once again, no firm decision can be made here. If, however, the latter reading is correct, the verse resolves the question with which the song began ("Why does Heshbon need building?") by stating that all that Sihon's conquering fire burned ("from Heshbon. . . . It devoured Ar of Moab . . . the heights of Arnon," v. 28) Israel's conquering fire has now burned *(Heshbon . . . Dibon . . . Nophah . . . Medeba).*[51]

31–32 These verses take material from v. 24 and restate it as a conclusion to the incident with Sihon and an introduction to the incident with Og of Bashan in vv. 33–35.

And Israel settled . . . Like the statement *and Israel . . . took possession of his* [Sihon's] *land . . .* (v. 24), the current verse looks forward to the conquest of the land under Joshua and is a summary statement. This means that the whole section probably dates from a time after the conquest.

32 This verse is a transition to vv. 33–35. It introduces the character of Moses into the narrative for the first time since 21:16 (really since 21:4–9). Moses sent spies who evidently brought a report, after which he sent a contingent of troops to take Jazer and environs.

Jazer. On the possible location of this site, see above on v. 24. The Hebrew text does not state that Jazer itself was taken, only that its *villages* were. It would be surprising, however, if v. 31 would state that the Israelites settled down in the land of the Amorites if Jazer itself had not fallen. Furthermore, since 32:34–36 lists Jazer among the cities that the Gadites (re)built, one may assume that it did eventually fall to the Israelites. Since Jazer is on the way north to Og's territory, the battle for Jazer and environs may have happened on the way. Nowhere does the text state that the whole Israelite force went on this northern march, although, since Moses accompanied the force, one may assume that it consisted of the main force of the army.

33–35 The story of the conquest of Og's territory has a close parallel in Moses' recapitulation of it in Deut. 3:1–11. The parallel

51. Hanson ("Song of Heshbon," 306) conjectures a reading that, although interesting, is unnecessary: "the high places of Chemosh, from Nophah as far as Medeba, are deserted" *(nāšammû bāmôṯ komuš nōp̱ḥâ ʿᵃḏê mêḏᵉḇâ).* Wenham seems to prefer this option (p. 162 n. 5).

between vv. 33–34 and Deut. 3:1–2 is striking; they are the same except that the current passage is in the third person, while Deut. 3 is in the first. The parallels between v. 35 and Deut. 3:3 are also close in content, but they differ a bit more in phraseology. On the basis of these close parallels many scholars have concluded that the author of the current text simply used Deut. 3:1–3.[52] For most of these scholars, this conclusion carries with it the assumption that both Num. 21 and Deut. 3 are centuries later than the events narrated. On the basis of the claim of the texts themselves that they have some connection with the time of Moses, this assumption may be questioned. If the texts do have some connection with the time of Moses (whether in an oral or written sense), then the fact that Num. 21:33–35 should be very similar to Deut. 3:1–3 is of less consequence. The similarities between vv. 33–34 and Deut. 3:1–2 make literary dependence of one on the other likely. The same is quite probably true of v. 35 and Deut. 3:3. There is no absolutely objective way of discovering which text is prior. The Numbers text is shorter than the text of Deut. 3 and is as likely to have shortened the latter as the other way around.

33 *the way of Bashan.* Most times the term *Bashan* occurs with the definite article, as here ("the Bashan," *habbāšān*).[53] *Bashan* is located in Transjordan and is bordered on the west by the territories of Geshur and Maacah (Josh. 12:5), on the south by the River Yarmuk (Deut. 3:10 continues this border from Edrei to Salecah), on the north by the slopes of Mt. Hermon, and on the east by the volcanic slopes of the Hauran range. The route is to the northeast of Israel's location in Sihon's land.

Og the king of Bashan. No extrabiblical record of this king is known. It is possible that he was not considered Amorite. Deut. 3:11; Josh. 12:4; 13:12 call him the last of the Rephaim (in Moabite called Emim [Deut. 2:11], in Ammonite, Zamzummim [2:20]). It is a matter of debate whether the term *Rephaim* is an ethnic or a descriptive term ("sunken [i.e., powerless] one").[54] The Rephaim are connected with the Anakim, the

52. For a summary of some scholarly conclusions in this matter, see Budd, pp. 243–44.

53. E.g., Num. 32:33; Deut. 1:4; 3:1, 3, 10–11, 13–14; 4:47; 29:6; 32:22; Josh. 9:10; 12:4–5; 13:11, 30; 1 K. 4:19; Isa. 2:13; Amos 4:1.

54. See BDB, p. 952a. Articles on the Rephaim include: J. Gray, "The Rephaim," *PEQ* 81 (1949) 127–39; idem, "DTN and RPUM in Ancient Ugarit," *PEQ* 84 (1952) 39–41; A. Jirku, "Rapa'u, der Fürst der Rapa'uma-Rephaim," *ZAW* 77 (1965) 82–83; A. Caquot, "Les rephaim ougaritiques," *Syria* 37 (1960) 75–93; J. C. de Moor, "Rāpi'ūma-Rephaim," *ZAW* 88 (1976) 323–45; R. Schnell, *IDB,* IV:35; S. Parker, *IDBSup,* p. 739; P. K. McCarter, Jr., *ISBE,* rev., IV:137.

"giants" of pre-Israelite Canaan (Deut. 2:10–11; see above on 13:28). In any case, Deut. 3:11 includes a note that Og's huge sarcophagus[55] (about 13.5 by 6 ft.) was on display in Rabbath-ammon. If the size of his sarcophagus is accurate and reflects his size, he must have been a frightening opponent.

Edrei. Apparently modern Der'ā, which is located on a tributary of the Yarmuk, about 30 mi. east of the Sea of Tiberias (Galilee), 30 mi. west of the Hauran range, and about 23 mi. west-northwest of Bozrah.[56] With Ashtaroth (Tell Aštarta) Edrei was Og's capital city (Deut. 1:4).

34 Yahweh here assures Moses that he has no reason to fear Og. Since no such assurance was given concerning Sihon in 21:21–31, it may be that Og was much stronger than Sihon (cf. the tradition of his large sarcophagus in Deut. 3:11). But the literary dependence of this passage on Deut. 3 makes it possible that this assurance is simply the literary expression of Deuteronomy (on Sihon, cf. Deut. 2:24–25, 31, 33), which expression is simply not found in the Numbers version of the Sihon narrative. The theology that it is Yahweh, not Israelite might, that gives the victory is made clear in this way.

just as you did to Sihon. It is not clear at this point just what Israel did to Sihon. One might conclude that what is meant is that "Israel smote him with the edge of the sword and took possession of his land" (v. 24). This is undoubtedly a general description of what went on, but Deut. 2:34–35 makes clear that Israel put him and his country to the ban (*ḥerem,* see v. 35 below).

35 This verse describes the downfall of Og's kingdom. While it is true that the phrase *and his sons* is not found in Deut. 3:3, that text does say that "no survivor was left to him" (*ʿaḏ-biltî hiš'îr-lô śārîḏ,* as also here). This phrase here may be thought of as simply making explicit that Og's dynasty came to an end with him.

22:1 This verse ends the journey of the Israelites as far as the book of Numbers is concerned. The journey is taken up again in terms

55. The word *ʿereś* is often translated as "bedstead" (AV, RV, NASB, NJPV, NKJV) or "bed" (NIV), but is probably better rendered by "sarcophagus" (Moffatt, NEB, NIV mg.; cf. GNB). See, e.g., G. A. Cooke, *A Text-book of North-Semitic Inscriptions* (Oxford: Clarendon, 1903), p. 187; A. D. H. Mayes, *Deuteronomy,* NCBC (Grand Rapids: Eerdmans, 1981), p. 144; J. A. Thompson, *Deuteronomy,* TOTC (Downers Grove: InterVarsity Press, 1974), p. 98.

56. A remarkable system of underground dwellings and tunnels has been found at this site. See, e.g., Budd, p. 247; Snaith, p. 174; Milgrom, *JPST,* p. 194; D. Pecosta, *ISBE,* rev., II:21; G. A. Smith, *Historical Geography*, pp. 340–41 n. 2.

similar to those in 21:10–11. The place of departure is not stated here (nor in 21:10), but in 33:48 is given as the mountains of Abarim.

the plains of Moab (ʿarᵉḇôṯ mô'āḇ) are the flat and fertile strip of country (about 5–6 mi. wide) north and east of the Dead Sea. The term is used in 26:3, 63; 31:12; 33:38–50; 35:1; 36:13; Deut. 34:1, 8; Josh. 13:32. It is at this place that Israel heard the final addresses of Moses contained in Deuteronomy, although the place is identified simply as "beyond the Jordan in the land of Moab" in Deut. 1:5.

on the other side of the Jordan of Jericho. The point of view is from inside the land of Canaan, which, of course, means that the standpoint of the verse is post-conquest. The *Jordan of Jericho* indicates that part of the Jordan River by the city of Jericho, modern Tell es-Sultan, in the same way that "the waters of Megiddo" (Judg. 5:19) indicate waters in that vicinity.

V. ON THE PLAINS OF MOAB (22:2–36:13)

A. STORY OF BALAAM (22:2–24:25)

Chapters 22–24 begin a new section of the book. They are the first narratives that take place on the plains of Moab, the locale throughout Deuteronomy. But these chapters are not totally separate from the travel narratives in chs. 20–21, for they detail the attempt of Balak, the king of another Transjordanian power (Moab), to cope with the Israelites' presence. Since Sihon and Og had attempted military victory and failed, Balak decided, with help from Midian, to defeat Israel by having them cursed by the famous seer Balaam, who would be able to curse the Israelites in the name of their own God Yahweh (22:2–7). Balaam speaks in Yahweh's name in 22:8, and calls Yahweh "my God" in 22:18.

Balak sends emissaries with fees for divination to persuade Balaam to come and curse Israel. At Yahweh's direction, Balaam refuses (22:8–14). Offended but undaunted, Balak sends forth a more distinguished (and evidently more financially amply endowed) group of messengers to try to convince Balaam, who makes it clear that it is not the amount of money but obedience to Yahweh's word that will determine whether he comes to Balak. He instructs the emissaries to spend the night, and, after being told to go by Yahweh, accompanies them in the morning (22:15–21).

While on the journey Yahweh becomes angry with Balaam and blocks his way with an armed angel. Balaam himself cannot see the heavenly adversary, but his donkey can. Three times the dumb and stubborn beast of burden turns from the roadway to avoid the angel, and three times Balaam steers her back to the road by beating her — thus insisting (unwittingly) on heading for disaster. Finally Balaam's donkey speaks, and Balaam himself is enlightened as to the real situation and repents of his foolishness (22:22–35).

When Balaam arrives in Moab he is taken to a place where Balak offers sacrifices and prepares to show him the people of Israel (22:36–40). In the morning, Balaam blesses the people rather than cursing them in four oracles delivered at various sites (23:7–10, 18b–24; 24:3–9, 15b–19). The first three oracles climax in the fourth, which is not only a blessing on Israel but a curse on Moab. Balaam concludes his blessings with four brief curses on various peoples (24:20–24) and departs for home (24:25).

The story is full of rich interconnections among its various parts, and these must receive emphasis in due course,[1] since, here as elsewhere, one must interpret the whole text in its final form, not putative fragmentary ancestors of it. Nonetheless, these chapters have some undeniable characteristics that have led many interpreters to conclude that they consist in a combination of a variety of sources that are not always reconcilable.

The first of these is the variation in the 51 occurrences of divine names.[2] The only section that seems to prefer one name over another is the story of Balaam's donkey (22:22–35), where the name Yahweh clearly prevails; the other sections show a fairly even distribution of names. The LXX agrees with the MT in 30 of these readings and disagrees in 22; half of these disagreements come in 22:22–35.[3] The case for making a division

1. See the commentary below; see also J. Licht, *Storytelling in the Bible* (Jerusalem: Magnes, 1978), pp. 69–74; Wenham, pp. 164–69; etc.

2. This literary feature has been noticed and treated with care because of the important role the alternation of divine names has played in the evolution of the documentary hypothesis in the first place. The names occur as follows:

Passage	Yahweh	Elohim	El	Shadday	Elyon
22:2–21, 36–41	4	6	0	0	0
22:22–35	12	1	0	0	0
23:1–30	8	3	4	0	0
24:1–25	5	1	4	2	1
Totals	29	11	8	2	1

(See, e.g., Gray, pp. 310–14.)

3. LXX has 52 divine names, inserting *ho theos* in 23:15 where MT has no divine name. The other disagreements are 22:13, 22–28, 31–32, 35; 23:3, 5, 8 (twice), 12, (15), 16, 26; 24:4, 13, 16. LXX translates "the angel of Yahweh" *(mala'ḵ YHWH)* by "the angel of God" *(ho angelos tou theou)* 8 times in ch. 22. Twice a more literal rendering of "angel of the Lord" *(angelon kyriou)* occurs (22:31, 34). LXX also renders Yahweh by *theos* 2 times in the chapter (vv. 28,

of sources by means of the use of various divine names is weak, except for 22:22–35, which stands out (and even this point is vitiated somewhat by the LXX).[4] The divine names may vary for stylistic reasons. Twelve of the occurrences of Yahweh are found in Balaam's speeches (about 41%), and three more speak of Yahweh with regard to these speeches (23:5, 16; 24:1). Ten occurrences of the name are in the phrase "the angel of Yahweh" in 22:22–35.

The only remaining occurrences of divine names in the pericope are 22:28, 31; 23:17; and 24:11. The first two of these refer to Yahweh's opening of the donkey's mouth and Balaam's eyes in miracles of perception. The latter two are in speeches by Balak, who, in the process of Balaam's oracles, has heard him refer to God by the name Yahweh. In fact, Balaam uses the generic term *Elohim* to refer to God only twice (22:38; 23:37). The point here may well be the apologetic one of stating to an Israelite audience that even a pagan seer may be inspired by Yahweh (see below).

Scholars also perceive inconsistencies in the narrative. Most of these are minor,[5] but a major one can be summarized by saying that 22:22–35 do not seem to fit well in the present literary context. For example, in v. 20 God says to Balaam, "Rise and go with them" (i.e., Balak's messengers). In v. 21 Balaam obeys, only to find in v. 22 that "God's wrath was kindled, since he was going." Again, in v. 21 Balaam goes with the Moabite princes, while the very next verse states that Balaam was with his two servants. Of course, it is possible that the princes were present but were not mentioned. Had this been the case, however, it is all the more remarkable that these messengers of Balak would not have reported the incident upon arriving home. Finally, the whole story could

---

31). In v. 22 where *Elohim* is rendered by *theos,* Sam. Pent. reads Yahweh. This shows the tradition, as reflected in MT, to be variable and not a good criterion for isolating sources.

4. Most modern scholars seem less ready to offer a compartmentalization of the chapters into sources on this (or any other) grounds than those of the last part of the 19th and early part of the 20th cents., when source criticism was at its zenith (see, e.g., Gray, pp. 309–13; McNeile, pp. 123–24). For an overview of scholarly research on the chapters, see Budd, pp. 256–65, with his own conclusions on pp. 261–65. Such scholars as Noth, pp. 171–75; Sturdy, pp. 156–58; A. W. Jenks (*The Elohist and North Israelite Traditions,* SBLMS 22 [Missoula, Mont.: Scholars Press, 1977], pp. 55–57), and W. F. Albright ("The Oracles of Balaam," *JBL* 63 [1944] 207–33, esp. 207–8) are not inclined to divide the narrative by source on the basis of the divine names.

5. See, e.g., Gray, p. 309.

be excised without damaging the main thrust of the story of Balaam and Balak (but see below). Thus it seems reasonable to conclude that 22:22–35 probably form an independent story about Balaam that has been brought into the present narrative about Balaam and Balak at some point in the stream of tradition, although how and when this happened is unclear, and one must still take 22:22–35 as part of a new whole in its present literary context.

It is now appropriate to make a few general comments about the goal and point of the whole Balaam cycle in its present literary context. Many commentators have spent a great deal of time discussing Balaam's character. Was he a sinner or saint?[6] It seems important to begin with the current chapters themselves rather than any later judgments on Balaam, biblical or postbiblical, and from this perspective one cannot make Balaam into either a sinner or a saint. Commentators have tried, but have only succeeded insofar as they have imported, e.g., character motivations, into the text; then they have succeeded in proving whichever option they set out to prove.[7] The text of chs. 22–24 is not concerned to pronounce on the matter. Balaam's character is incidental to the story.

It is clear from 31:16 that, in the end, Balaam fell by seducing the children of Israel into the sin at Baal-Peor (ch. 25), paying for this sin with his life (31:8). When subsequent biblical texts refer to the matters in chs. 22–24, their judgment on Balaam seems at least as neutral as these chapters (see Deut. 23:5–6 [Eng. 4–5]; Josh. 24:9–10; Mic. 6:4–5; Neh. 13:2). When the reference is to what Balaam later did, the judgment is clearly negative (Josh. 13:22). The NT picks up the negative judgment in 2 Pet. 2:15–16; Jude 11; Rev. 2:14, although the precise referents of these passages are unclear. Postbiblical Jewish tradition is almost wholly negative on Balaam's character as well.[8]

Nonetheless, it must be stressed that, whatever Balaam finally did, and whatever later tradition judged him to be, on the basis of the current text only a neutral judgment can be made. Balaam clearly participated in pagan rites (22:40–23:3a; 23:14–15, 29–30) and was involved in looking

6. See G. W. Coats, "Balaam: Sinner or Saint?" *Biblical Research* 18 (1973) 21–29.

7. One recent attempt is by Wenham (pp. 167–68), who seems concerned to defend the sinner side of Balaam's character. He succeeds only in stating possibilities, however, as he himself would admit.

8. One exception is in *Sifre* on Deut. 34:10 ("there has not arisen in Israel a prophet like Moses"): "but among the heathen there has, viz. Balaam." See Gray, p. 321.

for omens (24:1; forbidden to Israelites in Deut. 18:9–14), so that he cannot be made into a great devotee of Yahweh. Nonetheless, he did speak Yahweh's true word, defending it to Balak as irresistible (22:18, 38; 23:3b, 12, 26; 24:12–13), and not succumbing to Balak's blandishments (22:18; 24:13). The best judgment that one can make is that Balaam was inspired by God to speak his true word, although Balaam's devotion to Yahweh was partial at best and failed him in the end.

As the old saying goes, "The Lord can strike a mighty blow with a crooked stick," and one should look for the point of the passage along the lines of this saying. The conflict in the story is between Israel and Moab (and Midian). The characters of Balaam and Balak are simply representatives of this conflict. Yahweh is Israel's champion, hence the conflict is, more accurately, between Yahweh and those who oppose him and his purposes. Nothing these opponents do will be of any use. Opposition to Yahweh is doomed to fail, doomed to bring a curse on the opponent. Yahweh can draw non-Israelites in as tools to accomplish his purpose (so Melchizedek, Pharaoh, Rahab, Nebuchadnezzar, Cyrus, etc.). God may confirm his will through the mouth of a pagan such as Balaam. But in order to keep Israelites from finding Balaam too exalted a character, the story in 22:22–35 shows that this famous seer is not quite as perceptive as his donkey when left unenlightened by Yahweh. As in other narratives in Numbers, the final judgment of Moab (the curse of 24:17) comes because Balak of Moab has pushed Balaam to utter a curse on what God has decided to bless. In the action of Balaam there is also a further turning away from the punishment of Israel's past (the wandering years) to the blessing of its future (the conquest and settlement). All this the Balaam story accomplishes with literary skill and beauty.

These chapters contain narrative as well as four longer poetic oracles (23:7–10, 19–24; 24:3b–9, 15b–19) and four shorter oracles (24:20–24). One cannot know for sure whether the oracles and the narratives were composed at the same time. It seems most likely, however, that the narratives were composed to provide a setting for the oracles. No Israelite was present at these events, hence one must posit time for these narratives to have come into Israelite hands. The present text clearly presents Israelite theology to an Israelite audience, whatever the background of the texts that went into it might have been.

Balaam's social roles overlap those of the Mesopotamian diviner/seer (Babylonian *bārû*) and exorcist (Babylonian *ašipu*). The former role is seen, e.g., in the reports of God's nocturnal visits to Balaam in 22:7–21. The latter role is seen, e.g., in the narrative concerning sacrifice at seven altars in 22:40–23:7. In a stimulating study using contemporary role theories as paradigms, M. Moore has concluded that one reason for ambiguous attitudes toward Balaam in later tradition originate in the overlap of Balaam's roles as diviner/seer, which was accepted, and exorcist, which was not well, or widely, accepted.[9]

As for the age of the materials here, Albright posited that they could be from the mid-13th to the late 10th cents., with a preference for a date in the earlier period.[10] When they came into their present context is unknown, but there seems no reason to posit a very late date, certainly no later than the 10th cent. B.C. The discovery of an extrabiblical Balaam text has given new comparative material.

The text was discovered in 1967 at Tell Deir ʿAllā, the biblical Succoth, located in Transjordan near the confluence of the River Jabbok (modern Naḥr ez-Zerqā) and the Jordan River. It was found in a small, partially roofed, room with a floor that slopes toward the center of the room and benches on each side. The room is part of a larger complex that was destroyed (perhaps by earthquakes) in the early to mid-8th cent. B.C. and may have been part of a non-Israelite sanctuary. The text was written in black and red ink on lime plaster and, because of the curved shape of the fragments, was probably attached on the wall of the room on a stele. The fragments found on the floor probably fell away from the wall. These fragments have been arranged into two Combinations and thirteen other

9. See M. Moore, *The Balaam Traditions: Their Character and Development,* SBLDS 113 (Atlanta: Scholars Press, 1990), esp. pp. 109–22. The whole monograph may be read with profit. Unfortunately it arrived too late to be fully incorporated into the discussion. On prophecy in Mesopotamia, in addition to Moore, *Balaam Traditions,* pp. 20–65, see R. R. Wilson, *Prophecy and Society in Ancient Israel* (Philadelphia: Fortress, 1980), pp. 90–124, esp. 90–98 on the role of the *bārû;* see also Wilson's discussion of the Balaam pericope on pp. 147–50. The identification of Balaam as a *bārû* was evidently first made by S. Daiches in "Balaam, a Babylonian *bārû:* The Episode of Num. 22.2–24.24 and Some Babylonian Parallels," *Assyriologische und archaeologische Studien Hermann von Hilprecht gewidmet* (Leipzig: Hinrichs, 1909), pp. 60–70, and reiterated in "Balaam — A Babylonian Bārû," in *Bible Studies* (London: Edward Golston, 1950), pp. 110–19. See also H. B. Huffmon, "Prophecy in the Mari Letters," *Biblical Archaeologist Reader* (Garden City, N.Y.: Doubleday, 1970), III:199–224; idem, "Prophecy in the Ancient Near East," *IDBSup,* pp. 697–700. For other literature on the topic, see Moore, *Balaam Traditions,* pp. 124–36. On the Balaam story, see J. Lindblom, *Prophecy in Ancient Israel* (Philadelphia: Fortress, 1962), pp. 90–95.

10. Albright, "Oracles of Balaam," pp. 226–27; so also Wilson, *Prophecy and Society,* p. 148, etc.

smaller groupings. The larger of the two main Combinations (Combination I) was probably located near the top of the original stele, while Combination II was nearer the bottom.[11]

The text was first dated in the Persian period.[12] The dating was later modified to c. 725–675 B.C.,[13] and some scholars now place it earlier in the eighth, or even in the second half of the ninth cent. B.C.[14] The original publishers identified the text as Aramaic, and some scholars still hold to that identification.[15] Others have noted the text's affinities with (South) Canaanite.[16] The linguistic debate still continues, and may, in fact, show that the division of Semitic languages into Aramaic and Canaanite branches is a concept that needs revision, since the Balaam text clearly

11. On the location and physical description of the text and its surroundings, see, e.g., J. Hackett, *The Balaam Text from Deir ʿAllā,* HSM 31 (Chico, CA: Scholars Press, 1984), pp. 1–4, 21; M. Ibrahim and G. van der Kooij, "The Archaeology of Deir ʿAllā Phase IX," in J. Hoftijzer and G. van der Kooij, eds., *The Balaam Text from Deir ʿAllā Re-Evaluated: Proceedings of the International Symposium held at Leiden, 21–24 August 1989* (Leiden: Brill, 1990), pp. 16–29, esp. pp. 20, 28 (henceforth referred to as *Proceedings, 1989*); G. van der Kooij, "Book and Script at Deir ʿAllā," *Proceedings, 1989,* pp. 239–62, esp. 239–44.

12. H. J. Franken, "Texts from the Persian Period from Tell Deir ʿAllā," *VT* 17 (1967), 480–81.

13. E.g., by Hackett, *Balaam Text,* p. 2. This was substantially the date proposed by van der Kooij in the primary edition of the text; J. Hoftijzer and G. van der Kooij, *Aramaic Texts from Deir ʿAllā. With Contributions by H. J. Franken, V. R. Mehra, J. Voskuil, J. A. Mosk. Preface by P. A. H. de Boer,* Documenta et Monumenta Orientis Antiqui 19 (Leiden: Brill, 1976), p. 96; henceforth ATDA.

14. For the eighth-cent. date, see, e.g., B. Levine, "The Plaster Inscriptions from Deir ʿAllā: General Interpretation," in *Proceedings, 1989,* pp. 58–72, esp. 59. Levine's article contains much of value besides a discussion of the date. The ninth-cent. date was proposed by M. Weippert, "The Balaam Text from Deir ʿAllā and the Study of the Old Testament," *Proceedings, 1989,* p. 176.

15. E.g., D. Pardee, "The Linguistic Classification of the Deir ʿAllā Text written on Plaster," in *Proceedings, 1989,* pp. 100–105, esp. 105. So, earlier, among others, A. Caquot and A. Lemaire, "Les textes araméenes de Deir ʿAllā," *Syria* 54 (1977), 208; H.-P. Muller, "Einige alttestamentliche Probleme zur aramäischen Inschrift von Deir ʿAllā," *ZDPV* 94 (1978) 56; P. K. McCarter, "The Balaam Texts from Deir ʿAllā," *BASOR* 239 (1980) 50–51.

16. E.g., Hackett, *Balaam Text,* pp. 109–24, esp. 123–24; J. Greenfield has called the text "Gileadite," a local dialect close to the Canaanite of its time, but affected as well by Aramaic: "Philological Observations on the Deir ʿAllā Inscription," in *Proceedings, 1989,* pp. 109–20, esp. 118. Also McCarter, "The Dialect of the Deir ʿAllā Texts," *Proceedings, 1989,* pp. 91–94. Milgrom, *JPST,* p. 474, calls it "a dialect of Hebrew."

shows affinities with both branches.[17] It is clear that the language of the text is archaic, i.e., it conserves many features found in the supposed Northwest Semitic parent language, and a literary language, i.e., formulaic, poetic, and traditional.[18] The script is also unique, but has close affinities with Ammonite.[19]

The texts consist in 34 more or less legible lines with many gaps. Neither the translation nor the interpretation of the texts is agreed at present, but a general summary of content is as follows: Balaam, son of Beor, receives a message from the gods in a night visitation. The gods express displeasure over the state of affairs on earth (lines 1–2). On the next morning Balaam is disturbed by his message from the gods (lines 3–4). When asked why he is upset he passes on a message of doom (lines 5–16). Combination II consists in a group of ritual comments, perhaps on death, related to the god's reflection of the bad state of affairs on earth mentioned in Combination I (lines 1–18).[20]

With texts as framentary and unsure in linguistic, cultural, and religious contexts as these, one must be cautious in the extreme about claiming that they demonstrate this or that parallel with the biblical Balaam stories in Num. 22–24. The Deir ʿAllā texts do not demonstrate or even confirm that this Balaam was a historical character as the Bible portrays him.[21] The following are some obvious and limited points-of-contact between the Deir ʿAllā texts and Num. 22–24.

First, the Deir ʿAllā texts do demonstrate that Balaam, son of Beor, was a known literary character in the Transjordan, in an area within a few miles from where the biblical stories are set, in and before the eighth cent.

17. E.g., P. K. McCarter, *Proceedings, 1989,* pp. 88–99, esp. 91–94; see also Greenfield, *Proceedings, 1989*, pp. 117–18.

18. P. K. McCarter, "The Balaam Texts from Deir ʿAllā: The First Combination," *BASOR* 239 (1980), 50–51.

19. Hackett, *Balaam Text,* p. 10. Hackett's teacher, F. M. Cross ("Notes on the Ammonite Inscription from Tell Siran," *BASOR* 212 [1973] 12–15) held that the script has affinities with the Ammonite script as well. Other scholars, e.g., J. Naveh, "The Date of the Deir ʿAllā Inscription in Aramaic Script," *IEJ* 17 (1967) 256–58, have held that the script is basically Aramaic.

20. A convenient transliterated text may be found in Hackett, *Balaam Text,* pp. 25–26. The original publication of the texts was in ATDA, pp. 99–167. Hackett has made some useful, and now widely accepted modifications to the text as found in the primary edition, e.g., she moves fragments VIIId + XIIc at the end of lines 3–5 (Hackett, *Balaam Texts,* pp. 21–22). Combination II is very difficult, and no consensus exists on its meaning.

21. So, e.g., Harrison, p. 293.

B.C. It is reasonable to assume that both the biblical and the Deir ʿAllā Balaam cycles existed in oral form before they were written, so that both sets of stories can be said to be very old. The traditional Jewish position on these stories is that they entered Israelite tradition from the outside. The Deir ʿAllā Balaam texts would confirm that conclusion.[22]

Second, the social and religious roles of Balaam as both a diviner/seer *(bārû)* and an exorcist *(ašipu)* in both Balaam cycles is similar. For examples in the OT, see above on the social roles.[23]

Third, the divine names used in the Deir ʿAllā Balaam texts and the biblical texts are similar. The chief god in the Deir ʿAllā texts is *'il.* The cognate Hebrew name El is found 8 times in the Hebrew stories. The intermediaries between *'il* and Balaam are simply called the *'ilahin* ("gods"). These intermediaries are also called the *šaddayin (šdyn)* when they are members of *'il*'s council. The cognate divine names in the Hebrew stories are *'ᵉlōhîm* (used for the *one* God, 14 times) and *šadday* (2 times in ch. 24). On the basis of the parallel use of the divine names in both the Hebrew and Deir ʿAllā Balaam texts, it is not a surprise when, in 24:4, Balaam says that he is the one who sees the vision of *šadday.*[24]

Last, Balaam is subject to a revelation by night (Combination I, lines 1–2 [*wy'tw . 'lwh . 'lhn . blylh . wyḥz . mḥzh.* (2) *kmš' . ' l,* "and the gods came to him at night and he saw a vision (2) like a vision of El"]; Num. 22:20 [*wayyāḇō' 'ᵉlōhîm 'el bilʿām layᵉlâ wayyō'mer lô,* "and God came to Balaam at night and he said to him . . ."]), after which he rose up in the morning to give his message (Combination I, line 3 *[wyqm . blʿm . mn . mḥr,* "and Balaam rose on the next day"]; Num. 22:21*[wayyāqom bilʿam babbōqer,* "and Balaam rose in the morning"]). It is not only that the motifs are the same, but they occur next to one another in the text.[25]

22. See, e.g., the Babylonian Talmud, tractate *Baba Batra* 14b; Greenstone, p. 236; Milgrom, *JPST,* p. 185.

23. See references to Moore, *The Balaam Traditions,* in note 9 above. This monograph compares the socio-religious roles played by Balaam in both cycles of stories on pp. 66–109 and concludes that the exorcist/sorcerer role, which included bringing curses on one's enemies (e.g., 22:6, 11, 17, etc.), became dominant in the later interpretive tradition concerning Balaam. Since such passages as Deut. 18:9–14 forbade such rites for Israelites, a negative judgment grew up surrounding Balaam's role (see esp. pp. 115–16).

24. On the matter of the *šadday* in being the specific name for *'ilahin* in the divine council, see Hackett, *Balaam Text,* pp. 85–89.

25. Other parallels between the biblical and Deir ʿAllā Balaam texts may be found, e.g., in J. Hoftijzer, ATDA, pp. 173–282; H.-P. Muller, "Einige alttestamentliche Probleme zur aramäische Inschrift von Deir ʿAllā," *ZDPV* 94

1. ENCOUNTER BETWEEN BALAK AND BALAAM (22:2–40)

a. Messengers Find Balaam (22:2–21)

2 *And Balak son of Zippor saw all that Israel had done to the Amorites.*
3 *And Moab was very fearful of the people because they were numerous, and Moab was in dread of the children of Israel.*
4 *And Moab said to the elders of Midian, "Now this assembly will lick up all around us, as the ox licks up the greenery of the field." So Balak son of Zippor, king of Moab at that time,*
5 *sent messengers to Balaam son of Beor, to Pethor, which is by the River in the land*[1] *of the children of Amaw,*[2] *to call him, saying, "Behold, a people has come out of Egypt; and behold, it covers the eye of the land, and they are dwelling close in front of me.*
6 *And now, come, please, and curse*[3] *this people for*[4] *me, for they are mightier than I. Perhaps I might be able to smite*[5] *them and*

(1978) 56–67; idem, "Die aramäische Inschrift von Deir ʿAllā und die älteren Bileamsprüche," *ZAW* 94 (1982) 214–244; M. Delcor, "Le texte de Deir ʿAllā et les oracles bibliques de Balaʿam," *Congress Volume Vienna 1980,* SVT 32 (Leiden: Brill, 1981), pp. 52–73. On the more general relation of OT studies to the Deir ʿAllā texts, see M. Weippert, "The Balaam Text from Deir ʿAllā and the Study of the Old Testament," *Proceedings,* 1989), pp. 151–84.

1. In the construction *hannāhār ʾereṣ* both words are in the absolute state (as shown by the definite article and the pointing). The preposition "in" is unexpressed. See Driver, *Tenses,* § 191 Obs.

2. Reading *ʿamāw* (a place between Aleppo and Carchemish) for MT *ʿammô* ("his people"). Although MT makes sense, this emendation requires no change in consonants and results in a better meaning. A number of Hebrew mss., Sam. Pent., Pesh., and Vulg. read *ʿammôn* (Ammon); so also Gray, p. 326. See comments below on various options.

3. On the form of this imperative (*ʾārâ,* with paragogic *-â*) in double *ʿayin* verbs, see GKC, § 67o.

4. The *l*^e^ here expresses interest or advantage; see Williams, *Syntax,* § 271.

5. MT *ʾûlay ʾûḵal nakkeh-bô waʾ*^a^*gāršennû min-hāʾāreṣ*. The word *nakkeh* is best read as a Piel infinitive construct, which acts as a complementary infinitive to the verb *ʾûḵal,* "to be able" (on the complementary infinitive, see GKC, § 114m). Other alternatives include taking the clause as GKC, § 120c, does: "Peradventure I shall prevail (that) we may smite them, and (that) I might drive them out of the land" (which takes *nakkeh* as a Hiphil first common sing. imperfect); or to assume a textual corruption of *ʾûḵal* from *nûḵal* (after *ʾûlay*) (see *BHS*). After the adverb *ʾûlay* (often expressing hope), the conjunction *w*^e^ ("and") and the imperfect express purpose: "Perhaps I might be able" (Davidson, *Syntax,* § 53 Rem. 1).

drive them out from the land. For I know that the one whom[6] *you bless is blessed, and the one whom*[7] *you curse is cursed."*

7 *And the elders of Moab and the elders of Midian went off, and fees for divinations were in their hands. And they came to Balaam and spoke the words of Balak to him.*

8 *And he said to them, "Spend the night here and I will bring back a word to you, as Yahweh speaks to me." And the princes of Moab stayed with Balaam.*

9 *And God came to Balaam and he said, "Who are these men with you?"*

10 *And Balaam said to God, "Balak son of Zippor, king of Moab, has sent to me,*

11 *'Behold, the people who came out of Egypt are now covering the eye of the land, so now come and curse them for me; perhaps I will be able to fight against them and drive them out.' "*

12 *And God said to Balaam, "Do not go with them, do not curse the people, for they are blessed."*

13 *And Balaam arose in the morning and said to Balak's princes, "Go to your land, for Yahweh has refused to give me leave*[8] *to go*[9] *with you."*

14 *And the Moabite princes arose and came to Balak and said, "Balaam refused to come with us."*

15 *So Balak once again sent princes,*[10] *more numerous and distinguished than these,*

16 *and they came to Balaam and said to him, "Thus says Balak son of Zippor, 'Do not allow yourself to be kept from coming to me.*

17 *For I will surely do you great honor, and anything that you say to me I will do; so please come and curse this people for me.' "*

18 *And Balaam answered and said to the servants of Balak, "Even if*[11]

6. The combination *’ēṯ ’^{a}šer,* "the one whom," is a kind of independent relative clause. See GKC, § 138e; Williams, *Syntax,* § 464.

7. The second *’^{a}šer* is without *’eṯ,* but in the context it means "the one whom" just as the previous one does.

8. On the infinitive construct *l^{e}ṯittî,* "to give me leave," see GKC, § 115c; Davidson, *Syntax,* § 91 Rem. 4.

9. The form of the infinitive construct *l^{e}h^{a}lōḵ* is usually *leḵeṯ,* as if from a verb *wālaḵ.* See GKC, § 69x.

10. Lit., "and Balak again added to send princes" *(wayyōsep̄ ‘ôḏ bālāq š^{e}lōaḥ śārîm).* On the elimination of the *l^{e}* on the infinitive construct *š^{e}lōaḥ,* see Williams, *Syntax,* § 226.

11. On the hypothetical nature of the condition here (unlikely of fulfillment) with *’im* plus the imperfect in both the protasis and apodosis, see Driver, *Tenses,* § 143.

Balak were to give me his house full of silver and gold, I would not be able to transgress the utterance of Yahweh my God, to do little or much.

19 *But now, please stay also this night, that I might truly know what more Yahweh might speak to me."*[12]

20 *And God came to Balaam at night and he said to him, "Since the men have come to summon you,*[13] *rise, go with them; but only the word that I speak to you, that will you do."*

21 *So Balaam arose in the morning, saddled his donkey, and went with the Moabite princes.*

2–6 The Moabites make common cause with their neighbors, the Midianites, because of the perceived threat by Israel. Together they decide to approach a Mesopotamian seer named Balaam to curse Israel so that they might be weakened enough for Moab to defeat them and send them from the land.

2 *Balak son of Zippor.* Both names are unique in the OT, although the fem. form of *Zippor* (i.e., Zipporah) is the name of Moses' Midianite wife. *Balak* means "destroyer" and *Zippor* "sparrow" (related to a word meaning "chirp"), but this information is of little value, since parents in the ancient Near East named their children before their personalities or life's work became apparent. The meaning of names is, many times, therefore, irrelevant to the story. Names are usually given only for identification.

Amorites. As mentioned previously, the OT uses this term in various ways. Here it includes at least Sihon (21:21–31), but perhaps also Og of Bashan (21:33–35), who is called an Amorite in Deut. 3:8; 31:4; Josh. 2:10; 9:10; 24:12.

3 Moab (probably in the person of Balak) *was very fearful (wayyāg̱ār . . . m^{e}'ōḏ) and was in dread (wayāqāṣ)* of Israel because of its many people. Both terms indicate a kind of fear. The first means to be in

12. Lit., "what Yahweh might add to speak to me" *(mah-yyōsēp̱ YHWH dabbēr 'immî)*. According to GKC, § 109d, the form *mah-yyōsēp̱* may well be jussive in order to express the contingency of the matter (but cf. Davidson, *Syntax,* § 63 Rem. 3).

13. Heb. *'im-liqrō' l^{e}ḵā bā'û hā'^{a}nāšîm.* The construction with *'im* plus the perfect in the protasis of a conditional clause shows the supposition of an actual past fact anterior to the narrator's position in time; i.e., it is a fact well known and assumed to be true that the messengers have come to summon Balaam (vv. 16–17). Therefore the translation of *'im* by "since" is better than the common "if"; see Davidson, *Syntax,* § 130 (b).

awe of someone, hence unsure of how that person will use power (cf. 1 Sam. 18:15). It may also be used of dread before God (Deut. 9:19; Ps. 119:39), an enemy (Jer. 22:25; 39:17), or even disease (Deut. 22:28, 60; Job 3:28; 9:25). The second is a strong term that may mean "to have a loathing for" (Gen. 27:46; Lev. 20:23; Num. 21:5; 1 K. 11:25; Prov. 3:11) as well as "to dread" (Exod. 1:12; Isa. 7:16).[14] Though some commentators see the use of these two terms as unnecessarily repetitive, repetition is a common device for emphasis in Hebrew; one does not need to resort to doublets and composite narratives to explain it here.[15]

4 The Moabites communicate their concern to the elders of Midian. The Midianites lived both in the Sinai (Exod. 2:15–16; 3:1; Num. 10:29–30) and on Moab's border (Gen. 36:35). The Midianites were defeated in ancient times by Edom (Gen. 36:35), and were vassals of Sihon (Josh. 13:21), as were the Moabites (21:26). The Midianites were finally defeated by Gideon (Judg. 6–7). That both Midianites and Moabites had been under the domination of Sihon until recently makes their communication natural at this point. That the present story mentions the Midianites only in vv. 4 and 7 has led some to relegate the Midianites to a later redactional connection to 31:16, where they are made responsible for Israel's sin at Baal-Peor.[16] The present story tells only of the Moabite relation to Balaam (although the Midianites appear superficially in the story, the story is not about them). The story of the Midianite relations with Balaam is found in ch. 25, although this relation is made explicit only in 31:8, 16.

The *elders [zᵉqēnîm] of Midian* could be the same as those called "kings" *(mᵉlākîm)* in 31:8 or those called "princes" *(nᵉśîʾîm)* in Josh. 13:21. It is impossible to know why the fact that Balak was *king of Moab at that time* should be introduced at this point in the narrative rather than at v. 2, where it would be more natural. It may be because he became the king of Moab only after the fall of Sihon.

5–6 On the office or role of Balaam, see the introduction to chs. 22–24 above. The name *Balaam son of Beor (bilʿām ben-bᵉʿôr)* is very

14. For more on "fear" in the OT, see, e.g., W. Eichrodt, *Theology of the Old Testament,* OTL, 2 vols., tr. J. Baker (Philadelphia: Westminster, 1961, 1967), II: 268–77; G. Lee, *ISBE,* rev., II:289–92; neither Eichrodt nor Lee deals with the second verb in this passage *(qûṣ).* On this verb, see the brief note by L. Coppes in *TWOT,* II:794.

15. As, e.g., Gray (p. 323), McNeile (p. 125), Binns (p. 152), and Noth (p. 175) do. See Sturdy, p. 160; Budd, p. 265.

16. See, e.g., Noth, p. 176.

similar to Bela son of Beor *(belaʿ ben-bᵉʿôr),* the first king of Edom (Gen. 36:32). Although no biblical text identifies the two men, a few scholars have attempted to make a connection.[17] This leads to transforming Balaam into an Edomite, thus emending *ʾᵃrām* in 23:7 to *ʾᵉḏ ōm,* but what is to be done with the phrase "the eastern mountains" in the same verse, since Edom is south, not east, of Moab? Most scholars have rejected the identification as baseless.[18]

Pethor, which is by the River. The term *the River (hannāhār),* without any accompanying designation, usually denotes the Euphrates (e.g., Gen. 31:21; Exod. 23:31; Josh. 24:2–3, 14–15). The only exception seems to be Isa. 19:2, which refers to the Nile. Such an exception, however, is not enough to overturn the rule. *Pethor* is almost universally agreed to be ancient Pitru (modern Tell el-Aḥmar), a site on the Sajur, a tributary of the Euphrates, about two miles from its confluence with the Euphrates, and about 12 mi. south of Carchemish. Pitru is mentioned in a report of Shalmaneser II's (ca. 859–824) first campaign against Damascus, and even earlier by the Egyptian pharaoh Thutmose III (15th cent.).[19] The distance between Pethor (Pitru) and the plains of Moab would be over 370 miles. The journey would take an estimated 20–25 days, hence the four journeys in the story about 90 days.[20] The biblical narrative ignores the length of the journeys, choosing rather to structure the narrative on three pairs of days (days 1–2: 22:2–14; days 3–4: 22:15–35; days 5–6: 22:36–24:35).[21]

in the land of the children of Amaw (ʾereṣ bᵉnê-ʿamāw). The MT reads *ʾereṣ bᵉnê-ʿammô,* "in the land of the children of his people." Although this reading is possible, and simply means that Pethor was Balaam's native land, it seems awkward at best. The ancient versions that add the one letter *n* to the Hebrew consonants in the text, yielding *ʿammôn,* "Ammon," make Balaam a native of, and Pethor a site in, Transjordan rather than Mesopotamia, hence contrary to Deut. 23:4. This change also means that the *River* here must be identified with some stream that flows

17. The identification was taken up, e.g., by Gray (p. 324); A. H. Sayce, "Who Was Balaam?" *ExpTim* 15 (1903–1904) 405–6; and S. Mowinckel, "Der Ursprung der Bileamsage," *ZAW* 48 (1930) 233–71.

18. E.g., McNeile, p. 125; Noordtzij, p. 199; Sturdy, p. 161; Budd, p. 265.

19. On the inscription, see Gray, pp. 325–26; W. F. Albright, "The Home of Balaam," *JAOS* 35 (1917) 386–90.

20. Gray, p. 326.

21. Wenham, pp. 165–66; the weakest part of this structure, as Wenham himself admits, is in days 5–6, where the structure is implicit rather than explicit.

through the Transjordan, contrary to its usual meaning. The benefit of adopting this reading is that the trip between Pethor and Moab would be much shorter. The disadvantages are that one is forced to posit a confusion in sources, with one source preferring a Mesopotamian homeland for Balaam (reflected in Deut. 23:4) and the other a Transjordanian homeland.[22]

Others concur with A. S. Yahuda in pointing the Hebrew consonants *ʿmw* as *ʿamû* or *ʿamāw,* which is a place-name, located by Yahuda in northern Mesopotamia.[23] A fifteenth-century B.C. inscription from Alalakh refers to Amau as a territory between Aleppo and Carchemish, and thus in the same area as posited above for Pethor.[24]

Following an old suggestion by A. H. Sayce, Noordtzij has taken the consonants to refer to a north Syrian deity named Amu/Ammu, hence not clarifying where Pethor (or the River) was, but what Balaam was like. He lived in the land of (the god) Ammu (and worshiped him).[25]

With this kind of uncertainty, dogmatism is unwarranted. It seems best to take the slight modification to the MT, as in the translation above, or to keep the MT.[26]

Behold, it covers the eye of the land (hinnēh k̲issâ ʾet̲-ʿên hāʾāreṣ). In Exod. 10:5, 15 this same clause describes the great number of locusts that will afflict Egypt if Pharaoh fails to release the Israelites. The text of

22. The discovery of the Balaam text at Deir ʿAllā (ancient Succoth, just north of the Jabbok) in Transjordan provides a strong link between a Balaam tradition and this area, although the existence of a Balaam story there in the 8th/7th cent. (the text is dated c. 850–675 B.C.) may or may not speak of the origins of Balaam in the area some centuries earlier. See the discussion of the Deir ʿAllā text above.

23. A. S. Yahuda, "The Name of Balaam's Homeland," *JBL* 64 (1945) 547–51. See, e.g., Snaith, pp. 175–76; Sturdy, p. 161; Wenham, p. 169; Budd, pp. 249, 254, 265. Cf. NEB "the land of the Amavites"; GNB, RSV "the land of Amaw" (the latter is less accurate because it omits Heb. *b^e^nê,* lit., "sons," i.e., "children," from the translation). The discovery of the Deir ʿAllā Balaam text in the Transjordan means, at the very least, that there was an active literary tradition about Balaam around the eighth century B.C. and probably quite a bit before. J. Hackett has proposed that Balaam was the leader of a rival cult whom the Hebrew Balaam cycle makes out to be completely dependent on Yahweh. J. Hackett, "Some Observations on the Balaam Tradition at Deir ʿAllā," *BA* 49 (1986) 216–22, esp. 220.

24. See W. F. Albright, "Some Important Recent Discoveries: Alphabetic Origins and the Idrimi Statue," *BASOR* 118 (1950) 16 n. 13.

25. Noordtzij, p. 201.

26. See, e.g., Noth, pp. 173, 176.

Exod. 10:5 explains the idiom, "so that no one is able to see the land" *(wᵉlōʾ yûḵal lirʾōṯ ʾeṯ-hāʾāreṣ).* So here, the Israelites are said to be so numerous that they cover the land completely (e.g., like locusts).

6 The Bible shares Balak's view that curses and blessings have a real and lasting effect on human life once they have been uttered.[27]

7–14 The joint delegation of elders goes to Balaam. In a night visitation, Yahweh forbids him either to go with the elders or to curse Israel.

7 *fees for divinations.* The MT reads only *divinations (qᵉsāmîm),* although scholars widely agree that, in the same way that *bᵉśōrâ* means both "good news" (2 Sam. 18:20, 25) and "wages paid to the bearer of good news" (2 Sam. 4:10; 18:22), so *qᵉsōnîm* here can mean both the divinations and fees for them.[28] Although the OT clearly condemns *divination* itself (Deut. 18:10; 1 Sam. 15:23; 2 K. 17:17), collecting a fee for similar work seems to have been accepted by those who practiced it. Fees were collected by such men as Samuel (1 Sam. 9:7–8), Ahijah (1 K. 14:3), and Elijah (2 K. 8:8–9). Such men as Amos (7:12) do not look positively on such fees, but that attitude appears to have developed only later. This fee may be looked on as a consultation fee paid in advance of any cursing or blessing done by the seer.

8 After the elders arrived they reported to Balaam what Balak wanted him to do, and Balaam requested that they stay the night with him so that he could consult Yahweh and bring them an answer. *I will bring back a word to you, as Yahweh speaks to me.* This surely means that Balaam thought that he could contact Yahweh that night, although whether this was because it was his custom to have revelations in night visitations,

27. For materials on the biblical view of cursings and blessings, see J. Hempel, "Die israelitischen Anschauungen von Segen und Fluch im Lichte altorientalischer Parallelen," *ZDMG* n.f. 4 (1925) 20–110; J. Pedersen, *Israel: Its Life and Culture* (4 vols. repr. in 2; London: Oxford, 1926, 1940), I–II:182–212; Eichrodt, *Theology of the OT,* I:173–74; cf. 457–58; II:69–70, 72. H. C. Brichto, *The Problem of "Curse" in the Hebrew Bible* (Philadelphia: Society of Biblical Literature and Exegesis, 1962); C. Westermann, *Blessing in the Bible and the Life of the Church,* tr. K. Crim, OBT (Philadelphia: Fortress, 1978). For the definition and description of the genre of blessing, see, e.g., B. O. Long, *1 Kings; with an Introduction to the Historical Literature,* FOTL (Grand Rapids: Eerdmans, 1984), p. 245. On blessing, see above on 6:22–27.

28. So Dillmann, p. 143; Keil, p. 166; Gray, p. 329; Binns, p. 154; Heinisch, p. 89; Noordtzij, p. 203; Noth, p. 176; Snaith, p. 176; Sturdy, p. 163; de Vaulx, p. 266; Budd, pp. 249, 265; Harrison, p. 295. On the NJPS translation, see Milgrom, *JPST,* p. 187. AV, RV, RSV, NASB, NEB, NIV, NKJV.

or whether this was simply convenient at this point is not said (another night visitation happens in v. 20).[29]

As was mentioned above in the introduction to these chapters, Balaam himself uses the name *Yahweh* (22:8, 13, 18–19; 23:3, 12; 24:13), while the narrator uses *Elohim* (22:9–10, 12, 20). Noordtzij maintains that one should see this variation as the narrator's comment on Balaam's religious character, viz., he claimed knowledge of Yahweh, when in fact it was Elohim who came to him. Furthermore, Noordtzij understands *Elohim* not as a synonym for *Yahweh* but in its other sense of "pagan god." But *Elohim* is a pl. that means either God (i.e., Yahweh) or gods (pagan deities). References to a single pagan deity by the so-called intensive plural all occur either with suffixes or in the construct state rather than in the absolute state as would be required by Noordtzij's theory. In addition, v. 18 seems to require an equation of Yahweh and Elohim when Balaam says, *Yahweh my God (YHWH 'ĕlōhāy).* Had the narrator intended to convey that Balaam was fraudulently claiming visions from Yahweh, while actually being inspired by a pagan "evil spirit," he could have been much plainer about it. It seems best, therefore, to assume the usual equivalence of *Yahweh* and *Elohim* here. It is difficult to say what the name Yahweh meant on a pagan's lips. It seems to mean at least that Balaam knew that the name Yahweh would be the effective name with the Israelites. It may mean that Balaam was a worshiper of (or seeker after) Yahweh (the text seems to bear that meaning in 22:18). This would mean that, from time to time, Yahweh reveals himself to those outside Israel, usually for the benefit of Israel (see Melchizedek in Gen. 14). That Balaam finally fell into a fatal error (31:8, 16) is no sign that he did not at least revere Yahweh and that they did not communicate at this point.

Balak's messengers are styled *princes* in v. 8b, but this change in terminology need not indicate a composite text any more than their being called "elders" in v. 7 did.

9–11 *And God came to Balaam (wayyaḇō' 'ᵉlōhîm 'el-bilʿām)* — God comes to Balaam for the first time in these stories to give him an oracle (the message is delivered to Balaam in v. 12). The name for God here is *'ᵉlōhîm,* which is a cognate term for the *'ilahin* ("gods") that come

29. That the present visitation is at night can be seen by comparing vv. 8a and 13a. V. 20 clearly says it is at night. Documentarians claim that the present passage is E, and that revelation in dreams is characteristic of this source. See both Gray, pp. 327–28; Binns, pp. 152–13. On the night visitation, compare the Deir ʿAllā text, Combination I, line 1, where the visitation is clearly "at night" *(blylh).*

to Balaam in Combination I, line 1 of the Deir ʿAllā text. In v. 20 below God clearly comes to Balaam *by night.* Since Balaam has already asked the messengers to *spend the night* in v. 8, it may probably be assumed that God came at night here as well. In response to God's question, Who are these men with you? Balaam gives a summary of Balak's request to him (see vv. 5b–6a), but in a different tense and with small differences in vocabulary.[30] The words of Balak's messengers are not given in the text. They may have made such modifications in their master's instructions, Balaam himself may have substituted these words in his report to God, or the narrator may have done so for variety. The ancient versions match Balak's words more closely, but the MT is preferable.

12–14 Yahweh forbids Balaam to do two things: to go with Balak's messengers, and to curse Israel. In the morning Balaam reports to the messengers only that Yahweh will not let him go with them. The messengers then return to inform Balak of Balaam's rejection of his offer.

15–21 Balak sends more princes with greater promises of reward to Balaam. Again, Balaam consults Yahweh, who this time gives him permission to go with the messengers, with the proviso that he do only what Yahweh commands him to do.

16–18 *Thus says Balak.* This so-called messenger formula indicates that the person comes with an official word. Later on the prophets of Israel used this formula to mark their word as from Yahweh ("thus says Yahweh," *kōh 'āmar YHWH).*[31]

The speech of Balak (via his messengers) and his new and more distinguished delegation of messengers reveal his assumption that, whatever Balaam's given reason, his rejection of Balak's request was only a device to negotiate for a higher price. But the text itself says nothing about greed being Balaam's motive. Balaam's own statement is that it would not matter how much he were offered (even Balak's *house full of silver and gold*), because he was under constraint to report only what Yahweh said to him. Again, the narrator gives us no real reason to see this statement as anything but factual; i.e., it gives no basis for finding a hidden base motive for Balaam's action.[32]

30. Two different words for "to curse" are used (*'ārar* in v. 5b, *qāḇaḇ* in v. 11), and "to fight against" *(nilḥam)* is used in v. 11 in place of "to strike" *(nakkeh)* in v. 6.

31. See C. Westermann, *Basic Forms of Prophetic Speech,* tr. K. Crim (Philadelphia: Westminster, 1967), esp. pp. 90–95; R. R. Wilson, "Form Critical Investigation of the Prophetic Literature," SBLSP (1973), pp. 100–109, 114–20.

32. Many commentators do derive this meaning from the text (e.g., Keil,

little or great. This is a figure of speech, not uncommon in the Bible (e.g., 1 Sam. 20:2; 22:15; 25:36), called *merism* (or *merismus*). It includes the little things, the great things, and all the things in between.[33] It is a way of expressing totality by naming the extremes. That Balaam here uses Yahweh as a divine name may mean that he has somehow already become familiar with the Israelite God. It is more likely, however, that this is a point at which the current author made an Israelite contribution to a non-Israelite story. The theological point becomes that whatever the divine name used, whether El, Elohim or Shadday, it is really Yahweh that is meant by all of these. And Yahweh is in control of the story.[34]

19 Balaam encourages the messengers to spend the night. The words he uses are interesting: *that I might truly know what more Yahweh might speak to me.* The verbal forms (cohortative and jussive) are moods to express potentiality and show Balaam's wish (i.e., "that I might [be allowed to] know what Yahweh might speak to me"). The implication is that Balaam knows and wants the messengers to know that Yahweh has already pronounced his will in the matter of cursing the Israelites, but that Balaam is open to seeing whether the situation has changed. Again, there seems nothing evil or base in this response, but rather a healthy awareness that changed situations sometimes call for changed strategies.

20 This time the vision is clearly said to be at night (for other night visitations in the OT, see, e.g., Job 4:12–16; Zech. 1:8; Deir ʿAllā text, Combination I, line 1). Here, as in v. 9, God initiates the conversation. The narrator is not interested to tell what, if anything, was necessary in order to bring Yahweh and Balaam into contact. This time,

---

p. 167; Cook, p. 735; Noordtzij, p. 205), but one must question whether they do not read this into the text in order to justify other passages in the Bible that judge Balaam harshly.

33. See A. M. Honeyman, "Merismus in Biblical Hebrew," *JBL* 71 (1952) 11–18.

34. On the idea that other divine appellations are absorbed by Yahweh, see, e.g., A. Alt, "The God of the Fathers," in *Essays on Old Testament History and Religion,* tr. R. Wilson (Oxford: Blackwell, 1966), pp. 1–100; O. Eissfeldt, "Götternamen und Gottesvorstellungen bei den Semiten," *ZDMG* 83 (1929) 21–36; G. von Rad, *Old Testament Theology,* 2 vols., tr. D. Stalker (New York: Harper & Row, 1962, 1965), I:179–87; D. N. Freedman, "Divine Names and Titles in Early Hebrew Poetry," in *Pottery, Poetry and Prophecy* (Winona Lake, Ind.: Eisenbrauns, 1980), pp. 77–129 (this is a repr. of *Magnalia Dei: The Mighty Acts of God,* ed. F. M. Cross, et al. [New York: Doubleday, 1976], pp. 55–107); B. W. Anderson, *IDB,* II:407–17.

Balaam is allowed to go with them. Thus the first prohibition of v. 12 is cancelled.

but only the word that I speak to you, that will you do (w^{e}'aḵ 'eṯ-haddāḇār '^{a}šer-'^{a}ḏabbēr 'ēleyḵā 'ōṯô ṯa'^{a}śeh). Yahweh's command (*haddāḇār,* lit., "the word") includes not only what Balaam must say but also what he must do. Cursing and blessing were not seen as mere words, but as having active power to accomplish things in the real world.

The second prohibition of v. 12 is thus restated in a different way. Balaam must obey God. The reader may wonder just what God will tell Balaam to say and do. He has said that Israel is blessed (v. 12), but he has also said that Balaam could not even go, and now he has changed his mind on that point. Will he also change his mind on the second point and allow Balaam to curse Israel? Surely not! But has God himself not punished the Israelites in the past (see chs. 12–19)? This kind of ambiguity maintains reader interest and prolongs the drive to the climax of the story (as does the story of the donkey that follows in vv. 22–35).

21 The reader is introduced to a character that will be important in the following story: the donkey. The word for *donkey* here *('āṯôn)* is fem., and presumably refers to a female donkey. Such beasts were used for riding only in Judg. 5:10 and 2 K. 4:22. The male donkey *(ḥ^{a}môr)* was usually used (Exod. 4:20; Josh. 15:18; 1 Sam. 25:20; 2 Sam. 16:2; 17:23; 19:27; 1 K. 2:40; 13:13; Zech. 9:9). These beasts were used by all classes of people, as the passages above show.

b. Balaam and the Donkey (22:22–35)

22 *But God's anger was kindled, as he was going,*[1] *and an angel of Yahweh took his stand*[2] *in the road as an adversary to him. (And he was riding upon his donkey and his two servants were with him.)*

1. Several English versions translate the Hebrew participle *hôlēḵ* as a past tense, "he went" (AV, RV, RSV, NIV, NKJV), perhaps on the basis of Sam. Pent., which seems to read a perfect here (cf. LXX and Pesh.). Moffatt, NEB, NASB, GNB, and NJPS read "was going" (i.e., a true participle) on the basis of MT.

2. In Job 2:1 *hiṯyaṣṣeḇ* is used to describe the entrance of the adversary *(haśśaṭan)* and others entering into the divine council for formal prosecution of Job. According to a study of the divine council scenes in the OT (1 K. 22:19–23; Isa. 6:1–2; Ps. 29; 82:1–8; 89:6–9; Job 1:6 and 2:1), E. T. Mullen concluded that *hiṯyaṣṣeḇ* is, among other things, a technical term for participating in the divine assembly. Here the verb may have some of the technical nuances, as this particular adversary "takes his stand" in Balaam's way. See E. T. Mullen, *The Assembly of the Gods: The Divine Council in Canaanite and Early Hebrew Literature*, HSM 24 (Chico: Scholars Press, 1980), p. 231.

23 *When the donkey saw the angel of Yahweh standing in the road with his drawn sword in his hand, the donkey turned off the road and went into the fields, but Balaam hit the donkey to turn her back to the road.*

24 *Then Yahweh's angel stood in a closed-in*[3] *road among the vineyards, a wall on this side and a wall on that.*

25 *And the donkey saw Yahweh's angel and squeezed herself over to the wall, and pressed Balaam's foot against the wall, and again he started to beat her.*

26 *And again Yahweh's angel went over and stood in a narrow place where there was no way to turn right or left.*

27 *When the donkey saw Yahweh's angel, she lay down under Balaam. Balaam's anger was kindled and he struck the donkey with his riding stick.*[4]

28 *Then Yahweh opened the donkey's mouth, and she said to Balaam, "What have I done to you that you have struck me so, three times?"*[5]

29 *And Balaam said to the donkey, "Because you have dealt so shabbily*[6] *with me; if I had a sword in my hand, I would surely have killed you."*[7]

3. Heb. *mišʿôl* is a hapax legomenon. It is related to the word *šōʿal,* "hollow of the hand" (Isa. 40:12) and "handful" (1 K. 20:10). The walls on either side made the road seem like a "hollow place" perhaps. See BDB, p. 1043.

4. Heb. *maqqēl* was apparently a stick used for various functions. It may refer to a branch or a twig (like the "almond twig" in Jer. 1:11), or to a stick or staff used in journeying (Gen. 32:11; Exod. 12:11). Along with a sling, it is part of David's weaponry against Goliath (1 Sam. 17:40). The likelihood is that *maqqēl* is a general term that is specified by its use in a context. Here the "riding stick" was probably used both as a weapon and a sort of riding crop to encourage the donkey to go in a particular direction.

5. On *rᵉgālîm* (lit., "feet") for "times," see Davidson, *Syntax,* § 38 Rem. 5 (it occurs in Exod. 23:14; Num. 22:28, 32–33).

6. Heb. *hiṯʿallēl* is related to Arab. *ʿalla,* "to divert oneself with," thence "to entertain oneself at someone's expense." It is used of Yahweh's making sport of the Egyptians in Exod. 10:2, and of the Philistines making sport of Saul's dead body in 2 Sam. 31:4 (= 1 Chr. 10:4; Jer. 38:19); in Judg. 19:25 it is used of the sexual abuse of a woman in Gibeah. Balaam accuses his donkey of doing her own will at the expense of his, with no thought for his welfare or destination. The accusation, of course, shows how little Balaam really understands the situation. See BDB, p. 759b.

7. The construction *lû* plus the perfect connotes a wish that something had happened in the past (cf. 14:2; *lû maṯᵉnû,* "O that we had died"; also 20:3; Josh. 7:7. Here, "O if I had . . ." or "If there were *(lû yēš)* a sword in my hand now, had I surely killed thee!" See GKC, § 151e n. 1; also Williams, *Syntax,* § 548; Davidson, *Syntax,* § 131.

30 *And the donkey said to Balaam, "Am I not your donkey upon which you have ridden from your beginning until this day?*[8] *Has it ever been my custom to treat you so?" And he replied, "No."*

31 *Then Yahweh uncovered Balaam's eyes, and he saw Yahweh's angel standing in the road with his drawn sword in his hand, and he bowed down and prostrated himself upon his face.*

32 *And Yahweh's angel said to him, "Why have you struck your donkey these three times? Behold, I went out as an adversary, because your way was evil*[9] *before me.*

33 *And the donkey saw me and turned before me these three times, for had she not turned from before me*[10] *I would surely now have killed you and left her alive."*

34 *Then Balaam said to Yahweh's angel, "I have sinned, for I did not know that you were standing against me in the road. And now, since it is a bad thing in your sight,*[11] *let me return home."*

35 *And Yahweh's angel said to Balaam, "Go with the men, but you will speak only*[12] *the word that I speak to you." So Balaam went with the princes of Balak.*

8. This literal reading of *me῾ôḏᵉḵā,* "from your beginning," may be compared with *mē῾ôḏî* in Gen. 48:15, "ever since I was." The statement is hyperbole.

9. MT *kî yāraṭ hadderek̠ lᵉneḡdî,* "because the way in front of me is steep," makes little sense here. The clause is probably textually corrupt. Long ago Dillmann, p. 147, proposed changing *yāraṭ* to *yāraṭṭā* (second masc. sing. perfect) and translating: "because you precipitated the journey before (i.e., ahead of) me" (see BDB, p. 437b). This meaning is somewhat unusual for *yāraṭ,* but, since it is such a rare word (it occurs elsewhere only in Job 16:11), no confident decision can be made as to its semantic range. On the basis of Sam. Pent., LXX, and Vulg., *BHS* proposes reading *yēra῾* (from *rā῾a῾,* "to be evil, bad"). This same verb occurs in v. 34. Also following Sam. Pent., LXX, and Vulg., *BHS* suggests reading *darkᵉḵā,* "your way," for MT *hadderek̠,* which is another small change that makes good sense contextually. Thus the evidence, textually and contextually, supports the reading adopted above.

10. Lit., "perhaps she turned from before me" *(ʾûlay naṭᵉnâ mippānay).* Most authorities agree that, instead of *ʾûlay,* "perhaps," one should read *lûlê,* "unless," here (e.g., *BHS;* BDB, p. 530a; Davidson, *Syntax,* § 131a; Driver, *Tenses,* § 141). With *lûlê* plus the perfect in both the protasis and apodosis, the matter would be considered unlikely to have ever happened.

11. The verb *ra῾* (root *r῾῾*) is used here impersonally, "to be amiss to" (with *lᵉ*); so also Gen. 21:12; 2 Sam. 19:8; Jer. 7:6. The opposite *(ṭôḇ lᵉ-)* is found, e.g., in 1 Sam. 16:16; Hos. 10:1; Jer. 7:23; see Davidson, *Syntax,* § 109.

12. The particle *ʾep̱es* is used only here as a particle of limitation meaning "only"; see BDB, p. 67a; Williams, *Syntax,* § 427; Davidson, *Syntax,* § 153.

The story of Balaam's talking donkey raises many questions that go beyond the scope of a biblical commentary. Are there really angels? Can donkeys really talk? More generally, what is the nature of the miraculous? Modern questions concerning the reality of all these things go far beyond what the biblical text says to questions of belief about the text, to philosophical and systematic theology and apologetics. The text states clearly that there is at least one angel of Yahweh, that at least on this occasion a donkey talked.

I argued above that there are reasons to see vv. 22–35 as a narrative that was originally separate from its present context in the Balaam story. Many scholars see it as the remnant of a J narrative that, before its combination with E, comprehended the whole story of Balaam from its own point of view. Sturdy sees it as a story that originally referred to someone else, but was applied to Balaam when the present text was put together.[13] Indeed, vv. 22–35 may be left out entirely and 22:2–21, 36–40 make sense as a complete whole. But whatever one may say about its separate origin from the present context (and the grounds cited may be fairly convincing), this story is now part of the Balaam story as a whole and some sense must be made of it where it now stands; indeed, whoever put these chapters together intended that this be done. The very roughness (e.g., between the attitude of God in vv. 20 and 22) may be attributed as well to one author, who left the rough edges and antinomies in the story for his own reasons, as to a redactor who would likely have eliminated them.[14]

22 The most common question about this verse is the motive for God's anger with Balaam. At the very least it seems capricious for God to tell Balaam to go on his way in v. 20 and then to become angry with Balaam because he was going in v. 22. The question is whether the particle *kî* (usually translated "because, since" in this verse) should not have another of its well-attested meanings, viz., "when" or even "as" with the participle. This construction is somewhat rare, but not unknown in Biblical Hebrew.[15] If one translates temporally, as above, then God no longer becomes angry with Balaam on the grounds of his going (since God had given him permission to go in v. 20), but *as he was going,* i.e., somewhere on the journey for an unspecified reason. This view admittedly sidesteps

13. Sturdy, p. 165.

14. E. F. Sutcliffe, "A Note on Numbers XXII," *Bib* 18 (1937) 439. See also his earlier "De unitate litteraria Num. XXII," *Bib* 7 (1926) 3–39.

15. See Num. 31:51; 34:2; Deut. 11:31; 18:9; BDB, p. 473a.

the issue of the motive for God's wrath, but, if the translation proposed is correct, so does the text itself.[16]

angel of Yahweh. Many commentators see the angel of Yahweh (or angel of God) as a temporary manifestation of God himself, rather than a distinct heavenly being.[17] Many times this kind of distinction is built on a fixed idea of when a doctrine of a heavenly court full of angels could have developed in Israel. These arguments are tenuous at best. Although in other contexts God's angels seem to be more a manifestation of God himself (e.g., Gen. 16:7; 22:11, 15), in the current context the angel (Heb. *mal'āḵ,* "messenger") is distinguished from God by v. 31,[18] although it is also clear that what Yahweh's angel says is truly what Yahweh says (compare 22:20, 35).

an adversary to him (lᵉśāṭān lô). The term *śāṭān* here simply means "an opponent." In Job 1–2 "The Satan" (a title) is a member of the heavenly court whose job it is to test and try people's loyalty to God. In Zech. 3:1 he is a prosecutor of deviant humans. In 1 Chr. 21:1 he has become the enemy of the righteous. Finally, in the NT he is the enemy of all goodness and the embodiment of all evil. In the current passage the word is a common noun rather than a proper name.[19]

his two servants were with him. Much has also been made of the fact that the parenthetical remark about Balaam's two servants precludes the fact that he was with the Moabite princes, thus marking out a contradiction between the source of vv. 2–21 and that of the present narrative. But this is surely hyper-criticism. Traveling with servants was a common practice in the ancient world,[20] and one could make much of the Moabite

16. This suggestion is offered modestly, since no major modern commentator has seemed to adopt it. I found the translation suggested, but not supported with argument, in Samuel Cox, *Balaam: An Exposition and a Study* (London: Kegan Paul, Trench, 1884), p. 53. The case of God's seemingly unmotivated wrath is also seen in Exod. 4:24–26, which has also long perplexed commentators. Contrast Driver, *Tenses,* § 135 (4).

17. E.g., Gray, p. 333; McNeile, p. 128; Binns, p. 156; Noordtzij, p. 208; Noth, p. 179; Snaith, p. 176.

18. Sturdy, p. 166. See below on v. 35.

19. See, e.g., W. Foerster, G. von Rad, *TDNT,* II:72–81; VII:151–65; P. Day, *An Adversary in Heaven:* śāṭān *in the Hebrew Bible,* HSM 43 (Cambridge: Harvard Univ. Press, 1988), esp. pp. 45–67. The English versions have avoided any difficulty in attributing a post-OT view of Satan into the text by using the term *adversary* (AV, RV, RSV, NASB, NKJV, NJPS) or by paraphrasing completely (e.g., Moffatt "to hinder him"; GNB, NEB "to bar his way"; NIV "to oppose him").

20. See, e.g., the stories of the travels of the patriarchs in Gen. 12–50 or Naaman in 2 K. 5.

princes not having servants with them. The narrator does mention the Moabite princes in v. 35, but the point is that they, their servants (if they had any), and the servants of Balaam (who are mentioned only here) are irrelevant to the main line of the story. The story has only four principal characters: Yahweh, his angel, Balaam, and the donkey. That the narrator did not tell the reader why Balaam was traveling with his servants rather than with the princes is asking the story to tell what the narrator has not disclosed.

23–27 These verses narrate, in an ascending pattern, a threefold threat to Balaam from an armed angel of Yahweh. Three times the angel blocks Balaam's way, three times Balaam does not perceive the danger, and three times his donkey does. When the donkey tries to avert the danger, three times Balaam responds by beating the animal and directing it back toward the unseen adversary. Each time the blockage of Balaam's way is more absolute, but Balaam the seer cannot see it.

23 First, the angel simply stands in the road as Balaam travels through the open country (*haśśāḏeh,* Judg. 9:32, 42–44; 19:16; 1 Sam. 19:3; 20:5, 11, 24, 35; 2 K. 7:12; Mic. 4:10; etc.). The donkey turns off the road and into the fields to avoid the angel. Balaam brings his beast back to the road by beating it.

24–25 Next, the angel stands in a *closed-in road among the vineyards, a wall on this side and a wall on that (bᵉmišʿôl hakkᵉrāmîm gāḏēr mizzeh wᵉgāḏēr mizzeh).* There was not much room, but the donkey squeezed herself over to the wall in an attempt to get around the angel, pinching Balaam's foot against the wall in the process. This also brought a beating for the hapless beast. That *vineyards* are mentioned means that the setting is not the desert, but either at the very beginning or more probably toward the end of Balaam's journey to Moab.

26–27 In the climactic third scene, the angel stood *in a narrow place (bᵉmāqôm ṣār),* i.e., one where there was no way to get around the danger. The beast simply sat down with Balaam. At this point Balaam's *anger was kindled (wayyiḥar 'ap̱),* and he began to beat the donkey *with his riding stick (bammaqqēl).*The fact that the same expression *(and his anger was kindled)* is used of God (v. 22) and Balaam (v. 27) invites comparison. I have argued above that God's motive for anger is not revealed. Here Balaam's motive is his donkey's refusal to go in the way he wants her to go. Is it possible that God's motive for anger is Balaam's similar refusal to go where God wants him to go? Of course listeners to this story would know that Balaam's donkey had a reason to refuse to go into the path of the angel. Balaam's eyes were still closed to the reason (see v. 31). Balaam's staff was simply a stick or rod that he had with him and used, at this point, to beat his animal. Like the more commonly used parallel word for "staff" (*maṭṭeh;* 136 times in Numbers), the *maqqēl* could be used as a walking stick (Gen. 32:11) or a weapon (1 Sam. 17:40). Hos. 4:12 uses *maqqēl* for the staff used in divining oracles (rhabdomancy). It is, therefore, possible that this staff had a cultic/magical function for Balaam.[21]

The point of this whole story is that, in contrast to the important status of Balaam as a seer (see vv. 2–21), he is more blind to the presence of a messenger from Yahweh than his supposedly dumb beast. In his natural state (i.e., with "covered eyes"; see below on v. 31) Balaam was unaware of the reality of the spiritual world in spite of his professional reputation. This kind of statement would not be lost on an Israelite audience that might have been uncomfortable with a non-Israelite soothsayer being the vehicle of God's word.

28–30 In response to the three ever more constrictive threats, Yahweh causes a twofold loosening or opening; he *opens (pāṯaḥ)* the donkey's mouth (v. 28) and he *uncovers (gālâ)* Balaam's eyes (v. 31).

28 *Then Yahweh opened the donkey's mouth.* The same phrase is used of opening a prophet's mouth in Ezek. 3:27; 33:22. Since speaking animals were apparently unusual in Israel, the narrator makes it clear that this is an act of Yahweh himself. To discuss whether donkeys have sufficient vocal cords to speak overlooks the fact that this is an act of Almighty Yahweh. The question of how the donkey could speak does not concern the narrator.

What is most surprising is the seemingly calm way Balaam answers the question asked by his donkey. The reader must enter into the world of the story at this moment. The narrator is not concerned to have Balaam question the possibility of the donkey's speaking, but rather to report a rational conversation between the only two nonheavenly characters in the story. The only other biblical example of a talking animal,

21. On *maqqēl,* see *HALAT,* p. 593b. Hosea 4:12 probably deals with foreign cults, as is seen in the idiom "to play the harlot" used in the verse. See P. Bird, "To Play the Harlot": An Inquiry into an Old Testament Metaphor," in *Gender and Difference in Ancient Israel,* ed. P. Day (Minneapolis: Fortress, 1989), pp. 75–94, esp. 83–88. E.g., F. I. Andersen and D. N. Freedman, *Hosea,* AB (Garden City, N.Y.: Doubleday, 1980), pp. 342–79; H. W. Wolff, *Hosea,* Hermeneia, tr. G. Standsell (Philadelphia: Fortress, 1974), pp. 70–93. On rhabdomancy as part of the function of a diviner in the ancient Near East, and of Balaam himself in the Deir ʿAllā texts, see M. Moore, *The Balaam Traditions,* pp. 71–78.

the serpent in Gen. 3, also brings forth no astonishment from the human partner, but only rational dialogue.

29 The donkey asked Balaam what she had done to cause him to strike her three times. Balaam replied that the donkey was worthy of death because she had *dealt shabbily with* him, i.e., made sport of him.

30 The donkey asked Balaam whether, in all the time he had owned her (which is what *from your beginning until this day* means), she had ever refused to follow his instructions three times in succession, in spite of knowing what he wanted. He had to admit that she had not. The donkey does not tell Balaam that she had turned from the way to avoid danger, but leaves that for the angel in vv. 32–33. The point of the dialogue is that, when God opens the mouth, even a donkey can speak, so the Israelites need not fear this foreign seer. Yahweh is in control. Balaam was brought under conviction by the word of his donkey. His admission that his donkey's behavior was unique in his experience leads to the next scene.

31–35 The second act of loosening is the *uncovering* of Balaam's eyes so that he can perceive the spiritual reality.

31 *Then Yahweh uncovered Balaam's eyes.* The act of uncovering human eyes is no less Yahweh's act than that of opening the mouth of a dumb beast. The verb *gālâ,* "to uncover, reveal," is also used in this sense in 24:4, 16 (cf. Ps. 119:18). Its meaning is similar to another verb for opening the eyes *(pāqaḥ),* found in 2 K. 6:17, 20. It means to allow one to see things as they are, especially things that are not ordinarily visible to humans (as the angel was not).[22]

and he bowed down and prostrated himself upon his face (wayyiqqōḏ wayyištaḥû lᵉ'appāyw). The two verbs are used together in Gen. 24:26, 48; 43:28; Exod. 4:31; 12:27; 34:8; 1 Sam. 24:9; 28:14; 1 K. 1:16, 31; 1 Chr. 29:20; 2 Chr. 20:18; 29:30, always of someone lesser before someone greater, ten times of a person before Yahweh.[23]

32–33 Yahweh's angel addresses Balaam. The angel starts by picking up the donkey's question from v. 28. Why has Balaam struck his donkey three times when it was not the donkey who was against Balaam, but the angel of Yahweh (and this means opposition of the one who sent the angel, Yahweh himself).

your way was evil. If this translation is correct, then one must

22. On *gālâ,* see, e.g., H.-J. Zobel, *TDOT,* II:476–88; on *pāqaḥ,* see, e.g., V. Hamilton, *TWOT,* II:732–33.

23. They are found with *'appayim* ("nose," "face") in Exod. 34:8; 1 Sam. 24:9; 28:14; 1 K. 1:31. *HALAT,* pp. 283b–84a.

differentiate between what Yahweh's angel says here and what Balaam claims in v. 34. The angel says that Balaam's way was bad or evil *before me (lᵉnegdî),* i.e., it is "contrary to my will." What Balaam claims in v. 34 is that his way has been evil in the angel's sight *(bᵉʿêneykā),* i.e., the angel does not approve of it. The first statement is much stronger than the second. It is perhaps natural that Balaam sought to ameliorate the situation in v. 34.[24] The angel was prepared to slay Balaam and leave the donkey alive.

34 Balaam confesses that he had been in the wrong. He had tacitly admitted this already to his donkey in v. 30.

I have sinned (ḥāṭā'ṯî). The word *ḥāṭā'* does not involve a willful transgression of Yahweh's will and way, but rather a missing of the right way, a mistake (cf. Judg. 20:16; Job 5:24; Prov. 8:36; 19:2).[25] Balaam is simply saying that he made a mistake by not perceiving Yahweh's angel in the road. He now assumes that the reason the angel was blocking the way was that Yahweh did not want him to go to Balak: *since it is a bad thing in your sight, let me return home.* But the angel was not there to prevent him from going, but rather to make sure that he understood that without Yahweh's inspiration he could not hope to see (i.e., to perceive) anything. With Yahweh's inspiration even a donkey is more perceptive than a professional seer.

35 At the end of the passage the word of v. 20 is repeated in similar terms, except that what Yahweh himself has said in v. 20, Yahweh's angel says here. Although the characters of Yahweh and his angel are distinct, the latter is the servant of the former and would only speak his word. An Israelite audience, who believed in only one all-powerful God, would see a small difference beetween the words of Yahweh and the words of his angel just because they believed in one all-powerful God.[26] Balaam

24. See P. Haupt's note in Paterson, p. 56.

25. The mistake may be against other creatures (e.g., Gen. 20:9) or, far more commonly, against God (e.g., Lam. 5:7). On "sin" see, e.g., S. J. DeVries, *IDB,* IV:361–76, esp. 361; also E. Jacob, *Theology of the Old Testament,* tr. A. Heathcote, P. Allcock (New York: Harper & Row, 1958), pp. 281–97; W. Eichrodt, *Theology of the Old Testament,* OTL, tr. J. Baker, 2 vols. (Philadelphia: Westminster, 1961, 1967), I:374–81; G. von Rad, *Old Testament Theology,* tr. D. Stalker, 2 vols. (New York: Harper & Row, 1962, 1965), I:154–60, 262–72; on *ḥāṭā'* itself, see K. Koch, *TDOT,* IV:309–19.

26. The Deir ʿAllā Balaam text (Combination I, lines 1–2) has an oracle of El coming to Balaam through the mediation of the *'ilahin* ("gods"). Israelite theology would not countenance such "gods," but would permit "messengers" or "angels" *(mᵉlā'ḵîm)* to convey God's words. The parallel between the two texts

may go with the men, but when he gets to his destination he must do only what Yahweh says to him. This lesson has been driven home by the incident.

Whether or not Balaam understood all this, the reader may get the point that the story of Balaam and his donkey prefigures the way Balak will treat Balaam; the story will be reenacted in chs. 23–24. Just as the donkey has been caught three times between seeing a vision of an armed and dangerous angel of Yahweh on the one hand and feeling the stick of the blind Balaam on the other, so Balaam, who now sees that Yahweh's will for him is to bless Israel, will soon be caught, in three ever tighter situations, between doing Yahweh's will on the one hand, and succumbing to Balak's pressure to curse Israel on the other. The "sword" is now in Yahweh's hand; to ignore his will is fatal (cf. 31:8, 16). Balaam has become the donkey who can now see the divine danger, and whose mouth will be opened by God, in spite of the stick of Balak (perhaps it is more subtle than a stick — it is the carrot of riches). Anyone who resists Yahweh, even though he be considered wise, is a fool!

c. Balak Meets with Balaam (22:36–40)

36 *When Balak heard that Balaam was coming, he went out to meet him at the city of Moab, which is in the region*[1] *of the Arnon, at the extremity of that region.*

37 *And Balak said to Balaam, "Did I not surely send to you to summon you to me? Why did you not come to me? Was I not, in truth, able to honor you?"*

38 *And Balaam said to Balak, "Behold, I have come to you now. Am I, indeed, able to speak anything to you? The word that God may place in my mouth, that will I speak."*

39 *And Balaam went*[2] *with Balak, and they came to Kiriath-huzoth.*[3]

---

is an example of different theologies requiring different expressions. See Hackett, *Balaam Text,* pp. 25, 85–89.

1. Heb. *g*^{e}*ḇûl* can mean either "border" or "territory." The latter, more general meaning seems more appropriate here, although most English versions translate by "border." See BDB, pp. 147b–48a. The translation "border" gives a more exact location (cf. RSV "on the boundary formed by the Arnon, at the extremity of the boundary").

2. Sam. Pent., Targ., and Pesh. read "he brought [or led] him" (*way*^{e}*ḇi'ēhû,* Hiphil third masc. sing. perfect with third masc. sing. suffix), making Balak the one who led Balaam.

3. Targ. has understood Kiriath-huzoth as "into his city" *(lqryt mḥwzwhy),*

40 *Then Balak sacrificed cattle and sheep, and sent to Balaam and to the princes who were with him.*

This short passage concludes the main story of Balak's summoning of Balaam to curse Israel. It picks up the story of v. 21 by once again mentioning Balak. That Balak was last mentioned in v. 21 may mean that vv. 22–35 were an independent unit set into the rest of ch. 22. However, in the final form of the text, which one must interpret, vv. 36–40 are dependent on and assume the story of Balaam and his donkey in vv. 22–35.

36 *When Balak heard that Balaam was coming.* Perhaps the princes (v. 35) had set off ahead of Balaam, and met Balak before Balaam. This may be another reason why no mention of them was made in vv. 22–34. The princes simply are not literarily significant at this point, and are only mentioned in passing in v. 40.

the city of Moab (ʿîr môʾāḇ). Most scholars assume that this should be read as a proper name, Ir-Moab, and, furthermore, should probably be equated with Ar-Moab in 21:15, 28. Two relative clauses identify this site. The first one *(which is in the region of the Arnon)* places the site at the Arnon River, which formed the northern frontier of Moab at this time (cf. 21:13, 26). The second clause *(at the extremity of that region)* places it at the eastern edge of that territory (cf. 23:7). This is consistent with what has been said about the site of Ar-Moab above.

37 When Balaam arrives a small power struggle ensues. Balak chides him for not coming immediately when summoned. As in 22:15, 17 above, Balak assumes that Balaam at first declined to come because the promised reward was not sufficient. This is taken as an insult to the wealth and character of a king of Moab.

38 For his part, Balaam attempts to dominate the relationship by pointing clearly to the fact that he, by himself, cannot say anything but is wholly dependent upon what God says to him. Therefore, Balaam is not at the beck and call of Balak or any other human agent, but is under the control of God alone (*The word that God may place in my mouth, that I will speak;* cf. 1 K. 22:14).[4] This is essentially what Balaam had also told Balak's messengers in Pethor. Balaam here uses the term *Elohim,* the more general title (not really a proper name) for God, rather than the specific

---

and LXX has understood it as "dwelling" (*epauleōn,* which presupposes Heb. *ḥaṣērôṯ*).

4. The clause "Yahweh placed a word . . . in (my, his) mouth" is also found below in 23:5, 12, 16 (cf. Exod. 4:15). For this view of the prophet as the receiver and transmitter of what God says, see Exod. 7:1–2.

name *Yahweh,* which he had used with Balak's messengers in vv. 2–21. This is appropriate for a first meeting with one whose religious practices may be unfamiliar. He is in Balak's socio-religious sphere now, whereas when the messengers had come to him in Pethor, they were in his.

39 When the preliminaries were out of the way Balaam went with Balak to Kiriath-huzoth (lit., "town of streets"). This site is unknown unless it is the same as Kiriathaim (32:37), which has been identified as modern el-Qereiyât, northwest of Dibon. The placement of this site is suitable for the identification, but no certainty is possible on the point.[5]

40 *Then Balak sacrificed cattle and sheep (wayyizbaḥ bālāq bāqār wāṣō'n).* The verb *zāḇaḥ* does not necessarily mean that Balak offered these animals as sacrifices (see 1 Sam. 28:24; Ezek. 34:3; 2 Chr. 18:2; etc., where the verb means "to slaughter for food"), but most probably he did.

and sent to Balaam and to the princes who were with him (wayᵉ-šallaḥ lᵉḇilʿām wᵉlaśśārîm 'ᵃšer 'ittô). It is unclear whether the verb "to send" *(šillaḥ,* Piel) is transitive here (as in Neh. 8:12), and the object of the sending understood from the context (i.e., the sacrifices),[6] whether it means that Balak made the sacrifices in private and then sent for Balaam and the princes to join him (which would seem to demand reading the Qal instead of the Piel), or, perhaps, after the sacrifices, he sent Balaam and the princes away for the night.[7] The first option has good support from commentators and translators, and is possible syntactically. One might inquire about the kind of sacrifices that Balak shared with Balaam and the princes here. If we were dealing with the Israelite cult here, then the answer might be the peace offerings. There is no proof, however, that the Moabite cult was anything like the Israelite cult in sacrificial matters. We are probably safest in concluding that these sacrifices were meant to be a kind of welcome for Balaam.[8] Whether they were intended to be thanksgivings for his safe arrival or to seek the good offices of Balak's gods is not known.

5. See *Westminster Historical Atlas,* p. 65; also May, ed., *Oxford Bible Atlas,* 3rd ed., pp. 57, 61, 63, 69, 73; Gray (pp. 338–39) doubts the identification of Kiriath-huzoth and Kiriathaim.

6. So, e.g., Gray, p. 339; McNeile, p. 130; Binns, p. 158; Moffatt; NASB; GNB; NEB; NIV; NJPS; cf. Noth, p. 181; Wenham, p. 171. Parallels to this feast are possibly seen in 1 Sam. 9:12–26; 16:2–12; Neh. 8:9–12.

7. See BDB, pp. 1018–19. Sturdy (p. 167) seems to follow this line. AV, RV, and RSV translate more literally (and ambiguously), e.g., "and sent to Balaam and the princes who were with him" (RSV).

8. This is the conclusion of M. Moore, *Balaam Traditions,* pp. 104–5.

2. FIRST AND SECOND ORACLES (22:41–23:30)

a. Introductory Preparations (22:41–23:6)

41 *And in the morning Balak took Balaam and he brought him up on Bamoth-baal, and he showed him the outskirts of*[1] *the people from there.*

23:1 *And Balaam said to Balak, "Build seven altars for me here and furnish seven bulls and seven rams for me*[2] *here."*

2 *And Balak did as Balaam had spoken, and Balak and Balaam*[3] *offered a bull and a ram on each*[4] *altar.*

3 *And Balaam said to Balak, "Stand near your whole burnt offering and I will go; perhaps Yahweh will come to meet me. Whatever*[5] *matter he might show me, I will declare to you."*[6] *And he went to a bare height.*[7]

1. MT *qᵉṣeh,* lit., "end of." Vulg. reads "the full extent," followed by NEB; so also Noordtzij, p. 214. LXX simply reads *meros ti,* "some part," which is followed by NASB, NIV, GNB, NJPS. RSV "nearest of" presumes it was the near end of the people (so also Gray, p. 341). The above translation is closer to RSV, but attempts to convey some of the ambiguity of the text.

2. The twofold occurrence of *lî* here is to show interest or advantage (as in 22:6); see Williams, *Syntax,* § 271.

3. MT has a sing. verb *(wayyaʿal)* with a pl. subject, "Balak and Balaam"; in v. 30 the same expression occurs without the pl. subject. A few Heb. mss. and LXX do not have the pl. subject in v. 2; LXX reads *kai anēnenken,* "and he offered," in both v. 2 and v. 30. This may be the original reading; many commentators, e.g., Gray and Noth, eliminate "Balak and Balaam" as a gloss here.

4. MT has no clear grammatical indication of a distributive sense here, although the preposition *bᵉ-* may indicate it (Williams, *Syntax,* §§102, 254). It is most likely that only the context decides the matter; i.e., there were seven bulls, seven rams, and seven altars. When only one of each animal is named (both *pār* and *'ayil* are sing.), one assumes that one bull and one ram were offered on each altar.

5. The interrogative *mah* here has the indefinite meaning "whatever," as in 1 Sam. 21:4; see BDB, p. 553a (e); GKC, § 137c; Davidson, *Syntax,* § 8; Williams, *Syntax,* § 125.

6. This translation follows Gray, p. 344. It shows that Balaam does expect Yahweh to speak; he is only unsure about what he will say. Here as before Balaam clearly tells Balak that whatever the content of Yahweh's message — be it weal or woe for Moab — he will speak it. The alternative is to read it as hypothetical: "If he shows me anything, I will tell you" (cf. 1 Sam. 16:2; Driver, *Tenses,* § 149).

7. MT *šep̄î* occurs only here (unless the Ketib of Job 33:21 is accepted), though the pl. form (*šᵉpāyîm* or *šᵉpāyim*) is not uncommon (Isa. 41:18; 49:9; Jer. 3:2, 21; 4:11; 7:29; 12:12; 14:6). The versions clearly did not read "a bare height" (LXX *eutheian,* "straightaway"; Vulg. *velociter,* "swiftly"), but it is uncertain

4 *Then God came to meet Balaam. And he said to him, "I have prepared seven altars and have offered a bull and a ram on each altar."*
5 *And Yahweh*[8] *put a word in Balaam's mouth, and he said, "Return to Balak and there you shall speak."*
6 *And he returned to him, and, behold, he was standing by his whole burnt offering, he and all the princes of Moab.*[9]

These verses narrate the preparations made by Balaam and Balak for the reception of the first oracle. One must remember that Balak was a pagan, offering sacrifices to other gods than Yahweh, and that, no matter what the source of the original Balaam story, in the form in which it is now preserved, the story was written by an Israelite for Israelites. In the current text, therefore, details of a non-Israelite sacrificial system are related in terms of the Israelite system. It is not possible to draw far-reaching conclusions on what Balak or Balaam may have thought the actual sacrifices themselves meant or what the specific techniques were.

41 *And in the morning.* This is the only time indicator for the four oracles of Balaam, along with all the cultic preparations for their reception. If one assumes that all this — altar building, sacrifice, and reception of revelation — occurred in only one day, that would be a very busy day indeed. Perhaps this phrase is meant to set these oracles in a literary frame rather than a chronological one. In that case, these events may have been spread over several days.

Bamoth-baal may be the same place as Bamoth, which is in the right general area (see above on 21:19). It may also be a generic place-name, "the high places of Baal," of which there must have been many (cf. Isa. 15:2; 16:12; Jer. 48:35).[10] The important thing seems to be that from this vantage point Balaam could see at least part of the Israelites' encampment. It was apparently important to be able to see what was going to be cursed.

outskirts of the people (qᵉṣēh hāʿām). The word *qāṣeh* means

---

whether they were trying to make sense of *šᵉp̱î* or were reading some other Hebrew word. See the commentary below.

8. Sam. Pent. reads *malāʾḵ-YHWH,* "the angel of Yahweh," here. LXX reads *ho theos,* "God." *BHS* says to delete the proper name here, but gives no reason why this should be done. If one follows *BHS,* one has to read *wayyāśem* as an impersonal verb.

9. LXX adds the explanation: "and the spirit of God came upon him" *(kai egenēthē pneuma theou ep' autō).*

10. So, e.g., Noth, p. 182; Noordtzij, p. 214.

"end." The question is, which end — the near end (i.e., only those closest) or the far end (i.e., the whole people)? On the basis of the more likely reading of 23:13, the former seems slightly preferable.[11]

23:1–2 Since the matters to follow are clearly cultic and revelatory, Balaam the seer takes charge of the situation and gives Balak instructions that he then simply executes.

seven altars . . . seven bulls . . . seven rams. The number seven is sacred not only in the OT but in the ancient Near East generally.[12] In the OT, e.g., the creation narrative is given a seven-day framework (Gen. 1:1–2:3), the week is seven days long, the seventh month contains three special periods (New Year, Yom Kippur, Feast of Booths; Num. 29:1–39), etc. The altars were most probably built from materials found at the site of Bamoth-baal, which was already a sacred site dedicated to a particular god (as were the others named in 23:14, 28).[13]

Israel used *bulls* and *rams* for the most important sacrifices (Lev. 4:1–21; 5:14–6:7), and Moab may have done similarly. Balak simply does as he was told in the hope that correct performance of the prescribed rituals will issue in the desired curse on Israel.

Balak and Balaam offered. Even if, as is possible, the names Balak and Balaam are glosses in the present text,[14] it is known that both the one offering sacrifices and the diviner had a role in oracular sacrifice; thus the pl. subject may reflect the intended meaning of the text.[15]

3 It is interesting that the text calls these pagan sacrifices *whole burnt offerings (ʿōlôṯ),* a particular type of Hebrew sacrifice. Whether this means that the Moabites had a similar type of sacrifice or that the narrator is simply tying these sacrifices to something familiar to Israelite readers, the *whole burnt offering* is the one sacrifice that is not shared with the priest or the worshiper but wholly consumed on the altar (Lev. 1:3–17;

11. See n. 1 above on the translation, and the commentary below on 23:13.

12. For the significance of the number seven in the ancient Near East, see, e.g., J. Hehn, "Zur Bedeutung der Siebenzahl," in *Festschrift für Karl Marti,* BZAW 41 (1925), pp. 128–37; M. H. Pope, *IDB,* IV:294–95; B. C. Birch, *ISBE,* rev., III:559.

13. See Smith, *Historical Geography,* p. 382; Gray, pp. 341–42.

14. See n. 3 to the translation above.

15. Cf. Binns, p. 160. In v. 4, Balaam states that *he* has offered these sacrifices. On the shared nature of the offerings in the ancient Near East, see, e.g., S. Daiches, "Balaam, a Babylonian *bārû:* The Episode of Num. 22.2–24.2 and Some Babylonian Parallels," *Assyriologische und archaeologische Studien Hermann von Hilprecht Gewidmet* (Leipzig: Hinrichs, 1909), p. 62; Moore, *Balaam Traditions,* pp. 104–9.

6:1–6 [Eng. 8–13]). It is appropriate that costly sacrifice would be used for those instances in which a god was called on to speak to his representative.

Although Balaam may have thought that these seven sacrifices on seven altars would help to guarantee that God would meet him (see his word to God in v. 4b), he says here *perhaps Yahweh will come to meet me.* The verb "to meet" *(niqrâ)* is used of divine-human meeting elsewhere (e.g., vv. 15–16; Exod. 3:18). The text does not say that Balaam thought that he would meet with Yahweh in divination of natural signs; on the contrary, he had met Yahweh at home, and there Yahweh had brought a word of revelation. There was no reason why he might not do so now. The particle *perhaps ('ûlay)* simply gives God the option to speak or not, i.e., it gives God an invitation to speak. *Whatever (mah)* Yahweh decides to say to Balaam, he will report it faithfully to Balak. This is no more than has already been said in 22:8, 18, 38 (cf. 23:12, 26).

And he went to a bare height (wayyēlek̲ šep̲î). This is the only occurrence of the sing. *šᵉp̲î* (unless the one accepts the Ketib of Job 33:21). The pl. (*šᵉpāyîm* or *šᵉp̲āyim*) means "bare places, heights" (Isa. 41:18; 49:9; Jer. 3:2, 21; 4:11; 7:29; 12:12; 14:6). Although there is no other occurrence of the sing. (except perhaps Job 33:21), it should be kept in mind how rare a word this is in the OT (it occurs only 8 or 9 times). Long ago A. Kuenen suggested that the original text should be *wylk lkšpyw,* "and he went off to his enchantments" (haplography of the last two consonants of *wayyēlek̲*). Noordtzij follows this suggestion, which fits with his hypothesis that Balaam was an active *baru* practicing his sorceries here.[16] But as Gray states, in spite of all the interpretational difficulties, there is no proof that the versions read anything but *šᵉp̲î* and were trying to make sense of it.[17] Therefore *bare height,* i.e., a vantage point ideal for meeting with God, still makes the most sense of the options that have been brought forth. Noth suggests that by moving the action to this bare height, the narrator placed as much distance as possible between Balak's pagan sacrifice and Balaam's reception of God's revelation.[18]

4–6 When God does meet with Balaam, the first thing the seer does is to point to the seven altars with their offerings. Balaam may have thought that these sacrifices guaranteed a good word from God, although

16. Noordtzij, p. 215. Gray rightly rejects this emendation. For other suggestions on the meaning of *šᵉp̲î,* see Binns, p. 160.

17. See Gray, p. 344.

18. Noth, p. 182.

he is adamant with Balak that Yahweh will utter what he will, with no conditions. Or Balaam may have been pointing out to God that proper ritual has been followed. He states that he has prepared and offered these sacrifices. If the reading of the MT is kept in v. 2 (see above), both he and Balak were involved in the sacrifices. If only Balak offered the sacrifices (as seems to be the case in vv. 13, 30), however, then Balaam is speaking as the professional responsible for the whole process and not in a personal sense.

Some scholars insist that Balaam was looking for a portent in the natural world that he would then have to interpret to Balak.[19] Such divination would be different from the previous contact between God and Balaam (see 22:9, 20). This theory is more likely based on the desire of these scholars to make Balaam a villain than it is on the text of chs. 22–24.

Whatever Balaam's expectations were (and "divination" is mentioned in 24:1), *Yahweh put a word in Balaam's mouth* —i.e., he told Balaam precisely what he was to say by direct revelation (cf. also v. 16). This idiom is also used of the prophets of Israel (e.g., Deut. 18:18; Jer. 1:9). When Balaam receives Yahweh's word, he is commanded to speak it to Balak. He returns to Balak and finds him standing guard, along with all the princes of Moab, over the whole burnt offering he had made.

b. First Oracle (23:7–12)

7 *And he took up his oracle and said:*
"From Aram he brought[1] *me,*
The king of Moab, from the eastern mountains.[2]

19. E.g., Keil, pp. 176–77; Cook, pp. 739–40; Noordtzij, p. 215.

1. Davidson (*Syntax,* § 45 Rem. 2) and Driver (*Tenses,* § 27a) parse *yanḥēnî* as an imperfect and translate it by a historical present. It is probably not an imperfect, however, but a preterite, a true past tense; see Williams, *Syntax,* §§ 176–77; C. L. Seow, *A Grammar for Biblical Hebrew* (Nashville: Abingdon, 1987), p. 158. More complex discussion of the Hebrew preterite may be found in, e.g., G. R. Driver, *Problems of the Hebrew Verbal System* (Edinburgh: T. & T. Clark, 1936); see also L. McFall, *The Enigma of the Hebrew Verbal System: Solutions from Ewald to the Present Day,* Historic Texts and Interpreters in Biblical Scholarship, 2 (Sheffield: Almond, 1982), esp. pp. 127–30 (see a critique of Driver's views on pp. 136–51); S. Moscati, ed., *An Introduction to the Comparative Grammar of the Semitic Languages,* Porta Linguarum Orientalium (Wiesbaden: Harrassowitz, 1969), §§ 16.28–16.31.

2. On the poetic form of the pl. construct of *har,* "mountain," see GKC, § 93aa.

'Come, curse[3] Jacob for me,
And[4] come, denounce[5] Israel!'
8 *How shall I curse whom El has not cursed?*
How shall I denounce whom Yahweh has not denounced?
9 *For, from the top of the mountains I see,*[6]
And from the hills I behold.
Lo, a people dwelling alone,
And not considering itself among the nations.
10 *O that someone could count[7] the dust of Jacob?*
Or number[8] the dust cloud[9] of Israel?
Let my soul die the death of upright people,[10]
and may my end[11] be like his."

3. On the form of this imperative, see GKC, § 67o; Davidson, *Syntax,* § 60.

4. Albright ("The Oracles of Balaam," *JBL* 63 [1944] 212 n. 17) rejects the "and" *(*w^{e}*-)* in early poetry.

5. On the form of this imperative, see GKC, § 63c.

6. Albright ("Oracles," p. 212 n. 23) reads *'r'n* (i.e., without suffix) instead of MT *'er'ennû,* taking the final *nun* as energic. The reason for this reading is that neither this verb nor its parallel "to behold" (*'*^{a}*šûrennû,* which is also read as *'šrn* with energic *nun*) has a clear antecedent. His translation, then, is "From the peak of the mountains I see, And from the hill-tops I behold." The object of these verbs becomes "a people" *(ʿām)* from the next couplet.

7. The question conveys a wish; see GKC, § 151a. The perfect tense is used to express the fact that the speaker imagines this counting as done, and is amazed that it could be; see Davidson, *Syntax,* § 41 Rem. 2; Driver, *Tenses,* § 19 (2). Albright ("Oracles," p. 224) translates as a simple perfect.

8. MT *ûmispār 'eṯ-rōḇaʿ,* "a number, a fourth part." If this reading is correct, it would be an accusative of closer definition (so, e.g., Keil, p. 180). The reading adopted here follows Sam. Pent. and LXX, which presuppose *mî sāpar,* "who can number," in parallel to *mî mānâ,* "who can count," in the previous line. *BHS,* Davidson (*Syntax,* § 91 Rem. 3), Albright ("Oracles," p. 213 n. 27), and many commentators (e.g., Gray, pp. 347–48; Snaith, p. 178; de Vaulx, p. 276; Milgrom, *JPST,* p. 196) adopt this reading.

9. Most older commentators (e.g., Dillmann, p. 151; Gray, p. 348; McNeile, p. 132; Binns, p. 162; also BDB, p. 914a) emend *rōḇaʿ,* "fourth part," to *riḇ*^{e}*ḇōṯ,* "myriad," as in 10:36. LXX has *dēmous,* "clans." Albright ("Oracles," p. 213 n. 28) reads *trbʿt,* which is related to Akk. *turbu'tu,* "dust cloud" (possibly an Aramaic loanword in Akkadian; see Albright, "Oracles," p. 213 n. 28). Sam. Pent. reads *mrbʿt,* thus transmitting the final *ṯ* of the proposed reading. The initial *ṯ* of the proposed reading was later misread by the Masoretes as the sign of the definite direct object *('eṯ),* which is less usual in poetry. *HALAT,* pp. 1101b–2a, follows Albright and posits a Hebrew root *rbʿ* meaning "dust."

10. The substantive *y*^{e}*šārîm* is pl., thus referring to a whole group of individual Israelites. Albright ("Oracles," p. 213 n. 28a) refers to the final *m* as enclitic *mem,* not the sign of the masc. pl. (see also pp. 215 n. 45, 219 n. 83).

11. Binns (p. 162) refers to a 7th-cent. Aramaic inscription that uses the

11 *And Balak said to Balaam, "What have you done to me? I brought you to curse my enemies, and behold, you have done nothing but utter a blessing!"*[12]

12 *And he answered and said, "Shall I not be careful to speak that which Yahweh might put in my mouth?"*

Balaam's first oracle is written in seven tightly parallel couplets. Albright proposed a composition date between the mid-13th cent. and the end of the 12th, and a writing date of the 10th or early 9th century.[13] This date is probable.

7–8 *And he took up his oracle (wayyiśśā' mᵉšālô).* The word rendered *oracle (māšāl)* usually means "proverb," and it is used of the wisdom utterances (both longer and shorter) in the book of Proverbs (whose title in Hebrew is *mᵉšālîm*). But, as Gray points out, it can also refer to other kinds of utterances.[14] In Job 27:1 and 29:1 a *māšāl* is a declaration of woe. In Isa. 14:4; Mic. 2:4; and Hab. 2:4 the noun, likewise, indicates a recitation of woe "over" or "against" *('al)* an enemy. In the latter three passages *māšāl* is translated "taunt song."[15] The term here may speak more of the style of the speeches than of their form.[16] In this context the word *oracle* (NEB, NIV) is as good a translation as any. The verb "to take up" *(nāśā')* means "to give formal utterance to."

At the beginning of the oracle proper, the person shifts from third to first. Balaam is now speaking in his formal role as an oracle speaker.

---

term *end* (Heb. *'aḥᵃriṯ*) in just the same way: *wthnsny śhr wnkl wnśk ihb' šw mmtth w'ḥrth t'br,* "May Sahar and Nikal and Nusk make his death miserable, and may his posterity perish." See Cooke, *Textbook of North-Semitic Inscriptions,* p. 190; no. 65, lines 9–10. Cooke also points to some Nabatean inscriptions that use the term in the same way (pp. 217, 226; no. 79, line 2; no. 82, line 3). He also refers to Num. 24:20.

12. The Piel has two forms of the infinitive absolute: one that is morphologically identical with the infinitive construct *(bārēḵ),* and one that has the form *bārôḵ* (Josh. 24:10). The present case (also v. 25 below) uses the first form. Sam. Pent. reads the second in both cases. The infinitive absolute following its cognate finite verb usually indicates duration; cf. Davidson, *Syntax,* § 86 Rem. 3.

13. Albright, "Oracles," p. 213.

14. For a discussion of *māšāl* see Gray, pp. 344–45.

15. On Job, see, e.g., N. Habel, *The Book of Job,* OTL (Philadelphia: Westminster, 1985), p. 379; on the translation "taunt-song" in the prophets, see, e.g., J. D. W. Watts, *Isaiah 1–33,* WBC (Waco, Tex.: Word, 1985), 203, 207–08; L. Allen, *The Books of Joel, Obadiah, Jonah and Micah,* NICOT (Grand Rapids: Eerdmans, 1976), p. 290; J. J. M. Roberts, *Nahum, Habakkuk & Zephaniah: A Commentary,* OTL (Louisville: Westminster/Knox, 1991), pp. 117–18.

16. See the commentary above on 21:27.

The first couplet tells why Balaam is where he is, viz., he was brought by Balak from his homeland, *Aram.* In Hos. 12:13 (Eng. 12) the phrase "the country of Aram" *(śᵉḏēh ʾᵃrām)* occurs, and the current expression may be a shortened form of this expression. The land is sometimes called Aram-naharaim ("Aram of the two rivers," e.g., Deut. 23:4, which names this as Balaam's home) or Paddan-aram (e.g., Gen 28:2); it indicates the area northeast of Israel in northeast Syria and northwest Mesopotamia. This area is consonant with the location of Pethor suggested above in 22:5.[17] Thus *the eastern mountains* are the mountains that run through the eastern Syrian-Arabian desert up toward Pitru/Pethor.

The second couplet gives the reason for which Balak brought Balaam to Moab: to curse Israel. *curse . . . denounce.* The first of these verbs *(ʾārar)* is the common verb that means "to utter a curse" and in the present context probably means something like "to put under an evil spell."[18] The second of these verbs *(zāʿam)* is a less-well-attested word that, at base, oscillates in meaning between "to threaten" and "to injure."[19] When taken together the two words indicate that Balaam's job was to put Israel under an evil spell that would threaten or injure it. Israel believed, in common with other ancient Near Eastern peoples, that words uttered by someone were effective agents to accomplish the purpose for which they were uttered.[20]

8 In the third couplet Balaam states that he has no real power (nor does the text indicate he had a desire) to curse those whom El/Yahweh has not cursed. Here the ancient Semitic generic term for God *(El)* is identified with Yahweh,[21] much as Jacob and Israel are identified in v. 7. One should not read an ignoble motive into Balaam's feeling of compulsion here, any more than one might with Jeremiah (Jer. 20:7–12) or Peter and John (Acts 4:19–20), who express the same kind of feeling in even stronger terms.

9–10a The next three couplets give further reasons why Balaam

17. There is no need to emend MT *ʾᵃrām,* "Aram," to *ʾᵉḏôm,* "Edom," here. See Albright, "Oracles," pp. 211–12 n. 15.

18. H. C. Brichto, *The Problem of "Curse" in the Hebrew Bible* (Philadelphia: Society of Biblical Literature, 1963), pp. 99–100. Brichto holds that one important basic meaning for *ʾārar* is "to banish" (see pp. 77–99). See also J. Scharbert, *TDOT,* I:405–18.

19. Brichto, *Problem,* 202–3; H. Ringgren, *TDOT,* IV:106–12.

20. See, e.g., J. Pedersen, *Israel: Its Life and Culture, I–II,* pp. 411–52.

21. Thus further complicating the case, Noordtzij, p. 217, wishes to maintain that Yahweh and Elohim are different.

cannot curse Israel, and what it means that Israel has been blessed by Yahweh.

9a Balaam states that he can see Israel *from the top of the mountains . . . from the hills.* The word *mountains (ṣurîm)* indicates rocky crags.[22] It is parallel to the common word for *hills (gᵉḇāʿôṯ).*[23] It is probable that the words *from the top of (mērōʾš)* should be understood with both nouns. These two images are united by their height, but divided by the roughness of the mountains as opposed to the smoothness of the rounded hills. As in much poetry, the image is more than physical; Balaam is speaking of his current elevated state where he not only physically sees Israel but spiritually sees them as well.

9b The fifth couplet tells what Balaam sees in Israel: *a people dwelling alone.* This phrase broadly hints that Israel is in some way solitary among the nations. The term *alone (lᵉḇāḏāḏ)* can indicate security and safety (Deut. 33:28; Jer. 49:31; Mic. 7:14), but could also indicate a singleness of election among the nations of the earth (cf. Exod. 19:5). When this clause is compared with its parallel, *not considering itself among the nations,* the likelihood increases that Israel's aloneness consists in its special relationship with Yahweh. Balaam asserts that this nation is alone and is aware of this aloneness.

10a The sixth couplet describes the outward sign of Israel's election and blessing of God: its numerical strength, which is a fulfillment of the promise of Gen. 13:16. The numerical strength of Israel is, of course, the reason why the Moabites were fearful and decided to call Balaam in the first place (22:3–6). Here Balaam sees that strength as no mere accident, but as the sign of Israel's separate status, i.e., its blessing by Yahweh.

or number the dust cloud of Israel. The MT reads *ûmispār ʾeṯ-rōḇaʿ yiśrāʾēl,* "and a number, a fourth part of Israel." Keil offered the best explanation of the MT. He suggested that the "fourth part of Israel" be connected with the four camps of ch. 2, only one of which was visible to Balaam.[24] But this translation is replete with difficulties not only of syntax but of meaning, and the emendations suggested in the translation

22. *HALAT,* pp. 952b–53a; see Albright, "Oracles," p. 212 n. 22, who also identifies it with Aram. *ṭûr,* "mountain." The parallelism of *ṣr* and *gbʿt* also occurs in Ugaritic.

23. The noun occurs 63 times in Biblical Hebrew (cf. BDB, pp. 148b–49a), 10 times referring to an illicit cultic site (e.g., 1 K. 14:23; 2 K. 17:10; Jer. 2:20).

24. Keil, p. 180; cf. Cook, p. 741. For Keil's explanation of *ûmispār,* see n. 8 to the translation above.

above make the couplet more readable as well as synonymously parallel *(who can number/who can count; dust/dust cloud; Jacob/Israel).*

10b The last couplet closes the first oracle with a personal reflection by Balaam. He concludes his vision of Israel by wishing that, at the end of his own life, he could be as blessed as Israel was. In the light of the fact that Israel's blessing was shown by great numbers, it may be that Balaam is speaking of his posterity here sharing the same happy fate as Israel, a nation made up of *upright people.* In this wish he may be invoking upon himself the kind of blessing found in Gen. 12:3, that through Abraham and his offspring, all nations of the earth will bless themselves. This couplet is ironic in the light of the circumstances of Balaam's death recorded in 31:8, 16.

11–12 As one might expect, Balak is furious with Balaam, but Balaam reminds him of what he has said all along: he can say nothing apart from the will of Yahweh (23:5; cf. 22:38). M. Moore has seen in the clash between Balak and Balaam here a fundamental difference in role expectation. Balaam sees his own role primarily as a reciter of divine oracles. Balak, on the other hand, sees the role of Balaam as a sorcerer who will simply incant a spell to curse the Israelites. The tension is not resolved, here or later, and the whole enterprise comes to nothing but a negative outcome for Balak and Balaam.[25]

c. Second Oracle (23:13–26)

13 *And Balak said to him, "Come now with me to another place from where you can see them;*[1] *you will see only their extremity, but their entirety you will not see, and you will curse them for me from there."*

14 *And he took him to*[2] *the field of Zophim, to the top of the Pisgah, and he built seven altars and offered a bull and a ram on each altar.*

15 *And he said to Balak, "Stand there by your whole burnt offering, and I will meet Yahweh*[3] *over there."*

25. M. Moore, *The Balaam Traditions,* pp. 113–16.

1. Here and below, the pronouns referring to Israel are masc. sing. in Hebrew. They are translated as pl. to make a better English translation.

2. Heb. *wayyiqqāḥēhû śāḏeh.* The accusative of place is sometimes, as here, expressed without any preposition; see GKC, § 118f.

3. The MT reads only *wᵉʾānōḵî ʾiqqāreh kōh,* "and I will meet." Some divine name is obviously intended by the context to be the object of the verb "to meet." LXX reads *poreusomai eperōtēsai ton theon,* "I shall go off to meet God." The likelihood is that the name Yahweh should be inserted, since that is the name that occurs in the parallel verse (23:3) and in the next verse, which describes what

16 *And Yahweh[4] met with Balaam, and placed a word in his mouth, and said, "Return to Balak and speak thus."*
17 *And he came to him, and behold, he was standing beside his whole burnt offering, and the princes of Moab were with him. And Balak said to him, "What did Yahweh say?"*
18 *And he took up his oracle and said:*

"Rise, O Balak, and hear!
Give ear to me,[5] O son[6] of Zippor!
19 *God is not[7] human that he should fail,[8]*
nor of the human kind that he should change his mind.
Has he said and he will not do it?
Or[9] spoken[10] and will not bring it to stand?[11]
20 *Behold, I have received instruction[12] to bless;*
since he has blessed, I cannot revoke it.[13]

---

happened in this verse. See GKC, § 51p, for the Niphal first person sing. imperfect (*'iqqāreh*) with an *i* in the preformative rather than the more common *e* (i.e., *'eqqāreh*).

4. LXX reads *ho theos* instead of Yahweh here, and this reading is, according to *BHS,* followed by a few Hebrew mss. as well.

5. Albright ("Oracles," p. 214 n. 31) reads *'ēḏî,* "my witness, my testimony," instead of MT *'āḏî,* "unto me," which is an unusual preposition with this verb. MT stresses the sense of the vividness of the indirect object.

6. For MT *b^{e}nô* ("his son"), the *Sebir* note reads simply *bēn* ("son"). The *-ô* may be the remnant of a case ending. See 23:18; 24:3, 15; Gen. 1:24; Ps. 50:10; 79:2; 104:11, 20; Isa. 56:9; Zeph. 2:14. See GKC, §§ 90n, o; 96.

7. The negative particle *lō'* exerts its force over the whole succeeding verse without being repeated in the second clause (Davidson, *Syntax,* § 128 Rem. 6), and thus the *w^e-* on the noun *ben* should be translated as "or" (ibid., § 152).

8. The verb *wîḵazzēḇ* is a jussive; see GKC, § 109i; Davidson, *Syntax,* § 65 (c); Driver, *Tenses,* § 64.

9. Albright ("Oracles," p. 214 n. 34) omits the conjunction *w^e-*, "and, or," as often in poetry. LXX also eliminates the conjunction.

10. Heb. *'āmar . . . w^{e}ḏibber* are two perfects connected by a simple conjunctive *w^e-*. This construction shows a simple repetition of another idea already present rather than a progression in thought. See GKC, § 166a; Davidson, *Syntax,* §§ 58 (a), 150; Driver, *Tenses,* § 132.

11. Albright ("Oracles," p. 214 n. 35) reads *yqmn,* with an energic *nun* without the pronominal suffix. See the note on 23:9 above.

12. The verb *lāqaḥ* here means "to receive mentally," or "receive instruction," as in Exod. 22:10; Prov. 24:32; Jer. 2:30; etc.; see BDB, p. 543a (4f). Alternatively, one could point *lqḥty* as a passive *(luqqaḥtî),* "I have been brought hither (to bless)," as Albright suggests, although this seems less likely. See Albright, "Oracles," p. 214 n. 38.

13. MT *ûḇērēḵ w^{e}lō' '^{a}šîḇennâ* is a conditional sentence with no introductory particle, a *waw*-consecutive perfect in the protasis and imperfect (because

21 *Trouble is not perceived*[14] *in Jacob,*
and difficulty is not seen in Israel.
Yahweh his God is with them,
and rejoicing for a king[15] *is among them.*
22 *God brings them out of Egypt,*
He has something like the horns of the wild ox.[16]
23 *Surely,*[17] *there is no*[18] *enchantment against*[19] *Jacob,*
and no divination against Israel.
Now[20] *it is said*[21] *of Jacob*
and of Israel — 'What has God done!'
24 *Behold, a people arises like a lioness,*
and, like a lion, it lifts itself.

---

of *lō'*) in the apodosis; see GKC, § 159g; Davidson, *Syntax,* § 132 (a). Albright follows Sam. Pent. and LXX in reading *'brk wl' 'šbn,* the first-person sing. imperfect of *brk* ("I will bless") instead of MT third sing. perfect consecutive; so also Gray, p. 352; Binns, p. 164; but MT makes sense and should be retained. Albright also eliminates the pronominal suffix from *'ᵃšiḇennâ* and reads an energic *nun,* as in 23:9, 19. See Albright, "Oracles," p. 214 nn. 38a–39.

14. Both the verb *hibîṭ,* "to perceive," in this line and the verb *rā'â,* "to see," in the next are to be taken as impersonal constructions (viz., "one does not perceive," etc.), which are often circumlocutions for the passive; see Davidson, *Syntax,* § 108. Understanding the verbs as passive seems a better course than following Albright ("Oracles," p. 214 n. 42) in pointing them as passives (i.e., *hubbāṭ; rᵉ'î*).

15. For MT *tᵉrû'aṯ,* "noise of," Albright ("Oracles," p. 215 n. 43) proposes *tôra'aṯ,* "majesty of," from a root *yr',* "to fear" (i.e., that which causes awe or fear). This reading agrees with LXX *endoxa,* "notable," and Pesh. *tišbōḥtâ,* "majesty." See the commentary below on v. 21.

16. See the commentary below on this difficult clause. Albright ("Oracles," p. 224) translates it: "It is El who brought him from Egypt, while he stormed like a bull." The "he" of the second line is Israel (cf. p. 215 nn. 45, 47).

17. BDB, p. 472b, takes *kî* in this sense in this verse (cf. Williams, *Syntax,* § 449). An alternative might be to take it as explicative ("since"); cf. BDB, p. 473b.

18. The Hebrew negative *lō'* may be taken in this way; see Williams, *Syntax,* § 399 (4).

19. Quite a few scholars do not think that the preposition *bᵉ-* here may be taken in the sense of "against" (esp. Gray, pp. 355–56), but such a usage for this preposition is not uncommon (cf. *bāgaḏ bᵉ-; mā'al bᵉ-; rîḇ bᵉ-; nilḥam bᵉ-;* etc.); Williams, *Syntax,* § 242. Since one would expect *'ên,* not *lō',* as the negative in this clause, Albright ("Oracles," p. 215 n. 49) points *nḥš* and *qsm* as passives (*nuḥḥaš* and *qᵉsîm*); but this seems unnecessary. See the commentary below on this verse.

20. The compound *kā'ēṯ* means "now, at the present time"; see BDB, p. 453b; *HALAT,* p. 852b.

21. Another impersonal construction, with the Niphal of *'āmar* (cf. Davidson, *Syntax,* § 109).

It does not lie down until it eats the prey,
and drinks the blood[22] *of the slain."*

25 *And Balak said to Balaam, "Neither curse nor*[23] *bless*[24] *them at all!"*

26 *And Balaam answered and said to Balak, "Did I not speak to you, saying, 'All that Yahweh*[25] *speaks to me, that will I do'?"*

The oracle itself consists of eleven couplets, again of mainly synonymously parallel lines. Several ambiguities in interpretation here make this oracle more difficult than the first.

13 *another place.* Just as Balak had been persistent in trying to hire Balaam in the first place, and this persistence had brought Balaam to him by a supposed change in God's permission, so here it is perhaps true that Balak hopes, by changing the venue of the next oracle, to manipulate God into changing his mind and cursing his own people.

you will see only their extremity, but their entirety you will not see. If Balaam could see only part of the people from here, it is hard to see any advantage of this new site over the previous site of Bamoth-baal (see above on 22:41). For this reason and because the meaning of the words here is uncertain, scholars have explained the text variously. Keil said that the text means that "thou seest only the end of it, but not the whole of it (*sc.* here upon Bamoth-Baal)."[26] But this interpretation surely reads into the text what is not there. Others have held that at Bamoth-baal Balaam was overwhelmed by seeing the whole people, whereas, at this second site (as yet unnamed), he would see only part of them.[27] Gray held that the whole statement is a later gloss to explain why, after the failure of this second oracle to produce the desired curse, Balak and Balaam proceeded to yet a third site (23:27–28).[28] Whether or not Gray's gloss theory is correct, his explanation of the purpose of the line in the present context is

22. Heb. *dām,* "blood," in the sing. (as here) refers to the organic material found in the body. In the pl. *(dāmîm)* it refers to "bloodshed." See GKC, § 124n.

23. On *gam . . . gam* meaning "neither . . . nor" after a negative, see BDB, p. 169a.

24. On the use of the infinitive absolute of *bārēḵ* (Piel), see Davidson, *Syntax,* § 86 Rem. 3, and above on the translation of 23:11.

25. Sam. Pent., LXX, and Vulg. apparently read "God" *(hāʾᵉlōhîm)* here instead of Yahweh.

26. Keil, p. 181.

27. E.g., Noordtzij, p. 219; also those who follow the NEB text, e.g., Sturdy, p. 172.

28. Gray, pp. 349–50.

convincing. The site was not selected because Balaam could see any more of the people from it, but for another reason, which is not given in the text. Perhaps the second site was simply closer to the Israelite camp than the previous one. In any case, Balaam is told to curse Israel from this new site.

14–17 *field of Zophim (śᵉḏēh ṣōp̱îm).* Most translations render the Hebrew pl. participle *ṣōp̱îm* (from the verb *ṣāp̱â,* "to watch, spy")[29] as a proper name; NEB translates the name, "Field of the Watchers." Although this site is not named elsewhere and is unknown, this name must indicate a place known for its visibility, from which Balaam could see at least part of the plains of Moab. Some scholars have also posited that Zophim was a site already set apart for seeking omens such as the flight of birds, hence a natural site for what Balak had in mind.[30]

the top of the Pisgah. This place could be the same as the one mentioned in 21:20 (see the commentary there). Mt. Nebo, another peak in the Pisgah, commanded a view of all the land of Canaan (Deut. 3:27; 34:1). Balak was commanded to undergo the same ritual as before (see 23:1–5), which he did.

Stand there . . . I will meet Yahweh over there (hiṯyaṣṣēḇ kōh . . . wᵉʾānōḵî ʾiqqāreh YHWH kōh). As noted above, a divine name is missing here, but is clearly intended from the context. The word translated as both *there* and *over there* is *kōh,* usually translated as "thus." Some have concluded that this is the meaning here as well so that Balaam is instructing Balak how to stand rather than where.[31] Others have contended that these particles are local, as in 11:31 and Exod. 2:12.[32] Although the latter usage is rarer, it seems preferable in this context, which discusses the site of the ritual.

The scene climaxes, as in 23:5, as Yahweh places a divine word in Balaam's mouth. When Balaam returns to Balak and finds him standing with his princes by the burnt offering, Balak asks him directly, *What did Yahweh say?* Perhaps Balak was accustomed to hearing the name Yahweh by this time so that he used it here.

18–19a *Rise (qûm)* cannot simply be a call for Balak physically to stand up in Yahweh's presence, since, according to v. 17, he was already *standing beside his whole burnt offering.* More likely, the imperative is

29. See 1 Sam. 14:16; 2 Sam. 18:25, 27; 2 K. 9:17; Isa. 52:8; BDB, p. 859.
30. E.g., Dillmann, p. 152; Binns, p. 163; Noordtzij, p. 219.
31. See Keil, p. 182.
32. See Gray, p. 350.

simply a call to attention, equivalent, as Snaith says, to the German *Achtung!* (see the parallel in Isa. 32:9, "rise . . . hear . . . give ear").[33] Beyond this, it may be a call for Balak to allow his thoughts to be elevated to a higher spiritual reality in order to hear the word of Almighty Yahweh. Literarily, the word *qûm,* "to rise, stand," frames vv. 18b–19.[34]

God is not a human that he should fail (lōʾ ʾîš ʾēl wîḵazzēḇ). The first part of the line establishes a basic tenet of Hebrew thought: God and humankind are not the same. The assertion is even more vivid than that: God is not to be confused with a creature. The word used here is *ʾîš,* which does not generally mean humankind, but a single example of it, a man (even a male). God is definitely not a man. He is the Creator, not a creature. Of the many predications that could have been chosen here, *that he should fail* points to a very basic distinction between the Creator and a creature. Although the translation *lie* is common, the context shows that the primary thought is not that God does not utter untruths (although that is true), but that his purposes are utterly true and reliable, and that his nature does not disappoint or fail, as is the case with human creatures.[35]

This meaning is further illustrated by the parallel line *nor of the human kind that he should change his mind (ûḇen-ʾāḏām wᵉyiṯneḥām).* The words *human kind* are equivalent to "the son of man(kind)," mean "mere mortal" here,[36] and generalize on the term *human* in the first line. God is not a creature; furthermore, he is not even of the creature kind.

that he should change his mind. The basic meaning of the root *nḥm* appears to be "to change the mind, be sorry for." The Hithpael may be taken here as reflexive, "to change one's own mind."[37] It is well known

33. See Snaith, p. 178.

34. The last word of v. 19 is *yᵉqîmennâ,* "he will bring it to stand (or establish it)."

35. See Isa. 58:11, where *kizzēḇ* is used of a spring of water failing. A similar contrast between the Creator and the creature is found, e.g., in Isa. 40:6–8; Ps. 103:15–18.

36. BDB, p. 9. The terms *ʾîš* and *ben-ʾāḏām* are parallel elsewhere, e.g., in 2 Sam. 7:14; Jer. 49:18, 33; 50:40; 51:43; Ps. 80:18 (Eng. 17); Job 35:8 (cf. *ʾĕnôš* and *ben-ʾāḏām* in Ps. 8:5 [Eng. 4]).

37. Snaith, p. 179; the older view of D. Winton Thomas ("A Note on the Hebrew Root *nḥm,*" *ExpTim* 44 [1932–33] 191–92) and esp. N. Snaith ("The Meaning of 'The Paraclete,' " *ExpTim* 57 [1945–46] 47–50) must be modified in many points by the antietymologizing comments of J. Barr (*The Semantics of Biblical Language* [London: Oxford Univ. Press, 1961], pp. 116–17), but may still be used with caution; cf. also M. Wilson, *TWOT,* II:570b–71a; *HALAT,* pp. 650–51a.

that in some passages God repents or changes his mind (e.g., Gen. 6:6), but one must remember that all such language about God is anthropopathic and thus only an analogy. Many of these so-called changes of mind are in response to a change in human behavior (e.g., Jer. 18:8; 26:3), or in response to intercession (e.g., Exod. 32:14; Amos 7:3, 6). Although in many places Scripture asserts God's changelessness (e.g., 1 Sam. 15:29 [paraphrasing the present verse]; Mal. 3:6; Rom. 11:29; Jas. 1:17), one must be careful to read in these an invariability in purpose rather than a modern, pseudoscientific kind of unapproachable immutability, which in the end denies God any real relationship with his creation. It is important for a biblical doctrine of God's constancy that both these kinds of affirmations be held simultaneously. Although God's larger purposes do not change, as a Being in relationship his ways of dealing with others in that relationship will vary in specific cases. People are unreliable and fickle; Yahweh is neither.

19b–20 These verses explain v. 19a in greater depth: what Yahweh has said will be performed without fail, and what Yahweh has said is that Israel is blessed (see 23:7–10). This theological picture, of course, would contradict Balak's picture of God. His whole motive in moving the site of the second oracle was to force God to change his blessing into a curse. Balaam thus rebukes Balak for his idea of God, and in essence tells him that his plan is a failure now. No human — seer or otherwise — can contradict the utterance of the revealed will of Yahweh.

I have received instruction to bless; since he has blessed, I cannot revoke it. Balaam acknowledges that he cannot overrule Yahweh.

21a One may legitimately take the terms *trouble . . . difficulty ('āwen . . . 'āmāl)* in either the physical sense or in an ethical and spiritual sense.[38] In the first case, Balaam is saying that no physical or political problems are found in Jacob/Israel that would lead to cursing; in the second case, that the Israelites have no moral failings that would lead to cursing. Most scholars follow the translation adopted here.[39] The most interesting thing about either affirmation is its relationship to the wilderness wandering tradition in chs. 11–19, where Israel shows forth plenty of both kinds of problems.[40]

38. For the physical sense see, e.g., RSV, NIV. For the ethical and spiritual sense see, e.g., AV "iniquity" and "perverseness" respectively; NEB "iniquity" and "mischief"; see also RV, NKJV, Keil, p. 183.

39. So also Moffatt, NASB, NJPS, GNB, Dillmann, p. 153; Gray, p. 353; McNeile, p. 134; Binns, p. 164; Noordtzij, pp. 221–22.

40. Cf. Sturdy, p. 172.

Two comments should be made about this relationship. First, the point of view of chs. 11–19 is internal to Israel, whereas chs. 22–24 are clearly external, from the point of view of a foreign people and a foreign seer. It is highly unlikely that any Israelite even knew that this drama was being played out at the time. Although Israel had rebelled against God, and was in fact under the sentence of death, Israel was still, in spite of it all, Yahweh's chosen people. That God was neither unreliable nor fickle applied here as well. Second, this more positive point of view of Israel reflects the fact that a whole new day was dawning. The old generation would soon be dead (see the new census in ch. 26). Then Yahweh's plan for his people would again go forward.

21b The positive side of the reason why Yahweh had decided to bless Israel (the negative side of which is in v. 21a) is that God is present in the midst of his people. *rejoicing for a king (tᵉrûʿaṯ meleḵ).* The word *tᵉrûʿâ* can refer to a trumpet blast to call the people to war (e.g., Josh. 6:5; 2 Chr. 13:12), or to begin their march (Num. 10:5–6; 31:6), or to call them to ritual occasions (e.g., Yom Kippur, Lev. 25:9). It can also refer to a human shout (of joy) (1 Sam. 4:5–6; 2 Sam. 6:15 [= 1 Chr. 15:28]; 2 Chr. 15:14; Ezra 3:11–13; Job 8:21),[41] and it is probably to the last of these that the present clause refers. This joyful shout is *for a king,* i.e., on account of the fact that Israel's true king is Yahweh (Exod. 15:18; Deut. 33:5; Judg. 8:23; 1 Sam. 8:7; 12:12; Isa. 33:22), and that this divine king is not in a remote palace, but is in their very midst. His presence is, of course, pictured in the setup and arrangement of the tabernacle (Exod. 25–31; 35–40; esp. 25:8) and the Israelite camp around the tabernacle (Num. 2).

22 That King Yahweh is in Israel's midst is reflected in the Exodus from Egypt. *God brings them out (ʾēl môṣîʾām).* God's action is here described by means of a participle in typical hymnic form; the action of God's bringing Israel out from Egypt was not something that was completed historically until the conquest. The hymnic participle, however, describes action as ever in progress — God is always bringing his people out of Egypt; it is always a present reality.

This much of the verse is clear; the second clause, however, is anything but clear. *He has something like the horns of the wild ox (kᵉṯôʿᵃpōṯ rᵉʾēm lî,* lit., "like horns of a wild ox are to him"). Every word needs elucidation.

horns (tôʿᵃpōṯ). This pl. noun occurs only three other times in the OT: 24:8, where, once again, it refers to part of the wild ox; Ps. 95:4, where

41. BDB, pp. 929b–30a.

it refers to tops of mountains; and Job 22:25, where the reference is perhaps to piles of silver.[42] Thus the basic reference may be to the best or top part of something. The versions did not seem to know what to make of the word; LXX reads "like glory" *(hōs doxa),* and Vulg. and Targs. have readings meaning "in strength."

wild ox (rᵉʾēm) is equivalent to Akk. *rîmu* and Ugar. *r'um,* evidently a large, fierce, powerful wild bovine of the species *bos primigenius,* the now-extinct ancestor of modern cattle (cf. Num. 24:8; Deut. 33:17; Isa. 34:11; Job 39:9; Ps. 22:22 [Eng. 21]; 29:6; 92:11 [Eng. 10]). It is probable that the wild ox was already extinct in the Middle Bronze Age, and that the allusions in the Bible are derived from long-transmitted stories about it.[43] In Deut. 33:17 "the horns of the wild ox" *(qarnê rᵉʾēm)* uses the more common term for "horn" *(qeren).* One may probably assume that *tôʿᵃpōṯ rᵉʾēm* is equivalent to *qarnê rᵉʾēm* in Deut. 33:17 and means "horns of a wild ox," but one must still ask the meaning of such a phrase.

In the OT a horn may be a symbol of strength and vitality (Deut. 33:17; 2 Sam. 22:3 [= Ps. 18:3 (Eng. 2)]), might and dignity (1 Sam. 2:1, 10; Lam. 2:17; Ps. 75:11 [Eng. 10]; 89:18, 25 [Eng. 17, 24]; 92:11 [Eng. 10]; 112:9), or even haughtiness (Ps. 75:5–6 [Eng. 4–5]). Ps. 132:17 reads: "I will make a horn to sprout for David" (RSV), i.e., exalt and dignify the Davidic dynasty.[44] The metaphor, then, seems to refer to the might and power of the fabled wild ox.

The final question is, To whom does the word *lô (to him)* refer — to God or to Israel? The Hebrew is ambiguous, and translators and commentators are divided. Albright (and RSV and NIV) referred the horns to Israel: "It is El who brought him from Egypt, while he stormed like a bull."[45] Many others have seen in this second line a description not of the object of the first line (Israel), but rather of the subject: God (as would be more normal). In fact, only here does the oracle refer to Israel by a pl. rather than a sing. pronoun (i.e., *God brings them out ['ēl môṣîʾām]*). This pl. suffix may not be carelessness, or even looseness of expression, but an intentional attempt to distinguish Israel (which could be referred to in either sing. or pl.) from

42. See J. Hartley, *The Book of Job,* NICOT (Grand Rapids: Eerdmans, 1988), p. 332, who translates it "huge piles."

43. See esp. R. K. Harrison, *ISBE,* rev., IV:1061–62.

44. See A. A. Anderson, *Psalms,* 2 vols., NCBC (Grand Rapids: Eerdmans, 1981), 1:885; cf. Dan. 7:7–8, 24, where horns represent kings.

45. Albright, "Oracles," p. 224; cf. 215 nn. 45, 47. Albright was preceded in this identification by Keil, p. 184, and McNeile, p. 134; and followed in it by Noth, p. 187; Budd, p. 255; and Milgrom, *JPST,* p. 200.

God (who could not). The meaning here proposed is: "God brings them out of Egypt with horns (viz., might) like that of the wild ox."[46]

23 A number of scholars have perceived a roughness and lack of connection between v. 23 and the context and have concluded that it, or part of it, is a later gloss on the text.[47] One must, however, attempt to make some sense of the verse whether it it be a gloss or not.

enchantment . . . divination (naḥaš . . . qesem) refer to two methods of seeking the divine will, the first by a general use of omens (e.g., Gen. 44:5, 15), and the second by the drawing of lots, such as arrows (Ezek. 21:26–27 [Eng. 21–22]). Although the terms do not necessarily refer to ways of working evil against someone, they may be.

There are two interpretations of v. 23a, depending upon the translation of the inseparable preposition b^e- on the words *Jacob* and *Israel* *(b^eya'^{a}qōḇ . . . b^eyiśrā'ēl)*. The first takes the preposition in its most common sense of "in" or "among," and interprets the verse to mean that omens and lots are not acceptable or necessary methods of discovering the divine will in Israel. Indeed, both were forbidden early in Israel's history (Exod. 22:17 [Eng. 18]), although they continued to be practiced (e.g., Lev. 19:31; 20:6, 27; Deut. 18:10–11; Isa. 2:6; 3:2; 8:19; 44:25; Hos. 4:12; Mic. 3:6–7; Jer. 27:9; 29:8; Ezek. 13:6–23; Zech. 10:2).[48] The other approach takes the less common meaning of "against" (as in, e.g., Gen. 16:12; Num. 12:8).[49] The meaning would then be that no omen or lot would be able to work any evil against Israel.[50] Since Balak has been seeking to harm Israel by means of a curse, the latter alternative seems preferable.

Whereas v. 23a was negative (as was v. 21a), v. 23b is positive (as was v. 21b). No omens or lots harm Israel because Israel itself is an accomplished act of Yahweh himself *(what has God done!)*.

24 The two terms for lion (*lāḇī'* and *'^{a}rî*) are two of seven He-

46. Cf. NEB. Also following this line are the AV, RV, Moffatt, NASB, GNB, NJPS, NKJV, as well as Gray, pp. 354–55; Binns, pp. 164–65; Noordtzij, p. 222; Snaith, p. 179; and Wenham, pp. 175–76.

47. E.g., see Gray (pp. 355–56) for a summary of the case (see also McNeile, pp. 134–35; Binns, p. 165).

48. So Keil, p. 184; Dillmann, p. 154; Gray, p. 355; McNeile, p. 134; Binns, p. 165; Heinisch, p. 95; also LXX, Vulg., RV, Moffatt, NEB, NJPS.

49. The preposition often has this meaning with verbs (e.g., *rîḇ* b^e-, "to complain against"; *nilḥam* b^e-, "to fight against," etc.); cf. BDB, p. 89a (4a).

50. So Cook, p. 742; Budd, p. 268; Noordtzij, p. 222; Albright, "Oracles," p. 215 n. 49; Noth, p. 187; de Vaulx, p. 280; Wenham, p. 176; also AV, NKJV, RV mg., RSV, NASB, GNB, NEB mg., NIV.

brew words within this general semantic range. The second term is the most common one in the OT (35 times; the related term *'aryēh* is found 42 times. The first term is translated, e.g., by RSV, NEB, and the current translation, as *lioness,* but this is really a conjecture, and there is a related term *lᵉḇiyyā'* (Ezek. 19:2), which may actually mean *lioness.* Botterweck has concluded that *lāḇī'* might indicate the Asiatic lion, but that is based on conjecture.[51] The lion is a symbol of fierceness, strength, and power. It can be used as a symbol of Israel, as here (so also, e.g., Gen. 49:9; Deut. 33:20; Jer. 2:30; 12:8; Mic. 5:7), Israel's enemies (e.g., Isa. 5:29; Jer. 2:14–15; Amos 3:12), or God (e.g., Jer. 49:19; Hos. 5:14; 13:7–8; Amos 1:2), among other referents.[52] This verse simply states that because Israel is both indwelt and empowered by Yahweh, it is invincible; thus, Balak's plan to curse Israel by the name of Yahweh continues to be a failure. For similar images see 24:8–9; Gen. 49:9, 27; Deut. 33:20; Mic. 5:8.

25–26 The prose conclusion to the second oracle functions in the same way that 23:11–12 did. Balak is again angered by Balaam's defiance of his entreaty to curse Israel. *Neither curse nor bless them at all!* i.e., "Shut up!" Balak would prefer silence to the words of blessing. Balaam, once again, reminds Balak that he can speak only what Yahweh commands him to speak (22:18, 38; 23:12).

On the basis of the documentary hypothesis, some scholars have assumed that this verse was the end of the story, and that Balak is here saying good-bye to Balaam.[53] Apart from the theory, there is no reason to assume this meaning for Balak's words. The attempt to wheedle a curse out of Balaam and Yahweh continues in ch. 24.

3. THIRD, FOURTH, AND FINAL ORACLES (23:27–24:25)

a. Third Oracle (23:27–24:13)

27 *And Balak said to Balaam, "Come now, please,*[1] *I will take you to another place, perhaps it will be pleasing in the eyes of God that you should curse them for me from there."*

51. G. J. Botterweck, *TDOT,* I:377; *HALAT,* pp. 491b–92a.

52. Botterweck, *TDOT,* I: 374–88.

53. The E version of the story ends here, followed, after some linking verses, in ch. 24 by the J version. See, e.g., Gray, p. 358; McNeile, p. 135; Noth, p. 187.

1. *Come now, please (lᵉḵâ-nnā')* — this construction consists of the emphatic imperative of the verb *hālaḵ* used as an interjection, "Come now!" (GKC, §105b). To this interjection is added the emphatic particle *nā',* which adds a note of entreaty (GKC, §§105b n. 1; 110d).

28 *And Balak took Balaam to the top of the Peor, which overlooks the face of Jeshimon.*

29 *And Balaam said to Balak, "Build seven altars for me here and furnish seven bulls and seven rams for me here."*

30 *And Balak did as Balaam had said, and offered a bull and a ram on each altar.*

24:1 *When Balaam saw that it was good in Yahweh's eyes to bless Israel, he did not go, as at other times,*[2] *to encounter divinations, but he set his face to the wilderness.*

2 *Then Balaam lifted up his eyes and saw Israel dwelling by its tribes; and the spirit of God came upon him.*

3 *And he lifted up his oracle and said:*

"Utterance of Balaam, son[3] *of Beor,*
and utterance of the[4] *man of opened*[5] *eye —*
4 *Utterance of the hearer of*[6] *El's sayings,*[7]
who sees[8] *a vision of Shaddai;*
falling,[9] *but with uncovered eyes.*

2. The plurality of things is sometimes conveyed by the repetition of key words, as here: *k^e paʿam b^e paʿam,* lit., "as a time in a time," i.e., "as at other times"; see GKC, § 123c.

3. MT *b^enô* looks like the noun *ben* with the third masc. sing. suffix (i.e., "his son"), but the *-ô* is the remnant of the nominative case here; see GKC, §§ 90o; 96 (p. 285). The *Sebir* note reads *bēn.* Albright ("Oracles," p. 216 n. 54) sees this nominative case ending as evidence for an early date for the poem.

4. Albright ("Oracles," p. 216 n. 55) takes the definite article as a demonstrative article, "that man."

5. This translation depends to some extent on Pesh., which translates *š^eṯum* by *[d] gly',* "[which is] open" (so AV, RSV, NASB, NKJV). In contrast, Vulg. translates by *obduratus,* "shut" (Heb. *s^eṯum*) (so RV). Instead of MT *š^eṯum hāʿāyin,* Wellhausen (*Composition des Hexateuch,* p. 351) posited a relative particle *še-* here, well known in other places (e.g., the Song of Deborah), hence "whose eye is perfect" *(še-tāmâ ʿayin).* This reading is supported by LXX *(ho alēthinōs horōn).* Albright ("Balaam," p. 216 n. 56) and *BHS* follow this reading as well, as do NEB, NIV, GNB, and NJPS. Many of the English versions recognize variants in the margin.

6. On the construct passive participle, see GKC, § 116k.

7. Albright ("Balaam," p. 217 n. 59) posited that the clause "knower of Elyon's knowledge" (*yōḏēaʿ daʿaṯ ʿelyôn,* 24:16) ought to be found here as well. *BHS* and many scholars concur. The textual grounds for this addition are very slim (one Kennicott ms.), although it offers good parallelism.

8. According to Driver (*Tenses,* §§ 32–33), the imperfect here suggests a habit; Balaam habitually sees the vision of Shaddai, and whether the text says this is doubtful. It is, therefore, more likely that the imperfect is used in the poetry here in order to bring home the vividness of the act of seeing (i.e., as if it were still going on); cf. Davidson, *Syntax,* § 45 Rem. 2.

9. Albright ("Balaam," p. 217 n. 61) vocalizes *nōp̄ēl* as an intransitive parti-

5 *How good*[10] *are your tents, O Jacob,*
your dwelling places, O Israel.
6 *As wadis stretch themselves out,*
as gardens beside a river,
as aloes Yahweh has planted,
as cedars beside the waters,
7 *water flows from his buckets,*
and his seed in many waters.[11]
So that his kingship[12] *may be higher than Agag,*[13]
and his kingdom exalted.[14]
8 *God brought him out*[15] *of Egypt,*
he has like the horns of the wild ox;[16]
he devours nations, his adversaries,
and he breaks their bones,[17]
and with his arrows he wounds them.

---

ciple (*nap̲îl*) and refers the matter to a trance or lack of consciousness; he translates "in a trance" (p. 224). This position is supported by LXX, *en hypnō,* "in sleep."

10. The interrogative particle *mah* (plus a daghesh forte in the following word, i.e., *mah-ṭṭōḇâ*) introduces an exclamatory sentence, and expresses astonishment or admiration; see GKC, § 148b; Williams, *Syntax,* § 127.

11. LXX reads *exeleusetai anthrōpos ek tou spermatos autou kai kyreiusei ethnōn pollōn,* "a man will issue from his seed and will rule over many nations." This reading is apparently messianic, as also are Pesh. and Targ. (see the commentary below). *BHS* proposes that the text be read: *yizzallû l*^{e}*ʾummîm mēḥêlô ûz*^{e}*rōʿô ḇ*^{e}*ʿammîm,* "they will flow to the nations from his strength and his arm among the peoples."

12. See Albright, "Balaam," p. 218 n. 70.

13. Sam. Pent. and LXX read Gog here. Heb. *ʾ*^{a}*gāg* may remind the poet of *gāg,* "roof," so that the idiom is "higher than the roof."

14. The verb *w*^{e}*ṯinnaśśēʾ* is Hithpael (cf. GKC, § 54c). In verbs that begin with *nun* the Hithpael may either assimilate the infixed *t* or not. *BHS* suggests either *w*^{e}*ṯiṯnaśśēʾ* (an unassimilated Hithpael) or *w*^{e}*ṯinnāśēʾ* (Niphal), presumably with an unchanged meaning.

15. A few Hebrew mss., Pesh., and Targs. read *môṣîʾām* ("brought *them* out"), as in 23:22. Albright ("Balaam," p. 218 n. 72) follows Sam. Pent. and reads *nāḥâ,* "to guide," here. Since the verb *yāṣāʾ* occurs frequently in texts related to the Exodus, while the verb *nāḥâ* does not, Albright accepts the originality of Sam. Pent. as the more difficult (and therefore more likely) reading. Against this reading is the parallel with 23:22 above.

16. For this expression see the commentary above on 23:22.

17. The verb *gērēm* (Piel) occurs only here (unless the MT of Ezek. 23:34 is kept, which is unlikely; cf. G. A. Cooke, *A Critical and Exegetical Commentary on the Book of Ezekiel,* ICC [Edinburgh: T. & T. Clark, 1936], pp. 255–56; J. W. Wevers, *Ezekiel,* NCBC [Grand Rapids: Eerdmans, 1982], p. 138); see also the Qal in Zeph. 3:3. This text is also unsure; see *BHS* and K. Elliger, "Das Ende der

9 *He crouched, he lay down like a lion,*
and like a lioness;
who will rouse him up?
The ones who bless you are blessed,
but the ones who curse you are cursed."[18]

10 *And Balak's anger burned against Balaam, and he clapped his hands together. And Balak said to Balaam, "I summoned you to curse my enemies, and behold, you have done nothing but bless*[19] *them these three times."*

11 *So now, flee to your place! I said that I would surely do you honor, but Yahweh has held you back from honor."*

12 *And Balaam said to Balak, "Did I not also speak to your messengers whom you sent to me, saying,*

13 *'If he should give me his house full of silver and gold, I would not be able to transgress the mouth of Yahweh*[20] *to do good or evil by myself; what Yahweh says, that will I say!' "*

27–30 *Come now please* — on Balak's entreaty to Balaam contained in these words see the note to the translation above. *The top of the Peor, which overlooks the face of the Jeshimon (rō'š happ^{e}'ôr hannišqāp̱ 'al-p^{e}nê hay^{e}šîmōn)* — the major difference between this site and the site of Israel's encampment in 21:20 is the substitution of the words *the Peor* here for *the Pisgah* there. Neither site can be identified with certainty. *The Peor* — "the open place." Peor itself was probably close to Baal-Peor (24:3, 5) and to Beth-Peor. Israel encamped in Beth-Peor (Deut. 3:29; 4:46) and Moses was buried there (34:6).[21] *The Jeshimon* — see the commentary on 21:20. The same general area on the eastern side of the lower Jordan valley is indicated here. A site for *the top of the Peor* in the

---

'Abendwölfe' Zeph. 3,3 Hab 1,8," in *Festschrift Alfred Bertholet zum 80. Geburtstag,* hrsg. W. Baumgartner et al. (Tübingen: Mohr, 1950), pp. 158–75. It is a denominative verb from *gerem,* "bone, self" (Gen. 49:14; 2 K. 9:13; Prov. 17:22; 25:15); in Job 40:18 it parallels *'eṣem,* the common word for "bone" also found in the present verse. The rarity of the verb perhaps caused LXX to use a rare verb of its own, *ekmyelizō,* "to suck marrow from," which also conveys the image of the wild animal.

18. The parallel clauses here *(m^{e}ḇār^{a}ḵeyḵā ḇārēḵ w^{e}'ōr^{e}reyḵā 'ārûr)* begin with a pl. participle and end with a sing. (passive) participle. The pl. participles are each construed with a sing. in order to individualize the whole matter; see also Gen. 27:29; Jer. 22:4; etc. See Davidson, *Syntax,* § 116 Rem. 1.

19. On the use of the infinitive absolute here, see GKC, § 113r.

20. LXX reads *ho theos* here; cf. *BHS.*

21. In later days the site belonged in the territory of Reuben (Josh. 13:20).

northern Abarim range near Pisgah is likely.[22] Although the same general procedure of building seven altars and finding bulls and rams for them is the same here as in vv. 29–30, 23:1–4 and 14–17, there are some specific differences.

24:1–2 At least three major differences in the specific cultic practice are made explicit. First, Balaam did not go off and leave Balak and the princes standing by the sacrifices, but rather stayed with them (24:1). Second, Balaam also did not involve himself in divinations as he had done previously (24:1). Third, the mode of reception was different (*the Spirit of God came upon him;* 24:2). The reader is nowhere told why *Balaam saw that it was good in Yahweh's eyes to bless Israel;* perhaps it was because of his experiences as reported in ch. 23.

In any case, *he did not go, as at other times, to encounter divinations (wᵉlōʾ-hālaḵ kᵉpaʿam bᵉpaʿam liqraʾṯ nᵉḥāšîm).* The meaning of this clause seems to be that Balaam acted contrary to custom here in not engaging in *divinations,* such as casting lots (on this term see above on 23:23). The idiom *as at other times* may mean either "as in the immediately preceding times" (e.g., 1 Sam. 3:10) or "at times in the past," i.e., "customarily" (e.g., 1 Sam. 20:25).[23] The previous two narratives have not said explicitly that Balaam did engage in divination or magical practices, although both these earlier narratives use the verb *to meet* (*qārâ* or *qārāʾ;* 23:3, 15–16), which here is linked with divination.[24] The current verse, then, simply makes explicit what has been implicit previously. If *as at other times* referred only to a general custom, and not the immediately preceding episodes, it is hard to see why the comment should be made here at all.

Instead of engaging in divination, Balaam simply *set his face to the wilderness (wayyāšeṯ ʾel-hammiḏbār pānāyw).* A few scholars have seen this *wilderness* as different from the Jeshimon (23:28),[25] but this is

22. See, e.g., the siting of Beth-Peor (and Baal-Peor) as west-northwest of Heshbon in *Oxford Bible Atlas,* p. 63. For ancient attempts to identify the site, see the citations from Eusebius in Gray, p. 358; and Cook, p. 742.

23. Cf. Gray, p. 359; the idiom is also found in Judg. 16:20; 20:30, 31; see BDB, p. 822a.

24. The procedure of altar-building, etc. finds parallels in extrabiblical divinitory rites, such as the *bit rimki* purification ritual. The verbal forms of *qrh* or *qr'* are likewise found in divinatory contexts. According to M. Moore the altar-building procedure and the use of *qrh/qr'* are evidence of Balaam's role as an exorcist. See Moore, *The Balaam Traditions,* pp. 36–38, 105–6.

25. E.g., Dillmann, p. 156 (cf. Targ.). According to Snaith (p. 180) Rashi

unnecessary. Balaam turned to look toward the west and beheld the children of Israel encamped *by their tribes* (24:2), viz., as set forth in the regulations of ch. 2.

It is important to note that Balaam here received revelation in a way different from ch. 23, where a word was placed in his mouth (vv. 5, 16). Here *the Spirit of God came upon him.* While some scholars have held that this difference and the others noted above indicate different sources for chs. 23 and 24, it is as likely that these differences reflect matters of fact. In the previous two oracles, the focus was on Israel's past election by God, while in the third and fourth oracles the focus is on Israel's future as empowered by God. The different mode of reception may be called for by the fact that Balaam here does not engage in enchantments. It is impossible to know precisely the nature of the experience expressed by the words *the spirit of God came upon him.* All that can be said is that this powerful experience was not unique; it happened several times in the OT (e.g., Num. 11:17; Judg. 14:6; 1 Sam. 10:10; 11:6). From what follows one may conclude that when the spirit of God came upon Balaam it put him into some kind of ecstatic or, at least, visionary state (see, e.g., the descriptions in 24:3–4, 15–16), and that both his oracles in ch. 24 are the results of such a state.

3–4 These verses form the introduction to the oracle. With one exception in the MT,[26] they are identical to vv. 15–16.

He lifted up his oracle. This is the same expression used in 23:7. Three times in vv. 3–4 the word *utterance (n^{e}'um)* occurs. This noun (in the form of a passive participle) is almost always used of Yahweh's words, and is a regular feature of prophetic oracles (e.g., Isa. 14:22; Ezek. 13:6–7; Hos. 2:15, 18, 23 [Eng. 13, 16, 21]; Jon. 2:12; Mic. 4:6). It is used with a human subject only here, in vv. 15–16, and in 1 Sam. 23:1; Prov. 30:1 (Ps. 36:2 [Eng. 1] is textually difficult). The formula is quite uncommon at the beginning of an oracle (cf. 2 Sam. 23:1; Isa. 1:24; Ps. 110:1); it is usually a medial (e.g., Isa. 49:18; Amos 3:10) or concluding (e.g., Isa. 54:17; Amos 2:11; 4:3) formula. It is possible that it formed a stock idiom in

---

also held that the wilderness meant the wilderness east of Moab whence Israel had come. Balaam was looking back toward the golden calf for the inspiration for his oracles. This comment shows how much many commentators are determined to read into the narratives. Gray (p. 359) mentions the possibility that the wilderness here is that to the east in the separate document J, but in the present harmonized documents, the wilderness is the Jeshimon.

26. I.e., the occurrence of the clause "and knower of Elyon's knowledge" *(w^{e}yōḏēaʿ daʿaṯ ʿelyôn)* in v. 16; see n. 6 on the translation above.

oracular speech. Since the Spirit of God has come upon Balaam it is truly God's utterance (as in the overwhelming number of usages of *n*ᵉ*'um*).

the man of opened eye (haggeḇer šᵉṯum hā'āyin). If this translation is correct — and it is a conjecture — then the prophet is claiming that his inner "eye" of perception has been opened by God's spirit. The *open eye* is explained by other perceptual metaphors; Balaam hears what El has given him to hear (i.e., his sayings) and sees what Shaddai has given him to see (and, if *knower of Elyon's knowledge* does belong here [v. 16], then he knows what Elyon has given him to know); i.e., Balaam's inner perception has been tuned to understand and communicate what Yahweh wants.[27]

The divine names El and Shaddai are archaic. The former is the generic Semitic name for God, while the second is of uncertain meaning.[28] The common English translation "the Almighty" comes from LXX *(ho pantokratōr)* and Vulg. *(omnipotens).* Scholars do not agree on the original meaning of the name, and, in a sense, it does not matter, for in Israel it became simply an alternate designation for Yahweh. The three divine names found in vv. 2 and 4 are *'ᵉlōhîm* (v. 2), *'el,* and *šadday* (v. 4). In the Deir 'Allā Balaam text, Balaam receives a night-vision that is described as "like an oracle of El" (I:2). The vision is mediated to him by "the gods" (*'lhn;* I:1, 5). I:5–6 reads (in part): "The gods *('lhn)* gathered together, the *Šaddayin (šdyn)* took their places in the assembly."[29] Hackett has concluded that the *Šaddayin* are the "gods" *('lhn)* in El's council.[30]

Hackett goes on to argue that, since *Šadday* is a title given to El in the Old Testament (e.g., Gen. 17:1; 28:3; 35:11; Exod. 6:3; Ezek. 10:5), and since the *Šaddayin* are the gods met together in El's council, perhaps the title *Šadday* is applied to El in the Bible in his role as head of the divine council.[31] There are adequate examples of a god whose name in the plural signifies a

27. Noordtzij (p. 225) seems to take these genitives to mean that, e.g., Balaam sees what the Almighty (i.e., Shaddai) sees, so that in his ecstasy he perceives as God does. This interpretation seems to go beyond the evidence. Balaam all along has only claimed to say what God has given him to say. The present claim is the same although put in a different idiom because of the different mode of revelation.

28. For a discussion of the original meaning of *šadday,* see, e.g., BDB, pp. 994b–95a; KB, p. 950a; V. Hamilton, *TWOT,* II:907; see also W. F. Albright, "The Names Shaddai and Abram," *JBL* 54 (1935) 173–93; M. Walker, "A New Interpretation of the Divine Name 'Shaddai,'" *ZAW* 72 (1960) 64–66; Hackett, *The Balaam Text,* pp. 85–89.

29. J. Hackett, *The Balaam Text,* p. 29.

30. Ibid., p. 86.

31. Ibid., p. 87.

group of gods. At Ugarit, e.g., the gods in El's assembly are simply called by the plural *'lm.* In Ps. 82:1 the term *'^elōhîm* is used as El's (= Yahweh's) council. Hackett concludes:

> Since El and *Šadday* can be used to refer to the same deity in the Hebrew Bible, and since we now have a text where *šdyn* and *'lhn* are used interchangeably when referring to "the gods" in the council of El, it is reasonable to suggest that *Šadday* was the epithet applied to El as head of the council in the region where the gods in that council were known as *šdyn.*[32]

The divine names used in this passage are the very ones attested in an extrabiblical Balaam story. This cannot be an accident, although no direct literary dependence of the biblical story on the Deir ʿAllā text is suggested.

falling, but with uncovered eyes (nōp̄ēl ûg^elûy ʿênāyim). Most interpreters have concluded either that Balaam fell into some kind of ecstatic state (induced by meditation or other means), or that he fell as a result of the spirit's coming upon him in power (cf. Saul in 1 Sam. 19:24).[33] It is impossible to judge which of these applies here, but it is clear that in this "fallen" state Balaam's eye of perception was "uncovered" by God.[34] The word *uncover (gālâ)* is used of divine revelation.[35]

5–7a These verses form an aside to Israel. V. 5 simply states that Israel's tents or dwellings (symbolic of their dwellings in the land of promise) are (will be) good and appropriate. V. 6 consists of a fourfold agricultural metaphor, which must be understood as poetry, not botany. V. 7a concludes the agricultural metaphor begun in v. 6. In v. 7b the image changes from luxuriance and abundance to kingship and power.

6 *As wadis stretch themselves out (kin^eḥālîm niṭṭāyû).* Some scholars have proposed that, instead of *wadis (n^eḥālîm),* "palm trees" (from a root found in Arabic as *naḥîlun*) be read. These scholars claim that the whole verse deals with trees (since trees are found in an oriental garden).[36] But, as Gray pointed out, the comparison in v. 6a is not between

32. Ibid. On Ps. 82:1, see, e.g., A. A. Anderson, *Psalms 73–150,* NCBC (Grand Rapids: Eerdmans, 1972), p. 593; M. Tate, *Psalms 51–100,* WBC (Waco, Tex.: Word, 1990), pp. 329, 334–35, 340–41.

33. For the former see, e.g., McNeile, p. 137; Noth, p. 190; Budd, p. 269. For the latter see, e.g., Dillmann, p. 157; Keil, p. 187; Cook, pp. 743–44.

34. Vulg. makes this clear in its translation: "he fell and thereby his eyes were opened" *(cadit, et sic aperiuntur oculi).*

35. Thus LXX reads *apokekalymmenoi,* from *apokalyptō,* "to reveal."

36. So Snaith, p. 181; NEB, NJPS.

trees at all but between different kinds of land (wadi/garden), so that the emendation is unnecessary.[37] The comparison between a well-watered garden (cf. Isa. 58:11) and a verdant wadi is apt here. The point of the comparison is the luxuriance of both as analogies to the great growth of Israel in its dwelling place in Canaan.

as aloes Yahweh has planted (ka'ᵃhālîm nāṭaʿ YHWH). To the comparison between tracts of land in v. 6a is added a further comparison between trees in v. 6b. The exact species of the tree named here is unknown (aloe or lign-aloe has become traditional), but most have taken it to be either the eaglewood *(Aquillaria agallocha)* or the sandalwood *(Santalum album)* trees,[38] which were imported from Southeast Asia (cf. Prov. 7:17; Cant. 4:14). Because these trees are not native to Israel, some scholars have concluded that the text is corrupt and have suggested emendations.[39]

as cedars beside the waters (kaʿᵃrāzîm ʿᵃlê māyim). T. K. Cheyne noted that, since cedars do not grow by rivers but in the mountains, and since Ps. 104:16 speaks of Yahweh's planting *(nāṭaʿ)* them, the tree names in these two poetic lines should be reversed.[40] But rearrangement and modification of a poetic text are not justified on the supposed grounds that the poetry is not scientifically accurate. Israel is here compared to fragrant, exotic, and strong trees. Why should the image not be kept? That cedars do not grow by rivers misses the poetic metaphor as well. In the second line of each couplet in the verse water is mentioned as an image of a life source. If for no other reason than this, the cedar is placed by the water in v. 6b. The river/waters here enhance the image of luxuriance. If a cedar is a grand and mighty tree without an abundant life source (water), how much stronger will it be with that life source added?[41]

7 This verse is very difficult in the MT. The first part of the verse deals with Yahweh's blessings for Israel, while the second part deals with the power of Israel as it faces its enemies in and around Canaan.

37. See Gray, pp. 362–63.

38. On the former see Snaith, p. 181; R. K. Harrison, *ISBE,* rev., I:99. On the latter see J. Trever, *IDB,* I:88.

39. T. K. Cheyne ("Some Critical Difficulties in the Chapters on Balaam," *ExpTim* 10 [1898–99] 401) suggested "poplars" (ʿᵃ*rāḇîm;* Isa. 44:4; Ps. 137:2; the emendation is pure conjecture); and Dillmann (p. 157) "terebinths" or "palms" (*'êlîm;* Gen. 14:6; Exod. 15:27).

40. Cheyne, "Difficulties," p. 401; followed, e.g., by Gray, p. 363; Albright, "Balaam," p. 217 n. 65; Binns, p. 164; McNeile, p. 137.

41. See Wenham, p. 177.

7a The obscurity of the first couplet has led to many emendations and conjectures. Perhaps the oldest interpretation is the LXX, which made the whole verse messianic.[42] The most radical modern proposal is that of Cheyne, which was developed by Gray, and followed, at least in part, by *BHS.*[43] Although the MT is difficult and obscure (and possibly corrupt), the focus here will be on its explanation rather than resorting to textual conjecture.

Water flows from his buckets (yizzal-mayim middālyāw). The meaning seems to be that water overflows from two irrigation buckets (*dālyāw* is dual), perhaps conceived of as placed on opposite ends of a carrying pole. In the previous agricultural image, water was symbolic of the abundance of life, and it makes sense to keep the same imagery here.

and his seed in many waters (wᵉzarʿô bᵉmayim rabbîm). The line has no verb; the verb from the first line ("to flow," *yizzal*) should probably be understood as applying to the second line as well. It is also possible that the verb "to be" could be implied. As was said of the water source for

42. LXX *exeleusetai anthrōpos ek tou spermatos autou, kai kyrieusei ethnōn pollōn, kai hypsōthēsetai ē Gōg basileia autou, kai auxēthēsetai hē basileia autou,* "A man shall issue from his seed and he shall have dominion over many nations; and he shall be higher than the kingdom of Gog and his kingdom shall be exalted." It is probable that the LXX of Numbers was completed no later than the end of the 2nd cent. B.C. (e.g., B. J. Roberts, *The Old Testament Text and Versions* [Cardiff: Univ. of Wales, 1951], pp. 115–16). From the beginning of the 2nd cent., at least, there was intense messianic speculation. Many apocalyptic works were published at this time (see J. H. Charlesworth, ed., *The Old Testament Pseudepigrapha: Vol. 1, Apocalyptic Literature and Testaments* [Garden City, N.Y.: Doubleday, 1983], esp. pp. xxix–xxxiv, 3–765). On messianism in the 2nd/1st cents. B.C., see, e.g., E. Rivkin, *IDBSup,* 588–91; M. de Jonge and A. S. van der Woude, *TDNT,* IX:509–27. On the LXX translation, see Gray, pp. 363–66.

43. Cheyne ("Difficulties," p. 401) conjectures the reading *yirgᵉzû lᵉʾummîm mēḥêlô/ûzᵉrōʿô ḇᵉʿammîm rabbîm,* "Peoples shall tremble at his might, and his arm shall be on many peoples" (developed by Gray, p. 363; and followed, at least in part, by Binns, p. 169, and Noordtzij, p. 227). To start with the second line first, there is no particular difficulty in repointing the consonants *zrʿw* from *zarʿô* ("his seed") to *zᵉrōʿô* ("his arm"). It is more problematic to conclude that an *ʿayin* has dropped out of the text so that MT *bᵉmayim* ("in/by waters") be read *bᵉʿammîm* ("on peoples"). As expansive as the LXX is, however, it does not give support to such an emendation (it reads *ethnōn,* "nations"). The problem is that once one has concluded that this is the correct reading in the second half of the verse, one is forced to change the first half of the verse radically. These adjustments are made by conjecture and carry much less conviction. For an argument in favor of this emendation, see Gray, p. 363.

the gardens and cedars in v. 6b, so Israel will have a life source that brings great abundance to it in its good future in the land of promise. The *seed* is Israel's proliferating population, which will be nourished and nurtured by *many waters* (the life and blessing of Yahweh).[44]

7b *So that his kingship may be higher than Agag (w^e^yārōm mē'^a^g̱ag̱ malkô).* The verb "to be high" *(yārōm)* is jussive here; thus some commentators have taken it as a wish that the human kingship of Israel, promised to the people, e.g., in Gen. 17:6, 16; 35:11, be "higher" (better, more exalted) than Agag's. Most commentators and English translations, however, have taken the verb as a simple imperfect that states the future fact of such a kingship.[45] The jussive suggests the result of the blessing of God on Israel as explained in vv. 6–7a. Because Israel is firmly connected to God as a life source, its human kingship may ("will be able to") be more exalted than Agag's.

Agag. The presence of this personal name has been the occasion of great difficulty for commentators and translators. The long-standing nature of the difficulty is witnessed by the LXX and Sam. Pent., which read *Gog* (cf. Ezek. 38–39). Modern commentators have expressed various views. First, some see in this reference the name of the Amalekite king defeated by Saul in 1 Sam. 15. Of these, certain scholars see it as a specific prediction of that event, hence the defeat of Israel's oldest enemy (Exod. 17:14–16).[46] Second, others hold that this passage (or at least this verse) must date within memory of that event.[47] Third, still other scholars deny that Agag is a personal name here, and take it as an Amalekite dynastic name, or as a title, like "pharaoh" in Egypt.[48] Fourth, a few scholars have simply found the text to be corrupt and either left it at that or, like the LXX before them, posited other names to insert.[49]

44. So Keil, p. 189; Wenham, p. 177; cf. Sturdy, p. 176.

45. Two commentators who take the clause to express a wish are Keil (p. 189) and McNeile (p. 138); see also BDB, p. 926b. Commentators and translators who take the clause as expressing a future fact are, e.g., Gray, p. 366; Budd, p. 252; Milgrom, *JPST,* p. 204; Allen, *EBC,* p. 906; Harrison, pp. 316, 318–19; AV; RV; Moffatt (although Moffatt follows Sam. Pent. and LXX in reading Gog for Agag); RSV; NEB; NASB; NIV; NJPS; NKJV.

46. So, apparently, Wenham, pp. 177–78.

47. So Noth, p. 191; Sturdy, p. 176.

48. So Keil, p. 189; Cook, p. 744; S. Cox, *Balaam: An Exposition and Study* (London: Kegan Paul, Trench, 1884), p. 111; Noordtzij, p. 228.

49. So Gray, p. 366; Cheyne ("Difficulties," p. 401) proposes Og.

All these views have problems. The first makes this biblical prediction more specific than most are, including the future-oriented prophecies of 24:15–24. The second could be extended logically to conclude that there is no such thing as predictive prophecy (in contradiction to the evidence of many OT texts). The third is no more than a guess, because no evidence is cited to show that Agag and Pharaoh are comparable titles. The fourth view is simply descriptive of the state of the text, and makes little attempt at interpretation at all. It is little wonder, then, that many commentators have simply listed the options.[50]

If one were forced to choose from among the present options, one might choose the third, if provable, and failing that, simply say that, in the light of the patently corrupt nature of the present text, it might not be surprising had the name Agag been placed in the text (perhaps a gloss) when Saul's victory over the Amalekites was a fresh memory and taken to be a fulfillment of the promises given to Israel through Balaam, especially concerning the victory over the Amalekites (24:20), who were Israel's first attackers (Exod. 17:14–16). Admittedly, however, any of these options (or another) could be correct.

and his kingdom shall be exalted. The last line of the verse is the simplest. It is a general parallel to the previous line, stating that Israel's kingship will be an important one.

8 The first two lines are very similar to 23:22.[51] The present power of Israel grows out of the power of the God who brought it up from Egypt in the immediate past. God's power is not, however, confined to past or present, but extends into the future (the tense of the three verbs in this verse is imperfect — incomplete, ongoing action).

he devours nations, his adversaries (yōʾkal gôyim ṣārāyw). The words *nations* and *his adversaries* are in apposition. The image of eating will eventually lead to the image of a lion (v. 9); even now that wild animal seems to be in view. Not only does God through his people Israel devour "the flesh" of the adversary nations, but *breaks their bones,* i.e., crunches them up with his teeth.

Albright at first ("Balaam," p. 218 n. 69) kept MT and evidently took it as a title, related to the word for "roof," hence a pun of sorts. Later on, however, he preferred to read Gog with the Greek versions (*Yahweh and the Gods of Canaan,* p. 16 n. 40).

50. E.g., Binns, p. 169; Budd, p. 269.

51. See the commentary above on 23:22. The only difference is that the present text reads *môṣîʾô,* "he brought him out," where 23:22 reads *môṣîʾām,* "he brought them out"; cf. *BHS* at both verses.

and with his arrows he wounds them (wᵉḥiṣṣāyw yimḥāṣ). This is a very difficult clause (lit.: "and his arrows, he wounds"). The verb *māḥaṣ* is a fairly common verb meaning "to smite, shatter, wound."[52] Although the syntax of the two previous lines might lead one to expect that *his arrows* would be the direct object of the verb, it cannot be so unless the *his* refers to someone other than Israel, perhaps a hunter ("he [Israel] shatters his [a hunter's] arrows").[53] But this interpretation does not fit the text as it stands, for the only possible antecedents are Israel and Yahweh. If one is to keep the MT, one must see *his arrows* as an accusative of means or instrument, i.e., "with his arrows."[54] The line may be taken, as above, *he wounds them,* the pronominal suffix being shared with the noun *and their bones* in the previous line *(wᵉʿaṣmōṯêhem).* Several scholars have preferred to follow the Pesh., which read "(and he will shatter) his loins" *(waḥᵃlāṣāyw),* and long ago Dillmann proposed "(and he will shatter) his adversaries" *(wᵉlōḥᵃṣāyw).*[56] Neither emendation is necessary, but both offer a little improvement with the parallelism, in the first case with the line just previous *(and he breaks their bones),* in the second case with *he devours nations, his adversaries* two lines previous.[56] Virtually all major modern English translations keep the MT with all its difficulties.

9 As has been said, all the images of devouring and bone crunching are a propos of a wild animal, and this becomes obvious in v. 9a, where the image of a lion is repeated from 23:24 (although the content of the saying is different here). V. 9a reflects the Blessing of Jacob in Gen. 49:9b with only two variants.[57] In the days that follow the conquest of

52. See BDB, p. 563b. The cognate noun *maḥaṣ* means "a wound" in Isa. 30:26; cf. Paterson, p. 56.

53. So Noth (p. 191), although he dismisses this phrase from the text as a later addition without further comment.

54. See GKC, §§ 118m-r; Davidson, *Syntax,* §§ 70, 71 Rem. 2.

55. For the former see Snaith, p. 181; Binns, p. 170; NEB. For the latter see Dillmann, p. 159.

56. See Gray (p. 366) for more detailed comment.

57. Gen. 49:9b reads *rāḇaṣ* where the present text reads *šāḵaḇ* and *'aryēh* for *'ᵃrî* (Sam. Pent. reads *'ryh* in both places). H. M. Orlinksy ("RĀḆAṢ for ŠĀḴAḆ in Num. 24:9," *JQR* 35 [1944–45] 173–77) argued that *rāḇaṣ* was original here in Num. 24 as well as in Gen. 49; *rāḇaṣ* is used of animals (and symbolically of humans) lying down, while *šāḵaḇ* is used only of humans. LXX apparently read *rāḇaṣ,* since it has *anapauō* here, and elsewhere this verb translates *rāḇaṣ*. If, indeed, *šāḵaḇ* is original to this text, it must mean that the author was thinking not of a lion but of the humans in Israel symbolized by the lion.

Canaan, Israel, in its own land, will be like a lion/lioness resting in its den. The nations round about will rouse it at their own peril.

The ones who bless you are blessed, but the ones who curse you are cursed. This may be a stock formula (Gen. 27:29 has the same words in reverse order). If one believes that these oracles passed through Israelite hands before being incorporated into the text of Numbers (which is virtually certain), then, whatever Balaam may have meant, the Israelite author will have had in mind a promise such as that found in Gen. 12:3: "I will bless those who bless you, and the one who curses you, that one will I curse, and in you all the families of the earth will be blessed." In other words, the way in which a foreign nation deals with Israel is the ground of that nation's own weal or woe in the world.

10–13 Balak still does not understand the import of what Balaam has said. He thinks that he has paid to get a competent diviner to curse his enemies in the name of their own god. From his perspective Balaam has broken their contract. This diviner had taken on a responsibility and been unable or unwilling to carry it out.

10–11 *Balak's anger burned (wayyiḥar-'aḇ)* — the same description is given to God's anger (22:22) and Balaam's (22:27). Now all the major characters have been angry. On this idiom, see above on 22:22, 27. *Balak clapped his hands together* — this gesture expresses emotion. In the present context it expresses Balak's anger and disgust at the apparent incompetence and unethical practice of this seer (see this same gesture in Job 27:23; Lam. 2:15).[58] So he sends Balaam home (cf. Amos 7:12). He shows that he is ignorant of the whole matter when he says, with no little irony: *I said that I would surely do you honor* — i.e., pay Balaam a large fee (an honorarium) — *but Yahweh has held you back from honor* — i.e., "This god in whose name you claim to speak has cost you your fee!" This statement is intended to reflect, once again, on Balaam's competence as one whose job it was to bend the divine will to human will. But instead it reflects on Balak's different frame of reference.

58. *HALAT,* p. 722; on Job 27:23, see, e.g., N. Habel, *The Book of Job: A Commentary,* OTL (Philadelphia: Westminster, 1985), p. 361; J. Hartley, *The Book of Job,* NICOT (Grand Rapids: Eerdmans, 1988), p. 361; on Lam. 2:15, see, e.g., T. J. Meek, "Lamentations: Introduction and Exegesis," in *IB* (New York: Abingdon, 1956), VI:20.

12–13 Balaam's only response is to repeat what he had already said to Balak's princes back in Mesopotamia: no amount of money would make Balaam able to transgress Yahweh's word to speak either good or evil on his own. Balaam's original reply in 22:18 was that he could say nothing either "small or great." The moral nature of his reply here *(good or evil)* makes a reply to Balak's charge of incompetence and unethical practice. Whatever Balak's view of the appropriateness (i.e., *good*) of what he had said, Balaam claimed to say only what Yahweh had instructed him to say. Just as God's people Israel was invincible and irresistible, so neither Balak nor Balaam could overcome the power of Israel's God.

b. Fourth Oracle (24:14–19)

14 *"And now, behold, I am going to my people. Come, I will counsel you on that which this people will do to your people in the latter days."*

15 *And he took up his oracle and said:*

"Utterance of Balaam, son of Beor,
and utterance of the man of opened eye —
16 *Utterance of the hearer of El's saying,*
and knower of Elyon's knowledge;
who sees a vision of Shaddai,
falling, but with uncovered eyes.[1]
17 *I see him,*[2] *but not now,*
I behold him,[3] *but not nearby.*
A star[4] *will go out*[5] *from Jacob,*
a scepter[6] *will rise up from Israel;*

1. For vv. 15–16, see the commentary above on vv. 3–4.

2. LXX reads *deixō autō,* "I show him." Driver (*Tenses,* § 27) refers the verb to a single action in the present time, but expressed in the imperfect for emphasis.

3. LXX reads *makarizō,* "I pronounce happy."

4. Targs. read *mlk',* "the king," here.

5. LXX reads *anatelei,* "he will make (it) rise." In Hebrew the perfect tense sometimes deals with future actions that are considered as good as done. This so-called prophetic perfect is found here. The verbs that continue the thought are in the perfect consecutive and clearly refer to future events; cf. Davidson, *Syntax,* § 51 Rem. 2; Driver, *Tenses,* § 14 (a).

6. LXX reads *anthrōpos,* "human," for Heb. *šēḇet,* "staff," "scepter." Pesh. reads *ryš',* "the ruler," and Targs. *mšyḥ',* "the messiah."

and it will pierce the temples[7] *of Moab,*
and the crown of the head of[8] *all the sons of Sheth.*[9]
18 *And Edom will be a possession,*
and Seir, his enemies, will be a possession;[10]
and Israel does mightily.[11]
19 *Let dominion be exercised from Jacob,*[12]
he will destroy the remnant from the city."[13]

The fourth oracle (24:14–19), as well as the brief series of three oracles that follow (24:20–25), are difficult textually, hermeneutically, and theologically. On the one hand, they climax the whole series (they arise from the mention of a "king" in 24:7); on the other hand, these oracles are different from what has gone before in that they are wholly concerned with the future. Such predictive passages are usually difficult for the following reasons: (1) They may use specific terms, names, etc., that are not explained in the text itself and that could have more than one

7. According to Albright ("Oracles," p. 220 n. 86), the word *pa'ᵉṯê* means "temples, sides of the head," although it could also mean "frontiers," as in Ugar. *pi'âtu madbari,* "edges of the desert" (Keret A, 105). LXX reads *tous archēgous,* "the princes"; so also Pesh., Targs., Vulg.

8. Most scholars emend the so-called Pilpel verb *wᵉqarqar* ("to tear down," BDB, p. 326a) to *wᵉqoḏqōḏ* ("the crown of the head") with Sam. Pent. and the parallel passage in Jer. 48:45.

9. Albright ("Oracles," p. 220 n. 89) identifies *št* as the Šutu people of a 20th–19th-cent. B.C. Egyptian execration text. According to this text, the Šutu people were nomads in Palestine. This identification would be a strong attestation of the antiquity of the present poetic line.

10. Albright ("Oracles," p. 221 n. 92) points the consonants *yrš* (MT *yᵉrēšâ*) as a Qal passive participle *yārûš.* His translation is, as is common for the verb *yāraš,* "to dispossess": "and Edom shall be dispossessed, and dispossessed shall be Seir" (p. 225).

11. Albright ("Oracles," p. 221) proposed that v. 19a ("let dominion . . . Jacob") be inserted before v. 18b. This rearrangement seems unnecessary, since sense can be made of the text without it.

12. Albright ("Oracles," p. 221 n. 93) redivides *yrd my'qb* as *yrd-m* (enclitic *mem*) *y'qb,* inserts the word *'ybw* ("his foes") from v. 18b, where it does not fit very well (cf. *BHS*), and translates: "Jacob shall rule over his foes" (p. 225). It is possible that Israel (v. 18b) should be taken as the subject here and the verb be pointed *yirdeh,* "he will exercise dominion from Jacob" (see *BHS*).

13. For *'îr,* "city," some scholars read Ar, as mentioned above in 21:28. Albright moves the line "he will destroy the remnant from the city" to v. 17b after "all the sons of Sheth" ("Oracles," p. 220 n. 91); cf. *BHS.*

application. This usage tends to give these passages an opaque (or, at best, ambiguous) quality (cf. also Ezek. 38–39; Dan. 10–12; etc.). (2) The ambiguity that already inheres in this kind of text is heightened here by the fact that the MT is corrupt in spots, and that this corruption is not eased by recourse to the ancient versions, which mostly either interpret the text periphrastically or simply translate the MT, difficulties and all. (3) Also contributing to the difficulty is what later biblical texts and interpreters in church and synagogue have drawn from these oracles. How much of their interpretation can be read, even in an incipient form, back into the Balaam oracles themselves? The modern interpreter's own approach to such questions as the reality of biblical prediction will also be a factor in how one handles these verses.

The point of view taken here is that, while Balaam's predictions undoubtedly had some near-term fulfillment(s), and, while it may be possible to isolate one or more of these, such things are neither easy nor sure. This lack of certainty over the author's exact meaning ought to keep the interpreter from making definitive pronouncements on the specific referent of the text. Such texts as the present one often point as much to a *type* of fulfillment, a *kind* of action, as to a definite historical meaning that can be said to fulfill them. Taken within the whole of biblical theology, a fuller (not a different) meaning may become clearer as these texts are read and interpreted in the light of further biblical revelation. One must first suggest what the MT, as far as this is intelligible, meant, then recognize that these oracles will have a fuller meaning as they are placed in their wider biblical context. Although a near-term historical meaning may be primary, at some point the fuller meaning may be ultimate. An axiom of interpretation in predictive texts is that the specification of the prediction is in the statement(s) of fulfillment rather than in the prediction itself.[14]

14 Balaam tells Balak that he is going away as ordered (v. 11). Balak had wanted Moab's relationship with Israel to be governed by his own will as exercised over Israel's God through Balaam. But such has proved impossible because Balaam's God cannot be controlled by Balak (or by Balaam). Balak has shown great persistence in wanting to control the future, and now Balaam *will give an oracle to* Balak on what the relationship between Moab and Israel will look like *in the latter days*

14. The present approach is similar to that taken by such modern scholars as de Vaulx (p. 294) and Wenham (pp. 179, 182–83). Noordtzij (p. 232) also comes from much the same perspective, but puts his conclusions a bit more negatively than seems necessary.

*(b^{e}'*ah*^{a}*rît hayyāmîm). Give an oracle to you ('î'āṣ*^{e}*ḵā)* — a more usual translation of this verb is "to counsel, advise" (see, e.g., NASB, NKJV at this verse). In fact there is a rough balance between the meanings of "to advise" (16 times, e.g., Exod. 18:19; 2 Sam. 17:11, 15; Job 26:3; see also the participle *yô'ēṣ,* "counsellor, 22 times, e.g., Prov. 11:14; 24:6) and "to plan" (17 times, e.g., Ezek. 1:12; Mic. 6:5; Hab. 2:10). Other English translations render the verb here as "to advertise" (AV, RV), "to let you know" (RSV), "to warn" (NEB, NIV), and "to inform" (NJPS). W. Albright concluded on the basis of his study of the Proto-Sinaitic Inscriptions that the basic meaning of *y'ṣ* there was "to utter an oracle" (especially concerning the future).[15] L. Ruppert followed Albright in this conclusion.[16] The present interpretation follows both scholars, and fits the present context well. Since people who sought an oracle could use it as a guide, the meaning "to advise" developed. The content of the "advice" consists in the revealed "plan" of the deity, and so the meaning "to plan" developed as well. The phrase *the latter days* can simply refer to the future (Jer. 23:20), but can also indicate a time at the very end of the historical process, when a new age is ushered in by God (perhaps Gen. 49:1; Deut. 4:30; Isa. 2:2 = Mic. 4:1; Dan. 2:28).[17] The phrase itself is ambiguous and includes both perspectives, and might better be thought of as looking at the future from the perspective of what God purposes to do up to and including "the end."[18]

15–16 The clause *and knower of the knowledge of Elyon* is not found in vv. 3–4 (which otherwise closely parallel vv. 15–16), perhaps because in the earlier context Balaam's oracle was, more or less, a word for the present with some future implications, while here the whole of the oracle is directed to the more distant future, thus requiring the knowledge that Elyon gives. *Elyon* is an ancient divine name found 29 times in the OT, usually translated "Most High."[19] Originally an adjective meaning "high" (and so used 22 times in the OT), it is occasionally found in

15. W. F. Albright, *The Proto-Sinaitic Inscriptions and Their Decipherment,* Harvard Theological Studies 22 (Cambridge, Mass.: Harvard Univ., 1969), pp. 21, 43.

16. L. Ruppert, *TDOT,* VI:158.

17. For the former see Noordtzij (p. 230); NEB, NASB, NIV, NJPS, GNB. For the latter see AV, RV, RSV, NKJV.

18. Cf. G. W. Buchanan, "Eschatology and the End of Days," *JNES* 20 (1961) 188–93; E. Lipiński, "*b'ḥryt hymym* dans les textes préexiliques," *VT* 20 (1970) 445–65.

19. GKC, § 133g, calls it a superlative derived ultimately from the verb *'ālâ,* "to go up." LXX translates *Hypsistos,* "highest."

combination with other divine names such as *'ēl* (Gen. 14:18–20, 22), *'ĕlōhîm* (Ps. 57:3 [Eng. 2]; 78:56), or *Yahweh* (Ps. 7:18 [Eng. 17]; 47:3 [Eng. 2]).[20] The name may have had pagan origins as the highest god in a particular pantheon, but if so, in the OT it assimilated to Yahweh.[21]

17 *I see him but not now ('er'ennû wᵉlō' 'attâ).* The verb "to see" is used here to indicate a different kind of seeing than that of 22:41; 23:13; 24:2, which is physical. This is a spiritual seeing that Balaam perceives with his inner or spiritual "eye" opened (vv. 3–4).[22] In this spiritually elevated or ecstatic state Balaam makes out a figure *(him),* but his vision is *not now,* i.e., it is removed in time. The parallel clause does not merely repeat the thought, but enriches the chronological idea of *not now* with the spatial or situational idea of *not nearby (lō' qārôḇ).*

The identity of this *him* is purposely ambiguous. It may be the one(s) called the *star* and *staff* (or *scepter*) in the next lines, or it may be Israel as a people.[23] Whether the figure is individual or corporate, it must represent Israel in order to fulfill what Balaam claimed as the purpose of his oracle in v. 14b.

a star. Although it is relatively uncommon to use this image to refer to a royal figure in Israel (Isa. 14:12, which refers to the Babylonian king; cf. Ezek. 32:7; Rev. 22:16), it seems common in the ancient Near East.[24] The royal reference is confirmed by the parallel term *scepter (šēḇeṭ;* Amos 1:5, 8; Ps. 45:7 [Eng. 6]).[25]

This royal figure will *pierce the temples of Moab.* That the noun *pa'ᵃṯê* means *temples (of),* not just "sides (of)" (which is the basic meaning

20. The title *bᵉnê-'elyôn* in Ps. 82:6 is parallel to *'ĕlōhîm;* cf. A. A. Anderson, *Psalms,* 2 vols., NCBC (Grand Rapids: Eerdmans, 1981), I:595.

21. BDB, p. 751a; S. R. Driver, *The Book of Genesis,* Westminster Commentaries (London: Methuen, 1904), p. 165; G. L. Della Vida, "El Elyon in Genesis 14:18–20," *JBL* 63 (1944) 1–29; L. R. Fisher, "Abraham and His Priest King," *JBL* 81 (1962) 264–70; E. Jacob, *Theology of the Old Testament,* tr. A. W. Heathcote and R. Allcock (New York: Harper & Row, 1958), p. 47 n. 2; Eichrodt, *Theology of the OT,* I:181–82.

22. R. Alter sees this verb (*rā'â* and its synonyms) as a constant factor or motif that runs through the whole of chs. 22–24, giving the entire passage cohesion and unity (*The Art of Biblical Narrative* [New York: Basic Books, 1981], pp. 104–7, esp. p. 105).

23. For the former see Dillmann, p. 159; Keil, p. 192; Cook, p. 745; Noordtzij, pp. 230–31; Noth, p. 192; Wenham, pp. 178–79 (although Wenham discusses both views, he slightly favors the former). For the latter see Gray, p. 369; McNeile, p. 139; Binns, pp. 171–72.

24. See references in, e.g., Cook, p. 745; Binns, pp. 171–72.

25. Clearly to be preferred over NEB "comet."

of *pā'â*), may be concluded from the fact that the verb "to pierce" *(māḥaṣ)* usually takes a personal object, and from the phrases "side of the face" (*p*ᵉ*'aṯ pānāyw,* Lev. 13:41) and "side of the head" (*p*ᵉ*'aṯ rō'š,* Lev. 19:27), both of which mean the "temple." That the word is dual here means that it refers to the whole head. A good parallel to this meaning is gained by emending the Hebrew text very slightly, from the rare and obscure verb *qarqar,* "to tear down" (cf. Isa. 22:5), to *crown of the head (qoḏqōḏ),* as in Sam. Pent. and in Jer. 48:45, which cites the present verse.[26] The reference is, then, to those at the "head" of Moab, i.e., the leaders.

all the sons of Sheth. Some have interpreted the word *šēṯ* as the proper name Seth, to which it is identical, and then argued that, since Seth was the one designed to replace the slain Abel to carry on Adam's line (Gen. 4:25), the reference here is to the whole human race.[27] If one takes the verse as indicative that the main role of this future figure will be destruction rather than simple dominion (as the verb *māḥaṣ* probably indicates), then it is not likely that the whole of the human race is a suitable meaning. It is true, however, that Moab is an offspring of Seth (through Lot), and it is also true that the verb *māḥaṣ* does not necessarily indicate destruction, but only wounding (thus *maḥaṣ* in Isa. 30:26 is "a wound"),[28] so that it is possible to interpret *šēṯ* here as Seth, although it is an inclusive parallel and one would expect a better term could be found.

If one follows Sayce's conjecture (as developed by Albright) that *šēṯ* refers to the Šutu, a nomadic Palestinian tribe,[29] then one would have a suitable parallel here. If this is correct, however, Jer. 48:45, which cites this line in the 7th cent. B.C., had already forgotten this meaning. That text reads "the sons of tumult" *(b*ᵉ*nê šā'ôn).* This parallel passage has led many scholars to see *šēṯ* as a contraction of *ś*ᵉ*'ēṯ,* a rare word taken to mean "uproar" in Lam. 3:47. Gray questions this meaning and derives *šēṯ* from *ś*ᵉ*'ēṯ,* "pride," citing the pride of the Moabites in Isa. 16:6; 25:11; Zeph. 2:10.[30] Of these options, the tribal-name conjecture of Sayce and Albright may well be the best, but no certainty is possible.[31]

26. So virtually all modern commentators (except Keil), although most modern English translations follow MT (except Moffatt and NIV) instead.

27. So Targ. Onkelos and Rashi.

28. In Deut. 32:39 and Job 5:18 the verb means "to strike" and is contrasted to the verb "to heal" *(rāpā').*

29. See n. 9 on the translation above.

30. Gray, p. 371.

31. Such modern commentators as Sturdy (p. 179), Budd (p. 269), and Wenham (p. 179) follow Albright.

The stated purpose of Balaam's oracle in v. 14b has been completed: a future figure (either Israel or a representative of Israel) will destroy or subdue Moab. If the oracle stopped here it would be appropriate to ask further after the identity of this figure, but rather unexpectedly the oracle goes on in v. 18 to include Edom, perhaps because of the treatment received by Israel in 20:14–21, so inquiry on this topic is best postponed.

18 The first two lines of the verse state clearly that Edom/Seir will be dispossessed, or made into someone's (Israel's) possession. *Seir* is the ancient name for the land itself (Gen. 32:4) and the chief mountain range (cf. Deut. 33:2), while *Edom* refers to the people. The two names function simply as parallel terms here, as in Judg. 5:4. Edom/Seir is called *his enemies.* In the context of the entire poem (esp. vv. 17–19) this *his* refers to the star/scepter of v. 17, which has been identified here either with Israel or with one who represents Israel. Again, the actions of Edom in 20:14–21 are enough to rank them as enemies. Although at the present time Israel was not allowed to fight against Edom (Num. 20:14–21; Deut. 2:4–5), in the future the dispossession of these enemies would be accomplished while Israel *does mightily,* i.e., goes from strength to strength.

19 The MT undoubtedly read a jussive verb, *w^{e}yērd,* lit., "let him (it) exercise dominion." The verb here is to be understood impersonally, "let one exercise dominion," which then becomes a circumlocution for the passive.[32] The second verb, although not a jussive, continues the jussive force,[33] "let one destroy the remnant." This twofold wish that dominion be exercised and enemies destroyed is probably to be understood to mean that when the former is exercised the latter will be destroyed (cf. Mic. 5:8; Isa. 60:12; Zech. 12:6). The source from which the dominion will be exercised is *Jacob* (i.e., Israel), whereas the source of those who are destroyed is the parallel *the city,* which could also be translated as "Ar" (or perhaps "Ir"), i.e., the city in Moab where Balaam met with Balak in the first place (22:36; cf. 21:28). This line rounds off the oracle by bringing it back to the primary subject of Moab (v. 14b), after a brief excursus on Edom.

It is now appropriate to inquire as to the historical referent of the main actor in the oracle. It has been widely recognized that David's

32. See, e.g., Davidson, *Syntax,* § 109. The present translation uses passives as less awkward than the literal impersonal constructions.

33. The perfect consecutive *w^{e}he'^{e}b̂îḏ* is what might normally be expected to follow a jussive; see GKC, § 112q; Davidson, *Syntax,* § 55 (a); Driver, *Tenses,* § 113 (2).

victories over both Moab and Edom satisfy some of the contents of the oracle (2 Sam. 8:2, 13–14; 1 K. 11:15–16), and some scholars want to stop with David. One's theological convictions as well as critical methods would then determine whether the oracle dates before David's time or after it. If, however, David fulfilled the requirements here set forth, it was only a temporary fulfillment, since both Moab and Edom regained their independence and were reconquered at several points through Israel's history.[34] This lack of permanent possession of these enemies led the prophets of Israel to talk about a future conquering of both.[35] Indeed, these two may be thought to represent powers hostile to Yahweh and his people.

It is only natural that in this process this passage should be interpreted messianically. Already Targ. Onkelos translated *star* by "the king" *(mlk')* and *scepter* (v. 17) by "the anointed one" *(mšyḥ')*.[36] It is interesting that the messianic pretender of the early or mid-2nd cent. A.D. was called Bar-Kochba, "son of the star" (cf. v. 17). In Rev. 22:16 the risen Jesus calls himself "the bright and morning star." The so-called Star of Bethlehem (Matt. 2:2, 7, 9–10) may well have been based on expectation that a literal star would point the way to a scepter (i.e., a ruler, the Messiah).[37] From the early synogogue and church to the present day there have been those who have held that the ultimate reference of this passage is to the Messiah. It is doubtful that this text was originally understood messianically, and whether it can, in isolation from the rest of Scripture, be read in that way. It surely does give some of the first glints of messianic hope, even if only in a highly indirect form, and, when placed in the context of the whole canon of Scripture, some adumbration of the future victory of God such as came to be represented in the Messiah may be seen.[38]

34. On Moab: before David, Judg. 3:12–14; 1 Sam. 14:47; after David, the evidence of the Mesha Inscription; 2 K. 1:1; 3:4–5; 3:21–27; 13:20. On Edom: 1 K. 11:14, 17–22; 2 K. 8:20; 14:7, 22; 2 Chr. 28:17; Ps. 137.

35. On Moab: Isa. 15:1–16:14; Ezek. 25:8–11; Amos 2:1–3; Zeph. 2:8–11. On Edom: Isa. 34:5–17; 43:1–6; Jer. 49:7–22; Ezek. 25:12–14; Amos 9:11–12; Obad. 1–21. Both appear in Isa. 11:14.

36. See the comparative chart on the interpretations of three Targs. and LXX in Riggans, pp. 249–51.

37. This interpretation perhaps grows from a view of Hebrew poetry that saw in every word the conveying of exact information rather than a view that allows parallelism and indirect language, etc. Cf. Kugel, *Idea of Biblical Poetry,* pp. 96–170.

38. For similar conclusions, see Noordtzij, p. 232; de Vaulx, pp. 293–94, with remarks on Qumran; Wenham, pp. 178–79; W. S. LaSor, D. A. Hubbard, and F. W. Bush, *Old Testament Survey* (Grand Rapids: Eerdmans, 1982), p. 174.

c. Final Oracles (24:20–25)

20 *And he looked at Amalek, and took up his oracle and said:*
"Amalek was head of the nations,
But his end will be unto destruction."[1]
21 *And he looked at the Kenite, and took up his oracle and said:*
"Enduring is your dwelling place,[2]
your nest is placed[3] *in the rock;*
22 *nevertheless,*[4] *Kain will be for burning,*
while[5] *Asshur*[6] *takes you captive."*[7]

1. *BHS* suggests reading *ʿᵃḏê ʾāḇāḏ*, "to destruction," for MT *ʿᵃḏê ʾōḇēḏ*, "to the one who destroys." Albright ("Oracles," p. 221 n. 98), following Sam. Pent., redivides the consonants to *ʿd yʾbd*, and translates: "his end is to perish forever!" (p. 225). *BHS* seems more likely, because it retains the longer form of the preposition *ʿᵃḏê*. Far from being a late poetic form (so Gray, p. 376), this longer form may be early, related to Akk. *adi* (*HALAT*, p. 743a).

2. *BHS* (following Albright, "Oracles," p. 222 n. 99) inserts the name Kain here instead of where it occurs in MT (v. 22a).

3. Qal passive participle from *śîm*, "to put, place"; see GKC, § 73f.

4. The combination *kî ʾim* usually forms a contrast to a previous negation, but occasionally it may provide the contrast without it (so also in Gen. 40:14; Job 42:8; see BDB, p. 475a; Albright, "Oracles," p. 226). Keil (p. 197) posits that the line is an indirect question: "Is it (the case) that . . . ," but this seems less likely.

5. Here I follow Albright ("Oracles," p. 222 n. 103), who redivides MT *ʿdm(h)* (lit., "until what"; cf. RSV "how long") to *ʿdm* (preposition *ʿd* plus enclitic *mem*), "while." See also de Vaulx, p. 294; Wenham, p. 181. Others have seen the particle *mâ* as a fragment of a place-name to which Asshur carried captives, i.e., "Asshur will take you captive unto Ma — " (McNeile, p. 141; Binns, p. 174).

6. According to Albright ("Oracles," p. 222 n. 104) the word *ʾaššûr* has nothing to do with the country of Asshur (Assyria), but is rather the verb "to behold" *(šûr)* as found, e.g., in 23:10; 24:17, and should be pointed *ʾāšûr*, "I will behold." He later modified his position so as to see Asshur as a place parallel to Eber (*Yahweh and the Gods of Canaan* [Garden City, N.Y.: Doubleday, 1968], p. 16 n. 40). See the commentary below on v. 24.

7. MT *tišbekā*, lit., "she will take you captive," is strange because Asshur is usually masc. (but see Ezek. 32:22; cf. GKC, § 122h). Albright ("Oracles," p. 222 n. 105) repoints as *tōšāḇêḵā*, "your sojourners." His complete translation is: "The while I gaze, your sojourners (become fuel)." LXX *genētai tō Beōr neosia panourgias*, "he shall be to Beor a nest of knavery," perhaps reflects Heb. *qēn-ʿormâ*. *BHS* proposes that the consonant *r* was mistaken for *d* and that the two words read as *ʿaḏ-mâ* should be redivided and repointed as *ʿᵃrēmâ*, "a heap." The complete proposal is to read *ʿᵃrēmâ wᵉʾašpōṯ mōšāḇeḵā*, "your dwelling will be a heap and a rubbish dump" (following W. Rudolph, "Zum Text des Buches Numeri," *ZAW* 52 [1934] 115). The clause is very difficult and no certainty is possible.

23 *And[8] he took up his oracle and said:*
"Alas, who[9] will live[10] when God determines this?[11]
24 *And ships[12] from the coast of Kittim[13]*
will afflict Asshur, and afflict Eber;[14]
but he also will come to destruction."
25 *And Balaam rose and went back to his place. And also Balak went on his way.*

8. LXX prefixes the verse with the statement *kai idōn ton gōg,* "and he saw Gog." Picking up on the LXX reading of Gog for Agag in 24:7, Albright ("Oracles," p. 222 n. 106) inserted "And he saw Agag" here. In a later book he took the reading of LXX: "and he saw Gog" (*Yahweh and the Gods of Canaan,* p. 16 n. 40).

9. Albright ("Oracles," p. 222 n. 107) read MT *'ôy mî* as *'ym,* i.e., *'îyîm,* "islands."

10. On the basis of cognate languages, Albright ("Oracles," pp. 222–23 n. 108) posited a verb *ḥwy,* meaning "to gather," here in the passive, for MT *yiḥyeh,* "will live." Albright's translation of the clause to this point is: "The isles will be gathered." Sam. Pent. reads *yihyeh,* "will be."

11. For *śûm (miśśumô)* as "to determine," see Isa. 44:7; Hab. 1:12. *BHS* suggests several alternate readings for MT *miśśumô 'ēl,* lit., "from the placing of it (by) El." The apparatus in *BHS* is related to Albright's proposals. He read *miśś^{e}mō'l,* which on the basis of cognate languages he relates to *sim'al,* "north," in Syrian documents ca. 1700 B.C. ("Oracles," p. 223 n. 109). He thus reads "from the north," and the whole clause "the isles will be gathered from the north" (p. 226). That the preposition *min* can carry such a meaning as "when" (or even "after"), see, e.g., Williams, *Syntax* § 316 (Lev. 9:22; Isa. 44:7; Ps. 73:20). The suffix *(-ô)* has been taken as a neuter following LXX *(tauta),* and refers in a general way to God's actions as reflected in vv. 22–23. See the commentary on this clause (Gray, p. 378).

12. Sam. Pent. reads Heb. *ṣîm,* "ships," as a verb, *yôṣî'ēm,* "he will bring them out," which GKC, § 93y, follows. LXX basically agrees with this reading (*kai exeleusetai,* which may reflect Heb. *w^{e}yōṣ^{e}'îm*). Pesh. reads "and legions will march out." In spite of these variants, it is possible to keep MT here (see below).

13. MT *mîyaḏ kittîm.* Albright ("Oracles," p. 223 n. 111) proposed reading *myrkty ym* (substituting *r* for *d* again); i.e., *miyyark^{e}ṯê yām,* "from the farthest reaches of the sea" (cf. p. 226). Various versions specify locales other than Kittim (Cyprus) here; e.g., Vulg. "from Italy"; Targ. "from Rome."

14. Albright ("Oracles," p. 223 nn. 112–13) originally proposed that the text be read "and while I gaze they pass over" *(w' dm(?) 'šr 'br),* calling this "the first drastic emendation I have proposed in these oracles." Later, he changed his reading to one closer to the MT: "but they shall harass Aššûr and harass 'Eber" (*Yahweh and the Gods of Canaan,* p. 16 n. 40). The latter reading follows Sam. Pent., which has a pl. verb for MT's sing. Piel (cf. *BHS*). Albright also did not consider Aššûr to be Assyria but a synonym for Eber, who were nomads or "caravaneers" (ibid.). LXX understands Eber to be the Hebrews *(Hebraious),* whereas Targ. understands them to be residents across the Euphrates *(l' br prt).*

Three smaller oracles concerning the Amalekites (v. 20), the Kenites (vv. 21–22), and an unnamed power (vv. 23–24) conclude the Balaam narratives. Even so conservative a scholar as Noordtzij saw little or no connection between these verses and what has gone before. Many before and since have concurred in this judgment.[15] Although some of the key words that run through the oracles continue here (e.g., the verb *rā'â,* "to see," and the noun *māšāl,* "oracle"), nothing in the subject matter of these oracles relates them directly either to Moab or to Israel (the main actors in the Balaam narratives). De Vaulx simply mentions the fact that these oracles bring the number of Balaam oracles to seven, the ancient number of completeness.[16] Although these brief oracles may be related to Babylonian omen texts,[17] in the present context they are more clearly associated with the oracles against foreign nations (as vv. 17–19 were).

Since, in the final form of the text, these verses are related to the last oracle or Balaam, it is best to see them as beginning with the picture of Israel's future in vv. 17–19, although it is unclear how these oracles relate specifically to Israel's future. These verses clearly belong together in their present form since the last words of v. 24 ("but he also will come to destruction," *w^egam hû' ʿ^aḏê 'ōḇēḏ*) assume the last words of v. 20 ("but his end will be unto destruction," *w^e'aḥ^arîṯ ʿ^aḏê 'ōḇēḏ*).

20 *And he looked at (wayyar').* In this verse and the next the verb "to see" continues to refer to visionary seeing, as in v. 17. Thus comments on whether Balaam could see the lands of the Amalekites and the Kenites in the Negeb from his vantage point (in the final form of the narrative, assumed to be the same place as in 23:28) are irrelevant.

Amalek. The tribal ancestor of the Amalekites is here used as a synonym for the tribe (see the commentary above on 13:29; 14:25, 33–35). The oracle itself is without verbs (lit., "first of nations Amalek, his last unto being destroyed"), so that any time reference for the statement is a guess. The literary peg on which the oracle is hung is the play between the words *head* (*rē'šîṯ,* lit., "first") and *his end* (*'aḥ^arîṯô,* or "his last"). Three suggestions have been made regarding the meaning of *rē'šîṯ:* strength (cf. the same phrase in Amos 6:1), age, or primary opponent. Wenham thinks it possible that the self-estimate of the Amalekites may

15. E.g., Gray, p. 373; Binns, p. 173; Noth, p. 193; Sturdy, p. 180; de Vaulx, p. 295.

16. De Vaulx, p. 295.

17. Ibid.

18. Wenham, p. 181. Cf. Gray, p. 374.

be in view here.[18] There is little evidence that, judged from an external point of view, the Amalekites were ever a very powerful group, although the command in Num. 14:25 to avoid them must mean that they were considered a powerful foe from Israel's point of view. The second solution is somewhat more likely in that the Amalekites were known as the Melluḫḫa even as early as the 3rd millennium B.C.[19] It is also true that the Amalekites were the first to oppose Israel (Exod. 17:8–16). Thus, the term "first" fits in all three categories. Again, the play on words between "first" and "end" is primary.

his end will be unto destruction. The Amalekites were defeated by Saul (1 Sam. 14:48; 15:1–3) and David (27:8; 30:1–31; 2 Sam. 8:12), and seem to disappear from history after their defeat in the time of Hezekiah (1 Chr. 4:42–43).

21–22 These verses concern the Kenites. Their background is obscure; Gen. 15:19–20 mentions them as a Canaanite tribe who will be dispossessed from the land. They are frequently pictured as friendly toward Israel (Judg. 1:16; 5:24; 1 Sam. 27:10; 30:29). They evidently lived in the same general area as the Amalekites, with whom they may have had a covenant relation (cf. 1 Sam. 15:6; see also the fact that they are named in the context of David's pursuit of the Amalekites, 1 Sam. 27:9–10; 30:29). Hobab is called a Kenite in Judg. 1:16; 4:11, whereas other times Jethro (probably his father) is called a Midianite (e.g., Exod. 3:1); hence these two groups may be related (see above on 10:29–32).

21 *and he looked at* is the same phrase as in v. 20.

The word *Kenite* is derived from *qayin* (v. 22), which means "smith" (cf. Gen. 4:22), and Albright (and others) posited that the Kenites were originally metalworkers, although this thesis has been challenged.[20] The literary device that unites this oracle is the wordplay among the terms *Kenite (qênî), nest (qēn),* and the tribal ancestor *Kain* (or Cain, Heb. *qayin*).

The second and third lines of the verse are fairly easily interpreted: the Kenites are secure in their dwelling place. The terms *enduring (ʾêṯān)* and *rock (selaʿ)* indicate the impregnability of their home, and perhaps refer to the Kenites' point of origin in the mountains of Midian, or to the

19. De Vaulx, p. 295; cf. the contrary view of G. Landes, *IDB,* I:101.

20. See, e.g., Albright, *Yahweh and the Gods of Canaan,* pp. 41–42; N. Glueck, "Kenites and Kenizzites," *PEQ* 72 (1940) 22–24; idem, *Rivers in the Desert: A History of the Negev* (New York: Norton, 1959), p. 153. For challenges to this thesis see I. Kalimi, "Three Assumptions About the Kenites," *ZAW* 100 (1988) 386–93, esp. 386–89.

place where they dwelled in Canaan, which was also known as Kain, southeast of Hebron (Josh. 15:57).

22 This verse is unclear. If it is parallel to the other oracles, it should concern the downfall of the Kenites, and although it is very obscure, the MT seems to do so.[21] Why a nation that had been friendly with Israel should come in for such a discussion is unknown. The oracle, of course, does not predict that Israel would be involved in the fall of this friendly power.

Kain is a proper name functioning as a synonym for the tribe, much as Amalek substituted for the Amalekites in v. 20. The name may refer to Cain ben Adam (Gen. 4:1, etc.), to which its form is identical, although this is uncertain and is irrelevant for our purposes.

The second line of v. 22 is corrupt (see notes on the translation above). *Asshur ('aššûr).* The word is identical to the name for Assyria. Some have assumed that the mention of Asshur here dates the oracle (at least in its present form) to a time of 900 B.C. or later, during the Neo-Assyrian period.[22] Even if the Assyrian empire is meant here, it is clear that this empire existed much earlier than the 1st millennium, probably stretching back into the early second or late third.[23] It is more likely, however, that *Asshur* here is not Assyria at all but the Canaanite tribe called the Asshurim (Gen. 25:3 [cf. v. 18, NIV, NEB]; 2 Sam. 2:9; Ps. 83:9 [Eng. 8]). As far as can be determined, the Asshurim lived in an area adjoining the territories of the Amalekites and the Kenites. So the text is speaking of the oppression of one small tribal group by another.[24]

23–24 The last oracle has no addressee in the MT. *Alas, who will live when God determines this ('ôy mî yiḥyeh miśśumô 'ēl).* Although this is a fair translation of the MT, it makes little sense in the context, and the line is probably corrupt. Does *this* (a masc. sing. suffix in Hebrew) refer to a thing or to a person? The LXX and Vulg. have understood the text to mean something like "who will live from the time that God determines to do this thing?"[25] But what thing? If the suffix is taken to refer to a person, it may be either Asshur (v. 22), or the same one referred to in the last line

21. Keil (pp. 196–97) and Cook (pp. 747–48) attempted to make the statement a positive one.

22. E.g., Noth, p. 193.

23. See the overview by H. W. F. Saggs, "The Assyrians," in *Peoples of Old Testament Times,* ed. D. J. Wiseman (Oxford: Clarendon, 1974), pp. 156–78.

24. So, e.g., de Vaulx, p. 295; Wenham, p. 181; cf. Budd, p. 270.

25. LXX *hotan thēi tauta ho theos* ("when[ever] God might appoint these things"); Vulg. *quando faciet ista Deus* ("when God does that").

of v. 24 below ("but he also will come to destruction"), which is the power that afflicts Asshur and Eber.

While Albright's conjecture of "and the isles will be gathered from the north" eases many problems (see note on the translation above), it makes the first line of v. 24 in the MT read less well and requires emendation there too. One might conjecture that someone wrote this ominous comment in the margin of the text on the basis of reading *'aššûr* as Assyria, and that early in the textual tradition this comment slipped into the text itself, thus making a triplet instead of the more usual couplet. Although one cannot be sure of such a proposal, it is true that the clause as it stands in the MT does not fit into the context very smoothly.

24 *from the coast of* (*mîyaḏ,* lit., "from the hand of") means "from the vicinity of"; see also Gen. 34:21; Judg. 18:10; Isa. 22:18; 1 Chr. 4:40; Neh. 7:4; Ps. 104:25.[26]

Kittim was originally a city in Crete known as Kition, from which the island took its name. In Isa. 23:1, 12 the Kittim are the inhabitants of the island. By the time of Jer. 2:10 and Ezek. 37:6, Kittim could mean any of the western maritime powers. According to the LXX of Dan. 11:30, the term refers to the Romans, and in 1 Macc. 1:1, 8; 8:5, it refers to the Greeks (these passages allude to the present oracle). The MT is usually explained to mean that raiders in warships from the western Mediterranean will invade Assyria. Since no known attack of Cypriots on Assyria occurred, many other historical settings have been suggested, one of the most common being Alexander the Great's attack on the Persian Empire (which is called "Assyria" in Ezra 6:22). Some have brought the setting down to the age of the Seleucids or even the Romans.[27]

If the reference to Asshur is not to the Assyrians but to the Asshurim, as suggested above, then none of the above historical contexts is relevant; rather, the reference may be to the invasion of the so-called Sea Peoples, who arrived from the western Mediterranean to put pressure on both Egypt and Canaan in the 13th and 12th cents. B.C., about the same time as the Israelites did.[28] In Canaan the Philistines formed part of this

26. See BDB, p. 390b.

27. For a discussion of these views, see Dillmann, pp. 165–67; Gray, pp. 378–79.

28. On the Philistines and the other Sea Peoples, see the overview of K. A. Kitchen, "The Philistines," in *Peoples of OT Times,* pp. 53–78; more detail may be had in N. K. Sandars, *The Sea Peoples, Warriors of the Ancient Mediterranean, 1250–1150 B.C.* (London: Thames & Hudson, 1978); idem, *The Cambridge Ancient History, Vol. II/2: The Middle East and the Aegean Region c. 1380–1000*

group. If this is correct, then one may continue to see an early date for these oracles. Albright's conjecture for vv. 23b–24a ("the isles will be gathered from the north, from the farthest reaches of the sea") may point to an invasion of the Sea Peoples or Philistines as well.[29]

These powers will afflict the Asshurim as well as *Eber.* The meaning of the verb "to afflict" *(ʿānâ)* in the Qal is "to be in a low or humble position" (see the related words *ʿānāw,* "humble," *ʿanāwâ,* "humility," *ʿānî,* "the humble/poor," *ʿonî,* "affliction"). The Piel (as here) means "to inflict a low state on someone." The verb is used in personal relations, as a description of what Sarah did to Hagar (Gen. 16:6). It is used in national relations, as a description of the physical and spiritual pain that Egypt inflicted on Israel (Exod. 1:11–12). It is used to describe what God does to his enemies (e.g., Deut. 26:6). When the subject is God, the purpose of affliction is repentance (e.g., Deut. 8:1–10), but it is debatable whether repentance is the goal of human affliction of others. Here the context is battle. The goal of the battle is the destruction *(ʾōḇēḏ)* of Asshur and Eber by the Kittim.[30] Some scholars conjecture that Eber is a neighboring tribe to Asshur. Albright identified them as nomads of sorts.[31] De Vaulx saw Eber *(ʿēḇer)* as the Hebrews *(ʿiḇrî),* which agrees with the LXX *(Hebraious).* It is tempting to try to identify *Eber* as *ʿēp̱er* (Epher), one of the sons of Midian in Gen. 25:4, and relative of the Asshurim in 25:3, but there is no evidence for this identification.

But he also will come to destruction. The *he* is the power that oppresses Asshur and Eber. The last two oracles run together and say that the Kenites will be taken captive by Asshur, and that in turn Asshur (and Eber) would be oppressed by another power (possibly from the west, possibly the Philistines), but that this power too would go down to defeat. If all this is true (much of it is conjecture), then the whole of vv. 15–24 points to events that had at least partial fulfillment in the time of David (i.e., the Moabites, Edomites, other Canaanites, and Philistines were all subdued; see, e.g., the summary in 2 Sam. 8). It is therefore

---

BC, 3rd ed. (Cambridge: Cambridge Univ. Press, 1975), pp. 366–78, 507–16. Documentary evidence from one of the Harris Papyri indicates that the Sea Peoples put pressure on Egypt in the time of Ramses III (ca. 1182–1151); see *ANET,* pp. 262–63; de Vaulx, p. 296. For more on the relation between the Sea Peoples and Egypt, see A. Nibbi, *The Sea Peoples and Egypt* (Park Ridge, N.J.: Noyes, 1975).

29. See de Vaulx, p. 296; Wenham, p. 182.

30. See. L. Coppes, *TWOT,* II:682–93; E. Bammel, *TDNT,* VI:888–94.

31. See n. 14 on the translation above; Wenham (p. 182) follows this line of interpretation.

likely, though not provable, that the instrument of the destruction of this last power is Israel, or God through his instrument Israel. If David begins the fulfillment, however, all these powers may only represent those who are hostile to God and his people. Dan. 11:30 refers this passage to another time and to other events than those outlined here. Again, it becomes a *kind* of action in which God engages on behalf of his people. In the end, for Christians, "the kingdoms of the world" (Moab, Edom, Rome, the United States, Canada, Russia, and so on) "have become the kingdom of our Lord, and of his Christ, and he shall reign forever and ever" (Rev. 11:15).

25 *And Balaam rose and went back to his place* (*wayyāqom bilʿām wayyēlek̲ wayyāšob̲ limqōmô,* lit., "Balaam rose and went and returned to his place"). For the idiom itself see Gen. 18:33; 32:1. If this statement were taken in isolation from the rest of the book, it would simply mean that Balaam went back to Pethor. Exact destinations are not important at this point in the story (hence *And also Balak went on his way*). Later on, however, Balaam's destination will become important and be made explicit. Balaam enticed the Israelites to commit sin at Baal-Peor and was finally slain by them (Num. 31:8, 16; Josh. 13:22). The question is not whether chs. 22–24 and ch. 31 come from different sources (which may be the case), but whether the person who put the book of Numbers together would not expect his readers to remember 24:25 when they came to 31:8, 16. In the context of the final form of the text this statement means something like, "Balaam went off to another place, where he stayed." The vagueness of the statement tantalizes the reader into wondering what ever happened to him. The later material fills in this blank.

B. INCIDENT OF BAAL-PEOR (25:1–18)

1 *And Israel dwelt in Shittim. And the people began to commit fornication with*[1] *the daughters of Moab.*

2 *And they invited the people to the sacrifices of their gods, and the people ate and bowed themselves down*[2] *to their gods.*

1. For the preposition *ʾel* with this verb, cf. Ezek. 16:26, 28.

2. The verb *wayyištaḥ*^{a}*wwû* is traditionally parsed as from *šāḥâ* (BDB, p. 1005), but it is a (H)ishtaphel imperfect consecutive from *ḥāwâ;* cf. *HALAT,* pp. 283b–84a. The meaning of the verb is "to bow oneself down." The context of the action determines whether the verb simply implies a polite and deferential greeting (e.g., Gen. 23:7; 33:3, 6), worship of Yahweh (e.g., Ps. 5:6; 99:5, 9) or, as in the present text, (illegitimate) worship of gods other than Yahweh (also Exod. 20:5;

3 *And Israel bound itself to Baal-Peor. And Yahweh's anger burned against Israel.*

4 *And Yahweh said to Moses, "Take all the leaders*[3] *of the people and hang*[4] *them before Yahweh in the sun so that the fierce anger of Yahweh may turn from Israel."*

5 *And Moses said to the judges of Israel, "Slay, each one, his men who have bound themselves to Baal-Peor."*

6 *And behold, a man from the children of Israel came and brought a Midianite woman*[5] *to his brothers in the sight of Moses and in the sight of the whole congregation of the children of Israel, while they were weeping at the door of the tent of meeting.*

7 *And Phinehas the son of Eliezar, the son of Aaron the priest, saw it, and he rose up from the midst of the congregation and took a spear in his hand.*

Deut. 5:9). When the object of the verb is a deity, it is often found together with the verb *ʿāḇaḏ,* "to serve" (e.g., Deut. 8:19; 11:16; Jer. 8:2). So, although the verb itself designates only the outer action, certain contexts (e.g., the worship of other gods) justify taking it as indicative of an inner attitude as well. See, e.g., H. Preuss, *TDOT,* IV:248–57; also D. R. Ap-Thomas, "Notes on Some Terms Relating to Prayer," *VT* 6 (1956) 225–41, esp. 229; W. Zimmerli, "Das Zweite Gebot," in *Festschrift für Alfred Bertholet zum 80. Geburtstag;* hrsg. W. Baumgartner, et al. (Tübingen: Mohr, 1950), pp. 550–63, esp. 552–54.

3. On *rōš,* "leader," see the commentary above on 14:4.

4. The verb *yāqaʿ* occurs only four times in the Qal (Gen. 32:26; Jer. 6:8; Ezek. 23:17–18), three times in the Hiphil (Num. 25:4; 2 Sam. 21:6, 9), and once in the Hophal (2 Sam. 21:13). The versions reflect the uncertainty concerning its meaning: Aquila, "to impale" *(anapēzon);* Symmachus, "to hang" *(kremason);* Vulg., "to suspend" *(suspende);* Pesh., "to make known, expose" *(wprsʾ);* LXX, "to make an example of" *(paradeigmatison). BHS* recommends "to put out of joint," perhaps on the basis of the meaning of the Qal in Gen. 32:26, where Jacob's thigh is put out of joint. According to BDB, the verb denotes some form of execution (p. 429). W. Robertson Smith suggested (on the basis of Arab. *waqaʿa,* "to fall down," and *ʾauqaʿa,* "to cause to fall down") that the meaning should be "to cast down" (so NEB) (*Religion of the Semites,* p. 398), but this is unlikely, since the text that most clearly speaks of execution by throwing someone off a rock (2 Chr. 25:12) does not use *hôqaʿ*. English translations have either paraphrased (e.g., NIV "to kill and expose"; NASB, GNB, Moffatt "to execute") or followed the versions (mostly Vulg. and Targs.; AV, RV, RSV, NKJV "to hang up," NJPS follows Aquila, "to impale"). Perhaps "to hang" is as good a translation as any (cf. Driver, *Samuel,* p. 351).

5. The prefix *ha(m)* on *hammiḏyānîṯ,* usually the sign of the definite article, here may indicate that the term is generic, expressing a group or class of people; see Davidson, *Syntax,* § 22; Williams, *Syntax,* § 92. It is not necessarily because this Midianite woman had been named before in the part of the story now lost (cf. Noordtzij, p. 237).

8 *And he went after the man of Israel into the tent and pierced the two of them, the man of Israel and the woman in her stomach,*[6] *and the plague on the children of Israel was checked.*

9 *Nevertheless, those who died in the plague were twenty-four thousand.*

10 *And Yahweh spoke to Moses, saying:*

11 *"Phinehas the son of Eleazar, the son of Aaron the priest, turned away my wrath from upon the children of Israel when he was zealous with my own zeal among them, so that I did not destroy the children of Israel in my zeal.*

12 *Therefore say, 'Behold, I am about to give him my covenant of peace.*[7]

13 *He and his descendants will have a covenant of everlasting priesthood because*[8] *he was zealous for his God and made atonement for the children of Israel.' "*

14 *And the name of the slain man who was slain with the Midianite woman was Zimri the son of Salu, a leader of a Simeonite father's house.*[9]

15 *And the name of the Midianite woman was Kozbi the daughter of*

6. Many scholars have suggested that *'el-q^{o}ḇāṯāh,* "in her stomach," is a gloss that mirrors the words *'el-haqqubbâ,* "into the tent," from the first part of the verse (see, e.g., *BHS*). The word *q^{o}ḇāṯāh* occurs only here, and is thought to mean "inner parts" (BDB, p. 867a; *HALAT,* p. 992b). The word is probably the suffixed form of *qēḇâ,* which is found only in Deut. 18:3, and explained as the stomach of a sacrificial animal that (along with the shoulder and the two cheeks) was taken by the priest. If this word is a gloss, one must still explain its placement in the text. It seems more likely that the word is part of a wordplay with *qubbâ.*

7. Heb. *b^{e}rîṯî šālôm* appears to be a construct-genitive with a suffix on the noun in the construct state, which traditional grammar would forbid. (The normal way to express "my covenant of peace" is *b^{e}rîṯ-š^{e}lômî.*) GKC, §§ 128d; 131r n. 4 speak of the construction as an appositive — "a covenant, i.e., peace." While this is possible, it is more likely that this is another example of what D. N. Freedman has called the broken construct chain (cf. Hab. 3:8), which should simply be understood as a normal construct-genitive (D. N. Freedman, "The Broken Construct Chain," *Bib* 53 [1972] 534–36; repr. in *Pottery, Poetry, and Prophecy: Collected Essays on Hebrew Poetry* [Winona Lake, Ind.: Eisenbrauns, 1980], pp. 339–41).

8. Note the use of the preposition *taḥaṯ* (lit., "under") to introduce a causal clause (Williams, *Syntax,* §§ 353, 534).

9. Heb. *bêṯ-'āḇ laššim'ōnî,* lit., "a house of a father with regard to Simeon." The *l^{e}*- circumscribes the "father's house" as a single or indefinite one within Simeon. Were the construction simply done with the normal construct-genitive relationship one would translate "*the* father's house of the Simeonites"; cf. Davidson, *Syntax,* § 28 Rem. 5.

Zur. He was a head of tribes, that is, of a father's house,[10] *in Midian.*

16 *And Yahweh spoke to Moses, saying:*

17 *"Oppress*[11] *the Midianites, and all of you will strike them,*

18 *For they have been oppressors to you in their trickery with which they tricked you in the matter of Peor and in the matter of Kozbi, the daughter of a leader in Midian, their sister, who was slain on the day of the plague, on account of the matter of Peor."*

Chapter 25 is another complex narrative. It opens with Israel's engaging in sexual immorality leading to worship of "other gods" (vv. 1–2). The main god in question is named Baal of Peor, and Israel's worship of this god provoked Yahweh to order the death of Israel's leaders, although this sentence is not carried out (vv. 3–5). For a certain Israelite man (Zimri *ben* Salu, v. 14) brings a Midianite woman (Kozbi *baṯ* Zur, v. 15) into the camp right under the noses of the community, which is lamenting both their sin and God's punishment of it (which is revealed as a plague in v. 8). Phinehas, son of Eleazar the high priest, was incensed by this display and killed both the Israelite and the Midianite in their tent. This action halted the plague, which had already killed 24,000 (vv. 6–9). Phinehas's action showed Yahweh's own zeal for his honor, leading Yahweh to grant Phinehas and his descendants an everlasting tenure in the priesthood (vv. 10–13). Finally, the Midianites' trickery (rather than that of the Moabites) is used as a rationale for attacking them (vv. 16–18; see ch. 31).

Many scholars have accounted for the admitted anomalies in the story on the basis of editorial combination of more than one source.[12] It is likely that two stories have been amalgamated in the present text: the first a general tale of physical and spiritual fornication between Israel and foreigners, the second a more specific account of Zimri, Kozbi, and

10. Many scholars see the words *father's house (bêṯ-'āḇ)* as a gloss that should be eliminated; e.g., Paterson, p. 60; Gray, p. 387; de Vaulx, p. 300; Budd, p. 275.

11. The difficulty in finding an infinitive absolute when one would expect an imperative (or at least a finite verb) can be seen in the variant in Sam. Pent., which reads *ṣrrw,* probably the imperative. Occasionally, however, the infinitive absolute may be found in place of finite verbs, including imperatives (GKC, § 113bb; Davidson, *Syntax,* § 88 (b); Williams, *Syntax,* § 211). This kind of infinitive absolute may be followed by a finite verb (Davidson, § 88 Rem. 3).

12. Those who subscribe to the documentary hypothesis ascribe vv. 1–5 to JE and vv. 6–18 to P (though with complexities even within the documents); see the summary in Budd, pp. 275–79.

Phinehas. Together these stories make the point that Israel's priesthood must be pure in order to continue, and that Israel must be as pure as its priesthood in order to continue. It seems fruitless to speculate what the two stories might have looked like in their independent states, since they exist only in combination. In the process of producing the present text, details were most probably summarized and must sometimes be inferred from the whole text (i.e., only in vv. 8–9 does one learn that "Yahweh's wrath" in v. 2 meant "a plague").[13] The point of commenting on the unit is not to judge how well the present narrative seems to fit together, but to attempt to make sense of it as it stands before the reader. For the final form of the text, Wenham's analysis of the chapter seems sound: the sin, the plague, and its end (vv. 1–9); the outcome of Phinehas's actions (vv. 10–15); the judgment on Midian (vv. 16–18).[14]

The chapter is placed between the Balaam oracles and the second census account for theological and literary reasons. In relation to the Balaam oracles it shows that, even while God was blessing Israel through Balaam on the heights of Peor, below on the plains of Moab Israel was showing its weak and sinful character. The parallel between this incident and that of the Torah at Sinai and the golden calf (Exod. 20–32) is obvious.[15] God's blessing is because of his grace, not because of his people's merit. The juxtaposition of God's blessing his people and their sin is jarring. This chapter brings the reader back to earth after the oracular utterances of Balaam. These Israelites are, after all, the generation condemned to die in the wilderness for faithlessness (ch. 14). Even though God has a plan and a future for Israel, these particular Israelites are doomed. In ch. 26, a new census is taken because the old generation has finally died (cf. 26:63–65). Ch. 25 narrates the final plague that extinguished the old generation for its iniquity. Lest the reader think that this iniquity is only the old sin of the spies, this chapter spells out that Israel's sins, like God's mercies, seem new every morning. The chapter also prepares the reader to enter the new day in ch. 26.

13. Cf. Noordtzij, pp. 237–38.

14. See Wenham, p. 185.

15. Wenham (p. 184) has listed several parallels between the stories. Both involve worship of other gods (Exod. 32:8; Num. 25:2); God's wrath is appeased by an immediate slaughter (Exod. 32:26–28; Num. 25:7–8); the tribe of Levi is made priests, and Phinehas and descendants are guaranteed the priesthood (Exod. 32:29; Num. 25:11–13). In addition, Israel clearly did not know what was going on at Sinai (32:1), and it is highly unlikely that they were aware of Balaam's blessings, or they would have taken some military action.

1–2 *And Israel dwelt.* For this idiom, see 20:1; 21:25, 31.

in Shittim (baššiṭṭîm). The Hebrew word has the definite article, and so means "the acacias." The full name is given in 33:49 as Abel-shittim ("acacia meadows"). This was the site on the plains of Moab from which Joshua sent the spies into Jericho (Josh. 2:1; 3:1). Josephus connected the place with Abila (from the proper noun Abel),[16] a couple of miles east of the Jordan. More modern scholars have placed it at Tell el-Ḥammâm, which is located at the entrance of Wadi Kefrein into the Jordan Valley, about 10 mi. east-southeast of Jericho.[17]

began to commit fornication (wayyāḥel hāʿām liznôṯ). In addition to its literal meaning of "to commit fornication" (e.g., Gen. 38:24; Lev. 21:9; Deut. 22:21; Hos. 4:13–14; Amos 7:17), the verb *zānâ* can mean "to engage in idolatrous worship" (e.g., Isa. 57:3; Jer. 2:20; Ezek. 16:15; Hos. 2:7).[18] It is not necessary to choose which meaning is relevant here, since, in this introductory sentence, the meaning is purposely vague. The first acts may have been physical, but they quickly led to cultic and spiritual acts.

with the daughters of Moab (ʾel-bᵉnôṯ môʾāḇ). Although the land north of the Arnon had been under Amorite control (21:13, 26), there is no evidence that the Amorites had eliminated the more native population of Moabites. The place may be called "the plains of Moab" (*ʿarbôṯ-môʾāḇ;* 22:1; etc.) or "the land of Moab" (*ʾereṣ-môʾāḇ;* Deut. 1:5; etc.). That the Moabites and Midianites were a mixed population in this territory is also the witness of 22:4, 7. Chs. 22–24 highlighted Moab's attempt to overthrow Israel; Midian played a minor role in these chapters. Here the reverse is true — Midian is the chief actor, with Moab taking a supporting role.[19]

And they invited. The Moabite women invited the Israelites. Once the sexual union was consummated, it was natural for interests to be shared, and one of these interests was religious faith.

to the sacrifices of their gods (lᵉziḇḥê ʾᵉlōhêhen) refers to feasts where the worshipers ate sacrificial animals. The best way to take the text here is that the Israelites went to the sacrificial rites and *then* partook of meat that had been offered to the Moabite gods, and *then bowed them-*

16. I.e., Khirbet el-Kefrein; Josephus, *Ant.* 4.8.1; 5.1.1.

17. Cf. *Oxford Bible Atlas,* 3rd ed., p. 63.

18. See P. Bird, "'To Play the Harlot': An Inquiry into an Old Testament Metaphor," in *Gender and Difference in Ancient Israel,* ed. P. L. Day (Minneapolis: Fortress, 1989), pp. 75–94. See above on 14:33.

19. There is no need to posit separate sources, with Moab appearing in one (J) and Midian in another (E/P); cf. Gray, pp. 380–81.

selves down to these gods (i.e., worshiped them). Although the particular god in question will be named in v. 3 as Baal-Peor, one should probably read the pl. "gods" as a sing. here (as in Judg. 11:24; 1 K. 11:23). The statement is general and will be specified in a moment.

3 *And Israel bound itself.* The verb "to bind [or yoke] oneself" *(ṣāmaḏ)* is found only here and in the allusion to this event in Ps. 106:28. The term may conceal some technical cultic meaning now lost. The LXX translated the verb by *teleō,* which may mean "to initiate into the mysteries" (i.e., of the mystery religions, Gnosticism), or it may indicate a sexual union.[20]

It is clear that, after sexual relationships had led to participation in the pagan sacrificial feasts, the next step was a formal association with a particular god. That god was *Baal-Peor.* Baal was the name of the great Canaanite god of vegetation.[21] It was common to speak of him in various local manifestations. In combinations such as the present one, the second term is often the place-name where that local Baal was worshiped, hence this Baal was worshiped at (Beth) Peor (cf. Deut. 3:29; 4:46; on this site, see above on 23:38). For other biblical examples, see Baal-hermon (Judg. 3:3) and Baal-hazor (2 Sam. 13:23).[22] It is ironic that the Israelites may have joined themselves to a foreign god at the very site where Balaam uttered his startling third and fourth blessings of Israel (ch. 24).

4 Yahweh commands Moses to execute all the leaders of Israel *(rō'šê yiśrā'ēl).* The Sam. Pent. attempted to escape this text by paraphrasing that only the guilty were to be slain. Similarly, Keil holds that *them* in v. 4 should be understood as the idolators of v. 5, but this is not clear from the text itself.[23]

20. For the former see LSJ, 1772a (III). For the latter see Sturdy, p. 181.

21. For more on Baal in general, see E. O. James, *The Ancient Gods: The History of the Diffusion of Religion in the Ancient Near East and the Eastern Mediterranean* (London: Weidenfeld & Nicholson, 1960), pp. 87–90; J. Gray, *The Legacy of Canaan: The Ras Shamra Texts and Their Relevance to the Old Testament,* VTSup 5, rev. ed. (Leiden: Brill, 1965), pp. 163–69; A. S. Kapelrud, *The Ras Shamra Discoveries and the Old Testament* (Oxford: Blackwell, 1962), pp. 32–56; J. C. L. Gibson, *Canaanite Myths and Legends,* 2nd ed. (Edinburgh: T. & T. Clark, 1978), pp. 3–19.

22. For extrabiblical examples such as Baal-Lebanon, Baal-Tarsus, and Baal-Tyre, Baal-Sidon, see G. A. Cooke, *Textbook of North Semitic Inscriptions* (Oxford: Clarendon, 1903), passim (see index).

23. See Keil, pp. 204–5; Cook, p. 750. Dillmann (p. 169) held the same position, only on the basis that, in the conflation of J and E, the referent of "them" became confused.

and hang them . . . in the sun (wᵉhôqaʿ ʾôṯām . . . neḡeḏ haššāmeš). If "hanging" is the right meaning here, then *in the sun* probably refers to the public nature of the punishment (cf. 1 Sam. 12:12), although Wenham thinks of the nonburial of the corpses of the executed leaders.[24]

before Yahweh (lYHWH). This idiom also occurs in 2 Sam. 21:6 (with *hôqaʿ*) and possibly in Deut. 13:17 (Eng. 16) and Josh. 6:7. 2 Sam. 21:9 has *lip̄nê YHWH* (also meaning "before Yahweh") with the same verb. This expression may mean that the execution is done for the satisfaction of the honor of Yahweh or, more simply, *to* him, as the person to whom the leaders were given (as in the ban, *ḥērem*). This execution of the whole corps of Israelite leaders may seem unjust to a modern Western individualism (and perhaps to Moses as well; see below). It must be remembered, however, that these men were the divinely appointed representatives of the people. In v. 3 it was Israel (as a whole group) that bound itself to Baal-Peor, so that either the whole group must pay the price of God's wrath, or a representative group must. It is a serious thing to be a leader.

fierce anger (ḥᵃrôn ʾap̄-YHWH). These terms together always refer to Yahweh's anger. This outpouring from God always demands a heavy penalty: death (e.g., Exod. 32:12; Num. 25:4; Josh. 7:26; 1 Sam. 28:18; Job 20:23; Ps. 78:49) or exile (e.g., 2 K. 23:26; 2 Chr. 28:11; Jer. 4:8, 26; 12:13; 25:37–38; 30:24; Ps. 85:4; Lam. 1:12; 4:11). The words are found parallel to terms for destruction (Hos. 11:9) and indignation (Nah. 1:6; Zeph. 3:8). Milgrom has pointed out that the terms *qāṣap̄*, "to be wrathful," and *nāḡap̄*, "to smite" (i.e., with a plague, *maggēp̄â*), are simply parallels for this reflex action of God when he is met with such a blatant evil as idolatry. The current phrase might be seen as another synonym that would imply a pestilence from God, but this is not demonstrable.[25]

5 Moses commands judges to slay those who had bound themselves *(hanniṣmāḏîm)* to Baal-Peor. Each judge was responsible for carrying out the sentence on the guilty parties within their jurisdictions. It is possible that these *judges (šōp̄ᵉṭîm)* are the leaders *(rōʾšîm)* of thousands, hundreds, fifties, and tens who judged *(šāp̄aṭ)* the Israelites in Exod. 18:25–26. The question then becomes how these judges are related to the "leaders of the people" *(rōʾšê hāʿām)* who were to be executed in v. 4. If they were the same group, how would Moses carry out God's command to have them hung up before Yahweh and then slain if they were guilty?

24. Wenham (p. 186).

25. See Milgrom, *Studies in Levitical Terminology,* I:21 n. 75; p. 30 n. 109.

Keil attempted to see both sentences as being inflicted on the guilty parties.[26] But this view not only reverses the order of the text, in that the guilty were slain first and then hung up in the sun, but it also assumes that the guilty parties of v. 5 are the same as the "leaders of the people" in v. 4, which is very unlikely. Even if one sees vv. 4–5 as doublets due to a conflation of sources,[27] one must still decide what the meaning of the redacted text is. It is not clear, however, that these verses may be taken as doublets. In v. 4 Yahweh commanded Moses to execute all the leaders of the people; in v. 5 Moses commands judges to slay those who had bound themselves to Baal-Peor. The two commands are different. The best solution seems to be that Moses here, perhaps under the pressure of practicality, saw no way to accomplish Yahweh's command and so decided that only the guilty would be slain. W. H. Gispen suggested that this was the beginning of the plague, in which many more people died than was necessary.[28]

6 Neither God's nor Moses' sentence was carried out. The scene shifts abruptly to *the door of the tent of meeting,* where *Moses . . . and the whole congregation of the children of Israel . . . were weeping.* This action, because of its cultic locale, probably describes a formal lament of the community such as is found, e.g., in the Psalter.[29] Because the current chapter is a combination and summary of two stories (see above), it is difficult to know the exact cause of the lamentation. At this point in the combined narrative the cause is probably to be understood as the national sin and Yahweh's death sentence on the leaders. If the plague had already broken out (the reader knows nothing of the plague at this point), that also would be a reason for lamentation.

Into this cultic situation of mourning and lamentation an Israelite man *brought a Midianite woman to his brothers (wayyaqrēḇ 'el-'aḥāyw 'eṯ-hammiḏyānîṯ).* Phinehas's reaction to this event indicates that it was a blatant sin. Commentators have been divided on what this sin was: illicit

26. See Keil, p. 205.

27. Many scholars have assigned v. 4 to J and v. 5 to E; cf., e.g., Dillmann, pp. 167–69; Holzinger, pp. 126–31; Baentsch, pp. 622–24; Gray, p. 381.

28. As cited by Wenham, p. 187; Gispen's commentary, *Het boek Numeri* I–II, is unavailable to me.

29. Community laments are found in Pss. 12; 44; 58; 60; 74; 79; 80; 83; 85; 89:38–51; 90; 94; 123; 126; 129; 137; Lam. 5. These laments arose out of such times of community disaster as are narrated in Num. 25:1–5; Deut. 1:45; Judg. 20:23, 26; cf. Joel 2:12–16. See B. W. Anderson, *Out of the Depths: The Psalms Speak for Us Today,* rev. ed. (Philadelphia: Westminster, 1983), pp. 63–105, esp. 70–73; Noth, p. 198.

sex, foreign marriage, or some cultic offense.[30] All three factors seem to apply. Foreigners were seen as the source of the trouble, which began with illicit sexual relations leading to cultic violations (vv. 1–3a). That this act was done out in the open (i.e., *in the sight of Moses and in the sight of the whole congregation of the children of Israel*) contributed to its blatant appearance. The Midianite woman could be one of those called a daughter of Moab in v. 1, since the Midianites and Moabites are connected elsewhere (see above on v. 1).

7–9 This offense was the proverbial last straw. *Phinehas* is an Egyptian name *(pi-nḥas)* meaning "the dark-skinned one." His priestly lineage is traced back to Aaron to make it clear who he was (he is previously mentioned only in the genealogy of Exod. 6:25).[31] He stood up in the midst of the lamenting congregation and took a spear in his hand (the reader is not told where the spear came from). From what follows it is not surprising that 1 Chr. 9:20 speaks of him as the chief gatekeeper for the tabernacle.[32]

Phinehas pursued the couple *into the tent ('el-qubbâ).* This word, which occurs only here, comes from a root that means "vaulted," or "arched."[33] The Vulg. translated it as "brothel" *(lupanar),* which it can also mean in postbiblical Hebrew.[34] But there is no reason to see this meaning here. Some scholars understand the word to indicate an inner section of the tent, perhaps the women's quarters or even a bridal chamber,[35] but this is a guess. An Arabic word from a root *qbh* is a portable tent shrine of the pre-Islamic period.[36] The reference, then, could be to the tabernacle itself,

30. For the first see Keil, p. 205; Cook, p. 750. For the second see Baentsch, pp. 624–25; Binns, p. 178; Noordtzij, p. 241; Noth, p. 198; Sturdy, p. 184; Budd, p. 280. For the third see de Vaulx, p. 299; Wenham, p. 187; Milgrom, *JPST,* pp. 212, 214, 476–80; S. C. Reif, "What Enraged Phinehas?" *JBL* 90 (1971) 100–106; F. M. Cross, *Canaanite Myth,* pp. 201–3.

31. Later references to Phinehas are found in Num. 31:7 (Eng. 6); Josh. 22:13, 30–32; 24:33; Judg. 20:28; 1 Chr. 5:30; 6:35 (Eng. 6:4, 50); 9:20; Ezra 7:5; 8:2; Ps. 106:30; Sir. 45:23; 1 Macc. 2:26; 4 Macc. 18:12.

32. Eli the priest at Shiloh named one of his sons Phinehas, perhaps to legitimate his priesthood; cf. 1 Sam. 1:3; 2:24; 4:4, 11, 17, 19; 14:3. See, e.g., H. W. Hertzberg, *I & II Samuel: A Commentary,* tr. J. Bowden, OTL (Philadelphia: Westminster, 1964), pp. 23–24, 36, 46–51, 111–12.

33. See BDB, p. 866.

34. See Jastrow, *Dictionary,* p. 1323a.

35. See Cook (p. 750), for the inner section of the tent; Keil (p. 206) and Noordtzij (p. 241), for women's quarters; Noth (p. 198), for the bridal chamber.

36. From the Arabic, through Moorish influence in Spanish (with the definite article *'al*), comes the word *alcove.* On Arab. *qubbah,* see de Vaux, *Ancient Israel,* II:296–97, 501.

or to another shrine nearby.[37] Although one cannot eliminate the cultic connection out of hand, if the site were the tabernacle, the words *tent of meeting* would probably have been used (as in v. 6), and the evidence for another shrine is not convincing. The translation *tent* is vague, but our knowledge of the meaning of the word is vague as well.[38]

Phinehas pierced both the man and the woman with the spear. *in her stomach ('el-qᵒḇāṯāh).* The words *qubbâ (tent)* and *qᵒḇāṯāh (stomach)* were probably used together because of their similar sounds. Later Jewish interpretation held that Phinehas found the two in the act of sexual intercourse and pierced both of them through the sex organs (cf. above on 5:21–22) — the punishment fits the crime![39]

the plague . . . was checked. The act of Phinehas turned aside Yahweh's anger, much as the dramatic action of Aaron ended the plague in 17:13–15 (Eng. 16:46–48). It is unknown why Phinehas undertook this task rather than his father the high priest, although it has been suggested that, as in 16:36–40 (Hebrew 17:1–5), this task was not fit for the high priest, since the law that forbade him from coming in contact with corpses was stricter than for the ordinary priest (Lev. 21:1, 11).[40]

This is the first mention of *the plague (hammaḡēpâ)* in the narrative. The plague may have started when Yahweh became angry (v. 3), or when he saw that his death sentence on the leaders was not being carried out (v. 5). The reader must now adjust his or her interpretation of what it meant that *Yahweh's anger burned against Israel* in v. 3. This is a legitimate literary strategy, although it is possible that an earlier reference to the plague existed in a fuller account of the happenings of which the present chapter is a summary. Even though Phinehas's act stopped the plague, 24,000 people had already died.[41]

10–11 A new section begins with Yahweh's command that Moses

37. For the tabernacle see Sturdy, pp. 184–85; for another shrine see Budd, p. 280; Reif, "Phinehas," pp. 100–106; Cross, *Canaanite Myth,* pp. 201–3.

38. So also AV, Moffatt, NASB, GNB, NIV, NKJV. RSV and NEB have "inner room"; cf. RV "pavillion"; NJPS "chamber."

39. T.B. *Ḥullin* 134b; Snaith, p. 184.

40. E.g., Gray, p. 385; Milgrom, *JPST,* p. 215.

41. As is well known, in 1 Cor. 10:8 Paul gives the figure as 23,000. This contradiction has never been satisfactorily explained, and attempts at harmonizing the accounts raise more questions than they solve. Keil (p. 206) suggested that Paul's 23,000 did not include the leaders that were hanged, but only those who died by the plague. But the text does not say that any number of leaders were killed at all. See G. D. Fee, *The First Epistle to the Corinthians,* NICNT (Grand Rapids: Eerdmans, 1987), pp. 455–56.

speak to Phinehas. Phinehas turned Yahweh's wrath aside from the Israelites (i.e., checked the plague) *when he was zealous with my own zeal among them (bᵉqan'ô 'eṯ-qin'āṯî bᵉṯôḵām).* The words *zealous (qannā')* and *zeal (qin'â)* may also be translated as "jealous" and "jealousy."[42] Here the words indicate that fundamental attitude of Yahweh which defends his own honor, and the actions he takes to defend it. It hardly needs to be said that these terms are anthropomorphisms; thus one must not assume that God's jealousy or zeal is like human jealousy or zeal. It may be true that in certain, admittedly defective, ways (because of sin), human zeal may be like God's. God himself confessed that Phinehas's zeal was as if it were his own. Because Phinehas had acted in this way and with this spirit, he had satisfied God's honor. That Yahweh did not command this act of Phinehas was clear (his command was sterner still), but that he approved of it is just as clear. Phinehas's zeal became famous and was the pattern for such exceptional acts as Samuel's slaying of Agag (1 Sam. 15) or Mattathias's slaying of the Jew at the altar (1 Macc. 2:23–27) that touched off the Maccabean revolt.

12–13 Phinehas had showed that he could act with Yahweh's own zeal in difficult situations. This act won him God's promise of wholeness *(my covenant of peace, 'eṯ-bᵉrîṯî šālôm).* The word *covenant* here has the meaning of a "bond" of obligation. Basic to the sense of covenant throughout the OT is this sense of "bond" or "obligation" rather than "mutuality between parties." The covenant is, further, called *my* (viz., God's) *covenant.* The bond of obligation, therefore, is as absolute and dependable as God.[43] The material principle of this promise — its content and result — is *šālôm,* "wholeness."[44] This covenant was not limited to Phinehas alone, for his descendants are included in what v. 13 calls *a covenant of everlasting priesthood (bᵉrîṯ kᵉhunnaṯ 'ôlām).* This phrase

42. See BDB, p. 888. In the context of the ritual for the suspected adulteress (5:11–31) the terms have been translated "suspicious" and "suspicion." That translation is justified by the context, as the present one is (see above on 5:11–31). For more on *qin'â, qānā', qannā',* etc., see L. Coppes, *TWOT,* II:802–3; A. Stumpff, *TDNT,* II:878–80, 883–84; see also the brief but excellent article by N. J. Opperwall, R. J. Wyatt, *ISBE,* rev., II:971–73. From the perspective of systematic theology, Bernard Ramm stated that God's *zeal* was the outworking of the attention he gave to the cosmos he created. God does not view the cosmos with detachment, but with intense (jealous/zealous) care (B. Ramm, *Special Revelation and the Word of God* [Grand Rapids: Eerdmans, 1961], p. 90).

43. The literature on "covenant" *(bᵉrîṯ)* is massive. Good representative discussions with bibliographies may be found in M. Weinfeld, *TDOT,* II:253–79; G. Quell, *TDNT,* II:106–24.

44. On *šālôm,* see the commentary above on 6:26.

should be taken as synonymous with *my covenant of peace* in v. 12. It gives the formal principle *(everlasting priesthood)* that would shape the content of wholeness *(šālôm)*.

Of course, the beneficiaries of this everlasting priesthood would be not only Phinehas and his descendants, because a priest's work is as a mediator between God and people. In a situation of extreme crisis, Phinehas had acted in a way that made it possible for him to make the people beneficiaries of this covenant of wholeness: *he made atonement for the children of Israel (wayᵉḵappēr ʿal-bᵉnê yiśrāʾēl).*[45] The term *to make atonement* indicates the mediatorial work of the priest that averts God's wrath, usually by means of some sort of offering, here the sacrifice of the Israelite man and his Midianite consort (rather than the usual animal substitute for the human offender). It is possible that the basis of the term *kippēr* here is *kôp̱er,* "the ransom price," and that the death of Zimri and Cozbi in some way paid this price for the Israelites, i.e., allowed them to receive a lighter sentence than was deserved (in this case, death to the whole nation).[46] The outcome of Phinehas's zealous mediation was the end of the plague and a restored communion ("wholeness," *šālôm*) with Yahweh.

The priesthood itself had been promised to all the descendants of Aaron, not just the offspring of Eleazar (cf. Lev. 10; Num. 3:2–4; 1 Chr. 24:1–6; Ezra 8:2). It is not necessary to see the present passage as eliminating the descendants of Ithamar from that priesthood, since it is clear from such passages as 1 Chr. 24:1–6 that they still functioned as priests later than this period. It is also clear from Num. 20:24–29 that the succession to the high priesthood was not, to this point, automatically passed from father to son. The high priest could simply be called "the priest" (as Aaron is many times, and as Phinehas himself is in Josh. 22:13). Here it is established that, henceforth, the high priest would come from the descendants of Phinehas (cf. 1 Chr. 5:27–41 [Eng. 6:4–15]).[47]

14–15 These two verses give the names and families of the two slain people. They were perhaps not given until now because insertion of them in vv. 6–9 would have deflected the main point of those verses, which was not connected with the specific identity of the pair but with their sin,

45. See the close parallel to this passage in 17:11 (Eng. 16:46), where the same verb is used; cf. also the commentary on 8:19 above and on 31:50 below.

46. See Wenham, *Leviticus,* pp. 27–28, 59–61; also the commentary below on 31:50.

47. So also Cook, p. 751; Noordtzij, pp. 242–43; Noth, p. 199; Wenham, p. 188. Apart from a short period during Eli's time, the succession seems to have happened in the way set forth here (1 Sam. 1–3; 14:3).

its consequences, and Phinehas's reaction. Listing the names at the end of the narrative gives them a certain emphasis. Some scholars have seen the absence of the names in vv. 6–9 as a sign that vv. 14–15 are later compositions.[48]

Zimri the son of Salu (zimrî ben-sālû'). For the name Zimri see 1 K. 16:9–20; 2 K. 9:31; 1 Chr. 2:6; 8:36; 9:42. These particular individuals are not named again (but cf. 1 Macc. 2:26).

a leader of a Simeonite father's house (nᵉśî' bêṯ-'āḇ laššim'ōnî). (On *father's house* see the commentary above on 1:2.) Simeon as a tribe suffered an immense population loss between the first and second censuses (from 59,300 to 22,200). The decline in population may be connected to the plague reported here. It may well be that the Simeonites were the chief culprits in this matter, but, of course, this is speculative.

Kozbi the daughter of Zur (kozbî baṯ-ṣûr). Her name is found only here and in v. 18. *Zur* is a leader *(rō'š)* here, a chief *(naśî')* in v. 18 and Josh. 13:21, while in Num. 31:8 he is listed as one of the five *kings (mᵉlāḵîm)* of Midian. The term may mean no more than a local leader.

head of tribes (rō'š 'ummôṯ). The latter word is found only three times in the OT. In Ps. 117:1 it parallels "nations" *(gōyim)*; hence some kind of political or ethnic unit may be in view. If *father's house* here is a gloss, as, e.g., Paterson held, then the expression *head of tribes* may be a Midianite expression that is equated with this smaller unit of the Hebrew clan.[49] The construct chain "head of the peoples of a father's house" is an alternative way to read the whole without recourse to the hypothetical glossator.

16–18 These verses summarize and repeat the salient points of the story. They unify various elements in the chapter. The mention of Peor refers to the incident that formed scene one of the story (vv. 3, 5), and the mention of Kozbi refers to the incident that forms the center of the second scene (vv. 6–9, 15). The phrase *in the matter of ('al-dᵉḇar)* is repeated.[50] The element that the verses do not repeat is the everlasting tenure of the descendants of Phinehas in the (high) priesthood. These verses also set up the conflict that will arise in ch. 31, the attack on Midian.

48. E.g., Gray, p. 384; Noth, p. 199; Sturdy, p. 185; de Vaulx, p. 300; Budd, p. 280.

49. Paterson, p. 60.

50. As in the translation above, the first two instances of this phrase should be translated as "in the matter of" (viz., Peor and Kozbi), and the third "on account of the matter of (Peor)," giving the reason for the slaying of Kozbi; cf. Gray, p. 387.

C. THE SECOND CENSUS (25:19–26:65)

19 *And, after the plague, it happened*
26:1 *that Yahweh spoke to Moses and to Eleazar the son of Aaron the priest, saying:*
2 *"Calculate the total of all the congregation of the children of Israel, from twenty years old upward, by their fathers' houses, all in Israel going out to the army."*
3 *And Moses and Eleazar the priest spoke to them in the plains of Moab, over against the Jordan by Jericho, saying:*
4 *"From twenty years old and upward," as Yahweh had commanded Moses.*[1] *And the children of Israel who came out of the land of Egypt:*
5 *Reuben, Israel's firstborn: the sons of Reuben:*[2] *of*[3] *Hanoch, the clan of the Hanochites; of Pallu, the clan of the Palluites;*
6 *of Hezron, the clan of the Hezronites; of Carmi, the clan of the Carmites.*
7 *These are the clans of the Reubenites; and their numbers were 43,730.*
8 *And the son*[4] *of Pallu: Eliab.*
9 *And the sons of Eliab: Nemuel and*[5] *Dathan and Abiram. These are Dathan and Abiram, chosen*[6] *by the congregation, who struggled against Moses and Aaron in the congregation of Korah, when they struggled against Yahweh.*
10 *And the ground opened up its mouth and swallowed them and Korah, when the company died and the fire consumed two hundred fifty men and became a warning sign.*
11 *But the sons of Korah did not die.*

1. *BHS* wants to place the end of the verse here. Since MT makes sense and *BHS* offers no textual support for the emendation, MT is retained.

2. *BHS* proposes to add the word *l^{e}mišp^{e}ḥōṯām,* "according to their clans," here as in vv. 12, etc. Paterson (p. 60) says that this is the more necessary in the beginning of the list.

3. For MT *ḥ^{a}nôḵ, BHS* proposes reading *laḥ^{a}nôḵ,* "of Hanoch," here.

4. MT reads *ûḇ^{e}nê,* "and the sons of," but the *Sebir* note reads the sing., which makes sense since only one son is named.

5. *BHS* and many others propose deleting the name Nemuel and the following "and" on the name Dathan. Nemuel is found in v. 12. Of course, two persons could have the same name.

6. The Ketib is *q^{e}rû'ê,* a masc. pl. passive construct participle, while the Qere is a masc. pl. construct adjective. The reverse of the present situation occurs in 1:16.

12 *The sons of Simeon, according to their clans: of Nemuel,*[7] *the clan of the Nemuelites; of Jamin,*[8] *the clan of the Jaminites; of Jakin,*[9] *the clan of the Jakinites;*

13 *of Zerah,*[10] *the clan of the Zerahites; of Shaul, the clan of the Shaulites.*

14 *These are the clans of the Simeonites:*[11] *22,200.*

15 *The sons of Gad,*[12] *according to their clans: Of Zephon,*[13] *the clan of the Zephonites; of Haggi, the clan of the Haggites; of Shuni, the clan of the Shunites;*

16 *of Ozni,*[14] *the clan of the Oznites; of Eri, the clan of the Erites;*

17 *of Arod,*[15] *the clan of the Arodites; of Areli, the clan of the Arelites.*

18 *These are the clans of the sons of Gad, according to their numbers: 40,500.*

19 *The sons of Judah: Er and Onan; and Er and Onan died in the land of Canaan.*

20 *The sons of Judah, according to their clans were: of Shelah, the clan of the Shelanites; of Perez, the clan of the Perezites; of Zerah, the clan of the Zerahites.*

21 *And the sons of Perez were: of Hezron, the clan of the Hezronites; of Hamul,*[16] *the clan of the Hamulites.*

22 *These were the clans of Judah, according to their numbers: 76,500.*

7. Pesh. reads "of Jemuel" here; cf. Gen. 46:10; Exod. 6:15.

8. In Gen. 46:10 and Exod. 6:15 Ohad is in the third place, preceded by Jamin. One suspects either that the Ohadites died out (perhaps Zimri was the head of that clan, 25:14) or that some different traditions have been transmitted here.

9. In 1 Chr. 4:24 the name is Jarob.

10. Both Gen. 46:10 and Exod. 6:15 have Zohar *(ṣōḥar)* instead of Zerah *(zeraḥ).*

11. *BHS* proposes insertion of *lipquḏêhem,* "according to their numbers," as in v. 18, etc. (cf. v. 7). The LXX reads "from their numbers" *(ek tēs episke-pseōs).* It is judged more likely that the proposed insertion is secondary in the interest of textual uniformity.

12. LXX has vv. 15–18 on the Gadites after v. 27 (Zebulunites), as in Gen. 46. It is likely that LXX modified the order for uniformity with Gen. 46. Retain MT.

13. In Gen. 46:16 MT reads *ṣip̱yôn,* Ziphion, rather than *ṣ^{e}p̱ôn,* Zephon, as here. This is a spelling variant.

14. In Gen. 46:16 MT reads *'eṣbôn,* Ezbon, rather than *'oznî,* Ozni, as here.

15. In Gen. 46:16 MT reads *'^{a}rôḏî,* Arodi, rather than *'^{a}rôḏ,* Arod, as here. This is a spelling variant.

16. Instead of Hamul *(ḥāmûl)* and Hamulites *(ḥāmûlî)* Sam. Pent. has Hamuel and Hamuelites; LXX has *Iamouēl* and *Iamouēli.* These are spelling variants.

23 *The sons of Issachar, according to their clans: of*[17] *Tola, the clan of the Tolaites; of Puvah,*[18] *the clan of the Punites;*
24 *of Jashub,*[19] *the clan of the Jashubites; of Shimron, the clan of the Shimronites.*
25 *These are the clans of Issachar, according to their numbers: 64,300.*
26 *The sons of Zebulun, according to their clans: of Sered, the clan of the Seredites; of Elon, the clan of the Elonites; of Jahleel, the clan of the Jahleelites.*
27 *These are the clans of the Zebulunites, according to their numbers: 60,500.*
28 *The sons of Joseph, according to their clans:*[20] *Manasseh and Ephraim.*
29 *The sons of Manasseh: of Machir, the clan of the Machirites; and Machir fathered Gilead; of Gilead, the clan of the Gileadites.*
30 *These are the sons of Gilead: of Iezer,*[21] *the clan of the Iezerites; of Helek, the clan of the Helekites;*
31 *and of Asriel, the clan of the Asrielites; and of Shechem,*[22] *the clan of the Shechemites;*
32 *and of Shemida, the clan of the Shemidaites; and of Hepher,*[23] *the clan of the Hepherites.*

17. *BHS* proposes to read *l^eṯôlaʿ*, "of Tola," with a few Hebrew mss., Sam. Pent., and LXX. A letter *(l)* has dropped out of the Hebrew.

18. Many Hebrew mss. read *puwwâ*, Puvvah, instead of *puwâ*, Puvah, here. Sam. Pent., LXX, Pesh., and Vulg. evidently read Puah and Puhites (cf. 1 Chr. 7:1). The Hebrew consonant *waw (w)* was pronounced differently in different geographical areas. The different spellings are attempts to reflect these different pronunciations.

19. In Gen. 46:13 the name is *yôḇ*, Iob. The name Jashub may be a longer version of Iob.

20. *BHS* proposes transposing the word *l^emišp^{e}ḥōṯām*, "according to their clans," after "Manasseh" in v. 29. Since the tribe of Joseph is (uniquely) further divided into two half-tribes (Manasseh and Ephraim), which, then, each take on the status of a full tribe, this statement is consistent with the rest of the census document. *BHS* also offers no textual support for the proposal. Retain MT.

21. For MT *'îʿezer*, "Iezer," Sam. Pent. and LXX read "Ahiezer and the Ahiezerites." Some LXX mss. also read *tō Achiezer*. *BHS* proposes that *l^e'îʿezer*, "of Iezer," be read. Josh. 17:2 reads *'^{a}ḇîʿezer*, Abiezer, of which Iezer may be an abbreviation. The translation accepts *BHS*'s proposal (cf. v. 23 note).

22. For MT *w^e'aśrî'ēl* and *w^ešeḵem* LXX reads *tō Esriēl* and *tō Sychem;* on this basis, *BHS* proposes that *l^e'aśri'ēl* and *l^ešeḵem* be read here. The translation accepts this proposal (cf. notes on vv. 23, 30).

23. LXX reads *tō Sumaer* and *tō Omer* here; on this basis, *BHS* proposes that *liš^{e}mîḏâ* and *l^eḥēper* be read here. LXX obviously carries alternate names here as well. See the previous note.

33 *Now Zelophehad son of Hepher had no sons, but rather daughters; and the names of Zelophehad's daughters: Mahlah, Noah, Hoglah, Milcah, and Tirzah.*
34 *These are the clans of Manasseh, according to their numbers: 52,700.*
35 *These are the sons of Ephraim, according to their clans: of Shuthelah, the clan of the Shuthelahites; of Becher, the clan of the Becherites;*[24] *of Tahan,*[25] *the clan of the Tahanites.*
36 *And these are the sons of Shuthelah: of Eran, the clan of the Eranites.*[26]
37 *These are the clans of the sons of Ephraim, according to their numbers: 32,500. These are the sons of Joseph, according to their clans.*
38 *The sons of Benjamin, according to their clans: of Bela, the clan of the Belaites; of Ashbel,*[27] *the clan of the Ashbelites; of Ahiram, the clan of the Ahiramites;*
39 *of Shephupham,*[28] *the clan of the Shuphamites; of Hupham, the clan of the Huphamites.*
40 *The sons of Bela were Ard*[29] *and Naaman;*[30] *the clan of the Ardites;*[31] *and of Naaman, the clan of the Naamites.*
41 *These are the sons of Benjamin, according to their clans; and their numbers:*[32] *45,600.*
42 *These are the sons of Dan, according to their clans: of Shuham,*[33]

24. LXX does not have "of Becher, the clan of the Becherites" here. See the commentary on this verse.

25. According to LXX his name is Tanach, which seems to transpose two consonants in the Hebrew name.

26. Sam. Pent., LXX, and Pesh. read Edan instead of Eran.

27. LXX reads *Asybēr*.

28. LXX reads *Sōphan*. *BHS* proposes reading *l^e šû pām* with a few Hebrew mss., some LXX mss., Pesh., Targ., and Vulg. In Gen. 46:21 the sons of Benjamin are Bela, Becher, Ashbel, Gera, Naaman, Ehi, Rosh, Muppim, Huppim, and Ard. Gray (p. 393) proposed that Ehi, Rosh, and Muppim have arisen from a faulty division (and metathesis) of the Hebrew consonants *'ḥyrm špwpm* as *'ḥy (w)r(')š mppm,* and should be read as Ahiram and Shephupham as here.

29. LXX reads Adar (cf. 1 Chr. 8:3); Pesh. reads *'adôr*. This is, again, due to a metathesis of consonants.

30. Sam. Pent. omits the first clause of the verse.

31. This phrase is missing in LXX. Perhaps the word *l^e'ard,* "of Ard," should be inserted before this phrase (as in Sam. Pent.).

32. *BHS* proposes that *ûp^e qud̲êhem,* "and their numbers," be emended to read *lip^e qud̲êhem,* "according to their numbers," with Pesh. (as in v. 50 below).

33. According to Gen. 46:23 the name is Hushim *(ḥušîm);* cf. 1 Chr. 7:12. This is a matter of a simple metathesis of consonants.

the clan of the Shuhamites. These are clans of Dan, according to their clans.

43 *All the clans of the Shuhamites, according to their numbers: 64,400.*[34]

44 *The sons of Asher, according to their clans: of Imnah,*[35] *the clan of the Imnites;*[36] *of Ishvi,*[37] *the clan of the Ishvites; of Beriah, the clan of the Beriites.*[38]

45 *The sons of Beriah: of Heber, the clan of the Heberites; of Malchiel, the clan of the Malchielites.*

46 *And the name of Asher's daughter was Sarah.*

47 *These are the clans of the sons of Asher; according to their numbers: 53,400.*

48 *The sons of Naphtali, according to their clans: of Jahzeel, the clan of the Jahzeelites; of Guni, the clan of the Gunites;*

49 *of Jezer, the clan of the Jezerites; of Shillem, the clan of the Shillemites.*

50 *These are the clans of Naphtali according to their clans;*[39] *and their numbers:*[40] *45,500.*

51 *These are the numberings of the children of Israel: 601,730.*

52 *And Yahweh spoke to Moses, saying:*

53 *"To these let the land be divided in inheritance by the number of names.*

34. The fact that only one clan has been named for Dan (the tribe with the second largest population), along with the phrase (unique to this list) "all the clans of" *(kol mišpᵉḥōṯ),* has led many scholars to propose that vv. 42–43 are corrupt (e.g., Paterson, p. 60). *BHS* proposes that the words *lᵉmišpᵉḥōṯām kol-mišpᵉḥōṯ haššûḥāmî,* "according to their clans, all the clans of the Shuhamites," be excised as additions to the text.

35. LXX reads *Iamin.*

36. LXX reads *Iamini,* rather than MT *hayyimnâ.* One ms. of Sam. Pent. reads *hayyimnî.*

37. For MT *hayyišwî* Sam. Pent. reads *yišwậ.* Gen. 46:17 has both *yišwâ* and *yišwî,* Ishvah and Ishvi. LXX reads *Iesou, Iesoui.* It is likely that Ishvi arose by dittography (Cook, p. 755; Gray, p. 394), or that alternate traditions are included at Gen. 46:17.

38. LXX places the verses on Asher (44–47) after the verses on Gad (15–18), which LXX has after the verses on Zebulun (ending in v. 27). See n. 12 above.

39. *BHS* proposes that the word *lᵉmišpᵉḥōṯām,* "according to their clans," be deleted with Pesh.

40. *BHS* proposes that the word *ûp̄ᵉquḏêhem,* "and their numbers," be emended to read *lip̄ᵉquḏêhem,* "according to their numbers," with Pesh. (as in v. 41).

54 *For the many, you shall make their inheritance great; and to the few, you shall make their inheritance small, their inheritance will be given to them, every one according to their numbers.*
55 *But the land will be divided by lot. They shall inherit by the names of their fathers' tribes.*
56 *Their inheritance will be divided between the many and the few according to the lot.*
57 *And these are the numbers of the Levites; according to their clans: of Gershon, the clan of the Gershonites; of Kohath, the clan of the Kohathites; of Merari, the clan of the Merarites.*
58 *These are the clans of Levi: the clan of the Libnites, the clan of the Hebronites; the clan of the Mahlites; the clan of the Mushites; the clan of the Korahites.*[41] *And Kohath was the father of Amram.*
59 *And the name of Amram's wife was Jochebed, the daughter of Levi, who was born*[42] *to Levi in Egypt. And she bore Aaron, Moses, and Miriam their sister to Amram.*
60 *And Nadab, Abihu, Eleazar, and Ithamar were born to Aaron.*
61 *But Nadab and Abihu died when they offered strange fire before Yahweh.*[43]
62 *And their numbers were 23,000, every male from one month of age and upward. For they were not counted*[44] *in the midst of the children of Israel because an inheritance in the midst of the children of Israel had not been given to them.*
63 *These are the numberings of Moses and Eleazar the priest who numbered the children of Israel on the plains of Moab over against the Jordan by Jericho.*
64 *But among these there was not a one from the numberings of the children of Israel that Moses and Aaron made in the wilderness of Sinai.*

41. LXX reads *dēmos ho Kore kai dēmos ho Mousi,* "the clan of the Korahites and the clan of the Mushites."

42. MT *'ᵃšer yālᵉḏâ 'ōṯāh,* lit., "which she bore her," is problematic. The verb *yālᵉḏâ* ("she bore") is the third person fem. sing., which here may be taken impersonally as a circumlocution for the passive, i.e., "who was born," referring to Jochebed (see also 1 K. 1:6); see Davidson, *Syntax,* § 108 Rem. 1. Other suggestions include: *BHS* and Keil, p. 212, follow Targ. Pseudo-Jonathan in reading "her mother" *('immāh)* instead of MT *'ōṯāh;* Cook (p. 757) noted that some have even suggested taking the consonants *'th* as a proper name, Athah; Pesh. and Vulg. have repointed the verb *yālᵉḏâ* as the passive *yullᵉḏâ,* which is equivalent to what has been suggested here.

43. LXX adds the phrase *en tē herēmō Sina,* "in the wilderness of Sinai," as in v. 64, and so, again, makes the text more complete and uniform. MT is, therefore, more likely to be original.

44. On the form of the verb *hoṯpāqᵉḏû,* see GKC, § 54l.

65 *For Yahweh had said to them that they would surely die in the wilderness, and not a one of them would be left except Caleb the son of Jephunneh and Joshua the son of Nun.*

The last of the old generation died in the plague of ch. 25, thus bringing the punishment announced in 14:29–30 to fulfillment (26:64–65). A census of the new generation was appropriate, therefore, in order to replace that of chs. 1, 3, and 4. The approximate time of this new census is given in 25:19 as "after the plague." Vv. 3, 63 give the site of the census as "the plains of Moab" (*b*$^{e\text{c}}$*ar*^{e}*ḇōṯ mô'āḇ,* v. 3), as opposed to the first census, which took place "in the wilderness of Sinai" (*b*^{e}*miḏbar sînāy;* cf. 1:1), from which census only Caleb, Joshua, and Moses were left alive (cf. v. 65). One purpose of this second census was military (cf. "all in Israel going out to the army," *kol–yōṣē' ṣāḇā' b*^{e}*yiśrā'ēl,* v. 3; cf. 1:3, 20, 22, etc.). The Israelites had just been given orders to go to war with Midian (25:16–18), and beyond that lay the conquest of Canaan. So, although this second census marks a new beginning, it takes the reader back to 1:1, as if the events of the wilderness (10:11–25:18) had not happened.[45] A further, more important purpose for this census is the division of the land of Canaan into tribal allotments based, at least in part, on the population numbered in this census (vv. 52–56).

The list itself follows the makeup and order of ch. 1,[46] except that the order of Manasseh and Ephraim is reversed here, perhaps because of the former's growth and the latter's decline. Unlike ch. 1, the major occupation of this list is the division of the tribes into clans *(mišp*^{e}*ḥōṯ).* The list of Jacob's sons in Gen. 46:8–26 forms the basis of this clan list, with the names of the sons transformed into clan names (as the regular repetition of the words *according to their clans* shows). Gen. 46:8–26 has the superscription "the names of the children of Israel who came into Egypt" *(š*^{e}*môṯ b*^{e}*nê–yiśrā'ēl habbā'îm miṣray*^{e}*mâ),* while the present list begins "the children of Israel who came out of Egypt" *(b*^{e}*nê yiśrā'ēl hayyōṣ*^{e}*'îm mē'ereṣ miṣrāyim,* v. 4), i.e., at the exodus. One cause of the differences between these two lists (e.g., alternate spellings, related but different names for the same clan, the disappearance of the clan of Ohad

45. On the importance of chs. 1 and 26 to the structure of Numbers, see D. T. Olson, *The Death of the Old and the Birth of the New: The Framework of the Book of Numbers and the Pentateuch,* BJS 71 (Chico, Calif.: Scholars Press, 1985), esp. pp. 83–124.

46. See the commentary above on ch. 1. Generally, Levi is left out of the list of tribes and the number is brought back to twelve by the splitting of Joseph into Manasseh and Ephraim.

from Simeon) is probably events in the years between the descent into and the exodus from Egypt. On the basis of the claims of the text itself there would be an even longer time between the current list and those of 1 Chr. 2–8. Some differences between Num. 26 and 1 Chronicles may be understood in the same way. Other differences may be explained by positing different purposes for the various lists.

Numbers 26 is interested in the clans rather than the founders of the clans, all of whom were long dead, and one must reckon with the probability of variant traditions concerning these clans as distance from the actual events increased. The basic word used to describe the relationship of the names in the list is *son (bēn)*. The term can either be used of a first-generation offspring (e.g., Hanoch "son" of Reuben, 26:5) or of a second-(or later) generation of offspring (e.g., Eliab the "son" of Pallu, the "son" of Reuben, 26:8) — a more distant, if just as direct, relation to the "father." The political reality behind the term *son* in Num. 26 is probably the clan (e.g., Hanoch "son" of Reuben, 26:5), and behind a "grandson" a subclan (e.g., Eliab the "son" of Pallu, the son of Reuben, 26:8). Often, due to the fact that the word *ben,* "son," may mean no more than "descendant," there is a variant in the tradition as to whether one of these groups was a "son" or a "grandson."[47] One suspects that whether a clan was listed as a "son" or "grandson" had to do with its political importance, size, etc., which would vary from time to time, so that what seemed important (a "son") at one time might seem less so (a "grandson") at others. The most important item seems to be tribal lineage, on which Gen. 46 and Num. 26 agree for the most part.[48] But if the present forms of the lists in Gen. 46 and Num. 26 are the products of the postexilic age (hence not all that far in time from those of the Chronicler), then the differences are less easy to explain.

The current census gives the total number of people, listed not by clan but by tribe. It may be assumed that these totals were computed by adding the figures for each clan. The totals of five tribes decrease (Reuben, 2,770 less; Simeon, 37,100; Gad, 5,150; Ephraim, 8,000; Naphtali, 8,000), for a total decrease of 61,020. The totals of seven tribes increase (Judah, 1,900 more; Issachar, 9,900; Zebulun, 3,100; Manasseh, 20,500; Benjamin, 10,200; Dan, 1,700; Asher, 11,900), for a total increase of 59,200.

47. Cf. Gen. 47:21, where Naaman and Ard are sons of Benjamin; and Num. 26:40, where they are his grandsons through Bela. See the commentary below on Manasseh.

48. For specific differences between the two lists (and some references to the later lists of Chronicles), see the notes to the translation above as well as the comments below.

The net decrease is only 1,820 in spite of the judgment of God on Israel in the period between the two censuses.[49]

Some incidental notes that have no direct relevance to a census document are added to the present passage. See, e.g., the notes on Reuben's being firstborn (v. 5a); on the rebellion of Dathan, Abiram, and Korah (vv. 9–11); on Judah's sons (v. 19); on Zelophehad's and Asher's daughters (vv. 33, 46). Of these, the second and fourth refer to incidents that have taken place or will take place in Numbers (chs. 16–17; 27; 36). The others also occur in Gen. 46:9, 12, 17, and may have been transmitted for that reason.

One might assume that both the clan lists and the total figures are reported because the division of the land was to be based not only on the number of people in a tribe but also on the number of clans in it. Vv. 52–56 set out the bases for the division of the land: proportionality to numbers (vv. 53–54), and casting the sacred lot (v. 55). One cannot be sure how these two procedures were related (see below).

Since the Levites are not to have a physical inheritance in the land of Canaan itself (cf. 18:20), they are not included in the census with the other twelve tribes but have their own numbering in vv. 57–62. V. 63 is a conclusion that rounds off the list. Vv. 64–65 are an editorial comment that differentiates the current census from the first one and reminds the reader that the curse of 14:29–30 has come to be a fulfilled reality.

25:19–26:4a The instructions to Moses are summarized in terms similar to 1:2–3, 18–19 to connect the second census to the first. The purpose here is also military (see above). The high priest by now is Eleazar (the rationale for his high priesthood is explained again in v. 61), and the site is the plains of Moab. This, along with the general date *(after the plague),* differentiates the second census from the first.

4a *From twenty . . . Moses* is difficult. Whether something has fallen out of the MT or it was intended to be only a partial repetition of Yahweh's command is unknown. Commentators have offered many emendations of the text, the best of which seems to be Paterson's: "and Moses and Aaron *numbered* them[50] on the plains of Moab over against the Jordan by Jericho, from twenty years old and upward."

49. On the large numbers, see the "Excursus on Large Numbers" above.

50. This emendation follows Pesh., and involves reading MT *wayᵉḏabbēr,* "and he spoke," as *wayyip̱qōḏ,* "and he numbered," and eliminating the word *lēʾmōr,* "saying," as a gloss inserted to make sense of the verb "to say." Those who accept this emendation include Paterson, p. 60; *BHS;* cf. Moffatt, NEB, GNB. Most English versions simply insert the missing words from v. 3, i.e., "take a census of all males"; cf. AV, RV, RSV, NIV. The difference between the two positions is slight.

the Jordan by [lit., "of"] *Jericho.* This idiom, found again in v. 63, indicates the portion of the Jordan River that flowed near the city of Jericho.

4b This sentence should not be taken as a second object for the verb "to command" (as in AV, RV, NKJV), but as a separate sentence that forms the superscription for the clan lists to follow in vv. 5–51.

who came out of the land of Egypt. Some scholars have held that this clause is careless or unoriginal because they insist on seeing the clan names in vv. 5–51 as contemporary with the author of the chapter.[51] But the list is a traditional one, based on the list in Gen. 46:8–26, differing from it in that the latter gives the names of those who went *into* Egypt (Gen. 46:8). Num. 26 also differs from Gen. 46 in that it is not a list of individuals at all, but of Israelite *clans (mišpeḥōṯ)* at the time of the Exodus (perhaps updated to the author's time). As was said above, the people in this list from whom clans and subclans were named were long dead. Thus the author was using a traditional list wherever one would work, and adding to it where it did not reflect the current reality. Unfortunately it is not always possible to differentiate the traditional list from the contemporizations.

5–11 *the sons of Reuben.* Vv. 5–7 form the basic Reubenite clan list, which matches fairly closely that of Gen. 46:9. Vv. 8–11 add a whole group of clans to the list in order to tie the story of Dathan, Abiram, and Korah to the Reubenites (ch. 16). The reason for the addition of the section may be to amplify 16:1: "Dathan and Abiram, the sons of Eliab, chosen from the congregation." Cf. 1:16; 16:2.

the congregation of Korah. Cf. 16:5. The description of what happened to these rebels in v. 10 shows verbal reminiscences of 16:32, 35, but adds an important element when it claims that the deaths of Korah and his 250 men *became a warning sign (wayyehî lenēs).* Num. 17:3, 5 (Eng. 16:38, 40) teach that the "censers" used by the 250 men became "a sign" *('ôṯ)* and "a reminder" *(zikkārôn)* for Israel; the word *warning sign (nēs)* is not used. In fact, the word has the meaning of *warning* only here in the OT, although it took on that meaning commonly in postbiblical Hebrew.[52] The word *nēs* usually means a conspicuous or visible reminder or sign. It is used in an oracle conerning Egypt (Isa. 30:17) to picture the people of Judah, conspicuous and alone on a hilltop. The parallel term in that verse is "signal-pole" *(tōren).*[53] Elsewhere in Numbers the word is

51. E.g., Sturdy, p. 189; Budd, p. 292.

52. Cf. Jastrow, *Dictionary,* pp. 914b–15a.

53. On *nēs,* see *HALAT,* pp. 662b–63a; M. Wilson, *TWOT,* II:583. On *tōren,* see *HALAT,* pp. 1650b–51a.

used, e.g., to indicate the bronze serpent on the pole, i.e., something to which Israel can look (21:4–9).[54] Here the death of Dathan, Abiram, Korah, and the others is said to be this same kind of thing to which Israel could look, not for healing (as in ch. 21) but for warning. From 16:32–33 one might conclude that all of Korah's family perished with him, but 26:11 denies that his line was cut off. In the postexilic period the Korahites were certainly present (1 Chr. 26:1–9). A number of Psalms are attributed to the sons of Korah, a Levitical guild of temple singers (Pss. 42–49; 84; 85; 87; 88).

12–14 *Simeon.* The list is similar to that of Gen. 46:10; Exod. 6:15 (cf. 1 Chr. 4:24). It would be surprising if some of the clan names had not varied in the time between Gen. 46 and the book of Numbers. Further variations come in by the time of the Chronicler (1 Chr. 4:24). The clan of Ohad in the Genesis and Exodus lists may have died out. It is even possible that Zimri (25:6, 14) was a leader of the Ohadite clan, and that the plague destroyed the clan entirely. Simeon's population dropped by nearly two-thirds between Num. 1 and 26, and it is not hard to believe that some disaster such as recorded in ch. 25 accounts for the tribe's decimation. Gen. 46:10 and Exod. 6:15 state that *Shaul* (v. 13) is the offspring of a Canaanite woman, so contacts with non-Israelites were not new to Simeon.

15–18 *Gad.* The differences between this clan list and the list of names in Gen. 46:16 are minor. The population of Gad also fell quite remarkably in the wilderness period.

19–22 *Judah.* The notice of Er and Onan's deaths occurs in Gen. 38:7, 10 and again in Gen. 46:12. The author of Numbers probably took the information over from the latter source. It may also be included here to give a more complete view of the Judahite clans.

23–25 *Issachar.* Cf. Gen. 46:13; 1 Chr. 7:1.

26–27 *Zebulun.* Cf. Gen. 46:14.

28–37 *Joseph.* This forms the most complex section of the clan list and must have been of special interest to the author. Other than the notice of the two sons Manasseh and Ephraim in Gen. 46:20, that source offers no help. The elimination of Levi as one of the twelve and the concomitant splitting of Joseph into two is a mark of the book of Numbers. Because the section is fuller than some of the rest, principles may be seen at work here that probably underlie the other sections of vv. 5–51 as well. The genealogical list in the current chapter differs from the other lists in

54. For other usages, cf. BDB, pp. 651b–52a.

Numbers by its placement of Manasseh ahead of Ephraim.[55] J. Sasson has suggested that the rationale for such a change was that, occasionally, the order of genealogical lists was altered to place a certain individual in the seventh (or special) place.[56] Here the seventh place belongs to Manasseh, who is the ancestor of Zelophehad (v. 33), whose daughters will figure prominently in chs. 27 and 36.[57]

It is likely (as both Gray and Noordtzij point out) that geography is being discussed here in terms of clans and genealogy.[58]

29–34 *Manasseh.* Put in political terms, the Machirites (Manasseh's "son") are the "father" of Gilead, i.e., the clan took the land in the area of Gilead (and Bashan) in Transjordan (32:39–40; Deut. 3:13–15; Josh. 13:29–31). In this political and geographic setting, the other clans took their origin and moved, in due course, over into west Manasseh. A name such as *Shechem (šeḵem)* is undoubtedly related to the west Manassite town *(š^e ḵem)* (even though the two words are vocalized a bit differently in the MT, the consonants are the same). Judg. 6:11 speaks of Abiezer as a site in west Manasseh, and it is probably to be identified with *Iezer* in 26:30. One may speculate that the east Manassite sites (in Transjordan, Gilead) were settled first, the west sites a bit later (cf. 27:1; 36:1; Josh. 17:3).

The general nature of family terms such as "brother" and "son" when discussing clans may be seen by looking at Josh. 17:1–2, where it is far less clear that (Ab)iezer, Helek, Asriel, Shechem, Hepher, and Shemida are Gilead's actual sons. They are simply called "sons" of Manasseh, and so "brothers" of Machir. Yet other schema for the organization of Manasseh are found in 1 Chr. 2:21–24 and 7:14–19 (e.g., 7:19 calls Shechem the "son" of Shemida, while in Num. 26 both Shechem and Shemida are "sons" of Gilead and "great-grandsons" of Manasseh). Without going further, the point is clear. The family relationships asserted here (and elsewhere) in genealogical language should probably be taken to indicate importance at the time of a particular list. The variants between these lists of names should not make the reader distrust the basic relationships between clan groups, but should caution against pressing these family terms beyond what they were intended to convey.

55. The list of 13:4–5 may be in need of reconstruction; see the commentary.

56. J. Sasson, "A Genealogical 'Convention' in Biblical Chronography," *ZAW* 90 (1978) 171–72.

57. Sasson, "Genealogical 'Convention,'" pp. 181–82; the whole article (pp. 171–85) may be consulted with profit.

58. Gray, pp. 391–92; Noordtzij, pp. 247–48.

The names of *Zelophehad* and his *daughters* are included in v. 33 in order to pave the way for 27:1–11 (and 36:1–13). It is possible that the political reality behind the word "daughters" is the town.[59] *Tirzah* was an important town northeast of Shechem in Manasseh (Josh. 12:24; 1 K. 15:21).[60] A place known as Beth-hoglah is mentioned in Josh. 15:6; 18:19, 21.[61] According to Noordtzij, the fact that all these Manassite names are mentioned together is evidence that the list originated at a time before Manasseh was divided into east and west.[62]

35–37 *Ephraim.* Three clans (Shuthelah, Becher, Tahan) are thought of as major or primary, and one (Eran) as a descendant, hence minor or secondary (in political terms). According to Gen. 46:26 and 2 Sam. 20:1 *Becher* was a son of Benjamin rather than Ephraim. Of course, two men could have had the same name, and both could have founded clans, but Becher is not a Benjaminite in Num. 26. It is possible that, in the time between the entry to and the exodus from Egypt, a clan could have changed its identification from one tribe to another, but whether this did in fact happen is unknown. The list in 1 Chr. 7:20–29 has a Bered as an Ephraimite in v. 20, and this may be an alternate name for Becher.[63] The population of the tribe fell quite seriously between the censuses, and this reduction may explain why the current list reverts to the birth order of Joseph's sons (unlike ch. 1, which names Ephraim first).

38–41 *Benjamin.* Cf. Gen. 46:21; 1 Chr. 7:6–12; 8:1–40. Gen. 46:21 lists Becher as a son of Benjamin rather than of Ephraim (see above). The differences between the Genesis list and the current one probably reflect some historical changes. Both Gen. 46:21 and 1 Chr. 8:3 name Gera as a "son" of Benjamin. It is unknown why this name should be eliminated here. Perhaps no known clan members were counted, although, from 1 Chr. 8, the clan appears to have resurfaced in the postexilic period. Gen. 46:21 also lists both Ard and Naaman as full sons of Benjamin, while the current list makes them grandsons through Bela (see the principles discussed in the paragraphs on Manasseh above). 1 Chr. 8 lists Benjaminite clans known nowhere else.

42–43 *Dan.* Gen. 46:23 agrees that only one clan existed in Dan:

59. On the word *bat̠,* "daughter," meaning "village," see the commentary above on 21:25, 32.

60. See the excellent article by A. F. Rainey in *ISBE,* rev., IV:860–61.

61. See further in Gray, p. 392.

62. Noordtzij. p. 249.

63. This list in 1 Chr. 7:20–29 is unclear; see, e.g., H. G. M. Williamson, *1 and 2 Chronicles,* NCBC (Grand Rapids: Eerdmans, 1982), pp. 80–82.

Shuham (or Husham; see the note on the translation). In the light of the large population of Dan (second only to Judah), it is hard to believe that some less important Danite groups were not sorted out here. 2 Chr. 2–8 give no genealogy of Dan (or Zebulun).

44–50 The clan lists of *Asher* (vv. 44–47) and *Naphtali* (vv. 48–50) are in general agreement with those of Gen. 46:17, 24 respectively (cf. 1 Chr. 7:30–31; 7:13 respectively).

The tribes that have variants and problems are those which have been dealt with in some way by the book of Numbers, or those which became the more important ones (Reuben, Simeon, Manasseh, Ephraim, and Benjamin; Judah should be included in this list of important tribes even though its list is quite normal here). The less important tribes (Gad, Issachar, Zebulun, Asher, and Naphtali) are simply listed in Num. 26 with a minimum of variants. The total of the tribes is down just a bit from that of the previous census. In the MT the total is 601,730 (perhaps 596 tribal units with a total of 5,830 men, plus women and children).[64]

52-56 These verses give the major reason for conducting the second census: the division of the land of Canaan among the twelve tribes. This division will proceed on two bases. First, the population of the tribes will be taken into consideration; the land will be given *To these (lā'ē lleh),* i.e., the just-named tribal/clan groups in proportion to their population, as an *inheritance* (*naḥ^{a}lâ,* vv. 53–54, 56). It is because of this first rule that these verses follow the census document. Second, the principle of division by casting the sacred lot (v. 55) is enjoined (cf. Josh. 14:1; 15:1; 16:1; 17:1; etc.). The sacred lot *(gôrāl)* was thought to be a way of allowing God to reveal his will (Prov. 16:33).

They shall inherit by the names of their fathers' tribes (lišmôṯ maṭṭôṯ-'^{a}ḇōṯām yinḥālû). The phrase *their fathers' tribes* (1:16–17; 13:2; 33:54; 36:4) is a circumlocution for "their ancestral tribe," i.e., Judah, Benjamin, etc. The whole sentence probably means that each individual Israelite and therefore each clan inherited on the basis of tribe rather than on the basis of smaller units. This procedure would ensure that all related clans of a single tribe would live in one place and thus increase the political importance of the whole tribe. V. 56 puts the two principles together without explaining how they mesh. Some scholars have suggested that the area of the land in which a tribe was to live was determined by lot, whereas the size of the tribal inheritance within that general area was proportional.[65]

64. See the "Excursus on Large Numbers" above.

65. So, e.g., Dillmann, p. 175; Keil, p. 211; Gray, p. 395; Snaith,

57–62 Because the Levites were to serve in the tent of meeting, they were not included in the first census (1:47–54; 3:14–39; 4:1–49). A different reason will be given for their exclusion here, but not before the clan list is given. V. 57 gives the traditional list of Levi's offspring (cf. Gen. 46:11; Num. 3:17), put, as with the other tribal lists, into a clan list. The list of Levitical clans and subclans from 3:18–37 is: Gershon (the Libnites, the Shimeites), Kohath (the Amramites, the Izharites, the Hebronites, the Uzzielites), and Merari (the Mahlites and the Mushites), i.e., eight subclans from three clans. Again, by the time of the second census, all the men who founded the clans were long dead. As before, it is *clans, not individuals,* that are in view here.

The current Levitical clans (v. 58a) were: the Libnites (Gershon), the Hebronites (Kohath), the Mahlites (Merari), the Mushites (Merari), and the Korahites (probably Kohath; see below). Other than Amram, who will be mentioned in v. 58b, the Shimeites (through Gershon) and the Izharites and Uzzielites (through Kohath) are left out. The Korahites may simply be an alternate name for the Izharites, since Korah was the descendant of Izhar (16:1). It may be that the Shimeites and Uzzielites were too small in number to be counted as separate clan units at this time. V. 58a may contain only a list of operational subclans at the time. The statements in v. 58a intrude somewhat into the structure of vv. 57, 58b–61, and may be an attempt to widen the background of the Levites to include more information than vv. 58b–61 provide. The latter verses provide another account of the lineage of Aaron, Moses, and Miriam.

And Kohath was the father of Amram. Cf. 3:19; Exod. 6:14–25 (esp. v. 18). V. 58b takes up where v. 57 left off. This Amram is not to be confused with the man of the same name who appears in the next verse (and elsewhere) as the father of Aaron, Moses, and Miriam, many years later. Because the names are the same, the lists of Exod. 6, Num. 26, and 1 Chr. 6:3 fuse the two men by the principle of catchword, viz., putting units with like words (in this case a name) together. The phrase "his father's sister" in Exod. 6:20 and "the daughter of Levi" in Num. 26:59, both describing Jochebed, mean only that she, like the later Amram, was a member of the tribe of Levi. The probability is that these three passages (also, to an extent, Exod. 2:1) pass over the generations between the

---

p. 185. This proposal makes better sense than Noordtzij's conjecture (pp. 249–50) of three lots: one for the general location, another for the specific location within that area, and yet another for the location within that tribal area. Noordtzij himself admits the difficulty of the scheme.

original Amram and Moses' father in order to make the point absolutely clear that Moses (and Aaron and Miriam) were Kohathite Levites, and so entitled to the privileges of Kohathite Levites (e.g., the priesthood). Vv. 60–61 refer to the incident in Lev. 10:1–7 (cf. Num. 3:1–4) and explain again why Aaron's younger sons succeeded him in the high priesthood. It is possible that the current verses, like the so-called extraneous notes in vv. 5–51 (e.g., 8–11, 19, etc.), may have been found in the tradition that the author had before him.

62–63 In the first census the Levites reported 22,000 men of one month of age and older. Here the population increases by 1,000 in spite of the problems of the years of the wilderness wandering. The rationale for including the Levites' clan list after the clan list of the other tribes (vv. 5–51) and after the basis for the census (vv. 52–56) is that they had no land inheritance in Canaan (see above; cf. 18:20), although in 35:1–8 the Levites are given 40 villages (see below). V. 63 is a concluding formula that rounds off the document with the repetition of some information found in the introduction.

64–65 After the conclusion of the census document itself, the whole is placed within the theological framework of the years of the wilderness wandering. At the beginning, the death sentence was pronounced on the entire Exodus generation (14:29–30). Here at the end of the period, the comment is made that the death sentence had been carried out; only Caleb and Joshua (and Moses) were left from the names counted in the first census. The census was written proof that God kept his word. This census also marked the beginning of a new day for God's people. How it would work out only time would tell.

D. DAUGHTERS OF ZELOPHEHAD (27:1–11)

1 *And the daughters of Zelophehad the son of Hepher, the son of Machir, the son of Manasseh, of the clan of Manasseh the son of Joseph, approached. And these are the names of his daughters: Mahlah, Noah, Hoglah, Milcah, and Tirzah.*

2 *And they stood before Moses and before Eleazar the priest and before the leaders and the whole congregation at*[1] *the door of the tent of meeting, saying:*

3 *"Our father died in the wilderness, and he was not a member of*[2]

1. Heb. *peṯaḥ* is a construct noun used locatively, almost as a preposition; see Williams, *Syntax,* § 54.

2. Lit., "in the midst of" *(b^{e}ṯôḵ).*

the congregation who gathered against Yahweh, in the congregation of Korah, but died because of[3] *his own sin. And he had no sons.*
4 *Why should our father's name be lost from membership in his clan? Since he had no sons, give us a possession in the midst of our father's brothers."*
5 *And Moses presented their case before Yahweh.*
6 *And Yahweh spoke*[4] *to Moses, saying:*
7 *"The daughters of Zelophehad are speaking what is right. You will surely give them possession of an inheritance in the midst of their father's brothers, and you will pass over their father's inheritance to them.*[5]
8 *And you will speak to the children of Israel, saying: 'If a man should die without a son, then you will pass over his inheritance to his daughter.*
9 *And, if he had no daughter, then you will give his inheritance to his brothers.*
10 *And, if had no brothers, then you will give his inheritance to his father's brothers.*
11 *And if his father had no brothers, then you will give his inheritance to his nearest relative from his own clan, and he will possess it. And this will become a statutory ordinance for the children of Israel, as Yahweh commanded Moses.' "*

In the census of ch. 26 the tribes had been given the basis for the division of Canaan (made explicit in vv. 52–56). One of the notes in ch. 26 concerns the daughters of the Manassite Zelophehad. The reason for the inclusion of that note now becomes apparent. Although it may be true that these daughters founded clans or towns west of the Jordan, here they are treated as individuals.[6]

These five daughters came to Moses, Eleazar, the tribal leaders, and the congregation at the door of the tent of meeting, the place where

3. Lit., "in his own sin" *(b^e^ḥeṭ'ô),* but the preposition *b^e^-* can mean "because of" (Gen. 18:28; 1 K. 18:18); see Williams, *Syntax,* § 247.

4. MT *wayyō'mer YHWH . . . lē'mōr,* lit., "and Yahweh said . . . saying." Two Hebrew mss., Sam. Pent., and LXX presuppose *way^e^ḏabbēr,* "and he spoke," probably for variety.

5. The verse mixes masc. and fem. suffixes when referring to the daughters (2 masc.: *lāhem,* "to them"; *'^a^ḇîhem,* "their father"; 2 fem.: *'^a^ḇîhen,* "their father"; *lāhen,* "to them"). This is not uncommon in Hebrew; see GKC, § 135o; Davidson, *Syntax,* § 1 Rem. 3.

6. See the commentary above on 26:33.

judgments were issued, with a request and a proposal. Since their father had died without sons, in order that his name not be lost from membership in the clan[7] these daughters proposed that they be allowed to inherit their father's portion of land in Canaan in due course. They supported their case with the assurance that their father had not been connected with Korah's rebellion, but had died in the wilderness along with the rest of the Exodus generation as a fulfillment of God's curse (14:29–30). These daughters, therefore, ought to be on the same legal footing as any other member of their generation (vv. 1–4).

Since this request was unprecedented, Moses took the matter before Yahweh (as before, e.g., in Lev. 24:10–23; Num. 9:6–14; 15:32–36), who decided in favor of the women, allowing that, in the case of a father (and mother; see below) who died without sons, the daughter(s) could inherit the family property (vv. 5–7). This legislation did not cover the matter of the heiress who chose to marry outside her tribe, which would cancel the purpose of the legislation to keep land within the various clans and tribes; hence it had to be modified in ch. 36. A good deal of Hebrew case law was probably formed in the community in a way similar to that narrated here.[8] In the time of a new generation the case of the daughters

7. H. C. Brichto claims that at an early time the afterlife was conceived as the dead living on in male descendants attached to the family land. A dead parent had a good afterlife if his children prospered on the family property (Brichto, "Kin, Cult, Land, and Afterlife: A Biblical Complex," *HUCA* 44 [1973] 1–54, esp. 48). This view of the afterlife is not common, and Brichto's suggestion that this concept existed at an early time is virtually unique.

8. The form of vv. 8–11 is that of case (or casuistic) law: an opening conditional statement (with the particles *'im* or *kî*), followed by more definite circumstances and further conditions along with the action to be taken in the particular circumstances. The opening verses are the narrative framework that gives the occasion for the legislation. Examples of this kind of law are widespread in both the ancient Near East (e.g., the Code of Hammurabi) and the OT (e.g., in the Book of the Covenant [Exod. 20:22–23:33]: 21:2–11; 21:18–22:17; 22:25–27; 23:4–5, 23–33). On the subject of law, see, e.g., the classic essay by A. Alt, "The Origins of Israelite Law," in *Essays on Old Testament History and Religion,* tr. R. A. Wilson (Garden City, N.Y.: Doubleday, 1966), pp. 101–71; E. Gerstenberger, *Wesen und Herkunft des "Apodiktischen Rechts,"* WMANT 20 (Neukirchen-Vluyn: Neukirchener, 1965); H. J. Boecker, *Law and the Administration of Justice in the Old Testament and the Ancient East,* tr. J. Moiser (Minneapolis: Augsburg, 1980); D. Patrick, *Old Testament Law* (Atlanta: Knox, 1985); R. Sonsino, *Motive Clauses in Hebrew Law,* SBLDS 45 (Chico, Calif.: Scholars Press, 1980), esp. pp. 1–152. Gerstenberger criticized Alt's formulation of the so-called apodictic ("command") law, and Patrick divided Alt's casuistic law into two subgroups: primary (as here) and remedial (see Patrick, *OT Law,* pp. 23–24).

of Zelophehad would not be unique, but rather common, and this may be why the matter is included in the Torah, and why vv. 8–11 go beyond the specific case to set forth general legislation in matters of this nature.

The following is the order of inheritance: son, daughter, brother, paternal uncle, nearest clan kin. This same order is followed (with the exception of the daughter) in Lev. 25:48–49, dealing with the different case of redemption of land in the Jubilee year. Thus this general order (again, with the exception of the daughter) may well have been traditional.

This question would probably not have arisen much before the point at which the land of Canaan was divided. From the time of the descent into Egypt the question of the inheritance of land had been irrelevant, but with the conquest of Canaan it became a live issue. In the ancient Near East of the 3rd and 2nd millennia the possibility of daughters' inheriting land existed in several forms: they could inherit (as here) in the absence of sons, or after the sons in a family, or among the sons (as in Job 42:15).[9] It seems that the normal practice in Israel was that daughters did not inherit property, but joined the clan of their husbands after being given a dowry by their fathers (cf., e.g., Gen. 29:24, 29; Judg. 1:13–15; 1 K. 9:16).[10] As the Jubilee legislation showed, the principle was that land was to be kept in the family, clan, and tribe (Lev. 25:10, 13, 25–28), and that, in essence, the families, clans, and tribes assigned to the land were only sojourners on it — the land belonged to Yahweh (Lev. 25:23).[11]

9. See the summaries in Z. Ben-Barak, "Inheritance by Daughters in the Ancient Near East," *JSS* 25 (1980) 22–33; J. Paradise, "A Daughter and Her Father's Property at Nuzi," *JCS* 32 (1980) 189–207. One should not infer that daughters always inherited, or even normally inherited, property; but the possibility was well known across a wide span of time and culture. The date of Job is debated, with scholars arguing for dates between the late 2nd millennium (e.g., W. J. Urbock, "Oral Antecedents to Job, A Survey of Formulas and Formulaic Systems," *Semeia* 5 [1976], 111–37, esp. p. 132) and ca. 400 B.C. (M. Jastrow, *The Book of Job* [New York: Lippincott, 1920], p. 36). Neither Habel (*The Book of Job,* OTL [Philadelphia: Westminster, 1985], pp. 40–42) nor Clines (*Job 1–20,* WBC [Waco, Tex.: Word, 1989], p. lvii) will commit to a specific date. J. Hartley finally commits to a 7th-cent. date (*The Book of Job,* NICOT [Grand Rapids: Eerdmans, 1988], pp. 17–20). In any case the passage in 42:15 is in the epilogue to the book, which, with the prologue, may antedate the final form of the book by centuries.

10. See Boecker, *Law and the Administration of Justice,* p. 118; de Vaux, *Ancient Israel,* I:53–54.

11. This is an important theological affirmation. The affirmation that the land is God's gift to Israel (e.g., Gen. 15:7; 17:8; 24:7; Exod. 6:4; Lev. 20:4; 25:2; Deut. 5:16, 31; 9:6; 11:17) affirms his ownership of it. The observance of the sabbatical year (e.g., Exod. 23:10–11; Lev. 25:1–7; Deut. 15:1–11; 31:10–13), the

A number of scholars have concluded that the current law is later than and perhaps in contradiction to the law of levirate marriage in Deut. 25:5–10.[12] The levirate is undoubtedly old, since the narrative of Gen. 38 is based on the practice, as is the book of Ruth (set in the period of the Judges, although probably written quite a bit later). Whether this requires that the law of Deut. 25:5–10 be earlier than the current passage is debatable. That the two passages contradict one another, as suggested, e.g., by Snaith,[13] is not the case; the two passages concern different situations. Although not said directly, here one may assume that both father and mother are dead (since they were both part of the Exodus generation), and that no further heir is possible, as Noth has seen.[14] Deut. 25 assumes that only the father is dead and thus an heir may be given through the institution of the levirate.

Snaith concluded that this narrative is not about inheritance rights at all, but about how the Manassites came to inhabit territory west of the Jordan. (It is stated that they did so when this whole matter comes up again in Josh. 17:3–6.) Snaith interprets the inheritance "in the midst of our father's brothers" (Num. 27:4) to mean in the midst of the other tribes west of the Jordan.[15] This may have been a secondary use of such a story, but if this were the main aim, one might wonder (with Budd) why the narrator would introduce the complexifying factor of this story about women at all (even to the point of having it inserted in the census

---

Jubilee year (Lev. 25:8–55), and the offering of the firstfruits (e.g., Exod. 34:22; Lev. 23:15–22; Num. 28:26; Deut. 14:22–29; 26:9–15) institutionalize or sacramentalize that ownership. Even the distribution of the land by the sacred lot (Num. 26:55; Josh. 14:2; 18:1–10) points to the fact that God decides the allotments. See, e.g., W. Brueggemann, *The Land,* OBT (Philadelphia: Fortress, 1977); W. D. Davies, *The Gospel and the Land: Early Christianity and Jewish Territorial Doctrine* (Berkeley: Univ. of California Press, 1974); G. von Rad, "Promised Land and Yahweh's Land," in *The Problem of the Hexateuch and Other Essays,* tr. E. W. Trueman Dicken (1943; repr. Edinburgh: Oliver & Boyd, 1966), pp. 79–93.

12. E.g., Gray, pp. 397–98; Binns, p. 188; McNeile, p. 151; Snaith, pp. 185–86; Sturdy, p. 193; Budd, pp. 300–301. Noth (p. 212) and Sturdy allow that an older legal tradition may be behind the general legislation in vv. 8–11.

13. See Snaith, p. 186.

14. See Noth, p. 211.

15. Snaith (pp. 185–86) does not know what to make of this passage. He says it cut across what is known about inheritance in Israel and was a "bad law" (because it had to be modified in ch. 36). Part of this confusion comes from Snaith's adherence to the documentary hypothesis, which required that Deut. 25 be earlier than Num. 27, and part from his failing to see that the two passages refer to different cases. See also Snaith, "The Daughters of Zelophehad," *VT* 16 (1966) 124–27, esp. 126–27.

document of ch. 26).[16] It is far more likely that this narrative does in fact deal with a real concern of the new generation, viz., inheritance rights for daughters in certain cases. This view is strengthened by the fact that ch. 36 clearly deals with inheritance matters and clearly seeks to modify this legislation.

1–4 This section sets the conditions of the request. As stated above, the norm seems to be that daughters did not inherit land, although the complaint of Laban's daughters in Gen. 31:14 might indicate that they could have been given a portion had the father desired it.

the door of the tent of meeting. This was the place where Yahweh met his people for judgment (cf. 6:13; 10:3; 12:5; 16:18–19; 17:15 [Eng. 16:50]; 20:6). Any idea that God was concerned only with laws that affected the spiritual well-being of the nation conflicts with passages like this one. The division of law into things concerning God and things concerning only humans is modern and betrays a view of God as unconcerned with his world that has no basis in the Scriptures.

the congregation of Korah. This congregation was not made up solely of Levites but was a mixed group (see 26:9; cf. 16:5, 11, 16; 17:5 [Eng. 16:40]).[17]

The daughters began their proposal with a statement of facts. Their father was dead, he had not sided with Korah, and he died leaving no sons. The middle term in this statement is significant to show that Zelophehad had not rebelled against God and Moses as Korah had; i.e., he had not committed one of the sins with a high hand (cf. 15:30). This reference may indicate that persons who had been found guilty of such offenses were deprived of their property rights.[18] This statement was to indicate that the basic inheritance was not encumbered by a disqualifying crime. Zelophehad had *died because of his own sin,* i.e., he was guilty of that which every other member of the Exodus generation was guilty of and had paid the price. Therefore the question was only of the daughters' suitability as heirs, since he had no sons.

The daughters argue that current Israelite inheritance practices would cause Zelophehad's name to *be lost from membership in his clan (yiqqāraʿ . . . mittôḵ mišpaḥtô).* The verb basically means "to be taken away" (as in 36:3–4). The implication is that the current practice would

16. See Budd, p. 301.
17. See the commentary above on 16:1–2.
18. See J. Weingreen, "The Case of the Daughters of Zelophehad," *VT* 16 (1966) 518–21.

actually take Zelophehad's name away from its place among the clans of Manasseh. The daughters' request is that they be put on an equal footing with their *father's brothers,* i.e., the other Manassite clans.

a possession (ʾ^{a}ḥuzzâ). This term is commonly used of an inheritance of land (e.g., Gen. 47:11; Lev. 14:34; 25:10, 13, 25, 27–28, 33, 41, 45–46; Num. 32:5, 22, 29; 35:8). With the noun "land" *(ʾereṣ)* it means "possessed land" (e.g., Gen. 36:43; Lev. 14:34; 25:24; Num. 35:28).[19]

5–11 *Moses presented their case before Yahweh* (see 9:8; 15:34; cf. Exod. 18:19; Lev. 24:12–13). Since there was apparently no legal precedent upon which to base a decision, Moses took the matter before Yahweh, who is not only the ultimate arbiter of the law but its source. The process by which God and Moses communicated is not specified, but one might point to 12:8 as a general statement of it.

God declared that what these women had asked was *right* (*kēn,* which means "firm," "upright," or "dependable").[20] They were to be given a landed inheritance among the Manassite clans (i.e., *among their father's brothers,* v. 7; cf. v. 4). The instruction is that Moses *pass over (heʿ^{e}ḇîr)* Zelophehad's land to them. This verb means lit. "to cause to pass over," and in this legal context it implies the "passing over" of property to an heir.[21]

In vv. 8–11 this specific precedent is made into a general prescription. In cases such as vv. 3–4 set forth, the order of inheritance will be: son, daughter, brother, paternal uncle, next of kin in the same clan. This order shows some similarity to that of Lev. 25:48–49, although the case there is different. The current prescription was not meant to replace the normal line of descent through the male heirs, but to make an appropriate exception when the conditions warranted. This general rule is given the force of a *statutory ordinance (ḥuqqaṯ mišpāṭ),* a term used only here and in 35:29 (concerning the Levitical cities) to describe an authoritative statute or a rule of law.[22]

E. JOSHUA NAMED AS MOSES' SUCCESSOR (27:12–23)

12 *And Yahweh said to Moses, "Come up on this Mount Abarim and see the land that I have given to the children of Israel.*

19. See BDB, p. 28b.
20. See BDB, p. 467a; in modern Hebrew, *kēn* means "yes."
21. See BDB, p. 718b (1c).
22. See, e.g., McNeile, p. 153; Weingreen, "Daughters of Zelophehad," p. 519; Sonsino, *Motive Clauses in Hebrew Law,* p. 78.

13 *And, when you have seen it, then you also will be gathered to your kinfolk, just as your brother Aaron was gathered,*
14 *since you rebelled against my command to sanctify me*[1] *in the waters before their eyes in the wilderness of Zin in the contention of the congregation." (These were the waters of Meribah of Kadesh in the wilderness of Zin.)*
15 *And Moses spoke to Yahweh, saying:*
16 *"Let Yahweh, the God of the spirits of all flesh, appoint a man over the congregation*
17 *who can go out before them and come in before them, who can bring them out and bring them in, that the congregation of Yahweh might not be like sheep that have no shepherd."*
18 *And Yahweh said to Moses, "Take Joshua the son of Nun, a man in whom the spirit is, and lay*[2] *your hand upon him.*
19 *And you shall present him before Eleazar the priest and before the whole congregation, and you shall charge him in their sight.*
20 *And you will give some*[3] *of your authority to him, so that the congregation might obey.*
21 *And he shall stand before Eleazar the priest, and he shall inquire for him by means of the Urim before Yahweh. They will go out according to his command and according to his command they will come in, he and all the children of Israel, the whole congregation, with him."*
22 *And Moses did as Yahweh had commanded him, and he took Joshua and presented him before Eleazar the priest and before the whole congregation.*
23 *And he placed his hands upon him and charged him, as Yahweh had spoken by the agency of Moses.*[4]

Just as the censuses of chs. 1, 3, and 4 led to a flurry of preparations for departure from Sinai, so the second censuses in ch. 26 lead to preparations for departure from the plains of Moab and entry into the land of Canaan.

1. Cf. Gray, p. 400.

2. Heb. *sāmaḵ* can also mean "lean"; see BDB, pp. 701b–2a; cf. KB, p. 661.

3. This is the partitive *min,* which is quite common (e.g., Gen. 4:3–4; Exod. 16:27); see Williams, *Syntax,* § 324.

4. MT *bᵉyāḏ-mōšeh* is unusual; a number of versions (including LXX, Targ. Pseudo-Jonathan) presuppose *ka'ᵃšer ṣiwwâ YHWH 'eṯ-mōšeh,* "as Yahweh had commanded Moses," which is the more common expression. Sam. Pent. adds, "and he [Yahweh] said to him [Moses]," and then adds Deut. 3:21b–22. This whole clause reads like an addition to the text in MT. For *bᵉyāḏ* as "by the agency of," see 4:37, 45; BDB, p. 846a.

Thus 5:1–10:10 should be seen as parallel in main thrust to 26:52–36:13 (and on through Deuteronomy). Once the theory for the division of the land had been laid down (26:52–56), a specific problem had arisen for the daughters of Zelophehad (27:1–11). A modification of the rule concerning that group ends this section of the book (ch. 36) as well.

An important, albeit somewhat painful, issue is still to be resolved: a leader to replace Moses. The Exodus generation, with the exception of Moses, Joshua, and Caleb, had now died in the wilderness in fulfillment of the judgment passed on them by God for their unbelief (14:29–30). Of these three men, only Joshua and Caleb were to enter the land. Moses, too, was to perish outside of it on account of his rebellion at Meribah-kadesh (20:12; 27:14). Aaron and Miriam had already died (ch. 20), and Moses was soon to follow.

Scholars usually divide these verses into two distinct units (vv. 12–14, 15–23), often without much attempt at relating them,[5] but the two are closely related, as will be shown below. At the center of the first unit is an announcement of Moses' death (v. 13). In his study of death reports in Gen. 12–50, G. Coats found that they may contain some or all of the following parts: (1) a summary formula noting the age at the time of death, etc.; (2) a death notice (sometimes including the cause of death); (3) a burial notice; (4) a notice of mourning; (5) some notice of the continuance of the line of descent in spite of the death.[6]

Numbers 27 has a few of these parts, but it is more closely related to a special variation on the death report reserved for Aaron, Moses' brother, the other leader of early Israel (20:22–29). Aaron's death report shows the following structure: (1) a geographical indicator (Mt. Hor, vv. 22–23); (2) God's announcement of Aaron's death beforehand, along with the reason for his death (v. 24); (3) the appointment of a successor (vv. 25–26); (4) the execution of the successor's appointment (vv. 27–28a); (5) the actual death report (v. 28b); (6) the mourning rites (v. 29).

The current passage is similarly structured: (1) a geographical indicator (also a mountain, vv. 12–13a); (2) God's announcement of Moses' death beforehand, along with the reason (vv. 13b–14); (3) the appointment of a successor (vv. 15–21); (4) the execution of the succes-

5. So, e.g., Binns, p. 189.

6. See G. W. Coats, *Genesis; with an Introduction to Narrative Literature*, FOTL I (Grand Rapids: Eerdmans, 1983), pp. 163–65 (23:1–20); 172–73 (25:7–11); 174–75 (25:17–18); 238 (35:8); 240–42 (35:16–20); 245–46 (35:27–29); 300–303 (47:28–50:14); 313–15 (50:22–26).

sor's appointment (vv. 22–23). The major difference is that 27:12–23 does not go on to narrate Moses' death. That account is not found in the book of Numbers at all, but in Deut. 34:4–8.[7] The focus here is not on Moses' death but on the need to appoint a successor to Moses to lead the people into Canaan,[8] caused by his imminent death. The two passages are two halves of one reality; one gives the cause, the other the effect.

Many scholars have been surprised by the amount of intervening material between this announcement of Moses' death and his actual death in Deut. 34.[9] In the light of the volume of this intervening material it is not surprising that the command of Num. 27:12–14 is repeated (in a bit greater detail) in Deut. 32:48–52. A number of scholars have concluded that Moses' death report originally followed rather shortly after its announcement (much as in the case of Aaron).[10] First the material in Deuteronomy was added, and later the material in Num. 28–36 (some of the latest material in the Pentateuch) in a kind of miscellany.[11] While this sort of explanation is possible, it is just as plausible to hold that the author of Numbers had known of a number of final deeds and acts of Moses after this announcement and had narrated these in chs. 28–36, concluding with a narrative of Moses' death at the end of ch. 36.[12] When the material of the book of Deuteronomy came to be attached to Numbers, these further words of Moses caused the original ending of Numbers to be removed and added, in expanded form,[13] after the conclusion of Moses' third speech in Deut. 30:20. The whole of Deut. 31–34 forms a coda to the book that focuses on the twin themes of Moses' death and Joshua's succession to the leadership.

7. The structure in Deut. 34:4–8 is very similar to what Coats discovered in the patriarchal stories of Genesis: (1) death notice (vv. 4–5), (2) burial notice (v. 6), (3) summary formula on Moses' death (v. 7), (4) mourning rites (v. 8).

8. There may be some relationship here to the so-called installation genre (cf. D. J. McCarthy, "An Installation Genre?" *JBL* 90 [1971] 31–41), but, if so, the relationship seems to be indirect.

9. Most do not mention, however, that this announcement of Moses' death is really the second announcement of it, and that all the material from 20:13 on to Deut. 34 intervene, not just the material in Num. 28–36 and Deut. 1–30.

10. See Holzinger, pp. 136–37; Baentsch, pp. 637–40; Gray, pp. 399–400; McNeile, p. 153; de Vaulx, pp. 321–25; Budd, pp. 305–6.

11. E.g., Noth, pp. 4–10, 213.

12. This proposal would give chs. 27 and 36 parallel structures; both begin with the case of inheritance rights for women (Zelophehad's daughters) and conclude with the death of Moses.

13. Such passages include a summary of Num. 27:12–14 (Deut. 32:48–52) as well as vv. 15–23 (Deut. 31:1–8, 14–15, 23). Even in Deut. 31–34, Moses' death is postponed by the blessing of Moses (ch. 33).

In effect, the theme of Moses' death becomes a way of prolonging the climax of the story from Num. 20:12 (where it is first announced) until Deut. 34:4–8, where it is narrated. Here in Num. 27:12–23 the tension is heightened by reintroducing the fact that Moses must die before Israel goes into the land. When will he die? That question draws the reader forward through the rest of the book of Numbers and beyond into Deuteronomy, where it is mentioned at least twice (in 1:37–38 and 3:25–28) as a basis for further exhortation (2:1ff.; 4:1ff.). The climax is finally reached just before the Jordan is crossed. Num. 27:12–23 reintroduces this theme as a way of moving the narrative forward to the character of Joshua while keeping the story tied to its roots in Moses.[14]

12–14 *Mount Abarim* (i.e., "the mountain of the parts beyond [the Jordan]"). This is the range of mountains on the western border of Moab that descends to the Jordan Valley near the northeast tip of the Dead Sea. Deut. 32:49; 34:1 are more precise in locating the peak at Mt. Nebo (usually identified as Jebel en-Nebā, about 12 mi. west-northwest of the mouth of the Jordan).[15] There Moses will be allowed to survey the land of promise. Lest the fact that he is allowed to see the land should raise any hope of entering, v. 13 underlines that Moses will not be permitted to go into the land, and the reason why: once he has seen the land he will die.

be gathered to your kinsfolk. The same expression occurs in 20:24. The clause is often found together with the similar "and he breathed his last and died" (Gen. 25:8, 17; 35:29) or simply "he died" (Num. 20:26; Deut. 32:50), and is similar to "to be gathered to one's fathers" (e.g., Judg. 2:10). The reference to the incident at Meribah-kadesh (Num. 20:10–13) is made clear by verbal reminiscences[16] and the reference to Aaron, who died on a mountain as well (20:22–29). The last sentence of v. 14 makes the identification explicit, and may be a later gloss. The rebellion of Moses and Aaron (so called here by that name) will forbid Moses from entering the land, just as it had forbidden Aaron to do so.

the wilderness of Zin. See the commentary above on 13:21.

15–17 Moses' prayer is not for himself but for his people. He has

14. For more detailed conclusions on this section and its relationship to the last part of the book of Numbers as well as the book of Deuteronomy, see G. Myatt, "Numbers 27–30," M.Div. Honours Thesis, Acadia University, 1985, pp. 30–51, 101–5.

15. Snaith, p. 186; see also E. Grohman, *IDB,* III:528–29; S. Saller, M. Piccirillo, *ISBE,* rev., II:504–6.

16. E.g., Meribah *mᵉrîṯem,* "you rebelled"; Kadesh *lᵉhaqdîšēnî,* "to sanctify me." See the commentary above on 20:12.

not always been so concerned about the needs of others (cf. his statements in 11:11–15, 21–22; 20:10), but at this point in his life, he has perhaps learned compassion. In the light of his approaching demise, the timing of which has not been announced and is uncertain, Moses requests a competent leader to take over and lead Israel through the crucial days ahead.

God of the spirits of all flesh. The only other place this divine title is used is 16:22. At the rebellion of Korah, Dathan, and Abiram, when Yahweh had threatened to wipe out the whole congregation, Moses appealed both to his sovereignty and his grace.[17] Here God's sovereignty over his creation is underlined, and, once again in a crisis of leadership that could end disastrously (as the Korahite rebellion had), Moses prays that God will be gracious and show himself committed to his people by appointing a leader to succeed him.

Moses' request is for a leader *who can go out before them and come in before them, who can bring them out and bring them in* (*'ᵃšer-yēṣē' lip̱nêhem wa'ᵃšer yāḇō' lip̱nêhem wa'ᵃšer yôṣî'ēm wa'ᵃšer yᵉḇî'ēm*). These expressions, although not necessarily military in reference (e.g., 2 K. 11:8), are predominantly so (e.g., Deut. 31:2–3; Josh. 14:11; 1 Sam. 18:13, 16; 29:6; 1 K. 3:7), and the military connotation is appropriate to the context. The major task of Moses' successor would be the predominantly military one of conquest and division of Canaan.

before them. Moses' successor must be able to perform in the public eye (*lip̱nêhem,* lit., "to their faces") and to provide real leadership for the people in the coming days.

Unless a leader of this sort is found, Israel will be *like sheep without a shepherd* (*kaṣṣō'n 'ᵃšer 'ên-lāhem rō'eh*). This simile is used as a figure of speech for a scattered, helpless, and defeated people (as in 1 K. 22:17; cf. Ezek. 34:6; Zech. 1:7–8; 13:7), thus continuing the military imagery.

18–21 Yahweh responds to Moses' request by selecting Joshua, and prescribes the procedure by which the leadership is to be transferred. *Joshua* is a man who is qualified for the leadership. Not mentioned explicitly here is his long service to Moses and Israel (e.g., Exod. 17:8–16; 24:13–14; 32:15–20; 33:7–11; Num. 11:26–30; 13:1–14:38), but this is not necessarily a sign that such matters were unknown to the author. In fact, the designation of Joshua as *a man in whom the spirit is* may, in part, refer to these exploits. The use of *spirit* (*rûaḥ*) here links this verse with v. 16, which identifies God as "the God of the spirits of all flesh," i.e., the

17. See the commentary above on 16:22.

sovereign God. Here it simply indicates Joshua's divine endowment for leadership (cf. Gen. 48:14). This spirit was not something that now came upon Joshua, or was temporary (such as the coming of the spirit on the elders in 11:17, 25–26); it already existed in Joshua and was the basis of God's choice of him. Deut. 34:9 applies the phrase "full of the spirit of wisdom" to Joshua, confirming the thought here.

Moses is charged to recognize Joshua's endowment for leadership in three ways. First, he confirms this inner endowment by an external recognition or ceremony: he lays his hand(s) on Joshua. Whether Moses laid one hand or two on Joshua on this occasion cannot be said with certainty, since v. 18 reads the sing. and v. 23 the pl. (as does Deut. 34:9),[18] and the number may not be relevant. The meaning of the ritual is certainly more significant here. Laying a hand (or hands) on someone can accompany a blessing (as in Gen. 48:14), a sacrificial offering (e.g., Exod. 29:10, 15, 19; Lev. 1:4), or a dedication to office (e.g., Num. 8:10). The last sense is most relevant to the present case.[19] The sense basic to all these rituals may be the transfer of something (a blessing, guilt, leadership) from someone to someone (or something) else. In later times the laying on of hands accompanied one's admittance to the office of rabbi, and in Christian practice it accompanied designation of leaders (cf. Acts 6:6; 13:3; 1 Tim. 3:14; 2 Tim. 1:6). (One must be careful not to read later synagogue or church practice back into this text, but having taken note that this passage stands earlier in the stream of tradition than most of the rituals practiced today, one may comment that the theological similarities in the setting apart of leaders for God's people in any age transcend the differences.)

Second, Moses is to *present Joshua before Eleazar the priest.* A literal translation is "you shall cause him [viz., Joshua] to stand before Eleazar the priest." The verb *ʿāmaḏ* (Hiphil) + *lip̄nê* is used 12 times in the OT for an official act of "presentation" of one person before another. In Num. 3:6 and 8:13 the Levites are "presented" to Aaron for service. In 5:16, 18, 30 the suspected adulteress is presented by the priest or her husband before Yahweh for judgment. In Gen. 47:7 Jacob is presented before Pharaoh. In Lev. 14:11 the cleansed leper is presented to Yahweh at the door of the tent of meeting. The common theme in all these passages is the formal act of presentation. Joshua is about to be installed

18. LXX reads the pl. in all three passages.

19. See the commentary above on 8:10. Cf. R. Péter, "L'imposition des mains dans l'Ancien Testament," *VT* 27 (1977) 48–55, esp. 54–55.

as Moses' successor. The formal ceremony begins by Moses' presenting him not only before Eleazar, the religious representative of the people, but also before the whole congregation. The leadership of God's people had been shared by Moses and his brother Aaron, and, as of Num. 20, by Moses and Eleazar, Aaron's son. It was now time for the old generation to give way to the new; Joshua would replace Moses as Eleazar had replaced Aaron. Eleazar is a witness to these proceedings to underline the fact that the leadership is to be cooperative and shared. This shared leadership will be of even more significance in v. 21 (see below). Moses also lays his hand(s) on Joshua before the whole congregation, because it is the congregation who will be a vital part of the success of Joshua's leadership.

Third, Moses is to *charge (ṣiwwâ)* Joshua. This verb means "to command," and is used of Yahweh's directives through Moses to Israel (see, e.g., 27:11, 22). Here the "command" has the sense of a commission to Joshua. Deut. 31:7–8, 23 may be reminiscences of this charge.[20]

Moses will give *some of* his *authority (mēhôḏᵉḵā)* to Joshua. This is the only occurrence of the word *hôḏ* in the Hexateuch. Elsewhere the word is used of the "honor" or "majesty" due to God or a king.[21] Noth thinks that the term must indicate a kind of visible token of Moses' leadership; he translates it "vitality."[22] Most English translations have settled for "authority,"[23] since the purpose is that the people of the congregation *might obey.* This is the first hint that Joshua's leadership will be on a different level than Moses'. If Moses takes *some* of his authority and places it on Joshua, the latter has less authority than the former, and, in fact, derives authority from him (see further on v. 21 below).

Eleazar was a witness to this rite, but he was much more. Moses had been able to communicate directly with God (cf., e.g., 12:8), but Joshua would need to inquire of the high priest, who in turn would *inquire*

20. This passage in Deuteronomy fulfills the criteria for the installation genre set forth by McCarthy ("Installation Genre," pp. 31–41): (1) Encouragement Formula, (2) Description of Task, (3) Assistance Formula. In Num. 27, the most that can be made out is a description of the task in vv. 17b, 21b; cf. Myatt, "Num. 27–30," p. 40.

21. The term is used of God's majesty, e.g., in Ps. 21:6 (Eng. 5); 104:1; and of the king's in, e.g., Ps. 45:4 (Eng. 3); 1 Chr. 29:25 (Solomon's majesty is a gift from God). It is often found in combination with *hāḏār,* "splendor." See BDB, p. 217a; *HALAT,* p. 230; G. Warmuth, *TDOT,* III:335–41.

22. Noth, p. 215.

23. So RSV, NEB, NASB, NIV, NJPS, NKJV, GNB, Moffatt. AV and RV have "honour."

for him by means of the Urim before Yahweh. Joshua would need to depend upon Eleazar and the means of knowing God's will rather than direct communication with Yahweh (but cf. Josh. 20:1). This is the second hint that Joshua's leadership is of a lesser order than Moses'.

The antecedents of two pronouns in v. 21 are unclear. The *he* who is the subject of the verb "to inquire" is Eleazar, since the use of the Urim (and Thummim) was in the hands of the high priest (see below). The pronominal suffix *his* on the word *command* (*pîw,* lit., "his mouth") could refer to Joshua, Eleazar, or Yahweh. The nearest antecedent is Yahweh, and this makes the best sense as well.[24] When, at Joshua's request, Eleazar seeks the will of Yahweh through the Urim, it is finally God who makes the decision no matter who the human agent may be.

the Urim. Except for here and 1 Sam. 28:6, this term is always found with "the Thummim" *(tummîm).* The etymologies of the terms are unreliable guides to their meaning.[25] The Urim and Thummim are often conceived of as flat-surfaced stones entrusted by God to the Levites (Deut. 33:8) and kept in a pocket of the high priest's breastplate (Exod. 28:30; Lev. 8:8). Some scholars conjecture that each side of these stones had one of two colors. The high priest threw them in order to determine God's will in questions answerable by yes or no. If both stones were of one color, the answer would be yes; of the other color, no; and if different colors came up, no answer would be given.[26] In the absence of concrete data, this conjecture may be as good as any, but must be loosely held, as all conjectures should be.[27] The point is that Joshua is dependent on God (through Eleazar) for exercise of his leadership.

In the rite performed by Moses in the presence of Eleazar, both the old generation (Moses) and the new generation (Eleazar) cooperate in the transfer of the leadership to Joshua, the man in the middle, who belongs to the old (Exodus) generation but was exempted from the death sentence

24. Noordtzij (p. 257), Gray (p. 402), and Noth (p. 215) opt for Eleazar (although Noth admits the possibility that it may be Yahweh).

25. Cf. BDB, pp. 22a, 1070b; Snaith, p. 52.

26. E.g., Snaith, pp. 52, 187; Sturdy, pp. 197–98; Budd, p. 307; E. Lipiński, "'Ūrīm and Tummīm," *VT* 20 (1970) 495–96.

27. See the excellent summary by C. van Dam in *ISBE,* rev., IV:957–59, which comes to different conclusions. See further J. Lindblom, "Lot Casting in the Old Testament," *VT* 12 (1962) 164–78, esp. 170–78; E. Robinson, "Urim and Thummim: What Are They?" *VT* 14 (1964) 67–74; J. Maier, "Urim und Tummim. Recht und Bund in der Spannung zwischen Königtum und Priestertum im alten Israel," *Kairos* n.f. 11 (1969) 22–38; Lipiński, "'Ūrīm and Tummīm," pp. 495–96; W. Dommershausen, *TDOT,* II:450–56, esp. 452–54.

passed on that generation and, like the new generation, is going into the land of promise. Thus Joshua provides both continuity with the past and development of a new kind of leadership for the future. It is clear, however, that, even though the leadership has been passed ritually to Joshua, Moses continues to exercise the leadership as long as he is alive. Moses and Joshua may be partners in leadership from now until the end of Deuteronomy,[28] but Moses is clearly the senior partner; Joshua himself will not come into the leadership until "Moses my servant is dead" (Josh. 1:2).

22–23 The commands of Yahweh through Moses were carried out immediately and exactly. These verses apply only to the transfer of leadership to Joshua, not to Moses' going to the mountaintop to survey the land before his death, which, again, does not happen until Deut. 32:48–52 and 34:1–8.

F. FURTHER LEGISLATION (28:1–30:17 [Eng. 16])

1. CULTIC CALENDAR (28:1–30:1 [Eng. 29:40])

1 *And Yahweh spoke to Moses, saying:*

2 *"Command the children of Israel and say to them, 'You shall be careful to offer my offering,*[1] *my food for fire offerings of pleasing aroma to me at their appointed feasts.'*[2]

3 *And you will say to them, 'This is the fire offering which you must offer to Yahweh: two perfect yearling male lambs daily as a continual whole burnt offering.*

4 *The one lamb you shall offer in the morning, and the second lamb you shall offer between the two evenings;*[3]

5 *also one-tenth*[4] *ephah of fine flour for a meal offering mixed with one-quarter hin of beaten oil,*

28. Wenham (p. 195) calls it a coregency.

1. *BHS* reads the pl. *'eṯ-qorbānay* on the basis of LXX *(ta dōra mou),* rather than MT sing. *'eṯ-qorbānî.* The difference is whether one looks at *qorbān* as including all the offerings that follow or whether each offering is called a *qorbān.* MT takes the former view, LXX the latter. Read MT.

2. Reading pl. with Sam. Pent. for MT sing. *b^{e}mô‘^{a}ḏô,* "in its appointed time." Cf. LXX *en tais heortais mou,* "in my appointed feasts," perhaps reflecting Heb. *b^{e}mô‘^{a}ḏāy.*

3. On the phrase *bēn hā‘arbāyim,* "between the two evenings," see the commentary above on 9:3 (also below in 28:8).

4. LXX *kai poiēseis to dekaton,* "and you shall offer a tenth," presupposing a Hebrew original of *w^{e}‘āśîṯā ‘^{a}s'îrîṯ,* which perhaps became *wa‘^{a}śîrîṯ* by haplography.

6 *as a continual whole burnt offering,*[5] *which was instituted at Mount Sinai, for a pleasing aroma, a fire offering to Yahweh.*

7 *And its drink offering will be one-quarter hin*[6] *for each lamb. You will pour out a drink offering of strong drink*[7] *to Yahweh in the holy place.*[8]

8 *You will offer the second lamb between the two evenings. You will offer a like meal offering and drink offering as in the morning.*[9] *It is a fire offering, a pleasing aroma, to Yahweh.*

9 *And on the Sabbath day you will offer*[10] *two perfect yearling male lambs and two-tenths ephah of fine flour for a meal offering, mixed with oil, and its drink offering.*

10 *The whole burnt offering of each Sabbath is over and above*[11] *the continual whole burnt offering and its drink offering.*

11 *And at the beginnings of your months you shall offer as a whole*

5. The phrase *ʿōlaṯ tāmîḏ,* "continual whole burnt offering" (also in 28:10, 15, 23–24, 31; 29:6, 11, 16, 19, 22, 25, 28, 31, 34, 38), is an example of the adjective used as a genitive in apposition to the construct noun (cf., e.g., "in the ninth year," *bišnaṯ hatt*^{e}*šîʿîṯ,* 2 K. 17:6); see Williams, *Syntax,* § 42.

6. Paterson (p. 61) proposed that *baqqōḏeš hassēḵ neseḵ šēḵār lYHWH,* "you shall pour out to Yahweh a drink offering of strong drink in the sanctuary," be eliminated as a late gloss and that the word *yayin,* "wine," be inserted in the text after *hahîn,* "hin" (loss due to haplography), as in LXX. The reconstructed text would then read: *w*^{e}*niskô r*^{e}*ḇîʿiṯ hahîn lakkeḇeš hāʾeḥāḏ,* "and its drink offering: one-quarter hin of wine for each lamb." Gray (p. 409) agrees that v. 7b (and v. 6) is a gloss; so also Noth, p. 221.

7. For MT *šēḵār,* "strong drink," Targ. *(ḥ*^{a}*mar ʿattîq)* and Pesh. *(d*^{e}*ʿaṯîqâ)* read "old wine." Keil (p. 219) and Dillmann (pp. 182–83) think of "strong drink" as anything other than plain water; Binns (p. 194) takes it as a term that perhaps means wine; de Vaulx simply translates as "a fermented beverage."

8. On *baqqōḏeš* meaning "holy place, sanctuary," see Milgrom, *Studies in Levitical Terminology,* p. 39 n. 149.

9. This translation of *k*^{e}*minḥaṯ habbōqer ûḵ*^{e}*niskô taʿ*^{a}*śeh* is followed by, e.g., NIV, NEB, and NJPS. AV, RV, NASB, and RSV take this sentence in what seems a more difficult way, e.g., "like the cereal offering of the morning, and like its drink offering, you shall offer it." Budd (p. 316) also translates in the latter way, and explains that the term *minḥâ* in this context means both the whole burnt offering and the meal offering accompanying it. This seems a very strange way of taking *minḥâ* in a context where elsewhere it clearly means simply and only the meal offering. Here I have chosen to translate the preposition *k*^{e}- as indicating "a similar or like (thing)" (cf. BDB, pp. 453–54, esp. 453 [1a]). Cf. Williams, *Syntax,* § 261. This meaning seems more consistent with the context by keeping the meaning of *minḥâ* as "meal offering," and is followed by a number of modern English translations (noted above).

10. LXX here adds *prosaxete,* "you will offer"; cf. Gray, p. 412.

11. For *ʿal* as "over and above," see Williams, *Syntax,* § 292.

burnt offering to Yahweh two young bulls, one ram, and seven perfect yearling male lambs;

12 *and three-tenths ephah of fine flour for a meal offering mixed with oil for each bull, and two-tenths ephah of fine flour mixed with oil for the one ram,*

13 *and one-tenth of fine flour for a meal offering mixed with oil for each lamb. It is a whole burnt offering, a pleasing aroma, a fire offering to Yahweh.*

14 *And its drink offerings: one-half hin of wine per bull, one-third hin of wine per ram, and one-quarter hin per lamb. This is the whole burnt offering for each month, at its new moon, through the months of the year.*

15 *Also one male goat for a purification offering to Yahweh. It shall be over and above the continual whole burnt offering and its drink offering.*

16 *And in the first month, on the fourteenth day of the month, is Yahweh's Passover.*

17 *And on the fifteenth day of this month will be a festival; for seven days unleavened bread will be eaten.*

18 *And on the first day will be a sacred convocation; you will do no occupational work.*[12]

19 *And you will offer a fire offering, a whole burnt offering, to Yahweh: two young bulls, one ram, and seven yearling male lambs; they must be perfect for you.*

20 *And their meal offering: fine flour mixed with oil; you will offer three-tenths ephah per bull and two-tenths ephah per ram.*

21 *You will offer one-tenth for each lamb of the seven lambs,*

22 *and one male goat as a purification offering to make atonement on your behalf.*

23 *You will offer these besides the whole burnt offering of the morning, that is, of the continual whole burnt offering.*

24 *In the same way you will offer these every day for seven days, the food of a fire offering, a pleasing aroma to Yahweh; it will be offered over and above the continual whole burnt offering and its drink offering.*

25 *And on the seventh day will be a sacred convocation for you; you will do no occupational work.*

26 *And on the day of firstfruits, when you offer a meal offering of new grain to Yahweh, at your Feast of Weeks, there will be a sacred convocation, and you will do no occupational work.*

12. This is the way Milgrom translates *kol-m*^{e}*le'ḵeṯ* ‘^{a}*ḇōḏâ lō' ṯa*‘^{a}*śû* (*Studies in Levitical Terminology,* I:80–81 n. 297).

27 *And you shall offer a whole burnt offering for a pleasing aroma to Yahweh: two young bulls, one ram, seven yearling male lambs;*[13]

28 *and their meal offering: fine flour mixed with oil; three-tenths ephah for each bull, two-tenths ephah for the one ram,*

29 *one-tenth for each lamb of the seven lambs,*

30 *one male goat*[14] *to make atonement on your behalf.*

31 *You will offer these besides the continual whole burnt offering, its meal offering, and its drink offerings. They must be perfect for you.*[15]

29:1 *And in the seventh month, on the first of the month will be a sacred convocation for you; you shall do no occupational work; it will be a day of trumpet blowing for you.*

2 *And you will offer a whole burnt offering for a pleasing aroma to Yahweh: one young bull, one ram, seven perfect yearling male lambs;*

3 *and their meal offerings: fine flour mixed with oil; three-tenths ephah per bull, two-tenths ephah per ram,*

4 *and one-tenth for each lamb of the seven lambs;*

5 *and one male goat for a purification offering to make atonement on your behalf,*

6 *besides the whole burnt offering of the new moon and its meal offering, and the continual whole burnt offering and its meal offering, and their drink offerings, according to their statute; for a pleasing aroma, a fire offering to Yahweh.*

7 *And on the tenth of this seventh month will be a sacred convocation for you, and you will humble yourselves; you will engage in no work.*[16]

13. *BHS* follows Sam. Pent. and LXX in adding the phrase *tᵉmîmîm yihyû lāḵem,* "they must be perfect to you," as in 28:19.

14. *BHS* inserts *lᵉḥaṭṭā'ṯ,* "for a purification offering," with a few Hebrew mss., Sam. Pent., and LXX, as in v. 15, etc.

15. It is possible that this clause should be deleted here and inserted at the end of v. 27 (see n. 13 above); so *BHS.* The current translation has not done so, since MT does make sense as it stands.

16. For MT *kol-mᵉlā'ḵâ lō' ṯa'ᵃśû* a few Hebrew mss., some LXX mss., Pesh., Targ. Pseudo-Jonathan, and Vulg. read *kol-mᵉlā'ḵâ 'ᵃḇōḏâ lō' ṯa'ᵃśû,* as in vv. 12, 35, etc. This reading eliminates the difference between the Day of Atonement and the other sacred convocations. But the point of the text seems to be that there is a difference. On Yom Kippur no work at all is to be done, while on Unleavened Bread (28:18, 25), Weeks (28:26), and trumpet blowing (29:1) the work forbidden is "occupational" only, i.e., having to do with the everyday matters of daily life. See Milgrom, *Studies in Levitical Terminology,* I:80–81 n. 297.

8 *And you will offer a whole burnt offering to Yahweh, a pleasing aroma: one young bull, one ram, seven yearling male lambs; they shall be perfect for you;*
9 *and their meal offering: fine flour mixed with oil; three-tenths ephah for the bull, two-tenths ephah for the one ram,*
10 *one-tenth for each lamb of the seven lambs,*
11 *one male goat for a purification offering, besides the Kippur purification offering, the continual whole burnt offering and its meal offering, and their drink offerings.*
12 *And on the fifteenth day of the seventh month will be a sacred convocation for you; you will do no occupational work, and you will celebrate a feast to Yahweh for seven days.*
13 *And*[17] *you will offer a whole burnt offering, a pleasing aroma to Yahweh: thirteen young bulls, two rams, fourteen yearling male lambs; they must be perfect.*
14 *And their meal offerings:*[18] *fine flour mixed with oil; three-tenths ephah for each bull of the thirteen bulls, two-tenths ephah for each ram of the two rams,*
15 *and one-tenth for each lamb of the fourteen lambs,*
16 *and one male goat for a purification offering, besides the continual whole burnt offering, its meal offering, and its drink offering.*
17 *And on the second day: twelve young bulls, two rams, fourteen perfect yearling male lambs,*
18 *and their meal offerings and their drink offerings; for the bulls, for the rams, for the lambs, by their numbers, according to the statute.*
19 *And one male goat for a purification offering, besides the continual whole burnt offfering, its meal offerings, and their drink offerings.*
20 *And on the third day: eleven bulls, two rams, fourteen perfect yearling male lambs,*
21 *and their meal offering and their drink offerings; for the bulls, for the rams, for the lambs, by their numbers, according to the statute.*
22 *And one male goat for a purification offering, besides the continual whole burnt offering, its meal offerings, and its drink offering.*
23 *And on the fourth day: ten bulls, two rams, fourteen perfect yearling male lambs.*

17. In order to be consistent with the rest of the passage, LXX inserts *tē hēmera tē prōtē,* "on the first day," at the beginning of the verse.

18. The drink offerings are probably left out inadvertently here, since they are included in vv. 18, 21, 24, 27, 30, 33. Sam. Pent. mentions them at the end of v. 15; cf. *BHS;* Gray, p. 412.

24 *Their meal offering and their drink offerings; for the bulls, for the rams, for the lambs, by their numbers, according to the statute.*
25 *And one male goat for a purification offering, besides the continual whole burnt offering, its meal offering, and its drink offering.*
26 *And on the fifth day: nine bulls, two rams, fourteen perfect yearling male lambs,*
27 *and their meal offering and their drink offerings, for the bulls, for the rams, for the lambs, by their numbers, according to the statute.*
28 *And one male goat for a purification offering, besides the continual whole burnt offering, its meal offering, and its drink offering.*
29 *And on the sixth day: eight bulls, two rams, fourteen perfect yearling male lambs,*
30 *and their meal offering and their drink offerings; for the bulls, for the rams, for the lambs, by their numbers, according to the statute.*
31 *And one male goat as a purification offering, besides the continual whole burnt offering, its meal offering, and its drink offerings.*
32 *And on the seventh day: seven bulls, two rams, fourteen perfect yearling male lambs,*
33 *and their meal offering and their drink offerings, for the bulls, for the rams, and for the lambs, by their numbers, according to their statute.*
34 *And one male goat for a purification offering, besides the continual whole burnt offering, its meal offering, and its drink offering.*
35 *And on the eighth day will be a sacred assembly for you; you will do no occupational work.*
36 *And you will offer a whole burnt offering, a fire offering, a pleasing aroma to Yahweh: one bull, one ram, seven perfect yearling male lambs.*
37 *Their meal offering and their drink offerings; for the bull, for the ram, and for the lambs, by their numbers, according to the statute.*
38 *And one male goat for a purification offering, besides the continual whole burnt offering, its meal offering, and its drink offering.*
39 *You will offer these to Yahweh at your appointed feasts in addition to your votive offerings and your freewill offerings, for your whole burnt offerings, your meal offerings, your drink offerings, and your peace offerings.' "*
30:1 *And Moses said to the children of Israel according to all that*
(29:40) *Yahweh had commanded Moses.*

Chapters 28–29 contain a specific list of amounts for whole burnt offerings and purification offerings to be offered as the people's offerings at the public festivals of the Hebrew year. These purposes make these lists unique in the OT, although partial parallels may be found (e.g., Exod. 29:38–42; Lev. 1–7; 23; Num. 15:1–16; cf. Ezek. 45:18–46:15). This passage seems to assume all the previous passages in the Pentateuch concerning sacrifices, feasts, and the calendar. The majority of scholars deem this passage post-Ezran, or at least postexilic.[19] But the number of parallels between the present list and an Ugaritic ritual calendar of the 14th cent. B.C. suggest that this late dating may be unnecessary.[20]

The purposes of this list are clearly set forth in the superscription and subscription (28:1–2; 29:39–30:1 [Eng. 29:40]). First, this list concerns only Yahweh's offering (28:2), i.e., those sacrifices that belong wholly to him, the whole burnt offering and the purification offering (with appropriate meal and drink offerings following the scale of Num. 15). That, e.g., Lev. 23:17–19 contains additional offerings not mentioned here is not because of differences in the age of two documents, but because Num. 28–29 deals only with whole burnt offerings and purification offerings.[21] Second, this list concerns the people's offerings (28:1: "you [pl.] shall be careful to offer"; 28:2: "you [pl.] must offer"; 28:2; 29:3:

19. E.g., Dillmann (pp. 180–85), Gray (p. 403), Holzinger (pp. 140–41), Baentsch (pp. 640–41), and McNeile (p. 155) see it as post-Ezran. De Vaulx (pp. 326–28), Noth (pp. 219–20), Sturdy (pp. 200–201), Budd (pp. 314–15), and Binns (p. 192) see it as postexilic.

20. See L. R. Fisher, "A New Ritual Calendar from Ugarit," *HTR* 63 (1970) 485–501; cf. B. A. Levine, "The Descriptive Tabernacle Texts of the Pentateuch," *JAOS* 85 (1965) 307–18, esp. 315–18. Many scholars consider such texts "late" simply because they are more definitive and formal than other texts dealing with feasts. But, as I have mentioned before, there is little evidence to suggest that all literature proceeds necessarily from simple to complex and from informal to formal. This is an assumption of many scholars since the 19th cent., but it is not a demonstrable fact, and the contrary can be documented quite often. See, e.g., Gray's remarks comparing this list to the earlier ones in the Pentateuch and esp. in Ezek. 45–46: "The simple fact that quantities are *fixed* distinguishes this law from the earlier codes. . . . The first specification of quantities for public sacrifices is found in Ezekiel. . . . A mere comparison of the two tables scarcely proves P's posterior to Ezekiel's, but that it is so may be assumed in view of the wider arguments for the posteriority of P to Ezekiel" (Gray, pp. 404–5). This is speculation, not fact!

21. The fact that Lev. 23:18 and Num. 28:27 have slightly different quantities of animals is discussed below. On the matter of the different documents, see, e.g., Gray, pp. 403–7; see also the discussion in Budd, pp. 312–15.

"their [your] appointed feasts"). It is assumed that the people themselves were to provide these sacrifices from that which Yahweh had given them. This characteristic makes Num. 28–29 different from the list in Ezek. 45:18–46:15, in which the prince clearly provides and offers the sacrifices on behalf of the people (e.g., 45:17, 22, 25; 46:2, 4, 12–13, 16), hence the differences between the latter list and Num. 28–29 are not directly relevant here. Finally, Num. 28–29 sets forth the quantities for the public offerings for the public feasts of the Hebrew year, using the framework of Lev. 23. Any private offerings that are made at any time (including at these public feasts) are clearly additional (29:39).[22]

Both the feasts themselves and the quantities of sacrifices are organized around the number seven, the sacred number of wholeness and well-being. There were seven feasts: Sabbath, New Moon, Unleavened Bread, Weeks (day of firstfruits), day of trumpet blowing, Day of Atonement, and Tabernacles. The two most important (Unleavened Bread and Tabernacles) were each seven days long. During these feasts on seven days sacred convocations were called in which rest was enjoined: first and last of Unleavened Bread, Weeks, day of trumpet blowing, Day of Atonement, first of Tabernacles, and the day after Tabernacles (28:18, 25–26; 29:1, 7, 12, 35). As the seventh day (the Sabbath) was more sacred than the other six (28:9–10), the seventh month was more sacred than the others, with no fewer than three feasts or fasts in it (ch. 29). Similarly, elsewhere one learns that the seventh (sabbatical) year was special (Exod. 23:10–11; Deut. 15:1–18), as was the year after seven times seven years, the Jubilee year (Lev. 25).

In the matter of the quantities of the offerings, the number seven is also conspicuous: in all the yearly feasts the number of lambs sacrificed was either 7 or 14 per day; in the Feast of Unleavened Bread there were 14 bulls (7 × 2), 7 rams, and 49 lambs (7 × 7) offered as whole burnt offerings, plus 7 male goats as purification offerings. At the Feast of Tabernacles a total of 70 bulls (7 × 10), 14 rams, and 98 lambs (14 × 7 or 7 × 7 × 2) were offered, plus the 7 male goats as purification offerings, etc.

The arrangement of the chapter itself is taken from the calendar of feasts in Lev. 23. The order is simple, moving from the daily sacrifice

22. These same principles apply when discussing the relationship of the current chapters to Deut. 16. That Deut. 16 does not specify amounts, etc., may be not because it knew nothing of such but because it assumed that these amounts were already known and there was no need for massive repetition. The hortatory character of Deuteronomy must also be taken into account here.

(28:3–8) to the weekly (28:9–10), the monthly (28:11–15), and the yearly (28:16–29:38). The yearly feasts and fasts are arranged to follow the calendar, beginning in the first month (28:16–25) and progressing to the seventh (ch. 29). Finally, the sacrifices in these lists are additive, e.g., the offering for the Sabbath day is in addition to the continual offering (see 28:10, 15, 24, 31; 29:6, 11, 16, 19, 22, 25, 28, 31, 34, 38).

The following chart lists the offerings for the various feasts and fasts as found in these chapters:

		Whole Burnt Offerings*			**Purification Offerings**
Feasts		Bulls	Rams	Lambs	Male Goat
Continual		—	—	2	—
Sabbath		—	—	2	—
New Moon		2	1	7	1
Unleavened Bread		2	1	7	1
Day of Firstfruits		2	1	7	1
Trumpets		1	1	7	1
Day of Atonement		1	1	7	1
Tabernacles	Day 1	13	2	14	1
	Day 2	12	2	14	1
	Day 3	11	2	14	1
	Day 4	10	2	14	1
	Day 5	9	2	14	1
	Day 6	8	2	14	1
	Day 7	7	2	14	1
Day after Tabernacles		1	1	7	1

*The whole burnt offerings are accompanied by meal offerings of fine flour mixed with oil in the following quantities: 0.1 ephah per lamb, 0.2 ephah per ram, 0.3 ephah per bull. The drink offering to accompany the whole burnt offering was as follows: 0.25 hin per lamb, 0.33 hin per ram, 0.5 hin per bull. This is the schedule set out in Num. 15:1–16.

It is possible that these chapters are a narrative account of information found in some sort of sacrificial bookkeeping ledger, such as was suggested for the bulk of ch. 7. The major difference between ch. 7 and the current chapters is that here the ledger is made into a prescription rather than being a report. The date of such a ledger is unknown, but it may surely be of an early preexilic date. Parallels of such documents are known to have existed before the Mosaic age in the ancient Near East.[23]

23. See the commentary above on ch. 7. See also B. Levine, "The

1–2 The superscription introduces the whole list of sacrifices.

2 *my offering (qorbānî).* This term includes all the sacrifices and gifts that follow. The term *qorbān* literally means "that which is brought near" (i.e., "offered") to God. It naturally occurs most commonly in those passages that deal with matters of offerings and sacrifices (e.g., of the 38 occurrences of the term in Numbers 27 are in ch. 7).[24]

my food . . . fire offerings . . . pleasing aroma. See the commentary above on 15:3.

3–8 These verses discuss the regular or daily offering or *tāmîḏ.* This is the basic offering; all others are called *mûsāp̱,* or additional. The other offerings are added to this basic offering, which is brought to Yahweh every day of the year.

3 *perfect (tāmîm)* means without blemish and mature, as in 6:14 and 19:2.

5 *fine flour . . . ephah . . . hin (sōleṯ . . . 'êp̱â . . . hîn).* See the commentary above on 15:4.

beaten oil (šemen kāṯîṯ). The word *kāṯîṯ* occurs only five times in the OT (Exod. 27:20; 29:40; Lev. 24:2; Num. 28:5; 1 K. 5:25) and twice refers to the oil for the lamp in the tabernacle. The related verb means "to crush by beating."[25] This oil was evidently made by beating the olives rather than by pressing them (hence NIV "oil from pressed olives" is misleading).

6 *instituted at Mount Sinai* refers to Exod. 29:38–42 and gives the current law the full authority of Sinaitic legislation. Both the meal and drink offerings are given according to the schedule of 15:4.

7 *strong drink (šēḵār).* Elsewhere the drink offerings are wine (Num. 15:5, 7, 10; 28:14). Some scholars have proposed that *strong drink* here should be related to an Akkadian word for libations found in Babylonian cultic ceremonies *(šikaru).*[26] An alternative is that *strong drink* here

---

Descriptive Tabernacle Texts of the Pentateuch," *JAOS* 85 (1965) 307–18; A. F. Rainey, "The Order of Sacrifices in Old Testament Ritual Texts," *Bib* 51 (1970) 485–98.

24. See above on 5:15. On *qorban,* see further K. Rengstorf, *TDNT,* III:860–64. On the nuances of *qārāb,* see J. Milgrom, *Studies in Levitical Terminology,* I:33–43, esp. p. 37 n. 141.

25. BDB, p. 510.

26. See Gray, p. 409; Snaith, p. 189. Cf. Sturdy, p. 201, who thinks that this term was derived from the Babylonian environment of the Exile. He does not explain why it should appear in relation to the drink offering only in this text. See also Budd, p. 316.

is any intoxicant made from fruit or grain, i.e., a generic term, as perhaps in 6:3 above. Deut. 14:26 names both wine and strong drink as offerings, and this may mean that the book of Deuteronomy assumes that the strong drink mentioned here was different from wine and to be offered in addition to it.

in the holy place (baqqōḏeš). This term is a general one for the court where the altar of burnt offerings was located. A similar but less technical use of this term may be seen in 18:10, where a site like this is called a "most holy place." The court of the tent of meeting is called "a holy place" *(māqôm qāḏōš)* in Lev. 6:9, 19 (Eng. 16, 26). At a much later time, libations of red wine were poured out at the foot of the altar of burnt offerings (Sir. 50:15).

8 *You will offer a like meal offering and drink offering as in the morning.* The meaning is simply that the evening lamb is offered with the same amounts of meal and drink offerings as specified for the morning lamb.

9–10 As noted above, the number seven is special in this list. The seventh day was holy to Yahweh. Rest on the Sabbath day is set within the theology of creation (Gen. 2:2–3) and is basic to the covenant life of Israel (Exod. 20:8–11).[27] The Sabbath and the Day of Atonement are the two days on which all work is prohibited, as opposed to *occupational work* (Lev. 23:3; Num. 29:7). On this holiest day of the week, in addition to the two lambs of the regular daily offering, two more yearling male lambs without blemish were offered. Num. 28:23 seems to indicate that these additional offerings were sacrificed after the regular sacrifice in the morning.

11–15 The celebration of the beginning of the lunar month or new moon is instituted here (it is not found in Lev. 23), although, since it is assumed in Num. 10:10, perhaps it is not so much the marking of the passage of the month but this specific sacrifice that is instituted. The Hebrews celebrated the new moon throughout the life of the nation (1 Sam. 20:5; 2 K. 4:23; Isa. 1:13; Ezek. 46:6–7; Hos. 2:13 [Eng. 11]; 13:1–16; Amos 8:5; 1 Chr. 23:31; etc.); the new moon was an important feature of the life of the ancient Near East.[28]

27. The ordinance is explained in more detail than any other in the Decalogue, containing 55 words in the Hebrew text. The only other ordinance that comes close is found in vv. 4–6, which detail the prohibition against images of God (43 words).

28. See, e.g., de Vaux, *Ancient Israel,* I:183–86, esp. 183–84.

The amounts to be sacrificed as whole burnt offerings are: two bulls, one ram, and seven lambs, the same amounts as for each of the days of the Feast of Unleavened Bread (vv. 17–25) and on the day of firstfruits (vv. 26–31). The bulls and rams are mentioned for the first time here, and so amounts for the meal and drink offerings are given in vv. 12–14. The scale followed for the amounts of meal and drink offerings is that of 15:4–12 (see the commentary on these verses). The details of the meal offering are repeated up until the seven days of the Feast of Tabernacles (29:15), but those of the drink offering are assumed after this point.

The *purification offering (ḥaṭṭā'ṯ)* consisted of one male goat, and was required for every festival in the current list other than the Sabbath. Although the purification offering is listed after the whole burnt offering, other texts suggest that it was sacrificed prior to it (see, e.g., Lev. 9; 16; Num. 6:11, 16).[29]

16–25 The major feast of the March-April season, as far as the current passage is concerned, is Unleavened Bread (vv. 17–25), but in order to be complete the Feast of Passover is mentioned in v. 16. As mentioned above, the purpose of the present chapters is the listing of the amounts of public offerings. Since the Passover was a family feast, celebrated in the home without public offerings (Exod. 12:3–14), no further notice of it was necessary. Passover was celebrated on the fourteenth day of the first month. The next day began a feast that, although unnamed here, is clearly connected with the Feast of Unleavened Bread (Exod. 23:15; 34:18; Lev. 23:6; Deut. 16:16). One may assume that the readers of these chapters would already be familiar with the feasts themselves. The identity of the feast is made clear by mention of the fact that *for seven days unleavened bread will be eaten* (v. 17). Like the Passover, Unleavened Bread looked back to the Exodus from Egypt (Exod. 12:15–20).

On both the first and seventh days of the feast a *sacred convocation (miqrā' qōḏeš)* was held (so also Lev. 23:7). These days were marked by abstinence from *occupational work*, i.e., those forms of work that had to do with commerce and the business of everyday life. This kind of abstinence from work contrasts with the stricter kind of rest enjoined on the Sabbath (Lev. 23:3) and on the Day of Atonement (29:7). No further

29. A. F. Rainey ("Order of Sacrifices," pp. 485–98) discusses different orders for lists of sacrifices (see also Levine, "Descriptive Tabernacle Texts," pp. 307–18). On the purification offering itself, see the commentary above on 6:11; 19:9, 17.

explanation of this convocation is given. The offerings themselves are the same as on the day of New Moon and the day of firstfruits: two young bulls, one ram, seven yearling lambs without blemish, and one male goat for a purification offering. Again, these offerings are in addition to the continual whole burnt offerings, and according to v. 23 are to be offered after the morning *tāmîḏ*.

26–31 The offering here (uniquely) called the *day of firstfruits* is elsewhere called the Feast of the Harvest (Exod. 23:16) or the Feast of Weeks (Exod. 34:22; Deut. 16:10; v. 26). Firstfruits were, generally, the earliest parts of the fruit and grain crops that were given to Yahweh (Exod. 16:19; 34:26), as a sign that the whole crop was his. Earlier, the offering had been fixed as two loaves of bread (Lev. 23:17). Firstfruits of wine and oil are required in Num. 18:12, but the time is unspecified. By putting firstfruits on a *day,* the time of the celebration is fixed.[30] V. 26 is not intended to set a new day for the celebration of the day, but only to refer to familiar legislation such as Lev. 23:15–16, which set the time as fifty days after the presentation of the first of the grain (Lev. 23:9–14). The feast was later called Pentecost (from Gk. *pentekosta,* "fifty"). The calendar dates differed as to the results of the harvest, of course.

The day itself was a *sacred convocation,* which stressed abstinence from *occupational work* (cf. 28:18, 25). Lev. 23:17–21 is interesting in that it contains the only prescriptions for the amounts of the offerings in that list, and it differs from Num. 28:28–30. In the Numbers passage the offerings are the same as for the day of New Moon and for each day of Unleavened Bread (two young bulls, one ram, seven yearling lambs, one male goat for a purification offering). The Leviticus passage has two loaves of bread, two male lambs for a peace offering, one young bull, two rams, seven yearling lambs for the whole burnt offering, and one male goat for a purification offering. The two loaves and the peace offerings are not within the purview of the Numbers list and are simply eliminated because they are private. The purification offering and the number of perfect yearling male lambs are the same.

The most significant difference is the reversal in numbers between young bulls and rams. Three explanations of the discrepancy have been offered. First, it may be a textual corruption in Lev. 23 or Num. 28.[31]

30. On this passage, see Milgrom *JPST,* pp. 244–45; W. Eichrodt, *Theology of the Old Testament,* OTL, tr. J. Baker (Philadelphia: Westminster, 1967), I:152–53.

31. Cook, p. 761.

Second, the two passages may reflect a real difference in tradition.[32] Third, it is also possible that the offerings of Lev. 23 were thought of as wholly private, hence additional to the continual offering and to the offerings of Num. 28:27–30, which were public.[33] The problem with the first suggestion is that, while plausible in documents of this sort, no textual evidence supports it. No immediate rationale is obvious that would make one think of the second explanation. The third solution would mean that every worshiper had to bring a costly sacrifice, which is doubtful since the average Israelite could not afford it (one bull, two rams, nine lambs, one male goat, two loaves). Seeing these sacrifices as private would also produce a great number of sacrificial victims to be offered on the one altar. Although evidence for textual corruption is lacking, if the current chapters are narratives based on a ledger of prescribed quantities of sacrifices,[34] then such textual slips would be easy to make.

29:1–38 Most of ch. 29 deals with the seventh, and most sacred, month of the Hebrew year. The sacrifices of the three minor feasts that provide a framework for the month (i.e., on the first, tenth, and twenty-second days of the month) require whole burnt offerings of one bull, one ram, and seven lambs (with appropriate meal and drink offerings), plus a purification offering of one male goat. The main festival of the month is the Feast of Tabernacles (also called Booths or Sukkoth). The sacrifices for this seven-day feast are much greater than for the other feasts, marking Tabernacles as the major feast of the year.

1–6 Cf. Lev. 23:23–25. As the seventh day is especially sacred, so is the first day of the seventh month. That day was to have a *sacred convocation* marked by abstinence from *occupational work* (the fourth such convocation of the year).

it will be a day of trumpet blowing for you (yôm tᵉrûʿâ yihyeh

32. If one takes these texts as documents of the Mosaic age, then they would be about 40 years apart. But if Lev. 23 is from source H (7th/6th cent.) and Num. 28 is a late supplement to P (5th/4th cent.), then the distance is considerably greater, and a case for a real difference in tradition could be made. A. R. S. Kennedy thought that Lev. 23:18–20 (H) was revised by a Priestly editor (p. 154; so also Gray, p. 411; de Vaulx, p. 337), but if so, it was badly revised, since it did not match with the P document's list in Num. 28:27. Most scholars who follow this latter course do not mention the discrepancy, or simply note it without explanation.

33. Keil, p. 221.

34. As has been suggested above for the current chapters and ch. 7; cf. Levine, "Descriptive Tabernacle Texts," pp. 317–18; Rainey, "Order of Sacrifices," pp. 495–96. Textual variants concerning numbers are quite common.

lāḵem). The blowing of trumpets at appointed feasts is assumed by 10:10, and mentioned in connection with this day by Lev. 23:24. The name *day of trumpet blowing* is unique here. As early as Seleucid times (ca. 3rd–2nd cent. B.C.) this feast was connected with Rosh Hashanah or New Year. It is uncertain whether this text speaks of a New Year feast, and the evidence for such a feast is unclear.[35] The major activity of the day seems to be the blowing of the trumpet. The offerings (see above) are additional not only to the daily continual offering but also to the sacrifices offered on the day of the new moon. This fact meant a total whole burnt offering of three bulls, two rams, and sixteen lambs (plus appropriate meal and drink offerings, vv. 3–4), plus two male goats for the purification offering. The scale of meal offerings for this day is given in vv. 4–5; the drink offerings are probably on the scale of 28:7, 14. The meal and drink offerings for the continual offering and the New Moon offering are said to be *according to their statute* (*k^e mišpāṭām*, v. 6), which means according to the scale worked out in the statutes already given (e.g., 28:7, 12–14 as well as 15:4–11).

7–11 The tenth day of the seventh month is called the Day of Atonement *(yôm hakkippurîm)* in Lev. 23:27. The detailed legislation for this day is found in Lev. 16. The day is marked by a *sacred convocation* (the fifth), but, unlike the others, this day is marked by abstinence from all work rather than simply from the daily matters of business, etc. (called *occupational work*). In this matter the Day of Atonement is like the Sabbath day, which is also marked by stricter abstinence (Lev. 23:3).

35. On balance the evidence of the OT favors a New Year in the spring rather than the autumn. There is no direct OT evidence for a New Year festival within Judaism at all; other feasts seem to displace the New Year celebration. Later Judaism worked the details out in Mish. *Roš Haššana* (see Danby, *Mishnah,* pp. 188–94). For a good summary of the discussion on the matter, see D. Block, *ISBE,* rev., III:529–32; de Vaux, *Ancient Israel,* II:502–6. More complex discussions may be found in, e.g, S. Mowinckel, *Psalmenstudien II: Das Thronbesteigungsfest Jahwäs und der Ursprung der Eschatologie,* in *Skrifter utgitt av Det Norske Videnskaps-Akademi i Oslo, II, His.-Filos. Kl.* (1922); idem, *Psalms in Israel's Worship,* tr. D. R. Ap-Thomas, 2 vols. (Nashville: Abingdon, 1962), I:94–95, 106–92; I. Engnell, "New Year Festivals," in *Critical Essays on the Old Testament,* tr. J. T. Willis (London: SPCK, 1970), pp. 180–84; H. Ringgren, *Israelite Religion,* tr. D. E. Green (Philadelphia: Fortress, 1966), pp. 185–200; A. R. Johnson, *Sacral Kingship in Ancient Israel,* 2nd ed. (Cardiff: Univ. of Wales Press, 1967); N. H. Snaith, *The Jewish New Year Festival: Its Origin and Development* (London: SPCK, 1949); E. J. Young, *The Book of Isaiah,* 3 vols. (Grand Rapids: Eerdmans, 1965, 1969, 1972), I:494–99; H. J. Kraus, *Worship in Israel,* tr. G. Buswell (Oxford: Blackwell, 1965), pp. 61–66; G. Fohrer, *A History of Israelite Religion,* tr. D. Green (Nashville: Abingdon, 1972), pp. 142–45, 202–5.

The command to *humble yourselves (wᵉʿinnîṯem ʾeṯ nap̄šōṯêḵem)* probably has to do with fasting (as in Ps. 35:13; Isa. 58:3, 5).

The offerings will be as for the day of trumpet blowing. These are in addition to the Kippur purification offering and the continual daily offering. Of course, appropriate meal and drink offerings are to be offered as well.[36] The Kippur *purification offering* probably includes the goat that is the purification offering on behalf of the people's sin (Lev. 16:7–9, 15–19), and possibly the bull offering on behalf of the sin of the priest's own house (Lev. 16:6, 11–14).[37]

12–34 Cf. Exod. 23:16b; 34:22b; Lev. 23:33–36; Deut. 16:13–15. Elsewhere the feast beginning on the fifteenth day of the seventh month is called the Feast of Ingathering (*ḥag hāʾāsîp̄,* Exod. 23:16b; 34:22b) or the Feast of Tabernacles (*ḥag hassukkōṯ,* Lev. 23:33; Deut. 16:13). It was celebrated for seven days (also Deut. 16:15; Ezek. 45:25), from the fifteenth to the twenty-first days of the seventh month (also Lev. 23:34; Ezek. 45:25). On the first day of the feast a *sacred convocation* was held (the sixth), and all *occupational work* was forbidden, as in 28:18, 25–26; 29:1 (also Lev. 23:35). According to Lev. 23:39–43 and Deut. 16:13–15, the Feast of Tabernacles was celebrated by offering sacrifices, by living in huts or impermanent structures that reminded the people of their wilderness days,[38] and by rejoicing before Yahweh. This feast was to be celebrated with more public offerings by far than any other feast in Israel, thus making it the major feast of the year. Indeed, more bulls and rams are offered during Tabernacles than during the rest of the festivals of the year combined. Coming as it did at harvest time, it offered a good opportunity for the Israelites to show their gratitude to God for the bounty with which he had blessed them. The huge size of the prescribed public

36. On Lev. 16, see Wenham, *Leviticus,* pp. 225–38.

37. Snaith (*Jewish New Year Festival,* p. 139) marks the Day of Atonement as the old New Year's Day, but his evidence is far from conclusive.

38. The instructions concerning the construction of booths are not mentioned here, in Lev. 23:33–36, or in Deut. 16:13–15, but only in Lev. 23:40, 42, which, according to scholars, may be a later addition to the text or at least be incorporated from a different source, and in such later passages as Neh. 8:13–18. See, e.g., A. Noordtzij, *Leviticus,* tr. R. Togtman, Bible Student's Commentary (Grand Rapids: Zondervan, 1983), p. 241; M. Noth, *Leviticus: A Commentary,* tr. J. Anderson, OTL (Philadelphia: Westminster, 1965), pp. 175–76. That the Leviticus passage may be composite does not mean, however, that its composition needs to be brought down to the time of Nehemiah. The name of the Festival of Tabernacles was clearly fixed by the time of Deut. 16. Of course, the date of Deuteronomy is debated, but, in any case, it is before the time of Nehemiah.

offerings makes the theological point that the land of Canaan, into which the Israelites were coming, was a land so fertile that these large public offerings could be provided for thanksgiving to Yahweh.

The number of bulls (the costliest sacrifice) offered during the feast began with thirteen and descended one per day until seven bulls are offered on the seventh day of the feast. Scholars have attempted several explanations of this phenomenon, none of them convincing.[39] It is best simply to see the number of bulls as worked out so as to come to seven on the seventh day.[40] The number of lambs (14) and rams (2) remains constant day to day. When all the totals are added, they are all divisible by seven. In addition to these whole burnt offerings and their appropriate meal and drink offerings, one male goat per day is to be sacrificed as a purification offering.

35–38 On the day immediately following the conclusion of Tabernacles (i.e., the eighth day) another *sacred assembly* was to be held (the seventh) with the same regulations as for the first day of the feast. The name given to this last solemn gathering of the Israelites is different from the other six (*miqrāʾ*, 28:18, 25–26; 29:1, 7, 12). The word *ʿᵃṣereṯ* (also *ʿᵃṣārâ*) means lit. "that which is held in" (related to the verb *ʿāṣar,* "to restrain, retain").[41] It is used to describe a gathering that is "held" for divine worship (of Yahweh, Isa. 1:13; Amos 5:21; of Baal, 2 K. 10:20). In Deut. 16:8 the term refers to the sacred convocation held on the last day of the Feast of Unleavened Bread, which is called a *miqrāʾ* in Num. 28:25 (thus showing that the two terms *ʿᵃṣereṯ* and *miqrāʾ* are interchangeable for practical purposes). Here as well as in Lev. 23:36 and Neh. 8:18 the word describes the day after the seventh day of Tabernacles. In postbiblical Hebrew the term came to refer to the Feast of Weeks (as did its Aramaic equivalent *ʿᵃṣartāʾ* in Targs.). Although this eighth day is separated from the feast itself by the number of offerings given, its proximity in time probably explains why such passages as 1 K. 8:2, 65–66 speak of Tabernacles lasting eight days. The offerings are the same as for the first and tenth days of the seventh month.

29:39–30:1 (29:40) This passage fulfills two purposes. First, it simply states that the offerings here were *public offerings.* Any private

39. Binns (pp. 198–99) sees the declining number as following the waning moon; Sturdy (p. 201) sees it as indicating that the joy of the Israelites was at its peak on the first day and declined in each succeeding day (so also, with less certainty, Noth, p. 223).

40. So, e.g., Keil, p. 222.

41. BDB, pp. 783b–84a.

sacrifices such as might be offered on any occasion (e.g., offerings made at the discharge of a vow, other whole burnt offerings, meal offerings, drink offerings, or peace offerings; cf., e.g., Lev. 22:17–25; Num. 15:3, 8; Deut. 16:10, 17; 2 Chr. 29:21; Ezra 8:35) are over and above the offerings listed here. Second, 30:1 (Eng. 29:40) indicates that Moses transmitted accurately to the Israelites all that Yahweh had revealed to him. This is in line with other concluding formulae in Numbers (e.g., 1:19, 54; 2:33–34; 3:51; 4:37, 41, 45, 49; 5:4; 9:4a, 22b; 14:39a; 15:36b; 27:12, 23).

2. WOMEN'S VOWS (30:2–17 [Eng. 1–16])

2 (1) *And Moses spoke to the leaders of the tribes of the children of Israel, saying: "This is the word that Yahweh has commanded:*

3 (2) *If a man vows a vow to Yahweh, or swears an oath to take an obligation upon himself,*[1] *he shall not violate his word. He must do according to all that has gone out of his mouth.*

4 (3) *But if a woman vows a vow to Yahweh and takes an obligation upon herself in her father's house in her youth,*

5 (4) *but her father hears of her vow and the obligation that she took upon herself, and her father remains silent, then to her all her vows will stand and every obligation that she took upon herself will stand.*

6 (5) *But if her father restrained*[2] *her when he heard it, none of her vows or her obligations that she took upon herself will stand, and Yahweh will forgive her since her father restrained her.*

7 (6) *And if she should become married to a man*[3] *while she is under*

1. The infinitives construct *hiššāḇaʿ* ("to swear") and *leʾsōr* ("to take an obligation," or "to bind") follow after the finite verb in the imperfect *(yiddōr)* and the conjunction *ʾô*. The finite verb has already suggested the personal circumstances and kind of action of the situation. See also, e.g., Lev. 25:14; Deut. 14:21 (cf. Gen. 17:10; Exod. 12:48; Deut. 15:2; 2 K. 4:43); see Davidson, *Syntax,* § 88 Rem. 1; Williams, *Syntax,* § 209.

2. With the perfect in the protasis, the condition may be thought of as realized and actual. Compare the perfect here with the imperfect in v. 9 (Eng. 8). The condition there is more hypothetical. See Davidson, *Syntax,* § 130.

3. The construction with the imperfect tense of the verb *hāyâ* and *ʾim* in the protasis of a condition indicates the genuinely conditional nature of the sentence. The infinitive absolute of the same verb *(hāyô)* also places emphasis on the importance of the condition upon which the consequence (v. 8 [Eng. 7]) depends. This kind of construction is relatively common in conditional sentences; cf. Exod. 15:26; 19:5; 21:5; 22:3, 11–12, 16, 22; 23:22; Num. 21:2; Judg. 16:11; 1 Sam. 1:11; 12:25; 20:6, 9, 21; 2 Sam. 18:3. See GKC, § 113o (2); Davidson, *Syntax,* § 86 (a).

her vows or a rash utterance of her lips that she took upon herself,

8 (7) *and her husband hears of it and is silent to her when he hears of it, then her vows will stand and her obligations that she took upon herself will stand.*

9 (8) *But if, when he hears his wife, he restrains her, then he will void her vow that is upon her and the rash utterance of her lips that she bound upon herself,*[4] *and Yahweh will forgive her.*

10 (9) *As for the vow of a widow or the divorced woman:*[5] *all that she has taken upon herself will stand over her.*

11 (10) *And if she vows in her husband's house or takes upon herself an obligation by oath,*

12 (11) *and her husband hears of it and is silent to her, and he does not restrain her, then all her vows will stand, and every obligation that she bound upon herself will stand.*

13 (12) *But if in fact her husband voids them when he hears them, all that comes out from her lips concerning her vows and concerning her obligations of herself will not stand; her husband has voided them, and Yahweh will forgive her.*

14 (13) *Any vow and any oath of obligation to humble herself, her husband may establish and her husband may void.*

15 (14) *But if in fact her husband is silent to her from day to day, then he establishes all her vows or all her obligations that are upon her. He established them because he was silent to her when he heard it.*

16 (15) *But if in fact he voids them after he hears of it, then he will bear her guilt."*

17 (16) *These are the statutes that Yahweh commanded Moses; in the relation between a man and his wife, in the relation between a father and his daughter in her youth in her father's house.*

The practice of making promises or vows to God seems ancient, both in Israel (Gen. 28:20–22) and in the rest of the ancient Near East.[6] Vows may be positive promises to do or perform something (Judg. 11:30–31; 1 Sam.

4. LXX adds *ou menousin, hoti ho anēr aneneusen ap' autēs* ("they will not remain, since the husband has restrained her").

5. MT *g^erûšâ* is a Qal fem. sing. passive participle from the verb *gāraš*, which means "to expel." Thus a divorcee is thought of as one who is driven out (viz., of her husband's house, Deut. 24:1). This category is placed together with that of the widow *('almānâ)* in Lev. 21:14; 22:13 and Ezek. 44:22 as well as the current passage.

6. See a sample of votive materials in, e.g., Beyerlin, ed., *Near Eastern Religious Texts,* pp. 30–35, 228–37.

1:11), or they may be negative promises to abstain from something (Num. 6). In general, the Hebrew word that encompasses both kinds of promises is *neḏer.*[7] The present text uses *neḏer* only to express the positive vow. The negative vow is expressed, uniquely in ch. 30, by *'issār*.

The pentateuchal legislation concerning vows is in the form of specific legislation growing out of specific needs rather than dealing with vows in a comprehensive or philosophical manner. For example, the legislation of Lev. 5:4 speaks of the rash oath, 7:16–18 speaks of the eating of certain votive offerings, 22:17–25 insists that votive (and other) offerings be free of blemish, 27:1–31 gives the cost of not fulfilling vows, Num. 6:2–21 speaks of men and women taking Nazirite vows, Num. 15:1–10 speaks of meal and drink offerings to accompany vows, and Deut. 23:22–24 (Eng. 21–23) mention the principle that vows must be speedily fulfilled. Just so, Num. 30:2–17 (Eng. 1–16) is another example of specific principles for specific situations; in this case, the binding nature of vows made by certain classes of women. The reason for the nature of the pentateuchal laws may be that the Israelites *assumed,* with much of the culture around them, that vows were a legitimate expression of devotion to one's god(s), hence only specific ordinances governing the vows were seen as necessary.

Behind the legislation of this chapter lie several suppositions. First, women could make vows to God (cf. Num. 6:2; 1 Sam. 1:11). Second, vows that were put in words made to God were normally to be discharged as soon as possible ("He must do according to all that has gone out of his mouth," Num. 30:3b [Eng. 2b]; cf. Deut. 23:22, 24 [Eng. 21, 23]; Eccl. 5:3–5 [Eng. 4–6]). Even rashly uttered and ill-thought-through vows were binding (Lev. 5:4; cf. Gen. 27; Num. 30:7, 9 [Eng. 6, 8]). Third, a woman in the house of her father or of her husband was under his authority. It may have been the clash of these suppositions that led to the promulgation of the present legislation.

The form of the legislation (as is common in other passages dealing with vows) is casuistic or case law, which amounted to legal precedents drawn from specific cases.[8] The basic principle for males is set forth in v. 3 (Eng. 2): vows are binding. The question of women's vows, however, is more complex because of the third presupposition above. The passage concludes that, although a woman may make a vow to Yahweh

7. Cf. BDB, pp. 623b–24a; L. Coppes, *TWOT,* II:557b–58; de Vaux, *Ancient Israel,* II:465–66; G. H. Davies, *IDB,* IV:792–93; T. Cartledge, *ISBE,* rev., IV:998–99.

8. See the commentary above on 27:8–11.

(vv. 4, 7, 10–11, 14 [Eng. 3, 6, 9–10, 13]), if she is living in the house of (i.e., under the authority of) either her father or her husband, they can void the vow at the time they first hear about it (vv. 6, 9, 13 [Eng. 5, 8, 12]). The principle is, however, that if these men say nothing when they first hear about the vow, they establish it (i.e., silence is consent, vv. 5, 8, 12, 15 [Eng. 4, 7, 11, 14]), and can not later void the vow without incurring Yahweh's punishment (v. 16 [Eng. 15]). The principle of the inviolability of vows is upheld in that even when the father or husband voids the vow, its nonperformance incurs guilt that Yahweh must forgive or remit (vv. 6, 9, 13 [Eng. 5, 8, 12]).

Four classes of women are mentioned: (a) the young marriageable girl who still lives in her father's house (vv. 4–6 [Eng. 3–5]); (b) the woman who has taken an oath in her father's house but marries before the vow is fulfilled (vv. 7–10 [Eng. 6–9]);[9] (c) the widowed or divorced woman (v. 10 [Eng. 9]); (d) the married woman living in her husband's house (vv. 11–16 [Eng. 10–15]). This last case is broken into two further subcases: the woman whose husband voids her vow without penalty (vv. 11–13 [Eng. 10–12]) and the woman whose husband voids her vow but incurs a penalty (vv. 14–16 [Eng. 13–15]). According to Wenham, the laws may be arranged in two groups of three parallel cases.[10] Here again, the specificity of the case laws involved is clear. The cases of minor male children who were also under the authority of fathers or of unmarried older women are not mentioned.

The connection of ch. 30 with its context is not immediately obvious, and Noth, e.g., saw none at all.[11] Others (e.g., Sturdy and de Vaulx) have attempted to see the connection between chs. 28–29 and 30 in the connection between vows and the offerings that often accompanied them (cf. Lev. 7:16–18).[12] The offerings mandated in chs. 28–29 are public offerings, however, and have nothing to do with vows as such. The subject of votive offerings is mentioned in 29:39, and this mention may form a slender connection. Wenham concluded that vows were connected with sacrifices, and sacrifices might best be given at the time of one of the pilgrim festivals of the year. These festivals are prominent parts of the subject matter of chs. 28–29.[13] One might also see this section

9. Some scholars hold that this case deals with betrothed women who, while living under their husbands' authority (cf. Deut. 22:23–25), still live in their fathers' houses (see the commentary below on vv. 7–9 [Eng. 6–8]). See nn. 27-28.

10. Wenham, p. 206.

11. Noth, p. 224.

12. Sturdy, p. 209; de Vaulx, pp. 346–47.

13. Wenham, p. 205.

as rounding off chs. 27–30 by returning to the same general subject as 27:1–11, viz., women's rights. Ch. 36 will return to this subject yet again, so one might very well see the chapter in its place as giving a structure to chs. 27–30 and, in turn, to chs. 27–36. At the beginning, middle, and end of this unit the rights of a normally underprivileged group are addressed. Yahweh's land would be a place where all God's people would find rest.

The majority of commentators see this chapter as a late addition to P, although some admit that the traditions contained in it are ancient.[14] This text probably assumes some previous legislation on vows and deals with a specific issue not covered elsewhere. As concluded above, vow making was ancient in Israel. It is recorded that Jacob made vows long before Israel went down into Egypt (Gen. 28:20–22),[15] and there is no indication that this passage introduced an innovation, although this is an argument from silence. The subject of women's vows could legitimately have been raised any time after the practice began to conflict with at least one of the cultural suppositions listed above, and might well have been crucial at the time of the conquest, when fathers or husbands would likely be absent on military maneuvers for longer periods of time. But the subject is relevant at most any time, and this law could have been transmitted (and occasionally updated) in Israel for centuries. In a situation of domestic strife, an angry wife might vow away her son in order to punish a husband. The current law would make such rash vows difficult to achieve, as the husband could void such a vow as soon as he heard of it. From the other side, a bullying husband might so dominate his wife's life that she was not allowed any real religious freedom at all. Ch. 30 reinforces the right of women to make vows to Yahweh, and limits a husband's right to void a vow by requiring that his objection be made when he first hears of his wife's vow and not after a long period of reflection.[16]

2–3 (1–2) The introduction to the passage (v. 2 [Eng. 1]) is clear enough, even though it is literarily unusual. First, normally Yahweh is said to speak to Moses (or Aaron) in direct speech, whereas here he is reported to have spoken only by Moses *(This is the word that Yahweh has com-*

14. Those who see it as a late addition include Dillmann, pp. 185–87; Holzinger, p. 146; Baentsch, p. 648; Gray, p. 413. Sturdy (p. 209) admits that it may contain ancient traditions.

15. Some critics consider Gen. 28:20–22 passage to be E or JE; see, e.g., O. Eissfeldt, *Hexateuch-Synopse* (Leipzig: Hinrichs, 1922), p. 92; G. Fohrer, *Introduction to the Old Testament,* tr. D. Green (Nashville: Abingdon, 1968), p. 153; E. Speiser, *Genesis,* AB (Garden City, N.Y.: Doubleday, 1964), p. 217.

16. The rabbis discussed these matters in Mish. *Nedarim* 10–11.

manded).[17] The indirect speech does not reduce the force of the divine imperative, but merely expresses it in an unusual way.

Second, it is unusual that Moses should address the *leaders* [*rō'šê,* lit., "heads"] *of the tribes (hammaṭṭôṯ).* This phrase occurs elsewhere only in 1 K. 8:1 and 2 Chr. 5:2, although a related phrase, "the heads of the fathers of the tribes" *(rō'šê 'aḇôṯ hammaṭṭôṯ),* occurs in Num. 32:28 and Josh. 14:1; 21:1. Again, the meaning is clear enough, even though the words are unusual. This is the group of leaders (although not the specific men) appointed in 1:4, 16; 7:2; etc. Why Moses should address only the *leaders* here rather than the whole congregation is unknown.

The first principle stated has to do with vows for males.[18] When a male made a vow, it had to be kept (although redemption was possible, Lev. 27). As stated above, two words for vows are used here: *neḏer* for the positive vows and *'issār* for the negative. The latter word is unique to this chapter, but it is related to a common verb, *'āsar,* "to tie, bind, imprison."[19] In the Mishnah *'îssār* commonly meant "a prohibition or vow of abstinence."[20] In Biblical Aramaic and Syriac the cognate word means "an interdict" (Dan. 6:8–10, 13–14, 16).[21] The rareness of the term in Biblical Hebrew, together with the lateness of such cognates as exist, has led some scholars to confirm their already existing view that this passage is late postexilic.[22] All that can be said with certainty, however, is that ch. 30 uses a special vocabulary word not found elsewhere in the OT. The fact that a word occurs rarely in the OT does not indicate that it was a rare word in the spoken (or even written) language of the day, only that a use for it was not commonly found in the exant literature, or that examples of it have not survived.

He shall not profane his word (lō' yaḥēl deḇārô). The verb *ḥālal*

17. For the usual expression, see, e.g., "And Yahweh spoke to Moses," 1:1; 2:1; 3:5, 11, 14, 40, 44; 4:1, 17, 21; 5:1, 5, 11; 6:1, 22; 8:1, 5; 9:1, 9; 10:1; 11:16; 13:1; 14:11; 15:1; 17:16 (Eng. 1); 19:1; 26:1; 27:6, 12; 28:1; 31:1; 34:1; 35:1. The closest parallels to the present mode of speech are found in Exod. 16:16, 32; 35:4; Lev. 8:5; 9:6; 17:2.

18. Although the word *'îš* may occasionally be translated generically as "humankind" (e.g., Judg. 9:49; Isa. 2:9, 11, 17; etc.), here it has its basic meaning, "man" or "male," as the occurrence of the contrasting word *'iššâ,* "female," "woman," makes clear in v. 4 (Eng. 3). See N. Bratsiotis, *TDOT,* I:222–35, esp. 222–25.

19. See BDB, pp. 63b–64a.

20. See Jastrow, *Dictionary,* p. 57a.

21. See BDB, p. 1082a.

22. E.g., Snaith, p. 192.

(in the Niphil, Piel, and twice in the Hiphil, as here) has to do with the profanation of the sacred. "To profane" something means to use what has been set aside ("consecrated") for a holy purpose for other-than-holy ("common") use. God's name (i.e., his person and character) may be profaned by willful disobedience of his commandments (e.g., Amos 2:7; Jer. 34:16). Likewise the divine sanctuary may be profaned by pagans who do not know or obey God's ordinances (e.g., the Babylonians, Ezek. 7:21–24; Ps. 74:7) or disobedient Israelites (e.g., Ezek. 23:39; Mal. 2:11). The Sabbath may be profaned by ignoring its basic purposes (e.g., Ezek. 20:13, 16, 21, 24; 22:8; 23:38; cf. Num. 15:32–36).[23] The basic purpose of the vow is a positive promise to Yahweh (see above). To profane such a vow would entail failure to fulfill it. Such an act would put something holy to an unholy purpose. Once again, we see the seriousness with which the Israelites took the spoken word. A vow, once spoken, had an independent existence and was binding.[24]

4–16 (3–15) The binding nature of the male vow is not the point of the present law, however, but only a principle against which the issue of vows for certain classes of women may be approached. The structure of the sections dealing with those classes of women whose vows may be voided by father or husband is similar:

a. Particular type of woman cited (vv. 4, 7, 11 [Eng. 3, 6, 10])
b. Condition for validation of the vow (vv. 5, 8, 12, 15 [Eng. 4, 7, 11, 14])
c. Condition for voiding of the vow (vv. 6a, 9a, 13a, 15 [Eng. 5a, 8a, 12a, 14])
d. Consequences of voiding the vow (vv. 6b, 9b, 13b, 16 [Eng. 5b, 8b, 12b, 15])

The condition for the validation of the vow is the same in all cases: the silence of the father or husband when he first hears about the woman's vow. The condition for voiding the vow is likewise the same throughout:

23. W. Dommershausen, *TDOT*, IV: 409–17.

24. Cf. the unfortunate case of the word of Isaac in blessing Jacob by mistake (Gen. 27), which could not be changed, or the tragic case of Jephthah's rash vow (Judg. 11:35–36), which had to be fulfilled because uttered; cf. Num. 32:24; Ps. 66:13–14; Jer. 44:17. The rabbis put an end to this practice by declaring that the intent and the words had to match before a vow was binding (Mish. *Terumoth* 3:8; cf. also Jesus in Matt. 5:33–37). On *dāḇār* ("word," "thing") see J. Bergman, H. Lutzmann, W. Schmidt, *TDOT,* III:85–125. On the independent existence of spoken words such as vows, curses, and blessings, see above on 22:7.

if the man objects immediately after he first hears about the woman's vow. Three times the consequences of voiding the vow are that Yahweh will remit punishment for the unfulfilled vow because the father or husband forbade the woman. The last case is a bit different (see below on v. 16 [Eng. 15]).

4–6 (3–5) This is the case of a woman who makes a vow while she is *in her father's house,* i.e., under his authority, *in her youth (bin'ureyhā).* Although the Talmud (*Nedarim* 47b) makes this term refer to the time just before a young woman reaches puberty, this seems to be a postbiblical usage. In the OT the *na'ar* (and its fem. equivalent *na'ᵃrâ*) may even include infants (cf. Exod. 2:6; 1 Sam. 1:22; 4:21; Job 31:18), and rarely includes only virgins (cf. Judg. 19:3; Amos 2:7). It is therefore a general term that must be defined by its context. Here the woman in question has not yet been married, hence she was living at home. One must here think of one old enough to make a vow in the first place. Therefore the reference must be to young unmarried women of marriageable age.

In order to void the vow the father must object when he *hears the vow (wᵉšāma' 'eṯ-niḏrāh).* This does not mean that the father had to hear the actual vow itself, but only about the vow. The idiom used for the father's objection is that *he restrained her (hēnî' . . . 'ōṯāh),* which means "to show successful opposition to (her conduct in making the vow)."[25] The outcome of such opposition is that no vow or obligation that she may have taken on herself may *stand.* The verb *qûm* ("to stand") has the sense of "to be valid" all through this passage.[26] The young woman living in her father's house does not have the final legal say on binding herself to a vow.

7–9 (6–8) Some scholars have applied this section to a woman who was betrothed or engaged to be married, citing Deut. 22:23–25 as evidence that betrothed women were considered under the authority of their husbands.[27] But the idiom "to be for (to) a man" *(hayᵉṯâ lᵉ'îš)* means generally "to be(come) married" (Lev. 21:3; 22:12; Deut. 24:2; 25:5; Jer. 3:1; Ruth 1:12–13). It seems more likely, therefore, that the woman in question was one who took a vow while unmarried and that vow remained

25. See BDB, p. 626a; Gray, p. 416. The only derivative of the verb in the OT is *tᵉnû'â,* which is translated as "opposition" in 14:34 (see the commentary above) and Job 33:10.

26. It occurs in vv. 5–6, 8, 12 (Eng. 4–5, 7, 11); cf. Gen. 23:17, 20; Lev. 27:19; BDB, p. 878a. The Hiphil in vv. 14–15 (Eng. 13–14) has the meaning of "to make stand," "to validate."

27. So Cook, p. 765; Snaith, p. 193; Sturdy, p. 210; Budd, p. 323.

unfulfilled when she married.[28] The natural question would then be whether her new husband (under whose authority she now is) would have anything to say about the vow (of which her father must have already approved). The answer is yes, but the same rule applies as for the father in the first case: *when he hears his wife* (lit. "on the day of hearing his wife," i.e., immediately), he must *restrain her* or his silence is taken as consent to the performance of the vow, even if that vow was *a rash utterance of her lips (mibṭāʾ śᵉpāṯeyhā),* i.e., even if she took the vow without thinking.[29] If he does object, then *he will void her vow (wᵉhēpēr ʾeṯ-niḏrāh).* The verb *pārar* (Hiphil) is used to describe the violation of a covenant (Lev. 26:44; Judg. 2:1; Jer. 14:21) or rejection of advice (making it ineffectual; 2 Sam. 15:34; 17:14; Isa. 4:27). Here it simply means to abrogate or make void the vow that the woman took upon herself.[30] This statement is parallel to *none of her vows or her obligations that she took upon herself will stand* in v. 6 (Eng. 5), except that the active role of the husband is stressed here. Again, the nonperformance of the vow incurs guilt, but since the woman has been prevented from fulfilling the vow by a higher authority, Yahweh absolves her of it.

10 (9) A few scholars have concluded that this verse is a later interpolation or gloss,[31] but there is no textual evidence for this conclusion (see below on v. 17 [Eng. 16]). Some have held that v. 10 (Eng. 9) interrupts the sequence of vv. 7–9 and 11–16 (Eng. 6–8 and 10–15), both of which deal with married women. As pointed out above, however, vv. 7–9 (Eng. 6–8) deal with a specific kind of married woman — one who had taken a vow when unmarried and brought that unfulfilled vow with her to the marriage. Vv. 11–16 (Eng. 10–15) deal with women who make vows *after* marriage. There is a kind of progression in dealing with these cases: those never married, those married while under a vow, those who

28. So, e.g., Keil, p. 224; Gray, p. 416; McNeile, p. 162; Binns, p. 200; Noordtzij, p. 268; Noth, p. 225; and Wenham, p. 208. GNB brings this sense out clearly: "If an unmarried woman makes a vow . . . and then marries."

29. Heb. *mibṭāʾ* is found only in this section (vv. 7, 9 [Eng. 6, 8]). It is derived from a rare verb (*bāṭāʾ* or *bāṭâ*) that means "to speak rashly." In the Qal it is used of the fool who babbles on and on (Prov. 12:18), and in the Piel of vows that are uttered without thought (Lev. 5:4) and of Moses' words to the Israelites at Meribah in Ps. 133:33 (Eng. 32) (cf. Num. 20:2–13). That rash words and vows may have been a problem in Israel can be seen by the frequency with which they are mentioned (Prov. 20:25; Eccl. 5:1, 3–5 [Eng. 2, 4–6]; Sir. 18:23; Mish. *Nazir* 1:1–9:5, *Nedarim* 1:1–11:12).

30. See BDB, p. 830.

31. E.g., Holzinger, p. 147; Heinisch, p. 117; de Vaulx, p. 347.

have been widowed or divorced. All these are leading up to what must have been by far the most common: those who were married and living with their husbands (vv. 11–16 [Eng. 10–15]).

The widow or the divorcee might normally be expected to return to her father's house, if he were alive (cf., Gen. 38:11; Lev. 22:13; Ruth 1:8), or to be cared for by one of her sons.[32] The question would then be under whose authority such a woman would be. It might be thought that she would be under the authority of her father (once again) or her son. But according to the current legislation, once a married woman had become single, either by the death of her husband or by divorce, she was on the same ground vis-à-vis vows as the male in v. 3 (Eng. 2); *all that she has taken upon herself will stand over her*—she must fulfill any vow or obligation that she has taken on.

11–13 (10–12) Verses 11–16 (Eng. 10–15) deal with the largest class of women, those who were married and living in their husband's house (i.e., under his authority) and who took vows after their marriage. Snaith remarks that the Babylonian Talmud called such women "fully married."[33] The same principle obtained: if the husband objected when he first heard of the vow, he was allowed to void it, but if he said nothing immediately, the vow was established (i.e., it stood). Because of the nonperformance of the vow it was still necessary to cancel the wife's guilt, but Yahweh did this as before (vv. 6, 9 [Eng. 5, 8]).

14–16 (13–15) In the cases here considered guilt is incurred, but it belongs to the husband, not the wife.

to humble herself (leʿannōṯ nāp̄eš). The word *humble (ʿānâ)* is commonly related to fasting, but here it may include other vows of abstinence as well.[34] The husband may either establish or void these vows. The way in which he established them is, as above, by saying nothing to his wife.

from day to day (miyyôm ʾel-yôm). This phrase is probably another way of stating that the husband had to oppose the vow immediately or not at all (i.e., when he heard about her vow, vv. 5, 6, 8, 9, 12, 13 [Eng. 4, 5, 7, 8, 11, 12]). If he simply let it go and said nothing, then

32. On widows, see de Vaux, *Ancient Israel,* I:40; P. S. Hiebert, "Whence Shall Help Come to Me? The Biblical Widow," in *Gender and Difference in Ancient Israel,* ed. P. L. Day (Minneapolis: Fortress, 1989), pp. 125–41. On divorce and divorced women, see de Vaux, *Ancient Israel,* I:34–36.

33. Snaith, p. 193; the reference is to T.B. *Nedarim* 70a.

34. See the commentary above on 29:7.

the vow was established. He could only void it by stating his opposition immediately.

But if, in fact, he voids them after he hears of them (w^{e}'im hāpēr yāpēr 'ōṯām 'aḥ^{a}rê šom'ô). This clause may imply a longer period of reflection.

he will bear her iniquity (w^{e}nāśā' 'eṯ-'^{a}wōnāh). The guilt that devolves on the person who did not perform the vow (the woman) would be transferred to the man who, after deliberation, voids his wife's vow.[35]

17 (16) This verse forms the conclusion to the unit. It mentions in summary form that the regulations concern husband and wife as well as father and daughter. Some who have concluded that v. 10 (Eng. 9) is a later gloss remark that the widow and the divorcee are not included in this summary.[36] This conclusion carries some force, but in order to carry conviction it would be necessary to show that concluding summaries must mention minor as well as major parts of the passage summarized. But this is surely not the case (see, e.g., the concluding Torah subscript in 5:29–30,[37] or the shorter subscript in 1:44, etc.).

G. WAR WITH MIDIAN (31:1–54)

1 *And Yahweh spoke to Moses, saying:*

2 *"Vindicate the people of Israel with regard to the Midianites; afterward you will be gathered to your kinfolk."*[1]

3 *And Moses spoke to the people, saying: "Let men of war be armed among you that they may be against Midian in order to inflict the vindication of Yahweh upon Midian.*

4 *You shall send one thousand from each tribe*[2] *among all the tribes to the battle."*

35. On *nāśā' 'āwōn* meaning that one will bear divine punishment, see the commentary above on 5:31; see also W. Zimmerli, "Die Eigenart der prophetischen Rede des Ezechiel," *ZAW* 66 (1954) 1–26, esp. 8–11.

36. See, e.g., Holzinger, p. 147; de Vaulx, pp. 347–48.

37. See the commentary above on 5:11–31; see also M. Fishbane, "Accusations of Adultery: A Study of Law and Scribal Practice in Numbers 5:11–31," *HUCA* 45 (1974) 25–45, esp. 31–35.

1. MT reads pl. *('ammeykā).* Some versions read sing. *('amm^{e}kā),* but this is unnecessary. See the note to the translation of 20:24.

2. The distributive is here expressed by repeating the whole phrase *'elep lammaṭṭeh 'elep lammaṭṭeh,* lit., "one thousand for the tribe"; see GKC, § 134q; Davidson, *Syntax,* §§ 28 Rem. 8; 38 Rem. 4.

5 *So there were provided*[3] *from the thousands of Israel, one thousand per tribe, twelve thousand men armed for battle.*
6 *So Moses sent them, one thousand from each tribe, to the battle, they and Phinehas the son of Eleazar the priest to the battle, and the vessels of the sacred place and the trumpets for blowing were in his care.*
7 *And they waged war against Midian just as Yahweh had commanded Moses, and they killed every male.*
8 *And they killed the kings of Midian in addition to*[4] *the others who were slain; Evi, Rekem, Zur, Hur, and Reba, the five*[5] *kings of Midian. They also killed Balaam the son of Beor with the sword.*
9 *And the children of Israel took the Midianite women and children captive, and took all their beasts, cattle, and wealth as plunder.*
10 *And all their cities in the places they lived and all their encampments they burned with fire.*
11 *And they took all the spoil and all the booty from both human and beast.*
12 *And they brought the captives, the booty, and the spoil to Moses and to Eleazar the priest and to the congregation of the children of Israel, to the plains of Moab, which is by the Jordan that flows by Jericho.*
13 *And Moses and Eleazar the priest and all the leaders of the congregation went out*[6] *to meet them outside the camp.*
14 *And Moses became angry with the officers of the force, the*

3. MT *wayyissāp̱erû* is a Niphal from *māsar,* "to offer," here with *maʿal,* which may mean "trespass, transgression," hence "offer [i.e., commit] a trespass." This verb occurs only twice in the OT (here and in v. 16), though it is common in postbiblical Hebrew and Aramaic, where it means "deliver, transmit, surrender" (see Jastrow, *Dictionary,* pp. 810–11; cf. Gray, p. 421). Here it makes little sense. The versions read different texts here: LXX *kai exērithmēsan,* presupposing Heb. *wayyisāp̱erû,* "and they were chosen [or provided]" (similarly, Pesh. and Targs.). The Vulg. reads *dederunt,* "they gave," perhaps presupposing *wayyimserû.* Both *BHS* and BDB (p. 588) follow LXX, which makes the most sense and has been followed.

4. For the preposition *ʿal* in the sense of "in addition to," see BDB, p. 755 (4b); Williams, *Syntax,* § 292.

5. The numerals 2–10 are substantives that may precede a numbered object in the construct state, the object then being in the pl. of the genitive of material. See Williams, *Syntax,* § 95.

6. MT *wayyēṣeʾû.* The more usual form is the sing. verb in agreement with the first subject only; cf. Davidson, *Syntax,* § 114 (b) (see v. 54 below). When the predicate comes first, however, the verb may be in the pl. as here. Cf. Davidson, *Syntax,* § 114 (a).

commanders of thousands and the commanders of hundreds, who were coming from fighting the war.
15 *And Moses said to them, "Have you let every woman live?*
16 *Surely, these were the ones who caused the children of Israel to commit a trespass against Yahweh*[7] *at the word of Balaam, in the matter of Peor, so that a plague came upon the congregation of Yahweh.*
17 *So, now, kill every male among the children, and every woman who has known a man by lying with a male you shall also kill.*
18 *But any of the children among the women who have not known lying with a man you shall preserve alive for yourselves.*
19 *And you — all of you who killed a person or who touched a slain body — cleanse yourselves and your captives on the third day and on the seventh day.*
20 *And you will cleanse*[8] *every garment, every article made of hide, every work of goat hair, and every article of wood."*
21 *And Eleazar the priest said to the men of the army, those who came to the battle:*[9] *"This is the statute of the ordinance that Yahweh commanded Moses:*
22 *Only the gold and the silver, the copper, the iron, the tin, and the wood,*
23 *everything that may go into the fire, you will pass through the fire,*[10] *and it will become ceremonially clean; nevertheless, it must*

7. MT *limsor maʿal bYHWH.* Here is the other occurrence of the verb *māsar,* discussed above in v. 5. Again it is problematic. LXX reads *tou apostēsai kai hyperidein to rhēma kyriou,* "who rebelled and ignored the word of the Lord," as does Pesh. *(wmrrw wʾʿlyw bmrʾ). BHS* suggests reading either *limʿōl maʿal bYHWH,* "committed a transgression against Yahweh," or *lāsûr mēʿal YHWH,* "to turn from [upon] Yahweh." Paterson, p. 63, and Gray, p. 423, have adopted the former reading (see *HALAT,* p. 575b). If one retains MT, one must posit a meaning for *māsar* that is elsewhere attested only in the disputed v. 5 above until the postbiblical period (see note above). In the light of the difficulty the ancient versions have with *māsar* here and in v. 5, it is preferable to accept the reading *limʿōl maʿal bYHWH* while recognizing that there is, to date, no wholly convincing explanation of how MT arose.

8. MT *tiṯḥaṭṭāʾû,* a Hithpael, which means "you will cleanse yourselves." *BHS* suggests the Piel *ṭᵉḥaṭṭēʾû* instead, since it yields a better meaning.

9. On "those who came to the battle" *(hābbāʾîm lammilḥāmâ),* see Keil, p. 227.

10. LXX omits the clause "you will pass through the fire" *(taʿᵃḇîrû ḇāʾēš),* perhaps through homoioteleuton (according to *BHS*). Homoioteleuton is a scribal error in which the scribe omits a line with the same ending as a previous line. Here the second occurrence of *bāʾēš taʿᵃḇîrû* is dropped.

also be cleansed by the waters of impurity. But anything that may not go into the fire you will pass through the waters.[11]

24 *When you scrub your garments on the seventh day, you will become ceremonially clean. And afterward you may come into the camp."*

25 *And Yahweh said to Moses, saying:*

26 *"Take a count*[12] *of the captured booty, both of human and beast, you and Eleazar the priest and the leaders of the fathers of the congregation.*

27 *You will divide the booty between the warriors who go to the battle and the whole congregation.*

28 *And you will set aside a levy for Yahweh from the men of war who go out to the battle, one*[13] *life in five hundred, from humans, from the cattle, from the donkeys,*[14] *and from the sheep.*

29 *And you*[15] *shall take it from their half and give it to Eleazar the priest as a contribution for Yahweh.*

11. Heb. *bammāyim.* The definite article marks the waters as those mentioned earlier in the verse (GKC, § 126d). So, e.g., Budd, p. 326; Heinisch, p. 118; Noordtzij, p. 274; AV, RV, RSV, NASB, NIV, GNB, NEB. NEB and GNB read the Hebrew text to mean that only the metals are cleansed with fire; everything else is cleansed by the waters of purification. This interpretation requires reading the particle *'aḵ* ("nevertheless") as "everything else" (GNB) or "other things" (NEB). It also means that the last clause *(wᵉḵōl 'ᵃšer lō'-yāḇō' bā'ēš taʿᵃḇîrû ḇammāyim)* is epexegetical ("i.e., everything else which cannot go into the fire must be passed through the waters"). GNB paraphrases at this point. The current translation seems a better handling of the Hebrew text and follows the majority of commentators and translations as noted above.

12. For discussion of the idiom "to take a count of" *(śā' 'ēṯ rō'š),* see the discussion in the note at 1:2.

13. The numeral "one" *('eḥāḏ)* precedes the substantive here as it does most often in Aramaic; so also in Neh. 4:11; Dan. 8:13; Cant. 4:9 (see GKC, § 134d; Davidson, *Syntax,* § 35 Rem. 1).

14. Albright contended that the fact that donkeys were listed here rather than camels, which were not used for caravaning until the very end of the Late Bronze Age or beginning of the Iron Age, is a mark that the narrative here has at least an archaic base and is founded on actual happenings rather than being simply midrashic fiction. See *Yahweh and the Gods of Canaan,* pp. 70–73, 179, 270–71; and esp. idem, "Midianite Donkey Caravans," in *Translating and Understanding the Old Testament: Essays in Honor of H. G. May,* ed. H. Frank and W. Reed (Nashville: Abingdon, 1970), pp. 197–205.

15. MT reads the pl. *(tiqqāḥû).* The sing. (*tiqqaḥ,* as in vv. 27–28) is more likely; so Sam. Pent. and Pesh. The pl. could include the whole congregation along with Moses.

30 *And from the half of the children of Israel, take one drawn*[16] *from each fifty, from humans, from the cattle, from the donkeys, from the sheep, from all the beasts; and you will give them to the Levites who are standing guard over the tabernacle of Yahweh."*

31 *And Moses and Eleazar the priest did according to all that Yahweh had commanded Moses.*

32 *And the booty remaining from the plunder that the people of the army had taken was: sheep, 675,000.*

33 *And cattle, 72,000.*

34 *And donkeys, 61,000.*

35 *And humans from among the women who had not known lying with a man, the total persons, 32,000.*

36 *And the half, the share of those who had gone out into the battle was, by number: sheep, 337,500.*

37 *And the levy for Yahweh from the sheep was 675.*

38 *And the cattle, 36,000, of which Yahweh's levy was 72.*

39 *And the donkeys, 30,500, of which Yahweh's levy was 61.*

40 *And humans, 16,000, of which Yahweh's levy was 32 persons.*

41 *And Moses gave the levy, the offering for Yahweh, to Eleazar the priest, as Yahweh had commanded Moses.*

42 *And from the half of the children of Israel that Moses divided from that of the men who waged war,*

43 *that is, the half belonging to the congregation: from the sheep, 337,500.*

44 *And cattle, 36,000.*

45 *And donkeys, 30,500.*

46 *And humans, 16,000.*

47 *And Moses took from the half of the children of Israel one drawn*[17] *from each fifty, from humans and from beasts, and he gave them to the Levites who were standing guard over the tabernacle of Yahweh, as Yahweh had commanded Moses.*

48 *And those appointed over the thousands of the army, commanders of thousands and commanders of hundreds, drew near to Moses,*

49 *and said to Moses, "Your servants have taken a count of the men of war who were under our command; not a man is missing from us.*

16. LXX, Pesh., and Vulg. omit the word *drawn ('āḥuz);* see also v. 47 below.

17. LXX, Pesh., and Vulg. omit the word *drawn ('eṯ-hā'āḥuz);* see also v. 30 above.

50 *And we have brought Yahweh's offering, what each man found, articles of*[18] *gold, armlets and bracelets, signet rings, earrings, and ornaments, to make atonement for ourselves before Yahweh."*

51 *And Moses and Eleazar the priest received the gold from them, all wrought articles.*

52 *And all the gold of the contribution to Yahweh that was offered by the commanders of thousands and the commanders of hundreds was 16,750 shekels.*

53 *(The men of the army had taken plunder, each for himself.)*

54 *And Moses and Eleazar the priest received the gold from the commanders of the thousands and the hundreds*[19] *and brought it to the tent of meeting, a memorial for the children of Israel before Yahweh.*

Although the war with Midian is the first subject dealt with in ch. 31, it is not the main interest of the chapter, which rather lies in the cultic matters of waging the Yahweh war (i.e., inflicting the ban or *ḥērem,* vv. 13–18), cleansing the soldiers (vv. 19–24), dividing the booty (vv. 25–47), and bringing an offering to Yahweh (vv. 48–54). These cultic matters explain the placement of the chapter next to a legal/cultic section (chs. 28–30).

The present chapter takes up matters discussed in many other passages in the book and weaves them into the narrative: vengeance on Midian (vv. 2–3; cf. 25:16–18), Moses' coming death (v. 2; cf. 27:13), the trumpets (v. 6; cf. 10:2–10), Zur the Midianite (v. 8; cf. 25:15), Balaam (vv. 8, 16; cf. chs. 22–24), the incident of Baal-Peor (v. 16; cf. 25:6–9, 14–15), purification after contact with the dead (vv. 19–24; cf. 19:11–19 [also Lev. 11:32]), care for priests and Levites (vv. 28–47; cf. 18:8–32), costly offerings (vv. 48–54; cf. chs. 7, 28–29). In addition, the counting or mustering that takes place in vv. 3–5, 26, 32–47 reflects the theme of chs. 1–4; 26. Thus the chapter is a summary and conclusion of much that has gone before.

Many scholars have taken ch. 31 as a late addition to P, or even to the completed pentateuchal narrative, hence dependent on several

18. MT *k^e lî* is sing., but the *Sebir* note and a number of mss. read the pl. construct *(k^e lê),* which makes more sense in the context. In an unpointed text both terms would be identical.

19. MT *śorê hāʾ^a lāp̱îm w^e hammēʾôṯ,* "commanders of the thousands and the hundreds," may stand for *śorê hāʾ^a lāp̱îm w^e śorê hammēʾôṯ,* "commanders of the thousands and commanders of the hundreds," which occurs in v. 48. The same slightly shortened expression occurs in 1 Chr. 13:1.

other texts.[20] The army of 12,000 men drawn from the tribes is said to recall Judg. 21:10–12. The exploits of Gideon are recalled in the total destruction of the enemy (Num. 31:7; cf. Judg. 8:12) and the taking of spoil (Num. 31:48–54; cf. Judg. 8:24–27). The division of the spoil between the fighters and those who remained in camp is said to reflect David's practice in 1 Sam. 30:24–25. Of course, if Num. 31 is older than the passages in Judges and 1 Samuel, then the dependency would be the other way.[21] Matters of literary relationships among different texts are seldom as simple as sheer dependence of one on another. It suffices for the present context to point to similarities among the passages mentioned.

Scholars widely hold the story to be midrash rather than history. Midrash is generally considered a kind of devotional or homiletical meditation on a scriptural theme or passage, such as became common in the later rabbinic midrashim (e.g., *Sifre* on Numbers). Some of the methods that later became incorporated in midrash seem to be present here, most importantly the reflections on the earlier passages in the book (mentioned above). The word *midrash* (from the verb *dāraš,* "to seek") is used twice in the OT itself (2 Chr. 13:22 and 24:27), both times referring to sources that the Chronicler considered as historical.[22] The conclusion is that the techniques of midrash, even as practiced later, do not necessarily impugn the basic historical integrity of a narrative. That the author of ch. 31 wrote using motifs from other passages means only that this was his literary method, not that the event of vv. 1–12 could not have happened.[23]

Nonetheless, several factors in this chapter remain puzzling. First,

20. For the view that it is a late addition to P, see Dillmann, pp. 187–92; Holzinger, pp. 148–50; Baentsch, pp. 650–51; Gray, pp. 418–19; McNeile, pp. 163–64; Binns, p. xxxvi; Snaith, p. 193; Sturdy, pp. 214–16; Budd, pp. 329–30. Noth (pp. 228–29) holds that it is a late addition to a completed narrative.

21. Those who argue for a priority for Num. 31 include Keil, p. 226; Noordtzij, pp. 271–72; and Wenham, pp. 209–10.

22. The term is variously translated by the English versions in the two passages: "story," "commentary" (RSV); "story," "annals" (NEB); "annotations" (NIV); "treatise" (NASB); "history," "commentary" (GNB); "annals" (NKJV); etc. See, e.g., J. M. Myers, *II Chronicles,* AB (Garden City, N.Y.: Doubleday, 1965), pp. 79, 81, 139; H. G. M. Williamson, *1 and 2 Chronicles,* NCBC (Grand Rapids: Eerdmans, 1982), pp. 255, 326; R. B. Dillard, *2 Chronicles,* WBC (Waco: Word, 1987), pp. 109–10, 194.

23. See, e.g., Gray, pp. 417–19; Binns, pp. 201–2; Sturdy, pp. 214–16; Noth, pp. 228–29.

the report is that the Israelites "killed every male" in Midian, whereas later, in Gideon's day, Midian was a problem again (Judg. 6–8). The statement in v. 7 need mean nothing more than that the Israelites killed every male they found when they attacked the Midianites. Details of the war are really nonexistent here, but the impression given is of one surprise attack rather than a long war waged on many fronts. The Midianites are associated with many other peoples in the OT (e.g., the Ishmaelites, the Moabites, the Amalekites), mostly as a nomadic people. They may have been a league of separate tribes who came together for religious and political purposes around specific sites such as Kadesh and Elath, rather than a unified people at all.[24] If this were the case, then it may have been only the Moabite contingent of the Midianites that the Israelites destroyed here. This conjecture surely makes at least as much sense as that a postexilic editor (who should have known that the Midianites were a problem later) simply invented a story in the hope that no one would compare the narratives of Numbers with Judges.

Second, the fact that not a single Israelite warrior was slain in the war (v. 49) has raised questions. Such a claim is unquestionably remarkable; indeed, it was intended to be a witness to the supernatural care of Yahweh. Similar incidents are reported both inside and outside the Bible.[25]

Third, the number of animals seems very high, and perhaps some adjustment in our understanding of these figures is necessary.[26]

In all these matters all one really has to go on is one ancient text. All the claims in the text are theoretically possible by natural means, let alone supernatural. The question of what could have happened (or must have happened) cannot be decided by what the modern interpreter thinks is possible. On similar philosophical grounds most if not all miracles, and

24. See W. J. Dumbrell, "Midian — A Land or a League?" *VT* 25 (1975) 323–37. Dumbrell supports the basic historicity of the narrative, as does Albright, "Midianite Donkey Caravans," pp. 197–205.

25. See, e.g., Judg. 7:1–25; 1 Sam. 14:6–52. Keil (p. 230 n. 1) gives some extrabiblical parallels from Tacitus, wherein the Romans slaughtered their enemies without losing a single man in taking a Parthian castle, and from Strabo, who relates the killing of 1,000 Arabs with the loss of only two Romans at a particular battle. The veracity of these narratives is unknown. That they are cited here simply shows that other ancient authors also carried reports of battles wherein small losses were encountered.

26. See the excursus above on large numbers. The amount of booty is high when compared with that in other documents detailing the amount of spoil taken by war; cf. *ANET,* pp. 234–41, esp. 237–38.

theism itself, could finally be ruled out of court. One must only say that the case here is remarkable, and, if it happened in this way, was a witness to Yahweh's power on behalf of his people, which is the theological point the author is attempting to make. In the repetition of the story itself, Yahweh's power may be felt.

What use does such a passage as this have in the modern world? Only the briefest of notes must suffice here. It is clear that this law was given for the kingdom of God in national form (Israel), that this kingdom was intended to be a theocracy, and that this theocracy was in the ancient Near East. First, for Christians, the kingdom of God is no longer a national entity, else the NT is a meaningless document. Rather, the kingdom now extends over all national boundaries to embrace all who accept the Lordship of Christ. Second, the kingdom as such is still a theocracy, but the successor to Israel is the church, not a national entity (Gal. 6:16; 1 Pet. 2:9–10). No nation has the automatic right to assume these rules of war for itself as if it was the successor to Israel's mission. Third, the modern world, which has enough force to annihilate the planet many times over, is very different from the ancient Near East, with its limited possibilities for human destruction. Peter Craigie wrote:

> The transformation in the concept of the Kingdom means that the laws of war cannot simply be translated to fit a new context. In the new context the recognition of the principle of violence between states remains. But citizens of the Kingdom of God must not be bound by the necessity of violence; they must transcend the order of necessity. The death of Jesus, which is the death of God, demonstrated that the transcending of violence involved becoming the victim of violence. In a sense this may all seem very clear; we must receive violence, not employ it. Yet it is not quite so simple, for the Christian is not only a citizen of the Kingdom of God. He is also a citizen of a particular human state. The human state to which he belongs is bound by the order of necessity, of violence; it is caught in the same dilemma which characterized the existence of the ancient state of Israel, and the Old Testament has made it clear that that is an inevitable dilemma. No state can exist free from the necessity of violence or liberated from the possibility of war. And the dilemma for the Christian will be in determining how to understand the relationship between his two citizenships.[27]

1–3 The command to make war on the Midianites (25:16–18) is taken up again. This time the campaign is put in terms of vindication for

27. P. Craigie, *The Problem of War in the Old Testament* (Grand Rapids: Eerdmans, 1978), p. 102. This whole book may be read with profit.

the people of Israel (*n*[e]*qōm niqmaṯ b*[e]*nê yiśrā'ēl,* v. 2) and *the vindication of Yahweh* (*niqmaṯ YHWH,* v. 3). The more usual translation of the root *nqm* is "vengeance," but as Mendenhall has shown, punitive (or perhaps defensive) vindication is a better translation.[28] What is meant is an executive action on behalf of Yahweh, carried out through Israel, to vindicate the honor of Yahweh and Israel, which had been sullied by the matter of Baal-Peor. This phrase, as well as material in vv. 6–7 below, shows that this war is to be considered a Yahweh war in which the ban or *ḥērem* was to be carried out.

4–5 *You shall send one thousand.* The term *thousand ('elep̱)* in this context has been criticized as an unrealistic or ideal element in the story on account of the great differences in population of the tribes (cf. ch. 26), and their consequent different abilities to provide military aid for the project.[29] It could be, however, that the word *'elep̱* here has the meaning of "clan unit" (as in, e.g., Josh. 22:14; Judg. 6:15) or "military contingent," as Mendenhall has suggested.[30] If so, then the objection disappears. What would be asserted in this case would be that *out of the clans of Israel (mē'al*[e]*p̱ê yiśrā'ēl)* "military contingents" of undetermined size were provided, one per tribe. This understanding might easily allow for differing sizes in contingents based on the size, etc. of the tribe.

6–7 The fundamentally religious nature of this vindicative action is seen, first, in the fact that *Phinehas the son of Eleazar the priest* was involved in the battle. The reason why Phinehas rather than Eleazar was involved is unknown, but was probably analogous to the reason why Eleazar rather than Aaron was set the task of dealing with the unclean censers (17:1–5 [Eng. 16:36–40]), viz., the risk of cultic contamination of the high priest. A further reason may be that Phinehas's zeal in killing the daughter of Zur the Midianite clan chief had earned him a reputation and right to act in the matter.

the vessels of the sacred place and the trumpets for blowing were in his care. This is further evidence of the religious nature of the undertaking, although just what these *sacred vessels* were is a matter of debate.

28. G. Mendenhall, "The 'Vengeance' of Yahweh," in *The Tenth Generation* (Baltimore: Johns Hopkins Univ. Press, 1973), pp. 69–104, esp. 99. One need not agree with Mendenhall on the dating of the material in this chapter to appreciate his suggestions.

29. E.g., by Noth, p. 229; Sturdy, p. 216; Budd, p. 330.

30. See the excursus above on large numbers.

Snaith thinks they may stand for the ark of the covenant,[31] although since the term is pl. it must include more than the ark. Others are sure that it cannot include the ark.[32] Keil thought that the *vessels* were more closely defined by the term *and* (in its epexegetical sense of *i.e.*) *the trumpets.*[33] Dillmann followed Delitzsch in suggesting that the holy garments of the high priest are intended (for *k*ᵉ*lî* as "garment," see Deut. 22:5).[34] Targ. Pseudo-Jonathan and Noordtzij think that Urim and Thummim are meant (so also NJPS).[35] This suggestion is unlikely because these were kept by the high priest, and it is doubtful that he would have lent them out even for such a purpose.[36] Since the phrase *vessels of the sanctuary* is used, e.g., in 3:31; 4:15; 18:3; 1 K. 8:4; 1 Chr. 9:29; and 2 Chr. 5:6 to indicate the anointed furnishings of the tabernacle in general, it is likely to indicate the anointed furnishings in general here as well, probably including the ark. The trumpets (cf. 10:2–10) were not anointed and hence could not be called *vessels of the sanctuary.*[37]

In the battle the Israelites *killed every male* Midianite. As mentioned above, this phrase probably means that they killed every Midianite male that they found. This kind of slaughter is congruent with what is known about the ban *(ḥerem),* although that word is not actually used for this action.[38]

8 The names of the five slain Midianite kings occur again, in the same order, in Josh. 13:21. There they are designated as "leaders" *(n*ᵉ*śî'îm)* and "princes" (or "installed leaders," i.e., "vassals," *n*ᵉ*sîḵîm*) of Sihon. These men may be the same group designated as "elders" *(z*ᵉ*qēnîm)* in Num. 22:4. In 25:15 the leader Zur is simply designated the "head of a tribe" (i.e., a "father's house"). These other passages show the flexibility in the designation *king (meleḵ),* which here means no more than a local overlord.

31. Snaith, pp. 194–95.
32. E.g., Noth, p. 229; Budd, p. 330.
33. Keil, pp. 225–26; Cook, p. 767.
34. Dillmann, p. 189; Gray (p. 420) also considered it possible.
35. Noordtzij, p. 271.
36. See Dillmann, p. 189; McNeile, p. 164.
37. See Milgrom, *Studies in Levitical Terminology,* I:49 n. 186.
38. Although the detailed prescriptions for the ban are given their clear legal formulation in Deut. 7 and 20, one may conclude that this was only the codification of (and perhaps modification of) a well-known practice, not only in Israel, but in the ancient Near East generally (see a probable reference to the practice in Exod. 23:31–32; 34:13). On the ban, see the commentary above on 21:2–3.

These five names form one of the few concrete details found in this narrative, which, admittedly, was told for religious and nationalistic purposes. It is likely that these names are historical. *Evi* and *Reba* occur only here and in Josh. 13:21, while *Hur* occurs as the name of an Israelite chief in Exod. 17:10. The name that occurs most often in the ancient world is *Rekem.* An Israelite named Rekem is mentioned in 1 Chr. 2:43–44; 7:16, and it is the name of a Benjaminite town in Josh. 18:27. Nabatean inscriptions and Josephus point to the name as the original title for Petra.[39]

Balaam. Num. 24:25 states that Balaam *went back to his place.* The current passage indicates that he must have stopped on his way among the Midianites, perhaps to inform them in the matter of Baal-Peor (v. 16). Other than Josh. 13:21, which repeats this information, no text sheds any light on the differences between the current material and 24:25. Some scholars have concluded that the present text has simply drawn an inference from the fact that Midianites were involved in the original approach to Balaam (22:4, 7) and in ch. 25, which is placed immediately after chs. 22–24 to connect the incidents literarily.[40] Of course, such a conclusion is possible, but it is difficult to explain why an editor should invent a death for Balaam here, especially in the light of the fact that 24:25 has already ended his involvement in the narrative quite adequately. It seems just as possible that the current text narrates what actually took place, and that chs. 22–25 must be read as connected. It may be that the literary connection between the chapters dealing with the Moabites (chs. 22–24) and that dealing with the Midianites (ch. 25) reflects the way things really happened.

9–12 The term *captive* (*šᵉḇî,* vv. 12, 19; cf. the verb *šāḇâ,* "to take captives," v. 9) refers to humans. The other terms, *to take plunder* (*bāzaz,* vv. 9, 52), *plunder* (*bāz,* v. 32), *spoil* (*šālāl,* vv. 11–12), and *booty* (*malqôaḥ,* vv. 11–12, 26–27), are not greatly differentiated in the chapter and are probably used for variety to refer to what are called "the spoils of war": the animals and possessions of the defeated population.[41]

The places where the Midianites lived were burned. Two kinds of

39. Josephus, *Ant.* 4.7.1. For a further discussion of these names, see G. Mendenhall, "The 'Sea Peoples' in Palestine," in *Tenth Generation,* pp. 167–69.

40. E.g., Noth, p. 231; Sturdy, p. 213.

41. E.g., *malqôaḥ* means only "that which is seized," and is a general term. Some scholars, e.g., Keil (p. 226) and Snaith (p. 195), differentiate the booty into categories on the basis of vocabulary. Gray (pp. 421–22) and Budd (p. 331) agree with the position taken in the present commentary.

dwellings places are mentioned: *cities* and *encampments.* The other dwellings are *cities,* which are naturally a more permanent kind of dwelling. The term *cities* is modified by the phrase *in the places where they lived (b^e môš^e ḇoṯām).* The participle *môš^e ḇoṯ,* "dwelling places," is derived from the verb *yāšaḇ,* "to dwell, live." It is difficult to see why such a term would be attached to the word *cities* if it were not to imply that the Midianites had not built these cities but merely lived in them. Josh. 13:21 says that the five Midianite kings named in this verse were vassals of Sihon. Other passages style the Midianites as travelers or wanderers (see, e.g., Gen. 37:25–36; Exod. 2:17), and some scholars have, as has already been said, held that the Midianites were a league of tribes.[42] The spoils of war were brought from the battle site (which is unknown) to the place where the Israelites were camped in 22:1, i.e., *on the plains of Moab, which is by the Jordan that flows by Jericho.*

13–18 This admittedly vague battle report is the historical peg on which three related narratives are hung: the carrying out of the ban (vv. 13–18), the cleansing of warriors (vv. 19–24), and the division (and annotation) of booty (vv. 25–54).

13-14 *And Moses . . . went out . . . outside the camp.* The warriors had become ceremonially unclean by contacting the corpses of the slain (ch. 19) and could not be readmitted to Yahweh's camp (5:1–4). Moses became angry with the army's leaders for their conduct of the campaign.

The word *ḥayîl* is a common one for army. The basic meaning of the term is "power, strength," and thus the translation *force.*[43] The *officers* are, lit., "the numbered ones (of)" *(p^e qûḏê).* The passive participle of *pāqaḏ,* "to number," is used 66 times for the people who were numbered or set apart in the censuses (chs. 1–4, 26). The leaders are not designated simply by the term *p^e qûḏê,* and 7:2 differentiates between the leaders and "those numbered." The conclusion is that "those numbered of the army" is a general term that could refer to any soldier, or to a specific group of soldiers. Here and in v. 48 the word is qualified by others, viz., commanders of *(śārê)* thousands and commanders of hundreds, i.e., the men appointed by Moses to head up contingents of the army (Exod. 18:25), or *officers.*

15 The reason for Moses' anger was that the soldiers had allowed the women to live. It was the women who had tempted the Israelites to sin in the incident of Baal-Peor.

42. See Dumbrell, "Midian," 323–27.
43. H. Eising, *TDOT,* IV:349.

16–18 *at the word of Balaam.* The plan against Israel was Balaam's (see above on v. 8). This translation is to be preferred to NEB "on Balaam's departure."[44] The males had all been killed, but the women and children had been taken as booty after the manner found in Deut. 20:13–14 for peoples outside Canaan (as Midian was). God insisted that the male children be killed in order to destroy the means of future rebellion in Midian, and that all the women who were capable of sexual intercourse be killed in order to cut off the future population and to emphasize the nature of the sin of Baal-Peor. Thus only the young girls would be left alive, and these the Israelites were to keep for themselves, either as wives or slaves. If the former, then the view of foreigners at this time period allowed outsiders to join Israel (Deut. 21:10–14; Judg. 21:10–14). This is a far cry from the exclusivism of the time of Ezra (from which the P narrative has supposedly emanated). Moses' command was more in line with the stricter enforcement of the ban reserved for those peoples within Canaan and codified in Deut. 20:16–18.

19–24 The execution of Moses' command does not form part of the purpose of the narrative; perhaps that is why it is not mentioned. The theme of the death of these people, however, does link well to the next section. All warriors become unclean because of their contact with the dead, and must be purified before they can reenter society (i.e., in the book of Numbers, the camp). The procedures for cleansing here are based on those of 19:2, 9, 12, 14–19, but go beyond them. The section breaks into two subsections: the general rule (the preexistent statute) (vv. 19–20) and the new rule (vv. 21–24).

19–20 The army is to remain outside the camp for seven days (19:16–17; cf. Lev. 12:7; 13:5–6, 21, 26, 32–34; 15:24), cleansing itself as well as its prisoners on the third and seventh days (19:12–13, 23). They must cleanse their clothing (19:14–15) and any articles made of hide (i.e., leather; cf. Lev. 13:47–59), goat hair (cf. 1 Sam. 19:13, 16), or wood. Again, it is not surprising that parallels for these rituals are not complete; the Bible does not deal with every possible matter of common religious practice in Israel.

21–24 Eleazar now gives a new instruction. The fact that the

44. Cf. RSV, NIV, NASB, NJPS, etc. Even Sturdy (whose job it is to comment on NEB) chooses to depart from NEB here (p. 217). NEB based its reading on the proposed meaning of the Hebrew root *dbr* as "to go away," "to go behind." See, e.g., BDB, p. 180a; KB, p. 199b; *HALAT,* p. 201b; W. Schmidt, *TDOT,* III:94–97; Budd, p. 331.

statute of the ordinance (*ḥuqqaṯ hattôrâ;* see the commentary above on 19:2) came from Yahweh through Moses is reported, but indirectly (see the commentary above on 30:1).

22 *Only ('āḵ).* This particle is usually found in a limitation of something previously given.[45] The new ordinance is that any nonflammable item taken as booty must be passed through the fire to make it ceremonially clean *(ṭāhôr).* This new "baptism by fire" (cf. Matt. 3:11)[46] was in addition to the cleansing by *the waters of impurity* (see the commentary above on 19:9).

23 Anything flammable had only to be passed *through the waters (bammāyim).* Translators and commentators dispute whether the proper translation is with or without the definite article. Those who argue the latter case take the Hebrew definite article as generic, like the article on *the fire (hā'ēš).*[47] The meaning would then be "through water," i.e., through any clean, running water, as in 19:17.[48] But the clearest antecedent for *the waters* in v. 23b is *the waters of impurity* in v. 23a, and had the author intended to indicate other waters, he could have been clearer by using "running [or 'living'] waters" *(mayim ḥayyîm),* as in 19:17.

24 This verse summarizes the content of vv. 19–20 in the fashion of a Torah subscript (see the commentary above on 19:20–23; 5:11–31). It uses the vocabulary of garment scrubbing found in 19:7–8, 10, and especially 19.

25–54 These verses deal with the booty in a variety of ways: dividing it (vv. 25–27), the levy for Yahweh (vv. 28–31), the count of the booty (vv. 32–47), and the contribution of the commanders (vv. 48–54).

25–31 *Take a count.* The count was to be performed by Moses, Eleazar, and the leaders of the congregation. A similar group was responsible for the first census (1:2–16, 44). Only Moses and Eleazar are named as responsible for the second census (26:1), but one may assume the help of the other leaders.

26 *captured booty (malqôaḥ haššᵉḇî)* is an expression used

45. E.g., Noth, p. 231. BDB also notes that, occasionally, *'āḵ* may be asseverative, "surely" (p. 36b).

46. Later Jewish tradition required that nonflammable items bought from Gentiles be passed through the fire (Mish. *Abodah Zarah* 5:12). Yahweh himself was said to have been purified after the burial of Moses by such a baptism of fire. See Binns, p. 205.

47. GKC, §§ 126m, n.

48. So, e.g., Keil, pp. 227–28 (?); Dillmann, p. 191; Holzinger, p. 151; Gray, pp. 422–23; McNeile, p. 167; Wenham, p. 212; Moffatt, NJPS, NKJV.

generally to describe living things, both humans and animals (see above on vv. 9–12).

27 *You will divide the booty.* The spoils are divided equally between the warriors and those who stayed in the camp (as also in Josh. 22:8; 1 Sam. 30:24–25). Of course, those who see this passage as a late addition to the pentateuchal narrative will assert that this passage depends upon and is later than those of Joshua and 1 Samuel.[49]

28 The *levy* or "tax" *(meḵes)* is not set forth in earlier passages nor carried out in later ones. The word itself occurs only in this chapter in the OT, but in the postbiblical period it commonly designates a tax.[50] The verbal form *(kāsas)* simply means "to compute" or "count."[51] The purpose of the levy was to provide for the priests and the Levites. The care of priest and Levite is a theme found elsewhere in Numbers (e.g., 5:9–10; 6:19–20; 18:8–32). The levy was one out of 500 (0.2%) of both humans and animals from the half of the soldiers for the support of the priests, and one out of 50 (2%) from the half of the congregation for the support of the Levites. This 1:10 ratio is about the same as for the tithe (cf. 18:26). Since the soldiers took the lion's share of the risks in war, their share was larger than that divided among the rest of the population, and the amount given to support the priests was less.

29 *as a contribution for Yahweh (tᵉrûmaṯ YHWH).* See the commentary above on 5:9.

30 *standing guard.* See the commentary above on 1:53.

31 *And Moses . . . did according to all that Yahweh had commanded.* Here again is the formula of compliance (see also 30:1 [Eng. 29:40]; etc.).

It is hard to judge whether the current section was meant to be normative for all capture of booty in the future or only applicable to this one occasion. It seems more likely that the former is the case even in the face of the lack of biblical evidence that such a levy was ever carried out again. The whole passage seems to sum up former materials (see above) in a way that looks forward to similar incidents in the land of Canaan.

32–47 The heart of this section is in the lists of total numbers of living things in various groups: the totals for Israel (vv. 32–35), the half

49. E.g., Gray, pp. 417, 423; Budd, pp. 327–30.

50. Jastrow, *Dictionary,* p. 783b; a *môḵēs* was a "tax-collector" (p. 741b). The word is also found in Aramaic (*miḵsā',* p. 784a) and Syriac (*maḵsā',* BDB, p. 493b).

51. Found only in Exod. 12:4; BDB, p. 493b.

of the warriors and the priests' levy (vv. 36–41), the half of the congregation and the Levites' levy (vv. 42–47). Cook proposed that this section was based on the numbers of the levy for the priests in vv. 37–40, the larger numbers being then mathematically calculated.[52] This is a reasonable conclusion, but no certainty is possible. That the levy comes out in even numbers every time might lead one in this direction. Alternatively, the totals might have been rounded off before the levies were figured.

32–35 The grand totals are given first rather than last in this list. They are: 675,000 sheep, 72,000 cattle, 61,000 donkeys, and 32,000 maidens. It is understood that this is a list of *the booty remaining (hammalqôaḥ yeṯer),* which likely means the portion that was still alive after the march back from the battle site to the plains of Moab and after the action of 31:17 had been carried out. On the wealth of the Midianites, see Judg. 6:5; 8:24–26.

36–41 The booty was divided in half. The totals belonging to the soldiers or the congregation are easily calculated by dividing the numbers in vv. 32–35 by two. The levy to go to the priests is also easily calculated by multiplying the total numbers in these portions by the appropriate percentage (0.2% in the case of the priests, 2% in the case of the Levites). It is impossible to know what happened to the young girls; they probably either became wives for the men or, in the case of those levied for the priests and Levites, those who carried out their tasks in and around the tabernacle (Exod. 38:8; cf. 1 Sam. 2:22). Later on such people were called servants of the temple (e.g., 1 Chr. 9:2; Ezra 2:43; Neh. 3:26). Although the calculation of the levy for the Levites is not contained in the text, it may easily be calculated as ten times the levy for the priests, i.e., 6,750 sheep, 720 cattle, 610 donkeys, and 320 maidens.

42–47 In v. 47, *from the half* refers to v. 42; vv. 43–46 are technically parenthetical. The numbers in vv. 43–46 are the same as in vv. 36–40. The levies in the congregation's share of the booty are according to the ratio set out in v. 30.

48–54 This section begins with a statement of Yahweh's miraculous care for Israel. The commanders of the army took a count of their men and discovered that none had been lost in the assault on Midian. Vv. 25–47 dealt only with the living booty captured in the war, and this left all the precious metal that would have been taken from the Midianite warriors. Vv. 48–54 deal with this booty, which had not been counted in the previous section. Some scholars have concluded from v. 52 that the

52. Cook, p. 769. See also the "Excursus on Large Numbers" above.

soldiers of the rank and file had no part in this offering, but it is likely that v. 52 means that the golden articles that had been found and taken by every soldier (vv. 50, 53) were given through the officers as an *offering* (v. 50) or *contribution* (v. 52) to Yahweh.

50 The purpose of the offering to Yahweh is *to make atonement for ourselves before Yahweh (l^e^kappēr ʿal-napšōṯênû lip̄nê YHWH).* The exact meaning of this clause is debated. The center of the debate is the translation of the infinitive construct *l^e^kappēr (to make atonement).* In nonsacrificial contexts the verb may be translated "to pay the ransom price" *(kôp̄er).*[53] The ransom price was the amount paid that allowed a guilty person to receive a lesser penalty than was deserved. For example, in 25:13, Phinehas's slaughter of Zimri and Cozbi is said to "pay the ransom price for the children of Israel," i.e., to allow Israel to escape with less than total destruction. In ch. 25 the reason for such a ransom price is clear. What is it in the current chapter?

The best answer is to associate vv. 48–49 with their nearest OT parallel, Exod. 30:11–16. In that passage a census is taken to pay the ransom price (or "make atonement") for the self *(l^e^kappēr ʿal-hannep̄eš),* and this ransom price is presented before Yahweh *(lip̄nê YHWH)* as a remembrance for the children of Israel (*zikkārôn liḇnê yiśrāʾēl,* Exod. 30:16; Num. 31:50, 54).[54] That which is averted in Exod. 30:11 is the plague from Yahweh, his judgment. The way in which this plague is averted is by paying a one-half shekel ransom per person numbered in the census. The reason for the ransom price in Exod. 30 is the census. In a way that is not clear today, a census was thought to entail danger (cf. 2 Sam. 24).[55] The parallels in vocabulary between Exod. 30 and Num. 31

53. See Wenham, *Leviticus,* pp. 27–28, 59–61.

54. Milgrom, *Studies in Levitical Terminology,* I:30 n.108.

55. Some commentators have seen the sin in the knowledge of the number of the people, which knowledge was fit only for God; others have looked to David's ambition to explain the sin and danger in 2 Sam. 24 (e.g., A. R. S. Kennedy, *I and II Samuel,* Century Bible [Edinburgh: Jack, n.d.], p. 314). In a comparison between biblical idioms for taking censuses and those at Mari, E. A. Speiser concluded that the counting and recording of names brought danger since, "on periodic occasions, the higher powers made lists which determined who among the mortals was to live and who was to die." The word for census taking at Mari *(tēbibtum/ubbubum)* was also connected with "purification." This may show a contact with the ransom price in Exod. 30:12 and here in Num. 31:50. See Speiser, "Census and Ritual Expiation in Mari and Israel," *BASOR* 149 (1958) 17–33; repr. in *Oriental and Biblical Studies,* ed. J. J. Finkelstein and M. Greenberg (Philadelphia: Univ. of Pennsylvania Press, 1967), pp. 171–86.

indicate that some connection between these texts is likely. If there is a connection, however, it is not direct, because the actual weight of the golden objects given to Yahweh was 16,750 shekels, which should have provided ransom for 33,500 Israelites. The 12,000 soldiers (assuming the text to be a literal counting for the moment) would require only 6,000 shekels as a ransom price.

Because of the differences between the two texts, some scholars have posited other reasons for the offering: e.g., because the soldiers had disregarded the ban in the war, or because the soldiers had been recipients of the unmerited favor of Yahweh in the war.[56] Though these explanations are possible, the contact with Exod. 30:11–16 seems to provide the best (if not the completely satisfactory) solution.[57]

The items taken from the Midianites are first summed up as *articles of gold* (*kᵉlê zāhāḇ*), which are then enumerated as *armlets* (*'eṣʿāḏâ,* 2 Sam. 1:10; cf. *ṣᵉʿāḏâ,* Isa. 3:20), *bracelets* (*ṣāmîḏ,* Gen. 24:22, 30, 47; Ezek. 16:11; 23:42), *signet rings* (*ṭabbaʿaṯ,* e.g., Gen. 41:42; Esth. 3:12), *earrings* (*ʿāgîl,* Ezek. 16:12), and, perhaps, *ornaments* (*kûmāz,* Exod. 35:22). The meaning of this last term is the least sure in the list. BDB refers to the cognate Arabic term *kumzat,* which means "bunch" or "heap."[58] Snaith therefore concludes that clusters of beads is a satisfactory translation.[59] It is possible that this term is meant to be a general term for "other" items of gold.

51 This verse is a statement that Moses and Eleazar received the gold as set forth in v. 50, and is, once again, designed to state that all was done in obedience to a divine command. The wrought articles *(kᵉlî maʿaseh)* refer to those articles which were "made" *(asa)* by artisans, viz., those articles named in v. 50.

52–54 The total weight of the gold offered to Yahweh was 16,750

This explanation is still not wholly convincing, but in the present state of studies, we do not know why the census should be thought of as dangerous or potentially so. On Exod. 30:11–16, see esp. U. Cassuto, *A Commentary on the Book of Exodus,* tr. I. Abrahams (Jerusalem: Magnes, 1967), pp. 392–95. That the census was looked upon as a time of danger and potential sin can be seen from the Chronicler's interpretation of David's census (2 Sam. 24), where Satan incited David to take it (1 Chr. 21:1).

56. On the first see, e.g., Keil, p. 229; Noordtzij, p. 276. On the second see, e.g., Cook, p. 770; cf. Sturdy (p. 217), who connects the offering with thanksgiving rather than a ransom price.

57. So, e.g., Dillmann, p. 192; Gray, p. 425; Binns, p. 207; Heinisch, p. 120; Snaith, p. 196; Noth, p. 232; Wenham, p. 212; Budd, p. 332.

58. See BDB, p. 484b.

59. Snaith, p. 196.

shekels or about 600 pounds. Each fighting man had taken his own plunder and donated it to the officers for this *contribution (tᵉrûmâ)* to Yahweh.[60] Like the altar plates (17:5 [Eng. 16:40]), the gold was to be used as a *reminder (zikkārôn)*. Many scholars think that it was the Israelites who were to be reminded of the war against the Midianites.[61] But how would the average Israelite see or know anything about this offering once it was donated to the treasury? For this reason some scholars have concluded that this offering was a visual aid for Yahweh, so that he might remember the Israelites (as in NEB).[62] The gold was a sign that the Israelites had taken care to pay the ransom price at the appropriate time. One need not decide between the two alternatives. On the one hand, the gift could cause Israel to remember Yahweh's deliverance and be urged to further generosity toward the support of the tabernacle as a result. On the other hand, this mark of a willingness to fulfill the duty of the ransom price (or, perhaps, of a freewill offering) might be, for Yahweh, the mark of loyalty on the part of his people.[63]

H. TRANSJORDANIAN INHERITANCE (32:1–42)

1 *Now the children of Reuben*[1] *and the children of Gad*[2] *had a great many cattle. And they looked at the land of Jazer and the land of Gilead, and the place was truly a place for cattle.*

2 *And the children of Gad and the children of Reuben*[3] *came in and said to Moses and to Eleazar the priest and to the leaders of the congregation, saying:*

3 *"Ataroth, Dibon, Jazer, Nimrah, Heshbon, Elealeh, Sebam, Nebo, and Beon,*[4]

60. On *tᵉrûmâ,* see the commentary above on 5:9.

61. So, e.g., Snaith, p. 196.

62. So, e.g., Sturdy, p. 217.

63. Cf. Budd, p. 332.

1. The naming of Reuben before Gad here is unusual; elsewhere Gad is always named first. LXX keeps the present order in vv. 2, 25, 29, 31, and Pesh. and Sam. Pent. keep it throughout the whole chapter (vv. 6, 25, 29, 31, 33). These are later attempts to standardize the text.

2. Sam. Pent. adds the phrase "and the half-tribe of Manasseh" *(wᵉlaḥᵃṣî šēḇeṭ hammᵉnaššeh)* here as well as after Reuben's name in v. 2, and in vv. 6, 25, 29, 31. MT has the name at v. 33, and one assumes that the name was added for uniformity.

3. LXX and Pesh. invert the order of the two tribes to match that of v. 1. See n. 1 above.

4. For Beon *BHS* reads *bêṯ mᵉʿôn,* which is the same as *baʿal mᵉʿôn* in v. 38. See below on v. 38.

4 *the land that Yahweh smote before the congregation of Israel is a land for cattle, and your servants have cattle."*

5 *And they said, "If we have found favor in your sight, let this land be given*[5] *to your servants for an inheritance; do not make us cross over the Jordan."*

6 *But Moses said to the children of Gad and to the children of Reuben, "Will your brothers go in to the battle while you dwell here?*[6]

7 *Why would you restrain*[7] *the heart of the children of Israel from going over into the land that Yahweh has given to them?*

8 *So your fathers did when I sent them from Kadesh-barnea to see the land,*

9 *and they went up into the Valley of Eshcol and saw the land. Then they discouraged the heart of the children of Israel not to go into the land that Yahweh had given them.*

10 *And Yahweh's wrath was kindled in that day, and he took an oath, saying:*

11 *'The men who went up from Egypt, from twenty years old and upward,*[8] *will never see the land that I swore to Abraham, to Isaac, and to Jacob, for they have not fully followed me,*

12 *except Caleb the son of Jephunneh the Kenizzite and Joshua the son of Nun, for they have fully followed me.'*

13 *And the anger of Yahweh was kindled against Israel and he caused them to wander*[9] *in the wilderness forty years, until the whole generation who did evil in Yahweh's sight was finished.*

14 *Now, behold, you have risen in place of your fathers, a brood of*

5. GKC, § 150m, sees *yuttan* as a passive Qal rather than a Hophal because no corresponding Hiphil or Hophal perfect exists; so also Williams, *Syntax*, § 159.

6. MT *ha'aḥêḵem yaḇō'û lammilḥāmâ wᵉ'attem tēšᵉḇû pōh.* The *hê* interrogative is attached to two coordinate clauses, the first of which should really be subordinated to the second, so that the *hê* interrogative really affects only the second. See GKC, § 150m.

7. The Qere *(tᵉnî'ûn)* is a Hiphil, while the Ketib *(tᵉnû'ûn)* is a Qal, from the verb *nû'*, "to hinder, restrain, discourage." The difference in meaning between the Qal and the Hiphil is unknown since the Qal does not occur elsewhere in the OT. The Qere simply changes the form to the more common Hiphil. See BDB, p. 626a; *HALAT*, p. 640a.

8. LXX adds the following gloss: *hoi epistamenoi to kakon kai to agathon,* "those who were acquainted with evil and good."

9. MT *wayᵉni'ēm* is a Hiphil of *nāwa'*, hence "he caused them to wander." This meaning is found only two other times in the OT (1 Sam. 15:20; Ps. 59:12 [Eng. 11]). The Qal participle means "vagabond" in Gen. 4:12, 14 (of Cain). More frequently the Qal means "to vibrate" or "to quiver" (e.g., Isa. 7:2), and the Hiphil "to toss about" (Amos 9:9). See BDB, p. 631b.

sinful people, to increase[10] *still further the burning wrath of Yahweh against*[11] *Israel.*

15 *If you turn from following him, he will again leave them in the wilderness, and you will destroy this whole people."*[12]

16 *And they drew near to him and said, "Let us build sheepfolds for our animals here and cities for our little ones.*

17 *Then we will go equipped in battle array*[13] *before the children of Israel until*[14] *we have brought them into their place. But our little ones will stay in the fortified cities on account of the inhabitants of the land.*

18 *We will not return to our homes until each one of the children of Israel has taken his portion as a possession.*

19 *For we will not inherit with them across*[15] *the Jordan yonder,*[16] *for our inheritance has come to us across the Jordan to the east."*

20 *And Moses said to them, "If you will do this thing, if you will go armed before Yahweh to the battle,*

10. The infinitive construct *lispôṯ* should probably be repointed as *lāsepeṯ* here and in Deut. 29:18; Isa. 31:1 to conform to the more regular formation of the infinitive construct in Pe-Waw verbs; see GKC, § 69h n. 1; *BHS,* etc.

11. The preposition *'el* can be adversative, expressing disadvantage (Gen. 4:8; Jer. 21:13; 33:26); cf. Williams, *Syntax,* § 303.

12. MT *lᵉḵol-hā'ām hazzeh.* The direct object of the verb sometimes uses the preposition *lᵉ-*, instead of *'eṯ,* esp. with the Hiphil and Piel stems. This is also the case in Aramaic. See Davidson, *Syntax,* § 73 Rem. 7.

13. MT *ḥušîm,* "in haste," which does not seem to fit the context. LXX has *prophylaktēn,* "in the vanguard." Most scholars suggest reading *ḥᵃmušîm,* a Qal passive participle derived from a denominative verb either meaning "to be arranged in groups of fifty" (e.g., GKC, § 72p; BDB, p. 332b; *HALAT,* pp. 317b–18a; Dillmann, p. 196; Paterson, p. 64; Gray, p. 432; McNeile, p. 172; Binns, p. 211; Heinisch, p. 122; Snaith, pp. 197–98; de Vaulx, p. 366; Sturdy, p. 223; Budd, p. 344; cf. M. Noth, *The History of Israel,* tr. P. Ackroyd, 2nd ed. [New York: Harper & Row, 1960], p. 108 n. 1) or referring to organizing the army in five main groups: the vanguard, the rear guard, the middle, and two flanks (cf. LXX above; *HALAT,* pp. 317b–18a). In any case, the word came to mean something like "equipped in battle array" (BDB, p. 332b) or "organized on a war footing" (Noth, *History,* p. 108 n. 1). Cf. de Vaux, *Ancient Israel,* I:216–17. The term is also found in Exod. 13:18; Josh. 1:14; 4:12; Judg. 7:11 in the pl., as here.

14. MT *'aḏ 'ᵃšer 'im.* The word *'im,* technically pleonastic with *'aḏ 'ᵃšer,* introduces an element of doubt into the matter. See Williams, *Syntax,* § 457. So also in Gen. 28:15; Isa. 6:11 (both with the perfect); cf. Gray, p. 432.

15. The preposition *min* in *mē'ēḇer* expresses a distance from the speaker in one direction or another; see Williams, *Syntax,* § 323.

16. Heb. *wāhālᵉ'â.* Here the noun has the *hê* locale or accusative ending, which indicates a direction toward. So also in, e.g., Deut. 3:17, 27; 4:49.

21 *and every armed man of you will cross over the Jordan before Yahweh, until he has dispossessed his enemies before him,*
22 *and the land is subdued before Yahweh, then afterward you may return and be free of obligation before*[17] *Yahweh and Israel; and this land will be your possession before Yahweh.*
23 *But if you do not do thus, behold you have sinned*[18] *before Yahweh; and know that your sin will find you.*
24 *Build for yourselves cities for your little ones and folds for your flocks, and do all that has gone out of your mouth."*
25 *And the children of Gad and the children of Reuben said to Moses, saying: "Your servants will do as my lord commands.*
26 *Our little ones, our wives, our cattle, and all our animals will remain there*[19] *in the cities of Gilead.*
27 *Your servants will cross over, every armed man of the army, before Yahweh to the battle as my lord speaks."*[20]
28 *And Moses commanded Eleazar the priest and Joshua the son of Nun and the heads of the fathers' houses of the tribes of the children of Israel regarding them.*
29 *And Moses said to them, "If the children of Gad and the children of Reuben pass over the Jordan with you, every man armed for war before Yahweh, and the land is subdued before them, then you may give them the land of Gilead as a possession.*
30 *But if they do not go over armed with you, then they will have possessions in your midst in the land of Canaan."*[21]
31 *And the children of Gad and the children of Reuben answered,*

17. MT *mēYWHW ûmîyiśrā'ēl.* For this use of *min,* meaning "from the power of" or "at the hands of," see Job 4:17; BDB, p. 579b; Gray p. 431.

18. In a conditional sentence *'im* in the protasis expresses what is possible in present or future time. The apodosis with the perfect here represents the time when the consequence will already have taken place (GKC, § 159q).

19. LXX, Pesh., and Vulg. dealt with the awkwardness of MT *yihyû šām* (lit., "they will be there") by omitting *šām. BHS* emends to read "and we will cause our little ones . . . to dwell" *(wᵉnôšᵉḇēm . . .).* This emendation makes sense, but there is little textual support for it.

20. The verb *dāḇar,* "to speak," is found in the Qal only in the participle, as here (also Exod. 6:29 and some 36 others) and once in the infinitive (Ps. 51:6 [Eng. 4]), although this reading is disputed (cf. A. Weiser, *The Psalms,* tr. H. Hartwell, OTL [Philadelphia: Westminster, 1962], p. 400, with F. Delitzsch, *Biblical Commentary on the Psalms,* tr. D. Eaton, 2nd ed., Foreign Theological Library [London: Hodder & Stoughton, 1902], II:156–57); see BDB, p. 180b.

21. LXX adds: *kai diabibasete tēn aposkeuēn autōn kai tas gynaikas autōn kai ta ktēnē autōn protera hymōn eis gēn Chanaan,* "and you will bring their little ones and their wives and their animals over before you into Canaan." Cf. v. 26.

saying: "That which Yahweh has spoken to your servants, thus we will do.

32 *Indeed, we*[22] *will cross over armed before Yahweh into the land of Canaan; and our possessed inheritance will remain with us beyond the Jordan."*

33 *And Moses gave the kingdom of Sihon king of the Amorites and the kingdom of Og king of Bashan to the children of Gad and to the children of Reuben and to the half-tribe of Manasseh the son of Joseph, the land as regards its cities with their territories, the cities of the surrounding country.*

34 *And the children of Gad built Dibon, Ataroth, Aroer,*

35 *Atroth-shophan, Jazer, Jogbehah,*

36 *Beth-nimrah, and Beth-haran, fortified cities and sheepfolds.*

37 *And the children of Reuben built Heshbon, Elealeh, Kiriathaim,*

38 *Nebo, Baal-meon (name to be changed),*[23] *and Sibmah; and they gave new names to the cities they built.*

39 *And the sons of Machir the son of Manasseh went to Gilead and captured and dispossessed the Amorites who were in it.*

40 *And Moses gave Gilead to Machir the son of Manasseh, and he dwelled in it.*

41 *And Jair the son of Manasseh went and captured their villages and called them Havvoth-jair.*

42 *And Nobah went and captured Kenath and its villages and called it*[24] *Nobah after his name.*

Chapter 32 is a composite text, one part dealing with Reuben and Gad (vv. 1–38), and the other with a segment of Manasseh (vv. 39–42).[25] These

22. The personal pronoun *(naḥnû)* is for emphasis. The shortened form occurs only five times in the OT (Gen. 42:11; Exod. 16:7, 8; Num. 32:32; Lam. 3:42). In Arabic *năḥnu* is the regular form of the pronoun. In Aramaic *naḥnā'* is a common abbreviation for *'anaḥnā'*. See GKC, § 32d; BDB, p. 59b.

23. MT *mûsabbōṯ šēm* is probably a gloss. See above on v. 3. The reading perhaps should be sing. *(mûsaḇaṯ šēm)* (so *BHS*). (On the gerundive force of the passive participle here see Davidson, *Syntax,* § 97 Rem. 1; cf. also 2 K. 23:34.) Then the reference is to Baal-meon only. If the pl. is kept, it refers to both Nebo and Baal-meon, both of which contain the names of foreign deities and both of which are either to be changed by the Israelites (Beon may represent just such a change), or by the readers when they come to these words.

24. LXX reads pl. here *(autas)*. The sing. of MT refers to the whole region of Kenath/Nobah.

25. For a survey of modern scholarly research on the formation of the passage, see Budd, pp. 337–41.

two units are connected by the introduction of Manasseh at v. 33, within the Gadite/Reubenite section. The probability is that the lists of Gadite and Reubenite cities (vv. 34–38) form the core of the first section. Vv. 1–33 narrate events that led to the rebuilding of the cities in vv. 34–38. The tribes of Gad and Reuben were attracted to the area in and around Gilead because of its potential for cattle raising, and approached Moses with the request that they be allowed to settle there (vv. 1–5). Since this was a change from the plan that dictated that all twelve tribes settle west of the Jordan in Canaan, Moses saw it as a threat to the unity of Israel that would turn the Israelites away from taking the land of Canaan, as they had been turned from it in the days of the spies (chs. 13–14), and vociferously rejected the request (vv. 6–15). This rejection led to the Gadite/Reubenite proposal that, if they were allowed to secure their inheritance in Transjordan and leave their dependents there, they would cross the Jordan to help the other tribes in the conquest of Canaan (vv. 16–19). Moses formulated this proposal into a covenant agreement (vv. 20–24), to which Gad and Reuben formally agreed (vv. 25–27), and brought it before witnesses for enforcement (vv. 28–32). The outcome is the general report that Gilead was given to these two tribes (v. 33).

At some point in the compilation of the book, this narrative, which was originally told only of the Transjordanian portions of Gad and Reuben, was expanded to complete the picture in Transjordan by inclusion of an independent unit about conquests made in the northern part of the area by certain Manassite elements (vv. 39, 41–42), leading to Moses' gift of part of Transjordan to them as well (v. 40; cf. v. 33). Manasseh's portion in Transjordan, although it appears as an addition to the basic story of the settlements of Gad and Reuben here, is a well-attested OT tradition (Deut. 3:14–15; 4:43; 29:8; Josh. 12:6; 13:29; 14:3; 18:7). For further discussion of themes and problems in the chapter, as well as a possible time frame for the final form of the text, see below on the individual units.

1–5 The Gadites and Reubenites come to Moses, Eleazar, and the leaders of the people and request that they be allowed to settle in the Transjordan. To understand this proposal, one must remember that the consistent biblical definition of Canaan (the promised land) was limited to the territory west of the Jordan.[26] The proposal meant, therefore,

26. See, e.g., Num. 34; cf. Gen. 12:5; 23:2, 19; 35:6; 48:3, 7; 49:30; Exod. 16:35; Deut. 32:49; Josh. 5:12; 14:1; 21:2; 22:9–11, 32; 24:3; Judg. 21:12. On the extrabiblical definition of Canaan (which also excluded the Transjordan), see C. Libolt, *ISBE,* rev., pp. 585–91.

nothing short of a divided Israel, with part of Israel settling outside the land of promise.

1 *the land of Jazer.* Elsewhere Jazer is a city (see 21:24 above). The best interpretation of this phrase is to refer it to the territory around that city (now probably Khirbet Jazzir). This kind of identification might easily mean that the term *Gilead* is also to be taken in the very specific sense of the mountain or town of Gilead (Khirbet Jelʿad) a few miles north of Jazer.[27]

As is well known, the meaning of the term *Gilead* varies in the OT. Sometimes the reference seems to be to the whole of the conquered area east of the Jordan, as opposed to Canaan on the west (e.g., Josh. 22:9, 13). This territory is sometimes called the two halves of Gilead (Deut. 3:12–13; Josh. 12:2, 5; 13:31). Other times Gilead indicates only the southern half of the territory between the Arnon and the Yarmuk (e.g., all the towns in Num. 32:3, 34–37 are south of the Jabbok; also v. 29; Josh. 13:25). Other times only the northern half of the territory is intended (e.g., Num. 32:39; Josh. 17:1, 5–6). Geographical designations are not always as exact in the ancient world as moderns might like. One might also expect that people who did not know the geography of a place would be more likely to be vaguer than natives in their usage. A modern example of a similar phenomenon might be New York, which may either be a city (or part of a city) or a state, depending on the context. If the specific reference suggested above is not correct here, then one may assume either a general reference to the whole land or to the southern part of it.

the children of Reuben and the children of Gad. This order is followed only here in this chapter; vv. 2, 6, 25, 29, 31, 33 reverse the order. Reuben may be named first in this introductory verse because he is the firstborn (1:5, 20). It is clear, however, even from the Blessing of Moses, that Reuben is in danger of extinction as a tribe (Deut. 33:6). By contrast, in the same passage Moses makes much of the leadership of Gad (33:21). Later King Mesha of Moab did not mention the Reubenites, but said that "people of Gad" had long lived in Ataroth (cf. Num. 32:3).[28] The later order of putting Gad first, therefore, represents that tribe's actual leadership and importance. It is highly unlikely that the difference in order results from the conflation of two different sources.[29]

27. Noth, p. 237.

28. See the Mesha (Moabite) Inscription, line 10, in Beyerlin, ed., *Near Eastern Religious Texts,* p. 239; *ANET,* p. 320; *DOTT,* p. 196. The Mesha Inscription is ca. 830 B.C.

29. It has been the view of many scholars that this was the case: e.g., Gray, p. 427; Noth, p. 235.

2 *Moses, Eleazar . . . the leaders.* This is the same group referred to in 31:12–13 (with the same phrase in 31:13). This group, with the addition of Joshua, will be responsible for dividing the land in ch. 34.

3 Most of the cities named here can be located with some degree of confidence today.[30] *Ataroth (ʿᵃṭārôṯ)* is widely agreed to be Khirbet ʿAṭṭārûs, which is about 7.5 mi. north of Dibon and 8 mi. west of the Dead Sea. *Dibon (dîḇōn)* is modern Dhiḇân, which is about 4 mi. north of the Arnon and 12 mi. west of the Dead Sea. On *Jazer (yaʿzēr),* see above on v. 1. *Nimrah (nimrâ)* is called *Beth-nimrah* in v. 36 and is probably to be located at Tell el-Bleibil about 11 mi. east of the Jordan and 27 mi. west of ancient Rabbah. *Heshbon (ḥešbôn)* is agreed to be Tell Ḥešbân about 13 mi. east and a little north of the north end of the Dead Sea. *Elealeh (ʾelʿālēh)* is el-ʿÂl just northeast of Heshbon. *Sebam (śᵉḇām)* is called *Sibmah (śiḇmâ)* in v. 38. Several modern scholars have located it at Qurn el-Kibš, about 5 mi. south-southwest of Heshbon.[31] *Nebo (nᵉḇô)* is probably located at Khirbet el-Mekhaiyeṭ just south of Mt. Nebo *(nēbâ),* and a couple of miles south-southwest of Qurn el-Kibš. Finally, *Beon (bᵉʿôn)* is most probably the same as Baal-meon in v. 38, which is generally agreed to be at Maʿîn, northeast of Ataroth, about 5 mi. southwest of Medeba and 10 mi. south-southwest of Heshbon.

4–5 These sites are all said to be within *the land which Yahweh smote,* viz., in the conflict with Sihon (21:21–35), and therefore without any overall ruler to unify the various smaller villages and towns. The request *do not make us go over the Jordan (ʾal-taʿᵃḇirēnû ʾeṯ-hayyardēn)* could be taken in two ways. The first would be as a simple wish to settle in the Transjordan while helping the other ten tribes in the conquest of Canaan. (This is, in fact, the agreement that is finally reached [cf. vv. 16–19, 25–27].) The second would be as a request to settle in Transjordan and to opt out of the conquest of Canaan. Moses takes the proposal in the second way and thus responds scathingly in vv. 6–15. The text as it stands probably wants the reader to conclude that Gad and Reuben also intended the second meaning.

6–15 Moses rejects the request as a breach of Israel's unity. He likens this request to the incident of the spies in chs. 13–14. As the people in that day were turned from the conquest by the report of the majority of the spies, so a breakdown in the unity of the twelve tribes might turn the

30. See, e.g., *Oxford Bible Atlas,* 3rd ed., p. 63.
31. See Noth, p. 240.

people away from going in to conquer the land because of their reduced numbers. This disunity would only lead to a further delay in God's plan and disaster for the Israelites.

6–7 *Will your brothers go into battle while you dwell here?* The word *dwell* (*tēšᵉḇû,* from *yāšaḇ*) basically means "to stay," and may also mean "to sit."[32] One major difference between "sitting" and "dwelling" is the length of time one "stays." Moses' question, first, attacks the problem of "staying" in the short term. Do Reuben and Gad intend to "sit" in the Transjordan while their fellow tribes risk their lives to conquer Canaan? Then, Moses' question attacks the problem of "staying" in the long term, i.e., "dwelling" in the Transjordan. The whole of Canaan (not the Transjordan) has been promised to the whole of Israel (not part of it). If Reuben and Gad *dwell* outside Canaan, it threatens the unity of Israel. The same negative reaction to perceived disunity within the tribes is seen in the Song of Deborah (Judg. 5:15–17).

The disunity will *restrain the heart* of the rest of the Israelites. The verb *hēnîʾ* (see note to translation, above) may mean "to discourage." Modern readers tend to think of discouragement as "a sad feeling"; therefore this translation is avoided here. The verb means "to hold in, restrain," as in 30:6 (Eng. 5). The lands east of Jordan were conquered because Sihon opposed the Israelites' progress; they were not part of the promised land (see above). Therefore, Moses opposed any turning from the plan of settling in God's promised land toward a plan that dictated settling in a different land.

8–13 Instead, Moses argues that this stratagem is like the rebellion of the people following the mission of the spies into Canaan in chs. 13–14. That disaster led to the loss of one generation and forty years in the wilderness.

8 *your fathers* refers to the Exodus generation, not just the ancestors of Gad and Reuben.

Kadesh-barnea. This is the same place earlier called Kadesh (see the commentary above on 13:26; 20:13). This full form of the name is more common in Deuteronomy and deuteronomistic literature (e.g., Deut. 1:19; 2:14; 9:23; Josh. 10:41; 14:6–7).

9 *Valley of Eshcol.* See the commentary above on 13:21, 23.

10 *and he took an oath.* The content of what Yahweh swore is condensed in vv. 10–11 from 14:21–24, 29–34.

11 *twenty years old and upward.* This phrase is used in the census

32. BDB, p. 443.

lists (1:3, 18, 20, 22, 24, 26, 28, 30, 32, 34, 36, 38, 40, 42, 45; 26:2, 4) as well as in the oath Yahweh took in 14:29.

the land that I swore ('ēṯ hā'ᵃḏāmâ 'ᵃšer nišbaʿtî). This same expression occurs in 11:12. In 14:23 and Deut. 1:24 the word for land is *'ereṣ* rather than *'ᵃḏāmâ.* The two terms are broad synonyms, and no great weight should be attached to the use of the different terms.

for they have not fully followed me (kî lō' -mil'û 'aḥᵃrāy). A similar expression occurs in 14:24 (see the commentary there).

12 *Caleb* is called a Kenizzite in Josh. 14:6, 14; Judg. 1:13. He is called a Judahite in Num. 13:6 and 34:19 (see the commentary above on 13:1–15). 1 Chr. 4:1–23 encompass the offspring of Kenaz within the offspring of Judah, which shows that by the time of the Chronicler the two groups were considered to be closely related.

13 This verse summarizes the content of 14:33–35.

he caused them to wander (wayᵉniʿēm) — see the note to the translation above.

the whole generation (kol-haddôr) is the whole Exodus generation that passed away in the wilderness. The phrase *the whole generation* is used with reference to Joseph's generation in Exod. 1:6.

was finished (tōm). This same verb is used in 14:33, 35.

14–15 Moses draws the comparison down to the contemporary time. He calls the Israelites *a brood of sinful people (tarbûṯ 'ᵃnāšîm ḥaṭṭā'îm).* The first word *(tarbûṯ)* is a hapax legomenon that is related to the verb *rāḇâ* ("become great"); in this clearly pejorative context, it probably means "something that has grown large," much like the related term *(marbîṯ)* in 1 Sam. 2:33.[33]

If you turn from following him. See 14:43 for a similar expression.

this whole people. At the end of the unit, as at the beginning, Moses stresses the unity of the people. The actions of Gad and Reuben could cause Yahweh in his wrath to destroy the whole people if they, once again, refused to accept their inheritance in Canaan. Cf. the similar reaction when the unity of the people is threatened by the building of an altar when the tribes went home to Transjordan (Josh. 22:18).

16–19 The Gadites and Reubenites enter into negotiations in order to get the land they want. They promise to help in the conquest of Canaan and not to go home until that project is complete.

33. BDB, p. 916a. The word is translated as "brood" by RSV, NASB, NIV, NEB, NKJV, Moffatt; "breed" by NJPS; "generation" by GNB; and "an increase" by AV, RV.

16 *And they drew near to him (wayyigg^e^šû 'ēlāyw).* The term *nāgaš* is used to indicate a lesser party coming into the presence of a greater (Gen. 43:19; 45:4; 2 K. 5:13). In legal or quasi-legal settings it is used of coming into court to argue a case (Isa. 41:1, 21; 45:20–21; 50:8; cf. Exod. 24:14; Deut. 25:1; Josh. 3:9; 1 K. 18:30). Here it marks the institution of formal negotiations between Moses (representing Eleazar and the other leaders, who in turn represent the people) and Gad and Reuben.

The first detailed proposal is that they be allowed to fortify certain settlements of Transjordan for the benefit of their families and animals. *sheepfolds* (*gid̲rōt̲ ṣō' n,* lit., "sheep walls") are usually made of piled-up stones (1 Sam. 24:4 [Eng. 3]).[34]

The term *our little ones (ṭappēnû)* not only indicates the children of the families (as in, e.g., 14:3) but also the wives (as in, e.g., Gen. 34:29 [children and elderly]; 43:8 [women and children]), i.e., in modern terms, the dependents.

The *cities ('ārîm)* that they were to fortify for these dependents could not have been built from the ground up because of the limited amount of time. Rather, the word *bānâ* ("to build") with reference to the cities must mean either "rebuild" (after the war with Sihon; cf. Josh. 6:26) or "fortify" (so that their dependents could be left in safety).[35] The Gadites and Reubenites promise that they will take a conspicuous part in the conquest after they have established themselves in the Transjordan.

17 *Then we will go equipped in battle array before the children of Israel (wa'^a^naḥnû nēḥālēṣ ḥ^a^mušîm lip̱nê b^e^nê yiśrā'ēl).* The Gadites and Reubenites actually promise to go *before the children of Israel,* i.e., in a position of leadership, which may indicate a change in marching order from that set up in 2:16, where Reuben and Gad were in the second group to set out. Or the idiom may indicate only a willingness to take leadership in the conquest.

18 They promise not to go home (i.e., back to Transjordan) until the conquest is completed.

19 The motivation for all this is set forth here: *For we will not inherit with them across the Jordan yonder.* The verb "to inherit" *(nāḥal),* here in the imperfect, has a sense not only of incomplete action (futurity) to it, but also of the exercise of the will, i.e., "we do not wish to inherit," as well as "it will not come to be a fact that we will inherit."[36]

34. BDB, pp. 154b–55a.
35. See BDB, pp. 124–25a, for the uses of the word *bānâ.*
36. See Williams, *Syntax,* §§ 167, 171; Driver, *Tenses,* §§ 23, 37.

across the Jordan (mēʿēḇer layyardēn). Virtually the same words refer to the lands west and east of the Jordan, showing that the expression is vague in itself. The present position of the speakers is taken into consideration when Canaan is called literally "across the Jordan and beyond" *(mēʿēḇer layyardēn wāhālᵉâ).*[37] The land east of the Jordan is called "across the Jordan toward the sunrise" *(mēʿēḇer hayyardēn mizrāḥâ).*[38]

20–24 These verses contains Moses' direct reply to Gad and Reuben. He sets up a balance between blessing and curse. If Gad and Reuben will do as they have proposed and take an active role in the conquest until all the other Israelites have their possessions in the land of Canaan, then they will be allowed to return to Transjordan to settle according to their wishes. If they either will not go at all or, having gone, renege on any of the promises they have undertaken, then they will have committed a sin that will carry its own inescapable consequences. As Noordtzij has pointed out, this passage narrates the conclusion of a covenant (although the technical word *bᵉrîṯ,* "covenant," does not occur here). Blessings and curses are typical parts of a covenant formulary.[39]

The key phrase throughout the unit is *before Yahweh (lip̄nê YHWH),* found no less than four times (vv. 20–22).[40] Mustering the army (v. 20), crossing the Jordan (v. 21a), dispossessing the inhabitants (v. 21b), and subduing the land of Canaan (v. 22) are all done, literally, "to(ward) the face of Yahweh," i.e., he is vitally involved in the whole process with his people. The war is Yahweh's war. Cf. vv. 27, 29; 21:14; Josh. 4:13; Judg. 5:23. Keil may well be right in concluding that the visible sign of the presence of Yahweh was the ark (as in Josh. 4:10b–14 with reference to the same event as is referred to here).[41]

21 *until he has dispossessed his enemies before him.* Again, Yahweh is the one who dispossesses his enemies; the Israelites are but his agents. The verb "to possess" *(yāraš)* in the Hiphil *(hôrîš,* as here) means

37. On the term as a time reference, see 15:23: "from the day which Yahweh commanded and onward." See BDB, p. 229.

38. See 2:2; 3:38; 21:11; etc.

39. Noordtzij, p. 281. See, e.g., G. Mendenhall, "Covenant Forms in Israelite Tradition," *BA* 17 (1954) 50–76, repr. in *The Biblical Archaeologist Reader,* III, ed. E. F. Campbell and D. N. Freedman (Garden City, N.Y.: Anchor, 1970), pp. 25–53.

40. The word *mippānāyw,* lit., "from his face," in v. 21b clearly refers to Yahweh.

41. Keil, p. 235.

"to cause (others) to possess," i.e., "to dispossess" (so also in, e.g., Judg. 5:31).

22 *and be free of obligation (wihᵉyîṯem nᵉqîyîm).* The verb *nāqâ* means "to be clean," and the related adjective *nᵉqîyîm* "clean." Deut. 24:5 uses the term as meaning free of the obligation to do military service. The meaning here probably includes that, but also simply means "you will have discharged the duties of this covenant."

23–24 *know that your sin will find you (ûḏᵉʿû ḥaṭṭaʾṯᵉḵem ʾᵃšer timṣāʾ ʾeṯᵉḵem).* This statement has become proverbial in its AV dress: "Be sure your sin will find you out." Sin itself is virtually personified as one who will wend its way through any obstacles to find the guilty. See Gen. 4:7, where sin is said to be a demon crouching by the door waiting to spring upon the one coming outside.[42] In other words, the consequences of sin are unavoidable. This sentence constitutes the "curse" part of the covenant formulary. The implication is that because Yahweh is involved in the war, a failure to make good on this promise would result in sin, which Yahweh would punish. Only after the blessing and curse are pronounced does Moses agree to allow Gad and Reuben to billet their dependents and fortify the villages and towns in the area (v. 24).

25–27 The Gadites and the Reubenites formally ratify their agreement with the rest of Israel. Many commentators have pointed out that Moses is addressed in vv. 25, 27 as a king might be addressed (i.e., *your servants, my lord*), and that this is typical of deuteronomic style. This royal style is typical of formal ratification of covenant documents; it occurs both in this passage and especially in Deuteronomy.[43] It is note-

42. On this verse see, e.g., U. Cassuto, *Commentary on the Book of Genesis,* Part I, *From Adam to Noah,* tr. I. Abrahams (Jerusalem: Magnes, 1961), pp. 209–12; E. A. Speiser, *Genesis,* AB, 3rd ed. (Garden City, N.Y.: Doubleday, repr. 1986), pp. 32–33; G. Wenham, *Genesis 1–15,* WBC (Waco: Word, 1988), pp. 104–6; V. Hamilton, *The Book of Genesis, Chapters 1–17,* NICOT (Grand Rapids: Eerdmans, 1990), pp. 225–28; C. Westermann, *Genesis 1–11: A Commentary,* tr. J. Scullion (Minneapolis: Augsburg, 1984), pp. 282, 298–301.

43. For the connection with royal language, see, e.g., Sturdy, p. 223; de Vaulx, p. 368; Budd, pp. 339, 342, 349; cf. Snaith, p. 197. For the covenant structure of the book of Deuteronomy, see, e.g., P. C. Craigie, *Book of Deuteronomy,* NICOT (Grand Rapids: Eerdmans, 1976), pp. 22–24. At more length, see M. G. Kline, *Treaty of the Great King* (Grand Rapids: Eerdmans, 1963); idem, *The Structure of Biblical Authority* (Grand Rapids: Eerdmans, 1972); K. A.

worthy in this regard that the words *my lord ('ᵃḏōnî)* are used by the representatives of the whole Gadite and Reubenite populations as if they were a single person. The arrangement is basically quid pro quo: the Gadites and Reubenites will be allowed to settle in Transjordan and to fortify the settlements there (cf. v. 16), and in exchange for this settlement they will go armed into battle *before Yahweh* (see above on vv. 20–23) on behalf of Israel in the conquest of Canaan (cf. vv. 17–18).

28–33 The covenant ceremony moves to its conclusion. Moses summons the rest of the representatives of Israel (i.e., Eleazar the priest, Joshua, and the other leaders of the tribes) to witness the agreement. The stipulations of the covenant are repeated formally in their hearing, so that the covenant may be made. The repetition here is not necessarily the mark of a composite narrative;[44] it may simply be the mark of a formal covenant that has various parties involved. The end of the covenant in v. 33 is the assignment of the territory of Sihon and Og to Gad, Reuben, and, for the first time, the half-tribe of Manasseh.

28–30 The group that Moses summons as witnesses is the same group that will divide the land in 34:16–29. *Moses commanded.* He brought this group in not only as witnesses to the agreement between Israel and Gad and Reuben, but also as the people who would be responsible for carrying out the stipulations of the covenant, since he was soon to die (cf. 27:12–14). If Gad and Reuben comply with the terms as agreed, then Eleazar, Joshua, and the other leaders are to make sure that they are allowed to return to Transjordan to their dependents there, receiving it as their inheritance.

If they do not go over armed with you, then they will have possessions in your midst in the land of Canaan. It is unknown what sanctions are in view here, since no specific sanctions are mentioned. The text is best interpreted to mean that Gad and Reuben will be forced (by the rest of the tribes?) to bring their dependents over from Transjordan and to live in Canaan, i.e., on the west side of the Jordan River. Noth is probably right in suggesting that all this means is that their request for an inheritance in the Transjordan will be denied if they fail in their portion of the covenant agreement.[45]

Kitchen, *Ancient Orient and Old Testament* (Downers Grove: InterVarsity, 1966); M. Weinfeld, *Deuteronomy and the Deuteronomic School* (Oxford: Clarendon, 1972).

44. See, e.g., Sturdy, pp. 222–23; Budd, pp. 337–42.

45. Noth, p. 239.

31–32 Having been brought before witnesses, and having heard the agreement repeated before them, Gad and Reuben repeat their own promise to comply with Moses' stipulation to participate actively in the conquest and their understanding that their *possessed inheritance* (*'ᵃḥuzzaṯ naḥᵃlāṯēnû*) will be in Transjordan.

33 The major difficulty in this verse is the abrupt mention of *the half-tribe of Manasseh the son of Joseph* (*wᵉlaḥᵃṣî šēḇeṭ mᵉnaššeh ḇen-yôsēp̱*). Nothing in the previous narrative has prepared the reader for this reference. The Manassites are dealt with in vv. 39–42 below, and it is likely that these verses once formed a separate account that has been edited in its current place in the chapter by v. 33, which forms an editorial link to unify the account of the Manassites with that of the Reubenites and Gadites. The view that Manasseh had a share in the Transjordan along with Gad and Reuben is common in the OT (e.g., Deut. 3:12–15; 4:43; 29:7–8; Josh. 12:6; 13:29, 31; 14:3; 18:7).

The matter of the approximate date of Manasseh's military activity is discussed below on vv. 39–42. There is no reason to find in this tradition a late or fabricated account. The traditions about Gad and Reuben told only part of the story of the settlement in the Transjordan; Manasseh was also settled there. In order to tell the whole story of settlement east of the Jordan the narratives about Gad and Reuben were added to those of Manasseh. At the time these two were placed together, v. 33 or at least the phrase on Manasseh was added. No exact land assignments are made in v. 33. These come only in Josh. 13:8–32.

34–37 These verses consist of a list of towns *built* (i.e., rebuilt or fortified) by the Gadites. The list does assign the territory around these settlements to Gad, so that comments by scholars that this list of towns does not coincide with lists in Joshua is really beside the point.[46] These are the towns in which the Gadites left their dependents. Later some would be reassigned to Reuben. Of the eight sites listed here, Dibon, Ataroth, and Jazer were listed above in v. 3.

Aroer (*ʿᵃrōʿēr*) is usually identified as modern ʿArâʿîr, about 1 mi. north of the Arnon at the edge of the Arnon gorge, or 3 mi. south of Dibon. The site of *Atroth-Shophan* (*ʿaṭrōṯ šôp̄ān*) is unknown. Most scholars identify *Jogbehah* (*yogbᵒhâ*) as el-Jubeihât (or ʿajbeihât), about 6 mi. north-northwest of modern Amman and about 14 mi. east of es-Salt (cf. Judg. 8:11). *Beth-haran* (*bêṯ hārān*) is called Beth-haram in Josh. 13:27. Some

46. E.g., Gray, pp. 433–44; McNeile, p. 174; Binns, p. 213; Noth, p. 240; Sturdy, p. 224.

modern scholars have identified the site with Tell Iktanu on the east edge of the Jordan Valley, a couple of miles south of Beth-nimrah.[47] This identification means that the Gadite settlements were not only in the southern part of the area (Dibon and Aroer are just north of the Arnon), but also in the northern part (Jazer and Jogbehah), as well as in the Jordan Valley.

37–38 The only site name in the Reubenite list not mentioned in v. 3 above is *Kiriathaim (qiryāṯāyim),* which can probably be identified either with Khirbet el Qureiyeh, about 9 mi. southeast of Heshbon, or el-Qereiyât (Kerioth), about 3 mi. southwest of Attarus.[48] This means that the Reubenite territory is gathered around the Heshbon area in the midst of the settlements fortified by Gad.

(name to be changed) (mûsabbōṯ šēm). The reason for this gloss in the text is most probably that the names Nebo and Baal-meon, which immediately precede the gloss, contain the names of foreign deities that the Israelites are to read in some other way. It is probable that Beon in v. 3 is such a change (most probably for Baal-meon).[49] That this gloss should be read as a proper name, as Noordtzij attempted to do, is highly unlikely.[50]

39–42 These verses undoubtedly once formed an independent tradition concerning conquests of certain Manassites in the Transjordan. In order to complete the picture of early settlement there, the final form of the text barely unites these verses with what precedes by means of v. 33. Apparently only a portion of the Manassites made conquests in Transjordan.

Jair is here said to be a descendant of Machir, and it is probable that Nobah was as well. What was said with regard to genealogical language relating to clans in ch. 26 above must be remembered here. In nongenealogical language Jair (and Nobah) are Manassite clans (i.e., they are "descended from" Manasseh). The genealogical picture of Manasseh is quite confusing. Most times Machir is the only named son of Manasseh, although Josh. 17:1 calls Machir "Manasseh's firstborn" and possibly considers Abiezer, Helek, Asriel, Shechem, Hepher, and Shemida as other sons of Manasseh (in Num. 26:29–30 they are the sons of Gilead, the

47. See, e.g., *Oxford Bible Atlas,* p. 63. Other scholars identify it with Tell er-Rameh in the same vicinity (e.g., Noth. p. 240).

48. For the former see *Oxford Bible Atlas,* p. 63; cf. Gray, p. 436. For the latter see, e.g., Budd, p. 345.

49. So Gray, p. 437; McNeile, p. 175; Binns, p. 214; de Vaulx, p. 370; Sturdy, p. 224; Wenham, p. 216; Budd, p. 345; Harrison, pp. 399–400; Milgrom, *JPST,* p. 275.

50. Noordtzij, p. 283.

grandsons of Machir, and the great-grandsons of Manasseh).[51] V. 41 calls Jair the son of Manasseh in the same way that Machir is called son in vv. 39–40. 1 Chr. 7:14 names Asriel as another son of Manasseh, but this passage is so difficult textually that it is impossible to be sure just what is meant.[52] In any case, otherwise unattested offspring of Manasseh are named in this passage from the Chronicler.

39 The reference is general and quite simply states that Machirites captured and dispossessed Amorite settlements within Gilead. The text does not specify which Amorite settlements, what segment of the Machirites, or even what part of Gilead is meant, although it may be that only the northern half of that territory is referred to here (see above). The text also does not state when these conquests took place. If v. 40 is part of the original text, the conquests must have been sometime during the wars against Sihon and Og, but the position of v. 40 is not secure (see below).

40 This verse seems to be a parenthesis, for it interrupts the flow of vv. 39 and 41. As it stands in the final form of the text, it places the assignment of areas of the Transjordan to the Manassites in the hand of Moses. This is also the point of view in Deut. 3:15 for Gilead, and in Josh. 13:8–32 for the whole of the territory east of the Jordan. Although Eleazar, Joshua, and the other leaders actually divide the land, it was Moses who had been in charge. The allotment of Canaan, although carried out by lot (cf. Num. 26:55–56), was also by means of Moses' command (Josh. 14:2). It seems clear that v. 40 looks backward from that act. Thus the chapter in its final form probably came together after the period of the conquest and allotment of the land. Many scholars have concluded that v. 40 is an interpolation here, not only because vv. 39 and 41 flow better without this strictly extraneous matter, but also because the antecedent of *their villages* (v. 41) is clearly the Amorites (v. 39; but see below).[53]

41 That *Jair* is called *the son of Manasseh* should cause no puzzlement (he is also called son of Manasseh in Deut. 3:14 and son of Machir

51. See the discussion, e.g., in T. Butler, *Joshua,* WBC (Waco: Word, 1983), pp. 191–92; cf. another point of view in M. Woudstra, *Book of Joshua,* NICOT (Grand Rapids: Eerdmans, 1981), pp. 263–67.

52. On 1 Chr. 7:14–17 one must refer to the commentaries. H. G. M. Williamson accepts the reconstruction of the text on the basis of Num. 26 as proposed by Rudolph (*1 & 2 Chronicles,* NCBC [Grand Rapids: Eerdmans, 1982], p. 79); cf. also R. Braun, *1 Chronicles,* WBC (Waco: Word, 1986), pp. 110–12; J. Myers, *I Chronicles,* AB (Garden City, N.Y.: Doubleday, 1965), pp. 54–55.

53. So, e.g., Gray, p. 439; McNeile, p. 175; Binns, p. 215; Budd, pp. 342, 345.

in 1 Chr. 2:23; none of these should be taken as indicating direct genealogical sonship). The term *ben* (lit., "son") means no more than "descendant," and "descendant" may have social as well as genealogical ramifications.[54]

In 1 Chr. 2:21–22 Hezron of Judah marries the daughter of Machir, who bore Segub father of Jair, who took 23 cities in Gilead. Added together with those of Kenath (see below), the total of cities is 60. It is probable that the 60 Manassite towns in Josh. 13:31 are to be understood as a total of those of Jair and those of Kenath (Nobah). Jair was Machirite through his mother's side. How he came to be attached to his mother's tribe rather than his father's is unknown.

The territory Jair took and renamed is said to be in *Gilead*, perhaps used here as a general term for the Transjordan. In Deut. 3:14 Jair's conquests are said to be in the region of the Argob — "that is, Bashan, as far as the border of the Geshurites and the Maacathites." The Argob is north of the Yarmuk; Geshur and Maacah are just east of the Sea of Galilee and Lake Ḥuleh.[55] It seems unwise to try to make the term *Gilead* less elastic, and to see a contradiction between Deut. 3:14 and Num. 32:41. 1 K. 4:13 confirms Jair's activity along with the 60 cities in Solomon's time. Judg. 10:3, 5 mention a so-called minor judge, Jair the Gileadite. He judged Israel for 22 years, had 30 sons, and controlled 30 cities in Gilead. Some scholars are convinced that the two Jairs are in some sense the same. If so, then the date for the final form of the current passage can be no earlier than the middle of the period of the Judges. One must admit that the scattered conquests are pictured here in a way very similar to the more or less independent expeditions narrated in Judg. 1. But multiple individuals with the same names are well attested in the OT, and no proof of the identity of these two can be claimed. If, of course, the name Jair in this text is a clan name, as Machir surely is (*sons of Machir* [v. 39] = *Machir* [v. 40]), then this problem is not so acute.[56]

54. See, e.g., Mendenhall, *Tenth Generation,* pp. 174–97.

55. See, e.g., *Oxford Bible Atlas,* p. 65.

56. On the connection between the two Jairs, see, e.g., Gray, pp. 438–39; cf. Noordtzij, pp. 284–85. See, e.g., the two Israelite kings named Jeroboam who reigned many years apart (1 K. 12:20; 2 K. 14:23); the two other individuals named Jair (2 Sam. 21:19/1 Chr. 20:5; Esth. 2:9). A glance at such a work as H. H. Rowley, *Dictionary of Bible Personal Names* (London: Nelson, 1968), will multiply the examples. Many scholars are not convinced that the Jair of the present text is to be identified with the judge Jair: e.g., J. Gray, *Joshua, Judges, Ruth,* NCBC, rev. ed. (Grand Rapids: Eerdmans, 1986), p. 311. G. B. Gray (p. 440) thought of Jair in Judg. 10 as an individualization of the clan of Jair. Budd (p. 345) says that Judg. 10:3 calls

their villages (ḥawwōṯêhem). As has been said above, several scholars have concluded that v. 40 is an interpolation in part because the antecedent for *their* is the Amorites back in v. 39. Another interpretation, which alleviates the problem, is to repoint and divide the word so as to read "the villages of Ham" *(ḥawwōṯê ham).*[57] Ham is a site mentioned in Gen. 14:5, and is generally located about 25 mi. east of the Jordan, northwest of Ramoth-gilead.[58]

Havvoth-jair (*ḥawwōṯ yā'îr,* lit., "tent villages of Jair"). The word *ḥawwâ* is related to Arab. *ḥiwā',* "circle of tents." Other than in 32:41a, where the reading is "their tent villages," the term is always found in the compound name Havvoth-jair (also in Deut. 3:14; Josh. 13:30; Judg. 10:4; 1 K. 4:13; 1 Chr. 2:23). These passages locate these settlements either in Gilead (in the general sense; Num. 32:41; Judg. 10:4; 1 Chr. 2:23) or in the Argob in the northern Transjordan (Deut. 3:14; Josh. 13:30). 1 K. 4:13 seems to differentiate Gilead from the Argob, and places Havvoth-jair in the former.[59] These settlements were probably scattered over the territory on both sides of the Yarmuk, but especially north toward Geshur.[60]

42 *Nobah.* In Judg. 8:11 (the only other occurrence of the name), it is a site near Jogbehah.

Kenath. The original place-name was renamed Nobah after this clan. The earlier name of Kenath may well have been revived after a period of time, since 1 Chr. 2:23 uses it. Many scholars have identified the site as el-Qanawât on the northwest slopes of Mt. Hauran. If this is the actual site, then it must have formed the northeast border of Manasseh.[61] The association of Nobah with Jogbehah in Judg. 8:11 must then refer to a different site. The alternative is that the Nobah of the Judges passage is the same as Kenath here,[62] which would mean Manassite conquests quite a bit south of where the others were. Thus it seems preferable to identify Kenath with the northern alternative.

Jair "Jair the Gileadite," and that in this passage he is a judge. Thus Budd seems to see the two Jairs as identical persons (or personifications).

57. So Snaith, p. 198; Noordtzij, p. 285; so also NEB, NJPS mg.

58. Snaith, p. 198; *Oxford Bible Atlas,* p. 63.

59. On the nature of the text in 1 K. 4:13, see, e.g., J. Gray, *I & II Kings,* OTL, 2nd ed. (Philadelphia: Westminster, 1970), pp. 135, 138–39; G. H. Jones, *1 and 2 Kings,* NCBC, 2 vols. (Grand Rapids: Eerdmans, 1984), I:142–43.

60. *Oxford Bible Atlas,* p. 63.

61. So, e.g., Keil, p. 239; Cook, p. 773; Binns, p. 213; *Oxford Bible Atlas,* p. 136; and with less assurance, Gray, p. 437; Budd, p. 345.

62. So, e.g., Noth, p. 240; Snaith, p. 198.

I. TRAVEL ITINERARY (33:1–49)

1 *These are the stages of the journey of the children of Israel when they went out from the land of Egypt by their hosts under the leadership of Moses and Aaron.*

2 *And Moses wrote down their starting points, stage by stage,*[1] *at the command of Yahweh; and these are the stages of their journey according to their starting points:*

3 *They departed*[2] *from Rameses in the first month, on the fifteenth day of the first month, on the day after the Passover the children of Israel went out with a raised hand before the eyes of all the Egyptians,*

4 *while the Egyptians were burying those whom Yahweh struck down among them, all their firstborn.*[3] *Yahweh also executed judgments on their gods.*

5 *And the children of Israel departed from Rameses and encamped at Succoth.*

6 *And they departed from Succoth and encamped at Etham, which is on the edge of the wilderness.*

7 *And they departed from Etham, but turned back toward Pi-hahiroth, which is east of Baal-zephon, and they encamped before Migdol.*

8 *And they departed from Pi-haḥiroth and crossed over through the middle of the sea into the wilderness. And they went a three days' journey in the wilderness of Etham, and encamped at Marah.*

1. MT *l^{e}mas'êhem*, lit., "according to their stages." On the distributive use of the preposition *l^{e}*-, see Williams, *Syntax*, § 281.

2. MT *wayyisû.* The imperfect consecutive here simply begins a new stage in the narrative and is not meant to indicate a sequence in time with what has gone before. See Driver, *Syntax*, § 76a.

3. It is unusual syntactically to have the order of the words as they are translated here (*'ēṯ' ^{a}šer hikkâ YHWH bāhem kol-b^{e}ḵôr*). The more normal order would have the sign of the definite direct object (*'ēṯ*) immediately preceding the object of the verb (*kol-b^{e}ḵôr*). Pesh. and Vulg. both move the direct object so as to yield a reading "all firstborn which Yahweh struck down among them." *BHS* has proposed transposing the words *kol-b^{e}ḵôr* to a place after the particle *'ēṯ* to conform to the more common word order. It is true, however, that the particle *'ēṯ* is used before phrase and clauses with *'^{a}šer,* both when *'^{a}šer* means "the one(s) who," and when it introduces a that clause (for the former see, e.g., 1 Sam. 16:3, for the latter, e.g., Deut. 9:7; Waltke and O'Connor, *Biblical Hebrew Syntax,* 10.3.1.a). The less smooth reading adopted above emphasizes both that Yahweh struck these people down and that these people were all the firstborn (sons) of Egypt. On the syntax of *'ēṯ*, see, e.g., Waltke and O'Connor, *Hebrew Syntax,* 10.3; GKC, § 117 a-m; Davidson, *Syntax,* § 72. Of these, Waltke and O'Connor is the most up to date, of course.

9 *And they departed from Marah and came to Elim. Now in Elim were twelve springs of water and seventy date palms, and they encamped there.*

10 *And they departed from Elim and encamped beside the Reed Sea.*

11 *And they departed from the Reed Sea and encamped in the wilderness of Sin.*

12 *And they departed from the wilderness of Sin and encamped at Dophkah.*

13 *And they departed from Dophkah and encamped at Alush.*

14 *And they departed from Alush and encamped at Rephidim. And there was no water for the people to drink there.*

15 *And they departed from Rephidim and encamped in the wilderness of Sinai.*

16 *And they departed from the wilderness of Sinai and encamped at Kibroth-hattaavah.*

17 *And they departed from Kibroth-hattaavah and encamped at Hazeroth.*

18 *And they departed from Hazeroth and encamped at Rithmah.*

19 *And they departed from Rithmah and encamped at Rimmon-perez.*

20 *And they departed from Rimmon-perez and encamped at Libnah.*

21 *And they departed from Libnah and encamped at Rissah.*

22 *And they departed from Rissah and encamped at Kehelathah.*[4]

23 *And they departed from Kehelathah and encamped at the mountain of Shepher.*

24 *And they departed from the mountain of Shepher and encamped at Haradah.*

25 *And they departed from Haradah and encamped at Makheloth.*

26 *And they departed from Makheloth and encamped at Tahath.*[5]

27 *And they departed from Tahath and encamped at Terah.*

28 *And they departed from Terah and encamped at Mithkah.*

29 *And they departed from Mithkah and encamped in Hashmonah.*[6]

30 *And they departed from Hashmonah*[7] *and encamped at Moseroth.*

31 *And they departed from Moseroth and encamped at Bene-jaakan.*

32 *And they departed from Bene-jaakan and encamped at Hor-haggidgad.*

4. LXX reads *Makellath* here and in v. 22a.

5. LXX reads *Kataath* here and in v. 27a.

6. LXX reads *Selmōna* here and in v. 30a.

7. *BHS* proposes that vv. 36b–41a be inserted here. See, e.g., Noth, pp. 243–45.

33 *And they departed from Hor-haggidgad and encamped at Jotbathah.*

34 *And they departed from Jotbathah and encamped at Abronah.*

35 *And they departed from Abronah and encamped at Ezion-geber.*

36 *And they departed from Ezion-geber and encamped in the wilderness of Zin, that is, at Kadesh.*

37 *And they departed from Kadesh and encamped at Mount Hor on the edge of the land of Edom.*

38 *And Aaron the priest went up onto Mount Hor at the command of Yahweh, and he died there in the fortieth year after the exodus of the children of Israel from the land of Egypt, in the fifth month, on the first of the month.*

39 *And Aaron was one hundred twenty-three years old when he died on Mount Hor.*

40 *And the Canaanite, the king of Arad, who was dwelling in the Negeb, in the land of Canaan, heard of the coming of the children of Israel.*

41 *And they departed from Mount Hor and encamped at Zalmonah.*

42 *And they departed from Zalmonah and encamped at Punon.*

43 *And they departed from Punon and encamped at Oboth.*

44 *And they departed from Oboth and encamped at Iye-abarim at the border of Moab.*

45 *And they departed from Iyim and encamped at Dibon-gad.*

46 *And they departed from Dibon-gad and encamped at Almon-diblathaim.*

47 *And they departed from Almon-diblathaim and encamped in the mountains of the Abarim opposite Nebo.*

48 *And they departed from the mountains of the Abaraim and encamped on the plains of Moab, opposite the Jordan by Jericho.*

49 *And they encamped by the Jordan from Beth-jeshimoth as far as the Abel-shittim in the plains of Moab.*

These verses consist of a list of Israelite campsites from Egypt to the plains of Moab. To this list a number of geographical and historical allusions connected with particular sites (vv. 6b, 7b, 9b, 14b, 36b, 37b, 38–39, 40) have been added, along with an introduction (vv. 1–4) that informs the reader of the nature of the list (v. 1), the author (v. 2), the geographical and chronological framework for the beginning of the journey (v. 3), and the circumstances attending the beginning of that journey (v. 4). This is the only passage in the book of Numbers that claims direct Mosaic authorship, although his presence dominates the whole book.[8] This claim probably means that Moses is credited with the list that formed the basis of the current chapter.[9] That list, which is paralleled in ancient Near Eastern annals reaching back into the early 2nd millennium B.C., probably had the simple form of: "and they departed from *x* and encamped at *y*."[10] At some time the author or an editor incorporated the introduction and historical notes. There is no way of discerning the length of the interval between the compiling of the list itself, the composition of this chapter, and its incorporation into the present book. The placement of the list is in the pre-conquest period before Dibon, which according to 32:34 was rebuilt or fortified by Gad and given to Reuben as part of its inheritance (Josh. 13:17; cf. Dibon-gad, Num. 33:45). As elsewhere in this commentary the focus will be on the text as we have it today.

The itinerary breaks into three sections: from Egypt to Sinai (11 campsites, vv. 5–15), from Sinai to Kadesh (21 campsites, vv. 16–36), and from Kadesh to the plains of Moab (9 campsites, vv. 37–49). Thus, counting Rameses, 42 different sites are mentioned. Of these the names Dophkah, Alush, the camp by the Reed Sea, Rithmah, Rimmon-perez, Libnah, Rissah, Kehelathah, Mt. Shepher, Haradah, Makheloth, Tahath, Terah, Mithkah, Hashmonah, Abronah, and Zalmonah are unique to the current chapter.[11] Other campsites are mentioned, e.g., in Num. 21:10–20, and neither list (or those in the book of Exodus) was meant to name all Israelite campsites. Wenham has pointed out that the 42 names break down into six

8. Other passages in the Pentateuch that mention Moses' writing are Exod. 17:14; 24:4; 34:28; Deut. 31:9, 22, 24.

9. Whether this claim is to be taken at face value is another matter, of course. Dillmann thought that this claim meant at least that the source of the list was older than the basic P document (pp. 202–3). It seems unwise not to consider the possibility that the single document in the book of Numbers that directly claims Mosaic authorship could derive from the great Israelite leader. That there may be additions to his work is possible, of course.

10. See G. I. Davies, "The Wilderness Itineraries," *TynBul* 25 (1974) 46–81. This valuable article concludes that ancient itineraries were either made looking back on a campaign or ahead to it. Num. 33:1–49 is of the former type (e.g., p. 78). Although the parallels are widespread from both Mesopotamia and Egypt, the closest affinities with the present list seem to be in the Assyrian royal military annals from the 9th cent. B.C. describing journeys of Tukulti-Ninurta II (890–884 B.C.) and Ashurnasirpal II (883–859 B.C.) among others (see pp. 57–60).

11. That is, if Moseroth, Bene-jaakan, and Hor-haggidgad are the same sites as Moserah, Beeroth Bene-jaakan, and Gudgodah in Deut. 10:6–7, and Almon-diblathayim is the same as Beth-diblathayim in Jer. 48:22, as seems likely.

lists of seven names each, and that this looks like an intentionally chosen number (much as the names in Jesus' genealogy in Matt. 1:1–17 are artificially structured into three groups of 14 names each).[12] Nevertheless, it is difficult, at this distance in time, to reconstruct the significance of the parallels to be derived from this list, and at this point Wenham indulges in speculation that may or may not capture the ancient purpose. The artificial structure is there, but its exact significance eludes modern scholarship.

Although a great deal in this chapter is paralleled elsewhere in the story to this point, the 17 otherwise unknown names show that the narrative is much more than simply a summary of extant sources. There has been a great deal of conjecture on the location of these sites, but none of it carries much conviction. Modern scholars have no basis upon which to decide how these sites were named in the first place, and if, as seems likely, the names were selected by the Israelites, the chances of such names remaining when they had passed by or the chances of recognizing a site by name were it rediscovered today are virtually nonexistent. All this uncertainty holds not only for those unknown sites (mostly in the middle section of the itinerary) but for many of the more familiar sites as well. For a discussion of individual sites, see below.

Another problem in the study of this text has been brought about by the commitment of many scholars to an approach to the literature that sees it as a patchwork of sources, put together in an age much later than the Mosaic age. Many times the sources as delineated do not agree with one another, and, what is worse, the editor did not always understand the sources. Scholars who work from this perspective have noted that the current chapter has names that occur only in P (Pi-hahiroth, wilderness of Sin, Sinai, wilderness of Zin, Mt. Hor, Oboth, Iye-abarim, mountains of Abarim, plains of Moab) side by side with those that occur only in JE (Marah, Kibroth-hattaavah, Moseroth, Bene-jaakan, Hor-haggidgad, Jotbathah, Ezion-geber, Shittim). To this problem may be added the fact that there are sites mentioned elsewhere by JE that do not occur here (wilderness of Shur, Taberah, Hormah, Valley of Zered, other side of the Arnon, Beer, Mattanah, Nahaliel, Bamoth, Moab by the top of the Pisgah), and 17 sites that do not occur in any source. The conclusion of most of these scholars is that the present unit must have been written at a very late date after the combination of JE and P and the other source of the unknown names.[13] But this conclusion, in fact, states only that 33:1–49 rests on the

12. Wenham, pp. 217–19.
13. See, e.g., Gray, pp. 443–44; Budd, pp. 350–53.

more-or-less completed form of certain texts that precede it (e.g., Exod. 13–19; Num. 20–21), and the conclusion is true whether the author was using recent or centuries-old texts.

A problem inherent in the whole documentary approach is that it divides texts into pieces and then concludes that the very pieces eliminated by the analysis do not exist in the source delineated by the analysis and may contradict that source. The very piece of information necessary to correct the supposed contradiction can most often be supplied by the piece cut out by the method in the first place. All this is a way of raising again the issue raised many times previously in this commentary, that most of the tensions in a text are resolved when the text is treated holistically rather than atomistically. It seems reasonable that an author will write or edit texts in such a way that these texts make a cogent whole. It makes sense that the author of this chapter thought that the text was understandable as the Israelite route from Egypt to the plains of Moab, and, with the possible exception of the middle section, it will be treated so here.[14]

The question of the theological purpose of the unit remains. What could possibly be the edificatory use of such a list? How does it witness to the grace of God? It will be helpful to summarize the context: the Exodus generation is dead (ch. 25), the new generation has been counted (ch. 26), and thoughts have turned, once more, to life in the land of promise (chs. 27–31). Indeed, the inheritance of two and one-half tribes has already been granted in the Transjordan (ch. 32). Before turning to matters concerning division of the land of Canaan itself (33:50–36:12), there is time to cast the eye back over the way that has been crossed. The list of sites has the effect of levelling all the happenings of the last 40 years — the important sites (Pi-hahiroth, Sinai) and the (to later generations) unknown sites (Rissah, Mithkah, etc.) are all merely stopping places on the road to Canaan. And each stopping place is a witness not only to the leadership of Moses (who is about to die; cf. 27:12–23), but also to the mighty grace of God who led the people on, in spite of all, toward the promised land. The motif of "the journey of life" is a powerful one in the Bible,[15] and it is helpful, at points throughout the journey, but especially

14. See Wenham, who also follows the holistic approach, for a statement of the problem and a solution to it ("Additional Note on the Route of the Israelites," pp. 220–30). On the middle section of the itinerary, see the commentary below.

15. E.g., see the references to the journey in the book of Hebrews (e.g., 3:7–4:16), or the journey motif in Luke-Acts (e.g., Luke 9:51–18:14; Acts 12:1–24). On Luke-Acts, see, e.g., S. Garrett, "Exodus from Bondage: Luke 9:51 and Acts 12:1–24," *CBQ* 52 (1990) 656–80.

toward its end, to look back and reflect. This supposedly bare list of site-names is a device to help the people of God remember.

1–4 These verses form the introduction to the list. The claim of Mosaic authorship is put in the third person (*And Moses wrote down,* v. 2), and vv. 3–4 anticipate the beginning of the list of campsites in v. 5. It is likely, therefore, that these verses were added to form an introduction to the Mosaic list that began with the mention of Rameses in v. 5.

1 *stages of the journey of the children of Israel (masʿê bᵉnê-yiśrāʾēl).* The noun "stages" is related to a verb meaning "to pull up (tent pegs)" *(nāsaʿ);* thus it may represent the places from which the Israelites went when they broke camp — i.e., campsites. It is the same root that is found in the verb "to depart" throughout the unit.

by their hosts (lᵉṣiḇʾōṯām). This is basically a military term here.[16]

under the leadership of Moses and Aaron (lit., "at the hand of Moses and Aaron"). This phrase may also be military metaphor (cf. 31:49; 2 Sam. 18:2). The ancient Near Eastern parallels to this itinerary are all military documents, and this kind of terminology here may mean that the journey of Israel out of Egypt was seen in this way as well.[17] Moses and Aaron were the human leaders, but Yahweh himself was the supreme commander.

2 *Moses wrote down.* This is the only place in Numbers that mentions Moses writing.

Rameses. Most scholars are agreed that this is probably to be identified with the Pi-Ramesē of Egyptian texts. This city was undertaken by Seti I and completed by Rameses II, and is to be located at Tanis, Qantir, or perhaps even both sites.[18]

3 *in the first month, on the fifteenth day of the first month, on the day after Passover.* Passover occurred on the fourteenth day of the first month (Exod. 12:6, 18; Lev. 23:5; Num. 9:3, 5; 28:16; Josh. 5:10; Ezek. 45:21; Ezra 6:19; 2 Chr. 30:15; 35:1), and the Exodus on the next morning, which would later be designated as the first day of Unleavened Bread (e.g., Lev. 23:6). This dating concurs with the narrative of Exod. 12, although it is not specifically stated there.[19]

16. On the meaning of *ṣāḇāʾ* see the commentary above on 1:3.

17. Davies, "Wilderness Itineraries," p. 80.

18. So Davies, *Way of the Wilderness,* p. 79; Kitchen, *Ancient Orient and OT,* pp. 57–59; Wenham, p. 224; Budd, p. 354. Snaith (p. 199) opts for Qantir.

19. Many of the other ancient Near Eastern itineraries also begin with statements as to the date of the start of the mission or campaign; see Davies, "Wilderness Itineraries," pp. 53–57.

with a raised hand (b^e yāḏ rāmâ). The same expression occurs in Exod. 14:8. It probably means "defiantly" (so RSV in Exod. 14:8), treating the Egyptians as of no importance. See the same phrase in "the sin with the high hand" in Num. 15:30.

before the eyes of all the Egyptians. Exod. 12:33 does not mention that the Israelites went out of the land *while the Egyptians were burying all their firstborn* (v. 4), but the general mood of haste created by Exod. 12:28–31 is recreated here by using a participial clause (i.e., "action in progress").

Yahweh also executed judgments on their gods (ûḇē' lōhêhem 'āśâ YHWH š^e pāṭîm). This is a third-person report of what Yahweh himself said about Egypt's gods in Exod. 12:12 ("and on all of the gods of Egypt, I will execute judgments, I am Yahweh," *ûḇ^e ḵol-'^ĕ lōhê miṣrayim 'e^ĕ śeh š^e pāṭîm '^a nî YHWH*).

5–15 This section of the itinerary marks the journey from Egypt to Mt. Sinai. The southern location of Mt. Sinai at Jebel Musa is traditional and still probable, but by no means universally accepted.[20] Identification of sites along the way, especially after the crossing of the Reed Sea, depends on which direction Sinai was. Many sites are simply unknown (in spite of their locales being given in some Bible atlases).

5 *Succoth* (see Exod. 12:37). An Egyptian equivalent *(Ṯkw)* exists in Wâdī Tumilat west of the modern town of Ismailia at Tell el-Mashkhûṭa.

6 *Etham* (see Exod. 13:20). It has been traditional to connect Etham with an Egyptian word for "wall" or "fortress" *(ḫtm)* and Heb. *'ēṯām.* The wilderness of the *ḫtm* would be equivalent to the wilderness of Shur (Heb. *šûr,* "wall") of Exod. 15:22. Etham would then be one of a number of fortresses that lined Egypt's northeastern frontier. G. I. Davies questions the equivalency of *ḫtm* and Heb. *'tm,* since *ḫ* does not usually come into Hebrew as *'*. This would involve a mispronunciation of the Egyptian by Hebrews (not unheard-of), but the caution is worth noting.[21]

7 The literature on the crossing point of the sea by the Hebrews is truly enormous. It is undoubtedly true that the author intends to give an

20. See the discussion in Davies, *Way of the Wilderness,* pp. 62–69 (with notes and bibliography) and in Wenham (pp. 224–27). Wenham by no means accepts the tradition that Mt. Sinai is Jebel Musa, but argues for a more northerly locale at Jebel Sin Bisher, about 30 mi. southeast of Suez. See Davies's critique of such a view (*Way of the Wilderness,* pp. 67–69).

21. Davies, *Way of the Wilderness,* pp. 79–80.

exact location by his threefold placing of the event at *Pi-hahiroth, which is east of Baal-zephon, and they encamped before Migdol.* Not one of these sites is known with certainty. A north Egyptian site for Baal-zephon (at Mons Casius) seems less likely because the Hebrews were forbidden to go to Canaan by the northerly route (i.e., the "way of the Philistines," Exod. 13:17). Davies mentions a Migdol of Pharaoh Seti-Merneptah south of Wâdī Tumilat, but this identification is uncertain.[22] The most likely sites for the crossing of the sea are either at the southern end of Lake Menzaleh or a few miles to the south in the vicinity of the Bitter Lakes.[23]

8 *Marah.* This site is usually identified with ʿAin Ḥawâra located about 25 mi. down the eastern coast of the Gulf of Suez.

9 *Elim* (see Exod. 15:27). This may be located at Wâdī Gharandel about 75 mi. south of the Bitter Lakes.

10 *the Reed Sea (yam-sûp̱).* It is surprising that the *yam-sûp̱* is not mentioned until three stops after the crossing through the midst of the sea. This has led some to conclude that the tradition connecting the Reed Sea with the place of deliverance through the water is a later combining of traditions that did not originally belong together.[24] It is true that some texts speak of going through the sea but do not mention *yam-sûp̱* at all (e.g., Exod. 14:16, 22–23, 27–30; 15:1, 21; Num. 33:8). It is also true that a great deal of biblical tradition does make this connection (e.g., Exod. 15:4; Deut. 11:4: Josh. 2:10; 4:23; Neh. 9:9; Ps. 106:7 [the text is difficult], 9, 22; 136:13, 15). If one concludes that one must interpret these texts as a whole, then the places that merely mention going through the sea must be interpreted in the light of those that make the connection with *yam-sûp̱,* which clearly became the dominant biblical tradition. If this is the case, then, the present reference is to another encampment.

The meaning of *yam-sûp̱* is debated. While the words are clearly used to describe the Gulf of Aqabah, they may also designate the Gulf of Suez. Davies concurs with this judgment. But he does not think that they can also designate the area north of the Gulf of Suez, including the Bitter Lakes as well as Lakes Timsah and Menzaleh. Thus he must view the crossing of the sea as a literary motif rather than a historical fact.[25]

22. Ibid., p. 81.

23. For the former, see, e.g., *Westminster Historical Atlas,* map V. For the latter, see, e.g., *Oxford Bible Atlas,* p. 59; Davies, *Way of the Wilderness,* p. 82.

24. E.g., Snaith, p. 199; Budd, p. 354.

25. Davies, *Way of the Wilderness,* pp. 72–74. Since the current text does not claim a crossing at *yam-sûp̱,* that question must be referred to specialized works and commentaries on the book of Exodus. A selection of commentaries is:

11 The *wilderness of Sin* has not been definitely identified; some identify it as Dibbet er-Rammleh.[26] If one assumes a southern location for Sinai, this identification cannot be far off.

12–13 *Dophkah* and *Alush* cannot be identified with any certainty either, although some have suggested Serabit el-Khâdim and Wâdī el-ʿEšš respectively.[27]

14 Most have agreed that *Rephidim* is to be identified as Wâdī Refâyid about 30 mi. north of the tip of the Sinai Peninsula.

15 Finally, as has already been stated, Jebel Musa is as good a site for Mt. Sinai as has been proposed. The *wilderness of Sinai,* then, would be the territory of the plain of Râḥa and environs.

16–36 This stage of the itinerary starts at the wilderness of Sinai and extends to Kadesh. The current text of Numbers holds that Kadesh was the site of the rebellion of the spies (ch. 14) from which the Israelites were sent to wander in the wilderness (14:25). It also holds that they returned to Kadesh toward the end of the wandering period and, once again, set out for Canaan from there (20:1, 22). It may be that their wanderings brought them back into the vicinity of Kadesh from time to time throughout the thirty-eight years, but this is a conjecture. The present itinerary from Sinai to Kadesh does not report two (or more) visits to Kadesh. The only sites known from other biblical texts are Kibroth-hattaavah and Hazeroth (vv. 16–17), Moseroth, Bene-jaakan, Hor-haggidgad, and Jotbathah (vv. 30–33), Ezion-geber (vv. 35–36), and

---

U. Cassuto, *A Commentary on the Book of Exodus,* tr. I. Abrahams (Jerusalem: Magnes, 1967), pp. 167–68; J. P. Hyatt, *Exodus,* NCBC (Grand Rapids: Eerdmans, 1971), pp. 156–61; B. Childs, *Exodus: A Critical, Theological Commentary,* OTL (Philadelphia: Westminster, 1974), pp. 229–30; J. Durham, *Exodus,* WBC (Waco, Tex.: Word, 1987), pp. 182, 185. A selection of articles and monographs suffice here: O. Eissfeldt, *Baal Zephon, Zeus Kasios und der Duchzug der Israeliten durchs Meer* (Halle: Niemeyer, 1932); M. Noth, "Der Schauplatz des Meereswunders," *Festschrift Otto Eissfeldt,* ed. J. Fück (Halle: Niemeyer, 1948), pp. 181–90; W. Albright, "Baal Zephon," *Festschrift Alfred Bertholet zum 80. Geburtstag gewidmet,* ed. W. Baumgartner, et al. (Tübingen: Mohr, 1950), pp. 1–14; H. Cazelles, "Les localisations de l'Exode et la crítique littéraire," *RB* 62 (1955) 321–64; G. I. Davies, *The Way of the Wilderness,* pp. 56–57, 60–61, 70–74; idem, "The Wilderness Itineraries and the Composition of the Pentateuch," *VT* 33 (1983) 1–13; B. F. Batto, "The Reed Sea, Requiescat in Pace," *JBL* 102 (1983) 27–35.

26. *Westminster Historical Atlas,* p. 127.

27. E.g., Snaith, p. 200; on the dubiousness of the latter identification especially, see Davies, *Way of the Wilderness,* p. 84.

Kadesh itself (v. 36). Of these, Kibroth-hattaavah and Hazeroth are sites known from the beginning of the wandering period (Num. 11:34–35). Moseroth, Bene-jaakan, Hor-haggidgad, and Jotbathah are known in a different order and form from the fragment in Deut. 10:6–7. The complexities of the latter text are many, but the author of the passage clearly places these sites at the end of the wandering period, since he connects Moserah (Moseroth) with the site of Aaron's death, which Num. 20 locates at Mt. Hor (10:6; cf. Num. 20:22–29). It is possible that Hashmonah (v. 30) is to be connected with Heshmon in southern Judah (Josh. 15:27) and Bene-jaakan (v. 31) with a site in the southern Negeb.[28] All this may show that the current section of the itinerary blends together the journey from Sinai to Kadesh with the wandering in the wilderness. If this is the case, then this section of the text really does not give the route of a journey so much as a list of campsites in the wilderness of unknown geographic relation to one another.[29]

16 *Kibroth-hattaavah* is unknown (see above on 11:34).

17 *Hazeroth* (see above on 11:35). This site may be identified as ʿAin/Wâdī Ḥudeirat, about 40 mi. northeast of Jebel Mûsa.

18–30 For the sites between *Rithmah* (v. 18) and *Moseroth* (v. 30), no sure identifications have been made.[30] If these sites record the wilderness wanderings, one cannot even plot general directions.

31 *Moseroth.* If this site is identified with Moserah of Deut. 10:6, then it is the site of Aaron's death. But this identification seems to conflict with Num. 33:38, which names Mt. Hor as the place where Aaron died. Several explanations of the alternate traditions have been attempted. Some scholars find alternate (i.e., irreconcilable) traditions here, much as in the Sinai/Horeb passages elsewhere.[31] It is possible that Mt. Hor and Moserah/Moseroth may be alternate names for the same site, or sites in the same vicinity. Harrison has posited that Moserah in Deut. 10:6 is not to be read as a place-name at all, but as a common noun *môsērâ,* which he translates as "chastisement." Thus the passage gives the reason for Aaron's death, not the site.[32]

28. See Davies, *Way of the Wilderness,* pp. 86–87.

29. This point of view was suggested at least as long ago as Keil, pp. 242–43; also Cook, p. 776; Gray, p. 443; also mentioned by Wenham, p. 227.

30. For suggestions, see, e.g., Davies, *Way of the Wilderness,* pp. 85–86, as well as the older conjectures in such works as Cook, p. 776.

31. So, e.g., Gray, p. 447; Snaith, p. 200; Budd, p. 355; A. D. H. Mayes, *Deuteronomy,* NCBC (Grand Rapids: Eerdmans, 1981), pp. 205–6.

32. R. K. Harrison, *Introduction to the Old Testament* (Grand Rapids:

31 *Bene-jaakan* is called more fully Beeroth Bene-jaakan (lit., "the wells of the children of Jaakan") in Deut. 10:6. In Gen. 36:27 Akan (= Jaakan in 1 Chr. 1:42) is a Horite who lived in the Edomite area, i.e., close to Kadesh. It is likely that the four sites in Deut. 10:6–7 are in the same vicinity. If Mt. Hor is also in the vicinity of Kadesh, as was held above on 20:22, then Moserah/Moseroth and Mt. Hor are in the same vicinity, and the likelihood of alternate names or nearby sites becomes greater, but further than this one cannot go.[33] Long ago, H. Ewald suggested that vv. 36b–41a had been misplaced in the text and should be relocated to a place following v. 30a. This relocation would place Mt. Hor and Moseroth in adjacent places on the list and further suggest their geographic proximity.[34] The problem with the conjecture is the lack of textual support for it.

32 *Hor-haggidgad.* This is simply called Gudgodah in Deut. 10:7. It probably means "the cave of Gidgad/Gudgod." The site is unknown.

33 *Jotbathah.* D. Baly identifies the site tentatively as Bir Tabā in the southern Arabah.[35]

34 *Abronah.* The site is unknown.

35 *Ezion-geber* (Deut. 2:8; 1 K. 9:26; 22:49; 2 Chr. 8:17; 20:36). N. Glueck, among others, identified this site as Tell el-Kheleifeh near Elath, just north of the head of the Gulf of Aqabah.[36] More recently this

---

Eerdmans, 1969), p. 511. The suggestion is not particularly convincing since the passage in Deuteronomy lists sites, and, if one accepts Harrison's suggestion, Aaron's death has no site in the narrative.

33. E.g., Cook, p. 777. Keil makes an attempt to harmonize Deut. 10:6–7 and Num. 33 (pp. 245–46). S. R. Driver made a basically negative assessment of such harmonizations in *A Critical and Exegetical Commentary on Deuteronomy,* ICC (Edinburgh: T. & T. Clark, 1895), pp. 118–21.

34. H. A. W. Ewald, *Geschichte des Volkes Israel,* 3rd ed. (Göttingen, 1864–68), II:283–85 (esp. p. 285 n. 2); mentioned by, e.g., Davies, *Way of the Wilderness,* p. 108 n. 10. Noordtzij (p. 290) adopts this conjecture. *BHS* also mentions it.

35. D. Baly, *Geographical Companion to the Bible,* p. 174.

36. N. Glueck made the identification in several publications; some of the more important were: "Ezion-Geber: Solomon's Naval Base on the Red Sea," *BA* 1 (1938) 13–16; "Ezion-geber: Elath: City of Bricks with Straw," *BA* 3 (1940) 51–55; "The First Campaign at Tell el-Kheleifeh (Ezion-geber)," *BASOR* 71 (1938) 3–17; "The Topography and History of Ezion-geber and Elath," *BASOR* 72 (1938) 2–13; "The Second Campaign at Tell el-Kheleifeh (Ezion-Geber: Elath)," *BASOR* 75 (1939) 8–22; idem, "The Third Season of Excavation at Tell el-Kheleifeh," *BASOR* 79 (1940) 2–18; *Rivers in the Desert* (New York: Norton, 1959), pp. 31–32, 157–168. Snaith (p. 200), Budd (p. 385), Davies (*Way of the*

identification has been challenged, in particular by B. Rothenberg and G. Pratico.[37] An attractive alternate site for Ezion-geber is Jezeirat Faraun, a small island a couple of miles south of the head of the Gulf, a few hundred yards offshore.[38] No decision on which site may be identified with Ezion-geber can be made at least until more excavation can take place at Jezeirat Faraun.[39]

36 *Kadesh.* See above on 13:26.[40]

37–49 This stage of the journey is well attested from other sources in the book of Numbers and elsewhere. Two fairly lengthy notes interrupt the narrative in a way that does not happen elsewhere in the list (vv. 38–39, 40). It is unknown just how long after the composition of the original list these notes were added. There is no reason why this section, like vv. 5–15, cannot be seen as the actual itinerary from Kadesh through to the plains of Moab, from which the assault on Canaan would eventually be launched (Josh. 3:1–17).

37–39 *Mount Hor.* See above on 20:22.

38 *fortieth year after the exodus . . . fifth month . . . first of the month.* This information is not given elsewhere. It serves to mark the fact that at Aaron's death the forty years of punishment were nearly at an end. According to 20:1 the Israelites came back to Kadesh *in the first month,* but with no day or year given. It is possible, as was noted above, that the fortieth year was intended. This would mean that Israel remained at Kadesh for three to four months before moving off for Mt. Hor.

39 *Aaron was one hundred twenty-three years old.* This figure

---

Wilderness, p. 86), *Oxford Bible Atlas* (p. 129), and *Westminster Historical Atlas* (p. 124) all mention Tell el-Kheleifeh as the likely site for Ezion-geber.

37. Glueck's findings have been questioned by B. Rothenberg, "Ancient Copper Industries in the Western Arabah," Part II, "Tell El-Kheleifeh; Ezion-Geber; Eilath," *PEQ* 94 (1962) 5–71. On the basis of Rothenberg's paper, Glueck modified his stance considerably in "Ezion-geber," *BA* 28 (1965) 70–73. See also G. Pratico, "Nelson Glueck's 1938–1940 Excavations at Tell el-Kheleifeh: A Reappraisal," *BASOR* 259 (Summer 1985) 1–32; "Where is Ezion-Geber? A Reappraisal of the Site Nelson Glueck Identified as King Solomon's Red Sea Port," *Biblical Archaeology Review* 12 (1986) 24–35. Pratico gives a brief overview in *ISBE,* rev., IV:748–50.

38. See the discussion in Davies, *Way of the Wilderness,* pp. 85–86.

39. See A. Flinder, "Is This Solomon's Seaport"? *Biblical Archaeology Review* 15 (1989) 32–43, which identifies Jezeirat Faraun as Ezion-geber. To date, no hard data for dating the remains located on the island have been found, so the identification remains conjectural.

40. For a discussion and rejection of J. Koenig's hypothesis (to an extent, following Noth) that the sites from Sinai to Kadesh were along a pilgrim route through northwestern Arabia, see Davies, *Way of the Wilderness,* pp. 87–89.

tallies with the 40 years since the Exodus and the 83 years of Aaron's age in Egypt at about the time of the Exodus (Exod. 7:7).

40 This addition, taken (with slight variations in wording) from 21:1, is placed here immediately following the account of Aaron's death as it is in the fuller account of chs. 20–21. It is possible that the narrative of chs. 20–21 is one source for the notes in the current chapter.

41 *Zalmonah.* This site is unknown. Mt. Zalmon in Judg. 9:48 is possibly either Mt. Ebal or Mt. Gerizim, and the mountain named in Ps. 68:15 (Eng. 14) is unknown but conjectured to be Jebel Ḥaurân.[41] The Zalmonah of the present text is probably not to be identified with either peak, especially the former.

42 *Punon.* Most scholars agree that Punon is Khirbet Feinan north of Petra, on the eastern edge of the Arabah at the junction of Wâdī el-Gheweir and Wâdī eš-Šeger, about 28 mi. south of the Dead Sea. There are signs of occupation of this copper smelting site back to ca. 2,000 B.C.[42]

43 *Oboth.* See above on 21:10.

44 *Iye-Abarim.* See above on 21:11.

45 *Dibon-gad.* See above on 21:30 and 32:2. The name takes notice that Gadites rebuilt or fortified the site (32:34).

46 *Almon-diblathaim.* This site is probably to be identified with the Beth-diblathaim of Jer. 48:22, in the prophet's oracles against Moab, and in the Mesha Inscription (line 30). It has been tentatively identified as Khirbet Deleilât eš-Šerqiyeh, which is near both Medeba and Baal-meon (with which Mesha mentions Beth-diblathaim).[43]

47 *mountains of the Abarim.* See on 27:12 as well as 21:11 on Abarim.

49 *Beth-jeshimoth* is mentioned again in Josh. 12:3; 13:20; and Ezek. 25:9. It has been identified as Tell el-ʿAzeimeh about 12 mi. southeast of Jericho on the east side of the Jordan, just north of the Dead Sea.[44]

Abel-shittim. See above on 25:1.

41. For Mt. Ebal see J. A. Soggin, *Judges: A Commentary,* tr. J. Bowden, OTL (Philadelphia: Westminster, 1981), p. 191. For Mt. Gerizim see J. Gray, *Joshua, Judges, Ruth,* NCBC, rev. ed. (Grand Rapids: Eerdmans, 1986), p. 309. On Ps. 68 see A. A. Anderson, *Psalms,* NCBC, 2 vols. (Grand Rapids: Eerdmans, 1981), I:490; M. Dahood, *Psalms,* AB, 3 vols. (Garden City, N.Y.: Doubleday, 1965, 1968, 1970), I:142.

42. See, e.g., *Oxford Bible Atlas,* p. 59 U-2; 138; N. Glueck, *Explorations in Eastern Palestine,* AASOR 15 (1934–35), II:32–35.

43. See, e.g., *Oxford Bible Atlas,* p. 63 Y-5.

44. Snaith, p. 200; *Oxford Bible Atlas,* p. 63 Y-5.

J. REGULATIONS FOR LIVING IN CANAAN (33:50–36:13)

The promised land has been Israel's goal throughout the book of Numbers. It is only fitting, therefore, that the last section of the book (33:50–36:13) deals specifically with settlement in Canaan. Many of the themes that are mentioned here are developed in the deuteronomistic literature (Deuteronomy, Joshua–Kings). In a way, 33:50–36:13 anticipates and introduces this deuteronomistic literature.

The section breaks down into two groups of three laws each, carefully introduced by the clause "and Yahweh spoke to Moses" (*way^{e}ḏabbēr YHWH 'el-mōšeh,* 33:50; 34:1, 16; 35:1, 9; cf. 36:6) and surrounded by the phrase "on the plains of Moab by the Jordan at Jericho" (*b^{e}'ar^{e}ḇōṯ mô'aḇ 'al-yardēn y^{e}rēḥô,* 33:50; 35:1; 36:13).[1]

1. INTRODUCTION: CANAANITES MUST BE EXPELLED (33:50–56)

50 *And Yahweh spoke to Moses on the plains of Moab by the Jordan at Jericho, saying:*

51 *"Speak to the children of Israel, and say to them: 'When you cross over*[1] *the Jordan into the land of Canaan,*

52 *you will dispossess all the inhabitants of the land from before you, and you will destroy all their carved figures, and all their molten images you will destroy, and all their high places you shall demolish.*

53 *And you will possess the land and dwell in it, for I have given the land to you to possess.*

54 *And you will receive the land as an inheritance by lot according to your clans; for the many you will make their inheritance large, and for the few you will make their inheritance small; wherever it goes out to him, there his lot will be. You will inherit according to your fathers' tribes.*

55 *But if you do not dispossess the inhabitants of the land from before you, then it will be that those of them you allow to remain will be*

1. On the series of three as a common structure in the Pentateuch, see G. J. Wenham and J. G. McConville, "Drafting Techniques in Some Deuteronomic Laws," *VT* 30 (1980) 248–52.

1. The temporal construction *kî* plus participle is a bit unusual, although it does occur in the present context twice more (34:2; 35:10); also Judg. 12:5; cf. BDB, p. 473a; Williams, *Syntax,* §445; Davidson, *Syntax,* §145; GKC, §164d.

as splinters[2] *in your eyes and thorns*[3] *in your sides. And they will trouble you in the land in which you dwell.*
56 *And it will be that I will do to you what I purposed to do to them.' "*

Numbers 33:50–56 introduces the last section of the book by giving the presupposition of the whole: the expulsion of the Canaanites and the eradication of all signs of their religion from the land. It is only when this task is completed that Israel will inherit the land in perpetuity. As elsewhere in Numbers, exact obedience of Yahweh's commandments is the prerequisite for his blessings. If Israel will keep his word, it will endure in the land. If not, its existence will be cursed, not only by defeat at the hands of the remaining Canaanites, but also by God himself.

50–51 *the plains of Moab.* See the commentary above on 22:1; cf. 26:3; 35:1; 36:13.

when you cross over the Jordan into the land of Canaan. This clause is more or less repeated in 35:10 (cf. Deut. 11:31).

52 Israel must dispossess all the Canaanites and destroy all remnants of their religious systems from the land. *their carved figures (maśkîyōṯām).* In Lev. 26:1 this word is used to describe something made of stone, parallel to "idols" *('ᵉlîlim),* a "graven image" *(pesel),* and a "pillar" *(maṣṣēḇâ),* all objects of worship. Gray translates it as "figured stones," meaning stones on which were carved pagan religious symbols.[4] The meaning of *maśkiṯ* is not completely clear, but probably it is another cult object. Both LXX and Targ. conclude that the *maśkîṯ* is the place of worship.[5] It is more likely, however, that, here as elsewhere, the *high place (bāmâ)* is the place of worship (see below). Here, the *maśkîṯ* is connected

2. Heb. *śikkîm* (a hapax legomenon) apparently refers to any small, sharp object. This can be established by looking at the cognate languages: Arab. *šawkat,* "thorn" (see Snaith, p. 201), perhaps Akk. *šikkatu,* "a point," and Syr. *skt',* "a nail." See BDB, p. 968a. Two rare words in Hebrew may also be related: *śukkâ* (Job 40:31), "a point," and *mᵉśûkkâ* (Isa. 5:5), "a [thorn] hedge."

3. Heb. *ṣᵉnînim* is probably related to *ṣinîm,* "thorns, hooks" (Job 5:5; Prov. 22:5; see BDB, p. 856b), and may be related to *ṣᵉnôṯ* (Amos 4:2), although some have related this word to *ṣinnâ,* "shield" (BDB, p. 857a). Again, a small, sharply pointed object is intended.

4. Gray, p. 450.

5. In postbiblical Aramaic the verb *sᵉḵā'* means "to look out" or "to watch" (Jastrow, *Dictionary,* p. 989b). It is possible that LXX's *skopias* ("a lookout," esp. on a hilltop) thought that *maśkîyōṯām* was derived from a Hebrew cognate and, so, "a place of watching." Targ. also associates *maśkîṯ* with a place by translating *sᵉnîḏā',* "place of worship." See Gray, p. 452.

with *molten images (ṣalmê maśśēḵōṯām)* (see below), and is probably, like them, a cult image or object, perhaps even the figure of a god or goddess.

their molten images (ṣalmê massēḵōṯām). Cf. Exod. 34:17; Lev. 19:4; 1 Sam. 6:5, 11; Ezek. 16:17; 23:14. These were probably cast-metal images of the earthly shape of a god or a goddess. These are also found in the prohibition of Exod. 34:17. This is the only place in the Pentateuch where the word *image (ṣelem)* designates a pagan idol, although such a usage is found in, e.g., Amos 5:26; Ezek. 7:20; 16:17.

their high places (bāmōṯām). These are probably the Canaanite hill shrines that are so thoroughly condemned by the Deuteronomist (e.g., 1 K. 13:2, 32, 38; 2 K. 12:4; 14:4; 15:4, 35; 23:5–20). Sometimes the *bāmâ* is a legitimate place for the worship of Yahweh (e.g., 1 Sam. 9:12–25), and sometimes it is not (1 K. 11:7; 2 K. 23:8; Jer. 19:5). The sites were probably at least partially artificial since they could be built *(bānâ),* pulled down *(nāṯaṣ),* and removed *(sûr).* By the time of Jer. 7:31, the *bāmôṯ* were not necessarily even on hills. It is impossible to know exactly what sense the term has here. Sturdy thinks that they are better thought of as "cultic platforms."[6]

53–54 That Yahweh has given Israel Canaan as a possession is also the witness of, e.g., Gen. 15:17; Lev. 20:24; 25:46. The specific way in which the land is to be divided is *by lot.* V. 54 is strongly reminiscent of 26:54–55, and depends upon this material for its meaning.

wherever it goes out to him, there his lot will be (ʾ^{a}šer yēṣēʾ lô šāmmâ haggôrāl lô yihyeh). This line is quite vague. The first *it* is probably the lot as it is thrown and goes out. The *him* is not the individual, but the *many (raḇ)* and the *few (m^{e}ʿaṭ)* earlier in the verse, viz., the members of *your clans (mišp^{e}ḥōṯēḵem).* Thus the *him* might be paraphrased by "the clan." The meaning is that each clan's land claim will be settled by the throwing of the lot. The relative size of the clan will determine the size of the allotment. It is not always easy to see how these two principles go together (see above on 26:52–56). The word *clan* here may be taken in the loose sense of the tribe, as suggested by the last sentence of the verse *(You will inherit according to your fathers' tribes),* which is meant to define the earlier word *clans.* On *fathers' tribes,* see above on 26:55.[7]

55–56 The result of failing to dispossess the Canaanites is

6. Sturdy, p. 231; cf. the commentary above on 21:19.

7. See also N. Gottwald, *The Tribes of Yahweh: A Sociology of the Religion of Liberated Israel, 1250–1050 B.C.E.* (Maryknoll, N.Y.: Orbis, 1979), pp. 285–87, 288–92.

spelled out here. This warning is not surprising in the light of the previous rebellions of Israel. It is the warning of a curse, such as is found in covenant documents (cf. Deut. 28:15–68; see also Exod. 23:33; 34:11–13; Deut. 7:1–6; Josh. 23:12–13; Ezek. 28:24). If the Israelites fail to drive out the Canaanites and eradicate their religious observances and cultic sites from the land, then those Canaanites who are allowed to remain will be as *splinters* in the eyes and *thorns* in the side of Israel, viz., trouble (cf. the similar figures of speech in Josh. 23:13; Ezek. 28:24). As the splinter or thorn is small but sharp and can cause more than discomfort, including infection and (in the eyes) blindness, so even a small remnant of Canaanites will cause great problems in Israel's future. It therefore will be foolish to allow the Canaanites to remain in the land.

Indeed, v. 56 implies that it will be more than foolish — it will be sinful to allow them to remain. Again and again the Pentateuch (not only in Numbers) stresses the importance of obedience to God. God will repay disobedience, as he has in the past, with a punishment related to the context of the sin itself. Just as Miriam's criticism of Moses' Cushite wife was met with the whiteness of leprosy (ch. 12), and the disobedience because of fear of death in the wilderness brought that very kind of death (ch. 11), so here God promises to punish Israel with what he had intended for the Canaanites — expulsion from the land.

2. BORDERS OF THE LAND (34:1–15)

1 *And Yahweh spoke to Moses, saying:*

2 *"Command the children of Israel and say to them, 'When you come to to the land of Canaan,*[1] *this is the land that will fall to you by inheritance, the land of Canaan, with regard to its boundaries.*

3 *And your south side will be from the wilderness of Zin beside the edge of Edom, and your southern border will be from the end of the Salt Sea on the east.*

4 *Then your border will turn south toward the ascent of Akrabbim,*[2] *and cross over to Zin, and its extremities will be*[3] *south of*

1. As MT stands, the two nouns *hā'āreṣ k^{e}nā'an* are not a construct-genitive, "the land of Canaan," but two absolute nouns in apposition (Davidson, § 29a). The *Sebir* note and a few mss. of Sam. Pent. read *'ereṣ k^{e}na'an,* the normal construct-genitive. GKC, § 131f, posits that *k^{e}na'an* is a gloss and should be deleted (so also Williams, *Syntax,* § 70; Driver, *Tenses,* § 190; *BHS*).

2. For MT *'aqrabbîm* Pesh. reads *s^{e}parwayim.*

3. Read pl. with the Qere *(w^{e}hāyû).*

Kadesh-barnea; then it will go out to Hazer-addar[4] *and pass on to Azmon.*
5 *Then the border will turn from Azmon toward the Brook of Egypt, and its extremities will be at*[5] *the sea.*
6 *Also*[6] *a western border: it will be the Great Sea and its coast; this will be your western border.*
7 *And this will be your northern border: from the Great Sea you will mark out for yourselves as far as Mount Hor.*
8 *From Mount Hor you will mark it out to Lebo-Hamath. And the extremities of the border will be Zedad.*
9 *And the border will go out to Ziphron;*[7] *and its extremity will be at Hazar-enan.*[8] *This will be your northern border.*
10 *Now you will measure out your eastern border: from Hazar-enan to Shepham.*
11 *And then the border will descend from Shepham to Riblah*[9] *on the east side of Ain.*[10] *The border descends and strikes the shoulder of the Sea of Chinnereth on the east.*
12 *Then the border will descend to the Jordan, and its extremities will be the Salt Sea. This will be the land with its borders on all sides.' "*
13 *And Moses commanded the children of Israel, saying: "This is the land which you will inherit by lot, which Yahweh has commanded to give to the nine tribes and the half-tribe.*
14 *For the tribe of the children of the Reubenites according to their fathers' houses and the tribe of the children of the Gadites according to their fathers' houses have received their inheritance, as has half the tribe of Manasseh received their inheritance.*
15 *The two tribes and the one half-tribe received their inheritance on*

4. For MT *ḥ*^{a}*ṣar-ʼaddār* LXX reads Arad. Josh. 15:3 mentions two sites, Hezron and Addar, for the single Hazer-addar here. It is likely that a single site should be read in Joshua. *Oxford Bible Atlas* (3rd ed., p. 130) suggests Khirbet el-Qudeirat as the site, but this is admittedly a conjecture.

5. Read *hayyām* with Sam. Pent. and LXX (so also *BHS*) instead of MT *hayyāmâ*.

6. The word w^{e} is adjunctive ("also") here; Williams, *Syntax*, § 441.

7. LXX reads *Dephrōna*.

8. LXX reads *Asernain*.

9. For MT *hāriḇlâ* some mss. of Sam. Pent. read *hʼrblh;* LXX reads *Arbēla*. Gray (p. 461) conjectures *harbēlâ*, "to Harbel," with the so-called *hê* locale indicating motion toward, as in vv. 4–5, 8–10, 12, etc. He identified Harbel as either Harmel at the source of the Orontes River or Arbin, about 3 or 4 mi. northeast of Damascus.

10. Gray (pp. 461–62) posited that Ain was a mistake for a place-name *ʿîyôn;* cf. *BHS*.

the other side of the Jordan by Jericho, to the east, toward the rising sun."

These verses outline the borders of Israel. They are limited to the land west of the Jordan for the nine and one-half tribes. Many scholars point to the ideal nature of this boundary list.[11] It is true that Israel did not inhabit the territory outlined here; e.g., Israel's western border was not the Mediterranean Sea until ca. 144 B.C. under Simon Maccabeus (1 Macc. 14:5). But this passage presents a fairly accurate picture of the land of Canaan as found in Near Eastern texts from the middle of the 15th cent. B.C. on, and matches particularly well with the territory in the Egyptian district of Canaan in the second half of the 13th cent. B.C., at least according to Y. Aharoni.[12] Here as elsewhere many of these sites remain unknown at the present time, especially on the north and northeast borders.

Other lists of Israel's borders are found in various places in the OT. The most common designation for the whole land is "from Dan to Beer-sheba" (e.g., 1 Sam. 3:20), which comprises a smaller territory north to south than the present passage. Gen. 15:18 expands the land from the River of Egypt (as here, v. 5) to the Euphrates. Closer parallels to the present passage are found in Josh. 15:1–4 for the southern border, and in Ezek. 47:13–20 for the whole territory. Some scholars have concluded that the Numbers passage is based on one or both of these passages.[13] Indeed, the Numbers passage was probably written at a time after the conquest of Canaan, in which case a passage like Josh. 15:1–4 may have been used as a source document. It is also possible, however, that the passage in Ezekiel may have used both Joshua and Numbers as a source.

1–2 These verses introduce the whole narrative. They give Yahweh the initiative for setting out the boundaries of the land to be given to Israel.

the land that will fall to you by inheritance (hā'āreṣ 'ašer tippōl

11. E.g., Gray, pp. 452–53; Snaith, p. 201; Sturdy, p. 204; de Vaulx, pp. 388–89; Budd, p. 365.

12. See, e.g., Y. Aharoni, *The Land of the Bible: A Historical Geography,* ed. and tr. A. F. Rainey, rev. ed. (Philadelphia: Westminster, 1979), pp. 67–77, esp. 75–77; R. de Vaux, "Le Pays de Canaan," *JAOS* 88 (1968) 23–30; cf. M. Weippert, *IDBSup,* p. 126; Wenham, pp. 231–32.

13. E.g., A. G. Auld, *Joshua, Moses and the Land: Tetrateuch, Pentateuch, Hexateuch in a Generation Since 1938* (Edinburgh: T. & T. Clark, 1980), pp. 74–79. Budd (p. 365) concludes that the author of Numbers used both Josh. 15:1–4 and Ezek. 47:13–20 at different points in the construction of the narrative.

lāḵem b^{e}naḥ^{a}lâ). Cf. 26:52–56. The land of Canaan is commonly called an "inheritance" in Josh. 13–15.

3–5 These verses set out the southern border. They are closely related to Josh. 15:1–4, which sets out the border of Judah, the southernmost tribe. V. 3a gives a general outline of the border as facing the wilderness of Zin (cf. the commentary above on 13:21) and the territory of Edom. *the edge of Edom* must indicate the western edge of Edomite territory. Vv. 3b–5 take up the specific border posts. The known spots in the list are the *end (q^{e}ṣēh)* —the southern extremity — *of the Salt Sea,*[14] i.e., the Dead Sea, on the east, and *the River of Egypt (naḥlâ miṣrāyim),* i.e, Wâdī el-ʿArish, and on to the Mediterranean Sea on the west.[15] Between these two points the boundary first goes west-southwest from the Dead Sea to *the ascent of Akrabbim* ("scorpion pass"), probably modern Naqb eṣ-Safa, and, beyond that, in a more southerly direction through *Zin* (here probably the wilderness named in full in v. 3a) to *Kadesh-barnea,* probably Ain Qedeis or Ain Qudeirat (see the commentary above on 13:21), or possibly the whole area. From here the line begins to go back northwest toward Wâdī el-ʿArish, passing through Hazer-addar (an unknown site) and Azmon (also unknown, but possibly Qeṣeimeh),[16] and finally linking up with the River of Egypt on its northwesterly course to the Mediterranean Sea.

6 The western border of Canaan is the Mediterrranean and its coast. As has been pointed out, the Israelites did not dislodge the Philistines from this land during the OT period.

7–9 These verses set forth the northern border and are full of uncertainty. Ezek. 47:15–17 relates similar borders for the land, but the sites in that passage are also uncertain for the most part. The first difficulty is that one cannot be sure just how far north on the Mediterranean coast

14. The Dead Sea is called the Salt Sea *(yām hammelaḥ)* in Gen. 14:3; Num. 34:3, 12; Deut. 3:17; 4:49; Josh. 3:16; 12:3; 15:2, 5; 18:19. The name is fitting, since, with approximately 25–30 percent salinity, the Salt Sea is the most saline natural body of water in the world. See H. Ellison, *ISBE,* rev., I:881–82. Other than the Gen. 14 reference and the two in the current chapter, all the occurrences of this name are in the deuteronomistic literature, another connection between the end of the book of Numbers and the deuteronomistic material (see above on 33:16–36, 50–56).

15. On the River of Egypt, see Josh. 15:4, 47; 1 K. 8:65; 2 K. 24:7; 2 Chr. 7:8; Isa. 27:12.

16. Aharoni (*Land of the Bible,* p. 72) identifies Hazer-addar as Ain Qedeis and Ain Muweiliḥ as Azmon. He identifies Qeṣeimeh as Karka of Josh. 15:3.

to begin tracing the border line. This difficulty is compounded by the fact that the *Mount Hor* named here must be different from the Mt. Hor in 20:22 and 33:38 where Aaron died, since a site in the north for Aaron's death does not fit in with the context in either chs. 20 or 33.

8 *Lebo-Hamath.* See the commentary above on 13:21. The site is probably to be identified with Lebweh on the Orontes River, due east of Byblos (Gebal) on the coast, about 60 mi. north-northeast of Beth-rehob.[17]

Zedad is most probably Ṣadâd, about 35 mi. northeast of Lebweh on the edge of the desert.

9 *Ziphron* cannot at present be identified.

There is no agreement on the site of *Hazar-enan,* which is where the northern and eastern borders converge. Some have identified this last site with Qaryatein, a site east-southeast of Ṣadâd.[18] Ezek. 47:17 locates Hazar-enan as at or near the "northern border of Damascus."

10–12 The eastern border cannot be traced with any certainty north of the Sea of Chinnereth.

10 *Shepham* is otherwise unknown.

11 *Riblah* is certainly not the city on the Orontes River of that name (2 K. 25:6). Since the Hebrew noun has the definite article here *(hāriḇlâ),* it may be a corruption of another name. LXX reads Arbela (presupposing Heb. *'arb^{e}lâ*). An Arbela in Galilee is mentioned in 1 Macc. 9:2, identified with Khirbet Irbid just west of the widest part of the Sea of Chinnereth, and while this Arbela is in the area being discussed in these verses, it is impossible to be certain whether it is the site referred to here. The sight of *Ain* is likewise unknown, but Gray conjectured that the Hebrew letters *'yn* should be revocalized as Iyyon.[19] If this is correct, the site could be associated with Ijon (Tell ed-Dibbin) at the source of the Jordan.

the shoulder of the Sea of Chinnereth (keṯep yām-kinnereṯ). The noun *kāṯep* can mean the "shoulder" of a human (1 Sam. 17:6) or a beast (Ezek. 34:21), but it is also used to refer to a group of hills in Josh. 15:8, 10–11; 18:12–13, 16, 18–19. Here it probably refers to the hills northeast of the *Sea of Chinnereth.* This body of water (also in Josh. 13:27) was

17. See, e.g., Aharoni, *Land of the Bible,* pp. 72–73.

18. E.g., *Westminster Historical Atlas,* p. 51; Snaith, p. 202; Wenham, p. 232. Aharoni (*Land of the Bible,* p. 73) locates Ziphron at Ḥawwarin and Hazar-enan at Qaryatein. These two sites are two desert oases beyond Ṣadâd to the east.

19. See Gray, pp. 461–62.

named after the town in what would become the tribal holding of Naphtali (Deut. 3:17; Josh. 19:35). The small triangular plain on the northwestern shore of the sea is called the plain of Chinnereth in 1 K. 15:20. This body of water is also referred to as the Sea of Chinneroth (Josh. 13:3) and in the NT as the Lake of Gennesaret (Luke 5:1) or the Sea of Tiberias (John 21:1). It is nearly 13 mi. long and up to about 7 mi. wide.

12 South of the sea, the eastern border becomes the Jordan River, and finally, once again, the Dead Sea *(Salt Sea).*

13–15 These verses link this narrative with other parts of Numbers. V. 13 connects this story with the narrative in 26:52–56. Vv. 14–15 tie this story with ch. 32, which relates the apportionment of land east of the Jordan for the tribes of Reuben, Gad, and half of Manasseh.

3. LEADERS TO DRAW ISRAEL'S BORDERS (34:16–29)

16 *And Yahweh spoke to Moses, saying:*

17 *"These are the names of the men who will mark out*[1] *the land for possession for you: Eleazar the priest and Joshua the son of Nun.*

18 *And you will choose one leader from each tribe*[2] *to mark out the land for possession."*

19 *And these are the names of the men: For the tribe of Judah, Caleb the son of Jephunneh.*

20 *And for the tribe of the children of Simeon: Shemuel the son of Ammihud.*

1. Several commentators (e.g., Dillmann, p. 213; Paterson, p. 65; Gray, p. 463; cf. BDB, p. 635b) and *BHS* propose to change the vowel pointing on the Qal *yinḥalû* to read the Piel *y*ᵉ*naḥelû*. The argument is that the Qal means "to inherit," and the required meaning here is "to mark out for inheritance," since the leaders named in this passage do the latter, not the former. *for the Israelites* (see v. 29). If it be true that the Qal may not mean "to mark out for inheritance," then the emendation should be made, especially since the Piel does occur in v. 29. On the other hand, the Qal of this verb occurs not only in this verse, but also in the next one and in Josh. 19:49. All three of these passages require the meaning "to mark out for inheritance." One wonders whether the better course is not to posit that the Qal may mean both "to inherit" and "to mark out for inheritance" rather than to emend three readings to fit another pattern. The Akkadian cognate verb in the basic stem *(inḫilu)* occurs with the meaning "to assign an inheritance" (*HALAT,* p. 648a). Milgrom, *JPST,* p. 288 n. 20, allows either Qal or Piel. The Hebrew consonants are the same in either case.

2. The distributive "one leader from each tribe" is here expressed by repeating the phrase *nāśî 'eḥāḏ*. See Davidson, *Syntax,* § 38 Rem. 4.

21 *And for the tribe of Benjamin: Elidad the son of Chislon.*
22 *And for the tribe of the children of Dan, a leader: Bukki the son of Jogli.*
23 *And for the children of Joseph; for the tribe of the children of Manasseh, a leader: Hanniel the son of Ephod.*[3]
24 *And for the tribe of the children of Ephraim, a leader: Kemuel the son of Shiphtan.*
25 *And for the tribe of the children of Zebulun, a leader: Elizaphan the son of Parnach.*
26 *And for the tribe of the children of Issachar, a leader: Paltiel the son of Azzan.*[4]
27 *And for the tribe of the children of Asher, a leader: Ahihud*[5] *the son of Shelomi.*
28 *And for the tribe of the children of Naphtali, a leader: Pedahel the son of Ammihud."*[6]
29 *These are the ones whom Yahweh commanded to mark out the land of Canaan for the inheritance of the children of Israel.*

The new day has dawned. A new census has been taken (ch. 26), and the land of Canaan has been divided. In many ways the Israelites stand at the same position they did at the beginning of the book of Numbers, before their rebellion and the punishment of the wilderness years took place. Now, as then, it would be important for lay leadership to assist in the task at hand, which was marking out the boundaries of the land. In the preparations of 1:5–15 God appointed the leaders, and he does here again. In that earlier list, two God-appointed leaders were at the head of the people: Aaron the priest and Moses. Here, Aaron is already dead, and Moses is soon to die (27:12–23), so that new leaders — Eleazar the priest and Joshua — are at the head of the people. Of the other leaders in the old lists, only Caleb the son of Jephunneh is listed here; his survival is a reward for his faithful service at the time of the original mission to spy out the land (cf. 14:24, 30, 38).

The current list of leaders has only ten names, since the tribes of Reuben and Gad had no part in this matter (ch. 32). As was said on 1:5–15 above, it is very difficult to argue whether a particular name in a particular list is ancient. Noordtzij concluded that, since none of the names in the

3. LXX reads *Ouphi(d)*.

4. LXX reads *Oza* and Pesh. reads *'āzôr*.

5. LXX reads *Achiōr*.

6. LXX reads *huios Benamioud,* which presupposes Heb. *ben,* "son of," both in its own right (i.e., *huios*) and as the first part of the proper name *Ben*amioud.

current list was combined with Yahweh, the list could be considered very old. This theory is possible, but it is impossible to prove.[7] The order of the tribes is totally new, as is fitting for the new beginning; it is basically the same as the order in Josh. 13–19. It is at least possible that the order here is dependent upon the order of the actual conquest as narrated in Joshua. This, of course, would imply that the current passage was finally composed at a time after the conquest. The major difference between the lists is that the current list reverses the common order of Ephraim and Manasseh, perhaps on the basis of the census list in 26:28–37.

The tribes are listed in approximately the geographical position in which they would settle in the land, from south to north. The southern four tribes, Judah, Simeon, Benjamin, and Dan, are listed in vv. 19–22. It should be noted that the tribe of Dan is still in its more southern position, which may well speak for the antiquity of this list.[8] The central two tribes (the Joseph tribes, Manasseh and Ephraim) are next (vv. 23–24), and the northern tribes of Zebulun, Issachar, Asher, and Naphtali are found in vv. 25–28. The pericope ends with a formula restating (as v. 18 does) that these men were appointed by Yahweh to mark out the boundaries of Canaan.

4. CITIES OF THE LEVITES (35:1–8)

1 *And Yahweh spoke to Moses on the plains of Moab by the Jordan at Jericho, saying:*

2 *"Command the children of Israel that they should give to the Levites from their inherited possession cities to dwell in, and the land surrounding the cities you will give to the Levites.*

3 *And the cities will be for them to dwell in, and their lands*[1] *will be for their cattle and their flocks and for all their beasts.*

4 *And the lands of the cities that you will give to the Levites will be from the city wall outward one thousand*[2] *cubits all around.*

5 *And you will measure from the outside of the city on the east side two thousand cubits, and on the south side two thousand cubits, and on the west side two thousand cubits, and on the north side*

7. Others, e.g., Noth (p. 251), see the list itself as relatively recent, although some of the names themselves may be ancient. Again, this is very difficult to prove.

8. The narrative of Dan's migration to the far north is found in Judg. 18.

1. MT reads a masc. suffix here *(ûmigr^{e}šêhem),* referring to the lands of the Levites. Sam. Pent. has a fem. suffix *(ûmiḡr^{e}šêhen),* referring to the lands of the cities. Either reading is possible.

2. LXX reads *dischilious* ("two thousand") in order to bring this reading into line with those in v. 5. MT, as the more difficult reading, is to be preferred.

two thousand cubits. And the city will be in the midst. These will be the lands of the cities for them.[3]

6 *And the cities you will give to the Levites are the six cities of refuge to which you may designate that a manslayer may flee. And, in addition to them, you will give forty-two cities.*

7 *All the cities which you will give to the Levites are forty-eight cities; all with their lands.*[4]

8 *As for the cities which you will give from the possession of the children of Israel: From a larger tribe you will take a larger number, and from a smaller tribe you will take a smaller number, each in proportion to*[5] *its inheritance which it inherits it will give from its cities to the Levites."*

1 *the plains of Moab by the Jordan at Jericho.* For this common expression see 22:1; 26:63; 31:12; 33:48, 50; 36:13 (cf. 33:49).

2 *cities to dwell in.* The verb *to dwell in (lāšāḇeṯ)* here seems to indicate that the author did not want to contradict the principle that the Levites would have no landed inheritance in Canaan (18:23; cf. Deut. 10:9; 12:12; 14:27, 29; Josh. 14:4; 18:7), but would have tithes (18:24; Josh. 13:14) and Yahweh (Deut. 10:9; 18:2; Josh. 13:33) for their inheritance. Indeed, the terms *inherit (nāḥal), inheritance (naḥ*^{a}*lâ),* and *portion (ḥēleq),* usually used of the tribes' landed property in Canaan, are avoided here.[6] The meaning is most likely, therefore, that the Levites were not to own the towns, but only to live in them. They were perhaps also not to be the sole residents in these towns, since passages like Lev. 25:32–35 speak only of the Levites' redemption of *houses* in these towns, not of the towns themselves.[7] This conclusion is strengthened by the fact that, although

3. MT reads *lāhem,* "for them." The *Sebir* note, many mss. and printed editions of the Hebrew Bible, as well as Sam. Pent., LXX, Pesh., and Targ. Pseudo-Jonathan read *lāḵem,* "to you," in order to bring the construction into parallelism with the 2nd person. In this text, however, the 2nd person pl. denotes Moses (and the other leaders). Retain MT.

4. The word *'eṯ* marks the predicate here, as many times in verbless clauses. See GKC, § 117m; B. Waltke and M. O'Connor, *Introduction to Biblical Hebrew Syntax* (Winona Lake, Ind.: Eisenbrauns, 1990), § 10.3.2c.

5. On this meaning for *k*^{e}*pî,* see BDB, p. 805b; also 6:21; 7:5, 7–8.

6. For *nāḥal,* see Num. 18:20, 23–24; 26:55; 32:19; Josh. 16:4; 17:6; 19:9; Judg. 11:2. For *naḥ*^{a}*lâ,* see Num. 16:14; 36:2; Josh. 14:3; 17:4, 14; 19:49. For *ḥēleq* see Num. 18:20, 23; Josh. 18:5–7, 9; 15:3; 19:9.

7. Noordtzij (p. 296) compares the Levitical cities to the Hittite "cities of the gods," which were governed by temple personnel but not inhabited exclusively by them.

Josh. 21:11 assigns Hebron as one of the Levitical cities, 21:12 reports that the fields *(śāḏeh)* surrounding the city and all the villages attaching to it had been given to the non-Levitical family of Caleb. Further evidence for a mixed population in one of these Levitical cities (Shechem) may be seen in Judg. 9.

the land surrounding the cities (migrāš leʿārîm sᵉḇîḇōṯêhem). Although Josh. 21:11–12 and 1 Chr. 6:40–41 (Eng. 55–56) differentiate between the *land (migrāš)* surrounding a city and the "fields" *(śāḏeh),* the purpose of the *migrāš* here is said to be wholly for grazing (v. 3, *for their cattle and their flocks and for all their beasts*). Originally such lands were probably thought of as places "to drive" cattle (the verb *gāraš* means "to drive"). Lev. 25:35 states that these lands belong to the Levites and may not be sold.

4–5 Scholars do not agree on how to understand the figures in these verses, since v. 4 gives the figure one thousand cubits (about 500 yds.), while v. 5 gives twice that distance as the measure of the pasturelands surrounding the towns. LXX reads two thousand cubits in both vv. 4 and 5, probably an early attempt to reconcile the two. The two verses were presumably noncontradictory to the editor(s) of the final form of this text; otherwise it is hard to explain why some such expedient as is found in LXX is not followed (and the verses seem textually stable, with the exception of some LXX mss.).

M. Greenberg suggested that v. 4 gives the actual distance from the city wall in every direction (i.e, 1,000 cubits), while v. 5 is a theoretical verse that concludes that the total measurement of frontage on every side with the minimum-sized town would be 2,000 cubits.[8] This theoretical verse would be one way to give a regulation while recognizing that the actual size of the measurements would vary with the size of the town, the terrain, etc., and this suggestion seems reasonable. Terrain permitting, the actual size of the frontage of pasturelands in these towns would be 2,000 cubits *plus* the size of the town itself.

6–8 These verses link vv. 1–8 to what follows in vv. 9–34. The Levites are to be given six so-called cities of refuge (see the commentary below on vv. 9–34) as well as forty-two others from all tribal holdings, an average of four from each tribe, although the actual number of cities given

8. M. Greenberg, "Idealism and Practicality in Numbers 35:4–5 and Ezekiel 48," *JAOS* 88 (1968) 59–66. Wenham (p. 235) also follows Greenberg. Noordtzij (p. 296), Budd (p. 378), and Milgrom (*JPST,* pp. 502–4) suggest similar solutions, as did Keil (pp. 259–60) long ago.

from each tribe was to be worked out proportionally on the principle established in 26:54 and 33:54. According to Josh. 21, nine cities were given from Judah and Simeon, and four each from all the other tribes except Naphtali, which gave only three.

One must admit that this means that the principle of proportionality was not well followed. For example, at the second census (ch. 26) Naphtali had a larger population than Reuben, Simeon, Gad, or Ephraim, but gave fewer cities than any of these (except possibly Simeon, who was combined with Judah; Josh. 21:9–16, 20–22, 38–39). Issachar had roughly twice the population of Ephraim, but both were expected to cede four cities to the Levites (21:20–22, 28–29). It should be pointed out that the fulfillment of this legislation is looked to as future here, and, from the point of view of this text, no city was in Israelite hands. It probably took some time for many of the cities named in Josh. 21 to be conquered.[9] Noordtzij suggests that the tribes first decided which cities would be ceded to the Levites, and then looked at which tribal areas in which these cities were to be found.[10] It is a puzzle why such cities as Nob and Shiloh (called "cities of priests" in, e.g., 1 Sam. 21:1; 22:9) would not be in the list of Josh. 21.[11]

5. CITIES OF REFUGE (35:9–34)

9 *And Yahweh spoke to Moses, saying:*

10 *"Speak to the children of Israel and say to them, 'When you cross over the Jordan into the land of Canaan,*

11 *then you will select cities for yourselves. They will be cities of refuge for you to which the one who inadvertently slays another human being may flee.*

12 *And they will be cities for your refuge from the avenger,*[1] *that the*

9. E.g., Gezer (Judg. 1:29; 1 K. 9:16); Taanach (Judg. 1:27); Nahalal (Judg. 1:30); Rehob (Judg. 1:31).

10. Noordtzij, p. 296.

11. See commentaries on Josh. 21:1–42; e.g., T. Butler, *Joshua,* WBC (Waco, Tex.: Word, 1983), pp. 218–23; J. Gray, *Joshua, Judges, Ruth,* NCBC (Grand Rapids: Eerdmans, 1986), pp. 162–68; J. A. Soggin, *Joshua: A Commentary,* OTL, tr. R. A. Wilson (Philadelphia: Westminster, 1972), pp. 199–206; M. Woudstra, *The Book of Joshua,* NICOT (Grand Rapids: Eerdmans, 1981), pp. 303–13; D. Madvig, "Joshua," in *EBC* (Grand Rapids: Zondervan, 1992), III:348–53.

1. Here Sam. Pent., LXX, and Targ. read "the avenger of blood," i.e., they add the word *haddām,* as in vv. 19, 21, 25, 27. Gray (p. 470) prefers this reading. Absolute uniformity is not necessary. Read with MT.

slayer might not die until he stands before the congregation for judgment.

13 *And the cities that you will give will be your six cities of refuge.*

14 *You will give three cities in Transjordan and you will give three cities in the land of Canaan; these will be your cities of refuge.*

15 *There will be these six cities for refuge for the children of Israel, for the stranger, and for the sojourner in their midst, that anyone who slays another human being inadvertently may flee there.*

16 *But if he struck him down with an instrument of iron so that he died, he is a murderer; the murderer shall be put to death.*

17 *And if he struck him with a stone in the hand by which one may die, and he died, he is a murderer; the murderer shall be put to death.*

18 *Or if he struck him with a piece of wood in the hand by which one may die, and he died, he is a murderer; the murderer shall be put to death.*

19 *The avenger of blood, he may put the murderer to death; when he meets him he may put him to death.*

20 *And if he pushed him in hatred, whether*[2] *he threw something at him while lying in wait, and he died,*

21 *or, if he struck him with his hand in hostility, and he died, then the one who struck the blow will be put to death; he is a murderer. The avenger of blood may put the murderer to death when he meets him.*

22 *But if he pushed him suddenly without hostility, whether he threw something at him without lying in wait,*

23 *or he caused any stone by which one may die to fall upon him without*[3] *seeing him, and he died, and he was not an enemy to him and was not seeking*[4] *his harm,*

2. Here in vv. 20–21, as well as in vv. 22–23 below, the two dependent clauses, introduced by *'ô* (lit., "or . . . or," but here "whether . . . or"), are intended to be two alternative acts considered under the general category of the main clause introduced by *'im* ("if"), i.e., pushing a person in hatred may be either accomplished by throwing something or striking with the hand. See Driver, *Tenses,* § 138 ii Obs.; cf. Waltke and O'Connor, *Biblical Hebrew Syntax,* § 39.2.6b (example 4). Gray (p. 474) simply sees the "or" as expressing three protases to which there is only one apodosis in v. 24 (and possibly v. 21b).

3. The *lō'* in *b*^{e}*lō' r*^{e}*'ôṯ* (as well as below *lō'-'ôyēḇ lô,* and *w*^{e}*lō' m*^{e}*ḇaqqēš rā'āṯô*) is privative: "without seeing . . . without being his enemy . . . without seeking his harm." See Williams, *Syntax,* § 400.

4. The predicate participle *m*^{e}*ḇaqqēš* is negated by *lō'* here, which is quite unusual in Biblical Hebrew; Davidson, *Syntax,* § 100 Rem. 3; Driver, *Tenses,* § 162 n. 2.

24 *then the congregation will judge between the one who has struck him and the avenger of blood according to these ordinances.*
25 *And the congregation will rescue the slayer from the hand of the avenger of blood, and the congregation will return him to his city of refuge to which he had fled, and he will stay in it until the death of the high priest who has been anointed by the holy oil.*
26 *But if the slayer should, at any time, go beyond the border of his city of refuge to which he had fled,*
27 *and the avenger of blood finds him outside the border of his city of refuge, and the avenger of blood kills the slayer, he will have no bloodguilt.*
28 *For he must remain in his city of refuge until the death of the high priest. But after the death of the high priest, the slayer may return to his possessed land.*
29 *And these things will be statutes of judgment and ordinances for you throughout your generations, in all your dwelling places.*
30 *As for any who takes the life of a human, the murderer shall be put to death at the word of witnesses, except that no one shall be put to death on the word of one.*
31 *And you shall not take a ransom for the life of a murderer who is guilty of death; rather he must surely be put to death.*
32 *Also you shall not take a ransom for the life of the one who fled*[5] *to his city of refuge so that he might return to his dwelling in the land before the death of the priest.*[6]
33 *And you shall not pollute the land in which you are, for blood pollutes the land. And no atonement may be made for the land for the blood shed in it, except by the blood of the one who shed it.*
34 *And you shall not defile the land in which you are living, since I am dwelling in your midst; for I, Yahweh, am dwelling in the midst of the children of Israel.' "*

9–15 These verses legislate the establishment of six cities, from the forty-eight cities that are to be given to the Levites (see v. 6), for the refuge

5. The phrase *w^e lōʾ ṯiq^e ḥû ḵōper lānûs ʾel-ʿîr miqlāṭô* is difficult. Paterson (p. 66) reads *lannās,* a masc. sing. participle, which may also be read as "with regard to the one who flees." It seems clear, however, that LXX read the infinitive *(lytra tou phygein),* and there seem to be no significant textual variants to *lānûs.* The infinitive construct may be taken as a gerund with the article here, lit., "for the fleeing (one)"; cf. Waltke and O'Connor, *Biblical Hebrew Syntax,* §§ 36.1.1; 36.2.

6. Sam. Pent., LXX, and Pesh. read "high priest," i.e., they add the word *haggāḏôl* as in vv. 25, 28.

of people who have killed another human inadvertently. This law is meant to take effect *When you* [the Israelites] *cross over the Jordan into the land of Canaan,* as was also the case, e.g., in 33:51.

11 *you will select cities for yourselves (wᵉhiqrîṯem lāḵem ʿārîm).* The verb *qārâ* in the Hiphil means "to cause [something] to occur."[7] Here the meaning seems to develop to something like "to cause the right [cities] to appear before yourselves," i.e., "to choose" these cities. LXX translates *hiqrîḇ* by the verb *diastellō,* "to appoint,"[8] and most English versions have followed this translation.

cities of refuge (*ʿārê miqlāṭ,* lit., "cities of intaking"). In the OT the term *miqlāṭ* is always used either in connection with these six cities or with refugees who flee to these cities.[9] The concept of asylum for unintentional killing is known to be ancient in Israel (cf., e.g., 1 K. 1:50–53; 2:28–31). The law of Exod. 21:13–14 allowed for temporary asylum but did not designate the place (except to say that it may be at an altar) or define how long the asylum may last. The current passage more carefully distinguishes murder from unintentional killing (vv. 16–18, 20–23), puts responsibility for determining guilt or innocence in the hands of *the congregation* (*hāʿēḏâ,* vv. 12, 24–25), and defines the time period of the guilty party's stay in a city of refuge (vv. 25–28, 32). Deut. 19:1–13 gives other examples of unintentional killing and lays further stress on the responsibility of the community (this time in the persons of the elders of that community). Finally, Josh. 20 sets apart and names six specific cities to function as cities of refuge. These passages emphasize different aspects of the concept of asylum. The cities of refuge here legislated would not necessarily replace asylum at an altar. The present legislation may be seen to supplement such a practice.[10]

12 *avenger (gōʾēl).* Although this translation fits the present

7. See BDB, p. 899b; *HALAT,* p. 1062a.

8. Cf. Deut. 19:2, 7, where LXX also uses *diastellō* to translate *hiḇdîl* ("to distinguish, denominate").

9. See Num. 35:6, 11–15, 25–28, 32; Josh. 20:2–3; 21:13, 21, 27, 32, 38; 1 Chr. 6:42, 52 (Eng. 57, 67); cf. BDB, p. 886a.

10. So M. Greenberg, "The Biblical Conception of Asylum," *JBL* 78 (1959) 125–32, esp. 130. This article may still be consulted with profit. De Vaulx (pp. 396–403) gives a five-step process in the development of the custom stretching into the postexilic age, where he places both Num. 35 and most of Josh. 20. De Vaulx is followed, with minor modifications, by Budd (pp. 381–82). One should remember (following Greenberg), however, that it is not possible to conclude that the *custom* of asylum as reflected in Num. 35 is as recent as the postexilic era, whatever one's view of the age of the present text.

context, the basic meaning of the term *gō'ēl* is "near kin," and refers to the person chosen by a family to deal with a loss suffered by that family. The *gō'ēl* does not engage in revenge, but in redemption of family loss, and thus comes to mean "redeemer." The duties of the *gō'ēl* may be to contract Levirate marriage (Ruth 3:13),[11] to receive money payable to a dead family member on behalf of the family (Num. 5:8), to buy a family member out of slavery brought on by poverty (Lev. 25:48), to buy property that has passed out of the family under similar conditions (Lev. 25:25), or to buy property to keep it from passing out of the family (Jer. 32:7–15). The *gō'ēl* may also restore the loss a family has suffered when a member has been killed. When such becomes the task of the *gō'ē l,* the usual term is "avenger of blood" *(gō'ēl-haddām),* as in vv. 19, 21, 24–25, 27.

13–14 Three of the six cities of refuge are to be placed in Transjordan,[12] and three in Canaan proper. Josh. 20 names the six cities as Kedesh (Naphtali) in the north, Shechem (Ephraim) in the center, and Kiriath-arba or Hebron (Judah) in the south of Canaan, Bezer (Reuben) in the southeast, Ramoth-gilead (Gad) in the center, and Golan (Manasseh) in the north of Tranjordan.[13]

15 These cities are to be for the use of native-born Israelites as well as for those whose dwelling is more temporary in the land: the *stranger* (*gēr;* see the commentary above on 9:14) and the *sojourner (tôšāḇ).* The latter is probably a nonnative who is in some manner attached to a Hebrew family in a less permanent way than a *stranger,* but more permanent than a hired worker *(śāḵîr).*[14] These same two terms are found together in Gen. 23:4; Lev. 25:23, 35, 47. On the other hand, in a law parallel to the present one, Josh. 20:9 uses only the term *gēr.* Several scholars have suggested, therefore, that *gēr wᵉṯôšāḇ* is to be understood as a hendiadys = "resident aliens." Kellermann suggests that a *tôšāḇ*

11. On the custom of marriage and the function of the *gō'ēl* in the book of Ruth, see esp. R. Hubbard, *The Book of Ruth,* NICOT (Grand Rapids: Eerdmans, 1988), pp. 51–63, 185–89, 211–13, etc. This commentary has much of value in it on the whole institution of the *gō'ēl.*

12. According to Deut. 4:41–43, Moses designated the sites in Transjordan before his death.

13. Many scholars locate these sites as follows: Kedesh is Tell Qedesh, in Galilee, northwest of Lake Ḥuleh; Shechem is Tell Balaṭa by Mt. Gerizim; Hebron is el-Khalil, west of the Dead Sea; Bezer is Umm el-ʿAmad (possibly); Ramoth-gilead is Tell Ramit; Golan is Salem el-Jolan, north of the River Yarmuk. See, e.g., *Oxford Bible Atlas,* pp. 62–63.

14. Gray, p. 472; cf. BDB, p. 444b; Exod. 12:48. D. Kellerman, *TDOT,* II:439–49.

(stranger) describes in economic terms what *gēr (sojourner)* describes in legal terms.[15]

inadvertently (bišᵉgāgâ). See the commentary above on 15:22–26.

16–24 The following sections deal with the kinds of killing that qualify a killer to seek asylum in a city of refuge on the basis of the type of weapon or instrument used (vv. 16–18) and whether malice was involved in the killing (vv. 20–23). The avenger of blood is given the task of executing the murderer (v. 19; cf. v. 12), and the congregation is given the task of deciding whether a killer is guilty or innocent of murder (v. 24; cf. v. 12).

16–18 The principle, repeated three times for emphasis, is *the murderer shall be put to death (môṯ yûmaṯ hārōṣēaḥ)*, which underlines the principle in Gen. 9:6: "the shedder of human blood, his blood by the human will be shed" *(šōpēḵ dam hā'āḏām bā'āḏām dāmô yiššāpēḵ)*. Certain weapons connote hostility by their use. Any instrument of iron that causes death, along with a stone or piece of wood large enough to be held *in the hand*[16] is considered a murder weapon by definition, and its user is condemned to die as a murderer.

19 Here the full title *avenger of blood (gō'ēl haddām)* is given. On the *gō'ēl*, see above. This passage still puts the responsibility for carrying out the death sentence in the hands of the family rather than making it a function of the state. This kind of sociological model would operate better in premonarchic Israel than later.

20–21 The matter of the relationship between the killer and the victim comes into the picture here. Both *hate* (*śinâ*, v. 20) and *hostility* (*'êḇâ*, v. 21) are basic terms that indicate a state of enmity between the killer and victim.[17] If one acts with these motives and the actions result in the death of the victim (*and he died*, vv. 20–21), then the killer is summarily declared to be *a murderer* (*rōṣēaḥ*, v. 21), and is to be executed by the *avenger of blood* (*gō'ē l haddām*, v. 21).

On the basis of the context, the word *pushed (hāḏap)* seems to mean

15. See Kellerman, *TDOT*, II:448; Milgrom, *JPST*, p. 292; D. Block, *ISBE*, rev., IV:561–64.

16. The phrases *'eḇen yāḏ*, "stone in the hand," and *kᵉlî 'ēs-yāḏ*, "piece of wood in the hand," more likely indicate the size of the instrument (cf. *maqqēl yāḏ*, "staff in the hand," Ezek. 39:9) than Wenham's suggestion (p. 237; following a note by J. L. Saalschütz, *Das Mosäische Recht mit Berücksichtigung des spätern Jüdischen* [1853], p. 527) that "hand" here should be taken as "handle."

17. Literarily, therefore, the terms for enmity frame the regulation and give it shape.

"does away with" (cf. Isa. 22:19).[18] It is defined by the more particular clauses *he threw something at him while lying in wait (hišlîḵ ʿālāyw biṣᵉḏîyâ)* or *he struck him with his hand (hikkāhû ḇᵉyāḏô),* i.e., "did away with him, whether from a hiding place (clandestinely) or out in the open."

22–23 The opposite case is set forth here. The killer acts *without hostility* (*bᵉlōʾ ʾêḇâ,* v. 22), *without lying in wait (bᵉlōʾ ṣᵉḏiyyâ,* v. 22), *without seeing him* (*wᵉlōʾ rᵉʾôṯ,* v. 23), *was not an enemy to him* (*lōʾ-ʾôyēḇ lô,* v. 23), and *was not seeking his harm* (*lōʾ mᵉḇaqqēš rāʿāṯô,* v. 23). Although the result of the killer's action is the same as in the previous section (i.e., the victim died, v. 23), the outcome is different because of the attitude or intention of the killer.

24 This verse forms the conclusion to vv. 16–23 (not just vv. 22–23).[19] Both kinds of killings are adjudicated by *the congregation (hāʿēḏâ).* In most cases, this must have been a group representative of the whole congregation (as in Deut. 19:12 and Josh. 20:4). The fact that *the congregation* is not defined here suggests that this legislation probably assumes an older, well-known, procedure, and may also show that the writer of the current law is at least familiar with those of Deut. 19 and Josh. 20 and the current law was written after them. The motive of the killer (whether it was with or without hostility) is what the congregation must decide here. If, on the one hand, hostility can be proved to have existed between the killer and the victim, or if a lethal weapon was used (which, again, shows hostility), then the sentence of v. 19 (cf. vv. 16–18) is carried out. If not, then the procedure summarized in v. 25 and more closely defined in vv. 26–28 comes into play.

25–29 The job of the representatives of the congregation is, first, to *rescue the slayer from the hand of the avenger of blood.* This description indicates that the killer has fled to the nearest city of refuge and has been found guilty of inadvertent killing (vv. 22–23). The actual trial of the accused would probably have been held outside the city of refuge, since the congregation is said to *return* the inadvertent killer there for safety from the avenger of blood, although commentators have speculated on the matter of the site.[20] All one can say for sure is that the text implies it was away from the city of refuge. This seeming lack of precision is further evidence that the present

18. BDB, p. 213b.

19. See Gray, p. 475.

20. Budd (p. 383) gives three likely sites: the killer's home town, Jerusalem (so also Sturdy, p. 242), or the town nearest the scene of the crime (Noordtzij, p. 300). Wenham (p. 238) speculates that the site may have been just outside the city of refuge, which is as likely as any hypothesis.

legislation assumes previous practice. The other legal texts on the matter (e.g., Exod. 21:12–14 and Deut. 19:1–13) do not give more detail.

The last sentence of v. 25 gives the killer's term of detention in the city of refuge as *until the death of the high priest who has been anointed with holy oil.*[21] If, before that time, the killer goes outside the city of refuge, the avenger of blood may still kill him without incurring bloodguilt (i.e., risking the attack of another avenger of blood on him, vv. 26–28). We raise two questions: is the term of stay in the city of refuge seen as atoning for the death of the victim, and why is the death of the high priest seen as the end of that term?

The simplest and best view seems to be that the death of the high priest marks the end of an old era and the beginning of a new one.[22] Noth connected this verse with the custom of amnesty to prisoners at the accession of a new monarch.[23] But the term of detention in the city of refuge ended not with the anointing of a new high priest but at the death of the old one.[24] It is possible that the death of the high priest expiated the death of the victim and hence brought the bloodguilt of the killer to an end. His death may have been understood as fulfilling the principle that shed human blood can only be expiated by shed human blood (Gen. 9:6). In this case, the high priest's death was on behalf of the killer, much as the priest offers sacrifices on behalf of the people elsewhere.[25] The Talmud also takes the passage in this way — it is the death of the high priest rather than the term of confinement in the city of refuge that expiates the death of the victim.[26] This view is also consistent with vv. 32–33, which do not allow any ransom to buy off the blood of the victim. The clause *who has*

21. This whole title is found outside the current passage only in Lev. 21:10 (in a bit different form); these are the only places in the Pentateuch where the title high priest occurs. Outside the Pentateuch the term "high priest" *(hakkōhēn haggāḏōl)* occurs in Josh. 20:6; 2 K. 12:10; 22:4, 8; 23:4; 2 Chr. 34:9; Neh. 3:1, 20; 13:28; Hag. 1:1, 12, 14; 2:2, 4; Zech. 3:1, 8; 6:11. The term "anointed priest" *(hakkōhēn haammāšîaḥ)* is used of the high priest in Lev. 4:3, 5, 16; 6:15 (cf. 16:32). The term "head priest" *(hakkōhēn hārō'š)* is found in 2 K. 25:18 (= Jer. 52:24); 2 Chr. 19:11; 24:11; 26:40; 31:10; Ezra 7:5.

22. Noordtzij, p. 301.

23. Noth, p. 255. In the postexilic period, where Noth places this passage, the high priest takes over the role of the king.

24. See further criticism in Greenberg, "Biblical Conception of Asylum," p. 127.

25. So, e.g., Keil, p. 265; Sturdy, p. 242; Budd, p. 384.

26. T.B. *Makkot* 11b; see Greenberg, "Biblical Conception of Asylum," pp. 128–29; so also Wenham, p. 238.

been anointed by holy oil underlines the fact that the high priest has been set apart to this kind of ministry (cf. Exod. 29:1–46; Lev. 8:1–36).

29 The procedures outlined in vv. 10–28 will be applicable to Israel after the conquest of Canaan (v. 10) always and everywhere (i.e., *throughout your generations, in all your dwelling places).* In Num. 15:14, 15, 18, 21, 23, 38 the phrase *throughout your* (or their) *generations* occurs in summaries of the applicability of legal material beyond the immediate context. Although the term *statute of judgment,* which Milgrom applies to civil law,[27] occurs only here and in Lev. 27:11, the term *statute (ḥōq/ḥuqqâ)* is common in Numbers in summaries of the nature of legislation (i.e., it is a "statute," a "command").[28] Since the two terms *generations* and *statutes* are also used here, it is probable that this verse should simply be seen as a summary of the nature and applicability of the legislation concerning cities of refuge. Such a conclusion may imply that vv. 30–34 are either later interpretations of vv. 10–28, or from a different corpus of Israelite laws.[29]

30–34 These verses answer questions that might easily come up when the previous legislation was applied in specific cases. They deal with two main issues: the matter of witnesses in a capital case (v. 30) and the matter of accepting ransoms in lieu of the lives of either the murderer or inadvertent killer (vv. 31–32). The section ends with a general statement of theological principles (vv. 33–34).

30 The ancient Near East generally required more than one witness in order to obtain a murder conviction.[30] This law agrees with that tradition. Deut. 17:6 sets the number as at least two witnesses in all cases, especially capital ones.

31 The principle is that shed human blood must be atoned for by shed human blood (Gen. 9:5–6; Exod. 21:12; Lev. 24:17; cf. Deut. 19:11–13). This principle is assumed here in two ways. First, it is forbidden for a *ransom (kōp̄ēr)* in money to be taken in place of the life of the convicted murder (i.e., by the procedures outlined above). The *avenger of blood* must carry out the sentence. That *kōp̄ēr* can mean a money payment is shown by reference to 2 Sam. 21:1–14. David asks the Gibeonites, "what *atonement* shall I make"? (or "what payment shall I

27. Milgrom, *JPST,* p. 294.

28. On *statute,* see, e.g., above on 9:3; H. Ringgren, *TDOT,* V:139–49. It occurs in 9:3, 12, 14; 10:8; 15:15, 18, 23; 18:8, 11, 19; 19:2, 10, 21; 23:21; 27:11; 30:7; 35:29.

29. See, e.g., Gray, p. 475; Binns, p. 234; Noth, p. 256.

30. See the Code of Hammurabi, §§ 9–11 (*ANET,* p. 166); cf. Deut. 19:15; John 8:17; 2 Cor. 13:1; Heb. 10:28.

make"? *bammâ 'ᵃḵappēr,* v. 3), to which the Gibeonites respond, "It is not a matter of silver or gold to us" *('ên lānû kesep̱ wᵉzāhāḇ).*[31] The practical reason behind this law may very well be, as Noordtzij suggested, to avoid giving the rich who could afford such payments a loophole to commit murder at will, or a method of making an incident of human death an occasion for enrichment. The law thus upholds the principle of the importance of human life.[32]

32 V. 32 forbids the inadvertent killer to pay money in order to leave his city of refuge before the death of the high priest. This provision also assumes the seriousness of the loss of human life to the community. Even though inadvertent killers are not guilty of premeditated murder, they are still guilty of depriving the community of human life.

33–34 These verses give the theological rationale for the penalties attached to taking human life. The shedding of blood *pollutes* (Hiphil of *ḥānap̱*) the land.[33] The one who shed the blood (inadvertently) is kept confined in the city of refuge not only to keep him safe from the avenger of blood but also to keep the land isolated from the pollution of the act until the death of the high priest atones the shed blood and removes the bloodguilt. Both murder and inadvertent killing pollute the land. Murder is atoned for by the death of the murderer, inadvertent killing by the death of the high priest on behalf of the killer. Failing to observe these principles will *defile* (*tammē'*, lit., "make unclean") the land. Defilement of the land would put the whole people into the realm of the unclean, which would be unthinkable because Yahweh himself (the Holy One of Israel) was dwelling in their midst. If the people allowed the land to be defiled, then holy Yahweh would no longer dwell in their midst, and they would be lost.[34]

31. On *kōp̄ēr,* meaning "ransom price," see Milgrom, *Studies in Levitical Terminology,* I:27–31; Wenham, *Leviticus,* pp. 25–29.

32. Noordtzij, pp. 301–2.

33. Jer. 3:2, 9 use the same verb to describe the land's pollution by idolatry.

34. Illicit sexual relations, such as practiced by the Canaanites, are also said to pollute the land (Lev. 18:25–28), as does allowing a hanged person to remain hanging overnight (Deut. 21:23). The prophets use the word *ṭāmē'* (usually in the Piel), "to make unclean," to describe Israel's love affair with other gods and foreign nations (see Jer. 2:1–3:5; Ezek. 36:17–18; 43:7–8; etc.).

6. ADDITIONAL LEGISLATION FOR DAUGHTERS OF ZELOPHEHAD (36:1–13)

1 *And the heads of the fathers' houses*[1] *of the clan*[2] *of the children of Gilead, the son of Machir, the son of Manasseh, from the clans of the sons of Joseph drew near and spoke before Moses*[3] *and before the leaders, heads of the fathers' houses of the children of Israel.*

2 *And they said, "Yahweh commanded my lord to give the land as an inheritance by lot*[4] *to the children of Israel, and my lord was commanded by Yahweh to give the inheritance of Zelophehad our brother to his daughters.*

3 *Now, if they should become married to any from the sons of other tribes of the children of Israel, then their inheritance will be taken away from their father's inheritance and will be added*[5] *onto the inheritance of the tribe into which they come, and our lot of inheritance will be diminished.*[6]

4 *And when the Jubilee of the children of Israel comes, then their inheritance will be added onto the inheritance of the tribe into*

1. The word *'āḇôṯ* here substitutes for the fuller *bêṯ 'āḇôṯ*, as in Exod. 6:25; cf. 1 K. 8:1; 1 Chr. 6:4; 7:11; etc. See BDB, p. 3b.

2. It is possible that the word pointed as *lᵉmišpaḥaṯ* in MT should be pointed as a pl. *(mišpᵉḥōṯ)*, since there were many Gileadite clans (so Gray, p. 477). The only alternative is to read *mišpaḥaṯ* as indicating the whole of the Gileadites, and this is more inclusive than *mišpaḥa* usually is.

3. LXX and Pesh. add the words "and before Eleazar the priest." This would imply a Hebrew text of *wᵉlip̱nê 'elʿāzār hakkōhēn*. This reading is most likely an attempt to reconcile the current text with 27:2, but it is not necessary since ch. 36 is clearly a supplement.

4. The *bᵉ*- indicates agency here and below: "by Yahweh" *(bYHWH)*. See Williams, *Syntax,* § 245.

5. The 3rd person masc. sing. verb *(wᵉnôsap)* is often used impersonally. So, in the present verse, "an addition will be made," even when the noun to which the verb is connected is of the fem. gender (inheritance, *naḥᵃlâ*); see also Gen. 27:42 (cf. 2 Sam. 21:11; 1 K. 18:13; GKC, §121a). On the other hand, the same verb in v. 4 is found in the 3rd person fem. sing. *(wᵉnôsᵉpâ)*, which is, of course, in concord with *naḥᵃlâ*. Sam. Pent. reads 3rd fem. sing. in both vv. 3 and 4, but since the more difficult reading is usually preferred, and because the impersonal 3rd masc. sing. is a common construction, MT should be retained.

6. The hypothetical construction without conditional particles such as *'im* or *kî* may be formed by using a *wᵉ* plus a double perfect consecutive (as here; cf. Driver, *Tenses,* §§ 147–49) as well as the double jussive (or hypothetical imperative) (ibid., §§ 150–53). The time reference may be to the future (as here; ibid., § 149), to the past, or the present (ibid., § 148).

which they come, and their inheritance will be taken away[7] *from the inheritance of the tribe of our father."*
5 *And Moses commanded the children of Israel, saying: "The sayings of the children of Joseph are right."*
6 *This is the thing that Yahweh has commanded as regards the daughters of Zelophehad, saying: "Let them become married to whoever is the best in their own eyes, only let them become married within the clan of their father's*[8] *tribe.*
7 *The inheritance of the children of Israel will not change about from tribe to tribe, for every one of the children of Israel will hold onto the inheritance of their fathers' tribe.*
8 *And every daughter possessing an inheritance from the tribes of the children of Israel will be married to one from the clan of the tribe of her father so that the children of Israel may each one possess the inheritance of his fathers.*
9 *And no inheritance may change about from a tribe to another tribe, for each of the tribes of the children of Israel will hold onto its inheritance."*
10 *The daughters of Zelophehad did as Yahweh had commanded Moses.*
11 *That is, Mahlah, Tirzah, Hoglah, Milcah, and Noah,*[9] *the daughters of Zelophehad, became married to the sons of their uncles.*
12 *And they were married to those from the clans of the children of Manasseh, the son of Joseph. And their inheritance remained in the tribe of the clan of their father.*
13 *These are the commandments and the ordinances that Yahweh commanded by means of Moses to the children of Israel on the plains of Moab by the Jordan at Jericho.*

The last chapter of Numbers is clearly a supplement to 26:33–34 and especially 27:1–11.[10] The clan of Zelophehad had come to Moses concerned about the fact that they had no male heirs to inherit property (27:1–4). Yahweh, through Moses, decreed that in the absence of male heirs female heirs could inherit property in Canaan (27:5–10). As is often

7. For the masc. verb form *(yiggārâ)* with a fem. noun *(naḥ^{a}lâ),* see, e.g., Davidson, *Syntax,* § 113b; GKC, § 144b.

8. MT *'^{a}ḇîhem;* on the use of masc. pl. suffixes to refer to fem. subjects, see GKC, § 135o.

9. In Sam. Pent. the order of these names is as in 26:33 and 27:1, viz., Mahlah, Noah, Hoglah, Milcah, and Tirzah.

10. Cf. the commentary on these verses above.

the case when legislation is promulgated, further legislation becomes necessary. This chapter begins with a reminder by Zelophehad's daughters of the precedent (vv. 1–4). Readers are not told how long Moses took to reach the decision, but Moses — in Yahweh's name — brings a slight modification to marriage rules for inheriting daughters (vv. 5–7), which is then applied to all the tribes (vv. 8–9). The case ends with the implementation of what had been decreed (vv. 10–12). V. 13 is a closing formula not only for this case but also for the last section of Numbers (22:2–36:12).

1–4 In vv. 1–2 the leaders of the Gileadite clans in the tribe of Manasseh come before Moses and cite the precedent of the decision reached in 27:1–11. The problem that probably had already presented itself was that when inheriting daughters married into another tribe, their inheritance went over to the tribe of their husband. Such practice would break up the geographical unity of the tribe's inheritance by placing islands of non-Manassite holdings in the midst of their tribal lands, as well as reducing the amount of land in the Manassite inheritance (v. 3). Noth thought that v. 4 is irrelevant both literarily and factually, but the Jubilee legislation was, in many ways, the great remedy for ills concerning land and property in Canaan. The point of v. 4 is that even this legislation will do nothing to remedy the problem of inheriting females marrying outside their tribe, since that legislation dealt only with purchased property, not inherited property (see Lev. 25:13–55). Unless there is new legislation, real damage will be done to the Manassite inheritance, which is what 27:1–11 was designed to prevent in the first place.

5–9 These verses take a legal decision that limits inheriting females to marriage within their father's (i.e., ancestral) tribe, in this case Manasseh. This decision prohibits the transference of inherited land from one tribe to another and thus prevents both problems mentioned above. In vv. 8–9 these same principles are applied across the whole of Israel, and prevents such transference of property throughout the whole nation.

10–12 The daughters of Zelophehad obeyed Yahweh's word through Moses and married their cousins.

13 This concluding formula is similar to those found in Lev. 7:37–38; 26:46; 27:34. It ends a section of legal material. The formula is intended to conclude the whole section that began when Israel arrived on the plains of Moab in 22:1.

The last section of Numbers (33:50–36:12) dealt with matters of property and land *within the land of promise*. Thus the book ends on a forward-looking and open-ended note. What will happen in the land of Canaan? There is one major event to take place before the people can cross over the Jordan under the leadership of Joshua (cf. 27:18–23): Moses must die and entrust the leadership to a new generation. Preparation for life in the land of Canaan without Moses is a major theme of Deuteronomy.

INDEX OF SUBJECTS

INDEX OF AUTHORS

Authors simply footnoted are not included.

INDEX OF SCRIPTURE REFERENCES

This index includes only passages discussed in the text.

APOCRYPHA

NEW TESTAMENT